Source Readings in Music History

Source Readings in Music History

From Classical Antiquity through the Romantic Era

Selected and Annotated by

OLIVER STRUNK

PRINCETON UNIVERSITY

W · W · NORTON & COMPANY · INC · New York

Musical examples by Gordon Mapes

ISBN 0 393 09742 0

PRINTED IN THE UNITED STATES OF AMERICA
FOR THE PUBLISHERS BY THE VAIL-BALLOU PRESS, INC.

To the Memory of
CARL ENGEL
1883–1944

ACKNOWLEDGMENTS

THE EDITOR wishes to acknowledge with thanks the co-operation of the following publishers who have granted permission to quote from works copyrighted by them: the Harvard University Press, for the selections from Plato, *The Republic*, Aristotle's *Politics*, Athenaeus, *The Deipnosophists*, Clement of Alexandria, and St. Augustine's *Confessions*, all from the Loeb Classical Library; the Clarendon Press, Oxford, for a part of *The Harmonics of Aristoxenus* in the translation by Henry S. Macran; the Oxford University Press, London, for F. T. Arnold's translation of Viadana's preface to the *Cento concerti ecclesiastici*, first published in Arnold's *The Art of Accompaniment from a Thorough-Bass*; and J. M. Dent & Sons, Ltd., London, for the translation by Eric Blom of Gluck's dedication to *Alceste*.

ABBREVIATIONS

Grad. Vat.	*Graduale . . . de tempore et de sanctis* (Tournai, 1938)
Ant. Vat.	*Antiphonale . . . pro diurnis horis* (Rome, 1912)
	J. P. Migne, *Patrologia cursus completus.*
PL	—*Series latina.* 221 vols. (Paris, 1844–1855)
PG	—*Series graeca.* 166 vols. (Paris, 1857–1866)
GS	Martin Gerbert, *Scriptores ecclesiastici de musica.* 3 vols. (San Blasianis, 1784)
CS	C. E. H. Coussemaker, *Scriptorum de medii aevi nova series.* 4 vols. (Paris, 1864–1876)

Throughout the book, small letters refer to notes by the authors of the individual selections, arabic numerals to editor's notes.

Contents

I
THE GREEK VIEW OF MUSIC

1. Plato — *From the* Republic   *page*   3
2. Aristotle — *From the* Politics   13
3. Aristoxenus — *From the* Harmonic Elements   25
4. Cleonides — Harmonic Introduction   34
5. Athenaeus — *From the* Sophists at Dinner   47

II
THE EARLY CHRISTIAN VIEW OF MUSIC

6. Clement of Alexandria — *From the* Exhortation to the Greeks   59
7. St. Basil — *From the* Homily on the First Psalm   64
8. St. John Chrysostom — *From the* Exposition of Psalm XLI   67
9. St. Jerome — *From the* Commentary on the Epistle of Paul to the Ephesians   71
10. St. Augustine — *From the* Confessions   73

III
MUSIC AS A LIBERAL ART

11. Boethius — *From the* De institutione musica   79
12. Cassiodorus — *From the* Institutiones   87
13. Isidore of Seville — *From the* Etymologiarum   93

IV
MUSICAL THEORY IN THE MIDDLE AGES

14. Odo of Cluny — Enchiridion musices   103
15. Guido of Arezzo — Prologus antiphonarii sui   117

16. Guido of Arezzo — Epistola de ignoto cantu   121
17. Anonymous — *From the* Scholia enchiriadis   126
18. Franco of Cologne — Ars cantus mensurabilis   139
19. Marchetto da Padua — *From the* Pomerium   160
20. Jean de Muris — *From the* Ars novae musicae   172
21. Jacob of Liége — *From the* Speculum musicae   180

V

MUSICAL THEORISTS OF THE RENAISSANCE

22. Joannes Tinctoris — Proportionale musices — *Dedication*   193
23. Joannes Tinctoris — Liber de arte contrapuncti — *Dedication*   197
24. Bartolomé Ramos — *From the* Musica practica   200
25. Pietro Aron — *From the* Trattato della natura e cognizione di tutti
    gli toni di canto figurato   205
26. Heinrich Glarean — *From the* Dodecachordon   219
27. Gioseffe Zarlino — *From the* Istituzioni armoniche   228
28. Pietro Cerone — *From* El melopeo y maestro   262
29. Thomas Morley — *From* A Plain and Easy Introduction to Prac-
    tical Music   274

VI

MUSIC IN RENAISSANCE LIFE AND THOUGHT

30. Baldassare Castiglione — *From* Il cortegiano   281
31. Pierre de Ronsard — Livre des mélanges — *Dedication*   286
32. Giovanni de' Bardi — Discorso mandato a Giulio Caccini   290
33. Vincenzo Galilei — *From the* Dialogo della musica antica e della
    moderna   302
34. G. P. da Palestrina — Motettorum liber quartus — *Dedication*   323
35. Orlando di Lasso — Cantiones sacrae of 1593 — *Dedication*   325
36. William Byrd—Gradualia — *Dedications and forewords*   327
37. Henry Peacham — *From* The Compleat Gentleman   331

VII

REFORMATION AND COUNTER-REFORMATION

38. Martin Luther — Wittemberg Gesangbuch — *Foreword to the first
    edition*   341

39. Johann Walther — Wittemberg Gesangbuch — *Foreword to the revised edition* 343
40. Jean Calvin — Geneva Psalter — *Foreword* 345
41. Claude Goudimel — Geneva Psalter — *Foreword to the edition of 1565* 349
42. Thomas Cranmer — Letter to Henry VIII 350
43. Thomas East — The Whole Book of Psalms — *Dedication and preface* 352
44. Jacob de Kerle — Preces speciales — *Dedication* 355
45. Pope Gregory XIII — Brief on the Reform of the Chant 357

VIII

"SECONDA PRATICA" AND "STILE RAPPRESENTATIVO"

46. Pietro de' Bardi — Letter to G. B. Doni 363
47. Ottavio Rinuccini — Euridice — *Dedication* 367
48. Giulio Caccini — Euridice — *Dedication* 370
49. Jacopo Peri — Euridice — *Foreword* 373
50. Giulio Caccini — Le nuove musiche — *Foreword* 377
51. G. M. Artusi — *From* L'Artusi, ovvero, Delle imperfezioni della moderna musica 393
52. Claudio Monteverdi — Il quinto libro de' madrigali — *Foreword with the "Declaration" of His Brother G. C. Monteverdi* 405
53. Claudio Monteverdi — Madrigali guerrieri ed amorosi — *Foreword* 413

IX

MUSICAL PRACTICE IN THE BAROQUE AGE

54. Lodovico Grossi da Viadana — Cento concerti ecclesiastici — *Preface* 419
55. Agostino Agazzari — Del sonare sopra il basso 424
56. Heinrich Schütz — Symphoniae sacrae — *Dedications and forewords* 432
57. Georg Muffat — Florilegia *and* Auserlesene Instrumental-Music — *Forewords* 442
58. F. E. Niedt — Musikalische Handleitung — *Foreword* 453

xii   CONTENTS
OPERATIC RIVALRY IN FRANCE: PRO AND CONTRA LULLY
59. François Raguenet — Parallèle des Italiens et des Français   473
60. Le Cerf de La Viéville, Seigneur de Freneuse — *From the* Comparaison de la musique italienne et de la musique française   489
CRITICAL VIEWS OF ITALIAN OPERA: ADDISON AND MARCELLO
61. Joseph Addison — *From* The Spectator   511
62. Benedetto Marcello — *From* Il teatro alla moda   518
THE REFORMULATION OF THE THEORY OF HARMONY AND COUNTERPOINT
63. J. J. Fux — *From the* Gradus ad Parnassum   535
64. J. P. Rameau — *From the* Traité de l'harmonie   564
THE TRANSITION TO THE MUSICAL PRACTICE OF THE CLASSICAL PERIOD
65. J. J. Quantz — *From the* Versuch einer Anweisung die Flöte traversière zu spielen   577
66. Leopold Mozart — *From the* Versuch einer gründlichen Violinschule   599
67. C. P. E. Bach — *From the* Versuch über die wahre Art, das Clavier zu spielen   609
OPERATIC RIVALRY IN FRANCE: THE "QUERELLE DES BOUFFONS"
68. F. W. von Grimm — Le petit prophète de Boehmisch-Broda   619
69. J. J. Rousseau — Lettre sur la musique française   636

XV

CRITICAL VIEWS OF ITALIAN OPERA: ALGAROTTI AND GLUCK

70. Francesco Algarotti — *From the* Saggio sopra l'opera in musica   657
71. C. W. von Gluck — Alceste — *Dedication*   673
72. F. L. Du Roullet — Letter to M. d'Auvergne   676
73. C. W. von Gluck — Letter to the Editor of the "Mercure de France"   681

XVI

THE EUROPEAN SCENE

74. Charles Burney — *From* The Present State of Music in France and Italy   687
75. J. F. Reichardt — *From the* Briefe eines aufmerksamen Reisenden   699
76. A. E. M. Grétry — *From the* Mémoires   711
77. J. F. Reichardt—*From the* Briefe geschrieben auf einer Reise nach Wien   728

XVII

LITERARY FORERUNNERS OF MUSICAL ROMANTICISM

78. Jean Paul — *From the* Vorschule der Aesthetik   743
79. W. H. Wackenroder — The Remarkable Musical Life of the Musician Joseph Berglinger   750
80. Jean Paul—*From the* Hesperus   764
81. E. T. A. Hoffmann — Beethoven's Instrumental Music   775
82. E. T. A. Hoffmann — The Poet and the Composer   782

XVIII

COMPOSER-CRITICS OF THE NINETEENTH CENTURY

83. C. M. von Weber — On the Opera "Undine"   801
84. Hector Berlioz — Rossini's "William Tell"   808
85. Robert Schumann — Davidsbündlerblätter   827
86. Franz Liszt — *From* Berlioz and His "Harold" Symphony   846
87. Richard Wagner — *From* Das Kunstwerk der Zukunft   874
Index   905

Foreword

THIS BOOK began as an attempt to carry out a suggestion made in 1929 by Carl Engel in his *Views and Reviews*—to fulfil his wish for "a living record of musical personalities, events, conditions, tastes . . . a history of music faithfully and entirely carved from contemporary accounts." It owes something, too, to the well-known compilations of Kinsky and Schering and rather more, perhaps, to Andrea della Corte's *Antologia della storia della musica* and to an evaluation of this, its first model, by Alfred Einstein.

In its present form, however, it is neither the book that Engel asked for nor a literary anthology precisely comparable to the pictorial and musical ones of Kinsky and Schering, still less an English version of its Italian predecessor, with which it no longer has much in common. It departs from Engel's ideal scheme in that it has, at bottom, a practical purpose—to make conveniently accessible to the teacher or student of the history of music those things which he must eventually read. Historical documents being what they are, it inevitably lacks the seemingly unbroken continuity of Kinsky and Schering; at the same time, and for the same reason, it contains far more that is unique and irreplaceable than either of these. Unlike della Corte's book it restricts itself to historical documents as such, excluding the writing of present-day historians; aside from this, it naturally includes more translations, fewer original documents, and while recognizing that the somewhat limited scope of the *Antologia* was wholly appropriate in a book on music addressed to Italian readers, it seeks to take a broader view.

That, at certain moments in its development, music has been a subject of widespread and lively contemporary interest, calling forth a flood of documentation, while at other moments, perhaps not less critical, the records are either silent or unrevealing—this is in no way remarkable, for it is inherent in the very nature of music, of letters, and of history. The beginnings of the classical symphony and string quartet passed virtually unnoticed as developments without interest for the literary man; the beginnings of the opera and cantata, developments which concerned him immediately and deeply, were heralded and reviewed in documents so numerous that, even in a book of this size, it has been possible to include only the most significant. Thus, as already suggested, a documentary history of music cannot properly exhibit even the degree of continuity that is possible for an iconographic one or a collection of musical monuments, still less the degree expected of an interpretation. For this reason, too, I have rejected the simple chronological arrangement as inappropriate and misleading and have preferred to allow the documents to arrange themselves naturally under the various topics chronologically ordered in the Table of Contents and the book itself, some of these admirably precise, others perhaps rather too inclusive. As Engel shrewdly anticipated, the frieze has turned out to be incomplete, and I have left the gaps unfilled, as he wished.

For much the same reason, I have not sought to give the book a spurious unity by imposing upon it a particular point of view. At one time it is the musician himself who has the most revealing thing to say; at another time he lets someone else do the talking for him. And even when the musician speaks it is not always the composer who speaks most clearly; sometimes it is the theorist, at other times the performer. If this means that few readers will find the book uniformly interesting, it ought also to mean that "the changing patterns of life," as Engel called them, will be the more fully and the more faithfully reflected.

At the same time the book has of itself a natural unity and continuity of another sort. From Plato's characterization of music in the third book of his *Republic*, criticized by Aristotle and later referred to as authoritative by Zarlino, Bardi, Caccini, and the brothers Monteverdi, to the musical rhapsodies of Jean Paul and E. T. A. Hoffmann, quoted with approval by Liszt-Wittgenstein, these readings bring out with telling effect the dependence of man upon man, of age upon age. Isidore of Seville lifts whole passages bodily from Cassiodorus; Guido of Arezzo commends Odo's *Enchiridion* to his readers; Marchetto da Padua and Jean de Muris take Franco of Cologne and his *Ars cantus mensurabilis* as their point of departure; Peri quotes Aristoxenus and is quoted in turn by Algarotti; Jacob of Liége quarrels with Jean de Muris, Galilei with Zarlino, Monteverdi with Artusi, the Seigneur de Freneuse with the Abbé Raguenet. Thus in many instances one selection completes and justifies another. But even where this is not the case, the inclusion of a particular author, sometimes even of a particular selection, was often inevitable. Without Boethius, without Quantz, Leopold Mozart, and C. P. E. Bach, without Tinctoris and his historical asides, without the dedication of the *Alceste*, no book of this kind could prove really useful. This does not mean, however, that the entire contents of the book is of this order. In certain cases another selection or another author might have served equally well. Where this is true, the final choice was seldom made without considerable experiment, so that for this part of the contents the number of rejected items is considerably greater than the number now published. In general, the aim has been to do justice to every age without giving to any a disproportionate share of the space.

It was never my intention to compile a musical Bartlett, and I have accordingly sought, wherever possible, to include the complete text of the selection chosen, or—failing this—the complete text of a continuous, self-contained, and independently intelligible passage or series of passages, with or without regard for the chapter divisions of the original. But in a few cases I have made cuts to eliminate digressions or to avoid needless repetitions of things equally well said by earlier writers; in other cases the excessive length and involved construction of the original has forced me to abridge, reducing the scale of the whole while retaining the essential continuity of the argument. All cuts are clearly indicated, either by a row of dots or in annotations.

Of the eighty-seven items which the book includes, only six (29, 37, 42, 43, 61, and 74) were originally written in English. Here and there (30, 50, 59, and 70) it proved possible to use a contemporary translation, and where satisfactory modern translations were available (chiefly for a part of the contents of Chapters I and II, but also for single items in Chapters IX and XV), these have always been given the preference. In a few instances, satisfactory English versions became available only after I had made my own—in particular those of Fux by Alfred Mann (1943), of Schumann by Paul Rosenfeld (1946), of Marcello by R. G. Pauly (1948), of Leopold Mozart by Editha Knocker (1948), and of C. P. E. Bach by William J. Mitchell (1949). Even so, about three-fourths of the book consists of writings not previously published in English translation, or hitherto published only in unsatisfactory versions, some of them grotesquely inadequate.

In the translations here published for the first time, I have sought above all to find for every age and for every man an individual solution, accurate and appropriate. Reichardt writes in one style in 1774, in quite another one in 1810; if this is due in part to the formal differences between his two books and to the natural differences between the writing of a man barely twenty and a man nearly sixty, it is also due in part to the unparalleled political, social, and cultural changes that had taken place in the intervening thirty to forty years and to their effect upon the outlook, personality, and literary style of a man whom they had profoundly stirred. And just as one can often recognize a certain general affinity between the musical and literary styles of a particular time, so—whether one thinks of Lassus or Monteverdi, or Schütz or Muffat, of Rameau or Grétry, of Berlioz, Schumann, or Wagner—one can often recognize a more specific affinity between the musical and literary styles of a particular individual. To have sought to find a common denominator for these characteristic modes of expression would have been to falsify and to rob the book of a part of its potential usefulness. For much the same reason I have not sought to cover up or gloss over the plain fact that among the influential writers on music there have been some who were long-winded and pompous, some who were quarrelsome and malicious, some who were barely literate, some who were ill-informed, just as there have also been musicians whose literary gifts equalled or surpassed their gifts as composers or performers.

Particularly in the chapters devoted to ancient and medieval authors, the translation of technical terms proved a major difficulty. Certain of the older terms are lacking in precision; for others the exact meaning is controversial; sometimes an older writer defines a term for us in the light of its real or fancied etymology; at other times the etymological meaning of a term helps us to understand what an older writer has said or why he has said it. Among later authors, Zarlino and Rameau have evolved individual terminologies with which it would be useless and even hazardous to tamper. Thus, with a view to sparing the reader the necessity for constant reference to the original texts, and in order to avoid translations in the light of this or that hypothesis, useful to few, it has seemed wisest to allow each author to use his own terminology, however inconsistent, even though this has meant that in the earlier part of the book such words as "harmony," "melody," "system," "symphony," and "modulation" will be found in unusual or wholly unprecedented meanings. Names of instruments, too, have generally been left untranslated unless a completely satisfactory English equivalent presented itself. I am particularly grateful to the Clarendon Press and to the Harvard University Press, as representatives of the Loeb Classical Library, for having permitted me, in reprinting translations from Plato, Aristotle, Aristoxenus, Athenaeus, and Clement of Alexandria, to alter an occasional word or two with a view to bringing these translations into agreement with my general policy.

Still more debatable, perhaps, is my retention of other features of ancient and medieval terminology—of the designations "diatessaron," "diapente," and "diapason," and of the Guidonian nomenclature for the notes of the several hexachords. But being obliged, in any case, to retain the ancient and medieval names of the proportions and of the figures of the mensural notation, I have not wished to introduce an incongruous element.

In compensation I have used modern English and foreign spelling throughout, excepting in those rare cases where the retention of an archaic spelling seemed distinctly preferable. For the musical examples I have used modern clefs, excepting for plainsongs and for examples illustrating the use of the mensural notation, and, when the sense of the music seemed to require it, I have reduced the note-values. In Chapters VIII and IX, the realizations of the thorough basses are my own, excepting for Agazzari's third and final illustration, which was worked out by the author himself.

In determining what and how to annotate I have tried to steer a middle course, avoiding the all-too-obvious on the one hand and the excessively technical on the other. I have thought it my duty to identify the sources of most quotations and allusions and to explain each author's references to other parts of his writings. Here and there I have attempted to clarify a difficult passage, and when it seemed to me that no translation could adequately convey an author's meaning, I have often provided a note setting forth what I took his meaning to be. But I have not thought it appropriate to tire the reader by repeating familiar definitions and biographical data easily found in any dictionary of music. Nor have I thought it worthwhile, in Chapters IV and V, to provide text-critical footnotes enumerating the dozens of conjectural emendations required for the translations from the musical theorists of the tenth to fifteenth centuries. In their own day, the monumental collections of medieval writings on music published by Gerbert (1784) and Coussemaker (1864 to 1876) were notable—indeed heroic—achievements. This is not the place to point out their shortcomings.

Without the lively encouragement and patient sympathy of the late William Warder Norton my work on this book would never have been begun. Nor is it at all likely that I would ever have finished it without the active collaboration of my father, William Strunk, Jr., Emeritus Professor of English at Cornell University, whose expert assistance and sound advice were constantly at my disposal during the earlier stages of its preparation and who continued to follow my work on it with the keenest interest until 1946, the year of his death. A considerable number of the translations now published for the first time are largely his work [1] and there are few to which he did not make some improving contribution.

My warmest thanks are due to Professor Otto Kinkeldey, of Cornell University, and to Professor Alfred Einstein, of Smith College, for their extraordinary kindness in consenting to read the entire book in proof and for the many indispensable corrections and suggestions that they have sent me; again to Alfred Einstein, and to Paul Hindemith, for a number of constructive recommendations which grew out of their experiments with sections of the manuscript in connection with their teaching; likewise to Donald C. Mackenzie of the Department of Classics at Princeton University, who was good enough to go over with me my translation from Cleonides, and to my old friends Paul Lang, Arthur Mendel, and Erich Hertzmann, who have always been ready to listen and to advise.

Acknowledgment is due, also, to Dr. Dragan Plamenac, who prepared the greater number of the brief biographical notes which accompany the single readings; to Harvey Olnick, for his excellent notes on the selections by Grimm, Rousseau, and Grétry; to two of my students—Philip Keppler, Jr., who relieved me of some part of the proofreading and J. W. Kerman, who prepared the index; to Gordon Mapes, for his careful work on the autographing of the musical examples; and to Miss Katherine Barnard, Miss Florence Williams, and the entire staff of W. W. Norton & Co., Inc., for their unflagging interest and innumerable kindnesses.

Often, in the course of my reading, I have run across memorable things said by writers on music which, for one reason or another, were not suited for inclusion in the body of this book. One of these, however, is eminently suited for inclusion here. It is by Thomas Morley, and it reads as follows:

> But as concerning the book itself, if I had, before I began it, imagined half the pains and labor which it cost me, I would sooner have been persuaded to anything than to have taken in hand such a tedious piece of work, like unto a great sea, which the further I entered into, the more I saw before me unpassed; so that at length, despairing ever to make an end (seeing that grow so big in mine hands which I thought to have shut up in two or three sheets of paper), I laid it aside, in full determination to have proceeded no further but to have left it off as shamefully as it was foolishly begun. But then being admonished by some of my friends that it were pity to lose the fruits of the employment of so many good hours, and how justly I should be condemned of ignorant presump-

---

1 Largely his are the following: Items 7, 12 and 13, 22 and 23, 31, 34 to 36, 41, 44, 60, 62, 68 and 69, 72 and 73, 76; partly his are   Items 11, 14, 21, 32 and 33, 40, 46 to 53, 55 and 56, 63.

tion—in taking that in hand which I could not perform—if I did not go forward, I resolved to endure whatsoever pain, labor, loss of time and expense, and what not? rather than to leave that unbrought to an end in the which I was so far engulfed.

OLIVER STRUNK

The American Academy in Rome

I

The Greek View of Music

1. Plato

The great ancient Greek philosopher was born in 427 B.C. and died in 347 B.C. He must be considered the real founder of a philosophy of the arts in the modern sense of the word, although he derived his main ideas and method from the teachings of his eminent master Socrates.

After Socrates' death in 399 B.C., Plato started on extensive journeys, in the course of which he studied with Euclid. But he soon returned to Athens and began his career as a philosopher with writings in which he attacked the fallacious ideas on education propagated by the sophists. A crowd of students and enthusiastic followers gathered around him. About 390 Plato went to Sicily to become thoroughly acquainted with the Pythagorean doctrine and was well received at the court of Dionysius of Syracuse. After various unpleasant experiences, however, Plato returned to Athens, where he founded the so-called "Academy," a kind of school of higher studies, and spent his later life in restless scientific activity.

Plato's chief philosophical writings are not written in systematic form but take the shape of highly poetic and often dramatically vivid dialogues. The important figures of Greek public life in Plato's time make their appearance in them as representatives of their respective ideas. Socrates is regularly introduced as the moderator. One of the most famous dialogues from Plato's mature period is the one entitled *The Republic*. In this work the philosopher expounds his ideas about the organization of the ideal state. In such a state, as Plato conceives it, education is paramount and art derives its main value as a means of attaining this educational ideal. In this connection, Plato regards music as highly important; its lofty purpose is to serve, not for superficial entertainment, but to help in building up a harmonious personality and in calming the human passions.

From the Republic [1]

"And now, my friend," said I, "we may say that we have completely finished the part of music that concerns speeches and tales. For we have set forth what is to be said and how it is to be said." "I think so too," he replied.

10. "After this, then," said I, "comes the manner of songs and melodies?" "Obviously." "And having gone thus far, could not everybody discover what we must say of their character in order to conform to what has already been said?" "I am afraid that 'everybody' does not include me," laughed Glaucon; "I cannot sufficiently divine offhand what we ought to say, though I have a suspicion." "You certainly, I presume," said I, "have a sufficient understanding of this—that the melody is composed of three things, the words, the harmony, and the rhythm?" [2] "Yes," said he, "that much." "And so far as it is words, it surely in no manner differs from words not sung in the requirement of conformity to the patterns and manner that we have prescribed?" "True," he said. "And again, the harmony and the rhythm must follow the words." "Of course." "But we said we did not require dirges and lamentations in words." "We do not." "What, then, are the dirge-like harmonies? Tell me, for you are a musician." [3]

---

1 Text: *The Republic*, I (London, W. Heinemann, 1930), 245–269, 287–295. Translated for the Loeb Classical Library by Paul Shorey. Reprinted by permission of Harvard University Press.

The speaker is the Platonic Socrates; in this discussion of the place of music in the education of the "guardians" he addresses himself to Glaucon, son of Ariston.

2 Cf. "And again, the harmony and the rhythm must follow the words"; "The rhythm and harmony follow the words and not the words these" (pp. 4 and 7 below). These remarks of Plato's are frequently cited in the sixteenth and seventeenth centuries as arguments against what Monteverdi calls "The First Practice"; see pp. 256, 295, 378, 406 note d, and 414 below.

3 In the passage that follows, Plato enumerates six "harmonies," four of which he rejects on ethical grounds as unsuited for use in education. It should be read in the light of the comments of Aristotle in his *Politics* (1340B, 1341B–1342B, pp. 19, 23–24 below) and of Plutarch in his *De musica* (1136C–1137A).

The "harmonies" in question are precisely defined for us by Aristides Quintilianus, who writes them out in the vocal and instrumental notations

in the first book of his *De musica* (Meibom, pp. 21–22), where he has this to say of them:

"There are also other divisions of the tetrachord, and these the very oldest of the ancients used as harmonies. Sometimes they filled out the complete octochord; occasionally there was one that exceeded the scale of six tones; often there was one that fell short of it. For they did not always include all the notes; later on we shall give the reason why.

"To the Lydian scale they gave this form: diesis, ditone, tone, diesis, diesis, ditone, diesis; this was the complete scale.

"The Dorian had this form: tone, diesis, diesis, ditone, tone, diesis, diesis, ditone; this exceeded the diapason by a tone.

"The Phrygian had this form: tone, diesis, diesis, ditone, tone, diesis, diesis, tone; this was a complete diapason.

"To the Iastian they gave this form: diesis, diesis, ditone, trihemitone, tone; this fell short of the diapason by a tone.

"The Mixolydian had this form: two successive dieses, tone, tone, diesis, diesis, tritone; this was the complete scale.

"The so-called intense Lydian had this form: diesis, diesis, ditone, trihemitone.

"The Mixolydian," he said, "and the intense Lydian, and others similar to them." "These, then," said I, "we must do away with. For they are useless even to women who are to make the best of themselves, let alone to men." "Assuredly." "But again, drunkenness is a thing most unbefitting guardians, and so is softness and sloth." "Yes." "What, then, are the soft and convivial harmonies?" "There are certain Ionian and also Lydian ones that are called relaxed." "Will you make any use of them for warriors?" "None at all," he said; "but it would seem that you have left the Dorian and the Phrygian." "I don't know the harmonies," I said, "but leave us that [4] harmony that would fittingly imitate the utterances and the accents of a brave man who is engaged in warfare [5] or in any enforced business, and who, when he has failed, either meeting wounds or death or having fallen into some other mishap, in all these conditions confronts fortune with steadfast endurance and repels her strokes. And another for such a man engaged in works of peace, not enforced but voluntary, either trying to persuade somebody of something and imploring him—whether it be a god, through prayer, or a man, by teaching and admonition—or contrariwise yielding himself to another who is petitioning or teaching him or trying to change his opinions, and in consequence faring according to his wish, and not bearing himself arrogantly, but in all this acting modestly and moderately and acquiescing in the outcome. Leave us these two harmonies—the enforced and the voluntary—that will best imitate

"Thus the enharmonic diesis was to be heard in them all.

"To make things clear, a diagram of the scales is given below.

| LYDIAN |
| DORIAN |
| PHRYGIAN |
| IASTIAN |
| MIXOLYDIAN |
| SYNTONOLYDIAN |

"It is of these scales that the divine Plato speaks in his Republic, where he says that the Mixolydian and intense Lydian are dirge-like and the Iastian and Lydian convivial and too relaxed. Then he adds: 'You seem to be leaving out the Dorian and Phrygian.'

"For it was in this way that the ancients sought to explain their harmonies, matching the qualities of the sounds to the given material of the moral characters. On this point we shall speak more precisely later on."

For discussions of this testimony of Aristides, see J. F. Mountford's essays "Greek Music in Its Relation to Modern Times," in Journal of Hellenic Studies, XL (1920), 13–42 (especially 24–28), and "The Musical Scales of Plato's Republic," in Classical Quarterly, XVII (1923), 125–136; also R. P. Winnington-Ingram, Mode in Ancient Greek Music (Cambridge, 1936), pp. 21–30. Mountford, calling attention to Plutarch, De musica, 1136E, suggests that Aristides may have derived his information from the lost De musica of Aristoxenus; Winnington-Ingram connects the passage with the later remarks of Aristides (Meibom, pp. 95–96) on the nature of the harmonies "handed down" by Damon, Plato's authority in musical matters.

The testimony of Aristides is, of course, irreconcilable with the "pure-key view" of Greek music, and it is accordingly rejected as based upon forgery or misunderstanding by Monro, The Modes of Ancient Greek Music (Oxford, 1894), pp. 94–100, and Gombosi, Tonarten und Stimmungen der antiken Musik (Copenhagen, 1939), pp. 111–113.

4 ἐκείνην (that) may mean, but does not say, Dorian. [Shorey]

5 Monteverdi tells us (p. 413 below) that this characterization of the harmony suited to the brave man engaged in warfare prompted his discovery of the stile concitato.

the utterances of men failing or succeeding, the temperate, the brave—leave us these." "Well," said he, "you are asking me to leave none other than those I just spoke of." "Then," said I, "we shall not need in our songs and melodies an instrument of many strings or one on which all the harmonies can be played." "Not in my opinion," said he. "Then we shall not maintain makers of the trigonon, the pectis, or any other instrument which has many strings and can be played in many harmonies." "Apparently not." "Well, will you admit to the city makers and players of the aulos? Or is not the aulos the most 'many-stringed' of instruments and do not the pan-harmonics themselves imitate it?" "Clearly," he said. "You have left," said I, "the lyre and the cithara. These are useful in the city, and in the fields the shepherds would have a syrinx to pipe on." "So our argument indicates," he said. "We are not innovating, my friend, in preferring Apollo and the instruments of Apollo to Marsyas and his instruments." "No, by heaven!" he said, "I think not." "And by the dog," said I, "we have all unawares purged the city which a little while ago we said was wanton." "In that we show our good sense," he said.

11. "Come then, let us complete the purification. For upon harmonies would follow the consideration of rhythms: we must not pursue complexity nor great variety in the basic movements, but must observe what are the rhythms of a life that is orderly and brave, and after observing them require the foot and the melody to conform to that kind of man's speech and not the speech to the foot and the melody. What those rhythms would be, it is for you to tell us as you did the harmonies." "Nay, in faith," he said, "I cannot tell. For that there are some three forms from which the feet are combined, just as there are four in the notes of the voice whence come all harmonies, is a thing that I have observed and could tell. But which are imitations of which sort of life, I am unable to say." "Well," said I, "on this point we will take counsel with Damon, too,[6] as to which are the feet appropriate to illiberality, and insolence or madness or other evils, and what rhythms we must leave for their opposites; and I believe I have heard him obscurely speaking of a foot that he called the enoplios,[7] a composite foot, and a dactyl and an heroic foot, which he arranged, I know not how, to be equal up and down in the interchange of long and short,[8] and unless I am mistaken he used the term iambic, and there was another foot that he called the trochaic, and he added the quantities long

---

6 Damon (see p. 4 above, note 3), the leading Athenian authority on music in Plato's time, is mentioned again in Book IV of the *Republic* (424C) as one who holds that musical styles cannot be disturbed without unsettling fundamental political and social conventions. There are further references to him in Plato's *Alcibiades I* (118C) and *Laches* (200B).
7 Literally "in armor"—the rhythm of a warlike dance.
8 Cf. the discussion of warlike and peaceful dancing in the *Laws*, 815E–816D.

and short. And in some of these, I believe, he censured and commended the tempo of the foot no less than the rhythm itself, or else some combination of the two; I can't say. But, as I said, let this matter be postponed for Damon's consideration. For to determine the truth of these would require no little discourse. Do you think otherwise?" "No, by heaven, I do not." "But this you are able to determine—that seemliness and unseemliness are attendant upon the good rhythm and the bad." "Of course." "And, further, that good rhythm and bad rhythm accompany, the one fair diction, assimilating itself thereto, and the other the opposite, and so of the apt and the unapt, if, as we were just now saying, the rhythm and harmony follow the words and not the words these." "They certainly must follow the words," he said. "And what of the manner of the diction, and the speech?" said I. "Do they not follow and conform to the disposition of the soul?" "Of course." "And all the rest to the diction?" "Yes." "Good speech, then, good accord, and good grace, and good rhythm wait upon a good disposition, not that weakness of head which we euphemistically style goodness of heart, but the truly good and fair disposition of the character and the mind." "By all means," he said. "And must not our youth pursue these everywhere if they are to do what it is truly theirs to do?" "They must indeed." "And there is surely much of these qualities in painting and in all similar craftsmanship—weaving is full of them and embroidery and architecture and likewise the manufacture of household furnishings and thereto the natural bodies of animals and plants as well. For in all these there is grace or gracelessness. And gracelessness and evil rhythm and disharmony are akin to evil speaking and the evil temper, but the opposites are the symbols and the kin of the opposites, the sober and good disposition." "Entirely so," he said.

12. "Is it, then, only the poets that we must supervise and compel to embody in their poems the semblance of the good character or else not write poetry among us, or must we keep watch over the other craftsmen, and forbid them to represent the evil disposition, the licentious, the illiberal, the graceless, either in the likeness of living creatures or in buildings or in any other product of their art, on penalty, if unable to obey, of being forbidden to practise their art among us, that our guardians may not be bred among symbols of evil, as it were in a pasturage of poisonous herbs, lest gazing freely and cropping from many such day by day they little by little and all unawares accumulate and build up a huge mass of evil in their own souls. But we must look for those craftsmen who by the happy gift of nature are capable of following the trail of true beauty and grace, that our young men, dwelling as it were in a salubrious region, may

receive benefit from all things about them, whence the influence that emanates from works of beauty may waft itself to eye or ear like a breeze that brings from wholesome places health, and so from earliest childhood insensibly guide them to likeness, to friendship, to harmony with beautiful reason." "Yes," he said, "that would be far the best education for them." "And is it not for this reason, Glaucon," said I, "that education in music is most sovereign, because more than anything else rhythm and harmony find their way to the inmost soul and take strongest hold upon it, bringing with them and imparting grace, if one is rightly trained, and otherwise the contrary? And further, because omissions and the failure of beauty in things badly made or grown would be most quickly perceived by one who was properly educated in music, and so, feeling distaste rightly, he would praise beautiful things and take delight in them and receive them into his soul to foster its growth and become himself beautiful and good. The ugly he would rightly disapprove of and hate while still young and yet unable to apprehend the reason, but when reason came the man thus nurtured would be the first to give her welcome, for by this affinity he would know her." "I certainly think," he said, "that such is the cause of education in music." "It is, then," said I, "as it was when we learned our letters and felt that we knew them sufficiently only when the separate letters did not elude us, appearing as few elements in all the combinations that convey them, and when we did not disregard them in small things or great and think it unnecessary to recognize them, but were eager to distinguish them everywhere, in the belief that we should never be literate and letter-perfect till we could do this." "True." "And is it not also true that if there are any likenesses of letters reflected in water or mirrors, we shall never know them until we know the originals, but such knowledge belongs to the same art and discipline?" "By all means." "Then, by heaven, am I not right in saying that by the same token we shall never be true musicians, either—neither we nor the guardians that we have undertaken to educate—until we are able to recognize the forms of soberness, courage, liberality, and high-mindedness and all their kindred and their opposites, too, in all the combinations that contain and convey them, and to apprehend them and their images wherever found, disregarding them neither in trifles nor in great things, but believing the knowledge of them to belong to the same art and discipline?" "The conclusion is inevitable," he said. "Then," said I, "when there is a coincidence of a beautiful disposition in the soul and corresponding and harmonious beauties of the same type in the bodily form—is not this the fairest spectacle for one who is capable of its contemplation?" "Far the fairest." "And surely the fairest is the most lovable." "Of course." "The true musician, then, would love by preference persons of this sort; but if there were disharmony he would not love this." "No," he said, "not if there was a defect in the soul; but if it were in the body he would bear with it and still be willing to bestow his love." "I understand," I said, "that you have or have had favorites of this sort and I grant your distinction. But tell me this—can there be any communion between soberness and extravagant pleasure?" "How could there be," he said, "since such pleasure puts a man beside himself no less than pain?" "Or between it and virtue generally?" "By no means." "But is there between pleasure and insolence and license?" "Most assuredly." "Do you know of greater or keener pleasure than that associated with Aphrodite?" "I don't," he said, "nor yet of any more insane." "But is not the right love a sober and harmonious love of the orderly and the beautiful?" "It is indeed," said he. "Then nothing of madness, nothing akin to license, must be allowed to come nigh the right love?" "No." "Then this kind of pleasure may not come nigh, nor may lover and beloved who rightly love and are loved have anything to do with it?" "No, by heaven, Socrates," he said, "it must not come nigh them." "Thus, then, as it seems, you will lay down the law in the city that we are founding, that the lover may kiss and pass the time with and touch the beloved as a father would a son, for honorable ends, if he persuade him. But otherwise he must so associate with the objects of his care that there should never be any suspicion of anything further, on penalty of being stigmatized for want of taste and true musical culture." "Even so," he said. "Do you not agree, then, that our discourse on music has come to an end? It has certainly made a fitting end, for surely the end and consummation of culture is the love of the beautiful." "I concur," he said.

13. "After music our youth are to be educated by gymnastics?" "Certainly." "In this too they must be carefully trained from boyhood through life, and the way of it is this, I believe; but consider it yourself too. For I, for my part, do not believe that a sound body by its excellence makes the soul good, but on the contrary that a good soul by its virtue renders the body the best that is possible. What is your opinion?" "I think so too." "Then if we should sufficiently train the mind and turn over to it the minutiae of the care of the body, and content ourselves with merely indicating the norms or patterns, not to make a long story of it, we should be acting rightly?" "By all means." "From intoxication we said that they

must abstain. For a guardian is surely the last person in the world to whom it is allowable to get drunk and not know where on earth he is." "Yes," he said, "it would be absurd that a guardian should need a guard." "What next about their food? These men are athletes in the greatest of contests, are they not?" "Yes." "Is, then, the bodily habit of the athletes we see about us suitable for such?" "Perhaps." "Nay," said I, "that is a drowsy habit and precarious for health. Don't you observe that they sleep away their lives, and that if they depart ever so little from their prescribed regimen these athletes are liable to great and violent diseases?" "I do." "Then," said I, "we need some more ingenious form of training for our athletes of war, since these must be as it were sleepless hounds, and have the keenest possible perceptions of sight and hearing, and in their campaigns undergo many changes in their drinking water, their food, and in exposure to the heat of the sun and to storms, without disturbance of their health." "I think so." "Would not, then, the best gymnastics be akin to the music that we were just now describing?" "What do you mean?" "It would be a simple and flexible gymnastic, and especially so in the training for war." "In what way?" "One could learn that," said I, "even from Homer. For you are aware that in the banqueting of the heroes on campaign he does not feast them on fish, though they are at the sea-side on the Hellespont, nor on boiled meat, but only on roast, which is what soldiers could most easily procure. For everywhere, one may say, it is of easier provision to use the bare fire than to convey pots and pans along." "Indeed it is." "Neither, as I believe, does Homer ever make mention of sweetmeats. Is not that something which all men in training understand—that if one is to keep his body in good condition he must abstain from such things altogether?" "They are right," he said, "in that they know it and do abstain." "Then, my friend, if you think this is the right way, you apparently do not approve of a Syracusan table and Sicilian variety of made dishes." "I think not." "You would frown, then, on a little Corinthian maid as the *chère amie* of men who were to keep themselves fit?" "Most certainly." "And also on the seeming delights of Attic pastry?" "Inevitably." "In general, I take it, if we likened that kind of food and regimen to music and song expressed in the 'pan-harmonic' and in every variety of rhythm it would be a fair comparison." "Quite so." "And there variety engendered licentiousness, did it not, but here disease? While simplicity in music begets sobriety in the souls, and in gymnastic training it begets health in bodies." "Most true," he said. "And when licentiousness and disease multiply in a city, are not many courts of law and dispensaries opened, and the arts of chicane and medicine give themselves airs when even free men in great numbers take them very seriously?" "How can they help it?" he said.

. . . . .

"And so your youths," said I, "employing that simple music which we said engendered sobriety will, it is clear, guard themselves against falling into the need of the justice of the courtroom." "Yes," he said. "And will not our musician, pursuing the same trail in his use of gymnastics, if he please, get to have no need of medicine save when indispensable?" "I think so." "And even the exercises and toils of gymnastics he will undertake with a view to the spirited part of his nature to arouse that rather than for mere strength, unlike ordinary athletes, who treat diet and exercise only as a means to muscle." "Nothing could be truer," he said. "Then may we not say, Glaucon," said I, "that those who established an education in music and gymnastics had not the purpose in view that some attribute to them in so instituting, namely to treat the body by one and the soul by the other?" "But what?" he said. "It seems likely," I said, "that they ordained both chiefly for the soul's sake." "How so?" "Have you not observed," said I, "the effect on the disposition of the mind itself of lifelong devotion to gymnastics with total neglect of music? Or the disposition of those of the opposite habit?" "In what respect do you mean?" he said. "In respect of savagery and hardness or, on the other hand, of softness and gentleness?" "I have observed," he said, "that the devotees of unmitigated gymnastics turn out more brutal than they should be and those of music softer than is good for them." "And surely," said I, "this savagery is a quality derived from the high-spirited element in our nature, which, if rightly trained, becomes brave, but if overstrained, would naturally become hard and harsh." "I think so," he said. "And again, is not the gentleness a quality which the philosophic nature would yield? This if relaxed too far would be softer than is desirable but if rightly trained gentle and orderly?" "That is so." "But our requirement, we say, is that the guardians should possess both natures." "It is." "And must they not be harmoniously adjusted to one another?" "Of course." "And the soul of the man thus attuned is sober and brave?" "Certainly." "And that of the ill adjusted is cowardly and rude?" "It surely is."

18. "Now when a man abandons himself to music to play upon him and pour into his soul as it were through the funnel of his ears those sweet, soft, and dirge-like harmonies of which we were just now speaking, and gives his entire time to the warblings and blandishments of song, the first result is that the principle of high spirit, if he had it, is softened like

iron and is made useful instead of useless and brittle. But when he continues the practice without remission and is spellbound, the effect begins to be that he melts and liquefies till he completely dissolves away his spirit, cuts out as it were the very sinews of his soul and makes of himself a 'feeble warrior.' " "Assuredly," he said. "And if," said I, "he has to begin with a spiritless nature he reaches this result quickly, but if a high-spirited, by weakening the spirit he makes it unstable, quickly irritated by slight stimuli, and as quickly quelled. The outcome is that such men are choleric and irascible instead of high-spirited, and are peevish and discontented." "Precisely so." "On the other hand, if a man toils hard at gymnastics and eats right lustily and holds no truck with music and philosophy, does he not at first get very fit and full of pride and high spirit and become more brave and bold than he was?" "He does indeed." "But what if he does nothing but this and has no contact with the Muse in any way, is not the result that even if there was some principle of the love of knowledge in his soul, since it tastes of no instruction nor of any inquiry and does not participate in any discussion or any other form of culture, it becomes feeble, deaf, and blind, because it is not aroused or fed nor are its perceptions purified and quickened?" "That is so," he said. "And so such a man, I take it, becomes a misologist and a stranger to the Muses. He no longer makes any use of persuasion by speech but achieves all his ends like a beast by violence and savagery, and in his brute ignorance and ineptitude lives a life of disharmony and gracelessness." "That is entirely true," he said. "For these two, then, it seems there are two arts which I would say some god gave to mankind, music and gymnastics for the service of the high-spirited principle and the love of knowledge in them—not for the soul and the body except incidentally, but for the harmonious adjustment of these two principles by the proper degree of tension and relaxation of each." "Yes, so it appears," he said. "Then he who best blends gymnastics with music and applies them most suitably to the soul is the man whom we should most rightly pronounce to be the most perfect and harmonious musician, far rather than the one who brings the strings into unison with one another." "That seems likely, Socrates," he said. "And shall we not also need in our city, Glaucon, a permanent overseer of this kind if its constitution is to be preserved?" "We most certainly shall."

2. Aristotle

One of the most influential and versatile of thinkers, Aristotle was a "philosopher, psychologist, logician, moralist, political thinker, biologist, the founder of literary criticism." He was born in 384 B.C. in Stagira, a Greek colonial town on the Aegean Sea, and became a pupil and later a teacher at Plato's Academy in Athens. In 343 he was invited by Philip of Macedonia to supervise the education of Philip's son Alexander. After Alexander's ascension to the throne Aristotle returned to Athens and founded there the so-called "Peripatetic School" in the Lyceum. After Alexander's death Aristotle was obliged to leave Athens for political reasons and died in 322 B.C. on his country estate near Chalcis on the island of Euboea.

Aristotle's preserved works were probably written during the last twelve years of his life. They encompass nearly the entire range of the knowledge of his day. The *Politics* is a fragment of an extensive work on the *Constitutions*.

The influence of Aristotelian doctrine in the history of philosophy of the Western world has been immense. In the Middle Ages, Aristotle became the supreme philosophical authority. Yet his ideas remained imperfectly understood until the beginnings of textual criticism in the Renaissance.

From the Politics [1]

2. IT is therefore not difficult to see that the young must be taught those useful arts that are indispensably necessary; but it is clear that they should not be taught all the useful arts, those pursuits that are liberal being kept distinct from those that are illiberal, and that they must participate in such among the useful arts as will not render the person who participates in them vulgar. A task and also an art or a science must be deemed vulgar if it renders the body or soul or mind of free men useless for the employ-

1 Text: *The Politics* (London, W. Heinemann, 1932), pp. 637–645, 649–675. Translated for the Loeb Classical Library by H. Rackham. Reprinted by permission of Harvard University Press.

ments and actions of virtue. Hence we entitle vulgar all such arts as deteriorate the condition of the body, and also the industries that earn wages; for they make the mind preoccupied and degraded. And even with the liberal sciences, although it is not illiberal to take part in some of them up to a point, to devote oneself to them too assiduously and carefully is liable to have the injurious results specified. Also it makes much difference what object one has in view in a pursuit or study; if one follows it for the sake of oneself or one's friends, or on moral grounds, it is not illiberal, but the man who follows the same pursuit because of other people would often appear to be acting in a menial and servile manner.

The branches of study at present established fall into both classes, as was said before. There are perhaps four customary subjects of education, reading and writing, gymnastics, music, and fourth, with some people, drawing; reading and writing and drawing being taught as being useful for the purposes of life and very serviceable, and gymnastics as contributing to manly courage; but as to music here one might raise a question. For at present most people take part in it for the sake of pleasure; but those who originally included it in education did so because, as has often been said, nature itself seeks to be able not only to engage rightly in business but also to occupy leisure nobly; for—to speak about it yet again—this is the first principle of all things. For if although both business and leisure are necessary, yet leisure is more desirable and more fully an end than business, we must inquire what is the proper occupation of leisure. For assuredly it should not be employed in play,[2] since it would follow that play is our end in life. But if this is impossible, and sports should rather be employed in our times of business (for a man who is at work needs rest, and rest is the object of play, while business is accompanied by toil and exertion), it follows that in introducing sports we must watch the right opportunity for their employment, since we are applying them to serve as medicine; for the activity of play is a relaxation of the soul, and serves as recreation because of its pleasantness. But leisure seems itself to contain pleasure and happiness and felicity of life. And this is not possessed by the busy but by the leisured; for the busy man busies himself for the sake of some end as not being in his possession, but happiness is an end achieved, which all men think is accompanied by pleasure and not by pain. But all men do not go on to define this pleasure in the same way, but ac-

---

2 The distinction between "play," "sport," or "amusement" (παιδιά) and "pastime" or "entertainment" (διαγωγή) is essential to Aristotle's argument. "Amusement" is recreation, a restful and relaxing activity in spare time; "entertain-ment" is the employment of leisure. "Amusement" belongs to the worker, "entertainment" to the free man; "amusement" is useful, "entertainment" liberal.

cording to their various natures and to their own characters, and the pleasure with which the best man thinks that happiness is conjoined is the best pleasure and the one arising from the noblest sources. So that it is clear that some subjects must be learnt and acquired merely with a view to the pleasure in their pursuit, and that these studies and these branches of learning are ends in themselves, while the forms of learning related to business are studied as necessary and as means to other things. Hence our predecessors included music in education not as a necessity (for there is nothing necessary about it), nor as useful (in the way in which reading and writing are useful for business and for household management and for acquiring learning and for many pursuits of civil life, while drawing also seems to be useful in making us better judges of the works of artists), nor yet again as we pursue gymnastics for the sake of health and strength (for we do not see either of these things produced as a result of music); it remains therefore that it is useful as a pastime in leisure, which is evidently the purpose for which people actually introduce it, for they rank it as a form of pastime that they think proper for free men. For this reason Homer wrote thus:

> But him alone
> 'Tis meet to summon to the festal banquet; [3]

and after these words he speaks of certain others

> Who call the bard that he may gladden all.[4]

And also in other verses Odysseus says that this is the best pastime, when, as men are enjoying good cheer,

> The banqueters, seated in order due
> Throughout the hall may hear a minstrel sing.[5]

3. It is clear therefore that there is a form of education in which boys should be trained not because it is useful or necessary but as being liberal and noble; though whether there is one such subject of education or several, and what these are and how they are to be pursued, must be discussed later, but as it is we have made this much progress on the way, that we have some testimony even from the ancients, derived from the courses of education which they founded—for the point is proved by music. And it is also clear that some of the useful subjects as well ought to be studied by the young not only because of their utility, like the study of reading and writing, but also because they may lead on to many other

[3] Corresponds to *Odyssey*, XVII, 385, but not exactly. [Rackham]

[4] This line is not in our *Odyssey*, but apparently followed XVII, 383. [Rackham]

[5] *Odyssey*, IX, 5–6.

branches of knowledge; and similarly they should study drawing not in order that they may not go wrong in their private purchases and may avoid being cheated in buying and selling furniture, but rather because this study makes a man observant of bodily beauty; and to seek for utility everywhere is entirely unsuited to men that are great-souled and free. And since it is plain that education by habit must come before education by reason, and training of the body before training of the mind, it is clear from these considerations that the boys must be handed over to the care of the wrestling-master and the trainer; for the latter imparts a certain quality to the habit of the body and the former to its actions.

·   ·   ·   ·   ·

About music on the other hand we have previously raised some questions in the course of our argument, but it is well to take them up again and carry them further now, in order that this may give the key so to speak for the principles which one might advance in pronouncing about it. For it is not easy to say precisely what potency it possesses, nor yet for the sake of what object one should participate in it—whether for amusement and relaxation, as one indulges in sleep and deep drinking (for these in themselves are not serious pursuits but merely pleasant, and "relax our cares," as Euripides says [6]; owing to which people actually class music with them and employ all of these things, sleep, deep drinking, and music, in the same way, and they also place dancing in the same class); or whether we ought rather to think that music tends in some degree to virtue (music being capable of producing a certain quality of character just as gymnastics are capable of producing a certain quality of body, music accustoming men to be able to rejoice rightly); or that it contributes something to intellectual entertainment and culture (for this must be set down as a third alternative among those mentioned). Now it is not difficult to see that one must not make amusement the object of the education of the young; for amusement does not go with learning—learning is a painful process. Nor yet moreover is it suitable to assign intellectual entertainment to boys and to the young; for a thing that is an end does not belong to anything that is imperfect. But perhaps it might be thought that the serious pursuits of boys are for the sake of amusement when they have grown up to be men. But if something of this sort is the case, why should the young need to learn this accomplishment themselves, and not, like the Persian and Median kings, participate in the pleasure and the education of music by means of others performing it? for those who have made music a business and profession must necessarily perform better than those who practise

6 *Bacchae*, 378.

only long enough to learn. But if it is proper for them to labor at accomplishments of this sort, then it would also be right for them to prepare the dishes of an elaborate cuisine; but this is absurd. And the same difficulty also arises as to the question whether learning music can improve their characters; for why should they learn to perform edifying music themselves, instead of learning to enjoy it rightly and be able to judge it when they hear others performing, as the Spartans do? for the Spartans although they do not learn to perform can nevertheless judge good and bad music correctly, so it is said. And the same argument applies also if music is to be employed for refined enjoyment and entertainment; why need people learn to perform themselves instead of enjoying music played by others? And we may consider the conception that we have about the gods: Zeus does not sing and harp to the poets himself. But professional musicians we speak of as vulgar people, and indeed we think it not manly to perform music, except when drunk or for fun.

5. But perhaps these points will have to be considered afterwards; our first inquiry is whether music ought not or ought to be included in education, and what is its efficacy among the three uses of it that have been discussed—does it serve for education or amusement or entertainment? It is reasonable to reckon it under all of these heads, and it appears to participate in them all. Amusement is for the sake of relaxation, and relaxation must necessarily be pleasant, for it is a way of curing the pain due to laborious work; also entertainment ought admittedly to be not only honorable but also pleasant, for happiness is derived from both honor and pleasure; but we all pronounce music to be one of the pleasantest things, whether instrumental or instrumental and vocal music together (at least Musaeus says, "Song is man's sweetest joy," [7] and that is why people with good reason introduce it at parties and entertainments, for its exhilarating effect), so that for this reason also one might suppose that the younger men ought to be educated in music. For all harmless pleasures are not only suitable for the ultimate object but also for relaxation; and as it but rarely happens for men to reach their ultimate object, whereas they often relax and pursue amusement not so much with some ulterior object but because of the pleasure of it, it would be serviceable to let them relax at intervals in the pleasures derived from music. But it has come about that men make amusements an end; for the end also perhaps contains a certain pleasure, but not any ordinary pleasure, and seeking this they take the other as being this because it has a certain resemblance to the achievement of the end of their undertakings. For the end is desirable not for the sake of anything

---

7 A semi-legendary bard, to whom a number of oracular verses that were current were attributed. [Rackham]

that will result from it, and also pleasures of the sort under consideration are not desirable for the sake of some future result, but because of things that have happened already, for instance labor and pain. One might then perhaps assume this to be the reason which causes men to seek to procure happiness by means of those pleasures; but in the case of taking part in music, this is not because of this reason only, but also because performing music is useful, as it seems, for relaxation. But nevertheless we must examine whether it is not the case that, although this has come about, yet the nature of music is more honorable than corresponds with the employment of it mentioned, and it is proper not only to participate in the common pleasure that springs from it, which is perceptible to everybody (for the pleasure contained in music is of a natural kind, owing to which the use of it is dear to those of all ages and characters), but to see if its influence reaches also in a manner to the character and to the soul. And this would clearly be the case if we are affected in our characters in a certain manner by it. But it is clear that we are affected in a certain manner, both by many other kinds of music and not least by the melodies of Olympus; [8] for these admittedly make our souls enthusiastic, and enthusiasm is an affection of the character of the soul. And moreover everybody when listening to imitations is thrown into a corresponding state of feeling, even apart from the rhythms and melodies themselves.[9] And since it is the case that music is one of the things that give pleasure, and that virtue has to do with feeling delight and love and hatred rightly, there is obviously nothing that is more needful to learn and become habituated to than to judge correctly and to delight in virtuous characters and noble actions; but rhythms and melodies contain representations of anger and mildness, and also of courage and temperance and all their opposites and the other moral qualities, that most closely correspond to the true natures of these qualities (and this is clear from the facts of what occurs—when we listen to such representations we change in our soul); and habituation in feeling pain and delight at representations of reality is close to feeling them towards actual reality (for example, if a man delights in beholding the statue of somebody for no other reason than because of its actual form, the actual sight of the person whose statue he beholds must also of necessity give him pleasure); and it is the case that whereas the other objects of sensation contain no representation of character, for example the objects of touch and taste (though

---

8 Phrygian melodies; see p. 19 below, where the Phrygian harmony is said to have the power of arousing enthusiasm.

9 A probable correction of the Greek gives "by the rhythms and melodies themselves, even apart from the words." [Rackham].

Unlike Plato, Aristotle considers purely instrumental music a legitimate "mode of imitation" (cf. *Poetics*, i, 4–5; *Problems*, 919B [Problem 27]).

the objects of sight do so slightly, for there are forms that represent character, but only to a small extent, and not all men participate in visual perception of such qualities; also visual works of art are not representations of
character but rather the forms and colors produced are mere indications
of character, and these indications are only bodily sensations during the
emotions; not but what in so far as there is a difference even in regard to
the observation of these indications, the young must not look at the works
of Pauson, but those of Polygnotus [10] and of any other moral painter or
sculptor), pieces of music on the contrary do actually contain in themselves
imitations of character; and this is manifest, for even in the nature of the
mere harmonies there are differences, so that people when hearing them
are affected differently and have not the same feelings in regard to each
of them, but listen to some in a more mournful and restrained state, for
instance the harmony called Mixolydian, and to others in a softer state
of mind, for instance the relaxed harmonies, but in a midway state and
with the greatest composure to another, as the Dorian alone of harmonies
seems to act, while the Phrygian makes men enthusiastic; [11] for these
things are well stated by those who have studied this form of education,
as they derive the evidence for their theories from the actual facts of experience. And the same holds good about the rhythms also, for some have
a more stable and others a more emotional character, and of the latter
some are more vulgar in their emotional effects and others more liberal.
From these considerations therefore it is plain that music has the power of
producing a certain effect on the moral character of the soul, and if it has
the power to do this, it is clear that the young must be directed to music
and must be educated in it. Also education in music is well adapted to the
youthful nature; for the young owing to their youth cannot endure anything not sweetened by pleasure, and music is by nature a thing that has a
pleasant sweetness. And we seem to have a certain affinity with harmonies
and rhythms; owing to which many wise men say either that the soul is
a harmony or that it has harmony. [12]

6. We ought now to decide the question raised earlier, whether the
young ought to learn music by singing and playing themselves or not.
It is not difficult to see that it makes a great difference in the process of
acquiring a certain quality whether one takes a part in the actions that impart it oneself; for it is a thing that is impossible, or difficult, to become a

10 "Polygnotus represented men as better than
they really were, Pauson as worse." (*Poetics,*
1448A)
11 This fourfold classification of the "harmonies" according to their ethical character repeats
the classification of Plato (*Republic,* 398D–399A,
pp. 4–6 above).

12 Cf. Plato, *Republic,* 401D (pp. 8–9 above);
also *Republic,* 443D–443E; *Timaeus,* 47D–47E;
Phaedo, 85–95; for Aristotle's criticism see his
De anima, 407B–408A.

good judge of performances if one has not taken part in them. At the same time also boys must have some occupation, and one must think Archytas's rattle [18] a good invention, which people give to children in order that while occupied with this they may not break any of the furniture; for young things cannot keep still. Whereas then a rattle is a suitable occupation for infant children, education serves as a rattle for young people when older. Such considerations therefore prove that children should be trained in music so as actually to take part in its performance; and it is not difficult to distinguish what is suitable and unsuitable for various ages, and to refute those who assert that the practice of music is vulgar. For first, inasmuch as it is necessary to take part in the performances for the sake of judging them, it is therefore proper for the pupils when young actually to engage in the performances, though when they get older they should be released from performing, but be able to judge what is beautiful and enjoy it rightly because of the study in which they engaged in their youth. Then as to the objection raised by some people that music makes people vulgar, it is not difficult to solve it by considering how far pupils who are being educated with a view to civic virtue should take part in the actual performance of music, and in what melodies and what rhythms they should take part, and also what kinds of instruments should be used in their studies, as this naturally makes a difference. For the solution of the objection depends upon these points, as it is quite possible that some styles of music do produce the result mentioned. It is manifest therefore that the study of music must not place a hindrance in the way of subsequent activities, nor vulgarize the bodily frame and make it useless for the exercises of the soldier and the citizen, either for their practical pursuit now or for their scientific study later on. And this would come about in respect of their study if the pupils did not go on toiling at the exercises that aim at professional competitions, nor the wonderful and elaborate performances which have now entered into the competitions and have passed from the competitions into education, but also only practised exercises not of that sort until they are able to enjoy beautiful melodies and rhythms, and not merely the charm common to all music, which even some lower animals enjoy, as well as a multitude of slaves and children. And it is also clear from these considerations what sort of instruments they should use. The auloi must not be introduced into education, nor any other profes-

---

18 A Pythagorean philosopher, mathematician, statesman, and general of Tarentum, contemporary with Plato. He was interested in mechanics; but one tradition ascribes the toy in question to a carpenter of the same name. [Rackham]
To Archytas are also due the earliest divisions of the tetrachord that have come down to us, and Reinach plausibly attributes to him or to his circle the fixation, if not the actual invention of the Greek musical notation (cf. his *Musique grecque*, Paris, 1926, pp. 26 and 163).

sional instrument, such as the cithara or any other of that sort, but such instruments as will make them attentive pupils either at their musical training or in their other lessons. Moreover the aulos is not a moralizing but rather an exciting influence, so that it ought to be used for occasions of the kind at which attendance has the effect of purification rather than instruction. And let us add that the aulos happens to possess the additional property telling against its use in education that playing it prevents the employment of speech. Hence former ages rightly rejected its use by the young and the free, although at first they had employed it. For as they came to have more leisure because of their wealth and grew more high-spirited and valorous, both at a still earlier date and because after the Persian wars they were filled with pride as a result of their achievements, they began to engage in all branches of learning, making no distinction but pursuing research further. Because of this they even included aulos-playing among their studies; for in Sparta a certain chorus-leader played the aulos to his chorus himself, and at Athens it became so fashionable that almost the majority of freemen went in for aulos-playing, as is shown by the tablet erected by Thrasippus after having provided the chorus for Ecphantides. But later on it came to be disapproved of as a result of actual experience, when men were more capable of judging what music conduced to virtue and what did not; and similarly also many of the old instruments were disapproved of, like the pectis and the barbitos and the instruments designed to give pleasure to those who hear people playing them, the heptagonon, the trigonon, and the sambyca, and all the instruments that require manual skill. And indeed there is a reasonable foundation for the story that was told by the ancients about the auloi. The tale goes that Athene found a pair of auloi and threw them away. Now it is not a bad point in the story that the goddess did this out of annoyance because of the ugly distortion of her features; but as a matter of fact it is more likely that it was because education in aulos-playing has no effect on the intelligence, whereas we attribute science and art to Athene.

7. And since we reject professional education in the instruments and in performance [14] (and we count performance in competitions as professional, for the performer does not take part in it for his own improvement, but for his hearers' pleasure, and that a vulgar pleasure, owing to which we do not consider performing to be proper for free men, but somewhat menial; and indeed performers do become vulgar, since the object at which they aim is a low one, as vulgarity in the audience usually in-

---

[14] The Greek should probably be altered to read "reject some instruments and professional education in performance." [Rackham]

fluences the music, so that it imparts to the artists who practise it with a view to suit the audience a special kind of personality, and also of bodily frame because of the movements required)—we must therefore give some consideration to harmonies and rhythms, and to the question whether for educational purposes we must employ all the harmonies and all the rhythms or make distinctions; and next, whether for those who are working at music for education we shall lay down the same regulation, or ought we to establish some other third one (inasmuch as we see that the factors in music are melody and rhythm, and it is important to notice what influence each of these has upon education), and whether we are to prefer music with a good melody or music with a good rhythm. Now we consider that much is well said on these matters by some of the musicians of the present day and by some of those engaged in philosophy who happen to be experienced in musical education, and we will abandon the precise discussion as to each of these matters for any who wish it to seek it from those teachers, while for the present let us lay down general principles, merely stating the outlines of the subjects. And since we accept the classification of melodies made by some philosophers, as ethical melodies, melodies of action, and passionate melodies, distributing the various harmonies among these classes as being in nature akin to one or the other,[15] and as we say that music ought to be employed not for the purpose of one benefit that it confers but on account of several (for it serves the purpose both of education and of purgation—the term purgation we use for the present without explanation, but we will return to discuss the meaning that we give to it more explicitly in our treatise on poetry—and thirdly it serves for amusement, serving to relax our tension and to give rest from it), it is clear that we should employ all the harmonies, yet not employ them all in the same way, but use the most ethical ones for education, and the active and passionate kinds for listening to when others are performing (for any experience that occurs violently in some souls is found in all, though with different degrees of intensity—for example pity and fear, and also religious excitement; for some persons are very liable to this form of emotion, and under the influence of sacred music we see these people, when they use melodies that violently arouse the soul, being thrown into a state as if they had received medicinal treatment and taken a purge; the same experience then must come also to the compassionate and the timid and the other emotional people generally in such degree as befalls each individual of these classes, and all must undergo a purgation and a pleasant

---

15 Literally "ethical, practical, and enthusiastic." Beyond characterizing the Dorian as "ethical" (p. 15 below) and the Phrygian as "enthusiastic" (pp. 18–19 above), Aristotle does not tell us how the harmonies are to be distributed among these classes.

feeling of relief; and similarly also the purgative melodies afford harmless delight to people). Therefore those who go in for theatrical music must be set to compete in harmonies and melodies of this kind (and since the audience is of two classes, one freemen and educated people, and the other the vulgar class composed of mechanics and laborers and other such persons, the latter sort also must be assigned competitions and shows for relaxation; and just as their souls are warped from the natural state, so those harmonies and melodies that are intense and irregular in coloration are deviations, but people of each sort receive pleasure from what is naturally suited to them, owing to which the competitors before an audience of this sort must be allowed to employ some such kind of music as this); but for education, as has been said, the ethical class of melodies and of harmonies must be employed. And of that nature is the Dorian harmony, as we said before; but we must also accept any other harmony that those who take part in the pursuit of philosophy and in musical education may recommend to us. Socrates in the *Republic* does not do well in allowing only the Phrygian harmony along with the Dorian, and that when he has rejected the aulos among instruments; for the Phrygian harmony has the same effect among harmonies as the aulos among instruments—both are violently exciting and emotional. This is shown by poetry; for all Bacchic versification and all movement of that sort belong particularly to the aulos among the instruments, and these metres find their suitable accompaniment in melodies in the Phrygian harmony among the harmonies; for example the dithyramb is admittedly held to be a Phrygian metre, and the experts on this subject adduce many instances to prove this, particularly the fact that Philoxenus when he attempted to compose a dithyramb, "The Mysians," in the Dorian harmony was unable to do so, but merely by the force of nature fell back again into the suitable harmony, the Phrygian.[16] And all agree that the Dorian harmony is more sedate and of a specially manly character. Moreover since we praise and say that we ought to pursue the mean between extremes, and the Dorian harmony has this nature in relation to the other harmonies, it is clear that it suits the younger pupils to be educated rather in the Dorian melodies. But there are two objects to aim at, the possible as well as the suitable; for we are bound rather to attempt the things that are possible and those that are suitable for the particular class of people concerned; and in these matters also there are dividing lines drawn by the ages—for instance, those whose powers have waned through lapse of time cannot easily sing the intense harmonies, but to persons of that age nature suggests the relaxed

16 For the "Mysians," see J. F. Mountford in *Journal of Hellenic Studies*, XL (1920), 21–22.

harmonies. Therefore some musical experts also rightly criticize Socrates because he disapproved of the relaxed harmonies for amusement, taking them to have the character of intoxication, not in the sense of the effect of strong drink, for that clearly has more the result of making men frenzied revellers, but as failing in power. Hence even with a view to the period of life that is to follow, that of the comparatively old, it is proper to engage in the harmonies and melodies of this kind too, and also any kind of harmony that is suited to the age of boyhood because it is capable of being at once decorous and educative, which seems to be the nature of the Lydian most of all the harmonies. It is clear therefore that we should lay down these three canons to guide education—moderation, possibility, and suitability.

3. Aristoxenus

A pupil of the Pythagoreans and later of Aristotle, born about 350 B.C. at Tarentum in southern Italy, Aristoxenus is the most important of the ancient Greek writers about music. Of his numerous works only two books of the *Harmonic Elements* and fragments of the *Elements of Rhythmics* have come down to us. Aristoxenus' thought has a distinct empirical tendency. For example, he clearly perceives that listening to a musical composition presupposes an activity of collecting and building up impressions in one's memory. Aristoxenus also holds that the notes of a scale are to be judged, not by mathematical ratio, but by the ear. This empirical turn of mind makes Aristoxenus the first ancient writer to lay the foundation for a scientific aesthetics of music.

From the Harmonic Elements [1]

IT WILL be well perhaps to review in anticipation the course of our study; thus a foreknowledge of the road that we must travel will enable us to recognize each stage as we reach it, and so lighten the toil of the journey; nor shall we be harboring unknown to ourselves a false conception of our subject. Such was the condition, as Aristotle used often to relate, of most of the audience that attended Plato's lectures on the Good. They came, he used to say, every one of them, in the conviction that they would get from the lectures some one or other of the things that the world calls good; riches or health, or strength, in fine, some extraordinary gift of fortune. But when they found that Plato's reasonings were of sciences and numbers, and geometry, and astronomy, and of good and unity as predicates of the finite, methinks their disenchantment was complete. The result was that some of them sneered at the thing, while others vilified it. Now to what was all this trouble due? To the fact that they had not waited

1 Text: *The Harmonics of Aristoxenus,* as translated by H. S. Macran for the Clarendon Press (Oxford, 1902), pp. 187–198. Departures from Macran's wording are indicated by italics.

to inform themselves of the nature of the subject, but after the manner of the sect of word-catchers had flocked round open-mouthed, attracted by the mere title "good" in itself.

But if a general exposition of the subject had been given in advance, the intending pupil would either have abandoned his intention or if he was pleased with the exposition, would have remained in the said conviction to the end. It was for these very reasons, as he told us, that Aristotle himself used to give his intending pupils a preparatory statement of the subject and method of his course of study. And we agree with him in thinking, as we said at the beginning, that such prior information is desirable. For mistakes are often made in both directions. Some consider *harmonics* a sublime science, and expect a course of it to make them musicians; nay some even conceive it will exalt their moral nature. This mistake is due to their having run away with such phrases in our preamble as "we aim at the construction of every style of melody," and with our general statement "one class of musical art is hurtful to the moral character, another improves it"; while they missed completely our qualification of this statement, "in so far as musical art can improve the moral character." Then on the other hand there are persons who regard *harmonics* as quite a thing of no importance, and actually prefer to remain totally unacquainted even with its nature and aim. Neither of these views is correct. On the one hand the science is no proper object of contempt to the man of intelligence— this we shall see as the discussion progresses; nor on the other hand has it the quality of all-sufficiency, as some imagine. To be a musician, as we are always insisting, implies much more than a knowledge of *harmonics*, which is only one part of the musician's equipment, on the same level as the sciences of *rhythmics*, of *metrics*, of *organics*.

We shall now proceed to the consideration of *harmonics* and its parts. It is to be observed that in general the subject of our study is the question, In melody of every kind what are the natural laws according to which the voice in ascending or descending places the intervals? For we hold that the voice follows a natural law in its motion, and does not place the intervals at random. And of our answers we endeavor to supply proofs that will be in agreement with the phenomena—in this unlike our predecessors. For some of these introduced extraneous reasoning, and rejecting the senses as inaccurate, fabricated rational principles, asserting that height and depth of pitch consist in certain numerical ratios and relative rates of vibration—a theory utterly extraneous to the subject and quite at variance with the phenomena; while others, dispensing with reason and demonstration, confined themselves to isolated dogmatic statements, not being successful either in their enumeration of the mere phenomena. It is our endeavor that the principles which we assume shall without exception be evident to those who understand music, and that we shall advance to our conclusions by strict demonstration.

Our subject-matter then being all melody, whether vocal or instrumental, our method rests in the last resort on an appeal to the two faculties of hearing and intellect. By the former we judge the magnitudes of the intervals, by the latter we contemplate the functions of the notes. We must therefore accustom ourselves to an accurate discrimination of particulars. It is usual in geometrical constructions to use such a phrase as "Let this be a straight line"; but one must not be content with such language of assumption in the case of intervals. The geometrician makes no use of his faculty of sense-perception. He does not in any degree train his sight to discriminate the straight line, the circle, or any other figure, such training belonging rather to the practice of the carpenter, the turner, or some other such handicraftsman. But for the student of musical science accuracy of sense-perception is a fundamental requirement. For if his sense-perception is deficient, it is impossible for him to deal successfully with those questions that lie outside the sphere of sense-perception altogether. This will become clear in the course of our investigation. And we must bear in mind that musical cognition implies the simultaneous cognition of a permanent and of a changeable element, and that this applies without limitation or qualification to every branch of music. To begin with, our perception of the differences of the genera is dependent on the permanence of the containing, and the variation of the intermediate notes. Again, while the magnitude remains constant, we distinguish the interval between hypate and mese from that between paramese and nete; here, then, the magnitude is permanent, while the functions of the notes change; similarly, when there are several figures of the same magnitude, as of the *diatessaron,* or *diapente,* or any other; similarly, when the same interval leads or does not lead to modulation, according to its position. Again, in matters of rhythm we find many similar examples. Without any change in the characteristic proportion constituting any one genus of rhythm, the lengths of the feet vary in obedience to the general rate of movement; and while the magnitudes are constant, the quality of the feet undergoes a change; and the same magnitude serves as a foot and as a combination of feet. Plainly, too, unless there was a permanent quantum to deal with there could be no distinctions as to the methods of dividing it and arranging its parts. And in general, while rhythmical composition employs a rich variety of movements, the movements of the feet by which we note the rhythms are always simple and the same. Such, then, being the nature of music, we must in matters of harmony also accustom both ear and intellect to a correct judgment of the permanent and changeable element alike.

These remarks have exhibited the general character of the science called *harmonics;* and of this science there are, as a fact, seven parts.[2] Of these one and the first is to define the genera, and to show what are the permanent and what are the changeable elements presupposed by this distinction. None of our predecessors has drawn this distinction at all; nor is this to be wondered at. For they confined their attention to the enharmonic genus, to the neglect of the other two. Students of instruments, it is true, could not fail to distinguish each genus by ear, but none of them reflected even on the question, At what point does the enharmonic begin to pass into the chromatic? For their ability to discriminate each genus extended not to all the shades, inasmuch as they were not acquainted with all styles of musical composition or trained to exercise a nice discrimination in such distinctions; nor did they even observe that there were certain loci of the notes that alter their position with the change of genus. These reasons sufficiently explain why the genera have not as yet been definitely distinguished; but it is evident that we must supply this deficiency if we are to follow the differences that present themselves in works of musical composition.

Such is the first branch of *harmonics.* In the second we shall deal with intervals, omitting, to the best of our ability, none of the distinctions to be found in them. The majority of these, one might say, have as yet escaped observation. But we must bear in mind that wherever we come upon a distinction which has been overlooked, and not scientifically considered, we shall there fail to recognize the distinctions in works of melodic composition.

Again, since intervals are not in themselves sufficient to distinguish notes—for every magnitude, without qualification, that an interval can possess is common to several musical functions—the third part of our science will deal with notes, their number, and the means of recognizing them; and will consider the question whether they are certain points of pitch, as is vulgarly supposed, or whether they are musical functions, and also what is the meaning of a musical "function." Not one of these questions is clearly conceived by students of the subject.

The fourth part will consider *systems,* firstly as to their number and

2 In another order, the seven parts of harmonics are discussed at greater length by Cleonides in the selection that follows.

nature, secondly as to the manner of their construction from intervals and notes. Our predecessors have not regarded this part of the subject in either of these respects. On the one hand, no attention has been devoted to the questions whether intervals are collocated in any order to produce *systems*, or whether some collocations may not transgress a natural law. On the other hand, the distinctions in *systems* have not been completely enumerated by any of them. As to the first point, our forerunners simply ignored the distinction between "melodious" and "unmelodious"; as to the second, they either made no attempt at all at enumeration of *system-distinctions*, confining their attention to the seven *octachords* which they called harmonies; or if they made the attempt, they fell very short of completeness, like the school of Pythagoras of Zacynthus, and Agenor of Mitylene. The order that distinguishes the melodious from the unmelodious resembles that which we find in the collocation of letters in language. For it is not every collocation but only certain collocations of any given letters that will produce a syllable.

The fifth part of our science deals with the *tones* in which the *systems* are placed for the purposes of melody. No explanation has yet been offered of the manner in which those *tones* are to be found, or of the principle by which one must be guided in enunciating their number. The account of the *tones* given by the harmonists closely resembles the observance of the days according to which, for example, the tenth day of the month at Corinth is the fifth at Athens, and the eighth somewhere else. Just in the same way, some of the harmonists hold that the Hypodorian is the lowest of the *tones;* that a *semitone* above lies the Mixolydian; a *semitone* higher again the Dorian; a tone above the Dorian the Phrygian; likewise a tone above the Phrygian the Lydian. The number is sometimes increased by the addition of the Hypophrygian [3] at the bottom of the list. Others, again, having regard to the boring of finger-holes on the *auloi*, assume intervals of three *dieses* between the three lowest *tones*, the Hypophrygian, the Hypodorian, and the Dorian; a tone between the Dorian and Phrygian; three *dieses* again between the Phrygian and Lydian, and the same distance between the Lydian and Mixolydian. But they have not informed us on what principle they have persuaded themselves to this location of the *tones*. And that the close packing of small intervals is unmelodious and of no practical value whatsoever will be clear in the course of our discussion.

Again, since some melodies are simple, and others contain a modulation,

---

3 At the suggestion of my friend Whitney J. Oates of Princeton University, I omit the word "aulos," which seems not to belong in the text.

we must treat of modulation, considering first the nature of modulation in the abstract, and how it arises, or in other words, to what modification in the melodic order it owes its existence; secondly, how many modulations there are in all, and at what intervals they occur. On these questions we find no statements by our predecessors with or without proof.

The last section of our science is concerned with the actual *composition* of melody. For since in the same notes, indifferent in themselves, we have the choice of numerous melodic forms of every character, it is evident that here we have the practical question of the employment of the notes; and this is what we mean by the *composition* of melody. The science of harmony having traversed the said sections will find its consummation here.

It is plain that the apprehension of a melody consists in noting with both ear and intellect every distinction as it arises in the successive sounds —successive, for melody, like all branches of music, consists in a successive production. For the apprehension of music depends on these two faculties, sense-perception and memory; for we must perceive the sound that is present, and remember that which is past. In no other way can we follow the phenomena of music.

Now some find the goal of the science called *harmonics* in the notation of melodies, declaring this to be the ultimate limit of the apprehension of any given melody. Others again find it in the knowledge of the *auloi*, and in the ability to tell the manner of production of, and the agencies employed in, any piece rendered on the *aulos*.

Such views are conclusive evidence of an utter misconception. So far is notation from being the perfection of harmonic science that it is not even a part of it, any more than the marking of any particular metre is a part of metrical science. As in the latter case one might very well mark the scheme of the iambic metre without understanding its essence, so it is with melody also; if a man notes down the Phrygian scale it does not follow that he must know the essence of the Phrygian scale. Plainly then notation is not the ultimate limit of our science.

That the premises of our argument are true, and that the faculty of musical notation argues nothing beyond a discernment of the size of intervals, will be clear on consideration. In the use of signs for the intervals no peculiar mark is employed to denote all their individual distinctions, such as the several methods of dividing the *diatessaron*, which depend on the differences of genera, or of the several figures of the same interval which result from a variation in the disposition of the simple intervals. It is the same with the musical functions proper to the natures of the different tetrachords; the same notation is employed for the tetrachords hyperbolaion, neton, meson, and hypaton. Thus the signs fail to distinguish the functional differences, and consequently indicate the magnitudes of the intervals, and nothing more. But that the mere sense-discrimination of magnitudes is no part of the general comprehension of music was stated in the introduction, and the following considerations will make it patent. Mere knowledge of magnitudes does not enlighten one as to the functions of the tetrachords, or of the notes, or the differences of the genera or, briefly, the difference of *incomposite* and *composite* intervals, or the distinction between modulating and non-modulating *systems*, or the *styles* of melodic *composition*, or indeed anything else of the kind.

Now if the harmonists, as they are called, have in their ignorance seriously entertained this view, while there is nothing preposterous in their motives, their ignorance must be profound and invincible. But if, being aware that notation is not the final goal of *harmonics*, they have propounded this view merely through the desire to please amateurs, and to represent as the perfection of the science a certain visible activity, their motives deserve condemnation as very preposterous indeed. In the first place they would constitute the amateur judge of the sciences—and it is preposterous that the same person should be learner and judge of the same thing; in the second place they reverse the proper order in their fancy of representing a visible activity as the consummation of intellectual apprehension; for, as a fact, the ultimate factor in every visible activity is the intellectual process. For this latter is the presiding and determining principle; and as for the hands, voice, mouth, or breath—it is an error to suppose that they are very much more than inanimate instruments. And if this intellectual activity is something hidden deep down in the soul, and is not palpable or apparent to the ordinary man, as the operations of the hand and the like are apparent, we must not on that account alter our views. We shall be sure to miss the truth unless we place the supreme and ultimate, not in the thing determined, but in the activity that determines.

No less preposterous is the above-mentioned theory concerning the *auloi*. Nay, rather there is no error so fatal and so preposterous as to base the natural laws of harmony on any instrument. The essence and order of harmony depend not upon any of the properties of instruments. It is not because the *aulos* has finger-holes and bores, and the like, nor is it because it submits to certain operations of the hands and of the other parts naturally adapted to raise and lower the pitch, that the *diatessaron*, and the *diapente*, and the *diapason* are *symphonies*, or that each of the other intervals possesses its proper magnitude. For even with all these conditions present, players on the *aulos* fail for the most part to attain the exact order of melody; and whatever small success attends them is due to the employment of agencies external to the instrument, as in the well-known expedients of drawing the two *auloi* apart, and bringing them alongside, and of raising and lowering the pitch by changing the pressure of the breath. Plainly, then, one is as much justified in attributing their failures as their success to the essential nature of the *aulos*. But this would not have been so if there was anything gained by basing harmony on the nature of an instrument. In that case, as an immediate consequence of tracing melody up to its original in the nature of the *aulos*, we should have found it there fixed, unerring, and correct. But as a fact neither the *auloi* nor any other instrument will supply a foundation for the principles of harmony. There is a certain marvellous order which belongs to the nature of harmony in general; in this order every instrument, to the best of its ability, participates under the direction of that faculty of sense-perception on which they, as well as everything else in music, finally depend. To suppose, because one sees day by day the finger-holes the same and the strings at the same tension, that one will find in these harmony with its permanence and eternally immutable order—this is sheer folly. For as there is no harmony in the strings save that which the cunning of the hand confers upon them, so is there none in the finger-holes save what has been introduced by the same agency. That no instrument is self-tuned, and that the harmonizing of it is the prerogative of the sense-perception is obvious, and requires no proof. It is strange that the supporters of this absurd theory can cling to it in face of the fact that the *auloi* are perpetually in a state of change; and of course what is played on the instrument varies with the variation in the agencies employed in its production. It is surely clear then that on no consideration can melody be based on the *auloi;* for, firstly, an instrument will not supply a foundation for the order of harmony, and secondly, even if it were supposed that harmony should be based on some instrument, the choice should not have fallen on the *aulos,* an instrument especially liable to aberrations, resulting from the manufacture and manipulation of it, and from its own peculiar nature.

This will suffice as an introductory account of harmonic science; but as we prepare ourselves to enter upon the study of the *Elements* we must at the outset attend to the following considerations. Our exposition cannot be a successful one unless three conditions be fulfilled. Firstly, the phenomena themselves must be correctly observed; secondly, what is prior and what is derivative in them must be properly discriminated; thirdly, our conclusions and inferences must follow legitimately from the premises. And as in every science that consists of several propositions the proper course is to find certain principles from which to deduce the dependent truths, we must be guided in our selection of principles by two considerations. Firstly, every proposition that is to serve as a principle must be true and evident; secondly, it must be such as to be accepted by the sense-perception as one of the primary truths of harmonic science. For what requires demonstration cannot stand as a fundamental principle; and in general we must be watchful in determining our highest principles, lest on the one hand we let ourselves be dragged outside the proper track of our science by beginning with sound in general regarded as air-vibration, or on the other hand turn short of the flag and abandon much of what truly belongs to *harmonics*.

4. Cleonides

Of Cleonides we know only that several early manuscripts name him as the author of the little treatise that follows. From his account of the keys, in which there is no mention of Hyperaeolian and Hyperlydian, his French translator Ruelle concludes that he must have lived before the time of Alypius and Aristides Quintilianus (1st century A.D.), the earliest writers to speak of these additions to the Aristoxenian system. Actually, this would seem to suggest just the opposite. As an abbreviator and popularizer of Aristoxenus, Cleonides has no reason to mention these additions; the significant thing is that in naming the keys he uses both the Aristoxenian and the later nomenclature. Since the later nomenclature is patently devised for the extended system of fifteen keys, he must have lived after the time when this system was introduced. For the rest, he adheres so closely to Aristoxenus, even in his terminology and wording, that his little abstract is in effect a compensation for the loss of that part of the Aristoxenian writing which has not been preserved. This is in itself enough to dispose of the attribution to Euclid, found in many of the sources, for the teachings of Aristoxenus and of Euclid, in his *Division of the Canon*, are diametrically opposed. In a Latin translation by Georgius Valla, the *Eisagoge* of Cleonides was printed in Venice as early as 1497. It thus became one of the sources from which the musicians of the Renaissance drew their information about the music of Classical Antiquity.

Harmonic Introduction [1]

1. HARMONICS is the speculative and practical science having to do with the nature of the harmonious. And the harmonious is what is made up of notes and intervals having a certain order. The parts of harmonics are

[1] Text: Karl von Jan, *Musici Scriptores Graeci* (Leipzig, 1895), pp. 179–207. There is a French translation by C. E. Ruelle (Paris, 1884).

seven: it has to do with notes, intervals, genera, systems (or scales), tones (or keys), modulations, and melodic composition.

A note is a harmonious incidence of the voice upon a single pitch.

An interval is what is bounded by two notes differing as to height and depth.

Genus is a certain division of four notes.

A system is what is made up of more than one interval.

A tone is any region of the voice, apt for the reception of a system; it is without breadth.

Modulation is the transposition of a similar thing to a dissimilar region.

Melodic composition is the employment of the materials subject to harmonic practice with due regard to the requirements of each of the subjects under consideration.

2. The things considered under quality of voice are these. It has two sorts of movements: one is called continuous and belongs to speech, the other is diastematic and belongs to melody. In continuous movement, tensions and relaxations occur imperceptibly and the voice is never at rest until it becomes silent. In diastematic movement, the opposite takes place; the voice dwells on certain points and passes over the distances between them, proceeding first in the one way, then in the other. The points on which it dwells we call pitches, the passages from pitch to pitch we call intervals. The causes of the difference between pitches are tension and relaxation, their effects are height and depth. For the result of tension is to lead toward the high, that of relaxation toward the low. And height is the effect resulting from tension, depth that resulting from relaxation. Pitches are also called notes: one calls them "pitches" (τάσεις) when they are produced by instruments that are struck, because of their being stretched (τετάσθαι); one calls them "notes" (φθόγγοι) when they are produced by the voice. For to be stretched is a property of both. Considered as pitches, the number of notes is infinite; considered as functions, there are in each genus eighteen.

3. The genera are three: diatonic, chromatic, and enharmonic. The diatonic is sung in descending by tone, tone, and semitone, but in ascending by semitone, tone, and tone. The chromatic is sung in descending by trihemitone, semitone, and semitone, but in ascending by semitone, semitone, and trihemitone. The enharmonic is sung in descending by ditone, diesis, and diesis, but in ascending by diesis, diesis, and ditone.

4. In the diatonic, chromatic, and enharmonic genera the notes are these:

Proslambanomenos	Proslambanomenos	Proslambanomenos
Hypate hypaton	Hypate hypaton	Hypate hypaton
Parhypate hypaton	Parhypate hypaton	Parhypate hypaton
Diatonic lichanos hypaton	Chromatic lichanos hypaton	Enharmonic lichanos hypaton
Hypate meson	Hypate meson	Hypate meson
Parhypate meson	Parhypate meson	Parhypate meson
Diatonic lichanos meson	Chromatic lichanos meson	Enharmonic lichanos meson
Mese	Mese	Mese
Trite synemmenon	Trite synemmenon	Trite synemmenon
Diatonic paranete synemmenon	Chromatic paranete synemmenon	Enharmonic paranete synemmenon
Nete synemmenon	Nete synemmenon	Nete synemmenon
Paramese	Paramese	Paramese
Trite diezeugmenon	Trite diezeugmenon	Trite diezeugmenon
Diatonic paranete diezeugmenon	Chromatic paranete diezeugmenon	Enharmonic paranete diezeugmenon
Nete diezeugmenon	Nete diezeugmenon	Nete diezeugmenon
Trite hyperbolaion	Trite hyperbolaion	Trite hyperbolaion
Diatonic paranete hyperbolaion	Chromatic paranete hyperbolaion	Enharmonic paranete hyperbolaion
Nete hyperbolaion	Nete hyperbolaion	Nete hyperbolaion

In the blending of the genera they are these:

Proslambanomenos

Hypate hypaton
Parhypate hypaton
Enharmonic lichanos hypaton
Chromatic lichanos hypaton
Diatonic lichanos hypaton

Hypate meson
Parhypate meson
Enharmonic lichanos meson
Chromatic lichanos meson
Diatonic lichanos meson
Mese

Trite synemmenon
Enharmonic paranete synemmenon

Chromatic paranete synemmenon
Diatonic paranete synemmenon
Nete synemmenon

Paramese
Trite diezeugmenon
Enharmonic paranete diezeugmenon
Chromatic paranete diezeugmenon
Diatonic paranete diezeugmenon
Nete diezeugmenon

Trite hyperbolaion
Enharmonic paranete hyperbolaion
Chromatic paranete hyperbolaion
Diatonic paranete hyperbolaion
Nete hyperbolaion

Of the notes enumerated some are fixed, others movable. The fixed notes are all those that remain unchanged and on the same pitches in the different genera. The movable notes are all those in the opposite case; these do not remain unchanged and on the same pitches in the different genera. The fixed notes are eight, namely the proslambanomenos, hypate hypaton, hypate meson, mese, nete synemmenon, paramese, nete diezeugmenon, and nete hyperbolaion; the movable notes are all those that lie between these.

Of the fixed notes some are barypykna, others lie outside the pykna and bound the perfect systems. Five are barypykna, namely the hypate hypaton, hypate meson, mese, paramese, and nete diezeugmenon. The other three lie outside the pykna and bound the perfect systems, namely the proslambanomenos, nete synemmenon, and nete hyperbolaion.

Of the movable notes some are mesopykna, others are oxypykna, others are diatonic. Five are mesopykna, namely the parhypate hypaton, parhypate meson, trite synemmenon, trite diezeugmenon, and trite hyperbolaion. In each genus five are oxypykna: in the enharmonic genus of enharmonic pykna, in the chromatic genus of chromatic pykna; the diatonic genus does not share in the pyknon. In the enharmonic they are these: the enharmonic lichanos hypaton, enharmonic lichanos meson, enharmonic paranete synemmenon, enharmonic paranete diezeugmenon, and enharmonic paranete hyperbolaion. In the chromatic they are these: the chromatic lichanos hypaton, chromatic lichanos meson, chromatic paranete synemmenon, chromatic paranete diezeugmenon, and chromatic paranete hyperbolaion. In the diatonic they are these: the diatonic lichanos hypaton, diatonic lichanos meson, diatonic paranete synemmenon, diatonic paranete diezeugmenon, and diatonic paranete hyperbolaion.

5. Of intervals the differences are five, in that they differ from one another in magnitude, and in genus, and as the symphonic from the diaphonic, and as the composite from the incomposite, and as the rational from the irrational. They differ in magnitude in so far as some intervals are larger and others smaller, for example the ditone, tone, semitone, diatessaron, diapente, diapason, and the like. They differ in genus in so far as some intervals are diatonic, others chromatic, and others enharmonic. They differ as the symphonic from the diaphonic in so far as some intervals are symphonic and others diaphonic. The symphonic intervals are the diatessaron, diapente, diapason, and the like. The diaphonic intervals are all those smaller than the diatessaron and all those lying between the symphonic intervals. The intervals smaller than the diatessaron are the diesis, semitone, tone, trihemitone, and ditone; those lying between the symphonic intervals are the tritone, the tetratone, the pentatone, and the like. And symphony is a blending of two notes, a higher and a lower; diaphony, on the contrary, is a refusal of two notes to combine, with the result that they do not blend but grate harshly on the ear. Intervals differ in composition in so far as some are incomposite and others composite. The incomposite intervals are those bounded by consecutive notes, for example the intervals bounded by the hypate and parhypate and by the lichanos and mese; the same applies to the remaining intervals. The composite intervals are those not bounded by consecutive notes, for example the intervals bounded by the mese and parhypate and by the mese and nete and by the paramese and hypate. Thus certain intervals are common to the composite and incomposite, namely those from the semitone to the ditone. For the semitone is composite in the enharmonic genus, but incomposite in the chromatic and diatonic; the tone is composite in the chromatic genus, but incomposite in the diatonic; the trihemitone is incomposite in the chromatic genus, but composite in the diatonic; the ditone is incomposite in the enharmonic genus, but composite in the chromatic and diatonic. All intervals smaller than the semitone are incomposite; all intervals larger than the ditone are composite. Intervals differ as the rational from the irrational in so far as some are rational and others irrational. The rational intervals are those whose magnitudes can be defined, such as the tone, semitone, ditone, tritone, and the like. The irrational intervals are those deviating from these magnitudes to a greater or lesser degree by some irrational quantity.

6. The genera are the three already enumerated. For every melody

will be either diatonic or chromatic or enharmonic or common or a mixture of these. The diatonic genus is the one using diatonic division, the chromatic genus the one using chromatic division, the enharmonic genus the one using enharmonic division. The common genus is the one made up of the fixed notes. The mixed genus is the one in which two or three generic characteristics reveal themselves, such as diatonic and chromatic, or diatonic and enharmonic, or chromatic and enharmonic, or diatonic, chromatic, and enharmonic. The differences of the genera arise in connection with the movable notes, for the lichanos is moved within the locus of a tone, the parhypate within that of a diesis. Thus the highest lichanos is that a tone distant from the upper boundary of the tetrachord, the lowest that a ditone distant. In the same way the lowest parhypate is a diesis distant from the lower boundary of the tetrachord, the highest a semitone distant.

7. Shade is a specific division of a genus. There are six distinct and recognized shades: one enharmonic, three chromatic, and two diatonic.

The shade of the enharmonic uses the division of the genus itself, for it is sung by a diesis equivalent to a quarter-tone, another diesis equal to it, and a ditone.

Of the chromatic divisions, the lowest is the shade of the soft chromatic; it is sung by a diesis equivalent to a third-tone, another diesis equal to it, and the equivalent of a tone plus a half-tone plus a third-tone. The hemiolic chromatic is sung by a hemiolic diesis equivalent to one and one-half times the enharmonic diesis, another diesis equal to it, and an incomposite interval equivalent to seven enharmonic dieses. The tonic chromatic uses the shade of the genus itself, for it is sung by semitone, semitone, and trihemitone. And the chromatic shades just enumerated take their names from their pykna: the tonic chromatic from the tone inherent in its pyknon as a composite interval; the hemiolic chromatic from the hemiolic diesis inherent in its pyknon, one and one-half times the enharmonic diesis; in the same way the soft chromatic is the one having the least pyknon, seeing that its pyknon is relaxed and tuned down.

Of the diatonic divisions one is called soft, the other syntonic. The shade of the soft diatonic is sung by a semitone, an incomposite interval equivalent to three enharmonic dieses, and an interval equivalent to five enharmonic dieses, likewise incomposite. That of the syntonic diatonic shares the division of the genus itself, for it is sung by semitone, tone, and tone.

The shades are also shown by numbers in this manner. The tone is assumed to be divided into twelve least parts, of which each one is called a twelfth-tone. The remaining intervals are also assumed to be divided in the same proportion, the semitone into six twelfths, the diesis equivalent to a quarter-tone into three twelfths, the diesis equivalent to a third-tone into four twelfths, the whole diatessaron into thirty twelfths. In terms of quantity, then, the enharmonic will be sung by 3, 3, and 24 twelfths, the soft chromatic by 4, 4, and 22, the hemiolic chromatic by 4½, 4½ and 21, the tonic chromatic by 6, 6, and 18, the soft diatonic by 6, 9, and 15, the syntonic diatonic by 6, 12, and 12.

8. Of systems the differences are seven. Four of these were found also in intervals; these are the differences in magnitude, in genus, of the symphonic and diaphonic, and of the rational and irrational. Three differences are peculiar to systems; these are the differences of the progression by step and by leap, of the conjunct and the disjunct, and of the non-modulating and the modulating. In magnitude the larger systems differ from the smaller, as the system of the diapason from that of the tritone or diapente or diatessaron or the like. In genus the diatonic systems differ from the enharmonic or chromatic, or the chromatic or enharmonic from the others. Considered as symphonic or diaphonic, the systems bounded by symphonies will differ from those bounded by diaphonies. Of the systems within the non-modulating system six are symphonic: the smallest is that of the diatessaron, of two tones and a half, for example that from the hypate hypaton to hypate meson; the second, that of the diapente, of three tones and a half, for example that from the proslambanomenos to hypate meson; the third, that of the diapason, of six tones, for example that from the proslambanomenos to mese; the fourth, that of the diapason plus diatessaron, of eight tones and a half, for example that from the proslambanomenos to nete synemmenon or diatonic paranete diezeugmenon; the fifth, that of the diapason plus diapente, of nine tones and a half, for example that from the proslambanomenos to nete diezeugmenon; the sixth, that of the double diapason, of twelve tones, for example that from the proslambanomenos to nete hyperbolaion. The synemmenon system goes only as far as the fourth symphony; in this system the first symphony is that of the diatessaron, the second that of the diapente, the third that of the diapason, the fourth that of the diapason plus diatessaron. But the region of the voice extends to the seventh and eighth symphonies, which are the double diapason plus diatessaron and the double diapason plus diapente. The diaphonic systems are those smaller than that of the diatessaron and all those lying between the symphonic systems.

9. Figures (or species) of a particular magnitude arise when the order of the simple parts of the given whole undergoes a change with respect to

some dissimilar constituent part, the magnitude and number of the parts remaining the same. For when the parts are all equal and similar there is no change in the figures.[2]

Of the diatessaron there are three species. The first is that bounded by barypykna, as is that from the hypate hypaton to hypate meson; the second that bounded by mesopykna, as is that from the parhypate hypaton to parhypate meson; the third that bounded by oxypykna, as is that from the lichanos hypaton to lichanos meson. Thus in the enharmonic and chromatic genera the figures are comprehended in accordance with the nature of the pyknon.

But in the diatonic genus the figures do not occur in connection with a pyknon, for this genus is divided into semitones and tones. The symphony of the diatessaron contains one semitone and two tones; in the same way the diapente contains one semitone and three tones and the diapason two semitones and five tones. In this genus, then, the figures are considered in accordance with the nature of the semitones. Thus in the diatonic genus the first species of the diatessaron is that in which the semitone lies below the tones, the second that in which it lies above the tones, the third that in which it lies between the tones. And these species begin and end with the same notes as in the other genera.

Of the diapente there are four figures. The first, bounded by barypykna, is that in which the tone is at the top; it extends from the hypate meson to paramese. The second, bounded by mesopykna, is that in which the tone is second from the top; it extends from the parhypate meson to trite diezeugmenon. The third, bounded by oxypykna, is that in which the tone is third from the top; it extends from the lichanos meson to paranete diezeugmenon. The fourth, bounded by barypykna, is that in which the tone is at the bottom; it extends from the mese to nete diezeugmenon or from the proslambanomenos to hypate meson.

In the diatonic genus the first figure is that in which the semitone lies at the bottom, the second that in which it lies at the top, the third that in which it is second from the top, the fourth that in which it is third from the top.

Of the diapason there are seven species. The first, bounded by barypykna, is that in which the tone is at the top; it extends from the hypate hypaton to paramese and was called Mixolydian by the ancients.

---

2 Cf. Aristoxenus, *Harmonic Elements* (Macran's edition, p. 222): "Such a difference [of species] arises when the order of the simple parts of a certain whole is altered, while both the number and magnitude of those parts remain the same"; also Aristotle, *Politics*, 1276B: "And similarly with any other common whole or composite structure we say it is different if the form (εἶδος) of its composition is different—for instance a harmony consisting of the same notes we call different if at one time it is Dorian and at another Phrygian." [Rackham]

The second, bounded by mesopykna, is that in which the tone is second from the top; it extends from the parhypate hypaton to trite diezeugmenon and was called Lydian.

The third, bounded by oxypykna, is that in which the tone is third from the top; it extends from the lichanos hypaton to paranete diezeugmenon and was called Phrygian.

The fourth, bounded by barypykna, is that in which the tone is fourth from the top; it extends from the hypate meson to nete diezeugmenon and was called Dorian.

The fifth, bounded by mesopykna, is that in which the tone is fifth from the top; it extends from the parhypate meson to trite hyperbolaion and was called Hypolydian.

The sixth, bounded by oxypykna, is that in which the tone is sixth from the top; it extends from the lichanos meson to paranete hyperbolaion and was called Hypophrygian.

The seventh, bounded by barypykna, is that in which the tone is at the bottom; it extends from the mese to nete hyperbolaion or from the proslambanomenos to mese and was called common or Locrian or Hypodorian.

In the diatonic genus the first species of the diapason is that in which the semitone is first from the bottom but fourth from the top; the second is that in which it is third from the bottom but first from the top; the third is that in which it is second from either end; the fourth is that in which it is first from the bottom but third from the top; the fifth is that in which it is fourth from the bottom but first from the top; the sixth is that in which it is third from the bottom but second from the top; the seventh is that in which it is second from the bottom but third from the top. And these species begin and end with the same notes as in the enharmonic and chromatic genera and were called by the same names.

Considered as rational and irrational, the systems made up of rational intervals will differ from those made up of irrational ones, for those made up of rational intervals are rational, those made up of irrational ones irrational.

Considered as progressing by step and by leap, the systems that are sung by consecutive notes will differ from those that are sung by notes that are not consecutive.

Considered as conjunct and disjunct, the systems put together from conjunct tetrachords will differ from those put together from disjunct. And a conjunction is the note common to two tetrachords of the same species, sung one after another; a disjunction is the tone between two tetrachords of the same species, sung one after another. There are in all three conjunctions: the middle, the highest, and the lowest. The lowest conjunction is that of the tetrachords hypate and meson; the note common to this conjunction is the hypate meson. The middle conjunction is that of the tetrachords meson and neton synemmenon; the note common to this conjunction is the mese. The highest conjunction is that of the tetrachords neton diezeugmenon and hyperbolaion; the note common to this conjunction is the nete diezeugmenon. There is one disjunction, that of the tetrachords meson and neton diezeugmenon; the tone common to this disjunction is that from the mese to paramese.

Of perfect systems there are two, of which one is lesser, the other greater. The Lesser Perfect System is that by conjunction, extending from the proslambanomenos to nete synemmenon. There are in this system three conjunct tetrachords, namely the hypaton, meson, and synemmenon, and there is a tone between the proslambanomenos and hypate hypaton; this system is bounded by the symphony diapason plus diatessaron.

The Greater Perfect System is that by disjunction, extending from the proslambanomenos to nete hyperbolaion. There are in this system four tetrachords, two conjunct pairs mutually disjunct, namely the hypaton and meson and the diezeugmenon and hyperbolaion, and there are two tones, one between the proslambanomenos and hypate hypaton, the other between the mese and paramese; this system is bounded by the symphony double diapason.

Of the five tetrachords in the non-modulating system, which is put together from the two perfect ones, two are common to both the perfect systems: the tetrachords hypaton and meson; peculiar to the conjunct system is the tetrachord neton synemmenon; peculiar to the disjunct system are the tetrachords neton diezeugmenon and hyperbolaion.

11. Considered as non-modulating and modulating, the systems will differ in so far as the simple systems differ from those that are not simple. The simple systems are those in harmony with one mese, the duple those in harmony with two, the triple those in harmony with three, the multiple those in harmony with many. To be a mese is the function of the note whose property it is, in disjunction, to have above it an incomposite tone (this part of the system remaining unaffected) but below it an incomposite or composite ditone; in conjunction, however, there being three conjunct tetrachords, it is its property to be the highest note of the middle tetra-

chord or the lowest note of the highest tetrachord. And it is from the mese that the functions of the remaining notes are recognized, for it is clearly in relation to the mese that each of them is thus or thus.[3]

12. The word "tone" is used in four senses: as note, interval, region of the voice, and pitch. It is used in the sense of note in the epithet "seven-toned" as applied to the phorminx, for instance by Terpander and Ion. The former says:

To thee we will play new hymns upon a phorminx of seven tones and will love the four-voiced lay no more; [4]

the latter:

Eleven-stringèd lyre with thy flight of ten steps into the place where the three concordant roads of Harmonia meet, once all the Greeks raised but a meagre music, playing thee seven-toned four by four.[5]

And not a few others have used the epithet. We use the word "tone" in the sense of interval whenever we say that it is a tone from the mese to para-mese.

We use it of the region of the voice whenever we speak of Dorian, or Phrygian, or Lydian, or any of the other tones. According to Aristoxenus there are 13 tones:

Hypermixolydian, also called Hyperphrygian;
Two Mixolydians, a higher and a lower, of which the higher is also called Hyperiastian, the lower Hyperdorian;
Two Lydians, a higher and a lower, of which the lower is also called Aeolian;
Two Phrygians, a higher and a lower, of which the lower is also called Iastian;
One Dorian;
Two Hypolydians, a higher and a lower, the latter also called Hypoaeolian;
Two Hypophrygians, of which the lower is also called Hypoiastian;
Hypodorian.

Of these the highest is the Hypermixolydian, the lowest the Hypo-dorian. From the highest to the lowest, the distance between consecutive tones is a semitone, between two parallel tones a trihemitone; with the distance between the remaining tones the case will be similar. The Hyper-mixolydian is a diapason above the Hypodorian.

---

3 On the function of the mese cf. Aristotle, *Metaphysics*, 1018B; *Politics*, 1254A; *Problems*, 1919A (Problem 20).
4 Translation by J. M. Edmonds; see his edition of the *Lyra Graeca* for the Loeb Classical Library, I (London, 1928), 33.

5 Translation by J. M. Edmonds; see his *Elegy and Iambus*, published in the Loeb Classical Library, I (London, 1931), 433.

We use the word "tone" in the sense of pitch when we speak of using a higher or lower or intermediate tone of voice.

13. The word "modulation" is used in four senses: with reference to genus, system, tone, and melodic composition. Modulation in genus takes place whenever there is a modulation from the diatonic genus to the chromatic or enharmonic, or from the chromatic or enharmonic to some one of the others. Modulation in system takes place whenever there is a modulation from the conjunct system to the disjunct, or vice versa. Modulation in tone takes place whenever there is a modulation from the Dorian tone to the Phrygian, or from the Phrygian to the Lydian or Hypermixolydian or Hypodorian, or in general whenever there is a modulation from any one of the thirteen tones to any other. Modulations begin with the semitone and proceed to the diapason, some of them being made by symphonic intervals, others by diaphonic. Those made by symphonic intervals and by that of the tone are melodious. Of the rest, some are more melodious than unmelodious, others less so. For the greater or less the community of elements, the more melodious or unmelodious the modulation, seeing that every modulation requires the presence of some common element, whether a note, an interval, or a system. But this community is determined by the similarity of the notes, for a modulation is melodious or unmelodious in so far as it involves the coincidence of notes that are similar or dissimilar with respect to their participation in a pyknon.

Modulation in melodic composition takes place whenever there is a modulation in ethos from the diastaltic to the systaltic or hesychastic, or from the hesychastic to some one of the others.[6] The diastaltic ethos in melodic composition is that which reveals heroic deeds and the grandeur and loftiness of a manly soul and an affection akin to these. It is most used in tragedy and in all things that border on this character. The systaltic ethos is that by which the soul is brought into dejection and an effeminate condition. Such a state will correspond to erotic affections and to dirges and expressions of pity and things resembling these. The hesychastic ethos is that which accompanies quietude of soul and a liberal and peaceful state. To it will correspond hymns, paeans, eulogies, counsels, and things similar to these.

14. Melodic composition is the use of the enumerated parts of harmonics, which have the function of subject-matter. Melodic composition is accomplished by means of four figures: succession, plexus or network, repetition or selection, and prolongation. Succession is a progression of the

---

6 Cf. the threefold classification of Aristotle, *Politics,* 1341B (p. 22 above).

melody by consecutive notes; plexus or network a placing of intervals side by side; repetition or selection a striking of a single tone, repeated several times; prolongation a dwelling for a greater time-interval on a single utterance of the voice.

5. Athenaeus

A Greek rhetorician and grammarian of Naucratis in Egypt, Athenaeus lived in Rome about 200 A.D. Of his works we still possess fifteen books of the *Deipnosophistai* (Sophists at Dinner)—originally thirty books—an immense mine of information on matters connected with everyday life, the table, music, songs, dances, games, literature, etc. Its value as source material cannot be overestimated, as it is filled with quotations from writers whose works have not been preserved. In all, Athenaeus refers to nearly 800 writers. The work professes to be an account given by the author to his friend Timocrates of a banquet held at the house of Laurentius, a scholar and wealthy patron of art.

From the Sophists at Dinner [1]

ON THE subject of music there was daily conversation, some saying things recorded here, others saying other things, but all joining in praise of this kind of amusement; and Masurius, in all things excellent and wise (for he is a jurist second to none, and he has always been devoted to music and has taken up the playing of musical instruments), said: The comic poet Eupolis, my friends, remarks: "Music is a matter deep and intricate," and it is always supplying something new for those who can perceive. Hence Anaxilas, also, says in *Hyacinthus*: "Music is like Libya, which, I swear by the gods, brings forth some new creature every year." To quote *The Harp-Singer* of Theophilus: "A mighty treasure, good sirs, and a constant one, is music for all who have learned it and are educated." For indeed it trains character, and tames the hot-tempered and those whose opinions clash. The Pythagorean Cleinias, for example, as Chamaeleon of Pontus records, whose conduct and character were exemplary,

1 Text: *The Deipnosophists*, VI (Cambridge, Mass., Harvard University Press, 1937), 361–387, 409–419. Translated for the Loeb Classical Library by Charles Burton Gulick. Reprinted by permission of Harvard University Press.

would always take his cithara and play on it whenever it happened that he was exasperated to the point of anger. And in answer to those who inquired the reason he would say, "I am calming myself down." So, too, the Homeric Achilles calmed himself with his cithara, which was the only thing Homer grants to him out of the booty taken from Eëtion, and which had the power of allaying his fiery nature. He, at least, is the only one in the *Iliad* who plays this kind of music. That music can also heal diseases Theophrastus has recorded in his work *On Inspiration:* he says that persons subject to sciatica would always be free from its attacks if one played the aulos in the Phrygian harmony over the part affected. This harmony was first discovered by the Phrygians and constantly used by them. For this reason, he says, aulos-players among the Greeks have names which are Phrygian and appropriate to slaves; such, for example, is Sambas, mentioned by Alcman, also Adon and Telus, and in Hipponax, Cion, Codalus, and Babys, who occasioned the proverb said of those whose aulos-playing grows ever worse and worse, "Babys is playing worse." Aristoxenus attributes its invention to the Phrygian Hyagnis.

Heracleides of Pontus, however, says in the third book of his work *On Music* that the Phrygian should not be called a separate harmony any more than the Lydian. For there are only three harmonies, since there are also only three kinds of Greeks—Dorians, Aeolians, and Ionians. There is no small difference in the characters of these three, for while the Lacedaemonians preserve better than all other Dorians the customs of their fathers, and the Thessalians (these are they who conferred upon the Aeolians the origin of their race) have always maintained practically the same mode of life, the great majority of the Ionians, on the other hand, have undergone changes due to barbarian rulers who have for the time being come in contact with them. Hence the melodic style which the Dorians constructed they called the Dorian harmony; Aeolian they called the harmony which the Aeolians sang; Ionian, they said of the third one, which they heard Ionians sing. Now the Dorian harmony exhibits the quality of manly vigor, of magnificent bearing, not relaxed or merry, but sober and intense, neither varied nor complicated. But the Aeolian character contains the elements of ostentation and turgidity, and even conceit; these qualities are in keeping with their horse-breeding and their way of meeting strangers; yet this does not mean malice, but is, rather, lofty and confident. Hence also their fondness for drinking is something appropriate to them, also their love-affairs, and the entirely relaxed nature of their daily life. Wherefore they have the character of the Hypodorian harmony, as it is called. This, Heracleides says, is in fact the one which they called Aeolian, as Lasus of Hermione does in the "Hymn to Demeter of Hermion" in the following words: "I celebrate Demeter and Kore, wedded wife of Pluto, raising unto them a sweet-voiced hymn in the deep-toned Aeolian harmony." These lyrics are sung by all in the Hypodorian. Since, then, the melody is Hypodorian, it naturally follows that Lasus calls the harmony Aeolian. Again, Pratinas says, I believe: "Pursue neither the intense Muse nor yet the relaxed Ionian, but ploughing rather the middle glebe play the Aeolian with your melody." And in what follows he says more plainly: "Verily the Aeolian harmony is the song that befits all the bold." [2] Formerly, then, as I have said, they called it Aeolian, but later Hypodorian, as some assert, because they thought that in the auloi it had a range below the Dorian harmony.[3] But I believe that people who observed the turgid quality and pretence of nobleness in the character of the Aeolian harmony, regarded it not as Dorian at all, but something which somehow resembled the Dorian; hence they called it Hypodorian, just as we say that what resembles white is rather (*hypo-*) white, or what is not sweet, yet nearly sweet, rather (*hypo-*) sweet: in similar fashion they called Hypodorian that which was not quite Dorian.

Next in order let us examine the Milesians' character, which the Ionians illustrate. Because of their excellent physical condition they bear themselves haughtily, they are full of irate spirit, hard to placate, fond of contention, never condescending to kindliness nor cheerfulness, displaying a lack of affection and a hardness in their character. Hence also the kind of music known as the Ionian harmony is neither bright nor cheerful, but austere and hard, having a seriousness which is not ignoble; and so their harmony is well-adapted to tragedy. But the character of the Ionians today is more voluptuous, and the character of their harmony is much altered. They say that Pythermus of Teos composed lyric scolia in this kind of harmony, and since the poet was an Ionian the harmony was called Ionian. This is the Pythermus mentioned by Ananius or Hipponax in their *Iambic Verses:* . . . And in another passage as follows: "Pythermus speaks of gold as if other things were naught." In fact Pythermus

---

2 On the interpretation of these lines of Pratinas see D. B. Monro, *The Modes of Ancient Greek Music* (Oxford, 1894), pp. 5-6, and Professor Gulick's note in the Loeb Library edition of his translation (VI, 369). Since Dorian, Aeolian, and Ionian are the only harmonies under discussion in this paragraph, we may perhaps take 'the high-strung Muse" as referring to Dorian— or at least assume that the phrase was so understood by Heracleides or Athenaeus. But no matter how we take it and regardless of whether we understand the lines in a modal or in a tonal sense, the characterization of Aeolian as intermediate will be unintelligible unless we assume, as Professor Gulick implies, that it refers, not to pitch or structure, but to ethical quality.

3 See Aristoxenus, *Harmonic Elements* (p. 29 above), where Aristoxenus explains that those predecessors of his who based their enumeration of the keys on the boring of the finger-holes on the auloi placed the Hypodorian key three dieses below the Dorian.

does speak of it thus: "Other things, after all, are naught compared with gold." And so, considering also this saying of his, it is to be believed that Pythermus, being from Ionia, made the style of his lyrics fit the character of the Ionians. Hence I assume that it was not the Ionian harmony in which Pythermus composed, but a curious variation of harmonic figure. So one should look with disdain on those who cannot see specific differences, but simply attend to the highness or lowness of notes, and assume a Hypermixolydian harmony and again another higher than that. Nor can I see, in fact, that the Hyperphrygian has a special character of its own. And yet some persons assert that they have discovered another new, Hypophrygian, harmony! But a harmony must have a specific character or feeling, like the Locrian; this was once employed by some who flourished in the time of Simonides and Pindar, but it fell into disrepute again.[4]

These harmonies, then, are three, as we said of them at the beginning, being as many as there are tribes of Greeks. The Phrygian and the Lydian harmonies, originating with the barbarians, came to be known to the Greeks from the Phrygians and Lydians who emigrated to Peloponnesus with Pelops. The Lydians accompanied him because Sipylus was a city of Lydia; the Phrygians came not only because they lived on the borders of Lydia but also because Tantalus ruled over them. You may see everywhere in Peloponnesus, but especially in Lacedaemon, large mounds, which they call the tombs of the Phrygians who came with Pelops. These musical harmonies, then, the Greeks learned from them. Hence also Telestes of Selinus says: "The first to sing the Phrygian nome in honor of the Mountain Mother, amid the auloi beside the mixing-bowls of the Greeks, were they who came in the company of Pelops; and the Greeks struck up the Lydian hymn with the high-pitched twanging of the pectis."

Polybius of Megalopolis says:[5] "One must not accept it as fact that music was introduced among men for purposes of deceit and quackery, as Ephorus asserts that it was; nor should one believe that the ancient Cretans and Lacedaemonians introduced the aulos and a marching rhythm into battle, instead of the trumpet, without good reason; nor was it by chance that the earliest Arcadians carried the art of music into their entire social organization, so that they made it obligatory and habitual not only for boys but also for young men up to thirty years of age, although in all other respects they were most austere in their habits of life. It is only

---

4 This polemic against those who presume to add to the established harmonies is well discussed by Winnington-Ingram (*Mode in Ancient Greek Music*, Cambridge, 1936, pp. 20–21).

5 *Histories* IV, xx, 5–21.

among the Arcadians, at any rate, that the boys, from infancy up, are by law practised in singing hymns and paeans, in which, according to ancestral custom, they celebrate their national heroes and gods. After these they learn the nomes of Timotheus and Philoxenus and dance them annually in the theatres with Dionysiac aulos-players, the boys competing in the boys' contests, the young men in the contests of adult males. And throughout their whole lives, in their social gatherings they do not pursue methods and practices so much with the aid of imported entertainments as with their own talents, requiring one another to sing each in his turn. As for other branches of training, it is no disgrace to confess that one knows nothing, but it is deemed a disgrace among them to decline to sing. What is more, they practise marching-songs with aulos accompaniment in regular order, and further, they drill themselves in dances and display them annually in the theatres with elaborate care and at public expense. All this, therefore, the men of old taught them, not to gratify luxury and wealth, but because they observed the hardness in every one's life and the austerity of their character, which are the natural accompaniment of the coldness of their environment and the gloominess prevailing for the most part in their abodes; for all of us human beings naturally become assimilated to the character of our abode; hence it is also differences in our national position that cause us to differ very greatly from one another in character, in build, and in complexion. In addition to the training just described, their ancestors taught the Arcadian men and women the practice of public assembly and sacrifice, also at the same time choruses of girls and boys, eager as they were to civilize and soften the toughness of their natures by customs regularly organized. But the people of Cynaetha came at the end to neglect these customs, although they occupied by far the rudest part of Arcadia in point of topography as well as climate; when they plunged right into friction and rivalry with one another they finally became so brutalized that among them alone occurred the gravest acts of sacrilege. At the time when they brought upon themselves the great massacre, into whatever Arcadian cities they went on their way through, all the others immediately barred them out by public proclamation, but the Mantinaeans, after their withdrawal, instituted a purification of their city, carrying the blood of slain animals round about their entire territory."

Agias, the writer on music, has said that storax, which is burned as incense in the orchestras at the festival of Dionysus, produces a "Phrygian" odor to those who smell it.

In ancient times music was an incitement to bravery. At any rate the poet Alcaeus, who certainly was very musical, if any one ever was, places deeds of bravery higher than the achievements of poetry, since he was more than ordinarily warlike. Wherefore, pluming himself on these activities, he says: "The great hall glistens with bronze; the whole roof is adorned by the War-god with shining helmets, and over them wave white plumes of horsehair, adornments for the heads of heroes; shining greaves of bronze, defence against the cruel missiles, hide the pegs on which they hang; corslets of new linen and hollow shields lie scattered on the ground, and beside them are Chalcidian swords, beside them, too, many sashes and tunics. These we must not forget, now that before all else we have set ourselves to this task." And yet it doubtless would have been more fitting for his house to be full of musical instruments. However, the men of old assumed that bravery is the highest of civic virtues, and to this they thought it right to allot most honors . . . not to other men. Archilochus, at any rate, who was an excellent poet, made it his first boast that he was able to take part in these civic rivalries, and only secondarily mentioned his poetic talents, saying: "I am the squire of the lord Enyalius, and I am versed, too, in the lovely gift of the Muses." Similarly Aeschylus also, for all the great repute which he enjoys because of his poetry, none the less thought it right to have his bravery recorded by preference on his tomb, having composed this inscription: "Of his glorious might the grove at Marathon could tell, and the long-haired Medes—for they know!"

Hence it is that the brave Lacedaemonians march to battle with the music of the auloi, the Cretans with the lyre, the Lydians with syrinxes and the auloi, as Herodotus records.[6] Many of the barbarians also conduct diplomatic negotiations to the accompaniment of the auloi and cithara to soften the hearts of their opponents. Theopompus, in the forty-sixth book of his *Histories*, says: "The Getae conduct negotiations holding citharas in their hands and playing on them." Whence it is plain that Homer observes the ancient Greek system when he says: "(We have satisfied our souls with the equal feast) and with the phorminx, which the gods have made the companion of the feast,"[7] evidently because the art is beneficial also to those who feast. And this was the accepted custom, it is plain, first in order that every one who felt impelled to get drunk and stuff himself might have music to cure his violence and intemperance, and secondly, because music appeases surliness; for, by stripping off a man's gloominess, it produces good-temper and gladness becoming to a gentleman, wherefore Homer introduced the gods, in the first part of the *Iliad*, making

6 *Histories*, I, 17.   7 *Odyssey*, VIII, 99; XVII, 270–271.

use of music. For after their quarrel over Achilles, they spent the time continually listening "to the beautiful phorminx that Apollo held, and to the Muses who sang responsively with beautiful voice." [8] For that was bound to stop their bickerings and faction, as we were saying. It is plain, therefore, that while most persons devote this art to social gatherings for the sake of correcting conduct and of general usefulness, the ancients went further and included in their customs and laws the singing of praises to the gods by all who attended feasts, in order that our dignity and sobriety might be retained through their help. For, since the songs are sung in concert, if discourse on the gods has been added it dignifies the mood of every one. Philochorus says that the ancients, in pouring libations, do not always sing dithyrambs, but when they pour libations, they celebrate Dionysus with wine and drunkenness, but Apollo, in quiet and good order. Archilochus, at any rate, says: "For I know how to lead off, in the lovely song of lord Dionysus, the dithyramb, when my wits have been stricken with the thunder-bolt of wine." And Epicharmus, also, said in *Philoctetes:* "There can be no dithyramb when you drink water." It is plain, therefore, in the light of what we have said, that music did not, at the beginning, make its way into feasts merely for the sake of shallow and ordinary pleasure, as some persons think. As for the Lacedaemonians, if they studied the art of music, they say nothing of it, but that they are able to judge the art well is admitted by them, and in fact they assert that they have saved the art three times when it was threatened with debasement.[9]

. . . . .

In olden times the feeling for nobility was always maintained in the art of music, and all its elements skillfully retained the orderly beauty appropriate to them. Hence there were auloi peculiarly adapted to every harmony, and every player had auloi suited to every harmony used in the public contests. But Pronomus of Thebes began the practice of playing all the harmonies on the same auloi. Today, however, people take up music in a haphazard and irrational manner. In early times popularity with the masses was a sign of bad art; hence, when a certain aulos-player once received loud applause, Asopodorus of Phlius, who was himself still waiting in the wings, said "What's this? Something awful must have happened!" The player evidently could not have won approval with the crowd otherwise. (I am aware that some persons have narrated this story with Antigeneidas as the speaker.) And yet the musicians

---

[8] *Iliad*, I, 603–604.   [9] Cf. Aristotle, *Politics*, 1339B (p. 17 above).

of our day set as the goal of their art success with their audiences. Hence Aristoxenus in his *Drinking-Miscellany* says: "We act like the people of Poseidonia, who dwell on the Tyrrhenian Gulf. It so happened that although they were originally Greeks, they were completely barbarized, becoming Tuscans or Romans; they changed their speech and their other practices, but they still celebrate one festival that is Greek to this day, wherein they gather together and recall those ancient words and institutions, and after bewailing them and weeping over them in one another's presence they depart home. In like manner we also (says Aristoxenus), now that our theatres have become utterly barbarized and this prostituted music has moved on into a state of grave corruption, will get together by ourselves, few though we be, and recall what the art of music used to be." So much for what Aristoxenus says.

In view of this it is plain to me also that music should be the subject of philosophic reflection. Pythagoras of Samos, with all his great fame as a philosopher, is one of many conspicuous for having taken up music as no mere hobby; on the contrary, he explains the very being of the universe as bound together by musical principles. Taking it all together, it is plain that the ancient "wisdom" of the Greeks was given over especially to music. For this reason they regarded Apollo, among the gods, and Orpheus, among the demigods, as most musical and most wise; and they called all who followed this art sophists, as Aeschylus has done: "Then the sophist wildly struck his tortoise-shell lyre with notes discordant." And that the men of old were disposed to treat music with the greatest familiarity is clear also from Homer; why, in setting all his poetry to music he often, without thought, composes verses which are "acephalous," or "slack," or even "taper off at the end." But Xenophanes, Solon, Theognis, Phocylides, also the Corinthian elegiac poet Periander and other poets who do not add melodies to their poetry, finish off their verses in respect of the counting and the arrangement of the metrical feet, and see to it that not one of them is either acephalous or slack or tapering. Acephalous verses are those which have the quality of lameness at the beginning: "When they had come to the ships and to the Hellespont." "A strap lay stretched upon it, made of a slaughtered ox's hide." Slack verses are lame in the middle, as for example: "Then quickly Aeneas, dear son of Anchises." "Their leaders, again, were the two sons of Asclepius." Tapering verses limp at the close: "The Trojans shivered when they saw the wriggling snake." "Fair Cassiepeia, like unto the gods in form." "With this wine I filled a mighty goat-skin and carried it, with provisions as well."

Of all the Greeks the Spartans have most faithfully preserved the art of music, employing it most extensively, and many composers of lyrics have arisen among them. Even to this day they carefully retain the ancient songs, and are very well taught in them and strict in holding to them. Hence Pratinas says: "The Spartan, that cicada ready for a chorus." Wherefore, also, their poets continually addressed songs in terms like these: "Leader of sweetest hymns," and "Mellifluous melodies of the Muses." For people were glad to turn from the soberness and austerity of life to the solace of music, because the art has the power to charm. With good reason, therefore, the listeners enjoyed it.

Demetrius of Byzantium, in the fourth book of his work *On Poetry*, says that they used to employ the term *choregi*, not, as today, of the men who hired the choruses, but of those who led the chorus, as the etymology of the word denotes.

Also, it was customary to practise good music and not violate the ancient rules of the art.

It happened that in ancient times the Greeks were music-lovers; but later, with the breakdown of order, when practically all the ancient customs fell into decay, this devotion to principle ceased, and debased fashions in music came to light, wherein every one who practised them substituted effeminacy for gentleness, and license and looseness for moderation. What is more, this fashion will doubtless be carried further if some one does not bring the music of our forebears once more to open practice. For in ancient times it was the acts of heroes and the praise of the gods that the poets put to song-music. Homer, for example, says of Achilles: "And he was singing the glorious deeds of men," [10] that is, of heroes. And of Phemius he says: "He knoweth many charms for mortals, deeds of men and of gods, which minstrels celebrate." [11] This custom was kept up also among the barbarians, as Dinon declares in his *Persian History*. It was the singers, for example, that foresaw the courage of the first Cyrus and the war he was to wage against Astyages. "It was at the time (says Dinon) when Cyrus requested permission to visit Persia (he had previously been in charge of Astyages' rod-bearers, and later of his men-at-arms) and had departed; Astyages, therefore, celebrated a feast in company with his friends, and on that occasion a man named Angares (he was the most distinguished of the singers) was invited, and not only began to sing other customary songs but also, at the last, he told how that a mighty beast had been let loose in the swamp, bolder than a wild boar; which beast, if it got the mastery of the regions round it, would soon contend against a multitude without difficulty. And when Astyages

---

[10] *Iliad*, IX, 189.   [11] *Odyssey*, I, 337.

asked, 'What beast?' he replied, 'Cyrus the Persian.' Believing, therefore, that his suspicion about him had been correct, he kept summoning him to return . . . it did no good."

Though I might say many things more on the subject of music, I hear the buzzing of the auloi, and will therefore bring my long-winded discourse to a close, after repeating the lines from *The Aulos-Lover* of Philetaerus: "Zeus, it's indeed a fine thing to die to the music of the auloi. For only to such is it permitted in Hades to revel in love affairs, whereas those whose manners are sordid, having no knowledge of music, must carry water to the leaky jar."

II

The Early Christian View of Music

6. Clement of Alexandria

Titus Flavius Clemens Alexandrinus, a Greek ecclesiastical scholar and teacher of unknown origin, lived in the second half of the second century A.D. and died before 216. Clement was originally a pagan but was later converted to the Christian faith. He undertook extensive trips and became a pupil of Pantaenus in the catechetical school of Alexandria. After his master's death he became Pantaenus' successor. Among his pupils were Origen and Alexander, bishop of Jerusalem.

In his writings, Clement shows equal familiarity with Greek epic, lyric, tragic, and comic poetry on one hand, and with Greek prose writers and philosophers on the other. His thought is a combination of ecclesiastical tradition with elements of Hellenistic philosophy. Clement regarded Christianity as a teaching that surpassed the pagan Greek philosophy in that it revealed in Christ the absolute and perfect truth. Of his works, *The Exhortation to the Greeks* is in the main a polemic against the crudities of pagan mythological stories.

From the Exhortation to the Greeks [1]

I.

AMPHION of Thebes and Arion of Methymna were both minstrels. Both are celebrated in legend, and to this day the story is sung by a chorus of Greeks how their musical skill enabled the one to lure a fish and the other to build the walls of Thebes. There was also a Thracian wizard,[2] —so runs another Greek legend,—who used to tame wild beasts simply by his song, yes, and to transplant trees, oaks, by music. I can also tell you of another legend and another minstrel akin to these, namely, Eunomus the Locrian and the Pythian grasshopper. A solemn assembly of Greeks,

1 Text: *Clement of Alexandria* (London, W. W. Heinemann, 1919), 3–17. Translated for the Loeb Classical Library by Rev. G. W. Butterworth. Reprinted by permission of Harvard University Press.

2 Orpheus.

held in honour of a dead serpent, was gathering at Pytho,[3] and Eunomus sang a funeral ode for the reptile. Whether his song was a hymn in praise of the snake, or a lamentation over it, I cannot say; but there was a competition, and Eunomus was playing the cithara in the heat of the day, at the time when the grasshoppers, warmed by the sun, were singing under the leaves along the hills. They were singing, you see, not to the dead serpent of Pytho, but to the all-wise God, a spontaneous natural song, better than the measured nomes of Eunomus. A string breaks in the Locrian's hands; the grasshopper settles upon the neck of the instrument and begins to twitter there as if upon a branch: whereupon the minstrel, by adapting his music to the grasshopper's lay, supplied the place of the missing string. So it was not Eunomus that drew the grasshopper by his song, as the legend would have it, when it set up the bronze figure at Pytho, showing Eunomus with his cithara, and his ally in the contest. No, the grasshopper flew of its own accord, and sang of its own accord, although the Greeks thought it to have been responsive to music.

How in the world is it that you have given credence to worthless legends, imagining brute beasts to be enchanted by music, while the bright face of truth seems alone to strike you as deceptive, and is regarded with unbelieving eyes? Cithaeron, and Helicon, and the mountains of Odrysians and Thracians, temples of initiation into error, are held sacred on account of the attendant mysteries, and are celebrated in hymns. For my own part, mere legend though they are, I cannot bear the thought of all the calamities that are worked up into tragedy; yet in your hands the records of these evils have become dramas, and the actors of the dramas are a sight that gladdens your heart. But as for the dramas and the Lenaean poets, who are altogether like drunken men, let us wreathe them, if you like, with ivy, while they are performing the mad revels of the Bacchic rite, and shut them up, satyrs and frenzied rout and all,—yes, and the rest of the company of daemons too,—in Helicon and Cithaeron now grown old; and let us bring down truth, with wisdom in all her brightness, from heaven above, to the holy mountain of God and the holy company of the prophets. Let truth, sending forth her rays of light into the farthest distance, shine everywhere upon those who are wallowing in darkness, and deliver men from their error, stretching out her supreme right hand, even understanding, to point them to salvation. And when they have raised their heads and looked up let them forsake Helicon and Cithaeron to dwell in Sion; "for out of Sion shall go forth the law, and the Word

---

3 Delphi. According to the Greek legend the serpent was the ancient guardian of the Delphic shrine and was slain by Apollo. [Butterworth]

of the Lord from Jerusalem," [4] that is, the heavenly Word, the true champion, who is being crowned upon the stage of the whole world. Aye, and this Eunomus of mine sings not the nome of Terpander or of Capio, nor yet in Phrygian or Lydian or Dorian; but the new harmony, with its eternal nome that bears the name of God. This is the new song, the song of Moses,

> Soother of grief and wrath, that bids all ills be forgotten.[5]

There is a sweet and genuine medicine of persuasion blended with this song.

In my opinion, therefore, our Thracian, Orpheus, and the Theban and the Methymnian too, are not worthy of the name of man, since they were deceivers. Under cover of music they have outraged human life, being influenced by daemons, through some artful sorcery, to compass man's ruin. By commemorating deeds of violence in their religious rites, and by bringing stories of sorrow into worship, they were the first to lead men by the hand to idolatry; yes, and with stocks and stones, that is to say, statues and pictures, to build up the stupidity of custom. By their chants and enchantments they have held captive in the lowest slavery that truly noble freedom which belongs to those who are citizens under heaven.

But far different is my minstrel, for He has come to bring to a speedy end the bitter slavery of the daemons that lord it over us; and by leading us back to the mild and kindly yoke of piety He calls once again to heaven those who have been cast down to earth. He at least is the only one who ever tamed the most intractable of all wild beasts—man: for he tamed birds, that is, flighty men; reptiles, that is, crafty men; lions, that is, passionate men; swine, that is, pleasure-loving men; wolves, that is, rapacious men. Men without understanding are stocks and stones; indeed a man steeped in ignorance is even more senseless than stones. As our witness let the prophetic voice, which shares in the song of truth, come forward, speaking words of pity for those who waste away their lives in ignorance and folly,—"for God is able of these stones to raise up children unto Abraham." [6] And God, in compassion for the great dullness and the hardness of those whose hearts are petrified against the truth, did raise up out of those stones, that is, the Gentiles who trust in stones, a seed of piety sensitive to virtue. Again, in one place the words "offspring of vipers" [7] are applied to certain venomous and deceitful hypocrites, who lie in wait against righteousness; yet if any even of these snakes chooses to repent,

---

4 Isaiah 2:3.
5 Homer, *Odyssey*, iv, 221.

6 Matthew 3:9; Luke 3:8.
7 Matthew 3:7; Luke 3:7.

let him but follow the Word and he becomes a "man of God." [8] Others are figuratively called "wolves" [9] clothed in sheepskins, by which is meant rapacious creatures in the forms of men. And all these most savage beasts, and all such stones, the heavenly song of itself transformed into men of gentleness. "For we, yea we also were aforetime foolish, disobedient, deceived, serving divers lusts and pleasures, living in malice and envy, hateful, hating one another," as the apostolic writing says; "but when the kindness of God our Saviour, and His love toward man, appeared, not by works done in righteousness, which we did ourselves, but according to His mercy He saved us." [10]

See how mighty is the new song! It has made men out of stones and men out of wild beasts. They who were otherwise dead, who had no share in the real and true life, revived when they but heard the song. Furthermore, it is this which composed the entire creation into melodious order, and tuned into concert the discord of the elements, that the whole universe might be in harmony with it. [11] The ocean it left flowing, yet has prevented it from encroaching upon the land; whereas the land, which was being carried away, it made firm, and fixed as a boundary to the sea. Aye, and it softened the rage of fire by air, as one might blend the Dorian harmony with the Lydian; and the biting coldness of air it tempered by the intermixture of fire, thus melodiously mingling these extreme notes of the universe. What is more, this pure song, the stay of the universe and the harmony of all things, stretching from the centre to the circumference and from the extremities to the centre, reduced this whole to harmony, not in accordance with Thracian music, [12] which resembles that of Jubal, but in accordance with the fatherly purpose of God, which David earnestly sought. He who sprang from David and yet was before him, the Word of God, scorned those lifeless instruments of lyre and cithara. By the power of the Holy Spirit He arranged in harmonious order this great world, yes, and the little world of man too, body and soul together; and on this many-voiced instrument of the universe He makes music to God, and sings to the human instrument. "For thou art my harp and my pipe and my temple" [13]—my harp by reason of the music, my pipe by reason of the breath of the Spirit, my temple by reason of the Word—God's purpose being that the music should resound, the Spirit inspire, and the temple

8 I Timothy 6:11.

9 Matthew 7:15.

10 Titus 3:3-5.

11 Having credited to the New Song the wonders attributed by Greek legend to Orpheus, Amphion, and Arion, Clement now goes on to identify with it the harmonic principle, in accordance with which the Pythagoreans held the cosmos and the human microcosmos to have been formed from the four elements—water, earth, fire, and air.

12 The music of Orpheus.

13 The source of this quotation is unknown. It may be a fragment of an early Christian hymn, the metaphors being suggested by such passages as Psalm 57:8; I Corinthians 6:19. [Butterworth]

receive its Lord. Moreover, King David the harpist, whom we mentioned just above, urged us toward the truth and away from idols. So far was he from singing the praises of daemons that they were put to flight by him with the true music; and when Saul was possessed, David healed him merely by playing the harp.[14] The Lord fashioned man a beautiful, breathing instrument, after His own image; and assuredly He Himself is an all-harmonious instrument of God, melodious and holy, the wisdom that is above this world, the heavenly Word.

What then is the purpose of this instrument, the Word of God, the Lord, and the New Song? To open the eyes of the blind, to unstop the ears of the deaf, and to lead the halt and erring into the way of righteousness; to reveal God to foolish men, to make an end of corruption, to vanquish death, to reconcile disobedient sons to the Father. The instrument of God is loving to men. The Lord pities, chastens, exhorts, admonishes, saves, and guards us; and, over and above this, promises the kingdom of heaven as reward for our discipleship, while the only joy He has of us is that we are saved. For wickedness feeds upon the corruption of men; but truth, like the bee, does no harm to anything in the world, but takes delight only in the salvation of men. You have then God's promise; you have His love to man: partake of His grace.

And do not suppose that my song of salvation is new in the same sense as an implement or a house. For it was "before the morning star"; [15] and, "in the beginning was the Word, and the Word was with God, and the Word was God." [16] But error is old, and truth appears to be a new thing. Whether then the Phrygians are really proved to be ancient by the goats in the story; [17] or the Arcadians by the poets who describe them as older than the moon; or, again, the Egyptians by those who dream that this land first brought to light both gods and men; still, not one of these nations existed before this world. But we were before the foundation of the world, we who, because we were destined to be in Him, were begotten beforehand by God. We are the rational images formed by God's Word, or Reason, and we date from the beginning on account of our connection with Him, because "the Word was in the beginning." Well, because the Word was from the first, He was and is the divine beginning of all things; but because He lately took a name,—the name consecrated of old and worthy of power, the Christ,—I have called Him a New Song.

---

14 I Samuel 16:23.
15 Psalm 110:3.
16 John 1:1.
17 See the story in Herodotus, ii, 2. Psammetichus, king of Egypt, being desirous of discovering which was the most ancient people, put two children in charge of a herdsman. Goats were to be brought to them for giving milk, but no articulate speech was to be uttered in their presence. The first articulate sound they made was taken to be the Phrygian word for bread; hence the king assumed that Phrygians were the primitive race. [Butterworth]

7. St. Basil

St. Basil was born at Caesarea, Cappadocia, about 330 A.D. Surnamed The Great, he studied at Constantinople and Athens, was baptized in 357, and after extensive travels retired to the desert of Pontus and there founded a monastic order called the Basilians. He became bishop of Caesarea in 370 and died in 378.

St. Basil was important as a preacher (*Homilies*) and a theologian, and earned a prominent name in the early life of the Church by his efforts to settle the Arian dispute and to develop monastic institutions. The liturgy of St. Basil is still used in the Eastern Church.

From the Homily on the First Psalm [1]

1. ALL SCRIPTURE is given by inspiration of God and is profitable [2] and was composed by the Holy Spirit to the end that, as in a common dispensary for souls, we may, all men, select each the medicine for his own disease. For the Scripture saith, "Medicine pacifieth great offenses." [3] The Prophets therefore teach certain things, the Histories others, the Law others, and the kind of counsel given in the Proverbs others. But the book of the Psalms embraces whatever in all the others is helpful. It prophesies things to come, it recalls histories to the mind, it gives laws for living, it counsels what is to be done. And altogether it is a storehouse of good instructions, diligently providing for each what is useful to him. For it heals the ancient wounds of souls and to the newly wounded brings prompt relief; it ministers to what is sick and preserves what is in health; and it wholly removes the ills, howsoever great and of whatsoever kind, that attack souls in our human life; and this by means of a certain well-timed persuasion which inspires wholesome reflection.

1 Text: Migne, *Patrologia graeca*, XXIX, 209–213.   2 II Timothy 3:16.   3 Ecclesiastes 10:4.

For when the Holy Spirit saw that mankind was ill-inclined toward virtue and that we were heedless of the righteous life because of our inclination to pleasure, what did He do? He blended the delight of melody with doctrines in order that through the pleasantness and softness of the sound we might unawares receive what was useful in the words, according to the practice of wise physicians, who, when they give the more bitter draughts to the sick, often smear the rim of the cup with honey. For this purpose these harmonious melodies of the Psalms have been designed for us, that those who are of boyish age or wholly youthful in their character, while in appearance they sing, may in reality be educating their souls. For hardly a single one of the many, and even of the indolent, has gone away retaining in his memory any precept of the apostles or of the prophets, but the oracles of the Psalms they both sing at home and disseminate in the market place. And if somewhere one who rages like a wild beast from excessive anger falls under the spell of the psalm, he straightway departs, with the fierceness of his soul calmed by the melody.

2. A psalm is the tranquillity of souls, the arbitrator of peace, restraining the disorder and turbulence of thoughts, for it softens the passion of the soul and moderates its unruliness. A psalm forms friendships, unites the divided, mediates between enemies. For who can still consider him an enemy with whom he has sent forth one voice to God? So that the singing of psalms brings love, the greatest of good things, contriving harmony like some bond of union and uniting the people in the symphony of a single choir.

A psalm drives away demons, summons the help of angels, furnishes arms against nightly terrors, and gives respite from daily toil; to little children it is safety, to men in their prime an adornment, to the old a solace, to women their most fitting ornament. It peoples solitudes, it chastens market places. To beginners it is a beginning; to those who are advancing, an increase; to those who are concluding, a support. A psalm is the voice of the church. It gladdens feast days, it creates the grief which is in accord with God's will, for a psalm brings a tear even from a heart of stone.

A psalm is the work of the angels, the ordinance of Heaven, the incense of the Spirit. Oh, the wise invention of the teacher who devised how we might at the same time sing and learn profitable things, whereby doctrines are somehow more deeply impressed upon the mind!

What is learned unwillingly does not naturally remain, but things which are received with pleasure and love fix themselves more firmly in our minds. For what can we not learn from the Psalms? Can we not learn the splendor of courage, the exactness of justice, the dignity of self-control, the habit of repentance, the measure of patience, whatsoever good things that you may name? Here is perfect theology; here is foretold the incarnation of Christ; here are the threat of judgment, the hope of resurrection, the fear of punishment, the assurances of glory, the revelations of mysteries; all things are brought together in the book of Psalms as in some great and common storehouse.

Although there are many musical instruments, the prophet made this book suited to the psaltery, as it is called, revealing, it seems to me, the grace from on high which sounded in him through the Holy Spirit, since this alone, of all musical instruments, has the source of its sound above. For the brass wires of the cithara and the lyre sound from below against the plectrum, but the psaltery has the origins of its harmonious rhythms above, in order that we may study to seek for those things which are on high and not be drawn down by the pleasantness of the melody to the passions of the flesh.[4] And I think that by reason of this structure of the instrument the words of the prophet profoundly and wisely reveal to us that those whose souls are attuned and harmonious have an easy path to things above. But now let us examine the beginning of the Psalms.

* * * * *

---

[4] For this comparison and the various symbolic interpretations placed on it by the Church Fathers see Hermann Abert, *Die Musikanschauung des* *Mittelalters* (Halle, 1905), pp. 215–218, and Théodore Gérold, *Les Pères de l'église et la musique* (Paris, 1931), pp. 126–130.

8. St. John Chrysostom

St. John was born in Antioch about 345 A.D. He studied with the rhetorician Libanius, was ordained a priest, and in 397 became Bishop of Constantinople. A famous Greek Father, patron of preachers, he was surnamed *Chrysostomos* ("the golden-mouthed") on account of his impressive oratorical skill. Because of his zealous efforts to improve the moral standing of laymen and clerics alike, Chrysostom was twice deposed and sent into exile. The second time, in 404, he was banished first to Armenia, later to Pontus, and died in exile in 407.

St. John Chrysostom was one of the most important preachers of early Christianity. In his writings, he was more concerned with the practical and moral aspects of theology than with its theoretical and dogmatic aspects. This fact accounts for his being considered the greatest moralist among the ancient Christian theologians.

From the Exposition of Psalm XLI [1]

WHEN GOD saw that many men were rather indolent, that they came unwillingly to Scriptural readings and did not endure the labor this involves, wishing to make the labor more grateful and to take away the sensation of it, He blended melody with prophecy in order that, delighted by the modulation of the chant, all might with great eagerness give forth sacred hymns to Him. For nothing so uplifts the mind, giving it wings and freeing it from the earth, releasing it from the chains of the body, affecting it with love of wisdom, and causing it to scorn all things pertaining to this life, as modulated melody and the divine chant composed of number.

To such an extent, indeed, is our nature delighted by chants and songs that even infants at the breast, if they be weeping or afflicted, are by reason of it lulled to sleep. Nurses, carrying them in their arms, walking to and

1 Text: Migne, *Patrologia graeca*, LV, 155–159.

67

fro and singing certain childish songs to them, often cause them to close their eyes. For this reason travelers also, driving at noon the yoked animals, sing as they do so, lightening by their chants the hardships of the journey. And not only travelers, but also peasants often sing as they tread the grapes in the wine press, gather the vintage, tend the vine, and perform their other tasks. Sailors do likewise, pulling at the oars. Women, too, weaving and parting the tangled threads with the shuttle, often sing a certain single melody, sometimes individually and to themselves, sometimes all together in concert. This they do, the women, travelers, peasants, and sailors, striving to lighten with a chant the labor endured in working, for the mind suffers hardships and difficulties more easily when it hears songs and chants.

Inasmuch as this kind of pleasure is thoroughly innate to our mind, and lest demons introducing lascivious songs should overthrow everything, God established the psalms, in order that singing might be both a pleasure and a help. From strange chants harm, ruin, and many grievous matters are brought in, for those things that are lascivious and vicious in all songs settle in parts of the mind, making it softer and weaker; from the spiritual psalms, however, proceeds much of value, much utility, much sanctity, and every inducement to philosophy, for the words purify the mind and the Holy Spirit descends swiftly upon the mind of the singer. For those who sing with understanding invoke the grace of the Spirit.

Hear what Paul says: "Be not drunk with wine, wherein is excess, but be filled with the Spirit." He adds, moreover, what the cause of this filling is: "Singing and making melody in your heart to the Lord." [2] What is the meaning of "in your heart"? With understanding, he says; not so that the mouth utters words while the mind is inattentive, wandering in all directions, but so that the mind may hear the tongue.

And as swine flock together where there is a mire, but where there is aroma and incense there bees abide, so demons congregate where there are licentious chants, but where there are spiritual ones there the grace of the Spirit descends, sanctifying mouth and mind. This I say, not only that you may yourselves sing praises, but also that you may teach your wives and children to do so, not merely while weaving, to lighten the work, but especially at the table. For since Satan, seeking to ensnare us at feasts, for the most part employs as allies drunkenness, gluttony, immoderate laughter, and an inactive mind; at this time, both before and after table, it is especially necessary to fortify oneself with the protection

---

2 Ephesians 5:18, 19.

of the psalms and, rising from the feast together with one's wife and children, to sing sacred hymns to God.

For if Paul, imprisoned, made fast in the stocks, and threatened with intolerable scourges, with Silas praised God continually at midnight, when sleep is most pleasant to everyone, and neither the place, nor the hour, nor his anxieties, nor the tyrant's slumbers, nor the pain of his labors, nor anything else could bring him to interrupt his singing,[3] so much the more ought we, who live pleasantly and enjoy God's blessings, to give forth hymns expressing thanks to Him.

What if drunkenness or gluttony does make our minds dull and foolish? Where psalmody has entered, all these evil and depraved counsels retreat.

And just as not a few wealthy persons wipe off their tables with a sponge filled with balsam, so that if any stain remain from the food, they may remove it and show a clean table; so should we also, filling our mouths with spiritual melody instead of balsam, so that if any stain remain in our mind from the abundance, we may thereby wipe it away.

And all standing, let us say together: "For thou, Lord, hast made me glad through thy work; I will triumph in the works of thy hands." [4] Then after the psalmody let there be added a prayer, in order that along with the mind we may also make holy the house itself.

And as those who bring comedians, dancers, and harlots into their feasts call in demons and Satan himself and fill their homes with innumerable contentions (among them jealousy, adultery, debauchery, and countless evils); so those who invoke David with his lyre call inwardly on Christ. Where Christ is, let no demon enter; let him not even dare to look in in passing. Peace, delight, and all good things flow here as from fountains. Those make their home a theatre; make yours a church. For where there are psalms, and prayers, and the dance of the prophets, and singers with pious intentions, no one will err if he call the assembly a church.

Even though the meaning of the words be unknown to you, teach your mouth to utter them meanwhile. For the tongue is made holy by the words when they are uttered with a ready and eager mind. Once we have acquired this habit, neither through free will nor through carelessness shall we neglect our beautiful office; custom compelling us, even against our will, to carry out this worship daily. Nor will anyone, in such singing, be blamed if he be weakened by old age, or young, or have a harsh voice, or no knowledge at all of numbers. What is here sought for is a sober mind, an awakened intelligence, a contrite heart, sound reason, and clear

---

3 Acts 16:25.   4 Psalms 92:4.

conscience. If having these you have entered into God's sacred choir, you may stand beside David himself.

Here there is no need for the cithara, or for stretched strings, or for the plectrum, or for art, or for any instrument; but, if you like, you may yourself become a cithara, mortifying the members of the flesh and making a full harmony of mind and body.[5] For when the flesh no longer lusts against the Spirit,[6] but has submitted to its orders and has been led at length into the best and most admirable path, then will you create a spiritual melody.

Here there is no need for art which is slowly perfected; there is need only for lofty purpose, and we become skilled in a brief decisive moment. Here there is no need for place or for season; in all places and at all seasons you may sing with the mind. For whether you walk in the market place, or begin a journey, or sit down with your friends you may rouse up your mind or call out silently. So also Moses called out, and God heard him.[7] If you are an artisan, you may sing sitting and working in your shop. If you are a soldier, or if you sit in judgment, you may do the very same. One may also sing without voice, the mind resounding inwardly. For we sing, not to men, but to God, who can hear our hearts and enter into the silences of our minds.

In proof of this, Paul also cries out: "Likewise the Spirit also helpeth our infirmities. And he that searcheth the hearts knoweth what is the mind of the Spirit, because he maketh intercession for the saints according to the will of God." [8] This does not mean that the Spirit groans; it means that spiritual men, having the gifts of the Spirit, praying for their kinsmen and offering supplications, do so with contrition and groanings. Let us also do this, daily conversing with God in psalms and prayers. And let us not offer mere words, but let us know the very meaning of our speeches.

---

5 For further examples of this figurative treatment of musical instruments, see Hermann Abert, *Die Musikanschauung des Mittelalters* (Halle, 1905), pp. 211–223.

6 Galatians 5:17.
7 Exodus 14:15.
8 Romans 8:26, 27.

9. St. Jerome

Eusebius Sophronius Hieronymus, Christian saint, Church Father, patron of the theologians, was born about 340 A.D. at Stridon in Dalmatia. He studied Latin literature and Greek philosophy under Donatus and other masters in Rome. Baptized in 360, Jerome returned to Stridon an accomplished scholar. He then started on extensive travels, first to Gaul, then to the East, in the course of which he resolved henceforth to devote his scholarship to the Holy Scriptures. In 379 he was ordained a presbyter in Antioch and went to Constantinople to perfect himself in Greek. In 382, he was called to Rome, where Pope Damasus suggested to him to revise the old Latin translation of the Bible. The result of Jerome's protracted labor was the Latin translation of the Scriptures, which later became known under the name of the Vulgate or Authorized Version. Most of this work was done in Palestine, where Jerome had retired after Pope Damasus' death in 384, and where he died in September 420.

St. Jerome is "the great Christian scholar of his age rather than the profound theologian." Besides being the author of the Vulgate with which his name is forever coupled, St. Jerome left other important works in various fields of knowledge. His *Commentaries* are valuable because of his knowledge of Greek and Hebrew, and he is considered a pioneer in the fields of patrology and of biblical archeology. His *De viris illustribus* is a kind of ecclesiastical literary history.

From the Commentary on the Epistle of Paul to the Ephesians [1]

"SPEAKING to yourselves in psalms and hymns and spiritual songs, singing and making melody in your heart to the Lord." [2]

He who has kept himself from the drunkenness of wine, wherein is

---

[1] Text: Migne, *Patrologia latina,* XXVI, 561–562. [2] Ephesians 5:19.

excess, and has thereby been filled with the Spirit, is able to accept all things spiritually—psalms, hymns, and songs. How the psalm, the hymn, and the song differ from one another we learn most fully in the Psalter. Here let us say briefly that hymns declare the power and majesty of the Lord and continually praise his works and favors, something which all those psalms contain to which the word "Alleluia" is prefixed or appended. Psalms, moreover, properly affect the seat of the *ethos* in order that by means of this organ of the body we may know what ought to be done and what ought not to be done. The subtle moralist, however, who inquires into these things and examines the harmony of the world and the order and concord of all creatures, sings a spiritual song. To express our opinion more clearly to the simple-minded, the psalm is directed toward the body, the song toward the mind. We ought, then, to sing and to make melody and to praise the Lord more with the heart than with the voice.

This, indeed, is what is written: "Singing and making melody in your heart to the Lord." Let youth hear this, let them hear it whose office it is to make melody in the church: Sing to God, not with the voice, but with the heart; not, after the fashion of tragedians, in smearing the throat with a sweet drug, so that theatrical melodies and songs are heard in the church, but in fear, in work, and in knowledge of the Scriptures. And although a man be *kakophonos*, to use a common expression, if he have good works, he is a sweet singer before God. And let the servant of Christ sing so that he pleases, not through his voice, but through the words which he pronounces, in order that the evil spirit which was upon Saul [3] may depart from those who are similarly troubled and may not enter into those who would make of the house of God a popular theatre.

---

3 I Samuel 16:23.

10. St. Augustine

Aurelius Augustinus, one of the most distinguished of the Church Fathers, was born at Tagaste in Numidia (North Africa) in 354 A.D. After a period of spiritual crisis in his youth, Augustine in 384 went to Milan, where he came under the influence of St. Ambrose, the bishop of that city, who converted him to the Christian faith and baptized him in 387, together with his pupil Alypius and his son Adeodatus. Augustine then returned to Africa, where his reputation had continued to grow and in 395 was made Bishop of Hippo Regius (now Bone in Algeria). There he died in 430.

St. Augustine is the author of numerous works which have exerted the most profound influence upon the development of the Catholic doctrine, indeed of all Christian doctrine. Most famous among his writings are his *Confessions*, in which Augustine gave an account of the intellectual and moral crises that led to his conversion, and the voluminous work *De civitate Dei*. St. Augustine's writings contain important references to musical practice in the early Christian Church, particularly to the so-called Ambrosian Chant. Book X of his *Confessions* deals, among other things, with problems of musical aesthetics. A tract by St. Augustine, preserved under the title *De musica*, is largely devoted to questions of meter and versification.

From the Confessions [1]

XXXIII. THE PLEASURES TAKEN IN HEARING

THE DELIGHTS of mine ears, verily, have heretofore more strongly inveigled and engaged me; but thou hast brought me off and freed me. Yet still at hearing of those airs which thy words breathe soul into, whenas they are sung with a well tuned and well governed voice, I do, I confess,

1 Text: *St. Augustine's Confessions,* II (London, W. Heinemann, 1912), 165–169. Translated by William Watts (1631) and reprinted in the Loeb Classical Library. Reprinted here by permission of Harvard University Press.

receive a little contentment; not so great though as that I am enchanted by it, but that I can go away when I please. But yet for all this, that those airs may together with these words (by virtue of which they receive life) gain full admission with me, do they aspire to be entertained into a place of no mean honor in this heart of mine, nor can I scarce afford them a room befitting for them. For sometimes forsooth, do I seem to myself to attribute more respect unto them than is seemly; yea, even whilst together with those sacred ditties I perceive our minds to be far more religiously and zealously blown up into a flame of devotion, whenas these ditties are thus sung, than they would have been, had they not been so sung: yea, and I perceive withal, how that the several affections of our spirit, have their proper moods answerable to their variety in the voice and singing, and by some secret association therewith they be stirred up. But this contentment of my flesh (unto which it is not fit to give over the mind to be enervated) doth very often beguile me: the sense going not so along with the reason, as patiently to come behind it; but having for reason's sake gained admission, it strives even to run before and be her leader. Thus in these things I sometimes sin at unawares, but afterwards am aware of it.

Again at another time, through an indiscreet weariness of being in-veigled, do I err out of too precise a severity: yea, very fierce am I some-times, in the desire of having the melody of all pleasant music, to which David's Psalter is so often sung, banished both from mine own ears, and out of the whole church too: and the safer way it seems unto me, which I remember to have been often told me of Athanasius Bishop of Alexandria,[2] who caused the reader of the psalm to sound it forth with so little warbling of the voice, as that it was nearer to speaking, than to singing. Notwithstanding, so often as I call to mind the tears I shed at the hearing of thy church songs, in the beginning of my recovered faith, yea, and at this very time, whenas I am moved not with the singing, but with the thing sung (when namely they are set off with a clear voice and suitable modulation), I then acknowledge the great good use of this institution. Thus float I between peril of pleasure, and an approved profitable custom: inclined the more (though herein I pronounce no irrevocable opinion) to allow of the old usage of singing in the Church; that so by the delight taken in at the ears, the weaker minds be roused up into some feeling of devotion. And yet again, so oft as it befalls me to be more moved with the voice than with the ditty, I confess myself to have grievously offended: at which time I wish rather not to have heard the music. See now in what

---

2 St. Athanasius (293–373).

a state I am! Weep with me, and weep for me, O all you, who inwardly feel any thoughts, whence good actions do proceed. As for you that feel none such, these things move not you. But thou, O Lord my God, look upon me, hearken, and behold, and pity, and heal me, thou in whose eyes I am now become a problem to myself; and that is my infirmity.

III

Music as a Liberal Art

11. Boethius

A Roman statesman, philosopher, and mathematician, Boethius—in full Anicius Manlius Torquatus Severinus—was born in Rome about 480 A.D. Descended from an old and distinguished family, he became Consul in 510 and subsequently counselor to Theodoric, king of the Ostrogoths, who threw him into prison and finally executed him in 524 on charges of treason.

Boethius, together with Cassiodorus, was the chief author who through his writings transmitted the knowledge of ancient Greek music to the Middle Ages. The numerous manuscript copies of his *De institutione musica* preserved in various libraries testify to the popularity of the work during those remote centuries. It was the first printed in 1491–92 in a complete edition of Boethius' writings.

From the De institutione musica [1]

Book One

I. INTRODUCTION

MUSIC IS RELATED TO US BY NATURE AND CAN ENNOBLE OR CORRUPT THE CHARACTER

THE PERCEPTIVE power of all the senses is so spontaneously and naturally present in certain living creatures that to conceive of an animal without senses is impossible. But a scrutiny of the mind will not yield to the same degree a knowledge and clear understanding of the senses themselves. It is easily understood that we use our senses in understanding sensible things, but what in truth is the nature of the actual senses in conformitv with which we act, and what is the peculiar property of sensible things,

---

[1] Text: Edited by Gottfried Friedlein (Leipzig, 1867), pp. 178–189, 223–225.

is not so apparent or intelligible save by proper investigation and reflection upon the facts.

For sight is common to all mortals, but whether it results from images coming to the eye or from rays sent out to the object of sight is doubtful to the learned, though the vulgar are unaware that such doubt exists. Again, any one seeing a triangle or square easily recognizes what he sees, but to know the nature of a square or triangle he must inquire of a mathematician.

The same may be said of other matters of sense, especially of the judgment of the ear, whose power so apprehends sounds that it not only judges them and knows their differences, but is often delighted when the modes are sweet and well-ordered, and pained when disordered and incoherent ones offend the sense.

From this it follows that, of the four mathematical disciplines, the others are concerned with the pursuit of truth, but music is related not only to speculation but to morality as well. Nothing is more characteristic of human nature than to be soothed by sweet modes and stirred up by their opposites. Nor is this limited to particular professions or ages, but is common to all professions; and infants, youths, and the old as well are so naturally attuned to musical modes by a kind of spontaneous feeling that no age is without delight in sweet song. From this may be discerned the truth of what Plato not idly said, that the soul of the universe is united by musical concord.[2] For when, by means of what in ourselves is well and fitly ordered, we apprehend what in sounds is well and fitly combined, and take pleasure in it, we recognize that we ourselves are united by this likeness. For likeness is agreeable, unlikeness hateful and contrary.

From this source, also, the greatest alterations of character arise. A lascivious mind takes pleasure in the more lascivious modes, or often hearing them is softened and corrupted. Contrariwise, a sterner mind either finds joy in the more stirring modes or is aroused by them. This is why the musical modes are called by the names of peoples, as the Lydian and Phrygian modes, for whatever mode each people, as it were, delights in is named after it. For a people takes pleasure in modes resembling its own character, nor could it be that the soft should be akin to or delight the hard, or the hard delight the softer, but, as I have said, it is likeness which causes love and delight. For this reason Plato holds that any change in music of right moral tendency should be especially avoided, declaring that there could be no greater detriment to the morals of a community than a gradual perversion of chaste and modest music.[3]

---

2 *Timaeus,* 37A.   3 *Republic,* 424B–424C.

For the minds of those hearing it are immediately affected and gradually go astray, retaining no trace of honesty and right, if either the lascivious modes implant something shameful in their minds, or the harsher modes something savage and monstrous.

For discipline has no more open pathway to the mind than through the ear. When by this path rhythms and modes have reached the mind, it is evident that they also affect it and conform it to their nature. This may be seen in peoples. Ruder peoples delight in the harsher modes of the Thracians; civilized peoples, in more restrained modes; though in these days this almost never occurs. Since humanity is now lascivious and effeminate, it is wholly captivated by scenic and theatrical modes. Music was chaste and modest so long as it was played on simpler instruments, but since it has come to be played in a variety of manners and confusedly, it has lost the mode of gravity and virtue and fallen almost to baseness, preserving only a remnant of its ancient beauty.

This is why Plato prescribes that boys should not be trained in all modes, but only in those which are strong and simple.[4] And we should above all bear in mind that if in such a matter a series of very slight changes is made, a fresh change will not be felt, but later will create a great difference and will pass through the sense of hearing into the mind. Hence Plato considers that music of the highest moral quality and chastely composed, so that it is modest and simple and masculine, and not effeminate or savage or ill-assorted, is a great guardian of the commonwealth.[5]

This the Lacedaemonians insured when Thaletas, of Gortyna in Crete, brought to their city at great expense, was training boys in the art of music.[6] This was customary among ancient peoples and long endured. When Timotheus of Miletus added a single string to those which he found already in use and made music more complicated, he was expelled from Laconia [7] by a decree which I give in the original Greek words, premising that Spartan speech has the peculiarity of converting the letter *sigma* into *rho*:

Whereas Timotheus the Milesian, having come to our city, has dishonored the ancient music; and whereas, by discarding the seven-stringed cithara and

---

4 *Ibid.*, 399C (p. 5 above).
5 *Ibid.*, 401D (p. 8 above).
6 Cf. Plutarch, *De musica*, 1146C.
7 Athenaeus (636E) tells this story in another form: "Artemon, in the first book of his work *On the Dionysiac Guild*, says that Timotheus of Miletus is held by most authorities to have adopted an arrangement of strings with too great a number, namely the magadis; wherefore he was even about to be disciplined by the Lacedaemonians for trying to corrupt their ancient music, and some

one was on the point of cutting away his superfluous strings when he pointed to a small image of Apollo among them holding a lyre with the same number and arrangement of strings as his own, and so was acquitted" (From the translation by C. B. Gulick for the Loeb Classical Library). According to Pausanias (III, xii), the Lacedaemonians hung the cithara of Timotheus in the Scias to express their disapproval of his innovation, the addition of four new strings to the seven old ones. See also Plutarch, *De musica*, 1144F.

introducing a multiplicity of tones, he corrupts the ears of the young; and whereas, by the use of many strings and by the novelty of his melody, he decks music out as ignoble and intricate instead of simple and orderly, embellishing the melody with the chromatic genus instead of the enharmonic . . . to the antistrophic response; and whereas further, invited to take part in the contest of the Eleusinian Demeter, he suggests unseemly thoughts to the young by tricking out unbecomingly the myth of the pangs of Semele;

It is decreed concerning these matters, with Divine favor, that the Kings and Ephors shall censure Timotheus and compel him to cut away the superfluous strings of the eleven, leaving the seven, in order that everyone, heeding the dignity of the city, may beware of introducing anything ignoble into Sparta and that the good name of the contests may never be impaired.[8]

This decree sets forth that the Spartans were indignant at Timotheus the Milesian, because by complicating music he had harmed the minds of the boys whom he had taken as pupils and had turned them from the modesty of virtue, and because he had perverted harmony, which he found modest, into the chromatic genus, which is more effeminate. Such was their zeal for music that they believed it to take possession of the mind.

Indeed, it is well known how often song has overcome anger, how many wonders it has performed in affections of the body or mind. Who is unaware that Pythagoras, by means of a spondaic melody, calmed and restored to self-mastery a youth of Taormina who had become wrought up by the sound of the Phrygian mode? For when, one night, a certain harlot was in his rival's house, with the doors locked, and the youth in his frenzy was about to set fire to the house and Pythagoras was observing the motion of the stars, as his custom was; learning that the youth, wrought up by the sound of the Phrygian mode, was deaf to the many pleas of his friends to restrain him from the crime, he directed them to change the mode, and thus reduced the youth's fury to a state of perfect calm.

Cicero, in his *De consiliis*, tells the story differently, in this manner: "But if I may compare a trifling matter to a weighty one, struck by some similarity, it is said that when certain drunken youths, aroused, as is wont to happen, by the music of the tibiae, were about to break into the house of a modest woman, Pythagoras urged the player to play a spondaic melody. When he had done this, the slowness of the measures and the gravity of the player calmed their wanton fury."

To add briefly a few more illustrations, Terpander and Arion of

---

8 Perhaps the oldest forged document known to musical history. Wilamowitz, who suggests some emendations in the text (*Timotheus: Die Perser,* Leipzig, 1903, pp. 69–71), places it in the second century B.C. and calls it "a potpourri of every conceivable dialectal anomaly."

Methymna rescued the Lesbians and the Ionians from the gravest maladies by the aid of song. Then Ismenias the Theban, when the torments of sciatica were troubling a number of Boeotians, is reported to have rid them of all their afflictions by his melodies. And Empedocles, when an infuriated youth drew his sword upon a guest of his for having passed sentence upon his father, is said to have altered the mode of the singing and thus to have tempered the young man's anger.

Indeed, the power of the art of music became so evident through the studies of ancient philosophy that the Pythagoreans used to free themselves from the cares of the day by certain melodies, which caused a gentle and quiet slumber to steal upon them. Similarly, upon rising, they dispelled the stupor and confusion of sleep by certain other melodies, knowing that the whole structure of soul and body is united by musical harmony. For the impulses of the soul are stirred by emotions corresponding to the state of the body, as Democritus is said to have informed the physician Hippocrates, who came to treat him when he was in custody as a lunatic, being so regarded by all his fellow townsmen.

But to what purpose all these examples? For there can be no doubt that the state of our soul and body seems somehow to be combined together by the same proportions as our later discussion will show to combine and link together the modulations of harmony. Hence it is that sweet singing delights even children, whereas any harsh sound interrupts their pleasure in listening. Indeed, this is experienced by all ages and both sexes; though they differ in their actions, they are united by their enjoyment of music.

Why do the sorrowing, in their lamentations, express their very grief with musical modulations? This is especially a habit of women, to make the cause of their weeping seem the sweeter with some song. It was also an ancient custom that the music of the tibia preceded funeral lamentations, as witness the lines of Statius:

> The tibia with curving end,
> Wont to lead the funeral rites of tender shades,
> Sounds a deep note.[9]

And he who cannot sing agreeably still hums something to himself, not because what he sings gives him pleasure, but because one takes delight in giving outward expression to an inner pleasure, no matter what the manner.

Is it not evident that the spirit of warriors is roused by the sound of the trumpets? If it is true that a peaceful state of mind can be converted into

---

[9] *Thebaid*, vi, 120–121.

wrath and fury, then beyond doubt a gentler mode can temper the wrath and passionate desire of a perturbed mind. What does it signify that when anyone's ears and mind are pleased by a melody, he involuntarily keeps time by some bodily motion and his memory garners some strain of it? From all this appears the clear and certain proof that music is so much a part of our nature that we cannot do without it even if we wish to do so.

The power of the mind should therefore be directed to the purpose of comprehending by science what is inherent by nature. Just as in the study of vision, the learned are not content to behold colors and forms without investigating their properties, so they are not content to be delighted by melodies without knowing by what proportion of sounds these are inter-related.

2. THE THREE KINDS OF MUSIC, WITH A CONSIDERATION OF THE POWER OF MUSIC

A writer upon music should therefore state at the beginning how many kinds of music those who have investigated the subject are known to have recognized. There are three kinds: the first, the music of the universe; the second, human music; the third, instrumental music, as that of the cithara or the tibiae or the other instruments which serve for melody.

The first, the music of the universe, is especially to be studied in the combining of the elements and the variety of the seasons which are observed in the heavens. How indeed could the swift mechanism of the sky move silently in its course? And although this sound does not reach our ears (as must for many reasons be the case), the extremely rapid motion of such great bodies could not be altogether without sound, especially since the courses of the stars are joined together by such mutual adaptation that nothing more equally compacted or united could be imagined. For some are borne higher and others lower, and all are revolved with a just impulse, and from their different inequalities an established order of their courses may be deduced. For this reason an established order of modulation cannot be lacking in this celestial revolution.

Now unless a certain harmony united the differences and contrary powers of the four elements, how could they form a single body and mechanism? But all this diversity produces the variety of seasons and fruits, and thereby makes the year a unity. Wherefore if you could imagine any one of the factors which produce such a variety removed, all would perish, nor, so to speak, would they retain a vestige of consonance. And just as there is a measure of sound in low strings lest the lowness descend to inaudibility, and a measure of tenseness in high strings lest they be broken by the thinness of the sound, being too tense, and all is congruous and fitting, so we perceive that in the music of the universe nothing can be excessive and destroy some other part by its own excess, but each part brings its own contribution or aids others to bring theirs. For what winter binds, spring releases, summer heats, autumn ripens; and the seasons in turn bring forth their own fruits or help the others to bring forth theirs. These matters will be discussed more searchingly later on.

What human music is, anyone may understand by examining his own nature. For what is that which unites the incorporeal activity of the reason with the body, unless it be a certain mutual adaptation and as it were a tempering of low and high sounds into a single consonance? What else joins together the parts of the soul itself, which in the opinion of Aristotle is a joining together of the rational and the irrational? [10] What causes the blending of the body's elements or holds its parts together in established adaptation? But of this I shall treat later.

The third kind of music is that which is described as residing in certain instruments. This is produced by tension, as in strings, or by blowing, as in the tibiae or in those instruments activated by water, or by some kind of percussion, as in instruments which are struck upon certain bronze concavities, by which means various sounds are produced.

It seems best in this work to treat first of the music of instruments. But enough of introduction. The elements of music themselves must now be discussed.

· · · · · ·

33. WHAT A MUSICIAN IS

This is now to be considered: that every art, and every discipline as well, has by nature a more honorable character than a handicraft, which is produced by the hand and labor of a craftsman. For it is far greater and nobler to know what someone does than to accomplish oneself what someone else knows, for physical skill obeys like a handmaid while reason rules like a mistress. And unless the hand does what the mind sanctions, it is vain. How much more admirable, then, is the science of music in apprehending by reason than in accomplishing by work and deed! As much more so, namely, as the body is surpassed by the mind, because the person destitute of reason has lived in servitude. But reason rules and leads to the right. For unless its rule is obeyed, the work destitute of reason will waver. Thus it is that reason's contemplation of working does not need the deed, while the works of our hands are nothing unless led

---

[10] *On the Soul*, 423A.

by reason. And how great the glory and merit of reason are can be understood from this: that the remaining physical craftsmen (so to speak) take their names, not from their discipline, but rather from their instruments. For the player of the cithara is so called from the cithara, the player of the aulos from the tibia, and the others from the names of their instruments. He however is a musician who on reflection has taken to himself the science of singing, not by the servitude of work but by the rule of contemplation—a thing that we see in the work of buildings and wars, namely in the opposite conferring of the name. For the buildings are inscribed and the triumphs held in the names of those by whose rule and reason they were begun, not of those by whose labor and servitude they were completed.

Thus there are three classes concerned with the musical art. One class has to do with instruments, another invents songs, a third judges the work of instruments and the song. But that class which is dedicated to instruments and there consumes its entire efforts, as for example the players of the cithara and those who show their skill on the organ and other musical instruments, are separated from the intellect of musical science, since they are servants, as has been said, nor do they bear anything of reason, being wholly destitute of speculation. The second class having to do with music is that of the poets, which is borne to song not so much by speculation and reason as by a certain natural instinct. Thus this class also is to be separated from music. The third is that which assumes the skill of judging, so that it weighs rhythms and melodies and the whole of song. And seeing that the whole is founded in reason and speculation, this class is rightly reckoned as musical, and that man as a musician who possesses the faculty of judging, according to speculation or reason, appropriate and suitable to music, of modes and rhythms and of the classes of melodies and their mixtures and of all those things about which there is to be discussion later on and of the songs of the poets.

12. Cassiodorus

Flavius Magnus Aurelius Cassiodorus was born at Scyllacium, in Lucania, about 485 A.D. He first occupied a distinguished position at the court of Theodoric and Athalaric, kings of the Ostrogoths, and later retired into the monastery at Vivarium which he had founded and developed into a center of learning. There he wrote his *Institutiones*, which contains a section on music written between 550 and 562.

Cassiodorus is one of the most important early writers on music and, with Boethius, one of the two great intermediaries between the music of the ancient world and that of the Middle Ages.

From the Institutiones [1]

5. OF MUSIC

1. A CERTAIN Gaudentius, writing of music, says that Pythagoras found its beginning in the sound of hammers and the striking of stretched strings.[2] Our friend Mutianus, a man of the greatest learning, has translated the work of Gaudentius in a manner attesting his skill. Clement of Alexandria in his *Exhortation to the Greeks* declares that music received its origin from the Muses, and takes pains to make clear for what reason the Muses themselves were invented: they were so named ἀπὸ τοῦ μῶσθαι, that is, from inquiring, because, as the ancients would have it, they were the first to inquire into the power of songs and the modulation of the voice.[3] We find also that Censorinus, in his treatise *De die natali*, addressed to Quintus Cerellius, has written things not to be overlooked

---

1 Text: As edited by R. A. B. Mynors for the Clarendon Press (Oxford, 1937), pp. 142–150.

2 *Eisagoge* (Meibom, pp. 13–15).

8 (ii, p. 65 in G. W. Butterworth's translation for the Loeb Classical Library). Clement reports that Alcman derived the origin of the Muses from Zeus and Mnemosyne; he does not speak of the origin of music. As for the etymology ἀπὸ τοῦ μῶσθαι, this is due to Plato, *Cratylus*, 406A.

concerning musical discipline, or the second part of mathematics,[4] for which reason it is profitable to read him, in order to implant those things more deeply in the mind by frequent meditation.

2. The discipline of music is diffused through all the actions of our life. First, it is found that if we perform the commandments of the Creator and with pure minds obey the rules he has laid down, every word we speak, every pulsation of our veins, is related by musical rhythms to the powers of harmony. Music indeed is the knowledge of apt modulation. If we live virtuously, we are constantly proved to be under its discipline, but when we commit injustice we are without music. The heavens and the earth, indeed all things in them which are directed by a higher power, share in this discipline of music, for Pythagoras attests that this universe was founded by and can be governed by music.

3. Music is closely bound up with religion itself. Witness the decachord of the Ten Commandments, the tinkling of the harp, the timbrel, the melody of the organ, the sound of cymbals.[5] The very Psalter is without doubt named after a musical instrument because the exceedingly sweet and grateful melody of the celestial virtues is contained within it.

4. Let us now discuss the parts of music, as it has been handed down from the elders. Musical science is the discipline which treats of numbers in their relation to those things which are found in sounds, such as duple, triple, quadruple, and others called relative that are similar to these.[6]

5. The parts of music are three: harmonics, rhythmics, metrics.[7]

Harmonics is the musical science which distinguishes the high and low in sounds.

Rhythmics is that which inquires whether words in combination sound well or badly together.

---

4 xiii, 1.
5 Cf. Psalm 150: 3–5.
6 *Musica scientia est disciplina quae de numeris loquitur. qui ad aliquid sunt his qui inveniuntur in sonis, ut duplum, triplum, quadruplum, et his similia quae dicuntur ad aliquid.* This definition is designed to indicate the relation of music to the other divisions of mathematics and is an expansion of one which Cassiodorus has already given (II, iii, § 21) in introducing the subject of the quadrivium. "Mathematical science (or, as we may call it in Latin, 'doctrinal' science) is that science which considers abstract quantity. By abstract quantity we mean that quantity which we treat in a purely speculative way, separating it intellectually from its material and from its other accidents, such as evenness, oddness, and the like. It has these divisions: arithmetic, music, geometry, astronomy. Arithmetic is the discipline of absolute numerable quantity. Music is the discipline which treats of numbers in their relation to those things which are found in sounds. Geom-

etry is the discipline of immobile magnitude and of forms. Astronomy is the discipline of the course of the heavenly bodies; it contemplates all figures and with searching reason considers the orbits of the stars about themselves and about the earth." Compare Boethius, *De institutione arithmetica,* I, i: "Arithmetical impartiality inquires into absolute multitude; the continence of musical modulation investigates relative multitude; geometry declares the knowledge of immobile magnitude; the competence of astronomical discipline lays claim to the science of mobile magnitude." From these definitions by Cassiodorus and Boethius is derived the terse definition usual in the later Middle Ages: *Musica est de numero relato ad sonos*—Music has to do with number as related to sounds.
7 For this classification see Lasus of Hermione, as quoted by Martianus Capella (Meibom, p. 181–182) and Aristides Quintilianus (Meibom, p. 8), also Plutarch, *De musica,* 1142D, as emended by Reinach.

Metrics is that which by valid reasoning knows the measures of the various metres; for example, the heroic, the iambic, the elegiac.

6. There are three classes of musical instruments: instruments of percussion, instruments of tension, wind instruments.

Instruments of percussion comprise cup-shaped vessels of bronze and silver, or others whose hard metal, when struck, yields an agreeable clanging.

Instruments of tension are constructed with strings, held in place according to the rules of the art, which upon being struck by the plectrum delightfully soothe the ear. These comprise the various species of cithara.

Wind instruments are those which are actuated to produce a vocal sound when filled by a stream of air, as trumpets, reeds, organs, pandoria, and others of this nature.

7. We have still to explain about the symphonies.[8] Symphony is the fusion of a low sound with a high one or of a high sound with a low one, an adaptation effected either vocally or by blowing or striking. There are six symphonies:

1) diatessaron	4) diapason and diatessaron together
2) diapente	5) diapason and diapente together
3) diapason	6) disdiapason

I. The consonance diatessaron results from the ratio 4:3 (epitrita) and includes four sounds, hence its name.

II. The consonance diapente results from the ratio 3:2 (emiola) and includes five sounds.

III. The consonance diapason, also called diocto, results from the ratio 2:1 (diplasia or dupla) and includes eight sounds, hence also the name it takes of diocto or diapason—since the citharas of the ancients had eight strings this consonance, including as it does all sounds, is called diapason (literally, through all).[9]

IV. The consonance diapason and diatessaron together results from the ratio which the number 24 has to the number 8 [10] and includes eleven sounds.

V. The consonance diapason and diapente together results from the ratio 3:1 (triplasia) and includes twelve sounds.

VI. The consonance disdiapason, that is double diapason, results from the ratio 4:1 (tetraplasia) and includes fifteen sounds.

---

8 This account of the "symphonies" is drawn largely from Gaudentius, *Eisagoge* (Meibom, pp. 11–13).

9 This is of course an incorrect explanation. Compare the pseudo-Aristotelian *Problems*, xix, 32 (920A): "Why is the octave called the 'diapason' instead of being called the diocto according to the number of the notes, in the same way as the terms used for the fourth and fifth? Is it because originally there were seven strings? Then Terpander took away the trite and added the nete, and at that time it was called the diapason, not the diocto, for there were seven notes." (From the translation by W. S. Hett for the Loeb Classical Library)

10 The correct ratio is 24:9, or 8:3.

8. Key is a difference or quantity of the whole harmonic system, consisting in the intonation or level of the voice. There are fifteen keys:

Hypodorian	Dorian	Hyperdorian
Hypoiastian	Iastian	Hyperiastian
Hypophrygian	Phrygian	Hyperphrygian
Hypoaeolian	Aeolian	Hyperaeolian
Hypolydian	Lydian	Hyperlydian

I. The Hypodorian key is the one sounding lowest of all, for which reason it is also called lower.

II. The Hypoiastian exceeds the Hypodorian by a semitone.

III. The Hypophrygian exceeds the Hypoiastian by a semitone, the Hypodorian by a tone.

IV. The Hypoaeolian exceeds the Hypophrygian by a semitone, the Hypoiastian by a tone, the Hypodorian by a tone and a half.

V. The Hypolydian exceeds the Hypoaeolian by a semitone, the Hypophrygian by a tone, the Hypoiastian by a tone and a half, the Hypodorian by two tones.

VI. The Dorian exceeds the Hypolydian by a semitone, the Hypoaeolian by a tone, the Hypophrygian by a tone and a half, the Hypoiastian by two tones, the Hypodorian by two tones and a half, that is, by the consonance diatessaron.

VII. The Iastian exceeds the Dorian by a semitone, the Hypolydian by a tone, the Hypoaeolian by a tone and a half, the Hypophrygian by two tones, the Hypoiastian by two tones and a half, that is, by the consonance diatessaron, the Hypodorian by three tones.

VIII. The Phrygian exceeds the Iastian by a semitone, the Dorian by a tone, the Hypolydian by a tone and a half, the Hypoaeolian by two tones, the Hypophrygian by two tones and a half, that is, by the consonance diatessaron, the Hypoiastian by three tones, the Hypodorian by three tones and a half, that is, by the consonance diapente.

IX. The Aeolian exceeds the Phrygian by a semitone, the Iastian by a tone, the Dorian by a tone and a half, the Hypolydian by two tones, the Hypoaeolian by two tones and a half, that is, by the consonance diatessaron, the Hypophrygian by three tones, the Hypoiastian by three tones and a half, that is, by the consonance diapente, the Hypodorian by four tones.

X. The Lydian exceeds the Aeolian by a semitone, the Phrygian by a tone, the Iastian by a tone and a half, the Dorian by two tones, the Hypolydian by two tones and a half, that is, by the consonance diatessaron, the Hypoaeolian by three tones, the Hypophrygian by three tones and a half, that is, by the consonance diapente, the Hypoiastian by four tones, the Hypodorian by four tones and a half.

XI. The Hyperdorian exceeds the Lydian by a semitone, the Aeolian by a tone, the Phrygian by a tone and a half, the Iastian by two tones, the Dorian by two tones and a half, that is, by the consonance diatessaron, the Hypolydian by three tones, the Hypoaeolian by three tones and a half, that is, by the consonance diapente, the Hypophrygian by four tones, the Hypoiastian by four tones and a half, the Hypodorian by five tones.

XII. The Hyperiastian exceeds the Hyperdorian by a semitone, the Lydian by a tone, the Aeolian by a tone and a half, the Phrygian by two tones, the Iastian by two tones and a half, that is, by the consonance diatessaron, the Dorian by three tones, the Hypolydian by three tones and a half, that is, by the consonance diapente, the Hypoaeolian by four tones, the Hypophrygian by four tones and a half, the Hypoiastian by five tones, the Hypodorian by five tones and a half.

XIII. The Hyperphrygian exceeds the Hyperiastian by a semitone, the Hyperdorian by a tone, the Lydian by a tone and a half, the Aeolian by two tones, the Phrygian by two tones and a half, that is, by the consonance diatessaron, the Iastian by three tones, the Dorian by three tones and a half, that is, by the consonance diapente, the Hypolydian by four tones, the Hypoaeolian by four tones and a half, the Hypophrygian by five tones, the Hypoiastian by five tones and a half, the Hypodorian by six tones, that is, by the consonance diapason.

XIV. The Hyperaeolian exceeds the Hyperphrygian by a semitone, the Hyperiastian by a tone, the Hyperdorian by a tone and a half, the Lydian by two tones, the Aeolian by two tones and a half, that is, by the consonance diatessaron, the Phrygian by three tones, the Iastian by three tones and a half, that is, by the consonance diapente, the Dorian by four tones, the Hypolydian by four tones and a half, the Hypoaeolian by five tones, the Hypophrygian by five tones and a half, the Hypoiastian by six tones, that is, by the consonance diapason, the Hypodorian by six tones and a half.

XV. The Hyperlydian, the newest and highest of all, exceeds the Hyperaeolian by a semitone, the Hyperphrygian by a tone, the Hyperiastian by a tone and a half, the Hyperdorian by two tones, the Lydian by two tones and a half, that is, by the consonance diatessaron, the Aeolian by three tones, the Phrygian by three tones and a half, that is, by the consonance diapente, the Iastian by four tones, the Dorian by four tones and a half, the Hypolydian by five tones, the Hypoaeolian by five tones and a half, the Hypophrygian by six tones, that is, by the consonance diapason, the Hypoiastian by six tones and a half, the Hypodorian by seven tones.

From this it appears that the Hyperlydian key, the highest of all, exceeds the Hypodorian, the lowest of all, by seven tones. So useful, Varro observes, is the virtue displayed in these keys that they can compose distraught minds and also attract the very beasts, even serpents, birds, and dolphins to listen to their melody.

9. But of the lyre of Orpheus and the songs of the Sirens, as being

fabulous matters, we shall say nothing. Yet what shall we say of David, who freed Saul from the unclean spirit by the discipline of most wholesome melody, and by a new method, through the sense of hearing, restored the king to the health which the physicians had been unable to bestow by the virtues of herbs? Asclepiades the physician, according to the ancients a most learned man, is recorded to have restored a man from frenzy to his former sanity by means of melody. Many other miracles have been wrought upon the sick by this discipline. It is said that the heavens themselves, as we have recalled above, are made to revolve by sweet harmony. And to embrace all in a few words, nothing in things celestial or terrestrial which is fittingly conducted according to the Creator's own plan is found to be exempt from this discipline.

10. This study, therefore, which both lifts up our sense to celestial things and pleases our ears with melody, is most grateful and useful. Among the Greeks Alypius, Euclid, Ptolemy, and others have written excellent treatises on the subject. Of the Romans the distinguished Albinus has treated it with compendious brevity. We recall obtaining his book in a library in Rome and reading it with zeal. If this work has been carried off in consequence of the barbarian invasion, you have here the Latin version of Gaudentius by Mutianus; if you read this with close attention, it will open to you the courts of this science. It is said that Apuleius of Madaura has also brought together the doctrines of this work in Latin speech. Also St. Augustine, a father of the church, wrote in six books *De musica*, in which he showed that human speech naturally has rhythmical sounds and a measured harmony in its long and short syllables. Censorinus also has treated with subtlety of the accents of our speech, declaring that they have a relation to musical discipline. Of this book, along with others, I have left a transcript with you.

13. Isidore of Seville

Born in Cartagena ("New Carthage," in southeastern Spain), Isidore was brought to Seville in early childhood and in 599 succeeded his brother Leander as archbishop of that city; he died in 636. Teacher, administrator, controversialist, and scholar, he made important contributions to chronology and historiography and, in his *Etymologiarum sive originum libri xx,* written between 622 and 633, compiled an encyclopaedic treatise on the arts and sciences in the form of an inquiry into the origins of their technical terms. In addition to the chapters which follow, devoted exclusively to music, Isidore's treatise also includes a chapter on the Divine Offices (VI, xix), with many definitions of interest to the student of liturgical music. Like Boethius and Cassiodorus, Isidore was one of those intermediaries from whose writings the early Middle Ages derived their impressions of the ancient world.

From the Etymologiarum[1]

Book Three

15. OF MUSIC AND ITS NAME

MUSIC IS an art of modulation consisting of tone and song, called music by derivation from the Muses. The Muses were so named ἀπὸ τοῦ μῶσθαι, that is from inquiring, because, as the ancients would have it, they inquired into the power of songs and the modulation of the voice. The sound of these, since it is an impression upon the sense, flows by into the past and is imprinted upon the memory. Hence it was fabled by the poets that the Muses were the daughters of Jove and Memory. Unless sounds are remembered by man, they perish, for they cannot be written down.[2]

---

1 Text: As edited by W. M. Lindsay for the Clarendon Press (Oxford, 1911).

2 Cf. St. Augustine, *De ordine,* II, xiv: "And since what the intellect perceives (and numbers

16. OF ITS INVENTORS

Moses says that the inventor of the art of music was Tubal, who was of the race of Cain, before the flood.[3] The Greeks say that Pythagoras found its beginnings in the sound of hammers and the striking of stretched strings. Others report that Linus the Theban and Zetus and Amphion were the first to become illustrious in musical art. After their time this discipline gradually came to be especially ordered and was expanded in many ways, and not to know music was as disgraceful as to be unlettered. It was not only introduced into sacred rites, but was used in all festivals and on all joyful or mournful occasions. For as hymns were sung in the worship of the gods, so hymenaeal songs were sung at weddings, and threnodies and lamentations to the sound of tibiae at funerals. At banquets the lyre or the cithara was passed from hand to hand, and festal songs were assigned to each guest in turn.

17. WHAT MUSIC CAN DO

Thus without music no discipline can be perfect, for there is nothing without it. For the very universe, it is said, is held together by a certain harmony of sounds, and the heavens themselves are made to revolve by the modulation of harmony. Music moves the feelings and changes the emotions. In battles, moreover, the sound of the trumpet rouses the combatants, and the more furious the trumpeting, the more valorous their spirit. Song likewise encourages the rowers, music soothes the mind to endure toil, and the modulation of the voice consoles the weariness of each labor. Music also composes distraught minds, as may be read of David, who freed Saul from the unclean spirit by the art of melody. The very beasts also, even serpents, birds, and dolphins, music incites to listen to her melody. But every word we speak, every pulsation of our veins, is related by musical rhythms to the powers of harmony.

18. OF THE THREE PARTS OF MUSIC

The parts of music are three: that is, harmonics, rhythmics, metrics. Harmonics is that which distinguishes the high and low in sounds. Rhythmics is that which inquires whether words in combination sound well or badly together. Metrics is that which by valid reasoning knows the

---

are manifestly of this class) is always of the present and is deemed immortal, while sound, since it is an impression upon the sense, flows by into the past and is imprinted upon the memory, Reason has permitted the poets to pretend, in a reasonable fable, that the Muses were the daugh-

ters of Jove and Memory. Hence this discipline, which addresses itself to the intellect and to the sense alike, has acquired the name of Music." From Isidore's concluding sentence it is clear that he has only partly understood his authority.

3 Genesis 4:21.

measures of the various metres; for example, the heroic, the iambic, the elegiac.

19. OF THE THREEFOLD DIVISION OF MUSIC

Moreover for every sound which forms the material of songs, there is a threefold nature. The first is the harmonic, which consists of singing; the second, the organic, which is produced by blowing; the third, the rhythmic, in which the music is produced by the impulse of the fingers. For sound is caused either by the voice, as with the throat, or by blowing, as with the trumpet or the tibia, or by an impulse, as with the cithara or with anything else which becomes resonant when struck.[4]

20. OF THE FIRST DIVISION OF MUSIC, CALLED HARMONIC

The first division of music, which is called the harmonic, that is, the modulation of the voice, is the affair of comedians, tragedians, and choruses and of all who sing. It produces motion of the mind and body, and from this motion sound. From this sound comes the music which in man is called voice.

Voice is air struck (*verberatus*) by the breath, from which circumstance words (*verba*) also receive their name. Voice is proper to man and to irrational animals. For sound in other things is called voice by a misuse and not properly, as, "The voice of the trumpet snarled," and

> Broken voices by the shore.[5]

For the proper locutions are that the cliffs of the shore should resound, and

> The trumpet with resonant brass a terrible sound afar
> Gave forth.[6]

Harmony is a modulation of the voice and a concordance or mutual adaptation of several sounds.

Symphony is a fusion of the modulation of low and high concordant sounds, produced either vocally or by blowing or striking. Through symphony low and high sounds are concordant, in such a way that if any one of them is dissonant it offends the sense of hearing. The opposite of this is diaphony, that is, discrepant or dissonant sounds.

---

4 Cf. St. Augustine, *De ordine,* II, xiv: "Reason has understood that the judgment of the ear has to do only with sound and that sound has three varieties: it consists either in the voice of an animate being, or in what blowing produces in instruments, or in what is brought forth by striking. The first variety it understands to be the affair of tragedians, comedians, choruses, and the like, and in general of all who sing. The second it understands to be allotted to the auloi and similar instruments. To the third it understands to be given the citharas, lyres, cymbals, and anything else which becomes resonant when struck."
5 Vergil, *Aeneid,* iii, 556.
6 *Ibid.,* ix, 503.

Euphony is sweetness of the voice; it is also called melody, from the word *mel* (honey), because of its sweetness.

Diastema is an interval of the voice composed of two or more sounds.

Diesis consists of certain intervals and diminutions of modulation and interpolations between one sound and another.

Key is a raised enunciation of the voice. For it is a difference and quantity of the harmony consisting in the intonation or level of the voice, of which musicians have divided the varieties into fifteen parts, of which the Hyperlydian is the newest and highest, and the Hypodorian the lowest of all.

Song is an inflecting of the voice, for sound is simple and moreover it precedes song.

Arsis is a lifting up of the voice, that is, a beginning.

Thesis is a lowering of the voice, that is, an end.

Sweet voices are fine, full, loud, and high.

Penetrating voices are those which can hold a note an unusually long time, in such a way that they continuously fill the whole place, like the sound of trumpets.

A thin voice is one lacking in breath, as the voice of children or women or the sick. This is as it is in strings, for the finest strings emit fine, thin sounds.

In fat voices, as those of men, much breath is emitted at once.

A sharp voice is high and thin, as we see in strings.

A hard voice is one which emits sound violently, like thunder, like the sound of an anvil whenever the hammer is struck against the hard iron.

A harsh voice is a hoarse one, which is broken up by minute, dissimilar impulses.

A blind voice is one which is choked off as soon as produced, and once silent cannot be prolonged, as in crockery.

A pretty (*vinnola*) voice is soft and flexible; it is so called from *vinnus*, a softly curling lock of hair.

The perfect voice is high, sweet, and loud: high, to be adequate to the sublime; loud, to fill the ear; sweet, to soothe the minds of the hearers. If any one of these qualities is absent, the voice is not perfect.

21. OF THE SECOND DIVISION OF MUSIC, CALLED ORGANIC

The second division is the organic, found in the instruments which are activated to produce a vocal sound when filled by a stream of air, such as trumpets, reeds, pipes, organs, pandoria, and similar instruments.

Organ is the generic name of all musical vessels. The Greeks have another name for the kind of organ to which bellows are applied, but their common custom is to call it the organ.

The trumpet was invented by the Etruscans. Virgil writes:

> And Etruscan clangor of trumpets seemed to resound
> Through the air.[7]

It was employed not only in battles, but in all festivals of special praise-giving or rejoicing. Wherefore it is also said in the Psalter:[8] "Sound the trumpet at the beginning of the month, and on the day of your great solemnity." For the Jews were commanded to sound the trumpet at the time of the new moon, as they still do.

The tibiae, according to report, were devised in Phrygia. They were long used only in funerals, and afterward in the sacred rites of the heathen. It is thought that they are called tibiae because they were first made from the leg-bones of deer and fawns, and that then, by a misuse of the term, the name was used of those not made of leg-bones. Hence it is also called *tibicen*, as if for *tibiae cantus* (song of the leg-bone).

The reed is rightly the name of a tree, called *calamus* from *calendo*, that is, giving out voice.

The pipe some think to have been invented by Mercury; others, by Faunus, whom the Greeks call Pan; some by Daphnis, a shepherd of Agrigentum in Sicily. The pipe (*fistula*) is also named from sending forth a sound, for in Greek voice is called φώς, and sent forth, στόλια.

The sambuca, among musicians, is a kind of drum. The word means a kind of fragile wood, from which tibiae are made.

The pandoria is named from its inventor, of whom Virgil says:

> Pan first taught men to join reeds together with wax;
> Pan cares for sheep and shepherds.[9]

For among the heathen he was the god of shepherds, who first adapted reeds of unequal length to music and fitted them together with studious art.

22. OF THE THIRD DIVISION OF MUSIC, WHICH IS CALLED RHYTHMIC

The third division is the rhythmic, having to do with strings and striking, to which are assigned the different species of cithara, also the tympanum, the cymbal, the sistrum, vessels of bronze and silver, or

---

7 *Ibid.*, viii, 526.
8 Psalm 81:3.

9 *Eclogues*, ii, 32.

others whose hard metal, when struck, yields an agreeable clanging, and other instruments of this nature.

Tubal, as was said before, is regarded as the inventor of the cithara and psaltery, but by the Greeks Apollo was believed to have first discovered the use of the cithara. According to their tradition, the form of the cithara was originally like that of the human chest, because it gives forth sound as the chest gives forth voice, and it received its name from that reason, for in Doric the chest was called κιθάρα. Gradually numerous species were invented, as psalteries, lyres, barbitae, phoenices, and pectides, and those which are called Indian citharae and are played by two musicians at once; also many others, some of square and others of triangular form. The number of strings was also increased and the type altered. The ancients called the cithara *fidicula* and *fidicen,* because the strings are in good accord with each other, as befits men among whom there is trust (*fides*).

The ancient cithara had seven strings; whence Virgil's phrase, "the seven distinctions of sounds"; [10] "distinctions" because no string gives the same note as its neighbor. The strings were seven because that number filled the range of the voice, or because the heavens sound with seven motions. The strings (*chordae*) are so called from *cor* (heart), because the striking of the strings of the cithara is like the beating of the heart in the breast. Mercury was their inventor, and he was the first to compel sound to reside in strings.

The psaltery, popularly called *canticum,* has its name from *psallendo* (singing), because the chorus answers its voice in consonance. It resembles a barbaric cithara in the form of the letter delta, but there is this difference between it and the cithara, that it has its wooden sound-box above, and the strings are struck below and sound above, while the cithara has the sound-box below. The Hebrews used a ten-stringed psaltery, because of the ten commandments of their law.

The lyre is so called ἀπὸ τοῦ ληρεῖν (from sounding folly), that is, from the variety of voices, because it produces dissimilar sounds. They say it was invented by Mercury in the following manner. When the Nile, retreating into its channels, had left various animals in the fields, a tortoise was left behind. When it had putrefied and its sinews remained stretched within its shell, it gave out a sound on being struck by Mercury. After this pattern he made the lyre and transmitted it to Orpheus, who applied himself studiously to it and is deemed not merely to have swayed wild beasts with this art, but to have moved rocks and forests with the modulation of his song. Musicians have feigned in their fables that the

10 *Aeneid,* vi, 646.

Lyre was placed among the constellations because of his love of study and the glory of his song.

The tympanum is a skin or hide stretched over one side of a wooden frame; it is a half-drum, shaped like a sieve. It is called tympanum because it is a half, for which reason a half-pearl is called a tympanum. It is struck with a stick as a drum is.

Cymbals are certain vessels which produce sound when struck together. They are called cymbals because they are struck together in time with dancing, since the Greeks call dancing συμβαλεῖν.

The sistrum is named from its inventress, for Isis, a queen of the Egyptians, is considered to have invented this species of instrument. Juvenal has:

> Let Isis with angry sistrum blind my eyes.[11]

Women use this instrument because a woman invented it. So among the Amazons the army of women was summoned by the sistrum.

The bell (*tintinnabulum*) is named from its sound, as are also the clapping (*plausus*) of hands and the creaking (*stridor*) of hinges.

Drum (*symphonia*) is the ordinary name of a wooden frame covered on both sides with stretched skin, which the musicians strike in one place and another with small sticks, and there results a most delightful sound from the concord of low and high.

23. OF MUSICAL NUMBERS

You obtain musical numbers in this manner. Having set down the extreme terms, as say 6 and 12, you see by how many units 12 exceeds 6, and it is by 6 units. You square this: 6 times 6 is 36. You then add together those first extremes, 6 and 12; together they make 18. You then divide 36 by 18, which gives 2. Add this to the smaller number, that is, 6; this will give 8, and it will be the harmonic mean between 6 and 12.[12]

From this it appears that 8 exceeds 6 by 2 units, that is, by one-third of 6, and 8 is exceeded by 12 by 4 units, one-third of 12. By the same fraction that it exceeds, it is exceeded.

But just as this ratio appears in the universe from the revolution of the

---

11 *Satires*, xiii, 931.

12 This method for finding the harmonic mean between two extremes will give the correct answer only when the greater term is twice the lesser. Isidore's error lies in directing that the difference between the extremes be squared. It must be multiplied by the lesser term. With this correction his method agrees with that given by Boethius, *De institutione musica*, II, xvii: "If we seek the harmonic mean, we add the extremes, for example 10 and 40, one to another, making 50. Their difference, which is 30, we multiply by the lesser term, that is 10, making 10 times 30, or 300. This we divide by 50, making 6. This we add to the lesser term, making 16. If now we place this number between 10 and 40, we have a harmonic proportion."

spheres, so in the microcosm it is so inexpressibly potent that the man without its perfection and deprived of harmony does not exist. And by the perfection of the same music, measures consist of arsis and thesis, that is, of raising and lowering.

IV

Musical Theory in the Middle Ages

14. Odo of Cluny

A writer of the tenth century and a pupil of Remi (Remigius) of Auxerre, St. Odo of Cluny was in 899 canon and choir-singer at St. Martin of Tours and later became abbot of various French monasteries. In 927 he became head of the famous abbey of Cluny, where he died in 942.

Odo is credited with a number of important writings on the theory of music, among them the *Enchiridion musices*, also called *Dialogus de musica*. The *Enchiridion* contains the first systematic use of letters for pitches in the meaning that was to become standard for the Middle Ages—the full gamut extending from A to g, with the addition of the low Γ and the high a'.

Enchiridion musices

[*ca. 935*]

A book, also called a dialogue, composed by Dom Odo and concisely, properly, and becomingly brought together for the benefit of readers.[1]

PROLOGUE

You HAVE insistently requested, beloved brothers, that I should communicate to you a few rules concerning music, these to be only of a sort which boys and simple persons may understand and by means of which, with God's help, they may quickly attain to perfect skill in singing. You asked this, having yourselves seen and heard and by sure evidence verified that it could be done. For indeed, being stationed among you, with God's help alone I taught certain actual boys and youths by means of this art so that some after three days, others after four days, and one after a single week of training in it, were able to learn several antiphons and in a short

---

1 Text: Gerbert, *Scriptores*, I, 251–259, 263–264. There is a German translation by Bohn in *Monatshefte für Musik-Geschichte*, XII (1880), No. 2–3.

time to sing them without hesitation, not hearing them sung by anyone, but contenting themselves simply with a copy written according to the rules. With the passage of not many days they were singing at first sight and extempore and without a fault anything written in music, something which until now ordinary singers had never been able to do, many continuing to practice and study singing for fifty years without profit.

When you were earnestly and diligently inquiring whether our doctrines would be of value for all melodies, taking as my helper a certain brother who seemed perfect in comparison with other singers, I investigated the Antiphoner of the blessed Gregory, in which I found that nearly all things were regularly set down. A few things, corrupted by unskilled singers, were corrected, both on the evidence of other singers and by the authority of the rules. But in the longer melodies, beloved brothers, we found sounds belonging to the high modes and excessive ascents and descents, contrary to the rule. Yet, since universal usage agreed in defending these melodies, we did not presume to emend them. We noted them as unusual, however, in order that no one inquiring into the truth of the rule might be left in doubt.

This done, you were kindled by a greater desire and insisted, with vehement entreaties and urgings, not only that rules should be made, but also that the whole Antiphoner should be written in useful notes and with the formulas of the tones,[2] to the honor of God and of His Most Holy Mother Mary, in whose venerable monastery these things were being done.

Deriving confidence, therefore, from your entreaties, and complying with the orders of our common father, I am neither willing nor able to discontinue this work. For among the learned of this age the doctrine of this art is very difficult and extensive. Let therefore whoever pleases cultivate the field further with unwilling labor and wall it in. He who of himself perceives this little gift of God will be satisfied with a simple fruit. And in order that this may be the better understood and that you may receive what is necessary in proportion to your true desire, let one of you come forward to converse or ask questions. These I shall not neglect to answer, in so far as the Lord has given me the power.

---

2 For the formulas of the tones—"Primum quaerite regnum Dei," "Secundem autem simile est huic," and so forth—see Dom Pothier, *Les mélodies grégoriennes* (Solesmes, 1881), p. 289-290, or W. H. Frere in *Grove's Dictionary of Music and Musicians*, 3rd ed., III (London, 1928), 481. Odo's reference to these formulas indicates that the Antiphoner of which he speaks will have been provided with a Tonarius or classified list of the antiphons and responds, arranged according to the eight modes and sub-arranged according to their differences.

1. OF THE MONOCHORD AND ITS USE

(Disciple) What is music?

(Master) The science of singing truly and the easy road to perfection in singing.

(D) How so?

(M) As the teacher first shows you all the letters in a table, so the musician introduces all the sounds of melody on the monochord.

(D) What is the monochord?

(M) It is a long rectangular wooden chest, hollow within like a cithara; upon it is mounted a string, by the sounding of which you easily understand the varieties of sounds.

(D) How is the string itself mounted?

(M) A straight line is drawn down the middle of the chest, lengthwise, and points are marked on the line at a distance of one inch from each end. In the spaces outside these points two end-pieces are set, which hold the string so suspended above the line that the line beneath the string is of the same length as the string between the two end-pieces.

(D) How does one string produce many different sounds?

(M) The letters, or notes, used by musicians are placed in order on the line beneath the string, and when the bridge is moved between the line and the string, shortening or lengthening it, the string marvelously reproduces each melody by means of these letters. When any antiphon is marked with the same letters, the boys learn it better and more easily from the string than if they heard some one sing it, and after a few months' training, they are able to discard the string and sing by sight alone, without hesitation, music that they have never heard.

(D) What you say is very marvelous. Our singers, indeed, have never aspired to such perfection.

(M) Instead, brother, they missed the right path, and failing to ask the way, they labored all their life in vain.

(D) How can it be true that a string teaches more than a man?

(M) A man sings as he will or can, but the string is divided with such art by very learned men, using the aforesaid letters, that if it is diligently observed or considered, it cannot mislead.

2. OF THE MEASUREMENT OF THE MONOCHORD

(D) What is this art, I inquire.

(M) The measurement of the monochord, for if it is well measured, it never deceives.

(D) Can I perchance learn the exact measurements, simply and in a few words?

(M) Today, with God's help; only listen diligently.

At the first end-piece of the monochord, at the point at which we have spoken above, place the letter Γ, that is, a Greek G. (This Γ, since it is a letter rarely used, is by many not understood.) Carefully divide the distance from Γ to the point placed at the other end into nine parts, and where the first ninth from Γ ends, write the letter A; we shall call this the first step. Then, similarly, divide the distance from the first letter, A, to the end into nine, and at the first ninth, place the letter B for the second step. Then return to the beginning, divide by four from Γ, and for the third step write the letter C. From the first letter, A, divide similarly by four, and for the fourth step, write the letter D. In the same way, dividing B by four, you will find the fifth step, E. The third letter, C, likewise reveals the sixth step, F. Then return to Γ, and from it and from the other letters that follow it in order, divide the line in two parts, that is, in the middle, until, without Γ, you have fourteen or fifteen steps.

When you divide the sounds in the middle, you must mark them differently. For example, when you bisect the distance from Γ, instead of Γ, write G; for A bisected, set down a second a; for B, a second ♮; for C, a second c; for D, a second d; for E, a second e; for F, a second f; for G, a second g; and for a, a second $\frac{a}{a}$; so that from the middle of the monochord forward, the letters will be the same as in the first part.

In addition, from the sixth step, F, divide into four, and before ♮, place a second round b; these two are accepted as a single step, one being called the second ninth step, and both are not regularly found in the same melody.

The figures, moreover, both sounds and letters, are thus arranged in order:

	Γ		
First step	A	Eighth step	a
Second step	B	First ninth step	b
		Second ninth step	♮
Third step	C	Tenth step	c
Fourth step	D	Eleventh step	d
Fifth step	E	Twelfth step	e
Sixth step	F	Thirteenth step	f
Seventh step	G	Fourteenth step	g
		Fifteenth step	$\frac{a}{a}$

(D) Thanks be to God, I understand well, and I am confident that I shall now know how to make a monochord.[3]

---

[3] A monochord made according to Odo's directions will give the so-called Pythagorean intonation, the semitone (256/243) being obtained by subtracting the sum of two whole tones (9/8 plus 9/8 equals 81/64) from the fourth (4/3). Somewhat differently worded, Odo's directions are given also by Guido in the *Micrologus* (GS, II, 4-5) and in the *Epistola de ignoto cantu* (GS,

3. OF TONE AND SEMITONE

But why is it, I entreat, that I see on the regularly measured mono-chord in one place smaller and in another place larger spaces and intervals between the steps?

(M) The greater space is called a tone; it is from Γ to the first step, A, and from the first step, A, to the second, B. The lesser space, such as that from the second step, B, to the third, C, is called a semitone and makes a more restricted rise and fall. By no measure or number may the space of a semitone amount to that of a tone, but when the divisions are made in their places by the ratio given above, tones and semitones are formed.

If you have marked all the steps to the last, you will marvel to find in all of them a ninefold division just as you found it at first from Γ to the first step, A, and from the first step, A, to the second, B. Yet the first and second ninth steps, b and ♮, form with respect to one another neither a tone nor a semitone, but from the first ninth step, b, to the eighth, a, is a semitone and to the tenth, c, a tone; conversely, from the second ninth step, ♮, to the eighth, a, is a tone and to the tenth, c, a semitone. Thus one of them is always superfluous, and in each melody you accept one and reject the other in order not to seem to be making a tone and a semitone in the same place, which would be absurd.

(D) It is most marvelous that, although I did not divide by nine, except from Γ to the first step, A, and from the first step, A, to the second, B, I have found that all the tones are equally based on a ninefold division. But show me, I pray you, whether there are other divisions of the mono-chord and whether they are found in all or in several places.

4. OF THE CONSONANCES

(M) Besides the division of the tone, there are three divisions which govern the natural position of sounds which I have mentioned above.

The first is the quaternary division, as from the first step, A, to the fourth, D, so called because it is a division by four; this has four pitches and three intervals, namely, two tones and one semitone. Therefore, wherever you find two tones and a semitone between two pitches on the monochord, you will discover on trial that the interval formed by these two pitches extends to the very end in quaternary division; for this reason it is called diatessaron, that is, "of four."

The second is the ternary division, as from the first step, A, to the

---

II, 46, here perhaps an interpolation). In the *Micrologus* and in the *Regulae rhythmicae* (GS, II, 26–27) Guido gives also a second method of obtaining the same results, quicker but more difficult to remember.

fifth, E, this contains five pitches and four intervals, namely, three tones and one semitone. Therefore, wherever you see three tones and one semitone between two pitches, the interval formed by these two pitches will extend to the end by successive divisions of one-third. This interval is called diapente, that is, "of five," because it encloses five pitches.

The third is what is divided by two, or in the middle; it is called diapason, that is, "of all." This, as was said above, you will plainly recognize from the likeness of the letters, as from the first step, A, to the eighth, a. It consists of eight pitches and seven intervals, namely, of five tones and two semitones, for it contains one diatessaron and one diapente, the interval from the first step, A, to the fourth, D, forming a diatessaron, that from the fourth step, D, to the eighth, a, forming a diapente. From the first step, A, to the eighth, a, the diapason is obtained in the following manner: A, B, C, D, E, F, G, a.

(D) In few words I have learned not a little about divisions. Now I wish to hear why the same letters are used both in the first and in the second part.

(M) The reason is, that since the sounds of the second part, beginning with the seventh step, G (but excepting the first ninth step, b), are formed from those of the first part by the diapason, both parts so agree with each other that whatever letters form a tone, semitone, diatessaron, diapente, or diapason in the first part will likewise be found to do so in the second part. For example, in the first part, from Γ to A is a tone, to B is a tone and a tone, that is, a ditone, to C a diatessaron, to D a diapente, to G a diapason; similarly, in the second part, from G to a is a tone, to ♮ is a tone and a tone, to c a diatessaron, to d a diapente, to g a diapason. From this it follows that every melody is similarly sung in the first and in the second part. But the sounds of the first part sound in concord with those of the second part, as men's voices with those of boys.

(D) I consider that this has been wisely done. Now I expect to hear first how I may note down a melody so that I may understand it without a teacher and so that, when you give me examples of the rules, I may recognize the melody better and, if anything completely escape my memory, have recourse to such notes with entire confidence.

(M) Place before your eyes the letters of the monochord as the melody ranges through them; then, if you do not fully recognize the force of the letters themselves, you may hear them and learn them, wonderful to relate, from a master without his knowing it.

(D) Indeed I say that you have given me a wonderful master, who, made by me, teaches me, and teaching me, knows nothing himself. Nay, for his patience and obedience I fervently embrace him, and he will never torment me with blows or abuse when provoked by the slowness of my sense.

(M) He is a good master, but he demands a diligent listener.

5. OF THE CONJUNCTIONS OF SOUNDS

(D) To what am I to direct especial diligence?

(M) To the conjunctions of sounds which form various consonances, so that, just as they are various and different, you may be able to pronounce each of them opportunely in a dissimilar and different manner.

(D) How many differences there are, I pray you to teach me and show me by examples in common use.

(M) There are six, both in descent and in ascent. The first conjunction of sounds is when we join two sounds between which there is one semitone, as from the fifth step, E, to the sixth, F, a consonance closer and more restricted than any other; for example, the first ascent of the Antiphon "Haec est quae nescivit" or, in descent, conversely, "Vidimus stellam." The second is when there is a tone between two sounds, as from the third step, C, to the fourth, D; in ascent: "Non vos relinquam" and in descent: "Angelus Domini." The third is when a tone and a semitone make the difference between two sounds, as between the fourth step, D, and the sixth, F; in ascent: "Joannes autem" and in descent: "In lege." The fourth is when between one sound and another there are two tones, as from the sixth step, F, to the eighth, a; in ascent: "Adhuc multa habeo" and in descent: "Ecce Maria." The fifth is by means of a diatessaron, as from the first step, A, to the fourth, D; in ascent: "Valde honorandus" and in descent: "Secundum autem." The sixth is by means of a diapente, as from the fourth step, D, to the eighth, a, thus: "Primum quaerite," or, in descent, from the seventh step, G, to the third, C, thus: "Canite tuba." [4] Other regular conjunctions of sounds are nowhere found.

Haec est quae ne-sci-vit

Vi-di-mus stel-lam e-jus

---

[4] In Gerbert's edition, the beginnings of the various melodies cited in this chapter are printed (often very incorrectly) in small and capital letters, immediately above their opening words. These illustrations are here replaced by incipits copied from the Vatican edition of the Antiphoner, from the Tonarius in Vol. 9 of the *Paléographie musicale*, and from Dom Pothier's *Les Mélodies grégoriennes* (Solesmes, 1881).

6. OF THE DISTINGUISHING OF TONE AND SEMITONE ACCORDING TO
THE MODES

Ordinary singers often fall into the greatest error because they scarcely consider the force of tone and semitone and of the other consonances. Each of them chooses what first pleases his ear or appears easiest to utter or to pronounce, and with many melodies a great error is made in the mode. (I use the term "mode" of all the eight tones and modes of all melodies composed in the formulas in order, for if I said "tone," it would be uncertain whether I was speaking of the tones of the formulas or of the tones formed by nine-fold disposition and division.) These singers, if you question them about the mode of any melody, promptly answer what they do not know as though they knew it perfectly. But if you ask them how they know it, they say falteringly: "Because at the beginning and end it is like other melodies of the same mode," although they do not know the mode of any melody at all. They do not know that a dissimilarity in a single sound forces the mode to change, as in the Antiphon "O beatum Pontificem," which, although in the second mode at the beginning and end, was most painstakingly emended to the first mode by Dom Odo, merely because of the ascent of the sound on which are sung the words "O Martine dulcedo." [5] You may test this more diligently in the Antiphon "Domine qui operati sunt," for if you begin, as many attempt to, on F, in the sixth mode, it will not depart from that mode until the semitone, at "in tabernaculo tuo," on one syllable. But since it is thus in use, and sounds well, it ought not to be emended. Let us inquire, then, whether it does not perhaps begin in another mode, in which all will be found consonant and in which there will be no need for emendation. Begin it, therefore, on G, that is, in the eighth mode, and you will find that it stands regularly in that mode. For this reason, some begin "Domine" as in "Amen dico vobis." [6] From this it is understood that the musician who lightly and presumptuously emends many melodies is ignorant unless he first goes through all the modes to determine whether the melody may perhaps not stand in one or another, nor should he care as much for its similarity to other melodies as for regular truth. But if it suits no mode, let it be emended according to the one with which it least disagrees. This also should be observed: that the emended melody either sound better or depart little from its previous likeness.

5 St. Martin's Day, Second Vespers, Magnificat Antiphon (*Ant. Vat.*, p. 766). In the Vatican edition the antiphon is given in a shortened form, omitting the passage to which Odo takes exception. But since the "ascent" at "O Martine dulcedo" is repeated at "O sanctissima anima" (retained in the shortened version), the medieval form of the melody need not be quoted here. The "painstaking emendation" of which Odo speaks is made in the Prohemium of his Tonarius, where we read (GS, I, 249a) that the many who take "O beatum pontificem" to be of the second tone are mistaken and that it is properly of the first tone and of the seventh difference. That Odo, in the *Enchiridion*, refers to himself in the third person has led to questions about the authorship of the treatise. It would seem perfectly possible, however, for a writer, particularly in a dialogue, to refer to himself in the third person when speaking of another of his works.

6 To clarify Odo's comments on this antiphon,

the current version of its opening phrase, as given in the *Liber responsorialis* (Solesmes, 1895), p. 382, is compared below with older versions from the monastic antiphoners of Lucca and Worcester (*Paléographie musicale*, Vols. 9 and 12) and with a reconstruction of the "emendation" proposed by Odo. As will be obvious from this comparison, the melody originally involved an E-flat at "in tabernaculo tuo"; this is the "departure" to which Odo objects. Not only has this tone no place in the theoretical system of his time; it also conflicts with his conception of mode in that it gives to the F octave (with b-flat) the internal structure of the G. To avoid these difficulties Lucca and Worcester transpose the melody up a fifth, and Lucca even goes so far as to take the cadence still a step higher; the *Liber responsorialis* simply suppresses the offending accidental. Odo, however, transfers the entire melody to Mode VIII, and to effect this he is obliged to substitute for the original opening, character-

(D) You have warned me well against the error of unskilled singers and have also given me in few words no little knowledge of the careful investigation of the regular monochord, of the verification of regular melodies, and of the emendation of false ones, matters usefully exercising the sense, as is necessary.

7. OF THE LIMITS OF THE MODES

(D) Now tell me of how many sounds a melody ought to be formed.

(M) Some say eight, others nine, others ten.

(D) Why eight?

(M) Because of the greater division, that is, the diapason, or because the citharas of the ancients had eight strings.

(D) Why nine?

(M) Because of the double diapente, which is bounded by nine pitches. For since from Γ to the fourth step, D, is one diapente, and from this same

---

istic of Mode VI (cf., for example, "O admirabile commercium," *Ant. Vat.*, p. 258), a new one in keeping with his new tonality. Hence his reference to "Amen dico vobis," an antiphon of Mode VIII (*Ant. Vat.*, p. 398).

Liber responsorialis

Do-mi-ne, qui o-pe-ra-ti sunt ju-sti-ti-am, ha-bi-ta-bunt in ta-ber-na-cu-lo tu- o,

Lucca

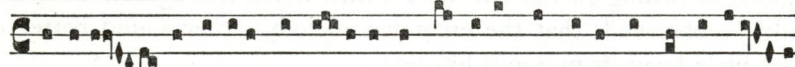

Do-mi-ne, qui o-pe-ra-ti sunt ju-sti-ti- am, ha-bi-ta-bunt in ta-ber-na- cu-lo tu - o,

Worcester

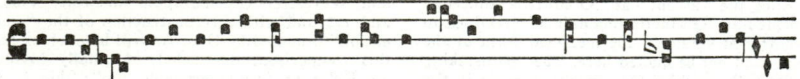

Do-mi-ne, qui o-pe-ra-ti sunt ju-sti-ti- am, ha-bi-ta-bunt in ta-ber-na- cu-lo tu-o,

Odo

Do-mi-ne, qui o-pe-ra-ti sunt ju-sti-ti-am, ha-bi-ta-bunt in ta-ber-na-cu-lo tu-o,

fourth step to the eighth, a, is another; from Γ to the eighth step, a, there are nine pitches.

(D) Why ten?

(M) Because of the authority of David's psaltery, or because the triple diatessaron is found at the tenth pitch. For from Γ to the third step, C, is one diatessaron, from the third step, C, to the sixth, F, is a second, from the sixth step, F, to the first ninth, b, is a third; from Γ, therefore, to the first ninth step, b, one counts ten pitches.

(D) May there also be fewer sounds in a melody?

(M) There may indeed be five or four, so situated, however, that the five produce the diapente and the four the diatessaron.

(D) The reasoning you have adduced and the evidence of nearly all melodies proves that what you say is true. Now explain what tone is, that which you more often call mode.

8. WHAT MODE IS, AND WHENCE IT IS DETERMINED OR DISTINGUISHED

(M) A tone, or mode, is a rule which classes every melody according to its final. For unless you know the final you cannot know where the melody ought to begin or how far it ought to ascend and descend.

(D) What rule does the beginning take from the final?

(M) Every beginning ought to concord with its final in one of the be-fore-mentioned six consonances. No sound may begin a melody, except it be the final itself or be consonant with it in some one of these six consonances. And whatever sounds agree with the final by means of these same six consonances may also begin a melody having this final, provided that a melody which ends on the fifth step, E, the first of the semitones in the third mode, is often found to begin on the tenth step, c, removed from the fifth step, E, by a diapente plus semitone.

The distinctions, too, that is, the places at which we repeatedly pause in a melody and at which we divide it, ought obviously to end in each mode with the same sounds with which a melody in that mode may begin. And where each mode best and most often begins, there as a rule it best and most suitably begins and ends its distinctions. Several distinctions ought to end with the sound which concludes the mode, the masters teach, for if more distinctions be made in some other sound than be made in this one, they desire the melody to be ended in that other sound and compel it to be changed from the mode in which it was. A melody, in other words, belongs most to the mode in which the majority of its distinctions lie. For the beginnings, too, are found most often and most suitably on the sound which concludes the melody. You may confirm what has been said by example in the Antiphon "Tribus miraculis":[7] this is one distinction; "ornatum diem sanctum colimus" is a second; "hodie stella Magos duxit ad praesepium" is a third; "hodie vinum ex aqua factum est ad nuptias" is a fourth; "hodie a Joanne Christus baptizari voluit" is the last. And so you see that in a regular melody several distinctions begin and end in the mode and that melodies begin and end on the same sound.

9. OF THE LIMITS OF THE MODES

(D) That these things are as you say is everywhere supported by the authority of singing masters. But proceed; what rule with regard to ascent and descent does a melody take from its final?

(M) In acute or high melodies, as in the first, third, fifth, and seventh modes, no melody ought to ascend further above its final than to the eighth sound, the sound having the same letter as the final, and this because of the special quality of the division which we call diapason: such a melody has below its final one sound. In lower melodies, as in the second, fourth, sixth, and eighth modes, let there be no descent below the final to any sound not joined to it by means of one of the six before-mentioned consonances; in ascent the progression is from the final by means of these same six consonances to the fifth sound, indeed sometimes as far as the sixth. On what sounds the melodies in all the modes most often begin, according to the present use, you will perceive in their formulas.

10. THE EIGHT MODES

(D) Now that you have shown that the melodies in all the modes take a rule from the final, it is time to explain how many modes, or tones, there are.

(M) Some count four modes.

(D) For what reason?

(M) Because every regular melody may end on any one of four of the sounds of the monochord.

(D) Which sounds are these?

(M) The fourth step, D, on which concludes the mode which we call Authentus Protus, that is, the first author or leader; the fifth step, E, on which concludes the mode which we call Authentus Deuterus, that is, the second author or leader; the sixth step, F, on which concludes the Authentus Tritus, that is, the third author or leader; and the seventh step, G, on which concludes the Authentus Tetrardus, that is, the fourth author or leader. These four, moreover, are divided into eight.

---

7 Epiphany, Second Vespers, Magnificat Antiphon (*Ant. Vat.*, p. 272).

(D) For what reason?

(M) For the sake of high and low melodies. For when a melody in the Authentus Protus is acute or high, we call the mode the Authentus Protus. But if in the same Authentus Protus it is grave or low, we call it the Plaga Proti.

(D) Why Plaga Proti?

(M) Plaga Proti, that is, a part of the first, because it ends on the same part, that is, on the same place or step of the monochord on which the Authentus Protus ended, the fourth, D. In a similar way, when a melody in the Authentus Deuterus is acute we call it the Authentus Deuterus, but if it is grave we name it the Plaga Deuteri. In the same manner, we say of the Authentus Tritus, Plaga Triti, and of the Authentus Tetrardus, Plaga Tetrardi. Usage teaches, moreover, to say, instead of Authentus Protus and Plaga Proti, first and second mode; instead of Authentus Deuterus and Plaga Deuteri, third and fourth mode; instead of Authentus Tritus and its Plaga, fifth and sixth mode; instead of Authentus Tetrardus and its Plaga, seventh and eighth mode. There are then eight modes, by means of which every melody, proceeding in different directions, is varied by eight dissimilar qualities.

(D) In what way shall I be able to perceive their differences and common characteristics?

(M) By means of tones and semitones. For where tones and semitones are formed alike, there also the remaining consonances are formed alike. Wherever there are two tones and a semitone, there also will be a diatessaron, and wherever three tones and a semitone are grouped together, there also the diapente will not be wanting. The remaining consonances are to be understood in a similar way.

.   .   .   .   .

(D) Since I have difficulty in finding even a few melodies which violate these rules, I have no doubt that their scarcity and, so to speak, furtive singularity are the work of presumptuous and corrupt singers.

(M) A rule, certainly, is a general mandate of any art; thus things which are singular do not obey the rules of art.

(D) But add, I pray you, according to the position of each sound, a few things more about the law of the modes.

(M) Your request deserves an answer. For each sound bears a resemblance to some one of the aforesaid modes.

For example, Γ, since it has above it two tones, adding after these a semitone and two tones and then a semitone and a tone, rightly bears a similarity to the seventh mode, for the final of the seventh mode also sounds the diapason to Γ. Likewise the first step, A, since it has below it a tone, but above it a tone, a semitone, and two tones, observes the rule of the first mode and is hence not without reason called first. But the second step, B, since one descends below it by two tones and ascends above it by a semitone and two tones, obeys the usual rule of the fourth mode. In addition, the third step, C, since it has below it a semitone and two tones, but above it two tones and a semitone and then three tones, is upheld by the property of the fifth or sixth mode.

Now, however, the eighth step, a, occupies the first place in similarity to the first step, whose diapason it is. On the other hand, if you consider it in connection with the first ninth step, b, it will have in descent a tone, but in ascent a semitone and three tones, like the third mode. The first ninth step, b, comprises in descent a semitone and two tones, like the sixth mode, but in ascent—either because three tones follow, or rather because it is not joined by any affinity to the following diatessaron—it has no regular resemblance to any mode and indeed cannot be formed by a diapason from the foregoing; consequently you will find that neither a melody nor a distinction may begin or end with it, except by a fault. The second ninth step, ♮, like the second step, B, resembles the fourth mode. The tenth step, c, like the third step, C, agrees with the fifth or sixth mode. But if it be deprived of the second ninth step, ♮, it will, in a different fashion, have below it a tone, a semitone, and two tones, but above it two tones and a semitone, on the analogy of the eighth mode, from whose final it marks a diatessaron.

The remaining sounds, which follow, are because of the similarity of their letters easily dealt with, as this diagram shows:

$$
\begin{array}{ccccccccccccccc}
& & & & & \text{III} & & & & & & & & & \\
\text{VII} & \text{I} & \text{V} & \text{I} & \text{III} & \text{V} & \text{VII} & \text{I} & & \text{V} & \text{I} & \text{III} & \text{V} & \text{VII} & \text{I} \\
\Gamma & \text{A} & \text{B} & \text{C} & \text{D} & \text{E} & \text{F} & \text{G} & \text{a} & \text{♮} & \text{c} & \text{d} & \text{e} & \text{f} & \text{g} & {}^{\text{a}}_{\text{a}} \\
\text{VIII} & \text{II} & \text{IV} & \text{VI} & \text{II} & \text{IV} & \text{VI} & \text{VIII} & \text{II} & \text{IV} & \text{VI} & \text{II} & \text{IV} & \text{VI} & \text{VIII} & \text{II} \\
& & & & & \text{VIII} & & & & & & & & & \\
\end{array}
$$

From what has been said, the diligent inquirer will, with the aid of Divine Grace, understand many other matters both concerning the modes and concerning the remaining rules of this art. But if he is negligent, or if he should presumptuously think to comprehend them by the keenness of his wit and not by Divine enlightenment, either he will comprehend them not at all or, so long as he does not return thanks to the Giver, he will become (God forbid!) the vassal of his pride and the less loyal to his Creator, who is blessed, world without end. Amen.

15. Guido of Arezzo

A Benedictine monk who made important contributions to the development of musical theory in the Middle Ages, Guido was probably born near Paris about 995 and received his education in the Benedictine abbey of St. Maur-des-Fossés. From there he went first to the abbey of Pomposa in northern Italy, and later to Arezzo. His reputation as a scholar in the field of musical theory brought Guido to Rome, where he convinced Pope John XIX of the excellence of the improvements that he had introduced into the teaching of music and singing. Guido became prior of the monastery at Avellano in 1029 and died about 1050.

Prologus antiphonarii sui [1]

[ca. 1025]

IN OUR TIMES, of all men, singers are the most foolish. For in any art those things which we know of ourselves are much more numerous than those which we learn from a master. As soon as they have read the Psalter attentively, small boys know the meanings of all books. Rustics understand the science of agriculture at once, for he who knows how to prune one vineyard, to plant one tree, to load one ass, does not hesitate to do in all cases as he did in the one, if not even better. But marvelous singers, and singers' pupils, though they sing every day for a hundred years, will never sing one antiphon, not even a short one, of themselves, without a master, losing time enough in singing to have learned thoroughly both sacred and secular letters.

And what is the most dangerous thing of all, many clerics and monks of the religious order neglect the psalms, the sacred readings, the nocturnal vigils, and the other works of piety that arouse and lead us on to

---

1 Text: Gerbert, *Scriptores*, II, 34–37.

everlasting glory, while they apply themselves with unceasing and most foolish effort to the science of singing which they can never master.

Who does not also bewail this (which is at once a grave error and a dangerous discord in Holy Church), that when we celebrate the divine office we are often seen rather to strive among ourselves than to praise God, in short, that scarcely one agrees with another, neither the pupil with his master, nor the pupil with his fellow pupils? It is for this reason that the antiphoners are not one, nor yet a few, but rather as many as are the masters in the single churches; and that the antiphoner is now commonly said to be, not Gregory's, but Leo's, or Albert's, or someone's else. And since to learn one is most difficult, there can be no doubt that to learn many is impossible.

In which matter, since the masters change many things arbitrarily, little or no blame should attach to me if I depart from common use in scarcely more than a few respects in order that every chant may return uniformly to a common rule of art. And inasmuch as all these evils and many others have arisen from the fault of those who make antiphoners, I strongly urge and maintain that no one should henceforth presume to provide an antiphoner with neumes except he understand this business and know how to do it properly according to the rules here laid down. Otherwise, without having first been a disciple of truth, he will most certainly be a master of error.

It is in this way, then, that I have decided, with God's help, to write this antiphoner so that hereafter, by means of it, any intelligent and studious person may learn singing and so that, after he has thoroughly learned a part of it through a master, he will unhesitatingly understand the rest of it by himself without one. As to this, should anyone doubt that I am telling the truth, let him come, make a trial, and see what small boys can do under our direction, boys who until now have been beaten for their gross ignorance of the psalms and vulgar letters, who often do not know how to pronounce the words and syllables of the very antiphon which, without a master, they sing correctly by themselves, something which, with God's help, any intelligent and studious person will be able to do if he try to understand the intention with which we have arranged the neumes.

The sounds, then, are so arranged that each sound, however often it may be repeated in a melody, is found always in its own row. And in order that you may better distinguish these rows, lines are drawn close together, and some rows of sounds occur on the lines themselves, others in the intervening intervals or spaces. Then the sounds on one line or in one space all sound alike. And in order that you may also understand to which lines or spaces each sound belongs, certain letters of the monochord are written at the beginning of the lines or spaces and the lines are also gone over in colors, thereby indicating that in the whole antiphoner and in every melody those lines or spaces which have one and the same letter or color, however many they may be, sound alike throughout, as though all were on one line. For just as the line indicates complete identity of sounds, so the letter or color indicates complete identity of lines, and hence of sounds also.

Then if you find the second row of sounds everywhere distinguished by such a letter or colored line, you will also know readily that this same identity of sounds and neumes runs through all the second rows. Understand the same of the third, fourth, and remaining rows, whether you count up or down. It is then most certainly true that all neumes or sounds similarly or dissimilarly formed on lines of the same letter or color sound alike throughout, the line being lettered or colored in the same way, and that on different lines or in different spaces even similarly formed neumes sound by no means alike. Hence, be the formation of the neumes as perfect as you please, without the addition of letters or colors it is altogether meaningless and worthless.

For we use two colors, namely yellow and red, and by means of them I teach you a rule that will enable you to know readily to what tone and to what letter of the monochord every neume and any sound belong, most useful if, as is very convenient, you make frequent use of the monochord and of the formulas of the tones.[2]

Now, as I shall show fully later on, the letters of the monochord are seven. Wherever, then, you see the color yellow, there is the third letter, C, and wherever you see the color red, there is the sixth letter, F, whether these colors be on the lines or between them. Hence in the third row beneath the yellow is the first letter, A, belonging to the first and second tone; above this, next to the yellow, is the second letter, B, belonging to the third and fourth tone; then, on the yellow itself, is the third letter or sound, C, belonging to the fifth and sixth tone; immediately above the yellow and third below the red is the fourth letter, D, belonging to the first and second tone; nearest the red is the fifth letter, E, belonging to the third and fourth tone; on the red itself is the sixth letter, F, belonging to the fifth and sixth tone; next above the red is the seventh letter, G, belonging to the seventh and eighth tone; then, in the third row above the

2 For the formulas of the tones see p. 104 above, note 2.

red, below the yellow, is repeated the first letter, a, belonging, as already explained, to the first and second tone; after this, differing in no respect from the
foregoing, are repeated all the rest; all which things this diagram [8] will teach
you quite clearly.

VII	I	III	V	I	III	V	VII	I	III	V	I	III	V	VII	I	III	V	I
															a	♮	c	d
Γ	A	B	C	D	E	F	G	a	♮	c	d	e	f	g	a	♮	c	d
VIII	II	IV	VI	II	IV	VI	VIII	II	IV	VI	II	IV	VI	VIII	II	IV	VI	II

Although each letter or sound belongs always to two tones, the formulas of the second, fourth, six, and eighth tones agree much better and more
frequently in the single neumes or sounds, for the formulas of the first,
third, fifth, and seventh agree only when the melody, descending from
above, concludes with a low note.[4]

Know, finally, that if you would make progress with these notes, you
must learn by heart a fair number of melodies so that through these single
neumes, modes, or sounds you may acquire through memory an understanding of all, of whatever sort they may be. For it is indeed quite another thing to know something by heart than it is to sing something by
heart, since only the wise can do the former while persons without foresight can often do the latter. As to the simple understanding of neumes,
let these things suffice.

How sounds are liquescent; whether they should be sung as connected
or as separate; which ones are retarded and tremulous, and which hastened; how a chant is divided by distinctions; whether the following or
preceding sound be higher, lower, or equal sounding; by a simple discussion all this is shown in the shape of the neumes itself, if the neumes
are, as they should be, carefully put together.

---

8 Guido's diagram should be compared with
Odo's (p. 116 above).

4 To put it differently, the final will as a rule
occur more frequently in plagal melodies than
in authentic ones. Thus the correspondence of a
given step to the appropriate plagal formula will
be greater than to the authentic formula with
which it is paired.

16. Guido of Arezzo

Epistola de ignoto cantu [1]

[ca. 1030]

To the most blessed and beloved Brother Michael, Guido, by many vicissitudes cast down and strengthened:

Either the times are hard or the judgments of the Divine ordinance are obscure when truth is trampled upon by falsehood and love is trampled upon by envy, which rarely ceases to accompany our order; by this means, the conspiring of the Philistines punishes the Israelitish transgression, lest if anything should promptly turn out according to our wishes, the mortal soul should perish in its self-confidence. For our actions are good only when we ascribe to the Creator all that we are able to accomplish.

Hence it is that you see me banished from pleasant domains and yourself suffocated so that you can scarcely breathe. In which plight I say that we are much like a certain artisan who presented to Augustus Caesar an incomparable treasure, namely, flexible glass. Thinking that because he could do something beyond the power of all others, he deserved a reward beyond all others, he was by the worst of fortunes sentenced to death, lest, if glass could be made as durable as it is marvelous, the entire royal treasure, consisting of various metals, should suddenly become worthless. And so from that time on, accursed envy has deprived mortals of this boon, as it once deprived them of Eden. For since the artisan's envy was unwilling to teach anyone his secret, the king's envy could destroy the artisan along with his art.[2]

For which reason, moved by a divinely inspired charity, I have brought to you and to as many others as I have been able a grace divinely bestowed on me, the most unworthy of men; namely, that those who come after

---

1 Text: Gerbert, *Scriptores*, II, 43–46, 50.
2 Cf. Petronius, *Satires*, 51; there are variants of the story in Pliny, *Naturalis historia*, xxxvi, 26, and Dio Cassius, *Roman History*, lvii, 21.

us, when they learn with the greatest ease the ecclesiastical melodies which I and all my predecessors learned only with the greatest difficulty, they will desire for me and for you and my other helpers eternal salvation, and by the mercy of God our sins will be remitted, or at least from the gratitude of so many will come some prayer for our souls.

For if at present those who have succeeded in gaining only an imperfect knowledge of singing in ten years of study intercede most devoutly before God for their teachers, what think you will be done for us and our helpers, who can produce a perfect singer in the space of one year, or at the most in two? Even if the customary baseness of mankind should prove ungrateful for such benefits, will not a just God reward our labors? Or, since this is God's work and we can do nothing without Him, shall we have no reward? Forbid the thought. For even the Apostle, though whatever is done is done by God's grace, sings none the less: "I have fought a good fight, I have finished my course, I have kept the faith. Henceforth there is laid up for me a crown of righteousness." [3]

Confident therefore in our hope of reward, we set about a task of such usefulness, and since after many storms the long-desired fair weather has returned, we must felicitously set sail.

But since you in your captivity are distrustful of liberty, I will set forth the situation in full. John, holder of the most high apostolic seat, who now governs the Roman Church,[4] hearing of the fame of our school and greatly wondering how, by means of our Antiphoner, boys could know songs which they had never heard, invited me through three emissaries to come to him. I therefore went to Rome with Dom Grunwald, the most reverend Abbot, and Dom Peter, Provost of the canons of the church of Arezzo, by the standards of our time a most learned man. The Pope, accordingly, was greatly pleased by my arrival, conversing much with me and inquiring of many matters. After repeatedly looking through our Antiphoner as if it were some prodigy, and reflecting on the rules prefixed to it, he did not dismiss the subject or leave the place where he sat until he had satisfied his desire by himself learning to sing a verse without hearing it beforehand, thus quickly finding true in his own case what he could hardly believe of others.

What need I say more? I was prevented by illness from remaining in Rome even a short time longer, as the summer heat in places swampy and near the sea was threatening our destruction. We finally came to the agreement that I should return later, at the beginning of winter, at which time

---

3 II Timothy 4:7–8.   4 John XIX, pope from 1024 to 1033.

I should reveal this work of mine more fully to the Pope and his clerk, who had enjoyed the foretaste of it.

A few days after this, desiring to see your spiritual father Dom Guido, Abbot of Pomposa, a man highly endeared to God and men by the merit of his virtue and wisdom, and a beloved friend, I paid him a visit. When he with his clear intelligence saw our Antiphoner, he at once recognized its value and had faith in it. He regretted that he had once given countenance to our rivals and asked me to come to Pomposa, urging upon me that monasteries were to be preferred to bishops' residences, especially Pomposa, because of its zeal for learning, which now by the grace of God and the industry of the most reverend Guido ranks foremost in Italy.

Swayed by the prayers of so eminent a father, and obeying his instructions, I wish first, God helping me, to confer distinction upon so notable a monastery by this work and further to reveal myself to the monks as a monk. Since nearly all the bishops have been convicted of simony, I should fear to enter into relations with any of their number.

As I cannot come to you at present, I am in the meantime addressing to you a most excellent method of finding an unknown melody, recently given to us by God and found most useful in practice. Further, I most reverently salute Dom Martin, the Prior of the Holy Congregation, our greatest helper, and with the most earnest entreaties commend my miserable self to his prayers, and I admonish Brother Peter, who, nourished by our milk, now feeds on the rudest barley, and after golden bowls of wine, drinks a mixture of vinegar, to remember one who remembers him.

．　．　．　．　．

To find an unknown melody, most blessed brother, the first and common procedure is this. You sound on the monochord the letters belonging to each neume, and by listening you will be able to learn the melody as if from hearing it sung by a teacher. But this procedure is childish, good indeed for beginners, but very bad for pupils who have made some progress. For I have seen many keen-witted philosophers who had sought out not merely Italian, but French, German, and even Greek teachers for the study of this art, but who, because they relied on this procedure alone, could never become, I will not say skilled musicians, but even choristers, nor could they duplicate the performance of our choir boys.

We do not need to have constant recourse to the voice of a singer or to the sound of some instrument to become acquainted with an unknown melody, so that as if blind we should seem never to go forward without a leader; we need to implant the differences and qualities of the individual sounds and of all descents and ascents deep in the memory. You will then have a most easy and approved method of finding an unknown melody, provided there is someone present to teach the pupil, not merely from a written textbook, but rather by informal discussion, according to our practice. For after I began teaching this procedure to boys, some of them were able to sing an unknown melody before the third day, which by other methods would not have been possible in many weeks.

If, therefore, you wish to commit any note or neume to memory so that it will promptly recur to you, whenever you wish, in any melody whatever, known or unknown to you, and so that you will be able to sound it at once and with full confidence, you must mark that note or neume at the beginning of some especially familiar melody; and to retain each and every note in your memory, you must have at ready command a melody of this description which begins with that note. For example, let it be this melody, which, in teaching boys, I use at the beginning and even to the very end:

C D F DE D	D D C D E E
Ut que-ant la - xis	re - so - na - re fi - bris
EFG E D EC D	F G a G FED D
Mi- ra ge-sto - rum	fa - mu - li tu - o- rum,
GaG FE F G D	a G a F Ga a
Sol - ve pol - lu - ti	la - bi - i re - a - tum,

GF ED C   E   D
San - cte   Jo - an - nes.

Do you not see how, in this melody, the six phrases begin each with a different note? If, trained as I have described, you know the beginning of each phrase so that you can at once and confidently begin any one you wish, you will be able to sing these notes in their proper qualities whenever you see them. Then, when you hear any neume that has not been written down, consider carefully which of these phrases is best adapted to the last note of the neume, so that this last note and the first note of your phrase are of the same pitch. And be sure that the neume ends on the note with which the phrase corresponding to it begins. And when you begin to sing an unknown melody that has been written down, take great care to end each neume so correctly that its last note joins well with the beginning of the phrase which begins with the note on which the neume ends. To sing an unknown melody competently as soon as you see it written down, or, hearing an unwritten melody, to see quickly how to write it down well, this rule will be of the greatest use to you.

I afterwards adapted short fragments of melody to the single sounds in order.[5] Closely examining the phrases of these, you will rejoice to find at the beginnings of the phrases all the ascending and descending progressions of each note in turn. If you succeed in singing at will the phrases of each and every one of these fragments, you will have learned, by a rule most brief and easy, the exceedingly difficult and manifold varieties of all the neumes. All these matters, which we can hardly indicate in any way with letters, we can easily lay bare by a simple discussion.

. . . . . .

The few words on the form of the modes and neumes which I have set down, both in prose and in verse, as a prologue to the Antiphoner [6] will perhaps briefly and sufficiently open the portals of the art of music. And let the painstaking seek out our little book called *Micrologus* [7] and also read the book *Enchiridion*,[8] most lucidly composed by the most reverend Abbot Odo, from whose example I have departed only in the forms of the notes, since I have simplified my treatment for the sake of the young, in this not following Boethius, whose treatise is useful to philosophers, but not to singers.

---

5 These "short fragments of melody" (*brevissimae symphoniae*) seem not to have been preserved.

6 In prose, pp. 117–120, in verse, GS, II, 25–34.

7 GS, II, 2–24, or edited by A. M. Amelli (1904). There are German translations by Raimund Schlecht in *Monatshefte für Musik-Geschichte*, V (1873), no. 9–11, and by Michael Hermesdorff (1876).

8 Pages 103–116.

17. From the Scholia enchiriadis

The polyphonic practice of the ninth and tenth centuries is known to us, not through practical monuments, but through theoretical writings which give rules for the improvisation of a simple counterpoint to a given plainsong. The earliest of these writings are the ninth-century *Musica enchiriadis*, its contemporary *Scholia*, or commentary, extracts from which are translated below, and the related "Cologne treatise" and "Paris treatise"; formerly ascribed to Hucbald of St. Amand (died 930), more recently to Otger, abbot of St. Pons de Tomieres (died 940), or to Hoger, abbot of Werden (died 902), they are now perhaps best left anonymous. The view of music set forth in this group of writings embraces a number of elements borrowed from Graeco-Roman authors, among them the concept of music as a branch of mathematics, the acceptance of Pythagorean number-theory and the Pythagorean division of the monochord, the rejection of "imperfect" consonance, the theoretical construction of a "system" from similar tetrachords, modeled on the "complete system" of ancient Greek music, and the use of a sign-notation based upon a misunderstanding of the notations of ancient Greek music (the so-called "Daseia" notation).

Of Symphonies [1]

[ca. 900]

(Disciple) What is a symphony?

(Master) A sweet blending of certain sounds, three of which are simple—diapason, diapente, and diatessaron—and three composite—double diapason, diapason plus diapente, and diapason plus diatessaron.

(D) Which is the symphony of the diapason?

---

[1] Text: Gerbert, *Scriptores*, I, 184–196. There is a German translation by Schlecht in *Monatshefte für Musik-Geschichte*, VI–VII (1874–75).

(M) That which is sung at the octave, six pitches intervening.

(D) Which is the diapente and which the diatessaron?

(M) The diapente occurs at the fifth, the diatessaron at the fourth, just as in pentachords and tetrachords the extremes agree with one another.

(D) Why is the diapason so called?

(M) Because the ancient cithara had only eight strings, the Greek word "diapason" being translated by the Latin "ex omnibus." [2]

(D) Why are the diapente and the diatessaron so called?

(M) The diapente is called "from five" because it contains five pitches; the diatessaron includes four pitches, being translated "from four."

(D) How is the diapason sung?

(M) Whenever in descending or ascending we pass from one sound to another in such a way that the higher and lower sounds are not so much consonant as equal-sounding, being by this agreement concordant, these sounds combine in the diapason; as when we descend from H to A or ascend from H to P, following the diagram given below.

A B C D E F G H I K L M N O P

| Relaxed | Intense |
| diapason | diapason |

For whether we take the one after the other at the octave, or whether we sing two in one with two sounds that are equal-sounding, we form the harmony of the simple diapason. And if we sing three in one with three such sounds we form the harmony of the double diapason. Furthermore, if we sing at the fifteenth, leaving out the inner sound, we shall also have the double diapason.

Let us sing them all in the way I have described.[3]

OF THE DIAPASON AND DOUBLE DIAPASON

This symphony, since it is easier and more open, is called greatest and first.

Nos qui vivimus, benedicimus Domino, ex hoc nunc et us-que in sae-cu-lum

---

2 Cf. Cassiodorus, *Institutiones*, II, v, § 7 (p. 89 above).

3 The given melody used in the examples which follow is the psalmody of the Tonus Peregrinus

OF THE DIAPENTE

The symphony of the diapente follows. This is formed whenever at the level of the fifth we take the one after the other or lead both in one in the way indicated below.

In this way the diapente is sung simply. The first composite symphony of the diapente is formed when the organal voice is doubled at the diapason so that the principal voice becomes a mean, as the fifth between prime and octave. I call principal the voice presenting the melody; organal, on the other hand, the one added below it for the sake of the symphony. Let us sing this in the way indicated below.

The second composite symphony of the diapente is formed when the voice which we have called principal is doubled at the diapason so that the organal voice becomes a mean, as the octave between fifth and twelfth.[4] Let us sing it in the way indicated below.

Nos qui vivimus, benedicimus Domino, ex hoc nunc et us-que in sae-cu-lum.

(or Tonus novissimus, as it is called by the author of the Commemoratio brevis, GS, I, 218). Although in the original notation the question is left open, we have assumed that the second tone of the given melody is to be understood as b-flat (not b-natural) and that a corresponding modification is to be made in the organum when it is at the fifth. Only on this basis do the examples

illustrating the organum at the fourth become intelligible. For a discussion of the melody of the Tonus Peregrinus, as given in the Scholia enchiriadis and Commemoratio brevis, see Dom Paolo Ferretti, Estetica gregoriana, I (Rome, 1934), 339, 355-363.

4 For inter quartam ac undecimam read inter quintam ac duodecimam; cf. p. 132 below,

The third composite symphony of the diapente is formed when the organal voice is doubled below at the diapason so that the principal voice is the highest, as the twelfth above octave and prime. This consonance at the twelfth is also concordant, the inner voice being left out.

The fourth composite symphony of the diapente is formed when the principal voice is doubled above at the diapason so that the organal voice is the lowest, as the prime below fifth and twelfth. This is concordant in a similar way, the inner voice being again left out.

The fifth composite symphony of the diapente is sung by a fourfold diversity of voices when both voices have been doubled at the diapason, as when to the fifth and twelfth the prime and octave supply the organum.

Let all be sung in the way indicated below.

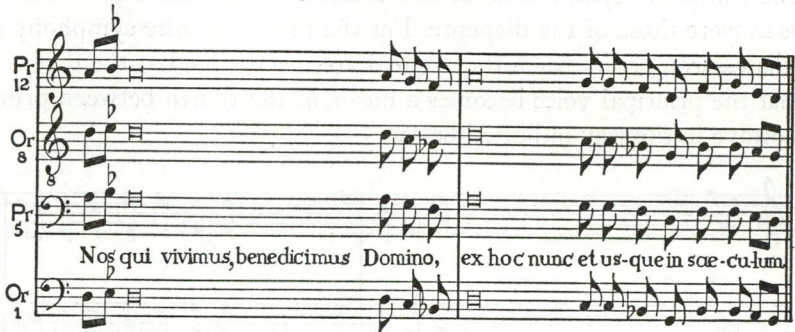

The sixth composite symphony of the diapente occurs when the organal voice is the highest, as the fifteenth above twelfth and fifth in the way indicated below.

Numerous further species of this same symphony can also be produced if either or both voices be tripled at the double diapason.

OF THE DIATESSARON

The symphony of the diatessaron follows. This occurs when at the level of the fourth we sing in one. Be it known, however, that this is not effected

where it is explained that in the second composite symphony of the diapente the principle voice stands a fourth below and a fifth above the inner organal voice. We have altered Gerbert's musical example to agree with the emended text.

as simply as at the other larger intervals, the organum being derived by a certain natural law about which we shall speak later. Nevertheless, if it be performed with the modest retardation most suitable to it and attended with proper diligence, there will be a most admirable smoothness of harmony.

The composite symphonies of the diatessaron are made in the same ways as were those of the diapente. For the first composite symphony of the diatessaron occurs when the organal voice is doubled at the diapason so that the principal voice becomes a mean, as the fourth between prime and octave in the way indicated below.

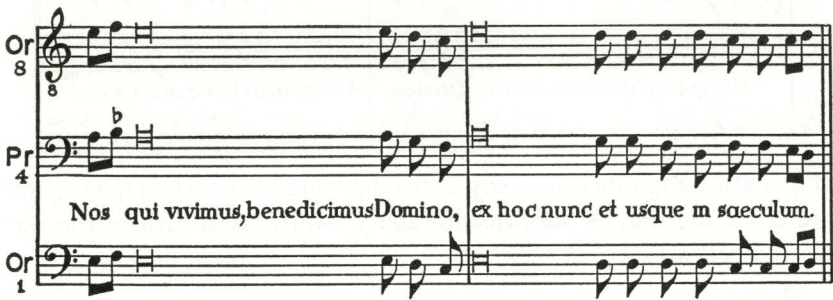

A second composite symphony of the diatessaron occurs when in the opposite way the principal voice is doubled at the diapason so that the organal voice becomes a mean, as the octave between fourth and eleventh.

The third composite symphony of the diatessaron occurs when the organal voice is doubled below at the diapason so that the principal voice becomes the highest, as the eleventh above octave and prime.

The fourth composite symphony of the diatessaron occurs when the principal voice is doubled above at the diapason so that the organal voice becomes the lowest, as the prime below fourth and eleventh.

The fifth composite symphony of the diatessaron occurs when both voices, namely principal and organal, are doubled at the diapason so that to the fourth and eleventh the prime and octave supply the organum.

Nos qui vivimus, benedicimus Domino, ex hoc nunc et usque in sae-cu-lum

The sixth composite symphony of the diatessaron occurs when the organal voice is the highest, as the fifteenth above eleventh and fourth. Let it be sung in the way indicated below.

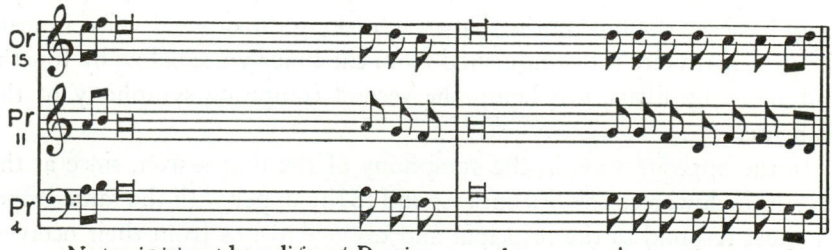

Nos qui vivimus, benedicimus Domino, ex hoc nunc et usque in sae-cu-lum.

And be it noted that whether the principal voice or the organal voice or both voices be doubled at the diapason the place of the highest voice can always be supplied by the voice of boys.

(D) What difference is there, I ask, between the first composite symphony of the diapente and the second of the diatessaron, when both here and there the extreme voices are separated from the inner voice by the same intervals? And similarly, what difference is there between the second composite symphony of the diapente and the first of the diatessaron?

(M) If you inquire why in the first composite symphony of the diapente the inner voice is principal rather than organal, while in the second composite symphony of the diatessaron the inner voice is organal rather than principal, when both here and there the inner voice is related to the extreme voices by the same intervals; and, on the other hand, why in the second composite symphony of the diapente the inner voice is called organal, while in the first composite symphony of the diatessaron it is principal; know that the reason is this: in the symphony of the diatessaron the organal voice does not accompany the principal voice so simply and absolutely as in that of the diapente, for by a certain natural law of its own it stands still in certain places and is unable to proceed further consonantly, just as in the diagrams already given it was shown how it does not descend below the fourth sound of the tetrachord.

Be it known, moreover, that in the composite symphonies already mentioned the diatessaron and diapente differ also by a certain other propriety. For since there is always a reversion of the tropes or tones at the fifth and octave, and in the symphony of the diapente, since at the fifth the lower voice responds to the upper with the same variety of trope, we must respond to either voice from its octave with the same trope.

Thus it follows that, when the organal voice has been doubled at the diapason, making the principal voice a mean, the organal voice is separated from the inner voice below by fifths and above by fourths, this being the first composite symphony of the diapente; moreover, when the principal voice has been doubled at the diapason, making the organal voice a mean, the principal voice is distinguished from the inner voice below by fourths and above by fifths, this being the second composite symphony of the diapente.

In the opposite way, in the symphony of the diatessaron, since at the fourth the lower voice does not respond to the upper with the same trope, we must respond to the principal and organal voices from their octaves, not with the same trope, but to each with its own.

Thus it follows that, when the organal voice has been doubled at the diapason, making the principal voice a mean, the organal voice is distant from the inner voice below by fourths and above by fifths, this being the first composite symphony of the diatessaron; moreover, when the principal voice has been doubled at the diapason, making the organal voice a mean, the principal voice is disjoined from the inner voice below by fifths and above by fourths, this being the second composite symphony of the diatessaron.

All of these are shown in the diagrams already given.

Have you a further question? [5]

(D) Inasmuch as you have said that in the symphony of the diapente the tropes sounded together are the same, while in the symphony of the diatessaron they are not, and that for this reason, in the already mentioned composite symphonies of both consonances, the inner voice, although separated from the extreme voices by the same intervals, is here principal but there organal, since the same trope does not occur both here and there; I ask what the difference is between the principal and organal voices in the symphony of the diapente, where the tropes are not dissimilar.

(M) Recall now what was said: in the symphony of the diapente, when the organal voice has been doubled at the diapason, if the inner voice were related to the extreme voices by the same interval, no difference between the principal and organal voices would be apparent. Now, however, since the organal voice stands below the principal voice at the fifth, but through the diapason above it at the fourth (just as vice versa in the symphony of the diatessaron the organal voice stands below the principal voice at the fourth, but through the diapason above it at the fifth), and since, when the principal voice has been doubled at the diapason, the situation is similar; since the inner voice is not related to the extreme voices by the same intervals, you can readily understand how the virtue of the symphony of the diapason, which multiplies both voices, also determines which voices are principal and which organal.

(D) Why cannot the organal voice in the symphony of the diatessaron agree with the principal voice so absolutely as is the case with the other symphonies?

(M) Since, as was said, the same tropes do not recur at the level of the fourth and the modes of different tropes cannot be maintained throughout or at the same time, for this reason in the symphony of the diatessaron the principal and organal voices do not agree throughout at the level of the fourth.

(D) I wish also to know how at the fourth the genus of the tropes is dissimilar.

(M) This you will easily perceive. For whether we transpose it one tone higher or to the fourth below, the mode of different tropes may be discerned by the attentive ear. Sing in the way indicated below: .

a	♮	c	d	c	♮	a
G	a	♮	c	♮	a	G
F	G	a	♮	a	G	F
E	F	G	a	G	F	E

---

5 Gerbert's assignment of this question to the disciple is emended by Schlecht.

(D) I discern plainly that by this transposition the authentic tone Protus passes over into the authentic Deuterus. But will you give now the reason why at some levels sounds are thus consonant, while at others they are either discrepant or not so much in agreement?

(M) Certainly one is at liberty to consider what reasons God has assigned, and thus in a delightful way we perceive a little the causes of the agreement and discrepancy of sounds, as well as the nature of the different tropes and why in transposing they pass over into other species or revert again to their own. For just as in counting absolutely the numerical series used (that is, 1, 2, 3, 4, and so forth) is simple and by reason of its simplicity easily grasped, even by boys, but when one thing is compared unequally with another it falls under various species of inequality; so in Music, the daughter of Arithmetic (that is, the science of number), sounds are enumerated by a simple order, but when sounded in relation to others they yield not only the various species of the delightful harmonies, but also the most delightful reasons for them.

(D) How is Harmony born of Arithmetic as from a mother; and what is Harmony, and what Music?

(M) Harmony we consider a concordant blending of unequal sounds. Music is the theory of concord itself. And as it is joined throughout to the theory of numbers, as are also the other disciplines of Mathematics, so it is through numbers that we must understand it.

(D) What are the disciplines of Mathematics?

(M) Arithmetic, Geometry, Music, and Astronomy.

(D) What is Mathematics?

(M) Doctrinal science.

(D) Why doctrinal?

(M) Because it considers abstract quantities.

(D) What are abstract quantities?

(M) Those which being without material, that is, without corporeal admixture, are treated by the intellect alone. In quantities, moreover, multitudes, magnitudes, their opposites, forms, equalities, relationships, and many other things which, to speak with Boethius,[6] are by nature incorporeal and immutable, prevailing by reason, are changed by the participation of the corporeal and through the operation of variable matter become mutable and inconstant. These quantities, further, are variously considered in Arithmetic, in Music, in Geometry, and in Astronomy. For these four disciplines are not arts of human invention, but considerable

6 This discussion of the quadrivium leans heavily on Cassiodorus. *Institutiones*, II, iii, § 21 (cf.
p. 88, note 6) and Boethius, *De institutione arithmetica*, I, i.

investigations of divine works; and by most marvelous reasons they lead ingenious minds to understand the creatures of the world; so that those who through these things know God and His eternal divinity are inexcusable if they do not glorify Him and give thanks.

(D) What is Arithmetic?

(M) The discipline of numerable quantities in themselves.

(D) What is Music?

(M) The rational discipline of agreement and discrepancy in sounds according to numbers in their relation to those things which are found in sounds.[7]

(D) What is Geometry?

(M) The discipline of immobile magnitude and of forms.

(D) What is Astronomy?

(M) The discipline of mobile magnitude which contemplates the course of the heavenly bodies and all figures and considers with inquiring reason the orbits of the stars about themselves and about the earth.

(D) How is it that through numerable science the three other disciplines exist?

(M) Because everything comprehended by these disciplines exists through reason formed of numbers and without numbers can be neither understood nor made known. For how can we learn what a triangle or quadrangle is, and the other concerns of Geometry, unless we already know what three and four are?

(D) In no way.

(M) Of what use is it in Astronomy to know the theory without knowing number? Whence do we know the risings and settings, the slowness and velocity of the wandering stars? Whence do we perceive the phases of the moon with its manifold variations, or what part of the zodiac is occupied by the sun or moon or any other planet you will? Is it not that as all things are set in motion by certain laws of number, without number they remain unknown?

(D) It is indeed.

(M) Why is it that, in Music, sounds are equal-sounding at the octave and consonant at the fourth and fifth? And why do they respond as equal-sounding at the fifteenth, as consonant at the twelfth and eleventh? What, moreover, are those measures which join sounds to other sounds so aptly that, if one be a little higher or lower than another, it cannot be concordant with it?

(D) It is surely marvelous that there be these commensurabilities in

---

[7] Cf. Cassiodorus, *Institutiones*, II, iii, § 21 (p. 88).

sounds by which the symphonies agree together so delightfully and the remaining sounds are joined together in order so appropriately. But it is for you to expound those things which you have proposed.

(M) I say that there is equal sound at the octave or diapason because sounds are here brought together by duple relationship (as 6 to 12, or 12 to 24). Similarly, there is equal sound at the fifteenth or double diapason because this symphony is in quadruple proportion (as 6 to 24). At the fifth or diapente, sounds respond consonantly to one another because they are in sesquialtera ratio, the lesser number containing two parts, the greater three (as 6 to 9, or 8 to 12). At the fourth or diatessaron, sounds are consonant because they are in epitrita or sesquitertia ratio, the lesser number containing three parts, the greater four (as 6 to 8, or 9 to 12). Brought together at the twelfth, they are concordant because the diapente responds to the diapason, or sesquialtera to duple (as 18 to 12 and 6, or 8 to 12 and 24), or because the twelfth is in triple proportion (as 18 to 6, or 24 to 8). At the eleventh, they are also consonant because the diatessaron responds to the diapason, or epitrita to duple (as 16 to 12 and 6, or 9 to 12 and 24). And because the diatessaron and the diapente are mutually related, the diatessaron including four sounds, the diapente five, sounds representing the difference between these symphonies are likewise concordant by this relationship, namely by the relationship of epogdous or sesquioctava, the difference between sesquialtera and sesquitertia being always epogdous (in which proportion are 8 and 9, making 16 and 18, making 32 and 36, and so on to infinity).

A diagram of what has been said.

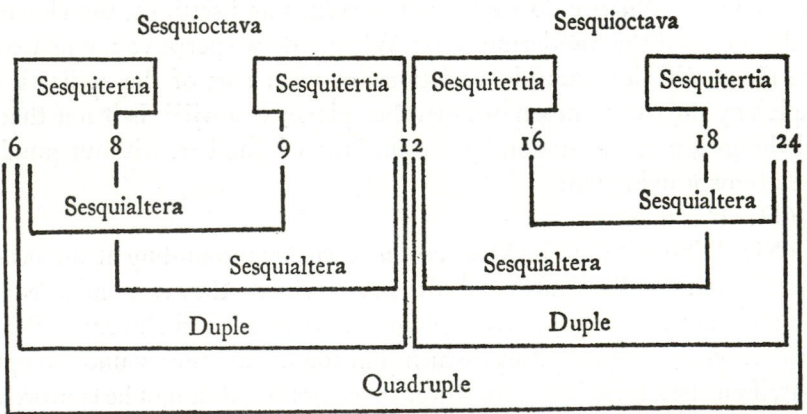

Aside from this, the symphonies of the diapason and double diapason are more perfect than those of the diatessaron and diapente because the former are of multiple inequality, the latter of superparticular, multiple inequality being more perfect than superparticular. Moreover, the sounds of these proportions, that is, of duple, triple, quadruple, sesquialtera, sesquitertia, and sesquioctava, doubtless form consonances or equal sounds because in all the disciplines they are the only commensurate and connumerate relative numbers. It is also on this account that they are assigned to the symphonies and other musical sounds, or rather, that by them the modulated sounds are created. Do you perceive now that Music can be explained only by arithmetical ratios?

(D) I perceive clearly that Arithmetic is necessary to an understanding of Music.

(M) Absolutely necessary, for Music is fashioned wholly in the likeness of numbers. Indeed, if you make one string or pipe twice as long as another of equal thickness (as 12 to 6, or 24 to 12), they will together sound the diapason. If you make another string or pipe of equal diameter longer by a third part of the smaller (as 8 to 6, or 16 to 12) or shorter by a fourth part of the larger (as 9 to 12 or 18 to 24), you will have the consonance of the diatessaron (8 to 6, or 16 to 12, and similarly 9 to 12, or 18 to 24). With 9 to 6, however, or 8 to 12, and similarly with 18 to 12, or 16 to 24, you will have the diapente. Thus it happens that, just as duple contains sesquialtera and sesquitertia (6 and 12, or 12 and 24 containing 8 and 9, or 16 and 18), namely, in an alternate way, so that the number in sesquialtera proportion to the smaller (as 9 to 6, or 18 to 12) is in sub-sesquitertia proportion to the larger (as 9 to 12, or 18 to 24) and on the other hand so that the number in sesquitertia proportion to the smaller (as 8 to 6, or 16 to 12) is in sub-sesquialtera proportion to the larger (as 8 to 12, or 16 to 24); so between two sounds sounding together the diapason, symphonies are always naturally disposed at the fourth and fifth, what is on the one side at the fourth being the diatessaron, what is on the other side at the fifth being the diapente, what there at the fourth sounds the diatessaron sounding here the diapente. Furthermore, just as in sesquioctava proportion 9 exceeds 8, as 18 does 16, and 36 does 32, so if the greater pipe or fiddle-string exceed the smaller by an eighth part, they will together sound the tone.

Whatever is delightful in song is brought about by number through the proportioned dimensions of sounds; whatever is excellent in rhythms, or in songs, or in any rhythmic movements you will, is effected wholly by number. Sounds pass quickly away, but numbers, which are obscured by the corporeal element in sounds and movements, remain. As St. Augustine says: [8]

8 De ordine, II, xiv–xv; see also his De libero arbitrio, II, xvi, translated into English by Richard McKeon in his Selections from Medieval Philosophers, I (New York, 1929), 58–61.

Thus reason has perceived that numbers govern and make perfect all that is in rhythms (called "numbers" in Latin) and in song itself; has examined them diligently; and has found them to be eternal and divine. Next surveying heaven and earth, reason has perceived that in them only beauty pleases it, in beauty only figures, in figures dimensions, and in dimensions numbers. These things, separated and ordered, reason has brought together in a discipline which it calls Geometry. Profoundly impressed by the movement of the heavens, reason has been further prompted to inquire diligently into this. Through the endless succession of the seasons, through the harmonious and regular courses of the stars, through the orderly extent of the intervening distances, reason has perceived that, here too, only dimension and numbers hold sway. Similarly putting these things in order by defining and dividing, reason brought forth Astronomy. In this way, then, all things present themselves in the mathematical disciplines as harmonious, as having to do with the immortal numbers which are apprehended by reflection and study, those which are perceived by the senses being mere shadows and images.

Who, therefore, would say that the theory of numbers was transient or that any art could exist without it?

(D) That not only Music but also the three other disciplines exist by the authority of numbers seems now sufficiently suggested. So I beg you to begin to treat the nature of numbers more fully, repeating the single points which have gone before, so that by way of numbers I may somehow arrive at a comprehension of the innermost secrets of musical theory.

18. Franco of Cologne

The biography of this central figure among the medieval theorists is virtually a complete blank. That he was a papal chaplain and a praeceptor of the Cologne Commandery of the Hospital of St. John of Jerusalem is set forth at the end of his treatise; the Anonymous of the British Museum (Coussemaker's Anonymous IV), writing in the last quarter of the thirteenth century, stresses the importance of Franco's contributions to the improvement and standardization of mensural writing; in the second quarter of the century that followed, the venerable Jacob of Liége recalls having heard a motet of Franco's sung in Paris.

Franco's one genuine writing, the *Ars cantus mensurabilis*, rests to a considerable extent upon the work of the theorists who immediately preceded him, and its teachings are in effect a compromise between an ideally logical system and the existing practice. For nearly a century its authority was enormous and unrivalled: there were several abridged versions; its text was made the subject of a number of commentaries, among them one by Simon Tunstede; Marchetto da Padua and Jean de Muris took Franco as their point of departure; and in the *Speculum* of Jacob of Liége the Franconian notation and the music for which it was devised found their last but most persuasive advocate.

Ars cantus mensurabilis [1]

[*ca. 1260*]

PROLOGUE

Now THAT philosophers have treated sufficiently of plainsong and have fully explained it to us both theoretically and practically (theoretically

1 Text: Coussemaker, *Scriptores*, I, 117–135. On the authorship see Besseler in *Archiv für Musikwissenschaft*, VIII (1926), 157–158; on the date and musical examples, Ludwig, *ibid.*, V (1923), 289–291. Wherever possible, Coussemaker's examples have been corrected to agree with the compositions from which they come. The text has been emended here and there with the help of Burney's quotations from the text of the MS. Oxford, Bodl. 842 (*A General History of Music*, II, 179–192).

above all Boethius, practically on the other hand Guido Monachus and, as to the ecclesiastical tropes, especially the blessed Gregory); supposing plainsong to have been most perfectly transmitted by the philosophers already mentioned, we propose—in accordance with the entreaties of certain influential persons and without losing sight of the natural order—to treat of mensurable music, which plainsong precedes as the principal the subaltern.

Let no one say that we began this work out of arrogance or merely for our own convenience; but rather out of evident necessity, for the ready apprehension of our auditors and the most perfect instruction of all writers of mensurable music. For when we see many, both moderns and ancients, saying good things about mensurable music in their "arts" and on the other hand deficient and in error in many respects, especially in the details of the science, we think their opinions are to be assisted, lest perchance as a result of their deficiency and error the science be exposed to harm.

We accordingly propose to expound mensurable music in a compendium, in which we shall not hesitate to introduce things well said by others or to disprove and avoid their errors and, if we have discovered some new thing, to uphold and prove it with good reasons.

I. OF THE DEFINITION OF MENSURABLE MUSIC AND ITS SPECIES

Mensurable music is melody measured by long and short time intervals. To understand this definition, let us consider what measure is and what time is. Measure is an attribute showing the length and brevity of any mensurable melody. I say "mensurable," because in plainsong this kind of measure is not present. Time is the measure of actual sound as well as of the opposite, its omission, commonly called rest. I say "rest is measured by time," because if this were not the case two different melodies—one with rests, the other without—could not be proportionately accommodated to one another.

Mensurable music is divided into wholly and partly mensurable. Music wholly mensurable is discant, because discant is measured by time in all its parts. Music partly mensurable is organum, because organum is not measured in all its parts. The word "organum," be it known, is used in two senses—in its proper sense and in the sense commonly accepted.[2] For organum in its proper sense is organum duplum, also called organum

---

[2] Cf. John of Garland (CS, I, 114a): "The word 'organum' is variously used—in a general sense and in a specific one"; Anonymous 4 (CS, I, 354b): "'Organum' is an ambiguous word." Wooldridge (*The Oxford History of Music*, I [1st ed., 1901], 177, 338–339) takes *organum communiter sumptum* to be a specific form.

purum. But in the sense commonly accepted organum is any ecclesiastical chant measured by time.

Since the simple precedes the complex, let us speak first of discant.

2. OF THE DEFINITION AND DIVISION OF DISCANT

Discant is a consonant combination of different melodies proportionately accommodated to one another by long, short, or still shorter sounds and expressed in writing as mutually proportioned by suitable figures. Discant is divided in this way: one kind is sounded simply; another, called hocket, is disconnected; another, called copula, is connected. Of these let us speak in turn. But since every discant is governed by mode let us explain first about the modes and afterwards about their signs or figures.

3. OF THE MODES OF EVERY DISCANT

Mode is the knowledge of sound measured by long and short time intervals. Different authorities count the modes differently, some allowing six, others seven.[3] We, however, allow only five, since to these five all others may be reduced.

The first mode proceeds entirely by longs. With it we combine the one which proceeds by long and breve—for two reasons: first, because the same rests are common to both; second, to put a stop to the controversy between the ancients and some of the moderns.[4] The second mode proceeds by breve and long, the third by long and two breves, the fourth by two breves and long, the fifth entirely by breves and semibreves.

But since sounds are the cause and principle of the modes, and notes are the signs of these, it is obvious that we ought to explain about notes, or about figures, which are the same. And since discant itself is governed both by actual sound and by the opposite, that is, by its omission,[5] and these two things are different, their signs are also different. And since actual sound precedes its omission, just as "habit" precedes "privation," let us speak of figures, which represent actual sound, before speaking of rests, which represent its omission.

---

8 John of Garland, who in this agrees with the authors of the *Discantus positio vulgaris* and *De musica libellus,* counts six modes (CS, I, 175a), adding (Jerome's text, CS, I, 97b): "Some add other modes, for example two longs and breve, but we need not count these, for with our six we have enough."

4 Cf. John of Garland (Jerome's text, CS, I, 98a): "Some would have it that our fifth mode is the first of all, and with good reason, for this mode precedes all the others. But as regards knowing the "tempora," the *modus rectus* takes precedence over the *modus obliquus;* thus the saying that the fifth mode is first does not hold." Pseudo-Aristotle (CS, I, 279a–281a) teaches a system of nine modes, beginning with Garland's fifth.

5 For the terms *vox recta* and *vox amissa* (or *omissa*) see John of Garland (CS, I, 176a) and Pseudo-Aristotle (CS, I, 278a); for the philosophical terms "habit" and "privation" Richard McKeon, *Selections from Medieval Philosophers,* II (New York, 1930), Glossary.

4. OF THE FIGURES OR SIGNS OF MENSURABLE MUSIC

A figure is a representation of a sound arranged in some mode. From this it follows that the figures ought to indicate the modes and not, as some have maintained, the contrary.[6] Figures are either simple or composite. The composite figures are the ligatures. Of simple figures there are three species—long, breve, and semibreve, the first of which has three varieties—perfect, imperfect, and duplex.

The perfect long is called first and principal, for in it all the others are included, to it also all the others are reducible. It is called perfect because it is measured by three "tempora," the ternary number being the most perfect number because it takes its name from the Holy Trinity, which is true and pure perfection. Its figure is quadrangular, with a descending tail on the right, representing length. ▜

The imperfect long has the same figure as the perfect, but signifies only two "tempora." It is called imperfect because it is never found except in combination with a preceding or following breve. From this it follows that those who call it "proper"[7] are in error, for that which is "proper" can stand by itself.

The duplex long, formed in this way: ▜ signifies two longs, combined in one figure in order that the line of plainsong in the tenor need not be broken up.

The breve, although it has two varieties, proper and altered, represents both by a quadrangular figure, without a tail: ■

Of the semibreve one variety is major, the other minor, although both are represented by the same lozenge-shaped figure: ◆

5. OF THE MUTUAL ARRANGEMENT OF FIGURES

Now the valuation of simple figures is dependent on their arrangement with respect to one another. This arrangement is understood, moreover, in that after a long follows either a long or a breve. Here be it also observed that the same is true of the valuation of breves and semibreves.

If long follow long, then the first long, whether it be a figure or a rest, is measured under one accent by three "tempora" and called perfect long:

In   Beth –   le – hem

---

6 This is at least implied by the definition of John of Garland (CS, I, 177b): "A figure is a representation of a sound according to its mode"; see also Pseudo-Aristotle (CS, I, 269b).

7 Cf. John of Garland (CS, I, 176a), who in this agrees with the author of the *De musica libellus* (CS, I, 378a).

But if breve follow long, the case is manifold, for there will be either a single breve or several of them.

If a single breve, then the long is of two "tempora" and called imperfect:

except between the two, namely between the long and the breve, there be placed that little stroke by some called "sign of perfection," by others "division of the mode." In this case, the first long is perfect, and the breve makes the following long imperfect:

If several breves, the case is again manifold, for there will be two, three, four, five, or more than five.

If only two:

then the long is perfect, except a single breve precede it:

Of the two breves, the first, moreover, is called a breve proper, the second an altered breve. (A breve proper is one which contains one "tempus" only. An altered breve, while the same as the imperfect long in value, differs from it in form, for both, though differently figured, are measured by two "tempora." What we call a "tempus" is that which is a minimum in fullness of voice.) But if between the aforesaid two breves be placed the stroke called "division of the mode":

then the first long is imperfect and the second also, while the breves will both be proper. This, however, is most unusual.

If only three breves stand between the two longs:

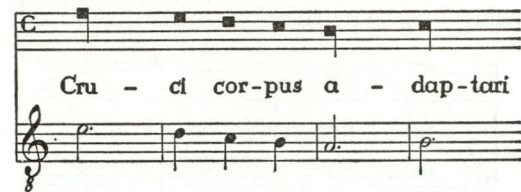

the case is the same as before, except that the one which we called altered breve in the first instance is here divided into two breves proper. But if between the first breve and the two following ones there be placed a "division of the mode":

then the first long is made imperfect by the first breve, and of the two following breves the first becomes a breve proper while the last is altered. Observe also that three "tempora," whether under one accent or under several, constitute a perfection.

If more than three breves:

then the first long is always imperfect except the "sign of perfection" be added to it:

Of the following breves, all are proper that are found in counting by the ternary number, which has been constituted perfection. But if at the end only two remain, the second is an altered breve:

while if only one remains, it will be proper and will make the final long imperfect:

Now the valuation of semibreves and breves is the same as in the rules already given. But observe that there cannot stand for a breve proper more than three semibreves (called minor semibreves, since they are the smallest parts of the breve proper):

or less than two (of which the first is called a minor semibreve, the second a major, since it includes in itself two minor ones):

But if three semibreves follow immediately on two standing for a breve proper, or vice versa:

then let a "division of the mode" be placed between three and two, or vice versa, as shown in the preceding example. For an altered breve, moreover, there cannot stand less than four semibreves:

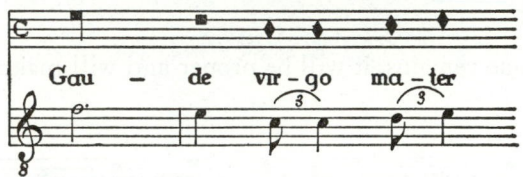

or more than six:

for the altered breve includes within itself two breves proper. From this appears the error of those who set for the altered breve at one time three semibreves and at other times two.

6. OF PLICAS IN SIMPLE FIGURES

Aside from these there are certain other simple figures, indicating the same things and called by the same names, but with the addition of what we call the plica.[8] Let us then consider what this is.

The plica is a note dividing the same sound into low and high. Plicas

---

[8] *Plica*, a fold, from *plicare*, to fold or double up.

are long, breve, and semibreve. But for the present we shall say nothing about the semibreve plica, for it cannot occur in simple figures, although, as will appear later on, it may be used in ligatures and groups of semibreves. Plicas, further, are either ascending or descending.

The long ascending plica is a quadrangular figure bearing on the right a single ascending stroke: ◢ or, more properly, bearing two strokes of which the right one is longer than the left: ◢ I say "more properly," for it is from these two strokes that the plica takes its name. The long descending plica likewise has two strokes, but descending ones, the right one longer than the left, as before: ◥

The breve ascending plica is that which has two ascending strokes, the left one, however, longer than the right: ◣ The descending breve plica has two descending strokes, the longer one on the left: ◥

Observe also that these plicas have a force similar to that of the simple figures already mentioned and that they are similarly regulated as to value.

7. OF LIGATURES AND THEIR PROPERTIES

Simple figures having been discussed, let us speak about those that are composite or, what amounts to the same thing, bound together, those that are rightly called ligatures.

A ligature is a conjunction of simple figures duly ordered by strokes. Ligatures are either ascending or descending. In an ascending ligature the second note is higher than the first; in a descending ligature the first note is higher than the second. Ligatures, moreover, are said to be "with propriety," "without propriety," or "with opposite propriety." And this is with respect to the beginning of the ligature. With respect to the end, however, they are said to be either "with perfection" or "without perfection."

Observe also that these differences are essential and specific to the ligature themselves. Hence a ligature "with propriety" differs essentially from one that is "without," just as a rational being differs from an irrational one, and the same is true of the other differences we have mentioned. Species is subordinate to genus. Yet to the species themselves no name is given, but the differences we have mentioned and the genus to which they belong define them. This agrees with what occurs in other real genera: "animate body," for example, defines a certain species to which no name is given.

With respect to the middle notes of ligatures no essential difference is found, from which it follows that all middle notes in ligature agree in significance. Hence it appears that the position of those is false who hold that in the ternary ligature the middle note is a long,[9] although in all others it is a breve. Now let us consider what is meant by "with propriety," "without propriety," and "with opposite propriety," also by "with perfection" and "without perfection," and what the significance of all these things may be.

"Propriety" is the note at the beginning of a ligature of primary invention, borrowed from plainsong; "perfection" means the same thing, but with respect to the final note. Whence follow the rules of the differences we have mentioned.

Every descending ligature having a stroke descending from the left side of the first note is called "with propriety." being so figured in plainsong. If it lack the stroke it is "without propriety." Further, every ascending ligature is "with propriety" if it lack the stroke. If, however, it have a stroke descending from the left side of the first note, or from the right side, which is more proper, it is "without propriety."

Further, every ligature, whether ascending or descending, bearing a stroke ascending from the first note, is "with opposite propriety."

Now with respect to the final note of a ligature these rules are given. Every ligature bearing the final note immediately above the penultimate is "perfect." A ligature is made "imperfect" in two ways: first, if the final note be rectangular, without a plica, the head turned away from (instead of being above) the penultimate; second, if the last two notes be combined in one oblique form, ascending or descending. In ascent, however, this last "imperfection" is out of use, nor is it necessary except, as will appear later on,[10] when the final breve in an ascending ligature is to take a plica.

Aside from these things be it known that, just as by these differences one ligature differs from another in form, so also in value. Whence follow the rules of every ligature.

In every ligature "with propriety" the first note is a breve, in every one "without propriety," a long. In every ligature "with perfection" the final note is a long, in every one "without perfection," a breve. In every ligature "with opposite propriety" the first note is a semibreve, to which we add, "and the following one," not in itself, but in consequence, for no semibreve may occur alone. Further, every middle note is a breve, except, as already explained, it be made a semibreve by "opposite propriety." Be it also understood that in ligatures the longs are made perfect

---

[9] Cf. John of Garland (CS, I, 179a–179b) on the expression of his second and fifth modes in ligature.

[10] Page 149 below.

in the way that was explained under simple figures and that the breves in a similar way become proper or are altered.

8. OF PLICAS IN COMPOSITE FIGURES

Aside from this be it known that any ligature, whether perfect or imperfect, may take the plica, and this with respect to its end. (What a plica is, has already been explained under simple figures.) For perfect ligatures may take the plica in two ways, ascending or descending. Imperfect ligatures may also take the plica in two ways. And observe that imperfect ligatures always take the plica in oblique imperfection, ascending or descending. And in such a case, where an imperfect ligature is to take a plica, the oblique form must be used in ascending, because the final note is to be made a breve. For if the rectangular imperfection take the plica, the plica will make it perfect, since it shares the rule of perfection.[11] Without the plica, the oblique imperfection is not to be used, for the position of rectangular imperfection suffices wherever there is no plica and is more proper and more usual. With this the plicas of all ligatures are manifest.

There are also certain combinations of simple figures and ligatures which share the nature, in part of ligatures, in part of simple figures, and which cannot be called either the one or the other.[12] For the valuation of such combinations we can give no rules other than those already given for simple figures and ligatures. Besides, there are other arrangements of simple figures and ligatures, distinguished by the rules of simple figures alone, which supply the defect of the combinations not governed by rule.

9. OF RESTS AND OF HOW THROUGH THEIR AGENCY THE MODES ARE CHANGED FROM ONE TO ANOTHER

The signs signifying actual sound having been discussed, let us consider the rests, which represent its omission. A rest is an omission of actual sound in the quantity proper to some mode. Of rests there are six species: perfect long, imperfect long (under which is included the altered breve, since they comprehend the same measure), breve proper, major semibreve, minor semibreve, and double bar (*finis punctorum*).

The rest of the perfect long is the omission of a perfect actual sound, comprehending in itself three "tempora." The rest of the imperfect long and altered breve is measured in a similar way by two "tempora" only.

---

11 That is, will give it the appearance of a long, being to the right, as in the long plica.
12 Franco refers here to the so-called *conjunctae*, conventional combinations derived from the *climacus* and other similar neumes, which appear to the theorists of the mensural notation to be made up of longs and semibreves, or of ligatures and semibreves.

The rest of the breve is the omission of a breve proper, including in itself a single "tempus." The major semibreve omits two parts of the breve proper, the minor a third part only. The double bar is called immensurable, for it occurs also in plainsong. This signifies simply that regardless of the mode the penultimate note is a long, even though it would be a breve if the mode were considered.

Aside from this, these six rests are subtly designated by six strokes, also called rests. Of these the first, called perfect, touching four lines, comprehends three spaces, since it is measured by three "tempora." For the same reason the imperfect rest, touching three lines, covers two spaces, the breve rest one space, the major semibreve rest two parts of one space, the minor semibreve rest one part only. The double bar, touching all lines, comprehends four spaces.

The formulae for all these are shown in the following example:

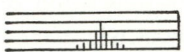

Observe also that rests have a marvelous power, for through their agency the modes are transformed from one to another. The proper rest of the first mode is the breve proper or perfect long; that of the second the imperfect long; those of the third and fourth properly perfect longs, though improperly breves proper or altered; the fifth ought properly to have the breve or semibreve. Now if the first mode, which proceeds by long, breve, and long, has after a breve an imperfect long rest:

Ma - ris stel - la   fer - vens

it is changed to the second. If the second mode, after a long, takes a breve rest:

O Ma - ri - a   ma - ter   de - i   flos

it is changed to the first.[13]

---

13 As Ludwig observes (*loc. cit.,* p. 290), these examples are poorly chosen: the mode does not change at all; it is simply that the form with up-beat is substituted for the form without. At the same time, the examples reveal the same confusion between quantity and accent that prompted the recognition of the fourth mode as a distinct variety of musical meter.

The fifth mode, when combined with the first in any discant, is governed by the rests of the first and takes a long note before a rest:

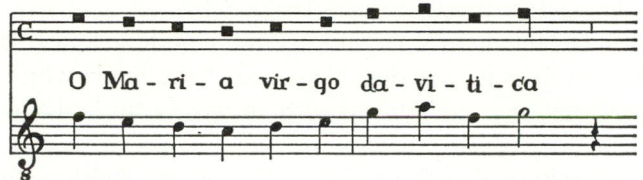

When combined with the second, it is governed by the rests of the second and takes a breve at the end before the rest:

When it is neither the one nor the other, it is governed by its own rests:

Observe also that all the modes may run together in a single discant, for through perfections all are reduced to one. Nor need one attempt to determine the mode to which such a discant belongs, although it may be said to belong to the one in which it chiefly or frequently remains.

Of rests and of the changing of the modes let these things suffice for the present.

10. HOW MANY FIGURES CAN BE BOUND AT ONE TIME?

Be it known that not to bind a figure that can be bound is a fault, but to bind a figure that cannot be bound a greater fault. Whence be it observed that longs cannot be bound together except in the binary ligature that is "without propriety" and "with perfection." Nor is it a fault if even in this situation they be unbound, for nowhere else are longs bound together. From this it follows that those who occasionally bind three longs together, as in tenors, err exceedingly, as do those who bind a long between two breves,[14] since, as we have seen, all middle notes become breves by rule.

---

14 Cf. p. 148 above and note 9.

Similarly, at one time more than two semibreves cannot be bound together, and then only at the beginning of the ligature, by which understand "of the ligature proper to semibreves."

Breves can be bound at the beginning, in the middle, and at the end.

From these things it is evident that, except the mode which proceeds entirely by longs, any mode taken without words can be bound.

The first mode, which proceeds by long and breve, first binds three "without propriety and with perfection," then two "with propriety and perfection," and as many more twos as desired, so that it concludes with two of this species, except the mode be changed.

Observe also that, as already explained under rests, the modes can be changed in several ways.

The second mode takes a binary ligature "with propriety and perfection," then two, two, and so forth, of the same species, a single breve remaining, except the mode be changed.

The third mode takes a four-note ligature "without propriety and with perfection," then three "with propriety and perfection," then three, three, and so forth, except the mode be changed.

The fourth mode first binds three "with propriety and perfection," then three, three, and so forth, of the same species, concluding with two "with propriety and without perfection," except the mode be changed.

The fifth mode ought to be bound as far as possible, concluding with breves or semibreves, except the mode be changed.

11. OF DISCANT AND ITS SPECIES

Figures and rests having been considered, let us speak of how discant ought to be written and of its species. But since every discant is governed by consonances, let us first consider the consonances and dissonances that are sounded at the same time and in different voices.[15]

By concord we mean two or more sounds so sounded at one time that the ear perceives them to agree with one another. By discord we mean the opposite, namely, two sounds so combined that the ear perceives them to be dissonant.

Of concords there are three species: perfect, imperfect, and intermediate.

---

[15] Franco's treatment of concord and discord is taken over, almost word for word, from John of Garland (Jerome's text, CS, I, 104b–106a). But, whereas Garland distinguishes three species of discord: perfect, imperfect, and intermediate— the intermediate discords ("which agree in part with the perfect, in part with the imperfect") being the tone and the diapente plus semitone— Franco distinguishes only two, assigning the tone to the imperfect species, the diapente plus semitone to the perfect. As to Garland's classification of the concords, this goes back in turn to the *De musica libellus* (CS, I, 382b).

Concords are perfect when two sounds are so combined that, because of the consonance, one is scarcely perceived to differ from the other. Of these there are two: unison and diapason.

Concords are imperfect when the ear perceives that two sounds differ considerably, yet are not discordant. Of these there are two: ditone and semiditone.

Concords are intermediate when two sounds are so combined that they produce a concord better than the imperfect, yet not better than the perfect. Of these there are two: diapente and diatessaron.

As to why one concord is more concordant than another, let this be left to plainsong.

Of discords there are two species: perfect and imperfect.

Discords are perfect when two sounds are so combined that the ear perceives them to disagree with one another. Of these there are four: semitone, tritone, ditone plus diapente, and semitone plus diapente.

Discords are imperfect when the ear perceives that two sounds agree with one another to a certain extent, yet are discordant. Of these there are three: tone, tone plus diapente, and semiditone plus diapente.

Observe also that both concords and discords can be endlessly extended, as in diapente plus diapason and diatessaron plus diapason, and similarly by adding the double and triple diapason, if it be possible for the voice.

Be it also known that immediately before a concord any imperfect discord concords well.

Discant is written either with words or with and without words. If with words, there are two possibilities—with a single text or with several texts. Discant is written with a single text in the cantilena, in the rondellus, and in any ecclesiastical chant. It is written with several texts in motets which have a triplum or a tenor, for the tenor is the equivalent of some text. It is written with and without words in the conduct and in the ecclesiastical discant improperly [16] called organum.

Observe also that except in conducts the procedure is the same in all these forms, for in all except the conduct there is first taken some cantus prius factus (called tenor, since it supports the discant and has its place from it). In the conduct, however, this is not the case, for cantus and discant are written by the same person. The word "discant," however, is used in two senses—first, as meaning something sung by several persons; second, as meaning something based on a cantus.

---

16 *Improprie,* Coussemaker's reading, is confirmed by Anonymous 1 (CS, I, 302b) and Jacob of Liége (CS, II, 395a), while Gerbert (GS, III, 12a) and Simon Tunstede (CS, IV, 294b and III, 361b) have *proprie.* If *improprie* is correct, the "ecclesiastical discant written with and without words" is organum "in the sense commonly accepted," not organum purum or duplum (cf. pp. 140–141 above).

In the former the procedure is as follows. The discant begins either in unison with the tenor:

or at the diapason:

or at the diapente:

or at the diatessaron:

or at the ditone:

or at the semiditone:

Vir - go vi - get me - li-us

Flos filius

proceeding then by concords, sometimes introducing discords in suitable places, so that when the tenor ascends the discant descends, and vice versa. Be it also known that sometimes, to enhance the beauty of a composition, the tenor and discant ascend and descend together:

A - ve ple - na gra - ti — a

Joanne

Be it also understood that in all the modes concords are always to be used at the beginning of a perfection, whether this beginning be a long, a breve, or a semibreve.

In conducts the procedure is different, for he who wishes to write a conduct ought first to invent as beautiful a melody as he can, then, as previously explained, using it as a tenor is used in writing discant.

He who shall wish to construct a triplum ought to have the tenor and discant in mind, so that if the triplum be discordant with the tenor, it will not be discordant with the discant, and vice versa. And let him proceed further by concords, ascending or descending now with the tenor, now with the discant, so that his triplum is not always with either one alone:

Dulcia

He who shall wish to construct a quadruplum or quintuplum ought to have in mind the melodies already written, so that if it be discordant with one, it will be in concord with the others. Nor ought it always to ascend or descend with any one of these, but now with the tenor, now with the discant, and so forth.

Be it observed also that in discant, as also in tripla and so forth, the equivalence in the perfections of longs, breves, and semibreves ought always to be borne in mind, so that there may be as many perfections in the discant, triplum, and so forth, as there are in the tenor, and vice versa, counting both actual sounds and their omissions as far as the penultimate, where such measure is not present, there being rather a point of organum here.

Of discant sounded simply let these things suffice for the present.

12. OF COPULA

A copula is a rapid, connected discant, either bound or unbound.

A bound copula is one which begins with a simple long and proceeds by binary ligatures "with propriety and perfection," as in the second mode, although it differs from the second mode in notation and in performance. It differs in notation, since the second mode does not begin with a simple long as the copula does:

If between the initial long and the following ligature be placed a division of the mode, it is no longer a copula, but is said to be in the second mode:

A –   men

In performance it differs also, since the second mode is performed with breve proper and imperfect long, while the copula is performed quickly to the end, as though with semibreve and breve.

An unbound copula is effected after the manner of the fifth mode, although it differs from the fifth mode in two respects—in notation and in performance. It differs in notation, since the fifth mode can be bound wherever there are no words, while the copula, although it is never used with words, is unbound:

In performance it differs also, since the fifth mode is performed with breves proper, while the copula is more quickly connected in performance.

Of copula let these things suffice.

13. OF HOCKET

A truncation is a sort of music sounded in a broken way by actual sounds and their omissions. Be it also known that a truncation can be effected in as many ways as the long, breve, and semibreve can be divided.

The long is divisible in numerous ways. First, it can be divided into long and breve, or breve and long, and from this division a truncation or hocket (for this is the same thing) is so effected that in one voice a breve is omitted, in the other a long:

(In seculum)

Then it can also be divided into three breves, or two, and into several semibreves, and from all these divisions a truncation is so sung by actual sounds and their omissions that when one voice rests, the other does not, and vice versa.

The breve, on the other hand, can be divided into three semibreves or two, and from this division a hocket is sung by omitting a semibreve in one voice and performing one in the other:

Be it also observed that from these truncations, by the omission and sounding of longs and breves, are made the vernacular hockets. Be it also observed that in them all the equivalence of the "tempora" and the concord of the actual sounds ought to be borne in mind. Be it also known that every truncation ought to be based on a cantus prius factus, whether it be vernacular or Latin.

Of hocket let this suffice.

14. OF ORGANUM

Organum, in the proper sense of the word, is a sort of music not measured in all its parts. Be it known that there can be no organum purum unless the tenor sustain a single tone,[17] for when the tenor takes several tones in succession, discant begins at once:

[Constan - - - tes e - sto - - - te]

The longs and breves of organum are distinguished by three rules.[18] The first is: Whatever is written as a simple long note is long; as a breve, short; as a semibreve, still shorter. The second is: Whatever is long requires concord with respect to the tenor; if a long occur as a discord, let the tenor be silent or feign concord: [19]

[Ju - dea]

---

17 Literally, "Except over a tenor where a single note is in unison."
18 Cf. John of Garland (CS, I, 114b).
19 Cf. Garland's commentator, Anonymous 4

(CS, I, 362b): "If (the organum) be concordant, the tenor will sing out; if not, the tenor will be silent or quiescent."

The third is: Whatever occurs immediately before the rest which we call double bar is long, for every penultimate is long.

Be it also observed that in organum purum, whenever several similar figures occur in unison, only the first is to be sounded; let all the rest observe the florid style.[20]

Of discant and its species, of signs (that is, of figures and rests), and of organum let the things said here suffice.

Here ends the great "Art of music" of that reverend man, Dominus Franco, Papal Chaplain and Praeceptor of the Cologne Commandery of the Hospital of St. John of Jerusalem.

---

20 Cf. *ibid.*, (CS, I, 363a): "Two notes of the same pitch, whether concordant or not, represent the florid long."

19. Marchetto da Padua

An elder contemporary of Jacopo da Bologna and Giovanni da Cascia, a native of Padua and later a resident of Cesena in the Romagna, Marchetto is the principal spokesman for the musicians of the Italian Trecento. In his chief writings, the *Lucidarium* (on plainsong) and the *Pomerium* (on mensural music), written in 1318, we have a full account of the state of musical knowledge in Italy at the beginning of the fourteenth century, with useful observations on the current practice of Marchetto's fellow countrymen and on the contemporary French practice. The *Pomerium*, in particular, provides us with our earliest theoretical exposition of duple time as an equally privileged variety of musical measure; in addition, it shows us clearly that, however much the musicians of fourteenth-century Italy may have been dependent upon France, they were in no way dependent upon the theory of the French Ars Nova, as first formulated in 1319 by Jean de Muris.

From the Pomerium [1]

[*1318*]

Book II

OF IMPERFECT TIME

SEEING THAT musical discipline has to do with opposites, now that we have considered perfect time in mensurable music, let us also, in a similar way, consider imperfect time. And in considering it, let us proceed in this order. We shall treat: first, of imperfect time in itself and absolutely, in so far as the comprehension of its essence is concerned; second, of imperfect

---

1 Text: Gerbert, *Scriptores*, III, 170–178, the musical examples from Marchetto's *Brevis compilatio*, Coussemaker, *Scriptores*, III, 5–8. For the date see the present editor's "Intorno a Marchetto da Padua," in the *Rassegna musicale* for October 1950.

time in its application to notes according to its totality and multiplication; third, of imperfect time in its application to notes according to its partibility and division.

I. OF IMPERFECT TIME IN ITSELF AND ABSOLUTELY

1. What imperfect time is, speaking musically.

In the first place we say that imperfect musical mensurable time is that which is a minimum, not in fullness, but in semi-fullness of voice. This definition we demonstrate as follows. It is certain that just as the perfect is that which lacks nothing,[2] so the imperfect is that which lacks something. But it is also certain, by the definition of perfect time already demonstrated, that perfect time is that which is a minimum in entire fullness of voice, formed in the manner there expounded.[3] It follows, therefore, that imperfect time, since it falls short of perfect, is not formed in entire fullness of voice.

But someone may say: You ought to derive the deficiency of imperfect time with respect to perfect, not from fullness of voice, but from lessness of time. Whence you ought to say that both times, perfect as well as imperfect, are formed in fullness of voice, but that fullness of voice is formed in less time when it is formed in imperfect time than when it is formed in perfect. Whence (our opponents say) that minimum which is formed in fullness of voice is imperfect time, not perfect.

But to this we reply that to be in fullness of voice and to be a minimum is necessarily perfect time, for perfect musical time is the first measure of all, for which reason also the measure of imperfect time is derived from it by subtracting a part, as will presently be explained. Therefore, since the minimum in any genus is the measure of all other things in it, as previously observed,[4] we conclude that minimum time is always perfect of itself, provided it be formed in fullness of voice, for as soon as we subtract from the quantity of perfect time we constitute imperfect. And so it appears that to define time by fullness of voice is to define it by essential excess or deficiency. Therefore our definition stands, namely that imperfect time is that which is a minimum, not in fullness of voice, but in semi-fullness. This much in the first place.

2. How are perfect and imperfect time essentially opposed?

In themselves, absolutely, and without reference to any division or multiplication of either, perfect and imperfect time are essentially op-

---

2 Cf. Aristotle, *Metaphysics,* 1021 B: "For each thing, and every substance, is perfect when, and only when, in respect of the form of its peculiar excellence, it lacks no particle of its natural magnitude." [Tredennick]

3 Cf. GS, III, 137b, where Marchetto names Franco as his authority for this definition.

4 Cf. GS, III, 137b, where Marchetto refers this statement to the authority of Aristotle.

posed, as is sufficiently clear from our definition. Nevertheless we also demonstrate this. It is certain that perfect and imperfect time are not wholly the same thing, for if they were, imperfect time could be called essentially perfect, and vice versa. Therefore they differ essentially. Now if two things differ essentially they differ actually, for the one is not the other. In this case they are opposed through "privation," for the one actually has something that the other has not. And from this it follows also that they are contradictory, for they can never both be true of the same thing at the same time. There can, then, be no time which could at once be essentially and actually perfect and imperfect.

And if someone say: Some time will be given which for various reasons will at once be perfect and imperfect; we reply that something or nothing will correspond to these reasons. If nothing corresponds, so much for the objection; if something, then one thing will at once be two things, which is impossible. It is therefore impossible for any musical time to be at once actually and essentially perfect and imperfect, as some pretend, for this implies a manifest contradiction, since it amounts to saying that someone is at once "man" and "not-man." And this much in the second place.

3. By how much does imperfect time fall short of perfect?

Imperfect time falls short of perfect by a third part, something we demonstrate as follows. It is certain that imperfect time is not as great in quantity as perfect, for if it were, it would not be imperfect. It is therefore necessary that it fall short of it by some quantity. It can, moreover, not fall short by less than one part, for if you say "by half a part," that half a part will be one part, even though it would be half of the remainder. Therefore, since the primary and principal parts of perfect time are three, for it was divided above by ternary division to obtain what is primary and principal, if imperfect time fall short of perfect, it cannot do so by less than a third part. It follows, therefore, that imperfect time in itself and essentially comprehends only two parts of perfect time.

II. OF THE APPLICATION OF IMPERFECT TIME TO NOTES ACCORDING TO ITS TOTALITY AND MULTIPLICATION

In itself and according to its totality and multiplication, imperfect time is in its application to notes wholly similar in every respect to perfect. Notes of three "tempora," of two "tempora," and of one "tempus" occur in the same way in imperfect time as in perfect and are also similarly figured. All accidents of music in imperfect time, such as rests, tails, and dots, are situated just as in perfect.

The reason is this: Since there can never be a material science, nor yet a sensible knowledge, of imperfect things, except by comparison to perfect (for never, whether through the intellect or through the senses, can we know a thing to be imperfect except we also know what is needed to make it perfect); so science, as regards those things that are apprehended by the intellect or the senses, has always to do with the perfect. Music, therefore, both with regard to its notes and with regard to its accidents, has always to do primarily and principally with perfect time. But by a subtraction made by the intellect of a part, namely of perfect time, music becomes a science of imperfect time. For if imperfect time were to have its own notes and accidents, different from those of perfect time, it follows that there would be primarily and principally a science and a sensible knowledge of imperfect things, having no relation to the perfect, something which, as we have said, is impossible both according to the intellect and according to the senses.

And if someone says: Very well, I shall be guided by the perfect, namely by comparing to its notes and accidents those of imperfect time; we reply that this will be in vain, for by such a comparison he can satisfy only in the notes and accidents of perfect time, namely by subtracting fullness and in consequence quantity from them. Thus he would make notes and accidents of imperfect time in vain.

But he may ask: How am I to know when music is in perfect time and when in imperfect if, as you say, they are completely alike, both in their notes and in their accidents? We reply that this is to be left entirely to the judgment of the composer, who understands the science of music thoroughly. In order, however, that one may know what the wish of the composer is, when music is to be sung in perfect time and when in imperfect, we say that when they are combined some sign ought to be added at the beginning of the music so that by means of it the wish of the composer who has arranged this varied music may be known. For as concerns the figured music and the notes no natural difference can be discovered.

It is demonstrated that any written composition can be written either in perfect time or in imperfect, for this difference in the manner of singing it is provided by the composer, namely for the sake of the harmony, and is not derived from the nature of the music. For this reason a sign indicating the difference need be added only when the composer so wishes, nor can any valid reason be found why one sign is preferable to another. For some use I and II to indicate the perfect and imperfect; others 3 and 2 to indicate the ternary and binary divisions of the "tempus"; others use other signs according to their good pleasure.

But since every composition of itself and naturally observes perfect time more than imperfect (for this is the reason why one is called perfect, the other imperfect), music is by its nature inclined, not toward imperfect time, but toward perfect. It is because of the wish of the composer and for the sake of harmony that music observes imperfect time, abandoning perfect, and for this reason be it observed that it is the composer who adds the sign indicating that his intention in the music is imperfect time.

III. OF THE APPLICATION OF IMPERFECT TIME TO NOTES ACCORDING TO ITS PARTIBILITY AND DIVISION

1. Into how many principal parts is imperfect time divided?

According to its partibility and division, imperfect time is so applied to notes that by primary division it is divided into two parts. Nor can it be divided into more, something we demonstrate as follows. In our first book it was demonstrated that by primary division perfect time is divided into three parts, no more, no less; we say "by primary and perfect division" for reasons already adduced. At the beginning of this second book it was also shown that imperfect time falls short of perfect and, as was likewise shown there, that it cannot fall short by less than a third part. There remain, then, two parts of imperfect time. It is clear, therefore, that by primary division imperfect time can be divided only into two parts, for otherwise it would in no respect fall short of perfect. And this is logical and appropriate, for just as to perfect time corresponds the more perfect division, which is into three, no more, no less, and this division comprehends all others; so to imperfect time corresponds the imperfect division, which is into two. And just as imperfect division is a part constituted within the ternary, so imperfect time is a part constituted within perfect.

By the first division of imperfect time there are then constituted two semibreves and not more [the "divisio binaria"]. These are equal, namely in value, and they equal two of the three semibreves of the first division of perfect time [the "divisio ternaria"]. For this reason they ought to be similarly figured, for they are equal to one another in value and in nature.

2. Of the binary division of imperfect time, according to the first way of dividing it.

But if either of the two semibreves be given a descending tail ♩♩=♩♪ ♩♩=♪♩ we go on to the second division of imperfect time [the "divisio quaternaria"], which is the division of each of our two parts into two others and not into three. For we have already explained and shown that imperfect time first observes imperfect division; if afterwards we were to divide our primary parts into three, it would to this end be necessary to repeat about threes. First let us say, then, that our parts of imperfect time are first divided into two others, making four. These four are equal in nature, and they equal eight parts of the twelve-part division of perfect time [the "divisio duodenaria perfecta"] ♩♩♩♩ = ♫♫ . But if of these four only three be given, the Italian practice is that the final one, being the end, will equal the first two. But if either one of the others be given a tail, the final one and the one without a tail will retain their natural value, the one with a tail equaling the two others "by art" (*via artis*) ♩♩♩ = ♩ ♫ ♩♩♩ = ♪ ♪. With three notes, two cannot be given tails, for the second one with a tail would be meaningless. And with four notes, if we remain in this division, it is unnecessary to give tails to any; if it be done, the note with a tail will belong either to the ternary division of the primary parts, which is the division of each of two into three [the "divisio senaria imperfecta"], or to the third division of imperfect time, which is the division of each of four into two [the "divisio octonaria"]. In this case the proportion between the notes with ascending and descending tails and those without, and between the final notes and the preceding ones, both "by art" and "by nature," is arrived at throughout as plainly demonstrated in our chapter on the semibreves of perfect time, and they will also be given the same names.

3. *On the secondary division of imperfect time.*

The principal parts of imperfect time, being two, can also be divided each one into three, thus constituting six notes [the "divisio senaria imperfecta"], and these six can again be divided in twos, making twelve [the "divisio duodenaria imperfecta"], or in threes, making eighteen [the "divisio octodenaria imperfecta"]. In the manner in which they are written and proportioned, in short, in all accidents and in their names, these are similar to those of perfect time.

From what has just been said has arisen a not inconsiderable error in mensurable music. For some have said: You say that I can divide the two parts of imperfect time in threes and thus have six. But these six have also been brought about by dividing the three parts of perfect time in twos. Therefore (our critics conclude) the "divisio senaria" is a mean between perfect and imperfect time.

We reply that, in dividing two things, a given number can always be found in both, and yet no part of either can ever be a mean between the one thing and the other; similarly, in dividing two lines by binary, ternary, and quaternary division, a given division can always be found in both, and yet no part of either can ever be a mean between the one line and the other. Thus, in dividing imperfect time into its parts, no matter how often you hit upon a number of parts which you arrived at in dividing perfect time into its parts, no part of imperfect time can ever be a mean between imperfect time and perfect, nor can all its parts together.[5]

And if someone says: You say that only the imperfect falls short of the perfect; we reply that this is true by the proportion of perfect time to imperfect, for in their essences the two times are distinct from one another, separate and opposite, as is clear from their opposed definitions, one being formed only in fullness of voice, the other in semi-fullness.

4. Of the disparity and difference between the French and the Italians when they sing in imperfect time, and of the question, which nation sings more rationally?

Be it known, moreover, that there is a great difference between the Italians and the French in the manner of proportioning notes in imperfect time, likewise in the manner of singing it. The Italians always attribute imperfection to the beginning, saying that the final note is more perfect, being the end. But the French say the opposite, namely that while this is true of perfect time; of imperfect time they say that the final note is always less perfect, being the end.

Which nation, then, sings more rationally? The French, we reply. The reason is that just as in anything perfect its last complement is said to be its perfection with respect to its end (for the perfect is that which lacks nothing, not only with respect to its beginning, but also with respect to its end), so in anything imperfect its imperfection and deficiency is understood with respect to its end (for a thing is called imperfect when it lacks something with respect to its end). If, therefore, we wish to sing or proportion sounds in the manner of singing in imperfect time, we ought rationally to attribute imperfection always to the final note, just as in the manner of singing in perfect time we attribute perfection to it. From this we conclude that in this manner of singing the French sing better and more reasonably than the Italians.

The manner of the Italians can, however, be sustained by saying that they imitate perfection in so far as they can (which is reasonable enough), namely by always reducing the imperfect to the perfect. Then, since the proportion of imperfect time is reduced to the perfection of perfect time (which amounts to reducing the imperfect to the perfect), the singing

---

[5] Cf. GS, III, 140b, where Marchetto resolves this confusion more simply: "Between contradictories there can never be a mean, according to the Philosopher; there can, then, never be a mean between perfect and imperfect time, speaking essentially, intrinsically, and *per se* of the nature of perfect and imperfect time." The reference is to Aristotle, *Metaphysics,* 1057A.

of the Italians in imperfect time can be sustained reasonably enough.

Be it said, however, that for the reason already given the French sing better and more properly.

5. Of the names and properties of the semibreves of imperfect time in the French and the Italian manner.[6]

If two semibreves be taken for the imperfect "tempus," in both the French and the Italian manner they are performed alike:

And since they are parts of the first division of imperfect time [the "divisio binaria"] they are called major semibreves "by nature," being comparable to two semibreves of the first division of perfect time [the "divisio ternaria"]. "By art," however, one of them can be given a tail; then in the Italian manner we go on to the second division of imperfect time [the "divisio quaternaria"], which is the division into four equal semibreves, and the semibreve with a tail, which is called major "by art," will contain three of four parts, the one without a tail retaining its natural value:

And since this second division of imperfect time is comparable in a partial way to the second division of perfect time [the "divisio senaria perfecta"], which is the division into six, its four equal semibreves are called minor semibreves "by nature."

But in the French manner, if one be given a tail, we go on at once to the ternary division of imperfect time [the "divisio senaria imperfecta"], which is

[6] Note that the French manner of dividing the imperfect "tempus," as described by Marchetto in this section, agrees throughout with that described by Philippe de Vitry in his *Ars nova* (CS, III, 18b–19a). But whereas de Vitry ob- tains his results "by art," Marchetto is chiefly concerned with a division "by nature"; his "French manner" corresponds roughly to that of the *Roman de Fauvel* (1314).

the division into six equal semibreves. These are called minims in the first degree, the semibreves having been divided beyond the division of minor semibreves. In this case the semibreve with a tail contains five of six parts "by art," the one without a tail retaining its natural value.

If three semibreves be taken for the imperfect "tempus," in the Italian manner the final one, being the end, will equal the two others in value:

But in the French manner, in order that the proportion and perfection of the whole measure may be preserved, the first note will contain three of six parts, the second two, and the third one, the notes being called major semibreve, minor semibreve, and minim.

When there are four semibreves, in the Italian manner they are performed alike:

But in the French manner (for in dividing imperfect time the French do not go beyond the "divisio senaria," even though they could) the first of these four contains two parts of six and the second one, the other two filling out the second half of the perfection in a similar way. This way of proportioning four notes among the six parts of the "tempus" was necessary in order that the French form might be generally observed. For, as will appear on reflection, in no other way can such a proportion or perfection be worked out without an excess or deficiency of perfection. For if each of the first two notes contain two parts of the "tempus," each of the remaining two containing only one, there will be no proportion between the parts, since in a division of this kind no mean proportion can ever rationally and naturally be found. This we call "by nature," for "by art" the same result can be obtained by adding the sign of art.

When there are five semibreves, in the Italian manner they belong to the third division of imperfect time [the "divisio octonaria"], which is the division into eight, comparable in a partial way to the division of perfect time into twelve [the "divisio duodenaria perfecta"], and the first two will be called minims in the second degree, the others remaining in the second division of imperfect time:

"By art," however, these minims can be placed otherwise among the five:

But in the French manner the first three are equal minims, the fourth containing two parts, the fifth one, for the French always place the more perfect immediately before the less perfect, proportioning them one to the other. Thus it ought always to be understood that the French attribute perfection to the beginning.

When there are six semibreves, in the Italian manner the first four are measured by four of eight parts of the "tempus," the last two remaining in the second division:

"By art," namely by giving them ascending tails, the minims can be placed otherwise:

But in the French manner all are equal and, as we have said before, they are called minims.

When there are seven semibreves, in the Italian manner the first six contain six parts of the "tempus," the last remaining in the second division:

except perchance it be artificially distinguished:

When there are eight semibreves, all are performed alike as minims:

But in the French manner, if one wished to take more than six semibreves for the imperfect "tempus," he would fall at once into its third division [the "divisio duodenaria imperfecta"], which is the division of six into twelve, and some of them would require ascending tails.

But he may ask: How can I know which of the semibreves with ascending tails belong to the third division, in twelve, and which to the second division, in six, when with six some are also given ascending tails in various ways? We reply that this depends on the number of notes being either less or greater than six.

And in order that it may be known which division of imperfect time we ought to follow in singing mensurable music, whether the French or the Italian, we say that at the beginning of any composition in the French manner, above the sign of imperfect time which is placed there, there should be placed a "G," denoting or indicating that the composition should be performed in the French manner [7] (just as in plainsong the founders of music placed a "Γ" at the beginning of the Guidonian hand to show that we had music from the Greeks), for we had this division of the imperfect "tempus" from the French. And if a single composition in imperfect time be proportioned according to the French and Italian manners combined, we say that at the beginning of the part in the French manner there should be placed a "G," but that in a similar way at the beginning of the part in the Italian manner there should be placed a Greek "I" ["Y"], which is the initial of their name.

---

[7] For a clear example of Marchetto's "French manner," headed "s.g." (Senaria Gallica), see the caccia "Or quà conpagni" in W. T. Marrocco's *Fourteenth-Century Italian Cacce* (Cambridge, 1942), pp. 46–47 and plate IV.

20. Jean de Muris

A native of Normandy, Jean de Muris was born before 1300 and died about 1351. He is known to have taught at the Sorbonne in Paris. He was a man of great learning, a philosopher and mathematician whose interest in music was distinctly secondary. Jean de Muris was on friendly terms with Philippe de Vitry, whose *Ars nova* he energetically endorsed and defended in his writings. He is credited with the authorship of the important *Ars novae musicae* and with a few other writings. Ironically enough, the voluminous *Speculum musicae*, a violent attack on his teachings, passed until quite recently as one of his own writings.

From the Ars novae musicae [1]

[*1319*]

II. MUSICA PRACTICA

SEEING THAT in the preceding discourse [2] we have touched lightly and in brief on the theory of music, it now remains to inquire at greater length into its practice, that part which is mensurable, since different practitioners think differently about this. As was shown in Book I, sound is generated by motion, since it belongs to the class of successive things.[3] For this reason, while it exists when it is made, it no longer exists once it has been made. Succession does not exist without motion. Time inseparably unites motion. Therefore it follows necessarily that time is the measure of sound. Time is also the measure of motion. But for us time is the measure of sound prolonged in one continuous motion, and this same definition of time we give also to the single time interval.

---

1 Text: Gerbert, *Scriptores*, III, 292–297, 300–301. Some emendations have been obtained by collating Gerbert's text with Coussemaker's Anonymous VI (CS, III, 398–401) and with his text of the *Conclusiones* (ibid., 109–113). On the De Muris texts in general see Besseler in *Archiv für Musikwissenschaft*, VIII (1926), 207–209.

2 Gerbert, *Scriptores*, III, 312, 256–258, 313–315.

3 *Ibid.*, p. 256.

According to one account, there are two sorts of time—greater and lesser,[4] greater time having longer motion, lesser time shorter. These do not differ in species, other things remaining the same, for greatness and lessness do not alter species. But to every time interval of measured sound our predecessors reasonably attributed a certain mode of perfection, prescribing this sort of time interval in order that it might support a ternary division, for they believed all perfection to be in the ternary number. For this reason they prescribed perfect time as the measure of all music, knowing that it is unsuitable for the imperfect to be found in art. Yet certain moderns believe themselves to have discovered the opposite of this, which is not consistent. Their meaning will be more clearly set forth in what follows.

That all perfection is implicit in the ternary number follows from many likely conjectures. For in God, who is most perfect, there is one substance, yet three persons; He is threefold, yet one, and one, yet threefold; very great, therefore, is the correspondence of unity to trinity. At first, in knowledge, are the separate and the concrete; from these, under the ternary number, the composite is derived. At first, in celestial bodies, are the thing moving, the thing moved, and time. Three attributes in stars and sun—heat, light, splendor; in elements—action, passion, matter; in individuals—generation, corruption, dissolution; in all finite time—beginning, middle, end; in all curable disease—rise, climax, decline. Three intellectual operations; three terms in the syllogism; three figures in argument; three intrinsic principles of natural things; three potentialities of the being that has not suffered privation; three loci of correlative distance; three lines in the whole universe. After one the ternary number is the first that is odd; by multiplying it by itself three times is generated also the first incomposite cubic number. Not two lines, but three, enclose a surface; the source of all polygonic figures is the triangle; first of all rectilinears is the triangular. Every object, if it is ever to stand, has three dimensions.[5]

Now, since the ternary number is everywhere present in some form or other, it may no longer be doubted that it is perfect. And, by the contrary of this proposition, the binary number, since it falls short of the ternary, also since it is thus of lower rank, is left imperfect. But any composite number formed from these may properly be considered perfect because of its similarity and correspondence to the ternary. For time, since

4 Compare Philippe de Vitry (CS, III, 21b–22b), who enumerates three varieties of perfect time—least, medium, and greater—and two of imperfect—least and greater.

5 For the role of the number three in the musical theory of the Middle Ages see Hermann Abert, *Die Musikanschauung des Mittelalters* (Halle, 1905), pp. 179–181.

it belongs to the class of continuous things, is not only again divisible by ternary numbers, but is also endlessly divisible to infinity.

Seeing, on the other hand, that sound measured by time consists in the union of two forms, namely the natural and the mathematical, it follows that because of the one its division never ceases while because of the other its division must necessarily stop somewhere; for just as nature limits the magnitude and increase of all material things, so it also limits their minuteness and decrease. For it is demonstrated naturally that nature is limited by a maximum and a minimum; sound, moreover, is in itself a natural form to which quantity is artificially attributed; it is necessary, therefore, for there to be limits of division beyond which no sound however fleeting may go. These limits we wish to apprehend by reason.

Prolonged sound measured by definite time is formed in the air not so much in the likeness of a point, line, or surface, as rather conically and spherically (in the likeness of a sphere, as light is formed in free space), something which may be tested by six listeners placed according to the six differences of proportion. And since such a sound is set in motion by the effort of the person striking, which is finite, for it proceeds from a finite being, its duration and continuation are necessarily limited, for sound cannot be generated in infinity or in an instant. Its limits are disposed in this way.

All music, especially mensurable music, is founded in perfection, combining in itself number and sound. The number, moreover, which musicians consider perfect in music is, as follows from what has been said, the ternary number. Music, then, takes its origin from the ternary number. The ternary number multiplied by itself produces nine; in a certain sense this ninefold number contains every other, for beyond nine there is always a return to the unit. Music, then, does not go beyond the nine-part number. Now the nine-part number again multiplied by itself produces 81, a product which is measured by the ternary number in three dimensions, just as sound is. For if we take three threes, two threes, and one three nine times, always multiplying the products again by three; then, as 3 times 3 produces 9, and 3 times 9 27, so 3 times 27 produces 81. From the unit, then, the third part of the ternary number, which is perfect, to 81, which is likewise perfect, these are, we say, the maximum and minimum limits of any whole sound, for the length of such a sound is included between these extremes. Within them, four distinct degrees of perfection may rationally be apportioned. This is done as follows.

No musical perfection exceeds the ternary number; it comprises and forms it. A perfection is that according to which something is called perfect. Perfect is that which is divisible into three equal parts, or into two unequal ones, of which the larger is twice the smaller. Unity, moreover, is indivisible and may be called neutral. In these, then, is comprehended the genus of divisibility, likewise of indivisibility. Now 81 is ternary and in this respect perfect; 54 is the corresponding binary number and in this respect imperfect; the corresponding unit is 27, making the perfect imperfect and the imperfect perfect. In these three numbers we distinguish the first degree; from 27 to 9 is the second; from 9 to 3 is the third; from 3 to 1 is the fourth; in any one of these we find again the perfect, imperfect, and neutral in the numbers 3, 2, and 1. There are then four degrees, no more, no less.

We have still to show by what figures, signs, or notes the things which we have said may be appropriately indicated or represented and by what words or names these may be called, for at this very time our doctors of music dispute daily with one another about this. And although signs are arbitrary, yet, since they should all be to a certain extent in mutual agreement, musicians ought to devise signs more appropriate to the sounds signified. In devising these, the wiser ancients long ago agreed and conceded that geometrical figures should be the signs of musical sounds.[6] Now the figure most suitable for writing music is the quadrilateral, for it arises from a single stroke of the pen, and in such a quadrilateral, as in a genus, all musical notes have their origin.[7] For the musical note is a quadrilateral figure arbitrarily representative of numbered sound measured by time. Moreover, the distinctions of this form are nine: rectangularity, equilaterality, the tail, the dot, the position, the right side, the left side, the upward direction, and the downward direction, as will be seen in the diagram to follow.

Now the ancients, while they wrote reasonably about the figures of the second and third degrees, had little to say about the first and fourth, although they made use of these remote degrees in their singing. For reasons which we shall pass over, their figures did not adequately represent what they sang. Nevertheless they gave us the means of accomplishing completely what they had incompletely accomplished. For they assumed the ternary and binary designated by a similar figure, the unit by a dissimilar one, inasmuch as the binary is closer to the ternary than the unit is.[8] Among things having a common symbol one passes more readily from one to another. And conversely.[9] From the ternary to the binary, that

---

6 Omitting *quos puncta . . . voluerunt appellare* with CS, III, 399b.

7 Omitting *per causam . . . explicatur* with CS, III, 399b.

8 Omitting *Quae autem . . . ut eadem* with CS, III, 399b.

9 Evidently a familiar axiom; in a different connection it is cited also by Jacob of Liége (CS, II, 420a).

is, from perfect to imperfect, and vice versa, one passes more readily than from the ternary to the unit; whatever the degree, therefore, the more similar figure ought to be common to those things the distinction between which is not perceived in themselves but is manifest rather in their relation to another thing. In the second degree, according to our predecessors, the quadrilateral, equilateral, rectangular figure with a tail to the right, ascending or descending, represents perfect and imperfect alike, that is, the ternary and binary. The same figure without a tail represents the unit in the second degree, the ternary and binary in the third. In this degree, on the other hand, the quadrilateral, equilateral, obtuse-angular figure represents the unit.

As to the first degree, the earlier authorities spoke about the binary and the unit, omitting the ternary or representing it by a figure similar to the one denoting the binary. In the fourth they abandoned the unit entirely or figured it implicitly in the ligatures. This is the last figure in the fourth degree, namely a quadrilateral, equilateral, obtuse-angular figure with a tail ascending. But in the first degree the first figure is similar to the second, namely a quadrilateral, non-equilateral, rectangular figure with a tail to the right, ascending or descending.

The differences of the first degree are between the non-equilateral figure and the equilateral; those of the second degree between the figure with a tail and the one without; those of the third between the rectangular figure and the obtuse-angular; those of the fourth between the obtuse-angular figure with a tail and the one without.

We have still to speak about the names of the figures which are called notes. In the first degree we may name them triplex long, duplex long, simplex long. In the second, following the terminology of the ancients, perfect long, imperfect long, breve. In the third, after the fashion of the preceding degree, perfect breve, imperfect breve, semibreve (so named not from equal division, but from being greater or lesser, so that the binary is called the greater part of three, the unit the lesser part, the lesser semibreve having been so called by the ancients also). In the fourth degree, following the terminology of the preceding ones, perfect semibreve, imperfect semibreve, least semibreve.

By others the notes are named otherwise, the same sense remaining. Omitting those of the first degree, which are named appropriately enough, we have long, semilong, breve, semibreve, minor, semiminor, minim. Or as follows, and more appropriately: longa, longior, longissima (that is, magna, major, maxima, beginning the comparison with the unit of the first degree); then, in the second, perfecta, imperfecta, brevis, brevior, brevissima (or parva), minor, minima.

First degree (Major mode)	▜ 81 Triplex long Longissima Maxima	▜ 54 Duplex long Longior Major	▜ 27 Simplex long Longa Magna
Second degree (Mode)	▜ 27 Perfect long Long Perfecta	▜ 18 Imperfect long Semilong Imperfecta	◼ 9 Breve Breve Brevis
Third degree (Time)	◼ 9 Perfect breve Breve Brevis	◼ 6 Imperfect breve Semibreve Brevior	◆ 3 Minor semi-breve Minor Brevissima
Fourth degree (Prolation)	◆ 3 Perfect semi-breve Minor Parva	◆ 2 Imperfect semi-breve Semiminor Minor	◆ 1 Minim Minim Minima

Perfection and imperfection are represented, as we have said, by the same figure, just as there may be in several forms the same general material; the distinction between them the authorities attribute to five modes (*modi*), as is evident in the second degree, the one about which they had most to say. Just as long before long is perfect, so also before two breves, before three breves, before a dot, before a long rest, long is always valued as three "tempora." And this distinction is called "from place or position." Imperfection is recognized in two modes—by the preceding unit or by the following unit. What has been said of the second degree is to be understood of the other degrees in their own way.

In any one of these degrees there may be distinguished the following species (*species*) of melody: one entirely in perfect notes or with the binary preceding and the unit following—as though one mode, these are identical in their rests; a second with the unit preceding and the binary following; a third combining the first and second, namely with the perfect note preceding and two units following; a fourth made in the opposite way; a fifth composed entirely of units and their divisions.

Of rests and ligatures new things might be said, but as to them let what is found in the canons of the ancients be sufficient, except that rests may now be arranged in the four degrees.

At the end of this little work be it observed that music may combine perfect notes in imperfect time (for example, notes equal in value to three breviores) with imperfect notes in perfect time (for example, notes equal in value to two breves), for three binary values and two ternary ones are made equal in multiples of six. Thus three perfect binary values in imperfect time are as two imperfect ternary ones in perfect, and alternating one with another they are finally made equal by equal proportion.[10] And music is sung with perfect notes in perfect time, or with imperfect ones in imperfect, whichever is fitting.

Again, it is possible to separate and disjoin perfections, not continuing them, as when a single breve occurs between two perfect notes, yet, the breves having been gathered together, the whole is reduced to perfection.[11] For what can be sung can also be written down.

Moreover, there are many other new things latent in music which will appear altogether plausible to posterity.

In this "Ars musicae" are included some things as it were obscured by being left implicit which, were they made explicit, would stop ever so many now disputing together about certain conclusions. It will be useful, then, if we, more from love of the disputants than for novelty's sake, were to demonstrate in an elegant way the truth of some conclusions regarding which there is among the masters growing doubt. And let no invidious critic rise up against us if, preserving the modes and other things which will be apparent, and observing always the bounds set by the ancients, we are obliged to lay down rules.

These are the conclusions.

1. That the long may be made imperfect by the breve.
2. That the breve may be made imperfect by the semibreve.
3. That the semibreve may be made imperfect by the minim.
4. That the long may be made imperfect by the semibreve.

---

10 Probably the first theoretical mention of the so-called *aequipollentiae*, in representing which the practical music of the fourteenth century makes use of the red (or colored) note. A specific example of the combination here described is the motet "Thoma tibi obsequia," cited by De Muris himself at the end of the *Quaestiones* (GS, III, 306a, and CS, III, 106a) and by Philippe de Vitry in his *Ars nova* (CS, III, 21a). On this example see Johannes Wolf, *Geschichte der Mensural-Notation* (Leipzig, 1904), I, 142; the motet itself was contained in a MS once the property of Philip the Good, discussed by Eugènie Droz and Geneviève Thibault in *Revue de musicologie*, X (1926), 1–8, and by Heinrich Besseler in *Archiv für Musikwissenschaft*, VIII (1926), 235–241.

11 Probably the first theoretical mention of syncopation.

5. That the breve may be made imperfect by the minim.
6. That the minim may not be made imperfect.
7. That the altered breve may be made imperfect by the semibreve.
8. That the altered semibreve may be made imperfect by the minim.
9. That the "tempus" may be divided into any number of equal parts.

. . . . . .

In these nine stated conclusions there are implicit many other special ones which application will make clear to the student.

Now, if these few things which we have said include anything which is seen to be inconsistent with truth, we ask you, venerable musicians (you in whom we have delighted because of music from earliest youth, for no science is hidden from him who knows music well), how far, from love of this work, you will correct and charitably tolerate our defects. For it is not possible for the mind of one man, unless he have an angelic intellect, to comprehend the whole truth of any science. Perhaps in the course of time there will happen to us what is now happening to the ancients, who believed that they held the end of music. Let no one say that we have concealed the state of music or its immutable end. For knowledge and opinion move in cycles, turning back on themselves in circles, as long as it pleases the supreme will of Him who has freely created and voluntarily segregated everything in this world.

21. Jacob of Liége

Since the publication in 1924 of Walter Grossmann's study of the introductory chapters of the treatise that follows, it has been generally recognized that the *Speculum musicae*, once supposed to be the work of Jean de Muris, is actually a violent attack on him, written sometime during the second quarter of the fourteenth century by a certain Jacob of Liége, about whom virtually nothing is known. Perhaps the most encyclopaedic of all medieval writings on music, the *Speculum* covers the entire range of the musical knowledge of its time; its last book, from which certain chapters are translated below, is at once an eloquent defence of the music of the Ars Antiqua and an impassioned tirade against the Ars Nova and all its works. As such, Jacob's *Speculum* becomes the prototype of Artusi's notorious attack on Monteverdi at the beginning of the seventeenth century.

From the Speculum musicae [1]

Prohemium to the Seventh Book

IN HIS commentary on the *Categories* of Aristotle, Simplicius says, commending the ancients: "We are not everywhere equal to discerning between true and false, yet in this we delight in attacking our betters." [2]

In this matter, just as it is profitable and praiseworthy to imitate things well done by the ancients, so it is pleasant and commendable to approve things well said by them, not to attack them, which last seems more the part of youths, for though youths are more inventive, old men are conceded more judicious. On this account, as the Master says in his *Histories*, youths and inexperienced persons, pleased by new things (for novelty is

---

1 Text: Coussemaker, *Scriptores*, II, 384–385, 427–432. On the authorship see Besseler in *Archiv für Musikwissenschaft*, VII (1925), 181.
2 *Commentaria in Aristotelem graeca*, VIII

(Berlin, 1907), 8. I am indebted to my friend Dr. W. J. Wilson of the National Archives for the identification of this reference.

congenial and enchanting to the ear), ought not so to praise the new that the old is buried.[3] For as a rule new teachings, although on first acquaintance they glitter outwardly, are seen to lack solid foundations within when they are well examined, are rejected and do not last long. For the rest, if it be unprofitable to accomplish by many means what can conveniently be accomplished by few, what profit can there be in adding to a sound old doctrine a wanton and curious new one, repudiating the former?

For it is written: Thou shalt not remove thy neighbor's landmark, which they of old time have set.[4]

Long ago venerable men (among them Tubal Cain, before the flood) wrote reasonably on plainsong; since that time many more (of whom we have already made mention) have done the same while many others (among whom stands out Franco, the German [*Teutonicus*], and a certain author who goes by the name of Aristotle)[5] have written on mensurable music. Now in our day have come new and more recent authors, writing on mensurable music, little revering their ancestors, the ancient doctors; nay, rather changing their sound doctrine in many respects, corrupting, reproving, annulling it, they protest against it in word and deed when the civil and mannerly thing to do would be to imitate the ancients in what they said well and, in doubtful matters, to defend and expound them. Considering these things in the modern manner of singing and still more in the modern writings, I was grieved. Disposed, then, to write certain things about mensurable music with the defense of the ancients as my primary and principal purpose, I afterwards, as a secondary purpose and from necessity, turned to plainsong and to theoretical and practical music. Having with God's help completed what was incidental, let me now, if I can, carry out my original design.[6]

And at this point I ask the benevolent reader to spare me and beg him condescend to me, for to my regret I am alone, while those whom I attack in this last satiric and controversial work are many. Not that I doubt that the modern way of singing and what is written about it displease many worthy persons, but that I have not noticed that there is anything written against it. I still belong to the ancient company which some of the moderns call rude. I am old; they are young and vigorous. Those whom I defend are dead; those whom I attack still living. They

---

3 Possibly a reference to Aristotle, *Nicomachean Ethics*, I, iii, 5.
4 Deuteronomy 19:14.
5 Magister Lambert, whose *Tractatus de Musica* is published by Coussemaker as the "Quidam Aristoteles" (*Scriptores*, I, 251–281).

6 The first six books of the *Speculum*, here called "incidental," amount to 473 chapters alone; see the tables of contents in CS, II, xvii–xxii, 193–196.

rejoice in having found nine new conclusions about mensurable music; [7] in this I am content to defend the ancient ones, which I deem reasonable.

"For knowledge and opinion move in cycles," they say, borrowing from Aristotle's *Meteorology*. For now it is earth where before it was water. And we are not to ascribe the modern attack on the ancients to presumption, for it is made from love of truth and of piety besides, for the moderns say also that they write from love of truth.

Where there are two friends it is most sacred to honor truth. "Socrates is my friend, but truth is still more my friend." [8] Whence St. Jerome, in his epistle against Rufinus, says on the authority of Pythagoras, who in this was repeating a divine teaching: "Let us cultivate truth, which alone brings men close to God." [9] For he who deserts truth deserts God, since God is truth.

It still seems pious to honor the ancients, who have given us a foundation in mensurable music; pious to defend them in what they said well and, in doubtful matters, to expound them, not to attack them; uncivil and reprehensible to attack good men after they are dead and unable to defend themselves. Let what I have said be my apology. For though in this work I am about to speak against the teachings of the moderns (in so far as they oppose the teachings of the ancients), I delight in their persons and from my youth have delighted in song, singers, music, and musicians.

·   ·   ·   ·   ·

43. A COMPARISON OF THE OLD ART OF MEASURED MUSIC WITH THE NEW, AS REGARDS PERFECTION AND IMPERFECTION

At this point, as I near the end of this work, let me draw certain comparisons, not lacking weight, from what has been already said. May what I have said and shall further say be as it appears to me, without prejudice of any kind. The facts are in no way altered by any assertion or denial of mine. May what is reasonable or more reasonable and what accords more fully with this art be retained, and what is less reasonable be rejected. There must be place for what accords with reason and with art, since this lives by art and reason in every man. Reason follows the law of nature which God has implanted in rational creatures. But since imperfections have at last come to be discussed, let us compare the ancient art of measured music with the modern, in order to continue with our subject.

---

7 For this and the following references to the "moderns," cf. Jean de Muris, *Ars novae musicae* (pp. 178–179 above). The reference to Aristotle's *Meteorology* is to 339B.

8 Proverbial, but ultimately derived from Aristotle, *Nicomachean Ethics*, I, vi, 1.

9 Migne, *Patrologia latina*, XXIII, 507.

To some, perhaps, the modern art will seem more perfect than the ancient, because it seems subtler and more difficult: subtler, because it reaches out further and makes many additions to the old art, as appears in the notes and measures and modes; for the word "subtle" is used of that which is more penetrating, reaching out further. That it is more difficult may be seen in the manner of singing and of dividing the measure in the works of the moderns.

To others, however, the opposite seems true, for that art appears to be more perfect which follows its basic principle more closely and goes against it less. Now the art of measured music is based on perfection, as not only the ancients but the moderns [10] declare. Therefore whichever makes the greater use of perfection appears to be the more perfect; but this is true of the ancient art, the art of Master Franco.

For the new art, as we have seen, uses manifold and various imperfections in its notes, modes, and measures. Everywhere, as it were, imperfection enters into it: not content with this imperfection in notes, modes, and measures, it extends the imperfection to the time. For the new art has what it calls imperfect time, and has breves which it calls imperfect in regard to time, a thing unknown to the old art, and it applies an imperfection arising from time to the notes of the individual degrees.

Not content with simple, duplex, and triplex longs and with breves, and some not content even with semibreves, the practitioners of this art are still inventing new ways of corrupting what is perfect with many imperfections: proximate or direct, as when the perfect simple long is made imperfect by the breve; remote, when the same note is made imperfect by the semibreve because it is the third part of a breve recta; more remote, when the same long is made imperfect by the minim. Nor are the moderns satisfied with making perfect notes imperfect and dragging them to imperfection; they must do this also with the imperfect notes, since a single imperfection does not suffice them, but only many.[11]

If the new art spoke of the said imperfections only in a speculative way, it would be more tolerable; but not so, for they put imperfection too much into practice. They use more imperfect notes than perfect; more imperfect modes than perfect; and consequently more imperfect measures. So that when the new art is said to be subtler than the ancient, it must be said also that, granting this, it is not therefore more perfect.

For not all subtlety is proof of perfection, nor is greater subtlety proof of greater perfection. Subtlety has no place among the degrees or orders

---

10 Cf. Jean de Muris, *op. cit.* (p. 173 above).   the conclusions of his *Ars novae musicae* (pp.
11 Cf. the terminology of Jean de Muris and   178-179 above).

or species of perfection, as is made clear in the fifth book of the *Metaphysics*,[12] nor is it sufficiently proved that the new art is subtler than the old. Even if we grant that it includes some new devices to which the old does not extend, the inclusion of many imperfections unknown to the old art does not prove it more perfect, but merely raises the question which of the arts under discussion is the more perfect.

As to the further assertion that the modern art is more difficult than the ancient, this, it must be said, does not make it more perfect, for what is more difficult is not for that simple reason more perfect. For though art is said to be concerned with what is difficult, it is nevertheless concerned with what is good and useful, since it is a virtue perfecting the soul through the medium of the intellect; for which reason authority says that the teaching of the wise is easy. But this will be discussed later on.

44. A COMPARISON OF THE OLD ART OF MEASURED MUSIC WITH THE NEW AS REGARDS SUBTLETY AND RUDENESS

Some moderns regard those singers as rude, idiotic, undiscerning, foolish, and ignorant who do not know the new art or who follow the old art, not the new, in singing, and in consequence they regard the old art as rude and, as it were, irrational, the new as subtle and rational. It may be asked, what is the source of this subtlety in the moderns and this rudeness in the ancients? For if subtlety comes from a greater and more penetrating intellect, who are to be reputed the subtler: those who discovered the principles of this art and found out what things are contrary to them, but have scrupulously followed these principles, or those who protest their intention of following them but do not, and seem rather to combat them? Let the judicious observe which party is offering a true judgment of this matter, without predilection, and what is the value of subtlety, what the value of difficulty, without utility. What is the value of subtlety which is contrary to the principles of science? Are not the subtlety and difficulty involved in the many diverse imperfections in notes, times, modes, and measures which they have contrived, incompatible with a science which is based on perfection? Is it great subtlety to abound in imperfections and to dismiss perfections?

Should the ancients be called rude for using perfections, the moderns subtle for using imperfections? Should the moderns be called subtle for introducing triplex longs, for joining duplex longs in ligature, for using duplex longs profusely, for using semibreves singly, for providing them

---

12 Aristotle, *Metaphysics*, 1021B.

with tails, for giving them the power of making longs and breves imperfect and at the same time another power which seems unnecessary to this art,[13] and for many other innovations which seem to contradict its basic principle? Should they further be called subtle for their new manner of singing, in which the words are lost, the effect of good concord is lessened, and the measure, as will be discussed later on, is confounded? And who are those who use many distinct sorts of music and manners of singing, who apply themselves to many distinct sorts of music and manners of singing? Do not the moderns use motets and chansons almost exclusively, except for introducing hockets in their motets? They have abandoned many other sorts of music, which they do not use in their proper form as the ancients did; for example, measured organa, organa not measured throughout, and the organum purum and duplum, of which few of the moderns know; likewise conducts, which are so beautiful and full of delight, and which are so artful and delightful when duplex, triplex, or quadruplex; likewise duplex, contraduplex, triplex, and quadruplex hockets. Among these sorts of music the old singers divided their time in rotation; these they made their foundation; in these they exercised themselves; in these they delighted, not in motets and chansons alone. Should the men who composed and used these sorts of music, or those who know and use them, be called rude, idiotic, and ignorant of the art of singing? For although they do not sing the modern sorts of music or in the modern manner, and do not use the new art of the moderns, they would know that art if they were willing to give their hearts to it and sing in the modern manner, but the manner does not please them, only the ancient manner, perhaps for the reasons previously discussed or others which can be discussed.

One modern doctor [14] says thus: "The duplex long in the perfect mode takes up six tempora. In this Franco and Petrus de Cruce and all the others are wrong: it should really take up nine." This doctor seems to be denouncing not merely the ancients, of whom he names two of great merit, but the moderns as well, since in that remark he says that not merely those two but all the others are wrong. He does not say, "the ancients," but says absolutely, "all the others," and in consequence says that he himself is wrong. For if all those men are rude so far as they are in error according to the statement to which I have replied above, and according to certain

---

13 Cf. Jean de Muris, *op. cit.*, Conclusion 7: "The altered breve may be made imperfect by the semibreve" (p. 179 above).
14 An otherwise unknown theorist whom Jacob

has previously quoted and criticized in Chapters 26 and 27 of the present book of the *Speculum* (CS, II, 410a–412a).

other statements of his previously discussed, he is still more in error; but I think that like all the other doctors, he believed himself to be speaking truth.

The old art, it is clear, must not be considered rude and irrational; first, because the arguments brought against it and some of the additions made to it by the moderns have been previously shown to be respectively contrary to reason or unnecessary to art; secondly, because even if the moderns have made good additions to the ancient art, it does not follow that the ancient art is in itself rude and irrational and its inventors and practitioners the same. Thus, granted that the doctors who have succeeded Boethius, as the monk Guido and the rest, have made many good additions to the art of tones or modes which he transmitted to us, the art of Boethius and Boethius himself should not on that account be reputed rude and irrational. For he laid the foundations of the art and furnished the principles from which others, following him, have drawn good and useful conclusions, consonant with the art and not contrary to or incompatible with those principles.

For if the moderns make many distinctions and use many designations with regard to semibreves, the ancients, as has been mentioned, seem to use more, so far as the facts go, however it may be with regard to the shapes. For when they used for the same equal tempus, that is, for the breve in its proper sense, now two unequal semibreves, now three, now four, five, six, seven, eight, or nine equal ones, these could be called semibreves secundae when they used two, because two such were the equivalent of the breve; semibreves tertiae when they used three, because three such equalled the breve in value; semibreves quartae when they used four, for a similar reason; semibreves quintae, when five; semibreves sextae, when six; semibreves septimae, when seven; semibreves octavae, when eight; semibreves nonae, when nine, for a similar reason, as stated above.[15] Though they made all these distinctions in semibreves, they never distinguished them in their shape and never gave them tails, but distinguished them sufficiently from each other by means of points.

45. A COMPARISON OF THE ANCIENT ART OF MEASURED MUSIC WITH THE NEW AS REGARDS LIBERTY AND SERVITUDE

The art of singing of the moderns seems to compare with the ancient art as a lady with a bondwoman or a housemaid, for now the new art seems to be mistress, the old art to serve; the new art reigns, the ancient is exiled.

---

15 Cf. VII, xvii (CS, II, 400b–402b), in which Jacob gives examples from Petrus de Cruce and an anonymous, illustrating the use of from four to nine semibreves for the perfect breve.

But it is contrary to reason that the art which uses perfections should be reduced to subjection and the art which uses imperfections should dominate, since the master should be more perfect than the slave.

Again, these arts seem to compare with one another as the old law with the new, except that in this comparison the art of the moderns seems to be in the position of the old law and the old music in that of the new law. For the new law is freer, plainer, more perfect, and easier to fulfill, for the new law contains fewer precepts and is less burdensome to observe. Wherefore our Lord saith in the Gospel: "My yoke is easy and my burden is light." [16] And St. James in his Epistle: "Whoso looketh into the perfect law of liberty." [17]

But the old law contained many and diverse moral, judicial, and ceremonial precepts which were difficult to fulfill. Whence St. Peter, in the Acts of the Apostles, speaking of the old law: "Why tempt ye God, to put a yoke upon the neck of the disciples which neither our fathers nor we were able to bear?" [18]

The teachings of the old law of measured music are few and clear as compared with those of the new. It would take long to recount how the moderns use rules for their various longs, breves, and semibreves, for their various measures and modes of singing; how they lay down various instructions for causing imperfections; how they use rules in distinguishing their sorts of music; nor are they wholly in agreement in their doctrines. For some of them indicate perfect time in their music with a round circle, because the round form is perfect, whereas others use three little strokes to denote this. These three strokes must touch one line and project a little on each side, to distinguish them from the strokes that denote rests.[19] And the prescriber of this rule upbraids those who ignore it, counting them as idiots and witless. For since here is obviously great learning, here is great wisdom, and let these things be positive. And perfect and imperfect time may be distinguished from each other in another way or other ways than these if combined with one another.[20] To denote the perfect mode they set down a quadrangle enclosing three little strokes; but to denote the imperfect mode, they set down a quadrangle enclosing two little strokes.[21] Others, to denote the imperfect, place a sign made up of two semicircles, and by such a sign they denote both the time and the mode. And as one of them says, they do not know how to denote the one without the other. Others presume to prefix *M* for the perfect mode and

---

16 Matthew 11:30.
17 James 1:25.
18 Acts 15:10.
19 Cf. Philippe de Vitry, *Ars nova* (CS, III, 19b).

20 That is, by means of the red (or colored) note; cf. Philippe de Vitry, *op. cit.* (CS, III, 21).
21 *Ibid.* (CS, III, 20b–21a).

N for the imperfect, saying that as O and C are used for variation of time, so M and N are used for recognition of the mode. Others, as if reversing matters, understand by O the perfect mode and perfect time, but by C the imperfect mode and imperfect time. Others say that a circle enclosing three little strokes may be used for the perfect mode and time, but to designate the imperfect mode and time they set down a semicircle enclosing two little strokes.[22]

These things and many others which the ancients never used the moderns use, and thus they drag this art to many burdens, and she who before was free from these burdens now seems a bondwoman as regards such matters, whereas, according to Seneca, liberty is one of the greatest goods, for which reason the poet says:

Not for all the gold in the world were liberty well sold.[23]

And since the old art is free from such burdens, the moderns do not permit her to rule. But since that is no right rule in which the free man who should be master is subject to him who is not free, the philosopher,[24] in his *Politics*, greatly disapproves of such government or rule.

46. A COMPARISON OF THE OLD ART OF MEASURED MUSIC WITH THE MODERN AS REGARDS STABILITY, AND OF THE OLD MODE OF SINGING WITH THE NEW

One important difference, among others, between perfect and imperfect work is that the perfect work is more stable than the imperfect; for the perfect work has no need of another; its existence does not depend on its being ordered with respect to something else; it has a firm foundation. That art, then, which is the more perfect of the two measured arts, the old and the modern, must be the one which is the more stable. Likewise, as has been mentioned above, we sometimes find certain new doctrines unstable, for though at first they are gladly and freely accepted because of their novelty, they displease and are rejected when well examined, lacking solid foundations, and there is a return to the more ancient teachers. Would it were thus with the modern measured art with respect to the old art!

For since the modern teachers are not fully in agreement with respect to the said art in their treatises, this is a sign of the instability of their art. For it is written that every kingdom divided against itself is brought to desolation,[25] for if one man oppose the other, how will their kingdom

---

22 *Ibid.* (CS, III, 21a).   24 Aristotle.
23 Proverbial.   25 Luke 11:17.

stand? Indeed if division spells evil and instability, then, according to the words of the prophet Hosea, their heart is divided; now shall they perish.[26]

Moreover, measured music seeks concord and shuns discord. It does not seek discordant teachers to attain these ends; indeed, all good things accord together. Would that it pleased the modern singers that the ancient music and the ancient manner of singing were again brought into use! For, if I may say so, the old art seems more perfect, more rational, more seemly, freer, simpler, and plainer. Music was originally discreet, seemly, simple, masculine, and of good morals; have not the moderns rendered it lascivious beyond measure? For this reason they have offended and are offending many judicious persons skilled also in music as Thales the Milesian offended the Spartans and Laconians,[27] a matter mentioned in our first book. Let the judicious take heed and decide what is true. For what purpose have the old music and method of singing and the practice of the old art been banished in favor of the moderns and the modern method of singing? What penalties had they incurred? Were they banished because of their goodness? But they do not please the satraps. As King Achish said to David: "Thou art upright and good, but thou dost not please the satraps." [28]

It is illegal that anyone should be an exile from his country save for sure and just cause, and that he should be cut off from the fellowship of the faithful, as if excommunicated, save by his own fault. I do not deny that the moderns have composed much good and beautiful music, but this is no reason why the ancients should be maligned and banished from the fellowship of singers. For one good thing does not oppose another, any more than one virtue opposes another.

In a certain company in which some able singers and judicious laymen were assembled, and where modern motets in the modern manner and some old ones were sung, I observed that even the laymen were better pleased with the ancient motets and the ancient manner than with the new. And even if the new manner pleased when it was a novelty, it does so no longer, but begins to displease many. So let the ancient music and the ancient manner of singing be brought back to their native land; let them come back into use; let the rational art once more flourish. It has been in exile, along with the corresponding method of singing, as if violently cast out from the fellowship of singers, but violence should not be perpetual. Wherein does this studied lasciviousness in singing so

---

26 Hosea 10:2.
27 Jacob seems to have confused Thales with Timotheus.
28 Cf. I Samuel 29:6.

greatly please, by which, as some think, the words are lost, the harmony of consonances is diminished, the value of the notes is changed, perfection is brought low, imperfection is exalted, and measure is confounded?

In a great company of judicious men, when motets in the modern manner were being sung, I observed that the question was asked, what language such singers were using, whether Hebrew, Greek, Latin, or some other, because it could not be made out what they were saying. Thus, although the moderns compose good and beautiful texts for their songs, they lose them by their manner of singing, since they are not understood.

This is what it has seemed needful to say in support of the old art of measured music and in defense of those who practice it. And since I have not found any previous teachers who have written of this matter, may I find successors and helpers who will write of it and will fortify with better arguments what I have touched upon.

V

Musical Theorists of the Renaissance

22. Joannes Tinctoris

A native of Flanders, perhaps of Poperinghe, a little town not far from Ypres, Joannes Tinctoris attended the University of Louvain in 1471 and before 1476 had established himself in Naples as chaplain to Ferdinand I (Don Ferrante) and tutor to Beatrice of Aragon, Ferdinand's daughter, afterwards the wife of Matthias Corvinus of Hungary. In 1487 Tinctoris traveled in France and Germany in search of singers for the royal chapel; he died in 1511, a canon of Nivelles. His principal writings include a treatise on the proportions; the *Diffinitorium musices*, our earliest dictionary of musical terms, written for his royal pupil before her marriage in 1476 but not printed until about 1495; a book on the nature and property of the modes, dedicated in 1476 to his distinguished contemporaries Ockeghem and Busnoys; and a book on the art of counterpoint, completed in 1477. Tinctoris is also the composer of a mass on the popular song "L'homme armé" and of a few motets and chansons, some of them printed by Petrucci in his earliest anthologies.

As a theorist, Tinctoris shows little originality. The real interest of his writings lies less in their detailed exposition of technical practices and procedures than in the historical observations with which he embellishes his forewords and in his many references to the works of the great masters of his day, with several of whom he was evidently on friendly terms.

Proportionale musices [1]

[ca. 1476]

The Proportional of Music, by Master Joannes Tinctoris, Licentiate in Laws, Chaplain to the Most Supreme Prince Ferdinand, King of Sicily and Jerusalem, begins with good omen.

---

[1] Text: CS, IV, 153b–155a. The treatise may be dated "before 1476," since Tinctoris refers to it in the prologue to his *Liber de natura et proprietate tonorum* (CS, IV, 16b–17b), completed on November 6, 1476.

DEDICATION

To THE MOST sacred and invincible prince, by the Divine Providence of the King of Kings and Lord of Lords, King of Sicily, Jerusalem, and Hungary, Joannes Tinctoris, the least among professors of music and among his chaplains, proffers humble and slavish obedience, even to kissing his feet.

Although, most wise king, from the time of the proto-musician Jubal, to whom Moses has attributed so much, as when in Genesis he calls him the first of all such as handle the harp and organ,[2] many men of the greatest fame, as David, Ptolemy, and Epaminondas (princes of Judaea, Egypt, and Greece), Zoroaster, Pythagoras, Linus the Theban, Zethus, Amphion, Orpheus, Musaeus, Socrates, Plato, Aristotle, Aristoxenus, and Timotheus bestowed such labor upon the liberal art of music that, on the testimony of Cicero,[3] they attained a comprehension of almost all its powers and its infinite material, and although for this reason many of the Greeks believed that certain of these men, and especially Pythagoras, had invented the very beginnings of music; nevertheless we know almost nothing of their mode of performing and writing music. Yet it is probable that this was most elegant, for they bestowed on this science, which Plato calls the mightiest of all,[4] their highest learning, so that they taught it to all the ancients, nor was anyone ignorant of music considered an educated man. And how potent, pray, must have been that melody by whose virtue gods, ancestral spirits, unclean demons, animals without reason, and things insensate were said to be moved! This (even if in part fabulous) is not devoid of mystery, for the poets would not have feigned such things of music had they not apprehended its marvelous power with a certain divine vigor of the mind.

But, after the fullness of time, in which the greatest of musicians, Jesus Christ, in whom is our peace, in duple proportion made two natures one, there have flourished in His church many wonderful musicians, as Gregory, Ambrose, Augustine, Hilary, Boethius, Martianus, Guido, and Jean de Muris, of whom some established the usage of singing in the salutary church itself, others composed numerous hymns and canticles for that purpose, others bequeathed to posterity the divinity, others the theory, others the practice of this art, in manuscripts now everywhere dispersed.

Lastly the most Christian princes, of whom, most pious King, you are

---

2 Genesis 4:21.
3 *De oratore*, I, iii, 10.

4 *Republic*, 401D (p. 8 above).

by far the foremost in the gifts of mind, of body, and of fortune, desiring to augment the divine service, founded chapels after the manner of David, in which at extraordinary expense they appointed singers to sing pleasant and comely praise to our God [5] with diverse (but not adverse) voices. And since the singers of princes, if their masters are endowed with the liberality which makes men illustrious, are rewarded with honor, glory, and wealth, many are kindled with a most fervent zeal for this study.

At this time, consequently, the possibilities of our music have been so marvelously increased that there appears to be a new art, if I may so call it, whose fount and origin is held to be among the English, of whom Dunstable stood forth as chief. Contemporary with him in France were Dufay and Binchoys, to whom directly succeeded the moderns Ockeghem, Busnoys, Regis and Caron, who are the most excellent of all the composers I have ever heard. Nor can the English, who are popularly said to shout while the French sing,[6] stand comparison with them. For the French contrive music in the newest manner for the new times, while the English continue to use one and the same style of composition, which shows a wretched poverty of invention.

But alas! I have perceived that not only these, but many other famous composers whom I admire, while they compose with much subtlety and ingenuity and with incomprehensible sweetness, are either wholly ignorant of musical proportions or indicate incorrectly the few that they know. I do not doubt that this results from a defect in arithmetic, a science without which no one becomes eminent, even in music, for from its innermost parts all proportion is derived.

Therefore, to the purpose that young men who wish to study the liberal and honorable art of music may not fall into similar ignorance and error in proportions, and in praise of God, by whom proportions were given, and for the splendor of your most consecrated Majesty, whose piety surpasses that of all other pious princes, and in honor of your most well-proportioned chapel, whose like I cannot easily believe to exist anywhere in the world, I enter, with the greatest facility my powers permit, upon this work, which with appropriateness to its subject I conclude should be called the Proportional of Music. If I have ventured in it to oppose many, indeed nearly all famous musicians, I entreat that this be by no means ascribed to arrogance. Contending under the banner of truth, I do not order that my writings should neces-

---

5 Psalm 147:1.
6 Cf. Ornithoparcus, *Musice active micrologus*

(Leipzig, 1516), IV, viii, or Pietro Aron, *Lucidario* (Venice, 1545), f. 31.

sarily be followed more than those of others. What in their writings I find correct, I approve; what wrong, I rebuke. If to my readers I seem to carry on this my tradition with justice, I exhort them to put their trust in me; if without justice, let them rather believe others, for I am as ready to be refuted by others as to refute them.

23. Joannes Tinctoris

Liber de arte contrapuncti [1]

[1477]

The Book of the Art of Counterpoint, by Master Joannes Tinctoris, Juris-consult, Musician, and Chaplain to His Most Serene Highness the King of Sicily, begins with good omen.

DEDICATION

To THE MOST sacred and glorious prince, Ferdinand, by the Grace of God King of Jerusalem and Sicily, Joannes Tinctoris, the least among his musicians, presents undying reverence.

Long ago, most sagacious King, I found in Horace's *Art of Poetry* this line, remarkable for its elegance and truth:

Understanding is both the first principle and the source of sound writing.[2]

For this reason, before undertaking to write about music, I have sought by listening, reading, and constant practice to obtain as full an understanding as I could of the various matters that have to do with it.

Though I have heard Wisdom herself cry out: "I love them that love me, and those who keep watch for me will find me," [3] and have approached my task with steadfast confidence, I confess that as yet I have scarcely swallowed a single drop from her fountain. And this drop, though it be one of the smallest, it is my task to impart to attentive and docile minds through the slender lines traced by my pen, not to deck myself thereby with glory, as Pliny [4] reproached the illustrious author Livy for having done, but to serve posterity, which Cicero [5] declares to

1 Text: CS, IV, 76b–77b. The treatise is dated Naples, October 11, 1477.
2 *Ars poetica*, 309.
3 Proverbs 8:17.
4 *Naturalis historia*, Praefatio, 12.
5 *Tusculan Disputations*, I, 35.

be the task of every excellent man in due proportion to his intellectual power, lest I should hide in the earth the talent given me by God,[6] who in the book of the Prophet is called the Lord of Knowledge,[7] and be cast into outer darkness, where is weeping and gnashing of teeth, as an unprofitable servant of the Lord.[8]

Now therefore, I have decided to set down in full, among other things, what little I have learned, through ever-watchful study, of the art of counterpoint for the benefit of all students of this honorable art, which, of the consonances declared by Boethius to govern all the delectation of music, is contrived for the glory and honor of His eternal majesty to whom, by this very counterpoint, pleasant and comely praise is offered, as commanded in the Psalm.[9]

Before carrying out this project, I cannot pass over in silence the opinion of numerous philosophers, among them Plato and Pythagoras and their successors Cicero, Macrobius, Boethius, and our Isidore, that the spheres of the stars revolve under the guidance of harmonic modulation, that is, by the consonance of various concords. But when, as Boethius relates,[10] some declare that Saturn moves with the deepest sound and that, as we pass by stages through the remaining planets, the moon moves with the highest, while others, conversely, ascribe the deepest sound to the moon and the highest to the sphere of the fixed stars, I put faith in neither opinion. Rather I unshakeably credit Aristotle [11] and his commentator,[12] along with our more recent philosophers, who most manifestly prove that in the heavens there is neither actual nor potential sound. For this reason it will never be possible to persuade me that musical concords, which cannot be produced without sound, can result from the motion of the heavenly bodies.

Concords of sounds and melodies, from whose sweetness, as Lactantius says,[13] the pleasure of the ear is derived, are produced, then, not by heavenly bodies, but by earthly instruments with the co-operation of nature. To these concords the ancient musicians—Plato, Pythagoras, Nicomachus, Aristoxenus, Philolaus, Archytas, Ptolemy, and many others, including even Boethius—most assiduously applied themselves, yet how they were accustomed to arrange and to form them is almost unknown to our generation. And if I may refer to my own experience, I have had in my hands

---

6 Matthew 25:25.
7 I Samuel 2:3.
8 Matthew 25:30.
9 Psalm 147:1.
10 *De institutione musica*, I, xxvii (Friedlein, p. 219).

11 *De caelo*, 290B.
12 Thomas Aquinas, *In libro Aristotelis de caelo et mundo expositio*, II, xiv (*Opera*, III [Rome, 1886], 173–177).
13 *Divinarum institutionum*, VI, xxi (Migne, *P.L.*, VI, 713).

certain old songs, called apocrypha, of unknown origin, so ineptly, so stupidly composed that they rather offended than pleased the ear.

Further, although it seems beyond belief, there does not exist a single piece of music, not composed within the last forty years, that is regarded by the learned as worth hearing. Yet at this present time, not to mention innumerable singers of the most beautiful diction, there flourish, whether by the effect of some celestial influence or by the force of assiduous practice, countless composers, among them Jean Ockeghem, Jean Regis, Antoine Busnoys, Firmin Caron, and Guillaume Faugues, who glory in having studied this divine art under John Dunstable, Gilles Binchoys, and Guillaume Dufay, recently deceased. Nearly all the works of these men exhale such sweetness that in my opinion they are to be considered most suitable, not only for men and heroes, but even for the immortal gods. Indeed, I never hear them, I never examine them, without coming away happier and more enlightened. As Virgil took Homer for his model in that divine work the *Aeneid*, so I, by Hercules, have used these composers as models for my modest works, and especially in the arrangement of the concords I have plainly imitated their admirable style of composing.

Finally, most excellent of kings, not unmindful what a rich outpouring of friendliness, by which I mean benevolence, you continue to bestow upon me in accordance with your exceptional humanity, I have undertaken to dedicate this little work to your most distinguished name, hoping that it will serve as dry wood by which the unfailing fire of the charity with which your most illustrious Majesty has heretofore favored me will long burn the more brightly. For it is most manifest that this proceeds from your virtue alone, than which, as Cicero says,[14] nothing is worthier of love.

---

14 *Laelius de amicitia liber,* viii, 28.

24. Bartolomé Ramos

The *Musica practica* of Bartolomé Ramos was printed in Bologna in 1482. Of the life of its author we know almost nothing. That he came from Baeza, near Madrid, and lectured in Bologna, after having previously lectured in Salamanca, is set forth in his book. Other sources tell us that, after leaving Bologna, he went to Rome, where he was still living in 1491.

From his pupil Giovanni Spataro we also learn that Ramos withheld parts of his book from the printer with a view to lecturing on them publicly; as we have it, the *Musica practica* is only a fragment. Those parts that were printed are none the less of extraordinary interest, for in them Ramos advances a novel division of the monochord which results in intervals largely identical with those of just intonation. Although he professes to owe this discovery to his reading of ancient authors, it seems on the whole more probable that he hit upon it empirically. He is himself scarcely aware of the implications of what he is advancing and claims no special virtue for his division beyond its ready intelligibility and the ease with which it can be carried out. Naturally enough, this radical break with tradition aroused a storm of protest. Ramos was violently attacked by Niccolo Burzio in his *Musices opusculum* (1487), just as his pupil Spataro was attacked later on by Franchino Gafori in his *Apologia* (1520). In the end, however, twice defended by Spataro, who replied both to Burzio and to Gafori, modified by Fogliano, and developed by Zarlino, the new teaching won out despite all opposition.

From the Musica practica [1]

[*1482*]

Part One—First Treatise

2. THE DIVISION OR COMPOSITION OF THE REGULAR MONOCHORD

THE REGULAR monochord has been subtly divided by Boethius [2] with numbers and measure. But although this division is useful and pleasant to theorists, to singers it is laborious and difficult to understand. And since we have promised to satisfy both, we shall give a most easy division of the regular monochord. Let no one think that we have found this with ordinary labor, we who have indeed discovered it reading the precepts of the ancients in many vigils and avoiding the errors of the moderns with care. And anyone even moderately informed will be able to understand it.

Let there be taken a string or chord of any length, and let this be stretched over a piece of wood having a certain concavity, and let the end to which the string is bound be marked at the point *a*. And let the end to which the string is drawn and stretched, placed in a straight line and at a distance, be marked at the point *q*. Now let the quantity *aq*, that is, the length of the whole string, be divided into two equal parts, and let the point of equal distance be marked with the letter *h*. The quantity *ha* we again divide in half, and in the middle of the division we put the letter *d*. The quantity *hd* is again bisected, and in the middle of the section the letter *f* is set down.

Understand the same to be done also with the other half of the string, that is, with *hq*, for in the first division the letter *p* will be inscribed at the midpoint, and in the division *hp* the letter *l* will be put equidistant from either end, and between *l* and *p*, when the same rule of intervals has been observed, we shall introduce the letter *n*. And when we divide *fn* by half we inscribe the letter *i*.

But we shall not go on to smaller parts by means of this division by half until we have made other divisions. Thus we divide the whole,

---

1 Text: The reprint of the original edition (Bologna, 1482) edited by Johannes Wolf in *Publikationen der Internationalen Musikgesellschaft, Beihefte*, II (Leipzig, 1901), 4–5, 96–99.

2 *De institutione musica*, IV, v.

aq, by three, and measuring from *q*, we put the letter *m* at the end of one third and the letter *e* at the end of two thirds. Then let *eq* be again divided by three, and going from *q* toward *e*, let the sign ♮ quadrum be set down at two thirds and, when the quantity ♮ quadrum to *q* has been doubled, let the letter *b* be inscribed.

Now we again bisect the quantity *mh*, and we mark the middle of the section with the letter *k*. And when we double the quantity *kq*, we put the letter *c* at the end of the duplication. Now between *e* and ♮ quadrum let the letter *g* stand equidistant from either end. Then when we divide *gq* into two equal parts, we inscribe the letter *o*.

Thus the whole monochord has been divided by a legitimate partition, as you will see in the diagram below.[8]

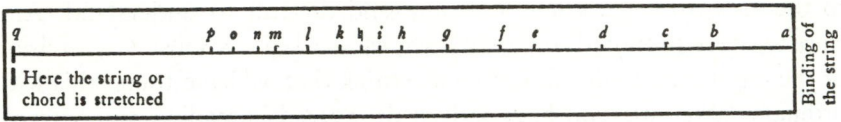

Here the string or chord is stretched

Binding of the string

Part Three—Second Treatise

3. IN WHICH THE DIVISIONS OF THE PRIMARY MONOCHORD ARE APPLIED TO NUMERICAL RATIOS

In the first division of our regular monochord we have said that Boethius subtly divided his by numbers and measure. We, however, for the sake of the young, have divided ours by vulgar fractions and with respect to continuous quantity in order that the student may not need first to know both arithmetic and geometry. For to require this would be to fall into the error which we have forbidden ourselves, seeing that we have said that he will need neither of these things to understand our teaching, provided only he be informed in the first rudiments. Thus we have said that a string was to be divided in half, or that a quantity was to be doubled, tripled, or divided by three, expressions most familiar to everyone.

Now, however, seeing that we have determined certain things about discrete quantity, that is, about numbers and numerical proportions, which we know to be most necessary to singers, applying to numerical ratio the same vulgar fractions of the string which we have put forward, we shall show the proportions in which these consist.

---

8 In I, ii, 5, Ramos gives additional directions for finding the lower b-flat and the half-steps e-flat, a-flat, f-sharp, and c-sharp of both octaves. These are of course obtained by proceeding in octaves, fourths, and fifths from *i* and *b*.

Let us assume that the whole length of the string, from *a* to *q*, is 24 inches. Then when we bisect it, marking the section with the letter *h*, *qh* with 12 inches corresponds to *qa* with 24 in duple relationship. Now if you will strike the whole length of the string, and when you have carefully considered the sound, you will put your finger on the point *h* and strike the string *hq*, you will perceive the sounding of the diapason. Thus the diapason is said to be in duple ratio [2:1]. But when we divide *ha* in half, inscribing the letter *d* in the middle, the string *dq* is left with 18 inches, which, compared to the whole, is governed by sesquitertia proportion [4:3]. Thus *d* to *a* is the symphony of the diatessaron. And when we bisect the quantity *hq*, putting the letter *p* in the middle of the section, *pq* is left with only 6 inches, which multiplied by four equals 24. Thus the ratio will necessarily be quadruple [4:1], and *p* to *a* will sound the melody of the double diapason. Then when *hp* has been divided in half and the section inscribed with the letter *l*, we duly perceive the quantity of *lq* to be 9 inches. And if we compare this to the whole we shall find duple superbipartient ratio [8:3], governing the symphony of the diapason plus diatessaron, which, as Boethius says,[4] only Ptolemy admits among the consonances. But we pass over these matters here, both because with the aid of experience we are about to show certain things in composition for three and four voices and because, a little later, with the aid of reason we shall say many things in speculation.

When dividing the whole string by three we put the letters *m* and *e* at one third and two thirds, going from *q* toward *e*, we show clearly that *mq* has 8 inches, which multiplied by three equals 24. Thus, governed by triple proportion [3:1], it sounds to the whole string the symphony of the diapason plus diapente. But *eq* is 16, which is found to be in sesquialtera ratio [3:2] to the whole. Thus it sounds the diapente to *aq*.

We now bisect the quantity *hd*, marking the section with the letter *f*. Seeing that *qd* has been shown to have 18 inches, we know for certain that *qf* has 15, which, compared to *qd*, we find in sesquiquinta ratio [6:5]. For 18 exceeds 15 by 3, which is one fifth-part of the smaller term. But if we compare it to *qh* we find it in sesquiquarta ratio [5:4]. From the latter comparison arises the consonance of the ditone or bitone, from the former the species semiditone or trihemitone, which, as has been shown, is formed from the perfect and imperfect tone.[5]

Now if we compare this same quantity, *qf*, to *qa* we find it in supertripartient quintas ratio [8:5]. For 24 exceeds 15 by three fifth-parts of

---

[4] *De institutione musica*, V, ix.

[5] In I, i, 3, after pointing out that the semitone is not strictly speaking a semitone at all, Ramos calls it an imperfect tone.

the smaller term. From this comparison arises the sound of the diapente plus semitone or minor sixth or minor hexad. But if we relate qf to ql we find it in superbipartient tertias proportion [5:3]. For 15 exceeds 9 by 6, which is exactly made up of two parts of nine. And this ratio gives rise to the major sixth or major hexad.[6]

Thus, since the fractions are vulgar and not difficult, we make all our divisions most easy. Guido, however, teaches the division of his monochord by nine steps, seeing that, as we have said, the tone is formed in sesquioctave proportion. But this clearly appears laborious and tedious to those who consider it, for it is more difficult to take an eighth part of any whole than to take a half or a third.[7] And the tone is found effectively by our division, just as it is by his, for example in the interval d to e, measured by the numbers 18 and 16, or in the interval l to m, expressed by the ambitus of the numbers 9 and 8.

But enough of these things. Let us now inquire which semitones of the monochord are to be sung and which are, as it seems, to be avoided, since one is found to be larger and the other smaller.[8]

---

6 The reader is advised to work out the entire scale for himself, adopting 288 as the length of the whole string in order that all measurements may be in integers. Without anticipating the results of this operation, it may be said that the scale of Ramos closely approximates the "pure scale" worked out later by Fogliano and Zarlino, and that in the octave F to f (with b-flat) it is actually identical with it. The C octave of Ramos, with its symmetrical construction, is even superior to the "pure scale" from a melodic point of view (cf. Joseph Yasser, *A Theory of Evolving Tonality*, New York, 1932, pp. 215–217).

7 "An eighth part" does not make sense in this context, for Guido, who gives two methods for dividing the monochord (cf. p. 106 above, note 6), divides by two, four, and nine, but not by eight. Perhaps Ramos is thinking of Boethius, who works from the higher pitches toward the lower ones, obtaining the tone (9:8) by adding eighths rather than by subtracting ninths.

8 The major and minor semitones of Ramos have the porportions 16:15 and 135:128.

25. Pietro Aron

Born about 1490 in Florence, Aron (also spelled Aaron) was one of the most important writers on musical theory in the first half of the sixteenth century. Thanks to the influence of a patron he was made a canon of the Cathedral at Rimini. In 1536, however, Aron became a monk of the order of the Bearers of the Cross, first at Bergamo, later at Padua and Venice; he died in 1545.

Aron's published works on musical theory comprise the *Libri III de institutione harmonica* (1516), the *Trattato della natura e cognizione di tutti gli toni di canto figurato* (1525), the *Lucidario in musica* (1545), and the *Compendiolo di molti dubbi* (without date). His chief writing, however, is the *Toscanello in musica* (1523, and four later editions), which contains the best exposition of contrapuntal rules to be found before Zarlino. Aron is the first theorist to recognize the practice of composing all voices of a composition simultaneously.

From the Trattato della natura e cognizione di tutti gli toni di canto figurato[1]

[*1525*]

I. AN EXPLANATION OF THE FINALS OF ALL THE TONES

JUST AS it is a credit and an honor to any artificer to comprehend and to know and to have a precise understanding of the parts and reasonings of

1 Text: The original edition (Venice, 1525). References to practical examples and certain parentheses of the original are given as author's notes. For a portrait, see Kinsky, p. 109, Fig. 2. As a convenience to the reader, the many examples that Aron cites are listed below in alphabetical order, with indications of the tones to which he assigns them and references to contemporary editions.

6 A l'audience	Heyne	Odhecaton 93
6 Allez regrets	Agricola	Odhecaton 57
5 Alma Redemptoris	Josquin	Corona, III
7 Ascendens Christus	Hylaere	Corona, I
8 Beata Dei Genitrix	Anon	Motetti C
1/2 Beata Dei Genitrix	Mouton	Corona, I
3 Benedic anima mea	Eustachio	Corona, II
6 Brunette	Stokhem	Odhecaton 5

his art, so it is a disgrace and a reproach to him not to know and to be in error among the articles of his faculty. Therefore, when I examined and considered the excellence and grandeur of many, many authors, ancient and modern, there is no manner of doubt that did not assail me inwardly as I reflected on this undertaking, especially since I knew the matter to be most difficult, sublime, and lofty to explain. None the less I intend to relate it to you, most gracious reader, not in a presumptuous or haughty style, but speaking humanely and at your feet. And knowing it to be exacting and strange, I judge that it was abandoned by the celebrated musicians already referred to not through ignorance but merely because it proved otherwise troublesome and exacting at the time. For it is clear that no writers of our age have explained how the many dif-

8 C'est possible	Anon		3 Miserere	Josquin	Corona, III
2 Ce n'est pas	La Rue	Canti B	1 Missa Ave maris stella	Josquin	Missarum, II
– Cela sans plus	Josquin	Odhecaton 61			
6 Celeste beneficium	Mouton	Corona, I	1 Missa D'un autre amer	Josquin	Missarum, II
1/2 Clangat plebs flores	Regis	Motetti a 5	– Missa de Beata Virgine	Josquin	Missarum, III
7 Comment peut	Josquin	Canti B	5, 7 Missa de Beata Virgine	La Rue	Missae
1/2 Congregati sunt	Mouton	Corona, II	2 Missa Hercules dux Ferrariae	Josquin	Missarum, II
2 D'un autre amer	De Orto	Canti B			
2 D'un autre amer	Heyne		7 Missa Ut sol	Mouton	
2 De tous biens plaine	Heyne	Odhecaton 20	7 Mittit ad Virginem	Anon	Motetti C
8 Disant adieu madame	Anon	Odhecaton 89	8 Mon mari m'a diffamée	De Orto	Canti B
8 E d'en revenez vous	Compère	Canti B	7 Multi sunt vocati	Zanetto	
8 E la la la	Anon	Canti B	8 Myn morgem ghaf	Anon	Canti B
6 Egregie Christi	Févin	Corona, I	1 Nobilis progenie	Févin	Corona, I
1 Fors seulement	La Rue	Canti B	1 Nomine qui Domini	Caen	Corona, II
1 Gaude Barbara	Mouton	Corona, I			
1 Gaude Virgo	Festa		3 Nunca fué pena mayor	Anon	Odhecaton 4
8 Hélas hélas	Ninot	Canti B	6 O admirabile commercium	Josquin	Antico, I
1 Hélas qu'il est à mon gré	Japart	Odhecaton 30	4 O Maria rogamus te	Anon	Motetti C
5 Hélas que pourra devenir	Caron	Odhecaton 13	8 O Venus bant	Josquin	Odhecaton 78
– Hélas m'amour	Anon		– Peccata mea Domine	Mouton	Corona, II
5 Illuminare Hierusalem	Mouton	Corona, II	1 Pourquoi fut fuie cette emprise	Anon	Canti B
3 Interveniat pro rege nostro	Jacotin	Corona, II	1 Pourtant si mon	Busnoys	
8 Je cuide si ce temps	Anon	Odhecaton 2	5 Quaeramus cum pastoribus	Mouton	Antico, I
1 Je dépite tous	Brumel	Canti B	1/2 Rogamus te Virgo Maria	Jacotin	Corona, II
6 Je ne demande	Busnoys	Odhecaton 42			
8 Je suis amie	Anon	Canti B	6 Sancta Trinitas	Févin	Corona, I
1/2 Judica me Deus	Caen	Corona, II	8 Si dedero	Agricola	Odhecaton 56
1 L'homme armé	Josquin	Canti B	2 Si mieux	Compère	Odhecaton 51
8 Ne l'oserai je dire	Anon	Odhecaton 29	5 Si sumpsero	Obrecht	Canti B
– La dicuplaisant	Anon		5 Stabat Mater	Josquin	Corona, III
1 La plus des plus	Josquin	Odhecaton 64	6 Tempus meum	Févin	Corona, I
5 La regretée	Heyne	Canti B	2 Virgo caelesti	Compère	Canti B
3 Laetatus sum	Eustachio	Corona, II	6 Vôtre bargeronette	Compère	Odhecaton 41
– Le serviteur	Anon	Odhecaton 35			
7 Madame hélas	Josquin	Odhecaton 66	1 Vulnerasti cor meum	Févin	Corona, I
3 Malheur me bat	Ockeghem	Odhecaton 63			
7 Mes pensées	Compère	Odhecaton 59			
3 Michael archangele	Jacotin	Corona, II			

ferent modes are to be recognized, although to their greater credit they have treated of matters which can be readily understood. I, therefore, not moved by ambition of any kind, but as a humble man, have undertaken this task, hoping that in humanity and kindliness my readers will all excuse whatever errors I may make. I show briefly what I know to be necessary, for I see that many are deceived about the true understanding, and regarding this I hope in some measure to satisfy them.

First I intend to explain what is meant by "final" and what by "species" and whether the final is always necessary and rational for the recognition of the tone or whether the tones are sometimes to be recognized from their species. Then I shall show what part the singer ought to examine and how the composer ought to proceed in his composition in accordance with his intention, touching also on certain other secrets which will surely afford you no little delight.

I say, then, that the final being diverse, that is, regular or irregular, it follows that each tone has a similarly diverse form.

From this it follows that at one time the final governs and at another time the species.

"Final" I define in this way: a final is simply a magisterial ending in music, introduced in order that the tone may be recognized. Musicians conclude such an ending regularly or irregularly in order that the nature and form of each tone may be the better understood. Thus the positions D *sol re*, E *la mi*, F *fa ut*, and G *sol re ut* have been constituted regular finals or ending steps for the first and second, third and fourth, fifth and sixth, and seventh and eighth tones, while the steps Gamma *ut*, A *re*, ♮ *mi*, C *fa ut*, A *la mi re*, B *fa* ♮ *mi*, and C *sol fa ut* are called irregular.

In accordance with this understanding, the final remains necessary, rational, and governing to every tone on the above-named regular steps.

The species, then, will govern sometimes regularly and sometimes irregularly.

"Species" is simply the arrangement of the sounds of the genus, varied in definite prescribed ways, as shown in the example.

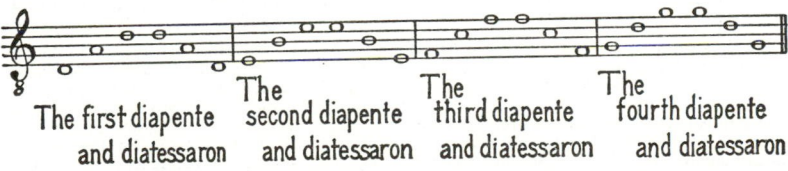

The first diapente and diatessaron   The second diapente and diatessaron   The third diapente and diatessaron   The fourth diapente and diatessaron

It follows, then, that the final is also necessary in the above-named irregular positions, namely A *la mi re*, B *fa* ♮ *mi*, and C *sol fa ut*. Here we shall consider it in two ways: first, with respect to confinality; second, with respect to the differences of the Saeculorum.[2] Thus, if a composition [a] ends in the position called A *la mi re* and there is no flat in the signature, the final will be common to the first and second tones with respect to confinality and also to the third with respect to difference,[3] provided—as you will understand from what follows—that the procedure in the composition be suited and appropriate to confinality or difference.[4] But if the composition has a flat in the signature, the final will be in my opinion neither necessary nor rational with respect to confinality, for it is clear that the form will differ from its previous state. For this reason, such compositions are to be judged by their species. The same will obviously apply to compositions ending on B *fa* ♮ *mi*, C *sol fa ut*, and all other steps on which the species may occur.

Therefore, the cognition derived from species is necessary understanding and not arbitrary to music. First, because this cognition is by definition true and necessary. Besides this, understanding that is necessary has something essential about it; but the cognition of species is essential and therefore necessary. Besides this, that which demands necessary cognition is *per se;* but the cognition of species is cognition *per se* and therefore necessary. Nor is it an objection that we are for the most part accustomed to base our cognition of music on the final, for I reply that this has been for the sake of readier understanding, inasmuch as those things that are at the end are customarily more closely observed than those that are at the beginning and in the middle.

And that our conclusion is true, we may demonstrate with these and other similar arguments. We say that man is defined as an animal rational and mortal; it is certain that rational and mortal are two differences for knowing what man is; of these, one is final and considered according to the end of man, namely mortal—the other is formal and considered according to the specific and formal being of living man, namely rational; the latter makes the essence of man better known than the former, which considers him according to his end, namely that man is mortal, for this is common both to man and to the other animals. Thus

---

a I speak always of masses, motets, canzoni, frottole, strambotti, madrigali, sonetti, and capitoli.

2 The confinals of the eight tones are, for Aron, the pitches a fifth above (or a fourth below) the established finals. He seems not to have thought it necessary to list the differences.

3 This step is also a difference in the fifth tone (see p. 216).

4 As Aron explains in Chapter 8, suitable and appropriate "procedure" turns largely on the choice of proper steps for medial cadences. In Chapters 9 to 12 these are said to be as follows: for the first tone—D, F, G, and a; for the second —A, C, D, F, G, and a; for the third—E, F, G, a, ♮, and c; for the fourth—C, D, E, F, G, and a; for the fifth—F, a, and c; for the sixth— C, D, F, a, and c; for the seventh—G, a, ♮, c, and d; for the eighth—D, F, G, and c.

the cognition of the end is not cognition *per se* and therefore not always necessary.

And this is demonstrated by certain compositions which, having the ordinary and regular final, but lacking the ascent and descent of some of its species, are not said to be of any tone but (as was shown in Chapter 30 of the first book of another work of mine, *De institutione harmonica*) are merely called *Canti euphoniaci*.

2. HOW THE SINGER OUGHT TO JUDGE THE TONE

The tenor being the firm and stable part, the part, that is, that holds and comprehends the whole concentus of the harmony, the singer must judge the tone by means of this part only. For we see that when a tenor and its cantus are far apart it causes, not pleasure, but little sweetness to those who hear it, something which arises from the distance that lies between the cantus and the contrabassus. The tenor being for this reason better suited to the natural progressions and more easily handled, every composition [b] is in my opinion to be judged by its tenor. For in the tenor the natural form is more readily considered than in the soprano, where, should you wish to form the seventh tone, you would need to find its diatessaron through the accidental course.[5] Thus we prescribe this manner and order for all compositions written at the composer's pleasure, whether upon a plainsong or without regard for one, also for compositions for five, six, seven, and more voices, in which it is usual to write a first and principal tenor. Each of the added parts will be governed by the nature of the tenor, and by means of the tenor the tone will be recognized unless the plainsong itself, which is primary and principal to such a recognition, be in some other part.[6]

---

b Whether Introit, Kyrie, Gloria, Gradual, Alleluia, Credo, Offertory, Sanctus, Agnus Dei, Postcommunion, Respond, Deo gratias, Psalm, Hymn, Magnificat, motet, canzone, frottola, bergerette, strambotto, madrigal, or capitolo.

5 We see, in other words, that when a tenor and its cantus belong to the same tone—and unless this is the case, the cantus can have no bearing on the tonality of the composition—they will lie far apart and the resulting texture will be disagreeable, particularly in view of the disparity between the cantus and the contrabassus. Thus the usual thing will be to make the tenor authentic and the cantus plagal, or vice versa, leaving the tenor as the sole determining factor. Aside from this, "in view of the inconvenience of the upward range," the cantus will seldom

ascend to the octave above the final in the seventh tone or (see p. 215 below) in the transposed third.

6 Cf. Jean Tinctoris, *Liber de natura et proprietate tonorum*, xxiv (CS, IV, 29a–29b): "When some mass or chanson or any other composition you please is made up of various parts, belonging to different tones, if you ask without qualification to what tone such a composition belongs, the person asked ought to reply without qualification according to the quality of the tenor, for in every composition this is the principal part and the basis of the whole relationship. But if it be asked specifically to what tone some single part of such a composition belongs, the person asked will reply specifically, 'To such and such a tone.'"

3. WAYS OF RECOGNIZING THE TONE OF DIFFERENT COMPOSITIONS

Reflecting alone for days and days, I recalled certain projects often in my mind. Wherefore, gracious reader, had not your gentle aspect and my eager wish for the desired end constrained me, I should more lightly have lowered the sails at the hard-won port. But since I think that you by no means blamed it, I wish to pursue the enterprise begun, not for those who turn a thing over and over, but solely for those familiar with this fare. Thus, having reached this point, I am left somewhat in doubt. Yet I intend rather to go on reasoning with you, seeking a rule by means of which you may arrive at a clear understanding of each of the tones in question.

In so far as compositions end in the positions D *sol re*, E *la mi*, F *fa ut*, and G *sol re ut*, they are to be judged according to their finals, and by means of these their true and proper species [c] will be recognized. These are the steps called regular to the first, second, third, fourth, fifth, sixth, seventh, and eighth tones, and on these steps the final will be necessary, rational, and governing.

Let me explain this to you more fully. First consider those compositions that have their final on D *sol re* and that at the beginning or in their course proceed with the species of the third, fourth, fifth, sixth, seventh, or eighth tone; all these are in my opinion to be judged only from their proper and regular final, provided that they contain contradictory and unsuitable procedures, for no other tone has a difference ending on this step. And as to those ending on E *la mi*, these are in my opinion subject in the same way only to their own form. Such compositions are best said to belong to mixed tones (*toni commisti*).[7]

But those compositions that end in the position called F *fa ut* are in my opinion subject not only to their own final and species but also to the nature and form of the first and fourth tones, in view of the difference which these tones sometimes exhibit on this step. Understand, however, that this is when they proceed in the way suited to the first and fourth tones, for otherwise they will remain of the fifth or sixth. Certain others end on G *sol re ut*; these are in my opinion subject to the

---

c Namely, from D *sol re* to the first A *la mi re* and from thence to D *la sol re*, from E *la mi* to B *fa* ♮ *mi* and from thence to high E *la mi*, from F *fa ut* to C *sol fa ut* and from thence to high F *fa ut*, and from low G *sol re ut* to D *la sol re* and from thence to the second G *sol re ut*.

7 Cf. Jean Tinctoris, *Diffinitorium musicae*, xviii (CS, IV, 190b): "A *tonus commixtus* is one which, if authentic, is mixed with a tone other than its plagal, if plagal, with a tone other than its authentic."

seventh and eighth tones and also to the first, second, third, and fourth, as you will understand from what follows.[8]

Certain other compositions end on the irregular steps A *la mi re*, B *fa ♮ mi*, and C *sol fa ut*; these we shall consider according to their procedure, their species, and the differences of the Saeculorum, for these considerations will govern them and yield the true recognition of the tone.

Certain other compositions end on D *la sol re*, E *la mi*, F *fa ut*, and G *sol re ut*; these steps are of the same nature as the regular steps previously named.

Certain other compositions, although they end regularly, have a flat signature; these are to be judged according to their species (excepting those ending on D *sol re*, F *fa ut*, etc.), for the final will now be neither necessary nor rational to the recognition of the tone.

Certain other compositions proceed at the beginning and in their course with the species suited to a given tone but end with species that contradict it; these are to be judged according to the species and differences previously mentioned, excepting (as was noted above) those ending on the regular finals.

Certain other compositions end irregularly and proceed inharmoniously without any complete diapente by means of which their true form might be recognized; these are to be judged by means of some species of diatessaron or by their own finals.

One will also find compositions arbitrarily written without regard to form or regular manner, comparable indeed to players of the game called *alleta,* who agree upon a certain goal at which they will take refuge and, chasing one after another, run back to that place or goal and are safe; of the composers of such works as these we say that they turn aimlessly round and round, progressing and digressing beyond the nature and the primary order that they have in mind until, by some trick, they arrive at an end of their own. Such harmonies or compositions can in my opinion be judged only by means of the final, and then only when they end without a flat signature.

In certain other compositions this signature appears only in the contrabassus, in others only in the tenor; such an arrangement is in our opinion neither permissible nor suitable in a harmony or composition unless it is used deliberately and introduced with art.[d]

---

8 Aron does not refer again to the possibility of endings on F in the first and fourth tones or on G (as difference) in the first, second, and fourth; for the ending on G in the third, see pp. 214–215 below.

d As by the excellent Josquin in the Patrem of his Mass of Our Lady and in a similar way by the divine Alexander [Agricola] in many of his compositions. [As published in Heft 42 of *Das Chorwerk*, the Credo of Josquin's *Missa de Beata*

Certain other compositions have a flat signature on low E *la mi*, the first A *la mi re*, B *fa* ♮ *mi*, and high E *la mi;* whether they end regularly or irregularly, these are in my opinion to be judged according to the species, not according to the final.[e]

4. AN EXPLANATION OF THE FIRST AND SECOND TONES

Every composition in which the tenor ends on D *sol re* is unhesitatingly to be assigned to the first or second tone, the more readily if the soprano end on D *la sol re* with the regular and rational final, clearly showing the natural form.[f] The same is also true of certain other compositions with a flat signature; the nature of these remains unchanged, in my opinion, for only the diatessaron, formed by the interval A *la mi re* to D *la sol re,* is altered. Seeing then that the diapente primary and natural to the tone is left intact, such compositions are also to be assigned to the first tone.[g]

And if sometimes, as has become the custom, the composer prolongs his work, amusing himself with additional progressions, you will, in my opinion, need to consider whether the final, as altered by the composer, is suited to and in keeping or out of keeping with his composition, for if reason guide him in what is suited to the tone he will at least see to it that some one part (namely, the tenor or cantus) sustains the final, while the others proceed as required by the tone, regular or irregular, with pleasing and appropriate progressions like those shown below, or in some more varied manner according to his pleasure and disposition.

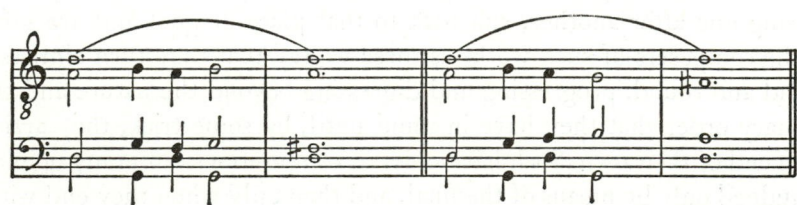

Virgine has no signatures whatever. But it is clear from Aron's comment and from the composition itself that the Tenor secundus, following the Tenor in canon at the fifth below, should have the signature one flat.—Ed.]

e For example, "Cela sans plus" by Josquin, "Peccata mea Domine" by Jean Mouton (in the *Motetti della corona*), "Le serviteur," "Hélas m'amour," "La dicuplaisant," &c. [Cf. Jean Tinctoris, *Liber de natura et proprietate tonorum,* xxiv (CS, IV, 29b): "If some one were to say to me, speaking in general, 'Tinctoris, I ask you to what tone the chanson *Le serviteur* belongs,' I would reply, 'Generally speaking, to the first

tone irregular,' since the tenor, or principal part, of this chanson belongs to this tone. But if he were to ask specifically to what tone the superius or contratenor belongs, I would reply specifically that the one and the other belong to the second tone irregular. But there is no one who doubts that a specific question about the tenor is to be answered as was the general one."—Ed.]

f As in the motets "Rogamus te virgo Maria" by Jacotin, "Judica me Deus" by A. Caen, "Congregati sunt" and "Beata Dei genitrix" by Jean Mouton, and "Clangat plebs flores" by Regis.

g As in the motet "Nomine qui Domini" by A. Caen, "Pourquoi fut fuie cette emprise," &c.

But since some will say, perhaps, that the position D *sol re* is common also to the second tone, I shall tell you that in figured music you will very seldom find a tenor with the procedure and downward range suited and appropriate to the second tone as ended in this way. Nevertheless, a composer may wish to proceed in accordance with the nature of the second tone; he will then take care to proceed at the beginning and in the course of his composition with some regard for its proper form, as observed and comprehended in the psalms and the Magnificat, where he is restricted and subject to the manner and order proper to the second tone.

Certain other compositions end on the step G *sol re ut;* with a flat signature, these are in my opinion only to be understood as of the first or second tone, even though this is the step ordinary and regular to the seventh and eighth. For this signature (or figure) alters the form or structure proper and natural to the seventh and eighth tones; at the same time, having acquired the species belonging to the first and second, the final becomes inactive and on this step is left arbitrary and as it were regular *per se,* not suited to the seventh and eighth tones, but necessary to the first and second.[h]

Certain other compositions, ending on this same step, are said to be of the second tone; these are readily recognized by their extended downward range.[i] And if this consideration seem to you not always to the purpose, do not be surprised, for composers sometimes observe the procedure of a given tone at the beginning and in the course of a composition, ending then in accordance with the difference of the plainsong, as you will understand from what follows.

Certain other tenors end on A *la mi re;* here you will need to consider and examine whether their procedure is suited and rational to such an ending, for if a tenor end irregularly in the first or second tone, not proceeding with its proper form, it may easily not belong to it, even though this step is one of its irregular finals and an ending of its Saeculorum or difference. As you will understand from what follows, this is because the third and fourth tones also use this step as a difference. For this reason, then, you will assign such a tenor to the first or second tone only when you find the proper form.[j]

h This is demonstrated by the following masses and motets, which are of the first tone in view of their procedure, structure, and complete diapason: *Ave maris stella* and *D'un autre amer* by Josquin, "Nobilis progenie" and "Vulnerasti cor meum" by Févin, &c.

i For example, "Virgo caelesti" by Loyset Compère, "D'un autre amer" and "De tous biens pleine" by Heyne, "Ce n'est pas" by Pierre de La Rue, and "D'un autre amer" by de Orto.

j As in "La plus de plus" by Josquin, which is of the first tone in view of the course of its diapente and its upward range, or in "Si mieux" by Loyset Compère, which is of the second, as will be readily evident.

Certain other compositions end on D *la sol re;* these are in my opinion to be assigned in the same way to the first and second tones, for it is clearly evident that from D *la sol re* to its diapason is the proper form of the first diapente and diatessaron, namely *re-la* and *re-sol.* When they ascend as far as the fifth or sixth step, and especially when they ascend still further, they will be of the first tone.[k] But when they lack this extension to the upper limit of the diapente, proceeding rather in the lower register, they will be of the second tone and not of the first.[l] This opinion of mine is supported by the venerable Father Zanetto, a musician of Venice.

5. AN EXPLANATION OF THE THIRD AND FOURTH TONES

The few who fish in these waters are in the habit of saying that every composition ending in the position E *la mi* is to be assigned to the fourth tone. They forget that this step is common also to the third, and in so doing seem to me to involve themselves in no little difficulty. Seeing that the difference often ends on this step in the fourth tone, many, thinking only of the ending of its Saeculorum, judge a composition to belong to it. Thus the greatest confusion may easily arise. It is accordingly necessary to consider at various times the final, the upward and downward range, the procedures, the intonations, and the differences, which, since they are of different sorts, end naturally in different ways.[m]

Certain other compositions ending in the position G *sol re ut* are said to be of the third tone, even though this is the step ordinary and regular to the seventh and eighth. You will need to give your most careful consideration to these and, above all, to their procedure, for unless they have the form and order due and appropriate to the third

k Whether with a flat signature, as in "Pourtant si mon" by Antoine Busnoys, "Gaude virgo" a motet by Costanzo Festa, "L'homme armé" *et sic de singulis* by Josquin, and "Hélas qu'il est à mon gré" by Japart; or without, as in "Fors seulement" by Pierre de La Rue, "Je dépite tous" by Brumel, and "Gaude Barbara" by Jean Mouton.

l For example, the mass *Hercules dux Ferrariae,* composed by Josquin, and many other works which I shall not enumerate, since you will readily understand them from their similarity to this one.

m Thus, in the motet "Michael archangele" by Jacotin, the first part is in my opinion of the irregular third tone while the second ends in the regular third tone, not in the fourth; the same is true of "Malheur me bat" by Ockeghem, "Interveniat pro rege nostro" by Jacotin, and many other compositions, similar to these and having the regular final and the required procedure and upward range.

tone, with this final they will never be assigned to it, but rather to the seventh or eighth. But where the natural form is found, they will always be assigned to the third tone, and not to the seventh or eighth, in view of their form and difference.[n] This opinion is likewise supported by the venerable Father Zanetto, Venetian musician.

You will also find certain other compositions ending on A *la mi re*; when these observe the appropriate procedure they will be assigned to the third tone.[o] But when they have a flat signature, they are in my opinion to be assigned to the third tone the more readily, even though at the beginning and in their course they fail to proceed in the due and appropriate way, for it is evident that the regular structure of the tone [p] will prevail. But because of the inconvenience of their upward range, few such pieces will be found, unless written for equal voices or *voci mutate*. Compositions of this sort are to be assigned to the third or fourth tone in view of their species and downward range, not because of their difference or procedure. Thus it may be inferred that, in view of their extended downward range, they will in preference be assigned to the fourth tone.[q]

6. AN EXPLANATION OF THE FIFTH AND SIXTH TONES

Spurred on by your affection and with my goal in sight, I turn to the question about which you may have been in doubt.[9] Thus, in beginning this part of my explanation, I ask you to observe that compositions ending in the position F *fa ut* are to be assigned to the fifth or sixth tone. On this point I should like to remove any remaining uncertainty, for seeing that such compositions very often—indeed, almost always—have the flat signature and that the form of the tone is altered, it would be easy for you to believe the contrary, in view of certain opinions that I have expressed above. Know, then, that in compositions such as these the older composers were more concerned with facility than with proper form and correct structure. For the fifth and sixth tones often require the help of the b-flat, although always to use it would be contrary to the tendencies of the mediations of these tones as laid down by the ancients. This opinion is likewise supported by the

n For example, "Nunca fué pena mayor," &c.

o For example, "Miserere mei Deus" by Josquin, "Laetatus sum" by Eustachio, "Benedic anima mea Dominum," in which the first part ends on the confinal, the second on the final, and the third on the difference, &c.

p Namely, *mi-mi* and *mi-la*, arising from the interval A *la mi re* to high E *la mi*, to which is added the upper diatessaron *mi-la*.

q For example, "O Maria rogamus te" in the *Motetti C* and many others which you will readily recognize on the same principle.

9 The reader, that is, having been told that in and D and F modes the flat signature does not effect a transposition (p. 211), and having seen that the explanation of this given for the D modes (p. 212) will not apply to the F, will have anticipated a difficulty at this point.

previously mentioned Venetian, Father Zanetto. For this reason, then, the older composers altered the third diapente, giving it the nature of the fourth, in order that the tritone which would otherwise occur in running through it might not cause inconvenience or harshness in their music.[r]

And if certain other compositions, ending on A *la mi re,* are to be assigned to the fifth tone, know that at the beginning and in their course these must observe a procedure suited to it; lacking this, the difference will have little force and, as previously explained, they may easily be of some other tone. Nevertheless, the composer may if he pleases observe this tone, but what is necessary will be recognized more clearly in the psalms and the Magnificat. The sixth tone we do not concede on this step, for it has neither the form nor the difference.

Certain other compositions ending on B *fa* ♮ *mi* are said to be of the fifth tone, but we do not approve this in the absence of the flat signature (or figure) which on this step produces the proper structure both ascending and descending. Here, then, the final is rational, necessary, and governing, and in this way the proper form is recognized.[s]

Certain other compositions, ending on C *sol fa ut,* are said to be of the fifth tone, both with and without the flat signature;[t] this is solely in view of the difference which the plainsong sometimes exhibits here. The sixth tone is lacking on this step, even though it is the confinal of the fifth and sixth tones regularly ended, for the step can bear no form or difference appropriate to it.

[r] This is uniformly demonstrated in the following compositions of the fifth tone, compositions which cannot be otherwise assigned in view of their upward range and procedure: "Stabat mater dolorosa" and "Alma Redemptoris" by Josquin, "Hélas que pourra devenir" by Caron, "Quaeramus cum pastoribus" and "Illuminare illuminare Jerusalem" by Jean Mouton, and the Sanctus and Agnus Dei of the Mass of Our Lady by Pierre de La Rue. Those which do not have this extended upward range, falling short of the diapente or hexachord, are to be assigned to the sixth tone as regularly ended, for example, "Brunette" by Stokhem, "Vôtre bergeronette" by

Compère, "Je ne demande" by Busnoys, "Allez regrets" by Agricola, "A l'audience" by Heyne, "Sancta Trinitas unus Deus" and "Tempus meum est ut revertar ad eum" by Févin, "Celeste beneficium" by Jean Mouton, "Egregie Christi" by Févin, &c.

[s] As demonstrated in the chanson "La regretée," composed by Heyne, which is of the fifth tone in view of its species, cadences, and upward range; or in "O admirabile commercium" by Josquin, which is said to be of the sixth, as are certain others similar to it, although there are few of these.

[t] For example, "Si sumpsero" by Obrecht.

7. AN EXPLANATION OF THE SEVENTH AND EIGHTH TONES

Certain persons have held that the seventh and eighth tones may end regularly and irregularly on three steps, namely Gamma *ut*, C *fa ut*, and G *sol re ut*, and regarding these endings many advance many different opinions, especially regarding those on Gamma *ut* and C *fa ut*. Compositions ending on these steps they assign rather to the seventh tone than to the eighth, and this because such a composition seldom if ever descends as the plagal form requires. In view of this confusion I shall tell you that I cannot admit such opinions, for it is clear that these compositions continue to observe the natural requirements of the proper and regular tones. Those ending on Gamma *ut*, in view of their acquired form, peculiar to the seventh tone, I take to be of this tone and not of the eighth when they are without the flat signature, but of the first or second when they have it. But those ending on C *fa ut*, for the reason given above and also because they do not have the proper diatessaron, I assign to the eighth tone and not to the seventh.[u] This opinion is likewise held by the previously mentioned musician, Father Zanetto.

Certain other compositions end in the position G *sol re ut;* these are naturally and regularly to be assigned to the seventh tone or to the eighth in view of their proper final and natural form.[v]

Certain other compositions end in the position C *sol fa ut;* these are in my opinion to be assigned in the same way to the seventh tone or to the eighth in view of their difference and procedure, the difference often ending on this step. Thus, if such a composition proceed in the appropriate way it will most certainly be of the seventh tone or of the eighth in view of its final, still more reasonably so if it has the flat signa-

---

[u] As demonstrated in the following compositions: "Mon mari m'a diffamée" by de Orto and the chanson called "E la la la"; following the same principle you will understand the rest.

[v] Thus the mass *Ut sol* by Jean Mouton and the Gloria of Our Lady by Pierre de La Rue are in our opinion to be assigned to the seventh tone in view of their species, their final, and their extended upward range; the same applies to "Multi sunt vocati pauci vero electi" by the venerable Father Zanetto of Venice and "Ascen-

dens Christus in altum" by Hylaere. But "Si dedero" by Alexander Agricola and "C'est possible que l'homme peut" will be of the eighth tone in view of their final and their procedure; the same is true of "O Venus bant" by Josquin, "Disant adieu madame," "Je suis amie," "Min morghem ghaf," "Hélas hélas" by Ninot, "E d'en revenez vous" by Compère, "Beata Dei genitrix," and many others which you will recognize on the same principle.

ture, for this will give it the proper structure, namely *ut-sol* and *re-sol*, the form peculiar to the seventh and eighth tones.[w]

Following these principles in your examinations and reflecting on the method set forth above, you will have a clear understanding of any other composition or tone suited and appropriate to figured music.

---

w Thus "Mes pensées" by Compère, "Madame hélas" and "Comment peut" by Josquin, and "Mittit ad virginem" can be assigned only to the seventh tone. But "Je cuide si ce temps" and "Ne l'oserai je dire" will be of the eighth tone and not of the seventh, as their form and extended downward procedure will show you.

26. Heinrich Glarean

Born in the Canton of Glarus in Switzerland in 1488, Glarean died in 1563 in Freiburg. Known as Glareanus, he was one of the great humanists of the sixteenth century. A friend of Erasmus of Rotterdam, he was a philosopher, theologian, philologist, historian, poet, and musical scholar, crowned poet laureate by Emperor Maximilian I. Among his works of interest to the musical reader, the most important is the *Dodecachordon* (i.e., the "instrument of twelve-strings"), which advocated four additions to the existing eight ecclesiastical modes. The book had a tremendous influence on the changing concept of the modal system. Glareanus also revised the works of Boethius, the edition being posthumously published by M. Rota in 1570. The *Dodecachordon* interests the historian not only because of its discussion of the ever-present problem of the modes but also because it contains many illuminating examples illustrating the intricate contrapuntal art of the time.

From the Dodecachordon

[1547]

Book Three—Chapter 24

Examples of the Paired Combinations of the Modes
together with
An Encomium of Josquin Desprez [1]

So MUCH for our examples of the twelve modes in that varied sort of music not (at least in our opinion) inappropriately called mensural, ex-

1 Text: The original edition (Basle, 1547). The musical examples are omitted. For the title page in facsimile, see Kinsky, p. 58, Fig. 3. German translation by Peter Bohn (with the musical examples in score) in *Publikationen älterer praktischer und theoretischer Musikwerke*, xvi (Leipzig, 1888).

amples cited with all possible brevity from various authors in proof of those things that have seemed to us in need of proof. It now remains for us to give examples of these same modes in combination,[2] not commonplace examples, to be sure, but weighty ones elegantly illustrating the matter. And since in our preceding book [3] we have sufficiently discussed the actual nature of these combinations, we shall refrain from re-examining it here. All our examples will be in the order seen in our last book; thus, having begun with Dorian and Hypodorian, we shall then add examples of the other paired combinations, briefly expressing our opinion about these, partly to show others a better way of judging and, as it were, to open men's eyes, partly to make known the merits of the ingenious in this art, merits which to certain sufficiently hostile judges seem commonplace, but which to us seem considerable and most worthy of admiration.

Now in this class of authors and in this great crowd of the ingenious there stands out as by far pre-eminent in temperament, conscientiousness, and industry (or I am mistaken in my feeling) Jodocus à Prato, whom people playfully (ὑποκοριστικῶς) call in his Belgian mother-tongue Josquin, as though they were to say "Little Jodocus." If this man, besides that native bent and strength of character by which he was distinguished, had had an understanding of the twelve modes and of the truth of musical theory, nature could have brought forth nothing more majestic and magnificent in this art; so versatile was his temperament in every respect, so armed with natural acumen and force, that there is nothing he could not have done in this profession. But moderation was wanting for the most part and, with learning, judgment; thus in certain places in his compositions he did not, as he should have, soberly repress the violent impulses of his unbridled temperament. Yet let this petty fault be condoned in view of the man's other incomparable gifts.

No one has more effectively expressed the passions of the soul in music than this symphonist, no one has more felicitously begun, no one has been able to compete in grace and facility on an equal footing with him, just as there is no Latin poet superior in the epic to Maro. For just as Maro, with his natural facility, was accustomed to adapt his poem to his subject so as to set weighty matters before the eyes of his readers with close-packed spondees, fleeting ones with unmixed dactyls, to use words

---

2 Examples, that is, in which the tenor, or principal part, has the combined plagal and authentic range.

3 II, xxviii–xxxv, pp. 138–161 (Bohn's translation, pp. 105–119).

suited to his every subject, in short, to undertake nothing inappropriately, as Flaccus says of Homer, so our Josquin, where his matter requires it, now advances with impetuous and precipitate notes, now intones his subject in long-drawn tones, and, to sum up, has brought forth nothing that was not delightful to the ear and approved as ingenious by the learned, nothing, in short, that was not acceptable and pleasing, even when it seemed less erudite, to those who listened to it with judgment. In most of his works he is the magnificent virtuoso, as in the *Missa super voces musicales* [4] and the *Missa ad fugam;* [5] in some he is the mocker, as in the *Missa La sol fa re mi;* [6] in some he extends himself in rivalry, [7] as in the *Missa de Beata Virgine;* [8] although others have also frequently attempted all these things, they have not with the same felicity met with a corresponding success in their undertakings.

This was for us the reason why in this, the consummation of our work, we have by preference cited examples by this man. And although his talent is beyond description, more easily admired than properly explained, he still seems preferable to others, not only for his talent, but also for his diligence in emending his works. For those who have known him say that he brought his things forth with much hesitation and with corrections of all sorts, and that he gave no composition to the public unless he had kept it by him for several years, the opposite of what we said Jacob Obrecht is reported to have done. Hence some not inappropriately maintain that the one may justly be compared to Virgil, the other to Ovid. But if we admit this, to whom shall we more fittingly compare Pierre de La Rue, an astonishingly delightful composer, than to Horace, Isaac than perhaps to Lucan, Févin than to Claudianus, Brumel to Statius? Yet I should seem foolish, and rightly, if I were to speak with so little taste of these men, and perhaps I should deserve to hear that popular saying, "Shoemaker, stick to your last!" Hence I proceed to the explanation and judging of the examples.

Of the first combination, that of Dorian and Hypodorian, let our example be the melody "Victimae paschali laudes," on the Blessed Resurrection of Christ, as set by this same author Josquin, [9] a melody that we

---

4 *Werken, Missen,* I (Amsterdam, 1926), 1–32.

5 *Missarum Josquin Liber III* (Venice, 1514). For a brief account of this work, see A. W. Ambros, *Geschichte der Musik,* III (3d ed., Leipzig, 1893), 220–221; the "Pleni sunt coeli" is given by Glarean (III, xiii, p. 258; Bohn's translation, pp. 204–205).

6 *Werken, Missen,* I (Amsterdam, 1926), 35–56.

7 With Antoine Brumel (see p. 225).

8 Das Chorwerk, VIII (Wolfenbüttel, 1936), Heft 42.

9 Glarean gives the complete musical text of the seven examples discussed in this chapter, and all of them are printed in score in Bohn's translation. We add, wherever possible, references to more recent and more readily accessible editions, in this instance to Josquin Desprez, *Werken, Motetten,* I (Amsterdam, 1926), 136–139.

have mentioned twice before and that we have further cited as an example of this combination in our second book.[10] In it, it will rightly be judged ingenious that the given theme is heard thus divided by intervals among the four voices, as is most fitting.[11] In its first part, the highest voice, borrowed from some well-known song,[12] presents the Hypodorian mode with an added ditone below. In the following part it is Dorian with an added diatessaron above. Here the ending is on the highest step of the diapason, whereas just the other way it ought to have been on the lowest; this part, however, is also borrowed,[13] and on this account he has not wished to alter it. The tenor is extended a ditone lower than the Hypodorian form requires, but the author does this with his usual license. The borrowed melodies he combines with other ancient ones, appropriately in the same mode, for melodies in other modes would not agree to this extent. At the same time, it was not difficult for this author to combine melodies belonging to different modes, even to do so gracefully, for he composed scarcely a single mass, be its mode what it may, without bringing in the Aeolian mode in the Nicene Creed,[14] something that others have attempted also, but not always with the same success. Each voice has something worthy of note, thus the tenor its stability, the bass its wonderful gravity, although I scarcely know whether it pleases everyone that he ascends as he does in the bass at the word "Galilaea." That this proceeds from the wantonness of his temperament we cannot deny; thus we must accept it gracefully as an addition. The cantus has an ancient flavor; the seventh note from the end is heard alone, with all the other voices pausing. Yet, in comparison with the genius of the man, all these things are wholly unimportant. Let us go on, then, to other examples.

Here, in the motet "De profundis," [15] I wish everyone to observe closely what the beginning is like and with how much passion and how much majesty the composer has given us the opening words; instead of transposing the modes from their natural positions to the higher register (as is elsewhere the usual custom), he has combined the systems of the two; at the same time, with astonishing and carefully studied elegance,

---

10 I, xiv, pp. 34–35; II, xxix, pp. 140–141 (Bohn's translation, pp. 26–27, 107).

11 Josquin treats the plainsong (*Grad. Rom.*, p. 242) as a "wandering cantus firmus," giving Stanza 1 to the tenor and, in Stanza 2, line 1 to the alto, line 2 to the bass, line 3 to the tenor, and so forth.

12 It is the superius of Ockeghem's chanson "D'un autre amer" (Eugénie Droz, *Trois chansonniers français*, I [Paris, 1927], 72–73).

13 It is the superius of Heyne's chanson "De tous biens plaine" (Knud Jeppesen, *Der Kopenhagener Chansonnier* [Copenhagen, 1927], pp. 7–8).

14 That is, without interpolating the Gregorian Credo, officially of Mode IV, but assigned by Glarean (II, xvii, pp. 104–109, Bohn's translation, pp. 82–86) to the Aeolian mode.

15 Hugo Riemann, *Handbuch der Musikgeschichte*, II, 1 (Leipzig, 1907), 258–268.

he has thrown the phrase [16] into violent disorder, usurping now the leap of the Lydian, now that of the Ionian, until at length, by means of these most beautiful refinements, he glides, creeping unobserved and without offending the ear, from Dorian to Phrygian. That this is difficult to do, especially in these two modes, the Dorian and Phrygian, we have already shown.[17] Thus, contrary to the nature of the modes, he has ended the combined systems of the Dorian and Hypodorian on E, the seat of the Phrygian. Yet there are other compositions in which he has done this also (nor is he alone in it), evidently from an immoderate love of novelty and an excessive eagerness to win a little glory for being unusual, a fault to which the more ingenious professors of the arts are in general so much given that, be it ever so peculiar to the symphonists, they still share it in common with many others. None the less the motet remains between A and d, respecting the limits of the Dorian and Hypodorian systems. And although by his unusual procedure he has sought nothing else, he has at least made it plain that, through the force of his temperament, he could bring it about that the charge customarily brought against the ancient musicians, namely, of progressing "From Dorian to Phrygian," [18] would be brought in vain against him by whom it was so learnedly accomplished, without the slightest offense to the ear. But enough of this motet.[19]

The second combination is that of the Hypophrygian and Phrygian modes, extending from B to e. But the combination rarely descends in this way to B without descending also to A; thus it usually lies between C and e. Yet our Josquin, in setting the Genealogy of Christ Our Saviour according to the Evangelists Matthew and Luke for four voices in harmony in this combination, descends to A re and ascends to f, adding here a semitone and there a tone, and this with his usual license.[20] The first one, according to Matthew, he has arranged in accordance with the true final close of the mode, namely on E; we show it here. The second one, taken from Luke, he has forced to end on G, but without

---

[16] The word "phrase" (*phrasis*) has for Glarean the special meaning "melodic idiom"; the "phrase" of a given mode consists for him partly in its tendency to emphasize its natural arithmetic or harmonic division at the fourth or fifth, partly in its use of certain characteristic tone-successions taken over from plainsong. Compare I, xiii, pp. 32–33 (Bohn's translation, pp. 24–25), where the leaps characteristic of the eight modes of plainsong are discussed and illustrated, also II, xxxvi (Bohn's translation, pp. 119–122). The leap characteristic of the Lydian mode is that from a to c; by "Ionian" leap Glarean must mean that from E to G.

[17] II, xi, pp. 90–93 (Bohn's translation, pp.

70–73), where the present example is also mentioned.

[18] Ἀπὸ δορίου ἐπὶ φρύγιον. Reinach, in his edition of Plutarch's *De musica* (Paris, 1900, p. 143, note on § 366), suggests that this proverb may be connected with the anecdote of the "Mysians" preserved by Aristotle (p. 23 above).

[19] Despite the range of its tenor, by which Glarean has evidently been misled, Josquin's "De profundis" is clearly Hypophrygian, or combined Phrygian and Hypophrygian; cf. Zarlino, *Istituzioni armoniche* (Venice, 1589), IV, xxiii.

[20] *Werken, Motetten*, I (Amsterdam, 1926), 59–69 (Matthew), 70–81 (Luke). The tenor descends to A in the Luke genealogy only.

altering the phrase of the modes at the time, and this also with his usual license.[21] The motet has great majesty, and it is wonderful that from material so sterile, namely, from a bare catalogue of men, he has been able to fashion as many delights as though it had been some fertile narrative. Many other things might be said, but let some of these be left for others to discuss.

The third combination, that of Lydian and Hypolydian, is unusual in this our age, for, as we have often remarked in the foregoing, all compositions in these modes are forced into the Ionian.[22] But in our example, the Agnus Dei from the *Missa Fortuna desperata*,[23] the reader may first admire the way in which a Lydian has been made from an Ionian, for the whole mass is sung in the Ionian mode. This is doubtless due to the bass, plunged into the lowest diapason. For in other compositions, as often as the tenor is Hypodorian, the bass is usually Dorian or Aeolian; again, just as a Phrygian tenor often has an Aeolian bass and cantus, here an Ionian bass has a Lydian tenor and alto.[24] But it is doubtful whether the author has done this by design or by accident. Aside from this, he talks nonsense with his canon, following the custom of the singers.[25] For who except Oedipus himself would understand such a riddle of the sphinx? He has humored the common singers, obeying the maxim, Ἀλωπεκίζειν πρὸς ἑτέραν ἀλώπεκα; that is, *Cum vulpe vulpinare tu quoque invicem*, as Master Erasmus has learnedly translated it, or, as the vulgar inelegantly put it, "Howl with the wolves, if you want to get along with them."

The fourth combination is that of the Mixolydian and its plagal, the Hypomixolydian; in our age it is seldom used. Nevertheless, once the symphonists had perceived the magnificence of these modes from ancient examples of ecclesiastical melody, roused as it were with enthusiasm,

---

21 On this ending see II, xxxvi, p. 163 (Bohn's translation, p. 121), also Pietro Aron, *Trattato della natura et cognizione*, v (pp. 214–215 above).

22 Cf. Pietro Aron, *op. cit.*, vi (p. 215 above).

23 Josquin Desprez, *Werken, Missen*, I (Amsterdam, 1926), 81–104.

24 Cf. III, xiii, pp. 250–251 (Bohn's translation, pp. 197–198), on the "mysterious relationship" of the modes, in which connection the present example is also mentioned. Here, as there, Glarean clearly has three distinct sorts of relationship in mind: (1) the natural relationship of any authentic mode to the plagal mode having the same final; (2) the special relationship of Phrygian to Aeolian, as a result of which a Phrygian composition may have marked Aeolian characteristics or an Aeolian composition a Phrygian final cadence; as an example of this relationship Glarean gives in III, xix, the motet "Tulerunt Dominum meum" (score in Bohn's translation,

pp. 272–278); cf. also Zarlino, *Istituzioni armoniche*, IV, xxx (pages 253–254 below); (3) the peculiar relationship of D-Dorian to D-Aeolian (transposed Aeolian) and of F-Lydian to F-Ionian (transposed Ionian), of which the present example is an illustration.

25 In Agnus I the bass is to invert his part, beginning it an eleventh lower than written and multiplying the time-values by four (double augmentation). Petrucci's editions, followed by Glarean, hint at this in the following distich, which Glarean heads "the riddle of the sphinx":

In gradus undenos descendant multiplicantes
Consimilique modo crescant Antipodes uno.

Let them descend by eleven steps with multiplied measure;
Then once more in like manner increase, to antipodes changing.

they tried in a certain most praiseworthy rivalry to do their utmost with the melody "Et in terra pax" on the Most Blessed Virgin and Queen of Heaven, Mary, Mother of Jesus Christ,[26] above all Antoine Brumel [27] and our Josquin Desprez, at a time when both were verging toward extreme old age.[28] Brumel, in his setting, has spared no pains to show the singers his skill, nay, he has strained every fibre of his temperament to leave behind for later generations a specimen of his ingenuity. Yet, in my opinion at least, Josquin has by far surpassed him in natural force and ingenious penetration and has so borne himself in the contest that Nature, mother of all, as though wishing to form from the four elements her most perfect creation, seems to me to have brought her utmost powers into play in order that it might be impossible to invent a better music. And thus the majority of the learned have not hesitated to award the first place to this composition, especially Joannes Vannius, whom we have mentioned in connection with the Hypomixolydian mode and to whose judgment we gladly subscribe, both because he gave it before us and because he outdid us in this matter by far. At the beginning, the tenor descends once to the Hypomixolydian diatessaron, otherwise the entire melody is Mixolydian, not Hypomixolydian. To me, the greatest passion seems to have been expressed at the word "Primogenitus" in the first part of the setting; others prefer the second part. But there is no part whatever that does not contain something that you may greatly admire.

Of the fifth combination, that of Aeolian and Hypoaeolian, we should not again be giving the same example if we had been able to obtain or discover another one anywhere among the symphonists of our age. Although in our previous book [29] we also produced other examples of the combination, this one [30] was by far the most enlightening, as one by many treated yet by all perverted and transposed from its natural position, even mutilated or altered with respect to its two diatessarons above and below, namely by Brumel and Josquin in their two so celebrated masses of the Virgin Mary, Mother of God; for this reason we have earnestly entreated that excellent man, Master Gregor Meyer, the distinguished organist of the cathedral at Solothurn in Switzerland, to treat the theme worthily, with all the skill at his command, in its natural position and with the two diatessarons proper to and born with the body of the melody.

---

26 *Grad. Rom.*, p. 32*.
27 Edited by Henry Expert (Paris, 1898) in the series *Maltres musiciens de la renaissance française*.
28 *Das Chorwerk*, VIII (Wolfenbüttel, 1936), Heft 42.

29 III, xviii, p. 304 (Bohn's translation, p. 259).
30 The Gregorian Kyrie "Cum jubilo" (*Grad. Rom.*, p. 32*), which Glarean has already discussed in II, xxxiii, pp. 152–156 (Bohn's translation, pp. 113–116).

In truth, we imagine this melody to be some splendid bird, whose body is the diapente re-la and whose two wings are the diatessarons mi-la. To sew to this body wings other than those with which it was born would be foolish, surely, unless like Aesop's crow it was to fly with strange plumage. We have prevailed upon him and, in all friendliness toward me and readiness to further liberal studies, he has sent us what we wanted; of this we now desire to make the reader a sharer. We do not at all hesitate to insert this composition among those of Josquin, such praise has been given to it; namely, the opinion of that learned man, Master John Alus, canon of the same cathedral and preacher of the Divine Word, who thinks that it would be no small ornament to the more serious studies, such as theology and sacred letters, if to these were added a knowledge of languages and of the mathematical disciplines, and that among these last it would most befit a priest of Holy Church if he knew music. Nor was the man mistaken in his opinion, for he had become versed in musical knowledge. We had his support in this work when he lived with us at Freiburg at the foot of the Black Forest and often refreshed us, now playing the organ, now joining to this the singing of things by Josquin. And so, since he has given the highest praise to this composition of our Gregor, he has easily won our approval and has been responsible for its coming into men's hands as worthy of the ears of the learned.

Of the sixth combination, that of Hyperaeolian and Hyperphrygian, we have deliberately omitted an example, for none is to be found anywhere and it would be foolish to invent one, especially with so great a choice of modes; the tenor, too, would have an outrageous ambitus, actually exceeding all the remaining combinations of the modes by an apotome. Aside from this, in our previous book we have given an invented example, less for imitation than for illustration, so that the matter might be understood, not so that something of the sort might be attempted by anyone, a thing we find that no one has attempted.

Of the seventh and last combination, namely of Ionian and Hypoionian, our example, "Planxit autem David," is again by Josquin Desprez,[31] the author of the examples of all the other combinations except the fifth. Of its beginning some will no doubt exclaim: "The mountain has labored and brought forth a mouse!" But they will not have considered that, throughout the motet, there is preserved what befits the mourner, who is wont at first to cry out frequently, then to murmur to himself, turning little by little to sorrowful complaints, thereupon

---

31 *Werken, Motetten,* I (Amsterdam, 1926), 95–104.

to subside or sometimes, when passion breaks out anew, to raise his voice again, shouting out a cry. All these things we see most beautifully observed in this composition, as will be evident to the attentive reader. Nor is there in it anything unworthy of its author; by the gods, he has everywhere expressed the passion in a wonderful way, thus, at the very beginning of the tenor, at the word "Jonathan."

27. Gioseffe Zarlino

Gioseffe Zarlino, easily the most influential personality in the history of musical theory from Aristoxenus to Rameau, was born at Chioggia, not far from Venice, in 1517. His teacher was the Venetian master Adrian Willaert, choirmaster at St. Mark's from 1527 to 1562. In 1565, on the departure for Parma of Cipriano Rore, his fellow-pupil and Willaert's successor, Zarlino fell heir to his old teacher's position at St. Mark's, a position that he continued to occupy until his death in 1590. The *Istituzioni armoniche*, his principal work, first published in 1558, was reprinted in 1562 and 1573; other writings are the *Dimostrazioni armoniche* (1571) and the *Sopplimenti musicali* (1588), this last in reply to the stand taken by Vincenzo Galilei, a rebellious pupil who had attacked Zarlino's entire teaching in his *Dialogo della musica antica e della moderna* (1581).

A true son of the Renaissance, Zarlino paints an ideal picture of the music of the Ancient World, takes pride in what his own time has done to create it anew, and flatly rejects the music of the Middle Ages, which seems to him a species of artistic sophistry. Professing to be more interested in the formulation of basic principles than in the laying-down of rules to govern particular cases, he looks on music as an imitation of nature and endeavors to derive his teachings from natural law. Starting from the ratios for the primary consonances, he succeeds in arriving at many of the conclusions that modern theory draws from the harmonic series, a phenomenon unknown to Zarlino and his time. He was the first to grasp the full implications of just intonation and to produce classical authority for it, the first to deal with harmony in terms of the triad rather than of the interval, the first to recognize the importance of the fundamental antithesis of major and minor, the first to attempt a rational explanation of the old rule forbidding the use of parallel fifths and octaves, the first to isolate and to describe the effects of the false relation; it was at his suggestion that the first printed edition of the *Harmonics* of Aristoxenus (in Latin translation) was undertaken. His writings bear witness to the extraordinary range and depth of his reading and to the understanding with which he read.

From *the* Istituzioni armoniche [1]

[*1558*]

Book Three

26. WHAT IS SOUGHT IN EVERY COMPOSITION; AND FIRST, OF THE SUBJECT [2]

I SHALL come now to the discussion of counterpoint, but before I begin this discussion it must be understood that in every good counterpoint, or in every good composition, there are required many things, and one may say that it would be imperfect if one of them were lacking.

The first of these is the subject, without which one can do nothing. For just as the builder, in all his operations, looks always toward the end and founds his work upon some matter which he calls the subject, so the musician in his operations, looking toward the end which prompts him to work, discovers the matter or subject upon which he founds his composition. Thus he perfects his work in conformity with his chosen end. Or again, just as the poet, prompted by such an end to improve or to delight (as Horace shows so clearly in his *Art of Poetry*, when he says:

Aut prodesse volunt, aut delectare poetae
Aut simul et iucunda et idonea dicere vitae), [3]

takes as the subject of his poem some history or fable, discovered by himself or borrowed from others, which he adorns and polishes with various manners, as he may prefer, leaving out nothing that might be fit or worthy to delight the minds of his hearers, in such a way that he takes on something of the magnificent and marvelous; so the musician, apart from being prompted by the same end to improve or to delight the minds of his listeners with harmonious accents, takes the subject and founds upon it his composition, which he adorns with various modulations and various harmonies in such a way that he offers welcome pleasure to his hearers.

---

1 Text: The edition published as the first volume of the *Opere* (Venice, 1589), collated with the first and second editions (Venice, 1558 and 1562). The postils of the original and some of the additions of 1589 are given as author's notes. For the title page in facsimile, see Kinsky, p. 110, Fig. 5.

2 The first half of this chapter is literally translated by Cerone in his *Melopeo* (Naples, 1613), XII, i.

3 Lines 333–334. "Poets aim either to benefit, or to amuse, or to utter words at once both pleasing and helpful to life." [Fairclough]

The second condition is that the composition should be principally composed of consonances; in addition, it should incidentally include many dissonances, suitably arranged in accordance with the rules which I propose to give later on.

The third is that the procedure of the parts should be good, that is, that the modulations [4] should proceed by true and legitimate intervals arising from the sonorous numbers,[5] so that through them may be acquired the usage of good harmonies.

The fourth condition to be sought is that the modulations and the concentus be varied, for harmony [6] has no other source than the diversity of the modulations and the diversity of the consonances variously combined.

The fifth is that the composition should be subject to a prescribed and determined harmony, mode, or tone (call it as we will), and that it should not be disordered.

The sixth and last (aside from the others which might be added) is that the harmony it contains should be so adapted to the speech, that is, to the words, that in joyous matters the harmony will not be mournful, and vice versa, that in mournful ones the harmony will not be joyful.

To assure a perfect understanding of the whole, I shall discuss these things separately as they become suited to my purpose and to my needs.

Beginning with the first, then, I say that, in every musical composition, what we call the subject is that part from which the composer derives

---

4 "A movement made from one sound to another by means of various intervals" (II, xiv). Zarlino distinguishes two sorts of modulation: "improper," as in plainsong, and "proper," as in figured music. "Proper modulation" has these further divisions: first, sol-fa or solmization; second, the modulation of artificial instruments; third, modulation in which words are adapted to the musical figures.

5 "Sonorous number is number related to voices and to sounds" (I, xix). For Zarlino, the sonorous (or harmonic) numbers are specifically the numbers 1 to 6, with their products and their squares. As he says in I, xv, the six-part number has its parts so proportioned that, when any two of them are taken, their relation gives us the ratio or form of one of the musical consonances, simple or composite. And these parts are so ordered that, if we take six strings stretched subject to the ratio of the numbers 1 to 6, when we strike them all together, our ear perceives no discrepancy and takes the highest pleasure in the harmony that arises; the opposite is the case if the order is changed in any respect. It should be noted that Zarlino does not say that the lengths of the strings correspond to the numbers 1 to 6; he says that they correspond to the ratios of these numbers. The relative lengths, as given in the *Dimostrazioni armoniche*, III, *Definizione* xliv, are 60, 30, 20, 15, 12, and 10; the resulting harmony will consist of unison, octave, twelfth, fifteenth, seventeenth, and nineteenth.

6 In II, xii, Zarlino defines harmony as having two varieties, "proper" and "improper." "Proper harmony" is a combination or mixture of low and high sounds, divided or not divided by intermediate sounds, which impresses the ear agreeably; it arises from the parts of a composition through the procedure which they make in accord with one another until they attain their end, and it has the power to dispose the soul to various passions. "Proper harmony" arises not only from consonances, but also from dissonances. It has two divisions: "perfect," as in the singing of many parts, and "imperfect," as in the singing of two parts only. "Improper harmony" arises when two sounds distant from one another with respect to the low and the high are heard divided by other intermediate sounds so that they give out an agreeable concentus, subject to several proportions. Musicians call such a combination a harmony. But, Zarlino says, it ought rather to be called a harmonious consonance, for it contains no modulation, and although its extremes are divided, it has no power to move the soul. "Improper harmony" has also two divisions: "simple," as in a combination of consonances arranged in harmonic proportion, and "by extension of meaning" (*ad un certo modo*), as in a combination otherwise arranged.

the invention to make the other parts of the work, however many they may be. Such a subject may take many forms, as the composer may prefer and in accordance with the loftiness of his imagination: it may be his own invention, that is, it may be that he has discovered it of himself; again, it may be that he has borrowed it from the works of others, adapting it to his work and adorning it with various parts and various modulations. And such a subject may be of several kinds: it may be a tenor or some other part of any composition you please, whether of plainsong or of figured music; again, it may be two or more parts of which one follows another in consequence [7] or in some other way, for the various forms of such subjects are innumerable.

When the composer has discovered his subject, he will write the other parts in the way which we shall see later on. When this is done, our practical musicians call the manner of composing "making counterpoint."

But when the composer has not first discovered his subject, that part which he first puts into execution or with which he begins his work, whatever it may be or however it may begin, whether high, low, or intermediate, will always be the subject to which he will then adapt the other parts in consequence or in some other way, as he prefers, adapting the harmony to the words as the matter they contain demands. And when the composer goes on to derive the subject from the parts of the work, that is, when he derives one part from another and goes on to write the work all at once, as we shall see elsewhere, that small part which he derives without the others and upon which he then composes the parts of his composition will always be called the subject. This manner of composing practical musicians call "composing from fantasy," although it may also be called "counterpointing," or as they say, "making counterpoint."

. . . . .

27. THAT COMPOSITIONS SHOULD BE MADE UP PRIMARILY OF CONSONANCES, AND SECONDARILY AND INCIDENTALLY OF DISSONANCES

And although every composition, every counterpoint, and in a word every harmony is made up primarily and principally of consonances, dis-

---

[7] "Consequence we define as a certain repetition or return of a part or the whole of a modulation; it arises from an order and arrangement of many musical figures which the composer makes in one part of his composition and from which, after a certain and limited space of time, there follow one or more other parts, low, high, intermediate, or in the same sound, at the diapason, diapente, diatessaron, or unison, these proceeding one after another by the same intervals. Imitation we shall define as a repetition or return which does not proceed by the same intervals but by wholly different ones, only the movements made by the parts and the figures being similar" (III, liv). Each has two varieties, strict and free, and may be either in direct or in contrary motion.

sonances are used secondarily and incidentally for the sake of greater beauty and elegance. Taken by themselves, these are not very acceptable to the ear; arranged as they regularly should be and in accordance with the precepts which we shall give, the ear tolerates them to such an extent that, far from being offended, it receives from them great pleasure and delight.

From this, among many other advantages, the musician derives two of no little value: we have already stated the first, namely, that with their aid he may pass from one consonance to another; [8] the second is that a dissonance causes the consonance which immediately follows it to seem more acceptable. Thus it is perceived and recognized with greater pleasure by the ear, just as after darkness light is more acceptable and delightful to the eye, and after the bitter the sweet is more luscious and palatable. And from everyday experience with sounds we learn that if a dissonance offends the ear for a certain length of time, the consonance which follows is made more acceptable and more sweet.

Thus the ancient musicians judged that they should admit in composition not only the consonances which they called perfect and those which they called imperfect, but dissonances also, knowing that their compositions would thus attain to greater beauty and elegance than they would without them. For if they were made up entirely of consonances, although beautiful sounds and good effects would issue from them, they would still be somehow imperfect, both as sound and as composition, seeing that (the consonances not being blended with dissonances) they would lack the great elegance that dissonance affords.

And although I have said that the composer is to use consonances principally and dissonances incidentally, he is not to understand by this that he is to use them in his counterpoints or compositions as they come to hand, without any rule or any order, for this would lead to confusion; on the contrary, he must take care to use them in a regular and orderly manner so that the whole will be profitable. Above all (apart from other things) he must keep in mind the two considerations upon which (in my judgment) all the beauty, all the elegance, and all the excellence of music depend: the movements which the parts of the composition make in ascending or descending in similar or contrary motion, and the arrangement of the consonances in their proper places in the harmonies. Of these things I propose with God's help to speak as may suit my purpose, for this has always been my chief intention.

And to introduce this discussion I propose to explain certain rules laid

8 III, xvii.

down by the ancients, who recognized the importance of such matters; teaching by means of these the regular procedure to be followed in using the consonances and dissonances one after another in composition, they went on to give rules about the movements, which they did imperfectly. Thus I shall state and explain these rules in order, and from this explanation I shall go on to show with evident reason what is to be done and how the rules are to be understood, adding also certain further rules, not only useful but also most necessary to those who seek to train themselves in a regular and well-ordered way of composing music of any kind in a learned and elegant manner, with good reasons and good foundations. In this way everyone may know in what part to arrange the consonances and in what place to use the major and the minor in his compositions.

· · · · ·

29. THAT TWO CONSONANCES SUBJECT TO THE SAME PROPORTION ARE NOT TO BE USED ONE AFTER ANOTHER, ASCENDING OR DESCENDING, WITHOUT A MEAN [9]

The ancient composers also avoided using one after another two perfect consonances of the same genus or species, their extremes subject to the same proportion, the modulations moving one step or more; thus they avoided using two or more unisons, two or more octaves, or two or more fifths, as seen in the following examples:

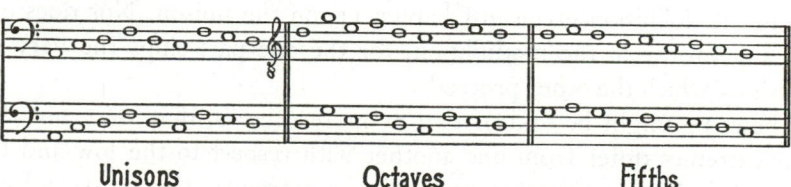

Unisons   Octaves   Fifths

For they knew very well that harmony can arise only from things that are among themselves diverse, discordant, and contrary, and not from things that are in complete agreement. Now if harmony arises from variety such as this, it is not sufficient that in music the parts of the composition be at a distance from one another with respect to the low and the high; the modulations must also be varied in their movements and must contain various consonances, subject to various proportions. And the more harmonious we judge a composition to be, the more we will find, between its several parts, different distances with respect to the

---

9 Having concluded the discussion of his first and second requirements, Zarlino now skips over to the fourth, leaving the third for Chapters 30 and 31.

low and the high, different movements, and different proportions. Perhaps the ancients saw that when consonances were not put together in the manner I have described, they were similar in their procedure and similar in the form of their proportions, although sometimes varied in their extremes with respect to the low and the high. Knowing, then, that such similarity can generate no variety in the concentus and judging (as was true) that perfect harmony consists in variety, not so much in the positions or distances of the parts of the composition as in the movements, the modulations, and the proportions, they held that in taking one after another two consonances similar in proportion, they were varying the position from low to high, or vice versa, without producing any good harmony, even though the extremes did vary one from another. Thus they did not wish that in composition two or more perfect consonances subject to the same proportion should be taken one after another, the parts ascending or descending together, without the mediation of another interval.

The unisons they especially avoided, for these sounds have no extremes and are neither different in position, nor at a distance from one another, nor productive of any variety in the procedure, but wholly similar in every respect. Nor in singing them does one find any difference with respect to the low and the high, for there is no interval between the one sound and the other, the sounds of the one part being in the same places as those of the other, as may be seen in the example above and in the definition given in Chapter 11, on the unison. Nor does one find any variety in the modulation, for the one part sings the very intervals by which the other proceeds.

The same might be said of two or more octaves, if it were not that their extremes differ from one another with respect to the low and the high; thus, being somewhat varied in its extremes, the octave affords the ear somewhat more pleasure than the unison.

And the same may be said of two or more fifths; since these progress by similar steps and proportions, some of the ancients were of the opinion that to a certain extent they gave rise rather to dissonance than to harmony or consonance.

Thus they held it as true that whenever one had arrived at perfect consonance one had attained the end and the perfection toward which music tends, and in order not to give the ear too much of this perfection they did not wish it repeated over and over again.

The truth and excellence of this admirable and useful admonition are confirmed by the operations of Nature, for in bringing into being the individuals of each species she makes them similar to one another in general, yet different in some particular, a difference or variety affording much pleasure to our senses. This admirable order the composer ought to imitate, for the more his operations resemble those of our great mother, the more he will be esteemed. And to this course the numbers and proportions invite him, for in their natural order one will not find two similar proportions following one another immediately, such as the progressions 1:1:1 or 2:2:2 or others like them, which would give the forms of two unisons, still less the progression 1:2:4:8, which is not harmonic but geometric and would give the forms of three consecutive octaves, and still less the progression 4:6:9, which would give the forms of two consecutive fifths. Thus he ought under no conditions to take one after another two unisons, or two octaves, or two fifths, since the natural cause of the consonances, which is the harmonic number, does not in its progression or natural order contain two similar proportions one after another without a mean, as may be seen in Chapter 15 of Part I. For although these consonances, taken in this manner, would obviously cause no dissonance between the parts, a certain heaviness would be heard which would displease.

For all these reasons, then, we ought under no conditions to offend against this rule, that is, we ought never to use the consonances one after another in the way described above; on the contrary, we should seek always to vary the sounds, the consonances, the movements, and the intervals, and in this way, from the variety of these things, we shall come to make a good and perfect harmony. Nor need it concern us that some have sought to do the opposite, rather (as we see from their compositions) from presumption and on their own authority than for any reason that they have had. For we ought not to imitate those who offend impertinently against the good manners and good rules of an art or science without giving any reason for doing so; we ought to imitate those who have conformed, conforming ourselves to them and embracing them as good masters, always avoiding the dreary and taking the good. And I say this for this reason: just as the sight of a picture is more delightful to the eye when it is painted with various colors than when it is painted with one color only, so the ear takes more pleasure and delight in the varied consonances which the more diligent composer puts into his compositions than in the simple and unvaried.

This the more diligent ancient musicians, to whom we are so much indebted, wished observed, and to it we add that, for the reasons already given, the composer ought not to use two or more imperfect consonances one after another, ascending or descending together, without a mean, such as two major or minor thirds, or two major or minor sixths, as seen in the example:

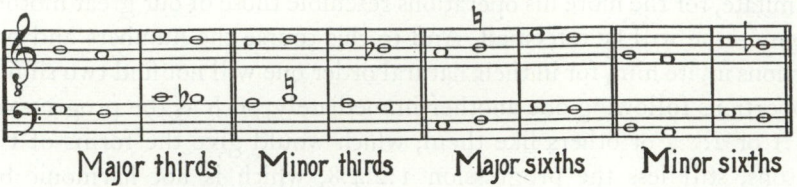

Major thirds   Minor thirds   Major sixths   Minor sixths

For not only do these offend against what I have said about the perfect consonances, but their procedure causes a certain bitterness to be heard, since there is altogether lacking in their modulations the interval of the major semitone, in which lies all the good in music and without which every modulation and every harmony is harsh, bitter, and as it were inconsonant. Another reason for this bitterness is that there is no harmonic relationship [10] between the parts or sounds of two major thirds or of two minor sixths, which makes these somewhat more dreary than the others, as we shall see later on. Thus in every progression or modulation which the parts make in singing together we ought to take special care that wherever possible at least one of them has or moves by the interval of the major semitone, so that the modulation and the harmony which arise from the movements which the parts of the composition make together may be more delightful and more sweet.[11] This is easily managed if the consonances taken one after another are diverse in species, so that after the major third or sixth will follow the minor, or vice versa, or so that after the major third will follow the minor sixth, or after the latter the former, and after the minor third the major sixth, or in the same way after the major sixth the minor third.[12] Nor is there more reason for forbidding the use, one after another, of two perfect consonances than of two imperfect ones, for although the former are perfect consonances, each of the latter is found to be perfect in its proportion. And just as it may not be said with truth that one man is more man than another, so also it may not be said that a major or minor third

10 Non-harmonic relationship or, as we should call it, false relation is defined and discussed in Chapters 30 and 31.

11 "The semitone is indeed the salt (so to speak), the condiment, and the cause of every good modulation and every good harmony" (III, x, with reference to the role of the semitone in the progressions major sixth to octave, major third to fifth, minor sixth to fifth, minor third to unison). "Guido places the semitone in the center of each of his hexachords, as though in the most worthy and most honored place, the seat of Virtue (as they say), for its excellence and nobility are such that without it every composition would be harsh and unbearable to hear, nor can one have any perfect harmony except by means of it" (III, xix).

12 As in the first part of the musical example at the top of p. 238 below.

or sixth taken below is greater or less than another taken above, or vice versa. Thus, since it is forbidden to use two perfect consonances of the same species one after another, we ought still less to use two imperfect ones of the same proportion, seeing that they are less consonant than the perfect.

But when two minor thirds, and similarly two major sixths, are used one after another, ascending or descending together by step, they may be tolerated, for although the major semitone is not heard in their modulations, and the thirds are naturally somewhat mournful and the sixths somewhat harsh, the slight difference that is heard in the movements of the parts gives a certain variety. For the lower part always ascends or descends by a minor tone and the upper by a major, or vice versa,[18] and this affords a certain satisfaction to the ear, the more so since the sounds of the parts stand in a harmonic relationship to one another. But when the parts move by leap we ought by no means to use two or more similar consonances one after another, ascending or descending, for apart from not observing the conditions touched on above, the sounds of the parts will not stand in a harmonic relationship to one another, as seen below:

Example of thirds   Example of sixths

Thus, to avoid the errors that may occur when it becomes necessary to take two thirds or two sixths one after another, we shall take care to take first the major and then the minor, or vice versa, taking them in whatever manner we wish, with movements by step or by leap, for everything will now agree. And we ought also to take care that, in taking the third after the sixth or the sixth after the third, we make one of them major and the other minor, as we can when there is movement in each of the parts, above and below. But when there is no movement in one or other of them, this rule cannot be observed without departing from the rules which, for the well-being of the composition, we shall give later on. Thus after the major third we shall have to take the major sixth and after the minor third the minor sixth, or vice versa, as seen in the example below:

---

18 In Zarlino's scale the minor tones are those from d to e and from g to a, all the others are major, including the tone b-flat to c.

Example of everything that has been said

We shall add that, it being forbidden to take two perfect or imperfect consonances in the way we have described, we ought also not to take two fourths in any composition whatever, as some do in certain short sections of their *canzoni* which they call *falso bordone*, for the fourth is without a doubt a perfect consonance.[14] But I shall discuss this point when I show how to compose for more than two voices.

30. WHEN THE PARTS OF A CANTILENA HAVE BETWEEN THEM A HARMONIC RELATIONSHIP, AND HOW WE MAY USE THE SEMIDIAPENTE AND THE TRITONE IN COMPOSITION

Before going on, I propose to explain what I have said above about the parts of the composition, namely, that sounds sometimes have and sometimes have not a harmonic relationship between them. It must first be understood that to say that the parts of a composition do not have between them a harmonic relationship is to say that between two consonances that two parts make one after another in singing, ascending or descending together, or ascending and descending together, there comes to be heard the augmented diapason, or the semidiapente, or the tritone. This occurs in the crossing of the first figure or note of the upper part with the second figure or note of the lower, or of the first of the lower with the second of the upper. Such a relationship, then, can occur only when we have at least four figures or notes, namely, the two lower and the two upper figures or notes of two consonances, as seen here: [a]

Augmented   Semidiapason   Semidiapente   Tritones
diapason

---

[a] But when two parts ascend together and the one or the other makes a movement which involves the semitone, it seems that because of this movement they are tolerated by the ear, as are the first cases of the augmented diapason and the semidiapente in the first and third sections of the example. [This sentence is not found in earlier editions of the *Istituzioni* and has accordingly been made a note.—Ed.]

14 III, lxi. "I am well aware that with many the authority of those who have taken this liberty

Thus, in order that our compositions may be correct and purged of every error, we shall seek to avoid these relationships as much as we can, especially when we compose for two voices, since these give rise to a certain fastidiousness in discriminating ears. For intervals like these do not occur among the sonorous numbers and are not sung in any sort of composition, even though some have held a contrary opinion. But be this as it may, they are most difficult to sing and they make a dreary effect.

And I am much astonished by those who have not hesitated at all to require the singing or modulation of these intervals in the parts of their compositions, and I cannot imagine why they have done so. And although it is not so bad to find this in the relationship between two modulations as to find it in the modulation of a single part, the same evil that was heard in the single part is now heard divided between two, and it gives the same offense to the ear. For unless the evil is diminished, little or nothing relieves the offensive nature of a fault, even though it be more offensive from one than from many.

Thus, in a composition for several voices, those intervals that are not admitted in modulation are to be so avoided that they will not be heard as relationships between the parts. This will have been done when the parts can be interchanged by means of harmonically proportioned intervals of the diatonic genus, that is, when we can ascend from the first sound of the lower part to the following sound of the upper, or vice versa, by a legitimate and singable interval. But this will not be the case when non-harmonic relationships are heard between the parts of the composition, whatever it may be, among four sounds arranged in the manner explained, for these cannot be changed unless with great disadvantage, as the intervals of the last example are changed in the example below:

Changes of the parts given above

Thus, whenever the parts of a composition or cantilena cannot be so interchanged that from this change there arises a procedure by true and legitimate singable intervals, we ought to avoid it, especially if our compositions are to be correct and purged of every error. But in composi-

---

will count more than the arguments I have put forward against it; let them do their worst by saying that what I hold in little esteem has been practised by many, for they are not capable of reason and do not wish to be."

tions for more than two voices it is often impossible to avoid such things and not to run into intricacies of this kind. For it sometimes happens that the composer will write upon a subject which repeatedly invites him to offend against this precept; thus, when necessity compels him, he will ignore it, as when he sees that the parts of his composition cannot be sung with comfort or when he wishes to adapt a consequent which may be sung with comfort, as we shall see elsewhere.[15] But when necessity compels him to offend, he ought at least to take care that he does so between diatonic steps and in steps which are natural and proper to the mode, for these do not give rise to so dreary an effect as do those which are accidental, being indicated within the composition by the signs ♮, ♯, and ♭.

Take note that I call those errors "natural" which arise in the way shown in the first example above, and that I call those "accidental" which arise when, between the true steps of the mode, there is inserted a step of another order, this step being the cause of the difficulty, as may happen in the Fifth Mode,[16] where the central step ♮ is often rejected in favor of the accidental ♭. Thus, between the ♭ and the ♮ preceding or following it, there will arise some one of the disorders in question, as seen in the first of the examples below. And this is the less agreeable since the ♮, which is the principal step of the mode, is absent from its proper place while the ♭, which is accidental, is present in its stead.

And although, for the reasons already given, we ought not to use these intervals in composition in this way, we may sometimes use the semidiapente as a single percussion if immediately after it we come to the ditone, for, as seen in the third of the examples below, the parts may be interchanged without disadvantage. This the better modern musicians observe, just as some of the more ancient observed it in the past.[17] And we are permitted to use not only the semidiapente, but in some cases the tritone also, as we shall see at the proper time. It will, however, be more advantageous to use the semidiapente than the tritone, for the consonances will then stand in their proper places, a thing which will not occur when the tritone is used. And we ought to take care that, in the parts involved, the semidiapente or tritone is immediately preceded by

15 III, lv, lxiii.
16 The Third Mode of the ecclesiastical system (Glarean's Phrygian). Having adopted Glarean's twelve modes in the earlier editions of the *Istituzioni* (1558 and 1562), by 1571, when the *Dimostrazioni* were first published, Zarlino had persuaded himself to renumber them, counting the authentic and plagal forms of the C mode as First and Second, and so forth. The various

arguments for this renumbering are set forth in the *Dimostrazioni* (V, Def. viii) and summarized by Hölger in his "Bemerkungen zu Zarlinos Theorie," *Zeitschrift für Musikwissenschaft*, IX (1926–27), 518–527. The principal argument is that, in numbering the species of any interval, the point of departure ought to be the natural scale resulting from the harmonic numbers.
17 III, lxi.

a consonance, no matter whether perfect or imperfect, for through the force of the preceding and following consonances the semidiapente comes to be tempered in such a way that, instead of making a dreary effect, it makes a good one, as experience proves and as is heard in the examples that follow.

First example   Second example   Third example

31. WHAT CONSIDERATION IS TO BE PAID TO RELATED INTERVALS IN COMPOSITIONS FOR MORE THAN TWO VOICES

Aside from this, the composer should bear in mind that, when they occur in counterpoints without being combined with other intervals, such relationships as the tritone, the semidiapente, the semidiapason, and the others that are similar to them are counted among the things in music that can afford little pleasure. Thus we should oblige ourselves not to use them in simple compositions, which (as I have said) are those for two voices, or in other compositions when two parts sing alone, for the same effects will obviously be heard in these. This is because there will not in either case be present what we have called "perfect harmony," in which a body of consonances and harmonies is heard, the extreme sounds being divided by other mean sounds; on the contrary, there will be present only what we have called "imperfect harmony," in which only two parts are heard singing together, no other sound dividing.[18] And since the sense of hearing grasps two parts more fully than three or four, we ought to vary the harmony between the two as much as we can and to take care not to use these relationships, a thing which may be done without any difficulty.

But in compositions for more than two voices this consideration is not so necessary, both because we cannot always observe it without great inconvenience, and because variety now consists not only in the changing of consonances, but also in the changing of harmonies and positions, a thing which is not true of compositions for two voices.

And I say this for this reason: just as there are ingredients in medicines and other electuaries, bitter and even poisonous in themselves, but in-

---

18 For "perfect" and "imperfect" harmony, Zarlino has "proper" and "improper," an obvious slip; cf. note 6, p. 230 above.

dubitably health-giving and less harsh when combined with other ingredients, so many things which in themselves are harsh and harmful become good and healthful when combined with others. Thus it is with these relationships in music. And there are other intervals which in themselves give little pleasure, but when combined with others make marvelous effects.

We ought, then, to consider these relationships in one way when we are about to use them simply and in another when we are about to use them in combination. For the variety of the harmony in such combinations consists not only in the variety of the consonances which occur between the parts, but also in the variety of the harmonies, which arises from the position of the sound forming the third or tenth above the lowest part of the composition. Either this is minor and the resulting harmony is ordered by or resembles the arithmetical proportion or mean, or it is major and the harmony is ordered by or resembles the harmonic.[19]

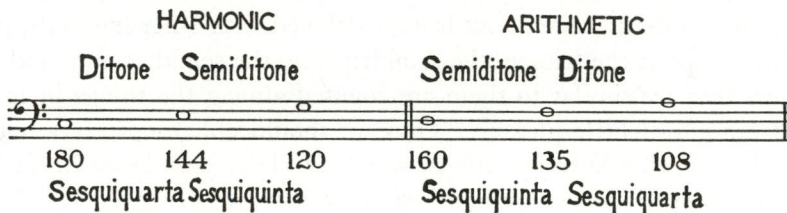

On this variety depend the whole diversity and perfection of the harmonies. For (as I shall say elsewhere) [20] in the perfect composition the fifth and third, or their extensions, must always be actively present, seeing that apart from these two consonances the ear can desire no sound that falls between their extremes or beyond them and yet is wholly distinct and different from those that lie within the extremes of these two consonances combined. For in this combination occur all the different sounds that can form different harmonies. But since the extremes of the fifth are invariable and always placed subject to the same proportion, apart from certain cases in which the fifth is used imperfectly, the extremes of the thirds are given different positions. I do not say different in proportion; I say different in position, for (as I have said elsewhere [b]) when the major third is placed below, the harmony is made joyful and when it is placed above, the harmony is made mournful. Thus, from the dif-

---

[b] Chapter 10.

[19] "Not with respect to the order of the proportions, which is actually arithmetic, but with respect to the proportions of the parts when the mean term has been interposed, for these are of the same quantity and proportion as are those produced by a harmonic mean term or divisor, although in the opposite order." (I, xv.)

[20] III, lix.

ferent positions of the thirds which are placed in counterpoint between the extremes of the fifth or above the octave, the variety of harmony arises.

If, then, we wish to vary the harmony and to observe in so far as possible the rule laid down in Chapter 29 (although this is not so necessary in compositions for more than two voices as it is in those for two) we must take the different thirds in such a way that, after first taking the major third, which forms the harmonic mean, we then take the minor, which forms the arithmetical. This we would not be able to observe so easily if we were to take the non-harmonic relationships into consideration, for while we were seeking to avoid them, we would be continuing the concentus in one division for some time without the mediation of the other; thus to no purpose we would cause the composition to sound mournful to words that carry joyfulness with them or to sound joyful to words that treat of mournful matters. I do not go so far as to say that the composer may not take two arithmetical divisions one after another, but I do say that he ought not to continue in this division for long, since to do so would make the concentus very melancholy. But to take two harmonic divisions one after another can never give offense, provided they be formed from natural steps, and with some judgment and purpose from accidental ones, for when its parts are thus arranged in order, harmony attains its ultimate end and makes its best effect.

But when two parts ascend or descend by one step or two steps we ought to use different divisions, especially when the tritone or semidiapente falls as a relationship between the two parts involved, that is, when in ascending or descending one step two major thirds are taken one after another, and when ascending or descending two steps two minor ones. But when the relationship is that of the semidiatessaron,[21] and it occurs between accidental signs, such as the ♯ and the ♭, or when only one of these signs is present, we need not avoid it at all, for the two divisions being harmonic it is obvious that they will make a good effect, even though they are not varied.

Nor need this astonish anyone, for if he will carefully examine the consonances arranged in the two orders, he will discover that the order which is arithmetical or resembles the arithmetical departs a little from the perfection of harmony, its parts being arranged out of their natural

---

21 For *semidiatessaron* (diminished fourth) we ought probably to read *diapente superflua* (augmented fifth); diminished fourths, fifths, and octaves occur as false relations between minor consonances, augmented ones between major consonances. Zarlino has already shown how the diminished fourth and augmented fifth occur as false relations in the musical example on p. 237.

Semidiatessaron   Augmented diapente

positions; on the other hand he will discover that the harmony which arises from or resembles the harmonic division is perfectly consonant, its parts being arranged and subject to the proper order of this proportion and according to the order which the sonorous numbers maintain in their natural succession, to be seen in Chapter 15 of Part I.

Let this be enough for the present; at another time, perhaps, I shall touch on this again in order that what I have said may be better understood.

·   ·   ·   ·   ·

40. THE PROCEDURE TO BE FOLLOWED IN WRITING SIMPLE COUNTERPOINTS FOR TWO VOICES, SUCH AS ARE CALLED NOTE AGAINST NOTE

To come now to the application of the rules that I have given, I shall show the procedure to be followed in writing counterpoints, beginning with those which are written simply and for two voices, note against note. From these the composer may go on to diminished counterpoints and to the usage of other compositions. Wishing then to observe what has been observed by all good writers and compilers on every other subject, I shall with reason begin with simple things, both to make the reader more submissive and to avoid confusion.

First observing what was said above in Chapter 26, the composer will choose a tenor from any plainsong he pleases, and this will be the subject of his composition, that is, of his counterpoint. Then he will examine it carefully and will see in what mode it is composed, so that he may make the appropriate cadences in their proper places and may know from these the nature of his composition. For if inadvertently he were to make these inappropriately and out of their places, mixing those of one mode with those of another, the end of his composition would come to be dissonant with the beginning and the middle.

But assuming that the chosen subject is the plainsong tenor given below, which is subject to the Third Mode,[22] he will above all else observe what was said in Chapter 28 above about the procedure in beginning a composition. Thus we shall place the first figure or note of our counterpoint at such an interval from the first of the subject that they will have between them one of the perfect consonances. This done, we shall combine the second note of our counterpoint with the second of the subject in a consonance, either perfect or imperfect, but in any case different from the preceding one, so that we shall not be offending against what

---

[22] The First Mode of the ecclesiastical system (Glarean's Dorian).

was said in Chapter 29, always having an eye to what was laid down in Chapter 38 [23] and observing the teaching of Chapter 37,[24] taking care that the parts of the composition are as conjunct as possible and that they make no large leaps, so that the interval between them will not be too great. This done, we shall come to the third figure or note of our counterpoint and combine it with the third of the subject, varying not only the steps or positions but also the consonances, taking perfect consonance after imperfect, or vice versa, or taking one after another two perfect consonances or two imperfect ones different in species, according to the rules given in Chapter 33 [25] and 34.[26] We shall do the same with the fourth note of our counterpoint and the fourth of the subject, and with the fifth, the sixth, and the others in order until we come to the end, where, following the rule given in the preceding chapter, we shall conclude our counterpoint with one of the perfect consonances.

But above all else we must take care that the contrapuntal part is not only varied in its different movements, touching different steps, now high, now low, and now intermediate, but that it is varied also in its consonances with the subject. And we should see to it that the contrapuntal part sings well and proceeds in so far as possible by step, since there lies in this a part of the beauty of counterpoint. And added to the many other things that one may ask (as we shall see), this will bring it to its perfection.

Thus he who will first exercise himself in this simple manner of composing may afterwards go on easily and quickly to greater things. For seeking to write various counterpoints and compositions upon a single subject, now below and now above, he will make himself thoroughly familiar with the steps and with the intervals of each consonance; then, following the precepts which I am about to give, he will be able to go on to the diminution of the figures, that is, to diminished counterpoint, writing the contrapuntal parts sometimes in consequence with his subject and sometimes imitating them or writing them in other ways, as we shall see; and from this he will be able to go on to compositions for more voices, so that, aided by our directions and by his own talents, he will in a short time become a good composer.

Take note, however, that in laying down a rule governing the procedure to be followed in writing a counterpoint upon a subject, I do

---

[23] How we ought to proceed from one consonance to another.

[24] That we ought to avoid as much as we can those movements that are made by leap, and in a similar way those distances that may occur between the parts of a composition.

[25] When two or more perfect or imperfect consonances, subject to different forms and taken one immediately after another, are conceded.

[26] That we do well to take imperfect consonance after perfect, or vice versa.

so, not in particular, but in general. Thus, with those rules which have been given before, the composer must use intelligence in deriving the counterpoint and must work with judgment, and in acquiring this, rules and precepts will have little value unless nature has aided him. Nor need this astonish him at all, seeing that it is true of every art and of every teaching.

For all who have sought to give instruction and to teach any art or science have always laid down general principles, seeing that science has to do, not with particulars, which are innumerable, but with general principles. This we see in the precepts of poetry and of oratory, as set down by Plato, Aristotle, Hermogenes, Demetrius Phalerius, Cicero, Quintilian, Horace, and others besides; these deal with the general and not with the particular. To give an example, I recall what Horace says, speaking in general of the order that poets are to follow in arranging their subject, which is history or fable, in the epic:

> Ordinis haec virtus erit et venus, aut ego fallor,
> Ut iam nunc dicat iam nunc debentia dici,
> Pleraque differat et praesens in tempus omittat.[c]

This rule was most familiar to the learned Virgil, as we shall see. For having chosen a particular subject, which was to describe the fall and burning of Troy and the voyage of Aeneas, he began at once with the voyage, interrupting the order, for the voyage came afterwards. But he understood that his poem would gain in art and in majesty if he were to cause the story to be told by Aeneas in Dido's presence, as he did, taking his occasion from the fortunes that had brought Aeneas to her in Carthage.[d] Such is the custom of the poets, and not only of the poets but also of the painters; these adapt history or fable as may best suit their purpose, for painting is simply silent poetry. Thus the painter, having once undertaken to depict a history or fable, adapts the figures and arranges them in his composition as they seem to him to stand best or to make the best effect, nor does he hesitate to place one of them rather in this way than in that—that is, to cause one of them to stand or to sit rather in one way than in another—as long as he observes the order of the history or fable which he is seeking to represent. And one sees that, although innumerable painters have depicted a single subject in innumerable manners, as I have often seen depicted the story of Roman Lucretia, the wife of Collatinus, the story of Horatius Cocles, and many others, all have had a single aim—that of representing the story. And

---

c *Ars poetica*, 42–44. ["Of order, this, if I mistake not, will be the excellence and charm: to say at the moment what at that moment should be said, reserving and omitting much for the present."—Fairclough]

d *Aeneid*, II.

one sees this done, not only by various painters of a single subject, but also by the single painter who has depicted a single subject in various ways.

Thus the musician must also seek to vary his counterpoint upon the subject, and if he can invent many passages he will choose the one that is best, most suited to his purpose, and most capable of making his counterpoint sonorous and orderly; the others he will set aside. And when he has invented a passage such as might be appropriate for a cadence, if it is not at the moment to his purpose he will reserve it for some other more suitable place. This he will do if the clause or period in the words or speech has not come to an end, for he must always wait until each of these is finished; in a similar way he will take care that it is in the proper place and that the mode in which his composition stands requires it.

He who wishes to begin in the right way with the art of counterpoint must observe all these things. But above everything else he must industriously exercise himself in this sort of composition in order that he may thus arrive more easily at the practice of diminished counterpoint, in which, as we shall see later on, there are many other things that he may use. And in order that he may have some understanding of all that I have said, I shall give below some varied counterpoints, note against note, upon the subject already mentioned; once he has examined these, he will readily understand the things that I shall show later on [27] and will be able to work with greater ease.

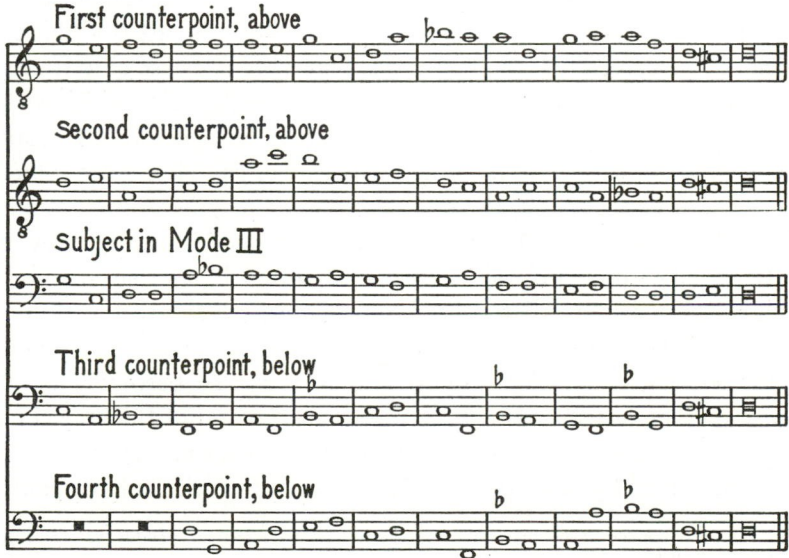

---

27 III, xlii–xliv.

Be advised, however, that to write counterpoint, note against note, appears to be and actually is somewhat more difficult than to write it diminished, for the one has not that liberty which the other has, seeing that in the one each note or figure may have one consonance only, while in the other it may have many of them, blended with dissonances according to the composer's pleasure and good judgment. Thus in the first sort the composer cannot at his pleasure arrange the parts so well that they will be without leaps, especially if he wishes to write upon a single subject many counterpoints which will be different throughout. But this need not discourage him, for if the root tastes somewhat bitter, he will before long enjoy the fruits which spring from it, and these are sweet, luscious, and palatable. Thus virtue (as the wise affirm) has to do with the difficult and not with the easy.

.   .   .   .   .

71. ON THE BENEFIT WHICH GOOD HARMONIES DERIVE FROM THE ACCIDENTS ENUMERATED

And now, before going further, let us determine to what extent good and sonorous harmonies derive benefit from the accidents enumerated.[28] And adopting a somewhat lofty manner of speaking for the sake of greater clarity: if the true object of sensation is the body which moves it through the mediation of the sensory organ, it must be understood that, in so far as we consider such bodies according to the different reasons of their movements, we must necessarily postulate in sensation different powers. For considered in so far as it may be seen, an object is called visible and may not be perceived by any other sense than vision. These objects are in fact of two sorts, for they are either primary, as is the color which we see before anything else, or they are commensurate (or shall we say proportionate), and not color, and inherent in many things that are not colored, such as the fire, the moon, the sun, the stars, and other similar things. Indeed these objects have for this reason no proper name; they are simply called visible, and this includes all those things that are visible through light, such as all the luminous bodies, which are those that I have named above. In so far as an object may be heard, as are the voices and the sounds, it is called audible and may not be perceived by any other sense than hearing. The same might also be said of the other kinds of objects. Such objects are called sensible particulars, since no one of them may be perceived by more than one of the senses which we have named.

---

28 In III, lxvii–lxx, on mode, time, prolation, perfection, imperfection, and the various species and effects of the point or dot.

To be sure, there are certain objects which are called common and which may be perceived by several senses; thus movement, rest, number, shape, and size may manifestly be seen, heard, and touched. Then there are certain other objects which are sensible by accident and which may not be perceived except through the mediation of something else; such are the sonorous bodies, which cannot be heard except through the mediation of the sound which is made in the air, as I have shown in Part II.[e]

The more pleasing and sweet these objects are to their particular sense, the more they are proportioned to it, and vice versa; thus the eye, looking at the sun, is offended, for this object is not proportioned to it. And what the philosophers say is true—that excess in the sensible object, if it does not corrupt the sense, at least corrupts the instrument.[f]

If, then, the particular sensible objects may not be perceived or judged by any other sense than that peculiar to them, as sound is by hearing, as color is by vision, and as the others are in order, let those who strive so hard and take such pains to introduce these intricacies into their compositions tell me (if they will) what and how much pleasure and benefit these may afford to the sense and whether these compositions of theirs are more beautiful and more sonorous than those that do not have such things, which are exclusively visible and fall under no other sense than vision and may not be heard in any way, since they are not common objects, perceptible to several senses, as were those mentioned above. If they have judgment, I know that they will reply that these things afford no benefit at all, for when they have been reduced to simple, ordinary notation and stripped of their ciphers, whatever and however great the harmony heard before, such and as great will be the harmony heard afterward. If, then, they are of no benefit at all in the formation of good harmonies, and if they afford no benefit at all to the sense, why to no purpose multiply the singer's duties and augment his vexations with things of this kind? For when he ought to be intent on singing cheerfully such compositions as are to the purpose, he must stand ready to consider chimeras of this sort, falling (according to the various accidents) under mode, time, and prolation, and he must allow nothing written to pass until he has examined it closely, seeing that if he does otherwise he will be thought (if I may say so) an awkward fellow and an ignoramus. And if these things afford no benefit, as they in truth do not, it seems to me sheer madness that anyone of lofty intelligence should have to end his studies and to waste his time and to vex himself about such irrelevant matters. Thus I counsel everyone to disregard these ciphers

---

e Chapter 10.   f Aristotle, *De anima*, 424A, 435B.

and to give his attention rather to those things that are productive of good harmonies and sweet ones.

Perhaps someone will say: "Is it not a fine thing to see a tenor well ordered under the signs of mode, time, and prolation, as contrived by the ancient musicians, who gave their attention to almost nothing else?"

It is indeed a fine thing, especially when it is written or painted, and miniatured too, by the hand of an outstanding scribe and miniaturist, using good inks, fine colors, and proportioned measures, and when (as I have seen) there is added to it a coat of arms, a miter, or a cardinal's hat, together with some other splendid object. But of what importance is this if a composition having a tenor written simply and without any intricacy is just as sonorous or as graceless as though it were full of such things?

Thus one may say with truth that this way of composing is simply an unnecessary multiplying of difficulty, and not a multiplying of harmony, and that it affords no benefit at all, since, as the philosophers hold, things are vainly multiplied when there is no purpose. For music, being the science which treats of the sounds and the voices, which are the particular objects of hearing, contemplates only the concord which arises from the strings and the voices (as Ammonius says [g]) and considers nothing else. Thus it seems to me that everything in music that is contemplative without being directed toward this end is vain and useless. For since music was indeed discovered to improve and to delight, as we have said at other times,[h] nothing in music has validity except the voices and the sounds which arise from the strings. These, as Aurelius Cassiodorus imagines, are so named because they move our hearts, a thing he shows most elegantly with the two Latin words *chordae* and *corda*.[i] Thus it is by this path that we perceive the improvement and delight that we derive from hearing harmonies and melodies.

From what has been said we may conclude, then, that this way of composing is not only useless but also harmful, as a loss of time, more precious than anything else, and that the points, lines, circles, semicircles, and other similar things depicted on the page are subject to the sense of vision and not to that of hearing, and that these are matters considered by the geometer, while the sounds and the voices (being in truth the particular objects of hearing) are matters primarily considered by the musician, although he incidentally considers many others.

---

g *In Praedicamentis.*
h I, iii.

i *Variae*, II, xl (Ad Boetium patricium).

Here, perhaps, someone will wish to reprehend and censure me, seeing that many learned and most celebrated ancient musicians, whose fame still lives among us, have practiced this way of composing and that I now wish to censure them.

To this I reply that if these critics will consider the matter, they will find that those compositions that are wrapped round with such restraints afford no greater benefit than they would if they were bare and plain, without any difficulty at all, and they will see that they complain with little reason, and they will understand that they themselves are to be censured, as persons opposed to truth. For although the ancients followed this fashion, they were well aware that such accidents can afford no augmentation or diminution of the harmony. But they practiced such things to show that they were not ignorant of the speculations put forward by certain idle theorists of that day, seeing that the contemplative part of the science then consisted rather in the contemplation of accidents of this sort than in the contemplation of the sounds, the voices, and the other things discussed in Parts I and II of these my labors.

And of this we have the testimony of many books, written by various authors; these treat of nothing but circles and semicircles, with and without points, whole or divided not only once but two and three times, and in them one sees so many points, pauses, colors, ciphers, signs, numbers against numbers, and other strange things that they sometimes appear to be the books of a bewildered merchant. Nor does one read in these books anything that might lead to the understanding of anything subject to the judgment of the sense of hearing, as are the voices and sounds from which the harmonies and melodies arise; they treat only of the things that we have named. And although the fame of some of these musicians still lives honorably among us, they have acquired their reputation, not with such chimeras, but with the good harmonies, the harmonious concentus, and the beautiful inventions which are seen and heard in their works. And although they disordered these with their intricacies, they obliged themselves also, if not through speculation, at least with the aid of practice and their judgment, to reduce their harmonies to the ultimate perfection they could give them, even if the matter was misunderstood and abused by many others, as the many errors committed by the practical musicians in their works bear witness.

Then as to the rational, that is, speculative part, we see that there were few who kept to the good road, for apart from what Boethius wrote in Latin about our science, and this too we find imperfect, there has been no one (leaving Franchino [29] and Faber Stapulensis [30] to one side, for one may say that they were commentators on Boethius) who has gone further in speculating on things pertaining to music, discovering the true proportions of the musical intervals, except Lodovico Fogliano [31] of Modena,[j] who having perhaps considered what Ptolemy left written on the syntonic diatonic,[32] spared no pains in writing a Latin book on this branch of the science, showing as well as he could the true proportions of the intervals involved. The rest of the theoretical musicians, clinging to what Boethius wrote of these matters, did not wish or were not able to go further and gave themselves over to describing the things that we have named; these they made subject to the quantitative genus, as they called it, under which come mode, time, and prolation, as may be seen in the *Recaneto di musica*,[33] the *Toscanello*,[34] the *Scintille*,[35] and a thousand other similar books.

Besides this there are also conflicting opinions on these questions and long disputations, of which there is no end, then many tracts, invectives, and apologies, written by certain musicians against certain others, in which (although one reads them a thousand times), having read, reread, and examined them, one finds nothing but the innumerable villanies and slanders which they immodestly address to one another (O what shame!) and in the end so little good that one is dumbfounded.

But we may in truth excuse these writers. There were sophists in those days, just as there were sophists in the time of Socrates and Plato, and they were as much esteemed, and this quantitative genus of theirs (one may truly call it an *Arte sofistica* in music and its musicians sophists) was as much practiced in its time as was sophistry in the time of the philosophers in question. Thus we ought continually to praise God and to thank Him that little by little (I know not how) this thing is almost spent and extinct and that He has put us into an age concerned only

---

[j] A note for the malicious. [This note, which does not appear in the earlier editions of the *Istituzioni*, is aimed at Vincenzo Galilei, who in his *Dialogo della musica antica e della moderna* (Florence, 1581), accuses Zarlino of appropriating Fogliano's ideas without giving him credit for them. Zarlino's defense may be seen in his *Sopplimenti*, III, ii.—Ed.]

[29] Zarlino refers here to Franchino Gafori's *Theoricum opus armonice discipline* (Naples, 1480).

[30] *Musica libris quatuor demonstrata* (Paris, 1496).

[31] *Musica theorica* (Venice, 1529); for a summary of Fogliano's contribution see Riemann,

Geschichte der Musiktheorie, 2d ed. (Berlin, 1920), pp. 334–336.

[32] In the syntonic diatonic of Ptolemy, the tetrachords of the Greater Perfect System are divided in the proportions 16:15, 9:8, 10:9. One of Zarlino's principal theses is that this division is the natural and inevitable one and the one actually used in the practical vocal music of his time.

[33] The *Recanetum de musica aurea*, by Stefano Vanneo (Rome, 1533).

[34] The *Toscanello in musica*, by Pietro Aron (Venice, 1523).

[35] The *Scintille, di musica* by G. M. Lanfranco (Brescia, 1533).

with the multiplying of good concentus and good melodies, the true end
toward which the musician ought to direct his every work.

. . . . .

Book Four

30. HOW THE MODES ARE TO BE JUDGED AND WHAT IS TO
BE OBSERVED IN COMPOSING IN THEM

Take note, to begin with, that although we have an almost infinite
number of compositions in each of the modes that have been discussed,
there are many that are written, not in the simple modes, but in the
mixed ones.[36] Thus we find the Fifth Mode mixed with the Twelfth,[37]
the Tenth with the First,[38] and so on with the others. An examination
of such compositions will make this clear, especially if we examine those
of the Fifth Mode that below, instead of the third species of the diapente,
E to ♮, have the third of the diatessaron, E to a, and that above, instead
of the third species of the diatessaron, ♮ to e, have the second of the
diapente, a to e, so that although the species lie within the same diapason,
E to e, one of the modes is harmonically divided and maintains the
form of the Fifth, while the other is arithmetically divided and maintains the form of the Twelfth. And since the species of the Twelfth Mode
are heard repeated over and over again, not only does the greater part
of the composition lose all relation to the Fifth Mode, but the whole
becomes subject to the Twelfth.

And that this is true will be clear from the following: when we combine these two species, the diatessaron E to a and the diapente a to e,
placing the former below and the latter above, we have without a doubt
the form of the Twelfth Mode, lying within the third species of the
diapason arithmetically divided; thus a composition that we judge to
be of the Fifth Mode comes to have nothing by which we might judge
that it is of the Fifth unless it is its ending on E, which is a most deceptive
thing. For although some would have us judge a composition by its
final (as by its end and not by what precedes it), seeing that everything
is rightly judged by or in its end, it does not follow from this that we
may come to recognize the mode on which a composition is based by this
alone. Thus we ought to believe, not that we may judge by this alone,
but that we must wait until the composition has reached its end and there

36 In IV, xiv, Zarlino defines a mixed mode
as one in which a fifth or fourth belonging to
another mode is heard often repeated.

37 Glarean's Phrygian and Hypoaeolian.
38 Glarean's Hypomixolydian and Ionian.

judge it rightly, that is, by its form, for the composition is then complete and has its form, which is the occasion of our judgment. Note, however, that this has two occasions: one is the form of the composition as a whole; the other is its end, that is, its final. But since form is that which gives being to a thing, it seems reasonable to me that our judgment should be based on the form of the whole and not, as some have wished, on the final alone.

And if a composition is to be judged from its form, that is, from its procedure, as is the obligation, it is not inconsistent that, rejecting the final, a principal mode may conclude on the central step of its diapason, harmonically divided, and in a similar way a collateral mode at either extreme of its diapason, arithmetically divided. How elegantly this can be done may be seen in the motet "Si bona suscepimus," composed for five voices by Verdelot,[39] and in the madrigal "O invidia nemica di virtute," likewise composed to be sung with five voices by Adriano; [40] although these have from beginning to end the procedure of the Eleventh Mode in the one case and of the Fourth in the other, they conclude, not on their true finals, but on their central steps.[41]

And what I say of the Fifth and Twelfth Modes is also true of the others which, for brevity's sake, I omit. Thus we should not be astonished if we often hear no difference between a composition ending on E and one ending on a, for they are written in mixed modes in the manner we have described; if they were composed in the simple ones there is no doubt that we would hear a great difference in harmony between them.

Thus in judging any composition, whatever it may be, we have to consider it most carefully from beginning to end and to determine the form in which it is written, whether in that of the First, or of the Second, or of some other mode, having an eye to the cadences, which throw a great light on this question; then we may judge it even though it concludes, not on its proper final, but on its central step or on some other that may prove to the purpose.

Nor is it inconsistent that we use this way of ending in our compositions, seeing that the ecclesiastics have used it also in their chants. This may be seen at the end of the Kyrie eleison called "For semidoubles" or "Of the apostles"; [42] although this clearly has the form of the Third Mode, it ends on a, the confinal, as they call it, and the central step of

---

39 *Motetti del fiore a 5*, II (Lyons, 1532), No. 18; reprinted by Maldeghem in his *Trésor musical, Musique religieuse*, 1892, pp. 8 ff.

40 *Musica nova di Adriano Willaert* (Venice, 1559), No. 24.

41 In other words, the motet by Verdelot is Aeolian, not Phrygian, while the madrigal by Willaert is Hypodorian, not Aeolian.

42 *Grad. Rom.*, p. 15*. (Cunctipotens Genitor Deus).

the diapason D to d within which the form of this mode lies. Then there is the offertory "Domine fac mecum," [43] from the mass for the Wednesday after the third Sunday in Lent, which lies between the extremes F and e; besides this there are two other chants: one is "Tollite hostias," [44] sung after the communion of the mass for the eighteenth Sunday after Pentecost, which lies between the extremes just mentioned; the other is "Per signum crucis," [45] sung on the solemn feasts of the Finding and Exaltation of the Holy Cross, which lies between the extremes F and g. These chants have the form of the Ninth Mode, for they contain the modulation of its diapente, G to d, and of its diatessaron, d to g; they conclude on ♮, the central step of the diapente. It is quite true that in the opinion of certain moderns [46] they are to be attributed to the Fourteenth, but I leave this to the judgment of anyone of intelligence. In some of the modern books these chants are found transposed, without ♭, from their natural position to the diapente below, either through the ignorance or carelessness of the copyists or through the arrogance of persons of little understanding. But in the good and correct copies, of which I have beside me an old one, written by hand, which may still be seen and examined, they lie between the extremes named above.

Note that what I call the form of the mode is the octave divided into its fifth and fourth, and that these two parts, arising from harmonic or arithmetic division, are heard repeated many times in their proper modes. Thus, when we compose, we may know what is to guide us in leading the parts of our composition and in putting the cadences at places suitable for the distinction of the words; as has been said, it is the mode. And in a similar way we may know how to proceed in judging a composition of any kind, whether plainsong or figured music.

* * * * *

32. HOW THE HARMONIES ARE ADAPTED TO THE WORDS PLACED BENEATH THEM

Seeing that the time and place require it, it now remains to be determined how one ought to combine the harmonies with the words placed beneath them. I say "to combine the harmonies with the words" for this reason: although (following Plato's opinion) we have said in

43 *Ibid.*, pp. 133–134.
44 *Ibid.*, pp. 374–375.
45 *Ibid.*, p. 492.
46 Namely Glarean (*Dodecachordon*, II, xxv,

III, xxi; Bohn's translation, pp. 101–102, 303–305), from whom Zarlino borrows all the examples of this paragraph.

Part II [47] that melody is a combination of speech, harmony, and rhythm,[k] and although it seems that in such a combination no one of these things is prior to another, Plato gives speech the first place and makes the other two parts subservient to it, for after he has shown the whole by means of the parts, he says that harmony and rhythm ought to follow speech. And this is the obligation. For if in speech, whether by way of narrative or of imitation (and these occur in speech), matters may be treated that are joyful or mournful, and grave or without gravity, and again modest or lascivious, we must also make a choice of a harmony and a rhythm similar to the nature of the matters contained in the speech in order that from the combination of these things, put together with proportion, may result a melody suited to the purpose.

We ought indeed to listen to what Horace says in his epistle on the *Art of Poetry:*

Versibus exponi tragicis res comica non volt; [48]

and to what Ovid says in this connection:

Callimachi numeris non est dicendus Achilles;
Cydippe non est oris, Homere, tui.[1]

For if the poet is not permitted to write a comedy in tragic verse, the musician will also not be permitted to combine unsuitably these two things, namely, harmony and words.[49] Thus it will be inappropriate if in a joyful matter he uses a mournful harmony and a grave rhythm, nor where funereal and tearful matters are treated is he permitted to use a joyful harmony and a rhythm that is light or rapid, call it as we will. On the contrary, he must use joyful harmonies and rapid rhythms in joyful matters, and in mournful ones, mournful harmonies and grave rhythms, so that everything may be done with proportion.

He who has studied what I have written in Part III and has considered the nature of the mode in which he wishes to write his composition will, I think, know precisely how to do this. In so far as he can, he must take

---

k *Republic,* III. [Page 4 above. Ambros, in his *Geschichte der Musik,* III, 3d ed. (Leipzig, 1893), 163, calls attention to an earlier sixteenth-century reference to this passage in the foreword by Johannes Ott to the *Missae tredecim* (Nuremberg, 1539): "Thus we see that learned musicians have diligently followed the rule that, in Plato, Socrates lays down for melodies: that the musician ought to make the melody follow the words, and not the words the melody. For since the greatest gravity resides in these words of the church, the composers clothe the musical sounds with a becoming gravity."—Ed.]

1 *Remediorum amoris,* 381–382. ["Achilles must not be told of in the numbers of Callimachus; Cydippe suits not thy utterance, Homer."—Mozley]

47 Chapter 12.

48 Line 89. "A theme for Comedy refuses to be set forth in the verses of Tragedy." [Fairclough]

49 The "Rules to be observed in dittying" given by Morley on pages 177 and 178 of his *Plain and Easy Introduction* (London, 1597) are in effect an abridged translation of the remainder of this chapter.

care to accompany each word in such a way that, if it denotes harshness, hardness, cruelty, bitterness, and other things of this sort, the harmony will be similar, that is, somewhat hard and harsh, but so that it does not offend. In the same way, if any word expresses complaint, grief, affliction, sighs, tears, and other things of this sort, the harmony will be full of sadness.[m]

Wishing to express effects of the first sort, he will do best to accustom himself to arrange the parts of his composition so that they proceed with such movements as are without the semitone, as are those of the tone and ditone, allowing the major sixth or thirteenth, which are naturally somewhat harsh, to be heard above the lowest tone of the concentus, and accompanying these with the syncope of the fourth or eleventh above this same tone, using rather slow movements; with these he may use the syncope of the seventh. But wishing to express effects of the second sort, he will use (always observing the rules that have been given) such movements as proceed by the semitone or semiditone or in some other similar way, often taking above the lowest tone of his composition the minor sixth or thirteenth, which are naturally soft and sweet, especially when they are combined in the right ways and with discretion and judgment.

Note, however, that the expression of these effects is to be attributed not only to the consonances that we have named, used as we have directed, but also to the movements that the parts make in singing, which are of two sorts—natural and accidental. The natural movements are those made between the natural steps of the music, where no sign or accidental step intervenes, and these have more virility than those made by means of the accidental steps, marked with the signs ♯ and ♭, which are indeed accidental and somewhat languid. In the same way there arises from the accidental movements a sort of interval called accidental, while from the natural movements arise the intervals called natural. We ought then to bear in mind that the natural movements make the music somewhat more sonorous and virile, while the accidental ones make it softer and somewhat more languid. Thus the natural movements may serve to express effects of our first sort, and the accidental ones may serve for the rest, so that combining with some judgment the intervals of the major and minor consonances and the natural and accidental movements, we will succeed in imitating the words with a thoroughly suitable harmony.

m Even though this be censured by some of our modern Aristarchs. [Namely, Vincenzo Galilei. See pages 88 and 89 of his *Dialogo della musica antica e della moderna* (pp. 315–316 below).—Ed.] But as to this, see Chapter 11 of Book VIII of our *Supplements*.

Then as to the observance of the rhythms, the primary consideration is the matter contained in the words: if this is joyful, we ought to proceed with swift and vigorous movements, that is, with figures carrying swiftness, such as the minim and semiminim; if it is mournful, we ought to proceed with slow and lingering movements.

Thus Adriano has taught us to express the one sort and the other in many compositions, among them "I vidi in terra angelici costumi," "Aspro core e selvaggio," and "Ove ch'i posi gli occhi," all written for six voices, "Quando fra l'altre donne" and "Giunto m'ha Amor" for five voices,[50] and innumerable others.

And although the ancients understood rhythms in another way than the moderns do, as is clear from many passages in Plato, we ought not only to keep this consideration in mind but also to take care that we adapt the words of the speech to the musical figures in such a way and with such rhythms that nothing barbarous is heard, not making short syllables long and long syllables short as is done every day in innumerable compositions, a truly shameful thing.[n] Nor do we find this vice only in figured music but, as is obvious to every man of judgment, in plainsong also, for there are few chants that are not filled with barbarous things of this kind. Thus over and over again we hear length given to the penultimate syllables of such words as *Dóminus, Angélus, Fílius, miráculum, glória*, and many others, syllables which are properly short and fleeting. To correct this would be a most praiseworthy undertaking and an easy one, for by changing it a very little, one would make the chant most suitable, nor would this change its original form, since this consists solely of many figures or notes in ligature, placed under the short syllables in question and inappropriately making them long when a single figure would suffice.

In a similar way we ought to take care not to separate the parts of the speech from one another with rests, so long as a clause, or any part of it, is incomplete and the sense of the words imperfect, a thing done by some of little intelligence, and unless a period is complete and the sense of the words perfect we ought not to make a cadence, especially one of the principal ones, or to use a rest larger than that of the minim, nor should the rest of the minim be used within the intermediate points. For this is in truth a vicious thing, and for all that it is practiced by some little re-

---

n But as to this, what has been said in Chapter 13 of Book VIII of our *Supplements* [On the three sorts of accents: grammatical, rhetorical, and musical.—Ed.] ought by all means to be carefully considered, so that all may go well and no error be committed.

50 *Musica nova di Adriano Willaert* (Venice, 1559), nos. 38, 33, 39, 26, and 30.

pentent practical musicians of our time, anyone inclined to heed the matter may easily observe and understand it.

Thus, since the matter is of great importance, the composer ought to open his eyes and not keep them closed so that he may not be thought ignorant of a thing so necessary, and he ought to take care to use the rest of the minim or semiminim (whichever suits his purpose) at the head of the intermediate points of the speech, for these have the force of commas, while at the head of the periods he may use whatever quantity of rest he chooses, for it seems to me that when the rests are used in this manner one may best distinguish the members of the period from one another and without any difficulty hear the perfect sense of the words.

33. THE PROCEDURE TO BE FOLLOWED IN PLACING THE MUSICAL FIGURES UNDER THE WORDS

Who will ever be able to recite, unless with great difficulty, the disorder and the inelegance that many practical musicians support and have supported and the confusion that they have caused in suitably adapting the musical figures to the words of the speech? When I reflect that a science that has brought law and good order to other things is in this respect so disorderly that it is barely tolerable, I cannot help complaining, for some compositions are indeed dumbfounding to hear and to see. It is not only that in the declamation of the words one hears confused periods, incomplete clauses, unsuitable cadences, singing without order, innumerable errors in applying the harmonies to the words, little regard for mode, badly accommodated parts, passages without beauty, rhythms without proportion, movements without purpose, figures badly numbered in time and prolation, and a thousand other disorders; one also finds the musical figures so adapted to the words that the singer cannot determine or discover a suitable way of performing them. Now he sees two syllables under many figures, now under two figures many syllables. Now he hears the singer of another part who, at some point where the words require it, uses the apostrophe or elides the vowels; wishing to do the same in his part, he succeeds in missing the beautiful and elegant manner of singing and in putting a figure that carries length under a short syllable, or vice versa. Now he hears the singers of the other parts make a syllable long which in his must necessarily be short. Thus, hearing all this diversity, he does not know what to do and remains thoroughly bewildered and confused.

And since the whole consists in adapting the musical figures to the words beneath them, and since in composition it is required that the musical figures be used to mark and note the pitches so that the sounds and the voices may be properly performed in every modulation; and seeing that it is by means of such figures that we perform the rhythm, that is, the length and brevity of the syllables of the speech, and that over these syllables there are often put, not one, two, or three, but even more such figures, as may be required by the accents suitably arranged in the speech; therefore, in order that no confusion may arise in adapting the figures to the syllables and to the words, and wishing (if I can) to end all this disorder; to the many rules I have already given in various places in accordance with the requirements of my materials, I now add these, which will serve both the composer and the singer and will at the same time be to my purpose.

1. A suitable figure is to be placed below each long or short syllable so that nothing barbarous will be heard. For in figured music each musical figure that stands alone and is not in ligature (apart from the semiminim and all those that are smaller than the semiminim) carries its own syllable with it. This rule is observed in plainsong also, for to each square figure is adapted a syllable of its own, excepting for the middle notes, which are sometimes treated like minims or even semiminims, as may be seen in many chants, especially in the chant for the Nicene Creed, "Credo in unum Deum," which they call the Credo cardinale.[51]

2. Not more than one syllable, and that at the beginning, is to be adapted to each ligature of several notes or figures, whether in figured music or in plainsong.

3. No syllable is to be adapted to the dot placed after the figures of figured music, although this is sung.

4. It is not usual to place a syllable below a semiminim, or below those figures that are smaller than the semiminim, or below the figure immediately following.

5. It is not customary to place any syllable below the figures immediately following a dotted semibreve or dotted minim, when these following figures are valued at less than the dots, as are semiminims after a dotted semibreve or chromas after a dotted minim; the same is true of the figures that immediately follow these.

6. Should it be necessary to place a syllable below a semiminim, one may also place another syllable below the figure following.

7. At the beginning of a composition, or after any rest in the middle, the first figure, whatever it may be, must necessarily carry with it a syllable.

8. In plainsong no word or syllable is ever repeated, although one some-

---

51 *Grad. Rom.*, pp. 67*–69* (Credo IV).

times hears this done, a thing indeed to be censured; in figured music such repetitions are sometimes tolerated—not of a syllable or of a word, but of some part of the speech whose sense is complete. This may be done when there are figures in such quantity that words may be repeated conveniently. But to repeat a thing many times over does not, in my opinion, go over well, unless it be done to give greater emphasis to words that have in them some grave sense and are worthy of consideration.

9. When all the syllables of a period or of one part of the speech have been adapted to the musical figures and there remain only the penultimate syllable and the last, the penultimate syllable will have the privilege of bearing a number of small figures—two, three, or some other quantity—provided, however, that it be long and not short, for if it were short a barbarism would occur. Singing in this way, there arises what many call a *neuma,* which occurs when many figures are sung above a single syllable. But when figures are placed in this way, they offend against our first rule.

10. The final syllable of the speech will fall below the final figure of the composition, if our rules are observed.

Seeing that the reader will find innumerable examples of all these things if he will examine the learned works of Adriano and of those who have been and are his disciples and observers of the good rules, I shall go on without giving further examples to the discussion of the ligatures formed from certain of the musical figures, for these are useful in this connection.

28. Pietro Cerone

An Italian writer for Spanish readers, Pietro Cerone was born in Bergamo, probably in the 1560's; in 1592 he visited Spain, where he later became a musician of the royal chapel, serving under Philip II and, after 1598, under his successor, Philip III. By 1609 he had returned to Italy; in this year he published a little treatise on plainsong in which he described himself as a musician of the royal chapel in Naples and informed his readers that a more extensive work of his, *El melopeo y maestro*, was about to appear. The book was not actually published until 1613.

El melopeo, which runs to 22 "books," 849 chapters, and 1,160 pages, is an undigested and often indigestible mass of information and misinformation about music, some of it useful, much of it useless. For its time it is distinctly conservative, even old-fashioned: it shows little understanding for Marenzio, and the names of Monteverdi and Marco da Gagliano are not so much as mentioned. Its tasteless pedantry was ridiculed with devastating effect by the eighteenth-century critic Antonio Eximeno, who called it "a musical monster" and, in his satiric novel *Don Lazarillo Vizcardi* (1802), treated it much as Cervantes had treated the romances of chivalry. Other critics have commended it for its sound musicianship, its admirable choice of examples, and its enlightening observations, such as those on the nature and meaning of the two- and three-part interludes of the sixteenth-century Mass and Magnificat, translated below. Neither verdict tells the whole story. The book is uneven and requires a discriminating reader; it has grave defects, but it also has redeeming merits.

From El melopeo y maestro [1]
[1613]

Book XII

12. THE MANNER TO BE OBSERVED IN COMPOSING A MOTET

You HAVE seen how many directions and how many considerations the contrapuntist, and still more the composer, must observe, both as regards the correct manner of singing and the greater convenience and ease of the singer and as regards what is proper to the workmanship. To be sure, one can neither give nor enumerate exactly all the directions which commonly occur in compositions. But those that I have mentioned are at least of such a nature and number that an elaborate composition may be written with fewer errors and fewer faults than some of those that one hears sung today in churches and in musical exercises. Apart from the aforesaid general directions I shall now give particular ones which will serve to order any kind of composition whatever in accordance with its proper style and in conformity with the true manner and with what has been observed by famous musicians.

When he wishes to write a motet, then, the composer must see to it that the voices sing with continual gravity and majesty, particularly the bass part, preserving this order in the parts from beginning to end, even though we see it disregarded in these times, particularly by those of my nation. These musicians dispose the lively parts and divisions in such a way that their compositions seem to be madrigals and sometimes canzonets; instead of the syncopated semibreve, they use the syncopated minim, suited neither to the gravity of the motet nor to its majesty; what is more, they use the semiminim rest and even the quaver rest, not only once, but continuing to the very end, a thing you will not find observed by those good ecclesiastical composers and excellent musicians Josquin, Phinot, Adriano,[2] Morales, Palestrina, Guerrero, Victoria, etc. And since the gravity which I say that motets must maintain might be so slow and heavy and broad that it would be unsuitable, unless for the Gloria Patri of the Magnificat, the "Et incarnatus est" of the Mass, the Lamentations

---

1 Text: The original edition (Naples, 1613),   2 Willaert.
pp. 685–691.

of Holy Week, or the Adoration of the Most Holy Sacrament of the Eucharist, I shall now set down here a few particular directions to be observed in composing a motet with the gravity and majesty of which I have spoken.

1. Let the gravity in motets be maintained in this manner: when several parts are singing and a breve occurs in one of them, let the other parts proceed with minims, or with semiminims, or with semibreves placed on the arsis of the measure, or with a dotted minim, also on the arsis, which is the better position; failing this, let them be on the thesis.

2. Because of their great rapidity and liveliness, quavers and semi-quavers are out of place here; too many semibreves are also out of place if all the parts continually run about in notes of this denomination above the aforesaid breve or semibreve on the arsis of the measure.

3. If the composition is for four or five voices (when all the parts are singing), let two or three parts sustain throughout one measure (when singing in the smaller measure) [3] or throughout several measures while the others proceed with minims and semiminims, but not with quavers and still less with semiquavers, and this (as I have said) in order not to fall into the style of madrigals or of secular chansons. And in this way the workmanship will have gravity and will preserve the true motet style.

4. Note that the aforesaid breve or semibreve should not always be placed in one and the same part (for thus it would come to form a plain-song), but now in one, now in another, the parts proceeding always with different motions and unequal values, provided the words do not demand that they be combined with gravity and majesty and with large and equal values, as we see sometimes in the works of excellent composers.

5. The invention of the motet should be newly invented, although many have composed motets upon the matter or principal motives of a madrigal, chanson, or *tiento*, a thing not wholly pleasing to me for the reasons given in Chapter 69 of Book 1 on page 198,[4] and because the workmanship in motets should be new throughout and in all respects, and also because such an order is permitted only in masses.

6. When the motet is divided into two sections and the closing words of the second section are the same as those of the first, the composer (if he wishes) may in a similar way repeat in the second section the same music that was sung in the first, a thing that as a rule occurs when the words are taken from the Responds and their Verses.[5]

---

3 See p. 270 below, where the "smaller" meas-ure is identified with "common" time, the "larg-er" with "alla breve."

4 That we ought to employ music in spiritual matters and not in profane ones.

5 When the words of a motet are those of a Respond and its Verse, the "prima pars" is regu-larly a setting of the Respond; in the "secunda pars" the setting of the Verse is normally fol-lowed by a return of the concluding line or lines

7. But it is true that, if the first section closes with an inconclusive cadence, the second should conclude, not with this final, but with the final of the tone in order to preserve the above-mentioned order of final cadences. The same license is used also in a motet in one section as often as it takes the same words, which is nearly always in the middle of the motet.[6]

8. The motet must close on the final of the tone in which it is composed in order that one may easily recognize what tone it is in. If it is divided into two sections, it is true that the first (if the composer wishes) may close with an inconclusive final, namely, on the step which bounds the diapente of the tone, provided the second section always closes with the final cadence proper to the tone.

9. And note that, if the motet is divided into three, four, or more sections, the composer must not fail to end the first and last sections on the true final, the other sections remaining at his pleasure.

10. But provided he does not make two inconclusive cadences in succession on the confinal of the tone.

Let these particular directions suffice for composing a motet with its necessary parts, never departing from the other rules and directions.

13. THE MANNER TO BE OBSERVED IN COMPOSING A MASS

The manner, or style, to be observed in composing a mass agrees with that of the motet as regards the slow movement which the parts should maintain, but not as regards the order, which is very different.

1. In the motet, the beginnings of the first, second, and following sections differ from one another, and the invention, provided it is appropriate to the mode, conforms to the composer's pleasure and fancy. But in composing a mass, it is perforce necessary and obligatory that the inventions at the beginnings of the first Kyrie, the Gloria, the Credo, the Sanctus, and the Agnus Dei should be one and the same; one and the same in invention, that is, but not in consonances and accompaniments. In other words, if the beginning of the invention of the first Kyrie runs *Ut re fa fa mi re*, the treble entering first, then the alto, then the tenor, and finally the bass, then not only the Gloria, but also the Credo, the Sanctus, and the Agnus Dei should begin with the same invention, namely, *Ut re fa fa mi re*, yet with different consonances and in different

---

of the Respond, usually in the same setting as before. For a conveniently accessible example of this very common procedure, see the motet "Ecce quomodo moritur justus," by Jacob Gallus, in Schering, *Geschichte der Musik in Beispielen* (Leipzig, 1931), No. 131.

6 See for example Palestrina's motets "Aegypte noli flere" and "Surge Petre," *Collected Works*, IV, 121 and 130.

manners. For example, if the treble began the imitation in the first Kyrie, let another voice (the tenor, alto, or bass) begin it in the Gloria, another in the Credo, another in the Sanctus, and still another in the Agnus Dei. And should it happen that the treble or some other part begins two or three times, take care that the other parts enter each time with consonances other than those with which they entered before. Thus all the aforesaid beginnings should maintain variety in the parts and consonances, but not in the invention or subject.

2. When the first Kyrie is finished, the Christe may be written upon some subsidiary motive from the same motet or madrigal (whichever it is) from which the principal subject was borrowed. Know also that the composer may here use some invention of his own, provided it is appropriate to the tone and not in another manner.

3. The beginnings of the last Kyrie and of the second and third Agnus Dei are in every respect at the composer's pleasure. Nevertheless, there is nothing to forbid his borrowing some other subsidiary motive from the motet or madrigal upon which the mass is composed.

4. The endings of the last Kyrie, the Gloria, the Credo, the Sanctus, the Osanna (for the Sanctus is always divided, for greater solemnity, into three or four sections), and the third Agnus Dei should perforce be in imitation, following the invention of the motet or madrigal upon which the mass is composed, preserving in each case the order which I have said should be preserved in the beginnings and imitations, namely, that all these endings should be the same in invention and termination, yet accompanied with different consonances and in different manners.

5. But the endings of the Christe, the Et in terra, the Patrem omnipotentem (dividing the Gloria and Credo into several sections), the Pleni sunt coeli or Benedictus (beginning or ending the section), and the second Agnus Dei may close on the confinal of the tone, provided two endings in succession do not close on the confinal, although they may do so on the final or principal.

6. In the course of the mass, the more use one makes (whether with or without imitation) of motives from the middle or inside of the composition upon which the mass is written, the better and the more praiseworthy the work will be.

7. When the mass is not ferial, or for week days, the Kyries, the Sanctus (with all that follows) and the Agnus Dei's should be solemnly ordered, repeating several times the motives of the imitation or invention of the subject; when it is ferial and without solemnity, it suffices to

use the invention two or three times at most, always closing with it, that is, without introducing new inventions or other matter.

8. The Gloria and Credo (provided they do not contain some duo or trio, which should be solemn, imitated, and ordered with much artifice) are composed as continuous movements, without solemnity and with less imitation of the parts, using imitations that are short, clear, familiar, and closely woven, unlike those of the Kyries, the Sanctus, and the Agnus Dei's, which (as I have said) should be long, elaborate, less familiar, and less closely woven.

9. It may be seen that good composers have taken care to make the parts sing all together, using such slow notes as the breve, semibreve, and minim, with devout consonances and with harmonious intervals, upon the words "Jesu Christe." This is done because of the reverence and decorum due to their meanings. The same is usually observed upon the words "Et incarnatus est" to "Crucifixus." To use imitations and lively progressions here, with other graces, is a very great error and a sign of great ignorance.

10. The composer (ending the section) is at liberty to write the Christe, the Crucifixus, the Pleni sunt coeli, the Benedictus, and the second Agnus Dei for fewer voices than are used in the work as a whole. In other words, if the mass is for five voices, the aforesaid sections may be written for four or for three; if the mass is for four voices, they may be written for three or even two. But it should be noted that, being written for fewer voices, these sections should be composed with greater artifice and greater learning and in a more lofty and more elegant style. These reduced parts are the flower of the whole work, so made in imitation of the perfect writer of comedy; [7] assuming that in the course of a comedy he uses verses of great elegance, learning, and savor, all leading up to the detail that a character recites some sonnet or madrigal, who does not know that this sonnet or madrigal is woven with greater artifice, elegance, and grace than all the rest of the comedy? A similar procedure is followed by learned and excellent composers in the duos and trios which they interpolate among the movements of their works.

11. And to conclude their work with greater harmony and greater sonority, composers usually write the last Agnus Dei for more voices, adding one or two parts to the regular parts of the composition, doubling as they find most convenient whichever part they please.

---

[7] Possibly a reference to Lope de Vega, who gives rules for the construction of these lyric interpolations in his *Arte nuevo de hacer comedias* (1609).

12. As a rule, the mass is usually composed upon some motet, madrigal, or chanson (as I have said), even though by another author; thus it afterwards takes its title from the first words with which the said motet, madrigal, or chanson, begins, thus "Missa Virtute magna," [8] "Missa Vestiva i colli," [9] "Missa En espoir." [10] If the composer does not wish to use the above-mentioned materials, but prefers to write his mass upon a new invention of his own, he may give it a title of another sort, thus "Missa sine nomine," or, if it is short, he may call it "Missa brevis" or "Missa L'hora è tarda." He may also name it from the subject of the composition, as was done by Pietro Ponzio, Pietro Vinci, and Morales, who, having contrived masses dependent upon the notes of the hexachord, gave them the title "Missa Ut re mi fa sol la"; others have used "Missa super voces musicales"; [11] and Josquin took for a subject or theme the five notes *La sol fa re mi*.[12] If the mass is composed upon the formulas of any tone it should take its title from the name of the tone to which the formulas belong, thus "Missa Primi toni," "Missa Secundi toni," etc. If it is written upon a plainsong, that is, if it is formed upon the notes of the Kyries, Glorias, Credos, Sanctuses, Agnus Dei's, or any other chant, but using the various figures of figured music, it should be named after the plainsong, namely, "Missa de Beata Virgine," "Missa Apostolorum," "Missa Dominicalis," "Missa Ecce sacerdos magnus," "Missa Ad coenam Agni providi." [13]

Take care always to observe the above-mentioned order in the beginnings, middle parts, and endings of the principal movements of the mass; failing this, know of a certainty that you will not be preserving the true order of composing masses which to this day we see used by the best composers and most excellent musicians.

Masses composed for several choruses should be written with short imitations, plain consonances, and less artifice.

---

8 Masses on the motet "Virtute magna," by Mathieu Lasson, were written by Clemens non papa and Palestrina.

9 Masses on Palestrina's madrigal "Vestiva i colli" were written by Palestrina himself and by a number of other composers, among them G. M. Nanino, Ruggiero Giovannelli, Giulio Belli, Felice Anerio, G. B. Cesena, Johannes Nucius, and Rudolf Lassus (see H. J. Moser, "Vestiva i colli," *Archiv für Musikforschung*, IV (1939), 129–156.

10 A mass on Gombert's chanson "En espoir" was written by Clemens non papa.

11 Other masses on the hexachord or *voces musicales* were written by Brumel, de Kerle, Palestrina, and Soriano.

12 *Werken, Missen*, I (Amsterdam, 1926), 35–36.

13 Masses on "Ecce sacerdos magnus" and "Ad coenam Agni providi" were included by Palestrina in his First Book of Masses (1554); there is another mass on "Ad coenam Agni providi" by Animuccia (1567).

14. THE MANNER TO BE OBSERVED IN COMPOSING PSALMS

Although in these kingdoms of Spain the singing of psalms in figured music is not customary, except in falso bordone, I do not wish to omit an explanation of what must be observed in writing them for the benefit of those who care to do so.

In composing psalms, even to omit imitating the psalmody will be no error, for if one were to imitate the plainsong in all the parts, repeating the motives, the verse would be very long, very elaborate, and overly solemn, solemnity being unsuited to psalmody. Yet there are Italians who have written psalms with more solemnity and with more art than they use in writing Magnificats, which is on due consideration a great error. But an imitation may very well be made in two parts, or even in one, in order that the mode may be more easily recognized, and if all the parts begin together, such a beginning will be equally free from blame.

Further, it is necessary to pattern the mediation of the figured music on the cadence of the mediation of the plainsong, in order that it may be immediately recognized as psalmody and also because the ancients (whose observations and precepts we are obliged to follow) always took care to do this, especially because these mediations are so necessary to distinguish this kind of composition from others. The final cadence should vary in conformity with the differences of the Euouae or Seculorum Amen.

Be it further observed that the music should be such as does not obscure the words, which should be very distinct and clear, so that all the parts will seem to enunciate together, no more, no less, as in a falso bordone, without long or elegant passages or any novelty other than ordinary consonances, introducing from time to time some short and commonplace imitation, following the practice we see observed by the choral composers, particularly by the Reverend Dom Matteo Asola and by the Reverend Dom Pietro Ponzio.[14]

Many composers (as I have said) have written psalms with much artifice, very finished and solemn, which, lacking the elements that I have mentioned, are considered good and learned as regards music, but neither good nor appropriate as regards psalmody; instead of being short, they were long; instead of using ordinary consonances, they used far-fetched and unauthorized passages; instead of setting the words clearly, they set them in a very obscure and cumbrous style; instead of making

---

14 For examples of the psalmodic style of Asola and Ponzio see Torchi, *L'arte musicale in* *Italia*, II, 373, and Burney, *A General History of Music*, III, 171.

them plain, they made them solemn and more imitated, repeating the imitations several times and continuing the plainsong in all the parts, which is the distinctive and particular style of the Magnificat.

It is true that, if the composer wishes, he may write the Gloria Patri in a more learned style, letting the plainsong continue in all the parts, adding one or two voices to those he had. In other words, if the other verses are for four voices, he may let the Gloria be for five or more. This may also be written in canon, but the whole should be succinctly ordered, leaving greater solemnity and greater artifice to the Gloria of the Magnificat and of the other canticles.

To conclude, I say that any invention used in the verses of the psalms should be very short, formed of few notes and these of small value, and also that the parts should enter in succession after rests of not more than one, two, three, or sometimes four measures. And this should be observed both to avoid making the verses long and to avoid falling into the style of the three privileged canticles.

Other particular directions and rules are given in Book 16, in treating of the tones of figured music.

15. THE MANNER TO BE OBSERVED IN COMPOSING THE THREE PRINCIPAL CANTICLES [15]

As is the custom, the three principal canticles, namely, the Magnificat, the Nunc dimittis, and the Benedictus Dominus Deus Israel, are always made solemn; for this reason, they must be composed in a more lofty style and with more art and more skill than the other canticles and the psalms. To this end the following order is observed.

In the first place, all the voices paraphrase the plainsong in imitation (although they sometimes sing some other imitation discovered by the composer), and these imitations should always be differently ordered. Herein lies the chief difficulty, for while the plainsong is always the same, the figured music must be ordered in different ways.

The parts may begin in succession after one, two, three, or four breve rests (the composition being in the larger or alla breve measure) or after the same number of semibreve rests (the composition being in the smaller or common measure), and this order should be strictly observed, at least by the first part, which should enter after a rest of not more than two measures; the other rests, coming later, are not observed with

---

[15] The three gospel-canticles Magnificat, Benedictus, and Nunc dimittis outrank the Old Testament canticles and psalms, and occupy fixed positions at Vespers, Lauds, and Compline.

the same rigor, for the remaining parts often rest beyond their prescribed limits, being unable to enter easily with the imitation. The same practice, I may say, is observed in beginning motets and the principal sections of the mass.

Take care to let one of the parts (the tenor is the most appropriate) sing the mediation of the plainsong with its proper cadence and the ending with its final cadence in accordance with the difference of the Seculorum which the composer has chosen.

1. Composers usually let all the parts imitate the intonation of the solemn plainsong [16] at the beginning of the verses, always varying the imitation and using different manners; this is the best plan.

2. It is also usual that, while two parts sing the intonation, the other parts sing some free and arbitrary invention, as may be seen in the Magnificat in the first tone by Morales, namely at "Anima mea Dominum." [17]

3. Sometimes, however, one lets all the parts sing certain inventions appropriate to the tone, disregarding the intonation of the plainsong, and it is the usual custom to pattern the end of the verse on the ending of the plainsong (at least in one part) in order that it may not end without giving to the canticle the solemnity of the ecclesiastical music, with its gravity and authority, and in order that it may be recognized for what it is.

4. There is also another very good order, often observed by good composers: one part sings the entire plainsong from beginning to end, interpolating rests from time to time, and upon this the other parts go on to sing various inventions, preserving always the gravity and the artifice belonging to the canticles and altogether disregarding the style of choral counterpoint, disregarding it, that is, without making the parts run about too much with consecutive minims and semiminims.

5. One may also let one part sing the plainsong up to the mediation of the verse, concluding it with its proper cadence; after this, all the parts sing in new manners to the end without imitating the plainsong at all, except to close on the final of the mode in accordance with the position of the Seculorum.

6. The opposite of this is also possible: after having reached the mediation of the verse without imitating the plainsong either more or less than this, one or two parts sing the ending of the plainsong.

16 That is, the gospel-canticle tone.

17 The procedure is equally well illustrated by the corresponding passage in Palestrina's Magnificat in Tone II, *Complete Works*, xxvii, 6.

Pedrell has published a Magnificat in Tone VIII by Morales in *Hispaniae schola musica sacra*, I, 20–23.

7. Another manner used is this: one part sings half the plainsong and another part finishes the remainder.

8. There is no doubt that Magnificats may also be written (as certain persons often write them today) without obligation either to plainsong or to inventions; these, however, will be taken by those expert in the musical profession for what they are, namely for things improperly and injudiciously written. This is because the composing of canticles in the manner of psalms is permitted for special use, on simple feasts and ferial days, in the services of those churches where figured music is sung every day, for although the text is privileged, the day does not require solemnity.

For greater decorum and gravity, the Gloria Patri is written with many breves and semibreves, interpolating occasional dissonances, and with all the parts singing continuously in order that the conclusion may be more full and sonorous. Thus it is unsuitable to end in fewer parts than were used in the composition as a whole, with two or three voices singing, as is done in other verses, except that, for the convenience of the music and of the composer, a rest of three or four measures is permitted. It may also be ordered in canon, adding one or more voices, as I have said of the Gloria Patri of the psalms; the same is true of the "Sicut erat," composed upon the even-numbered verses, namely, upon "Et exsultavit," etc.[18]

The composer is at liberty to write any one of the verses in the middle for fewer voices, and actually the usual thing is, in composing upon the odd-numbered verses, beginning with "Anima mea Dominum," to take the verse "Et misericordia eius" or "Deposuit potentes," but in composing upon the even-numbered verses, beginning with "Et exsultavit," to take as a rule the verse "Fecit potentiam" or "Esurientes implevit bonis." In the texture of these verses one uses greater industry and artifice, as was pointed out in section 10 of the chapter before last, in speaking of the sections of the mass that are usually written for fewer voices.

Thus all these particulars should be observed in composing the Magnificat, Benedictus, and Nunc dimittis.

Of the imitations and mediations and of the initial, medial, and final cadences of the psalms and canticles we shall treat in the book on the tones of figured music.

---

18 In their polyphonic settings of the gospel-canticles, the composers of the sixteenth century usually restrict themselves to alternate verses, leaving the remainder of the text to be chanted in unison. Thus, when the odd-numbered verses are set, "Gloria Patri" will be choral, "Sicut erat" unison; when the even-numbered verses (beginning with Verse 2, "Et exsultavit") are set, "Gloria Patri" will be unison, "Sicut erat" choral.

16. ON THE MANNER OF COMPOSING HYMNS AND THE LAMENTATIONS OF HOLY WEEK

Of the hymn there is nothing to be said except that it too is composed upon the plainsong with much solemnity, much artifice, and many repetitions (unless it is intended to be sung while walking in procession or on days of no solemnity); that the more it paraphrases the plainsong, the more beautiful it will be and the more carats it will have; and that any one of the verses in the middle may be sung with fewer voices, the last one for more voices (if so desired), in the manner spoken of in connection with the canticles.

The style for composing the Lamentations is such that all the parts proceed with gravity and modesty, nearly always singing together with such notes as the long, breve, semibreve, and minim, one part alone sometimes singing a few semiminims taken by step. In this kind of composition, more than in any other, the composer makes use of dissonances, suspensions, and harsh passages to make his work more doleful and mournful, as the sense of the words and the significance of the season demand. The usual custom is to compose them in the untransposed second, fourth, and sixth tones, these tones being naturally sad and doleful, and they are always sung by very low and heavy voices (only male voices taking part), with only one voice to a part. Of all varieties of composition, know that this is one of the most difficult to write judiciously and to make appropriate to the season and to the sense of the words. In each tone the positions of the initial, medial, and final cadences are the same as those of masses and motets (but with fewer divisions); those of the psalms and canticles are here of no use at all, for they usually end with the mediation of the verse or in accordance with the differences of the Seculorum.

In all the varieties of composition thus far explained, the syncopated minim and quaver are out of place, equally so the semiminim rest, for these, as I have pointed out at various times, are elements opposed to the gravity, majesty, and devout character required by ecclesiastical music, for all that many do the opposite today, either because they lack the knowledge necessary to the finished composer and excellent musician, or because, having it, they use it only to delight the sensual and to attract with their *firinfinfin* the vulgar throng.

29. Thomas Morley

One of the leading masters of the Elizabethan madrigal school and a remarkable musical theorist, Thomas Morley was born in 1557. He became a pupil of William Byrd, and in 1588 was awarded the degree of Mus.Bac. at Oxford. Subsequently, he became organist at St. Paul's in London and entered the Chapel Royal. He died in 1603.

Morley is particularly important as a composer of secular music; his madrigals, canzonets, ballets, and virginal pieces are remarkable for their consummate workmanship as well as for the grace and freshness of their melodic invention. Morley also left works of value in the field of religious music. His book, *A Plain and Easy Introduction to Practical Music* (1597), is one of the best-organized and most useful among sixteenth-century treatises.

From A Plain and Easy Introduction to Practical Music [1]

[*1597*]

THIS MUCH for motets, under which I comprehend all grave and sober music. The light music hath been of late more deeply dived into, so that there is no vanity which in it hath not been followed to the full, but the best kind of it is termed madrigal, a word for the etymology of which I can give no reason, yet use showeth that it is a kind of music made upon songs and sonnets such as Petrarcha and many other poets of our time have excelled in.

This kind of music were not so much disallowable if the poets who compose the ditties would abstain from some obscenities which all honest

---

1 Text: The original edition (London, 1597), as reproduced in *Shakespeare Association Facsimiles,* XIV (London, 1937), 179–181.

ears abhor, and sometimes from blasphemies to such as this, "ch'altro di te iddio non voglio," [2] which no man (at least who hath any hope of salvation) can sing without trembling. As for the music, it is next unto the motet the most artificial and to men of understanding most delightful. If therefore you will compose in this kind, you must possess yourself of an amorous humor (for in no composition shall you prove admirable except you put on and possess yourself wholly with that vein wherein you compose), so that you must in your music be wavering like the wind, sometimes wanton, sometimes drooping, sometimes grave and staid, otherwhile effeminate; you may maintain points [3] and revert them,[4] use triplas,[5] and show the very uttermost of your variety, and the more variety you show the better shall you please. In this kind our age excelleth, so that if you imitate any I would appoint you these for guides: Alfonso Ferrabosco for deep skill, Luca Marenzio for good air and fine invention, Horatio Vecchi, Stephano Venturi, Ruggiero Giovanelli, and John Croce, with divers others who are very good, but not so generally good as these.

The second degree of gravity in this light music is given to canzonets, that is, little short songs, wherein little art can be showed, being made in strains, the beginning of which is some point lightly touched, and every strain repeated except the middle, which is in composition of the music a counterfeit of the madrigal.

Of the nature of these are the Neapolitans, or *canzoni a la Napoletana,* different from them in nothing save in name, so that whosoever knoweth the nature of the one must needs know the other also, and if you think them worthy of your pains to compose them, you have a pattern of them in Luca Marenzio and John Ferretti, who as it should seem hath employed most of all his study that way.

The last degree of gravity (if they have any at all) is given to the *villanelle,* or country songs, which are made only for the ditty's sake, for, so they be aptly set to express the nature of the ditty, the composer (though he were never so excellent) will not stick to take many perfect chords of one kind together, for in this kind they think it no fault (as being a kind of keeping decorum) to make a clownish music to a clownish

---

2 "Other than thee I'll have no god" (in an erotic context).

3 "We call that [a point or] a fugue when one part beginneth and the other singeth the same for some number of notes (which the first did sing)."—p. 76.

4 "The reverting of a point (which also we term a revert) is when a point is made rising or falling and then turned to go the contrary way as many notes as it did at first."—p. 85.

5 "Is that which diminisheth the value of the notes to one third part: for three breves are set for one, and three semibreves for one, and is known when two numbers are set before the song, whereof the one containeth the other thrice, thus: 3/1, 9/2, 9/3."—p. 29.

matter, and though many times the ditty be fine enough, yet because it carrieth that name *villanella* they take those disallowances as being good enough for plow and cart.

There is also another kind more light than this which they term *balletti*, or dances, and are songs which being sung to a ditty may likewise be danced; these and all other kinds of light music saving the madrigal are by a general name called airs. There be also another kind of ballets, commonly called fa las (the first set of that kind which I have seen was made by Gastoldi; if others have labored in the same field I know not), but a slight kind of music it is, and as I take it devised to be danced to voices.

The slightest kind of music (if they deserve the name of music) are the *vinate*, or drinking songs, for as I said before there is no kind of vanity whereunto they have not applied some music or other, as they have framed this to be sung in their drinking, but that vice being so rare among the Italians and Spaniards, I rather think that music to have been devised by or for the Germans (who in swarms do flock to the University of Italy) rather than for the Italians themselves.

There is likewise a kind of songs (which I had almost forgotten) called *Giustinianas* and are all written in the Bergamasca language. A wanton and rude kind of music it is and like enough to carry the name of some notable courtesan of the city of Bergamo, for no man will deny that Giustiniana is the name of a woman.[6]

There be also many other kinds of songs which the Italians make, as *pastorellas* and *passamezos* with a ditty and such like, which it would be both tedious and superfluous to delate unto you in words. Therefore I will leave to speak any more of them and begin to declare unto you those kinds which they make without ditties.

The most principal and chiefest kind of music which is made without a ditty is the fantasy, that is, when a musician taketh a point at his pleasure and wresteth and turneth it as he list, making either much or little of it as shall seem best in his own conceit. In this may more art be shown than in any other music, because the composer is tied to nothing but that he may add, diminish, and alter at his pleasure. And this kind will bear any allowances whatsoever tolerable in other music, except changing the air and leaving the key, which in fantasy may never be suffered. Other things you may use at your pleasure, as bindings with

---

6 Morley's naive definition is wholly misleading. Strictly speaking, the *giustiniana* is a specifically Venetian form of the *mascherata;* the three singers, who invariably stutter, introduce themselves as old men in love; see Alfred Einstein, "The Greghesca and the Giustiniana of the Sixteenth Century," *Journal of Renaissance and Baroque Music,* I (1946–47), 19–32.

discords, quick motions, slow motions, proportions, and what you list. Likewise this kind of music is with them who practise instruments of parts in greatest use, but for voices it is but seldom used.

The next in gravity and goodness unto this is called a pavan, a kind of staid music, ordained for grave dancing, and most commonly made of three strains, whereof every strain is played or sung twice. A strain they make to contain 8, 12, or 16 semibreves as they list, yet fewer than eight I have not seen in any pavan. In this you may not so much insist in following the point as in a fantasy, but it shall be enough to touch it once and so away to some close. Also in this you must cast your music by four, so that if you keep that rule it is no matter how many fours you put in your strain, for it will fall out well enough in the end, the art of dancing being come to that perfection that every reasonable dancer will make measure of no measure, so that it is no great matter of what number you make your strain.

After every pavan we usually set a galliard (that is, a kind of music made out of the other), causing it to go by a measure which the learned call *trochaicam rationem*, consisting of a long and a short stroke successively, for as the foot *trochaeus* consisteth of one syllable of two times and another of one time, so is the first of these two strokes double to the latter, the first being in time of a semibreve and the latter of a minim. This is a lighter and more stirring kind of dancing than the pavan, consisting of the same number of strains, and look how many fours of semibreves you put in the strain of your pavan, so many times six minims must you put in the strain of your galliard. The Italians make their galliards (which they term *saltarelli*) plain, and frame ditties to them which in their mascarados they sing and dance, and many times without any instruments at all, but instead of instruments they have courtesans disguised in men's apparel who sing and dance to their own songs.

The alman is a more heavy dance than this (fitly representing the nature of the people whose name it carrieth), so that no extraordinary motions are used in dancing of it. It is made of strains, sometimes two, sometimes three, and every strain is made by four, but you must mark that the four of the pavan measure is in dupla proportion to the four of the alman measure, so that as the usual pavan containeth in a strain the time of sixteen semibreves, so the usual alman contains the time of eight, and most commonly in short notes.

Like unto this is the French *branle* (which they call *branle simple*), which goeth somewhat rounder in time than this, otherwise the measure is all one. The *branle de Poitou*, or *branle double*, is more quick in time (as being in a round tripla), but the strain is longer, containing most usually twelve whole strokes.

Like unto this (but more light) be the *voltes* and *courantes*, which being both of a measure are notwithstanding danced after sundry fashions, the *volte* rising and leaping, the *courante* trevising and running, in which measure also our country dance is made, though it be danced after another form than any of the former. All these be made in strains, either two or three, as shall seem best to the maker, but the *courante* has twice so much in a strain as the English country dance.

There be also many other kinds of dances (as hornpipes, jigs, and infinite more) which I cannot nominate unto you, but knowing these the rest cannot but be understood, as being one with some of these which I have already told you.

VI

Music in Renaissance Life
and Thought

30. Baldassare Castiglione

Born in 1478 near Mantua, the descendant of an old and distinguished family, Baldassare Castiglione is one of the representative figures of the Italian Renaissance. He served various princely courts and in 1525 went to Spain as an envoy of the Pope to the court of Charles V. He died at Toledo in 1529.

Castiglione is the author of poetry in Italian and Latin, and his letters are important as source material for the history of his time. His claim to lasting fame, however, rests upon *Il cortegiano* (1528), in which he endeavors to draw, in dialogues of great vivacity, a picture of the ideal courtier, giving at the same time a colorful description of contemporary society. The book professes to be an account of discussions held at the Ducal Palace in Urbino on four evenings in March 1507, each of the four books corresponding to one evening. The personages depicted are all more or less conspicuous historical figures, psychologically individualized and characterized. Castiglione leaves no doubt about the importance that music, song, and dance assumed at the court of Urbino and in the cultural frame of Renaissance society in general.

From Il cortegiano [1]

[*1528*]

[Translated by Sir Thomas Hoby, 1561]

AT THIS they all laughed. And the Count, beginning afresh:

"My lords (quoth he), you must think I am not pleased with the Courtier if he be not also a musician, and besides his understanding and cunning upon the book, have skill in like manner on sundry instruments. For if we weigh it well, there is no ease of the labors and medicines of

1 Text: The reprint of the original edition of the translation of Sir Thomas Hoby (London, 1561), as published in *Tudor Translations,* XXIII (London, 1900). Castiglione's *Cortegiano* was written in 1514 and first published in 1528. I have made some use of the notes of Michele Scherillo (Milan, 1928).

feeble minds to be found more honest and more praiseworthy in time of leisure than it. And principally in courts, where (beside the refreshing of vexations that music bringeth unto each man) many things are taken in hand to please women withal, whose tender and soft breasts are soon pierced with melody and filled with sweetness. Therefore no marvel that in the old days and nowadays they have always been inclined to musicians, and counted this a most acceptable food of the mind."

Then the Lord Gaspar:

"I believe music (quoth he) together with many other vanities is meet for women, and peradventure for some also that have the likeness of men, but not for them that be men indeed; who ought not with such delicacies to womanish their minds and bring themselves in that sort to dread death."

"Speak it not," answered the Count. "For I shall enter into a large sea of the praise of music and call to rehearsal how much it hath always been renowned among them of old time and counted a holy matter; [2] and how it hath been the opinion of most wise philosophers that the world is made of music, and the heavens in their moving make a melody, and our soul framed after the very same sort, and therefore lifteth up itself and (as it were) reviveth the virtues and force of it with music. Wherefore it is written that Alexander was sometime so fervently stirred with it that (in a manner) against his will he was forced to arise from banquets and run to weapon, afterward the musician changing the stroke and his manner of tune, pacified himself again and returned from weapon to banqueting.[3] And I shall tell you that grave Socrates when he was well stricken in years learned to play upon the harp.[4] And I remember I have understood that Plato and Aristotle will have a man that is well brought up, to be also a musician; and declare with infinite reasons the force of music to be to very great purpose in us, and for many causes (that should be too long to rehearse) ought necessarily to be learned from a man's childhood, not only for the superficial melody that is heard, but to be sufficient to bring into us a new habit that is good and a custom inclining to virtue, which maketh the mind more apt to the conceiving of felicity, even as bodily exercise maketh the body more lusty, and not only hurteth not civil matters and warlike affairs, but is a

---

2 Quintilian, *Institutio oratoria,* I, x, 9.

3 Variously reported, although not in this form, by Seneca, Dio Chrysostom, Plutarch, and Suidas, the musician being sometimes Xenophantes, sometimes Timotheus, and sometimes Antigenedes. As told by Castiglione and other writers of his time the story appears to come ultimately from St. Basil, *Ad adolescentes* (PG, XXXI,

580): "When on one occasion Timotheus played on the aulos in Phrygian to Alexander, it is said that he roused him to arms during the banqueting and, when he had relaxed the harmony, brought him back to the guests again." For the version of Suidas, see note 23, p. 319 below.

4 Quintilian, *op. cit.,* I, x, 14.

great stay to them. Also Lycurgus in his sharp laws allowed music.[5] And it is read that the Lacedemons, which were valiant in arms, and the Cretenses used harps and other soft instruments; [6] and many most excellent captains of old time (as Epaminondas) gave themselves to music; and such as had not a sight in it (as Themistocles) were a great deal the less set by.[7] Have you not read that among the first instructions which the good old man Chiron taught Achilles in his tender age, whom he had brought up from his nurse and cradle, music was one? And the wise master would have those hands that should shed so much Trojan blood to be oftentimes occupied in playing upon the harp? What soldier is there (therefore) that will think it a shame to follow Achilles, omitting many other famous captains that I could allege? Do ye not then deprive our Courtier of music, which doth not only make sweet the minds of men, but also many times wild beasts tame; and whoso savoreth it not, a man may assuredly think him not to be well in his wits. Behold, I pray you, what force it hath, that in times past allured a fish to suffer a man to ride upon him through the tempestuous sea. We may see it used in the holy temples to render laud and thanks unto God, and it is a credible matter that it is acceptable unto Him, and that He hath given it unto us for a most sweet lightening of our travails and vexations. So that many times the boisterous laborers in the fields in the heat of the sun beguile their pain with rude and carterlike singing. With this the unmannerly countrywoman that ariseth before day out of her sleep to spin and card, defendeth herself and maketh her labor pleasant. This is the most sweet pastime after rain, wind, and tempest unto the miserable mariners. With this do the weary pilgrims comfort themselves in their troublesome and long voyages. And oftentimes prisoners in adversity, in fetters, and in stocks. In like manner for a greater proof that the tunableness of music (though it be but rude) is a very great refreshing of all worldly pains and griefs, a man would judge that nature had taught it unto nurses for a special remedy to the continual wailings of sucking babes, which at the sound of their voices fall into a quiet and sweet sleep, forgetting the tears that are so proper to them, and given us of nature in that age for a guess of the rest of our life to come." [8]

Here the Count pausing awhile the Lord Julian said:

"I am not of the Lord Gaspar's opinion, but I believe for the reasons you allege and for many others, that music is not only an ornament, but

---

5 *Ibid.*, I, x, 15.

6 Often reported; cf. Plutarch, *De musica,* xxvi, and Athenaeus, 626B (pp. 50 and 52 above).

7 Cicero, *Tusculan Disputations,* I, ii, 4.

8 St. John Chrysostom, *Exposition of Psalm XLI* (pp. 67–69 above).

also necessary for a Courtier. But I would have you declare how this and the other qualities which you appoint him are to be practised, and at what time, and in what sort. Because many things that of themselves be worthy praise, oftentimes in practising them out of season seem most foolish. And contrariwise, some things that appear to be of small moment, in the well applying them are greatly esteemed."

. . . . . .

"Methink," answered Sir Frederick, "pricksong is a fair music, so it be done upon the book surely and after a good sort. But to sing to the lute [9] is much better, because all the sweetness consisteth in one alone, and a man is much more heedful and understandeth better the feat manner and the air or vein of it when the ears are not busied in hearing any more than one voice; and beside, every little error is soon perceived, which happeneth not in singing with company, for one beareth out another. But singing to the lute with the ditty [10] (methink) is more pleasant than the rest, for it addeth to the words such a grace and strength that it is a great wonder. Also all instruments with frets [11] are full of harmony, because the tunes of them are very perfect, and with ease a man may do many things upon them that fill the mind with the sweetness of music. And the music of a set of viols [12] doth no less delight a man, for it is very sweet and artificial. A man's breast giveth a great ornament and grace to all these instruments, in the which I will have it sufficient that our Courtier have an understanding. Yet the more cunning he is upon them, the better it is for him, without meddling much with the instruments that Minerva and Alcibiades refused,[13] because it seemeth they are noisome. Now as touching the time and season when these sorts of music are to be practised, I believe at all times when a man is in familiar and loving company, having nothing else ado. But especially they are meet to be practised in the presence of women, because those sights sweeten the minds of the hearers and make them the more apt to be pierced with the pleasantness of music, and also they quicken the spirits of the very doers. I am well pleased (as I have said) they flee the multitude, and especially of the unnoble. But the seasoning of the whole must be discretion, because in effect it were a matter unpossible to imagine all cases that fall. And if the Courtier be a righteous judge of himself, he

9 Castiglione has *il cantare alla viola*.
10 Castiglione has *il cantare alla viola per recitare*.
11 Castiglione has "all keyboard instruments" (*tutti gli instrumenti di tasti*).
12 Castiglione has *quattro viole da arco*.
13 The auloi; for the story, see Plutarch, *Life of Alcibiades*.

shall apply himself well enough to the time and shall discern when the hearers' minds are disposed to give ear and when they are not. He shall know his age, for (to say the truth) it were no meet matter, but an ill sight to see a man of any estimation being old, hoarheaded and toothless, full of wrinkles, with a lute in his arms [14] playing upon it and singing in the midst of a company of women, although he could do it reasonably well. And that because such songs contain in them words of love, and in old men love is a thing to be jested at, although otherwhile he seemeth among other miracles of his to take delight in spite of years to set afire frozen hearts."

Then answered the Lord Julian:

"Do you not bar poor old men from this pleasure, Sir Frederick, for in my time I have known men of years have very perfect breasts and most nimble fingers for instruments, much more than some young men."

"I go not about," quoth Sir Frederick, "to bar old men from this pleasure, but I will bar you these ladies from laughing at that folly. And in case old men will sing to the lute,[15] let them do it secretly, and only to rid their minds of those troublesome cares and grievous disquietings that our life is full of and to taste of that excellence which I believe Pythagoras and Socrates favored in music. And set case they exercise it not at all, for that they have gotten a certain habit and custom of it, they shall savor it much better in hearing than he that hath no knowledge in it. For like as the arms of a smith that is weak in other things, because they are more exercised, be stronger than another body's that is sturdy but not exercised to work with his arms, even so the ears that be exercised in music do much better and sooner discern it and with much more pleasure judge of it than other, how good and quick soever they be, that have not been practised in the variety of pleasant music; because those musical tunes pierce not, but without leaving any taste of themselves, pass by the ears not accustomed to hear them, although the very wild beasts feel some delight in melody. This is therefore the pleasure meet for old men to take in music. The selfsame I say of dancing, for indeed these exercises ought to be left of before age constraineth us to leave them whether we will or no."

. . . . .

---

[14] Castiglione has *con una viola in braccio*.   [15] Castiglione has *cantare alla viola*.

31. Pierre de Ronsard

The great French poet was born in 1524 and died in 1585. Ronsard strove to bring about a rebirth of lyric poetry in the ancient Greek sense of the term, as a musical expression of the soul in a state of emotion. As this ideal could be achieved only by a close co-operation of music and poetry, Ronsard set all his efforts in this direction. Thus, to the collected poems which appeared under the title *Les amours* (1552) he added a musical supplement containing settings of his poems by various musicians of the time. Considering Ronsard's views on the union of music and poetry, it is not surprising that he was one of the poets whose works were most frequently set to music. There exist entire collections of Ronsard's poems set to music by Philippe de Monte, Antoine de Bertrand, and other contemporary composers; but his verses are also found in a great number of miscellaneous collections of polyphonic chansons of the sixteenth century with musical settings by Jannequin, Goudimel, Certon, Lassus, Le Jeune, Costeley, etc. Important as a sort of manifesto is Ronsard's dedication to François II, prefixed to the *Livre des mélanges,* published in 1560 by Le Roy and Ballard.

Livre des mélanges [1]

[*1560*]

DEDICATION

EVEN, SIRE, as by the touchstone one tries gold, whether it be good or bad, so the ancients tried by music the spirits of those who are noble and magnanimous, not straying from their first essence, and of those who are numbed, slothful, and bastardized in this mortal body, no more

---

1 Text: *Oeuvres complètes,* ed. by Paul Laumonier (Paris, 1914–19), VII, 16–20. Laumonier gives the text of 1572; I have preferred to translate the text of 1560, which is easily restored with the help of Laumonier's note (see note 5, p. 289 below).

remembering the celestial harmony of heaven than the comrades of Ulysses, after Circe had turned them into swine, remembered that they had been men. For he, Sire, that hearing a sweet accord of instruments or the sweetness of the natural voice feels no joy and no agitation and is not thrilled from head to foot, as being delightfully rapt and somehow carried out of himself—'tis the sign of one whose soul is tortuous, vicious, and depraved, and of whom one should beware, as not fortunately born. For how could one be in accord with a man who by nature hates accord? He is unworthy to behold the sweet light of the sun who does not honor music as being a small part of that which, as Plato says, so harmoniously animates the whole great universe. Contrariwise, he who does honor and reverence to music is commonly a man of worth, sound of soul, by nature loving things lofty, philosophy, the conduct of affairs of state, the tasks of war, and in brief, in all honorable offices he ever shows the sparks of his virtue.

Now to tell here what music is; whether it is governed more by inspiration than by art; to tell of its concords, its tones, modulations, voices, intervals, sounds, systems, and transformations; of its division into enharmonic, which for its difficulty was never perfectly in use; into chromatic, which for its lasciviousness was by the ancients banished from republics; into diatonic, which was by all approved, as approaching nearest to the melody of the macrocosm; to speak of the Phrygian, Dorian, and Lydian music; and how certain peoples of Greece went bravely into battle inspired by harmony, as do our soldiers today to the sounds of drums and trumpets; how King Alexander was roused to fury by the songs of Timotheus, and how Agamemnon, going to Troy, left on purpose in his house I know not what Dorian musician, who by the virtue of the anapestic foot tempered the unbridled amorous passions of his wife Clytaemnestra, inflamed with love of whom Aegisthus could never attain to enjoyment until he had wickedly put the musician to death; to wish further to deduce how all things, as well in the heavens and in the sea as on the earth, are composed of accords, measures, and proportions; to wish to discuss how the most honorable persons of past ages, monarchs, princes, philosophers, governors of provinces, and captains of renown, were curiously enamored of the ardors of music; I should never have done; the more so as music has always been the sign and the mark of those who have shown themselves virtuous, magnanimous, and truly born to feel nothing vulgar.

For example I shall take solely the late King your father,[2] may God

---

2 Henri II.

absolve him, who during his reign made it apparent how liberally Heaven had endowed him with all graces and with gifts rare among kings; who surpassed, not only in grandeur of empire, but in clemency, liberality, goodness, piety, and religion, not only all the princes his predecessors, but all who have ever lived that have borne that honorable title of king; who, in order to reveal the stars of his high birth and to show that he was perfect in all virtues, so honored, loved, and esteemed music that all in France who today remain well-disposed toward this art, have not, all combined, so much affection for it as he had alone.

You also, Sire, as the inheritor both of his realm and of his virtues, show that you are his son, favored by Heaven, in so perfectly loving this science and its accords, without which nothing of this world could remain whole.

Now to tell you here of Orpheus, of Terpander, of Eumolpus, of Arion, these are stories with which I do not wish to burden the paper, as things well known to you. I will relate to you only that anciently the kings most eminent for virtue caused their children to be brought up in the houses of musicians, as did Peleus, who sent his son Achilles, and Aeson, who sent his son Jason, to the venerated cave of the centaur Chiron to be instructed as well in arms as in medicine and in the art of music, the more so as these three professions, joined together, are not unbefitting the grandeur of a prince; and there were given by Achilles and Jason, who were princes of your age,[3] such commendable examples of virtue that the one was honored by the divine poet Homer as sole author of the taking of Troy, and the other was celebrated by Apollonius of Rhodes as the first who taught the sea to endure the unknown burden of ships; and after he had passed the rocks Symplegades and tamed the fury of the cold Scythian Sea, he returned to his country enriched by the noble fleece of gold. Therefore, Sire, these two princes will be to you as patrons of virtue, and when sometimes you are wearied by your most urgent affairs, you will imitate them by lightening your cares with the accords of music, in order to return the fresher and the better-disposed to the royal burden which you support with such adroitness.

Your Majesty should not marvel if this book of miscellanies, which is very humbly dedicated to you by your very humble and obedient servants and printers Adrian Le Roy and Robert Ballard, is composed of the oldest songs that can today be found,[4] because the music of the ancients has

---

3 François II, husband of Mary Queen of Scots, was sixteen years old on January 19, 1560, and died on December 5 of the same year.

4 The composers most frequently represented are Willaert, Gombert, Lassus, Josquin, Leschenet, Arcadelt, Crequillon, Mouton, Certon, and Maillard.

always been esteemed the most divine, the more so since it was composed in a happier age, less contaminated by the vices which reign in this last age of iron. Moreover, the divine inspirations of music, poetry, and painting do not arrive at perfection by degrees, like the other sciences, but by starts, and like flashes of lightning, one here, another there, appear in various lands, then suddenly vanish. And for that reason, Sire, when some excellent worker in this art reveals himself, you should guard him with care, as being something so excellent that it rarely appears. Of such men have arisen within six or seven score years Josquin Desprez, a native of Hainaut, and his disciples Mouton, Willaert, Richafort, Jannequin, Maillard, Claudin, Moulu, Certon,[5] and Arcadelt, who in the perfection of this art does not yield to the ancients, from being inspired by Charles, Cardinal of Lorraine, his Apollo.

Many other things might be said of music, which Plutarch and Boethius have amply mentioned. But neither the brevity of this preface, nor the convenience of time, nor the subject permits me to discourse of it at greater length. Entreating the Creator, Sire, to increase more and more the virtues of Your Majesty and to continue you in the kindly affection which you are pleased to have for music and for all those who study to make flourish again under your sway the sciences and arts which flourished under the empire of Caesar Augustus, of which Augustus may it be God's will to grant you the years, the virtues, and the prosperity.

---

[5] For the remainder of this paragraph the edition of 1572 substitutes the following: ". . . and Arcadelt, and now the more than divine Orlando, who like a bee has sipped all the most beautiful flowers of the ancients and moreover seems alone to have stolen the harmony of the heavens to delight us with it on earth, surpassing the ancients and making himself the unique wonder of our time."

32. Giovanni de' Bardi

Born in Florence in 1534, descended from a wealthy family, a devoted amateur of the arts and an earnest student of music and poetry, Giovanni de' Bardi was in a position to dedicate himself almost exclusively to the work in which he was primarily interested, i.e., to bring about a musical renascence that would correspond to the humanistic spirit of the Renaissance. To attain this goal, Bardi gathered at his home in Florence the most prominent scholars and artists of the city—the so-called "Camerata"—and collaborated in the first experiments in conscious imitation of ancient Greek tragedy, experiments that were to result in the birth of a new art-form, the opera. Of the numerous documents bearing on the first experiments, the present discourse is perhaps the very earliest. It purports to be the work of Bardi himself; in reality, it will perhaps have been written for him by Galilei or some other member of his circle.

In 1592 Bardi abandoned Florence for Rome where he became chamberlain at the papal court, leaving his work in Florence to be continued by others.

Discourse on Ancient Music and Good Singing

ADDRESSED TO GIULIO CACCINI, CALLED ROMANO [1]

[ca. 1580]

SINCE I think that I shall be doing a thing not unpleasing to you, my very dear Signor Giulio Caccini, if I collect one by one the countless discussions of music which we have had together in various places and at various times and bind them up, like a little sheaf gleaned from the field of your intellect, I shall do it in such a way that you may comprehend

---

1 Text: As published in G. B. Doni, *Lyra Barberina* (Florence, 1763), II, 233–248. I have omitted two passages of secondary interest.

and consider them in one view, like a united and well-proportioned body. And I take pleasure in holding the present brief discourse, like those former ones, with you, for having been associated from your youth with so many noble and gifted members of the Florentine Academy, you have (not only in my opinion, but also in the opinion of those who understand the true and perfect music) reached such a point that there is not a man in Italy who surpasses you, nay, few—perhaps not one—who equals you.

I speak of that sort of music which today is sung to instruments, either in company with others, or alone. It would take too long and would perhaps become tedious to you and to him who reads this my discourse, were I to treat one by one of its principles and of the great men who have taken part in it, of whom to my knowledge at least fifty became great philosophers or most polished reciters of poetry. Thus I shall not stop now to tell of the wealth of instruments that these great scholars had. But, in order that I may well express their ideas, I shall treat very briefly of who it was that defined this music, of the twenty-seven tunings [2] that the ancients had, and of the seven modes that they called "harmonies," [3] like the architect who, to finish the house that he has planned in his mind, first provides himself with everything he needs for his labor. Thus the beginning of my discourse will be the definition of this music. For just as one could have only a poor notion of what a man is if one did not know that a man is an animal rational, visible, and sociable, or of what a city is if one did not know that a city is a union of a number of houses and quarters situated in one place in order that men may live well and justly, so one cannot pass judgment on practical music and on good singing if one does not know what sort of thing this music is.

---

[2] " 'Tuning' (spartimento or distribuzione) means to indicate by an exact number the difference between the semitone and the tone, and thus between one tone and another, in vocal and instrumental music" (p. 235 of the original).

[3] "To each of the seven species of the octave the ancients assigned a tone (by them called a 'harmony'), and these tones differed from one another not only in species but also in being sung each at its own pitch—low, intermediate, or high; thus some were sung and played in the lower notes of the double octave, others in the intermediate, and others in the higher, as will be seen in the demonstration we shall give of the seven tones" (p. 237 of the original). In this demonstration (p. 239 of the original), which is concerned solely with the teachings of Ptolemy, Bardi writes out the seven species of the double octave as a descending series (Hypodorian as highest, Mixolydian as lowest) and goes on to explain that, as actually sung, these form an ascending series with the Hypodorian as the lowest; a tone above this is the Hypophrygian, a tone above this the Hypolydian, and a semitone above this the Dorian, which is sung in the quintadecima ordinaria (A to a'); Phrygian, Lydian, and Mixolydian follow at the intervals tone, tone, and semitone. Up to a certain point Bardi presents the Ptolemaic teaching correctly: the species are correctly named and identified and the pitch-relationships of the mesai correctly stated. But the final outcome is an elaborate misunderstanding: mese is for Bardi always the Ptolemaic or "thetic" mese; thus his keys ascend, not by tone and semitone, but by thirds. Expressed in terms of our key-signatures, Bardi's identifications amount to this: Hypodorian, 2 sharps; Hypophrygian, 6 sharps; Hypolydian, 3 sharps; Dorian, no signature; Phrygian, 4 sharps; Lydian, 8 sharps; Mixolydian, 2 flats. It may be added that Galilei offers a similar but not identical misinterpretation of the Ptolemaic teaching in his Dialogo della musica antica e della moderna (Venice, 1581).

Music is defined by Plato in the third book of his *Republic*,[4] where he says that it is a combination of words and harmony and rhythm. But in order that the terms "harmony" and "rhythm" may be thoroughly understood, we shall briefly define them as well as we can.

Harmony is a general term, and in speaking of it, Pythagoras says, and after him Plato, that the world is composed of it. But let us come to the particular and treat of the harmony of music as defined by Plato, which harmony, according to Pausanias,[5] takes its name from Harmonia, the wife of Cadmus, at whose wedding the Muses sang. Harmony then is the proportion of the low and the high, and of words in rhythm, that is, well arranged with respect to the long and the short. And harmony is likewise in musical instruments, for in these too are the low, the high, and the intermediate, and also rhythm, that is, faster or slower movement of the long and the short.[6] Again, harmony may be composed of all these things combined, that is, of words well sung and having, as their accompaniment, this or that instrument.

Rhythm is likewise a general term, and in defining it, Aristides Quintilianus says that it is a system of times arranged in certain orders, a system being simply an ordering of things.[7] Discussing rhythm, Plato says that it is divided into three species, progressing either by harmony, or by bodily movement, or by words, bodily rhythm being manifest to the eye, the other two species to the ear.[8] But let us come to the rhythm of music, which is simply giving time to words that are sung as long and short, and as fast and slow, likewise to musical instruments.

Taken all together, these considerations show that practical music is a combination of words arranged by a poet into verses made up of various metres with respect to the long and the short, these being in their movement now fast and now slow, now low, now high, and now intermediate, approaching the sound of the words of the human voice, now sung by that voice alone, now accompanied by a musical instrument, which in turn should accompany the words with the long and the short, with fast and slow movement, and with the low, the high, and the intermediate.

Now that we have given the definition of music according to Plato (a definition in which Aristotle and the other scholars concur) and have said what music is, . . . let us turn to the marvels of music, in discussing which Damon, the teacher of Socrates, says that, being chaste, it has the

---

4 398D (p. 4 above).
5 *Description of Greece*, IX, xii, 3.
6 Plato, *Laws*, 665A, also *Symposium*, 187A-B, and *Philebus*, 17C.

7 Aristides Quintilianus, *De musica* (Meibom's ed., p. 31).
8 *Laws*, 672E–673A.

power of disposing our minds to virtue and, being the contrary, to vice.[9] And Plato says that there are two disciplines—one for the body, which is gymnastics, and one for the good of the mind, which is music; he also tells us that Thales the Milesian sang so sweetly that he not only influenced the minds of certain persons, but also cured illness and the plague.[10] And we read that Pythagoras cured drunkards with music, and Empedocles insane persons, and Socrates a man possessed.[11] And Plutarch tells us that Asclepiades cured delirious persons with the symphony, which is simply a mixture of song and sound.[12] And it is said that Ismenias cured sciatic persons and the fever with music.[11] And Aulus Gellius writes that those who suffered from sciatic gout were healed with the sound of the tibia, likewise those who had been bitten by serpents.[13]

But I should go far afield and beyond my intention if I were to give to music and all its marvels the praise that is their due, for my sole intention is to show you, as clearly as I can, how it is to be treated in practice. Thus, now that I have stated the definition of music and have said what rhythm is, and likewise harmony, both in general and in particular,[14] it is fitting that I show you how many and of what sort are the divisions of music and what their virtues are, for without discussing these things it would be difficult for me to attain the end that I have set before me.

I say, therefore, that the music of our times has two divisions—one which is called counterpoint and another which we shall call the art of good singing. The first of these is simply a combination of several melodies and of several modes sung at the same time—a combination, that is, of the low, the high, and the intermediate, and of the various rhythms of the several melodies. To take an example, if a madrigal is composed in four parts, then the bass will sing one melody, the tenor another, and the alto and soprano still other ones, different from theirs and in different modes. This we have shown above—we have shown, that is, that in every one of our musical compositions there are, in the low, the intermediate, and the high, various octave-species,[15] and various rhythms. And this, to take another example, because Messer Bass, soberly dressed in semibreves and minims, stalks through the ground-floor rooms of his

9 Aristides Quintilianus, *op. cit.,* (Meibom's ed., pp. 94–96).

10 *Laws,* 673A. Plato does not mention Thales the Milesian in a musical connection; Bardi is thinking, perhaps, of Plutarch's references to Thaletas (or Thales) of Crete.

11 Boethius, *De institutione musica,* I, i (pp. 82–83 above).

12 Not said by Plutarch, but often reported by others; cf., for example, Censorinus, *In die natali,* xii, Martianus Capella, *Satyricon,* ix, Isidore of Seville, *Etymologiae,* IV, xiii.

13 *Attic Nights,* IV, xiii.

14 For Bardi's definition of harmony "in particular," see note 3, p. 291 above.

15 Page 237 of the original: "Another error in the music of our time is that two species of the octave are always sung in every composition; in the Second Tone, for example, the bass sings the octave beginning d *sol re* and the soprano its octave duplication."

palace while Soprano, decked out in minims and semiminims, walks hurriedly about the terrace at a rapid pace and Messers Tenor and Alto, with various ornaments and in habits different from the others, stray through the rooms of the intervening floors. For in truth it would seem a sin to the contrapuntists of today (may they be pardoned these mixtures of several melodies and several modes!)—it would seem, I say, a mortal sin if all the parts were heard to beat at the same time with the same notes, with the same syllables of the verse, and with the same longs and shorts; the more they make the parts move, the more artful they think they are. This, in my opinion, is the concern of the stringed instruments, for, there being no voice in these, it is fitting that the player, in playing airs not suited to singing or dancing—it is fitting, I say, that the player should make the parts move and that he should contrive canons, double counterpoints, and other novelties to avoid wearying his hearers. And I judge this to be the species of music so much condemned by the philosophers, especially by Aristotle in the Eighth Book of his *Politics*,[16] where he calls it artificial and wholly useless, except as a contrast to its rivals, and unworthy of a free man for lacking the power to move a man's mind to this or that moral quality. Elsewhere, speaking of this same subject, he says that a man cannot be called a good musician who lacks the power to dispose the mind of another with his harmony to any moral quality.

But since we are so much in the dark, let us at least endeavor to give poor unfortunate Music a little light, for from her decline until now, and this means ever so many centuries, she has had not one artificer who has at all considered her case, but has been treated in another way, inimical to her, that of counterpoint. This light may be permitted to reach her only little by little, just as a man who has been afflicted with a very serious illness ought properly to be restored step by step to his former state of health, taking little food, and that nourishing and easily digestible.

For the present, the little food that we shall give to Music shall be to endeavor not to spoil the verse, not imitating the musicians of today, who think nothing of spoiling it to pursue their ideas or of cutting it to bits to make nonsense of the words, like a man who does not mind that the robe made from the cloth that he has is short and ill-fitting or even that his large and conspicuous slippers happen to have been cut from it. For, to take an example, while the soprano sings "Voi che ascoltate in rime," [17] the bass at the same time sings other words, thus mixing one idea with

---

16 1341B (pages 22-23 above).   17 Petrarch, *Rime*, i, 1.

another, which rightly considered is the torture and death of forsaken Music. This subject is discussed by all the great scholars and in particular by Plato, who says that the melody ought always to follow the verse that the poet has composed,[18] just as a good cook adds a little sauce or condiment to a dish that he has well seasoned, to make it seem more pleasing to his master.

In composing, then, you will make it your chief aim to arrange the verse well and to declaim the words as intelligibly as you can, not letting yourself be led astray by the counterpoint like a bad swimmer who lets himself be carried out of his course by the current and comes to shore beyond the mark that he had set, for you will consider it self-evident that, just as the soul is nobler than the body, so the words are nobler than the counterpoint. Would it not seem ridiculous if, walking in the public square, you saw a servant followed by his master and commanding him, or a boy who wanted to instruct his father or his tutor? The divine Cipriano, toward the end of his life, was well aware how very grave an error this was in the counterpoint of his day. For this reason, straining every fibre of his genius, he devoted himself to making the verse and the sound of the words thoroughly intelligible in his madrigals, as may be seen in one of those for five voices, "Poichè m'invita amore," [19] and in an earlier one, "Se bene il duolo," [20] and in still another, "Di virtù, di costume, di valore"; [21] also in those published very shortly before his death, in the one with the words "Un altra volta la Germania stride," in another beginning "O sonno, o della quiete umid'ombrosa," in "Schietto arbuscello," [22] and in the rest, by no means composed at haphazard. For this great man told me himself, in Venice, that this was the true manner of composing and a different one, and if he had not been taken from us by death, he would in my opinion have restored the music combining several melodies to a degree of perfection from which others might easily have returned it little by little to that true and perfect music so highly praised by the ancients.

But perhaps we have made too long a digression. So we shall say that, besides not spoiling the words, you will likewise not spoil the verse. Thus, wishing to set to music a madrigal or canzone or any other poem, you will carefully commit it to memory and consider whether the content

---

18 *Republic,* 400D (p. 7 above).
19 *Le Vive fiamme de'vaghi e dilettevoli madrigali* (Venice, 1565), No. 16.
20 Published in his *Quarto libro de' Madrigali a cinque voci* (Venice, 1557), No. 3 (quoted by Einstein in *The Italian Madrigal,* I, 420).

21 Published in his *Terzo libro de' Madrigali a cinque voci* (Venice, 1557).
22 *Il secondo libro de' Madrigali a quattro voci* (Venice, 1557), Nos. 1, 5, and 3. See the reprint by Gertrude Parker Smith, *Smith College Archives,* VI (Northampton, 1943).

is, for example, magnificent or plaintive. If it is magnificent, you will take the Dorian mode,[23] which begins on E *la mi* and has a *la mi re* as its mese, giving the entire melody to the tenor and turning about the mese as much as you can,[24] for (as we have said elsewhere) things that are sublime and magnificent are uttered in an agreeable and intermediate tone of voice. But if the content is plaintive, you will take the Mixolydian mode,[25] which begins on b *mi* and has e *la mi* as its mese; about this you will turn as much as you can, giving the principal melody to the soprano part. And in this way you will continue to regulate matters according to the other contents expressed in the words, always bearing in mind the nature of the slow, the fast, and the intermediate. Having, for example, to set to music the canzone beginning "Italia mia, ben che'l parlar sia indarno,"[26] you will take the Dorian mode mentioned above, giving the principal melody to the tenor, turning about the mese, and so adapting the rhythm, that is, the long and the short, that it will be neither too slow nor too fast but will imitate the speech of a man magnificent and serious. And in considering other cases, you will proceed just as we have directed in this one.

But since it is the usual thing nowadays to enliven musical performances by adding to the voice the delicate melody of instruments, it will not be inappropriate if with all possible brevity I say something about these. I say, then, that musical instruments are of two sorts, being either wind instruments or stringed instruments; of those like the drum I find no science, for in them there is no musical sound, only a percussion.

Wind instruments, as more nearly imitating the human voice, are given preference over the others by Aristotle in his *Problems*.[27] But to discuss this point is not to our purpose. We shall simply say that among the wind instruments there are some for playing compositions that are low-pitched and somnolent—these are the trombones; others apt for playing those that are high-pitched and lively, such as the *cornetti*; still others apt for playing those usual ones that lie in the intermediate register, such as the flutes and *pifferi allemani*. But seeing that I have not sufficient grasp of the wind instruments to use suitably

23 By "the Dorian mode" Bardi means the octave species as from E to e, sung in the register E to e (see note 3, p. 291 above).

24 Bardi understands the Ptolemaic or "thetic" *mese* (the fourth step within each modal octave) to have had the function of a tonic or tonal center in the music of the Greeks.

25 By "the Mixolydian mode" Bardi means the octave species as from B to b, sung in the regis-

ter a to a' (2 flats); the mese is d (transposed e *la mi*). It is because of this relatively high register that Bardi now assigns the principal melody to the soprano, having previously directed that in Dorian compositions it should be given to the tenor.

26 Petrarch, *Rime*, cxxviii, 1.

27 XIX, xliii (922A).

those that I know, I defer to the judgment of those who are skilled in this profession.

Next come the stringed instruments, their strings worked in two sorts, although we use them in many forms. For part of them are of brass or of some other metal; the others, taken from animals, we call gut. Strings of gut are used for the viols and harps, also for the lute and such other instruments as are similar to it, and as more nearly resembling the human voice, they will be the better suited to the intermediate modes, like the Dorian; the same may be said of the viols, which have much of the grave and the magnificent. Strings of metal are used for the *gravicembali* and citherns, and as more effective in the higher harmonies than the above, can be played in the low, the high, and the intermediate.

Besides this, it is necessary to take great care in combining these instruments, for not all of them are tuned according to the same tuning, the viol and lute being tuned according to the tuning of Aristoxenus,[28] the harp and *gravicembalo* making their modulations with other intervals. And more than once I have felt like laughing when I saw musicians struggling to put a lute or viol into proper tune with a keyboard instrument, for aside from the octave these instruments have few strings in common that are in unison, a circumstance that may detract from their usefulness, since until now this highly important matter has gone unnoticed or, if noticed, unremedied. In your consorts, then, you will as far as possible avoid combining lutes or viols with keyboard instruments or harps or other instruments not tuned in unison, but in various ways.

Before concluding my discussion of instruments, I have thought to make known to you an idea that has often occurred to me. Since you are to be the source of an unparalleled music, I would have you skilled in playing upon an instrument some beautiful melody partaking of the sublime and magnificent, perhaps one such as that composed by the philosopher Memphis,[29] to the sound of which Socrates illustrated all

---

28 By "the tuning of Aristoxenus" Bardi means equal temperament, by "other intervals" the intervals of meantone temperament or intervals closely approximating these. Cf. Galilei, *Discorso intorno all'opere di messer Gioseffe Zarlino* (Florence, 1589), p. 116: "If there were no other impediment, it might well be that we should be satisfied with the fifth that we hear on the keyboard instruments, which is not only smaller than the sesquialtera fifth, but smaller than the fifth sounded by the lute, which is the same as that of Aristoxenus, differences which if slight are nonetheless perceptible. Thus it appears that in a sense the Pythagorean fifth is somewhat high and that of the keyboard instruments somewhat low, while that of the lute, lying between these two, is the true one which, as we have said, is the same as that of Aristoxenus." Measured in "cents," the justly intoned (Pythagorean) fifth is 702, the equally tempered (Aristoxenian) fifth 700, the fifth of the meantone temperament 696.6.

29 Athenaeus, 20D: "The entire population of the world . . . united in naming the philosopher-dancer of our time (Agrippa, slave of Verus) 'Memphis,' quaintly comparing his bodily motions with the oldest and most royal of cities. . . . This 'Memphis' explains the nature of the Pythagorean system, expounding in silent mimicry all its doctrines to us more clearly than they who profess to teach eloquence." [Gulick]

the precepts of the Pythagorean philosophy without speaking a word. I add that, just as among Moors and Spanish women one may see shameless and wanton customs represented in music and dancing, so the virtuous and perfect musician can represent the contrary, that is, songs and dances filled with majesty and continence, as we read of that never-sufficiently-to-be-praised musician [30] who for so many years maintained the resolution of Penelope and preserved her from the importunity of her suitors until the wise and cunning Ulysses returned from his long exile to his native land.

But let us leave the sort of practical music that consists in good composing and playing and come to the sort that is used in good singing. This has two divisions—singing in company and singing alone. Thus, to bring our discussion to an end, we must again place before our eyes all that we have discussed thus far, for this is the foundation upon which our palace is to stand firm. Let us recall, then, that the tunings were devised by the ancient philosophers with the greatest care and in a determined number, since each sound in singing must fit its place exactly; that the same may be said of the highness and the lowness of the modes and of their quality, and of the distinctions of the octaves with their various semitones, and of the force of the harmonies that are low, intermediate, and high; that the Dorian mode, lying in the center of the sounds suited to human speech, was prized and revered more highly than the rest, while the lower and higher harmonies were less prized, the one being too sluggish, the other too agitated. We have shown that the verse is made up of the long and the short and that, in the opinion of Plato and others, the sound and the counterpoint (as we choose to call it) should follow the speech and not the contrary, and we have defined music, harmony, and rhythm.

. . . . .

Let us now speak of the great distinction that should be made between singing alone and singing in company and of how one should not imitate those who, when they sing in parts, as though the whole company had come only to hear their creaking, think only of making their own voices heard, not knowing or perhaps not remembering that good part-singing is simply joining one's voice with the voices of others and forming one body with these; the same may be said of those others who, to complete their passages, disregard the time, so breaking and stretching it that they

[30] Phemius.

make it altogether impossible for their colleagues to sing properly. The singer ought also to take care to enter softly after a rest, not imitating those who enter so noisily that they seem to be finding fault with you for some mistake, or those others who, to avoid the bass parts, sing so loudly in the high register that they seem like criers auctioning off the pledges of the unfortunate, like little snarling dogs stealing silently through the streets of others and imagining that they are making no end of noise.

When singing alone, whether to the lute or *gravicembalo* or to some other instrument, the singer may contract or expand the time at will, seeing that it is his privilege to regulate the time as he thinks fit. To make divisions upon the bass is not natural, for (as we have said) this part is by nature slow, low, and somnolent. Yet it is the custom to do this. I know not what to say of it and am not eager to praise or to blame it, but I would counsel you to do it as little as possible and, when you do, at least to make it clear that you do it to please someone, also taking care never to pass from the tenor to the bass, seeing that with its passages the bass takes away whatever magnificence and gravity the tenor, with its majesty, has bestowed.

Besides this, it is necessary to sing accurately and well, to give each tone and semitone its proper place, and to connect the sounds exactly. Rejecting the improper practices employed today by those who search for unusual sounds, you will seek to use only a few, turning about the mese of the mode and employing it as often as you can, bearing in mind that, in speaking, man seeks to use few sounds and seldom, perhaps never uses wide leaps unless stirred up by anger or some other violent passion. In this you will imitate the great musician Olympus, who, in the many hundreds of songs that he gave to the world, never touched more than four strings in the principal part.

Then you will bear in mind that the noblest function a singer can perform is that of giving proper and exact expression to the canzone as set down by the composer, not imitating those who aim only at being thought clever (a ridiculous pretension) and who so spoil a madrigal with their ill-ordered passages that even the composer himself would not recognize it as his creation.

Finally, the nice singer will endeavor to deliver his song with all the suavity and sweetness in his power, rejecting the notion that music must be sung boldly, for a man of this mind seems among other singers like a plum among oranges or like a man of fierce appearance showing the *giaro* among city dwellers and well-bred people. Speaking on this topic, Aristotle says in his *Politics* [31] that youths should be taught music as a thing seasoned with great sweetness; and Plato, that Thales the Milesian cured illness with his sweet manner of singing; and Macrobius, that, on leaving the body, the soul returns to its origin, which is heaven, through the sweetness of music; [32] and the poet:

> Musica dulcisono coelestia numina cantu [33]

with the rest of the passage; and Petrarch:

> Sweet song, O ladies virtuous and fair [34]

and at another time:

> Here sweetly sang and here sat down; [35]

and the divine poet Dante, in the second canto of his *Purgatorio*, in which he meets Casella, an excellent musician of his time:

> Then he began so sweetly
> That the sweetness still sounds within me [36]

and in his *Paradiso*, in the twenty-third canto:

> Then they remained there in my sight,
> Singing *Regina coeli* so sweetly
> That it has never left my heart [37]

and again in the twenty-seventh canto:

> To Father, Son, and Holy Ghost
> All Paradise took up the Glory
> So that the sweet song intoxicated me.[38]

From these things one may gather that music is pure sweetness and that he who would sing should sing the sweetest music and the sweetest modes well ordered in the sweetest manner.

Beyond this—and this will be the end of my discourse—you will bear in mind that in company a man ought always to be mannerly and courteous, not insisting on his own wishes but yielding to those of others, giving

---

31 1340B (p. 19 above).

32 *Commentary on the Somnium Scipionis*, II, xxiv, 6.

33 A setting of this poem for four voices by Cipriano da Rore was published in his *Vive fiamme de' vaghi e dilettevoli madrigali* (Venice, 1565).

34 *Rime*, cccxii, 8: *Dolce cantare oneste donne e belle.*

35 *Rime*, cxii, 9: *Qui cantò dolcemente, e qui s'assise.*

36 Lines 113–114:
Cominciò egli allor sì dolcemente,
che la dolcezza ancor dentro mi suona.

37 Lines 127–129:
Indi rimaser lì nel mio cospetto,
Regina coeli cantando sì dolce,
che mai da me non si partì il diletto.

38 Lines 1–3:
Al Padre, al Figlio, allo Spirito Santo
cominciò Gloria tutto il Paradiso,
sì che m'inebbriava il dolce canto.

satisfaction to the best of his ability as often as he is called on, not imitating those who always grumble and, if they perform a service, perform it so grudgingly and disagreeably that their compliance becomes a mortification and a burden. Thus your manners will be pleasing and gentle, always at the command of others. When you sing you will take care to stand in a suitable posture, so much like your usual one that your hearers will question whether the sound is coming from your lips or from those of someone else. And you will not imitate those who, with much ado, begin tuning their voices and recounting their misfortunes, saying that they have caught cold, that they have not slept the night before, that their stomach is not right, and other things of this sort, so tedious that before they begin to sing they have canceled the pleasure with their exasperating excuses.

I have come to the end of what I undertook to discuss. May God grant that it may be as helpful and pleasing to you as it was troublesome to me. And I have no doubt at all that it will prove of great service to you if you will be on your guard against those three horrible monsters that prey on virtue—Adulation, Envy, and Ignorance. Of Adulation, Dante says (through the person of Interminelli) in the eighteenth canto of his *Inferno*:

> Down to this have sunk me the flatteries
> Of which my tongue was never weary; [39]

of Envy, gentle Petrarch says:

> O envy, enemy of virtue,
> By nature hostile to fair principles; [40]

and of the Ignorant, Dante sings, in the third canto of *Inferno*, as follows:

> These have not hope of death,
> And their blind life is so base
> That they are envious of every other fate;

> Report of them the world allows not to exist;
> Mercy and Justice disdain them;
> Let us not speak of them, but look and pass. [41]

---

[39] Lines 125–126:
Quaggiù m'hanno sommerso le lusinghe,
ond'io non ebbi mai la lingua stucca.
[40] *Rime*, clxxii, 1–2:
O invidia nimica di vertute,
Ch'a'bei principii volentier contrasti.
[41] Lines 46–51:

Questi non hanno speranza di morte,
e lor cieca vita è tanto bassa,
che invidiosi son d'ogni altra sorte.

Fama di loro il mondo esser non lassa,
misericordia e giustizia gli sdegna:
non ragioniam di lor, ma guarda e passa.

33. Vincenzo Galilei

A Florentine nobleman, born circa 1533, Vincenzo was the father of Galileo Galilei, the famous astronomer and philosopher. He was an excellent musician, particularly as a player on the lute and viol, but he is chiefly remembered for the prominent role he played as a member of Bardi's "Camerata," the circle of musicians and amateurs that invented the new *stile recitativo*. Vincenzo's study of ancient Greek music provided him with a basis for his experiments in the new musical style and led to the writing of his *Dialogo della musica antica e della moderna* (1581), in which he attacks the elaborate polyphonic style of the sixteenth century. Galilei died at Florence in 1591.

From the
Dialogo della musica antica e della moderna [1]
[*1581*]

MUSIC was numbered by the ancients among the arts that are called liberal, that is, worthy of a free man, and among the Greeks its masters and discoverers, like those of almost all the other sciences, were always in great esteem. And by the best legislators it was decreed that it must be taught, not only as a lifelong delight but as useful to virtue, to those who were born to acquire perfection and human happiness, which is the object of the state. But in the course of time the Greeks lost the art of music and the other sciences as well, along with their dominion. The Romans had a knowledge of music, obtaining it from the Greeks, but they practiced chiefly that part appropriate to the theaters where tragedy and comedy were performed, without much prizing the part which is concerned with speculation; and being continually engaged in wars, they

---

1 Text: The original edition (Venice, 1581). I have translated pages 80 to 90 and the beginning and end of the dialogue, making a number of cuts. Some of the postils of the original and one parenthesis are given as author's notes.

paid little attention even to the former part and thus easily forgot it. Later, after Italy had for a long period suffered great barbarian invasions, the light of every science was extinguished, and as if all men had been overcome by a heavy lethargy of ignorance, they lived without any desire for learning and took as little notice of music as of the western Indies. And they persisted in this blindness until first Gafurius [2] and after him Glarean and later Zarlino [3] (truly the princes in this modern practice) began to investigate what music was and to seek to rescue it from the darkness in which it had been buried. That part which they understood and appreciated, they brought little by little to its present condition, but from what can be learned from countless passages in the ancient histories and in the poets and philosophers, it does not seem to any who are intelligent that they restored it to its ancient state, or that they attained to the true and perfect knowledge of it. This may have been owing to the rudeness of the times, the difficulty of the subject, and the scarcity of good interpreters.

None the less, these writers deserve the highest praise and the world owes them a perpetual debt; if for nothing else, at least for having given to many the occasion to devote greater labor to the subject, trying to discover how to bring it to perfection. This it seems, but only so far as pertains to theory, has been attained in our times by Girolamo Mei, [4] a man of worth, to whom all musicians and all men should give thanks and honor, and afterwards, in our own city, by the very illustrious Signor Giovanni Bardi de' Conti di Vernio, [5] who having long studied music, and

---

2 Galilei is presumably referring to the *De harmonia musicorum instrumentorum opus* (Milan, 1518).

3 Although Galilei had been a pupil of Zarlino's in the early sixties and had been in friendly correspondence with Zarlino as late as 1578, his dialogue is essentially a violent attack on the very foundations of Zarlino's teaching. Zarlino replied to this attack in his *Sopplimenti musicali* (Venice, 1588), quoting from his correspondence with Galilei, and Galilei returned to the attack in his *Discorso intorno all'opere di messer Gioseffo Zarlino* (Florence, 1589).

4 Mei is the author of an unpublished treatise on ancient music, *De modis musicis veterum libri quatuor*, the second book of which was published in 1602 in an abridged Italian translation by Pier del Nero. Burney (III, 173, note q) quotes some remarks of Doni's on Galilei's indebtedness to Mei and goes on to say that he has himself examined Mei's MS. In this he discovers "not only opinions similar to those of Galilei, but frequently the words in which they are expressed in his dialogue; particularly in a letter from Mei, dated Rome, 1572, in answer to two that he had received from Galilei, in which he seems to have been consulted concerning the usual difficulties which those have to encounter who undertake

to discuss the music of the ancients. I procured a copy of this letter entire, and considerable extracts from the other writings of Mei, which indeed contain the whole substance of Galilei's dialogue, except the musical scales and proportions of the ancients." It appears very likely that Bardi too owes much to Mei and that some of the similarities between Bardi's *Discorso* and Galilei's *Dialogo* are to be explained in this way. On this question see also Henriette Martin, "Le 'Camerata' du comte Bardi et la musique florentine du XVIe siècle," *Revue de musicologie*, XIII, 63–74, 152–161, 227–234; XIV, 92–100, 141–151.

5 Galilei dedicates his dialogue to Bardi, his "most considerate patron," and in his dedication has this to say about their relationship: "How shall I be able even to begin to repay you for the opportunity that you have given me and that has enabled me to attend with a quiet mind to those studies to which I have devoted myself since my youth and which without your help I should not now have brought to the state in which they are? To this add your readiness to have sent at my instance from the furthest parts of Europe those various books and instruments without which it would have been impossible to acquire that idea of music that by their means we have

finding great delight in it as in all the other sciences, has greatly ennobled it and made it worthy of esteem, having by his example incited the nobles to the same study, many of whom are accustomed to go to his house and pass the time there in cultivated leisure with delightful songs and laudable discussions.

Being therefore under great obligation to the courtesy of this most gracious gentleman, and consequently desiring to show him by some outward sign my inward wish to serve him, I have judged that I could not spend the time to better profit than by devoting my energies to this subject, since I hoped by so doing to give him some sign of gratitude and to aid the world not a little to escape from the darkness in which it has been enveloped since the above-mentioned loss. Be this, however, said without arrogance and with all respect for those who from Guido Aretino down to our times have written on this subject; although if I should attribute to myself some little glory in this action, I might perhaps not merit rebuke, since the inclination for these liberal studies given to me by nature, and the continual diligence I have employed for many years in preparing them, would with great reason justify my discussing them. But let the judgment of this be strictly reserved to those versed in the subject.

For this reason, apart from the one previously mentioned, and in order that I may not defraud the world of any benefit it might receive from my efforts, it has pleased me to publish some thoughts of mine on ancient music and that of our times, which until this day have been (in my opinion) little understood by any who have discussed them, a thing that without further testimony from me may serve as clear evidence of the difficulty of the subject. I therefore desire of the reader that he be prepared to pass judgment and to compare my writings with those of the other moderns with the greatest attention and with his mind free from any human passion, for it is clear that whoever has not wholly freed his mind from passion cannot form a perfect judgment of anything. I shall receive with pleasure every suggestion that is given to me by an understanding man and lover of truth, and shall be obliged to

acquired. And so that I might show this science to the world very much more clearly than, since its loss, perhaps, it has yet been shown, has it not seemed to you important to give me opportunity for travel and to confer on me your favor in every other necessary matter to seek out many places and thus to derive further and more accurate ideas from the manners of the inhabitants and from ancient memoirs and from men versed in musical science? . . . And what greater sign of your courtesy and benevolence could you have given me than often to put to one side your more serious and important affairs to explain to me *viva voce* the obscure meanings of ancient and important writers, whose ideas, understood by few, you set so precisely to rights that one would well have been able to believe that you had found yourself again in those happy centuries in which one had the most complete understanding of music."

him for it without being ashamed to learn from one who understands better than myself.

And now, since long continuous speaking, flowing on like a torrent, seems not to have that force and vigor in concluding sentences and arguments which dialogue has, I have judged it most to the purpose to treat my present discourses in that manner, and this I can easily believe to have been one of the potent causes that induced Plato to treat the subjects of divine philosophy in this way. I have accordingly chosen to discuss this subject the very illustrious Signor Giovanni Bardi, mentioned a little while ago, and with him Signor Piero Strozzi,[6] as being both most zealous for the true music and great lovers of such speculations as these and moreover qualified to sustain this or even a weightier argument.

· · · · ·

(S) May it please you to give me some further particulars, so that I may escape from my ignorance and also learn how to answer the practical musicians of today, who maintain that the music of the ancients was in comparison with their own a thing to be laughed at, and that the astonishment they caused with it in men's minds had no other source or origin than their coarseness and rudeness, but being proud of it, they afterwards made a great to-do over it in their books.

(B) Observe how bold they are, these men who laugh at the effects of a thing without knowing what it was, or what its nature and properties were, or how its effects could have been produced! What better argument do you wish, in order to convince them, than the miracles, to give them that name, that this music performed, miracles related to us by the worthiest and most famous writers, outside the profession of music, that the world has ever had?

But, leaving this to one side, let us turn to a clear and reasonable example, which will be this: from what I have been able to gather, it is certain that the present manner of singing several airs together has not been in use for more than a hundred and fifty years, although I do not know that there exists an authoritative example of the modern practice that is that old or that anyone wishes to have one. And all the best practical musicians agree in saying and believing that between that time and this, music has reached the highest perfection that man can imagine, indeed that since the death of Cipriano Rore, a musician truly unique in

6 Strozzi is also mentioned by Jacopo Peri (p. 375 below) in connection with his music for *Dafne* and *Euridice*.

this manner of counterpoint, it has rather declined than advanced. Now if in the hundred years, or a little more, that it has been practiced in this manner by people who are commonly of little or no worth, of unknown birthplace and parentage, so to speak, having no gifts of fortune, or else few, and hardly able to read, it has reached the pitch of excellence that they say, how much more astonishing and marvelous it must have been among the Greeks and Romans, where it lasted for centuries and centuries, continually in the care of the wisest, most learned, most judicious, and most wealthy men and of the bravest and most princely commanders that the world has ever had!

· · · · ·

For all the height of excellence of the practical music of the moderns, there is not heard or seen today the slightest sign of its accomplishing what ancient music accomplished, nor do we read that it accomplished it fifty or a hundred years ago when it was not so common and familiar to men. Thus neither its novelty nor its excellence has ever had the power, with our modern musicians, of producing any of the virtuous, infinitely beneficial and comforting effects that ancient music produced. From this it is a necessary conclusion that either music or human nature has changed from its original state. But what ancient music was, and what modern music is, and how this change could come about, this I shall show at the proper time.

(S) I take such pleasure in hearing these novelties which you advocate with such reasonable and living arguments, that if you are content, I shall be glad to hear all that you may wish to say further on the subject and shall not interfere with the order in which you have proposed to yourself to discuss the material.

(B) If that is your pleasure, it shall be mine as well, the more so because, having gone over it in advance, I shall not have to repeat the same thing several times. Let us then determine how much of the proposed material we can truly perceive, without fearing (since our only desire is for the public benefit) any imputation that may be cast on us for having been the first to dare to break this ice, so hard, thick, and plentiful. But observe this: if the practice of music—I mean now the true music which, as Polybius says,[a] is useful to all men, and not that music which, according to Ephorus, was invented to delude and deceive them—if the practice of music, I say, was introduced among men for the reason and

---

[a] In the preface to his *Histories*. [*Histories*, iv, 20; that part of the passage in question which relates to Ephorus is quoted by Athenaeus, xiv (p. 50 above).—Ed.]

object that all the learned concur in declaring, namely, if it arose primarily
to express the passions with greater effectiveness in celebrating the praises
of the gods, the genii, and the heroes,[b] and secondarily to communicate
these with equal force to the minds of mortals for their benefit and advantage, then it will be clear that the rules observed by the modern contrapuntists as inviolable laws, as well as those they often use from choice
and to show their learning, will be directly opposed to the perfection
of the true and best harmonies and melodies. It will not be difficult to
prove and demonstrate this to them convincingly, for when they recall
all that has thus far been said on this subject, they will set aside their
own interest and their envy, wrong practice, and ignorance.

As the foundation of this subject, then, I shall briefly mention only
two topics as principal and important, promising to explain them com-
prehensively a little further on. I say accordingly that the nature of the
low sound is one thing, that of the high sound another, and that of the
intermediate sound different from either of these. I say likewise that
fast movement has one property, slow movement another, and that intermediate movement is far from either.[7] Now if these two principles are
true, and they most certainly are, it may easily be gathered from them,
since truth is a unity, that singing in consonance in the manner that the
modern practical musicians use is an absurdity,[c] for consonance is nothing but a mixture of high and low sound which (as you know already)
strikes the ear inoffensively, or delightfully, or very sweetly.

For if we find this contrariety of passion between the extreme sounds
of the simple consonances, how much more the extended and composite
consonances will have, by reason of the greater distance between their
extremes, and how much more than these the consonances that are
several times extended and composite, which because of their greater
distance from their origin are less pure, less perceptible to the ear, and
less comprehensible to the intellect! None the less, the modern practical
musicians go industriously seeking them out on the artificial and natural
instruments. And if the diapason and diapente are as we have described
them, and if the extreme sounds of each of these are perfectly [8] combined, particularly those of the least multiple interval,[d] which because
of their mutual correspondence seem to be almost the same and to unite

---

b Just as the origin of our music for several
voices may be in part comprehended from the
plainsongs of the church.

c To the contrary, Zarlino says in his *Istituzioni*, II, i, xvi, xlix, that harmony is imperfect
without it.

d The diapason.

7 This line of argument is already familiar
from Bardi's *Discorso* (pp. 293–294 above).

8 Galilei writes "separately" (*separatamente*),
which makes little sense in this context; "perfectly" would seem to be required by the sequence of his ideas.

in a single term, how much more will the extremes of the imperfect consonances differ in nature, and how much more than these the dissonances of which their music is full! And if such diversity is found between only two parts which together sound a single interval, whether simple or composite, how much greater diversity there will be among four or six or more, often composite and of different natures, sounded together at the same time, as for the most part and to the greater ruin of true music is the custom of the contrapuntists in their *canzoni!*

After these impediments, caused by the diversity of sounds and the variety of voices, those that arise from the unequal movement of the parts are no less important, and these are that the soprano part often hardly moves because of the slowness of its notes, while on the contrary the bass part flies and those of the tenor and alto walk with leisurely pace, or while one of these fairly flies, the bass is proceeding at a walk and the soprano is almost motionless.[9] Thus while the nature of the movement and sound made by one of the parts would be attracting the listener, and the more so when combined with words conforming to this movement and sound, the other part, as its contrary, would be repelling him, not otherwise than would happen to a column, everywhere set evenly upon its base, if anyone, to overthrow it, were to attach two or more equal ropes to its capital, each pulled in an opposite direction from an equal distance with an equal force.[10] For it would not move at all from its place, for all the effort expended, unless perhaps it was somewhat weakened by some imperfection of its own, since the force on one side would counteract the opposite force. But if someone else were to attack it with the same appliances and the same forces, pulling from one side only, it would not be wonderful, to my thinking, if all that effort were strong enough to make it fall.

.   .   .   .   .

The present way of composing and singing several airs in consonance at the same time was derived, unless I am mistaken, from stringed instruments similar to the epigonion and the simicion, or from these very ones. Seeing that the strings of these were in their number and arrangement and in the manner of their stretching such as has been shown above, the cithara players of those times began—either for the purpose of somehow surpassing those who sang to the cithara or of escaping the need of

---

9 Cf. Bardi, *Discorso* (pp. 293–294 above); Mei also has this figure: "At the same moment, the soprano scarcely budges while the tenor flies and the bass walks as though with resoled shoes." (I translate the French of Mlle Martin.)

10 Mei also has this figure of the column; cf. the article by Mlle Martin, cited above.

always having a singer with them for the sake of the perfection of the melody that his voice and their instrument produced—they began, I say, with that little knowledge of music which they had and with no regard for the laws of Terpander or of any other approved and authoritative legislator, to seek a way of somehow delighting the ear with the mere sound of the instrument, without the aid of the voice. And they decided that the variety of consonances and harmonies would be an effective means of coloring this design. Before this time the use of these for the purpose we have mentioned had not been approved by anyone of sound mind, but greatly and with just cause abhorred, for it was well known that consonance had the power of arousing discord in listeners whose minds were well-ordered.

. . . . . .

Thus the cithara players, wishing to make up for their defect, introduced upon the artificial instruments this way of playing several airs together in consonance. Long practicing these, and looking always toward the prescribed end, they began, by long experience, to distinguish in them what displeased, what caused annoyance, and finally what delighted the ear. And to have a broader and more spacious field, they introduced not only the use of imperfect consonances (discreetly so called to make it seem rather that they were consonances) but also that of dissonances, seeing that with only the five consonances that the ancients esteemed (those now called perfect), the matter became tedious and difficult to manage.

. . . . . .

The practical players of those times therefore began to form, upon the instruments that I have mentioned to you above, their rules and laws. The first of these was, that when not more than two strings were sounded at once, it was forbidden to take, one after another, two of those consonances that are today called perfect, when these were of the same species and genus. For this there was no other reason than that with two strings only, these consonances, because of the simplicity of their extreme sounds, do not completely delight the ear, for hearing, like all the other senses, takes pleasure in the diversity of its proper objects. On the other hand they admitted two and three imperfect consonances as less simple and more varied, not because of the difference of the major or minor tone that is found between them, as some make bold to say,[e] but because

e Zarlino, *Istituzioni*, III, ii.

of the variety of their extremes, which do not blend so well in this respect as those of the perfect consonances. And it is clear that this rule of not taking two or more perfect consonances one after another under the conditions mentioned above was enacted by the legislators only for the situation in which two strings and not more were sounded at the same time, for when three, four, or more strings were sounded upon the artificial instruments, they allowed them, just as they are allowed today, without offense to the ear.

I am well aware that some pedants of our time (I know no politer name to call them by) make bold to say, to those simpler than themselves who listen to them as miracles, that on the keyboard instruments of which they make profession, changing the fingers conceals the two perfect consonances from the sight and not the hearing of those who observe them attentively. Notice, please, what unheard-of folly this is, to wish to make sight a competent judge of the different quality of sounds, which is equivalent to saying that hearing has a share in discerning the differences of colors.

It was from this way of playing in consonance, I say then, that practical musicians, a little before our grandfathers' time, derived the belief that it was also possible to compose and to sing in this manner, for the ancient and learned manner had been lost many, many years before as a result of wars or other circumstances. Of this ancient manner we shall speak a little further on, and we shall throw upon it, in addition to the light we have already thrown, the greatest light possible to our feeble powers, with the sole object of inciting great and virtuous minds to labor in so noble a science and to see to bringing it back to its first and happy state. This I do not consider impossible, knowing that it was not revealed by the stars to those who first discovered it and brought it to the height of perfection, but of a certainty acquired by industrious art and assiduous study. The ancient music, I say, was lost, along with all the liberal arts and sciences, and its light has so dimmed that many consider its wonderful excellence a dream and a fable.

After its loss they began to derive from the stringed and wind instruments and also from the organ, which was in use in those times, although somewhat different from ours, rules and a norm for composing and singing several airs together, just as they had played them on the instruments. And they adopted as laws the same practices that the cithara players and organists had previously been observing, excepting that of not using two perfect consonances of the same species when four or more voices were singing together; perhaps to make the matter more difficult, or to show that they had a more refined and delicate ear than their predecessors, or actually believing that the same conditions which govern the relations of two voices singing together also govern those of four or six or more.

This way of composing and singing, by the novelty which it introduced, along with the ease of quickly becoming a musician, pleased the generality of people, as usually happens, thanks to their imperfection and the little knowledge they always have of what is good and true, and gave opportunities for the artisans to indulge in wild fancies and to introduce further novel doctrines, for the latest comers were unwilling to follow in the footsteps of their predecessors and wholly to approve their work, lest they should seem to be almost confessing by silent consent their inferiority to them in industry and talent; all this with the aim of bringing music to the ruin in which we find it. For this reason they added to the rule that it was permissible to use two imperfect consonances, that these must necessarily be of different species,[11] and further, that in proceeding from imperfect to perfect consonance the progression should always be to the nearest,[12] always meaning in compositions for two voices.

Now you see how, little by little, lured by ambition, they went on without at all perceiving it, making reason subject to sense, the form to the material, the true to the false. Not content with this, men of our time have added to the way of proceeding from imperfect to perfect consonance and from imperfect to imperfect, the rule that one must take into consideration and indeed avoid the relations of the tritone and semidiapente which may arise between the one part and the other,[13] and they have therefore decreed that when a third follows a major sixth, it should always be minor (because the parts have changed position by contrary motion), and that when the major third is followed by a sixth, it should always be minor, and vice versa.[11] They decreed further that when four or more parts are singing together, the lowest part should never be without its third and fifth (or instead of the fifth, the sixth) or one of their extensions.[14]

There is no one who does not consider these rules excellent and necessary for the mere delight the ear takes in the variety of the harmonies, but for the expression of conceptions they are pestilent, being fit for nothing but to make the concentus varied and full, and this is not always,

11 Zarlino, *Istituzioni,* III, xxix (pp. 235–238 above).
12 *Ibid.,* III, xxxviii (How we ought to proceed from one consonance to another). The rule in question is of course much older than Zarlino's

statement of it, but it is presumably this statement that Galilei has in mind.
13 *Ibid.,* III, xxx (pp. 238–241 above).
14 *Ibid.,* III, xxxi (p. 242 above) and lix.

indeed is never suited to express any conception of the poet or the orator. I repeat, therefore, that if the rules in question had been applied to their original purpose, those who have amplified them in modern times would deserve no less praise than those who first laid them down, but the whole mistake is that the purpose today is different, indeed directly opposed to that of the first inventors of this kind of music, while what the true purpose is has long been evident. It was never the intention of the inventors that these rules should have to serve for the use of those harmonies that, combined with words and with the appropriate passion, express the conceptions of the mind; they were to serve for the sound of the artificial instruments alone, both stringed and wind, as may be gathered from what we have said thus far of their first authors. But the matter has always been understood in the opposite way by their successors, and this belief has endured so long that I think it will be most difficult, if not impossible, to remove and dispel it from men's minds, especially from the minds of those who are mere practitioners of this kind of counterpoint, and therefore esteemed and prized by the vulgar and salaried by various gentlemen, and who have been informing others about this practice, by them called music, down to the present day.

For if anyone wished to persuade such men as these that they were ignorant of the true music, he would need, not the rhetoric of Cicero or Demosthenes, but the sword of the paladin Orlando, or the authority of some great prince who was a friend to truth and who might abandon the vulgar music to the vulgar, as suited to them, and persuade the noble, by his example, to devote themselves to the music suited to them. This is the music that Aristotle calls honest and used with dignity, for in the well-ordered state, as he says in his Eighth Book,[t] those forms of music that are like the vulgar, corrupt and removed from the true form, are conceded to the vulgar, as are those so much admired and prized by them today, for each naturally seeks his like. But of this, enough said.

Consider each rule of the modern contrapuntists by itself, or, if you wish, consider them all together. They aim at nothing but the delight of the ear, if it can truly be called delight. They have not a book among them for their use and convenience that speaks of how to express the conceptions of the mind and of how to impress them with the greatest possible effectiveness on the minds of the listeners; of this they do not think and never have thought since the invention of this kind of music, but only of how to disfigure it still more, if such a thing be possible. And that in truth the last thing the moderns think of is the expression of the

---

t *Politics*, VIII. [Pages 22–23 above.]

words with the passion that these require, excepting in the ridiculous way that I shall shortly relate, let it be a manifest sign that their observances and rules amount to nothing more than a manner of modulating about among the musical intervals with the aim of making the music a contest of varied harmonies according to the rules stated above and without further thought of the conception and sense of the words. And if it were permitted me, I should like to show you, with several examples of authority, that among the most famous contrapuntists of this century there are some who do not even know how to read, let alone understand. Their ignorance and lack of consideration is one of the most potent reasons why the music of today does not cause in the listeners any of those virtuous and wonderful effects that ancient music caused.

. . . . .

If the object of the modern practical musicians is, as they say, to delight the sense of hearing with the variety of the consonances, and if this property of tickling (for it cannot with truth be called delight in any other sense) resides in a simple piece of hollow wood over which are stretched four, six, or more strings of the gut of a dumb beast or of some other material, disposed according to the nature of the harmonic numbers, or in a given number of natural reeds or of artificial ones made of wood, metal, or some other material, divided by proportioned and suitable measures, with a little air blowing inside them while they are touched or struck by the clumsy and untutored hand of some base idiot or other, then let this object of delighting with the variety of their harmonies be abandoned to these instruments, for being without sense, movement, intellect, speech, discourse, reason, or soul, they are capable of nothing else. But let men, who have been endowed by nature with all these noble and excellent parts, endeavor to use them not merely to delight, but as imitators of the good ancients, to improve at the same time, for they have the capacity to do this and in doing otherwise they are acting contrary to nature, which is the handmaiden of God.

Judicious and learned men, when they regard the various colors and shapes of objects, do not find satisfaction, like the ignorant multitude, in the mere pleasure that sight affords, but in investigating afterwards the mutual appropriateness and proportion of these incidental attributes and likewise their properties and nature. In the same way, I say that it is not enough merely to take pleasure in the various harmonies heard between the parts of a musical composition unless one also determines the proportion in which the voices are combined, in order not to be like the herbalist who in his simplicity knows nothing about simples except their names—and such are most of those who pass for musicians today among the vulgar.

Among their absurdities and novelties is also numbered that of sometimes transposing music originally composed according to natural, singable, and usual movements up or down to strange pitches that are unsingable, altogether out of the ordinary, and full of artifice (just as skilled organists are accustomed to transpose for the convenience of the chorus, using accidental signs, by a tone, a third, or some other interval), and this only in order to vaunt themselves and their achievements as miracles before those more ignorant than themselves. Add to this that among the more famous there are and always have been those who have first put notes together according to their caprice and have then fitted to them whatever words they pleased, not minding at all that there was the same incongruity between the words and their notes as that which has been said to exist between the dithyramb and the Dorian harmony,[15] or a greater one, for even men of worth are amazed that most modern compositions sound better when well played than when well sung, failing to perceive that their purpose is to be communicated to the hearer by means of artificial instruments and not of natural ones, since they are artifice itself and not at all natural. And to diminish still further their amazement and my trouble in so often reciting the words of others, let them read in this connection the tenth problem in Aristotle's Nineteenth Book,[16] which will dispose of them.

Beyond the beauty and grace of the consonances, there is nothing ingenious or choice in modern counterpoint excepting the use of the dissonances, provided these are arranged with the necessary means and judiciously resolved. For the expression of conceptions in order to impress the passions on the listener, both of them are not merely a great impediment, but the worst of poisons. The reason is this: the continual sweetness of the various harmonies, combined with the slight harshness and bitterness of the various dissonances (besides the thousand other sorts of artifice that the contrapuntists of our day have so industriously sought out to allure our ears, to enumerate which I omit lest I become tedious), these are, as I have said, the greatest impediment to moving the mind to any passion. For the mind, being chiefly taken up and, so to speak, bound by the snares of the pleasure thus produced, is not given time to under-

---

15 Aristotle, *Politics,* 1342B (p. 23 above).
16 "Why is it that—granting that the human voice is a pleasanter sound than that of instruments—the voice of one who sings without words—as do those who hum—is not so pleasant as the sound of aulos or lyre?" [Hett].

stand, let alone consider, the badly uttered words. All this is wholly different from what is necessary to passion from its nature, for passion and moral character must be simple and natural, or at least appear so, and their sole aim must be to arouse their counterpart in others.

(S) From what you have said thus far may be gathered, it seems, among other important things, that the music of today is not of great value for expressing the passions of the mind by means of words, but is of value merely for the wind and stringed instruments, from which the ear, it appears, desires nothing but the sweet enjoyment of the variety of their harmonies, combined with the suitable and proportioned movements of which they have an abundance; these are then made manifest to the ear by some practiced and skilled performer.

(B) What you say would always be the case if the various harmonies of the artificial instruments were fit only to divert and tickle the ears, as you say, and if the contrapuntists of our time were content to disfigure only the part of music that pertains to the expression of conceptions. But they have not been content with this and have treated no better the part having to do with the harmonies of the artificial instruments in themselves and concerned with the pleasure of the sense without going on to that of the mind. This too they have reduced to such estate that if it were to get the least bit worse, it would need rather to be buried than to be cured.

.   .   .   .   .

Finally I come as I promised to the treatment of the most important and principal part of music, the imitation of the conceptions that are derived from the words. After disposing of this question I shall speak to you about the principles observed by the ancient musicians.

Our practical contrapuntists say, or rather hold to be certain, that they have expressed the conceptions of the mind in the proper manner and have imitated the words whenever, in setting to music a sonnet, *canzone, romanzo,* madrigal, or other poem in which there occurs a line saying, for example:

> Bitter heart and savage, and cruel will,[17]

which is the first line of one of the sonnets of Petrarch, they have caused many sevenths, fourths, seconds, and major sixths to be sung between the

---

17 Petrarch, *Rime,* cclxv, 1: *Aspro core e selvaggio, e cruda voglia;* it will be recalled that Willaert's setting of this poem was cited by Zarlino in his *Institutions,* IV, xxxii (p. 258 above) as a model of correct musical expression.

parts and by means of these have made a rough, harsh, and unpleasant sound in the ears of the listeners.[g]

The sound is indeed not unlike that given by the cithara of Orpheus in the hands of Neantius, the son of Pittacus, the tyrant of the Greek island of Lesbos, where flourished the greatest and most esteemed musicians of the world, in honor of whose greatness it had been deposited there, we read, after the death of the remarkable cithara player Pericletus, the glorious winner in the Carneian festival of the Lacedaemonians. When this Neantius played upon the cithara in question, it was revealed by his lack of skill that the strings were partly of wolf-gut and partly of lamb-gut, and because of this imperfection [h]—or because of the transgression he had committed in taking the sacred cithara from the temple by deceit, believing that the virtue of playing it well resided in it by magic, as in Bradamante's lance that of throwing to the ground whomsoever she touched with it [18]—he received, when he played it, condign punishment, being devoured by dogs. This was his only resemblance to the learned poet, sage priest, and unique musician who as you know was slain by the Bacchantes.

At another time they will say that they are imitating the words when among the conceptions of these there are any meaning "to flee" or "to fly"; these they will declaim with the greatest rapidity and the least grace imaginable. In connection with words meaning "to disappear," "to swoon," "to die," or actually "to be extinct" they have made the parts break off so abruptly, that instead of inducing the passion corresponding to any of these, they have aroused laughter and at other times contempt in the listeners, who felt that they were being ridiculed. Then with words meaning "alone," "two," or "together" they have caused one lone part, or two, or all the parts together to sing with unheard-of elegance. Others, in the singing of this particular line from one of the sestinas of Petrarch:

And with the lame ox he will be pursuing Laura,[19]

have declaimed it to staggering, wavering, syncopated notes as though they had the hiccups. And when, as sometimes happens, the conceptions they have had in hand made mention of the rolling of the drum, or of the sound of the trumpet or any other such instrument, they have sought to represent its sound in their music, without minding at all that they

---

[g] Zarlino, *Istituzioni*, III, lxvi, IV, xxxii. [Page 257 above.]

[h] Fracastoro, *De antipathia et sympathia rerum*, i.

[18] Ariosto, *Orlando furioso*, VIII, xvii; XXX, xv.

[19] *Rime*, ccxxxix, 36: *E col bue zoppo andrem cacciando l'aura* (Galilei writes *andrà* and *Laura*). Cf. the setting of this line by Orlando di Lasso (*Sämmtliche Werke*, IV, 80).

were pronouncing these words in some unheard-of manner. Finding words denoting diversity of color, such as "dark" or "light" hair and similar expressions, they have put black or white notes beneath them to express this sort of conception craftily and gracefully, as they say, meanwhile making the sense of hearing subject to the accidents of color and shape, the particular objects of sight and, in solid bodies, of touch. Nor has there been any lack of those who, still more corrupt, have sought to portray with notes the words "azure" and "violet" according to their sound, just as the stringmakers nowadays color their gut strings. At another time, finding the line:

He descended into hell, into the lap of Pluto,

they have made one part of the composition descend in such a way that the singer has sounded more like someone groaning to frighten children and terrify them than like anyone singing sense. In the opposite way, finding this one:

This one aspires to the stars,

in declaiming it they have ascended to a height that no one shrieking from excessive pain, internal or external, has ever reached. And coming, as sometimes happens, to words meaning "weep," "laugh," "sing," "shout," "shriek," or to "false deceits," "harsh chains," "hard bonds," "rugged mount," "unyielding rock," "cruel woman," and the like, to say nothing of their sighs, unusual forms, and so on, they have declaimed them, to color their absurd and vain designs, in manners more outlandish than those of any far-off barbarian.

Unhappy men, they do not perceive that if Isocrates or Corax or any of the other famous orators had ever, in an oration, uttered two of these words in such a fashion, they would have moved all their hearers to laughter and contempt and would besides this have been derided and despised by them as men foolish, abject, and worthless. And yet they wonder that the music of their times produces none of the notable effects that ancient music produced, when, quite the other way, they would have more cause for amazement if it were to produce any of them, seeing that their music is so remote from the ancient music and so unlike it as actually to be its contrary and its mortal enemy, as has been said and proved and will be proved still more, and seeing that it has no means enabling it even to think of producing such effects, let alone to obtain them. For its sole aim is to delight the ear, while that of ancient music is to induce in another the same passion that one feels oneself. No person of judgment understands the expression of the conceptions of the mind by means of words in this ridiculous manner, but in another, far removed and very different.

(S) I pray you, tell me how.

(B) In the same way that, among many others, those two famous orators that I mentioned a little while ago expressed them, and afterwards every musician of repute. And if they wish to understand the manner of it, I shall content myself with showing them how and from whom they can learn with little pain and trouble and with the greatest pleasure, and it will be thus: when they go for their amusement to the tragedies and comedies that the mummers act, let them a few times leave off their immoderate laughing, and instead be so good as to observe, when one quiet gentleman speaks with another, in what manner he speaks, how high or low his voice is pitched, with what volume of sound, with what sort of accents and gestures, and with what rapidity or slowness his words are uttered. Let them mark a little what difference obtains in all these things when one of them speaks with one of his servants, or one of these with another; let them observe the prince when he chances to be conversing with one of his subjects and vassals; when with the petitioner who is entreating his favor; how the man infuriated or excited speaks; the married woman, the girl, the mere child, the clever harlot, the lover speaking to his mistress as he seeks to persuade her to grant his wishes, the man who laments, the one who cries out, the timid man, and the man exultant with joy. From these variations of circumstance, if they observe them attentively and examine them with care, they will be able to select the norm of what is fitting for the expression of any other conception whatever that can call for their handling.[20]

Every brute beast has the natural faculty of communicating its pleasure and its pain of body and mind, at least to those of its own species, nor was voice given to them by nature for any other purpose. And among rational animals there are some so stupid that, since they do not know, thanks to their worthlessness, how to make practical application of this faculty and how to profit by it on occasion, they believe that they are without it naturally.[21]

---

20 "O bel discorso, truly worthy of the great man he imagines himself to be! From it we may gather that what he actually wishes is to reduce music greatly in dignity and reputation, when, to learn imitation, he bids us go to hear the zanies in tragedies and comedies and to become out-and-out actors and buffoons. What has the musician to do with those who recite tragedies and comedies?" (Zarlino, Sopplimenti, VIII, xi).

21 "Thus in his opinion it is a shameful thing to be more man than beast, or at least to be more the modest man than the buffoon, because at the right time and place the songs of the buffoon may move his listeners to laughter. It is not perceived that such imitations belong rather to the orator than to the musician and that when the singer uses such means, he ought rather to be called an actor or a buffoon, than a singer. Everyone knows that the orator who wishes to move

When the ancient musician sang any poem whatever, he first considered very diligently the character of the person speaking: his age, his sex, with whom he was speaking, and the effect he sought to produce by this means; and these conceptions, previously clothed by the poet in chosen words suited to such a need, the musician then expressed in the tone [22] and with the accents and gestures, the quantity and quality of sound, and the rhythm appropriate to that action and to such a person. For this reason we read of Timotheus, who in the opinion of Suidas was a player of the aulos and not of the cithara,[23] that when he roused the great Alexander with the difficult mode of Minerva to combat with the armies of his foes, not only did the circumstances mentioned reveal themselves in the rhythms, the words, and the conceptions of the entire song in conformity with his desire, but in my opinion at least, his habit, the aspect of his countenance, and each particular gesture and member must have shown on this occasion that he was burning with desire to fight, to overcome, and to conquer the enemy. For this reason Alexander was forced to cry out for his arms and to say that this should be the song of kings.[24] And rightly, for provided the impediments have been removed, if the musician has not the power to direct the minds of his listeners to their benefit, his science and knowledge are to be reputed null and vain, since the art of music was instituted and numbered among the liberal arts for no other purpose.

· · · · ·

(S) I have only one remaining doubt, Signor Giovanni, which by your leave will serve as a seal for our discussion, and it is this: how does it happen that the compositions of many who are generally reputed to be great players, both of the lute and of the keyboard instruments, do not succeed when they play them on these instruments, and that other players, also of repute, have left no other memory than their names? And that on the other hand there are some of little repute with the general public who have succeeded excellently in writing in their chosen profes-

---

the passions must study them and must imitate not only the actor but any other sort of person who might help him to this end. This the great orator Cicero did, practicing continually with the actor Roscius and the poet Architus. But in this case, what becomes the orator does not become the musician." (Zarlino, *Sopplimenti*, VIII, xi).

22 Galilei is using the word "tone" (*tono*) in its technical sense.

23 *Lexicon*, under Timotheus: "When on one occasion Timotheus the aulos-player played on the aulos the nome of Athena called Orthios, they say that Alexander was so moved that, as

he listened, he sprang to arms and said that this should be the royal aulos-music."

24 "So that this Timotheus of his ought, if not to be, at least to seem the most perfect of zanies and buffoons. But who ever heard finer or sweeter discourse than this, all stuff and nonsense? Thus, leaving the *zanni*, the *zannini*, and the *zannoli* to one side, we shall now explain how one ought to speak in an imitation made by means of music" (Zarlino, *Sopplimenti*, VIII, xi). Zarlino goes on to a discussion of the references to music at the beginning of Aristotle's *Poetics*.

sion? And that other musicians are very learned and erudite, and for all that, on the practical side, their compositions have not been at all satisfactory when performed? And that others will hardly know how to read, and will have very little knowledge of practical matters, especially in music, and for all that they will succeed marvelously in counterpoint? And finally, which of these are to be more reputed and esteemed, and which less, and why?

(B) Properly to clear up your doubts, I should need your permission to speak freely (for at the beginning of our discussion you said that this befitted those who seek the truth of things), but since according to the flatterers of today it is ill-bred to name anyone and reproach him with reason in order that he may learn his error and mend his ways, I shall go over them in whatever random order occurs to me and say what I think of them with the greatest modesty at my command, not because what could be said of any is not pure truth, but in order not to be considered slanderous (even with complete injustice) by the envious and malicious.

I say then that in our times there have been and are many excellent players, both of the lute and of the keyboard instruments, among whom some have indeed known how to play well and how to write well, or let us say how to compose well, for their instrument, as for the keyboard instrument an Annibale Padovano and for the lute a Fabrizio Dentice, noble Neapolitan.

Others there have been and are who . . . will know how to write and to show their knowledge excellently and who will observe every slightest particular detail that is needed for good playing and good composition, but apart from this the imagination of one is so lacking in invention, and the fingers and hands of another, either from some natural defect, or from having exercised them little, or from some other circumstance, are so weak or so unskilled in obeying the commands given to them by reason, that he is unable to express the passions with them as he understands them and has engraved them in his thought; these are the reasons why neither the one nor the other gives entire satisfaction in what he does and why they give up the attempt, still seeking, like the orator, to remedy this defect with the pen, with which some of them have been remarkably successful.

Others there have been and are who will play well on one or the other instrument and yet will write badly. Of these a part, being more prudent, have never taken the pains to show their knowledge to the world with the pen, and if they have composed or written anything, have not published it, well aware that it was of little or no worth and that it would thus have brought discredit on them if it had come into the hands of this or that man of understanding.

There are others who have not known how to do the one thing or the other; none the less they have been and are reputed by many to be men of worth. And the same thing that has happened to players has likewise happened (as you will understand) to simple contrapuntists.

.   .   .   .   .

As to which of all these sorts of men deserve to be more esteemed than others, I think that one may safely say that those who play, compose, and likewise write excellently not only merit the highest praise, but deserve to be greatly esteemed and prized by every man of sound intellect.

Those who are more learned than these are no less deserving, although they may be less favored by nature in ready liveliness of hand and in contrapuntal invention, no less deserving, that is, when their knowledge not only makes up for this deficiency but exceeds that of the first sort. For those who teach us a virtue are much more to be esteemed, and the rarer and more excellent they are the more so, than those who merely delight us with their buffooneries; first because it is a greater and a higher thing to know what another does than to do what he does, and then because every purely sensual pleasure ends by satiating us (by reason of its inconstancy) and never makes us thirst for any knowledge. And I say that they are even more deserving when that knowledge of theirs is combined with the highest character, as these are the things chiefly to be desired in the perfect musician and in every follower of the arts, in order that with his learning and his character he may make those who frequent him and listen to him men of learning and good character. In addition I say that it is impossible to find a man who is truly a musician and is vicious, and that if a man has a vicious nature, it will be difficult, or rather impossible for him to be virtuous and to make others virtuous. And to say even more,[1] the man who has in his boyhood used every necessary means and proper care to learn the science of the true music, devoting to it all his labor and effort, will praise and embrace everything that accords with dignity and honesty and will denounce and flee from the contrary, and he will be the last to commit any ugly or unseemly action, and gathering from music most copious fruits, he will be of infinite advantage and utility

---

1 Plutarch, *De musica*, xli.

both to himself and to his state, nor will he ever, in any place or at any time, do or say any inconsiderate thing, but will continually be guided by decorum, modesty, and reverence.

I turn to those of the third circle and say that they should and can content themselves with being somewhat esteemed by persons who are inferior to them in knowledge. Their worth may be compared to the singing of boys, who are praised and caressed by everyone so long as they have their beautiful voices and throats, but when from any incidental cause their organ is impaired by losing or temporarily losing that little grace, beauty, and sonority of voice, they lose at the same time all their credit, reputation, and skill. None the less, whoever well considers it cannot deny the skill, nor can he deny the hoarseness and the change of voice. And the skill of these is like the fleeting beauty of woman, who, as long as her face retains that desirable disposition of lineaments and colors that combine to form its beauty, is admired by all the world, not for being learned or intelligent in some art or science, but for being beautiful because of the harmony of these incidental details. As these lineaments begin to be altered and cease to preserve that perfect proportion which formerly existed among them, that beauty withers like a garden flower.

With this conclusion, then, the most illustrious Signor Giovanni Bardi, a rare example of every royal virtue, gave his discourse an end.

34. G. P. da Palestrina

Giovanni Pierluigi da Palestrina was born about 1525 at Palestrina, not far from Rome. At first he occupied the position of organist and choirmaster in his native town; in later life he became *magister puerorum* at the Cappella Giulia in Rome. As a young man he sang in the choir of the Sistine Chapel, but after the death of Pope Marcellus II he was removed from this position. In 1555 Palestrina was appointed choirmaster at S. Giovanni in Laterano. In 1561 he exchanged this position with a similar one at S. Maria Maggiore, where he remained until 1571. Palestrina died at Rome in 1594.

Motettorum liber quartus [1]

[*Rome, 1584*]

Dedication

To OUR Most Holy Lord Gregory XIII, Supreme Pontiff:

There are too many poems with no other subject matter than loves alien to the Christian profession and name. These poems, written by men truly carried away by fury, corrupters of youth, a great many musicians have chosen as the material for their skill and industry, and while they have been distinguished by the praise of their talent, they have equally given offense to good and serious men. I blush and grieve to admit that I was once one of their number. But now, when past things cannot be changed and things done cannot be undone, I have changed my purpose. Therefore I have both already labored on those poems which have been written of the praises of our Lord Jesus Christ and his Most Holy Mother the Virgin Mary,[2] and at this time chosen those

---

1 Text: *Werke*, IV (Leipzig, 1874), v.
2 A reference to his first book of spiritual madrigals, published in 1581 (*Werke*. XXIX

[Leipzig, 1883], 1–92) and dedicated to Giacomo Boncompagni, Gregory's natural son.

which contain the divine love of Christ and his spouse the soul, indeed the Canticles of Solomon. I have used a kind of music somewhat livelier than I have been accustomed to use in ecclesiastical melodies, for this I felt that the subject itself demanded. It has been my wish, indeed, to offer this work, such as it is, to Your Holiness, who I doubt not will certainly be satisfied by the intent and the endeavor, if less so by the thing itself. But if (may it so befall!) I shall give satisfaction with the thing itself, I shall be encouraged to produce others which I shall expect to please Your Holiness. May God, as long as may be, preserve for us Gregory, the most vigilant shepherd, with the greatest love for his flock, and heap all felicity upon him.

His humble servant,
Giovanni Aloysio Palestrina.

35. Orlando di Lasso

Born at Mons in Belgium circa 1532, Di Lasso went as a boy to Sicily and Milan, where he stayed until 1550. From there he moved on to Naples and then to Rome, where he can be traced in 1553. A trip through France and England ended in Antwerp. In 1556 Di Lasso entered the service of Duke Albrecht V of Bavaria and in 1560 he was appointed choirmaster to the Bavarian court, a position he retained until his death, which occurred in 1594.

Cantiones sacrae [1]

[*1593*]

Dedication

To the Most Reverend and Illustrious Prince and Lord, Lord
Johann Otto, Bishop of Augsburg, his very benevolent
lord and patron

MOST THINGS in this universe so differ in men's judgments that some give more pleasure shortly after they have come into being and, as it were, while still in their vernal flower, others when they have grown to maturity, but none, or surely very few, gain favor when they are already failing and threaten to pass away. It is thus with the mastery of our harmonic art, music. In this age of annually renewed fertility, abounding in *cantiones* of every kind and in rival composers who daily come forward with the desire of pleasing, nay of winning for themselves the foremost place, it seems not easy to determine whether this divine art has attained its full growth, not to say the peak, the summit of its perfection, or whether it is decking itself with flowers after a new birth.

Indeed, if we rely solely on the judgment of our senses, disregarding the counsel of reason, then arbors covered with new vines, ornamented

---

[1] Text: *Sämmtliche Werke*, XIII (Leipzig, 1901), vii–viii.

with a luxuriant growth of shoots and tendrils, are more pleasing to the eye than old vines, set out in rows and tied to stakes and props, but with their stocks roughened and split open by age. Yet the first are virtually unfruitful, while the second yield a liquor which is most sweet to mankind, rejecting all that is useless. In the same way, in estimating the *cantiones* which I composed long ago, in the springtime of my life and the ardor of my years, and those which I produce now, in my old age, I have come to think that while the former are more likely to please, because they are more gay and festive, the latter reveal in their sound more substance and energy, and afford a profounder pleasure to the mind and the ear of the critic. Let the impartial auditor consider whether my measures, soon to withdraw from the theater of this world, are not like the light of day, which is wont to be sweeter just before sunset:

> *Ut esse Phoebi dulcius lumen solet*
> *Jam jam cadentis.*

Intending therefore to publish the present collection of *cantiones*, called motets, written for six voices, a venerable if less melodious music, I had need to seek a patron of sacred and distinguished name, to whom in accordance with my earnest desire, I might consecrate them. I immediately found you, Most Illustrious and Eminent Johann, Most Reverend Prince, being moved to this primarily by my admiration of your manifold and splendid virtues, especially directed toward men of my profession, and of the extreme inclination and liberality of your mind to this same art, and being moreover confident that your Most Reverend Eminence will receive with kindly and cheerful countenance and with attentive ears this music of Orlandus, perhaps my swan song, and would not reject the composer, who most humbly commends himself to you.

Munich, on the feast-day of Michael the Archangel
In the year 1593

To the Most Reverend, Illustrious, and Eminent
Johann

Most respectfully
Orlandus Lassus, Choirmaster to the Most
Serene Duke of Bavaria

36. William Byrd

Born in 1543, William Byrd died at Stondon, Essex, in 1623. A pupil of Thomas Tallis, he was appointed organist of Lincoln Cathedral in 1563, and in 1570 was sworn in as a member of the Chapel Royal. There he shared with Tallis the honorary post of organist. Byrd remained a Catholic throughout his life, as shown in his will, dated 1622.

Byrd is perhaps the most outstanding Elizabethan composer of sacred music and one of the chief writers for the virginals. Among his works are the two books of the *Gradualia*, the dedications and forewords of which are given below. Byrd's virginal pieces are preserved in many manuscript collections of English keyboard music. In the Fitzwilliam Virginal Book alone he is represented with seventy pieces.

Gradualia [1]

[1605–1607]

Dedications and forewords

To that Most Illustrious and Distinguished Man, and his
Right Honorable Lord, Henry Howard, Earl of Northampton, Warden of the Cinque Ports, and one of
the Privy Council of His Most Serene Majesty, James, King of Great Britain

THE SWAN, they say, when his death is near, sings more sweetly. However little I may be able to attain to the sweetness of that bird in these songs which I have judged should be dedicated to you, most illustrious Henry, I have had two defences or incentives of no common rate for emulating that sweetness in some sort at least. The one was the sweetness of the words themselves, the other your worthiness. For even as

1 Text: *Tudor Church Music*, VII (Oxford, 1927), facs. before pp. 3 and 209.

among artisans it is shameful in a craftsman to make a rude piece of work from some precious material, so indeed to sacred words in which the praises of God and of the Heavenly host are sung, none but some celestial harmony (so far as our powers avail) will be proper. Moreover in these words, as I have learned by trial, there is such a profound and hidden power that to one thinking upon things divine and diligently and earnestly pondering them, all the fittest numbers occur as if of themselves and freely offer themselves to the mind which is not indolent or inert. Truly your worthiness is as great as that of your most ancient family, which, long beaten by bitter storms and stricken, as it were, by the frost of adverse fortune, now in part flourishes again in your own person, and in part, encouraged by the King's Most Serene Majesty, sends out, by your labor and merits, rays of its ancient splendor to the eager eyes of all Englishmen. Since you are also of the King's Privy Council, you always suggest, always further, those things which tend to the greater glory of God, to the greatness of this entire realm, now happily united under one sovereign, James, and most particularly to the honorable tranquillity and peace of all honest private men. In these things the praise due to you is the greater for that in their accomplishment you direct and aim all your efforts, not at popular favor, which you deem vain, nor at the desire of gain, which you consider base, but to the honor only of God, who sees in dark places. And these matters are indeed public, and truly honorable, such as not merely by any songs of mine, but by the mouth and pen of all, will be transmitted to our posterity and to foreign nations, among whom your name is renowned.

But private reasons also impelled me to use my utmost industry in this matter. I have had and still have you, if I err not, as a most benevolent patron in the distressed affairs of my family. You have often listened with pleasure to my melodies, which from men like yourself is a reward to musicians and, so to speak, their highest honorarium. At your plea and request, the Most Serene King has augmented me and my fellows who serve His Majesty's person in music with new benefits and with increases of stipend. For this reason I have resolved that this work of mine (if by chance it shall be of such desert) shall stand as an everlasting testimony of the gratitude of all our hearts to His Majesty and to yourself, distinguished patron, and of my affectionate wishes for those eminent men, whom I love and honor as I perform this office for them. You see, Right Honorable Earl, with what defenders I am provided and by what incentives I am prompted in wishing (if only I could) to imitate the swan.

With truly excellent judgment Alexander forbade any but Apelles or Lysippus to paint him or to sculpture him in bronze. Nor has it been in any way granted to me to satisfy my task, save only that I have tried to ornament things divine with the highest art at my command and to offer nothing not wrought with care to so distinguished a man as yourself. If I have accomplished this, I shall declare these lucubrations of mine (for so without falsehood I may call the products of nightly toil) my swan songs. This they will surely be, if not for their sweetness, at least as proceeding from such age. While I indeed decided at the request of friends to work upon them and to spread them abroad, it was you alone that I set before me in my mind as shining above me like a star guiding me on a course beset with rocks. If in your judgment I have brought back wares not wholly without use, it will be the unique consolation of my old age to have brought into the light a work not unmeet for our Most Serene King, whose honor I have wished to augment in my epistle, nor for you, most generous Lord, skilled in the knowledge of human and divine letters, nor unworthy of my years, which I have all consumed in music. Farewell.

To your most Worshipful Honor,
William Byrd.

The Author
To the True Lovers of Music

For you, most high-minded and righteous, who delight at times to sing to God in hymns and spiritual songs, are here set forth for your exercising the Offices for the whole year which are proper to the chief Feasts of the Blessed Virgin Mary and of All Saints; moreover others in five voices with their words drawn from the fountain of Holy Writ; also the Office at the Feast of Corpus Christi, with the more customary antiphons of the same Blessed Virgin and other songs in four voices of the same kind; also all the hymns composed in honor of the Virgin; finally, various songs in three voices sung at the Feast of Easter. Further, to the end that they may be ordered each in its own place in the various parts of the service, I have added a special index at the end of the book; here all that are proper to the same feasts may easily be found grouped together, though differing in the number of voices.

If to these pious words I have set notes not unfitting (as I have wished and as they require), may the honor, as is just, be to God and the pleasure be yours. Howsoever this may be, give them fair and friendly judgment, and commend me to God in your prayers. Farewell.

To the Right Illustrious and Honorable
John Lord Petre of Writtle, his
most clement Maecenas,
Salutation

Since I have attained to such length of years, relying upon the divine mercy, that I have seen many of my pupils in music, men indeed peculiarly skillful in that art, finish their allotted time while I survived, and since also in my own house I consider that the benefits of the divine bounty have been directed toward me, indeed have been showered upon me, my mind is eager, remembering my faith, duty, and piety to God, to leave to posterity a public testimony, at least in some sort, of a heart grateful and referring all things, if this be counted a merit, to my Creator. Having attained to this age, I have attempted, out of devotion to the divine worship, myself unworthy and unequal, to affix notes, to serve as a garland, to certain pious and honeyed praises of the Christian rite to be sung by four, five, or six voices. These are adapted to the glorious Nativity of Christ our Savior, the Epiphany, the Resurrection, and finally to the Feast of Saints Peter and Paul.

These songs, most Christian Sir, long since completed by me and committed to the press, should in my judgment be dedicated to you above all others, for you are held renowned for the harmony of virtues and letters and distinguished by your love for all the daughters of the Muses and of science. Inasmuch as these musical lucubrations, like fruits sprung from a fertile soil, have mostly proceeded from your house (truly most friendly to me and mine), and from that tempering of the sky have brought forth more grateful and abundant fruits, receive, then, Right Honorable Lord, these little flowers, plucked as it were from your gardens and most rightfully due to you as tithes, and may it be no burden to you to protect these my last labors, to the end that they may go forth to the public under the auspices of your most renowned name, to the glory of God the Greatest and Best, to the greatness of your honor, and finally for the pleasure of all who properly cultivate the Muses. Meanwhile I pray from my soul that all present things may be of good omen to you and all future things happy. Farewell.

The third day of April in the year of man's salvation restored 1607.

Your Honor's most dutiful
William Byrde.

37. Henry Peacham

Born circa 1576, Henry Peacham settled in London in 1612 and spent the years 1613–14 traveling in France, Italy, Westphalia, and the Netherlands. He had many friends in musical circles, among them the lutenist and composer John Dowland. His most important book, *The Compleat Gentleman,* appeared in 1622 and was reissued in 1626 and 1627. Peacham was an ardent supporter of the royal cause, but his book teaches a more or less Puritan concept of duty. Thus *The Compleat Gentleman* may be called an English Puritan counterpart to Castiglione's *Cortegiano.* Peacham's last book was published in 1642, and he died soon thereafter.

From The Compleat Gentleman [1]

[*1622*]

OF MUSIC

Music, a sister to Poetry, next craveth your acquaintance, if your genius be so disposed. I know there are many who are *adeo* ἄμουσοι and of such disproportioned spirits that they avoid her company (as a great cardinal in Rome did roses at their first coming in, that to avoid their scent he built him an house in the champaign [*campagna*], far from any town) or, as with a rose not long since, a great lady's cheek in England, their ears are ready to blister at the tenderest touch thereof. I dare not pass so rash a censure of these as Pindar doth,[2] or the Italian, having fitted a proverb to the same effect, "Whom God loves not, that man loves not music"; but I am verily persuaded they are by nature very ill disposed and of such a brutish stupidity that scarce anything else that is good

---

1 Text: The Clarendon Press reprint of the edition of 1634 (Oxford, 1906), pp. 96–104. I have printed some of the postils of the original as author's notes. *The Compleat Gentleman* was first published in 1622.

2 Pythian Odes, I, 13–14: But all the beings that Zeus hath not loved, are astonished, when they hear the voice of the Pierides, whether on the earth, or on the resistless sea. [Sandys]

and savoreth of virtue is to be found in them. Never wise man, I think, questioned the lawful use hereof, since it is an immediate gift of heaven, bestowed on man, whereby to praise and magnify his Creator; to solace him in the midst of so many sorrows and cares, wherewith life is hourly beset; and that by song, as by letters, the memory of doctrine and the benefits of God might be forever preserved (as we are taught by that song of Moses [a] and those divine psalms of the sweet singer of Israel, who with his psaltery [b] so loudly resounded the mysteries and innumerable benefits of the Almighty Creator) and the service of God advanced (as we may find in 2 Samuel vi:5, Psalm 33, 21, 43, and 4, 108, 3,[3] and in sundry other places of scripture which for brevity I omit).

But, say our sectaries, the service of God is nothing advanced by singing and instruments as we use it in our cathedral churches, that is, by "antiphony,[c] rests, repetitions, variety of moods and proportions, with the like."

For the first, that it is not contrary but consonant to the word of God so in singing to answer either, the practice of Miriam, the prophetess and sister of Moses, when she answered the men in her song,[4] will approve; for repetition, nothing was more usual in the singing of the Levites, and among the psalms of David the 136th is wholly compounded of those two most graceful and sweet figures of repetition, symploce and anaphora. For resting and proportions, the nature of the Hebrew verse, as the meanest Hebrician knoweth, consisting many times of uneven feet, going sometime in this number, sometimes in that (one while, as St. Jerome saith,[5] in the numbers of Sappho, another while, of Alcaeus), doth of necessity require it. And wherein doth our practice of singing and playing with instruments in his Majesty's chapel and our cathedral churches differ from the practice of David, the priests, and Levites? [d] Do we not make one sign in praising and thanking God with voices and instruments of all sorts? "Donec," as St. Jerome saith,[6] "reboet laquear templi"; the roof of the church echoeth again, and which, lest they should cavil at as a Jewish ceremony, we know to have been practiced in the ancient purity of the church. But we return where we left.

The physicians will tell you that the exercise of music is a great lengthener of the life by stirring and reviving of the spirits, holding a secret sympathy with them; besides, the exercise of singing openeth the

---

a Deuteronomy 32.
b It was an instrument three square, of 72 strings, of incomparable sweetness.
c Answering one another in the choir.
d II Chronicles 5:12, 13.

3 Peacham's reference is not clear.
4 Exodus 15:20, 21.
5 Cf. *Epistola* LIII, 8.
6 Cf. *Epistola* LXXVII, 11: Et aurata Templorum tecta reboans.

breast and pipes. It is an enemy to melancholy and dejection of the mind, which St. Chrysostom truly calleth the Devil's bath; [e] yea, a curer of some diseases—in Apulia in Italy and thereabouts it is most certain that those who are stung with the tarantula are cured only by music. Beside the aforesaid benefit of singing, it is a most ready help for a bad pronunciation and distinct speaking which I have heard confirmed by many great divines; yea, I myself have known many children to have been holpen of their stammering in speech only by it.

Plato calleth it "a divine and heavenly practice," [f] profitable for the seeking out of that which is good and honest.

Homer saith musicians are "worthy of honor and regard of the whole world," [g] and we know, albeit Lycurgus imposed most straight and sharp laws upon the Lacedaemonians, yet he ever allowed them the exercise of music.

Aristotle averreth music to be the only disposer of the mind to virtue and goodness, wherefore he reckoneth it among those four principal exercises wherein he would have children instructed. [h]

Tully saith there consisteth in the practice of singing and playing upon instruments great knowledge and the most excellent instruction of the mind, and for the effect it worketh in the mind he termeth it "Stabilem thesaurum, qui mores instuit, componitque, ac mollit irarum ardores, &c."; a lasting treasure which rectifieth and ordereth our manners and allayeth the heat and fury of our anger, &c. [i]

I might run into an infinite sea of the praise and use of so excellent an art, but I only show it you with the finger, because I desire not that any noble or gentleman should (save at his private recreation and leisurable hours) prove a master in the same or neglect his more weighty employments, though I avouch it a skill worthy the knowledge and exercise of the greatest prince.

King Henry the Eighth could not only sing his part sure, but of himself composed a service of four, five, and six parts, as Erasmus in a certain epistle testifieth of his own knowledge. [j]

The Duke of Venosa, an Italian prince, [γ] in like manner of late years hath given excellent proof of his knowledge and love to music, having himself composed many rare songs which I have seen.

But above others, who carrieth away the palm for excellency, not only in music, but in whatsoever is to be wished in a brave prince, is the yet

e *In lib. de Angore animi.*
f Δαιμόνιον πρᾶγμα.—*Republic,* 531C.
g Τιμῆς ἔμμοροί εἰσι καὶ αἰδοῦς.—*Odyssey,* VIII, 480.
h *Politics,* 1337B (p. 14 above).

i Cicero, *Tusculan Disputations,* I. [Peacham's reference is not correct.—Ed.]
j In *Farragine Epistola.*

γ Carlo Gesualdo, Prince of Venosa.

living Maurice, Landgrave of Hesse, of whose own composition I have seen eight or ten several sets of motets and solemn music, set purposely for his own chapel, where, for the great honor of some festival and many times for his recreation only, he is his own organist. Besides he readily speaketh ten or twelve several languages, he is so universal a scholar that, coming (as he doth often) to his University of Marburg, what questions soever he meeteth with set up (as the manner is in the German and our universities), he will extempore dispute an hour or two (even in boots and spurs) upon them with their best professors. I pass over his rare skill in chirurgy, he being generally accounted the best bone-setter in the country. Who have seen his estate, his hospitality, his rich furnished armory, his grave stable of great horses, his courtesy to all strangers, being men of quality and good parts, let them speak the rest.

But since the natural inclination of some men driveth them as it were perforce to the top of excellency, examples of this kind are very rare; yea, great personages many times are more violently carried than might well stand with their honors and necessity of their affairs. Yet were it to these honest and commendable exercises, savoring of virtue, it were well; but many, neglecting their duties and places, will addict themselves wholly to trifles and the most ridiculous and childish practices. As Eropus, King of Macedonia, took pleasure only in making of candies,[k] Domitian his recreation was to catch and kill flies, and could not be spoken with many times in so serious employment.[l] Ptolomaeus Philadelphus was an excellent smith and a basket-maker, Alphonse Atestino, Duke of Ferrara, delighted himself only in turning and playing the joiner, Rodolph, the late emperor, in setting of stones and making watches. Which and the like much eclipse state and majesty, bringing familiarity and by consequence contempt with the meanest. I desire no more in you than to sing your part sure and at the first sight, withal to play the same upon your viol, or the exercise of the lute privately to yourself.

To deliver you my opinion, whom among other authors you should imitate and allow for the best, there being so many equally good, is somewhat difficult; yet as in the rest herein you shall have my opinion.

For motets and music of piety and devotion, as well for the honor of our nation as the merit of the man, I prefer above all others our phoenix, Mr. William Byrd, whom in that kind I know not whether any may equal, I am sure none excel, even by the judgment of France and Italy,

---

k Cuspinianus, *De Caesaribus et Imperatoribus*.   l Suetonius, *Lives of the Caesars*, VIII.

who are very sparing in the commendation of strangers in regard of that conceit they hold of themselves. His *Cantiones sacrae*,[8] as also his *Gradualia*,[9] are mere angelical and divine, and being of himself naturally disposed to gravity and piety his vein is not so much for light madrigals or canzonets, yet his "Virginelle" [10] and some others in his First Set cannot be mended by the best Italian of them all.

For composition I prefer next Ludovico de Victoria, a most judicious and a sweet composer; after him Orlando di Lasso, a very rare and excellent author who lived some forty years since in the court of the Duke of Bavaria. He hath published as well in Latin as French many sets; his vein is grave and sweet; among his Latin songs his *Seven Penitential Psalms* are the best, and that French set of his wherein is "Susanna un jour," [11] upon which ditty many others have since exercised their invention.[12]

For delicious air and sweet invention in madrigals, Luca Marenzio excelleth all other whosoever, having published more sets than any author else whosoever, and to say truth hath not an ill song, though sometime an oversight (which might be the printer's fault) of two eights or fifths escaped him, as between the tenor and bass in the last close of "I must depart all hapless," ending according to the nature of the ditty most artificially with a minim rest. His first, second, and third parts of "Tirsi," "Veggo dolce mio bene," "Che fa hogg'il mio sole," "Cantava," or "Sweet singing Amaryllis," are songs the muses themselves might not have been ashamed to have had composed.[13] Of stature and complexion he was a little and black man; he was organist in the Pope's chapel at Rome a good while; afterward he went into Poland, being in displeasure with the Pope for overmuch familiarity with a kinswoman of his (whom the Queen of Poland sent for by Luca Marenzio afterward, she being one of the rarest women in Europe for her voice and the lute). But returning, he found the affection of the Pope so estranged from him that hereupon he took a conceit and died.

Alphonso Ferabosco the father, while he lived, for judgment and depth of skill (as also his son yet living) was inferior unto none; what

8 *Collected Vocal Works*, I–III (London, 1937).

9 *Tudor Church Music*, VII (Oxford, 1927); *Collected Vocal Works*, IV–VII (London, 1938).

10 *The English Madrigal School* (London, 1920), XIV, No. 44 and 45; the words are translated from Ariosto.

11 *Works*, XIV, No. 64.

12 Cf. the settings by Ferabosco (*The Old English Edition*, XI, No. 1), Byrd (*The English Madrigal School*, XIV, No. 29, and XV, No. 8), Sweelinck (*Works*, VII, No. 8), and Farnaby (*The English Madrigal School*, XX, No. 12).

13 "Io partirò" ("I must depart all hapless"), "Tirsi," "Che fa hogg'il mio sole," and "Cantava" are reprinted in *Publikationen älterer Musik*, IV, i. The first three of these madrigals appeared with English text in Yonge's *Musica Transalpina* (1588); "Cantava" and "Veggo dolce mio bene" appeared in Watson's *Italian Madrigals Englished* (1590). The parallel fifths at the end of "Io partirò" occur in Yonge's reprint but not in the original composition.

he did was most elaborate and profound and pleasing enough in air, though Master Thomas Morley censureth him otherwise.[14] That of his, "I saw my lady weeping," [15] and the "Nightingale" (upon which ditty Master Byrd and he in a friendly emulation exercised their invention), [16] cannot be bettered for sweetness of air or depth of judgment.

I bring you now mine own master, Horatio Vecchi of Modena, beside goodness of air most pleasing of all other for his conceit and variety, wherewith all his works are singularly beautified, as well his madrigals of five and six as those his canzonets, printed at Nuremberg, wherein for trial sing his "Vivo in fuoco amoroso, Lucretia mia," where upon "Io catenato moro" with excellent judgment he driveth a crotchet through many minims, causing it to resemble a chain with the links. Again, in "S'io potessi raccor'i mei sospiri," the breaking of the word "sospiri" with crotchet and crotchet rest into sighs, and that "Fa mi un canzone, &c.," to make one sleep at noon, with sundry other of like conceit and pleasant invention.[17]

Then that great master, and master not long since of St. Mark's chapel in Venice,[m] second to none for a full, lofty, and sprightly vein, following none save his own humor, who while he lived was one of the most free and brave companions of the world. His *Penitential Psalms* are excellently composed and for piety are his best.

Nor must I here forget our rare countryman Peter Philips, organist to their Altezzas at Brussels, now one of the greatest masters of music in Europe. He hath sent us over many excellent songs, as well motets as madrigals; he affecteth altogether the Italian vein.

There are many other authors very excellent, as Boschetto [n] and Claudio de Monteverdi, equal to any before named, Giovanni Ferretti, Stephano Felis, Giulio Rinaldi, Philippe de Monte, Andrea Gabrieli, Cipriano de Rore, Pallavicino, Geminiano, with others yet living, whose several works for me here to examine would be over tedious and needless; and for me, please your own ear and fancy. Those whom I have before mentioned have been ever (within these thirty or forty years) held for the best.

I willingly, to avoid tediousness, forbear to speak of the worth and excellency of the rest of our English composers, Master Doctor Dowland,

m Giovanni Croce.

n Boschetto, his motets of 8 parts printed in Rome, 1594.

14 *A Plain and Easy Introduction*, p. 180 (p. 275 above).

15 *The Old English Edition*, XI, No. 2 and 3.

16 Ferabosco's setting is reprinted in *The Old English Edition*, XI, No. 9, Byrd's in *The English Madrigal School*, XV, No. 9; both are prompted by the Lassus chanson "Le rossignol" (*Works*, XIV, No. 82), printed with English text in Yonge's *Musica Transalpina* (1588).

17 Vecchi's "Fa mi un canzone" (properly "Fa una canzone") is reprinted in Alfred Einstein, *The Italian Madrigal* (Princeton, 1949), III, No. 87. It has this refrain:

Falla d'un tuono ch'invita al dormire,
Dolcemente facendola finire.

Thomas Morley, Mr. Alphonso, Mr. Wilbye, Mr. Kirbye, Mr. Weelkes, Michael East, Mr. Bateson, Mr. Deering, with sundry others, inferior to none in the world (however much soever the Italian attributes to himself) for depth of skill and richness of conceit.

Infinite is the sweet variety that the theorique of music exerciseth the mind withal, as the contemplation of proportion, of concords and discords, diversity of moods and tones, infiniteness of invention, &c. But I dare affirm there is no one science in the world that so affecteth the free and generous spirit with a more delightful and inoffensive recreation or better disposeth the mind to what is commendable and virtuous.

The commonwealth of the Cynethenses in Arcadia, falling from the delight they formerly had in music, grew into seditious humors and civil wars, which Polybius took especially note of,[o] and I suppose hereupon it was ordained in Arcadia that everyone should practise music by the space of thirty years.

The ancient Gauls in like manner (whom Julian [p] termed barbarous) became most courteous and tractable by the practise of music.

Yea, in my opinion no rhetoric more persuadeth or hath greater power over the mind; nay, hath not music her figures, the same which rhetoric? What is a revert but her antistrophe? her reports, but sweet anaphoras? her counterchange of points, antimetaboles? her passionate airs, but prosopopoeias? with infinite other of the same nature.

How doth music amaze us when of sound discords she maketh the sweetest harmony? And who can show us the reason why two basins, bowls, brass pots, or the like, of the same bigness, the one being full, the other empty, shall stricken be a just diapason in sound one to the other; or that there should be such sympathy in sounds that two lutes of equal size being laid upon a table and tuned unison, or alike in the Gamma, G *sol re ut,* or any other string, the one stricken, the other untouched shall answer it?

But to conclude, if all arts hold their esteem and value according to their effects, account this goodly science not among the number of those which Lucian placeth without the gates of hell as vain and unprofitable, but of such which are πηγαὶ τῶν καλῶν, the fountains of our lives' good and happiness. Since it is a principal means of glorifying our merciful Creator, it heightens our devotion, it gives delight and ease to our travails, it expelleth sadness and heaviness of spirit, preserveth people in concord and amity, allayeth fierceness and anger, and lastly, is the best physic for many melancholy diseases.

---

o *Histories,* IV. xx (quoted by Athenaeus, p *Epistola 71* (Hertlein).
p. 51 above).

VII

Reformation and Counter-Reformation

38. Martin Luther

The great German reformer was born at Eisleben in 1483 and died there in 1546. From 1522 on, a great deal of his attention was directed toward achieving a reform of the services of the church. Luther had long occupied himself with the idea of a German Mass, and during 1524 he worked on the realization of this project, assisted by two musical collaborators, Johann Walther and Conrad Rupff. The result of these efforts was the publication of Luther's "German Mass." At the same time, the reformer was turning his attention to writing and adapting hymns to be sung during the service. The Wittemberg Gesangbuch, which also appeared in 1524, has remained to our day the basis of the musical part of the service of the Evangelical church. And yet, none of the tunes introduced into Protestant church singing can be attributed to Luther himself with any degree of certainty, not even the most famous of them, "Ein' feste Burg ist unser Gott."

Wittemberg Gesangbuch [1]

[1524]

Foreword to the first edition

THAT THE singing of spiritual songs is a good thing and one pleasing to God is, I believe, not hidden from any Christian, for not only the example of the prophets and kings in the Old Testament (who praised God with singing and playing, with hymns and the sound of all manner of stringed instruments), but also the special custom of singing psalms, have been known to everyone and to universal Christianity from the beginning. Nay, St. Paul establishes this also, I Corinthians 14, and orders

---

1 Text: *Publikationen aelterer praktischer und theoretischer Musikwerke,* VII (Berlin, 1878), preceding p. 1 of score.

the Colossians to sing psalms and spiritual songs to the Lord in their hearts, in order that God's word and Christ's teaching may be thus spread abroad and practised in every way.

Accordingly, as a good beginning and to encourage those who can do better, I and several others have brought together certain spiritual songs with a view to spreading abroad and setting in motion the holy Gospel which now, by the grace of God, has again emerged, so that we too may pride ourselves, as Moses does in his song, Exodus 15, that Christ is our strength and song and may not know anything to sing or to say, save Jesus Christ our Savior, as Paul says, I Corinthians 2.

These, further, are set for four voices for no other reason than that I wished that the young (who, apart from this, should and must be trained in music and in other proper arts) might have something to rid them of their love ditties and wanton songs and might, instead of these, learn wholesome things and thus yield willingly, as becomes them, to the good; also, because I am not of the opinion that all the arts shall be crushed to earth and perish through the Gospel, as some bigoted persons pretend, but would willingly see them all, and especially music, servants of Him who gave and created them. So I pray that every pious Christian may bear with this and, should God grant him an equal or a greater talent, help to further it. Besides, unfortunately, the world is so lax and so forgetful in training and teaching its neglected young people that one might well encourage this first of all. God grant us His grace. Amen.

39. Johann Walther

Luther's friend and musical adviser, Johann Walther was born in 1496 and died in 1570 at Torgau, where he had become a choir singer to the Elector of Saxony in 1524 and choirmaster in 1525. He was sent to Dresden in 1548 and remained there until 1554 but subsequently returned to his home.

Walther assisted Luther in working out the musical part of the German Protestant Mass and the Wittemberg Gesangbuch. He published several collections of polyphonic church songs, and other compositions of his are found in various miscellaneous collections published by German music publishers of the sixteenth century.

Wittemberg Gesangbuch [1]

[1537]

Foreword to the revised edition

No WONDER that music is so utterly despised and rejected at this time, seeing that other arts, which after all we should and must possess, are so lamentably regarded by everyone as altogether worthless. But the Devil will have his way: now that, by the grace of God, we have overthrown against him the popish mass with all its trappings, he throws to the ground in turn, as best he can, all that God requires. Yet, in order that our fair art may not be thus wholly destroyed, I have—in God's praise and in pure defiance of the Devil and his contempt—brought out in print the spiritual songs formerly printed at Wittemberg, setting the greater part anew, insofar as God permitted me, carefully correcting and improving the rest, and further adding several little pieces for five and

---

1 **Text**: With Luther's foreword (see above).

six voices. So I pray that every pious Christian may bear with this my insufficiency and do the same or better for the glory of God and the furtherance of the art. And although these my songs will have many critics, I readily concede to anyone the honor of being my judge, seeing that I perhaps am still a student in this art. With this I commend all pious Christians to almighty God; may He grant us all his grace. Amen.

40. Jean Calvin

Jean Calvin (or Cauvin), the great Franco-Swiss religious reformer, was born at Noyon, France, in 1509, and died at Geneva in 1564. He lived first in Paris but was forced to leave because of his leanings toward the cause of reformation. He fled to Basle in 1534 and published in that city his *Institutio religionis christianae* (1536). Subsequently Calvin settled and taught in Geneva, where he spent the rest of his life building up a church community in accordance with his religious convictions. Here the French translation of the Psalter by Marot and Bèze, which was to assume such importance for the service of the Calvinist Church, was published in 1543.

Geneva Psalter [1]

[1543]

Foreword

THE EPISTLE TO THE READER

JEAN CALVIN to all Christians and lovers of God's Word, Salutation:

As it is a thing indeed demanded by Christianity, and one of the most necessary, that each of the faithful observe and maintain the communion of the Church in his neighborhood, attending the assemblies which are held both on the Lord's day and on other days to honor and serve God, so it is also expedient and reasonable that all should know and hear what is said and done in the temple, to receive fruit and edification therefrom. For our Lord did not institute the order which we must observe when we gather together in His name merely that the world might be amused by seeing and looking upon it, but wished rather that therefrom should

[1] Text: *Oeuvres choisies. Publiées par la Compagnie des pasteurs de Genève* (Geneva, 1909), pp. 169–170, 173–176.

come profit to all His people. Thus witnesseth Saint Paul,[2] commanding that all which is done in the Church be directed unto the common edifying of all, a thing the servant would not have commanded, had it not been the intention of the Master. For to say that we can have devotion, either at prayers or at ceremonies, without understanding anything of them, is a great mockery, however much it be commonly said. A good affection toward God is not a thing dead and brutish, but a lively movement, proceeding from the Holy Spirit when the heart is rightly touched and the understanding enlightened. And indeed, if one could be edified by the things which one sees without knowing what they mean, Saint Paul would not so rigorously forbid speaking in an unknown tongue and would not use the argument that where there is no doctrine, there is no edification.[3] Yet if we wish to honor well the holy decrees of our Lord, as used in the Church, the main thing is to know what they contain, what they mean, and to what end they tend, in order that their observance may be useful and salutary and in consequence rightly ruled.

Now there are in brief three things that our Lord has commanded us to observe in our spiritual assemblies, namely, the preaching of His Word, the public and solemn prayers, and the administration of His sacraments. I abstain at this time from speaking of preaching, seeing that there is no question thereof. . . . Of the sacraments I shall speak later.

As to the public prayers, these are of two kinds: some are offered by means of words alone, the others with song. And this is not a thing invented a little time ago, for it has existed since the first origin of the Church; this appears from the histories, and even Saint Paul speaks not only of praying by word of mouth, but also of singing.[4] And in truth we know by experience that song has great force and vigor to move and inflame the hearts of men to invoke and praise God with a more vehement and ardent zeal. It must always be looked to that the song be not light and frivolous but have weight and majesty, as Saint Augustine says,[5] and there is likewise a great difference between the music one makes to entertain men at table and in their homes, and the psalms which are sung in the Church in the presence of God and His angels.

Therefore, when anyone wishes to judge rightly of the form that is here presented, we hope that he will find it holy and pure, for it is entirely directed toward that edification of which we have spoken, however more widely the practice of singing may extend. For even in our homes and in the fields it should be an incentive, and as it were an organ

---

2 1 Corinthians 14:26.   4 1 Corinthians 14:15.
3 1 Corinthians 14:19.   5 Cf. *Epistola* LV, xviii, 34.

for praising God and lifting up our hearts to Him, to console us by meditating upon His virtue, goodness, wisdom, and justice, a thing more necessary than one can say. In the first place, it is not without reason that the Holy Spirit exhorts us so carefully by means of the Holy Scripture to rejoice in God and that all our joy is there reduced to its true end, for He knows how much we are inclined to delight in vanity. Just as our nature, then, draws us and induces us to seek all means of foolish and vicious rejoicing, so, to the contrary, our Lord, to distract us and withdraw us from the enticements of the flesh and the world, presents to us all possible means in order to occupy us in that spiritual joy which He so much recommends to us.[6] Now among the other things proper to recreate man and give him pleasure, music is either the first or one of the principal, and we must think that it is a gift of God deputed to that purpose. For which reason we must be the more careful not to abuse it, for fear of soiling and contaminating it, converting it to our condemnation when it has been dedicated to our profit and welfare. Were there no other consideration than this alone, it might well move us to moderate the use of music to make it serve all that is of good repute and that it should not be the occasion of our giving free rein to dissoluteness or of our making ourselves effeminate with disordered pleasures and that it should not become the instrument of lasciviousness or of any shamelessness. But there is still more, for there is hardly anything in the world with more power to turn or bend, this way and that, the morals of men, as Plato has prudently considered.[7] And in fact we find by experience that it has a secret and almost incredible power to move our hearts in one way or another.

Wherefore we must be the more diligent in ruling it in such a manner that it may be useful to us and in no way pernicious. For this reason the early doctors of the Church often complain that the people of their times are addicted to dishonest and shameless songs, which not without reason they call mortal and Satanic poison for the corruption of the world. Now in speaking of music I understand two parts, namely, the letter, or subject and matter, and the song, or melody. It is true that, as Saint Paul says, every evil word corrupts good manners,[8] but when it has the melody with it, it pierces the heart much more strongly and enters within; as wine is poured into the cask with a funnel, so venom and corruption are distilled to the very depths of the heart by melody. Now what is there to do? It is to have songs not merely honest but also holy, which will be

---

6 Here ends the preface in the first edition (1542). What follows is found only in the edition of 1545 and in those of the Psalter. [Choisy]

7 *Republic,* 401D (p. 8 above).
8 Ephesians 4:29.

like spurs to incite us to pray to God and praise Him, and to meditate upon His works in order to love, fear, honor, and glorify Him. Now what Saint Augustine says is true—that no one can sing things worthy of God save what he has received from Him.[9] Wherefore, although we look far and wide and search on every hand, we shall not find better songs nor songs better suited to that end than the Psalms of David which the Holy Spirit made and uttered through him. And for this reason, when we sing them we may be certain that God puts the words in our mouths as if Himself sang in us to exalt His glory. Wherefore Chrysostom exhorts men as well as women and little children to accustom themselves to sing them, in order that this may be like a meditation to associate them with the company of angels.[10] Then we must remember what Saint Paul says—that spiritual songs cannot be well sung save with the heart.[11] Now the heart requires the intelligence, and therein, says Saint Augustine, lies the difference between the singing of men and of birds.[12] For a linnet, a nightingale, a parrot will sing well, but it will be without understanding. Now the peculiar gift of man is to sing knowing what he is saying. After the intelligence must follow the heart and the affection, which cannot be unless we have the hymn imprinted on our memory in order never to cease singing.

For these reasons the present book, even for this cause, besides the rest which has been said, should be in singular favor with everyone who desires to enjoy himself honestly and in God's way, that is, for his welfare and to the profit of his neighbors, and thus it has no need to be much recommended by me, seeing that it carries its value and its praise. But may the world be so well advised that instead of the songs that it has previously used, in part vain and frivolous, in part stupid and dull, in part foul and vile and consequently evil and harmful, it may accustom itself hereafter to sing these divine and celestial hymns with the good King David. Touching the melody, it has seemed best that it be moderated in the way that we have adopted in order that it may have the weight and majesty proper to the subject and may even be suitable for singing in Church, according to what has been said.

Geneva, June 10, 1543.

---

9 *In Psalmum XXXIV Enarratio*, I, 1.
10 *Exposition of Psalm XLI* (pp. 68–70 above).
11 Ephesians 5:19.
12 *In Psalmum XVIII Enarratio*, II, 1.

41. Claude Goudimel

Born at Besançon circa 1505, Goudimel lost his life in 1572 as a victim of the Huguenot massacres at Lyon. His first compositions are found in the extensive collections of French chansons published in 1549 by Nicolas du Chemin in Paris. In 1557 and 1558 Goudimel published a Magnificat and four masses—his last music for the services of the Catholic Church. In all, Goudimel published three distinct settings of the tunes in the Huguenot psalters—one in motet-style between 1551 and 1566, and two for four voices, simply harmonized, in 1564 and 1565.

Geneva Psalter [1]

[*1565*]

Foreword to the edition of 1565

To our readers:

To the melody of the psalms we have, in this little volume, adapted three parts, not to induce you to sing them in Church, but that you may rejoice in God, particularly in your homes. This should not be found an ill thing, the more so since the melody used in Church is left in its entirety, just as though it were alone.

1 Text: The facsimile of the original edition (Geneva, 1565), published by the Bärenreiter-Verlag (Cassel, 1935).

42. Thomas Cranmer

An English churchman and one of the principal promoters of Reformation in his native country, Cranmer was born in 1489. He was appointed Chaplain to Henry VIII and became Archbishop of Canterbury in 1533. Cranmer played an important role in the early history of the Church of England, particularly in the publishing of the Book of Common Prayer. He died at the stake as a heretic in 1556, during Mary's reign.

Letter to Henry VIII [1]

[1544]

IT MAY please Your Majesty to be advertised that, according to Your Highness' commandment, sent unto me by Your Grace's secretary, Mr. Pagett, I have translated into the English tongue, so well as I could in so short time, certain processions to be used upon festival days if after due correction and amendment of the same Your Highness shall think it so convenient. In which translation, forasmuch as many of the processions in the Latin were but barren, as meseemed, and little fruitful, I was constrained to use more than the liberty of a translator: for in some processions I have altered divers words; in some I have added part; in some taken part away; some I have left out whole, either for because the matter appeared to me to be little to purpose, or because the days be not with us festival days; and some processions I have added whole because I thought I had a better matter for the purpose than was the procession in Latin. The judgment whereof I refer wholly unto Your Majesty, and after Your Highness hath corrected it, if Your Grace command some devout and solemn note to be made thereunto (as it is

1 Text: *Miscellaneous Writings and Letters* (Cambridge, 1846), p. 412.

to the procession which Your Majesty hath already set forth in English) [2] I trust it will much excitate and stir the hearts of all men unto devotion and godliness. But in my opinion, the song that should be made thereunto would not be full of notes, but, as near as may be, for every syllable a note, so that it may be sung distinctly and devoutly as be in the matins and evensong Venite, the hymns, Te Deum, Benedictus, Magnificat, Nunc dimittis, and all the psalms and versicles; and in the mass Gloria in excelsis, Gloria Patri, the Creed, the Preface, the Pater Noster, and some of the Sanctus and Agnus. As concerning the "Salva festa dies," the Latin note, as I think, is sober and distinct enough, wherefore I have travailed to make the verses in English and have put the Latin note unto the same. Nevertheless, they that be cunning in singing can make a much more solemn note thereto. I made them only for a proof, to see how English would do in song.[3] But because mine English verses lack the grace and facility that I wish they had, Your Majesty may cause some other to make them again that can do the same in more pleasant English and phrase. As for the sentence, I suppose will serve well enough. Thus Almighty God preserve Your Majesty in long and prosperous health and felicity!

From Bekisbourne, the 7th of October.
    Your Grace's most bounden
        chaplain and beadsman,
            T. Cantuarien

To the King's most excellent Majesty

---

[2] *An Exhortation unto Prayer* (London, Richard Grafton, June 16, 1544). The full title continues: "Thought meet by the King's Majesty and his clergy to be read to the people in every church afore processions. Also a litany with suffrages to be said or sung in the time of the said processions."

[3] Cranmer's translation seems not to have been published or preserved.

43. Thomas East

An important typographer and publisher, Thomas East (or Easte, Este), is remembered as the publisher of much Elizabethan music. Between 1588 and 1607, he printed a long series of works by Byrd, Yonge, Watson, Morley, Kirbye, Wilbye, Dowland, Jones, and other authors. His first publication was William Byrd's *Psalms, Sonnets and Songs of Sadness and Piety*. In 1592 he edited *The Whole Book of Psalms, With Their Wonted Tunes, in Four Parts*. Two other editions appeared in 1594 and 1604. This collection was one of the first to appear in score, rather than in separate part-books.

The Whole Book of Psalms [1]

[*1592*]

Dedication and preface

To the Right Honorable Sir John Puckering, Knight, Lord Keeper of the Great Seal of England:

The word of God, Right Honorable, delighteth those which are spiritually minded; the art of music recreateth such as are not sensually affected; where zeal in the one and skill in the other do meet, the whole man is revived. The mercies of God are great provoking unto thankfulness; the necessities of man are great, enforcing unto prayer; the state of us all is such that the publishing of God's glory for the edifying one of another cannot be overslipped; in all these the heart must be the workmaster, the tongue the instrument, and a sanctified knowledge as the hand to polish the work. The Psalms of David are a paraphrasis of

---

1 The original edition (London, 1592). A reprint, edited by E. F. Rimbault, was published in 1844 as Vol. 11 of the series brought out by the Musical Antiquarian Society.

the Scriptures; they teach us thankfulness, prayer, and all the duties of a Christian whatsoever; they have such comfort in them that such as will be conversant in the same cannot possibly lose their labor. Blessed is that man which delighteth therein and meditateth in the same continually. He that is heavy hath the Psalms to help his prayer; he that is merry hath the Psalms to guide his affections; and he that hath a desire to be seriously employed in either of these duties hath this excellent gift of God, the knowledge of music, offered him for his further help; that the heart rejoicing in the word and the ears delighting in the notes and tunes, both these might join together unto the praise of God. Some have pleased themselves with pastorals, others with madrigals, but such as are endued with David's heart desire with David to sing unto God psalms and hymns and spiritual songs. For whose sake I have set forth this work that they busy themselves in the psalms of this holy man, being by men of skill put into four parts that each man may sing that part which best may serve his voice.

In this book the church tunes are carefully corrected and other short tunes added which are sung in London and other places of this realm. And regarding chiefly to help the simple, curiosity is shunned. The profit is theirs that will use this book; the pains theirs that have compiled it; the charges his who, setting it forth, respecteth a public benefit, not his private gain. Now having finished it, in most humble manner I present it unto Your Honor as to a maintainer of godliness, a friend to virtue, and a lover of music, hoping of Your Lordship's favorable acceptance, craving your honorable patronage and countenance, and praying unto God long to continue Your Lordship a protector of the just and the same God to be a protector of Your Lordship's welfare forever.

Your good Lordship's most humbly at command

Thomas East.

The Preface

Although I might have used the skill of some one learned musician in the setting of these psalms in four parts, yet for variety's sake I have entreated the help of many, being such as I know to be expert in the art and sufficient to answer such curious carping musicians whose skill hath not been employed to the furthering of this work.[2] And I have not only set down in this book all the tunes usually printed heretofore with as

---

2 East's contributors were John Farmer, George Kirbye, Richard Allison, Giles Farnaby, Edward Blancks, John Dowland, William Cob-bold, Edmund Hooper, Edward Johnson, and Michael Cavendish.

much truth as I could possibly gather among divers of our ordinary psalm books, but also have added those which are commonly sung nowadays and not printed in our common psalm books with the rest. And all this have I so orderly cast that the four parts lie always together in open sight. The which my travail, as it hath been to the furtherance of music in all Godly sort and to the comfort of all good Christians, so I pray thee to take it in good part and use it to the glory of God.

T. E.

44. Jacob de Kerle

Born at Ypres, Belgium, in 1531, de Kerle died in 1591 at Prague. He was first organist or choirmaster at Orvieto in Italy, later in Bavaria, and subsequently in Ypres, Rome, Augsburg, Cambrai, and Cologne. From 1582 until his death he was court chaplain to Rudolph II.

De Kerle's biography is varied and interesting because of the important political and religious events in which he took part. The style of his music is elaborately polyphonic; at times he uses also the new devices of contemporary chromaticism. De Kerle left works in the different forms of religious music but did not altogether neglect madrigal writing. His *Preces speciales*, written for the Council of Trent, were published at Venice in 1562.

Preces speciales [1]

[*1562*]

Dedication

To the Most Illustrious and Reverend Lords Ercole Cardinal of
Mantua, Girolamo Cardinal Seripando, Stanislaus Cardinal
of Ermland, Lodovico Cardinal Simonetta, Mark Cardinal of Hohenems, Legates of the Tridentine
Council, His Most Worshipful Lords

THESE TEN forms of pious prayer under the title of responses, by Pietro Soto, a member of the Dominican Order and a man of apostolic life and doctrine, and accommodated to the figures and modes of music by me at the command of that best and most distinguished prince the Cardinal Bishop of Augsburg, my patron, I have thought best to send to you,

---

1 Text: *Denkmäler der Tonkunst in Bayern*, XXVI (Augsburg, 1926), lxviii.

most wise and illustrious Fathers, who preside over the public council of the Christian Church. For since whatever time remains free from the salutary affairs of the Republic you devote to divine matters and sacred offices, I have hoped that these prayers, not unrelated either to the praises of God or to the time of the Church, would not be displeasing to you. You will not, I think, reject the plan of joining musical numbers to these prayers, a plan which that most holy man David, the man after God's own heart, employed. If you less approve my own skill in the matter, you will surely not disapprove of my purpose; for what I can, I contribute to the glory of God in the sight of all. For if God judges the services and works of men not by the weight of the matter but by their minds, then the nearer to God you approach than other men, the more you are wishing to imitate His benignity. Oh, that it may only be possible for us to call down the mercy of God by pious prayers as we perceive is done by your wise actions! Given at Rome.

Your Most Illustrious and Reverend Lordships'
Most Humble and Devoted Servant,
Jacobus de Kerle

45. Pope Gregory XIII

The brief of Gregory XIII, entrusting Palestrina and his colleague Annibale Zoilo with the revision of the music of the Roman Gradual and Antiphoner, was a natural outgrowth of the publication, in 1568 and 1570, of the reformed Breviary and Missal ordered by the Council of Trent and approved by Gregory's predecessor, Paul V. The aim of this proposed revision was twofold: on the one hand, it was to bring the choir books into agreement with the liturgical revisions already made official; on the other, it was to rid the plainsong melodies of those "barbarisms, obscurities, contrarieties, and superfluities" which were offensive to Renaissance sensibilities. During the year 1578, as his correspondence shows, Palestrina was deeply preoccupied with this work of revision; later on, however, he seems to have set it aside, never to take it up again. In 1611, some years after his death, other hands were charged with the responsibility, and although it seems clear that the so-called "Editio Medicaea," published in 1614, is not very different from the revised version that Palestrina must have had in mind, it is on the whole unlikely that it actually includes any work of his.

Pope from 1572 to 1585, Gregory XIII (Ugo Buoncompagno) inaugurated important changes in the musical arrangements at St. Peter's. His revision of the calendar has made his name a household word. To him Palestrina dedicated his Fourth Book of Masses (1582) and his motets on the Song of Solomon (Book V, 1584).

Brief on the Reform of the Chant [1]

[*October 25, 1577*]

To Palestrina and Zoilo

BELOVED SONS:

Greetings and apostolic benediction!

Inasmuch as it has come to our attention that the Antiphoners, Graduals, and Psalters that have been provided with music for the celebration of the divine praises and offices in plainsong (as it is called) since the publication of the Breviary and Missal ordered by the Council of Trent have been filled to overflowing with barbarisms, obscurities, contrarieties, and superfluities as a result of the clumsiness or negligence or even wickedness of the composers, scribes, and printers: in order that these books may agree with the aforesaid Breviary and Missal, as is appropriate and fitting, and may at the same time be so ordered, their superfluities having been shorn away and their barbarisms and obscurities removed, that through their agency God's name may be reverently, distinctly, and devoutly praised; desiring to provide for this in so far as with God's help we may, we have decided to turn to you, whose skill in the art of music and in singing, whose faithfulness and diligence, and whose piety toward God have been fully tested, and to assign to you this all-important task, trusting confidently that you will amply satisfy this desire of ours. And thus we charge you with the business of revising and (so far as shall seem expedient to you) of purging, correcting, and reforming these Antiphoners, Graduals, and Psalters, together with such other chants as are used in our churches according to the rite of Holy Roman Church, whether at the Canonical Hours or at Mass or at other divine services, and over all of these things we entrust you for the present with full and unrestricted jurisdiction and power by virtue of our apostolic authority, and in order that you may pursue the aforesaid more quickly and diligently you have our permission to admit other skilled musicians as as-

---

1 Text: Raphael Molitor, *Die nach-Tridentinische Choral-Reform zu Rom*, I (Leipzig, 1901), 297–298.

sistants if you so desire. The Apostolic Constitutions and any other regulations that may be to the contrary notwithstanding. Given at St. Peter's in Rome under Peter's seal this twenty-fifth day of October, 1577, in the sixth year of our pontificate.

To our beloved sons Giovanni Pierluigi da Palestrina and Annibale Zoilo Romano, musicians of our private chapel.

VIII

"Seconda pratica" and "stile rappresentativo"

46. Pietro de' Bardi

The letter reproduced below was addressed by Pietro de' Bardi—the son of Giovanni, the patron and promoter of the first Florentine "Camerata"—to G. B. Doni (1594–1647), who had asked for information about the first attempts at realizing the new "representative" style which Pietro had witnessed as a youth in his father's home.

Letter to G. B. Doni [1]
[*1634*]

To MY very illustrious and revered patron, the Most Honored Signor Giovan Battista Doni:

My father, Signor Giovanni, who took great delight in music and was in his day a composer of some reputation, always had about him the most celebrated men of the city, learned in this profession, and inviting them to his house, he formed a sort of delightful and continual academy from which vice and in particular every kind of gaming were absent. To this the noble youth of Florence were attracted with great profit to themselves, passing their time not only in pursuit of music, but also in discussing and receiving instruction in poetry, astrology, and other sciences which by turns lent value to this pleasant converse.

Vincenzo Galilei, the father of the present famous astronomer, a man of a certain repute in those days, was so taken with this distinguished assembly that, adding to practical music, in which he was highly regarded, the study of musical theory, he endeavored, with the help of these virtuosi and of his own frequent vigils, to extract the essence of the Greek, the

---

1 Text: Angelo Solerti, *Le origini del melodramma* (Turin, 1903), pp. 143–147. Doni makes extensive use of this letter in Chapter 9 of his "Trattato della musica scenica," published posthumously in his collected works (Florence, 1763).

Latin, and the more modern writers, and by this means became a thorough master of the theory of every sort of music.

This great intellect recognized that, besides restoring ancient music in so far as so obscure a subject permitted, one of the chief aims of the academy was to improve modern music and to raise it in some degree from the wretched state to which it had been reduced, chiefly by the Goths, after the loss of the ancient music and of the other liberal arts and sciences. Thus he was the first to let us hear singing in *stile rappresentativo*, in which arduous undertaking, then considered almost ridiculous, he was chiefly encouraged and assisted by my father, who toiled for entire nights and incurred great expense for the sake of this noble discovery, as the said Vincenzo gratefully acknowledges to my father in his learned book on ancient and modern music.[2] Accordingly he let us hear the lament of Count Ugolino, from Dante,[3] intelligibly sung by a good tenor and precisely accompanied by a consort of viols. This novelty, although it aroused considerable envy among the professional musicians, was pleasing to the true lovers of the art. Continuing with this undertaking, Galilei set to music a part of the Lamentations and Responds of Holy Week, and these were sung in devout company in the same manner.

Giulio Caccini, considered a rare singer and a man of taste, although very young, was at this time in my father's "Camerata," and feeling himself inclined toward this new music, he began, entirely under my father's instructions, to sing ariettas, sonnets, and other poems suitable for reading aloud, to a single instrument and in a manner that astonished his hearers.

Also in Florence at this time was Jacopo Peri, who, as the first pupil of Cristofano Malvezzi, received high praise as a player of the organ and the keyboard instruments and as a composer of counterpoint and was rightly regarded as second to none of the singers in that city. This man, in competition with Giulio, brought the enterprise of the *stile rappresentativo* to light, and avoiding a certain roughness and excessive antiquity which had been felt in the compositions of Galilei, he sweetened this style, together with Giulio, and made it capable of moving the passions in a rare manner, as in the course of time was done by them both.

By so doing, these men acquired the title of the first singers and inventors of this manner of composing and singing. Peri had more science, and having found a way of imitating familiar speech by using few sounds

---

2 See p. 303 above, note 5.   3 *Inferno*, xxxiii, 4–75.

and by meticulous exactness in other respects, he won great fame. Giulio's inventions had more elegance.

The first poem to be sung on the stage in *stile rappresentativo* was the story of *Dafne*, by Signor Ottavio Rinuccini, set to music by Peri in few numbers and short scenes and recited and sung privately in a small room.[4] I was left speechless with amazement. It was sung to the accompaniment of a consort of instruments, an arrangement followed thereafter in the other comedies. Caccini and Peri were under great obligation to Signor Ottavio, but under still greater to Signor Jacopo Corsi,[5] who, becoming ardent and discontent with all but the superlative in this art, directed these composers with excellent ideas and marvelous doctrines, as befitted so noble an enterprise. These directions were carried out by Peri and Caccini in all their compositions of this sort and were combined by them in various manners.

After the *Dafne*, many stories were represented by Signor Ottavio himself, who, as good poet and good musician in one, was received with great applause, as was the affable Corsi, who supported the enterprise with a lavish hand. The most famous of these stories were the *Euridice* and the *Arianna;*[6] besides these, many shorter ones were set to music by Caccini and Peri. Nor was there any want of men to imitate them, and in Florence, the first home of this sort of music, and in other cities of Italy, especially in Rome, these gave and are still giving a marvelous account of themselves on the dramatic stage. Among the foremost of these it seems fitting to place Monteverdi.

I fear that I have badly carried out Your Most Reverend Lordship's command, not only because I have been slow to obey Your Lordship, but also because I have far from satisfied myself, for there are few now living who remember the music of those times. Nonetheless I believe that as I serve Your Lordship with heartfelt affection, so Your Lordship will confirm the truth of my small selection from the many things that might be said about this style of *musica rappresentativa* which is in such esteem.

But I hope that I shall in some way be excused through the kindness of Your Most Excellent Lordship, and predicting for Your Lordship

---

4 For the involved history of this work, see O. G. Sonneck's "'Dafne,' the First Opera," *Sammelbände der Internationalen Musik-Gesellschaft,* XV (1913–14), 102–110, or his note on the libretto in the Catalogue of *Opera Librettos Printed before 1800* (Washington, 1914), I, 339–345.

5 See the further references to this influential

patron and amateur by Rinuccini and Peri (pp. 368, 373 and 375 below). Corsi set at least two numbers from Rinuccini's *Dafne* to music; for a recent reprint of the second of these see Robert Haas, *Die Musik des Barock* (Potsdam, 1934), p. 23. An elegy on Corsi's death, set to music by Marco da Gagliano, was published in 1604.

6 Set to music by Monteverdi in 1608.

a most happy Christmas, I pray that God Himself, the father of all blessings, may grant Your Lordship perfect felicity.

Florence, December 14, 1634.
   Your Very Illustrious and Reverend Lordship's
      Most humble servant,
         Pietro Bardi, Conte di Vernio.

47. Ottavio Rinuccini

Ottavio Rinuccini, the librettist of the *Euridice*, was born in Florence in 1562, and if we except his brief stay in Paris following the marriage of Maria dei Medici and Henry IV of France, he remained a resident of Florence until his death in 1621. We first hear of him in a musical connection as the author of the texts for a group of madrigals performed in honor of the wedding of Virginia dei Medici and Cesare d'Este in 1587; two years later, in 1589, he provided the texts set to music by Marenzio for the intermezzo depicting Apollo's combat with the dragon, performed in honor of the wedding of Ferdinand dei Medici and Christine of Lorraine. His work for this intermezzo was later expanded in his *Dafne*, set to music by Peri and Corsi in 1594, by Marco da Gagliano in 1607, and—in a German translation by Martin Opitz—by Heinrich Schütz in 1627; it thus becomes the connecting link between the long series of Florentine intermezzi, which had begun in 1539, and the opera itself. Aside from his early wedding-pieces and his librettos for *Dafne* and *Euridice*, Rinuccini is also the author of two librettos written for Monteverdi in 1608—*Arianna* and *Il Ballo delle ingrate*—and of madrigals and canzonette set to music by Monteverdi, Marco da Gagliano, and other early monodists. His collected verses were published posthumously in 1622.

Euridice [1]

[1600]

Dedication

To THE most Christian Maria Medici, Queen of France and of Navarre.

It has been the opinion of many, most Christian Queen, that the ancient Greeks and Romans, in representing their tragedies upon the stage,

---

1 Text: Solerti, *op. cit.*, pp. 40–42.

sang them throughout. But until now this noble manner of recitation has been neither revived nor (to my knowledge) even attempted by anyone, and I used to believe that this was due to the imperfection of the modern music, by far inferior to the ancient. But the opinion thus formed was wholly driven from my mind by Messer Jacopo Peri, who, hearing of the intention of Signor Jacopo Corsi and myself, set to music with so much grace the fable of *Dafne* (which I had written solely to make a simple trial of what the music of our age could do) that it gave pleasure beyond belief to the few who heard it.

Taking courage from this, Signor Jacopo gave to this same fable a better form and again represented it at his house, where it was heard and commended, not only by the entire nobility of our favored state, but also by the most serene Grand Duchess and by the most illustrious cardinals Dal Monte and Montaldo.[2]

But much greater favor and fortune have been bestowed upon the *Euridice*, set to music by the aforesaid Peri with wonderful art, little used by others, for the graciousness and magnificence of the most serene Grand Duchess found it worthy of representation upon a most noble stage in the presence of Your Majesty, the Cardinal Legates, and ever so many princes and lords of Italy and France.[3]

For this reason, beginning to recognize with what favor such representations in music are received, I have wished to bring these two to light, in order that others, more skillful than myself, may employ their talents to increase the number and improve the quality of poems thus composed and cease to envy those ancients so much celebrated by noble writers.

To some I may seem to have been too bold in altering the conclusion of the fable of Orpheus,[4] but so it seemed fitting to me at a time of such great rejoicing, having as my justification the example of the Greek poets in other fables. And our own Dante ventured to declare that Ulysses was drowned on his voyage,[5] for all that Homer and the other poets had related the contrary. So likewise I have followed the authority of Sophocles in his *Ajax* [6] in introducing a change of scene, being unable to represent otherwise the prayers and lamentations of Orpheus.

May Your Majesty recognize in these my labors, small though they

2 Sonneck (see p. 365, note 4) argues that this later performance, in Corsi's palace, must have taken place not later than January 18, 1599.

3 The performance took place on October 6, 1600. It will be noticed that Rinuccini does not mention Caccini's connection with it.

4 In the original fable, Orpheus obtains Eurydice's release only on the condition that he shall not look back at her as she follows him. When he forgets this condition, Eurydice vanishes, and Orpheus is later torn to pieces by Thracian Maenads.

5 *Inferno*, XXVI, 139–142.

6 At line 815.

be, the humble devotion of my mind to Your Majesty and live long in happiness to receive from God each day greater graces and greater favors.

Florence, October 4, 1600.
　Your Majesty's most humble servant,
　　Ottavio Rinuccini.

48. Giulio Caccini

Born at Rome in 1550 and called "Romano" after his birthplace, Caccini settled in Florence in 1564. His importance in music history is twofold: on the one hand, he took an active part in the invention of the *stile rappresentativo* and the opera, and on the other, he applied the new style to the composition of vocal chamber music, i.e., monodic songs (arias, madrigals) with *basso continuo*. Primarily interested in singing, Caccini shunned dry musical recitation of the text; in his epoch-making collection of monodic songs *Le nuove musiche* (1602) he made abundant use of coloratura, and in so doing greatly influenced the music of the forthcoming monodic period. Caccini's setting of Rinuccini's *Euridice* was the first opera to be printed.

Euridice [1]

[*1600*]

Dedication

To THE most illustrious lord, Signor Giovanni Bardi, Conte di Vernio, Lieutenant-General of both companies of the Guard of Our Most Holy Father.

After composing the fable of *Euridice* in music in *stile rappresentativo* and having it printed, I felt it to be part of my duty to dedicate it to Your Illustrious Lordship, whose especial servant I have always been and to whom I find myself under innumerable obligations. In it Your Lordship will recognize that style which, as Your Lordship knows, I used on other occasions, many years ago, in the eclogue of Sannazaro, "Itene

---

[1] Text: Solerti, *op. cit.*, pp. 50–52.

all'ombra degli ameni faggi," [2] and in other madrigals of mine from that time: "Perfidissimo volto," "Vedrò il mio sol," "Dovrò dunque morire," [3] and the like. This is likewise the manner which Your Lordship, in the years when Your Lordship's "Camerata" was flourishing in Florence, discussing it in company with many other noble virtuosi, declared to be that used by the ancient Greeks when introducing song into the representations of their tragedies and other fables.

Thus the harmony of the parts reciting in the present *Euridice* is supported above a *basso continuato*.[4] In this I have indicated the most necessary fourths, fifths, sixths, and sevenths, and major and minor thirds, for the rest leaving it to the judgment and art of the player to adapt the inner parts in their places; the notes of the bass I have sometimes tied in order that, in the passing of the many dissonances that occur, the note may not be struck again and the ear offended. In this manner of singing I have used a certain neglect which I deem to have an element of nobility, believing that with it I have approached that much nearer to ordinary speech. Further, when two sopranos are making passages, singing with the inner parts, I have not avoided the succession of two octaves or two fifths, thinking thereby, with their beauty and novelty, to cause a greater pleasure, especially since apart from these passages all the parts are free from such faults.

I had thought, on the present occasion, to deliver a discourse to my readers upon the noble manner of singing, in my judgment the best for others to adopt, along with some curious points relating to it and with the new manner of passages and redoubled points, invented by me, which Vittoria Archilei, a singer of that excellence to which her resounding fame bears witness,[5] has long employed in singing my works. But since this has not at present seemed best to some of my friends (to whom I cannot and must not be disloyal), I have reserved this for another occasion,[6] enjoying, for the time being, this single satisfaction of having been the first to give songs of this kind and their style and manner to the press.[7] This manner appears throughout my other compositions, composed at various times going back more than fifteen years, as I have

---

[2] From his *Arcadia*. The line given is the beginning of the monologue of Montano in terza rima, following the "Prosa seconda." Caccini's music seems not to have been preserved.

[3] *Le nuove musiche*, nos. 6, 7, and 11. A modern reprint, edited by Carlo Perinello, was published in 1919 as Vol. 4 of the *Classici della musica italiana*.

[4] For examples of Caccini's *basso continuato*, see pp. 388–390 below.

[5] Vittoria Archilei, who had taken part in the Florentine intermezzi of 1589, sang the role of Eurydice at the first performance of the Peri-Caccini score (see also p. 375 below).

[6] The promised "discourse" was subsequently published as a foreword to the *Nuove musiche* (see pp. 377–392 below).

[7] Caccini has evidently rushed into print in order to anticipate the publication of Peri's score; his claim is that he is the first to have printed songs in the new style; Peri's claim (p. 376 below) is that his *Euridice* was performed before Caccini's was composed or printed.

never used in them any art other than the imitation of the conceit of the words, touching those chords more or less passionate which I judged most suitable for the grace which is required for good singing, which grace and which manner of singing Your Most Illustrious Lordship has many times reported to me to be universally accepted in Rome as good.

Meanwhile I pray Your Lordship to receive with favor the expression of my good will, etc., and to continue to grant me Your Lordship's protection, under which shield I hope ever to be able to take refuge, etc., and to be defended from the perils that commonly threaten things little used, knowing that Your Lordship will always be able to testify that my compositions are not unpleasing to a great prince who, having occasion to test all the good arts, can judge them supremely well. With which, kissing Your Illustrious Lordship's hand, I pray Our Lord to bestow happiness upon Your Lordship.

Florence, December 20, 1600.
    Your Illustrious Lordship's
        Most affectionate and beholden servant,
            Giulio Caccini.

49. Jacopo Peri

Born at Rome in 1561, but of Florentine extraction, Peri occupied the position of "general music manager" to the Florentine court. He was a distinguished member of Bardi's "Camerata" and collaborated in the first attempts at realizing the *stile rappresentativo*. In contrast to Caccini, who was a gifted writer of melodies, Peri was primarily interested in drama and declamation. The score of his opera *Euridice*, on Rinuccini's text, was not printed until 1601. Peri died in Florence in 1633.

Euridice [1]

[*1601*]

Foreword

To my readers:

Before laying before you, gracious readers, these my compositions, I have thought it fitting to let you know what led me to seek out this new manner of music, for in all human operations reason should be the principle and source, and he who cannot readily give his reasons affords ground for believing that he has acted as the result of chance.

Although Signor Emilio del Cavaliere, before any other of whom I know, enabled us with marvelous invention to hear our kind of music upon the stage, nonetheless as early as 1594, it pleased the Signors Jacopo Corsi and Ottavio Rinuccini that I should employ it in another guise and should set to music the fable of *Dafne*, written by Signor Ottavio to make a simple trial of what the music of our age could do.[2]

---

1 Text: Solerti, *op. cit.*, pp. 43–49.

2 Here, as elsewhere in his foreword, Peri borrows literally from Rinuccini's dedication.

Seeing that dramatic poetry was concerned and that it was therefore necessary to imitate speech in song (and surely no one ever spoke in song), I judged that the ancient Greeks and Romans (who, in the opinion of many, sang their tragedies throughout in representing them upon the stage) had used a harmony surpassing that of ordinary speech but falling so far below the melody of song as to take an intermediate form. And this is why we find their poems admitting the iambic verse, a form less elevated than the hexameter but said to be advanced beyond the confines of familiar conversation. For this reason, discarding every other manner of singing hitherto heard, I devoted myself wholly to seeking out the kind of imitation necessary for these poems. And I considered that the kind of speech that the ancients assigned to singing and that they called "diastematica" (that is, sustained or suspended) could in part be hastened and made to take an intermediate course, lying between the slow and suspended movements of song and the swift and rapid movements of speech, and that it could be adapted to my purpose (as they adapted it in reading poems and heroic verses) and made to approach that other kind of speech which they called "continuata," a thing our moderns have already accomplished in their compositions, although perhaps for another purpose.[3]

I knew likewise that in our speech some words are so intoned that harmony can be based upon them and that in the course of speaking it passes through many others that are not so intoned until it returns to another that will bear a progression to a fresh consonance. And having in mind those inflections and accents that serve us in our grief, in our joy, and in similar states, I caused the bass to move in time to these, either more or less, following the passions, and I held it firm throughout the false and true proportions [4] until, running through various notes, the voice of the speaker came to a word that, being intoned in familiar speech, opened the way to a fresh harmony. And this not only in order that the flow of the discourse might not distress the ear (as though stumbling among the repeated notes that it encountered because of the rapid succession of the consonances) and in order that it might not seem in a way to dance to the movement of the bass (especially where the subject was sad or grave, more cheerful subjects naturally calling for more rapid movements), but also because the use of the false proportions would either diminish or offset whatever advantage it brought us, because of

---

3 Peri borrows the terms "diastematica" and "continuata" from Aristoxenian theory (cf. Cleonides, *Introduction*, p. 35 above).

4 The "false proportions" are the non-harmonic tones that occur in a recitative over a sustained bass.

the necessity of intoning every note, which the ancient music may perhaps have had less need of doing.

And therefore, just as I should not venture to affirm that this is the manner of singing used in the fables of the Greeks and Romans, so I have come to believe that it is the only one our music can give us to be adapted to our speech. For this reason, having imparted my opinion to the gentlemen in question, I demonstrated to them this new manner of singing, which gave the highest pleasure, not only to Signor Jacopo, who had already composed some most beautiful airs for this fable, and to Signor Pietro Strozzi, to Signor Francesco Cini, and to other most learned gentlemen (for music flourishes today among the nobility), but also to that celebrated lady whom one may call the Euterpe of our age, Signora Vittoria Archilei. This lady, who has always made my compositions seem worthy of her singing, adorns them not only with those groups and those long windings of the voice, simple and double, which the liveliness of her talent can invent at any moment (more to comply with the usage of our times than because she considers the beauty and force of our singing to lie in them), but also with those elegances and graces that cannot be written or, if written, cannot be learned from writing. One who heard and praised her was Messer Giovan Battista Jacomelli, most excellent in every part of music, who has almost changed his name to Violino, being a marvelous violinist, and who, for the three successive years in which he appeared at the carnival, was heard with the greatest delight and received with the universal applause of those who attended.

But the present *Euridice* had an even greater success, not because it was heard by these same gentlemen and other worthy men whom I have named and further by Count Alfonso Fontanella and Signor Orazio Vecchi, noble confirmers of my belief, but because it was represented before so great a queen and before so many celebrated princes of Italy and France and because it was sung by the most excellent musicians of our times. Of these, Signor Francesco Rasi, a nobleman of Arezzo, represented Amyntas; Signor Antonio Brandi, Arcetro; and Signor Melchior Palantrotti, Pluto.[5] Behind the scenes, music was played by gentlemen illustrious by noble blood and excellence in music: Signor Jacopo Corsi, whom I have so frequently named, played a gravicembalo; Signor Don Grazia Montalvo, a theorbo; Messer Giovan Battista dal Violino, a lira grande; and Messer Giovanni Lapi, a large lute.

And although until then I had composed the work exactly as it is now

---

[5] Peri mentions only the "noble" members of the cast.

published, nonetheless Giulio Caccini (called Romano), whose extreme merit is known to the world, composed the airs of Eurydice and some of those of the shepherd and of the nymphs of the chorus, also the choruses "Al canto, al ballo," "Sospirate," and "Poi che gli eterni imperi," and this because they were to be sung by persons under his direction. These airs may be seen in his *Euridice*, composed and printed only after mine was represented before Her Most Christian Majesty.

Receive it then graciously, courteous readers, and although I have not arrived, with this manner, at the goal that I had thought it possible to attain, the consideration of novelty having been a brake upon my course, give it in every way a welcome and it may be that on another occasion I may show you something more perfect than this. Meanwhile I shall consider myself to have done enough, having cleared the road for others who, by their merit, may go on in my footsteps to that glory which it has not been granted me to reach. And I hope that the use of the false proportions, played and sung without hesitation, discreetly, and precisely, being pleasing to men so numerous and so distinguished, may not offend you, especially in the more mournful and serious airs of Orpheus, Arcetro, and Dafne, the part represented with so much grace by Jacopo Giusti, a little boy from Lucca.

And live happily.
Jacopo Peri.

50. Giulio Caccini

Le nuove musiche [1]

[*1602*]

Foreword

To MY readers:

If hitherto I have not put forth to the view of the world those fruits of my music studies employed about that noble manner of singing which I learned of my master, the famous Scipione del Palla, nor my compositions of airs, composed by me at different times, seeing them frequently practised by the most famous singers in Italy, both men and women, and by other noble lovers of this art, this has proceeded from my not esteeming them, as the said compositions have in my opinion received enough honor, indeed much more than they deserve. But seeing many of them go about maimed and spoiled; seeing ill used those long winding points, simple and double, that is redoubled or intertwined one with the other,[2] therefore devised by me to avoid that old manner of running division which has been hitherto used, being indeed more proper for wind and stringed instruments than for the voice; and seeing that there is made nowadays an indifferent and confused use of those excellent graces and ornaments to the good and true manner of singing which we call trills and groups, exclamations of increasing and abating

---

1 Text: The basis of the present translation is the abridged version printed in later editions of John Playford's *Introduction to the Skill of Music* under the title: "A brief discourse of the Italian manner of singing, wherein is set down the use of those graces in singing, as the trill and *gruppo*, used in Italy and now in England; written some years since by an English gentleman who had lived long in Italy, and being returned, taught the same here." Arnold Dolmetsch seems to have been the first to identify this as a translation of Cac-cini's foreword (see his *Interpretation of the Music of the XVIIth and XVIIIth Centuries* [London, 1915]). Using the 10th edition (London, 1693), I have corrected the old translation here and there and have completed it by translating those passages that it omitted. For the Italian text, cf. Solerti, *op. cit.*, pp. 55–70, or the facsimile reprint (Rome, 1934).

2 Quei lunghi giri di voci semplici e doppi, cioè radoppiate, intrecciate l'una nell' altra.

of the voice; [3] I have found it necessary and also have been urged by my friends to have my said compositions printed, in this my first publication to explain to my readers in this discourse the reasons which led me to this manner of singing for a solo voice, and in this my discourse, since compositions of that complete grace which I can hear in my mind have been hitherto unknown in modern times (so far as I know), to leave some footprints that others may attain to this excellent manner of singing, for "a great fire follows a little spark."

Indeed, in the times when the most virtuous "Camerata" of the most illustrious Signor Giovanni Bardi, Count of Vernio, flourished in Florence, and in it were assembled not only a great part of the nobility but also the first musicians and men of talent and poets and philosophers of the city, and I too frequently attended it, I can say that I learned more from their learned discussions than I learned from descant in over thirty years; for these most understanding gentlemen always encouraged me and convinced me with the clearest reasons not to follow that old way of composition whose music, not suffering the words to be understood by the hearers, ruins the conceit and the verse, now lengthening and now shortening the syllables to match the descant, a laceration of the poetry, but to hold fast to that manner so much praised by Plato and other philosophers, who declare that music is nothing other than the fable and last and not the contrary, the rhythm and the sound,[4] in order to penetrate the perception of others and to produce those marvelous effects, admired by the writers, which cannot be produced by descant in modern musical compositions, especially in singing a solo above a stringed instrument, not a word of it being understood for the multitude of divisions made upon long and short syllables and in every sort of music, though by the vulgar such singers were cried up for famous.

It being plain, then, as I say, that such music and musicians gave no other delight than what harmony could give the ear, for, unless the words were understood, they could not move the understanding, I have endeavored in those my late compositions to bring in a kind of music by which men might, as it were, talk in harmony, using in that kind of singing, as I have said at other times,[5] a certain noble neglect of the song, passing now and then through certain dissonances, holding the bass note firm, except when I did not wish to observe the common practice, and playing the inner voices on an instrument for the expression of some passion, these being of no use for any other purpose. For which reason,

---

3 Il crescere o scemare della voce, l'esclamazioni, trilli e gruppi.

4 *Republic,* 398D (p. 4 above).

5 See the dedication of his *Euridice* (p. 371 above).

having in those times made a beginning of such songs for a single voice and believing that they had more power to delight and move than the greatest number of voices singing together, I composed in those times the madrigals "Perfidissimo volto," "Vedrò il mio sol," "Dovrò dunque morire," and the like, and in particular the air based on the eclogue of Sannazaro, "Itene a l'ombra degli ameni faggi," [6] in that very style which later served me for the fables which were represented in song at Florence.

The affectionate applause with which these madrigals and this air were received in the "Camerata" and the exhortations to pursue by this path the end I had proposed to myself led me to betake myself to Rome to make trial of them there also.[7] At Rome, when the said madrigals and air were heard in the house of Signor Nero Neri by many gentlemen accustomed to gather there, and particularly by Signor Leone Strozzi, all can testify how I was urged to continue the enterprise I had begun, all telling me that they had never before heard harmony of a single voice, accompanied by a single stringed instrument, with such power to move the passion of the mind as those madrigals, both because of their style and because, when madrigals published for several voices were sung by a single voice, as was then a common practice, the single part of the soprano, sung as a solo, could have no effect by itself, so artificial were the corresponding parts.

Returning from Rome to Florence, and having in mind that in those times there were also in use among musicians certain canzonets, for the most part with despicable words which I considered unseemly and not such as would be esteemed by men of understanding, the thought also came to me to compose from time to time for the relief of my depressed spirits some canzonets to be used as airs in a consort of several stringed instruments. I imparted this thought of mine to many gentlemen of the city and was courteously gratified by them with many canzonets in various metres, and soon afterwards Signor Gabriello Chiabrera favored me with a great abundance, very different from all the rest, and provided me with great opportunity for variety.[8] All these canzonets, which from time to time I set to various airs, were not unpleasing even to all Italy. Now everyone wishing to compose for a single voice employs this style, particularly here in Florence, where, during the thirty years that I have

---

6 See p. 371 above, notes 2 and 3.

7 Caccini seems to have left Florence for Rome sometime after July 30, 1593 (see the documents published by Gandolfi, *Rivista musicale italiana*, III [1896], 718).

8 Chiabrera is the author of the words of several of the *ariette* included in the *Nuove musiche* (nos. 3, 9, and 10), also of the madrigal "Deh, dove son fuggiti" (see pp. 389–390 below); he was also the librettist for the *Rapimento di Cefalo* and the author of an elegy on Caccini's death ("Belle ninfe de' prati").

received a salary from these most serene princes, whoever has so wished has, thanks to their bounty, been able to see and hear at his pleasure all that I have accomplished in these studies throughout that time.

In which, as well in the madrigals as in the airs, I endeavored the imitation of the conceit of the words, seeking out the chords more or less passionate according to the meaning of them and what had especial grace, having concealed in them so much as I could the art of descant, and passed or stayed the consonances or chords upon long syllables, avoiding the short and observing the same rule in making the passages of division by some few quavers to notes and to cadences not exceeding the value of a quarter or half a semibreve at most, chiefly on short syllables. These are allowable because they pass soon and are, not divisions, but a means of adding grace and because in special cases judgment makes every rule suffer some exception. But, as I said before, those long windings and turnings of the voice are ill used; for I have observed that divisions have been invented, not because they are necessary unto a good fashion of singing, but rather for a certain tickling of the ears of those who do not well understand what it is to sing passionately; for if they did, undoubtedly divisions would have been abhorred, there being nothing more contrary to passion than they are. I have said that these long winding points are ill used because I introduced them for use in some kind of music less passionate or affectuous, and upon long syllables, not short, and in final cadences, for the rest these long points of division needing to observe no rule concerning the vowels than that the vowel "u" produces a better effect in the soprano voice than in the tenor, the vowel "i" a better effect in the tenor than the vowel "u," the others being all in common use, though the open vowels are more sonorous than the closed, as also easier and fitter for stirring up the disposition. And again, if some short points of division should be used, let this be according to the rules observed in my works, not at all adventures, but upon the practice of the descant, to think of them first in those things that a man will sing by himself and to fashion out the manner of them, but not to promise a man's self that this descant will bear it. For to the good manner of composing and singing in this way, the understanding of this conceit and the humor of the words, imitating it and giving it its flavor as well in passionate chords as passionate expressions in singing, doth more avail than descant, I having made use of it only to accord two parts together and to avoid certain notable errors and bind certain discords for the accompanying of the passion more than to use the art. And certain it is that an air composed in this manner upon the conceit of the words by one that hath a good fashion of singing will work a better effect and delight more than another made with all the art of descant, for which no better reason can be given than experience itself. Such then were the reasons that led me to this manner of singing for a solo voice and showed me where, and on which syllables and vowels, long points of division should be used.

It now remains to say why the increasing and abating of the voice, exclamations, trills, groups, and other effects above mentioned are used indifferently, for they are now said to be used indifferently whenever anyone uses them, whether in passionate compositions where they are most required, or in canzonets for dancing where the humor or conceit of the words is not minded.

The original of which defect (if I deceive not myself) is hence occasioned because the musician doth not well possess and make himself master of that which he is to sing. For if he did so, undoubtedly he would not run into such errors as most easily he falleth into who hath framed to himself a manner of singing, for example altogether passionate, with a general rule that in increasing and abating the voice, and in exclamations, is the foundation of passion, and who doth always use them in every sort of music, not discerning whether the words require it; whereas those that well understand the conceit and meaning of the words, know our defects and can distinguish where the passion is more or less required. Which sort of people we should endeavor to please with all diligence and more to esteem their praise than the applause of the ignorant vulgar.

This art admitteth no mediocrity; and how much the more curiosities are in it, by reason of the excellence thereof, with so much the more labor and love ought we, the professors thereof, to find them out. Which love hath moved me (considering that from writings we receive the light of all science and of all art) to leave behind me this little light in the ensuing notes and discourses, it being my intention to show so much as appertaineth to him who maketh the profession of singing alone to the harmony of the theorbo or other stringed instrument, so that he be already entered into the theory of music and play sufficiently. Not that this cannot also be attained by long practise (as it is seen that many, both men and women, have done, and yet this they attain is but unto a certain degree), but because the theory of the writings conduceth unto the attaining of that degree, and because in the profession of a singer (in regard of the excellence thereof) not only particular things are of use, but they all together do better it.

Therefore, to proceed in order, thus will I say that the chiefest foundations and most important grounds of this art are the tuning of the voice [9] in all the notes, not only that it be neither too high nor too low, but that there be a good manner of tuning it used. Which tuning being used for the most part in two fashions, we will consider both of the one and the other, and by the following notes will show that which to me seemeth more proper to other effects.

There are some, therefore, that in the tuning of the first note, tune it a third under; others tune the said first note in his proper tune, always increasing it in loudness, saying that this is the good way of putting forth the voice gracefully.

Concerning the first: Since it is not a general rule, because it agrees not in many chords, although in such places as it may be used it is now become so ordinary; that instead of being a grace (because some stay too long in the third note under, whereas it should be but lightly touched) it is rather tedious to the ear; and that, for beginners in particular, it ought seldom to be used; but instead of it, as being more strange, I would choose the second for the increasing of the voice.

Now, because I have not contained myself within ordinary terms and such as others have used, yea rather have continually searched after novelty so much as was possible for me, so that the novelty may fitly serve to the better obtaining of the musician's end, that is, to delight and move the affections of the mind, I have found it to be a more affectuous way to tune the voice by a contrary effect to the other, that is, to tune the first note in its proper tune, diminishing it; because exclamation is the principal means to move the affection, and exclamation properly is no other thing but the slacking of the voice to reinforce it somewhat more; whereas increasing of the voice in the treble part, especially in feigned voices,[10] doth oftentimes become harsh and insufferable to the hearing, as upon divers occasions I have heard. Undoubtedly, therefore, as an affection more proper to move, it will work a better effect to tune the voice diminishing it rather than increasing of it; because in the first of these ways now mentioned, when a man increases the voice to make an exclamation, it is needful that, in slacking of it, he increase it the more, and therefore I have said that it showeth harsh and rough; but in the diminishing of the voice it will work a quite contrary effect, because when the voice is slacked, then to give it a little spirit will always make it more passionate. Besides that also, using sometimes one, sometimes another, variety may

---

[9] L'intonazione della voce.   [10] Voci finte.

be used, which is very necessary in this art, so that it be directed to the said end.

So then, if this be the greatest part of that grace in singing which is apt to move the affection of the mind in those conceits, certainly where there is most use of such affections or passions, and if it be demonstrated with such lively reasons, a new consequence is hence inferred: that from writings of men likewise may be learned that most necessary grace which cannot be described in better manner and more clearly for the understanding thereof, and yet it may be perfectly attained unto. So that after the study of the theory and after these rules, they may be put in practice, by which a man grows more perfect in all arts, especially in the profession of a perfect singer, be it man or woman.

Of tuning, therefore, with more or less grace, and how it may be done in the aforesaid manner, trial may be made in the above-written notes, with the words under them "Cor mio, deh non languire." For in the first minim with the prick, you may tune "Cor mio," diminishing it by little and little, and in the falling of the crotchet increase the voice with a little more spirit, and it will become an exclamation passionate enough, though in a note that falls but one degree. But much more sprightful will it appear in the word "deh," by holding of a note that falls not by one degree, as likewise it will become most sweet by the taking of the greater sixth that falls by a leap. Which thing I have observed, not only to show to others what a thing exclamation is and from whence it grows, but also that there may be two kinds of it, one more passionate than the other, as well by the manner in which they are described or tuned in the one way or other, as also by imitation of the word when it shall have a signification suitable to the conceit. Besides that, exclamations may be used in all passionate musics, by one general rule in all minims and crotchets with a prick falling; and they shall be far more passionate by the following note, which runneth, than they can be in semibreves, in which it will be fitter for increasing and diminishing the voice without using the exclamations. Yet by consequence understand that in airy musics or courantes to dance, instead of these passions, there is to be used only a lively, cheerful kind of singing which is carried and ruled by the air itself. In the which, though sometimes there may be place for some exclamation, that liveliness of singing is in that place to be omitted, and not any passion to be used which savoreth of languishment. Whereupon we see how necessary a certain judgment is for a musician, which sometimes useth to prevail above art. As also we may perceive by the foregoing notes how much greater grace the four first quavers have upon the second syllable of the word "languire" (being so stayed by the second quaver with a prick) than the four last equal quavers, so printed for example.

But because there are many things which are used in a good fashion of singing which, because there is found in them a greater grace, being described in some one manner, make a contrary effect one to the other (whereupon we use to say of a man that he sings with much grace or little grace), these things will occasion me at this time: first, to demonstrate in what fashion I have described the trill and the group, and the manner used by me to teach them, to those who have been interested, in my house; and further, all other the more necessary effects, so that I leave not unexpressed any curiosity which I have observed.

Trill, or plain shake　　Gruppo, or double relish

The trill described by me is upon one note only. My only reason for demonstrating it in this fashion is that in teaching it to my first wife and then to my second wife, now living, and to my daughters, I have observed no other rule than that of its description, both as trill and as group, that is to say, to begin with the first crotchet and to beat every note with the throat upon the vowel "a" unto the last breve, as likewise the *gruppo*, or double relish. Which trill and *gruppo* was exactly learned and exquisitely performed by my former wife according to the aforesaid rule, as I shall leave to the judgment of anyone who has heard her sing and as I likewise leave to the judgment of others, for this can be heard, with what exquisiteness it is performed by my second wife, now living. So that if it be true that experience is the teacher of all things, I can with some confidence affirm and say that there cannot be a better means used to teach it nor a better form to describe it, as each is so expressed. Which trill and group, because they are a step necessary unto many things that are described, and are effects of that grace which is most desired for singing well, and (as is aforesaid) being described in one or other manner do work a contrary effect to that which is requisite, I will show not only how they may be used, but also all the effects of them described in two manners with the same value of the notes, that still we may know (as is aforementioned) that by these writings, together with practice, may be learned all the curiosities of this art.

From the notes written above in two manners it is to be observed in these graces that the second hath more grace in it than the first. And for your better experience we will in this following air describe some of these graces with words under, together with the bass for the theorbo, in which air is contained the most passionate passages, by practicing which you may exercise yourself in them and attain ever greater perfection in them.

And because in the two last lines, at the words "Ahi dispietato Amor" in the *aria di romanesca* and afterwards in the madrigal "Deh, dove son fuggiti," there are contained the best passions that can be used in this noble manner of singing, I have therefore thought good to set them down; both to show where it is fit to increase and abate the voice, to make exclamations, trills, and groups, and in a word all the treasures of this art, as also not to have to demonstrate this again in all the works which will follow later, and that they may serve for example, whereby men may take notice in the music of the places where they are most necessary according to the passions of the words; although I call that the noble manner of singing which is used without tying a man's self to the ordinary measure of time, making many times the value of the notes less by half, and sometimes more, according to the conceit of the words, whence proceeds that excellent kind of singing with a graceful neglect, whereof I have spoken before.[a]

Since, then, there are so many effects to be used for the excellency of this art, there is required (for the performing of them) necessarily a good voice, as also good wind to give liberty and serve upon all occasions where is most need. It shall therefore be a profitable advertisement that the professor of this art, being to sing to a theorbo or other stringed instrument and not being compelled to fit himself to others, that he so pitch his tune as to sing his clear and natural voice, avoiding feigned tunes of notes. In which, to feign them, or at the least to enforce notes, if his wind serve him well so as he do not discover them much (because for the most part they offend the ear), yet a man must have a command of breath to give the greater spirit to the increasing and diminishing of the voice, to exclamations and other passions, as is related. Therefore let him take heed that, spending much breath upon such notes, it do not afterward fail him in such places as it is most needful; for from a feigned

a Our author having briefly set forth this chief or most usual grace in singing called the trill, which, as he saith very right, is by a beating in the throat on the vowel "ah," some observe that it is rather the shaking of the uvula or palate on the throat in one sound upon a note. For the attaining of this, the most surest and ready way is by imitation of those who are perfect in the same. Yet I have heard of some that have attained it after this manner: In the singing a plainsong of six notes up and six down, they have in the midst of every note beat or shaked with their finger upon their throat, which by often practice came to do the same notes exactly without. It was also my chance to be in company with some gentlemen at a musical practice which sang their parts very well and used this grace (called the trill) very exactly. I desired to know their tutor; they told me I was their tutor, for they had never had any other but this my *Introduction*. That (I answered) could direct them but in the theory; they must needs have a better help in the practice, especially in attaining to sing the trill so well. One of them made this reply (which made me smile): I used, said he, at my first learning the trill, to imitate that breaking of a sound in the throat which men use when they lure their hawks, as *he-he-he-he-he*; which he used slow at first, and after more swift on several notes higher and lower in sound, till he became perfect therein.

The trill, being the most usual grace, is usually made in closes, cadences, and when on a long note exclamation or passion is expressed (there the trill is made in the latter part of such note), but most usually upon binding notes and such notes as precede the closing note. Those who once attain to the perfect use of the trill, other graces will become easy. [Note by Playford]

voice can come no noble manner of singing, which only proceeds from a natural voice, serving aptly for all the notes which a man can manage according to his ability, employing his wind in such a fashion as he command all the best passionate graces used in this most worthy manner of singing.

The love whereof, and generally of all music, being kindled in me by a natural inclination and by the study of so many years, shall excuse me if I have suffered myself to be carried further than perhaps was fit for him who no less esteems and desires to learn from others than to communicate to others what himself hath learned, and to be further transported in this discourse than can stand with that respect I bear to all the professors of this art. Which art, being excellent and naturally delightful, doth then become admirable and entirely wins the love of others when such as possess it, both by teaching and delighting others, do often exercise it and make it appear to be a pattern and true resemblance of those never ceasing celestial harmonies whence proceed so many good effects and benefits upon earth, raising and exciting the minds of the hearers to the contemplation of those infinite delights which Heaven affordeth.

Inasmuch as I have been accustomed, in all the compositions which have come from my pen, to indicate by figures above the bass part the major thirds and sixths where a sharp is set down and the minor ones where there is a flat, and in the same way to indicate that sevenths and other dissonances should be used in the inner voices for accompaniment, it now remains to be said that the ties in the bass part have been so used by me because after the consonance only the note indicated is to be struck again, it being the one most necessary (if I am not mistaken) for the theorbo in its special capacity and the easiest to use and put into effect, as that instrument is better fitted to accompany the voice, especially the tenor voice, than any other. For the rest, I leave to the discretion of the more intelligent the striking again, along with the bass, of those notes which may accord with their best judgment and which will best accompany the solo voice part, as it is not possible, so far as I know, to designate them more clearly without tablature.

51. G. M. Artusi

Born in 1540, Artusi was a canon of the church of San Salvatore at Bologna. He died in 1613. He was a distinguished theorist, well versed in the art of counterpoint but of a completely reactionary turn of mind. The innovations that had been introduced into polyphonic music by such great composers as Rore, Monteverdi, and Gesualdo were quite beyond his understanding. His *L'Artusi, ovvero, Delle imperfezioni della moderna musica,* shows to what lengths he could go in his fight against what he called the "imperfections" of the new music. From his limited point of view, however, as an ardent partisan of traditional polyphony, Artusi was perfectly consistent in his attacks, for the madrigal of his time had indeed begun to disintegrate.

From L'Artusi, ovvero, Delle imperfezioni della moderna musica [1]

[*1600*]

SECOND DISCOURSE

THE DAWN of the seventeenth day was breaking as Signor Luca left his house and proceeded toward the monastery of the reverend fathers of Santa Maria del Vado [2] where dwelt Signor Vario, in the service of the Most Illustrious and Reverend Signor the Cardinal Pompeo Arigoni, truly most illustrious for the many virtues, the goodness, the justice, and the piety which in that Most Illustrious and Reverend Signor universally shine in the service of persons of every quality. On his reaching the monastery, his arrival was announced to Signor Vario, who indeed was momentarily expecting him. Signor Vario immediately left his room and met Signor Luca at the head of the stairs, from whence, after

---

[1] Text: The original edition (Venice, 1600), ff. 39–44, 71v. The postils of the original have been omitted.

[2] The scene is laid in Ferrara.

due ceremonies and salutations, they went again to carry on their discussion, according to the arrangement adopted the day before, into a room sufficiently remote and conveniently free from disturbing sounds. After they had seated themselves, Signor Luca began.

(Luca) Yesterday, sir, after I had left Your Lordship and was going toward the Piazza, I was invited by some gentlemen to hear certain new madrigals. Delighted by the amiability of my friends and by the novelty of the compositions, I accompanied them to the house of Signor Antonio Goretti, a nobleman of Ferrara, a young virtuoso and as great a lover of music as any man I have ever known. I found there Signor Luzzasco and Signor Hippolito Fiorini,[3] distinguished men, with whom had assembled many noble spirits, versed in music. The madrigals were sung and repeated, but without giving the name of the author. The texture was not unpleasing. But, as Your Lordship will see, insofar as it introduced new rules, new modes, and new turns of phrase, these were harsh and little pleasing to the ear, nor could they be otherwise; for so long as they violate the good rules—in part founded upon experience, the mother of all things, in part observed in nature, and in part proved by demonstration—we must believe them deformations of the nature and propriety of true harmony, far removed from the object of music, which, as Your Lordship said yesterday, is delectation.

But, in order that you may see the whole question and give me your judgment, here are the passages, scattered here and there through the above-mentioned madrigals, which I wrote out yesterday evening for my amusement.

(Vario) Signor Luca, you bring me new things which astonish me not a little. It pleases me, at my age, to see a new method of composing, though it would please me much more if I saw that these passages were founded upon some reason which could satisfy the intellect. But as castles in the air, chimeras founded upon sand, these novelties do not please me; they deserve blame, not praise. Let us see the passages, however.[4]

(L) Indeed, in the light of what little experience I have in this art, these things do not seem to me to entitle their authors or inventors to build a four-story mansion (as the saying goes), seeing that they are contrary to what is good and beautiful in the harmonic institutions. They are

---

3 Goretti, Luzzasco, and Fiorini were of course real persons, prominent in the musical life of Ferrara. Luzzasco, in particular, is cited by Monteverdi as one of those who "renewed" the "Second Practice" (cf. p. 408 below).

4 See opposite page. "Passages" 8 and 9 are from the first and second parts of Claudio Monte-

verdi's "Anima mia perdona" (*Quarto libro a 5*), 1 to 7 from his "Cruda Amarilli" (*Quinto libro a 5*). These madrigals did not appear in print until 1603 and 1605, three to five years after the publication of Artusi's criticism. Artusi's examples differ in a few minor points from the editions later published by the composer.

harsh to the ear, rather offending than delighting it, and to the good rules left by those who have established the order and the bounds of this science they bring confusion and imperfection of no little consequence. Instead of enriching, augmenting, and ennobling harmony by various means, as so many noble spirits have done, they bring it to such estate that the beautiful and purified style is indistinguishable from the barbaric. And all the while they continue to excuse these things by various arguments in conformity with the style.

(V) You say well. But how can they excuse and palliate these imperfections, which could not possibly be more absurd?

(L) Absurd? I do not know how you can defend that opinion of yours. They call absurd the things composed in another style and would have it that theirs is the true method of composition, declaring that this novelty and new order of composing is about to produce many effects which ordinary music, full of so many and such sweet harmonies, cannot and never will produce. And they will have it that the sense, hearing such asperities, will be moved and will do marvelous things.

(V) Are you in earnest or are you mocking me?

(L) Am I in earnest? It is rather they who mock those who hold otherwise.

(V) Since I see that you are not mocking me, I will tell you what I think of them, but take note that I shall not be so ready to yield to their opinion. And, for the first argument against them, I tell you that the high is a part of the low and arises from the low and, being a part of it, must continue to be related to it, as to its beginning or as the cloud to the spring from which it is derived. That this is true, the experiment of the monochord will show you. For if two strings of equal length and thickness are stretched over one and the same equal space and tuned perfectly in unison (which is regarded by the musician as a single sound, just as two surfaces which are throughout in contact with each other are regarded by Vitello [5] as a single surface), and if you cut off a part from one of these or bring out a high sound from it by placing a bridge under it, I say that beyond doubt the high will be a part of the low. And if you would know that a part produces the high sound, strike the whole and then the part which is high with respect to the whole, and it will necessarily be related to the low, as the part to the whole or as to its beginning.

At the lowest note of the complete system, or of any composition, there may be represented an eye, sending forth various visual rays and regarding all the parts, observing in what proportion they correspond to their beginning and foundation. How then will the first, second, fourth, fifth, and other measures stand, if the higher part has no correspondence or harmonic proportion to the lower?

(L) They claim that they do observe harmonic relation, saying that the semiminim in the first measure, which is taken after the rest of the

---

5 Erasmus Vitello (Erazm Ciolek), Polish mathematician of the thirteenth century.

same value and which forms a sixteenth with the lower part, would already be dissonant if the cantus were to sing as follows:

for then the tenor, singing the first semiminim an octave lower, would cause the second one, which forms the dissonance, to be heard with it above; aside from this, they say, since the third of the four semiminims is consonant, what difference can it make if we cause a little more harshness to be heard by converting two semiminims, one consonant, the other dissonant, into one minim wholly dissonant; this is as though we were to sing four semiminims, alternately consonant and dissonant, following the rule for figures of this value. In this way they make all that they do more gross.

(V) Good! I follow you perfectly, and answer that the sense of hearing does not perceive what it does not hear and, not perceiving it, cannot present it to the intellect, there being nothing in the intellect that has not first been perceived by the senses. How absurd it is to say that the tenor sustains a note in one register while the soprano, immediately afterward in a higher register, produces the effect the tenor should have produced! Especially after the rest, how much more evident it is to the ear that the soprano sings a sixteenth and then a fourteenth! It is one thing that the ear should hear a dissonance in one part after a rest, another that, when several semiminims are successively taken by step, one after another, one is perceived to be consonant, another dissonant; one thing to hear two semiminims taken by step in the natural way, another to hear a minim, and that taken by leap, in place of the dissonant semiminim. This last offends the ear; the others do not, for the movement is by step.

(L) Well said. But they say that all this is called grace and is an accented singing.

(V) I do not remember having read in any author—and countless excellent ones have written of music—that there is such a thing as accented music. I shall welcome it if you will tell me what it is, according to the pretension of these modern composers.

(L) They say that the accents in compositions have a remarkable effect and that these accents occur only when a part ascends to a higher note; for example, that when four notes ascend by step, the accent is produced on the last note and not on the others, the voice beginning a third lower than the note on which the accent is to be produced and being carried gracefully to its level. But, to produce good accord always, this demands the greatest discretion and judgment in the singer for its execution. Here is an example:

(V) I will tell you two things. First, that these words do not explain in clear terms the nature, the peculiarity, and the essence of this manner of accented singing, but seem to be a circumlocution calculated to show, not that they are disposed to regulate all things with rules founded on truth, but rather that they wish to confuse them. We must define what this accent is; then we shall see whether the parts of our definition are mutually in accord, a thing which I do not know that any serious author has so far done. Second, this manner of singing which you call accented does not assume that the composers will employ barbarisms such as are seen in the examples you show me. It requires that the composers produce good accord (a point which you must note well and above all else) and that the singer use great discretion and judgment in "carrying the voice" on such occasions. And if you tell me that the effect which the tenor produces in the seventh measure tends to demonstrate this manner of accented singing, I will reply that the singer does not know at what point, in the opinion and intent of the composers, he should, with discretion, "carry the voice." For this reason there is necessarily an error in grammar. It would be better if, when they mean that the singer should, with judgment and discretion, "carry the voice," they introduced at that point some sign indicating their wish, in order that, perceiving the need, he might produce better accord and more pleasing harmony than he produces by singing along at his own will.

(L) Such an indication would not be unprofitable if one could reasonably discover a universal sign to indicate this manner of "carrying the voice" to the singer. But, while these new inventors are exhausting themselves in new inventions to make this manifest, they go on scattering these passages through their compositions, which, when sung or sounded on different instruments by musicians accustomed to this kind of accented music, full of things left implicit, yield a not unpleasing harmony at which I marvel.

(V) This may result from two things. First, that the singers do not sing what is written, but "carry the voice," sustaining it in such a way that, when they perceive that it is about to produce some bad effect, they divert it elsewhere, carrying it to a place where they think it will not offend the ear. Second, that sensuous excess corrupts the sense, meaning simply that the ear is so taken up with the other parts that it does not fully perceive the offense committed against it (as it would if the composition were for two, three, or four voices), while reason, which knows and distinguishes the good from the bad, perceives right well that a deception is wrought on the sense, which receives the material only in a certain confused way, even though it border on truth. This manifestly is clearly seen when the organist adds to his other registers that of the twelfth; here it is reason and not the ear that discovers the many dissonances which occur among them.

(L) It is known that the ear is deceived, and to this these composers, or new inventors, apply themselves with enthusiasm. They seek only to satisfy the ear and with this aim toil night and day at their instruments to hear the effect which passages so made produce; the poor fellows do not perceive that what the instruments tell them is false and that it is one thing to search with voices and instruments for something pertaining to the harmonic faculty, another to arrive at the exact truth by means of reason seconded by the ear.

(V) I should like to give you my opinion, but I suspect that it may displease you.

(L) Give it; I shall be glad to listen.

(V) It is my belief that there is nothing but smoke in the heads of such composers and that they are so enamored of themselves as to think it within their power to corrupt, spoil, and ruin the good old rules handed down in former times by so many theorists and most excellent musicians, the very men from whom these moderns have learned to string together a few notes with little grace. But do you know what usually happens to such works as these? What Horace says in the tenth ode of his second book:

> Saepius ventis agitatur ingens
> pinus et celsae graviore casu
> decidunt turres feriuntque summos
> fulmina montis.[6]

---

6 'Tis oftener the tall pine that is shaken by the wind; 'tis the lofty towers that fall with the heavier crash, and 'tis the tops of the mountains that the lightning strikes. [Bennett]

In the end, since they are built without foundation, they are quickly consumed by time and cast to the ground, and the builders remain deluded and mocked at.

(L) I grant you that all this is true. But tell me if this science can be advanced by new modes of expression. Why is it that you are unwilling to augment it, or that augmenting it displeases you or does not seem good to you? The field is large; everyone is occupied with new things; musicians too should expand their art, for making all compositions after one fashion sickens and disgusts the ear.

(V) I do not deny that discovering new things is not merely good but necessary. But do you tell me first why you wish to employ these dissonances as they employ them. If you do it in order to say, "I wish them to be plainly heard, but so that the ear may not be offended," why do you not use them in the ordinary way, conformable to reason, in accordance with what Adriano,[7] Cipriano,[8] Palestrina, Porta, Claudio,[9] Gabrieli, Gastoldi, Nanino, Giovanelli, and so many, many others in this academy have written? Have they perhaps failed to cause asperities to be heard? Look at Orlando di Lasso, Philippe de Monte, and Giaches de Wert, and you will find full heaps of them. If you do not wish the ear to be so much offended by them, you will find the manner and order of their use in the same authors. Now, even if you wish dissonance to become consonant, it remains necessary that it be contrary to consonance; by nature it is always dissonant and can hence become consonant only when consonance becomes dissonant; this brings us to impossibilities, although these new composers may perhaps so exert themselves that in the course of time they will discover a new method by which dissonance will become consonance, and consonance dissonance. And it is no great matter, for lofty intelligences like these, to be doing and inventing things of this kind exclusively.

(L) Their aim is precisely to temper to some degree the harshness of dissonance in another way than that used by their predecessors, and to this they devote their efforts.

(V) If the purpose can be attained by observing the precepts and good rules handed down by the theorists and followed by all the practitioners, what reason is there to go beyond the bounds to seek out new extravagances? Do you not know that all the arts and sciences have been brought under rules by scholars of the past and that the first elements, rules, and precepts on which they are founded have been handed down to us in

---

[7] Willaert.   [9] Merulo.
[8] Rore.

order that, so long as there is no deviation from them, one person shall be able to understand what another says or does? And just as, to avoid confusion, it is not permitted to every schoolmaster to change the rules bequeathed by Guarino,[10] nor to every poet to put a long syllable in verse in place of a short one, nor to every arithmetician to corrupt the processes and proofs which are proper to that art, so it is not permitted to everyone who strings notes together to deprave and corrupt music, introducing new modes of composing with new principles founded on sand. Horace says:

> Est modus in rebus, sunt certi denique fines
> Quos ultra citraque nequit consistere rectum.[11]

(L) The truth is that all the arts and sciences have been brought under rules. But still, since dissonances are employed in harmonies as nonessentials, it seems that musicians are entitled to use them at their pleasure.

(V) I do not deny that dissonances are employed as nonessentials in compositions, but I say none the less that, being by nature contrary to consonance, they can by no means agree in the same way and should not be employed in the same way. Consonances are used freely in harmonies, by leap or by step, without distinction, but dissonances, being of another nature, must be considered in another way; this way is demonstrated by Artusi in his *Art of Counterpoint*,[12] but not in the manner which these new masters follow.

(L) These musicians observe the rule that the part forming the dissonance with the lowest part has a harmonic correspondence with the tenor, so that it accords with every other part while the lowest part also accords with every other part. Thus they make a mixture of their own.

(V) I see that this rule of theirs is observed in the first, fourth, fifth, sixth, and seventh measures. But in the sixth measure the quavers have no harmonic relation, either with the bass or with the tenor. With what sort of rule do you think they can save themselves?

(L) I do not know how they can help themselves here. I see the observance of no rule, although I believe that the quavers are the result of perceiving, with instruments, that they do not greatly offend the ear because of their rapid movement.

---

10 The grammatical *Regulae* of the humanist Guarino Veronese (1374–1460), a resident of Ferrara after 1429.

11 There is a measure in all things. There are, in short, fixed bounds, beyond and short of which right can find no place (*Satires*, I, i, 106–107). [Fairclough]

12 Venice, 1586–89, and later editions.

(V) Are you not reminded of what Aristoxenus says of such men as these? Yesterday I gave you the substance of his thought; now I shall give you his very words. In the second book of his *Harmonics* he says: "It is therefore a very great and altogether disgraceful sin to refer the nature of a harmonic question to an instrument." [13] As regards the point that, because of their rapid movement they do not offend the ear, the intellect, recognizing the deception wrought upon the sense, declares that since these intervals are not consonant, but dissonant and placed at random, they can in no way be in a harmonic relation; that they can therefore cause no harmony pleasing to the ear; and that their rapidity, accompanied by so many parts making noise together, is nothing else than the sensuous excess which corrupts the sense.

(L) They think only of satisfying the sense, caring little that reason should enter here to judge their compositions.

(V) If such as these had read the ninth chapter of the first book of Boethius, and the first chapter of his fifth book,[14] and the first chapter of the first book of Ptolemy,[15] they would beyond doubt be of a different mind.

(L) They do not even think of looking at the volumes of Boethius. But if you would know what they say, they are content to know how to string their notes together after their fashion and to teach the singers to sing their compositions, accompanying themselves with many movements of the body, and in the end they let themselves go to such an extent that they seem to be actually dying—this is the perfection of their music.

(V) You have said the very thing. They and their activities die together. By the general judgment of the wise and learned, ignorance, more than anything else, is considered the greatest of the many accidents which makes uncertain for every workman the road of good work which leads to immortality. Through ignorance a man is unable to distinguish which activities are better and which worse, and as a result of this inability he commonly embraces many things from which he should flee and flees from many which he should follow and embrace. Of ignorance, then, are born compositions of this sort, which, like monstrosities, pass through the hands of this man and that, and these men do not know themselves what the real nature of these compositions is. For them it is enough to create

---

13 Cf. p. 31 above. Artusi quotes Aristoxenus in the Latin translation of Antonius Gogava (Venice, 1562).

14 "Not every judgment is to be pronounced by the senses, but reason is rather to be believed: wherein of the fallibility of the senses" (I, ix); "Of the nature of harmony, and what the means of judging it are, and whether the senses are always to be believed" (V, i).

15 "Of harmonic judgments."

a tumult of sounds, a confusion of absurdities, an assemblage of imperfections, and all springs from that ignorance with which they are beclouded.

(L) Ignorance has always been a cause of evil, the more so when accompanied by self-love. Horace says:

Est caecus Amor sui.[16]

It does not stop to discover its own imperfections, but believes that all it does and thinks is well done, as the drunkard thinks that he is sober and the sober man drunk.

(V) It is too onerous to discuss scientific questions with one who is ignorant of science. It is as when the countryman plows a field full of stalks and thorns and other things which hinder him from tilling the soil, instead of a field that has been well plowed before and has yielded fruits from the seed sown upon it. Observe how harsh and uncouth is this passage, which to their minds is exquisite. In the third measure, after the minim rest, the lowest part clashes with the highest in a semidiapente which leaves the singer in doubt whether he is making an error or singing correctly. All composers have employed this interval, but in a different way. I say "in a different way," because although they employ it in the first and second parts of the measure, called arsis and thesis, they do not use it in either case after a "privation" of sound; as Artusi demonstrates in his *Art of Counterpoint*, a sixth or some other consonance precedes it.

(L) I have never seen or heard the interval used as these composers use it. They imply that the minim rest serves as a consonance. But, as you have said, the ear does not judge what it does not hear. Cipriano uses this interval in his madrigal "Non gemme, non fin'oro,"[17] and Morales in his Magnificat in the fifth mode, at the verse "Sicut locutus est,"[18] but in the manner taught by our elders, of which they left fully a thousand examples. And it is truly marvelous that the ancients, with their great industry and diligence, have taught the way, not to make consonant those intervals which nature herself created dissonant, but so to use them that they seem properly to lose some of their harshness and to acquire sweetness. But when, by a departure from the manner taught by the ancients, they are used and taken absolutely, they cannot have a good effect.

---

16 Blind self-love (*Odes*, I, xviii, 14). [Bennett]

17 *Primo libro a 4*, No. 22, measure 4 (*Smith College Music Archives*, VI, 75).

18 Cf. *Ambros, Geschichte der Musik*, IV (Leipzig, 1878), 370.

(V) This is one of those things in which experience has taught them to recognize what is good and beautiful and what is bad.

(L) Beyond doubt, much experience about many particulars, of which this is but one, shows the truth.

(V) Our ancients never taught that sevenths may be used absolutely and openly, as you see them used in the second, third, fourth, fifth, sixth, and seventh measures, for they do not give grace to the composition and, as I said a little while ago, the higher part has no correspondence to its whole, beginning, or foundation.

(L) This is a new paradox.

(V) If this new paradox were reasonably founded on some reason, it would deserve much praise and would move onward to eternal life. But it is destined to have a short life, for demonstration can only show that truth is against it.

.   .   .   .   .

(L) I remain under great obligation to Your Lordship's amiability. I believe that we shall depart tomorrow morning without fail; it remains for me to pray that you will both retain me in your favor and consider me at your command. I shall go well content, for by Your Lordship's favor I take with me things that console and content me greatly.

(V) Signor Luca, it is my duty always to serve you, just as I pray you to command me. And if any doubt occurs to you concerning our discussions, let me know, for I shall gladly do what is necessary. So I remain at your service and pray the Lord to give you a pleasant journey.

(L) Signor Vario, I kiss your hand. Farewell.

52. Claudio Monteverdi

Born at Cremona in 1567, Monteverdi studied counterpoint with Marcantonio Ingegneri and entered the service of the dukes of Gonzaga at Mantua as a viol player. He waited until 1603 to be made choirmaster at the Mantuan court. In 1613 he left for Venice, where he assumed the position of *maestro di cappella* at St. Mark's, a post he held until his death in 1643.

The Fifth Book of Monteverdi's madrigals—there are nine books in all—is introduced by a foreword in which the composer replies to the bitter attacks that had been leveled against his art by the reactionary critic Artusi. The pieces contained in this book already show a strong tendency toward the new style. In the Eighth Book (*Madrigali guerrieri ed amorosi*, 1638), the pieces no longer have anything in common with the tradition. That Monteverdi should call such pieces "Madrigali" is an indication of the level to which the madrigal had sunk by the third decade of the seventeenth century.

Il quinto libro de' madrigali

[*1605*]

Foreword with the "Declaration" of His Brother G. C. Monteverdi [1]

[*1607*]

Some months ago a letter of my brother Claudio Monteverdi was printed and given to the public. A certain person, under the fictitious name of Antonio Braccini da Todi, has been at pains to make this seem to the world a chimera and a vanity.[2] For this reason, impelled by the love I bear my brother and still

---

1 Text: The original edition, printed at the end of Claudio's *Scherzi musicali* (Venice, 1607); published in facsimile by Malipiero in his edition of Monteverdi's works, X, 69–72.

2 Artusi had continued his attack on Monteverdi in his *Seconda parte dell' Artusi* (Venice, 1603), and on the publication of Monteverdi's

Quinto libro a 5 in 1605, had replied to it in a *Discorso musicale*, publishing it in 1606 or 1607 under the pseudonym Antonio Braccini. No copy of this abusive pamphlet is known to have been preserved. Subsequently (1608), Artusi published a *Discorso secondo musicale*, replying to the "Declaration" printed here.

more by the truth contained in his letter, and seeing that he pays attention to deeds and takes little notice of the words of others, and being unable to endure that his works should be so unjustly censured, I have determined to reply to the objections raised against them, declaring in fuller detail what my brother, in his letter, compressed into little space, to the end that this person and whoever follows him may learn that the truth that it contains is very different from what he represents in his discussions. The letter says:

Do not marvel that I am giving these madrigals to the press without first replying to the objections that the Artusi [a] *has brought against some*

[a] By the Artusi is to be understood the book bearing the title, *L'Artusi; or, Of the Imperfections of Modern Music,* whose author, disregarding the civil precept of Horace, *Nec tua laudabis studia, haud aliena reprendes* [Praise not your own studies; blame not those of others], and without any cause given by him, and therefore unjustly, says the worst he can of certain musical compositions of my brother Claudio.

very minute details [b] *in them, for being in the service of His Serene*

[b] These details, called "passages" by Artusi, which are seen so lacerated by him in his Second Discourse, are part of my brother's madrigal "Cruda Amarilli," and their harmony is part of the melody of which this is composed; for this reason he has called them details and not "passages."

Highness, I have not at my disposal the time that would be required. [c]

[c] This my brother said, not only because of his responsibility for both church and chamber music, but also because of other extraordinary services, for, serving a great prince, he finds the greater part of his time taken up, now with tourneys, now with ballets, now with comedies and various concerts, and lastly with the playing of the two *viole bastarde,* a responsibility and study which is not so usual as his adversary would have understood. And my brother has bided his time and continues to bide his time, not only for the reason and valid excuse set forth, but also because he knows that *properantes omnia perverse agunt* [the hasty do all things badly], that excellence and speed are not companions in any undertaking whatsoever, and that perfect excellence requires the whole man, the more so in attempting to treat of a matter hardly touched upon by intelligent harmonic theorists, and not, like his opponent, of a matter *nota lippis atque tonsoribus* [familiar to the blear-eyed and to barbers].

Nevertheless, to show that I do not compose my works at haphazard, [d]

[d] My brother says that he does not compose his works at haphazard because, in this kind of music, it has been his intention to make the words the mistress of the harmony and not the servant, and because it is in this manner that his work is to be judged in the composition of the melody. Of this Plato speaks as follows:

"The song is composed of three things: the words, the harmony, and the rhythm"; and, a little further on: "And so of the apt and the unapt, if the rhythm and the harmony follow the words, and not the words these." Then, to give greater force to the words, he continues: "Do not the manner of the diction and the words follow and conform to the disposition of the soul?" and then: "Indeed, all the rest follows and conforms to the diction." [3] But in this case, Artusi takes certain details, or, as he calls them, "passages," from my brother's madrigal "Cruda Amarilli," paying no attention to the words, but neglecting them as though they had nothing to do with the music, later showing the said "passages" deprived of their words, of all their harmony, and of their rhythm. But if, in the "passages" noted as false, he had shown the words that went with them, then the world would have known without fail where his judgment had gone astray, and he would not have said that they were chimeras and castles in the air from their entire disregard of the rules of the First Practice. But it would truly have been a beautiful demonstration if he had also done the same with Cipriano's madrigals "Dalle belle contrade," "Se ben il duol," "Et se pur mi mantieni amor," "Poiche m'invita amore," "Crudel acerba," "Un altra volta," [4] and, to conclude, with others whose harmony obeys their words exactly and which would indeed be left bodies without soul if they were left without this most important and principal part of music, his opponent implying, by passing judgment on these "passages" without the words, that all excellence and beauty consist in the exact observance of the aforesaid rules of the First Practice, which makes the harmony mistress of the words. This my brother will make apparent, knowing for certain that in a kind of composition such as this of his, music turns on the perfection of the melody, considered from which point of view the harmony, from being the mistress, becomes the servant of the words, and the words the mistress of the harmony, to which way of thinking the Second Practice, or modern usage, tends. Taking this as a basis, he promises to show, in refutation of his opponent, that the harmony of the madrigal "Cruda Amarilli" is not composed at haphazard, but with beautiful art and excellent study, unperceived by his adversary and unknown to him.

And since my brother promises, in refutation of his opponent, to show with writings that with respect to the perfection of the melody the writings of his adversary are not based upon the truth of art, let his opponent, in refutation of my brother's madrigal, show the errors of others through the medium of the press with a comparable practical performance—with harmony observing the rules of the First Practice, that is, disregarding the perfection of the melody, considered from which point of view the harmony, from being servant, becomes mistress; for *purpura juxta purpuram dijudicanda* [the purple is to be judged

[3] *Republic*, 398D (pp. 4 and 7 above). Monteverdi quotes Plato in the Latin translation of Marsilio Ficino.

[4] *Quinto libro a 5* (1566), No. 2 (reprinted by Walter Wiora in *Das Chorwerk*, Heft 5); *Quarto libro a 5* (1557), No. 3 (quoted by Einstein in *The Italian Madrigal*, I, 420); *Le vive fiamme* (1565), Nos. 18 and 16; *Secondo libro a 4* (1557), Nos. 9 (second part) and 1 (reprinted by Gertrude Parker Smith in *Smith College Music Archives*, VI, 127 and 90).

according to the purple]—for using only words to oppose the deeds of another is *nil agit exemplum litem quod lite resolvit* [the example that, settling one dispute by another, accomplishes nothing]. Then let him allow the world to be the judge, and if he brings forward no deeds, but only words, deeds being what commend the master, my brother will again find himself meriting the praise, and not he. For as the sick man does not pronounce the physician intelligent from hearing him prate of Hippocrates and Galen, but does so when he recovers health by his wisdom, so the world does not pronounce the musician intelligent from hearing him ply his tongue in telling of the honored harmonic theorists. For it was not in this way that Timotheus incited Alexander to war, but by singing. To such a practical performance my brother invites his opponent, not others, for he yields to them all, honors and reveres them all; his opponent he invites, once and for all, because he wishes to devote himself to music and not to writing, except as promised on this one occasion, and, following the divine Cipriano de Rore, the Signor Prencipe di Venosa, Emilio del Cavaliere, Count Alfonso Fontanella, the Count of the Camerata, the Cavalier Turchi, Pecci, and other gentlemen of that heroic school, to pay no attention to nonsense and chimeras.

I have written a reply which will appear, as soon as I have revised it, bearing the title, Seconda Pratica; [e] ovvero, Perfezioni della Moderna

[e] Because his opponent seeks to attack the modern music and to defend the old. These are indeed different from one another in their manner of employing the consonances and dissonances, as my brother will make apparent. And since this difference is unknown to the opponent, let everyone understand what the one is and what the other, in order that the truth of the matter may be more clear. Both are honored, revered, and commended by my brother. To the old music he has given the name of First Practice from its being the first practical usage, and the modern music he has called Second Practice from its being the second practical usage.

By First Practice he understands the one that turns on the perfection of the harmony, that is, the one that considers the harmony not commanded, but commanding, not the servant, but the mistress of the words, and this was founded by those first men who composed in our notation music for more than one voice, was then followed and amplified by Ockeghem, Josquin Desprez, Pierre de La Rue, Jean Mouton, Crequillon, Clemens non Papa, Gombert, and others of those times, and was finally perfected by Messer Adriano with actual composition and by the most excellent Zarlino with most judicious rules.

By Second Practice, which was first renewed in our notation by Cipriano de Rore (as my brother will make apparent), was followed and amplified, not only by the gentlemen already mentioned, but by Ingegneri, Marenzio, Giaches de Wert, Luzzasco, likewise by Jacopo Peri, Giulio Caccini, and finally by loftier spirits with a better understanding of true art, he understands the one that turns on the perfection of the melody, that is, the one that considers harmony not commanding, but commanded, and makes the words the mistress of the harmony. For reasons of this sort he has called it "second," and not "new," and he has called it "practice," and not "theory," because he understands its explanation to turn on the manner of employing the consonances and dissonances in actual composition. He has not called it "Musical Institutions" because he confesses that he is not one to undertake so great an enterprise, and he leaves the composition of such noble writings to the Cavalier Ercole Bottrigari and to the Reverend Zarlino. Zarlino used the title "Harmonic Institutions" because he wished to teach the laws and rules of harmony; my brother has used the title "Second Practice," that is, second practical usage, because he wishes to make use of the considerations of that usage, that is, of melodic considerations and their explanations, employing only so many of them as concern his defense against his opponent.

Musica.[f] *Some, not suspecting that there is any practice other than that*

[f] He will call it "Perfections of Modern Music" on the authority of Plato, who says: "Does not music also turn on the perfection of the melody?" [5]

taught by Zarlino, will wonder at this,[g] but let them be assured that,

[g] He has said "some," and not "all," to indicate only the opponent and his followers. He has said "they will wonder" because he knows for certain that these men are wanting, not only in understanding of the Second Practice, but (as he will make apparent) to a considerable extent in that of the First also. "Not suspecting that there is any practice other than that taught by Zarlino," that is, not suspecting that there is any practice other than that of Messer Adriano, for the Reverend Zarlino did not intend to treat of any other practice, as he indeed declares, saying: "It never was nor is it my intention to treat of the usage of practice according to the manner of the ancients, either Greeks or Latins, even if at times I touch upon it; my intention is solely to describe the method of those who have discovered our way of causing several parts to sound together with various modulations and various melodies, especially according to the way and manner observed by Messer Adriano." [6] Thus the Reverend Zarlino concedes that the practice taught by him is not the one and only truth. For this reason my brother intends to make use of the principles taught by Plato and practiced by the divine Cipriano and by modern usage, principles different from those taught and established by the Reverend Zarlino and practiced by Messer Adriano.

with regard to the consonances and dissonances,[h] there is still another

[h] But let the opponent and his followers be assured that, with regard to the consonances and dissonances, that is, with regard to the manner of employing the consonances and dissonances.

---

[5] *Gorgias*, 449D. [6] *Sopplimenti musicali*, I, i.

way of considering them, different from the established way,[1] *which,*

[1] By the established way of considering the consonances and dissonances, which turns on the manner of their employment, my brother understands those rules of the Reverend Zarlino that are to be found in the third book of his *Institutions* and that tend to show the practical perfection of the harmony, not of the melody, as is clearly revealed by the musical examples he gives there; these show in actual music the meaning of his precepts and laws, which are seen to have no regard for the words, for they show the harmony to be the mistress and not the servant. For this reason my brother will prove to the opponent and his followers that, when the harmony is the servant of the words, the manner of employing the consonances and dissonances is not determined in the established way, for the one harmony differs from the other in this respect.

with satisfaction to the reason and to the senses,[j] *defends the modern method of composing.*

[j] "With satisfaction to the reason" because he will take his stand upon the consonances and dissonances approved by mathematics (for he has said "with regard to the manner of employing them") and because he will likewise take his stand upon the command of the words, the chief mistress of the art considered from the point of view of the perfection of the melody, as Plato affirms in the third book of his *Republic* [7] (for he has said "Second Practice"). "With satisfaction to the senses" because the combination of words commanding with rhythm and harmony obedient to them (and I say "obedient" because the combination in itself is not enough to perfect the melody) affects the disposition of mind. Here is what Plato says: "For only melody, turning the mind away from all things whatsoever that distract, reduces it to itself"; [8] not harmony alone, be it ever so perfect, as the Reverend Zarlino concedes in these words: "If we take harmony absolutely, without adding to it anything else, it will have no power to produce any extrinsic effect," adding, a little further on: "In a certain way, it intrinsically prepares for and disposes to joy or sadness, but it does not on this account lead to the expression of any extrinsic effect." [9]

I have wished to say this to you in order that the expression "Second Practice" may not be appropriated by any one else,[k] *and further, that*

[k] My brother has made known to the world that this expression is assuredly his in order that it may be known and concluded that when his adversary said, in the second book of the Artusi: "This Second Practice, which may in all truth be said to be the dregs of the First," he spoke as he did to speak evil of my brother's works. This was in the year 1603, when my brother had first decided to begin writing his defense of himself against his opponent and when the expres-

---

[7] *Republic*, 398D (p. 4 above).   [9] *Istituzioni armoniche*, II, vii.
[8] Marsilio Ficino, "Compendium in Timaeum,"
XXX.

sion "Second Practice" had barely passed his lips, a sure indication that his adversary was desirous of defaming in the same vein my brother's words and his music as well, although they were still in manuscript. And for what reason? Let him say it who knows; let him see it who can find it on the map! But why does the adversary show so much astonishment in that discourse of his, saying further: "You show yourself as jealous of that expression as though you feared that someone would rob you of it," as though he meant to say, in his language: "You should not fear such a theft, for you are not worth imitating, let alone robbing"? I inform him that, if the matter has to be considered in this light, my brother will have not a few arguments in his favor, in particular the *canto alla francese* in the modern manner that has been a matter of marvel for the three or four years since it was published and which he has applied, now to motets, now to madrigals, now to canzonets and airs. Who before him brought this to Italy until he returned from the baths of Spa in the year 1599? Who before him began to apply it to Latin words and to words in our vulgar tongue? Has he not now composed his *Scherzi?* There would be much to say of this to his advantage, and still more (if I wished) of other things, but I pass over them in silence since, as I have said, the matter does not need to be considered in this light. I shall call it "Second Practice" with regard to the manner of its employment; with regard to its origin it might be called "First."

the ingenious may reflect meanwhile upon other secondary matters concerning harmony [1] *and believe that the modern composer builds upon*

---

[1] "Other matters," that is, not clinging obstinately to the belief that the whole requirement of art is to be found only in the rules of the First Practice on the ground that, in all varieties of composition, the harmony is always the same thing, having reached its limit, and that it is thus incapable of obeying the words perfectly. "Secondary matters," that is, matters concerning the Second Practice, or the perfection of the melody. "Concerning harmony," that is, concerning not merely the details or "passages" of a composition, but its fruit. For if the opponent had considered the harmony of my brother's madrigal "O Mirtillo" in this light, he would not, in that discourse of his, have uttered such extravagances with regard to its mode, although it appears that he speaks generally, his words being: "The Artusi has likewise explained and demonstrated the confusion introduced into composition by those who begin in one mode, follow this with another, and end with one wholly unrelated to the first and second ideas, which is like hearing the talk of a madman, who, as the saying goes, hits now the hoop and now the cask." Poor fellow, he does not perceive that, while he is posing before the world as preceptor ordinary, he falls into the error of denying the mixed modes. If these did not exist, would not the Hymn of the Apostles,[10] which begins in the sixth mode and ends in the fourth, strike now the hoop and now the cask; likewise the introit "Spiritus Domini replevit

---

10 "Exsultet coelum laudibus," *Ant. Rom.*, Hymni antiqui, p. 33.

orbem terrarum" [11] and especially the Te Deum laudamus? [12] Would not Josquin be an ignoramus for having begun his mass on "Faisant regrets" [13] in the sixth mode and finished it in the second? The "Nasce la pena mia" of the excellent Striggio,[14] the harmony of which composition (from the point of view of the First Practice) may well be called divine—would it not be a chimera, being built upon a mode consisting of the first, eighth, eleventh, and fourth? The madrigal "Quando signor lasciaste" of the divine Cipriano de Rore,[15] which begins in the eleventh mode, passes into the second and tenth in the middle, and ends in the first, the second part in the eighth—would not this thing of Cipriano's be a truly trifling vanity? And what would Messer Adriano be called for having begun in the first mode in "Ne projicias nos in tempore senectutis" (a motet for five voices to be found at the end of his first book), making the middle in the second mode and the end in the fourth? But let the opponent read Chapter 14 of the fourth book of the Reverend Zarlino's *Institutions* and he will learn.[16]

the foundation of truth.[m] *Farewell.*

[m] My brother, knowing that, because of the command of the words, modern composition does not and cannot observe the rules of practice and that only a method of composition that takes account of this command will be so accepted by the world that it may justly be called a usage, has said this because he cannot believe and never will believe—even if his own arguments are insufficient to sustain the truth of such a usage—that the world will be deceived, even if his opponent is. And farewell.

---

11 *Grad. Rom.,* p. 292.

12 *Ibid.,* p. 141*.

13 *Missarum Josquin liber III* (Venice, 1514), No. 2. Cf. Ambros, *Geschichte der Musik,* 3d ed., III (Leipzig, 1893), 220, and for the Osanna and Benedictus, Burney, *A General History of Music,* II (London, 1782), 499–500.

14 *Primo libro a 6* (1560), No. 3, reprinted by Charles van den Borren as an appendix to his edition of Philippe de Monte's *Missa Nasce la pena mia* (Düsseldorf, n.d.).

15 *Quarto libro a 5* (1557), No. 9.

16 "On the common or mixed modes."

53. Claudio Monteverdi

Madrigali guerrieri ed amorosi [1]

[*Venice, 1638*]

Foreword

I HAVE reflected that the principal passions or affections of our mind are three, namely, anger, moderation, and humility or supplication; so the best philosophers declare, and the very nature of our voice indicates this in having high, low, and middle registers. The art of music also points clearly to these three in its terms "agitated," "soft," and "moderate" (*concitato, molle,* and *temperato*).[2] In all the works of former composers I have indeed found examples of the "soft" and the "moderate," but never of the "agitated," a genus nevertheless described by Plato in the third book of his *Rhetoric* in these words: "Take that harmony that would fittingly imitate the utterances and the accents of a brave man who is engaged in warfare."[3] And since I was aware that it is contraries which greatly move our mind, and that this is the purpose which all good music should have—as Boethius asserts, saying, "Music is related to us, and either ennobles or corrupts the character"[4]—for this reason I have applied myself with no small diligence and toil to rediscover this genus.

After reflecting that according to all the best philosophers the fast pyrrhic measure was used for lively and warlike dances, and the slow spondaic measure for their opposites,[5] I considered the semibreve, and proposed that a single semibreve should correspond to one spondaic beat; when this was reduced to sixteen semiquavers, struck one after the other,

---

1 Text: The original edition (Venice, 1638). A facsimile of Monteverdi's Foreword is published in Vol. 8 of Malipiero's edition of the collected works.

2 Evidently a reference to Aristotle's threefold classification of melodies or to its reformulation by the school of Aristoxenus (pp. 22 and 45 above).

3 *Republic*, 399A (see p. 5 above).

4 *De institutione musica*, I, i (see p. 79 above).

5 Plato, *Laws*, 816C.

413

and combined with words expressing anger and disdain, I recognized in this brief sample a resemblance to the passion which I sought, although the words did not follow metrically the rapidity of the instrument.

To obtain a better proof, I took the divine Tasso, as a poet who expresses with the greatest propriety and naturalness the qualities which he wishes to describe, and selected his description of the combat of Tancred and Clorinda [6] as an opportunity of describing in music contrary passions, namely, warfare and entreaty and death. In the year 1624 I caused this composition to be performed in the noble house of my especial patron and indulgent protector the Most Illustrious and Excellent Signor Girolamo Mocenigo, an eminent dignitary in the service of the Most Serene Republic, and it was received by the best citizens of the noble city of Venice with much applause and praise.

After the apparent success of my first attempt to depict anger, I proceeded with greater zeal to make a fuller investigation, and composed other works in that kind, both ecclesiastical and for chamber performance. Further, this genus found such favor with the composers of music that they not only praised it by word of mouth, but, to my great pleasure and honor, they showed this by written work in imitation of mine. For this reason I have thought it best to make known that the investigation and the first essay of this genus, so necessary to the art of music, came from me. It may be said with reason that until the present, music has been imperfect, having had only the two general—"soft" and "moderate."

It seemed at first to the musicians, especially to those who were called on to play the *basso continuo*, more ridiculous than praiseworthy to strum on a single string sixteen times in one measure, and for that reason they reduced this multiplicity to one stroke to the measure, sounding the spondee instead of the pyrrhic foot, and destroying the resemblance to agitated speech. Take notice, therefore, that in this kind the *basso continuo* must be played, along with its accompanying parts, in the form and manner as written. Similarly, in the other compositions, of different kind, all the other directions necessary for performance are set forth. For the manners of performance must take account of three things: text, harmony, and rhythm.[7]

My rediscovery of this warlike genus has given me occasion to write certain madrigals which I have called *Guerrieri*. And since the music played before great princes at their courts to please their delicate taste is of three kinds, according to the method of performance—theater music,

---

[6] *La Gerusalemme liberata*, xii, 52–68.   [7] Plato, *Republic*, 398D (see p. 4 above).

chamber music, and dance music—I have indicated these in my present work with the titles *Guerriera, Amorosa,* and *Rappresentativa.*[8]

I know that this work will be imperfect, for I have but little skill, particularly in the warlike genus, because it is new and *omne principium est debile.* I therefore pray the benevolent reader to accept my good will, which will await from his learned pen a greater perfection in the said style, because *inventis facile est addere.* Farewell.

8 This seems to say, but cannot mean, that there is a correspondence between Monteverdi's three methods of performance and his three varieties of madrigal. Among the *Madrigali guerrieri,* for example, some are *teatrali,* some *da camera,* some *da ballo.* To put it differently, *guerriero* and *amoroso* correspond to kinds of music—*concitato* and *molle*—while *rappresentativo* corresponds to *teatrale,* a method of performance.

IX

Musical Practice in the Baroque Age

IX

54. Lodovico Grossi da Viadana

Born at Viadana near Mantua in 1564, Lodovico Grossi studied with Costanzo Porta and became in 1594 choirmaster at the Cathedral of Mantua, remaining there until 1609. About 1595 Viadana entered the Franciscan order. Later he lived at Rome, Padua, and Fano; he died near his birthplace in 1627.

Viadana published a number of volumes of sacred and secular music in the various polyphonic forms, but the work upon which his historical reputation chiefly rests is the collection *Cento concerti ecclesiastici* (for one to four voices with a bass for the organ), published at Venice in 1602. Viadana cannot be regarded as the inventor of the figured bass, as it had been advanced repeatedly before his time, but through his *Cento concerti* he exerted a lasting influence on the development of religious chamber music.

Cento concerti ecclesiastici [1]

[1602]

Preface

LODOVICO VIADANA to his kind readers.

There have been many reasons (courteous readers) which have induced me to compose concertos of this kind, among which the following is one of the most important: I saw that singers wishing to sing to the organ, either with three voices, or two, or to a single one by itself, were sometimes forced by the lack of compositions suitable to their purpose to take one, two, or three parts from motets in five, six, seven, or even eight; these, owing to the fact that they ought to be heard in conjunction with other

---

1 Text: As translated by F. T. Arnold in *The Art of Accompaniment from a Thorough-Bass* (London, Oxford University Press, 1931), pp. 3-4, 10-19. I have translated the last paragraph, omitted by Arnold, from the text printed by Max Schneider in his *Anfänge des Basso continuo* (Leipzig, 1918).

parts, as being necessary for the imitations, closes, counterpoints, and other features of the composition as a whole, are full of long and repeated pauses; closes are missing; there is a lack of melody, and, in short, very little continuity or meaning, quite apart from the interruptions of the words which are sometimes in part omitted, and sometimes separated by inconvenient breaks which render the style of performance either imperfect, or wearisome, or ugly, and far from pleasing to the listeners, not to mention the very great difficulty which the singers experience in performance.

Accordingly, having repeatedly given no little thought to these difficulties, I have tried very hard to find a way of remedying to some extent so notable a deficiency, and I believe, thank God, that I have at length found it, having, to this end, composed some of these concertos of mine for a single voice (soprano, alto, tenor, bass) and some others for the same parts in a variety of combinations, always making it my aim to give satisfaction thereby to singers of every description, combining the parts in every variety of ways, so that whoever wants a soprano with a tenor, a tenor with an alto, an alto with a cantus, a cantus with a bass, a bass with an alto, two sopranos, two altos, two tenors, two basses, will find them all, perfectly adapted to his requirements; and whoever wants other combinations of the same parts will also find them in these concertos, now for three, and now for four voices, so that there will be no singer who will not be able to find among them plenty of pieces, perfectly suited to his requirements and in accordance with his taste, wherewith to do himself credit.

You will find some others which I have composed for instruments in various ways, which makes the invention more complete and gives the concertos greater adaptability and variety.

Furthermore, I have taken particular care to avoid pauses in them, except so far as is necessitated by the character and scheme of the different pieces.

I have, to the very best of my ability, endeavored to achieve an agreeable and graceful tunefulness in all the parts by giving them a good and well-sustained melodic progression.

I have not failed to introduce, where appropriate, certain figures and cadences, and other convenient opportunities for ornaments and passagework and for giving other proofs of the aptitude and elegant style of the singers, although, for the most part, to facilitate matters, the stock passages have been used, such as nature itself provides, but more florid.

I have taken pains that the words should be so well disposed beneath the notes that, besides insuring their proper delivery, all in complete and due sequence, it should be possible for them to be clearly understood by the hearers, provided that they are delivered distinctly by the singers.

The other less important reason (in comparison with the one aforesaid) which has also made me hasten to publish this my invention is the following: I saw that some of these *Concerti*, which I composed five or six years ago when in Rome (happening then to bethink myself of this new fashion), found such favor with many singers and musicians that they were not only found worthy to be sung again and again in many of the leading places of worship, but that some persons actually took occasion to imitate them very cleverly and to print some of these imitations; wherefore, both for the above reason and also to satisfy my friends, by whom I have frequently been most urgently requested and advised to publish my said concertos as soon as possible, I have at last made up my mind, after having completed the intended number, to print them, as I am now doing, being convinced that this work need not be altogether displeasing to discerning singers and musicians, and that even though it possess no other merit, a willing and active spirit will, at least, not have been lacking, and since it provides, along with its novelty, more than ordinary food for thought, you cannot disdain to read the following instructions, which, in practice, will be of no slight assistance.

1. Concertos of this kind must be sung with refinement, discretion, and elegance, using accents with reason and embellishments with moderation and in their proper place: above all, not adding anything beyond what is printed in them, inasmuch as there are sometimes certain singers, who, because they are favored by nature with a certain agility of the throat, never sing the songs as they are written, not realizing that nowadays their like are not acceptable, but are, on the contrary, held in very low esteem indeed, particularly in Rome, where the true school of good singing flourishes.

2. The organist is bound to play the organ part simply, and in particular with the left hand; if, however, he wants to execute some movement with the right hand, as by ornamenting the cadences, or by some appropriate embellishment, he must play in such a manner that the singer or singers are not covered or confused by too much movement.

3. It will likewise be a good thing that the organist should first cast an eye over the concerto which is to be sung, since, by understanding the nature of the music, he will always execute the accompaniments better.

4. Let the organist be warned always to make the cadences in their proper position: that is to say, if a concerto for one bass voice alone is being sung, to make a bass cadence; if it be for a tenor, to make a tenor cadence; if an alto or soprano, to make it in the place of the one or the other, since it would always have a bad effect if, while the soprano were making its cadence, the organ were to make it in the tenor, or if, while someone were singing the tenor cadence, the organ were to make it in the soprano.

5. When a concerto begins after the manner of a fugue, the organist begins also with a single note, and, on the entry of the several parts, it is at his discretion to accompany them as he pleases.

6. No tablature has been made for these concertos, not in order to escape the trouble, but to make them easier for the organist to play, since, as a matter of fact, not every one would play from a tablature at sight, and the majority would play from the partitura as being less trouble; I hope that the organists will be able to make the said tablature at their own convenience, which, to tell the truth, is much better.

7. When passages in full harmony are played on the organ, they are to be played with hands and feet, but without the further addition of stops; because the character of these soft and delicate *concerti* does not bear the great noise of the full organ, besides which, in miniature *concerti*, it has something pedantic about it.

8. Every care has been taken in assigning the accidentals where they occur, and the prudent organist will therefore see that he observes them.

9. The organ part is never under any obligation to avoid two fifths or two octaves, but those parts which are sung by the voices are.

10. If anyone should want to sing this kind of music without organ or clavier, the effect will never be good; on the contrary, for the most part, dissonances will be heard.

11. In these concertos, falsettos will have a better effect than natural sopranos; because boys, for the most part, sing carelessly, and with little grace, likewise because we have reckoned on distance to give greater charm; there is, however, no doubt that no money can pay a good natural soprano; but there are few of them.

12. When one wants to sing a concerto written in the four usual parts,[2]

---

2 For "in the four usual parts" read "for equal voices" (*à voci pari*). Viadana follows the usual practice of his time, which applies the expression *à voci pari* not only to music in a single register, high or low, but also to music in which the over-all register is relatively restricted. Then in his "O sacrum convivium" *à voci pari* (Arnold, *op. cit.*, pp. 31–33) the four clefs are alto, tenor, tenor, and bass.

the organist must never play high up, and, vice versa, when one wants to sing a concerto of high pitch, the organist must never play low down, unless it be in cadences in the octave, because it then gives charm.

Nor let anyone presume to tell me here that the said concertos are a little too difficult, for my intention has been to make them for those who understand and sing well, and not for those who abuse their craft. And be in good health.

55. Agostino Agazzari

Born of a noble family at Siena in 1578, Agazzari was teaching in 1602 as *musicae praefectus* at the Germanic College in Rome. Ultimately, however, he returned to his native city and became choirmaster at its cathedral, a post he retained until his death in 1640.

Agazzari was an intimate friend of Viadana and one of the first to adopt the figured bass and to publish instructions concerning its realization. He sets forth his views in his *Del sonare sopra il basso*, 1607, and in the second book of his *Sacrae cantiones*, 1608. His musical publications are numerous and include an early opera, *Eumelio*, performed at the Roman Seminary, the Jesuit headquarters, in 1606.

Of Playing upon a Bass with All Instruments and of Their Use in the Consort [1]
[*1607*]

HAVING NOW to speak to you of musical instruments, I must first, for the sake of the order and brevity required in all discussions, classify them according to the needs of my subject and proposed material. I shall therefore divide them into classes, namely, into instruments like a foundation and instruments like ornaments. Like a foundation are those which guide and support the whole body of the voices and instruments of the consort; such are the organ, harpsichord, etc., and similarly, when there are few voices or solo voices, the lute, theorbo, harp, etc. Like ornaments are those which, in a playful and contrapuntal fashion, make the harmony more agreeable and sonorous, namely, the lute,

---

1 Text: The facsimile reprint of the original edition of 1607 (Milan, 1933); see also Otto Kinkeldey, *Orgel und Klavier in der Musik des 16 Jahrhunderts* (Leipzig, 1910), pp. 216–221.

theorbo, harp, *lirone*, cithern, spinet, *chitarrino*, violin, pandora, and the like.

Further, some are stringed instruments, others wind instruments. Of those of this second group (excepting the organ) I shall say nothing, because they are not used in good and pleasing consorts, because of their insufficient union with the stringed instruments and because of the variation produced in them by the human breath, although they are introduced in great and noisy ones. Sometimes in small consorts, when there are *organetti* in the octave above, the trombone replaces the double bass, but it must be well and softly played. All this I say in general, for in particular cases these instruments may be played so excellently by a master hand that they adorn and beautify the harmony.

In the same way, among the stringed instruments, some have within them a perfect harmony of the parts, such as the organ, harpsichord, lute, *arpa doppia*, etc.; others have an imperfect one, such as the common cithern, *lirone, chitarrino*, etc.; others have little or none, such as the viol, violin, pandora, etc. For this reason I shall speak in the first place of those instruments of the first class which are the foundation and have perfect harmony and in the second place of those which serve for ornament.

Having made this division and laid down these principles, let us come to the instructions for playing upon a bass. I say, then, that he who wishes to play well should understand three things. First he must know counterpoint (or at least sing with assurance, understand proportions and tempora, and read in all the clefs) and must know how to resolve dissonances with consonances, how to distinguish the major and minor thirds and sixths, and other similar matters. Second, he must know how to play his instrument well, understanding its tablature or score, and must be very familiar with its keyboard or finger board in order not to have to search painfully for the consonances and beats during the music, knowing that his eye is busy watching the parts before him. Third, he must have a good ear in order to perceive the movements of the parts in their relation to one another. Of this I do not speak, for I could not say anything that would help those poor in it by nature.

But to come to the point, I conclude that no definite rule can be laid down for playing works where there are no signs of any sort, it being necessary to be guided in these by the intention of the composer, who is free and can, if he sees fit, place on the first half of a note a fifth or sixth, or vice versa, and this a major or a minor one, as seems more suitable to him or as may be necessitated by the words. And even though some writers who treat of counterpoint have defined the order of progression from one consonance to another as though there were but one way, they are in the wrong; they will pardon me for saying this, for they show that they have not understood that the consonances and the harmony as a whole are subject and subordinate to the words, not vice versa, and this I shall defend, if need be, with all the reasons I can. While it is perfectly true that, absolutely and in general, it is possible to lay down definite rules of progression, when there are words they must be clothed with that suitable harmony which arouses or conveys some passion.

As no definite rule can be given, the player must necessarily rely upon his ear and follow the work and its progressions. But if you would have an easy way of avoiding these obstacles and of playing the work exactly, take this one, indicating with figures above the notes of the bass the consonances and dissonances used with them by the composer; for example, if on the first half of a note there is a fifth and then a sixth, or vice versa, or a fourth and then a third, as illustrated:

Further, you must know that all consonances are either natural or accidental to the mode. When they are natural, no accidental is written at all; for example, when b is natural, the third above G (otherwise b-flat or b-natural) is naturally major; to make it minor, you must write a flat above the note G, in which case the third is accidentally minor; conversely, when b is flat, to make the third major, you must write a sharp above the note G. I say the same of the sixths, reminding you that an accidental below or near a note refers to the note itself, while one above it refers to the consonance which it serves to indicate, as in the following example:

Since all cadences, whether medial or final, require the major third, some musicians do not indicate it; to be on the safe side, however, I advise writing the accidental, especially in medial cadences.

The instruments being divided into two classes, it follows that they have different functions and are differently used. An instrument that serves as foundation must be played with great judgment and due regard for the size of the chorus; if there are many voices one should play with full harmonies, increasing the registers, while if there are few one should use few consonances, decreasing the registers and playing the work as purely and exactly as possible, using few passages and few divisions, occasionally supporting the voices with low notes and frequently avoiding the high ones which cover up the voices, especially the sopranos or falsettos. For this reason one should take the greatest possible care to avoid touching or diminishing with a division the note which the soprano sings, in order not to duplicate it or obscure the excellence of the note itself or of the passage which the good singer executes upon it; for the same reason one does well to play within a rather small compass and in a lower register.

I say the same of the lute, harp, theorbo, harpsichord, etc., when they serve as foundation with one or more voices singing above them, for in this case, to support the voice, they must maintain a solid, sonorous, sustained harmony, playing now piano, now forte, according to the quality and quantity of the voices, the place, and the work, while, to avoid interfering with the singer, they must not restrike the strings too often when he executes a passage or expresses a passion.

Finally, my purpose being to teach how to play upon a bass (not simply how to play, for this must be known beforehand), I take for granted a certain number of principles and terms; for example, that imperfect consonances progress to the nearest perfect ones; that cadences require the major third, as is for the most part true; that dissonances are resolved by the nearest consonance, the seventh by the sixth and the fourth by the third when the part containing the resolution lies above, the opposite when it lies below. But these matters I shall not discuss at length; he who does not know them must learn them. At present I shall teach the conduct of the hand on the organ.

The bass proceeds in many ways, namely, by step, by leap, with conjunct divisions, or with disjunct notes of small value. When it ascends by step, the right hand must descend by step or by leap; conversely, when the left hand ascends or descends by a leap of a third, fourth, or fifth, the right hand must proceed by step. For it is not good for both to ascend or descend together; not only is this ugly to see and to hear, but there is in it no variety at all, for it will be all octaves and fifths. When the bass ascends with a conjunct division, the right hand must remain stationary; when the progression is disjunct, with notes of small value, each note must have its own accompaniment. Here is an example of the whole:

Having now spoken sufficiently of the instruments which serve as a foundation to enable a judicious man to obtain much light from this slender ray (for saying too much makes for confusion), I shall speak briefly of those which serve as ornaments.

These instruments, which are combined with the voices in various ways, are in my opinion so combined for no other purpose than to ornament and beautify, and indeed to season the consort. For this reason, these instruments should be used in a different way than those of the first class; while those maintained the tenor and a plain harmony, these must make the melody flourishing and graceful, each according to its quality, with a variety of beautiful counterpoints. But in this the one class differs from the other; while the instruments of the first class, playing the bass before them as it stands, require no great knowledge of counterpoint in the player, those of the second class do require it, for the player must compose new parts above the bass and new and varied passages and counterpoints.

For this reason, he who plays the lute (which is the noblest instrument of them all) must play it nobly, with much invention and variety, not as is done by those who, because they have a ready hand, do nothing but play runs and make divisions from beginning to end, especially when playing with other instruments which do the same, in all of which nothing is heard but babel and confusion, displeasing and disagreeable to the listener. Sometimes, therefore, he must use gentle strokes and repercussions, sometimes slow passages, sometimes rapid and repeated ones, sometimes something played on the bass strings, sometimes beautiful vyings and conceits, repeating and bringing out these figures at different pitches and in different places; he must, in short, so weave the voices together with long groups, trills, and accents, each in its turn, that he gives grace to the consort and enjoyment and delight to the listeners, judiciously preventing these embellishments from conflicting with one another and allowing time to each, especially when there are other similar instruments, a thing to be avoided, in my opinion, unless they play at a great distance or are differently tuned or of different sizes.

And what I say of the lute, as the principal instrument, I wish understood of the others in their kind, for it would take a long time to discuss them all separately.

But since each instrument has its own peculiar limitations, the player must take advantage of them and be guided by them to produce a good result. Bowed instruments, for example, have a different style than those plucked with a quill or with the finger. The player of the *lirone* must bow with long, clear, sonorous strokes, bringing out the inner parts well, with attention to the major and minor thirds and sixths, a matter difficult but important with his instrument. The violin requires beautiful passages, distinct and long, with playful figures and little echoes and imitations repeated in several places, passionate accents, mute strokes of the bow, groups, trills, etc. The *violone*, as lowest part, proceeds with gravity, supporting the harmony of the other parts with soft resonance, dwelling as much as possible on the heavier strings, frequently touching the lowest ones. The theorbo, with its full and gentle consonances, reinforces the melody greatly, restriking and lightly passing over the bass strings, its special excellence, with trills and mute accents played with the left hand. The *arpa doppia*, which is everywhere useful, as much so in the soprano as in the bass, explores its entire range with gentle plucked notes, echoes of the two hands, trills, etc.; in short, it aims at good counterpoint. The cithern, whether the common cithern or the *ceterone*, is used with the other instruments in a playful way, making counterpoints upon the part. But all this must be done prudently; if the instruments are alone in the consort, they must lead it and do everything; if they play in company, each must regard the other, giving it room and not conflicting with it; if there are many, they must each await their turn and not, chirping all at once like sparrows, try to shout one another down. Let these few remarks serve to give some light to him who seeks to learn. He who relies on his own efforts needs no instruction at all; I do not write for him—I esteem and honor him. But if perchance some wit desires to carry the discussion further, I am at his service.

Finally, one must know how to transpose music from one step to another that has all the consonances natural and proper to the given tone.[2] No other transposition is possible without a very disagreeable sound, for, as I have sometimes observed, in transposing a first or second tone, naturally pleasing because of its many b-flats, to some step whose tone requires b-natural, it will be difficult for the player to avoid stumbling

---

2 For a full discussion of this problem cf. Arthur Mendel, "Pitch in the 16th and Early 17th Centuries," *The Musical Quarterly*, XXXIV (1948), nos. 1–4.

against some conflicting note; thus, with this crudity, the consort is spoiled and the listeners are offended, while the natural character of the given tone does not appear. Most natural and convenient of all is the transposition to the fourth or fifth, sometimes to a step higher or lower; in short, one must see which transposition is most appropriate and suitable to the given tone, not as is done by those who pretend to play every tone on every step, for if I could argue at length, I could show these their error and the impropriety of this.

Having treated thus far of playing upon a bass, it seems to me desirable to say something about the bass itself, for it has, I know, been censured by some, ignorant of its purpose or lacking the soul to play it. It is, then, for three reasons that this method has been introduced: first, because of the modern style of composing and singing recitative; second, because of its convenience; third, because of the number and variety of works which are necessary for concerted music.

As to the first reason, I shall say that, since the recent discovery of the true style of expressing the words, namely, the imitation of speech itself in the best possible manner, something which succeeds best with a single voice or with few voices, as in the modern airs of certain able men and as is now much practiced at Rome in concerted music, it is no longer necessary to make a score or tablature, but, as we have said above, a bass with its signs suffices. And if anyone objects that a bass will not suffice to play the ancient works, I shall reply that music of this kind is no longer in use, both because of the confusion and babel of the words, arising from the long and intricate imitations, and because it has no grace, for, with all the voices singing, one hears neither period nor sense, these being interfered with and covered up by imitations; indeed, at every moment, each voice has different words, a thing displeasing to men of competence and judgment. And on this account music would have come very near to being banished from Holy Church by a sovereign pontiff had not Giovanni Palestrina found the remedy, showing that the fault and error lay, not with music, but with the composers, and composing in confirmation of this the mass entitled *Missa Papae Marcelli*.[3] For this reason, although such compositions are good according to the rules of counterpoint, they are at the same time faulty according to the rules of music that is true and good, something which arises from disregarding the aim and function and good precepts of the latter, such composers wishing to stand solely on the observance of canonic treatment and imitation of the notes,

---

[3] Probably the earliest reference to the salvation of church music through the agency of the *Missa Papae Marcelli*.

not on the passion and expression of the words. Indeed, many of them wrote their music first and fitted words to it afterwards. For the moment, let this suffice, for it would not be to the purpose to discuss the matter at length in this place.

The second reason is the great convenience of the method, for with little labor the musician will have a large stock for his needs; apart from this, the learner is free from tablature, a matter difficult and burdensome to many and likewise very liable to error, the eye and mind being wholly occupied with following so many parts, especially when it is necessary to play concerted music on the spur of the moment.

The third and last reason, namely, the number of works which are necessary for concerted music, is alone sufficient ground, it seems to me, for introducing this so convenient method of playing, for if he were to put into tablature or score all the works which are sung in the course of a year in a single church in Rome, wherever concerted music is professed, the organist would need to have a larger library than a Doctor of Laws.

There was then abundant reason for the introduction of this kind of bass, with the method described above, on the ground that there is no need for the player to play the parts as written if he aims to accompany singing and not to play the work as written, a matter foreign to our subject. Accept what I have said in place of all I might have said, my desire being to satisfy in brief your courteous demands, so many times repeated, and not my natural bent, which is rather to learn from others than to teach them. Take it as it is, then, and let the shortness of the time be my excuse.

56. Heinrich Schütz

Born in Saxony in 1585, Schütz is the composer who first introduced into German music the new style that was coming to the fore in Italy at the beginning of his career. As a chorister in the service of the Landgrave Moritz of Hesse, he was sent in 1609 to Venice, where he studied under Giovanni Gabrieli. In 1612, after Gabrieli's death, Schütz returned to Cassel and was appointed organist to the Landgrave. In 1614 he exchanged this post with that of choirmaster to the Elector of Saxony at Dresden. In 1628, Schütz set out on a second visit to Venice. The artistic results of this second journey to Italy are contained in the first part of his *Symphoniae sacrae*, published in 1629. A second and third part were added in 1647 and 1650. Among Schütz's later works are his German *Passions*, which paved the way for J. S. Bach's great works in this form. Schütz died at Dresden in 1672.

Symphoniae sacrae[1]

Dedications and forewords

PRIMA PARS—OPUS II

[*Venice, 1629*]

To the Eldest Son
of the Elector of Saxony in the Holy Roman Empire, the Most
Serene Prince and Lord, Lord Johann Georg, Duke of Saxony,
Jülich, Cleves, and Berg, Landgrave of Thuringia, Margrave
of Meissen, Count of the Mark and Ravensberg,
Lord of Ravenstein, etc.,

---

1 Texts: *Sämmtliche Werke*, V (Leipzig, 1887), 3; VII (Leipzig, 1888), 3–6; X (Leipzig, 1891), 3–5.

A youth of heroic nature, the splendor of the House of Saxony, the most desired hope of his country, the author's most clement lord,

Heinrich Schütz presents his greetings.

IN MY absence, best of Princes,[2] I am not absent from you, for I still feel that by your great father's [3] orders I am accompanying you through the charming fields of music. For just as when I sailed from my port the tried benignity of him who made this possible was to me constantly as a favoring breeze (I refer to the security of my fortunes), I may stray with you with the same security, since you also are a guiding star to me. I therefore rejoice marvelously to be making my entire sojourn abroad in company with your image, as if you were sharing it. When this comes to my mind (and it does so at almost every point of my journey) it brings before me your very distinguished intellectual adornments, derived from your eminent father. It is no marvel that these, like seeds that have been sown, should grow up marvelously with you in the flower of your youth in the fertile soil of your intelligence and portend everything marvelous to the happiness of the Saxon land.

For this reason I think it good that in preparation for my return I should consider bringing something to offer as a votive gift and hang up as a tablet to my divinity. But it first occurs to me that I must present you with something from my studies that would above all find approval with you. This indeed, most fortunately, is the case.

Let your clemency incline you to listen. When I arrived at Venice, I cast anchor here where as a youth I had passed the novitiate of my art under the great Gabrieli [4]—Gabrieli, immortal gods, how great a man! If loquacious antiquity had seen him, let me say it in a word, it would have set him above Amphions, or if the Muses loved wedlock, Melpomene would have rejoiced in no other spouse, so great was he in the art of awakening the modes. This fame reports, and indeed unvarying fame. I myself am a most trustworthy witness, having derived the highest benefit from full four years' association with him. But this I pass over.

Staying in Venice as the guest of old friends, I learned that the long unchanged theory of composing melodies had set aside the ancient rhythms to tickle the ears of today with fresh devices. To this method

2 Johann Georg II (1613–1680), Elector after 1656.
3 Johann Georg I (1585–1656), Elector after 1611.
4 Schütz, writing during his second stay in Venice (1628–1629), refers here to his first stay (1609–1613) and to his studies with Giovanni Gabrieli, undertaken with the support of Landgrave Moritz of Hesse-Cassel; see also the dedication of his Opus 1, the Italian madrigals of 1611 (*Sämmtliche Werke*, IX, 3).

I directed my mind and energies, to the end that, in accordance with my purpose, I might offer you something from the store of my industry, while this labor, such as it is, is being undergone, I see myself undertaking a perilous risk for you, a young man both trained in the other virtues worthy of a highly praised prince and so skilled in this art as to have unusual expectations. With you I include your most able prefect Volrad von Watzdorff, a master of the same art, unless, I might say, it should serve him, and you as well, as a refuge from severer cares, such as befall princes like yourselves. But consider, Prince, and you, most noble Volrad, while we in sincerity offer these gifts, that even the highest divinities look upon pure hands, not full ones, upon hands, that is, which the candor of the soul, not waters of the spring, keeps free from stain. When men like you, standing next to the gods, show themselves in such light to us, why should I not have confidence? But if these things of mine should provoke some distaste, I shall appeal to your clemency and to the graciousness of the prefect, and shall urge as excuses the shortness of the time, the inconveniences of travel, and a mind perhaps aspiring, in the hope of your gratitude, to too great a task.

Farewell, renowned ornament of your house, and continue, I earnestly pray, to cherish me in the bosom of your clemency as you have begun to do.

Venice, August 19.

Secunda Pars—Opus X

[Dresden, 1647]

To the most serene all-powerful high-born Prince and Lord

Lord Christian V

Prince in Denmark, Norway, and of the Wends and Goths; Duke of Schleswig, Holstein, Stormarn, and the Dithmarschen; Count of Oldenburg and Delmenhorst, etc.;

My most gracious Prince and Lord.

Most serene and all-powerful Prince and gracious Lord: [5] That, now two years ago in connection with my then most humbly rendered per-

---

[5] Prince Christian (1603–1647), who died in the year of this dedication and during the lifetime of his father, King Christian IV (1577–1648), was the son-in-law of Johann Georg I.

sonal attendance in Copenhagen, Your Princely Serenity received and accepted with uncommon grace the present insignificant little musical work, composed by me and at that time extant only in manuscript copies; that, out of inborn princely inclination toward all praiseworthy arts and especially toward noble music, you caused the same to be used and performed on several occasions; and also that you gave me real and conspicuous assurance of your gracious satisfaction in that, my humble dedication; all this I call to mind in everlasting and most respectful recollection and, in consequence, find myself obliged in turn, out of bounden gratitude, to celebrate at all times and to the best of my ability your heroic nature and outstanding princely virtues and to consider at each and every opportunity how the great and unmerited favor shown to me may, through most bounden attendance, be to some extent repaid.

Moreover, since for various reasons (some of them hereinafter stated in my memorial to the reader) this little work, thoroughly revised and somewhat enlarged and improved, is now through publication to be brought to light, I have regarded it as in all respects my duty not even this time to pass by Your Princely Serenity in silence but, with this now new and public edition, also to renew my first and earlier humblest dedication, thereby above all to demonstrate and reaffirm my unceasing and most bounden devotion.

May it then please Your Princely Serenity now, with your gracious hands and eyes, to accept anew, as you did before, my repeatedly mentioned unworthy little work (the which I herewith once more present to you in deepest humility) and, with princely indulgence and graciousness, to be further inclined, so always to remain, toward my insignificant person and toward the praiseworthy profession of music, which otherwise has thus far suffered during these upset martial times great loss of its patrons.[6]

May the All-Highest, whose honor, praise, and glory the heavenly hosts continually do sing, again lend unity and good harmony on all sides and to all stations and also long preserve in health and happiness, and in all prosperity pleasing to Him, Your Princely Serenity, together with Your Princely Spouse and the whole most praiseworthy crown of Denmark, to the honor of His holy name, to the improvement of the free arts and especially of beloved music, at present greatly deteriorated, and also to the advantage of my unworthy person in particular. I faithfully

---

6 Here, as elsewhere, Schütz refers to the effects of the Thirty Years' War (1618–1648).

and humbly commend Your Princely Serenity to His fatherly care, myself then to your perpetual and gracious affection.

Dresden, on the first day of the month of May in the year 1647.
Your Princely Serenity's
Most dutiful and humble
Servant,

Heinrich Schütz

Ad benevolum lectorem.

Dear gracious reader: How, in the year 1629, when I had come for the second time to Italy and had resided there a while, I composed, in conformity with the insignificant talent God has lent me and, be it said without vanity, in a short time, a little Latin work for one, two, and three vocal parts, with two subordinate violins or similar instruments, in the musical style I then met with there; and how I caused the same to be set up and printed in Venice under the title *Symphoniae sacrae;* none of this shall be concealed from you here.

Since, at that time, from copies of the work, part of which had been exported to Germany and had there fallen into the hands of musicians, there came to my ears a report that the work was there thought to be of real value, further, that it was being diligently performed in various distinguished places with German words in place of Latin adapted throughout; I regarded this as a special incentive to me to attempt another little work of the same sort in our German mother tongue; and, after a bold beginning, I accordingly finished the same at length, with God's help, together with other works of mine (such as are here included).

Since then, however, and up until the present, I have been no little dissuaded from giving these out in a public edition, not only by the wretched times which still continue unabated in our beloved fatherland, unfavorable no less to music than to the other free arts, but also, and indeed above all, by the modern Italian manner used therein, still hidden from the majority, both as regards the composition and the proper performance of it, by means of which (in the opinion of the keen-witted Signor Claudio Monteverdi in the foreword to the Eighth Book of his madrigals) music is thought to have at length attained its final perfection.[7]

Indeed (to admit the truth here reluctantly), experience has thus far repeatedly shown that this same modern music, whether Italian or after the Italian manner, together with the measure proper for it and for the

---

7 See pp. 413–415 above.

notes of lesser value therein introduced, will neither rightly adapt itself to most of us Germans on this side, as many of us as are not bred to it, nor yet becomingly depart from us; in that (doubtless even in those places where one has thought to have good music) things thus composed are often so abused, defamed, and as it were actually broken that to an intelligent ear they can occasion nothing less than disgust and annoyance, to the author and to the praiseworthy German nation a wholly unjustified disparagement, as though the latter were in fact unskilled in noble music (as indeed there is no lack of such accusations on the part of certain foreigners).

But inasmuch as this little work, completed some years ago, was at that time humbly presented as manuscript to the serene all-powerful Prince and Lord, Lord Christian V, Prince in Denmark, Norway, and of the Goths and Wends, etc., as is, with other matters, to be seen from the foregoing most humble dedication; and inasmuch as I have since learned how many pieces of my composition, carelessly and incorrectly copied, scattered far and wide (as is then usual), have come into the hands of distinguished musicians; I have been obliged, therefore, to take the same once more in hand myself, and, after carrying out a thorough revision, I communicate them herewith through publication to those who may seek pleasure in them.

Now, since I should needlessly address myself to competent musicians, trained in good schools, if I were to call to their attention the pains I have expended herein (and, after the glory of God, it is to please these alone that the present few copies are now come to light); and since the manner herein introduced will be by no means displeasing to them;

Then to the others, especially to those who neither know nor practice the proper beat for the afore-mentioned modern music and its notes of lesser value and also the steady broadened way of bowing the violin which we Germans have (but who may wish nonetheless to perform something of this), this my friendly request: that before they undertake to employ one or other of these pieces in public they will not be ashamed on this account to seek instruction in advance from those familiar with this manner and will spare themselves no pains in private practice lest perchance on the contrary there accrue to them and to the author himself, through no fault of his, instead of the expected thanks, an unexpected ridicule.

Further, inasmuch as in the concerto "Es steh Gott auf," etc., I have been guided, in some few details, by Signor Claudio Monteverdi's madrigal "Armato il cor," etc., and also by one of his chaconnes with two tenor voices, I leave the question of how far I have gone in this to those familiar with the afore-mentioned compositions.[8] But let no one on this account suspect my remaining work unduly, for I am not accustomed to dress my works in borrowed plumage.

Finally, I make this further offer: that, if God continue to prolong my life, I shall, with His help, publish without delay still others of my admittedly unworthy *opera*, and, first among these, works of such a sort that even those who neither are nor intend becoming musicians *ex professo* may use them, it is hoped, and with the better effect.

Vale.

Tertia Pars—Opus XII

[*Dresden, 1650*]

To the most serene high-born Prince and Lord

Lord Johann Georg
Duke of Saxony, Jülich, Cleve, and Berg; Arch Marshal and Elector
of the Holy Roman Empire; Landgrave in Thuringia;
Margrave of Meissen, also of Upper and Lower
Lausitz; Burgrave of Magdeburg; Count
of the March and Ravensberg;
Lord of Ravenstein.

Most gracious Elector and Lord: Just as Your Electoral Serenity can, I trust, graciously call to mind and recollect for how long a time, now thirty-five years, I have in most humble submission and due fidelity been your constant servant, and just as you will not be less likely to recall how I have at all times loyally and industriously offered up the little talent lent me by God and have waited upon you with it, both in Your Electoral Serenity's Court Chapel and also in connection with other events that have occurred within this time and with various past solemnities;

So similarly there remains constantly with me in vivid memory how, during the past tedious thirty-year succession of wars, Your Electoral Serenity has never entirely withdrawn your favor and helping hand, either from the other free arts, or yet from the noble art of music, but has continued to assist them to the utmost, and especially how (during

---

8 For the concerto by Schütz see his *Sämmtliche Werke*, VII, 87–97; Monteverdi's "Armato il cor" and "Zefiro torna" may be consulted in the Appendix of the same volume or in Vol. 9 of Malipiero's edition of Monteverdi's works. The bass of Monteverdi's "Zefiro torna" was also used by Benedetto Ferrari in 1637 and by Tarquinio Merula in the same year (cf. Hugo Riemann, *Handbuch der Musikgeschichte*, II, 2. Teil [2d ed., Leipzig, 1922], 55–61, 121–124, 489–492).

the continued unrest in our universally beloved fatherland, the German nation) you have shown my unworthy person evidences of favor of all sorts: that in the year 1628 and again in 1629, for the continuance of my profession, you not only graciously allowed me to visit Italy (in order that I might there inform myself about the new and now usual manner of music introduced since my first return thence) and greatly furthered this enterprise, but also graciously permitted me, this my journey completed, at the further request of His Majesty of Denmark, Christian IV, now at rest in God,[9] to spend some time at his Royal Chapel, to head the *Directorium* (at that time offered me unsolicited), and in this way to preserve my small knowledge of music through constant practice and bring to it further experience.

Nor ought in this connection to be passed over in silence the most gracious means granted me some time ago by Your Electoral Serenity whereby the publication or giving out of my musical work can in future be even further forwarded and its printing facilitated.

For this high and mighty benefit I shall for the rest of my life remain justly bound to express to Your Electoral Serenity my most humble thanks and shall in addition do my utmost, through further most humble attendance (as long as my now diminished powers permit), to deserve again Your Electoral Serenity's many-sided favor and to continue in the possession of this same consolation in future.

And to this end is also directed the most humble dedication of this, my twelfth little work, which, with Your Electoral Serenity's lofty name at its head, I send forth into the world herewith; not only as a public witness of my proper and constant gratitude, but also to make known to everyone, above all to those whom my compositions may please, through what circumstance, favor, and furtherance the same are now brought to light and (should God grant me life) may continue to appear in future, and that the thanks and the honor (should anything of value be found in them) is due to Your Electoral Serenity alone.

Hence then to yourself my most humble and most diligent request that you may graciously deign to receive and accept from me in electoral favor the well-intended and faithfully devoted dedication and presentation of this my unsolicited work, not completed without effort, and that you may continue to favor me, your old and faithful servant, with that mercy and grace which until now you have used toward me.

Whereupon, together with many thousands, I wish with all my heart

---

9 Christian IV had died in 1648, the year following the publication of the second part of the *Symphoniae sacrae.*

that, to the advantage of your great electoral house and as a consolation to your loyal subjects, almighty God may preserve Your Electoral Serenity in good and constant health for many years to come and that, after the heavy burden of war, so long endured, He may grant you to enjoy to the full the restoration of order [10] in your honorable land, brought about through His mercy (for which everlasting thanks) and to rejoice in this and apply and employ the same fruitfully in the furtherance of the glory of God and the preservation of the good free arts.

Dated, Dresden, on the Feast of St. Michael Archangel in the year 1650.

> Your Electoral Serenity's
> Most humble and dutiful
> Heinrich Schütz

Dear gracious reader:

For all that there is no doubt that competent and experienced musicians will know in advance and of themselves how properly to order and employ this my present musical work, as well as the others that have been published; since, however, this leaf will otherwise have to remain vacant or empty, I have deemed it good to cause some few memorials to be here listed, hoping that no one will object to hearing in some measure my opinion, as the author's, about it.

1. Thus the complementary parts added to this work *ad beneplacitum* are to be found in four separate books, and from the index to the thorough bass part is to be seen to what concertos they belong and how many of them belong to each, whereby in general this further point seems noteworthy, that although in the index just mentioned most complementary music is only listed as being in four parts and although only four printed parts are supplied, the same may (if copied out again) be doubled and as it were divided into two choirs, for example vocal and instrumental, and ordered with the others. The rest is left to the judgment of the competent conductor.

2. Above the bass for the organ I have had the signatures entered with all possible care. The Italians are for the most part accustomed today to use no figures in this connection, objecting that experienced organists do not need them and without them know how to play along according to the counterpoint, while the inexperienced will not find the musical concord or agreement even when one places a figure immediately above

---

10 A reference to the end of the Thirty Years' War (1648).

it. Which then in itself is doubtless true enough, for to play along properly above the thorough bass and to content a musical ear thereby is not such a simple matter, for all that many a one may think so. That, however, in my previously published compositions I make use of these same signatures follows the precept: *Abundans cautela non nocet.*[11]

3. The organ must be registered with discretion (according to whether the complementary parts are added or left out).

4. Finally, I wish in this place hereby once again to call attention to all that has previously been pointed out to the reader in the published second part of my *Symphoniae sacrae* regarding modern music or the present manner of composition and touching the proper and suitable beat for it.

Commending us all faithfully to Divine Providence in mercy.

The Author.

---

[11] Abundant caution does no harm.

57. Georg Muffat

Born about 1645, this South German composer was organist at the Strassburg Cathedral till 1674. From there he visited Paris where he studied Lully's style. About 1678 he became organist to the Bishop of Salzburg, visited Vienna and Rome, and in 1690 was made organist, and in 1695 choirmaster to the Bishop of Passau. Muffat published several important collections of suites for string orchestra with basso continuo; their forewords contain discussions of the French and Italian styles and instructions concerning the playing of stringed instruments and the execution of ornaments. Another well-known work of Muffat's is his *Apparatus musico-organisticus* (1690), of importance for the history of organ playing and organ music.

Georg Muffat was the father of an equally distinguished composer for the organ and harpsichord, Gottlieb (Theophil) Muffat.

Florilegia [1]

FLORILEGIUM PRIMUM
[*Augsburg, 1695*]

Foreword

THE AUTHOR'S FOREWORD TO THE GRACIOUS AMATEUR

HERE YOU have my pieces, composed in Salzburg before I came to Passau and conforming in the main to the French ballet style, now submitted to you, gracious amateur, for your entertainment and approval. Heard with pleasure by several princes and also praised by others of the higher nobility, they are published at the repeated entreaty of good friends and with the approbation of distinguished musicians, both Italian and Ger-

---

1 Texts: *Denkmäler der Tonkunst in Oester-* reich, I2 (Vienna, 1894), 10–11; II2 (Vienna, 1895), 19–20, 28; XI2 (Vienna, 1904), 8–10.

Muffat prints each of these forewords in four languages—Latin, German, Italian, and French.

man. To these importunities I have given in the more gladly, observing that in Germany the French style is gradually coming to the fore and becoming the fashion. This same style, which formerly flourished in Paris under the most celebrated Jean Baptiste Lully, I have diligently sought to master, and, returning from France to Alsace, from whence I was driven by the last war, I was perhaps the first to bring this manner, not displeasing to many professional musicians, into Austria and Bohemia and afterwards to Salzburg and Passau. Inasmuch as the ballet compositions of the aforesaid Lully and other things after his manner entirely reject, for the sake of flowing and natural movement, all other artifices —immoderate runs as well as frequent and ill-sounding leaps—they had at first the misfortune, in these countries, to displease many of our violinists, at that time more intent on the variety of unusual conceits and artificialities than on grace; for this reason, when occasionally produced by those ignorant of the French manner or envious of foreign art, they came off badly, robbed of their proper tempo and other ornaments. When, however, they were exhibited with greater perfection, first in Austria by certain foreign violinists, soon afterwards in Bavaria by His Electoral Serenity's excellent musicians, they were more maturely considered, and many, in order to conform to the genius of the princes and lords applauding such music, began to form a better opinion of it, to accustom themselves to its style and grace, and even to study it. No doubt they discovered the truth of what an extremely discerning prince once said to me, touching this style: namely, that what they had learned previously was more difficult than what, to charm the ear, they needed to have learned. Now that the ill-considered contempt for the aforesaid ballet style has gradually fallen off, it has seemed to me that I might the more confidently come forward with my admittedly insignificant pieces, which, though they appear simple, are the more in need of the artistry and favor of our violinists. To give reasons for the names prefixed to each fascicle seems needless, especially since these have been named, only to distinguish one from another, either for some cause, effect, or other circumstance peculiar to myself or for some state of the affections which I have experienced.[2]

It still remains for me to remind and request such musicians as are as yet unfamiliar with the aforesaid style that, when notes are enclosed in such brackets as these ⌐¬ ∟⌐ , they are to play the first time those notes which precede the sign of repetition ∫ :‖:, the second time omit-

---

[2] The Latin titles of the seven suites making up the *Florilegium primum* might be translated: Piety, The Joys of the Hopeful, Gratitude, Impatience, Solicitude, Flatteries, Constancy.

ting these altogether, straightway skipping over instead to those notes which follow immediately after the sign of repetition just mentioned :||:. This sign, f, whether at the very beginning or after the sign of repetition :||:, marks the note from which, omitting the preceding altogether, one must begin; it is also to be observed when it occurs near the middle of the second part or somewhat further from the end. Although I find not displeasing the practice of some who, having in this case first repeated the whole second part once more in its entirety, begin again at the aforesaid sign f and repeat this much alone a third time, this is a matter to be settled by the musicians before the performance. The beat or measure governed by the signs 2 and ₵, divided into two parts, must be given once again as fast as that following the sign C, divided into four. Moreover, the time of those pieces comprehended by the names *Ouverture*, *Prélude*, and *Symphonie* is to be beaten rather slowly when it is marked 2, a little more briskly for the *Ballet*, in any case more slowly than one beats at the sign ₵, which last, in the *Gavotte*, is not so precipitate as in the *Bourrée*. Further, although at the sign 2 the measure is very slowly divided into two parts, the notes have nearly the same value as they have with the Italians at the sign C and the additional direction "Presto," when the measure is divided into four; the difference between the two is simply that in the latter case one must not, as in the former and better, give to successive quavers a dotted rhythm, but must, on the contrary, play them evenly. The *Symphonie* of the fourth fascicle provides an example of this. As to the other signs, 3/2 requires a restrained movement, 3/4 a gayer one, yet uniformly somewhat slow in *Sarabandes* and *Airs*, lively in the *Rondeau*, very brisk in *Menuets*, *Courantes*, and many other dances, as also in the Fugues appended to the *Ouvertures*. The remaining pieces, such as are called *Gigues* and *Canaries*, need to be played the fastest of all, no matter what the time signature.

Gracious amateur, may it please you to accept this my *Florilegium primum*, protecting it from the envious and grudging, and excusing such errors of mine and of the press as may have crept in. Await what is promised at the end of the work. Farewell and favor him who would deserve your favor.

• • • • •

Friendly amateur, I had planned, for the better advancement and greater glory of our Germany in its higher flights into the musical arts, to append to these ballets certain observations perhaps not displeasing to you, touching the performance of the same, having promised—in my *Apparatus Musico-Organisticus,* delivered five years ago, at the time of his royal coronation, into the all-serenest hands of our invincible Emperor Leopold—to attach something noteworthy and useful of this nature to all my forthcoming musical works. But since the limited time allowed me to complete this work did not permit my properly arranging the aforesaid observations, I have put these off to append them to my *Florilegium secundum,* in precisely the same style as this, which, if the present work finds acceptance, shall follow it without delay. In this same *Florilegium secundum* you may expect my new pieces, composed in Passau no less for the fitting reception of distinguished visitors than for the better ballet exercise of the youthful higher nobility; in the meantime another work of instrumental music, in an unusual but lofty style, has begun to sweat under the Passau printing press.[8]

FLORILEGIUM SECUNDUM
[*Passau, 1698*]

Foreword

When I remarked, friendly reader, that the first garland of my ballet pieces, printed and published at Augsburg in 1695, early last year, as a precursor of various musical works of mine to follow in the future, had not only been kindly received by many, especially by those amateurs who prized its natural and flowing style and for whose entertainment it was after all chiefly designed, but had further given rise to a great demand for my other promised ballets; I thought it proper to submit for your worthy intellectual entertainment and kindly approval this my second garland, enriched by many pieces, more amusing—thanks to the variety of its inventions, and, it is to be hoped, more valuable—thanks to the utility of its added observations. It contains no small part of the ballets recently composed in Passau and performed with great applause at this illustrious court, both for dancing and at many instrumental concerts. The which, though also serving in various other connections—for example, as chamber music, table music, or night music—still owes its origin more to Your Reverend Highness' zealous concern for the education of the youthful higher nobility resident at your court than to my desire to tickle the ear.

---

[8] The *Auserlesene Instrumental-Music* of 1701 (see pp. 449–452 below).

For, when Your Reverend Highness proposed to determine what progress those high and well-born gentlemen, your nephews, and those noble gentlemen, your pages, had made in their studies and noble exercises, hence also in dancing, Herr Christian Leopold Krünner, groom of the chamber and most deserving court dancing-master to Your Reverend Highness aforesaid, besought me to compose entirely new airs for certain ingenious inventions which he had conceived in order that, enhanced by theatrical costumes and apparatus, the dancing might be the more impressive. And when I had complied with this request of his to the best of my meager ability, Your Reverend Highness regarded this our work with such gracious eyes that you ordered us to prepare, for a further exercise in dancing, more arrangements of the same kind and also to perform these even before princes and other distinguished visitors, yourself taking gracious pleasure in such things as often as they were produced.

All this I have wished to point out to you in advance, friendly reader, so that, if anything in these pieces should strike your ears as strange or vulgar, you will ascribe it, not at all to a sterility or rudeness of style, but to the exigencies of the natural representations belonging to the dance, of which you may form an idea from the engraving diligently printed at the head of the thorough bass and violin parts.[4]

Then, although I should unwillingly be reckoned among those who adopt every idea that occurs to them, regarding it as the more praiseworthy, the more extravagant it is; among those to whom these lines of Horace apply so well:

> Nimium patienter utrumque
> Ne dicam stulte mirati; [5]

it sometimes happens, nonetheless, that for the better suggestion of certain words, manners, or gestures, one must defer a little. For this reason, since to avoid all excess great caution is required, I have sought diligently to soften, by means of the sweetness of agreeable consonances, whatever seemed unusual in the upper voice, namely the violin, and also to lend distinction, by means of the artful setting of the inner voices and the bass, to whatever seemed overly vulgar.

Aside from this, you have in this second garland my first observation, promised to you in the foregoing, showing how such ballets ought properly to be played according to the ideas of the late Monsieur Jean

---

4 The engraving is not reproduced in the critical edition.

5 *The Art of Poetry*, 271–272. Too tolerant, not to say foolish, was their admiration of both. [Fairclough]

Baptiste de Lully; observations written at the request of those who, as yet insufficiently instructed in this proper manner, have a desire to know in what it chiefly consists or in how it may be distinguished from the manner and opinion of others. All of which I wish to state as briefly as possible, readily admitting, at the same time, that others (of whom already there are many in these parts), violinists by actual profession and in addition well versed in the aforesaid manner, might have ordered this business much better than I. And I protest that, in what I am about to say, there is no intention to detract in the least from the well-earned reputation of many other celebrated violinists (whose flourishing abundance in Germany I myself acknowledge most respectfully); nor are these to be regarded as of little competence, even though not used to this new manner, for they have other qualities which concern the art more directly and more highly, and would beyond a doubt not only equal but easily excel the foreigners, were they to add to the musical assurance, the manual dexterity, and the store of artifice already at their command, the animated and agreeable charm of the Lullists.

Finally, I have added at the end of this work a catalogue of these partitas, with their keys and the years of their performance, and of my other things, already published or still to follow; to this I would direct your attention, so that, if perchance you meet in the works of others things more or less similar to my ideas, you may discover from my chronology that the theft is not to be charged to my account, and so that, being apprised of what I plan to work on for your entertainment and further advantage in music, you may receive this my painstaking the more kindly. Farewell.

FIRST OBSERVATION
ON THE PERFORMANCE OF BALLETS IN THE LULLIAN-FRENCH MANNER

·   ·   ·   ·   ·

The art of playing ballets on the violin in the manner of the most celebrated Jean Baptiste Lully (here understood in all its purity, admired and praised by the world's most excellent masters) is so ingenious a study that one can scarcely imagine anything more agreeable or more beautiful.

To reveal to you, gracious reader, its chief secrets, know that it has at one time two aims: namely, to appeal to the ear in the most agreeable way and to indicate properly the measure of the dance, so that one may recognize at once to what variety each piece belongs and may feel in one's affections and one's feet, as it were without noticing it at all, an inclination to dance. For this there are, in my opinion, five considerations necessary. First, one must, for purity of intonation, stop the strings accurately. Second, the bow must be drawn in a uniform way by all the players. Third, one must bear constantly in mind the time signature, or tempo and measure, proper to each piece. Fourth, one must pay strict attention to the usual signs of repetition introduced and also to the qualities of the style and of the art of dancing. Fifth, one must use with discernment certain ornaments making the pieces much more beautiful and agreeable, lighting them up, as it were, with sparkling precious stones. Of which the following distich:

> Contactus, plectrum, tempus, mos, atque venustas
> Efficient alacrem, dulcisonamque chelyn.[6]

.   .   .   .   .

May it then please you, gracious amateur, to receive kindly this my first observation, until now kept secret, but now most diligently brought together in this brief order for your approval and communicated to you, and to protect the same generously, in accordance with your inborn inclination toward music, from all envious persons and from interpreters opposed to my ideas. Should you find in this work something defective, ascribe it to my want of ability, crediting its merits to Almighty God, as the dispenser of all grace, and praying Him that He may vouchsafe to the Christian world, and especially to our beloved Germany, more peaceful times, pleasing to the Muses; and that He may graciously grant to me—wandering about Parnassus, variously troubled, despite all envy —continued life and health under the all-serenest shadow of the Austrian eagle and the most gracious protection of the miter of Lamberg-Passau and also such a disposition of affairs and affections as is required for the better explanation of this subject and for the completion of further work designed for your pleasure.

---

6 Fingering, bowing, and tempo, usage, orna-
    mentation;
These to the viol will bring liveliness, sweet-
    ness of tone.

Auserlesene Instrumental-Music

[*Passau, 1701*]

Foreword

AFTER HAVING printed and published my two garlands, or *Florilegia*, of agreeable ballet pieces, the first at Augsburg in the year 1695, the second at Passau in the year 1698, I present to you, sympathetic reader, this first collection of my instrumental concertos, blending the serious and the gay, entitled "of a more select harmony" because they contain (in the ballet airs) not only the liveliness and grace drawn intact from the Lullian well, but also certain profound and unusual affects of the Italian manner, various capricious and artful conceits, and alternations of many sorts, interspersed with special diligence between the great choir and the trio of soloists. These concertos, suited neither to the church (because of the ballet airs and airs of other sorts which they include) nor for dancing (because of other interwoven conceits, now slow and serious, now gay and nimble, and composed only for the express refreshment of the ear), may be performed most appropriately in connection with entertainments given by great princes and lords, for receptions of distinguished guests, and at state banquets, serenades, and assemblies of musical amateurs and virtuosi.

The idea of this ingenious mixture first occurred to me some time ago in Rome, where I learned the Italian manner on the clavier from the world-famous Signor Bernardo [7] and where I heard, with great pleasure and astonishment, several concertos of this sort, composed by the gifted Signor Arcangelo Corelli, and beautifully performed with the utmost accuracy by a great number of instrumental players.

Having observed the considerable variety in these, I composed several of the present concertos, which were tried over at the house of the aforesaid Signor Arcangelo Corelli (to whom I am deeply indebted for many useful observations touching this style, most graciously communicated to me); then, with his approbation—just as was long ago the case with the Lullian ballet style on my return from France—I brought to Germany, as the first, some specimens of this harmony, until then unknown in these parts, and, increasing their number to twelve, performed them successfully on highly distinguished occasions at various times and

---

7 Pasquini.

places (as is then enigmatically implied in the titles prefixed to each concerto). The hearing granted in Vienna, at the imperial royal coronation in Augsburg, also in Munich, Salzburg, and Passau—*most graciously* by Their Imperial and Royal Majesties, *graciously*, however, by several electoral and other princes—to these my admittedly insignificant compositions; the great kindness generously shown on their account to my unworthy self; the approbation of a master most celebrated for his delicate discrimination; and the acclamation of my listeners, which has spread even to distant lands; all these things will easily console me for the fault-finding and envious persons who have risen up against this work and whose malicious undertakings have at all times foretold a happy issue for me. As to you, understanding reader, may it please you to make sympathetic trial of this first collection and to observe the observations which follow, in order that you may attain my herein intended goal and the full emphasis of the composition.

OF THE NUMBER AND CHARACTER OF THE PLAYERS AND INSTRUMENTS

1. Should you be short of string players, or wish to try over these concertos with only a few, you may form a perfect little trio, at all times necessary, from the following voices: Violino primo concertino, Violino secundo concertino, and Basso continuo e Violoncino concertino. Your bass, however, will go better on the small French bass than on the double bass used hereabouts, and to this may be added, for the greater ornamentation of the harmony, a harpsichord or theorbo, played from the very same part. Further, it is to be noted that, besides observing the directions *piano* and *forte*, all should play with a full tone at the direction *T* or *tutti*, softly and tenderly at the direction *S* or *solo*.

2. With four string players you may make music by adding to the three principal voices just mentioned the Viola prima, with five by adding to these the Viola secunda.

3. Should still more players be available, add to all the parts aforesaid the three remaining ones, namely, the Violino primo, Violino secundo, and Violone or Basso continuo of the concerto grosso (or great choir), assigning to each of these, as reason and the number of available musicians may dictate, either one, two, or three players. In this case, to make the harmony of the bass the more majestic, a large double bass will prove most serviceable.

4. But insofar as you may have a still greater number of musicians at your disposal, you may assign additional players, not only to the first and second violin parts of the great choir (concerto grosso), but also to the two inner viola parts and to the bass, further ornamenting this last

with the accompaniment of harpsichords, theorbos, harps, and similar instruments; as to the little choir or trio, for it is always to this that the word "concertino" refers, let it be played singly, but at the same time superlatively well, by your three best string players with the accompaniment of an organist or theorbo player, never assigning more to a part, unless in some unusually vast place where the players of the great choir are exceptionally numerous, then assigning two at the most.

5. Should there be among your musicians some who can play and modulate the French oboe or shawm agreeably, you may with the best effect use two of these instead of the two violins, and a good bassoon player instead of the French bass, to form the concertino or little trio in some of these concertos; provided you choose only concertos in those keys, or transposed to those keys, in which the instruments just mentioned are of some use, provided also that, if some few things therein should lie too high or too low, you replace these instruments with violins or transpose to a more convenient octave. In this fashion I have often performed successfully the first, third, fourth, eighth, ninth, and tenth concertos in their original keys and the seventh in a transposition from E-flat to E major.

OF THE MANNER TO BE OBSERVED IN PERFORMING THESE CONCERTOS

6. The note in the concerto grosso standing at the very beginning or entering after a rest or *suspirium* is to be sounded without hesitation, with a full tone, and boldly by each and every player, unless the word *piano* directs otherwise, for this note, were one to slight it or sound it only timidly, would weaken and obscure the whole harmony.

7. At the direction *piano* or *p* all are ordinarily to play at once so softly and tenderly that one barely hears them, at the direction *forte* or *f* with so full a tone, from the first note so marked, that the listeners are left, as it were, astounded at such vehemence.

8. In directing the measure or beat, one should for the most part follow the Italians, who are accustomed to proceed much more slowly than we do at the directions *Adagio, Grave, Largo,* etc., so slowly sometimes that one can scarcely wait for them, but, at the directions *Allegro, Vivace, Presto, Più presto,* and *Prestissimo* much more rapidly and in a more lively manner. For by exactly observing this opposition or rivalry of the slow and the fast, the loud and the soft, the fullness of the great choir and the delicacy of the little trio, the ear is ravished by a singular astonishment, as is the eye by the opposition of light and shade. Though this has often been reported by others, it can never be said or enjoined sufficiently.

9. To each voice, hence also to the inner and lower voices, should be assigned, not only the mediocre and weaker players, but also a few of the able ones, who should regard it as no disgrace to lead these voices for you as worthily as they would lead the others, contrary to the deep-rooted prejudice of certain haughty persons, who faint away on the spot if one does not assign them to the violin or some other prominent part.

10. In the opening sonatas and fugues and in the affecting Graves that are interpolated, the Italian manner is to be chiefly observed, and, in the suspensions, the note tied over, the note sounding the dissonance in another voice, and the note resolving the dissonance aforesaid (those experienced in this art will readily understand this) are to be played at all times with the same full tone, lifting the bow (in Italian, *staccato*), detaching them rather than weakening them by prolonging them timidly.

11. Inasmuch as the force and charm of these compositions largely depends on the connection between successive movements, special care is to be taken that, after a sonata, air, or interpolated Grave, no noticeable wait or silence, above all no annoying tuning of the violins, should interrupt the continuous order; on the contrary, provided only the last notes of the several periods be held out to their full value and the repetitions observed as otherwise usual, but so that the more serious airs are repeated twice only, the livelier ones three times on occasion, but the Graves never, it is earnestly requested that the listeners be maintained in continuous attention from beginning to end, until, at a given moment, all end the concerto together, forcibly and, as it were, unexpectedly.

12. Finally, since nothing is so exquisite or lofty that, if heard too often, it does not depreciate, and since it is to be presumed that there will be no lack of bunglers enamored of this style, who, if they merely misplace without judgment *forte* and *piano*, *solo* and *tutti*, and other such matters, piling up threadbare stupidities in disorder, will imagine that they have attained the zenith of art; it is my advice that these concertos should be performed neither too often nor one after another, two —still less, more than two—in succession, but rather in moderation— sometimes only one previously tried over in private—after a partita more usual in style (of which many may be found in my *Florilegia*), observing a suitable variety of key—at the end of an important function, and then with all possible ardor, ornament, and magnificence. Having considered all this duly, may it please you, understanding reader, to regard this work kindly and to await my *Florilegium tertium*, or third garland of ballet pieces,[8] and other works. Farewell.

---

[8] This promised continuation never appeared.

58. F. E. Niedt

Friedrich Erhardt Niedt describes himself in 1700 as a notary public living in Jena. Later on he became a resident of Copenhagen, where he died sometime before 1717. The first part of his principal writing, the *Musikalische Handleitung*, was published in Hamburg in 1700; a second part followed in 1706, and in 1717, after the author's death, the third part was brought out by Johann Mattheson.

Niedt was one of the first German writers to teach the art of accompaniment from a thorough bass. That his little treatise was well thought of in its day is evident not only from Mattheson's editorial work on the third part and from his reprint of the second, but also from the extracts copied from it by J. S. Bach and incorporated in his "Precepts and Principles," a collection of rules compiled in 1738 for the use of his pupils. One section from this compilation of Bach's is translated by David and Mendel in *The Bach Reader* (New York, W. W. Norton & Co., Inc., 1945); there is a complete translation in the third volume of the English Spitta (Appendix XII).

Before introducing his reader to the study of the thorough bass itself, Niedt entertains him with a foreword in the shape of a short satiric novel in which he reproves his German contemporaries for clinging obstinately to an antiquated system of musical notation and pokes fun at the arrogant incompetence of the old-fashioned provincial music-teacher. This is included here as a brief but characteristic specimen of a literary variety which enjoyed a widespread if short-lived popularity in Germany toward the end of the seventeenth century, as witness Johann Kuhnau's *Musikalischer Quacksalber* (1700) or the various similar productions published between 1676 and 1691 by Wolfgang Caspar Printz.

Musikalische Handleitung [1]

[1700]

Foreword

1. PHOEBUS IN HIS fiery chariot had by this time climbed so high along the heavenly ramparts that the white shroud of winter, shaming itself before him, had had once more to grant our quarter of the globe an open countenance. Already Flora had dressed the trees in gay attire; Pomona, too, had again bedecked the trees' bald crown with a becoming wig; and Ceres, hard at work, was helping the fields, already sown and teeming, to a joyous bearing of their fruits. At this season, all things are so alive and astir that I too was unwilling to sit longer imprisoned by my four walls; very early one morning I went out into the open country, thinking to contemplate with my five senses the wonderwork of nature. No sooner had I gone a little distance from the town than my nostrils were filled with the agreeable perfume of the loveliest flowers and plants; these at the same time gave no less pleasure to my eyes; I was tempted to touch and to pick a few of them and to taste them, some delightfully sweet, others agreeably sour; to my ears, however, the most pleasant thing of all was that the winged field musicians were making, with many variations, so gay a music. As though enchanted by these sensual pleasures I went on, knowing not where, until I arrived unexpectedly at a deep glen, through the midst of which a limpid stream swept by, putting a stop to my walk which, as it was, had already been rather a long one. Only then did I notice that I was somewhat tired. Accordingly I lay down for a moment, stretched out on the ground, and should actually have been overtaken by a gentle sleep had this not been prevented by a buzzing sound which presented itself, *per intervalla,* to my ears. At this I raised myself a little, looking toward the place from which this buzzing voice seemed to be coming. It was at my right—a cheerful wood with trees of every sort all thrown together. Seeing this, I surmised that a bittern might perhaps have settled there to act as *basso* to the other delightful songsters. But when the sound seemed to be coming nearer and nearer and to be growing louder and louder, I sprang up nimbly, thinking to run away, for I feared that there might by chance be in the neighborhood a satyr with a hunting horn, and I thought it inadvisable to await his arrival.

2. But, lo and behold, at that moment there came trotting right up to me two men on horseback, one of whom addressed me as follows: "Good friend, if you too are of our company, then follow us to the place agreed upon." My answer was that I knew nothing of any company, hence nothing of the place

---

1 Text: The second edition (Hamburg, 1706). I have omitted part of § 14 and all of § 15.

of which he spoke, but that I was thoroughly upset by an adventure that had befallen me. Questioned about this, I recounted it to them, whereupon they fell to laughing heartily at my expense. On my betraying some annoyance at this, the second horseman spoke, bowing politely to make good the presumed affront. "My friend," he said, "do not take our laughter amiss; we could not help it. I will soon relieve your fears by waking you from your dream. Know then that we are hastening to an appointed *collegium musicum* which the celebrated musician Florimon designs to hold today and at which he has invited us, as members, to appear. Now we may readily imagine that he will have caused his apprentices to bring all sorts of instruments to the place, above all a fine big positive organ on which he is to play the thorough bass himself. This he will at once have tested to see whether the removal and delivering of it from his home have put it out of tune. No doubt but what some uncouth sound or other found its way to your ears and that you fancied this to have come, first, from a bittern, but finally, from the actual horn of a forest deity. The flute that is peeking out of your pocket makes me think that you must be of our profession, or at least an amateur and friend to noble music. So do not begrudge the effort of following us thither. I assure you that you will count it fortunate that the scare you had will have been the cause of your enjoying the merry company with us and that Master Florimon will not be displeased to see us bringing you along *pro hospite*, especially when we tell him what a terrible fright he unwittingly gave you."

3. The great politeness of this person induced me to reply to him in kind, and I thanked him politely for his friendly offer. At the same time I gave him to understand that, while I was a devotee of music, I had not as yet so perfected myself in it (though my student days were long since over) that I could take part in everything extempore; that nothing more agreeable could befall me than to be permitted to see gathered in one place so great a number of musicians, doubtless all of them well drilled, and to listen to their harmonious exercises; and that this would spur me on to pursue the noble art the more industriously so that, if I studiously applied myself, I might one day reach such a point that I could take my place in the company of masters. "Then follow us confidently," replied my guide; "the way is short, but should you be pleased to mount my horse, I will the while accompany you on foot." This too great honor I declined, thanking him again, and with the two of them holding their horses to a leisurely pace on my account, I soon reached the middle of the wood. Here there stood a rather deserted palace and in this a great paved hall where Master Florimon, with the permission of the local authorities, had caused his instruments to be brought in great number so that the invited musicians and amateurs might use them according to their pleasure and preference.

4. After my two guides had given up their horses to be led out to pasture by a servant assigned to this task, they went up with me into the hall, where Master Florimon, standing at the door, gaily bade us welcome. The first of my companions, whose name was Tacitus, sought to apologize for my presence

and explained in a few words how and for what reasons he and his comrade had brought me along with them. "Gentlemen," Master Florimon replied, "no apologies are necessary—this man too shall be a welcome guest." With this he showed us to a long table, about which twelve musicians were already seated, awaiting Tacitus and his companion. We greeted them cordially, as they in turn did us, rising from their seats and asking us to be pleased to sit down in their company, something to which we offered no great objection. Master Florimon alone remained standing by the table at his positive organ, which had been set up facing the open window, so that its sound, when it was touched, might ring through the woods, sending back a doubled echo.

5. To make a long story short, the music was now to begin. Master Florimon, as director of the *chorus musicus*, distributed the parts, deciding who should play the first violin, who the second, and so forth; he himself remained at the thorough bass; I chose the role of a listener. First there was played an agreeable sonata, set by the director himself; this was followed by other things of his, composed with special art. Each participant was now busied in letting his skill be seen and heard, yet things did not go so smoothly but that from time to time one heard a little pig, even a full-grown sow; still, the whole came to an end without undue confusion, for it is written: *In fine videbitur cujus toni.* Master Florimon swallowed his displeasure as best he could, not wishing to shame those openly who had soiled his fine work with their swine. Instead, he caused his apprentices to pour out for each person a fair-sized glass of good wine; this all emptied together, *more Palatino*, for instrumentalists also know how to turn to their advantage the proverb: *Cantores amant humores.* After this they fell to making music again, but the parts were now differently distributed, so that he who had previously played a violin was given a *viola da braccio*, and vice versa. Master Florimon himself undertook to handle the *viola da gamba* and requested Tacitus to play the thorough bass; beside him, Mopsus took up his stand to reinforce him with a *violone*, and although I was also offered a part to play, the company was in the end content with the excuse of my incompetence— thus, once again, I could to my greater satisfaction be an observer. Everything went as before, except that after every piece there was a rest of one hundred full measures, during which time each player, if he cared to, sent for a glass of wine. I must admit that the composition was so beautiful and that the greater part of the company played, this time too, with such remarkable art and so valiantly, that Orpheus with his lyre, nay, Apollo with all his Muses, would have had to concede the prize to this assembly, if only Mopsus and Negligentius, and Corydon too, had not at times screwed up their art to rather too high a point.

6. The whole company had at length grown tired of making music, for nothing is so good and so pleasant to hear that the ear does not finally call a halt; one may have too much, even of a good thing: *Omne nimium vertitur in vitium.* Enough is as good as a feast. In my own case, however, the word was

Venter caret auribus; the belly has no ears, and it cannot make a meal of fleeting sounds. For by this time the sun was ready to set, and I had not had the least thing to eat since watching it rise. Who, then, was more cheerful than I when Master Florimon had a good cold supper brought in and served up? I fell to with a will at the piece of roast mutton that had been placed before me, at the same time forcing myself, as best I could, not to wolf everything down at once, lest I be taken for a shameless glutton. With the food there was also a good drink of wine, further an excellent malt liquor, and to this last we finally gave our preference.

7. With this, as the beer began to find its mark, there arose among the gentlemen musicians all sorts of discourse touching their art, just as sailors, when they meet, are wont to talk of their winds, peasants of their cattle, hunters of their dogs, and every man of what he can do and can understand. Yet, the rule being that he who has learned the least and has the fewest brains in his head will give himself out, when he drinks, as the cleverest master of all, we had here to have just this experience. Mopsus, who had previously been the worst music corrupter, wished now in his conceit to pass for the best organist and composer, in a word, for the most excellent *musicus.* He bragged a good deal of how he had served full eight years under a world-famous master and of how, with great and tireless industry, he had at length reached such a point that he could not only put everything into the German tablature by himself, but also, after a brief inspection, play it off. In this connection he had a fling at those who hold music to be an easy matter and boldly declared that a man may far more quickly become a *Magister,* nay, even a *Doctor* of all three faculties, than an accomplished *musicus.* His neighbors, to be sure—an organist named Fidelio from the town of Lauterbach—sought to contradict him, saying that he had heard that there was one famous master who set no store whatever by the laborious German tablature and could yet teach music, as though from the ground up, to an intelligent person so that in little time he need not be ashamed to play for anyone. At this Mopsus nearly jumped out of his skin. "Pray hold your tongue," said he to Fidelio; "you don't know what you're talking about; I too have heard all about the fellow who feeds you music with a spoon; what they say about him is foul and fabricated—nothing but big talk." With rather more modesty his good friend Corydon added: "After all, my dear Fidelio, you may safely believe what Master Mopsus says; to be sure, I too have heard great things of this master, but it is my opinion that, if they are true, they must be accomplished by forbidden, supernatural arts." Negligentius spoke up also and held that one ought just to keep the old way; that would be the best plan and our elders were after all no fools. The good Negligentius had been for fifty-six years organist at Springenfeld. At these words, the entire rest of the company would soon have come to blows, had not Master Florimon interposed his authority and kept at hand a few of his staff, who presented themselves at the entrance to the hall with some old hunting pikes, so that they might make peace,

should there perchance be fighting. Of these fellows Mopsus was so thoroughly afraid that on their appearance he began at once to pull in his horns.

8. When things had become more quiet, Florimon addressed himself to Tacitus, Capellmeister at Klingewoll, in this fashion: "Dear sir, I commend the modesty with which you have listened patiently to so many absurdities, you who in my opinion have a greater understanding of the art than any of us." "Master Florimon," Tacitus replied, "I have heard these precepts from my youth: 'No one speaks amiss by keeping silent,' and similarly, 'Never answer until you are asked.' What then? Says not the all-wisest of kings: 'Answer not a fool according to his folly, lest thou also be like unto him'?" [2] "Aha!" cried Corydon. "Now you mean me and my fellows; may you, etc!" "Come on, boys!" Florimon shouted. "This way with your hunting pikes!" They lost no time over it. Florimon, however, held them off, a little to one side of the table, with his arm. At this the trembling Corydon said: "Reverend Master Florimon, I will gladly keep still. It was only in jest that I spoke as I did. I pray you, do let Master Tacitus go on for a while with his talk. I myself know well enough that he speaks but little, yet, when at length the words begin to flow, what he says is worth hearing."

9. "I am ready," continued Tacitus, "to respect the prejudices of everyone, and I wish to quarrel with no one on this account; at the same time, it is annoying"—the gentlemen-at-arms, standing near the table with their boar-hunting halberds, made him somewhat bold, for Florimon was his friend—"to hear many pronouncing judgment on a matter they do not understand and to have Hans Lassdünkel bragging at all times and in all places. It would be much better if he were quiet as a mouse; thus he would often not even betray his lack of understanding and, did one not afterwards find him out a bungler, would remain a good *musicus*. As I know from my own case, at a time when I still had the least understanding of music, I was to my way of thinking the most excellent of masters; since having had my eyes opened by my last teacher, I have even been ashamed of myself." "Pardon me, sir, for interrupting you," said Florimon at this. "I am well aware that you have had two teachers who sought in various and contrary ways to teach you the musical *Fundamenta*; some say you owe your science largely to the first; others say, to the last; please be so kind as to tell us yourself what your frank opinion about this is." "Were I to do so," Tacitus objected, "I should have to tell the whole story of my life." "Just this," said Florimon, "will be the thing most pleasing to us to hear, and, sir, you will greatly oblige the whole company—especially, perhaps, Masters Mopsus and Corydon—if you will humor me in this." Tacitus replied: "To oblige Milord Florimon, it shall be willingly done. Yet I shall make this condition in advance: should I be forced to relate my own stupidities, let no one laugh up his sleeve at me who has perhaps been in his day—and may for that matter still be at this moment—a greater fool than I."

---

2 Proverbs 26:4.

10. As to my early childhood, then, I see no great necessity for speaking of it, and, to tell the truth, I have actually forgotten the greater part of it; this much, however, I do recall—that I had a father and mother of honorable descent who, with great care and diligence, kept me from my sixth year on at school and—besides reading, writing, and arithmetic —at music, that is, at singing and fiddling, for to this I had a great inclination. Then, when I was nearly twelve, my father (who could do no more and no better for me than to see to it that I learned something honest in my youth) brought me to a master who enjoyed throughout the countryside the reputation of being the best organist. He was called Orbilius—and the name suited him, for, as you will presently hear in detail, he was a horrible tormentor of his pupils; further, he had been made organist in the right place, namely, in Poltersheim—a place well known to some of you, though, should you not recall it at the moment, your womenfolk, when you get home, can doubtless show you where it lies. With this Orbilius I had first of all to make the acquaintance of the letters of the German tablature and of the crow's feet, written above and beside them, that purport to indicate the time, further, of the keys of the clavier. Before I had properly (and still not completely) grasped this, two years had already gone by. Meanwhile I reflected: "Alas, had you but known the organist's art was so difficult, you might well have given up your inclination to it. Look here! You already understand the notes by which one otherwise sings and fiddles; were your master to use these in teaching you at the clavier, it would no doubt be a good thing!" To be sure, this was not such a stupid idea on my part, but if I was an apprentice, it followed that my master must be still cleverer than I. My first piece, which was to teach me to place my fingers properly according to the *applicatur*, had the imposing title "Bergamasco"—the melody is otherwise a familiar country song, "Ripen Garsten wille wi meyen," etc., sung by the boys in the streets—and I cannot imagine what the special secret is that this piece hides and that makes it such a favorite with so many organists that they have their pupils learn it first of all. After this my master also taught me to play a couple of *sarabandes,* a *courante simple,* and a *ballo,* all with imposing titles, further, the chorale "Erbarm dich mein, O Herre Gott," etc. Then came dreadful long *praeludia, toccate, ciaconne, fughe,* and more such zoological marvels; these I was to learn by heart, since (as my teacher sternly told me) "unless you first master these admirable pieces perfectly, you good-fornothing, you will never in all the world learn one *basso continuo,* for it is from these splendidly worked-out written models that you, you lout,

you loafer, must learn the manner of the *basso continuo*." I still did not know that by this he meant thorough bass, which I had heard all about before in connection with singing; for this reason I wondered what sort of creature a *basso continuo* might be. In those days I had only a blind man to lead me; now, having had my eyes opened by my later teacher, I see that it is in thorough bass, and not in *toccate* and things of that sort, that science lies; that, provided he first have some understanding of the notes, a pupil who begins at once with thorough bass will grasp it as quickly—indeed, even more quickly—than one who has already played for several years from German tablature; what is more, that, once he has had some practice in it and knows how to vary it, he will be able to play off a *toccata* or a *fuga* or the like, of himself and, as they say, out of his own head, while he who has already put three whole books of *ciaconne* and more such things into tablature, and has learned to play them, will be unable to play half a line of thorough bass. But, to return to my story, I worked hard, and many a time, over those splendid pieces of writing, my master roughly boxed my ears, slapped my face, rapped me on the nose, pinched my ears, and pulled my hair; at other times I was treated to live coals, the strap, and more such delicacies. Willy-nilly, he was determined to beat music into my head. But, for all his good intentions, this would not do; the more he abused me, the more stupid I became; indeed, be it said in all modesty that, though I had to work for at least half a year over a single *toccata* or *praeludium* and *fuga*, when I came to play it—just when things were going splendidly and at their best— I stuck fast all of a sudden and could recall neither beginning nor end. At this, from my master's kindly fists there rained down on my ears some three score blows; meanwhile he consoled me with words like these: "May you be this, that, and the other, you bloodhound! Even the sparrows on the roof will learn before you do!" In this wise I had spent seven years with my master before I could play five *praeludia* and the chorale, or German psalm, in two parts.

11. "In truth," said Florimon, "I must confess that Master Tacitus did not advance any too quickly during his years of apprenticeship. It is my desire to know more about how he finally became the splendidly experienced musician that he is today, but, before I make him a formal request for this, he will be pleased to drink a glass of wine. After the impassioned story he has just told us, I know that it will do him no harm; each member of the company shall pledge him with his glass." No one could refuse this. Tacitus then went on with his story.

At length (he said) my master took up the thorough bass with me; from the first I was in terror, thinking "Now you will really begin to catch it!" I had noticed that whenever he and the cantor tried anything over together they often came to blows over the thorough bass; I could only conclude that my own head would still more often be the target. In instructing me, my master's procedure was as follows. He showed me neither rules nor figures—even to him the numerals standing above the bass were no better than towns in Bohemia; he simply played the bass through for me once or twice, saying: "You must play it thus and so—that's the way I learned it." But if I was not getting on, you would have been entertained to see the admirable means my master found to teach me the art after his own fashion. The *sexta* was situated behind my right ear, the *quarta* behind my left, the *septima* on my cheeks, the *nona* in my hair, the false *quinta* on my nose, the *secunda* on my back, the *tertia minor* across my knuckles, the *tertia major* and *quinta* on my shins; the *decima* and *undecima* were special sorts of boxes on the ear. Thus, from the whereabouts of the blow or kick, I was supposed to know what to play; the best part of it was that continual kicking in the shins made my feet right active on the pedals, the use of which I was also beginning to learn at this time. Besides this, my master showed me how to put thorough bass into tablature, provided I could get hold of the complete composition; at times, however, there was stuff in this that neither of us could play as it stood. Once he hit upon an extraordinary measure; since with no foundation none of his teaching could drive the thorough bass through my head, he actually decided to kick it into me. Seizing my hair, he pulled me down from the organ bench on which I was sitting before the keyboard, threw me to the ground, lifted me way up by the hair so that, when I fell back, my head struck sharply against the floor, and then trampled all over me, stamping on me for some time. At length, when the *basso continuo* had quite robbed him of his senses, he dragged me from the room toward a flight of stairs leading to the street, saying as he did so: "Here is an end to your apprenticeship and here you have your indentures (for I shall throw these in for good measure)!" So saying, he would have pushed me downstairs, so that with so much learning my head would probably have been crushed, once and for all, had I not misunderstood this too and grabbed him by the legs so that he tumbled with me down the stairs, head over heels into the street. No harm was done, although a reddish sap began to flow from our mouths and noses. At first I feared that my lesson might be flowing away with it, but I soon realized that it was only ordinary blood, the loss of which disturbed me the less when I saw that my teacher was in similar trouble and that people who (as usually happens) had come running up in droves were making fun of the crazy Orbilius, were tearing me from him (for they knew him as a Tartar), and were concerned lest he should actually beat me to death.

12. Bloody as I was, I let my teacher march back up the stairs with his wife and her maid, the two of whom had helped him to his feet after the bad fall that he had taken, for I thought: "I have no desire for further dealings of this sort with you—it is best that we should simply part company." At this I went in to the nearest house, where my neighbor gave me a cordial reception and advised me that, inasmuch as my parents, before their death, had settled in full with Orbilius for his teaching and, in addition to this, had left me a little money so that I might try my luck in the world, I ought, now that I had attained my majority, to betake myself elsewhere—with my understanding of my art, I would no doubt find a situation sooner or later. I followed this well-meant advice and sent to my teacher's house for my clothes and other belongings. Orbilius sought at first to prevent their being taken away, but when I began to threaten, telling him that I would bring a swarm of lawyers about his ears and that I had already engaged one for this purpose, he thought better of it, especially since he had many enemies in the council and elsewhere. In giving up my things, he sent word that, wherever I might go, I was to speak no ill of what had happened to me during my years of apprenticeship and that in particular I was to keep to myself the indentures he had given me at the end. "Good!" I thought. "Go on being yourself! I have now been with you for all of nine years and I know you like a book—I shall not advise any honest man to apprentice a child to you." The very next day I found work on a traveling van and set out into the world, I cared not whither, for now that all my friends were dead, I was as much at home in one place as in another.

13. After wandering for some time hither and yon I arrived at length in the province of Marcolphia where, one Sunday, I went into a village church. Here, on an old organ of five stops, a simple-hearted organist was prancing about in great style; sometimes he used his whole fist with all five fingers at once and, to make sure of a sufficient uproar, at every cadence he helped himself out with his nose. This was in his opinion a most artistic *secretum*, and he told me later on that, if he had known that I too was of his profession, he would have been unwilling to show it openly in my presence. After the sermon I begged that I might have the

honor of playing just once on his instrument. To this he at first turned a cold shoulder, but he soon changed his mind, for I had decked myself out in quite handsome clothes and there are many for whom clothes make the man. "Well, sir," he said to me, "perhaps it can be done if only you are sure of your business so that you won't stumble—but wait —I know what to do—I shall stand right here behind you so that if needs be I can help you out at the keyboard and assure your getting through without disgrace." I was somewhat annoyed with him for not taking me at once for a master; nevertheless I sat down and played one of my most artful *praeludia manualia* and, for a close, a *sonata* (such things I regularly carried with me in my pocket, ready for any emergency). Hearing these, the village organist thrust out his nose and pricked up his ears and the people in the church were on the point of dancing. At this I was so set up that I secretly thought even my old master Orbilius insignificant in comparison with myself, imagining that wherever a place as organist might be open, it must inevitably go to me while my competitors stood to one side. And to be sure, what I imagined actually came to pass, for on that very day a visiting nobleman was also in the church. After the service he sent for me and, when I had paid him my respects, he addressed me as follows. "My good friend, in church today your public performance on the organ gave me such great pleasure that with all my heart I should like to see you in a good position. I can even help in no small way to bring this about; inasmuch as in the town of Dantzfurt, which lies near my residence, the organist has just died, and inasmuch as I have some influence with the ancient and honorable council of that town, so that without my consent they will call no one to the post, I myself will help you to get it, but with the proviso that you marry my lady's chambermaid, who has faithfully served Her Ladyship—and myself too, although with perfect honesty—so that I may thus help two people to a livelihood at once." I accepted this proposal, thanked him most respectfully, and immediately set out with him for his estate, where we arrived that very evening.

. . . . .

14. To make a long story short, the marriage contract was drawn up the next day. Cornaria, my intended, gave me as a token a handsome gold ring and promised to supply me in future with abundant linens; I for my part engaged to deliver to her at the first possible moment, as a pledge of my love, a present that I would have made for her by a celebrated artist. In the meantime, letters were sent off to the ancient

and honorable town council of Dantzfurt, and the courier returned with a reply in writing, addressed to my lord patron. His recommendation would be given special weight and the ability of his celebrated master was not questioned (who was more puffed up by this than I?); nevertheless, since it was presumed that the citizens would not be willing to relinquish their traditional right and would insist upon the presentation of the candidate by the council, I was to be good enough to present myself for hearing and trial on the eighth day *a dato*, which would be St. Margaret's, at the beginning of the dog days. My Cornaria and I lived in a fool's paradise; with the permission of her noble mistress, she visited me in my room some six or seven times a day; there nothing was heard but amorous discourse, and at this Cornaria proved much more adept than I.

. . . . . .

16. Now the time came when I was to give my trial performance in Dantzfurt before assuming my new office. Fortunately for me, the town cantor was an old man who had forgotten what little he had ever known about music. Here "birds of a feather flocked together," as the saying goes, and I did not need to plague myself about the thorough bass, which I feared like the Devil himself. Thus, seeing that I could make my own choice and play what I pleased, the trial came off well, and people were at once congratulating me right and left on my appointment, of which, in the opinion of the ancient and honorable council, no one was worthier than I. Since the customary annual inventory was to take place that same evening, I was immediately invited; there, over the banquet table, after the pastors, the burgomasters, and the lord of the manor had praised my recent and duly delivered masterpiece, I began myself to brag of my art. I expressed my contempt for all the other masters I had heard of, pulled the most celebrated people to pieces, and knew how to find fault with everyone, now on this score, now on that, for example, for not holding such and such a finger properly, for not having any elegant movement and presence in their bodies when they played, for not being able to make any proper trills with their feet on the pedals, and many other such stupidities. One parson extolled a certain organist of his acquaintance from whom he had taken a few months' lessons on the clavier. By this time, after all, I was clever enough not to contradict him openly; still, this praise of someone else cut me to the quick and I began at once to fear that my authority would be somewhat the worse for it. My only desire was that everyone should

praise me alone, and to this end I gave all possible encouragement and opportunity. Well, I stayed from now on in the town, near the church, in the house in which the former organist had lived and in which, with my permission, his widow and children continued to live. I sent my dearest Cornaria an account of all that had happened, telling her in particular that I had come to the sort of place where there were people who understood music thoroughly and who looked on me as the most celebrated organist in the world. To tell the truth, I was actually a sorry bungler and knew nothing more presentable to play than what was written in my book.

17. But hear how the tables were turned. My dearest Cornaria sent me the melancholy tidings that that noble gentleman, my patron and champion, had suddenly died, from which I could readily conclude that I need no longer expect with my dear one any such generous portion as my lord had promised me. Into the bargain, the old cantor died the next week, and, when it was time to hear the new candidate, I was told to bring him the things that he should sing at his trial. I excused myself, saying that I did not as yet have my things with me, but the new cantor quickly disposed of this, replying: "Indeed! Then let him spend a few hours in composing something new!" At once it became the pleasure of all the overseers that I should do this and that it should likewise be a new trial of my art. The only one displeased with the arrangement was myself. For, having previously sought to pass myself off as the complete musician, to admit that I could not compose would have compromised my dignity. The trial was to take place the following day. I sat down and, scratching my head, debated with myself the course that I would take—whether to stay or to run away. At length I hit upon the remedy (so I imagined, at least)—I brought out all my fugues and hunted through them for one to which to fit the text *Laudate Dominum omnes gentes*. This I then arranged in such a way that, when on the organ I played the subject in the pedals, the cantor would sing the bass along with me, just as I played it. The following morning the trial was to be held in the church, in the presence, not only of the assembled gentry and overseers, but also of a great throng of citizens who of their own accord had gathered there. The new cantor had with him two instrumentalists who offered to play along on violins or zinks. I told them, however, that it was a trial of vocal music that was contemplated, not one of instrumental music, and that for this reason I had omitted the instruments in the new piece that I had composed. With this excuse they were obliged to content themselves. Told to begin, I first improvised a

praeambulum on the full organ; then, when it was time for the cantor to begin his *Laudate Dominum*, I left most of the stops out so that the organ might peal the more merrily. The cantor beat time with one hand and sang out boldly with a fine deep voice, while the instrumentalists, who were standing by, laughed up their sleeves until I thought they would burst. Seeing what was going on, I presumed that they were laughing at the cantor for rumbling so much. But when the cantor came to a rest, turned to them, and joined in the laughter—indeed, could not stop laughing, even after he began to sing again—I soon saw which way the wind was blowing, that the laughter must be aimed at me, and at this I was so overcome that I was ready to give up the ghost on the spot. When the piece was at an end, the cantor drew from his pocket various things for voices and instruments and asked me to play a thorough bass to them in order that the company in the church might have a further treat. There I stood in my true colors.

"Gentlemen, don't laugh at me so much"—here Tacitus betrayed a slight annoyance—"some one of you who is laughing now with the rest may one day have the same experience." So saying, he continued his narrative.

18. After this (he said) I had to come out with the truth, and so, seeking to cover up my ignorance as best I could, I answered the cantor as follows: "If only you had given me the things yesterday so that I could first have put them into tablature or, failing this, have looked them over once or twice, I should have been glad to accommodate you; having neglected to do this, you will not misinterpret it if I do not at once accept this closely figured bass to play." In the meantime a boy came running up to the organ, calling to the new cantor that the overseers wished to speak to him. As I learned later, they were well satisfied with his voice, but wished to go on listening to him; he might now choose some of his own things and tell the organist that, in accompanying them, he should save his art for another time and play softly so that they might hear better what was being sung (they assumed that it required special skill to get all the organ-pipes to play at one time). To this the cantor replied, with a somewhat contemptuous smile: "By all means, gentlemen; I should be glad to do so if only the bungler (by this he meant me) knew how to play." This struck them as very peculiar, and, thinking that the cantor would not thus speak behind his back of so excellent a master unless it was from envy, they immediately sent for me also and asked whether I was not able to play right off the things the cantor had with him. Here I offered again my previous excuses; I was ready to die

of shame, still more so when the cantor spoke up once more. "Gentlemen," he said, "we will perforce make shift, for one of the two instrumentalists who came here with me can play the thorough bass; let the other play one violin and I will engage both to sing and play the other." This was most agreeable to the entire company, so there was nothing for me to do but to remain in the lower church with the rest while the three of them, to my great dismay, played one thing after another—so sweetly that the citizens who were present began to grumble openly against the council for having been so quickly taken in by the Arch-Imposter (so they called me) whom they had accepted as organist. "They ought to chase the loafer back to where he came from!" Hearing this, I hurriedly made my decision and addressed myself to the assembled company, saying that, since there was evidently not room enough for both the cantor and myself, I would prefer asking to be released to being continually at odds with him. Thus I got out of the affair with little honor and danced merrily away from Dantzfurt again. The cantor, on the other hand, was at once engaged, together with his two instrumentalists (for until now the place had had no town musicians of its own). The arrangement was that one of the two should play the organ in church as organist, receiving for this the regular salary; in addition to this he was to be in attendance at weddings and other formal revelries with the other, to whom a given annual pension was assured in writing; the two were to divide the profits as they pleased.

19. Thus I had had all my trouble and vexation for nothing. My chief consolation in it was that I had not yet married Cornaria and could thus withdraw on the pretext that our courtship had been inspired by the promise that I should become organist in Dantzfurt and that, now that nothing had come of this, the council having, after my patron's death, set the cantor on me in order to rid themselves of me, my former promise was no longer binding. With this the good Cornaria was obliged to content herself and I, for my part, am as well satisfied, for in due course she married an elderly widower whose forehead, since this his second marriage, has put forth such shoots that, from his wife Cornaria, he has received the name Cornutus.

20. What next? What was I to do now? Passing myself off for a master of music had certainly turned out badly for me. I decided, accordingly, to apprentice myself all over again to Master Prudentius, the same organist of whom the parson previously mentioned had said in further praise that he was an extraordinarily able composer. And although he lived in the town of Schönhall, more than sixty miles away,

I preferred making this long journey to remaining the rest of my days an ignoramus and a ruined man. When I arrived, I found Master Prudentius at home, busily at work on his music; he received me most cordially, bade me sit down and, after a few moments' pause, desired me to let him know where I had come from. He took me for a likely fellow, and indeed I might well have passed for one if clothes could make a good-for-nothing into an honest man, for I had provided myself with a fine new suit and, although it was my entire capital, still had a little money left over. I told Prudentius candidly how matters stood with me, how very badly I had been disappointed in my expectations, and how I had come to him so that he might teach me something honest; if he were willing to oblige me in this and to give me sound instruction in music, I would not only pay him adequately for his trouble—I would also gratefully sing his praises the rest of my life. Master Prudentius then went on to ask who had been my teacher, how long I had studied, and what method my master had employed in teaching me. After I had answered all these questions modestly and had once more begged him to receive and accept me as his obedient apprentice, he gave me this heartening answer: "My friend, perceiving how very earnestly you desire to become a thorough musician, I cannot find it in my heart to send you away empty-handed, even though I have already a full day's work every day. And so, if you have money enough to maintain yourself here for a year, I will within that time so instruct you in the real fundamentals and in the organist's art that, from being a false organist (*Argenist*) you will become a true one (*Organist*). For my trouble I ask not one farthing, for if you will only promise me to be industrious and to employ your art to the glory of God I will instruct you for nothing, every morning from seven to eight. Aside from this, you may come to my house whenever you please and practice by yourself in a room where there are several claviers." Was ever man happier than I? The same day I arranged with a baker for my year's board, and the next morning and every other morning after that I went at the appointed time to Master Prudentius, who began at once by instructing me in thorough bass, saying: "In this lies the whole basis of practical music and of composition and with this I begin with all my pupils. Thus they have the advantage that, instead of having to plague themselves with the troublesome tablature, only to remain forever paper organists, even though they have studied for many years, they become in a short time good thorough musicians." Under my new teacher, I employed my time as industriously as I knew how; he, for his part, spared no pains to instruct me faithfully and, when the year was over, he addressed me as follows: "Now, my dear Tacitus, basing my teaching on the fundamentals, I have so instructed you in music that you may, from now on, bear the name, not of a false organist, but of a true one and of a thorough musician and composer. Go your way, employ your art to the glory of God, and should you meet with anyone who is desirous of learning music, impart it to him for nothing, just as you received it from me and just as I, at your entreaty, faithfully dictated it to you." Thus, with many tears and sincere protestations of gratitude, I took leave of Master Prudentius and found my way back to my fatherland, where—as you gentlemen are well aware—I have now been active for some years in my present capacity.

"To oblige Master Florimon I have had to make this story rather diffuse; If in so doing I have made myself irksome to any other member of this company, I shall be glad to ask his pardon."

21. Thus Tacitus ended his narrative, making good his long silence by his long speech. Master Florimon thanked him for it becomingly and, after the drinks had gone round again once or twice, addressed the company as follows: "I must admit that Master Prudentius began with Tacitus in the right way. I am acquainted with the man myself, and I know that he introduces his pupils to the thorough bass at once and that within one year, if only they already know their notes and can count twenty, they so perfect themselves in it that it becomes a joy. I also know that, as a part of his instruction, he shows them how to make fugues and other such things extempore and that from time to time, once they are fairly presentable in such music as requires the thorough bass, he gives them music that is fully written out—as though for an amusement and in order that they may be able to reproduce the embellishments in it. This is much easier for them to learn than the German tablature, and I have no patience with what some say against it—that one ought to keep the old way. All honor to our German ancestors, who in their day brought things to an extremely high point with the tablature! Sixty years ago, or perhaps a few years earlier, one could scarcely find a single German organist who played the thorough bass or read from notes. But now that a better, more correct, and easier way has been discovered, why should we not abandon the old one? The Italians never have had a German tablature, but have used notes since longer than one can remember; just this is the real reason why they were able to maintain so long their superiority in music over us Germans."

22. Master Negligentius interrupted Florimon at this point. "What you say is nonetheless offensive to many an honest German organist—let the Italians just dare to make a claim like that again!" To which Florimon modestly replied: "Very true! I too am well aware that there are today many German organists who are not much inferior to the foreigners—nay, are in certain respects superior to them. On this we agree. The reason is that they become

accustomed to play the thorough bass so very much earlier than formerly. Were they to follow the teaching of Prudentius, whom one can never praise enough, and to make this the very beginning, they would discover its excellent effect, even in their pupils. What is more, we should no longer hear the impudent assertion that anyone who has not studied for nine or ten years, but has acquired his art in a shorter time, must have been to school with a wizard. Uninformed pronouncements of this kind remind me of the peasant who, when asked to decide the quarrel between the nightingale and the cuckoo as to which was the better singer, delivered himself of the following bovinity: 'Both are excellent singers, but the cuckoo sings a better *choral* music, while the nightingale's voice is better suited to the *figural.*' Even so, he was not as inept a critic as the clown who, when chosen as their judge, gave to Pan, the shepherd-god with the reed pipes, the preference over Phoebus, who played artfully on instruments of all sorts, for which reason this uncouth fellow, whose name was Midas, was deservedly endowed by Phoebus with the ears of an ass."

23. What further topics Florimon and the others went on to discuss, how they made merry far into the night, and what other delightful compositions they sang and played, all this I shall pass over in silence, recording simply that not long after this I enrolled myself as a pupil of Master Tacitus, who faithfully instructed me, just as Prudentius had faithfully instructed him.

24. And now, just as my teacher faithfully instructed me, so—in this, the first part of my *Musical Tutor; or, Thorough-Bass Instructor,* as also in the second part to follow—I shall faithfully impart the whole to those of you who love music and seek learning, and, to begin with, how properly to play a thorough bass, hoping that I shall thus be rendering a conspicuous service to many, as I am bound by Christian charity to do, and ignoring what certain prejudiced critics may say of it.

X

Operatic Rivalry in France: Pro and Contra Lully

59. François Raguenet

With the Abbé François Raguenet (born at Rouen in 1660) began the impassioned and obstinate controversies about the opera that were to hold under their sway the artistic and literary circles in France throughout the eighteenth century. No matter whether the controversy was fought out between the followers and detractors of Lully, as was the case with Raguenet and Le Cerf de La Viéville; whether it was transferred to the field of comic opera, as in the "Querelle des Bouffons" (see Chapter XIV); or whether it assumed the aspect of a fight for or against the major operatic reform embodied in the works of C. W. von Gluck (see Chapter XV)—the underlying issue was fundamentally the same—should the musical expression in the opera be entirely autonomous, or should it be determined by the exigencies of the dramatic action?

Raguenet had visited Rome in 1698 and had there become an ardent admirer of Italian music. Returned to France, he published in 1702 his *Parallèle des Italiens et des Français en ce qui regarde la musique et les opéras,* in which he took Lully and his imitators severely to task while extolling the merits of Italian musicians. The date and circumstances of Raguenet's death are not known, but there are reports that he took his own life about 1722.

Parallèle des Italiens et des Français [1]

[*1702*]

THERE ARE so many things wherein the French music has the advantage over the Italian, and as many more wherein the Italian is superior to the French, that, without a particular examination into the one and the other, I think it impossible to draw a just parallel between 'em or entertain a

---

1 Text: The original edition of the anonymous English translation of 1709, attributed by Sir John Hawkins to J. E. Galliard. Only a very few of the translator's notes are reprinted here; all of these are included, however, in the edition prepared by the present editor for the *Musical Quarterly,* XXXII (1946), 411–436.

right judgment of either. The operas are the compositions that admit of the greatest variety and extent, and they are common both to the Italians and French. 'Tis in these the masters of both nations endeavor more particularly to exert themselves and make their genius shine, and 'tis on these, therefore, I intend to build my present comparison. But in this there are many things that require a particular distinction, such as the language, the composition, the qualifications of the actors, those of the performers, the different sorts of voices, the recitative, the airs, the symphonies, the chorus, the dance, the machines, the decorations, and whatever else is essential to an opera or serves to make the entertainment complete and perfect. And these things ought to be particularly inquired into before we can pretend to determine in favor either of the Italian or French.

Our operas are writ much better than the Italian; they are regular, coherent designs; and, though repeated without the music, they are as entertaining as any of our other pieces that are purely dramatic. Nothing can be more natural and lively than their dialogues; the gods are made to speak with a dignity suitable to their character, kings with all the majesty their rank requires, and the nymphs and shepherds with a softness and innocent mirth peculiar to the plains. Love, jealousy, anger, and the rest of the passions are touched with the greatest art and nicety, and there are few of our tragedies or comedies that appear more beautiful than Quinault's operas.

On the other hand, the Italian operas are poor, incoherent rhapsodies without any connection or design; all their pieces, properly speaking, are patched up with thin, insipid scraps; their scenes consist of some trivial dialogues or soliloquy, at the end of which they foist in one of their best airs, which concludes the scene. These airs are seldom of a piece with the rest of the opera, being usually written by other poets, either occasionally or in the body of some other work. When the undertaker of an opera has fixed himself in a town and got his company together, he makes choice of the subject he likes best, such as Camilla, Themistocles, Xerxes, &c. But this piece, as I just now observed, is no better than a patchwork, larded with the best airs his performers are acquainted with, which airs are like saddles, fit for all horses alike; they are declarations of love made on one side and embraced or rejected on the other, transports of happy lovers or complaints of the unfortunate, protestations of fidelity or stings of jealousy, raptures of pleasure or pangs of sorrow, rage, and despair. And one of these airs you are sure to find at the end of every scene. Now certainly such a medley as this can never be set in competition with our operas, which are wrought up with great exactness and marvelous conduct.

Besides, our operas have a farther advantage over the Italian in respect of the voice, and that is the bass, which is so frequent among us and so rarely to be met with in Italy. For every man that has an ear will witness with me that nothing can be more charming than a good bass; the simple sound of these basses, which sometimes seems to sink into a profound abyss, has something wonderfully charming in it. The air receives a stronger concussion from these deep voices than it doth from those that are higher and is consequently filled with a more agreeable and extensive harmony. When the persons of gods or kings, a Jupiter, Neptune, Priam, or Agamemnon, are brought on the stage, our actors, with their deep voices, give 'em an air of majesty, quite different from that of the feigned basses among the Italians, which have neither depth nor strength. Besides, the interfering of the basses with the upper parts forms an agreeable contrast and makes us perceive the beauties of the one from the opposition they meet with from the other, a pleasure to which the Italians are perfect strangers, the voices of their singers, who are for the most part castrati, being perfectly like those of their women.

Besides the advantages we claim from the beauty of our designs and the variety of voices, we receive still more from our chorus, dances, and other entertainments, in which we infinitely excel the Italians. They, instead of these decorations, which furnish our operas with an agreeable variety and give 'em a peculiar air of grandeur and magnificence, have usually nothing but some burlesque scenes of a buffoon, some old woman that's to be in love with a young footman, or a conjurer that shall turn a cat into a bird, a fiddler into an owl, and play a few other tricks of legerdemain that are only fit to divert the mob. And, for their dancers, they are the poorest creatures in the world; they are all of a lump, without arms, legs, a shape, or air.

As to the instruments, our masters touch the violin much finer and with a greater nicety than they do in Italy. Every stroke of their bow sounds harsh, if broken, and disagreeable, if continued. Moreover, besides all the instruments that are common to us as well as the Italians, we have the hautboys, which, by their sounds, equally mellow and piercing, have infinitely the advantage of the violins in all brisk, lively airs, and the flutes, which so many of our great artists [a] have taught to groan after so moving a manner in our moanful airs, and sigh so amorously in those that are tender.

In short, we have the advantage of 'em in dress. Our habits infinitely excel all we see abroad, both in costliness and fancy. The Italians them-

a Philbert, Philidor, Descouteaux, and the Hotteterres.

selves will own that no dancers in Europe are equal to ours; the Combatants and Cyclops in *Perseus*, the Tremblers and Smiths in *Isis*, the Unlucky Dreams in *Atys*, and our other entries are originals in their kind, as well in respect of the airs composed by Lully, as of the steps which Beauchamp has adapted to those airs. The theatre produced nothing like it till those two great men appeared; 'tis an entertainment of which they are the sole inventors, and they have carried it to so high a degree of perfection that, as no person either in Italy or elsewhere has hitherto rivaled 'em, so, I fear, the world will never produce their equal. No theater can represent a fight more lively than we see it sometimes expressed in our dances, and, in a word, everything is performed with an unexceptionable nicety; the conduct and economy, through the whole, is so admirable that no man of common understanding will deny but that the French operas form a more lively representation than the Italian and that a mere spectator must be much better pleased in France than Italy. This is the sum of what can be offered to our advantage in behalf of our music and operas; let us now examine wherein the Italians have the advantage over us in these two points.

Their language is much more naturally adapted to music than ours; their vowels are all sonorous, whereas above half of ours are mute or at best bear a very small part in pronunciation, so that, in the first place, no cadence or beautiful passage can be formed upon the syllables that consist of those vowels, and, in the next, the words are expressed by halves, so that we are left to guess at what the French are singing, whereas the Italian is perfectly understood. Besides, though all the Italian vowels are full and open, yet the composers choose out of them such as they judge most proper for their finest divisions. They generally make choice of the vowel *a*, which, being clearer and more distinct than any of the rest, expresses the beauty of the cadence and division to a better advantage. Whereas we make use of all the vowels indifferently, those that are mute as well as those that are sonorous; nay, very often we pitch upon a diphthong, as in the words *chaîne* and *gloire*, which syllables, consisting of two vowels joined together, create a confused sound and want that clearness and beauty that we find in the simple vowels. But this is not the most material part to be considered in music; let us now examine into its essence and form, that is, the structure of the airs, either distinctly considered or in relation to the different parts of which the whole composition consists.

The Italians are more bold and hardy in their airs than the French; they carry their point farther, both in their tender songs and those that are more sprightly as well as in their other compositions; nay, they often unite styles which the French think incompatible. The French, in those compositions that consist of many parts, seldom regard more than that which is principal, whereas the Italians usually study to make all the parts equally shining and beautiful. In short, the invention of the one is inexhaustible, but the genius of the other is narrow and constrained; this the reader will fully understand when we descend to particulars.

It is not to be wondered that the Italians think our music dull and stupefying, that according to their taste it appears flat and insipid, if we consider the nature of the French airs compared to those of the Italian. The French, in their airs, aim at the soft, the easy, the flowing and coherent; the whole air is of the same tone, or, if sometimes they venture to vary it, they do it with so many preparations, they so qualify it, that still the air seems to be as natural and consistent as if they had attempted no change at all; there is nothing bold and adventurous in it; it's all equal and of a piece. But the Italians pass boldly and in an instant from b-sharp to b-flat and from b-flat to b-sharp; [2] they venture the boldest cadences and the most irregular dissonance; and their airs are so out of the way that they resemble the compositions of no other nation in the world.

The French would think themselves undone if they offended in the least against the rules; they flatter, tickle, and court the ear and are still doubtful of success, though everything be done with an exact regularity. The more hardy Italian changes the tone and the mode without any awe or hesitation; he makes double or treble cadences of seven or eight bars together upon tones we should think incapable of the least division. He'll make a swelling [b] of so prodigious a length that they who are unacquainted with it can't choose but be offended at first to see him so adventurous, but before he has done they'll think they can't sufficiently admire him. He'll have passages of such an extent as will perfectly confound his auditors at first, and upon such irregular tones as shall instill a terror as well as surprise into the audience, who will immediately conclude that the whole concert is degenerating into a dreadful dissonance; and betraying 'em by that means into a concern for the music, which seems to be upon the brink of ruin, he immediately reconciles 'em by such regular cadences that everyone is surprised to see harmony rising again, in a manner, out of discord itself and owing its greatest beauties to those irregularities which seemed to threaten it with destruction. The Italians venture at everything that is harsh and out of the way, but then they do it like people that have a right to venture and are sure of success. Under a notion of being the greatest

b By the Italians called *messa di voce*.   2 That is, from major to minor and from minor to major.

and most absolute masters of music in the world, like despotic sovereigns they dispense with its rules in hardy but fortunate sallies; they exert themselves above the art, but, like masters of that art whose laws they follow or transgress at pleasure, they insult the niceness of the ear which others court; they master and conquer it with charms which owe their irresistible force to the boldness of the adventurous composer.

Sometimes we meet with a swelling to which the first notes of the thorough bass jar so harshly as the ear is highly offended with it, but the bass, continuing to play on, returns at last to the swelling with such beautiful intervals that we quickly discover the composer's design, in the choice of those discords, was to give the hearer a more true and perfect relish of the ravishing notes that on a sudden restore the whole harmony.

Let a Frenchman be set to sing one of these dissonances, and he'll want courage enough to support it with that resolution wherewith it must be sustained to make it succeed; his ear, being accustomed to the most soft and natural intervals, is startled at such an irregularity; he trembles and is in a sweat whilst he attempts to sing it. Whereas the Italians, who are inured from their youth to these dissonances, sing the most irregular notes with the same assurance they would the most beautiful and perform everything with a confidence that secures 'em of success.

Music is become exceedingly common in Italy; the Italians sing from their cradles, they sing at all times and places, a natural uniform song is too vulgar for their ears. Such airs are to them like things tasteless and decayed. If you would hit their palate, you must regale it with variety and be continually passing from one key to another, though you venture at the most uncommon and unnatural passages. Without this you'll be unable to keep 'em awake or excite their attention.

But to be more particular, as the Italians are naturally much more brisk than the French, so are they more sensible of the passions and consequently express 'em more lively in all their productions. If a storm or rage is to be described in a symphony, their notes give us so natural an idea of it that our souls can hardly receive a stronger impression from the reality than they do from the description; everything is so brisk and piercing, so impetuous and affecting, that the imagination, the senses, the soul, and the body itself are all betrayed into a general transport; 'tis impossible not to be borne down with the rapidity of these movements. A symphony of furies shakes the soul; it undermines and overthrows it in spite of all its care; the artist himself, whilst he is performing it, is seized with an unavoidable agony; he tortures his violin; he racks his body; he is no longer master of himself, but is agitated like one possessed with an ir-resistible motion.

If, on the other side, the symphony is to express a calm and tranquillity, which requires a quite different style, they however execute it with an equal success. Here the notes descend so low that the soul is swallowed with 'em in the profound abyss. Every string of the bow is of an infinite length, lingering on a dying sound which decays gradually till at last it absolutely expires. Their symphonies of sleep insensibly steal the soul from the body and so suspend its faculties and operations that, being bound up, as it were, in the harmony that entirely possesses and enchants it, it's as dead to everything else as if all its powers were captivated by a real sleep.

In short, as for the conformity of the air with the sense of the words, I never heard any symphony comparable to that which was performed at Rome in the Oratory of St. Jerome of Charity on St. Martin's Day in the year 1697 upon these two words—*Mille saette* ("A thousand thun-derbolts"). The air consisted of disjointed notes, like those in a jig, which gave the soul a lively impression of an arrow and that wrought so effectu-ally upon the imagination that every violin appeared to be a bow, and their bows were like so many flying arrows, darting their pointed heads upon every part of the symphony. Nothing can be more masterly or more happily expressed. So that, be their airs either of a sprightly or gentle style, let 'em be impetuous or languishing, in all these the Italians are equally preferable to the French. But there is one thing beyond all this which neither the French nor any other nation besides themselves in the world ever attempted; for they will sometimes unite in a most surprising manner the tender with the sprightly, as may be instanced in that cele-brated air, "Mai non si vidde ancor più bella fedeltà," &c.,[3] which is the softest and most tender of any in the world, and yet its symphony is as lively and piercing as ever was composed. These different characters are they able to unite so artfully that, far from destroying a contrary by its contrary, they make the one serve to embellish the other.

But if we now proceed from the simple airs to a consideration of those pieces that consist of several parts, we there shall find the mighty ad-vantages the Italians have over the French. I never met with a master in France but what agreed that the Italians knew much better how to turn and vary a trio than the French. Among us, the first upper part is generally beautiful enough, but then the second usually descends too low to deserve

3 From the opera *Camilla*, by M. A. Bononcini.

our attention. In Italy the upper parts are generally three or four notes higher than in France, so that their seconds are high enough to have as much beauty as the very first with us.[4] Besides, all their three parts are so equally good that it is often difficult to find which is the subject. Lully has composed some after this manner, but they are few in number, whereas we hardly meet with any in Italy that are otherwise.

But of compositions consisting of more parts than three, the advantages of the Italian masters will still appear greater.[5] In France, it's sufficient if the subject be beautiful; we very rarely find that the parts which accompany it are so much as coherent. We have some thorough basses, indeed, which are good grounds and which, for that reason, are highly extolled by us. But where this happens, the upper parts grow very poor; they give way to the bass, which then becomes the subject. As for the accompaniments of the violin, they are, for the most part, nothing but single strokes of the bow, heard by intervals, without any uniform coherent music, serving only to express, from time to time, a few accords. Whereas in Italy, the first and second upper part, the thorough bass, and all the other parts that concur to the composition of the fullest pieces, are equally finished. The parts for the violins are usually as beautiful as the air itself. So that after we have been entertained with something very charming in the air, we are insensibly captivated by the parts that accompany it, which are equally engaging and make us quit the subject to listen to them. Everything is so exactly beautiful that it's difficult to find out the principal part. Sometimes the thorough bass lays so fast hold of our ear that in listening to it we forget the subject; at other times the subject is so insinuating that we no longer regard the bass, when all on a sudden the violins become so ravishing that we mind neither the bass nor the subject. 'Tis too much for one soul to taste the several beauties of so many parts. She must multiply herself before she can relish and digest three or four delights at once which are all beautiful alike; 'tis transport, enchantment, and ecstasy of pleasure; her faculties are upon so great a stretch, she's forced to ease herself by exclamations; she waits impatiently for the end of the air that she may have a breathing room; she sometimes finds it

---

4 Freneuse replies to this objection of Raguenet's in his Second Dialogue (Jacques Bonnet, *Histoire de la musique* [Amsterdam, 1725], II, 69): "The first upper parts of the Italians squeak because they are too high; their second upper parts have the fault of being too close to the first and too far from the bass, which is the third part."

5 Compare Freneuse (*ibid.*, II, 74–75): "'Is it in the choruses that the advantage of the Italians is supposed to lie? . . . Everyone knows that choruses are out of use in Italy, indeed beyond the means of the ordinary Italian opera house.

. . . How many singers do you suppose an Italian company has?' 'Say twenty or twenty-five, Monsieur, as in our own.' 'Nothing of the sort, Madame; usually six or seven—seven or eight. Those marvelous opera companies in Venice, Naples, and Rome consist of seven or eight voices. . . . When the composer of an opera aspires to the glory of having included a chorus in his work, as a rarity, it is these seven or eight persons as a group who form it, all singing together—the king, the clown, the queen, and the old woman.' "

impossible to wait so long, and then the music is interrupted by an universal applause. These are the daily effects of the Italian composition which everyone who has been in Italy can abundantly testify; we meet with the like in no other nation whatsoever. They are beauties improved to such a degree of excellence as not to be reached by the imagination till mastered by the understanding, and when they are understood our imaginations can form nothing beyond 'em.

To conclude, the Italians are inexhaustible in their productions of such pieces as are composed of several parts, in which on the other side the French are extremely limited. In France, the composer thinks he has done his business if he can diversify the subject; as for the accompaniments you find nothing like it in them; they are all upon the same chords, the same cadence, where you see all at once, without any variety or surprise. The French composers steal from one another or copy from their own works so that all their compositions are much alike. Whereas the Italian invention is infinite, both for the quantity and diversity of their airs; the number of 'em may modestly be said to be without number; and yet it will be very difficult to find two among 'em that are alike. We are daily admiring Lully's fertile genius in the composition of so many beautiful different airs. France never produced a master that had a talent like him; this I'm sure no one will contradict, and this is all I desire to make it appear how much the Italians are superior to the French, both for the invention and composition; for, in short, this great man, whose works we set in competition with those of the greatest masters in Italy, was himself an Italian. He has excelled all our musicians in the opinion of the French themselves.[6] To establish, therefore, an equality between the two nations, we ought to produce some Frenchman who has in the same manner excelled the greatest masters in Italy, and that by the confession of the Italians themselves; but this is an instance we have not yet been able to produce. Besides, Lully is the only man ever appeared in France with a genius so superior for music; whereas Italy abounds in masters, the worst of which may be compared to him; they are to be found at Rome, Naples, Florence, Venice, Bologna, Milan, and Turin, in which places there has been a long succession of them. They have had their Luigi, their Carissimi, their Melani, and their Legrenzi; to these succeeded their Buononcini, their Corelli, and their Bassani, who are still living and charm all Europe with their excellent productions. The first seemed to have robbed the art of all her beauties; and yet those that followed have at least rivaled 'em in an infinite number of works of a stamp perfectly new; they grow up there every day

6 "In the opinion of the French themselves" should be "In the French style itself."

and seem to claim the laurel from their predecessors; they are flourishing in all parts of Italy, whereas in France a master like one of them is looked on as a Phoenix; the whole realm has been able to produce but one in an age, and 'tis to be feared no age hereafter will ever be able to supply the loss of Lully. 'Tis therefore undeniably evident that the Italian genius for music is incomparably preferable to that of the French.

We have had no masterly compositions in France since Lully's death, so that all true lovers of music must despair of any new entertainments among us; but if they take the pains to go into Italy, I'll answer for 'em; let their heads be never so full of the French compositions, they'll renounce 'em all that they may have room enough for the Italian airs, which bear not the least resemblance to those in France, though this is an assertion no one can rightly comprehend that has not been in Italy; for the French have no notion of anything fine in music that doth not resemble some of their favorite airs.

These are the advantages the Italians have over the French in point of music, generally considered. Let us now examine wherein they excel 'em in relation to the operas. And that some order may be observed in the examination of so many things as concur to the forming of an opera, I think it proper to begin first with the music, in which some judgment of the recitative and symphony is first to be made before we descend to the singers themselves, who are to be considered in a twofold sense, as musicians and actors; the instruments and those that touch them, the decorations, and machines will likewise require a place in this examination.

There is no weak part in any of the Italian operas, where no sense is preferable to the rest for its peculiar beauties; all the songs are of an equal force and are sure to be crowned with applause, whereas in our operas there are I know not how many languishing scenes and insipid airs with which nobody can be pleased or diverted.

It must be confessed that our recitative is much better than that of the Italians, which is too close and simple; it's the same throughout and can't properly be called singing. Their recitative is little better than downright speaking, without any inflection or modulation of the voice, and yet there is this to be admired in it—the parts that accompany this psalmody are incomparable, for they have such an extraordinary genius for composition that they know how to adapt charming concords, even to a voice that does little more than speak, a thing to be met with in no other part of the world whatsoever.

What has been said of their music in general, with regard to ours, will be of equal force if we consider their symphony in particular. The symphony in our operas is frequently poor and tiresome, whereas in Italy it's equally full and harmonious.

I observed in the beginning of this parallel how much we had the advantage over the Italians in our basses, so common with us and so rare to be found in Italy; but how small is this in comparison to the benefit their operas receive from their castrati, who abound without number among them, whereas there is not one to be found in all France. Our women's voices are indeed as soft and agreeable as are those of their castrati, but then they are far from being either so strong or lively. No man or woman in the world can boast of a voice like theirs; they are clear, they are moving, and affect the soul itself.

Sometimes you hear a symphony so charming that you think nothing in music can exceed it till on a sudden you perceive it was designed only to accompany a more charming air sung by one of these castrati, who, with a voice the most clear and at the same time equally soft, pierces the symphony and tops the instruments with an agreeableness which they that hear it may conceive but will never be able to describe.

These pipes of theirs resemble that of the nightingale; their long-winded throats draw you in a manner out of your depth and make you lose your breath. They'll execute passages of I know not how many bars together, they'll have echoes on the same passages and swellings of a prodigious length, and then, with a chuckle in the throat, exactly like that of a nightingale, they'll conclude with cadences of an equal length, and all this in the same breath.

Add to this that these soft—these charming voices acquire new charms by being in the mouth of a lover; what can be more affecting than the expressions of their sufferings in such tender passionate notes; in this the Italian lovers have a very great advantage over ours, whose hoarse masculine voices ill agree with the fine soft things they are to say to their mistresses. Besides, the Italian voices being equally strong as they are soft, we hear all they sing very distinctly, whereas half of it is lost upon our theatre unless we sit close to the stage or have the spirit of divination. Our upper parts are usually performed by girls that have neither lungs nor wind, whereas the same parts in Italy are always performed by men whose firm piercing voices are to be heard clearly in the largest theatres without losing a syllable, sit where you will.

But the greatest advantage the Italians receive from these castrati is that their voices hold good for thirty or forty years together, whereas our women begin to lose the beauty of theirs at ten or twelve years' end. So that an actress is hardly formed for the stage before she loses her voice and another must be taken to supply her place, who, being a stranger to the theatre, will at least be out in the action if she comes off tolerably well in the singing and won't be fit to perform any considerable parts under five or six years' practice. We think it a mighty matter in France if we can brag of five or six good voices among thirty or forty actors and actresses that are employed in the opera. In Italy they are almost all of equal merit; they seldom make use of indifferent voices where there is so great a variety of good ones.[7]

As for the actors, they must be considered either as musicians that have a part to sing or players that are to act on the theatre; in both these capacities the French are infinitely outdone by the Italians.

In all our operas we have either some insignificant actor that sings out of tune or time, or some ignorant actress that sings false and is excused, either because she is not as yet thoroughly acquainted with the stage or else she has no voice, and then she is borne with because she has some other way of pleasing the town and withal makes a handsome figure. This never happens in Italy, where there is not a voice but what may very well be liked; they have neither man or woman but what perform their parts so perfectly well that they are sure to charm an audience by their agreeable manner of singing though their voices are not extraordinary, for music is nowhere so well understood as in Italy. At which we are not to wonder when we consider that the Italians learn music as we do to read; they have schools among 'em where their children are taught to sing as soon as ours learn their A B C; they are sent thither whilst they are very young and continue there for nine or ten years, so that by that time our children are able to read true and without any hesitation, theirs have been taught to sing with the same judgment and facility. To sing at sight with them is no more than to read so with us. The Italians study music once for all and attain it to the greatest perfection; the French learn it by halves, and so making themselves never masters of it, they are bound always to be scholars. When any new piece is to be presented in France, our singers are forced to con it over and over before they can make themselves perfect. How many times must we practice an opera before it's fit to be performed; this man begins too soon, that too slow; one sings out of tune, another out of time; in the meanwhile the composer labors with hand and voice and screws his body into a thousand

---

7 Compare Freneuse (*ibid.*, II, 123): "Six or seven voices suffice for an Italian opera; it is thus not extraordinary that they should all be of more or less equal merit. Nevertheless they seldom are so, although one does in truth hear some who are admirable. In France, where we require forty or fifty, it is not necessary that the members of the chorus and those who have only a little air in passing should sing as beautifully as the others."

contortions and finds all little enough to his purpose. Whereas the Italians are so perfect and, if I may use the expression, so infallible, that with them a whole opera is performed with the greatest exactness without so much as beating time or knowing who has the direction of the music. To this exactness they join all the embellishments an air is capable of; they run an hundred sort of divisions in it; they in a manner play with it and teach their throats to echo in a ravishing manner, whereas we hardly know what an echo in music means.

In their tender airs they soften the voice insensibly and at last let it die outright. These are beauties of the greatest nicety, a nicety not only unknown to, but impracticable by the French, whose upper parts are so weak that when they come to soften 'em, they are quite smothered and you hear no more of 'em. However, these echoes, these abatements of the voice, add such a grace to the Italian airs that very often the composer finds 'em more charming in the mouth of the singer than they were at first in his own imagination. And in this the Italian operas have a double advantage over the French, since that which makes 'em better singers makes 'em also better actors. For playing, as it were, with the music and singing exactly true, without obliging themselves to attend either the person that beats the time or anything else, they have full leisure to adjust themselves to the action, and having nothing else to do but to express the passions and compose their carriage, they must certainly act much better than the French, who being not such thorough masters of the music, are wholly busied in the performance. We have not one man in all our operas fit to act a lover, except Dufrom, but, besides that he sings very false and has little or no skill in music, his voice is not comparable to that of the castrati. If a principal actress, such as La Rochoix, should step aside, all France can't afford another to supply her place.[8] Whereas in Italy, when one actor or actress is out of the way, they have ten as good ready to succeed 'em, for all the Italians are born comedians and are as good actors as they are musicians. Their old women are incomparable figures, and their buffoons excel the best of the sort we ever saw on our stage.

The Italians have this farther advantage over us, which is that their castrati can act what part they please, either a man or a woman as the cast of the piece requires, for they are so used to perform women's parts that no actress in the world can do it better than they. Their voice is as soft as a woman's and withal it's much stronger; they are of a larger size than women, generally speaking, and appear consequently more majestic. Nay,

8 I saw that woman at Paris; she was a good figure enough and had a tolerable voice, but then she was a wretched actress and sung insufferably out of tune. [Translator's note]

they usually look handsomer on the stage than women themselves. Ferinni, for example, who performed the part of Sybaris in the opera of *Themistocles* at Rome in the year 1685 is taller and more beautiful than women commonly are.[9] He had I know not what air of grandeur and modesty in his countenance; dressed, as he was, like a Persian princess, with his plume and turban, he looked like a real queen or empress, and probably no woman in the world ever made a more beautiful figure than he did in that habit. Italy abounds with these people; you'll find a great choice of actors and actresses in every town you come at. I saw a man at Rome who understood music as well as the best of our performers and at the same time he was as good an actor as our Harlequin or Raisin, yet by profession he was neither singer nor comedian. He was a solicitor and quitted his employment in the carnival time to perform a part in the opera; when that was done, he returned again to his business.[10] It's therefore much easier, as we have made it appear, to perform an opera in Italy than in France.

The Italians have, besides all this, the same advantage over us in respect of the instruments and the performers as they have in regard of the singers and their voices. Their violins are mounted with strings much larger than ours; their bows are longer, and they can make their instruments sound as loud again as we do ours. The first time I heard our band in the Opéra after my return out of Italy, my ears had been so used to the loudness of the Italian violins that I thought ours had all been bridled. Their archlutes are as large again as our theorbos and their sound consequently louder by half; their bass-viols are as large again as the French, and all ours put together don't sound so loud in our operas as two or three of those basses do in Italy. This is certainly an instrument much wanted in France; 'tis the basis on which the Italians in a manner build the whole consort; 'tis a sure foundation, equally firm as it is deep and low; it has a full mellow sound, filling the air with an agreeable harmony in a sphere of activity extending itself to the utmost bounds of the most capacious places. The sound of their symphonies is wafted by the air to the roof in their churches and even to the skies in open places. And for those that play on these instruments, we have very few can come near 'em here in France. I have seen children in Italy not above fourteen or fifteen years old play the bass or treble admirably well in symphonies they never saw before and in such symphonies as would puzzle the best of our masters,

---

9 Upon inquiry I'm informed that Ferinni never perform'd on any theatre in Rome but that of Tordinona and that the opera of *Themistocles* was never represented on that theatre, so that I believe the author has either mistaken or forgot the name of the opera.—[Translator's note] Pos-sibly the opera in question is Zannettini's *Temistocle in bando,* performed in Venice, 1683.

10 The lawyer here mention'd is called Paciani, a man well known at Rome; his performances on the theatre are purely for his pleasure. [Translator's note]

and this they do often over the shoulders of two or three others that stand between them and the score. 'Tis wonderful to see these striplings with a side look take off the most difficult pieces at first sight. They beat no time to the bands in Italy, and yet you never find 'em out in the measure or the tune. You must rummage all Paris to fit out a good band; 'tis impossible to find two such as that in the Opéra. At Rome, which is not a tenth part so populous as Paris, there are hands enough to compose seven or eight bands, consisting of harpsichords, violins, and theorbos, equally good and perfect. But that which makes the Italian bands infinitely preferable to those in France is that the greatest masters are not above performing in 'em. I have seen Corelli, Pasquini, and Gaetani play all together in the same opera at Rome, and they are allowed to be the greatest masters in the world on the violin, the harpsichord, and theorbo or archlute, and as such they are generally paid 300 or 400 pistoles apiece for a month, or six weeks at the most. This is the commonest pay in Italy, and this encouragement is one reason why they have more masters there than we have with us. We despise 'em in France as people of a mean profession; in Italy they are esteemed as men of note and distinction. There they raise very considerable fortunes, whereas with us they get but a bare livelihood. From hence it is that ten times more people apply themselves to music in Italy than France. Nothing is more common in Italy than performers, singers, and music. The singers in the Navona Square at Rome and those on the Rialto at Venice, which hold the same rank there as our ballad singers on Pont Neuf do with us, will often join three or four in a company; and one taking the violin, another the bass, and a third a theorbo or guitar, with these instruments they'll accompany their voices so justly that we seldom meet with much better music in our French consorts.

To conclude all, the Italian decorations and machines are much better than ours; their boxes are more magnificent; the opening of the stage higher and more capacious; our painting, compared to theirs, is no better than daubing; you'll find among their decorations, statues of marble and alabaster that may vie with the most celebrated antiques in Rome; palaces, colonnades, galleries, and sketches of architecture superior in grandeur and magnificence to all the buildings in the world; pieces of perspective that deceive the judgment as well as the eye, even of those that are curious in the art; prospects of a prodigious extent in spaces not thirty foot deep; nay, they often represent on the stage the lofty edifices of the ancient Romans, of which only the remains are now to be seen, such as the Colosseum which I saw in the Roman College in the year 1698 in the same perfection in which it stood in the reign of Vespasian, its founder, so that these decorations are not only entertaining, but instructive.

As for their machines, I can't think it in the power of human wit to carry the invention farther. In the year 1697 I saw an opera at Turin wherein Orpheus was to charm the wild beasts by the power of his voice.[11] Of these there were all sorts introduced on the stage; nothing could be more natural or better designed; an ape, among the rest, played an hundred pranks, the most diverting in the world, leaping on the backs of the other animals, scratching their heads, and entertaining the spectators with the rest of his monkey tricks. I saw once at Venice an elephant discovered on the stage, when in an instant that great machine disappeared and an army was seen in its place, the soldiers having, by the disposition of their shields, given so true a representation of it as if it had been a real living elephant.

The ghost of a woman, surrounded with guards, was introduced on the Theatre of Capranica at Rome in the year 1698; this phantom, extending her arms and unfolding her clothes, was with one motion transformed into a perfect palace, with its front, its wings, its body and courtyard all formed by magical architecture; the guards striking their halberds on the stage were immediately turned into so many water-works, cascades, and trees that formed a charming garden before the palace. Nothing can be more quick than were those changes, nothing more ingenious or surprising. And in truth the greatest wits in Italy frequently amuse themselves with inventions of this nature. People of the first quality entertain the public with such spectacles as these without any prospect of gain to themselves. Signor Cavaliere Acciajoli, brother to the cardinal of that name, had the direction of those on the Theatre Capranica in the year 1698.

This is the sum of what can be offered in behalf of the French or Italian music by way of parallel. I have but one thing more to add in favor of the operas in Italy which will confirm all that has been already said to their advantage; which is that, though they have neither choruses nor other diversions in use with us, their entertainments last five or six hours together and yet the audience is never tired, whereas after one of our representations, which does not hold above half so long at most, there are very few spectators but what grow sufficiently weary and think they have had more than enough.[12]

---

11 This was the *Orfeo* of Antonio Sartorio; Loewenberg gives the date of the first performance in Turin as March 20, 1697.

12 The Italian operas don't usually last five or six hours, as this author imagines, the longest being not above four. 'Tis true that sometimes at Vienna the late Emperor Leopold would have operas of the length the author mentions, provided they were good, being a great admirer of the Italian music; besides he composed himself and played on the harpsichord to perfection.—[Translator's note] Compare Freneuse (*ibid.*, II, 50): " 'That was a mighty short opera,' said the Countess when [Campra's] *Tancrède* was over. 'And that is already handsome praise,' the Chevalier said; 'you will not say as much for the Italian operas that last five or six hours and that will seem to you to have lasted eight or nine.' "

60. Le Cerf de La Viéville, Seigneur de Freneuse

Jean Laurent le Cerf de La Viéville, Lord of Freneuse, was born in 1647 and died in 1710. He was an ardent admirer of Lully and deeply affected by Raguenet's attack on him in his *Parallèle des Italiens et des Français*. Freneuse answered Raguenet in his *Comparaison de la musique italienne et de la musique française*, the first part of which first appeared in 1704. In the following year (1705) a second edition of this first part was brought out together with a second part containing the *Traité du bon goût en musique* which is reproduced below. Raguenet having published an answer to the writings of Freneuse in 1705, the latter reciprocated by adding a third part to his *Comparaison* in 1706. All three parts were then reprinted and added, in 1725, to the second edition of Pierre Bourdelot's and Jacques Bonnet's *Historie de la musique*.

From the Comparaison de la musique italienne et de la musique française

[*1705*]

"*Traité du bon goût en musique*" [1]

"YOU ARE methodical in your divisions, monsieur," replied Mademoiselle M. " 'To bring to the opera attention, a certain knowledge, a familiarity with these entertainments, and good taste.' Indeed, without attention there is no way of judging of things. One judges of them the better for

---

[1] Text: Jacques Bonnet, *Histoire de la musique* (Amsterdam, 1725), III, 258–262, 275–278, 280–283, 285–287, 292–294, 297–299, 301–309, 313–316, 318–322. The "Treatise on Good Taste" forms part of the sixth dialogue of the *Comparaison*. The speakers are the Marquis des E——, the Chevalier de —— (the author himself), the Comtesse du B——, and Mlle. M—— ——; the scene is the home of the Countess. Unless otherwise noted, the examples cited are from the operas of Lully.

being accustomed to see others of their kind and even for having several times seen the things which are under discussion. At the sixth performance of a play I discuss it better than at the first. And then, good taste. We can be attentive, monsieur, when we please, and no opera can be wholly new to us. May we have from you, if you please, that third thing so essential and so rare. Teach us what good taste is, the secret of acquiring it and keeping it, and the indications that one has acquired it and has kept it. Would not that be enough, madame?"

"Yes," said the Countess. "I shall be glad if anyone will teach me how to distinguish perfectly the beauties of music and their different value and how to become attached to them. Speak, monsieur le Marquis, and by so doing relieve us of the fatigue of our excursion into learning."

"I intend," said the Marquis, "to rely upon that lad there to take the pains to give you the explanation you have asked for. As I have never read any author who has treated of good taste, even of good taste in general, in a precise manner, and as I have never seen any who treated of good taste in music in any manner, I fear that my own ideas would not be sharply defined."

"And would mine be any more so?" asked the Chevalier. "If I am to say what I have imagined on the subject, I must have Madame's command. Without an absolute order to serve as my excuse for opening, for undertaking the discussion of so new and so difficult a matter, I should not have the boldness to do so."

The beautiful Countess smiled.

"See that smile," said the Marquis. "There is your order, a very pleasant one."

"It is small pay," replied the Chevalier, "if I must content myself with a smile for the danger I am about to incur. But as you have observed, the ladies are cruelly reserved in this age. I shall expound to you then, since Madame so commands me, what eight or ten years of attentive assiduity at the Opéra, long reflections at the close of performances, and my study of the nature of amusement have led me to conclude concerning good taste. You will find that it could be applied to several other fine arts: to painting, to eloquence, to poetry. I freely agree that all these arts have a bond of union which makes what can be said of each of them almost common to all, and I take for a good omen that what is said of any one is, in part, true of the others.

"But nevertheless, music will be found to have some particular and distinctive attribute of its own. Besides, monsieur le Comte was right, madame, in suspecting me of wishing to justify the principles of the ancients.[2] I am for the men of that age and the women of this. It is on the side of the principles of ancient music that I have all the while been seeking to enlist you; I praised them to you on purpose at the time of our second conversation;[3] I shall continue to follow them; and I am very well pleased that we have refuted M. Perrault's book,[4] in order to have the right to follow these principles with entire freedom.

"There are two great ways of knowing good and bad things: by our inward feeling and by the rules. We know the good and the bad only by these means. What we see and what we hear pleases us or displeases us. If one listens only to the inward feeling, one will say, 'It seems to me that that is good, or that it is not.' On the other hand, the masters, the skilled, following the observations they have made, have established precepts in every craft. These comprised whatever had seemed to them to be the best and the surest. The established precepts are the rules, and if one consults them regarding what one sees and what one hears, one will say that this is good or is not good, according to such and such a rule, or for such and such a reason. These masters were men; were they incapable of being deceived? The authority of the rules is considerable, but after all it is not a law. Inward feeling is still less sure, because each should distrust his own, should distrust that it is what it should be. Who will dare flatter himself that he has a fortunate nature, endowed with sure and clear ideas of the good, the beautiful, the true? We have all brought into the world the foundation of these ideas, more or less clear and certain, but since our birth we have received, and this it is sad and painful to correct, a thousand false impressions, a thousand dangerous prejudices, which have weakened and stifled within us the voice of uncorrupted nature.

---

2 Rightly understood, the controversy between Raguenet and Freneuse is not so much concerned with the rival claims of French and Italian music as with those of a "classic" and a "modern" style. As such, it is simply a part of the larger quarrel between the ancients and moderns, begun in France by Boileau, Fontenelle, and the brothers Charles and Claude Perrault, and continued in England by Temple, Wotton, and Swift. Raguenet's book is pro modern in that its title is an obvious paraphrase of Charles Perrault's *Parallèles des anciens et des modernes en ce qui regarde les arts et les sciences* (1688–97) and in that it appeared with an "Approbation" by Fontenelle. The reply of Freneuse is pro classic in that it repeatedly quotes with approval from Boileau, the chief partisan of the ancients, and in that it includes an attack on Claude Perrault. Cf. his first dialogue (Bonnet, *op. cit.*, II, 17–18): "M. de Fontenelle is entitled to his opinions. In comparison with the Italians, the French musicians are our ancients. Aside from this, M. de Fontenelle is interested only in exalting the French above other nations in poetry, physics, and the other sciences within his province; thus if he abandons the glory of France in music, this carries no weight." Cf. also his reply to Raguenet's *Defense du Parallèle* (Paris, 1705) in his third book (Bonnet, *op. cit.*, IV, 188): "When I say that, in comparison with the Italians, the French musicians are our ancients, this simply means that, compared with Italians, whose great vogue did not begin in France until ten years ago or thereabouts, our composers, to whom we have been attached for thirty, forty, sixty years, have had to share the disgrace of the ancients, if we are to believe M. de Fontenelle, who likes to prefer the latest arrivals. And our composers are also ancients in view of their character, their simplicity, and their naturalness, qualities which M. de Fontenelle is not accustomed to rating very highly. For all his attempts at dialectic, M. l'Abbé cannot prove my little jest to be far-fetched or obscure."

3 The fifth dialogue, a conversation on musical history, opera, and the life of Lully.

4 The present dialogue began with a discussion of Claude Perrault's "De la musique des anciens," first published in his *Essais de physique*, II (1680).

"I think that in this uncertainty and confusion the remedy is to lend to the inward feeling the support of the rules, that our policy should be to correct and strengthen the one by the other, and that it is this union of the rules and the feeling which forms good taste. To listen attentively to the inward feeling, to disentangle it, and then to purify it by the application of the rules; there is the art of judging with certainty, and therefore I am persuaded that good taste is the most natural feeling, corrected or confirmed by the best rules."

.   .   .   .   .

"Oh, monsieur, what are these rules? I cannot consult them unless you . . ."

"There are little ones and great ones, madame, and we have touched upon both sorts in our conversation. The little rules are those of composition, on which twenty treatises have been written, of which I do not cite a single one, because I am waiting for somebody to write a twenty-first one that will be good.[a] Just as faults of versification are condemnable and perceptible in the best poets (witness the saying of M. le Duc de Montausier that Corneille should be crowned as a poet and whipped as a versifier), the same is true of faults of composition in the best musicians. An air in which these are found loses something of its value. Our masters have sufficiently instructed us in the little rules, and a little reflection will make us remember to pay attention to them when they are violated . . ."

"An example, Chevalier, an example. Precepts without examples only disquiet and distress me . . ."

"But these examples can hardly be cited from memory, and besides, examples of faults and minutiae are not easy to find in Lully, the only composer I wish to cite here, and it is dangerous to propose to find them. No matter, madame, you will make a beautiful excuse for the audacity and the novelty of my criticisms. For example, then, it is a little rule of composition, founded in part on the necessity of expressing, of depicting, to use low notes or high notes with words which represent a low or a lofty object. Colasse has been praised for having observed this rule in very remarkable fashion in the passage of *Thétis et Pélée*,

Les cieux, l'enfer, la terre et l'onde [5]

On the contrary, at the end of the first act of *Acis et Galatée*, where Polyphemus says,

---

[a] Since that time, Etienne Roger has published that of Masson. [Masson's *Nouveau traité*, first published in Paris in 1694, was reprinted by Roger of Amsterdam about 1710.—Ed.]

[5] The skies and hell, the earth, the ocean.

Je suis au comble de mes voeux [6]

the note to which the word *comble* (summit) is sung is very low, the lowest note of all that line. *Comble* called for a high note, and strictly speaking, that negligence is assuredly a fault which detracts from the value of the admirable melody of that recitative. Little rules, which, for all that, enter into consideration.

"You know the great rules, mademoiselle," continued the Chevalier, turning toward Mademoiselle, who was amusing herself by looking at her scarf, "indeed we have gone over them to the point of weariness."

"Yes," she replied, "but go ahead as if I didn't know them." [b]

"Very well, mademoiselle. A piece of music should be natural, expressive, harmonious. In the first place, natural, or rather, simple, for simplicity is the first part, the first sign of the natural, which is almost equally an ingredient in these three qualities. In the second place, expressive. In the third place, harmonious, melodious, pleasing—take your choice. These are the three great, the three important rules which one must apply to the airs that the inward feeling has approved, and it is they which in the last resort decide."

" 'Fore heaven, monsieur le Chevalier," said Mademoiselle, "how greatly I should be obliged to you if you would just once define for me in precise words those terms which you use as a stand-by. 'Natural, simple.' What, in precise words, do you call simple and natural? . . ."

"Ah, well, I hate all obscurity just as you do, and I am delighted that you should prevent me from leaving those terms in any way obscure. I call natural, in the literal sense, the music which is composed of notes that present themselves naturally, which is not composed of notes that are farfetched or out of the ordinary. I call simple the music which is not loaded with ornaments, with harmonies. I call expressive an air of which the notes are perfectly suited to the words, and a symphony which expresses perfectly what it aims to express. I call harmonious, melodious, pleasing, the music which fills, contents, and tickles the ear.

.   .   .   .   .

"A last rule, which must be added to the little rules and the three great rules, and which clarifies and fortifies both groups, is always to abhor excess. Let us make it a habit and a merit to have contempt, distaste, and aversion without quarter for all that contains anything superfluous. Let us hate even an expression which is of the right character but which goes beyond the appropriate degree of force. And to return to where we were,

---

b *Le bourgeois gentilhomme,* Act I.   6 I reach the summit of my hopes.

when your inward feeling has caused you to enjoy an air, which moreover conforms to the minor rules, make sure, by examining it in the light of the three great rules and the rule of just proportion, that your heart and your senses have not been deceived. After which, mademoiselle, be at rest; be assured that the air is truly one to be esteemed.

"You are going to ask me for an example, an air which the great rules condemn. Gladly, madame, and from Lully, since it is a question of satisfying you. Listen to that air of *Phaëton*,[c]

> *Que l'incertitude*
> *Est un rigoureux tourment!*

It will flatter your ear, and I do not think that there are faults in it. An attentive ear will confirm the opinion that it is simple, agreeable, natural. Examine whether it is expressive; you will perceive that it is not. Lybia is lamenting the rigor of a sorrowful uncertainty. How does she lament it? In a gay tone and movement. How excuse the incongruity arising from this gaiety and from a sort of pleasantry caused by the repetition of the verses? Perhaps Quinault incited Lully to this vicious pleasantry. But why did Lully accept these words and follow them, increasing the defect? It would seem to me that, taking the words as they stand, the falsity of expression which prevails in the air makes it bad, and I should like neither to sing it nor to hear it, in spite of my veneration for its author."

"I have seen," said the Marquis, "a man of wit, who is a scholar and a musician, who likewise criticized the duet of the prologue of *Persée*,

> *La grandeur brillante*
> *Qui fait tant de bruit*, etc.,

finding in it a misplaced gaiety. If it were an ambitious man expressing in this tone the unhappiness of ambition, I too believe that the gaiety would be a grave fault. But it is a philosopher who is describing the evils from which he has sheltered himself, evils at which he laughs. Is he not right in depicting them gaily and laughingly? The words,

> *Notre sort est tranquille;*
> *C'est un bien qui nous doit rendre heureux*,

justify the movement and the amiable gaiety of the whole duet.

"Indeed, I have no doubt that constant adherence to these principles and exact care in applying them in detail to all the music that one hears will really lead one to good taste. One who took the pains to judge always

---

c Act II, Scene iii.

in this manner would in less than a year be able to judge without thinking about it."

"Trust us to do so," said the Countess. "But although we must not let ourselves be blinded by the reputation of composers, cannot their favorable or unfavorable reputation serve to give a certain assurance to the judgments we have already formed? Am I not justified in saying, 'My heart, my ear, all the rules agree in persuading me that "Bois épais" [7] is a charming air. And it is by Lully, a new pledge of the correctness of my taste. This other air does not flatter my ear, nor does it touch me; it has neither sweetness nor expression. And it is by Charpentier. [8] Yes, I am judging it rightly; it is bad.' Would that be bad reasoning, Chevalier?"

"Not at all, madame, anything but bad. It is clear that the reputation of the composers, which would be a dangerous guide before we judge, is excellent for confirming our opinions after we have judged. But the memory of Charpentier is greatly obliged for citing him so appositely. Apparently you are of the opinion of the Abbé de Saint Real, [d] that it is less forbidden to maltreat dead authors than living ones."

"But," said the Countess, "could there not be some other method of judging music, not so long and not so trying, some way of judging it at a glance and in a phrase? Try to find for me, Marquis, the secret of consoling my indolence, or rather my vivacity, which indeed accepts the principles which we have just run over, but which is hampered by them and tired of them."

"Yes, madame," the old noble promptly replied, "I will find for you the secret of judging in a phrase. I will make you judge by a silent and summary application of your principles. It will not be so sure, but it will ordinarily be just, and moreover, easy and convenient. You do not wish to take the pains to judge by reasoning. Judge by comparison, which is the method of courtiers, as La Bruyère, I believe, somewhere says. You will need to carry in your head two airs representing the two qualities, one good and one bad; that is, good and bad by almost unanimous consent, and two symphonies, one good and one bad, and you must have all their beauties and all their faults at the tip of your fingers. You must have the knowledge of the least of the beauties and faults of these two airs and these two symphonies ever at command and thoroughly familiar, and compare with these models the airs and symphonies you hear.

d *De la critique*, chap. ii.

7 From his *Amadis*, II, iv.

8 Born in Paris, Charpentier studied in Rome with Carissimi; he returned to France a partisan of Italian music and became Lully's principal adversary.

"These latter you will esteem in proportion to their resemblance to the others, and the idea of this resemblance alone, accordingly as it strikes you more or less forcibly, will cause you to say, with greater or less force, 'I like that air; that symphony does not please me.' I am convinced that the ablest connoisseur should not neglect to combine with the judgments based on reasoning these judgments by comparison, from which will be derived an additional clearness, well adapted to confirm our feelings. For a man of wit, a man of the world, who knows how to make the most of this taste derived from comparison, it will perhaps be sufficient. It is a facility which is flattering to indolence and a fortunate resource for ignorance. I shall praise every symphony which approaches the one that accompanies the air of *Acis et Galatée*, 'Qu'une injuste fierté,' of the passacaglia of *Armide*, etc. I shall admire every sad air which imitates 'Bois épais,' every lively air which resembles that of *Amadis*, which all France, from the princess to the serving maid in the tavern, has so often sung,

Amour, que veux-tu de moi?

And so on. The precept is not complicated, and its application will not be fatiguing."

.   .   .   .   .   .

"Now," said the Countess, "let us judge of the degrees of value of airs. So far we have not spoken of the degrees of beauty. But indeed, Chevalier, I understand that you are on the point of telling me that no one knows how to determine these degrees, that the more perfectly an air complies with the rules the better it is, and the further it departs from them the worse, and that it depends on the skill of the connoisseur to measure these degrees of perfection or of imperfection."

"Beyond doubt that will be my answer, madame," said the Chevalier. "Meanwhile there are precepts with regard to this matter. First, infringements of the little rules are as nothing in comparison with violations of the great ones. Listen to a lesson of Holy Week which begins with a sixth, but go out when one begins with a roulade. In the second place, the pleasures of the heart being, by the principles we have established, superior to those of the ear, an air which offends against the laws that are directed toward touching the heart offends more than one which disregards merely those which aim to satisfy the ear. Let us forgive two similar cadences which are too near to each other, or a poor thorough bass, and let us never forgive a melody which is cold and forced. There you have two ideas which will help us to make up our minds about the degrees of good and bad of a piece.

"In the third place, the most beautiful thing is that which is equally admired by the people and by the learned or by all the connoisseurs. Then, after this, I should admire more that which is generally admired by all the people. Finally, that which is admired by all the learned. Mademoiselle likes precise definitions. The learned are the masters of music, the musicians by profession, stubborn about the rules. The people is the multitude, the great mass, which has not risen to special knowledge and has only its natural feeling as its guide and as the warrant for its judgments. The connoisseurs are those who are neither altogether of the people nor altogether learned, half the one and half the other, a shade less learned than of the people, that is to say, crediting the rules a shade less than natural feeling; and this definition is my own.

.　.　.　.　.

"As to the half-learned, they are in music what they are in any art, in anything whatever, the most contemptible and the most insupportable of all men. Let us attach more importance to the opinion of a good bourgeois of the Rue St. Denis than to that of the apprentice-composers, these chevaliers of accompaniment, whose efforts and whose vanity have turned topsy-turvy the little taste they might have had;

> Of the folk who, attended by one scurvy lute,
> Say, 'my bass,' and make marvelous doctors.[a]

"Therefore, mesdames, I persist in maintaining the rank which I have assigned to the suffrages of those who judge of our operas: the people and the learned or the connoisseurs; the people alone; the connoisseurs alone; the learned alone. That order is good. I see in *Thésée* the first scene of the second act:

> *Doux repos, innocente paix*, etc.;

the third scene of the third act:

> *Princesse, scavez-vous ce que peut ma colère*, etc.;

the fifth scene of the fourth act:

> *Eglé ne m'aime plus, et n'a rien à me dire*, etc.;

admired equally by our people and by our learned. I believe without any difficulty that these scenes are the most beautiful, and I have verified that

[a] Imitated from Molière's *Les Fâcheux*, scene of the hunter, II, vii.

they will pass for such with the connoisseurs. I see the first and fourth scenes of the fourth act,

Cruelle, ne voulez-vous pas, etc.,

and

Faut-il voir contre moi tous les enfers armés, etc.,

loved by the people, who are moved to tenderness by them. I do not hesitate to prefer them greatly to

Prions, prions la déesse, etc.,

of Act I, Scene vi, and to the entire part of the Grand Priestess, a part so imbued with learning, which makes the learned esteem it in spite of its coldness. In this way there are in Lully two hundred expressive pieces which touch the multitude, and I should not hesitate to prefer them to the admirable trio, 'Le fil de la vie,' [f] one of the most perfect learned pieces and one of the most acceptable to the learned that Lully has left. I am ready to maintain against all comers that the public's favorite scenes in *Proserpine*,[g]

J'ai peine à concevoir d'où vient le trouble extrème, etc.,

and

Venez-vous contre moi défendre un téméraire, etc.,

are worth far more than the learned scenes of *Les Ombres heureuses*,

Loin d'ici, loin de nous, etc.

The despair of Roland is of far greater merit than the profound beauties of the part of Logistille, etc.[9]

．　．　．　．　．

"When I heard, for example, the air of *Amadis*,

Amour, que veux-tu de moi, etc.,

sung by all the kitchen maids of France, I was right in thinking that this air was already certain to have the approbation of everybody in France of a degree between that of princess and that of kitchen maid; that this air had passed through all those degrees to reach the lowest, and had captured the esteem and the suffrage of all people of quality, of all the learned, of that immense number of persons of distinction on whose lips it had been, and remarking that it had succeeded in touching the kitchen maid as it had succeeded in touching the princess, that it pleased equally

---

f *Isis*, Act IV. 　　　　9 Characters in Lully's *Roland*.
g Acts II and IV.

the learned and the ignorant, the intelligences of the highest order and of the lowest, I concluded that it must be very beautiful, very natural, very full of true expression, to have moved so many different hearts and flat-tered so many different ears. But an air of the Pont-Neuf, which has begun among the populace and which spreads among the populace, has only the approval of the populace, and the humbler folk of France, very unlike those of Athens and not attending the theater as those of Athens did, have not a natural feeling pure enough to entitle their suffrage to count when it stands alone. You will not count it, madame, except when it comes after your own. But you will please permit the more or less lively approbation of the populace to be a sixth measure, which I was forgetting, of the degree of beauty of musical works. These are our principles; all follows logi-cally."

"Yes," said the Marquis, "they bring you, willy-nilly, to that con-clusion. And that characterization of the people, the connoisseurs, and the learned makes me realize that we must listen to the reasoning of the learned, defer to the feeling of the connoisseurs, and study how the people are moved. I conceive that above all this, the study of how the people are moved by theatrical representations can infinitely clarify and facilitate our judgments and help us to make them true. At the first three representations of an opera, let us concern ourselves only with ourselves; it will keep us sufficiently occupied, unless long habituation leaves our minds exceptionally free. But at the fourth and later performances let us apply ourselves to studying in what manner and how greatly the people are touched. The value and the degree of value of pieces will certainly be revealed by the impression which they make on the heart of the people and by the vivacity of that impression. When Armida works herself up to stab Rinaldo in the last scene of the second act, I have twenty times seen everybody seized by terror, holding his breath, motionless, all the soul in the ears and eyes, until the air of the violin which ends the scene gave leave to breathe, then at that point breathing again with a murmur of delight and admiration. I had no need to reason. That unanimous re-sponse of the people told me with certainty that the scene was of over-powering beauty.[10] A number of times in Paris, when the duet of *Persée*, so learnedly written and so difficult,

Les vents impétueux, etc.,

was well given, I have seen the entire public, similarly attentive, remain for the half of a quarter-hour without breathing, with their eyes fixed

10 For this scene see Schering, *Geschichte der Musik in Beispielen* (Leipzig, 1931), No. 234. Rameau analyzes Armida's monologue in his *Nouveau système* (1726) and in his *Observations* (1754) replies to Rousseau's criticism of it in his *Lettre sur la musique française* (1753).

upon Phineus and Merope, and when the duet was finished, nod to each other to indicate the pleasure it had given them. Certainly a beautiful passage: expressive learning, beautiful roulades.

"I am so much of the Chevalier's opinion, namely, that the public is an oracle for the fine arts, that I could even like to study and put faith in the responses of a particular section of the public to certain things which come especially within their province, which concern them, and about which they have a particular feeling. I remember that at the beginning of a performance of *Hésione*,[11] in that scene, the fifth of the second act, in which Venus begs Anchises for his love, which he has refused (I don't know why, since Venus was hardly made to have refusals flung in her face, and since on the faith of the legend he was by no means cruel to her), and when he leaves her, saying,

> *À vos regards tout doit rendre les armes;*
> *Si je n'adore pas leur pouvoir éclatant,*
> *Je sens du moins qu'un coeur qui veut être constant*
> *Doit craindre de voir tant de charmes,*[12]

I remember, I say, that at these last verses, I saw all the ladies look at each other and smile. The ignoble advances of Venus had distressed their vanity; now a universal joy returned to their faces. I had no need of discussion to know that the language and the expression of the passage were most graceful. The natural response of those ladies, more skilled than we in matters of gallantry, their air, the contentment in their eyes, were my warrant, and I could rely upon them. Should one of the learned have asserted that the music did not match the words, I should have assured him that if the music had not been as graceful as the words, the passage would have made a less general and less lively impression on the ladies.

"Let us then add this to our other rules: to study at the Opéra the response of the public and of particular groups from the public, in so far as certain things are more within their range and their competence. Here is another secret for throwing a clear and immediate light on the subject of our thoughts, a secret likewise derived from our principles, to which we cannot adhere too closely. A thousand fashionables who daily judge music at haphazard and in a way to move pity do so only from having no

---

11 Opera by André Campra.

12 Your dazzling glances overcome all arms;
If I withhold the worship to them due,
At least I feel that one whose heart would
    fain be true
Should fear to gaze upon such potent
    charms.

principles to adhere to. Our principles are such that we may well adhere to them without reserve."

"While we are on the subject of these principles," replied Madame du B., "pray, give me also, messieurs, those which will enable me to judge of voices, singers, and players of instruments, so that I shall be able to pass on the merit of any of these with the same clearness and the same certainty as on the music which they execute. When we learn to sing or to play an instrument, our masters burden us with a quantity of little observations which become a confused jumble, because we are not taught to refer them to certain general principles."

"That is what the masters forget, madame," replied the Marquis, smiling. "But you are right; it would be clearer and more convenient later if they said, in so many words, that the perfection of a voice, of singing, and of the playing of an instrument depends only on this. I am going to explain the method which I have devised and adopted to judge of the players of instruments, the voices, and the singers that I hear; you may use it if it pleases you.

"A perfect voice should be sonorous, of wide range, sweet, exact (*nette*), lively, flexible. These six qualities, which nature combines only once in a century, are ordinarily present in half measure. A voice of wide range and of a beautiful tone (*son*), a touching tone, is a great, a beautiful voice, and the sweeter it is, in addition, a thing rarer in great voices than in others, the more beautiful I believe it to be. A lively and flexible voice is a pretty voice, a pleasing voice, and the more exact it is, in addition, the less, in my opinion, will it be subject to hoarseness and coughing, the frequent drawbacks of pretty voices, and the more I shall esteem it. Bacilly [h] esteems these little voices as much as the great ones; they interested him. My friend and I, who like noble, bold, penetrating tones, are of a different taste. We are for the great voices, and we shall allow the little voices to embellish their tunes ever so neatly with no regrets on our part.

"I reduce the merit of a singer to three things: accuracy, expression, neatness (*propreté*). I reduce the merit of a player upon an instrument to three other things: exactness (*netteté*), delicacy, getting the most out of his instrument. The first thing required of a singer is correct pitch. If he sings without accompaniment, he cannot sing off pitch except by insensibly raising or lowering the tone, so that at the end of the air he is higher or lower than he was at the beginning. The first of these faults is

---

h *Art de chanter,* Part I, ch. vii.

that of voices too loud or too shrill, the coarse basses and the voices of women; the second that of weak chests. If one is singing with accompaniment, one sings falsely by not taking or by leaving the pitch prescribed by the harmony which the accompaniment must create.

"Expression on the part of a singer consists in entering, in a spirited and appropriate manner, into the feeling of the verses he sings, to inform them with passion is the term, as one who understands them and is the first to feel them. On the whole, the recitative and the smaller airs should be sung lightly, the great airs more consciously (*en s'écoutant davantage*), bringing out the full force of each note. It is noticeable that the fault of beginners is to sing too fast, that of the good provincial singers to go a little too slowly. Neatness (*propreté*) is that great mass of little observations, unknown to the Italians but so well known to our own masters, and which by their combined effect afford great pleasure, I assure you. To open the mouth, to produce (*porter*) the tones in the right way, to prepare, ornament (*préparer, battre*), and finish a cadence gracefully, etc. I listen attentively to a singer; the number of minutiae which must be observed does not embarrass me because I arrange them each under one of these three heads, and in case he satisfies me under these three heads, I do not ask him for a fourth. Of the three qualities to which I reduce the merit of a player, exactness is the principal one, especially for the players of instruments which are played directly by the fingers, without a bow. Count that of five hundred players of the lute, the harpsichord, etc., there will not be one who succeeds in playing as exactly (*nettement*) as one has the right to ask. And without exactness, what is a piece for the lute or the harpsichord? A noise, a jangling of harmonies in which one understands nothing. I would sooner listen to a hurdy-gurdy. After this precious exactness comes delicacy. It is in instruments what neatness (*propreté*) is in singing. It is at capturing delicacy that all those little observations aim that your masters burden you with.

"Last, to get the most out of the instrument. It is certainly necessary that an instrument should sound (*parle*), and it is true that to make it sound well is an art and a most important talent, but let us not lose sight of the capital maxim of monsieur le Chevalier, the golden mean. In truth, mademoiselle, your Italians carry too far a certain desire to elicit sound from their instruments. My intelligence, my heart, my ears tell me, all at once, that they produce a sound excessively shrill and violent. I am always afraid that the first stroke of the bow will make the violin fly into splinters, they use so much pressure. Besides, you comprehend that the sovereign perfection of an instrumentalist and of a singer would be to ally the three qualities, and if they could, to combine them in equal proportions. But I think I have observed that they never have all three in equal measure; the best instrumentalist, the best singer exceeds in some one point and is mediocre as regards the other two; at best, he excels in two and is passable in the third. I must remember further to say to you that keeping the measure with inviolable precision is in singing a part of accuracy, and in the playing of instruments the principal cause of exactness."

"I tender you my thanks, monsieur," said the Countess. "What you have said will comfort me and enlighten me. Let us continue our exploration of good taste. To acquire it, then, we shall accustom ourselves to judge of everything by listening to our natural feeling, and by confirming this with the aid of the little and the great rules; we shall pay attention, after judging, to the reputation of the composers; we shall consider our judgments final only after hearing pieces for the third or fourth time; we shall combine judgment by comparison with that by reasoning. At the Opéra we shall study with care the responses of the spectators; and we shall let our own judgment and that of the public be confirmed by the decrees of time. Is that all? Has good taste been completely acquired?"

"One more little practice to observe, madame," said the Chevalier. "As, with all that, we shall not at once become good judges, but shall now and then be mistaken, we shall form the habit of observing and eliminating our misconceptions. We shall at times examine our judgments as strictly as we examine the works of others, and when we find that we have committed an error, we shall follow it step by step; we shall retrace our way to the origin of our misconception, and after finding it we shall make precise note of this cause. The better we shall have noted it, the less subject we shall be to falling into it again. This practice is of great utility in every way and leads very quickly and very directly to good taste.

· · · · ·

"But if it is agreeable to you, we shall agree that the greatest possible evidence of good taste is to give praise where praise is due. We are under no obligation to find fault when we hear a piece of music that shocks us. We can leave the hall or we can remain silent. But I think that praise is a tribute which one owes to whoever has deserved it.

> And grudging mortals only when compelled
> Will offer incense to the rarest virtues.[1]

"It is an injustice to those mortals who make a profession of being wits, and a right-minded man praises and even delights in praising when he

---

1 Antoine de La Fosse, *Polixène*, a tragedy, Act I, Scene ii.

feels that someone has succeeded in pleasing him. Lully took pleasure in applauding the music of others which satisfied him. He said a number of times that the symphony to which has been written that irreverent potpourri of words,

Je gage de boire autant qu'un Suisse, etc.,[18]

seemed to him to be one of the most graceful he knew for any kind of instrument, especially for wind instruments. (Indeed, take note of this, you will have difficulty in finding another which rolls along (*roule*) or rather leaps so agreeably.) And he praised Lambert [14] and old Boësset [15] every day. M. Ménage [j] answered the Cardinal de Retz, who had asked him for a little instruction in how to become a judge of poems, 'Monseigneur, always say the thing is worthless; you can hardly go wrong.' Still, Monseigneur le Cardinal de Retz would sometimes have gone wrong, for after all there are some good poems. There are also some good musical works.

"The exquisite mark of good taste, then, is to praise those and only those. And that is not enough; the degree of praise must correspond to the degree of value of the work. To praise more or less than this is bad taste, and I am persuaded that here is the reef on which the greatest number of people are wrecked. He who can praise with reason and in due proportion will be a perfect connoisseur; do not doubt it, but recognize him by this perilous test. Do you not often laugh, madame, at the terms which certain persons use to express approval and the grand words they fill their mouths with? Do not expect a moderate eulogy from them. Just as what displeases them is always detestable, frightful, abominable, so what pleases them is never less than admirable, incomparable, inimitable, and the poor Abbé R[aguenet] thereby became lamentably addicted to —————— we noticed it sufficiently at the time. But none the less, Ménage gave sensible advice, and we can see that one is more commonly and more shamefully wrong in praising too much than in praising too little. What torrents of ridiculous praise! How many Madelons in this world, who 'would sooner have written an "oh, oh" than an epic poem!' [k] How many learned ladies who are in love with a '*quoi qu'on die!*' [l] And the unfortunate thing about these exaggerated praises is that they dishonor those who receive them. Those stiff people,[m] from whom politeness never extorts

---

j Ménage, Vol. II, p. 280.
k *Les Précieuses ridicules*, Scene x.
l *Les Femmes savantes*, Act III, Scene ii.
m La Bruyère.

18 I wager I can drink as much as a Swiss, etc.
14 Michel Lambert, composer of several books

of airs, was Lully's father-in-law and collaborated with him on the music of the *Ballet des arts* (1663).
15 Antoine Boësset, composer of *airs de cour*, is for Freneuse one of the principal representatives of classicism in French vocal music.

a word more than they think is their duty, are or seem to be more polite in this respect than the others. One is fortunate to have the courage to reply, as Segrais once did to Mademoiselle: '*Mordi!* would your Highness be any the fatter for having made me say something silly?' "

"Monsieur le Chevalier," said Mademoiselle M., coldly, "be on your guard, you too, against that ugly habit of overpraising."

. . . . . .

"Come, mademoiselle," said the old noble, "let's convert each other. And let's convert each other good-naturedly and quickly, for we haven't the time to disagree. You see that that lad there is a conscientious man and that his good faith is rather dry than dubious. He is not singing master for the Français, and it does not appear that he has ever had a share in the profits of the Opéra. Indeed, I advise you to believe him."

"I am sorry to be still unable to surrender," replied Mademoiselle M. "But even if your reasoning were unanswerable, I have a resource which would stand me in lieu of everything. It is the example of so many persons of eminent rank who are enchanted by Italian music. I rely upon their taste, which constitutes an authority superior to all your arguments."

"In the matter of taste, mademoiselle," retorted the Chevalier, "great nobles are only men like ourselves, whose name proves little. Each has his voice and the voices are equal, or at least it is not their quality which will determine their weight. But in case you put your trust in authorities, we have one on our side to whom you can defer. The King—

> I should name another name to you, madame
> Knew I of any higher.[n]—

the King, I say, is on our side. But I am no courtier. I do not wish to stress that name, however great it may be, or to maintain that it decides. Let us put aside from the person of the King all the splendor which his rank and his reign bestow upon it, and let us regard him only as a private person in his kingdom. It is only rendering him the justice which one would not refuse to a minister out of favor to say that of all the men of Europe he is one of those born with the greatest sense and the most direct and just intelligence. He loves music and is a competent judge of it. The great number of ballets in which he has danced and of operas composed expressly for him or of his choice, the honor he has done to Lully and to so many other musicians in permitting them to approach him, attest that he loves music. That he is a good judge of it, this same love of the art, his

---

n *Britannicus,* Act II, Scene iii.

familiarity with it, and the personal qualities that no one could refuse to concede that he possesses, are the proof. It is certain that the fashion of hailing with rapture the beauty of the operatic pieces now brought to us from Italy in bales has not yet reached him. Even in Lully's lifetime the King enjoyed a beautiful Italian piece when one was presented to him. He had a motet of Lorenzani [16] sung before him five times. He was fond of the air of M. de La Barre, attributed to Luigi, etc.[o] He had, as he still has, among his singers some *castrati,* in order to have them sing airs from time to time, a thing in which I agree that they are excellent. But for all that he was attached to the opera of Lully, to the music and musicians of France, and since the death of Lully he has not changed his taste; he has stoutly adhered to it, though there have been attempts to make him change it."

"If the recent story which a thousand persons have been telling is true," said the Marquis, "it is specific and shows very well that the magnificence and the lively pace of the Italian symphonies have failed to please him. Don't you know the story, ladies? A courtier of some importance who had extolled these symphonies to the King, brought him little Batiste, a French violinist of surprising natural aptitude who had studied for three or four years under Corelli. The interests of Italy were in good hands. You can imagine that little Batiste had studied his lesson besides. He played rapid passages which would have made Mademoiselle faint with delight or terror before Madame gave the word. The King listened with all the attention that Italy could desire, and when Italy waited to be admired, said, 'Send for one of my violinists!' One came; his name is not given; apparently it was one of mediocre merit, who happened to be at hand.

" 'An air from *Cadmus,*' said the King.

"The violinist played the first one that occurred to him, a simple, unified air; and *Cadmus* is not, of all our operas, that from which one would have chosen to select an air if the incident had been premeditated.

" 'I can only say to you, sir,' said the King to the courtier, 'that is my taste; that is my taste.' "

"I had already heard the story," interposed Madame du B. "They say that nothing is truer, and they say too that after Monseigneur, whose extreme fairness is recognized by all France, had heard Batistin [17] and Marchand of the King's Band play the violoncello, he greatly preferred

---

o *Le Mercure galant,* August, 1678, p. 246. ["Dolorosi pensieri," by J. C. La Barre, mistakenly attributed to Luigi Rossi.—Ed.]

16 Paolo Lorenzani, Italian composer resident

in Paris from 1678 to 1694, was influential as a representative of Italian music in France.

17 Jean Baptiste Stuck, Italian-born violoncellist and composer of German extraction, a resident of Paris during the greater part of his life.

the Frenchman to the Italian, in spite of the efforts and the insinuations of those who had presented the latter to him."

"The grand total, messieurs the partisans of Italy," said the Marquis, "is this. Do you yield to reason? Reason pronounces for us. Do you respect the authority of illustrious connoisseurs?

We reign over a heart alone worth all the rest.[p]

And in consequence, reconcile yourselves to believing that not only are the Italian operas greatly inferior to ours on the stage, which was the first question, but that the Italian operas on paper, and divided into vocal part and symphonies, are always absolutely bad in the first respect and rarely good in the second, this being the fundamental subject of the last disputes of our pretty musician. She has said that she would give us the cards for a little game of omber. May she be pleased to do so. Mademoiselle, who does not play, will have to go halves with monsieur le Chevalier."

.   .   .   .   .

---

[p] Prologue to *Armide*.

XI

Critical Views of Italian Opera: Addison and Marcello

61. Joseph Addison

One of the greatest English essayists and men of letters, Addison (1672–1719) was the leading contributor to the periodicals *The Tatler, The Spectator* and *The Guardian,* published by his friend Richard Steele from 1709 to 1713. Particularly important are Addison's contributions to *The Spectator.* The paper stood for reason and moderation in an age of bitter party strife. In his essays, Addison shows himself an able painter of life and manners. His witty, distinguished writings exerted an important influence on criticism, not only in England but also in France and Germany.

From The Spectator [1]

Tuesday, March 6, 1711.
Spectatum admissi risum teneatis?—Hor.[2]

AN OPERA may be allowed to be extravagantly lavish in its decorations, as its only design is to gratify the senses, and keep up an indolent attention in the audience. Common sense, however, requires, that there should be nothing in the scenes and machines which may appear childish and absurd. How would the wits of King Charles's time have laughed to have seen Nicolini [3] exposed to a tempest in robes of ermine, and sailing in an open boat upon a sea of pasteboard! What a field of raillery would they have been let into, had they been entertained with painted dragons spitting wildfire, enchanted chariots drawn by Flanders mares, and real cascades

1 Text: As edited by G. Gregory Smith for Everyman's Library (London, 1907), I, 20–23, 49–52.
2 Could you, my friends, if favored with a private view, refrain from laughing?—*Ars poetica,* 5. [Fairclough]

3 Nicolini, who sang in London at the Theatre in the Haymarket during the seasons of 1708 to 1712 and 1715 to 1717, created the principal castrato roles in Handel's operas *Rinaldo* and *Amadigi.*

in artificial landscapes! [4] A little skill in criticism would inform us, that shadows and realities ought not to be mixed together in the same piece; and that the scenes which are designed as the representations of nature, should be filled with resemblances, and not with the things themselves. If one would represent a wide champaign country filled with herds and flocks, it would be ridiculous to draw the country only upon the scenes, and to crowd several parts of the stage with sheep and oxen. This is joining together inconsistencies, and making the decoration partly real and partly imaginary. I would recommend what I have here said to the directors, as well as to the admirers, of our modern opera.

As I was walking in the streets about a fortnight ago, I saw an ordinary fellow carrying a cage full of little birds upon his shoulder; and, as I was wondering with myself what use he would put them to, he was met very luckily by an acquaintance, who had the same curiosity. Upon his asking him what he had upon his shoulder, he told him, that he had been buying sparrows for the opera. Sparrows for the opera! says his friend, licking his lips; what, are they to be roasted? No, no, says the other; they are to enter towards the end of the first act, and to fly about the stage.

This strange dialogue awakened my curiosity so far, that I immediately bought the opera, by which means I perceived the sparrows were to act the part of singing birds in a delightful grove; though, upon a nearer inquiry, I found the sparrows put the same trick upon the audience, that Sir Martin Mar-all [5] practised upon his mistress; for, though they flew in sight, the music proceeded from a consort of flagelets and bird-calls [6] which were planted behind the scenes. At the same time I made this discovery, I found, by the discourse of the actors, that there were great designs on foot for the improvement of the opera; that it had been proposed to break down a part of the wall, and to surprise the audience with a party of an hundred horse; and that there was actually a project of bringing the New River into the house, to be employed in jetteaus and water-works. This project, as I have since heard, is postponed till the summer season; when it is thought the coolness that proceeds from fountains and cascades will be more acceptable and refreshing to people of quality. In the meantime, to find out a more agreeable entertainment for the winter season, the opera of *Rinaldo* is filled with thunder and lightning, illuminations

---

4 These references are without exception to the stage machinery of Handel's *Rinaldo*.

5 Character in Dryden's comedy of the same name. In Act V, Sir Martin acts out the singing of a serenade to the lute, while the actual singing and playing is done in an adjoining room by his man. The scheme miscarries.

6 Almirena's cavatina "Augelletti che cantate" (*Rinaldo*, I, vi) has an accompaniment for flauto piccolo (or "flageolett" as Handel calls it in his autograph score), two flutes, and strings.

and fire-works; which the audience may look upon without catching cold, and indeed without much danger of being burnt; for there are several engines filled with water, and ready to play at a minute's warning, in case any such accident should happen. However, as I have a very great friendship for the owner of this theatre, I hope that he has been wise enough to insure his house before he would let this opera be acted in it.

It is no wonder that those scenes should be very surprising, which were contrived by two poets of different nations,[7] and raised by two magicians of different sexes. Armida (as we are told in the argument) was an Amazonian enchantress, and poor Signor Cassani (as we learn from the persons represented) a Christian conjuror (Mago Christiano). I must confess I am very much puzzled to find how an Amazon should be versed in the black art; or how a good Christian (for such is the part of the magician) should deal with the devil.

To consider the poets after the conjurors, I shall give you a taste of the Italian from the first lines of his preface: Eccoti, benigno lettore, un parto di poche sere, che se ben nato di notte, non è però aborto di tenebre, mà si farà conoscere figliolo d'Apollo con qualche raggio di Parnasso. "Behold, gentle reader, the birth of a few evenings, which, though it be the offspring of the night, is not the abortive of darkness, but will make itself known to be the son of Apollo, with a certain ray of Parnassus." He afterwards proceeds to call Mynheer Hendel the Orpheus of our age, and to acquaint us, in the same sublimity of style, that he composed this opera in a fortnight. Such are the wits to whose tastes we so ambitiously conform ourselves. The truth of it is, the finest writers among the modern Italians express themselves in such a florid form of words, and such tedious circumlocutions, as are used by none but pedants in our own country; and at the same time fill their writings with such poor imaginations and conceits, as our youths are ashamed of before they have been two years at the university. Some may be apt to think that it is the difference of genius which produces this difference in the works of the two nations; but to show there is nothing in this, if we look into the writings of the old Italians, such as Cicero and Virgil, we shall find that the English writers, in their way of thinking and expressing themselves, resemble those authors much more than the modern Italians pretend to do. And as for the poet himself,[8] from whom the dreams of this opera are taken, I must entirely agree with Monsieur Boileau, that one verse in Virgil is worth all the clinquant or tinsel of Tasso.[9]

---

7 Aaron Hill and Giacomo Rossi.
8 Torquato Tasso, from whose *Gerusalemme liberata* the story of *Rinaldo* is drawn.
9 *Satire*, IX, 176.

But to return to the sparrows; there have been so many flights of them let loose in this opera, that it is feared the house will never get rid of them; and that in other plays they make their entrance in very wrong and improper scenes, so as to be seen flying in a lady's bed-chamber, or perching upon a king's throne; besides the inconveniences which the heads of the audience may sometimes suffer from them. I am credibly informed, that there was once a design of casting into an opera the story of Whittington and his cat, and that in order to do it, there had been got together a great quantity of mice; but Mr. Rich, the proprietor of the playhouse, very prudently considered, that it would be impossible for the cat to kill them all, and that consequently the princes of the stage might be as much infested with mice, as the prince of the island was before the cat's arrival upon it; for which reason he would not permit it to be acted in his house. And indeed I cannot blame him: for, as he said very well upon that occasion, I do not hear that any of the performers in our opera pretend to equal the famous pied piper, who made all the mice of a great town in Germany follow his music, and by that means cleared the place of those little noxious animals.

Before I dismiss this paper, I must inform my reader, that I hear there is a treaty on foot with London and Wise (who will be appointed gardeners of the playhouse) to furnish the opera of Rinaldo and Armida with an orange-grove; and that the next time it is acted, the singing birds will be personated by tom-tits: the undertakers being resolved to spare neither pains nor money for the gratification of the audience.

Thursday, March 15, 1711.
Dic mihi, si fias tu leo, qualis eris?—Mart.[10]

There is nothing that of late years has afforded matter of greater amusement to the town than Signor Nicolini's combat with a lion [11] in the Haymarket, which has been very often exhibited to the general satisfaction of most of the nobility and gentry in the kingdom of Great Britain. Upon the first rumor of this intended combat, it was confidently affirmed, and is still believed by many in both galleries, that there would be a tame lion sent from the Tower every opera night, in order to be killed by Hydaspes; this report, though altogether groundless, so universally prevailed in the upper regions of the playhouse, that some of the most refined

---

10 Tell me, if you became a lion, what sort of lion will you be?—*Epigrammata*, XII, xcii. [Ker]

11 In the opera *L'Idaspe fedele* by Francesco Mancini, first performed in London, April 3, 1710.

politicians in those parts of the audience gave it out in whisper, that the lion was a cousin-german of the tiger who made his appearance in King William's days, and that the stage would be supplied with lions at the public expense, during the whole session. Many likewise were the conjectures of the treatment which this lion was to meet with from the hands of Signor Nicolini: some supposed that he was to subdue him in recitativo, as Orpheus used to serve the wild beasts in his time, and afterwards to knock him on the head; some fancied that the lion would not pretend to lay his paws upon the hero, by reason of the received opinion, that a lion will not hurt a virgin; several, who pretended to have seen the opera in Italy, had informed their friends, that the lion was to act a part in High-Dutch, and roar twice or thrice to a thorough bass, before he fell at the feet of Hydaspes. To clear up a matter that was so variously reported, I have made it my business to examine whether this pretended lion is really the savage he appears to be, or only a counterfeit.

But before I communicate my discoveries, I must acquaint the reader, that upon my walking behind the scenes last winter, as I was thinking on something else, I accidentally justled against a monstrous animal that extremely startled me, and upon my nearer survey of it, appeared to be a lion rampant. The lion, seeing me very much surprised, told me, in a gentle voice, that I might come by him if I pleased: "For," says he, "I do not intend to hurt anybody." I thanked him very kindly, and passed by him. And in a little time after saw him leap upon the stage, and act his part with very great applause. It has been observed by several, that the lion has changed his manner of acting twice or thrice since his first appearance; which will not seem strange, when I acquaint my reader that the lion has been changed upon the audience three several times. The first lion was a candle-snuffer, who being a fellow of a testy, choleric temper, overdid his part, and would not suffer himself to be killed so easily as he ought to have done; besides, it was observed of him, that he grew more surly every time he came out of the lion, and having dropped some words in ordinary conversation, as if he had not fought his best, and that he suffered himself to be thrown upon his back in the scuffle, and that he would wrestle with Mr. Nicolini for what he pleased, out of his lion's skin, it was thought proper to discard him; and it is verily believed, to this day, that had he been brought upon the stage another time, he would certainly have done mischief. Besides, it was objected against the first lion, that he reared himself so high upon his hinder paws, and walked in so erect a posture, that he looked more like an old man than a lion.

The second lion was a tailor by trade, who belonged to the playhouse, and had the character of a mild and peaceable man in his profession. If the former was too furious, this was too sheepish for his part; insomuch that after a short, modest walk upon the stage, he would fall at the first touch of Hydaspes, without grappling with him, and giving him an opportunity of showing his variety of Italian trips. It is said, indeed, that he once gave him a rip in his flesh-colored doublet; but this was only to make work for himself, in his private character of a tailor. I must not omit that it was this second lion who treated me with so much humanity behind the scenes.

The acting lion at present is, as I am informed, a country gentleman, who does it for his diversion, but desires his name may be concealed. He says, very handsomely, in his own excuse, that he does not act for gain; that he indulges an innocent pleasure in it; and that it is better to pass away an evening in this manner than in gaming and drinking: but at the same time says, with a very agreeable raillery upon himself, that if his name should be known, the ill-natured world might call him, "the ass in the lion's skin." This gentleman's temper is made out of such a happy mixture of the mild and choleric, that he outdoes both his predecessors, and has drawn together greater audiences than have been known in the memory of man.

I must not conclude my narrative, without taking notice of a groundless report that has been raised to a gentleman's disadvantage, of whom I must declare myself an admirer; namely, that Signor Nicolini and the lion have been seen sitting peaceably by one another, and smoking a pipe together behind the scenes; by which their common enemies would insinuate, that it is but a sham combat which they represent upon the stage: but upon inquiry I find, that if any such correspondence has passed between them, it was not till the combat was over, when the lion was to be looked upon as dead, according to the received rules of the drama. Besides, this is what is practised every day in Westminster Hall, where nothing is more usual than to see a couple of lawyers, who have been tearing each other to pieces in the court, embracing one another as soon as they are out of it.

I would not be thought, in any part of this relation, to reflect upon Signor Nicolini, who in acting this part only complies with the wretched taste of his audience; he knows very well, that the lion has many more admirers than himself; as they say of the famous equestrian statue on the Pont Neuf at Paris, that more people go to see the horse than the king who sits upon it. On the contrary, it gives me a just indignation to see a person whose action gives new majesty to kings, resolution to heroes, and softness to lovers, thus sinking from the greatness of his behavior, and degraded into the character of the London Prentice. I have often wished, that our tragedians would copy after this great master in action. Could they make the same use of their arms and legs, and inform their faces with as significant looks and passions, how glorious would an English tragedy appear with that action which is capable of giving a dignity to the forced thoughts, cold conceits, and unnatural expressions of an Italian opera! In the meantime, I have related this combat of the lion, to show what are at present the reigning entertainments of the politer part of Great Britain.

Audiences have often been reproached by writers for the coarseness of their taste; but our present grievance does not seem to be the want of a good taste, but of common sense.

62. Benedetto Marcello

Born at Venice in 1686 to patrician parents, Marcello was distinguished both as a composer and as a writer. His most significant and best-known musical work is the *Estro poetico-armonico*, a collection, in eight volumes, of settings of fifty Psalms for one to four voices with *basso continuo* and a few instruments. Marcello was also a composer of instrumental music.

Among his literary works, the satire *Il teatro alla moda* (c. 1720) is the most famous. It marks, within the Italian scene, the spontaneous reaction of those concerned with the musical theater as a temple of dramatic art against all those—singers, composers, men of the stage—who wanted to use it for the gratification of their personal vanities. Although more than two centuries old, the witty work has lost none of its interest.

From Il teatro alla moda [1]

[*1720*]

THE

THEATER

A LA MODE

OR

Safe and easy METHOD of properly composing and producing Italian OPERAS according to modern practice
in which

1 Text: Tessier's edition (Venice, 1887), pp. 51–79. For a reproduction of the original title page and an explanation of its satiric vignette and imprint, see R. G. Pauly, "Benedetto Marcello's Satire on Early 18th-Century Opera," *Musical Quarterly*, XXXIV (1948), 222–233, with refer- ences to important studies by Malipiero and Rolandi. A complete translation of the *Teatro alla moda*, by Mr. Pauly, is published in the *Musical Quarterly*, XXXIV (1948), 371–403, and XXXV (1949), 85–105.

Are given useful and necessary recommendations to Poets, Composers
of Music, Singers of either sex, Impresarios,
Musicians, Designers and Painters of Scenes, Buffo parts,
Costumers, Pages, Supernumeraries, Prompters, Copyists,
Protectors and MOTHERS of Lady Singers, and other
Persons connected with the Theater

DEDICATED

BY THE AUTHOR OF THE BOOK

TO ITS COMPOSER

[Vignette]

Printed in the SUBURBS of BELISANIA for ALDIVIVA
LICANTE, at the Sign of the BEAR in the BOAT
For sale in CORAL STREET at the
GATE of ORLANDO'S PALACE
And will be reprinted each year with new additions

TO THE POETS

In the first place the modern poet will not need to read or ever to have
read the ancient Latin and Greek authors, because not even the ancient
Greeks or Romans ever read the moderns.

Likewise he will not need to profess any understanding of Italian meter
or verse, except for some superficial notion that a line is composed of seven
or eleven syllables, by the aid of which rule he may then make them, according to his whim, of three, five, nine, thirteen, and even of fifteen.

But he will say that he has pursued all the studies of mathematics,
painting, chemistry, medicine, etc., protesting that finally his genius has
forced him to take up poetry, not meaning by this the method of correctly accenting, rhyming, etc., etc., or the terms of poetry, or the fables,
or the histories, but rather, at most, introducing into his works some terms
of the sciences indicated above, or of other sciences which have nothing
to do with poetic training.

He will accordingly call Dante, Petrarch, Ariosto, etc., obscure, harsh,
and tedious poets, and therefore of no account or little to be imitated. But
he will have a stock of various modern poems, from which he will take

sentiments, thoughts, and entire lines, calling the theft praiseworthy imitation.

Before composing his opera the modern poet will seek to obtain from the impresario a precise note of the number and quality of the scenes the latter desires, in order to include them all in his drama, taking care, if there enter into it any elaborate effects of sacrifices or banquets or descending heavens or other spectacles, to come to an understanding with the stage hands as to how many dialogues, soliloquies, ariettas, etc., he must use to prolong the preceding scenes, to enable them to get all ready at their convenience, even at the risk of enfeebling the opera and intolerably boring the audience.

He will write the whole opera without formulating any plot, simply composing it line by line, in order that the public, having no understanding of the intrigue, may remain curious to the very end. Above all, let the good modern poet have a care that all his characters come on very often to no purpose, for then they must necessarily make their exits one by one, singing the customary *canzonetta*.

The poet will never inquire into the merits of the actors, but will rather ask whether the impresario will have a good bear, a good lion, a good nightingale, good thunderbolts, earthquakes, flashes of lightning, etc.

At the end of his opera he will introduce a magnificent scene, of striking appearance, to insure that the public will not walk out in the middle of the performance, and he will conclude with the customary chorus in honor of either the sun or the moon or else of the impresario.

In dedicating his book to some great personage, he will try to find one rather rich than learned, and will make a bargain to reward some good mediator, say the cook or the major domo of the patron himself, with a third of the proceeds of the dedication. From his patron he will ascertain in the first place the number and degree of the titles with which to adorn his name on the title page, augmenting the said titles by affixing "etc., etc., etc., etc." He will exalt the family and glories of his patron's ancestors, using frequently in his dedicatory epistle the terms "liberality," "generous soul," etc., and if (as sometimes happens) he finds in his personage no occasion for praise, he will say that he himself is silent in order not to offend the modesty of his patron, but that Fame with her hundred sonorous trumpets will sound his immortal name from pole to pole. Finally he will conclude by saying, in token of profoundest veneration, that he kisses the jumps of the fleas on the feet of His Excellency's dog.

It will be most useful to the modern poet to protest to the reader that he composed the opera in his most tender years; and if he can add that he did this in a few days (even if he has worked upon it for more than a few years), that will be a particularly good modern touch, showing that he has completely renounced the ancient precept,

Nonumque prematur in annum.[2]

In such a case he will be able to declare further that he is a poet only for his own amusement, to lighten the burden of more serious occupations; that he had no thought of publishing his work; but that by the advice of friends and the command of his patron he has been induced to do so, and not at all by any desire of fame or hope of gain. And further that the distinguished virtuosity of the cast, the renowned artistry of the composer of the music, and the dexterity of the supernumeraries and the bear will correct the defects of the drama.

In his account of the argument he will discourse at great length on the precepts of tragedy and the art of poetry, following the reflections of Sophocles, Euripides, Aristotle, Horace, etc. He will add, in conclusion, that the poet of today must abandon every good rule to adapt himself to the genius of the present corrupt age, the licentiousness of the theater, the extravagance of the conductor of the orchestra, the indiscretion of the musicians, the delicacy of the bear, the supernumeraries, etc.

But let him be careful not to neglect the customary explanation of the three most important points of every drama: the place, the time, and the action, indicating that the place is in *such and such a theater*, the time *from eight P.M. until midnight*, the action *the bankrupting of the impresario*.

It is not essential that the subject of the opera be historical. Rather, since all the Greek and Latin stories have been treated by the ancient Greeks and Romans and by the most select Italians of the good age, the task of the modern poet is to invent a fiction, contriving in it answers of oracles, royal shipwrecks, evil auguries from roast oxen, etc.; it being enough that among the dramatis personae some historic name should be offered to the public. All the rest may then be invented at the author's pleasure, taking care, above everything, that the text be not over 1,200 lines long, more or less, including the ariettas.

Then, to give his opera a greater reputation, the modern poet will aim to name it rather from one of the principal actions than from a character; e.g., instead of "Amadis" or "Buovo" or "Bertha at the Camp," he will call it "The Generous Ingratitude," "Vengeance at the Funeral," or "The Bear in the Boat."

2 And keep it back until the ninth year.—Horace, *Ars poetica*, 388. [Fairclough]

The incidental details of the opera will be prisons, stilettos, poisons, bear hunts, hunting the wild ox, earthquakes, sacrifices, settlements of contracts, mad scenes, etc., because by such unexpected things the public is extraordinarily thrilled; and if it should ever be possible to introduce a scene in which some of the characters should sit down and others should fall asleep in a grove or garden while a plot was being laid against their lives, and should wake up (something never seen in an Italian theater), that would reach the very acme of the marvelous.

The modern poet need not devote much labor to the style of his drama, reflecting that it must be heard and understood by the multitude, but in his desire to make it more intelligible he will leave out the customary articles and will use long periods, which are not customary, being lavish with epithets when he finds it necessary to fill out some line of a recitative or *canzonetta.*

He will provide himself, further, with a large number of old operas, from which he will take his subject and setting, changing only the verse and a few names of characters. He will do the same thing in adapting dramas from French into Italian, from prose into verse, or from tragic to comic, adding or taking out characters according to the needs of the impresario.

If he has no other resource, he will become a great schemer in order to compose operas, joining forces with another poet, furnishing the subject and writing a share of the verses, under an agreement to divide the proceeds of the dedication and the profits of publication.

But he will absolutely never allow the singer to make his exit without the customary *canzonetta,* especially when, by a vicissitude of the drama, the latter must go out to die, commit suicide, drink poison, etc.

He will never read the entire opera to the impresario, though he will recite snatches of some of the scenes to him and repeatedly recite bits from the scene of the poison or the sacrifice or the chairs or the bears or the settlements of contracts; adding that if such a scene as that deceives his expectations, there is no use in writing operas any more.

Let the good modern poet be careful to understand nothing at all of music, for such knowledge was characteristic of the ancient poets, according to Strabo, Pliny, Plutarch, etc., who did not separate the poet from the musician or the musician from the poet, as was true of Amphion, Philammon, Demodocus, Terpander, etc., etc., etc.

The ariettas should have no relation whatever to the recitative, but the poet should do his best to introduce into them for the most part the terms "butterfly," "mosquito," "nightingale," "quail," "bark," "canoe," "jessamine," "gillyflower," "saucepan," "cooking pot," "tiger," "lion," "whale," "crayfish," "turkey," "cold capon," etc., etc., etc., for in this way he reveals himself as a good philosopher, distinguishing the properties of animals, plants, flowers, etc., in his similes.

Before the opera is produced, the poet must praise the singers, the impresario, the orchestra, the supernumeraries, etc. If the opera, later, should not be well received, he must inveigh against the actors, "who did not perform it according to his conception, thinking only of singing"; against the composer, "who did not comprehend the force of the scenes, giving all his attention to the ariettas"; against the impresario, "who with excessive economy produced it with an inadequate setting"; and against the musicians and supernumeraries, "who were all drunk every evening, etc."; protesting further that he had composed the drama in another manner; that he consented to make cuts and additions at the whim of those in command and particularly of the insatiable prima donna and the bear; that he will make it possible to read it in the original version; that at present he hardly recognizes it as his own; and if anyone doubts this, let him ask the housemaid or the laundress, who read and considered it before anyone else.

At the rehearsals of the opera he will never disclose his intention to any of the actors, wisely reflecting that they desire to do everything in their own way.

If the requirements of the opera leave any member of the company without a part, he will add one for him as soon as the virtuoso himself or his patron requests it, having always ready to hand a few hundreds of ariettas for use in additions, alterations, etc., and will not neglect to fill the libretto with the customary superfluous verses enclosed between inverted commas.

If a husband and wife should be in prison and one of them should go out to die, the other must inevitably stay behind to sing an arietta. The words of this should be lively, to relieve the sadness of the audience and to make them understand that it is all in fun.

If two characters talk love or plan conspiracies, ambushes, etc., they must always do it in the presence of the pages and supernumeraries.

If any character needs to write, the poet will have the scene changed and a small table and an armchair brought in. After the letter is written, he will have the table taken away, for the said table must no longer be thought of as a part of the setting in which the writing is done. He will follow the same practice with the throne, and with chairs, sofas, grass seats, etc.

He will present dances of gardeners in the halls of the royal palace and dances of courtiers in groves, and will note that the dance of the Piraeus may be presented in a hall, in a courtyard, in Persia, in Egypt, etc.

In case the modern poet discovers that the singer enunciates badly, he must not correct him, because if the singer should remedy his fault and speak distinctly, it might hurt the sale of the libretto.

If members of the cast ask him on which side they should make their entrances and exits or in which direction they should make gestures and what they should wear, he will let them enter, exit, make gestures, and dress in their own way.

If the meters of the arias should not please the composer, the poet will be prompt to change them, introducing into them further, at the latter's caprice, winds, storms, fogs, siroccos, the Levanter, the Tramontane, etc. Many of the arias should be so long that the beginning will be forgotten before the end is reached.

The opera should be presented with only six characters, having due care that two or three parts are so introduced that in case of necessity they may be cut out without detriment to the action.

The part of the father or the tyrant, when it is the principal one, should always be entrusted to *castrati*, reserving tenors and basses for captains of the guard, confidants of the king, shepherds, messengers, etc.

Poets of little credit will have in the course of the year employment in the courts or on estates; they will have charge of accounts, copy parts, correct for the press, speak evil of each other, etc., etc., etc.

The poet will claim a box from the impresario, half of which he will sublet months before the opera is put on and for all the first nights, filling the other half with masks, whom he will bring into the theater free.

He will visit the prima donna frequently, because the success or failure of the opera usually depends upon her, and he will adapt the opera to her genius, lengthening or shortening her role or that of the bear or other characters, etc. But he will not allow himself to confide to her anything relating to the intrigue of the opera, for the modern virtuosa does not need to understand anything of that; giving instead, at the most, some little information on the subject to her mother, father, brother, or protector.

He will call upon the composer and will read the drama to him many times, and will inform him where the recitative is to proceed lento, where presto, where appassionato, etc., as the modern composer is not expected to perceive anything of that sort himself, and will then burden the arias with "very brief ritornelli and passages" (rather, many complete repetitions of the words), that the poetry may be the better enjoyed.

He will be extremely polite to the members of the orchestra, the costumers, the bear, the pages, the supernumeraries, etc., commending his opera to them all, etc., etc., etc., etc.

TO THE COMPOSERS OF MUSIC

The modern composer of music will not need to have any notion of the rules of good composition, apart from a few universal principles of practice.

He will not understand the numerical proportions of music, or the excellent effect of contrary movements, or the false relation of the tritone or of major sixths. He will not know the names and number of the modes or tones, or how they are classified, or what are their properties. Rather, he will say on that subject, "There are only two modes, major and minor; the major, the one which has the major third; the minor, the one which has the minor third," not rightly perceiving what the ancients meant by the major and minor mode.

He will not distinguish one from another the three genera: diatonic, chromatic, and enharmonic, but will confound at his whim the progressions of all three in a single *canzonetta*, to distinguish himself completely by this modern confusion.

He will use the major and minor accidentals at his own free will, confounding their signs at random. Likewise he will use the enharmonic sign in the place of the chromatic, saying that they are the same thing, because each of them adds a small semitone, and in this way he will show himself wholly unaware that the chromatic sign always belongs between tones, to divide them, and the enharmonic only between semitones, its especial property being to divide large semitones and nothing else. For this reason the modern composer, as has been said above, needs to be entirely in the dark as regards these matters and others like them.

Consequently he will have little facility in reading and still less in writing, and therefore will not understand Latin, even though he must compose church music, into which he will introduce sarabands, gigues, courantes, etc., calling them fugues, canons, double counterpoints, etc.

Turning now to our discussion of the theater, the modern master musician will understand nothing of poetry. He will not make out the meaning of the speeches; he will not distinguish the long and short syllables, or the force of the scenes, etc. Likewise he will not observe the special qualities of the stringed or the wind instruments if he plays the harpsichord, and if he is a player of stringed instruments, he will not take the pains to understand the harpsichord, being convinced that he can become a good composer in the modern manner without practical acquaintance with that instrument.

It will do no harm, however, if the modern composer should have been for many years a player of the violin or the viola, and also copyist for some noted composer, and should have kept the original manuscripts of his operas, serenades, etc., stealing from them and still others ideas for ritornelli, overtures, arias, recitatives, variations on "La Folia," choruses, etc.

Therefore, on receiving the opera from the poet, he will prescribe to him the meters and the number of lines of the arias, entreating him, further, to provide him with a fair copy, without omitting any full stops, commas, or question marks, etc., though in setting it to music he will show no regard for full stops, question marks, or commas.

Before putting hand to the opera, he will call upon all the ladies of the company, whom he will offer to serve according to their genius, i.e., with *arie senza bassi*,[3] with *furlanette*, with rigadoons, etc., all with violins, bear, and supernumeraries in unison.

He will take care, after that, never to read the entire opera, to avoid getting confused, but will set it line by line, remembering further to have all the arias quickly changed, using in them, then, motives already prepared in the course of the year, and if, as most often happens, the new words to the said arias fail to fit the notes felicitously, he will again pester the poet until he is wholly satisfied with them.

He will compose all the arias with an accompaniment for the instruments, taking care that each part moves forward with notes or figures of the same value, whether these be quarters, eighths, or sixteenths. For to compose well in the modern manner, one should aim at noise rather than at harmony, which latter consists principally in the different values of the figures, some of them tied over, others not, etc., but to escape harmony of this kind, the modern composer must not use any other suspensions than the usual fourth and third in the cadence, and if in this he still suspects himself of having too great a leaning toward the ancient, he will end his arias with all the instruments in unison.

Let him further see to it that the arias, to the very end of the opera, are alternatively a lively one and a pathetic one, without regard to the words, the modes, or the proprieties of the scene. If substantive nouns,

---

3 See, for example, in Handel's *Agrippina:* I, xviii, "Ho un non sò che nel cor" (Agrippina); III, x, "Bel piacere" (Poppea).

e.g., *padre, impero, amore, arena, regno, beltà, lena, core,* etc., etc., or adverbs, as *no, senza, già,* and others, should occur in the arias, the modern composer should base upon them a long passage; e.g., *paaa . . . impeeee . . . amoooo . . . areeee . . . reeee . . . beltàaaaa . . . lenaaaaa . . . ,* etc.; *nooo . . . seeeeen . . . giàaaaaa . . . ,* etc. The object is to get away from the ancient style, which did not use passages on substantive nouns or on adverbs, but only on words signifying some passion or movement; e.g., *tormento, affanno, canto, volar, cader,* etc., etc., etc., etc.

In the recitatives the modulation shall be at the composer's fancy, moving the bass with all possible frequency, and as soon as each scene is composed, he will have his wife hear it, in case he is married to a virtuosa; if not, his servant, his copyist, etc., etc., etc., etc.

All the ariettas should be preceded by very long ritornelli with violins in unison, composed ordinarily of eighth and sixteenth notes, and these will be played mezzopiano, to make them more novel and less tedious, having a care that the arias which follow have nothing to do with the said ritornelli.

The ariettas, further, should proceed *senza basso,* and to keep the singer on the pitch, have him accompanied by violins in unison, sounding also a few bass notes on the violas, but this is not essential.

When the musico has a cadenza, the composer will silence all the instruments, leaving it free to the virtuoso or virtuosa to carry on as long as he pleases.

He will not take much pains with duets or choruses, but will contrive to have them cut out.

For the rest, the modern composer will add that he composes with little study and with a vast number of errors in order to satisfy the audience, with this formula condemning the taste of the audience, which in truth now and then enjoys what it hears, even if it is not good, because it has no opportunity of hearing anything better.

He will serve the impresario for the smallest of pay, remembering the thousands of scudi that the virtuosi cost him, and for that reason will be content with less than the lowest of these receives, provided that he is not worse off than the bear and the supernumeraries.

In walking with singers, especially *castrati,* the composer will always place himself at their left and keep one step behind, hat in hand, remembering that the lowest of them is, in the operas, at least a general, a captain of the king's forces, of the queen's forces, etc.

He will quicken or retard the tempo of the arias to suit the genius of the virtuosi, covering up whatever bad judgment they show with the reflection that his own reputation, credit, and interests are in their hands, and for that reason, if need be, he will alter arias, recitatives, sharps, flats, naturals, etc.

All the *canzonette* should be made up of the same things, that is, of extremely long passages, of syncopation, of chromatic progressions, of alterations of syllables, of repetitions of meaningless words, e.g., *amore amore, impero impero, Europa Europa, furori furori, orgoglio orgoglio,* etc., etc., etc. Consequently, when the modern composer is writing an opera, he should always have before his eyes, for the sake of this effect, an inventory of all the aforesaid terms, without some one of which no aria will ever come to an end, and that in order to ecape as far as possible from variety, which is no longer in use.

At the end of a recitative in flats, he will suddenly attack an aria with three or four sharps in the signature and then return to flats in the following recitative; this by way of novelty.

Likewise the modern composer will divide the sentiment or meaning of the words, making the musico sing the first line, though by itself it has no meaning at all, and then inserting a long ritornello for violins, violas, etc., etc.[4]

If the modern composer should give lessons to some virtuosa of the opera house, let him have a care to charge her to enunciate badly, and with this object to teach her a great number of divisions and of graces, so that not a single word will be understood, and by this means the music will stand out better and be appreciated.

When the musicians play the bass without harpsichords or double basses, it makes no difference at all that the strings of the said bass (with regard to the voice and the bowed instrument) should drown out the singer's part, as usually occurs the more in the arias of the contralti, tenors, and basses.

The modern composer must also compose *canzonette*, especially for contralto or mezzo-soprano, which the basses will accompany by playing the same notes in the octave below and the violins, in the octave above, writing out all the parts in the score. In so doing he will regard himself as composing in three parts, though the arietta actually has only a single part, diversified only by the octave in low and high.[5]

If the modern composer wishes to compose in four parts, two of them must indispensably proceed in unison or in octaves; at the same time he

---

[4] A reference to the so-called "Devisen-Arie" or "Motto-Aria."

[5] See, for example, in Handel's *Agrippina:* II, xiv, "Col raggio placido" (Pallante).

will also diversify the movement of the subject; for example, if one part proceeds by half notes or quarter notes, let the other proceed by eighths or sixteenths, etc.

Basses proceeding by quarter notes (*crome*) will be called "chromatic basses" by the modern composer, for it would not be fitting for him to know the meaning of the word "chromatic." He will also take pains to know nothing at all of poetry, because knowledge of this kind was suitable to the ancient musicians, that is, to Pindar, Arion, Orpheus, Hesiod, etc., who according to Pausanias were most excellent poets, no less than musicians, and the modern composer must do his utmost to be unlike them, etc.

He will captivate the public with ariettas accompanied by pizzicati or muted instruments, marine trumpets, cymbals, etc.

The modern composer will claim from the impresario, in addition to his fee, the present of a poet, to make use of as he pleases, and as soon as the latter has written his text, he will read it to his friends, who understand nothing of it, and by their opinion he will regulate ritornelli, passages, appoggiaturas, enharmonic sharps, chromatic flats, etc.

Let the modern composer be careful not to neglect the customary chromatic or accompanied recitative, and to that end let him oblige the poet, presented to him by the impresario as above, to provide him with a scene of a sacrifice, a mad scene, a prison scene, etc.[6]

He will never compose arias with *basso solo obbligato*,[7] bearing in mind that this is out of date and that, further, in the time required to compose one such, he could compose a dozen accompanied by the instruments.

Desiring, then, to compose some arias with basses, he must make up the latter out of two or at most three notes, repeated or else tied together after the fashion of a pedal point, and must see to it, above all things, that all the second parts [8] are made up of secondhand stuff.

If the impresario should later complain about the music, the composer will protest that he is unjust in so doing, as the opera contains a third more than the usual number of notes and took almost fifty hours to compose.

If some aria should fail to please the virtuose or their protectors, he will say that it needs to be heard in the theater with the costumes, the lights, the supernumeraries, etc.

---

6 For accompanied recitatives of this kind see Handel's *Il Pastor fido*, III, vii (sacrifice), *Orlando*, II, xi (mad scene), and *Rodelinda*, III, iii (prison scene); in particular, the treatment of prison scenes in this style had by 1733 become so familiar that the *Beggar's Opera* could ridicule it effectively in the scene of MacHeath's soliloquy, suggested by the prison scene in Ariosti's *Coriolanus*.

7 "When the composer selects and restricts himself to a particular subject in the bass, maintaining it strictly throughout the whole piece without departing from it (unless ever so slightly or by bringing it at the fifth), so that the dominant or melodious part is accommodated to it."— Johann Mattheson, *Das neu-eröffnete Orchestre* (Hamburg, 1713), p. 182.

8 I.e., the middle sections of the da capo arias.

At the end of each ritornello, the conductor must nod to the virtuosi, in order that they may come in at the right time, which they will never know of themselves, because of the customary length and variation of the said ritornello.

He will compose some arias in bass style, for all that they are to be sung by soprani and contralti.

The modern composer will oblige the impresario to provide a great number of violins, oboes, horns, etc., preferring to let him economize on double basses, for these should not be used except in the preliminary tuning.

The Sinfonia will consist of a *tempo francese*, or *prestissimo* of eighth notes in the mode with the major third, which must be followed in the usual fashion by a *piano* in the same mode with the minor third, concluding finally with a minuet, gavotte, or gigue, again in the major mode, in this manner avoiding fugues, suspensions, *soggetti*, etc., as antiquities entirely excluded from modern practice.

The composer will arrange that the best arias fall to the prima donna, and if the opera needs cutting, he will not permit the removal of arias or ritornelli, but rather of entire scenes of recitative, of the bear, of earthquakes, etc.

If the second lady should complain that she has fewer notes in her part than the prima donna, he will manage to console her by making the number equal with the aid of passages in the arias, appoggiaturas, graces in good taste, etc., etc., etc.

The modern composer will make use of old arias composed in other countries, making profound reverences to the protectors of virtuosi, lovers of music, renters of stools, supernumeraries, stage hands, etc., and commending himself to all.

If *canzonette* must be changed, he will never change them for the better, and he will say of any arietta that fails to please that it is a masterpiece, but was ruined by the musicians, not appreciated by the public, taking care to put out the lights which he has at the harpsichord for the *arie senza basso*, to keep his head from getting too hot, and to relight them for the recitatives.

The modern composer will show the greatest attentions to all the virtuose of the operas, presenting them all with old cantatas transposed to fit their voices, in addition saying to each one that the opera owes its success to her talent. The same thing he will say to each man in the cast, to each member of the orchestra, to each supernumerary, bear, earthquake, etc.

Every evening he will bring in masks free of admission fee, whom he will seat near him in the orchestra pit, occasionally giving the cello or the double bass an evening off for the sake of his guests.

All modern composers will have the following words placed under the announcement of the cast:

The music is by the ever most archi-celebrated Signor N. N., conductor of the orchestra, of concerts, of chamber concerts, dancing master, fencing master, etc., etc., etc., etc.

XII

The Reformulation of the Theory of Harmony and Counterpoint

63. J. J. Fux

Born in Styria in 1660, Johann Joseph Fux died at Vienna in 1741. He became composer to the Imperial Court in 1698, second choirmaster at the Cathedral of St. Stephen in 1705, and first choirmaster at the Court in 1715. Fux wrote an important quantity of sacred music (including about 50 masses and 3 requiems); 10 oratorios and 18 operas; also a number of orchestral suites, trio-sonatas, etc., of which only a small part was published during his lifetime. Fux is still well remembered today as the author of the theoretical work *Gradus ad Parnassum* (1725), which has served generations as a textbook for strict counterpoint. Its system is based, in an ultra-conservative way, on the church modes.

From the Gradus ad Parnassum [1]

[1725]

Book Two

DIALOGUE

(Josephus) I COME TO YOU, revered master, to be instructed in the precepts and laws of music.

(Aloysius) What, you wish to learn musical composition?

(J) That is indeed my wish.

(A) Are you unaware that the study of music is a boundless sea, not to be concluded within the years of Nestor? Truly, you are planning to assume a burden greater than Aetna. For if the choice of a mode of life is universally a matter full of difficulty, since on this choice, rightly or

1 Text: The original edition (Vienna, 1725), pp. 43–81. A complete translation, by Alfred Mann, was published by W. W. Norton & Co., Inc., in 1943. In this dialogue between master and pupil, Fux names the master for Palestrina and modestly gives his own name to the pupil.

wrongly made, the good or bad fortune of all the rest of life depends, how much more cautious foresight must he who thinks of entering upon the path of this discipline use before he can venture to adopt a counsel and decide his own case! For a musician and a poet are born. You must think back, whether from tender years you have felt yourself impelled to this study by a certain natural impulse, and whether it has befallen you to be intensely moved by the delight of harmony.

(J) Yes, most intensely. For, from the time when I hardly had the power of reason, an unknowing child, I have been borne unwillingly onward, carried away by the force of this ardor, directing all my thoughts and cares toward music, and still burning with a wonderful zeal to learn it with full understanding. Day and night my ears seem to be filled with sweet modulation, so that there seems to me to be no ground whatever for doubting the genuineness of my vocation. Nor do I shrink from the severity of the task, which with nature's aid I am confident of mastering without difficulty. For I have heard it said by a certain old man that study is rather a pleasure than a task.

(A) I am wonderfully delighted to perceive how your nature is inclined. I shall raise just one more difficulty; if this can be resolved, I shall inscribe you among my disciples.

(J) Speak freely, honored master. But I am certain that I shall not be deterred from my purpose, either by the cause you have in mind or by any other.

(A) Are you perhaps tickled by the hope of future riches and of abundance of private possessions in wishing to embrace this mode of life? If that is the case, take my advice and change your purpose. For not Plutus but Apollo presides over Parnassus. Those who are inspired by covetousness and seek the way to wealth must follow a different road.

(J) Not at all. I wish you to be persuaded that the compass of my wish is none other than the very love of music, free from any desire of gain. In addition, I recall having been very often admonished by my teacher that if we are content with a modest way of life, we shall wish to be more zealous for virtue, fame, and distinction than for means, for virtue is its own reward.

(A) I am incredibly pleased to have found a youth after my own heart. But do you know all the things concerning intervals, the classification of consonances and dissonances, the varieties of motions, and the four rules,[2] which have been said in the preceding book?

---

2 The four "cardinal" rules are the following: (1) one proceeds from perfect consonance to perfect by contrary or oblique motion; (2) from perfect consonance to imperfect by all three motions (parallel, contrary, or oblique); (3) from imperfect consonance to perfect by contrary or oblique motion; (4) from imperfect consonance to imperfect by all three motions.

(J) So far as I know, I think that not one of them is hidden from me.

(A) Then let us proceed to our work, taking our beginning from God himself, thrice greatest, the fount of all sciences.

(J) Before we begin our lessons, permit me first, revered master, to ask what is to be understood by the name counterpoint, a very common word, which I so frequently hear from the lips not only of the skilled but even of those ignorant of music.

(A) You are right to ask, for this indeed is to be the chief object of our study and labor. You must know that in old times points were set down instead of the modern notes, so that a composition with points set down against points used to be called counterpoint. This term is now used in spite of the change in the notes, and the name of counterpoint is understood to mean a composition elaborated according to the rules of art. Counterpoint as a genus comprises a number of species, which we shall successively examine. Meanwhile, let us begin with the simplest species, namely:

First Exercise—First Lesson

OF NOTE AGAINST NOTE

(J) Through your kindness, my first question has been satisfactorily answered. Now tell me, simply, what this first species of counterpoint is— the species note against note.

(A) I shall tell you. It is the simplest combination of two or more voices and of notes of equal value, consisting wholly of consonances. The species of the notes is immaterial, provided all are of the same value. But inasmuch as the semibreve is the most readily understood, I have thought it advantageous for us to use it in these exercises. With God's help, therefore, let us begin with the combining of two voices, setting down as our foundation some cantus firmus, either freely invented or taken from a choir book. For example:

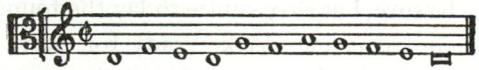

To each of these notes is to be given, in the cantus above, its particular consonance, observing the considerations of the motions and rules expressed at the end of the preceding book and employing chiefly contrary and oblique motion, through the use of which we shall not easily fall into error. Greater precaution will be necessary in progressing from one note to another in parallel motion, in which case, the danger of error being greater, we must also pay greater attention to the rules.

(J) From the clarity of the motions and rules, all that you have just said seems familiar to me. Yet I recall your making the distinction that, among the consonances, some are perfect, others imperfect; it seems to me, therefore, that I need to know whether some distinction is also to be made in using them.

(A) Have patience; I shall tell you all. There is indeed a great difference between the perfect and the imperfect consonances; here, however, aside from the consideration of motion and that more imperfect than perfect consonances are to be employed, their use is wholly identical, excepting at the beginning and end, both of which ought to consist of perfect consonance.

(J) Are you willing, beloved master, to explain the reasons why more imperfect than perfect consonances are to be employed in this connection and why the beginning and end ought to consist of perfect consonances?

(A) By your eagerness, praiseworthy as it is, I am virtually obliged to discuss certain things out of their turn. I shall discuss them none the less, but not fully, lest, overburdened at the outset by the variety of so many things, your mind be confused. Know, then, that for reasons to be discussed elsewhere, the imperfect consonances are more harmonious than the perfect. Hence, if a combination of this species, in two parts only and in other respects most simple, were to be filled with perfect consonances, it would necessarily appear empty and wholly devoid of harmony. As regards the beginning and end, accept this reasoning. The beginning is the sign of perfection, the end, of repose. Hence, since the imperfect consonances are both devoid of perfection and incapable of concluding an ending, the beginning and end ought to consist of perfect consonances. Observe, finally, that if the cantus firmus is situated in the lower part, a major sixth is to be given to the penultimate note, if in the upper part, a minor third.

(J) Are these things all that is required for this species of counterpoint?

(A) Not all, to be sure, but they suffice to lay the foundation. The rest will be made clear in correction. Make ready for work, therefore, and, having set down your cantus firmus as a foundation, try to erect above it in the soprano clef a counterpoint, following the procedure thus far explained.

(J) I shall do what I can.

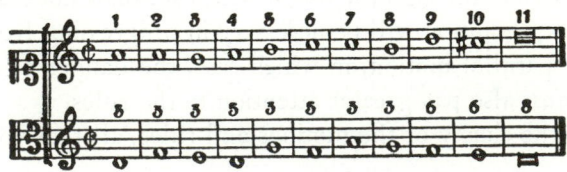

(A) You have hit the nail on the head. I marvel at your perspicacity and attention. But to what end have you placed figures both above the cantus and above the alto?

(J) By the figures placed above the alto I have wished to indicate the consonances employed, in order that, having before my eyes the motions from one consonance to another, I might depart less from the proper way of progressing. And those placed above the cantus, that is, 1, 2, 3, 4, 5, 6, 7, etc., merely indicate the numbering of the notes, to show you, revered master, that, if I hit the mark, I did this not by chance but by design.

You directed me to begin with perfect consonance; this I did, using a fifth. From the first note to the second, that is, from a fifth to a third, or from perfect to imperfect consonance, I progressed in oblique motion, although this might have been done in all three ways. From the second note to the third, namely, from a third to a third, or from imperfect to imperfect consonance, I employed parallel motion, following the rule which says: from imperfect to imperfect consonance in all three motions. From the third note to the fourth, or from a third, an imperfect consonance, to a fifth, a perfect one, I went in contrary motion, according to the rule saying: from imperfect to perfect consonance in contrary motion. From the fourth note to the fifth, or from perfect to imperfect consonance, I progressed in parallel motion, the rule permitting. From the fifth note to the sixth, that is, from imperfect to perfect consonance, the rule so directing, I employed contrary motion. From the sixth note to the seventh the progression was by oblique motion, not subject to any error. From the seventh note to the eighth, or from imperfect to imperfect consonance, I went on in parallel motion. From the eighth note to the ninth, as from imperfect to imperfect consonance, any motion was feasible. From the ninth note to the tenth the case was the same, for the tenth note, that is, the penultimate, forms a major sixth, as you directed, the cantus firmus being in the lower part. From the tenth note to the eleventh I continued by following the rule which teaches that, in proceeding from imperfect to perfect consonance, one uses contrary motion. The eleventh note, as final, is, as you have taught, a perfect consonance.

(A) In this you have proved an excellent judge. So be of good cheer; if you have so implanted the three motions and the four different rules in your memory that, having even a little reflected on them, you do not depart from them, an easy road to further progress lies open to you. Now continue, leaving the cantus firmus in the alto as it is, and set the tenor below as a counterpoint, with the difference, however, that, just as in the previous example you measured the relation of the consonances to the cantus firmus by ascending, you now measure it by descending from the cantus firmus to the bass.

(J) This seems to me more difficult to do.

(A) It seems so. I recall having also observed this same difficulty in other students; it will, however, be less difficult if you observe, as I have said, that the relation of the consonances is to be found by counting from the cantus firmus to the bass.

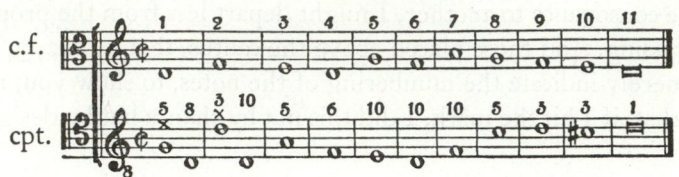

(J) Why is it, revered master, that you have marked my first and second notes with the sign of error? Have I not begun with a fifth, a perfect consonance? And have I not gone on to the second note, namely, a third, in parallel motion, as permitted by the rule which says: from perfect to imperfect consonance in any motion? Free me at once, I beg you, from the despair with which I am oppressed, for I am thoroughly ashamed!

(A) Do not despair, beloved son, for the first error did not occur through any fault of yours, since you had not yet been given the precept that the counterpoint must be adapted to the same mode in which the cantus firmus is, a rule I would have given to you now. For, in the preceding example, since the cantus firmus is in D la sol re, as evident from its beginning and end, and you have begun in G sol re ut, it is clear that you have led your beginning out of the mode; to correct this I have set, in place of your fifth, an octave, of the same mode as the cantus firmus.

(J) I rejoice that this error, from henceforth to be borne in mind, occurred through inexperience and not through carelessness. But what is the nature of my other error, indicated at the second note?

(A) In this case, the error is not with respect to the first note, but with respect to the third. You have progressed from a third to a fifth in parallel motion, contrary to the rule which says: from imperfect to perfect consonance in contrary motion; the error is easily corrected if the second note stands still below, in oblique motion, on D la sol re and forms a tenth, in which case the progression from the second note to the third, namely, from a tenth to a fifth, or from imperfect to perfect consonance, occurs in contrary motion, as the rule provides. I would not have you discouraged by this little error, for it is scarcely possible for the beginner to be so attentive that he commits no errors at all. Practice is the master of all things. In the meantime, be content that you have done the rest correctly, above all, that, the cantus firmus being in the upper part, you have given to the penultimate note a minor third, as I directed a little while ago.

(J) So that I may in time pay more attention to this rule and bear it more firmly in mind, are you willing to explain the reason why one is forbidden to go from imperfect to perfect consonance in parallel motion?

(A) I shall explain this. It is because in such case two fifths follow immediately on one another, one of them open or evident, the other closed or hidden, this last made manifest by division, as I shall show you now in an example:

The ability to make such divisions is an essential part of the art of singing, especially of solo singing. The same is also to be understood of the progression from the octave to the fifth in parallel motion, in which case two fifths again follow immediately on one another for the same reason, as the example shows:

Here you see how, by dividing the leap of the fifth, two fifths are disclosed, one of which, before the division, was hidden. From this can be concluded that the legislators of any art have ordained nothing needless or not founded on reason.

(J) I see this and am astonished.

(A) Now continue and, repeating this same exercise, go through all the modes contained within the octave, following the natural order step by step. You have begun with D; now there follow E, F, G, A, and C.

(J) Why have you omitted B, the note between A and C?

(A) Because it does not have a consonant fifth and for this reason cannot constitute a mode, as we shall explain more fully in the proper place. Let us look at an example:

Inasmuch as this fifth consists only of two tones and as many semitones, it is a false or dissonant fifth, for the true or consonant fifth, as explained in our first book, consists of three tones and a semitone.

(J) Can I not make a consonant fifth from this false one by adding a flat to the lower note or a sharp to the upper, as in this example:

(A) You can indeed, but in such case, your fifth being foreign to the diatonic genus, you will have no longer a natural mode, the only variety with which we are at present concerned, but a transposed one, regarding which in its proper place.

(J) Do these modes differ from one another?

(A) Indeed they do, and in the highest degree. For the different situation of the semitones of each octave also gives rise to a different species of melody, something which does not at present concern you. Come, therefore, and, resuming your exercise, build a counterpoint above the cantus firmus, which I shall now write out for you in E.

You have done it just right. Now, putting the cantus firmus in the upper part, contrive a counterpoint below in the tenor.

(J) What, have I erred again? If this is what happens to me in two-part writing and in the simplest species, what will happen in composition for three, four, and more voices? Tell me, please, what error is indicated by the slur drawn from the sixth note to the seventh, with a cross over it.

(A) Do not be displeased by an error which you could not avoid, having never been warned against it, and do not be tormented in advance by a dread of composition for many voices, for experience will in time make you more careful and more expert by far. I do not doubt that you have often heard the trite proverb, "Mi contra fa est diabolus in musica";

this is what you have done in proceeding from your sixth note, fa, to your seventh, mi, by a leap of an augmented fourth, or tritone, an interval forbidden in counterpoint as difficult to sing and ill-sounding. Be of good cheer and proceed from the E mode to that on F.

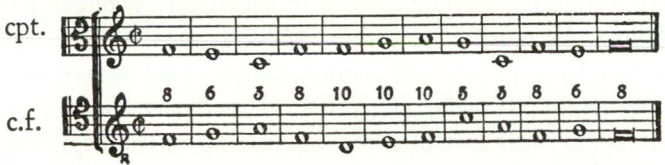

Excellent, from beginning to end!

(J) This time, for a change, you wrote out the cantus firmus for me in the tenor clef; has this some significance?

(A) None whatever; I intend only that the different clefs should gradually become more familiar to you. Whereby is to be noted, none the less, that one ought always to combine adjacent clefs, in order that the simple consonances may be more readily distinguished from the composite. Now, form a counterpoint below the cantus firmus, in the bass.

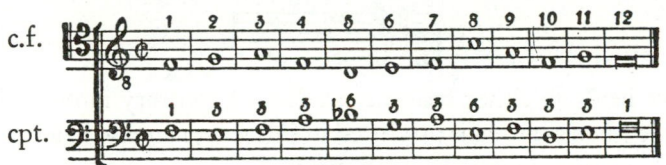

Excellent, to be sure; but why have you crossed over the cantus firmus with your counterpoint from the fourth note to the seventh?

(J) Because I should otherwise have been obliged to proceed this far in parallel motion, a less elegant style of singing.

(A) Most observant, especially in that, considering the cantus firmus, in this case the lower part, as your bass, you measured the relation of the consonances by ascending from it. Let us go on to the G mode.

(J) Though I fashioned this counterpoint with the greatest possible attention, I remark again two signs indicating errors, namely, from the ninth note to the tenth, and from the tenth note to the eleventh.

(A) You seem to me impatient; at the same time I am highly delighted with this eagerness of yours not to depart from the rules. How do you expect to avoid these minutiae, regarding which you have never been taught? From the ninth note to the tenth you have employed a leap of a major sixth, forbidden in counterpoint, in which variety of composition all things ought to be most easy to sing. Then, from the tenth note to the eleventh, you have progressed from a tenth to an octave in conjunct motion, that is, ascending by step in the lower part and descending by step in the upper; this sort of octave, occurring at the beginning of the measure, is called *ottava battuta* in Italian, *thesis* in Greek, and is prohibited. Nevertheless, though I have repeatedly reflected at length on the reason for this prohibition, I have never been able to discover the cause of the fault or any difference that could explain why the octave is approved in this example:

but rejected in this one:

the octave being in either case the product of contrary motion. The case is different when a unison is produced in this way, namely, in a progression from a third to a unison, for example:

for the unison, resulting from equal proportion, is barely audible here and seems, as it were, absorbed and lost, for which reason it ought never to be used in this species of counterpoint excepting at the beginning and end. But to return to the so-called *ottava battuta* mentioned above, I leave it to you to avoid or employ it as you please, for it is of little consequence. But if, as in this example, a descent to the octave, taken conjunctly, is made by a leap from some more remote consonance, I regard it as intolerable, even in composition for many voices.

bad   bad

The same applies also, and with more force, to the unison, for example:

bad   bad

In composition for eight voices, as will be explained in the proper place, such leaps are scarcely to be avoided, especially in the basses or in those parts which serve in their stead. You have still to put the counterpoint of the last example in the lower part.

(J) What is the meaning of the N.B. placed above the first note of the counterpoint?

(A) It indicates that, in any other case, the progression by leap from a unison to another consonance would be improper, as is also the similar progression from another consonance to a unison, as we said a moment ago. But inasmuch as, in this case, the leap is part of the cantus firmus, which cannot be altered, it may be tolerated here. The case would be different if, not hampered by consideration for a plainsong, you could do as you pleased, working of your free will. But why have you added a sharp, not usually employed in the diatonic genus, to your eleventh note?

(J) Here it was my aim to use a sixth. But when I learned the art of singing I was told that fa tends to descend, mi to ascend; accordingly, since the progression from this sixth to the following third was an ascending one, I added a sharp in order that this ascent might be made more valid. Aside from this, if the eleventh note, F, were taken without a sharp, there would result a somewhat unfavorable relation to the thirteenth note, F, taken with a sharp.

(A) You have been most observant. I believe that every stumbling block has been removed. Go on, therefore, to A and C, the two remaining modes.

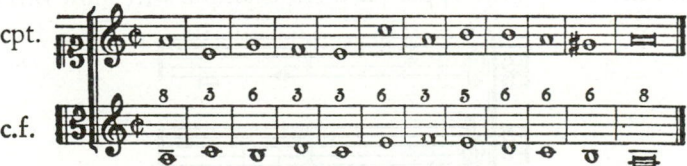

c.f.

cpt.

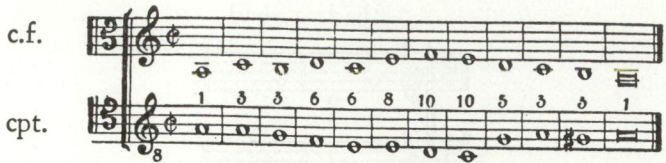

From these last two examples it is apparent that you have now noted everything one needs to know about this species. Therefore let us pursue the second species.

First Exercise—Second Lesson
OF THE SECOND SPECIES OF COUNTERPOINT

Before I undertake to explain this second species of counterpoint, know first that we are at present concerned with duple time, whose beat or measure is made up of two equal parts, one consisting in a lowering, the other in a raising of the hand. In Greek, the lowering of the hand is called *thesis*, the raising *arsis*, and for our greater convenience I propose that we use these two words alternately in the present exercise. This second species arises when against one semibreve are taken two minims, of which the one, occurring in the thesis, must always be consonant, while the other, in the arsis, may be dissonant if it moves by step from the preceding note to the following, but must be consonant if it results from a leap. Dissonance, then, is admitted in this species of counterpoint only by division, that is, when it fills the space intervening between two notes separated by a leap of a third. For example:

Diminution   Diminution

Nor need one consider whether this note of division is consonant or dissonant; it is sufficient that it fills the empty space between two notes separated by a leap of a third.

(J) Aside from this, is not what was taught in the first species of counterpoint about motion and progressions to be observed here also?

(A) Most strictly; except for the penultimate measure, which, in this species, should have first a fifth and then a major sixth, if the cantus firmus or plainsong is in the lower part, or first a fifth and then a minor third, if the cantus firmus is in the upper part. An example will show this clearly.

It will facilitate matters if you will consider the end before you begin to write. Now do you take the work in hand, employing the same cantus firmi as before.

(J) I shall do so. But I beg your indulgence should I fall into errors, for I have only a highly confused idea of this matter.

(A) Do what you can; I shall take nothing ill, and correction will readily dispel the darkness of obscurity.

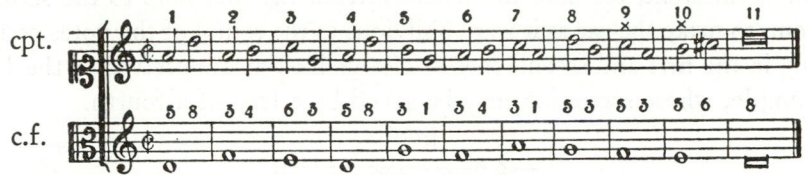

(J) Not unwarranted was my dread of erring, for I remark two signs of rebuke, neither of which I understand, the first at the first note of the ninth measure, the second at the first note of the tenth measure, although I have progressed throughout from imperfect to imperfect consonance in contrary motion.

(A) You reason correctly, for the cause of these two errors is one and the same, and I do not wonder at your not knowing it, never having been thus taught. Note, therefore, that a leap of a third can save neither two fifths nor two octaves, for the intervening note, occurring in the arsis, is regarded as nonexistent, its small value and narrow interval preventing its so modifying the sound that the relation of the two fifths or octaves will not be perceived by the ear. Let us look at the last example, beginning at the eighth measure.

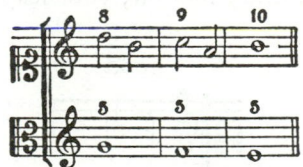

Now, if the note intervening, or occurring in the arsis, is regarded as non-essential, the situation stands thus revealed:

The same applies also to the octave.

idem

With a leap of a wider interval, for example, a fourth, fifth, or sixth, the case is different, for here the distance from the first note to the second seems to make the ear as it were oblivious to the sound of the notes occurring in the first and second theses. Let us look at the octaves of the last example, whose succession may be saved by a leap of a fourth.

good

For the same reason, it is because of this leap of a fourth that in your last exercise I marked the third to fourth measure with no sign of error, for leaving this note out of account, the situation stands thus:

This progression is contrary to the rule which says: from imperfect to perfect consonance in contrary motion; your leap of a fourth removes the error in this manner:

good

Let your preceding exercise be now corrected.

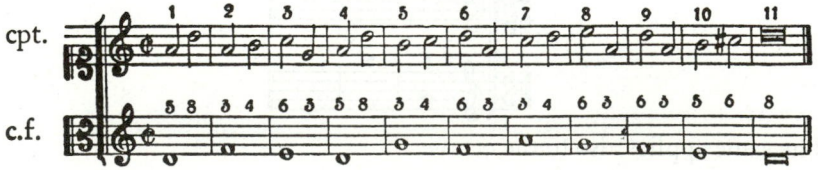

I see now that you have sufficiently in mind what has been said thus far. But before you take up the composition of this exercise with the counterpoint in the lower part, I shall propose to you certain things most useful to know, whose observance will greatly facilitate matters. First, in place of the first note of all you may put a rest of the value of half a measure; second, if it chance that the two parts are so close and so conjunct that you scarcely know which way to go and cannot possibly progress in contrary motion, you may manage by a leap of a minor sixth (which is permitted) or of an octave, as in the following examples:

Now continue, and build up the counterpoint of the preceding exercise in the lower part.

Now, again taking up all the cantus firmi set down in the first species of counterpoint, run through the remaining five modes, forming your counterpoint above and below.

(J) I recall your having said a little while ago that when a counterpoint of this species is in the lower part, the first note of the penultimate measure ought to be given a fifth; it appears, however, that in this variety of mode the fifth is not admitted, the relation *mi contra fa* making it a dissonance. For this reason I thought it wise to use the sixth in its place.

(A) Your observation pleases me exceedingly. Now continue, and pursue the same exercise through the remaining four modes.

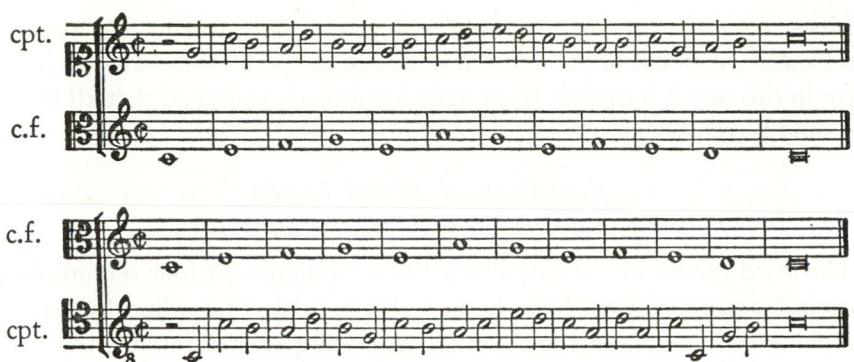

You have managed this quite well enough. Thus the gods bestow all things on the industrious; bear also this saying in mind: "The drop of water wears away the stone, not by its force, but by its constant falling," which teaches that untiring application to study is required for the attainment of the sciences, so that (as the saying goes) we should "allow no day to pass without its line." Aside from this, I have sought to teach you here to consider not only the measure in which you are working, but also those that follow.

(J) So you have indeed, revered master. For in composing the preceding exercises in counterpoint I should scarcely have known what to do if, considering one measure or another before deciding to write, I had not anticipated what was fitting there.

(A) Seeing you so wise, I rejoice marvelously and urge you again and again to overcome the great difficulty at the beginning by zealous and constant attention, not suffering yourself to be oppressed by the severity of your burden or to be enticed away from the assiduity of your study by flattery, as though you already understood a great deal. Do this, and little by little you will perceive the darkness giving place to light and the veil of obscurity being raised before you to some extent, and you will rejoice.

Here we ought also to speak of triple time, in which three notes are taken against one. Because of its facility, however, the matter is of little moment, and I do not think it worth while to devote a special lesson to it. You will find that a few examples only are sufficient for its understanding.

Here, since all three notes move by step, the intermediate one may be dissonant; it would be otherwise if one or other of the three were to leap, for in this case it is evident from what has already been said that all three should be consonant.

First Exercise—Third Lesson
OF THE THIRD SPECIES OF COUNTERPOINT

The third species of counterpoint is the combination of four semiminims against one semibreve. Note here, to begin with, that when five semiminims follow one another by step, ascending or descending, the first should be consonant while the second may be dissonant, the third must again be consonant while the fourth may be dissonant if the fifth is consonant, as in the examples:

The first situation suspending this rule is one in which the second and fourth notes chance to be consonant, in which case the third may be dissonant, as in the following examples:

Here, in each example, the third note is dissonant; we call it a division of the leap of a third. To lay bare the truth of this matter, let us reduce these examples to their essentials in this manner:

From this it is clear that the dissonant third note is nothing more than a division of the leap of a third, filling the space intervening between the second and third notes, which space is always open to division, that is, to being filled by the intervening note.

The second case in which we depart from the general rule is the changing note, in Italian *nota cambiata*, by means of which we progress by leap from a dissonant second note to a consonance, as seen in the following examples:

Strictly speaking, this leap of a third from the second note to the third ought to be made from the first note to the second, in which case the second note would form the consonance of the sixth in this manner:

In this situation, if a division were made from the first note to the second, the matter would stand thus:

But since in this species of counterpoint the quaver is not admitted, men of great authority have been pleased to approve the first example, in which the second note has the seventh, perhaps because of the greater elegance of the melody.

Finally it remains to show how the penultimate measure is to be contrived, for this measure presents much greater difficulty than the others. When the cantus firmus is in the lower part, it should be constituted in this manner:

But when the cantus firmus is in the upper part, it is to be made in the following way:

Now that you understand these things, together with those of which we have spoken previously in connection with the other species, I hope that this species of composition will be easy for you; at the same time, if you would avoid obstacles as you go along, I would admonish you again and again to have a special consideration for the measures that follow. Take up your work, then, pursuing in order all the cantus firmi set down in the first lesson.

Why have you sometimes used a b-flat, a sign scarcely usual in the diatonic genus with which we are concerned?

(J) It seemed to me that some harshness would otherwise proceed from the relation *mi contra fa*. Nor did I think it prejudicial to the diatonic genus, since it was introduced, not essentially, but accidentally and from necessity.

(A) Well noted; for the same reason, even sharps are sometimes to be employed, though one must use special judgment in considering when and where. From the preceding examples it appears that you have what is required for this species sufficiently in mind. To keep our discussion within bounds I leave the three modes still remaining, G, A, and C, for you to pursue on your own account. Let us go on, then, to the

First Exercise—Fourth Lesson
OF THE FOURTH SPECIES OF COUNTERPOINT

This species arises when against one semibreve are taken two minims, these placed on one and the same degree and bound together by a tie; the first must occur in the arsis, the second in the thesis. It is usually called *ligature* or *syncope* and has two varieties—the consonant and the dissonant.

A consonant ligature is one whose two minims, in the arsis and in the thesis, are both consonant. Examples will make the matter clear.

Consonant Ligatures

A dissonant ligature is one whose first note, in the arsis, is indeed consonant (an invariable rule), but whose second, in the thesis, is dissonant, as may be seen in the following examples:

Dissonant Ligatures

Further, since the dissonances here are not accidental or by division, as in the preceding species, but essential, occurring in the arsis; and since, as disagreeable to the ear, they are unable to cause any pleasure of themselves and must derive their charm from the consonances immediately following, in which they are resolved; for these reasons we must now speak

OF THE RESOLUTION OF DISSONANCES

Before I undertake to say how dissonances should be resolved, it will be useful to know that tied notes, bound as it were in chains, are nothing more than retardations of notes that follow, and that afterwards, as though liberated from their servitude, they are seen to enter into the free state. For this reason, dissonances should always be resolved in the nearest consonances, descending by step, as clearly seen in the following example:

Removing the retardation, the example stands thus:

From this may be concluded that it is easy to know in what consonance each dissonance should be resolved: namely, in the one found in the thesis of the measure immediately following when the retardation is removed. Whence it follows that, when the cantus firmus is in the lower part, the second must be resolved in the unison, the fourth in the third, the seventh in the sixth, and the ninth in the octave. This reasoning holds good to such an extent that it forbids a progression in ligature from a unison to a second or from a ninth to an octave, as seen in the following examples:

Removing the retardation in this manner, you will see a succession of two unisons in the first example, of two octaves in the second:

The opposite occurs when the progression is from a third to a second or from a tenth to a ninth, in this way:

These situations are correctly constituted, for they are valid even when the retardation or ligature is removed in the following manner:

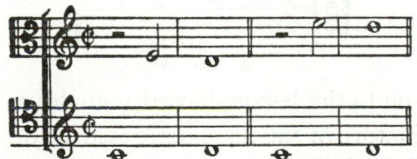

Having shown what dissonances may be employed and how they should be resolved when the cantus firmus is in the lower part, we have now to say what dissonances are admitted and by what means they should be resolved when the cantus firmus is in the upper part. I say, therefore, that one may here employ the second resolved in the third, the fourth in the fifth, and the ninth in the tenth. For example:

(J) Why do you omit the seventh here? Is it because it cannot be employed when the cantus firmus is in the upper part? May it please you to tell me the cause of this.

(A) I confess that I omitted the seventh here deliberately. But I can give scarcely any reason for this but the great authority of the classical authors, to whom much is to be conceded in practice and of whom barely one is to be found who used the seventh resolved in this manner in the octave.

One might say perhaps that the seventh resolved in this manner was avoided as resolving in a perfect consonance, the octave, from which it could derive very little harmony, were it not that one frequently finds in these same authors the second, which is the inversion of the seventh, resolved in the unison, from which, as the most perfect of the consonances, a dissonance can derive still less harmony. In this particular, then, I think that the usage introduced by the great masters should be taken into consideration. Let us look at an example of the inverted seventh, or second, resolved in the unison.

(J) Before I go on to the lesson, have I your leave to inquire whether the retardation or ligature of the dissonance is also admitted in ascending? Is not the nature of the following examples the same:

(A) You raise a question more difficult to disentangle than the Gordian knot, which you cannot now understand without being taken beyond the boundary of this discipline and which is therefore to be answered at another time. Even though, when you remove the retardation, the nature of the thirds appears the same, there none the less remains a certain difference, which, as I have said, I shall explain in the proper place. In the meantime, speaking ex cathedra, I tell you that all dissonances should be resolved by descending in the nearest consonance. Aside from this, when the cantus firmus is in the lower part, the penultimate measure in this species is to be concluded by a seventh resolved in a sixth, when the cantus firmus is in the upper part, by a second resolved in a minor third, which will progress at the end to a unison.

(J) Is each measure to be given its ligature?

(A) Generally speaking, wherever possible. But you will sometimes happen on a measure in which no ligature is admissible, in which case it will have to be filled with single minims until an opportunity of making ligatures again presents itself. Come, apply yourself to your ligatures.

You have indeed done well; but why did you omit the ligature in your fifth measure? There would have been one if, after your third, you had used the fifth; this would have been the first note of your ligature, and, keeping it on the same degree, you would have had the second note, namely, the sixth, in the thesis of the following measure. I have said, you know, that no opportunity is to be overlooked.

(J) To be sure, I could have made one; but I omitted it deliberately in order not to fall into an odious repetition, for immediately before, in the third and fourth measures, I had used the same ligatures.

(A) A sufficiently prudent observation, for one must yield not a little to the nature of the melody and to the elegance of the progression. Continue.

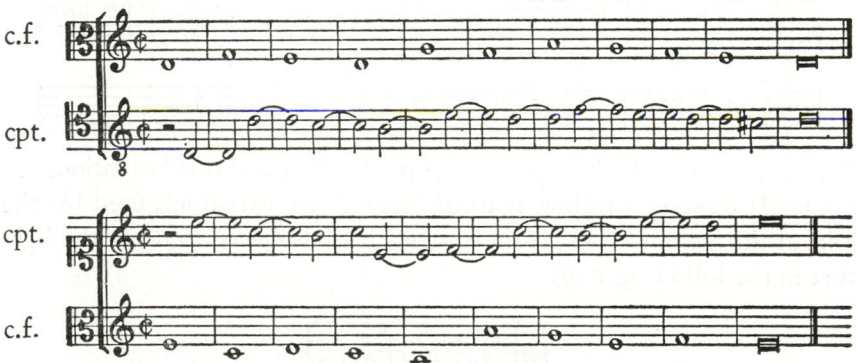

Let these examples suffice for the present. But since the ligatures contribute in no inconsiderable way to the seasoning of musical harmony, I recommend to you not only that you pursue in this manner the cantus firmi of the three remaining modes, but also that you invent others and give yourself further exercise in this species, in which you will never have exercise enough.

As a refinement belonging to the next species, I shall explain here in advance that the ligatures of which we have spoken thus far may also be made in another way; so made, they lose little of their essential character, yet bring to the harmony a means of a more lively movement. For example:

Original form   idem   Original form   idem

From these examples it is quite clear that the first and third situations are essential; those that follow, marked "idem," are variations, used for the sake of the melody or of the movement. It is also usual to break the ligature in the following way:

Aside from this, one may in the next species occasionally interpolate two quavers; these, however, are to be taken in the second and fourth parts of the measure, never in the first and third.

These things being understood, let us go on to the

First Exercise—Fifth Lesson

OF THE FIFTH SPECIES OF COUNTERPOINT

This species is called florid counterpoint, because it should bloom like a garden of little flowers with ornament of every kind, pleasant melody, graceful easy movement, and an elegant variety of figures. For just as in division we use all the other common species of arithmetic, such as counting, addition, subtraction, and multiplication, so this species is nothing more than an amassing and combining of the preceding species of counterpoint, nor is there about it anything new to be taught, aside from the elegance of the melody, with which I exhort and entreat you to take the utmost care and pains, never losing sight of it.

(J) As far as within my power, I shall take pains, but I scarcely trust myself to take up my pen, having no example before my eyes.

(A) Be of good cheer; I shall form the first example for you.

The counterpoints of the remaining cantus firmi I leave to you to be patterned after this model.

Your work is industrious enough, and what pleases me not inconsiderably is that you have paid no little attention to writing a good melodic line and that at the beginning of the thesis you have frequently employed oblique motion or syncope, a labor which I would have further commended to you, since it brings the utmost grace to the counterpoint.

(J) I am immeasurably delighted to learn that the result of my application and effort does not altogether displease you, and, encouraged by your flattery, I believe myself on the point of making no inconsiderable progress in little time. Am I to pursue the remaining three modes in your presence or on my own account?

(A) Inasmuch as this species is more useful than I can say, I shall indeed ask you to complete the aforesaid three modes in my presence; at the same time I would admonish you to exercise yourself unceasingly more and more in this variety of composition.

(J) I shall always observe your counsel as a law.

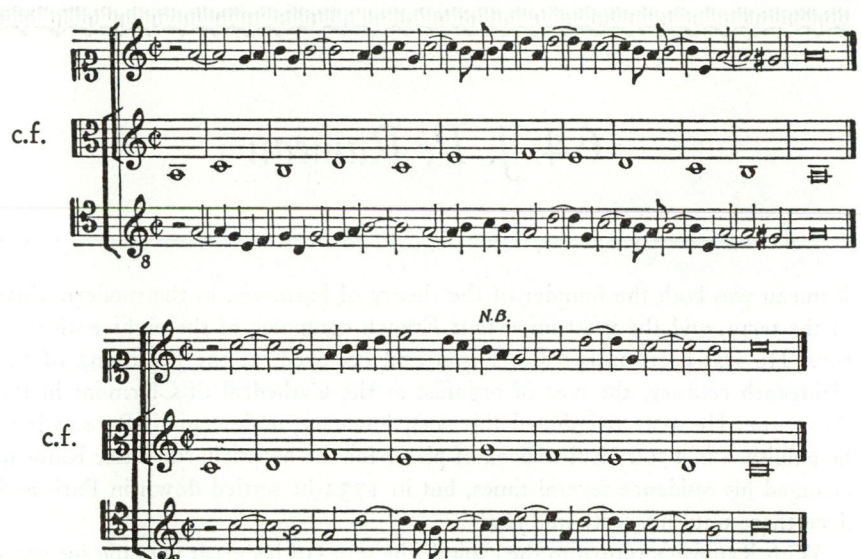

What is indicated by the N.B. placed above the cantus in the fifth measure of the last example?

(A) Do not distress yourself, for you have thus far heard nothing about this from me. I tell you now, not indeed as a rule, but rather as a counsel, that, when two semiminims are placed at the beginning of the measure without a ligature immediately following, the melody takes on the character of an ending. For this reason it will be advisable for you to employ two semiminims at the beginning of the measure only in connection with a following ligature or to make easier a continuation with two further semiminims as in the following example:

better

Now praise be to God, we have completed two-part writing, running through all five species with an underlying cantus firmus. Now we are to return to the beginning, namely to note against note in three parts, and to see what is to be observed in each species and in what manner the combining of three parts ought to be arranged.

64. J. P. Rameau

Rameau was both the founder of the theory of harmony, in the modern sense of the term, and the most important French composer of the eighteenth century. He was born in 1683 at Dijon and occupied, at the beginning of the eighteenth century, the post of organist at the Cathedral of Clermont in the Auvergne. He soon abandoned this post, however, and went to Paris, where he published in 1706 his first book of pieces for the harpsichord. Later Rameau changed his residence several times, but in 1732 he settled down in Paris and lived there until his death in 1764.

With Rameau's return to the capital, the series of his great operatic successes began: in 1733, *Hippolyte et Aricie*; in 1735, *Les Indes galantes*; in 1737, *Castor et Pollux*; in 1739, *Les Fêtes d'Hébé* and *Dardanus*, etc. Aside from operas Rameau wrote a number of cantatas and motets, also pieces for the harpsichord, alone and in conjunction with other instruments.

As a theorist, Rameau published in 1722 his epoch-making *Traité de l'harmonie*. It was the first in a long list of writings that appeared between 1722 and 1760.

From the Traité de l'harmonie [1]

[*1722*]

Preface

IN WHATEVER progress music has made thus far, it appears that the more sensible the ear becomes of its marvelous effects, the less curious the mind is to fathom its true principles, so that one may say that, while experience has here acquired a certain authority, reason has lost its rights.

Such writings as have come down to us from the ancients make it very clear that reason alone enabled them to discover the greater part of music's properties; yet, though experience still obliges us to approve most of the

---

1 Text: The original edition (Paris, 1722), preliminary leaves 2–3, pp. 125–128, 138–143.

rules which they passed on, we neglect today all the advantages we might derive from reason in favor of the experience of ordinary practice.

If experience can apprise us of the different properties of music, it is in other respects not capable alone of permitting us to discover the principle of these properties with all the precision that belongs to reason; the consequences we derive from it are often false, or leave us at least with a certain doubt that only reason can dispel. How, for example, shall we be able to prove that our music is more perfect than that of the ancients, when it no longer seems to us capable of the effects which they attributed to theirs? Will it be by saying that the more familiar things become, the less surprise they cause, and that the rapture into which they could throw us when they were new degenerates insensibly as we accustom ourselves to it, becoming in the end mere amusement? This would at most presume its equality, not its superiority. But if, by the statement of a self-evident principle, from which we subsequently derived the due and certain consequences, we could make it clear that our music had reached a final stage of perfection which the ancients were far from realizing (the reader may refer on this point to Chapter 21 of Book 2),[2] we would in that case know what to believe, we would better perceive the force of the previous reflection, and, knowing by these means the limits of the art, we would abide by them the more willingly; persons of superior taste and genius would no longer be fearful of lacking the knowledge necessary for proficiency; in a word, the light of reason, thus dispelling the doubts into which experience may plunge us at any moment, would be a sure guarantee of the success we could promise ourselves.

If modern musicians (that is to say, musicians since Zarlino [a]) had applied themselves as the ancients did to giving reasons for what they practiced, they would have abandoned many preconceived ideas which are not to their advantage, and this would even have led them to give up those with which they are still too much occupied and of which they are having great difficulty in ridding themselves. Experience, then, is too much in favor with them, it somehow seduces them until it is the cause of the little pains they take to inform themselves properly about the beauties which it leads them to discover daily; their knowledge is not common property, they have not the gift of communicating it, and, since they do not at all

---

a Zarlino, a celebrated writer on music who wrote nearly one hundred and fifty years ago and of whom one finds very feeble imitations in the works on this subject that have appeared since his.

["More than with anyone else we ought to occupy ourselves with this author, for he has served posterity as a model and in practical matters we are constantly being referred to him as to one who for some musicians is still the oracle and whom M. de Brossard himself calls the 'Prince of modern musicians.' "—*Traité*, p. 18.]

2 "On the modes."

perceive this, they are often more astonished at one's not understanding them than they are at their not making themselves understood. This reproach is somewhat harsh, I admit, but I include it here because I perhaps still deserve it myself, despite all I have done to avoid it. However this may be, I have always wished that it might make on others the effect it has made on me. It is, then, for this reason, and above all to revive that noble rivalry which formerly flourished, that I have risked communicating to the public my recent researches in an art to which I have sought to give all the simplicity which is natural to it in order that the mind may comprehend its properties as easily as the ear is sensible of them.

No one man is capable of exhausting a subject as profound as this one; it is almost impossible for him not to be constantly overlooking something, despite all his pains; but at least the new discoveries which he may join to those already made known on the subject are so many paths marked out for those who may be able to pursue them further.

Music is a science which ought to have certain rules; these rules ought to be derived from a self-evident principle; and this principle can scarcely be known to us without the help of mathematics. I ought, too, to admit that, notwithstanding all the experience I may have been able to acquire for myself in music through having practiced it during a considerable period of time, it was only with the help of mathematics that my ideas disentangled themselves and that light replaced an obscurity that I had not previously recognized as such. If I did not know how to distinguish the principle from the rule, the principle soon offered itself to me in a way at once simple and convincing; the consequences with which it next supplied me led me to recognize in them as many rules, related through them to the principle. The true sense of these rules, their proper application, their relation to one another, and the order they ought to observe among themselves (the simplest serving as introduction to the less simple, and so on by degrees), finally the choice of terms; all this, I say, of which I had formerly been ignorant, developed in my mind with so much clarity and precision that I could not avoid concluding that it would be desirable (as someone said to me one day when I was applauding the perfections of our modern music) if the knowledge of the musicians of this century were to correspond to the beauties of their compositions. It is, then, not enough to be sensible of the effects of a science or of an art; it is necessary beyond this to comprehend them in such a way that one may make them intelligible; and it is to this end that I have chiefly applied myself in the body of this work.

•　　•　　•　　•　　•

Book Two—Chapter 18

Observations on the Establishment of Rules, in Which is Taught the Method of Composing a Fundamental Bass

ARTICLE I

ON THE ESTABLISHMENT OF RULES

We may judge of music only through the intervention of hearing, and reason has authority in it only in so far as it agrees with the ear; at the same time, nothing can be more convincing to us than their union in our judgments. Our nature is satisfied by the ear, our mind by reason; let us then judge of nothing excepting through their co-operation.

Experience offers us a number of harmonies, capable of an infinite diversity, by which we should always be confused, did we not look to another cause for their principle; this diversity sows doubts everywhere, and each of us, imagining that his ear cannot be deceived, wishes to be himself the sole judge. Reason, quite the other way, sets before us a single harmony, whose properties it easily determines if experience assist. Once experience confirms what reason authorizes, the latter ought to be given the upper hand, for nothing is more convincing than its decisions, especially when they are drawn from a principle as simple as the one it offers us. Let us rely, then, on reason alone, if this is possible, calling experience to its aid only to corroborate its proofs.

The first musicians—in a word, all those who confined themselves solely to speculation—admitted only the triad as universal principle. If Zarlino, joining practice to theory, spoke of sixth chords and six-four chords, we know already that these arise from it also. Beyond this, it is only a question of determining whether the dissonances cannot similarly be reduced to it, something easily proved, for all of them are generated by a new sound added to the primary harmony, which is always present in its full perfection. Thus reason alone still suffices to authorize this addition and to determine its use, the addition being naturally made by a *rule of three* or (as pointed out in Book I, Chapter 7, page 29) [3] by a new multiplication of the numbers which gave us our primary harmony. Hence—the rules of music being concerned only with the consonances and feasible dissonances, these consonances being all of them contained in the triad, these dissonances in the same harmony and in the seventh added to it—it is evident that our rules ought to be based chiefly on the primary harmony and that which is formed by the added seventh. And if, after having derived the

---

[3] "On harmonic division or the origin of the harmonies."

consequences of a principle so simple and so natural, we follow step by step that which has been taught and practiced, especially where this has been skillfully done, accommodating ourselves always to that which experience leads us to approve, who can doubt for a moment that this principle is not the true object of our rules?

See to this end what Zarlino says on the subject of the fundamental bass and its progression, the progression it imposes on the other parts, and the progression of the thirds, the consonances in general, and the dissonances; note that he has omitted those dissonances which we call *major*,[4] that he has not properly defined the *interrupted cadence*,[5] that he does not speak at all of the *irregular cadence* [6] or of the inversion of harmonies (although he teaches its use by those of the sixth, second, etc.), that he cites without qualification the chord of the ninth (which we treat as inadmissible except *by supposition*),[7] that he is not on solid ground with his *modes*, that (as we shall see in Chapter 21) his music can accordingly not profit by the perfections with which ours is graced, and finally that his examples do not agree with his text. Examine his reasons, whether they be reasons or words and whence he derives them; examine his explanations, his comparisons, and the sources of his knowledge; after this, draw proper conclusions from them and you will actually discover that all harmony and all melody must turn on the two harmonies we have proposed and, what is more, on their lowest sound (which is in either case the same) and, as we have maintained to this point, on its progression. Then hear the music of the most skillful masters, examine it, and put it to the test by means of a fundamental bass, following the explanation we shall give at the end of this chapter; you will find only the triad and the chord of the seventh—you will find, I say, only the tonic note and its dominant, provided you are well acquainted with *modulation* and able to distinguish all the changes of key, it being further noted that the sixth step often replaces the dominant,[8] though only in minor keys.

---

4 "Dissonances are either major or minor, like the thirds from which they are derived and whose properties they share. The major are derived from the leading tone and become such only when combined with the minor dissonances, which are derived from the seventh."—*Table des termes.*

5 "A cadence is called 'broken' [or 'interrupted'] when the dominant, in the bass or in one of the other parts, ascends one step."—*Table des termes.*

6 "A cadence is called 'irregular' when the bass ascends a fifth. This succession results in a dissonance which proceeds irregularly but which can always be suppressed."—*Table des termes.* The dissonance to which Rameau refers is that of the "added sixth," as in the succession II $^6_5$—I. In later writings Rameau also calls this succession the "imperfect" cadence.

7 " 'Supposition,' a term . . . applied to sounds which alter the perfection of harmonies in that by their addition the harmonies exceed the compass of an octave. There are only two harmonies 'by supposition' and from these are derived two others."—*Table des termes.* The two harmonies "by supposition" are those of the ninth and eleventh; derived from them are those of the "augmented fifth" (III $^9_5$) and "augmented seventh" (I $^{11}_7$), as Rameau calls them. In his *Génération harmonique* (1737) Rameau explains "supposition" more precisely as resulting in "a dissonant harmony arranged by thirds, below which is added a third or a fifth." "Harmonies by supposition" are incapable of inversion.

8 Rameau first uses the term "subdominant" in his *Nouveau système* (1726).

The principle of harmony is present not only in the triad and in the chord of the seventh formed from it, but still more precisely in the lowest sound of these two harmonies, which is, so to speak, the *harmonic center* to which all other sounds must be related. This also is one of the reasons why we have found it necessary to base our system on the division of a single string, inasmuch as such a string, giving us our lowest sound, is the principle of all those that arise from its division, just as the unit with which it is compared is the principle of all the numbers.

To perceive that all the harmonies and their different properties originate in the triad and the chord of the seventh is not enough; beyond this it is necessary to note that all the properties of these two primary harmonies depend absolutely on the *harmonic center* and its progression. The intervals of which they are composed are intervals only in relation to this *center*, which makes use of the same intervals to form its progression, on which progression the order and progression of the two primary harmonies alone depend. These intervals are all comprised in the third, fifth, and seventh, for if others occur they are either inversions (like the sixth, fourth, and second), or extensions of one or the other (like the ninth and eleventh), or alterations (like the tritone and false fifth)—we make no mention of the octave, knowing that it is a mere duplication. This reduction of the intervals has yet another exact relation to that of the harmonies: the inverted intervals form inverted harmonies, the extended intervals form harmonies "by supposition," the altered intervals form harmonies "by borrowing," [9] the whole arising from our three primary intervals, from which the fundamental harmonies are formed, and related solely to our *harmonic center*.

Even this is not enough; the ear not only sanctions these fundamental harmonies but—once their progression has been determined by that of their lowest and fundamental sound—finds always agreeable and never otherwise everything that conforms to this fundamental, whether it be understood, inverted, "supposed," or "borrowed," reason and hearing agreeing in this to such an extent that not one exception is to be found.

How marvelous this principle is in its simplicity! So many harmonies, so many beautiful melodies, this infinite diversity, these expressions, so beautiful and so proper, these sentiments, so well contrived—all this arises from two or three intervals arranged in thirds whose principle is summed up in a single sound:

---

9 " 'Borrowing' is a new term, used to distinguish a particular class of harmonies which can occur only in minor keys."—*Table des termes.* "We call these harmonies 'borrowed' in that they borrow their perfection from a sound which they do not contain."—*Traité*, p. 43. The chief "borrowed" harmony is that of the diminished seventh; from this Rameau derives "by supposition" III $\frac{5}{4}$ and I $\frac{7}{6}$

	Fundamen-tal sound	Third	Fifth	Seventh
	1	3	5	7

The reader ought already to be persuaded by the foregoing remarks, and the rules which we shall establish on our principle will serve to convince him.

• • • • • •

Chapter 19

CONTINUATION OF THE PRECEDING CHAPTER, IN WHICH IT APPEARS THAT MELODY ARISES FROM HARMONY

At first sight it would seem that harmony arises from melody, inasmuch as the melodies which the single voices produce become harmony when they are combined; it has, however, been necessary to determine in advance a path for each of these voices in order that they may agree together. No matter, then, what order of melody we may observe in the individual parts, taken together they will scarcely form a tolerable harmony (not to say that it is impossible that they should do so) unless this order has been dictated to them by the rules of harmony. Nevertheless, to make the whole theory of harmony more intelligible, we begin by teaching the method of constructing a melody, and supposing that we have made some progress with this, whatever ideas we may have formed concerning it are set aside the moment it is a question of joining to it another part; we are no longer masters of the melody, and while we are occupied in seeking out the path which one part should follow in relation to another, we often lose sight of the one we proposed to ourselves, or are at least obliged to change it, lest the restraint this first part imposes on us prevent our always giving to the others a melody as perfect as we might wish. It is, then, harmony that guides us, not melody. A learned musician may indeed propose to himself a beautiful melody suitable for harmonization. But whence has he this happy faculty? Cannot nature have provided it? Assuredly. And if, on the other hand, nature has refused him this gift, how may he succeed? Only by means of the rules. But whence are we to derive these? This is what we must determine.

Does the first division of a string offer us at once two intervals from which we might form a melody? Surely not, for a man who sings only a given note and its octave can construct no very acceptable melody. The second and third divisions, from which arise the whole of harmony, do not furnish us with sounds more suitable for melody, for a melody composed only of thirds, fourths, fifths, sixths, and octaves would still be far from perfect. It is harmony, then, that is generated first; it is accordingly from harmony that we must necessarily derive our rules of melody, and we shall be doing just this if we single out the harmonic intervals of which we have spoken in order to form from them a fundamental progression. And although this is not yet melody, when these intervals are taken in succession above one of their number, following a natural diatonic course laid down for them by their very progression as they serve one another as mutual foundation, we derive from their consonant and diatonic progression all the melody we need. Hence we must know the harmonic intervals before the melodic ones, and all the melody one can teach a beginner (if we may call this melody) consists in these consonant intervals. We shall see in Chapter 21 that, although it arises from harmony, the ancients still derived their *modulation* from melody alone.

Once we are familiar with this consonant progression, it takes but little more effort to add three sounds above the sound which serves as bass than to add only one. This is how we account for the two procedures. Above a given bass you may place the third, fifth, or octave—or you may place the third, fifth, and octave; to make use of any one of these intervals you must know them all, and if you know them all it is no more difficult to use them together than to use them separately. Furthermore, if the bass descends a third, the part which had the third before now has the fifth— we can account for the matter in no other way. But if, in these different progressions of the bass, we find the third here, the fifth there, and the octave in a third place, we must always know what ought to follow, according to the momentary progression of the bass. Hence, without realizing it, we teach composition in four parts while we explain it only in two. Then, since I must know what follows each consonance, according to the momentary progression of the bass, each of the consonances occurring in turn, it is no more difficult to use them together than to use them individually. The more so since, if I am unable to distinguish them when they are together, I can only confine myself to each one individually. Thus, by one means or another, I find a way of composing a harmony perfect in its four parts, from which I then derive all the knowledge necessary for arriving at perfection. Besides, the explanation which we add makes mistakes impossible, if we may rely on the experience which various persons who knew only the notes have had in this, and who, after a second reading of our rules, have composed a harmony as perfect as one could wish.

Finally, if the composer can give himself the satisfaction of hearing his productions,[b] his ear will form itself little by little, and, once he has become sensible of the perfect harmony toward which his beginnings lead him, he may be certain of a success which depends without qualification on these primary principles alone.

After this, there can be no doubt that, when four parts are once familiar to us, we shall be able to reduce them to three and to two. But what rule can teach us to compose in two parts, even when we have thoroughly mastered it, something which is nearly impossible, seeing that we are guided in this by no foundation and that everything that can be taught about it is sterile, either because our memory is incapable of retaining it or because it is only with difficulty that everything is included, it being necessary to add at the end the words *Caetera docebit usus?* [10] Would we progress from two to three and four parts? What is taught about this is so little that we shall need genius and taste as consummate as that of the great masters themselves if we are to understand their teachings. On the subject of four-part writing, Zarlino [c] says that it can scarcely be taught on paper and that he leaves it to the discretion of the composers, who can form themselves on his previously stated rules for two and three parts. Our ideas are exactly opposite, for we have just said that harmony can only be taught in four parts, where all its properties are summed up (as we have maintained all along) in two harmonies, and that it is very easy to reduce these four parts to three and to two; whereas Zarlino, who does not even define his two and three parts precisely, admits his inability to define four, after having agreed that perfect harmony consists in four parts, which he compares (Chapter 58, fol. 281) [11] to the four elements. In conclusion we shall say that, if the reader has failed to obtain a perfect understanding of the rules of harmony which we have given thus far, the principle which we have adopted is a sure means of attaining such an understanding and will permit nothing to escape.

Chapter 20

OF THE PROPERTIES OF HARMONIES

It is certain that harmony can arouse in us different passions, depending on the particular harmonies that are employed. There are harmonies that are sad, languishing, tender, agreeable, gay, and striking; there are also

---

b It is partly with this in mind that we give rules for accompanying.

c *Istituzioni armoniche,* Part 3, Chapter 65, fol. 310. ["Necessary observations on compositions for four and more voices."—Ed.]

10 Experience will teach the rest.

11 "The method to be followed in composing music for more than two voices, and the names of the parts."

certain successions of harmonies for the expression of these passions; and although it is quite foreign to my purpose I shall give of this as full an explanation as experience has given me.

Consonant harmonies are to be found everywhere but should be employed most frequently in music expressing gaiety and magnificence; and, since we cannot avoid intermingling some dissonant harmonies, we must contrive that these arise naturally, that they are as far as possible prepared, and that the most prominent parts, the soprano and bass, are always consonant with respect to one another.

Sweetness and tenderness are sometimes well enough expressed by prepared minor dissonances.

Tender complaints sometimes require dissonances "by borrowing" and "by supposition," rather minor than major, such major dissonances as may occur being confined rather to the inner parts than to the outer.

Languishings and sufferings are perfectly expressed by dissonances "by supposition" and especially by chromatic progressions, regarding which we shall speak in our next book.

Despair and all passions having to do with anger or which have anything striking about them require unprepared dissonances of every kind; above all, the major dissonances should be situated in the soprano. In certain expressions of this nature it is even effective to pass from one key to another by means of unprepared major dissonances, yet in such a way that the ear is not offended by too great a disproportion; like all other such procedures, this can accordingly be carried out only with considerable discretion, for if we do nothing but pile dissonance on dissonance wherever there is place for it, it will be a much greater fault than allowing only consonance to be heard. Dissonance, then, is to be employed with considerable discretion, and, when we feel that its harshness is not in agreement with the expression, we ought even to avoid allowing it to be heard, in those harmonies that cannot do without it, by suppressing it adroitly, dispersing the consonances which make up the rest of the harmony through all the parts; for one ought always to bear in mind that the seventh, from which all the dissonances arise, is simply a sound added to the triad which does not at all destroy the basis of the harmony and may always be suppressed when we think it appropriate.

Melody has not less force than harmony in expression, but it is almost impossible to give certain rules for it, since good taste is here more influential than other considerations. Hence we leave to happy geniuses the pleasure of distinguishing themselves in this particular, the source of almost all the force of the sentiments, and hope that skillful persons, for whom we have said nothing new, will not resent our having revealed secrets of which they have wished, perhaps, to be the sole proprietors, for our limited intelligence does not permit us to rival them in this last degree of perfection, without which the most beautiful harmony becomes insipid and through which they are always in a position to excel. As we shall see in what follows, it is only when we know how to arrange a series of harmonies appropriately that we can derive from them a melody suited to the subject, but taste is, in this, always the prime mover.

It is here that the ancients would appear to have excelled, if we may believe their accounts: one by his melody made Ulysses weep, another obliged Alexander to take up arms, still another rendered a furious young man mild and gentle. In a word, one sees on every hand the astonishing effects of their music, regarding which Zarlino is most plausible when he says that with them the word "harmony" often signified nothing more than simple melody and that all these effects arose more from an energetic discourse whose force was intensified by their manner of reciting or singing it and which can certainly not have enjoyed all the diversity which perfect harmony, of which they were ignorant, has obtained for us today. Their harmony, he says further,[d] consisted only in a triad, which he calls a "symphony," above which they sang all sorts of melodies indifferently, very much like what is played on our musettes and vielles.

For the rest, a good musician ought to surrender himself to all the characters he wishes to depict and, like a skillful actor, put himself in the place of the speaker, imagine himself in the localities where the different events he wishes to represent occur, and take in these the same interest as those most concerned; he ought to be a good speaker, at least by nature; and he ought to know when the voice should be raised or lowered, by more or by less, in order to adapt to this his melody, his harmony, his modulation, and his movement.

---

d *Ibid.*, Chapter 79, fol. 356. ["Of the things which contribute to the composition of the genera." —Ed.]

XIII

The Transition to the Musical Practice of the Classical Period

65. J. J. Quantz

This outstanding flute player and composer for the flute began his career as an oboist in the Dresden royal orchestra in 1718. Quantz was born in 1697 and received his first training in counterpoint under Zelenka and Fux at Vienna. In 1724 he set out on a series of extended journeys: he visited Italy and studied in Rome with Gasparini and went in 1726 to Paris, where he stayed seven months and published several instrumental works, and to London, where he stayed three months. In 1728 Quantz entered into relations with Frederick the Great, who became a great admirer of his art and engaged him in 1741 as a flutist and composer to his court. He retained this position until his death in 1773.

Quantz was an extremely prolific composer: for the King alone he wrote three hundred concertos and two hundred other compositions. His best-known work, however, and the one that best testifies to the solidity of his musicianship, is his method for the flute, *Versuch einer Anweisung die Flöte traversière zu spielen* (1752). The book does not confine itself to flute playing but discusses questions of general importance for the musical practice and musical aesthetics of the time.

From the Versuch einer Anweisung die Flöte traversière zu spielen [1]

[*1752*]

HOW A PERFORMER AND A PIECE OF MUSIC OUGHT TO BE JUDGED

1. THERE IS perhaps no art so subject to every man's judgment as music. It would seem as though there were nothing easier than to judge it. Not only every musician, but also everyone who gives himself out as a musical amateur, wishes likewise to be regarded as a judge of what he hears.

---

1 Text: The original edition (Berlin, 1752), pp. 275–281, 293–308, 323–325, 328–329, 331–334.

2. We are not always satisfied that each performer whom we hear should be at pains to offer what lies within his powers; we often expect to hear more than we ourselves have ever been used to hearing. If, in a company, not all sing or play with equal perfection, we often attribute all the excellence to one performer, considering the others as of no account, without reflecting that one may have his merits in this style, another in that, one, for example, in Adagio, another in Allegro. We fail to consider that the attraction of music consists, not in equality or similarity, but in variety. If it were possible for all musicians to sing or play with the same ability and in the same taste, as a result of this lack of an agreeable variety the greater part of our enjoyment in music would be lost.

3. We are seldom guided by our own impression, which would after all be the surest guide, but we are at once anxious to hear which one is the ablest of those who are singing or playing, just as though we could at one time oversee and estimate the skill of several persons, like things that only show their worth and merit on the scales. And now we listen only to him who is in this fashion pronounced the ablest. A piece which he performs carelessly enough, often intentionally, and which is into the bargain a very poor one, is puffed up as a marvel; to another, for all the great industry with which he is at pains to perform some choice piece, we grant barely a few moments' attention.

4. We seldom allow a performer time enough to show his strength or weakness. We also fail to consider that a performer is not always in a position to offer what he understands; that often the slightest accident may easily cause him to lose all his self-possession; and that, as a result of this, we ought in fairness to hear him more than once before venturing to pass judgment on him. Some performers are forward and have perhaps a few pieces in which they can show everything that they can do and, so to speak, unburden themselves of their whole art at one time, so that we hear them once and for all. Others who are not thus forward and whose art cannot, as in the former case, be confined to a few pieces have not the same advantage. For most listeners are only too inclined to be hasty in their judgments and allow themselves to be altogether too much prepossessed by what they hear at first. Had they the patience and the opportunity to hear each performer several times, no great insight would be required as a rule; they would need only to be guided by their own feelings, without prejudice, and to see which performer gave them the most pleasure in the long run.

5. As regards composition, we are no better off. We are unwilling to be regarded as ignorant; at the same time we feel, no doubt, that we may

not always be competent to make a proper decision. Hence we are usually inclined to begin by asking who the composer is, in order to be guided by this in our judgment. Does the piece prove to be by someone to whom we have conceded our approval in advance, it is at once unhesitatingly pronounced beautiful. Does the contrary apply, or have we perhaps some objection to the author's person, the whole piece passes for worthless. Anyone who wishes to convince himself of this in a positive way need only publish two pieces of equal excellence under different names, one of which is in favor, the other out of favor. The ignorance of many judges will surely soon betray itself.

6. More modest listeners, who do not credit themselves with sufficient insight to judge a thing, often have recourse to a musician, whose word they accept as irrefutable truth. Assuredly, by listening to many good performances and to the judgment which experienced, instructed, and honest musicians pass on them, we can attain a certain degree of knowledge, especially when we ask also about the reasons why a piece is good or bad. This, then, ought to be one of the most reliable means of avoiding error. But are all those who make music their business at the same time musical experts or musical scholars? Have not ever so many of these learned their art as a mere trade? It can then easily happen that we address our questions to the wrong person and that the musician, quite as much as the amateur, is swayed in his decision by ignorance, envy, prejudice, or flattery. Like wildfire, such a verdict spreads abroad at once and so takes in the uninformed who rely on a supposed oracle of this kind that in the end there arises from it a prejudice which is not easily again removed. What is more, it is not even possible for every musician to be a competent judge of all that can occur in music. Singing requires its special insight. The variety of the instruments is so great that the powers and the lifetime of a single person would be insufficient for attaining insight into all their properties. Before placing his trust in the judgment of a musician, the musical amateur must therefore accurately determine whether his musician is really in a position to judge correctly. With one who has thoroughly mastered his art, we are on safer ground than with one who has only followed his good instincts; the latter, however, is also not to be entirely rejected. And because it is not easy for anyone to be so free from the passions that his judgments do not sometimes even run counter to his knowledge, the musical amateur must also in this respect accept the judgment of a musician with caution. There are some whom almost nothing pleases but what they have written themselves. Alas, then, for all music that has not the honor to thank their celebrated pens for its

existence! Whenever, to avoid scandal, they find themselves obliged to praise a thing, do they not do so in a way which, after all, betrays that to praise is difficult for them? Others, just the other way, praise everything indiscriminately, to fall out with nobody and to make themselves agreeable to everyone. Many a rising young musician regards nothing as beautiful but what has flowed from his master's inventive genius. Many a composer seeks his reputation in unrelieved remote modulations, obscure melodies, and other things of this sort. With him, everything is to be extraordinary and unusual. No doubt he has won applause by his real merits and also surreptitiously gained a following by other means. Does anyone expect him and those who blindly honor him to pronounce a thing beautiful which does not agree with this way of thinking? The older generation complains of the melodic extravagances of the younger; the younger generation makes fun of the dry style of the older. Nevertheless, we occasionally find musicians who grasp a thing impartially according to its real worth, who praise what ought to be praised, and who reject what ought to be rejected. Such musical scholars are the safest to trust. Yet the upright and able musician must be very much on his guard lest his passions lead him to commit some injustice and especially lest professional jealousy deceive him, for his judgment, to be sure, while it can be the most correct, can also, because of the reputation he enjoys, be the most dangerous.

7. Now since music is the sort of art which must be judged, not according to our own fancy, but, like the other fine arts, according to good taste, acquired through certain rules and refined by much experience and exercise; since he who wishes to judge another ought to understand at least as much as the other, if not more; since these qualities are seldom met with in those who occupy themselves with the judging of music; since, on the contrary, the greater part of these are governed by ignorance, prejudice, and passions which hinder correct judgment; many a one would do much better if he would keep his judgment to himself and listen with greater attention, if, without judging, he can still take pleasure in music. When he listens more to judge the performer needlessly than to enjoy the music, he arbitrarily deprives himself of the greater part of the pleasure which he would otherwise take in it. And when, even before the musician has finished his piece, our critic is already occupied in imposing his mistaken opinions on his neighbors, he makes the musician lose, not only his self-possession, but also his power to finish with a stout heart and to demonstrate his ability as he might otherwise have done. For who can remain insensible and self-possessed when, here and there among his listeners, he

sees expressions of disapproval? The hasty judge, moreover, is in constant danger of betraying his ignorance to others who are not of his opinion and perhaps understand more than he does; he can expect, therefore, no advantage from his judgment. From this, we may conclude how really difficult it is to take upon ourselves the office of a music critic and to discharge it honorably.

8. In judging music, besides obeying the usual dictates of reason and fairness, we should always pay particular attention to three points, namely, to the piece itself, to the performer, and to the listener. A fine composition may be mutilated by a bad performance; a poor composition, on the other hand, deprives the performer of his advantage; we must first determine, therefore, whether it is the performer or the composition that is responsible for the good or bad effect. With regard to the listener, as with regard to the performer, much depends on the various constitutions of the temperament. Some prefer the magnificent and lively style, some the mournful and profound, some the gay and delicate; each is governed by his inclinations. Some have considerable knowledge which others lack. We are not always carried away immediately the first time we hear this piece or that. It often happens that a piece pleases us today which tomorrow, if we chance to be in a different mood, we can scarcely sit through; on the other hand, a piece may displease us today in which tomorrow we discover beauties. A piece may be well written and well played; even so it fails to please everyone. A poor piece badly played may displease many; at the same time it finds a few admirers. The place in which a piece of music is performed can put many obstacles in the way of our judging it correctly. We hear, for example, one and the same piece, today from near by, tomorrow from far off. In each case we notice a difference. We may hear a piece intended for a vast place and a large orchestra in its proper setting. It will please us immensely. But if, at some other time, we hear the same piece in a room, performed perhaps by other persons, with a few instruments accompanying, it will have lost half its beauty. A piece that has well-nigh enchanted us in the chamber may be barely recognizable when we hear it in the theater. If, on the one hand, we were to ornament a slow movement, written in the French taste, with many arbitrary embellishments as though it were an Italian Adagio, or if, on the other hand, we were to perform an Italian Adagio in a good, dry, straightforward style with pretty, pleasing trills in the French taste; the former would become wholly unrecognizable—the latter would sound very plain and thin; as a result, neither one would please either the Frenchman or the Italian. Each piece, then, must be played in the style that belongs to it; unless

this is done, there can be no judgment. Supposing, further, that each piece were played, according to the taste proper to it, in these two ways, no Italian could judge the French and no Frenchman the Italian, for both are prepossessed by prejudices in favor of their country and their national music.

9. After this, everyone will grant me, I believe, that the correct and impartial judgment of a piece of music requires, not merely a little insight, but perhaps the highest degree of musical skill; that far more is involved than merely being able to sing or play a little ourselves; and that, as a result of this, if we would judge, we must apply ourselves assiduously to the attainment of that knowledge which reason, good taste, and art have placed within our reach. And further, I hope that no one will wish to dispute my contention that not every one of those who commonly set themselves up as judges of music is equipped with this knowledge and that, for this reason, there must arise a great detriment to music, musicians, and musical amateurs, who are kept thereby in a constant state of uncertainty.

10. I shall attempt to indicate, by means of certain characteristic signs, the chief qualities of the complete performer and of the well-written piece of music, in order that musicians, and musical amateurs as well, may have at least some guidance in forming their judgments and in determining to which performer or to which piece of music they may properly give their approval. Let everyone who seeks to judge try always to do so without prejudice, without passion, with fairness. Let him proceed cautiously and not hurry himself unduly. Let him regard the thing itself and not allow himself to be blinded by secondary considerations which have nothing to do with it; for example, whether the performer or composer is of this or that nationality, whether or not he has traveled abroad, whether he claims to be a pupil of a famous master, whether he is in the service of a great lord, or of a little one, or of no one at all, whether he has a musical character or no character, whether he is friend or foe, young or old, and so forth. In general, we shall not easily be unfair if, instead of saying of a performer or a piece of music, "It is worthless," we say only, "It does not please me." The latter everyone has the right to say, for no one is obliged to be pleased with anything. The former, however, we ought in fairness to leave solely to the real musical experts, who are in any case duty bound to indicate the reasons for their verdict.

.   .   .   .   .

28. To judge an instrumental composition properly, we must have an exact knowledge, not only of the characteristics of each species which may occur in it, but also, as already observed, of the instruments themselves. In itself, a piece may conform both to good taste and to the rules of composition, and hence be well written, but still run counter to the instrument. On the other hand, a piece may conform to the instrument, but be in itself useless. Vocal music has certain advantages which instrumental music must do without. The words and the human voice work to the composer's greatest advantage, with regard both to invention and to characterization. Experience clearly shows this when, in the absence of voices, arias are played on an instrument. Without words and without the human voice, instrumental music, quite as much as vocal music, should express certain passions and transport the listeners from one to another. But if this is to be properly managed, to compensate for the absence of words and of the human voice, neither the composer nor the performer may have a soul of wood.

29. The principal species of instrumental composition in which voices take no part are: the concerto, the overture, the sinfonia, the quartet, the trio, and the solo. In each of the following there are two varieties: the concerto, the trio, and the solo. We have concerti grossi and concerti da camera. The trios are, as the phrase goes, either elaborate or gallant. With the solos the case is the same.

30. The concertos were originated by the Italians. Torelli is said to have written the first ones. A concerto grosso consists in a mixture of various concerted instruments wherein, as an invariable rule, two or more parts—the number may sometimes run as high as eight or even higher—concert with one another. In the concerto da camera, however, there is only a single concerted instrument.

31. The qualities of a concerto grosso require, in each of its movements: (1) a magnificent ritornello at the beginning, which should be more harmonic than melodic, more serious than humorous, and relieved by unisons; (2) a skillful mixture of the imitations in the concerted parts, in order that the ear may be unexpectedly surprised, now by this instrument, now by that; (3) these imitations must be made up of short and pleasing ideas; (4) there must be a constant alternation of the brilliant and the ingratiating; (5) the inner tutti sections must be kept short; (6) the alternations of the concerted instruments must be so distributed that one is not heard too much and another too little; (7) now and then, after a trio, there must be woven in a short solo for one instrument or another; (8) before the end the solo instruments must briefly repeat what they had at

the beginning; and (9) the final tutti must conclude with the loftiest and most magnificent ideas of the first ritornello. Such a concerto requires numerous accompanying players, a large place, a serious performance, and a moderate tempo.

32. Of concertos with a single concerted instrument, the so-called "concerti da camera," there are likewise two varieties. Some, like the concerto grosso, require many accompanying players, others a few. Unless this is observed, neither the one nor the other has its proper effect. From the first ritornello one can gather to which variety a concerto belongs. If this is serious, magnificent, more harmonic than melodic, and relieved by many unisons, the harmony changing, not with eighth or quarter measures, but with half or full measures, many players must accompany. If, on the other hand, it consists in a fleeting, humorous, gay, or singing melody, the harmony changing rapidly, it will have a better effect with a few players accompanying than with many.

33. A serious concerto, that is, a simple one written for many players, requires the following in the first movement: (1) There should be a magnificent ritornello, with all the parts well elaborated. (2) There should be a pleasing and intelligible melody. (3) There should be regular imitations. (4) The best ideas of the ritornello may be broken up and used for relief within or between the solos. (5) The thorough bass should sound well and be suitable for use as a bass. (6) The composer should write no more inner parts than the principal part permits, for it is often more effective to double the principal melody than to introduce forced inner parts. (7) The progressions of the thorough bass and of the inner parts may neither impede the principal part in its liveliness nor drown out or stifle it. (8) A proportional length must be observed in the ritornello. This should consist of at least two main sections. The second of these, since it is to be repeated at the end of the movement as a conclusion, must be clothed with the finest and most magnificent ideas. (9) Insofar as the opening idea of the ritornello is neither singing nor wholly suitable for solo use, the composer must introduce a new idea, directly contrasted with the first, but so joined to it that it is not evident whether it is introduced from necessity or after due deliberation. (10) The solo sections must be in part singing, while the ingratiating should be in part relieved by brilliant, melodious, harmonious passages, always suited to the instrument, and also, to maintain the fire to the end, by short, lively, magnificent tutti sections. (11) The concerted, or solo, sections may not be too short or the inner tuttis too long. (12) The accompaniment to the solo must contain no progressions which might obscure the concerted part; on the contrary,

it must be made up alternately of many parts and few, in order that the principal part may now and then have room to come to the fore with greater freedom. In general, light and shade must be maintained throughout. When the solo passages permit it, or when the composer knows how to discover such as will, it is most effective that the accompanying parts should introduce beneath them something familiar from the ritornello. (13) The modulation must always be correct and natural, not touching on any key so remote that it might offend the ear. (14) The laws of meter, to which the composer has at all times to pay strict attention, must here, too, be exactly observed. The caesuras, or divisions of the melody, may not fall on the second or fourth quarter in common duple time, or on the third or fifth measure in triple. The composer must endeavor to maintain the meter with which he begins, whether it be by whole or half measures or, in triple time, by two-, four-, or eight-measure phrases; otherwise the most artful composition becomes defective. In triple time, in an arioso, if the melody permits frequent divisions, successive caesuras after three- and two-measure phrases are permitted. (15) The composer may not follow up the solo passages with uniform transpositions *ad nauseam;* on the contrary, he must imperceptibly interrupt and shorten them at the right time. (16) The ending may not be hurried unduly or bitten off too short; on the contrary, the composer should endeavor to make it thoroughly solid. Nor may he conclude with wholly new ideas; on the contrary, the last solo section must repeat the most pleasing of those ideas that have been heard before. (17) The last tutti, finally, must conclude the Allegro, as briefly as possible, with the second section of the first ritornello.

34. Not every variety of measure is suitable for the first movement of a magnificent concerto. If the movement is to be lively, the composer may employ common duple time, in which the smallest note is the sixteenth, permitting the caesura to fall on the second half of the measure. If it is likewise to be magnificent, he should choose a longer meter, one in which the caesura regularly occupies the full measure and falls only on the down beat. If, however, it is to be both serious and magnificent, he may choose for it, in common duple time, a moderate tempo in which the smallest note is the thirty-second, the caesura falling on the second half of the measure. The dotted sixteenths will in this case contribute much to the magnificence of the ritornello. The movement may be defined by the word *allegretto.* Notes of this kind can also be written in the moderate alla breve time. It is only necessary to change the eighths to quarters, the sixteenths to eighths, and the thirty-seconds to sixteenths. In this case, however, the caesura may always fall on the beginning of the measure. The ordinary

alla breve time, in which the smallest note is the eighth, is to be regarded as the equivalent of two-four time and is more suited to the last movement than to the first, for, unless one writes continually in the strict style, using all the voices, it is more expressive of the pleasing than of the magnificent. In general, triple time is little used for the first movement, unless in the form of three-four time with occasional sixteenths and a movement in eighths in the inner and lowest parts, the harmony changing, as a rule, only with full measures.

35. The Adagio must be distinguished from the first Allegro in every respect—in its musical rhyme-structure, its meter, and its key. If the Allegro is in one of the major keys, for example in C major, the Adagio may, as one prefers, be in C minor, E minor, A minor, F major, G major, or even G minor. If, on the other hand, the first Allegro is in one of the minor keys, for example in C minor, the Adagio may be in E-flat major, F minor, G minor, or A-flat major. These successions of keys are the most natural. The ear is never offended by them, and the same relationships apply to all keys, whatever they may be called. He who wishes to surprise the listener in a painful and disagreeable way is at liberty to choose, beyond these keys, such as may give pleasure to him alone. To say the least, considerable caution is necessary in this regard.

36. For the arousing and subsequent stilling of the passions the Adagio offers greater opportunity than the Allegro. In former times it was for the most part written in a plain dry style, more harmonic than melodic. The composers left to the performers what had been expected of them, namely, to make the melody singable, but this could not be well accomplished without considerable addition of embellishments. In other words, it was in those days much easier to write an Adagio than to play one. Now, as it may be readily imagined that such an Adagio did not always have the good fortune to fall into skillful hands, and since the performance was seldom as successful as the author might have wished, there has come of this evil some good, namely, that composers have for some time past begun to make their Adagios more singing. By this means the composer has more honor and the performer less of a puzzle; moreover, the Adagio itself can no longer be distorted or mutilated in such a variety of ways as was formerly often the case.

37. But since the Adagio does not usually find as many admirers as the Allegro among the musically uninstructed, the composer must endeavor in every possible way to make it pleasing even to those listeners without musical experience. To this end, he should above all strictly observe the following rules. (1) He must aim studiously at the greatest

possible brevity, both in the ritornellos and in the solo sections. (2) The ritornello must be melodious, harmonious, and expressive. (3) The principal part must have a melody which, though it permits some addition of embellishments, may still please without it. (4) The melody of the principal part must alternate with the tutti sections used between for relief. (5) This melody must be just as touching and expressive as though there were words below it. (6) From time to time something from the ritornello must be introduced. (7) The composer may not wander off into too many keys, for this is the greatest impediment to brevity. (8) The accompaniment beneath the solo must be rather more plain than figured, in order that the principal part may not be prevented from making ornaments and may retain complete freedom to introduce, judiciously and reasonably, many or few embellishments. (9) The composer, finally, must endeavor to characterize the Adagio with some epithet clearly expressing the passion contained therein, in order that the required tempo may be readily determined.

38. The final Allegro of a concerto must be very different from the first movement, not only in its style and nature, but also in its meter. The last Allegro must be just as humorous and gay as the first is serious. To this end, the following meters will prove useful: $\frac{2}{4}$, $\frac{3}{4}$, $\frac{3}{8}$, $\frac{6}{8}$, $\frac{9}{8}$, and $\frac{12}{8}$. In no case should all three movements of a concerto be written in the same meter. But if the first movement is in duple time and the second in triple, the last may be written either in triple or in two-four time. In no case, however, may it stand in common duple time, for this would be too serious and hence as little suited to the last movement as two-four or a rapid triple time to the first. Similarly, all three movements may not begin on the same step, but, if the upper part begins in the first movement on the keynote, it may begin in the second on the third and in the third on the fifth. And although the last movement is in the key of the first, the composer, to avoid similarity in the modulations, must still be careful not to pass through the same succession of keys in the last movement as he did in the first.

39. Generally speaking, in the last movement (1) The ritornello must be short, gay, fiery, but at the same time somewhat playful. (2) The principal part must have a simple melody, pleasing and fleeting. (3) The solo passages should be easy, in order that the rapidity of the movement may not be impeded. They may, further, bear no similarity to those in the first movement. For example, if those in the first movement are made up of broken notes and arpeggios, those in the last movement may be rolling or proceed by step. Or if there are triplets in the first movement,

the passages in the last movement may be made up of even notes, or vice versa. (4) The laws of meter must be observed with the utmost severity. For the shorter and more rapid the variety of measure, the more painful it is if these laws are violated. In ¾ and in rapid ¾, ⅜, and ⅝ time, the caesura, then, must always fall on the beginning of every second measure, the principal divisions on the fourth and eighth measures. (5) The accompaniment may not employ too many voices or be overcrowded; on the contrary, it must be made up of such notes as the accompanying parts can produce without undue movement or effort, for the last movement is as a rule played very rapidly.

40. To insure a proportional length, even in a concerto, consult a time-piece. If the first movement takes five minutes, the Adagio five to six, and the last movement three to four, the whole is of the proper length. And it is in general more advantageous if the listeners find a piece rather too short than too long.

41. He who now understands how to make a concerto of this sort will have no difficulty in contriving also a humorous little concerto da camera of the playful kind. It will, then, be unnecessary to discuss this separately.

42. An overture, played before an opera, requires a magnificent beginning, full of gravity, a brilliant, well-elaborated principal section, and a good combination of different instruments, such as flutes, oboes, or horns. Its origin is due to the French. Lully has provided excellent models. Some German composers, however, among them Handel and Telemann, have far surpassed him in this. Indeed, the French fare with their overtures very much as do the Italians with their concertos. Still, in view of their excellent effect, it is a pity that the overtures are not more usual in Germany.

43. The Italian sinfonias, having the same purpose as the overtures, naturally require, as regards magnificence, precisely the same qualities. But since most of them are contrived by composers such as have exercised their genius more in vocal than in instrumental music, we have thus far only a very few sinfonias, perfect in all respects, to use as models. Sometimes it seems as though the composers of opera, in contriving their sinfonias, went about it as do those painters who, in finishing a portrait, use the left-over colors to fill in the sky or the costume. In the meantime it stands to reason, as previously mentioned, that a sinfonia should have some connection with the content of its opera or at least with the first scene of it and not, as frequently occurs, conclude invariably with a gay minuet. I have no wish to set up a standard in this regard, for it is impossible to bring under a single head all the circumstances that may occur at the begin-

ning of an opera. At the same time, I believe that it should be very easy to find a mean. It is admittedly quite unnecessary that the sinfonia before an opera consist always of three movements; could the composer not conclude, perhaps, with the first or second? For example, if the first scene involved heroic or other fiery passions, he might end his sinfonia with the first movement. If mournful or amorous passions occurred in it, he might stop after the second movement. But if the first scene involved no particular passions at all, these appearing only in the course of the opera or at the end, he might close with the third movement. By so doing, he would have an opportunity to arrange each movement in a way suitable to the matter at hand. The sinfonia, moreover, would still retain its usefulness for other purposes.

44. A quartet, that is, a sonata for three concerted instruments and a thorough bass, is the real touchstone of the true contrapuntist, as it is also an affair wherein many a one not properly grounded in his art may come to grief. Its use has never become really common; as a result, it may not even be known to everyone. Indeed, it is to be feared that in the end this kind of music will have to suffer the fate of the lost arts. A good quartet implies: (1) pure four-part writing; (2) a good harmonious melody; (3) short, regular imitations; (4) a judicious combination of the concerted instruments; (5) a proper thorough bass suited for use as a bass; (6) ideas of the sort that are mutually invertible, so that one may build either above or below them, the inner parts maintaining an at least tolerable and not displeasing melodic line; (7) that it must not be obvious whether this part or that one has the advantage; (8) that each part, after a rest, must re-enter, not as inner part, but as principal part and with a pleasing melody (this, however, is to be understood as applying, not to the thorough bass, but only to the three concerted parts); (9) that if there is a fugue, it must be carried out in a masterly and at the same time tasteful fashion in all four parts, observing all the rules. A certain set of six quartets for various instruments, chiefly flute, oboe, and violin, composed quite some time ago by Herr Telemann, may serve as particularly beautiful models of this kind of music.

45. A trio, while it is a task less tedious for the composer than a quartet, nevertheless requires on his part almost the same degree of artistry, if it is in its way to be of the proper sort. Yet it has the advantage that the ideas introduced may be more gallant and pleasing than in the quartet, for there is one concerted part the less. In a trio, then, the composer must follow these rules: (1) He must invent a melody which will tolerate a singing counterpoint. (2) The subjects proposed at the beginning of each

movement may not be too long, especially in the Adagio, for in the imitations which the second part makes at the fifth, fourth, and unison, an overlong subject can easily become wearisome. (3) No part may propose any subject that the other cannot answer. (4) The imitations must be brief and the passages brilliant. (5) In the repetition of the most pleasing ideas a good order must be maintained. (6) The two principal parts must be so written that the thorough bass below may be natural and sound well. (7) If a fugue is introduced, it must be, as in the quartet, carried out in all the parts, not only correctly, observing all the rules of composition, but also tastefully. The episodes, whether they consist of passages or of other imitations, must be pleasing and brilliant. (8) While progressions of the two principal parts in parallel thirds and sixths are an ornament of the trio, they must not be overdone or run into the ground, but rather interrupted by passages or other imitations. (9) The trio, finally, must be so contrived that one can scarcely guess which of the two parts is the first.

46. To write a solo is today no longer regarded as an art. Almost every instrumentalist occupies himself in this way. If he has no ideas, he helps himself with borrowed ones. If he is lacking in knowledge of the rules of composition, he lets someone else write the bass for him. As a result, our time brings forth, instead of good models, many monstrosities.

47. As a matter of fact, it is by no means so easy to write a good solo. There are composers who understand composition perfectly and are successful in works for many voices, but who write poor solos. On the other hand, there are composers for whom the solos turn out better than the things for many voices. He who succeeds in both is fortunate. Little need as there is to have mastered all the innermost secrets of composition in order to write a good solo, there is as little chance of accomplishing anything reasonable of this kind without having some understanding of harmony.

48. If a solo is to reflect credit on the composer and the performer, then (1) its Adagio must be in itself singing and expressive; (2) the performer must have opportunities to show his judgment, invention, and insight; (3) the delicate must be relieved from time to time by something ingenious; (4) the thorough bass must be a natural one above which one can build easily; (5) no idea may be too often repeated, either in the same key or in a transposition, for not only can this make difficulties for the player, but it can also become tiresome for the listeners; (6) the natural melody must be interrupted occasionally by dissonances, to arouse the passions of the listeners in a suitable manner; (7) the Adagio must not be too long.

49. The first Allegro requires: (1) a flowing, coherent, and somewhat serious melody; (2) well-connected ideas; (3) brilliant passages, well unified melodically; (4) a good order in the repetition of the ideas; (5) choice and beautiful progressions at the end of the first part, so arranged that, in a transposition, they may conclude the second part also; (6) that the first part must be somewhat shorter than the second; (7) that the most brilliant passages must be reserved for the second part; (8) that the thorough bass must be natural, making such progressions as will maintain a continuous liveliness.

50. The second Allegro may be either very gay and rapid, or moderate and aria-like. In this, the composer must be guided by the first movement. If this is serious, the last movement may be gay. But if it is lively and rapid, the last movement may be moderate and aria-like. With regard to variety of measure, what was said of the concertos must also be observed here, lest one movement be like the other. In general, if a solo is to please everyone, it must be so contrived that it affords nourishment to each listener's temperamental inclinations. It must be neither purely cantabile nor purely lively from beginning to end. And just as each movement must be very different from any other, the individual movements must be in themselves good mixtures of pleasing and brilliant ideas. For the most beautiful melody will in the end prove a soporific if it is never relieved, and continuous liveliness and unmitigated difficulty arouse astonishment but do not move particularly. Indeed, such mixtures of contrasted ideas should be the aim, not merely in the solo, but in all kinds of music. If a composer knows how to hit this off properly and thereby to set in motion the passions of his listeners, one may truly say of him that he has attained a high degree of good taste and found, so to speak, the musical philosopher's stone.[2]

51. These, then, are the chief characteristics of the principal species of musical composition—characteristics which must be present in each according to its kind if a connoisseur is to pronounce it good and worthy of applause. Still there will always be left over a number of listeners who are unable to attain that insight into music which is necessary if our characteristic signs of the excellence of a piece are to be remarked in it. Such listeners, then, must confine themselves exclusively to secondary considerations touching, not the performer's person, but the music in general, considerations which can also to a certain extent afford an indication of the excellence of a piece. They will proceed most securely if, when music

---

2 Cf. Burney's characterization of John Christian Bach (*A General History of Music*, IV, 483): "Bach seems to have been the first composer who observed the law of contrast as a principle. Before his time, contrast there frequently was, in the works of others, but it seems to have been accidental. Bach, in his symphonies and other instrumental pieces, as well as his songs, seldom failed, after a rapid and noisy passage, to introduce one that was slow and soothing."

is sung or played at great assemblies (these, however, should be such assemblies as convene for no other purpose than to hear music—assemblies at which music is not regarded as a mere side issue and at which the listeners are made up both of connoisseurs and of the musically uninstructed), they will observe the expressions and gestures of the audience, endeavoring to determine: whether only a few or the majority of the company are aroused to attention; whether one listener or another gives signs of pleasure or displeasure; whether the performers are approached or ignored; whether there is silence or loud conversation; whether anyone nods his head in time to the music; whether anyone is desirous of knowing the author of the piece; whether the company, when the piece is over, shows a wish to hear it again. Finally, they must also inquire a little into their own feelings and determine whether the music they have heard has moved them, even though they cannot always give the reason for this. Then, if all the favorable considerations just enumerated are found in a piece of music, even the musically uninstructed listener may confidently conclude that it has been well written and well performed.

52. The divergence in taste which asserts itself in all the various nations that take any pleasure at all in art has the greatest influence on musical judgment, not only as regards essential matters, but still more as regards accidental ones. It is therefore necessary to inquire in still greater detail into this divergence, although, as the need arose, I have already commented on it to some extent at various points in the foregoing.

53. Every nation, unless it belongs among the barbarous, has in its music some one quality which pleases it pre-eminently and above others; at the same time this quality diverges in some cases so little from others and is in other cases of so little consequence that we cannot consider it worthy of special attention. In recent times, however, two nations have not only acquired special merit through their improvement of musical taste, but have also, in following their innate temperamental inclinations, come to diverge pre-eminently from one another in this respect. These nations are the Italian and the French. Other nations have most applauded the tastes of these two peoples and have endeavored to imitate one taste or the other and to adopt some part of it. As a result of this, the two peoples before mentioned have been seduced, as it were, into setting themselves up as arbiters of good taste in music, and, since for some time past no foreigner has objected, for several centuries they have actually been, so to speak, the musical lawgivers. From them, good taste in music was brought afterwards to other peoples.

54. Not to go back to its remotest origins, music, like the other fine

arts, was handed down in olden times from the Greeks to the Romans, and, after the decline of Roman splendor, it lay for a long time as though in the dust of oblivion; this much is certain. But which nation it was that first began to rescue music from its decline and to restore it in its renewed form is a question that has been much disputed. We may presume, however, that a really thorough and proper investigation would render a decision in favor of the Italians. To be sure, it took a long time to bring music to that approximation of perfection in which it stands today. It is possible that, at certain times, one nation was somewhat further advanced in this respect and that, at certain other times, another nation came to the fore, only to follow again later on. Charlemagne, at the time he was in Rome, already awarded the palm to the Italian musicians for their singing and even caused a number of them to come to his court. He endeavored to organize his music after Italian models.

55. There is good reason to believe that, long after the time of Charlemagne, the music of the Italians and the French was by no means as different as it is today. Lully—whom the French regard as almost a general in music, continuing to this day to approve his taste throughout all France, endeavoring indeed, whenever any of their countrymen wish to depart from it, to restore it with care and to maintain it, unaltered, in full sway— Lully, as is well known, was an Italian. I will admit that this celebrated man, having come to France very young, adapted himself, to some extent, to the older French music and adopted its taste. But no one will be able to show that it was possible for him to deny altogether the taste peculiar to his own nation, some notion of which he must have gathered in Italy after all. Since Lully's death, however, the taste in music has in Italy been constantly and very noticeably changing, as everyone knows, while in France it has remained precisely the same; for this reason, the divergence between the two has in the meantime really begun to show itself.

.   .   .   .   .

76. If, after this, we wished to characterize in brief the Italian and the French music and to draw a parallel between the divergent tastes of the one and the other, regarding each from its best side, the comparison would run, in my opinion, substantially to this effect:

The Italians, in composition, are broad-minded, magnificent, lively, expressive, profound, lofty in their way of thinking, somewhat bizarre, free, forward, audacious, extravagant, occasionally careless in their meter; at the same time, they are also singing, ingratiating, delicate, moving, and rich in invention. They write more for the connoisseur than for the amateur. The French, in composition, are lively, expressive, natural, pleasing and intelligible to the public, and more correct in their meter than the Italians; at the same time, they are neither profound nor bold but on the contrary very narrow-minded, servile, always the same, commonplace in their way of thinking, dry in invention; they continually warm over the ideas of their predecessors and write more for the amateur than for the connoisseur.

The Italian way of singing is profound and artful, at once moving and astonishing; it engages the musical understanding and is pleasing, charming, expressive, rich in taste and stylish delivery; it transports the listener in an agreeable way from one passion to another. The French way of singing is simple rather than artful, speaking rather than singing, exaggerated rather than natural in expressing the passions and in voice, wanting in taste and stylish delivery, and always the same; it is more for amateurs than for musical experts, better suited to drinking songs than to serious arias, and, while it amuses the senses, it leaves the musical understanding wholly disengaged.

The Italian way of playing is arbitrary, extravagant, artificial, obscure, likewise frequently audacious and bizarre, difficult in performance; it permits a considerable addition of embellishments and requires a fair knowledge of harmony; in the uninstructed it arouses less pleasure than astonishment. The French way of playing is servile but modest, clear, neat and pure in its delivery, easy to imitate, neither profound nor obscure, but intelligible to every man and suited to the amateur; it requires little knowledge of harmony, for the embellishments are for the most part prescribed by the composer; at the same time, it is, for the musical expert, little conducive to reflection.

In a word, the Italian music is arbitrary and the French narrow-minded; for this reason, the good effect depends, in the latter case, more on the composition than on the performance, in the former case, almost as much—indeed, in some pieces even more—on the performance than on the composition.

The Italian way of singing is preferable to their way of playing, the French way of playing preferable to their way of singing.

77. The qualities of these two kinds of music might easily be developed at greater length and more thoroughly examined. This, however, would be more suited to a separate and special treatise than to my present purpose. As it is, I have endeavored to enumerate in brief their principal truths and characteristic signs, as also their differences. I leave each of my readers at liberty to draw, from what has been said, his own conclu-

sions as to which taste properly deserves the preference. I am confident that my readers, in fairness to me, will be that much the less inclined to accuse me of partiality in this, since whatever degree of taste I may have acquired myself has flowed both from the Italian and from the French, since I have traveled in both countries with the express purpose of profiting in each from its good side, and since I am therefore an eye- and ear-witness of both kinds of music.

78. Now, if we were to make a thorough examination of the music of the Germans of more than a century ago, we should find that, even that far back, they had reached a very high point, not only in correct harmonic composition, but also in the playing of many instruments. Of good taste, however, and of beautiful melody we should find little trace, save for a few old chorales; on the contrary, we should find their taste and melody alike longer than their neighbors', rather plain, dry, thin, and simple.

79. In composition they were, as indicated, harmonious and many-voiced, but not melodious or charming.

Their writing was more artful than intelligible or pleasing, more for the eye than for the ear.

The very oldest introduced in their elaborate pieces too many superfluous cadences in succession and were accustomed scarcely to modulate from one key to another without first making a cadence, a straightforward procedure with which the ear was seldom surprised.

Their ideas were not well chosen or well connected.

To arouse and still the passions was something unknown to them.

·   ·   ·   ·   ·

82. However wretched the taste of German composers, singers, and instrumentalists may have been in former times, for all their thorough insight into harmony, it has now taken on, little by little, a very different appearance. For, if we cannot precisely say of the Germans that they have produced a taste of their own, wholly different from the music of other nations, they are the more capable of adopting one from outside, whichever they please, and they know how to profit by the good side of foreign music, whatever its kind.

83. As long ago as the middle of the last century a few celebrated men, some of whom had themselves visited Italy and France with profit, others of whom had taken the works and taste of distinguished foreigners as their models, began to work on the improvement of musical taste. The players of the organ and clavier, among the latter especially Froberger and after him Pachelbel, among the former Reincken, Buxtehude, Bruhns, and

several others, wrote almost as the first the most tasteful pieces of their time for their instruments. Above all, the art of playing the organ, for the most part taken over from the Netherlanders, was carried at this time to a very high point by those just named and a few other skillful men. More recently, this art was brought to its highest and final perfection by Johann Sebastian Bach, a man worthy of admiration. It is only to be hoped, in view of the small number of those who still take a certain pains with it, that with his death this art may not again tend toward decline, or even toward its downfall.

* * * * *

86. The Italians were formerly accustomed to call the German taste in music *un gusto barbaro*—"a barbarous taste." But now that it has come to pass that several German composers have been in Italy, where they have had opportunities to perform works of theirs with success, both operas and instrumental music, and since at the present time the operas which the Italians find most tasteful, and rightly so, are actually the productions of a German pen,[3] the prejudice has gradually been removed. It must be said, however, that the Germans are indebted—deeply to the Italians and somewhat to the French—for this favorable change in their taste. Everyone knows that, for more than a century, Italian and French composers, singers, and instrumentalists have been in service and have performed operas at various German courts—at Vienna, Dresden, Berlin, Hanover, Munich, Ansbach, and many others. Everyone knows that great lords have sent many of their musicians to Italy and France and that, as I have said before, many of the improvers of German taste have visited one or both of these countries. These have adopted the taste of the one or the other and have hit upon a mixture which has enabled them to write and to perform with success, not only German, but also Italian, French, and English operas and other Singspiele, each in its own language and taste. We cannot say as much of the Italian composers or of the French. It is not that they lacked the necessary talent, but rather that they gave themselves little pains to learn foreign languages and that they could not persuade themselves that, apart from them and without their language, respectable accomplishment in vocal music was still a possibility.

87. When we know how to select with due discrimination from the musical tastes of various peoples what is best in each, there arises a mixed taste which, without overstepping the bounds of modesty, may very well be called the German taste, not only because the Germans were the first

---

3 That of Johann Adolf Hasse.

to hit upon it, but also because, introduced many years ago in various parts of Germany, it still flourishes there, displeasing neither in Italy, nor France, nor any other country.

88. Now, provided the German nation does not again abandon this taste; if it will endeavor, as its most celebrated composers did in the past, to explore it further and further; if its composers of the new generation will apply themselves, as their predecessors did, more diligently than is unfortunately the case at present to mastering thoroughly, along with their mixed taste, the rules of composition; if, instead of stopping at mere melody and at the contriving of theatrical arias alone, they will exercise themselves also in the church style and in instrumental music; if, for the disposition of their pieces and the reasonable connecting and combining of their ideas, they will take as their models such composers as have received general applause, writing in their way and imitating their fine taste—yet not so that they accustom themselves thereby, as so often happens, to dress themselves in borrowed plumage, perhaps copying or warming over the principal section or the whole context from this or that composer; if, far from doing this, they will bend their own inventive faculties to show and clarify their talents without prejudice to others and to become composers instead of forever remaining mere copyists; if the German instrumentalists will refuse to permit themselves to be led astray by a bizarre and comic style, as we have called the Italian, but will take as their models the style of those who sing well and play with a reasonable taste; if finally the Italians and the French will imitate the Germans in their mixture of tastes as the Germans have imitated them; if, as I say, all these things are observed with one accord—then, in time, there may be introduced a general good taste in music. And this is something not at all improbable, for neither the Italians nor the French—though more the amateurs among them than the musicians themselves—are any longer wholly satisfied with their purely national taste alone, but show for some time past more pleasure in some foreign compositions than in their own.

89. In a taste consisting, like the present German taste, in a mixture of the tastes of various peoples, each nation finds something similar to its own—something, then, with which it cannot be displeased. Considering everything said up to this point about the divergence in taste, the purely Italian must have the preference over the purely French; yet, since the former is not now as thorough as it was, having become audacious and bizarre, and since the latter has remained all too simple, everyone will concede that a mixed taste, composed of what is good in both, must be unfailingly more general and more pleasing. For a music that is accepted

and pronounced good, not by a single country or by a single province or by this or that nation alone, but by many peoples—that is pronounced good, nay, that, for the reasons offered, cannot be pronounced other than good—must be, if based in other respects on reason and sound feeling, beyond all dispute the best.

66. Leopold Mozart

The father of Wolfgang Amadeus, himself an excellent violinist and a respectable composer, was born at Augsburg in 1719. He entered the service of the Prince-Bishop of Salzburg, served as a composer and assistant *maestro di cappella* to the episcopal court, and died at Salzburg in 1787.

Leopold Mozart was a prolific composer and wrote a large quantity of works in the most varied forms of sacred and secular music: masses, motets, symphonies, serenades, concertos, oratorios, operas, etc. His best-known work, however, is probably his method for the violin, *Versuch einer gründlichen Violinschule*, published in the year of Wolfgang's birth (1756), one of the oldest and most solid books of its kind. It is, with Quantz's method for the flute and C. P. E. Bach's method for keyboard instruments, an important source for the study of musical practice in the period immediately preceding the dawning of the classical era.

From the Versuch einer gründlichen Violinschule [1]

[*1756*]

Chapter Twelve

ON READING MUSIC CORRECTLY AND ON GOOD DELIVERY IN GENERAL

1. EVERYTHING turns on good performance—everyday experience confirms this rule. Many a half-composer is pleased and delighted when he hears his musical Galimathias performed by good players who know how to apply the passion, which he has not even thought about, in its proper place, how to make the greatest possible distinction in the characters, which has never occurred to him, and consequently how, by means of a good delivery, to render the whole wretched scribble tolerable to the ears

---

1 Text: The facsimile reprint of the original edition of 1756 (Vienna, 1922), pp. 252–264. A complete translation, by Editha Knocker, was published by the Oxford University Press in 1948.

of the listeners. But on the other hand, who does not know that the best composition is often so miserably performed that the composer himself has difficulty enough in recognizing his own work?

2. The good delivery of a composition in the present taste is not as simple as those people believe who think they are doing very well if, following their own ideas, they ornament and contort a piece in a truly idiotic fashion and who have no conception whatever of the passion that is supposed to be expressed in it. But who are these people? In the main they are those who, since they can scarcely play in time, even tolerably, begin at once with concertos and solos in order (as they stupidly imagine) to establish themselves as quickly as possible in the company of the virtuosi. Some actually reach such a point that, in a few concertos or solos that they have practiced thoroughly, they play off the most difficult passages with uncommon facility. These they know by heart. But if they are to perform even a few minuets in the cantabile style directed by the composer, they are in no position to do so—indeed one sees this already in the concertos they have studied. For as long as they play an Allegro, things still go well, but as soon as they come to an Adagio, they betray their gross ignorance and their poor judgment in every single measure of the piece. They play without order and without expression; they fail to distinguish the loud and the soft; the embellishments are applied in the wrong places, too thickly crowded and for the most part confused; sometimes, just the other way, the notes are too expressionless and one sees that the player does not know what to do. In such players one can seldom hope any longer for improvement, for of all people they are the most prepossessed in their own favor, and he would incur their highest displeasure who sought, out of the goodness of his heart, to persuade them of their mistakes.

3. To read correctly, as directed, the musical compositions of the good masters and to play each piece in accordance with the passion prevailing in it calls for far more art than to study the most difficult concertos and solos. To do the latter does not require much intelligence. And if the player is adroit enough to figure out the fingering he can learn the most difficult passages by himself, provided he practices them diligently. But to do the former is not as easy as this. For the player has not only to attend closely to every annotation and direction and to play the work as it is set down and not otherwise; he has also to enter into the passion that is to be expressed and to apply and to execute all the runs, the legatos and staccatos, the fortes and pianos, in a word, everything that bears in any way on the tasteful delivery of a piece, observing in this a certain good style that can be learned only by sound judgment through long experience.

4. Let the reader now decide for himself whether, among violinists, the good orchestral player ought not to be prized far more highly than the mere soloist. The soloist can play everything as he pleases and adjust its delivery to his own ideas, even to his own hand; the orchestral player must have the ability to grasp at once and to deliver properly the taste, the ideas, and the expression of different composers. The soloist, to bring things out cleanly, has only to practice at home—others must adapt themselves to him; the orchestral player must read everything at sight—often, indeed, passages such as run counter to the natural arrangement of the measure [a]—he must adapt himself to others. The soloist, if only he has a clean delivery, can in general play his concertos acceptably, even with distinction; the orchestral player, on the other hand, must have a considerable grasp of music in general, of the art of composition, and of differences in characters, nay, he must have a peculiarly versatile talent if he is to fill his office creditably, especially if he is ever to act as the leader of an orchestra. Are there some who believe that, among violinists, one finds more good orchestral players than soloists? They are mistaken. Poor accompanists are admittedly numerous enough, but there are very few good ones, for today everyone wants to be the soloist. But as to what an orchestra consisting entirely of soloists is like, I leave this to those gentlemen composers who have performed their works under such conditions. Few soloists read well, for it is their habit to be continually introducing details of their own invention and to regard themselves alone, paying little regard to others.[b]

5. Thus, until the player can accompany quite well, he must play no solos. He must first know exactly how to execute all the various strokes of the bow; he must understand how to apply the fortes and pianos in the proper place and to the proper degree; he must learn how to distinguish the characters of pieces and how to deliver each passage according to its required and peculiar taste; in a word, before he begins to play solos and concertos, he must be able to read the works of many gifted persons correctly and elegantly. From a painting, one sees at once whether he who has painted it is a master of drawing; in the same way, many a musician would play his solo more intelligently if he had ever learned to

---

a *Contra metrum musicum.* Of this I have already given notice in Chapter 1, Section 2, § 4, note *d*. And I do not know what I am to think when I see an aria, by one of those Italian composers who are so celebrated just now, which runs so counter to the musical meter that one would suppose it made by a pupil.

[In the note *d* to which Mozart refers, it is pointed out that common time ordinarily has two divisions only and that infractions of this rule are excused only in peasant dances or other unusual melodies.—Ed.]

b But what I say does not at all apply to those great virtuosi who, in addition to being extraordinarily gifted as players of concertos, are also good orchestral players. Such people are really deserving of the highest esteem.

deliver a symphony or trio in accordance with the good taste it required or to accompany an aria with the proper passion and in accordance with the character peculiar to it. I shall endeavor to set down some brief rules which the player can make profitable use of in the performance of a piece of music.

6. The player must of course tune his instrument carefully and exactly to those of his fellows; this he already knows and my mentioning the matter may seem somewhat superfluous. But since even those who wish to pass for first violinists often fail to tune their instruments exactly together, I find it absolutely necessary to mention the matter here, the more so since it is to the first violinist that the rest are supposed to tune. In playing with the organ or harpsichord, these determine the pitch; if neither one is present, the pitch is taken from the wind instruments. Some tune the A-string first, others the D. Both do well, if only they tune carefully and exactly. I would mention only one other point; in a warm room the pitch of the stringed instruments gradually falls, in a cold one it gradually rises.

7. Before beginning to play a piece, the player must thoroughly examine and consider it. He must discover the character, the tempo, and the sort of movement that it requires and must carefully determine whether there is not concealed in it some passage, seemingly unimportant at first sight, which will nonetheless be far from easy to play, demanding a special style of delivery and expression. Then, during the performance itself, he must spare no pains to discover and deliver correctly the passion that the composer has sought to apply and, since the mournful and the merry often alternate, he must be intent on delivering each of these in its own style. In a word, he must play everything in such a way that he will himself be moved by it.[c]

8. From this it follows that the player must pay the strictest attention to the prescribed pianos and fortes and not always be scraping away on one level. Nay, without direction and, as a rule, of himself, he must know how to relieve the soft with the loud and how to apply each of these in its proper place, for, following the familiar expression in painting, this is called light and shade. Notes that are raised by a sharp or natural he ought always to attack somewhat more vigorously, reducing his tone again for the continuation of the melody:

---

[c] It is bad enough that many a player never gives a thought to what he is doing and simply plays off his music as though in a dream or as though he were actually playing for himself alone. If such a player, at the beginning of a piece, gets a few beats ahead of the tempo, he does not notice it, and I will wager that he would finish the piece several measures before his fellows if his neighbor or the leader himself did not call his attention to it.

pia.   *for.*   *pia.*

In the same way he should differentiate in intensity a note that is momentarily lowered by a flat or natural:

p   *f*   *p*

With half notes that occur among shorter values, the invariable custom is to attack them vigorously and then to diminish the tone again:

fp   *fp*

Indeed, quarters are sometimes also played in just this way:

fp   *fp*   *fp*   *fp*

And this is the expression actually called for by the composer when he marks a note with an *f* or *p*, that is, with a forte or piano. But after the player has vigorously attacked the note, he must not let his bow leave the strings, as some clumsy players do; the stroke must be continued and consequently the tone still heard, though it will gently taper off.[d]

9. The accent,[e] expression, or intensity of the tone will fall as a rule on the strong or initial note that the Italians call the *nota buona*. But there are distinct varieties of these initial or "good" notes. The particularly strong notes are the following: in every measure, the note beginning the first quarter; in the half measure, the first note, or, in ¼ time, the first note of the third quarter; in ⁶⁄₄ and ⁶⁄₈ time, the first notes of the first and fourth quarters; in ¹²⁄₈ time, the first notes of the first, fourth, seventh, and tenth quarters. These, then, are the initial notes on which the maximum intensity of the tone will fall, wherever the composer has indicated no other expression. In the ordinary accompaniments for an aria or concerto, in which as a rule only eighth and sixteenth notes occur, they are

---

d Let the reader look up what I have said about this on p. 44, note *k*. [In this note (Chapter 1, Section 3, § 18), Mozart complains of those who cannot play a half note or even a quarter without dividing it into two parts.—Ed.]

e By the word "accent" I understand here, not

the French *port de voix*, which Rousseau tries to explain in his *Méthode pour apprendre à chanter*, p. 56, but a pressure (*expression*) or stress, an emphasis, from the Greek ἐν (*in*) and φάσις (*apparitio, dictio*).

usually written nowadays as separate notes or are at least marked for a few measures at the beginning with a little stroke:

The player must accordingly continue in this way to attack the first note vigorously until a change occurs.

10. The other "good" notes are those which are always distinguished from the rest by a slightly increased intensity, but to which this increased intensity must be very moderately applied. They are: in alla breve time, the quarters and eighth notes, and, in the so-called half triple time, the quarters; further, in common time and in 2/4 and 3/4 time, the eighth and sixteenth notes; finally, in 3/8 and 6/8 time, the sixteenth notes; and so forth. When several notes of this sort follow one after another, slurred two and two, the accent will fall on the first of each two, and this first note will not only be attacked somewhat more vigorously but will also be sustained somewhat longer while the second note will be bound to it, quite gently and quietly and somewhat retarded.[f] It often happens, however, that three, four, and even more such notes are bound together by a slur of this sort. In such a case, the player must attack the first of them somewhat more vigorously and sustain it longer and must bind the rest to it in the same bow, without the slightest stress, by reducing the intensity more and more.[g]

11. From Chapters 6 [2] and 7 the reader has seen how much the melody may be differentiated by the legatos and staccatos. The player, then, must not only pay the strictest attention to such legatos as are written out and indicated, but since in many a composition nothing is indicated at all, he must know how to apply the legato and staccato himself in a tasteful manner and in the proper place. The chapter on the many varieties of bowing, particularly in its second section, will serve to show the player how to go about making such alteration in this as he thinks proper, provided always that it is in keeping with the character of the piece.

12. Today, in certain passages, one finds the skillful composer apply-

---

[f] Let the reader look at the illustration of this in Chapter 7, Section 1, § 3, and in particular let him read § 5 in Chapter 7, Section 2, and look at the musical examples.

[Chapter 7, "On the many different sorts of bowing," deals in Section 1 with notes of equal value and in Section 2 with figures consisting of notes of unequal value.—Ed.]

[g] Let the reader call Chapter 7 to mind from time to time, especially what was said there in Section 1, § 20.

[The concluding paragraph (§ 20) of Section 1 explains that after mastering the various ways of bowing the examples that have been given, the student must learn to play them with taste and so that their variety is immediately perceptible.—Ed.]

[2] Chapter 6 is entitled "On the so-called triplets."

ing the expression in a quite special, unusual, and unexpected way which would puzzle many if it were not indicated.

For the expression and the intensity of the tone fall here on the last quarter of the measure, and the first quarter of the measure following is to be bound to it very quietly, without being stressed. The player, then, is by no means to distinguish these two notes by a pressure from the bow, but is to play them as though they formed a single half note.[h]

13. In gay pieces, to make the delivery really lively, the accent is usually applied to the highest note. This leads to the stress falling on the last note of the second and fourth quarters in common time and on the end of the second quarter in 2/4 time, especially when the piece begins with an upbeat.

But in pieces that are slow and sad, this may not be done, for here the upbeat must be, not detached, but sustained and delivered in a singing style.

14. In 3/4 and 3/8 time the accent may also fall on the second quarter.

15. The player will notice that, in the example last given, the dotted quarter (d) in the first measure is slurred to the eighth note (c) that follows. Accordingly, at the dot he must not bear down with his bow, but, as in all other situations of this kind, he must attack the quarter with a moderate intensity, hold out the time of the dot without stress, and very quietly bind the following eighth note to it.[i]

16. In the same way, such notes as these, which would otherwise be divided off according to the measure, must never be divided, nor may their division be indicated by a stress; on the contrary, the player must

---

h Here too let the reader call to mind § 18 and note *k* in Chapter 1, Section 3.

[The paragraph in question deals in greater detail with the correct performance of syncopa- tions like those just described; for Mozart's "Note *k*," see Note d above.—Ed.]

i I have already drawn attention to this in Chapter 1, Section 3, § 9.

simply attack them and sustain them quietly, exactly as though they stood at the beginning of the quarter.[j] This manner of delivery gives rise to a sort of broken tempo which makes a very strange and agreeable impression, since either the inner voice or the bass seems to separate itself from the upper voice; it has the further effect that in certain passages the fifths do not sound together, but are heard alternately, one after the other. Here, for example, are three voices.

17. Not only in the situation just discussed, but wherever a forte is prescribed, the player must moderate the intensity, not foolishly sawing away, above all in accompanying a concerto. Some people either do not do a thing at all or, in doing it, are certain to exaggerate it. The player must be guided by the passion. Sometimes a note requires a rather vigorous attack, at other times a moderate one, at still other times one that is barely perceptible. The first usually occurs in connection with a sudden expression that all the instruments make together; as a rule, this is indicated by the direction *fp*.

The second occurs in connection with those especially prominent notes that were discussed in §9 of this chapter. The third occurs in connection with all the remaining notes first enumerated in §10; to these the player must apply a barely perceptible stress. For even though he sees many fortes written into the accompaniment of a concerto, he must apply the intensity in moderation and not so exaggerate it that he drowns out the soloist. Quite the other way, such intensity, sparingly and briefly applied, must set off the solo part, give spirit to the melody, help out the soloist, and make easier for him the task of properly characterizing the piece.

18. The player, just as he must pay the strictest attention to the legatos, staccatos, fortes, and pianos required by the expression, must also avoid playing away continually with a dragging heavy bow and must be guided by the passion predominating in each passage. Gay and playful passages

j Let the reader just look at §§ 21, 22, and 23 in Chapter 4, where he will also find examples enough. Here belongs also what was said at the end of Chapter 1, Section 3, § 18, by no means forgetting note *k*.

[The several paragraphs in Chapter 4 deal with various ways of bowing such rhythms as eighth, quarter, eighth, or sixteenth, eighth, sixteenth; for Mozart's references to Chapter 1, see Notes d and h above.—Ed.]

must be distinguished by light short strokes and played off joyously and rapidly, just as pieces that are slow and sad must be delivered with long-drawn strokes, richly and tenderly.

19. As a rule, in accompanying a concerto the player must not sustain the notes but must play them off quickly, and in 6/8 and 12/8 time, to avoid making the delivery drowsy, must cut off the quarters almost as though they were eighth notes. But let him see to it that the tempo remains steady and that the quarters are more audible than the eighth notes.

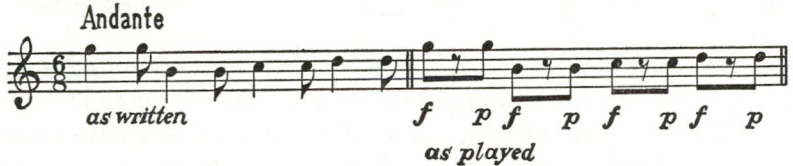

20. Many who have no notion of taste are never willing to maintain a steady tempo in accompanying a concerto, but are constantly at pains to yield to the soloist. These are accompanists for bunglers and not for masters. If the player has before him some Italian prima donna who cannot even carry off in the proper tempo what she has learned by heart, or any other fancied virtuoso of this sort, he must admittedly skip over whole half-measures if he is to prevent a public disgrace. But when he accompanies a true virtuoso, one who is worthy of this title, he must not allow himself to be seduced into hesitating or hurrying by the prolongations and anticipations of the notes that the soloist knows how to bring in so skillfully and touchingly, but must at all times continue to play in the same steady tempo. Otherwise what the soloist has sought to build up will be torn down again by his accompanying.[k]

21. Furthermore, if the performance is to be good, the players must pay strict attention to one another and especially to their leader in order that they may not only begin together but may also play throughout in the same tempo and with the same expression. There are certain passages in playing which one easily falls to hurrying.[l] Aside from this, the players must take care to play off the chords quickly and together, the short notes following a dot or a rest of small value somewhat after the beat and

k The skillful accompanist, then, must be able to judge his soloist. To a respectable virtuoso he must by no means yield, for to do so would ruin the soloist's *tempo rubato*. But what this "stolen time" is may be more easily demonstrated than described. Has he to do, on the contrary, with a fancied virtuoso? Then, in an Adagio cantabile, he may often sustain an eighth note for half a measure until the soloist comes to himself, as it were, after his paroxysm, and nothing goes in time, for the soloist plays in the style of a recitative.

l Let the reader just call to mind § 38 in Chapter 4. And in Chapters 6 and 7 I have stressed the importance of a steady tempo more than once. [Paragraph 38 of Chapter 4 deals with the bowing and correct performance of continuous sixteenths; for Chapters 6 and 7, see Notes f and 2 above.—Ed.]

rapidly.[m] If several notes are to be played as an upbeat or after a short rest, the usual thing is to take them in a down-bow, including the first note of the following quarter in the same stroke. Here the players must pay special attention to one another and not begin too early. This is an example with chords and rests of small value.

22. All that I have set down in this last chapter bears in particular on reading music correctly and in general on the clean and sensible delivery of a well-written piece of music. And all the pains that I have taken in the writing of this book have been directed toward one end: to set the beginner on the right path and to prepare him for the recognition and perception of a good musical taste. So I shall stop here, although I have still many things to say to the musical fraternity. Who knows? I may make bold to enrich the musical world with another book if I see that this my desire to serve the beginner has not been altogether useless.

---

m Let the reader look up what I have written in §§ 2 and 3 of Chapter 7, Section 2, also the musical examples given in this connection.

[These two paragraphs deal more explicitly with the correct performance of the short note or notes following a dot.—Ed.]

67. C. P. E. Bach

Johann Sebastian's second son, sometimes called the "Berlin" or "Hamburg" Bach, was born in 1714 at Weimar. In 1738 he moved to Berlin and in 1740 became harpsichordist to Frederick the Great. In 1767 Bach gave up this position to become Telemann's successor as director of church music at Hamburg. He died there in 1788.

As a composer, C. P. E. Bach is the foremost representative of the galant style in German music. Especially remarkable are the innovations he introduced into keyboard music, particularly the sonata. He wrote a great deal for instruments, but also much sacred music (Passions, cantatas, etc.).

His theoretical work, the *Versuch über die wahre Art, das Clavier zu spielen* (in two parts, 1753–1762) has remained to the present day a source of primary importance for the musical practice of the time.

From the Versuch über die wahre Art, das Clavier zu spielen [1]
[1753]

OF THE EMBELLISHMENTS IN GENERAL

1. No ONE, perhaps, has ever questioned the necessity of embellishments. We may perceive this from our meeting them everywhere in great abundance. Indeed, when we consider the good they do they are indispensable. They tie the notes together; they enliven them; they give them, when necessary, a special emphasis and weight; they make them pleasing and hence arouse a special attention; they help to clarify their content; whatever its nature, whether sad, gay, or of any other sort we please, they

1 Text: As edited by Walter Niemann from the second (1759) edition of the original (5th ed., Leipzig, 1925), pp. 24–31. A complete translation, by W. J. Mitchell, was published by W. W. Norton & Co., Inc., in 1949.

invariably contribute their share; they provide the correct manner of delivery with a considerable part of its occasion and material; a mediocre composition may be assisted by them, while without them the finest melody must seem empty and monotonous, the clearest content at all times unclear.

2. For all the good embellishments may thus do, they may do equal harm if we choose bad ones or apply them in an unskillful way, apart from their proper place and in excess of their due number.

3. For this reason, those who in their pieces clearly indicate the embellishments that belong to them have always followed a safer procedure than if they had left their things to the discretion of unskilled performers.

4. Also in this respect we must do justice to the French for being unusually careful in the marking of their pieces. In Germany, the greatest masters of our instrument have done the same, and who knows but what the reasonable choice and number of their embellishments may have given the occasion to the French today of no longer burdening, as formerly, almost every note with such an ornament, thereby concealing the necessary clarity and noble simplicity of the melody.

5. From this we see that we must learn to distinguish good embellishments from bad, to perform the good ones correctly, and to apply them in their proper place and in due number.

6. The embellishments lend themselves readily to a division into two classes. To the first I assign those customarily indicated either by certain accepted signs or by a few small notes; to the second may be assigned the rest, which have no signs and are made up of many small notes.

7. Since this second class of embellishments depends especially on musical taste and is hence all too subject to change, since in things for the clavier it is for the most part found written out, and since we can in any case spare it, in view of the sufficient number of the others, I shall treat it only briefly at the end in connection with the cadenzas and shall otherwise concern myself only with those of the first class, inasmuch as these have for some time past, so to speak, belonged to the very nature of clavier-playing and will no doubt always remain the fashion. To these familiar embellishments I shall add a few new ones; I shall explain them and, as far as possible, determine their position; I shall, for convenience' sake, give at the same time their fingering and, where it is noteworthy, the manner of their delivery; I shall illustrate with examples what cannot always be said with sufficient clarity; I shall say what needs to be said about certain incorrect or at least ambiguous signs, so that one may learn to distinguish them from the correct ones, likewise about embellishments to be rejected;

finally I shall refer my readers to the sample pieces, and shall hope, by all these means, to clear away more or less the false notion of the necessity of redundant fancy notes in clavier-playing which here and there has taken root.

8. Regardless of this, everyone who has the skill is at liberty to introduce embellishments more diffuse than ours. He need only take care, in so doing, that this occurs seldom, in the right place, and without doing violence to the passion of the piece. Of himself he will understand that, for example, the depiction of innocence or sadness will tolerate less ornamenting than the other passions. He who in this heeds what is needed may be allowed to have his way, for he skillfully combines, with the singing style of playing his instrument, the elements of surprise and fire in which the instruments have the advantage of the voice and, as a result, knows how to awaken and maintain with constant change a high degree of attention in his listeners. This difference between instrument and voice may be preserved unhesitatingly. He who in other respects bestows on these embellishments the care they need may be unconcerned as to whether what he plays can or cannot be sung.

9. At the same time, an overlavish treatment, even of our sort of embellishments, is to be avoided above all things. Let them be regarded as ornaments which can overload the finest structure, as spices which can spoil the finest food. Many notes, being of no consequence, must be spared them; many notes, sparkling enough in themselves, will likewise not tolerate them, for embellishments would only intensify their weight and artlessness, distinguishing them from others. Failing this, I should commit the same error as the speaker who places an emphatic stress on every word; everything sounds the same and is in consequence unclear.

10. We shall see in what follows that some situations permit more than one sort of embellishment; in such cases, let us take advantage of variation; let us apply, here an ingratiating embellishment, here a sparkling one, and sometimes, for variety's sake, let us use a wholly plain delivery when the notes permit it, without embellishment but in accordance both with the rules of good delivery, to be treated in the next part, and with the true passion.

11. It is difficult to determine the position of each embellishment with absolute precision, for each composer, provided he does no violence to good taste, is at liberty in his inventions to prescribe in most places any embellishment he pleases. In this we are content to instruct our readers by a few well-established rules and examples and by illustrating, in any case, the impossibility of applying particular embellishments; in those

pieces which indicate all embellishments there is no need for concern, while in those which indicate little or nothing the embellishments are customarily supplied in the regular way.

12. Since to this day I can name no one who has anticipated me in this difficult matter and who might have cleared for me this treacherous path, I trust that no one will blame me for believing that, even within certain well-established situations, there may perhaps be still a possibility of exception.

13. And since, to make a reasonable use of this material, he must attend to many small details, the reader should exercise his ear as much as possible by diligent listening to good performances and, the better to understand many things, must have mastered above all the art of thorough bass. Experience has shown that he who has no thorough understanding of harmony is, in applying the embellishments, always fumbling in the dark and that he has to thank mere chance, and never his insight, for the fortunate outcome. To this end, where necessary, I shall always add the bass of the examples.

14. Although the singers and the players of instruments other than ours, if they wish to play their pieces well, can no more do without most of our embellishments than we can ourselves, we players of the clavier have followed the more orderly procedure by giving certain signs to the embellishments, clearly indicating the manner of playing our pieces.

15. By not observing this praiseworthy precaution and by seeking, on the contrary, to indicate all things by few signs, not only has the theory of the embellishments been made sour to players of the clavier and even more so to others, but we have also seen the rise of many ambiguous, indeed false signs which sometimes, even today, cause many pieces to be performed unsuitably. For example, the mordent is in music a necessary and familiar embellishment, yet there are few, apart from players of the clavier, who know its sign. I know of a piece in which, as a result of this, a particular passage has often been ruined. This passage, if it is not to sound untasteful, must be played with a long mordent, something which no one would hit upon without an indication. The necessity of using as its indication a sign known only to players of the clavier, there being no other, has resulted in its being confused with the sign of a trill. We shall see in what follows, from the great difference between these two embellishments, how disagreeable an effect this has had.

16. Since the French are careful in placing the signs of their embellishments, it follows that, in hitherto departing altogether, as we have, unfortunately, from their things and from their way of playing the clavier,

we have at the same time also deviated from the precise indication of our embellishments to such an extent that today these once so familiar signs are already becoming unfamiliar, even to players of the clavier.

17. The notes comprised in the embellishments take their accidentals from the key signature. Nevertheless, we shall see in what follows that there are frequent exceptions to this rule, readily discovered by a practiced ear, caused sometimes by the preceding notes, sometimes by the following ones, and in general by the modulations of a melody into another key.

18. But in order that the reader may also overcome those difficulties that arise on this account, I have found it necessary to retain that practice according to which the accidentals are indicated along with the embellishments in all cases. One will find them in the sample pieces, wherever necessary, now singly, now in pairs.

19. All embellishments must stand in a proportioned relation to the value of their note, to the tempo, and to the content of the piece. Especially in those cases where various sorts of embellishments occur and where the passion is not too restricting, it should be remarked that the more notes an embellishment comprises, the longer the note to which it is applied must be, no matter whether this length arises from the value of the note or from the tempo of the piece. The player must avoid detracting from the brilliance that an embellishment is intended to produce by allowing too much of the value of its note to remain left over; at the same time, he must also avoid occasioning a lack of clarity by performing certain embellishments too quickly, something which occurs mainly when he applies many embellishments or embellishments of many notes to notes of small value.

20. Although we shall see in what follows that the player may sometimes intentionally apply to a long note an embellishment that does not wholly fill out its value, he may not release the last note of such an embellishment until the following note is due, for the chief aim of all embellishments should be to tie the notes together.

21. We see, then, that embellishments are used more in slow and moderate tempi than in rapid ones, more in connection with long notes than with short ones.

22. Whatever needs to be observed regarding the value of the notes, the signs, and the small notes, I shall always include as a part of my explanations. The reader, too, will find the small notes printed in the sample pieces with their actual values.

23. All embellishments indicated by small notes belong to the note that follows; the preceding note, in consequence, never diminishes in

value, while the following note loses as much as is made up by the small notes taken together. This observation is the more necessary in that it is commonly disregarded and in that I have been unable to avoid sometimes detaching certain small notes from their main note in the sample pieces, the space being so crowded with signs for fingering, embellishments, and delivery that it required this.

24. In accordance with this rule, then, these small notes are struck in place of the note that follows, together with the bass or with the other parts. Through them the player slides into the note following; this too is very often disregarded in that he pounces roughly upon the main note after having, in addition to this, unskillfully applied or produced the embellishments associated with the small notes.

25. Our present taste being what it is and the good Italian way of singing having made considerable contribution to it, the player cannot manage with the French embellishments alone; for this reason, I have had to compile my embellishments from more than one nation. To these I have added a few new ones. Apart from this, I believe that the best way of playing the clavier or any other instrument is that which succeeds in skillfully combining what is neat and brilliant in the French taste with what is ingratiating in the Italian way of singing. For this the Germans are particularly well adapted as long as they remain unprejudiced.

26. At the same time, it is possible that a few will not be wholly satisfied with this my choice of embellishments, having perhaps embraced one taste alone; I believe, however, that no one can be a thorough judge of anything in music unless he has heard all kinds and knows how to find what is best in each. What is more, I agree with a certain great man who declared that, while one taste has more good in it than another, there is none the less in every taste some particular thing that is good, no taste being as yet so perfect that it will not still tolerate further additions. By means of such additions and refinements we have reached the point at which we are and shall continue to go on and on. This, however, cannot possibly happen if we work at and, as it were, worship one sort of taste alone; on the contrary, we must know how to profit by whatever is good, wherever it may be found.

27. Therefore, since the embellishments together with the manner of their employment make a considerable contribution to fine taste, the player should be neither so changeable that without further inquiry he accepts at every moment each new embellishment, regardless of its sponsor, nor yet so prejudiced in favor of himself and his own taste that out of vanity he refuses to accept anything new whatever. He should of course

put the new thing to a rigorous test before he adopts it, and it is possible that in time the introduction of unnatural novelties will make good taste as rare as art. At the same time, to keep pace with the fashion, the player should be, if not the first, then not the last to take up new embellishments. Let him not oppose them if they do not always appeal to him at first. New things, attractive as they are occasionally, sometimes seem to us perverse. And this is often evidence of the worth of things which in the long run last longer than those which are overly pleasing in the beginning. These last are as a rule so run into the ground that they soon become nauseating.

28. While most of my examples of embellishments are for the right hand, I by no means deny these graces to the left; on the contrary, I urge every player to exercise each hand alone in all of them, for this brings with it a dexterity and lightness in the production of other notes. We shall see in what follows that certain embellishments also occur often in the bass. Apart from this, the player is obliged to reproduce all imitations to the last detail. In short, the left hand must have exercise in this to manage it skillfully; failing this, it will be better to omit the embellishments, which lose their charm if we perform them badly.

•　　•　　•　　•　　•

XIV

Operatic Rivalry in France: The "Querelle des Bouffons"

68. F. W. *von Grimm*

Born at Ratisbon in 1723, Grimm went in 1747 to Paris, where he soon made the acquaintance of Rousseau, d'Alembert, and Diderot, and became associated with the work on the great *Encyclopédie*. In 1776 he was made minister plenipotentiary for Gotha at Paris, a post he held until 1792, when the Revolution forced him to return to Germany. He died in 1807.

Grimm took an active part in the "Querelle des Bouffons" as one of the first and foremost partisans of the Italian *opera buffa*. One of his earliest contributions to this controversy is the little pamphlet *Le petit prophète de Boehmisch-Broda* (1753), which was a musical fable in a pseudo-Biblical style, with thinly disguised references to the contemporary scene. In the same year, 1753, Grimm began to issue periodical reports (the *Correspondance littéraire, philosophique et critique*), which circulated only in a few manuscript copies, sent to a few of the European princely courts. The *Correspondance* contains valuable material for the history of French opera. On the other hand, Grimm took no interest in instrumental music and devoted not a single word to the important changes that were taking place at his time in this field.

The Little Prophet of Boehmischbroda [1]

[*1753*]

Here are written the twenty-one chapters of the prophecy of Gabriel Joannes
Nepomucenus Franciscus de Paula Waldstorch, called Waldstoerchel,
native of Boehmischbroda in Bohemia, student of philosophy and
moral theology in the Greater College of the Reverend Jesuit
Fathers, son of a discreet and honorable person, Eustachius
Josephus Wolfgangus Waldstorch, master lutemaker and
maker of violins, living in the Judengass of the Old
Town at Prague, hard by the Carmelites, at the sign
of the Red Violin, and he has written them with
his own hand, and he calls them his vision:
in Latin, Canticum Cygni Bohemici.

---

1 Text: *Correspondance littéraire, philosophique et critique*, XVI (Paris, 1882), 313–336.

THE THREE MINUETS

AND I was in my garret which I call my chamber, and it was cold, and I had no fire in my stove, for wood was dear.

And I was wrapped in my cloak which once was blue, and which has turned white, seeing that it is worn threadbare.

And I was scraping on my violin to limber my fingers, and I foresaw that the carnival of the coming year would be long.

And the demon of ambition breathed upon my soul, and I said to myself:

Come, let us compose minuets for the ridotto of Prague, and may my glory be in every man's mouth, and be known to all the world and to all Bohemia.

And may they point a finger at me, calling me the Composer of Minuets κατ' ἐξοχὴν, which means above all others.

And may the beauty of my minuets be vaunted both by them that dance them and by them that play them, and may they be played in all the inns during the fair of Jubilate [2] at Leipzig, and may everyone say:

Behold the beautiful minuets of the carnival of Prague! Behold the minuets of Gabriel Joannes Nepomucenus Franciscus de Paula Waldstorch, student of philosophy! Behold the minuets of the great composer! Behold them!

And I abandoned myself to all the chimeras of pride, and I was intoxicated by the fumes of vanity, and I put on my hat aslant.

And I marched with long strides about my garret which I call my chamber, and in the intoxication of my ambitious projects I said:

Ah! how my father will glory in his illustrious son! My mother will bless the womb that has borne me and the breasts that have given me suck!

And I took pleasure in the extravagance of my ideas, and I did not tire of them, and I lifted up my head, which I am not wont to bear very high.

And ambition heated me, even though there was no wood in my stove, and I said:

Ah! how beautiful it is to have loftiness of soul, and what great things the love of glory makes one do!

And I lifted up my mantle which once was blue and which has turned white, seeing that it is worn threadbare, and I took my violin, and I composed on the spot three minuets one after the other, and the second was in a minor key.

---

2 The church festival of the third Sunday after Easter, so called from the first word of the Introit of that day.

And I played them on my violin and they pleased me exceedingly; I played them again and they pleased me even more; and I said: Ah! how fine it is to be an author!

THE VOICE

And suddenly my chamber, which is only a garret, was lighted up with a great light, even though there was but a farthing candle upon my table.

(For I burn a tallow candle when I make music, because I am gay,

And I burn rapeseed oil when I study philosophy, because I am sad.)

And I heard a voice which burst into laughter, and its laughter was louder than the sound of my violin.

And I was annoyed to be thus mocked at, for by nature I dislike mockery.

And the voice which I did not behold said:

Be appeased, for I make a mock of your anger, and by nature you dislike mockery.

And be quickly appeased, and renounce your projects of glory, for I have always confounded them, because they were contrary to mine.

And another will compose the minuets for the carnival of Prague, and your minuets will not be played at the Leipzig fair, because you will not have composed them.

For I have chosen and appointed you among all your comrades to proclaim hard truths to a frivolous and presumptuous people which will mock at you (even though by nature you dislike mockery), because it is untractable and flighty, and which will not believe you, because you will speak the truth.

And I have chosen you for this because I do what I please and because I am accountable to nobody.

And you will compose no minuets, for it is I who tell you so.

THE MARIONETTES

And a hand seized me by the hair of my head, and I felt myself borne through the air, and I was on the way from Thursday until Friday, and I was wrapped in my mantle which once was blue and which has turned white, seeing that it is worn threadbare.

And I arrived in a city of which I had never heard tell until that day, and its name was Paris, and I saw that it was very large and very dirty.

And it was afternoon, and it was the fifth hour of the day, and I found myself in a theatre to which people were thronging.

And my heart leapt with joy, for I love to see fine performances, and even though I am not rich, I think nothing of money when I go to them.

And I said to myself (for I love to talk to myself when I have the time):

Doubtless it is here that they play Tamerlane and Bajazeth [3] with great marionettes, for I found the hall too superb to be only a theatre for Polichinelle.[4]

And I heard the violins tuning up, and I said: Doubtless they will also give serenades, and they will make the little marionettes dance after the great ones have spoken their piece.

For I found the theatre to be large enough for that, and even though bringing out the marionettes might cause some confusion in the wings (for they were very narrow), I judged that as many as six marionettes could dance in the front row and that this ought to be very beautiful.

And although I had seen many booths for marionettes in my day, I knew of none more beautiful, seeing that the decorations were superb and the boxes richly decorated, all with much taste and very clean.

And in all the itinerant theatres of German comedy, I had seen nothing that came near it, even though men play in them and not marionettes.

And even though with us the decorations are more brilliant, because they are oiled with oil and expense is not spared, I found none the less that these would have been more beautiful than ours if they had been oiled as with us.

THE WOODCHOPPER [5]

And while I was saying this to myself (for I love to talk to myself when I have the time), I found that the orchestra had begun to play, without my having noticed it, and they were playing something which they called an overture.

---

[3] In the first half of the eighteenth century alone, there are no less than a dozen operas—the most famous are those by Handel and Vivaldi—which treat of the invasion (1402) of the Mongol Empire by the Turkish sultan Bajazet I, and his capture by Tamerlane, the famed descendant of Genghis Khan.

[4] The French counterpart of the English Punch and the Italian Pulcinella.

[5] A caricature of the time-beater, a man employed by the Opéra solely to mark the beat by striking a heavy stick (sometimes a cane or a thick sheaf of papers) against some solid object. Although not uncommon in other ensemble genres (especially church music), audible time-beating at the opera was rare and roundly condemned; it persisted nevertheless until the last decade of the century. Rousseau, in comparing it with Italian direction of opera from the keyboard, remarked

characteristically (1756) in his *Dictionnaire de musique*: "The Paris Opéra is the only theater in Europe where one beats the measure without following it" (cf. the article "Battre la mesure").

Rousseau's copy of "The Little Prophet" is annotated in manuscript by him (cf. Poulet-Malassis, *La Querelle des Bouffons*, Paris, 1876); annotations below attributed to Rousseau are based upon this document. At this point, he suggests in the margin that the "woodchopper" is Rebel, i.e., François Rebel (1701–1775), who was associated with the Opéra from 1733 to 1757, first as leader of the first violins and later as a director and manager. His father Jean Ferry Rebel (1666–1747), an equally famous composer and violinist, and one of the last surviving pupils of Lully, beat the time at the Opéra during the last decade and a half of his life.

And I saw a man who was holding a stick, and I believed that he was going to castigate the bad violins, for I heard many of them, among the others that were good and were not many.

And he made a noise as if he were splitting wood, and I was astonished that he did not dislocate his shoulder, and the vigor of his arm terrified me.

And I reflected (for I love to reflect when I have the time), and I said to myself:

Oh! how talents are misplaced in this world, and how genius displays itself none the less, even if it is out of its right place!

And I said: If that man had been born in my father's house, which is a quarter of a league from the forest of Boehmischbroda in Bohemia, he would make as much as thirty farthings a day, and his family would be rich and honored and his children would live in abundance.

And people would say: Behold the woodchopper of Boehmischbroda, behold him! And his talents would not be wasted, whereas in this booth he cannot earn enough to eat his bread and drink his water.

And I beheld that they called that "beating the time," and although it was beaten most forcibly, the musicians were never together.

And I began to regret the serenades that we sing, we pupils of the Jesuits, in the streets of Prague when night falls, for we keep together and we have no stick.

And the curtain rose, and I saw ropes at the back of the stage, and they were throwing them about;

And I said to myself: Doubtless they will fasten them to the head of Tamerlane, and there will be a great procession of other marionettes after him (for there were many ropes), and he will open the scene that way, and the spectacle will be magnificent.

And I found it wrong that they had not fastened the ropes before raising the curtain, as is done with us, for I have good judgment.

THE BLACK EYES

But not at all. And I saw a shepherd enter,[6] and the people cried: Behold the god of song, behold him! And I saw that I was at the French opera.

And his voice affected and flattered my ears, his laments touched me,

---

6 It was often held that the pastoral scene, providing the customary backdrop for early and middle eighteenth-century French opera, was hardly a "return to nature," but rather an affectation of it.

and he expressed with art everything that he wished, and although he sang slowly he did not bore me, for he had taste and soul.[7]

And I saw his shepherdess enter,[8] and she had great black eyes which she made tender to console him, for he had need of consolation, because he said so.

And her voice was light and brilliant, and its tone rang like silver, and it was as pure as the gold which issues from the furnace, and she sang very well her songs which were not well written, and her throat rounded out what was flat.

And although the music was feeble and poor, it did not seem so when she sang, and I said: Ah! the deceitful hussy! For she had art, and her skill wrought an illusion upon me.

And I said to myself (for I love to talk to myself when I have the time):

Doubtless that shepherd and that shepherdess have enemies who force them to sing in marionette booths to spoil their voices and to make them have weak chests.

For I could smell the odor of oil and tallow which was poisoning me, even though I was born in the forest of Boehmischbroda in Bohemia where the air is thick, and though I have pursued all my studies with the aid of a lamp fed with oil that is not good, for it costs only eight farthings; and I have done well in my studies, for I am a scholar.

And I began to curse the enemies of that shepherd and that shepherdess in the sincerity of my heart, for their voices and their singing caused me pleasure even though their music bored me, and I began to feel pity at their fate; and I continued to curse, for I am malicious when I am angered.

THE SORCERESS

And when my shepherdess, whom I call mine because she pleased me, had consoled my shepherd, whom I call mine because he gave me pleasure, and when they had well caressed each other and had no more to tell each other, they went away.

And I saw a woman come striding in,[9] and she came down to the front of the stage, and she frowned and shook her fists, and I judged that she was in a bad temper.

---

7 Identified at this point by Rousseau as Pierre Jélyotte (1713–1797), the most famous French tenor of his day. Although he sang the traditional French repertoire, his popularity with both French and Italian partisans permitted him to remain aloof from the controversy.

8 Identified by Rousseau as Marie Fel (1713–1794), a soprano whose fame equaled that of the tenor Jélyotte. She was also an intimate friend of Baron Grimm.

9 Identified here by Rousseau as Mlle. Chevalier, or more properly Marie Jeanne Fesch, whose career at the Opéra spanned the years from 1741 to 1765—a singer spoken well of by LaBorde. She sang many leading roles in Rameau's tragedies.

And it seemed to me that she was making threats, and I was annoyed, because I am quick of comprehension and I have a natural dislike of threats, and my neighbor said: No, it is I that she is angry with; and his neighbor said: No, it is I.

And I puzzled my head to find out why she was so furious, for her part was only pathetic, and I saw that it was impossible for me to divine the reason.

And she had in her hand a wand which was mysterious, because the poet had said so, and by means of that wand she could do everything and know everything, except how to sing, which she did not know at all, although she thought she did.

And I heard her utter frightful shrieks, and her veins became swollen and her face became as red as Tyrian purple and her two eyes started from her head, and she filled me with fear.

And I saw that those who sing in the church of St. Apollonia at Vyšehrad,[10] though they are well fed and their thirst is well quenched, could never match their lungs against those of the sorceress, and I said: Ah! why are they not here to hear the sorceress? They would not hold their heads so high, and when we take off our hats to them, we students, they would salute us more affably.

And with her voice, although it was off the pitch, she called up the dead, even though she put the living to flight, and I said to myself: Beyond a doubt, those who are dead and buried in this booth have by nature no ears for music.

And there came on an old man [11] whom the woman with the wand called young (for the poet had said so), although he was past sixty. And he gargled before the public and pretended to sing.

And I felt that this was irreverent, and his gargling continued all the time and his part was done; and I said: Since this man needs so many preliminaries before he can sing, they should say to him: Say your part without singing, for you will say it well; for I am judicious and of good counsel.

And his gargling made me laugh, and when I wished to mock at him, his acting overawed me, and I saw that he was a man worthy of veneration, for he had dignity and nobility and he waved his arms in a way no one could rival.

•　•　•　•　•

10 A settlement near Prague, centered about a medieval castle.
11 Claude de Chassé (1698–1786), a bass heard at the Opéra for over thirty years. He was a splendid actor but a poor singer.

And I saw that they called that in France an opera, and I noted it in my tablets to jog my memory.

And I was quite content to see the curtain fall, and I said: Ah! never again shall I see you rise!

And the voice which was my guide began to laugh, and I could tell that it was mocking at me, even though that annoyed me, for by nature I dislike mockery.

And it said to me: You will not depart for the ridotto of Prague, and you will not depart, for that is my design.

And you will spend the night here writing down my wishes which I shall dictate to you, and you will proclaim them to the people which I once cherished and which has become odious to me by the number of times it has deserted me.

· · · · ·

And the voice which had spoken to me became strong, vehement, and pathetic, and I wrote.

HERE BEGINS THE REVELATION

O walls which I have raised with my own hand to be a monument of my glory! O walls once inhabited by a people whom I called my own, because I had chosen them from the beginning to make of them the first people of Europe and to carry their glory and their fame beyond the limits which I have set to the universe!

O city which callest thyself the Great, because thou art immense, and the Glorious, because I have covered thee with my wings; listen, for I am about to speak.

And thou, O Place where they have erected the theatre of the Comédie Française, to whom I have given genius and taste for a possession in common, and to whom I have said: Thou shalt have not thine equal in the universe, and thy glory shall be carried from the East to the West and from the South to the North; listen, for I am about to speak.

And thou, frivolous and haughty theatre, thou who hast arrogated to thyself the title of Academy of Music, although thou art none, and although I have not given thee my permission to do so, listen, for I am about to speak.

O people frivolous and flighty! O people addicted to desertion and abandoned to the madness of your pride and your vanity!

Come, let me reckon with you, I who, if I wish, can reckon you as nothing; come, let me confound you in your own eyes and inscribe your baseness upon your haughty forehead with my own hand, in all the languages of Europe.

THE TRANSMIGRATION

You were festering in the mire of ignorance and barbarism; you were groping in the darkness of superstition and stupidity; your philosophers were without sense and your teachers were idiots. In your schools a barbarous jargon was spoken, and in your theatres mysteries were played. And my heart was moved with pity, and I said to myself: This is a pleasant people; I like its spirit, which is buoyant, and its ways, which are gentle; and I will make it my people, for it is my will, and it shall be the first of peoples, and there shall be no people so pretty.

And its neighbors shall behold its glory, which they shall be unable to attain. And when I have formed it according to my desire, it will amuse me, for it is pleasant and agreeable by nature, and I like to be amused.

And I have rescued your fathers from the nothingness in which they were, and I have brought on the day to enlighten you, and I have implanted in your heart the torch of sciences and letters and arts.

. . . . . .

THE FLORENTINE [12]

And even as I had brought the other arts from Italy to give them all to you, I wished to implant music in your hearts and adapt it myself to the genius of your language.

And I wished to create your musicians and to form them, and to teach them to make music that would satisfy my ear and my heart.

And you have scorned my favors, because I have showered them upon you in abundance.

And in the hardness of your hearts you have created an opera which has wearied me for twenty-four years and which is the laughingstock of Europe to this day.

And in your opinionated extravagance you have erected an Academy of Music, although it is none, which I have never recognized.

And you have chosen a Florentine for your idol without consulting me and although I had not sent him.

---

12 Jean Baptiste Lully (1632–1687), the creator of French opera (more properly the *tragédie lyrique*) and of two of its more important ingredients: the French *ouverture,* and a variety of accompanied recitative especially suited to the French language. Born in Florence, he left his native city as a lad of eleven and a half to come to France.

And because he had received a faint gleam of genius, you have dared to oppose him to me, because in my clemency I had given you my servant Quinault.[13]

And you have believed that his monotony would make me impatient and would force me to abandon you, because I am prompt of action and because you wished to tire me with the number of his works.

And you have shouted in the stupidity of your ignorance: Ah, behold the creator of song! Ah, behold him!

And because, with his poverty of ideas, he has done what he could, you call him a creator to this very day, when he has created nothing, and while the Germans have wearied my ears and made my head split for two hundred years, in their churches and in their vespers, with a kind of singing which you call your own recitative, whereas it is theirs (even though they do not boast of it, because they find it bad), and while in the imbecility of your ideas you believe it to have been invented by the Florentine [14] whom you call M. de Lully [15] to this day.

THE PRECURSOR

And notwithstanding your stubbornness and your opinionated dementia, I have not cast you off in my wrath as you deserved, and I have not delivered you to the contempt of your neighbors.

And I took pity on the childishness of your judgment and the dullness of your ear, and I undertook to lead you back to the right way by the very roads on which you had gone astray in the folly of your heart.

And I undertook to make distasteful to you the monotony of the Florentine and the insipidity of those who have followed him for more than forty years.

And I formed a man [16] for this purpose and I equipped his mind, and I animated him, and I said to him: Have genius; and he had it.

And when it was time I sent him and I said to him: Make yourself master of the stage which they call Academy of Music, although it is none, and purge it of all that bad music which they have had produced by people whom I have never avowed, beginning with the Florentine, whom

---

13 Philippe Quinault (1635–1688) was employed by Lully as his librettist. It was not an equal collaboration; the librettist was obliged to conform to the whims of an autocratic composer. Here it is Lully's music that is under attack, a reversal from the opening years of the century when it was held that poor drama owed its success to Lully's excellent music.

14 The identity of French and German recitative and a denial of the unique form and style of Lully's musical declamation cannot be objectively sustained. The comparison, whether justified or not, certainly reveals the then low esteem of the French avant-garde for German music.

15 Lully consistently avoided the Italian form (Giovanni Battista Lulli) of his name, and Grimm makes the most of the fact that even the "idol" of the supporters of native music is an Italian.

16 Identified at this point by Rousseau as Jean Philippe Rameau (1683–1764), the leading French composer of the time.

they call great, and down to little Mouret,[17] whom they call gay and pleasant.

And you will astonish them with the fire and the force of the harmony which I have put in your head and with the abundance of the ideas with which I have supplied you.

And they will call baroque that which is harmonious, as they call simple that which is flat. And after they have called you a barbarian for fifteen years, they will no longer be able to do without your music, for it will have opened their ears.

And you will have prepared the ways which I have imagined to give a music to that people which is not worthy of my benefits, for you are my servant.

.   .   .   .   .

THE EMISSARY [18]

That is why the vanity and insolence of your untractability have reached their limit and I am weary of enduring them.

And in another moment I shall sweep you away, as the south wind sweeps away the dust of the fields, and I shall plunge you again into the mire of barbarism from which I rescued your fathers in the movements of my clemency.

And behold the last miracle which I have resolved to perform, and I shall perform one such as I have never before performed, for I am beginning to despise you, because I no longer esteem you.

And I swear it and I say: Behold the last! And I choose for my emissary my servant Manelli, and I drag him out of the mud and I give him shoes, and I say: Cast off your sabots, and after you have traveled up and down through the provinces of Germany to have bread to eat and water to drink, I shall send you where praise awaits you and where you will do my will.

And I shall set Bourbons at your right and Bourbons at your left, and they will protect you, because I love them and I have given them a taste for beautiful things.[19]

And you will sing in the theatre which they call Academy of Music without my consent and, although it is none, you will force them to applaud you with delight, in spite of their resenting it.

---

17 Jean Joseph Mouret (1682–1738), composer of operas and ballets in the style of Lully.

18 Pierre Manelli, the leading singer of the Italian company. He dropped from sight with the return of the troupe to Italy.

19 A reference to the pro-Italian faction among the nobility; Rousseau cites two of the most prominent: the Duchesse d'Orléans and the Conte de Clermont.

And you will not know what to do with all your glory, and you will exclaim in the modesty of your heart: Not to me, not to me, for there are five hundred better than I in my country, and I am the last of my family.

But I have chosen you on purpose, despite the modesty of your heart, from out the five hundred who are better than you, to humiliate this vain and proud people which I am beginning to despise, because I no longer esteem it.

And you will bring it the music of my servant Pergolesi,[20] whom men to this day call divine, because I caused him to spring fully formed from my brain.

And it will be the time of signs and miracles.

And the philosopher will leave his study and the geometer his calculations and the astronomer his telescope and the chemist his retort and the wit his assemblies and the painter his brush and the sculptor his chisel; only their wives will not wish to go, for they will have no ears, and the boxes will be filled by men.

And they will all come to applaud you, and they will await your fair companion as the lover awaits with impatient heart her whom he loves; and they will be enraptured with joy, and they will lift up their hands toward heaven in the intoxication of their souls.

And they will kiss each other with joy, and stranger will clasp stranger in his arms, and they will congratulate each other on the pleasure they have received.

For I shall have opened their ears, and they will exclaim: Oh! Oh! what music! Oh! Oh! what music!

And after they have heard it for three months, they will no longer be able to endure the slowness and monotony of their singing, which they call recitative and I call plainsong.

And their monologues, which they call touching, will make them yawn; the scenes which they call interesting will weary them, and the scenes which they call gay will put them to sleep.

And a spirit of dizziness will seize them, and they will no longer know what they desire or what they do not desire.

---

20 Giovanni Battista Pergolesi (1710–1736), whose sprightly comic opera *La Serva padrona* (composed, 1733) was the first Paris offering of the Italian company (August 1, 1752). The performance at the Opéra, with an overture by Telemann, and on the same bill with Lully's *Acis et Galatée,* fanned the flames of a conflict already announced by Grimm's earlier polemic, his *Lettre sur Omphale.* The Paris première of *La Serva padrona* was, however, some years earlier (October 4, 1746). That event aroused no controversy although the work was well received; the argumentative French were still debating the merits of Rameau *vs.* Lully.

THE MARVELOUS [21]

O people bewildered in the intoxication of your errors, O people slow to understand, hearken to my voice, as I speak to you for the last time, and perceive the constancy of my warnings.

Banish from your Opéra the tediousness which prevents me from attending. Abandon the prejudices which you have sucked with your mother's milk and with which you still daily quench your thirst.

Deliver me from the childish genre which you call the marvelous, when it is marvelous only to you and to your children; be sincere in your repentance, and I will again stretch out my arms to you and will forget the iniquities of your fathers and your own.

And I will create for you an Opéra agreeing with my taste and my desires, and I shall call it Academy of Music, because it will be one.

And I shall be your inspector, and there will no longer be a woodchopper at the head of your orchestra nor any carpenters to direct your choruses.

And I shall be in your orchestra and I shall animate it, and I shall teach it to feel genius in order to reproduce it with taste, and I shall drive out the bad violins and I shall give you songs in their place.[22]

And I shall give you actors who will sing like my servant Jélyotte and like my servant Fel, and no longer will shrieks be heard in your theatre.

And I shall drive out from your theatre both the demons and the shades, and the fairies and the genii, and all the monsters with which your poets have corrupted it through the power which they have conferred upon wands in fits of their madness, without my consent.

And I shall consecrate your opera, like that of the Italians, to great portrayals of great subjects, and to the passions, and to the depiction of all characters, from the pathetic even to the comic.

And you will amuse yourselves no more making lightnings and thunders and tempests, for I shall teach you to make Meropes and Andromaches and Didos speak.

And I shall be with your poets and with your musicians, and I shall teach your poets to write texts and your musicians to write music.

---

21 "Within the pale of this term came scenic effects, decorations, ballets, *divertissements,* and *machines* [stage apparatus]. The purpose of all this paraphernalia was to create an illusion of splendor and magnificence, fit atmosphere within which the doings of gods and heroes were to be unfolded" (Alfred Richard Oliver, *The Encyclopedists as Critics of Music,* New York, 1948, pp. 47–53). Grimm thus satirizes the emphasis on pageantry and effect at the expense of the drama.

22 To replace violins, however bad, with songs is to imply not only a dearth of songs but a superabundance of orchestral forces as well. The charge that the orchestra is overpowering the singer recurs constantly in operatic criticism.

And I shall give your poets invention and imagination in common, so that they will have no more need of the wand or of spells.

And even as your musicians have written notes down to this day, so they will write music which will be music, and I will put genius in their scores and taste in their accompaniments, and I will deliver these from the weight of the notes with which they burden them, and I shall select them myself.

And I shall teach them to be simple without being flat, and they will no more call that which is monotonous beautiful simplicity. And I shall create your recitative, and I shall teach them to write music which will have character and exact and distinct movement, and which will not be void of expression.

And I shall work with them and my genius shall guide them, and I shall assign boundaries and distinctive character to each species, from the tragedy even to the interlude.

And as I have caused one to be performed by my servant Jélyotte and by my servant Fel, which gave you great pleasure because I had it written as I desired, by a man with whom I do what I please, though he rebels against me, for I govern him in spite of his resenting it, and I have named his interlude the *Devin du village*.[23]

So I shall teach your musicians to write pastorals and comedies and tragedies, and they will no more need to say: This is comic, and that is tragic, for it will clearly appear without their saying so, although they do well to say it today.

And your glory will be resplendent on every side, and I myself will spread it among all nations; you will be called the people above all others, and you will have no equal, and I shall not tire of looking upon you because it will be pleasing to me to see you.

And your genius and your wit and your taste and your graces and your charms and your amiability will make my heart leap for joy, for you shall be my people and there shall be no other like you.

THE TENNIS COURT

And if you do not take advantage of the moment while there is yet time, and of the miracle which I have wrought by the last of my emissaries, Manelli, my servant, to humiliate you for having refused to hear

---

23 Both words and music are by Jean Jacques Rousseau. The Fontainebleau performance for the court (October 18, 1752) was followed by an equally successful public première at the Opéra (March 1, 1753). The prestige of the composer held this amateurish work on the boards of the Opéra throughout the century and led to many performances elsewhere both in the original language and in translations. Among the numerous parodies that it inspired is Favart's *Bastien et Bastienne*, of which Weiskern's German version was set to music by the young Mozart (1768).

those whom I had sent to you in great number, and for having persisted in the willfulness of your false judgments and your childish prejudices;

And if the mission of my servant Manelli, the strangest of the miracles that I have ever wrought, cannot bring you back from your delusions and determine you to consecrate your theatre to good music and to banish from it tediousness and flatness;

And if, before mending your ways, you are waiting, in the vanity of your arrogance, for me to send you five hundred others who are better than he, even though I have no wish to do so;

Behold what I say: I will be avenged upon your strange blindness, and your measure shall be full to overflowing.

And I will make your ear as hard as the horn of the buffalo of the forest, and in your calculations you shall be as fierce as the wild ass of the desert.

And in my wrath I will permit you to hiss the music of my well-beloved Tartini and the playing of my servant Pagin.[24]

And I will prevent you from feeling the genius and the sublimity which I have put into Italian music, and in spite of that you will be unable to hear your own, for it will bore you, as it has bored me for eighty years.

And scales will cover your eyes, and you will drive out my servant Servandoni, and you will send for the decorators of the Pont Notre-Dame.[25]

And your theater, which you call Academy of Music without my consent and although it is none, will be deserted and abandoned, and you will go no more to converse, nor your wives to be seen.

And I will inspire my servant Jélyotte with plans of retirement, and in his place I will give you blacksmiths and locksmiths.

And I shall remove my servant Fel, and I will place her where I please, for I cherish her as the apple of my eye.

And the singing will be out of tune from the rising of the curtain even unto the falling of the curtain. And you will be forced to close your theatre, and its doors will not reopen until it has once more become what it was, namely, a tennis court.

---

24 A reference to an intrigue (1750) at the Concerts Spirituels against André Noël Pagin (1721–1785), a celebrated French violinist and pupil of Tartini. Pagin had championed the violin concertos of his teacher too persistently for the conservative clique. He was so humiliated by the experience as to resolve to play henceforth only in private. Dr. Burney heard him in the course of his Continental travels (1770) and reported very favorably.

25 The Florentine decorator and architect Servandoni (1695–1766), senior decorator at the Opéra from 1728 to 1743, was responsible for the introduction of asymmetrical backdrops at that theater. His bold diagonal lines and remarkable use of perspective gave to the tiny French stage an illusion of depth and space. His influence, obscuring another decorator at the Opéra, the French painter François Boucher, even outlasted his break with the directors of the Académie Royale de Musique. Cf. Jeanne Bouché, "Servandoni" (Gazette des Beaux-Arts, 1910, pp. 121–146).

THE SLAP

And I shall carry my vengeance still further. And I shall confound your proud vanity, in which you boast to your neighbors of the geniuses that I have created among you and of the philosophers that I have sent you; while you abuse them in your heart and while you insult me in their persons.

And I shall remember all your ignoble actions and they shall be before my eyes without ceasing:

From the day when you hissed the *Misanthrope* down to that on which you committed the unpardonable sin, preferring the *Carnaval du Parnasse* to *Zoroastre*; [26]

From the triumph of the *Phèdre* of Pradon over the *Phèdre* of Racine [27] down to the triumph of the Opéra Comique over the Comédie Française.[28]

And I shall take away the theatre of the Comédie Française, and I shall establish it in foreign lands, and you will have it no longer, for you will have reduced the actors to beggary.

And far-off peoples will see the masterpieces of your fathers; and they will see them in their theatres and will admire them without making mention of you; for your glory will be passed, and you will be in relation to your fathers what the Greeks of today are in relation to the ancient ones, that is, a barbarous and stupid people.

. . . . .

And coarse and licentious vaudeville [29] will be the delight of your spirit, and you will think it delicious.

And the indecency and the flatness of the dialogue will not shock you. And morality will be outraged with impunity among you, for you will

---

26 *Le Carnaval du Parnasse*, a *ballet heroïque* by Jean Joseph Mondonville (1711–1772), was produced at the Opéra on September 23, 1749, court protection assuring a favorable reception. Rameau's *Zoroastre* followed on December 5. The initial run of the latter work was curtailed by the activities of the partisans of Lully, and the false impression was given that the public preferred the works of Mondonville.

27 A reference to the servile copy of Racine's *Phèdre* by Nicolas Pradon (1632–1698). It was, however, the anti-Racine cabal which caused the failure of Racine's play.

28 What Grimm prophesies in jest turned out to be not far from the truth; by the end of the century the Opéra Comique ranked among the leading Paris theaters. At mid-century it was still a rude bourgeois enterprise (held at the fairs of Saint Laurent and Saint Germain) whose improvised entertainment was a mixture of song and speech. The Comédie Française was then the reigning seat of spoken French drama, although even at this time the "coarse and licentious vaudeville" (Grimm, see below) was known to have penetrated into that theater.

29 A short satirical poem set to unsophisticated music, or more properly, as in the vaudeville-comedy, a more extended poem or series of such poems given stage presentation. Grimm failed to recognize in the vaudeville-comedy, perhaps the prime ingredient of the then emerging *opéra comique*, the true French counterpart of Italian *opera buffa*.

have none, and you will no longer be conscious of what is good nor of what is evil.

And your philosophers will not enlighten you, and I will prevent them from writing, and the press shall be denied to them.

And they will no longer take pleasure in dwelling among you, for I shall no longer be there.

And the voice was silent.

And I, Gabriel Joannes Nepomucenus Franciscus de Paula Waldstorch, called Waldstoerchel, student of philosophy and moral theology in the Greater College of the Reverend Jesuit Fathers, native of Boehmisch-broda in Bohemia, I wept at the fate of that people, for I am tenderhearted by nature.

And I wished to intercede for it, because I am kindhearted and because I was tired of writing, for I had been writing a long time.

And I was wrong, for the voice was angry, and I received a slap, and my head was knocked against the pillar of the corner which to this day is called the corner on the Queen's side.

And I woke with a start, and I found myself in my garret which I call my chamber, and I found my three minuets, of which the second is in a minor key.

And I took my violin and I played them, and they pleased me as before, and I played them again, and they pleased me even more, and I said: Let us write the others quickly, for there have to be two dozen; and I no longer felt the force of genius, for the thing they call opera was always in my mind, and I wrote many notes, but no minuets at all, and in the bitterness of my heart I cried out: Why did I not finish the two dozen before the Vision?

69. J. J. Rousseau

Jean Jacques Rousseau was born at Geneva in 1712 and died in 1778 near Paris. With his battle cry, "Retournons à la nature," Rousseau exerted a deep and lasting influence on the music of his time. He was not technically trained as a musician, but this did not prevent him from taking a passionate interest in things musical. In the "Querelle des Bouffons" Rousseau fought with Grimm on the side of the partisans of the Italian *opera buffa*. His most important writing in this field is his *Lettre sur la musique française* (1753). Rousseau even tried his hand as composer of a comic opera on a French text in which he attempted to follow the principles of the *opera buffa*. The work—*Le Devin du village* (1752)—was extremely successful and played an important role in forming the style of French *opéra comique*. Rousseau was also the author of a valuable *Dictionnaire de musique* (1768).

Lettre sur la musique française [1]

[*1753*]

TO THE READER

Since the quarrel which arose last year at the Opéra produced nothing but abuse, bestowed by the one party with much wit and by the other with much animosity, I was unwilling to take any part in it, for that kind of contest was wholly unsuited to me and I was well aware that it was not a time to speak only reason. Now that the buffoons are dismissed, or the next thing to it, and there is no more question of cabals, I think I may venture my opinion, and I shall state it with my customary frankness, without fear of offending anyone by so doing. It even seems to me that in a subject of this kind, any reserve would be an affront to my readers, for I admit that I should have a poor opinion of a people who attached a ridiculous importance to their songs, who made more of their musicians than of their philosophers, and among whom one

---

1 Text: The original edition (Paris, 1753).

needed to speak more circumspectly of music than of the gravest questions of morality.

Do you remember, sir, the story, told by M. de Fontenelle,[2] of the Silesian infant who was born with a golden tooth? Immediately all the doctors of Germany exhausted themselves in learned disquisitions on how it was possible to be born with a golden tooth; the last thing that anyone thought of was to verify the fact; and it was found that the tooth was not golden. To avoid a similar embarrassment, it would be well, before speaking of the excellence of our music, to make sure of its existence, and to examine first, not whether it is made of gold, but whether we have one.

The Germans, the Spaniards, and the English have long claimed to possess a music peculiar to their own language; they had, in fact, national operas [3] which they admired in perfect good faith, and they were firmly persuaded that their glory would be at stake if they allowed those masterpieces, insupportable to any ears but their own, to be abolished. Pleasure has at last prevailed over vanity with them, or, at least, they have found a pleasure more easily understood in sacrificing to taste and to reason the prejudices which often make nations ridiculous by the very honor which they attach to them.

We still have in France the same feeling about our music that they had then about theirs, but who will give us the assurance that because we have been more stubborn, our obstinacy has been better grounded? Would it not then be fitting, in order to form a proper judgment of French music, that we should for once try to test it in the crucible of reason and see if it can endure the ordeal?

It is not my intention to delve deeply into this subject; that is not the business of a letter; perhaps it is not mine. I wish only to try to establish certain principles by which, until better have been found, the masters of the art, or rather the philosophers, may direct their researches; for, as a sage once said, it is the office of the poet to write poetry and that of the musician to compose music, but it is the province only of the philosopher to discuss the one and the other well.[4]

·   ·   ·   ·   ·

---

2 Bernard Le Bovier de Fontenelle (1657–1757), *littérateur*, perpetual secretary of the Académie des Beaux-Arts, and author of the famous remark, "Sonate, que me veux-tu?"

3 What is within limits true of Germany, and to a lesser extent of Spain, is not valid for the English scene. The period coincides with the decline of Italian opera in London and the rise of two indigenous substitutes, ballad opera and oratorio.

4 Omitted here is an extended section wherein Rousseau seeks to prove that the Italian language is best suited for musical setting.

The Italians pretend that our melody is flat and devoid of tune, and all the neutral nations [a] unanimously confirm their judgment on this point. On our side we accuse their music of being bizarre and baroque.[b] I had rather believe that both are mistaken than be reduced to saying that in countries where the sciences and the arts have arrived at so high a degree of perfection, music has still to be born.

The least partial among us [c] content themselves with saying that Italian music and French music are both good, each in its kind, each for its own language; but besides the refusal of other nations to agree to this parity, there still remains the question, which of the two languages is by its nature adapted to the best kind of music. This is a question much agitated in France, but which will never be agitated elsewhere, a question which can be decided only by an ear perfectly impartial, and which consequently becomes every day more difficult to resolve in the only country in which it is a problem. Here are some experiments on this subject which everyone is free to verify, and which, it seems to me, can serve to give the answer, at least so far as regards melody, to which alone almost the whole dispute is reducible.

I took, in the two kinds of music, airs equally esteemed, each in its own kind, and divesting them, the one of its *ports-de-voix* [5] and its perpetual cadenzas, the other of the implied notes which the composer does not trouble to write, but leaves to the discretion of the singer [d]; I sol-fa'd them exactly by note, without any ornament and without adding anything of my own to the sense or connection of the phrases. I will not tell you what effect this comparison produced upon my mind, because I have the right to offer my reasons but not to impose my authority. I merely report to you the means which I adopted to form my own opinion, in order that you, in turn, may employ them yourself if you find them good. I must warn you only that this experiment requires more precautions than one

---

a There was a time, says Milord Shaftesbury, when the practice of speaking French had made French music fashionable among us. But Italian music, by giving us a nearer view of nature, soon gave us a distaste for the other and made us see it as dull, as flat, and as doleful as it really is.

b It seems to me that people no longer dare make this reproach so frequently since it has been heard in our country. Thus this admirable music has only to show itself as it is in order to clear itself of all the faults of which it is accused.

c Many condemn the total exclusion of French music unhesitatingly pronounced by the amateurs of music; these conciliatory moderates would have no exclusive tastes, as if the love of what is good ought to compel a love of what is bad.

d This procedure gives all the advantages to the French music, for the implied notes in Ital-

ian music are no less of the essence of the melody than those which are written out. It is less a question of what is written than of what should be sung, and this manner of writing notes ought simply to pass as a sort of abbreviation; whereas the cadenzas and *ports-de-voix* of French music are indeed, if you will, demanded by the style, but are not essential to the melody; they are a kind of make-up which covers its ugliness without removing it and which only makes it the more ridiculous to sensitive ears.

5 A specifically French *agrément*, an upward resolving appoggiatura executed by means of a mordent. See musical illustration in Rousseau's *Dictionnaire de musique* (Paris, 1768), Plate B, Figure 13.

would think. The first and most difficult of all is that one must maintain good faith and be equally fair in choosing and in judging. The second is that, in order to attempt this examination, one must necessarily be equally acquainted with both styles; otherwise the one which happened to be the more familiar would constantly present itself to the prejudice of the other. And this second condition is hardly easier than the first, for of all those who are well acquainted with both kinds of music, no one hesitates in his choice, and one can tell from the absurdly confused arguments of those who have undertaken to attack Italian music, how much they know of it and of the art in general.

I must add that it is essential to proceed in exact time, but I foresee that this warning, superfluous in any other country, will be quite useless in France, and this sole omission necessarily involves incompetence in judgment.

With all these precautions taken, the character of each kind of music is not slow in declaring itself, and then it is quite hard not to clothe the phrases with the ideas which are suited to them and not to add to them, at least mentally, the turns and ornaments which one is able to refuse them in singing; nor must one rest the matter on a single trial, for one air may give more pleasure than another without determining which kind of music has the preference, and a rational judgment can be formed only after a great number of trials. Besides, by foregoing a knowledge of the words, one remains ignorant of the most important element in the melody, namely the expression, and all that can be determined in this way is whether the modulation is good and whether the tune is natural and beautiful. All this shows us how hard it is to take enough precautions against prejudice and what great need we have of reasoning to put us in a condition to form a sane judgment in matters of taste.

I made another experiment which requires fewer precautions and which may perhaps seem more decisive. I gave to Italians the most beautiful airs of Lully to sing, and to French musicians some airs of Leo [6] and of Pergolesi, and I observed that while the French singers were very far from apprehending the true taste of these pieces, they were still sensible of their melody and drew from them in their own fashion melodious, agreeable, and well-cadenced musical phrases. But the Italians, while they sol-fa'd our most pathetic airs with the greatest exactness, could never recognize in them either the phrasing or the time; for them it was not a kind of music which made sense, but only a series of notes set down with-

---

[6] Leonardo Leo (1694–1744), one of the opera composers of the Neapolitan school and the teacher of Jommelli, who is mentioned below.

out choice and as it were at random; they sang them precisely as you would read Arabic words written in French characters.[e]

Third experiment. I saw at Venice an Armenian, a man of intelligence, who had never heard any music, and in whose presence were performed, in the same concert, a French monologue which began with these words:

Temple sacré, séjour tranquille,[7]

and an air of Galuppi, which began with these:

Voi che languite
Senza speranza.

Both were sung, the French piece indifferently and the Italian badly, by a man familiar only with French music and at that time a great enthusiast for that of M. Rameau. I observed that during the French song the Armenian showed more surprise than pleasure, but everybody observed that from the first bars of the Italian air his face and his eyes grew soft; he was enchanted; he surrendered his soul to the impressions of the music; and though he understood little of the language, the mere sounds visibly enraptured him. From that moment he could not be induced to listen to any French air.

But without seeking examples elsewhere, have we not even among us many persons who, knowing no opera but our own, believe in good faith that they have no taste for singing and are disabused only by the Italian intermezzi? It is precisely because they like only the true music that they think they do not like music.

I allow that the great number of its faults has made me doubt the existence of our melody and has made me suspect that it might well be only a sort of modulated plainsong which has nothing agreeable in itself and which pleases only with the aid of certain arbitrary ornaments, and then only such persons as have agreed to consider them beautiful. Thus our music is hardly endurable to our own ears when it is performed by mediocre voices lacking the art to make it effective. It takes a Fel or a Jélyotte[8] to sing French music, but any voice is good in Italian music, because the beauties of Italian singing are in the music itself, whereas

---

[e] Our musicians profess to derive a great advantage from this difference. "We can perform Italian music," they say, with their customary pride, "and the Italians cannot perform ours; therefore our music is better than theirs." They fail to see that they ought to draw a quite contrary conclusion and say, "therefore the Italians have melody and we have none."

[7] From Rameau's *Hippolyte et Aricie* (text by Simon Joseph Pelegrin) performed in 1733: Act I, Scene I (*Oeuvres complètes*, VI, 53).

[8] Marie Fel (1713–1794) and Pierre Jélyotte (1713–1797), the two leading singers of the French lyric stage, are best known for their performances in traditional French opera. Although they sang in Rousseau's *Le Devin du village*, they avoided taking sides in the aesthetic battle of the time.

those of French singing, if there are any, are all in the art of the singer.[f]

Three things seem to me to unite in contributing to the perfection of Italian melody. The first is the softness of the language, which makes all the inflections easy and leaves the taste of the musician free to make a more exquisite choice among them, to give a greater variety to his combinations, and to provide each singer with a particular style of singing, so that each man has the character and tone which are proper to him and distinguish him from other men.

The second is the boldness of the modulations, which, although less servilely prepared than our own, are much more pleasing from being made more perceptible, and without imparting any harshness to the song, add a lively energy to the expression. It is by this means that the musician, passing abruptly from one key or mode to another, and suppressing, when necessary, the intermediate and pedantic transitions, is able to express the reticences, the interruptions, the falterings, which are the language of impetuous passion so often employed by the ardent Metastasio, which a Porpora, a Galuppi, a Cocchi, a Jommelli, a Perez, a Terradellas have so often successfully reproduced,[9] and of which our lyric poets know as little as do our musicians.

The third advantage, the one which gives to melody its greatest effect, is the extreme exactness of time which is felt in the slowest as well as in the liveliest movements, an exactness which makes the singing animated and interesting, the accompaniments lively and rhythmical; which really multiplies the tunes by making as many different melodies out of a single combination of sounds as there are ways of scanning them; which conveys every sentiment to the heart and every picture to the mind; which enables the musician to express in his air all the imaginable characters of words, many of which we have no idea of; [g] and which renders all the movements

---

[f] Besides, it is a mistake to believe that the Italian singers generally have less voice than the French. On the contrary they must have a stronger and more harmonious resonance to make themselves heard in the immense theaters of Italy without ceasing to keep the sound under the control which Italian music requires. French singing demands all the power of the lungs, the whole extent of the voice. "Louder," say our singing masters; "more volume; open your mouth; use all your voice." "Softer," say the Italian masters; "don't force it; sing at your ease; make your notes soft, flexible, and flowing; save the outbursts for those rare, brief moments when you must astonish and overwhelm." Now it seems to me that when it is necessary to make oneself heard, the man who can do so without screaming must have the stronger voice.

[g] Not to depart from the comic style, the only one known to Paris, consider the airs, "Quando sciolto avrò il contratto," "Io ho un vespaio," "O questo o quello t'hai a risolvere," "Ha un gusto da stordire," "Stizzoso mio, stizzoso," "Io sono una donzella," "Quanti maestri, quanti dottori," "I sbirri già lo aspettano," "Ma dunque il testamento," "Senti me, se brami stare, o che risa! che piacere!" all characters of airs of which French music has not the first elements and of which it is incapable of expressing a single word.

[9] Niccolo Antonio Porpora (1686–1766), Baldassare Galuppi, often called Buranello after his birthplace (1706–1785), Gioacchino Cocchi (1715–1804), Niccolo Jommelli (1714–1774), Davide Perez (1711–1778), Domenico Terradellas (1711–1751); with the exception of the buffa composer Galuppi, largely a list of the more prominent opera composers associated with the Neapolitan school. Galuppi was performed by the Italian

proper to express all the characters,[h] or at the will of the composer renders a single movement proper to contrast and change the character.

These, in my opinion, are the sources from which Italian music derives its charms and its energy, to which may be added a new and strong proof of the advantage of its melody, in that it does not require so often as ours those frequent inversions of harmony which give to the thorough bass a melody worthy of a soprano. Those who find such great beauties in French melody might very well tell us to which of these things it owes them or show us the advantages it has to take their place.

On first acquaintance with Italian melody, one finds in it only graces and believes it suited only to express agreeable sentiments, but with the least study of its pathetic and tragic character, one is soon surprised by the force imparted to it by the art of the composer in their great pieces of music. It is by the aid of these scientific modulations, of this simple and pure harmony, of these lively and brilliant accompaniments that their divine performances harrow or enrapture the soul, carry away the spectator, and force from him, in his transports, the cries with which our placid operas were never honored.

How does the musician succeed in producing these grand effects? Is it by contrasting the movements, by multiplying the harmonies, the notes, the parts? Is it by heaping design upon design, instrument upon instrument? Any such jumble, which is only a bad substitute where genius is lacking, would stifle the music instead of enlivening it and would destroy the interest by dividing the attention. Whatever harmony several parts, each perfectly melodious, may be capable of producing together, the effect of these beautiful melodies disappears as soon as they are heard simultaneously, and there is heard only a chord succession, which one may say is always lifeless when not animated by melody; so that the more one heaps up inappropriate melodies, the less the music is pleasing and melodious, because it is impossible for the ear to follow several melodies at once, and as one effaces the impression of another, the sum total is only noise and confusion. For a piece of music to become interesting, for it to convey to the soul the sentiments which it is intended to arouse, all the parts must concur in reinforcing the impression of the subject: the harmony must serve only to make it more energetic; the accompaniment

---

troupe, but few of the works of the others appeared on the Paris stage, their operas gaining standing by performances of isolated arias and by the accounts of those who had heard them elsewhere.

h I shall content myself with citing a single example, but a very striking one: the air, "Se pur d'un infelice," in *The Intriguing Chambermaid* [*La Finta cameriera*], a very pathetic air with a very lively movement, which lacks only a voice to sing it, an orchestra to accompany it, ears to hear it, and the second part, which should not be suppressed.

must embellish it without covering it up or disfiguring it; the bass, by
a uniform and simple progression, must somehow guide the singer and
the listener without either's perceiving it; in a word, the entire ensemble
must at one time convey only one melody to the ear and only one idea to
the mind.

This unity of melody seems to me to be an indispensable rule, no less
important in music than the unity of action in tragedy, for it is based on
the same principle and directed toward the same object. Thus all the good
Italian composers conform to it with a care which sometimes degenerates
into affectation, and with the least reflection one soon perceives that from
it their music derives its principal effect. It is in this great rule that one
must seek the cause of the frequent accompaniments in unison which are
observed in Italian music and which, reinforcing the idea of the melody,
at the same time render its notes more soft and mellow and less tiring
for the voice. These unisons are not practicable in our music, unless it be
in some types of airs chosen for the purpose and adapted to it. A pathetic
French air would never be tolerable if accompanied in this manner, because, as vocal and instrumental music with us have different characters,
we cannot employ in the one the same devices which suit the other without
offending against the melody and the style; leaving out of account that
as the time is always vague and undetermined, especially in slow airs, the
instruments and the voice would never be in agreement and would not
keep step well enough to produce a pleasing effect together. A further
beauty resulting from these unisons is to give a more sensible expression
to the vocal melody, now by letting it unexpectedly reinforce the instruments in a passage, now by letting it make them more tender, now by
letting it give them some striking, energetic phrase of the melody of which
it is itself incapable, but for which the listener, skillfully deceived, never
fails to give it credit when the orchestra knows how to bring it to the fore
at the right moment. From this arises also that perfect correspondence
between the ritornelli and the melody, as the result of which all the strokes
which we admire in the one are only the development of the other, so
that the source of all the beauties of the accompaniment is always to be
sought in the vocal part; this accompaniment is so wholly of a piece with
the singing and corresponds so exactly to the words that it often seems to
determine the action and to dictate to the actor the gesture which he is
to make,[1] and an actor who would be incapable of playing the part with

[1] Numerous examples may be found in the intermezzi which have been performed for us this
year, among others in the air "Ha un gusto di
stordire" in The Music Master [Il Maestro di
musica]; in that of "Son padrone" in The
Vain Woman [La Donna superba]; in that of
"Vi stò ben" in Tracollo; in that of "Tu non
pensi" in The Bohemian [La Zingara]; and in
nearly all of those which require acting.

the words alone might play it very correctly with the music, because the music performs so well its function of interpreter.

Besides this, the Italian accompaniments are very far from always being in unison with the voice. There are two very frequent cases in which the music separates them. One is when the voice, lightly singing a passage over a series of harmonies, so holds the attention that the accompaniment cannot share it; yet even then this accompaniment is made so simple that the ear, affected only by agreeable harmonies, does not perceive in them any harmony which could distract it.

The other case demands a little more effort to be comprehended. "When the musician understands his art," says the author of the *Letter on the Deaf and Dumb*,[10] "the parts of the accompaniment concur either in reinforcing the expression of the vocal part, or in adding new ideas demanded by the subject and beyond the capacity of the vocal part to express." This passage seems to me to contain a very useful precept, and this is how I think it should be understood.

If the vocal part is of such a nature as to require some additions, or as our old musicians used to say, some divisions, which add to the expression or to the agreeableness without thereby destroying the unity of the melody, so that the ear, which would perhaps blame them if made by the voice, approves of them in the accompaniment and allows itself to be gently affected without being made less attentive to the vocal part, then the skillful musician, by managing them properly and disposing them with taste, will embellish his subject and give it more expression without impairing its unity; and although the accompaniment will not be exactly like the vocal part, the two will nevertheless constitute only a single air and a single melody. For if the sense of the words connotes some accessory idea, the musician will superimpose this during the pauses of the voice or while it sustains some note, and will thus be able to present it to the hearer without distracting him from the idea expressed by the voice. The advantage will be still greater if this accessory idea can be expressed by a restrained and continuous accompaniment, producing a slight murmur rather than a real melody, like the sound of a river or the twittering of birds, for then the composer can completely separate the vocal part from the accompaniment, and assigning to the latter only the expression of the accessory idea, he will dispose his vocal part in such a way as to give frequent openings to the orchestra, taking care to insure that the instrumental part is always dominated by the vocal, a matter depending more upon the art of the composer than on the execution of the instruments;

10 One of the many anonymous pamphlets supporting Italian music.

but this demands a consummate experience, in order to avoid a double melody.

This is all that the rule of unity can concede to the taste of the musician in order to ornament the singing or to make it more expressive, whether by embellishing the principal subject or by adding to this another which remains subordinate. But to make the violins play by themselves on one side, the flutes on another, the bassoons on a third, each with a special motive and almost without any mutual relation, and to call all this chaos music is to insult alike the ear and the judgment of the hearers.

· · · · ·

I hope, sir, that you will pardon me the length of this article, out of consideration for the novelty and the importance of its aim. I have felt it my duty to enlarge somewhat upon so essential a rule as that of the unity of melody, a rule of which no theorist, to my knowledge, has to this day spoken, which the Italian composers alone have felt and practiced, perhaps without suspecting its existence, a rule on which depend the sweetness of the melody, the force of the expression, and almost all the charm of good music. Before I leave this subject, it remains for me to show you that from it result new advantages for harmony itself, at the expense of which I seemed to be bestowing all the advantages upon melody, and that the expression of the melody gives occasion to that of the harmony by forcing the composer to dispose them with art.

Do you recall, sir, having sometimes heard the son of the Italian impresario, a boy of ten years at the most, accompany the intermezzi which were given here at the Opéra this year? We were struck, from the first day, by the effect produced by his little fingers in the accompaniment on the harpsichord, and the whole audience perceived, from his exact and brilliant playing, that he was not the usual accompanist. I at once sought for the reasons of this difference, for I had no doubt that the Sieur Noblet [11] was a good harmonist and accompanied very exactly, but what was my surprise, as I watched the hands of the little fellow, to see that he almost never filled out the chords, and that he suppressed many notes, very often using only two fingers, one of which nearly always sounded the octave of the bass. "What!" said I to myself, "the complete harmony has less effect than the harmony mutilated, and our accompanists, filling out all the chords, produce only a confused sound, while this one, with fewer notes, creates more harmony, or at least makes his harmony

---

11 Charles Noblet, accompanist at the Opéra until 1762. He composed sacred music heard at the Concerts Spirituels and published two "livres de clavecin" (1754, 1756).

more distinct and more pleasing!" The problem perplexed me. I understood its importance even better, when upon further observation I saw that all the Italians accompanied in the same manner as the little boy, and that consequently this economy in their accompaniment must depend on the same principle as that which they follow in their score.

I well understood how the bass, being the foundation of all harmony, should always prevail over the rest, and that when the other parts stifle it or cover it up, this causes a confusion which makes the harmony less distinct; and I saw in this the reason why the Italians, so economical with the right hand in accompanying, ordinarily play the octave of the bass with the left; why they have so many double basses in their orchestras; and why they so often make their violas ʲ proceed with the bass, instead of giving them a separate part as the French never fail to do. But this, which accounted for the precision of the harmonies, did not account for their energy, and I soon saw that there must be some subtler and less obvious principle in the expressiveness which I observed in the simplicity of Italian harmony while I found our own so complicated, cold, and languid.

I remembered then to have read in some work of M. Rameau that each consonance has its particular character, that is to say, a manner peculiar to itself of affecting the soul; that the effect of the third is not at all the same as that of the fifth, nor that of the fourth the same as that of the sixth; similarly the minor thirds and sixths must affect us differently from the major. Granting this, it follows clearly enough that the dissonances and all the intervals possible will be in the same case. This experience is confirmed by reason, since whenever the relations are different the impressions cannot be the same.

Now in reasoning from this hypothesis I reflected: "I see clearly that two consonances added together inappropriately, although according to the rules of harmony, may, even while increasing the harmony, weaken, oppose, or divide each other's effect. If the whole effect of a fifth is required for the expression which I need, I may well risk weakening that expression if I introduce a third sound which, interposing two other intervals within this fifth, will necessarily modify its effect by adding that of the two thirds into which I have resolved it; and even if the whole combination makes a very good harmony, these thirds themselves, being of different species, may still reciprocally impair each other's effect. In

---

ʲ One can observe in the orchestra of our Opéra that in Italian music the violas almost never play their part when it doubles the bass at the octave; perhaps in these circumstances they do not deign to copy the bass. Are the conductors of the orchestra unaware that the lack of connection between the bass and the treble makes the harmony too dry?

like manner, if I needed the simultaneous impression of the fifth and the two thirds, I should weaken that impression and change it for the worse if I suppressed one of the three notes forming the consonance.

"This argument becomes even more apparent when applied to dissonance. Suppose that I have need of all the harshness of the tritone or all the colorlessness of the diminished fifth (a contrast, by the way, which shows how much the effect of an interval can be changed by inversion); if, in such circumstances, instead of conveying to the ear only two sounds which form the dissonance, I am minded to complete the chord with all the notes belonging to it, then I add to the tritone the second and the sixth and to the diminished fifth the sixth and the third; that is, by introducing into each of these chords a new dissonance, I introduce at the same time three consonances which must necessarily temper and weaken its effect by making one of these consonances more colorful and the other less harsh."

It is therefore a certain principle, and one based on nature, that all music in which the harmony is scrupulously filled out, every accompaniment in which all the harmonies are complete, must make a great deal of noise but have very little expression. This is precisely the character of French music. It is true that in regulating the harmonies and the part-leading, the selection becomes difficult and demands much experience and taste if it is always to be made suitably; but if there is one rule to help the composer acquit himself well on such occasion, it is surely that of the unity of melody which I have tried to establish, and which is in conformity with the character of Italian music and accounts for the sweetness of the melody together with the force of expression which prevails in it.

From all this it follows that after a thorough study of the elementary rules of harmony, the musician must not hasten to be inconsiderately lavish of it, nor believe himself ready to compose because he knows how to fill out the harmonies; but that before setting hand to the much longer and more difficult study of the various impressions which the consonances, the dissonances, and all the harmonies make on sensitive ears, he must often remind himself that the great art of the composer consists no less in knowing on occasion which notes to leave out than in knowing which to use. It is by studying and continually turning the pages of the masterpieces of Italy that he will learn how to make that delicate choice, if nature has given him enough genius and taste to feel its necessity. For the difficulties of the art are visible only to those who are born to overcome them, and such men will not be of a mind to look with disdain on the vacant spaces in a score, but seeing the ease with which a pupil could have filled them, they will suspect and look for the reasons for this deceptive simplicity, the more admirable because beneath a feigned negligence it conceals prodigies, and because *l'arte che tutto fa, nulla si scuopre* ("the art which does all remains invisible").

Here, in my opinion, is the cause of the surprising effects produced by the harmony of Italian music, although much less burdened than that of our own, which produces so few. This does not mean that the harmony must never be full, but that it must be made full only with selection and discernment. Neither is it to say that to make this selection the musician is obliged to go through this reasoning, but that he should be sensible of its result. It is for him to have the taste and the genius to discover the things that are effective; it is for the theorist to investigate the causes and to say why these things are effective.

If you cast your eye on our modern compositions and especially if you hear them played, you will soon recognize that our musicians have so little understood all this that in striving to arrive at the same goal they have followed the directly opposite road, and if I may be allowed to state my frank opinion, I find that the further our music advances toward apparent perfection, the more it is actually deteriorating.

It was perhaps necessary that it should reach its present state, in order that our ears might insensibly become accustomed to reject the prejudices of habit and to enjoy other airs than those with which our nurses sang us to sleep; but I foresee that to bring it to the very mediocre degree of merit of which it is capable, we shall sooner or later have to begin by once more descending (or reascending) to the state to which Lully brought it. Let us agree that the harmony of that famous musician is purer and less inverted; that his basses are more natural and proceed more directly; that his melody is more flowing; that his accompaniments, less burdened, spring more truly from the subject and depart from it less; that his recitative is much less mannered than ours, and consequently much better. This is confirmed by the style of the execution, for the old recitative was sung by the actors of that time in a way wholly different from that of today. It was livelier and less dragging; it was sung less and declaimed more.[k] In our recitative the cadenzas and *ports-de-voix* have been multiplied; it has become still more languid and has hardly anything left to distinguish it from what we call "air."

Now that airs and recitatives have been mentioned, you will permit me, sir, to conclude this letter with some observations on the one and the

k This is proved by the time of the representation of Lully's operas, much longer now than in his day by the unanimous report of those who have seen them long ago. Thus, whenever these operas are revived, they call for considerable cutting.

other which will perhaps throw some helpful light on the solution of the problem involved.

One may judge of the idea our musicians have of the nature of an opera by the singularity of their nomenclature. Those grand pieces of Italian music which ravish the soul, those masterpieces of genius which draw tears, which offer the most striking pictures, which paint the liveliest situations and fill the soul with all the passions they express, the French call "ariettes." They give the name of "airs" to those insipid little ditties which they interpolate in the scenes of their operas, and reserve that of "monologues" particularly to those long-drawn-out and tedious lamentations which if only sung in tune and without screams would put everybody to sleep.

In the Italian opera all the airs grow out of the situation and form a part of the scene. Now a despairing father imagines he sees the ghost of a son whom he has unjustly put to death upbraid him with his cruelty; now an easygoing prince, compelled to give an example of severity, entreats the gods to deprive him of his rule or to give him a less susceptible heart. Here a tender mother weeps to recover her son whom she thought dead; there we hear the language of love, not filled with that insipid rigmarole of "flames" and "chains," [12] but tragic, animated, ardent, and faltering, and befitting impetuous passion. Upon such words it is appropriate to lavish all the wealth of a music full of force and expression and to enhance the energy of the poetry by that of harmony and melody.

The words of our ariettes, on the contrary, always detached from the subject, are only a wretched medley of honeyed phrases which one is only too glad not to understand. They are a random assemblage of the small number of sonorous words that our language can furnish, turned and twisted in every manner except the one that might give them some meaning. It is upon such impertinent nonsense that our musicians exhaust their taste and knowledge and our actors waste their gestures and lungs; it is over these extravagant pieces that our women go into ecstasies of admiration. And the most striking proof that French music is incapable of either description or expression is that it cannot display the few beauties at its command except upon words which have no meaning.

Meanwhile, to hear the French talk of music, one would imagine that in their operas it depicts great scenes and great passions, and that only ariettes are found in Italian operas, to which the very word "ariette" and the ridiculous thing it signifies are equally unknown. We must not be sur-

---

12 The special attention given to the musical setting of such words in the *tragédie-lyrique* grew out of classical French declamation. Cf. Grétry, who has the same complaint (p. 715 below); or Diderot, in his *Neveu de Rameau* (*Oeuvres complètes*, V, 461 f.).

prised by the grossness of these prejudices: Italian music has no enemies, even among ourselves, but those who know nothing about it, and all Frenchmen who have tried to study it with the sole aim of criticizing it understandingly have soon become its most zealous admirers.[1]

After the "ariettes," which constitute the triumph of modern taste in Paris, come the famous monologues which are admired in our old operas. In this connection it is to be noted that our most beautiful airs are always in the monologues and never in the scenes, for, as our actors have no art of pantomime and the music does not indicate any gesture or depict any situation, the one who remains silent has no notion what to do with himself while the other is singing.

The drawling nature of our language, the little flexibility of our voices, and the doleful tone which perpetually reigns in our opera, give a slow tempo to nearly all our French monologues, and as the time or beat is not made perceptible either in the melody or in the bass or in the accompaniment, nothing drags so much or is so relaxed, so languid, as these beautiful monologues, which everybody admires while he yawns; they aim to be sad and are only tiresome; they aim to touch the heart and only distress the ear.

The Italians are more adroit in their Adagios, for when the time is so slow that there is any danger of weakening the sense of the rhythm, they make their bass proceed by notes of equal value which mark the movement, while the accompaniment also marks it by subdivisions of the beats, which, keeping the voice and the ear in time, make the melody more pleasing and above all more energetic by this exactness. But the nature of French music forbids our composers this resource, for if the actor were compelled to keep time, he would immediately be prevented from displaying his voice and his action, from dwelling on his notes, from swelling and prolonging them, and from screaming at the top of his lungs, and in consequence he would no longer be applauded.

But what still more effectively prevents monotony and boredom in the Italian tragedies is the advantage of being able to express all the passions and depict all the characters in whatever measure and time the composer pleases. Our melody, which in itself expresses nothing, derives all its expression from the tempo one gives to it. It is of necessity sad in a slow tempo, furious or gay in a lively one, serious in a moderate one; the melody itself counts for almost nothing in this; the tempo alone, or, to put it more accurately, the degree of rapidity alone determines the

---

[1] A presupposition little favorable to French music appears in this: those who despise it most are precisely those who know it best, for it is as ridiculous when examined as it is intolerable when heard.

character. But Italian melody finds in every tempo expressions for all characters, pictures for all objects. When the musician so chooses, it is sad in a slow tempo, and, as I have already said, it changes character in the same movement at the pleasure of the composer. Contrasts are thereby made easy, without depending for this on the poet and without the risk of conflicts with the sense.

Here is the source of that prodigious variety which the great masters of Italy were able to display in their operas without ever departing from nature, a variety which prevents monotony, languor, and ennui, and which French musicians cannot imitate because their tempi are prescribed by the sense of the words and they are forced to adhere to them unless they are willing to fall into ridiculous inconsistencies.

With regard to the recitative, of which it remains for me to speak, it seems to me that to judge it properly we must begin by knowing exactly what it is, for of all those who have discussed it I am so far unaware of any one who has thought of defining it. I do not know, sir, what idea you may have of that word; as for myself, I call recitative a harmonious declamation, that is, a declamation of which all the inflections are formed by harmonious intervals. It therefore follows that as each language has its own peculiar declamation, each language ought also to have its own peculiar recitative. This does not preclude one from very properly comparing one recitative with another to discover which of the two is the better, that is, the better adapted to its purpose.

Recitative is necessary in lyric drama, first, to connect the action and preserve the unity; second, to set off the airs, of which a continuous succession would be insupportable; third, to express a number of things which cannot be expressed by lyric, cadenced music. Mere declamation cannot be suitable for all that in a lyric work, because the transition from speech to song and especially that from song to speech has an abruptness which the ear does not readily accept, and presents a shocking contrast which destroys all the illusion and in consequence the interest.[18] For there is a kind of probability which must be preserved even at the Opéra, by making the language so homogeneous that the whole may at least be taken for a hypothetical language. Add to this that the aid of the harmonies augments the energy of musical declamation and compensates advantageously for what is less natural in its intonations.

It is evident, according to these notions, that the best recitative, in any language whatever, if this language fulfills the necessary conditions, is

---

[18] Rousseau refers to the Opéra Comique, which was then giving performances of mixed song and declamation (*comédies mêlées d'ariettes*) at the fairs of St. Germain and St. Laurent.

that which comes the nearest to speaking; if there were one which came so near to it as to deceive the ear or the mind while still preserving the required harmony, one might boldly pronounce that it had attained to the highest perfection of which any recitative is capable.

Let us now examine by this rule what in France is called "recitative." I pray you, tell me what relation you find between that recitative and our declamation. How can you ever conceive that the French language, of which the accent is so uniform, so simple, so modest, so unlike that of song, can be properly rendered by the shrill and noisy intonations of that recitative, and that there should be any relation whatever between the soft inflection of speech and these prolonged and exaggerated sounds, or rather these perpetual shrieks which form the tissue of that part of our music even more than that of the airs? For instance, let anyone who knows how to read recite the first four lines of the famous recognition scene of Iphigénie; you will barely detect a few slight inequalities, a few feeble inflections of the voice, in a tranquil recital which has nothing lively or impassioned, nothing which compels the speaker to raise or lower the voice. Then have one of our actresses deliver the same lines as set to music by the composer, and try, if you can, to endure that extravagant shrieking which shifts at each moment from low to high and from high to low, traverses without a subject the whole vocal register, and interrupts the recital in the wrong place to string some beautiful notes upon syllables without meaning, which correspond to no pause in the sense. Add to this the *fredons*,[14] cadenzas, and *ports-de-voix* which recur at every moment, and tell me what analogy there can be between speech and this pretended recitative, or at least show me some ground on which one may find reason to vaunt this wonderful French recitative whose invention is Lully's title to glory.

It is very amusing to see the partisans of French music take refuge in the character of the language and attribute to it the faults of which they do not dare to accuse their idol, whereas it is evident on all grounds that the recitative most suitable to the French language must be almost the opposite of that which is in use; that it must range within very small intervals, without much raising or lowering of the voice; with few prolonged notes, no sudden outbursts, still fewer shrieks; especially, nothing which resembles melody; little inequality in the duration or value of the notes or in their intensity either. In a word, the true French recitative, if one is possible, will be found only by a path directly opposite to that taken by Lully and his successors, by some new path which assuredly the French

---

14 Literally a short roulade, here implying excessive ornamentation.

composers, so proud of their false learning and consequently so far from feeling and loving what is true, will not soon be willing to seek and which they will probably never find.

Here would be the place to show you, by the example of Italian recitative, that all the conditions which I have postulated in a good recitative can actually be found there; that it can have at the same time all the vivacity and all the energy of harmony; that it can proceed as rapidly as speech and be as melodious as veritable song; that it can indicate all the inflections with which the most vehement passions animate discourse, without straining the voice of the singer or deafening the ears of the listeners. I could show you how, with the aid of a particular basic progression, one may multiply the modulations of the recitative in a way suitable to it and which contributes to distinguishing it from the airs when, in order to preserve the graces of the melody, the key must be less frequently changed; how, especially, when one wishes to give passion the time to display all its movements, it is possible, by means of a skillfully managed interlude, to make the orchestra express by varied and pathetic phrases what the actor can only relate—a master stroke of the musician's art, by which, in an accompanied recitative,[m] he may combine the most affecting melody with all the vehemence of declamation without ever confusing the one with the other. I could unfold to you all the numberless beauties of that admirable recitative of which in France so many absurd tales are told, as absurd as the judgments which people presume to pass on them, as if one could judge of a recitative without a thorough knowledge of the language to which it belongs. But to enter into these details it would be necessary, so to speak, to create a new dictionary, to coin terms every moment in order to present to French readers ideas unknown among them, and to address them in language which would seem meaningless to them. In a word, one would be obliged, in order to make oneself clear, to speak a language they understood, and consequently to speak of any science or art whatever except music alone. Therefore I shall not go into this subject with an affected detail which would do nothing to instruct my readers and concerning which they might presume that I owed the apparent force of my arguments only to their ignorance in this matter.

For the same reason I shall also not attempt what was proposed this

---

m I had hoped that Signor Caffarelli would give us, in the concert of sacred music, some example of grand recitative and of pathetic melody, in order to let the pretended connoisseurs hear for once what they have so long been passing judgment on, but I found, from his reasons for doing nothing of the kind, that he knew better than I the capacity of his hearers.

[Gaetano Majorano, called Caffarelli after his earliest protector (1703–1783), one of the leading Italian castrati. Louis XV engaged him to entertain the Dauphine, according to the *Mémoires du duc de Luynes* (XII, 471 and XIII, 10), and while in Paris he was also heard at the Concert Spirituel on November 5, 1753—an event which Rousseau presumably attended.—Ed.]

winter in a publication addressed to the "Little Prophet" and his opponents, a comparison between two pieces of music, the one Italian and the other French, which were there indicated.

·   ·   ·   ·   ·

I think that I have shown that there is neither measure nor melody in French music, because the language is not capable of them; that French singing is a continual squalling, insupportable to an unprejudiced ear; that its harmony is crude and devoid of expression and suggests only the padding of a pupil; that French "airs" are not airs; that French recitative is not recitative. From this I conclude that the French have no music and cannot have any; [n] or that if they ever have, it will be so much the worse for them.[15]

I am, etc.

---

[n] I do not call it having a music to import that of another language and try to apply it to one's own, and I had rather we kept our wretched and absurd singing than that we should still more absurdly unite Italian melody with the French language. This distasteful combination, which will perhaps from now on constitute the study of our musicians, is too monstrous to be accepted, and the character of our language will never lend itself to it. At most, some comic pieces will succeed in passing by reason of their orchestral part, but I boldly predict that the tragic style will never be attempted. At the Opéra Comique this winter the public applauded the work of a man of talent who seems to have listened with good ears, and who has translated the style into French as closely as is possible; his accompaniments are well imitated without being copied; and if he has written no melody, it is because it is impossible to write any. Young musicians who feel that you have talent, continue in public to despise Italian music; I am well aware that your present interest requires it; but in private make haste to study that language and that music if you wish to be able some day to turn against your comrades the disdain which today you affect for your masters.

[15] Rousseau's blanket condemnation of French music represents a sudden about-face. Only a few years before, in 1750 to be exact, he had sent Baron Grimm a comparison of French and Italian opera. In 1750 he had found many reasons for thinking French opera superior to Italian. Had the letter been generally available at the time, it would have been most embarrassing to its author. The document is reprinted in the appendix of Albert Jansen's *Jean-Jacques Rousseau als Musiker* (Berlin, 1884), pp. 455–463.

XV

Critical Views of Italian Opera:
Algarotti and Gluck

70. Francesco Algarotti

Algarotti was a man of many-sided and cosmopolitan culture. Born at Venice in 1712, he went in 1740 to Berlin on the invitation of Frederick the Great, and remained there for nine years in close touch with the King, assisting him in the translation of opera librettos. He returned to Italy in 1753 and died at Pisa in 1764.

The outstanding characteristic of Algarotti's writings is a kind of cosmopolitan dilettantism. His *Saggio sopra l'opera in musica* (1755) is of interest as the work of a highly cultured Italian, voicing critical views on contemporary Italian opera. Among his other writings, his *Lettere sulla pittura* command attention as a source of information and judicious criticism.

From the Saggio sopra l'opera in musica [1]
[*1755*]

I. OF THE POEM, ARGUMENT, OR BUSINESS OF AN OPERA

As SOON as the desired regulation shall have been introduced on the theatre it will then be incumbent to proceed to the various constituent parts of an opera in order that those amendments should be made in each whereof they severally now appear the most deficient. The leading object to be maturely considered is the nature of the subject to be chosen, an article of much more consequence than is commonly imagined; for the success or failure of the drama depends, in a great measure, on a good or bad choice of the subject. It is here of no less consequence than, in architecture, the plan is to an edifice, or the canvas, in painting, is to a picture; because thereon the poet draws the outlines of his intended representation, and its coloring is the task of the musical composer. It is therefore the poet's duty, as chief engineer of the undertaking, to give directions to the

---

[1] Text: The original edition of the anonymous English translation of 1768, pp. 14–52.

dancers, the machinists, the painters; nay, down even to those who are entrusted with the care of the wardrobe and dressing the performers. The poet is to carry in his mind a comprehensive view of the *whole* of the drama; because those parts which are not the productions of his pen ought to flow from the dictates of his actuating judgment, which is to give being and movement to the whole.

At the first institution of operas, the poets imagined the heathen mythology to be the best source from which they could derive subjects for their dramas. Hence Daphne, Eurydice, Ariadne, were made choice of by Ottavio Rinuccini and are looked upon as the eldest musical dramas, having been exhibited about the beginning of the last century. There was, besides, Poliziano's *Orpheus*,[2] which also had been represented with instrumental accompaniments, as well as another performance that was no more than a medley of dancing and music, contrived by Bergonzo Botta for the entertainment of a Duke of Milan in the city of Tortona.[3] A particular species of drama was exhibited at Venice for the amusement of Henry the Third; it had been set to music by the famous Zarlino.[4] Add to these some other performances, which ought only to be considered as so many rough sketches and preludes to a complete opera.

The intent of our poets was to revive the Greek tragedy in all its lustre and to introduce Melpomene on our stage, attended by music, dancing, and all that imperial pomp with which, at the brilliant period of a Sophocles and Euripides, she was wont to be escorted. And that such splendid pageantry might appear to be the genuine right of tragedy, the poets had recourse for their subjects to the heroic ages and heathen mythology. From that fountain, the bard, according to his inventive pleasure, introduced on the theatre all the deities of paganism; now shifting his scene to Olympus, now fixing it in the Elysian shades, now plunging it down to Tartarus, with as much ease as if to Argos or to Thebes. And thus, by the intervention of superior beings, he gave an air of probability to most surprising and wonderful events. Every circumstance being thus elevated above the sphere of mortal existence, it necessarily followed that the singing of actors in an opera appeared a true imitation of the language made use of by the deities they represented.

This then was the original cause why, in the first dramas that had been exhibited in the courts of sovereigns or the palaces of princes in order to

---

2 Performed at Mantua in 1472, or perhaps 1471; cf. Alfred Einstein, *The Italian Madrigal* (Princeton, 1949), I, 34–35.

3 The medley referred to was a festal play with music to celebrate the wedding of Gian Galeazzo Sforza and Isabella of Aragon. The performance of this unnamed work took place in 1488.

4 A reference to Cornelio Frangipane's *Proteo* of 1574, the music not by Zarlino but by Claudio Merulo; cf. Angelo Solerti, "Le rappresentazioni musicali di Venezia dal 1571 al 1605," *Rivista musicale italiana*, IX (1902), 503–558.

celebrate their nuptials, such expensive machinery was employed; not an article was omitted that could excite an idea of what is most wonderful to be seen either on earth or in the heavens. To superadd a greater diversity and thereby give a new animation to the whole, crowded choruses of singers were admitted, as well as dances of various contrivance, with a special attention that the execution of the ballet should coincide and be combined with the choral song; all which pleasing effects were made to spring naturally from the subject of the drama.

No doubt then can remain of the exquisite delight that such magic representations must have given to an enraptured assembly; for although it consisted but of a single subject, it nevertheless displayed an almost infinite variety of entertainment. There is even now frequent opportunity of seeing, on the French musical theatre, a spirited likeness to what is here advanced; because the opera was first introduced in Paris by Cardinal Mazarin, whither it carried the same magnificent apparatus with which it had made its appearance at his time in Italy.[5]

These representations must, however, have afterwards suffered not a little by the intermixture of buffoon characters, which are such ill-suited companions of the dignity of heroes and of gods; for by making the spectators laugh out of season, they disconcert the solemnity of the piece. Some traces of this theatric impropriety are even now observable in the eldest of the French musical dramas.[6]

The opera did not long remain confined in the courts of sovereigns and palaces of princes, but, emancipating itself from such thralldom, displayed its charms on public theatres, to which the curious of all ranks were admitted for pay. But in this situation, as must obviously occur to whoever reflects, it was impossible that the pomp and splendor which was attendant on this entertainment from its origin could be continued. The falling off, in that article, was occasioned principally by the exorbitant salaries the singers insisted on, which had been but inconsiderable at the first outset of the musical drama; as for instance, a certain female singer was called *La Centoventi*, "The Hundred-and-Twenty," [7] for having received so many crowns for her performance during a single carnival, a sum which hath been amazingly exceeded since, almost beyond all bounds.

Hence arose the necessity for opera directors to change their measures and to be as frugally economical on the one hand as they found themselves unavoidably profuse on the other. Through such saving, the opera may

---

5 For a list of the Italian operas performed in France between 1645 and 1662 see Alfred Loewenberg, *Annals of Opera* (Cambridge, 1943), p. 21.

6 Comic characters appear in the first three operas of Lully (*Cadmus*, 1673; *Alceste*, 1674; *Thésée*, 1675) but not in the later works.

7 This singer has not been further identified.

be said to have fallen from heaven upon the earth and, being divorced from an intercourse with gods, to have humbly resigned itself to that of mortals.

Thenceforward prevailed a general renunciation of all subjects to be found in the fabulous accounts of the heathen deities, and none were made choice of but those derived from the histories of humble mankind, because less magnificent in their nature, and therefore less liable to large disbursements for their exhibition.

The directors, obliged to circumspection for their own safety, were induced to imagine they might supply the place of all that costly pomp and splendid variety of decoration, to which the dazzled spectators had been accustomed so long, by introducing a chaster regularity into their drama, seconded by the auxiliary charms of a more poetical diction as well as by the concurring powers of a more exquisite musical composition. This project gained ground the faster from the public's observing that one of these arts was entirely employed in modeling itself on our ancient authors, and the other solely intent on enriching itself with new ornaments; which made operas to be looked upon by many as having nearly reached the pinnacle of perfection. However, that these representations might not appear too naked and uniform, interludes and ballets, to amuse the audience, were introduced between the acts; and thus, by degrees, the opera took that form which is now practised on our theatres.

It is an incontrovertible fact that subjects for an operatical drama, whether taken from pagan mythology or historians, have inevitable inconveniences annexed to them. The fabulous subjects, on account of the great number of machines and magnificent apparatus which they require, often distress the poet into limits too narrow for him to carry on and unravel his plot with propriety; because he is not allowed either sufficient time or space to display the passions of each character, so absolutely necessary to the completing of an opera, which, in the main, is nothing more than a tragic poem recited to musical sounds. And from the inconvenience alluded to here, it has happened that a great number of the French operas, as well as the first of the Italian, are nothing better than entertainments for the eyes, having more the appearance of a masquerade than of a regular dramatic performance; because therein the principal action is whelmed, as it were, under a heap of accessories, and, the poetical part being so flimsy and wretched, it was with just reason called a string of madrigals.

On the other hand, the subjects taken from history are liable to the objection of their not being so well adapted to music, which seems to exclude them from all plea of probability. This impleaded error may be observed every day upon the Italian stage. For who can be brought to think that the trillings of an air flow so justifiably from the mouth of a Julius Caesar or a Cato as from the lips of Venus or Apollo? Moreover, historical subjects do not furnish so striking a variety as those that are fabulous; they are apt to be too austere and monotonous. The stage, in such representations, would forever exhibit an almost solitary scene unless we are willing to number, among the ranks of actors, the mob of attendants that crowd after sovereigns, even into their closets. Besides, it is no easy matter to contrive ballets or interludes suitable to subjects taken from history; because all such entertainments ought to form a kind of social union and become, as it were, constituent parts of the whole. Such, for example, on the French stage, is the "Ballet of the Shepherds," that celebrates the marriage of Medoro with Angelica and makes Orlando acquainted with his accumulated wretchedness.[8] But this is far from being the effect of entertainments obtruded into the Italian operas, in which, although the subject be Roman and the ballet consist of dancers dressed like Roman soldiers, yet so unconnected is it with the business of the drama that the Scozzese or Furlana might as well be danced. And this is the reason why subjects chosen from history are for the most part necessitated to appear naked or to make use of such alien accoutrements as neither belong, nor are by any means suitable to them.

In order to obviate such inconveniences, the only means left to the poet is to exert all his judgement and taste in choosing the subject of his drama, that thereby he may attain his end, which is to delight the eyes and the ears, to rouse up and to affect the hearts of an audience, without the risk of sinning against reason or common sense. Wherefore the most prudent method he can adopt will be to make choice of an event that has happened, either in very remote times, or in countries very distant from us and quite estranged from our usages, which may afford various incidents of the marvellous, notwithstanding that the subject, at the same time, be extremely simple and not unknown, two desirable requisites.

The great distance of place where the action is fixed will prevent the recital of it to musical sounds from appearing quite so improbable to us. The marvellousness of the theme will furnish the author with an opportunity of interweaving therewith dances, choruses, and a variety of scenical decorations. The simplicity and notoriety of it will exempt his muse from the perplexing trouble and tedious preparations necessary to

8 In Lully's *Roland* (1685), II, v.

make the personages of a drama known, that, suitable to his notification, may be displayed their passions, the main spring and actuating spirit of the stage.

The two operas of *Didone* and *Achille in Sciro,* written by the celebrated Metastasio, come very near to the mark proposed here.[9] The subjects of these dramatic poems are simple and taken from very remote antiquity, but without being too far-fetched. In the midst of their most impassioned scenes, there is an opportunity of introducing splendid banquets, magnificent embassies, embarkations, choruses, battles, conflagrations, &c, so as to give a farther extension to the sovereignty of the musical drama, and makes its rightfulness be more ascertained than has been hitherto allowed.

The same doctrine may be advanced in regard to an opera on the subject of Montezuma, as much on account of the greatness, as of the novelty of such an action as that emperor's catastrophe must afford. A display of the Mexican and Spanish customs, seen for the first time together, must form a most beautiful contrast; and the barbaric magnificence of America would receive various heightenings by being opposed in different views to that of Europe.[a]

Several subjects may likewise be taken from Ariosto and Tasso, equally fitting as Montezuma for the opera theatre; for besides these being so universally known, they would furnish not only a fine field for exercising the passions, but also for introducing all the surprising illusions of the magic art.

An opera of Aeneas in Troy, or of Iphigenia in Aulis, would answer the same purpose; [10] and to the great variety for scenes and machinery, still greater heightenings might be derived from the enchanting *poetry* of Virgil and Euripides.

There are many other subjects to the full as applicable to the stage and that may be found equally fraught with marvellous incidents. Let then a poet who is judicious enough make a prudent collection of the subjects truly dramatic that are to be found in tracing the fabulous accounts of the heathen gods, and do the same also in regard to more modern times. Such

a Montezuma has been chosen for the subject of an opera, performed with the greatest magnificence at the Theatre Royal of Berlin. [Carl Heinrich Graun's *Montezuma,* a setting of G. P. Tagliazucchi's Italian version of a French libretto by Frederick the Great, was first performed on January 6, 1755, in Berlin. Algarotti signed the dedication of his *Saggio* on October 6, 1754. Yet this reference to the subject of Montezuma was surely written with the forthcoming performance in mind; Frederick had written to Algarotti about his plans for the opera as early as October 1753

(see his letter, quoted in part by Mayer-Reinach in his edition of the score for the *Denkmäler deutscher Tonkunst,* XV [1904]).—Ed.]

9 Metastasio's *Didone abbandonata* was first set to music by Domenico Sarro in 1724; the first setting of his *Achille in Sciro* (1736) was by Antonio Caldara.

10 Algarotti outlines an opera on the first of these subjects at the end of his *Saggio* and after this prints his own libretto on the second.

a proceeding, relative to the opera, would not be unlike what is oft-times found necessary in states, which it is impossible to preserve from decay and in the unimpaired enjoyment of their constitutional vigor without making them revert, from time to time, to their original principles.

2. ON THE MUSICAL COMPOSITION FOR OPERAS

No art now appears to stand so much in need of having the conclusive maxim of the preceding chapter put in practice as that of music, so greatly has it degenerated from its former dignity. For by laying aside every regard to decorum, and by scorning to keep within the bounds prescribed, it has suffered itself to be led far, very far astray in a bewildering pursuit of new-fangled whimsies and capricious conceits. Wherefore it would now be very seasonable to revive the decree made by the Lacedaemonians against that man who, through a distempered passion for novelty, had so sophisticated their music with his crotchety innovations that, from noble and manly, he rendered it effeminate and disgusting.

Mankind in general, it must be owned, are actuated by a love of novelty; and it is as true that, without it, music, like every other art, could not have received the great improvements it has. What we here implead is not a chaste passion for novelty, but a too great fondness for it; because it was that which reduced music to the declining state so much lamented by all true connoisseurs. While arts are in their infancy the love of novelty is no doubt essential, as it is to that they owe their being, and after, by its kindly influence, are improved, matured, and brought to perfection; but that point being once attained, the indulging this passion too far will, from benign and vivifying, become noxious and fatal. The arts have experienced this vicissitude in almost every nation where they have appeared, as, among the Italians, hath music at this time in a more remarkable manner.

On its revival in Italy, though in very barbarous times, this elegant art soon made its power be known throughout Europe; nay more, it was cultivated to such a degree by the tramontane nations that it may without exaggeration be asserted the Italians themselves were, for a certain period of time, glad to receive instructions from them.

On the return of music to Venice, Rome, Bologna, and Naples, as to its native place, such considerable improvements were made there in the musical art, during the two last centuries, that foreigners, in their turn, repaired thither for instruction; and such would be now the case were they not deterred from so doing by the raging frenzy after novelty that prevails in all the Italian schools. For, as if music were yet unrudimented and in its infancy, the mistaken professors spare no pains to trick out their art with every species of grotesque imagination and fantastical combination which they think can be executed by sounds. The public too, as if they were likewise in a state of childhood, change almost every moment their notions of, and fondness for things, rejecting today with scorn what yesterday was so passionately admired. The taste in singing, which, some years ago, enraptured audiences hung upon with wonder and delight, is now received with a supercilious disapprobation; not because it is sunk in real merit, but for the very groundless reason of its being old and not in frequent use. And thus we see that in compositions instituted for the representation of nature, whose mode is ever one, there is the same desire of changing as in the fluctuating fashions of the dresses we wear.

Another principal reason that can be assigned for the present degeneracy of music is the authority, power, and supreme command usurped in its name; because the composer, in consequence, acts like a despotic sovereign, contracting all the views of pleasing to his department alone. It is almost impossible to persuade him that he ought to be in a subordinate station, that music derives its greatest merit from being no more than an auxiliary, the handmaid to poetry. His chief business, then, is to predispose the minds of the audience for receiving the impression to be excited by the poet's verse, to infuse such a general tendency in their affections as to make them analogous with those particular ideas which the poet means to inspire. In fine, its genuine office is to communicate a more animating energy to the language of the muses.

That old and just charge, enforced by critics against operatical performances, of making their heroes and heroines die *singing,* can be ascribed to no other cause but the defect of a proper harmony between the words and the music. Were all ridiculous quavering omitted when the serious passions are to speak, and were the musical composition judiciously adapted to them, then it would not appear more improbable that a person should die singing, than reciting verses.

It is an undeniable fact that, in the earliest ages, the poets were all musical proficients; the vocal part, then, ranked as it should, which was to render the thoughts of the mind and affections of the heart with more forcible, more lively, and more kindling expression. But now that the twin sisters, poetry and music, go no longer hand in hand, it is not at all surprising, if the business of the one is to add coloring to what the other has designated, that the coloring, separately considered, appear beautiful; yet, upon a nice examination of the whole, the contours offend by not being properly rounded and by the absence of a social blending of the parts throughout. Nor can a remedy be applied to so great an evil otherwise but by the modest discretion of a composer who will not think it beneath him to receive, from the poet's mouth, the purport of his meaning and intention; who will also make himself a competent master of the author's sense before he writes a note of music and will ever afterwards confer with him concerning the music he shall have composed; and, by thus proceeding, keep up such a dependence and friendly intercourse as subsisted between Lully and Quinault, Vinci and Metastasio, which indeed the true regulation of an operatical theatre requires.

Among the errors observable in the present system of music, the most obvious, and that which first strikes the ears at the very opening of an opera, is the hackneyed manner of composing overtures, which are always made to consist of two allegros with one grave and to be as noisy as possible. Thus are they void of variation and so jog on much alike. Yet what a wide difference ought to be perceived between that, for example, which precedes the death of Dido and that which is prefixed to the nuptials of Demetrius and Cleonice. The main drift of an overture should be to announce, in a certain manner, the business of the drama and consequently prepare the audience to receive those affecting impressions that are to result from the whole of the performance, so that from hence a leading view and presaging notions of it may be conceived, as is of an oration from the exordium. But our present composers look upon an overture as an article quite detached and absolutely different from the poet's drama. They use it as an opportunity of playing off a tempestuous music to stun the ears of an audience. If some, however, employ it as an exordium, it is of a kindred complection to those of certain writers, who, with big and pompous words, repeatedly display before us the loftiness of the subject and the lowness of their genius; which preluding would suit any other subject as well and might as judiciously be prefixed for an exordium to one oration as another.[11]

After the overture, the next article that presents itself to our consideration is the recitative; and as it is wont to be the most noisy part of an opera, so is it the least attended to and the most neglected. It seems as if our musical composers were of opinion that the recitative is not of consequence enough to deserve their attention, they deeming it incapable of exciting any great delight. But the ancient masters thought in a quite different manner. There needs no stronger proof than to read what Jacopo Peri, who may be justly called the inventor of the recitative, wrote in his preface to *Euridice*.[12] When he had applied himself to an investigation of that

---

11 Compare the criticism of Quantz (p. 588 above).   12 See pp. 373–376 above.

species of musical imitation which would the readiest lend itself to theatric exhibitions, he directed his tasteful researches to discover the manner which had been employed by the ancient Greeks on similar occasions. He carefully observed the Italian words which are capable of intonation or consonance and those which are not. He was very exact in minuting down our several modes of pronunciation, as well as the different accents of grief, of joy, and of all the other affections incident to the human frame, and that in order to make the bass move a timing attendance to them, now with more energy, now with less, according to the nature of each. So nicely scrupulous was he in his course of vocal experiments that he scrutinized intimately the very nature of the Italian language; on which account, in order to be more accurate, he frequently consulted with several gentlemen not less remarkable for the delicacy of their ears, than for their being uncommonly skilled both in the arts of music and poetry.

The final conclusion of his ingenious inquiry was that the groundwork of all such imitation should be an harmony chastely following nature step by step; a something between common speaking and melody; a well-combined system between that kind of performance which the ancients called the *diastematica*,[b] as if held in and suspended, and the other, called the *continuata*.[c] Such were the studies of the musical composers in former times. They proceeded in the improvement of their art with the utmost care and attention; and the effect proved that they did not lose their time in the pursuit of unprofitable subtleties.

The recitative in their time was made to vary with the subject and assume a complection suitable to the spirit of the words. It sometimes moved with a rapidity equal to that of the text and at others with an attendant slowness; but never failed to mark, in a conspicuous manner, those inflections and sallies which the violence of our passions can transfuse into the expression of them. All musical compositions finished in so masterly a manner were heard with delight. Numbers now living must remember how certain passages of simple recitative have affected the minds of an audience to a degree that no modern air is able to produce.

However, the recitative, all disregarded as it may be, has been known to excite emotions in an audience when it was of the *obbligato* kind, as the artists term it, that is, when strictly accompanied with instruments.[13] Per-

---

b Diastematic implies, according to the sense of the ancients, a simple interval, in opposition to a compound one, by them called a system. [Note from translator's glossary]

c Continuata, in vocal music, means to continue or hold on a sound with an equal strength or manner, or to continue a movement in an equal degree of time all the way. [Note from translator's glossary]

13 Compare the comments of Marcello (p. 529 above); for Metastasio's views, see his letter to Hasse, published by Burney in his *Memoirs of the Life and Writings of the Abate Metastasio* (London, 1796), I, 315-330.

haps it would not be improper to employ it oftener than is now the custom. What a kindly warmth might be communicated to the recitative if, where a passion exerts itself, it were to be enforced by the united orchestra! By so doing, the heart and mind at once would be stormed, as it were, by all the powers of music. A more evincing instance of such an effect cannot be quoted than the greater part of the last act of *Didone*, set to music by Vinci, which is executed in the taste recommended here; and no doubt but Virgil's self would be pleased to hear a composition so animating and so terrible.

Another good purpose which must be derived from such a practice is that then would not appear to us so enormous the great variety and disproportion now observable in the *andamento* of the recitative and that of the airs; but, on the contrary, a more friendly agreement among the several parts of an opera would be the result. The connoisseurs have often been displeased with those sudden transitions where, from a recitative in the *andantissimo* and gentlest movement, the performers are made to skip off and bound away into ariettas of the briskest execution, which is to the full as absurd as if a person, when soberly walking, should all on the sudden set to leaping and capering.

The surest method to bring about a better understanding among the several constituent parts of an opera would be not to crowd so much art into the airs and to curb the instrumental part more than is now the custom. In every period of the opera these two formed the most brilliant parts of it; and, in proportion as the musical composition has been more and more refined, so have they received still greater heightenings. They were naked formerly in comparison of what we see them now and were in as absolute a state of simplicity as they had been at their origin, insomuch that, either in point of melody or accompaniments, they did not rise above recitative.

Old Scarlatti was the first who infused life, movement, and spirit in them. It was he who clothed their nakedness with the splendid attire of noble accompaniments, but they were dealt out by him in a sober and judicious manner. They were by no means intricate or obscure, but open and obvious; highly finished, yet free from all the minuteness of affectation; and that not so much on account of the vastness of the theatres, by means of which many of the minor excellencies in musical performances may be lost, as in regard to the voices, to which alone they should be made subservient.

But unwarrantable changes have happened, since that great master's time down to ours, in which all the bounds of discretion are wantonly over-

leapt. The airs now are whelmed under and disfigured by crowded ornaments with which unnatural method the rage of novelty labors to embellish them. How tediously prolix are those *ritornelli* that precede them;
nay, and are often superfluous! For can anything be more improbable than
that, in an air expressive of wrath, an actor should calmly wait with his
hand stuck in his sword-belt until the *ritornello* be over to give vent to
a passion that is supposed to be boiling in his breast? And after the
ritornello then comes on the part to be sung, but the multitude of fiddles,
etc., that accompany it in general produce no better an effect than to
astonish the faculty of hearing and to drown the voice of a singer. Why
is there not more use made of the basses, and why not increase the number
of bass viols, which are the shades of music? Where is the necessity for
so many fiddles, with which our orchestras are now thronged? Fewer
would do, for they prove in this case like too many hands on board of a
ship which, instead of being assistant, are a great impediment to its navi-
gation. Why are not lutes and harps allowed a place? With their light
and piercing notes they would give a sprightliness to the *ripienos*. Why
is the *violetta* excluded from our orchestras, since from its institution it
was intended to act a middle part between the fiddles and the basses in
order that harmony might thence ensue?

But one of the most favorite practices now, and which indeed makes
our theatres to resound with peals of applause, is, in an air, to form a contest between the voice and a hautboy or between the voice and a trumpet
so as to exhibit, as it were, a kind of musical tilting-match with the utmost
exertion on either side. But such a skirmishing of voices and instruments is
very displeasing to the judicious part of the audience, who, on the contrary, would receive the greatest delight from the airs being accompanied
by instruments differently qualified from the present in use, and perhaps
even by the organ, as hath been formerly practiced.[d] The consequence
then would be that the respective qualities of instruments would be properly adapted to the nature of the words which they are intended to accompany and that they would aptly glide into those parts where a due
expression of the passion should stand most in need of them. Then the
accompaniment would be of service to the singer's voice by enforcing
the pathetic affections of the song and would prove not unlike to the
numbers of elegant and harmonious prose, which, according to the maxim
of a learned sage, ought to be like the beating on an anvil by smiths, at
once both musical and skilfully labored.

These faults, however considerable, are not the greatest that have been

d In the orchestra of the theatre in the famous villa of Cataio an organ is now to be seen.

introduced in the composition of airs; we must go farther back to investigate the first source of this evil, which, in the judgment of the most able professors, is to be found in the misconduct of choosing the subject of an air, because rarely any attention is paid to the *andamento* of the melody being natural and corresponding to the sense of the words it is to convey; besides, the extravagant varieties which it is now made to shift and turn about after cannot be managed to tend to one common center or point of unity. For the chief view of our present musical composers is to court, flatter, and surprise the ears, but not at all either to affect the heart or kindle the imagination of those who hear them; therefore, to accomplish their favorite end, they frequently bound over all rules. To be prodigal of shining passages, to repeat words without end, and musically to interweave or entangle them as they please are the three principal methods by which they carry on their operations.

The first of these expedients is indeed big with danger when we attend to the good effect that is to be expected from melody, because through its middle situation it possesses more of the *virtù*. Moreover, music delights to make an use of acute notes in her compositions, similar to that which painting does with striking lights in her performances.

In regard to brilliant passages, common sense forbids the introduction of them excepting where the words are expressive of passion or movement; otherwise they deserve no milder an appellation than being so many impertinent interruptions of the musical sense.

The repeating of words, and these chiming rencounters that are made for the sake of sound merely and are devoid of meaning, prove intolerable to a judicious ear. Words are to be treated in no other manner but according as the passion dictates; and, when the sense of an air is finished, the first part of it ought never to be sung over again, which is one of our modern innovations and quite repugnant to the natural process of our speech and passions, that are not accustomed to thus turn about and recoil upon themselves.

Most people who frequent our Italian theatres must have observed that, even when the sense of an air breathes a roused and furious tendency, yet, if the words "father" or "son" be in the text, the composer never fails to slacken his notes, to give them all the softness he can, and to stop in a moment the impetuosity of the tune. Moreover he flatters himself, on such an occasion, that, besides having clothed the words with sentimental sounds suitable to them, he hath also given to them an additional seasoning of variety.

But in our sense he hath entirely spoiled all with such a dissonance of expression that will ever be objected to by all who have the least pretensions to judgment and taste. The duty of a composer is to express the sense, not of this or that particular word, but the comprehensive meaning of all the words in the air. It is also his duty to make variety flow from the several modifications the subject in itself is capable of, and not from adjuncts that adventitiously fasten themselves thereon and are foreign from, preposterous, or repugnant to the poet's intention.

It seems that our composers take the same mistaken pains which some writers do, who, regardless of connection and order in a discourse, bend all their thoughts to collect and string together a number of finely sounding words. But, notwithstanding such words are ever so harmonious, a discourse so written would prove an useless, vain, and contemptible performance. The same may be said of every musical composition which is not calculated either to express some sentiment or awaken the idea of some imagery of the mind.[e] Like what we have compared it to, it must turn out but an useless and a vain production, which, should it be received with a temporary and slight applause, must soon be consigned to perpetual silence and oblivion, notwithstanding all the art that might have been employed in choosing the musical combinations. On the contrary, those airs alone remain forever engraven on the memory of the public that paint images to the mind or express the passions, and are for that reason called the speaking airs because more congenial to nature, which can never be justly imitated but by a beautiful simplicity which will always bear away the palm from the most labored refinements of art.

Although poetry and music be so near akin to each other, yet they have pursued different views here in Italy. The muse presiding over harmony was too chaste in the last century to give in to those affectations and languishing airs which she is at present so fond of indulging. She then knew the way to the human heart and how to stamp permanent impressions thereon; she possessed the secret of incorporating herself, as it were, with the meaning of the words, and, that the probability might seem the greater, she was to the last degree simple, yet affecting, though at the same time the poetic muse had run away from all semblance of truth to make a parade of hyperbolical, far-fetched, fantastical whimsies. Since that time, by a strange vicissitude, as soon as poetry was made to return into the right path, music ran astray.

Such excellent masters as a Cesti and a Carissimi had the hard fate of

---

e "All music that paints nothing is only noise, and, were it not for custom that unnatures everything, it would excite no more pleasure than a sequel of harmonious and finely sounding words without any order or connection."—Preface of the *Encyclopédie*. [Algarotti's quotation is from the "Discours préliminaire" of d'Alembert.—Ed.]

composing music for words in the style of Achillino,[14] men who were equal to the noble task of conveying in musical numbers the sighs and love-breathings of a Petrarch. But now, alas, the elegant, the terse, the graceful poems of Metastasio are degraded into music by wretched composers. It must not, however, be hence concluded that no vestige of true music is to be perceived among us, because, as a proof against such an opinion, and that no small one, may be produced our intermezzi and comic operas, wherein the first of all musical requisites, that of expression, takes the lead more than in any other of our compositions; which is owing perhaps to the impossibility the masters found of indulging their own fancy in a wanton display of all the secrets of their art and the manifold treasures of musical knowledge, from which ostentatious prodigality they were luckily prevented by the very limited abilities of their singers. Wherefore, in their own despite, they found themselves obliged to cultivate simplicity and follow nature. Whatever may have been the cause, this style soon obtained the vogue and triumphed over every other although called plebeian.

To this kind of performance we owe the extending of our musical fame on the other side of the Alps among the French, who had been at all times our rivals in every polite art. The emulous contention which had so long subsisted between them and us for a pre-eminence in music is universally known. No means could be hit on by our artists to make their execution agreeable to Gallic ears, and the Italian melody was abhorred by them as much as had been, in former times, an Italian regency.

But no sooner was heard upon the theatre of Paris the natural yet elegant style of the *Serva padrona*,[15] rich with airs so expressive and duets so pleasing, than the far greater part of the French became not only proselytes to, but even zealous advocates in behalf of the Italian music. A revolution so sudden was caused by an intermezzo and two comic actors. The like had been attempted in vain in the most elaborate pieces of eminent composers through a long series of years, although bedizened over with so many brilliant passages, surprising shakes, etc. Nor did the repeated efforts of our most celebrated performers, vocal or instrumental, fare better.

Nevertheless, all the good musical composition modern Italy can boast of is not absolutely confined to the intermezzi and comic operas, for it must be confessed that in some of our late serious pieces there are parts not unworthy of the best masters and the most applauded era of music. Several

---

14 G. F. Achillini (1466–1538), prolific author   15 See p. 630 above, note 20.
of pedantic verse.

instances are to be found in the works of Pergolesi and Vinci, whom death too soon snatched from us, as well as in those of Galuppi, Jommelli, "Il Sassone," [16] that are deserving to be for ever in esteem.

Through the energy of the composition of these masters, music makes an audience feel sometimes from the stage the very same effects that were formerly felt in the chapels under the direction of Palestrina and Rodio.[17] We have likewise proofs of the like powerful influence in the skilful productions of Benedetto Marcello, a man second in merit to none among the ancients and certainly the first among the moderns. Who ever was more animated with a divine flame in conceiving and more judicious in conducting his works than Marcello? In the cantatas of Timotheus and Cassandra and in the celebrated collection of psalms [18] he hath expressed in a wonderful manner, not only all the different passions of the heart, but even the most delicate sentiments of the mind. He has, moreover, the art of representing to our fancy things even inanimate. He found out the secret of associating with all the gracefulness and charms of the modern the chaste correctness of ancient music, which in him appears like the attractive graces of a beloved and respected matron.

16 Johann Adolph Hasse.

17 Rocco Rodio, a Neapolitan composer of the sixteenth century and the author of a treatise, *Regole di musica*, published in 1609.

18 Marcello's "Timoteo" (1726) has the sub- title "Gli effetti della musica"; the four volumes of his *Estro poetico-armonico*, collected settings of fifty paraphrases from the Psalms, were first published in Venice from 1724 to 1727.

71. C. W. von Gluck

Born in 1714 near the German-Bohemian border, Gluck is the master who liberated the opera from the conventions of contemporary Italian *opera seria* and created a new operatic style based on truly dramatic expression. After studying for four years with Sammartini in Milan and visiting London and various cities on the Continent, Gluck settled in Vienna in 1750.

The opera *Orfeo ed Euridice*, written in 1762, marks a turning point in Gluck's career. Here he applied for the first time his new ideas, supported by his able and original librettist, Ranieri de' Calzabigi. Gluck gives an explanation of his aims in the forewords to the printed scores of his operas *Alceste* (1768) and *Paride ed Elena* (1770). In 1772, Gluck found a new and congenial collaborator in Le Bland Du Roullet, who had adapted Racine's *Iphigénie* as an opera libretto. The new score—*Iphigénie en Aulide*—was accepted by the Paris Opéra, and Gluck himself went to Paris to direct the rehearsals. After reinforcing his position with *Armide* (1777) and *Iphigénie en Tauride* (1779), Gluck returned, crowned with fresh laurels, to Vienna, where he died in 1787.

Alceste [1]

[1769]

Dedication

Your Royal Highness:

When I undertook to write the music for *Alceste*, I resolved to divest it entirely of all those abuses, introduced into it either by the mistaken vanity of singers or by the too great complaisance of composers, which have so

---

[1] Text: As translated by Eric Blom for Alfred Einstein's *Gluck* (London, J. M. Dent & Sons, Ltd., 1936), pp. 98–100.

long disfigured Italian opera and made of the most splendid and most beautiful of spectacles the most ridiculous and wearisome. I have striven to restrict music to its true office of serving poetry by means of expression and by following the situations of the story, without interrupting the action or stifling it with a useless superfluity of ornaments; and I believed that it should do this in the same way as telling colors affect a correct and well-ordered drawing, by a well-assorted contrast of light and shade, which serves to animate the figures without altering their contours. Thus I did not wish to arrest an actor in the greatest heat of dialogue in order to wait for a tiresome *ritornello*, nor to hold him up in the middle of a word on a vowel favorable to his voice, nor to make display of the agility of his fine voice in some long-drawn passage, nor to wait while the orchestra gives him time to recover his breath for a cadenza. I did not think it my duty to pass quickly over the second section [2] of an aria of which the words are perhaps the most impassioned and important, in order to repeat regularly four times over those of the first part, and to finish the aria where its sense may perhaps not end for the convenience of the singer who wishes to show that he can capriciously vary a passage in a number of guises; in short, I have sought to abolish all the abuses against which good sense and reason have long cried out in vain.

I have felt that the overture ought to apprise the spectators of the nature of the action that is to be represented and to form, so to speak, its argument; that the concerted instruments should be introduced in proportion to the interest and the intensity of the words, and not leave that sharp contrast between the aria and the recitative in the dialogue, so as not to break a period unreasonably nor wantonly disturb the force and heat of the action.

Furthermore, I believed that my greatest labor should be devoted to seeking a beautiful simplicity, and I have avoided making displays of difficulty at the expense of clearness; nor did I judge it desirable to discover novelties if it was not naturally suggested by the situation and the expression; and there is no rule which I have not thought it right to set aside willingly for the sake of an intended effect.

Such are my principles. By good fortune my designs were wonderfully furthered by the libretto, in which the celebrated author, devising a new dramatic scheme, for florid descriptions, unnatural paragons, and

---

2 By "second section" Gluck means the central or contrasting section of the da capo aria. In the eighteenth century the first section of such an aria regularly presented its full text twice and had then to be repeated after the central or contrasting section, hence Gluck's reference to repeating the words of the first part "four times over." Frederick the Great says much the same thing in a letter of May 4, 1754, quoted in *Denkmäler der Tonkunst in Österreich*, XV (1904), ix.

sententious, cold morality, had substituted heartfelt language, strong passions, interesting situations and an endlessly varied spectacle. The success of the work justified my maxims, and the universal approbation of so enlightened a city has made it clearly evident that simplicity, truth and naturalness are the great principles of beauty in all artistic manifestations. For all that, in spite of repeated urgings on the part of some most eminent persons to decide upon the publication of this opera of mine in print, I was well aware of all the risk run in combating such firmly and profoundly rooted prejudices, and I thus felt the necessity of fortifying myself with the most powerful patronage of YOUR ROYAL HIGHNESS, whose August Name I beg you may have the grace to prefix to this my opera, a name which with so much justice enjoys the suffrages of an enlightened Europe. The great protector of the fine arts, who reigns over a nation that had the glory of making them arise again from universal oppression and which itself has produced the greatest models, in a city that was always the first to shake off the yoke of vulgar prejudices in order to clear a path for perfection, may alone undertake the reform of that noble spectacle in which all the fine arts take so great a share. If this should succeed, the glory of having moved the first stone will remain for me, and in this public testimonial of Your Highness's furtherance of the same, I have the honor to subscribe myself, with the most humble respect,

Your Royal Highness's

Most humble, most devoted, and most obliged servant,

CHRISTOFORO GLUCK.

72. F. L. Du Roullet

Du Roullet was the young dilettante who adapted Racine's *Iphigénie* as an opera libretto for Gluck. His *Lettre à M. D., un des directeurs de l'Opéra de Paris* (1772) was reprinted in 1781, together with other writings called forth by the dispute between the partisans of Gluck and Piccinni, in *Mémoires pour servir à l'histoire de la révolution opérée dans la musique par M. le Chevalier Gluck*, by Gaspard Leblond.

Letter to M. d'Auvergne [1]

[*1722*]

Vienna in Austria, August 1, 1772

THE ESTEEM which is due to you, Sir,[2] both for your talents, certainly most distinguished, and for the uprightness of your character, with which I am particularly acquainted, has determined me to undertake to write to you, to inform you that the famous M. Glouch,[3] so well known throughout Europe, has composed a French opera which he would like to have given upon the Paris stage. This great man, after composing more than forty Italian operas, which have had the greatest success in all the theatres where that language is accepted, has been convinced by a thoughtful reading of the ancients and the moderns and by profound meditations upon his art that the Italians, in their theatrical compositions, have strayed from the true path; that the French style is the true style of musical drama; that if it has not yet attained to perfection, the reason must be sought less in the talents of French musicians than in the authors of the poems, who, entirely unacquainted with the scope of musical art, have in their composi-

---

1 Text: *Mercure de France*, Octobre 1772, pp. 169–174.

2 The Chevalier Antoine d'Auvergne.
3 Du Roullet uses this spelling throughout.

tions preferred wit to sentiment, gallantry to the passions, and sweetness and color of versification to the pathetic in style and in character.

In accordance with these reflections, having communicated his ideas to a man of much wit, talent, and taste,[4] he obtained from him two Italian poems which he set to music. He has himself directed these two operas in the theaters of Parma, Milan, Naples, etc. They have had incredible success there and have produced a revolution in this kind of work in Italy. Last winter, in M. Glouch's absence, the city of Bologna presented one of these operas, and when the proceeds were reckoned, Bologna had made by this production more than 80,000 ducats, about 900,000 French livres.[5] Upon his return here, M. Glouch, enlightened by his own experience, believed himself to have perceived that the Italian language, better adapted by its frequent repetition of vowels to what the Italians call passages, lacks the clearness and the energy of French; that the advantage which we have been conceding to the former was even destructive of the true musical-dramatic style, in which every passage is an anomaly or at least weakens the expression.

In accordance with these observations M. Glouch became indignant at the bold assertions of those of our French writers who have dared to calumniate the French language by maintaining that it is incapable of lending itself to great musical composition.[6] No one can be a more competent judge in this matter than M. Glouch; he has a perfect knowledge of the two languages; and although he speaks French with difficulty, he has made a special and thorough study of it. In short, he knows all its fine distinctions and especially its prosody, which he observes most scrupulously. For a long time he has been making trial of his skill in dealing with these two languages in works in different styles, and has won successes at a court where they are equally familiar, although for practical use French is preferred, at a court the better prepared to judge of talents of this kind because the ear and the taste are there constantly exercised.

After he had made these observations, M. Glouch was desirous of an opportunity of supporting his judgment in favor of the French language by a practical demonstration, when chance caused the tragedy-opera *Iphigénie en Aulide* to fall into his hands. He believed that in this work he had found what he was seeking. The author, or to speak more exactly, the adapter of this poem [7] seems to me to have followed Racine with the most scrupulous attention. It is his *Iphigénie* itself, converted into an

---

4 Ranieri de' Calzabigi, author of *Orfeo ed Euridice* (1762) and *Alceste* (1767), also of *Paride ed Elena* (1770).

5 There is no mention of any such performance in Loewenberg's *Annals.*

6 Particularly Jean Jacques Rousseau.

7 Du Roullet himself.

opera. To attain this result it was necessary to simplify the exposition and to eliminate the episode of Ériphyle. Calchas is introduced into the first act instead of the confidant Arcas; by this device the exposition is given by means of action, the subject is simplified, and the action, more closely knit, advances more rapidly to its goal. The interest has not been diminished by these changes; it has even seemed to me as complete as the tragedy of Racine. Since after the episode of Ériphyle had been removed the denouement of the play of this great man could no longer serve for the opera in question, it has been replaced by a denouement in action which should produce a very good effect, and of which the idea has been furnished to the author by the Greek tragic writers, as well as by Racine himself in the preface to his *Iphigénie*.[8]

The whole work has been divided into three acts, a division which seems to me to be the most favorable for the kind of work which calls for great rapidity of action. In each act the author has naturally introduced a brilliant *divertissement*, derived without effort from the subject and so connected with it as to seem one of its parts, which augments or completes the action. He has taken great pains to oppose situation to situation and character to character, producing thereby a piquant variety, necessary to hold the spectator's attention and to interest him throughout the duration of the performance. He has found a means of presenting a noble and magnificent spectacle to the eye without resorting to machines and without requiring considerable expenditure. I do not believe that any one has ever produced a new opera which called for less expense and was at the same time more imposing.

The author of this poem, of which the entire performance, including the *divertissements*, ought to take at the most no longer than two and a half hours, has made it his obligation to use the thoughts and even the lines of Racine when the nature of the work, although different, has allowed. The subject of *Iphigénie en Aulide* has seemed to me so much the better chosen in that the author, by following Racine as closely as possible, has made sure of the effect of his work, and that by the certainty of success he is amply compensated for whatever he may have lost on the side of self-esteem.

M. Glouch's name alone would absolve me, Sir, from speaking of the music of this opera, if the pleasure it has given me on repeated hearing permitted me to remain silent. It seemed to me that this great man has in this composition exhausted all the resources of his art. Simple, natural

---

8 What Racine actually does in his preface is to report the classical tradition for Diana's inter- vention and to reject this ending as too absurd and incredible for the theater of his time.

song, always guided by the truest, the most affecting expression and by the most ingratiating melody; an inexhaustible variety in his subject and in his turn of phrase; the grandest effects of harmony, employed equally in the terrible, the pathetic, and the graceful; a recitative that is rapid, yet noble and expressive of the style; airs for dances of the greatest variety, in a new style and of the most agreeable freshness; choruses, duets, trios, quartets equally expressive, touching, and well-declaimed; the prosody of the language scrupulously observed—everything in this composition seemed to me to be in our style; nothing seemed foreign to my French ear; it is the work of a talent; everywhere M. Glouch is poet and musician; everywhere in it one recognizes the man of genius and at the same time the man of taste; nothing in it is weak or neglected.

You know, Sir, that I am not an enthusiast, and that in the quarrels which have arisen concerning the preference between the musical styles I have preserved an absolute neutrality. I consequently flatter myself that you will not be prejudiced against the eulogy which I am here bestowing on the music of the opera of *Iphigénie*. I am convinced that you will be eager to applaud. I know that no one desires more than you the progress of your art, to which you have already greatly contributed by your productions and by the applause which I have seen you give to those who distinguished themselves therein. You will therefore be pleased, both as a man of talent and as a good citizen, to see a foreigner as famous as M. Glouch employed in working in our language and in avenging it, in the eyes of all Europe, of the calumnious imputations of our own authors.

M. Glouch desires to know whether the management of the Académie de Musique would have enough confidence in his talents to decide to give his opera. He is ready to make the journey to France, but wishes to be assured in advance both that his opera will be represented and at what time, approximately, this can take place.

If you have nothing determined on for the winter, for Lent, or for the reopening after Easter, I believe that you could not do better than to assign him one of those periods. M. Glouch has been most pressingly invited to Naples for the month of May; he has been unwilling to make any engagement in that quarter, and is resolved to sacrifice the profits which are offered him if he can be assured that his opera will be accepted by your Academy, to which I beg you to transmit this letter, and to send me word of the decision which will fix that of M. Glouch. I should be greatly flattered to share with you, Sir, the distinction of making known to our nation all that it can promise itself to the advantage of its language embellished by the art which you profess. With these sentiments I am, Sir,

Your very humble and obedient servant.

P. S. If the management has not enough confidence in the opinion which I have formed of the words of the opera, I will send it to you on the first occasion.

I forgot to tell you, Sir, that M. Glouch, very disinterested by nature, does not ask for his work more than the sum fixed by the management for the authors of new operas.

73. C. W. von Gluck

Letter to the Editor of the "Mercure de France"[1]

[1773]

Sir:

I SHOULD be liable to just reproaches and I should bring very serious reproaches against myself if after reading the letter, written from here to one of the directors of the Académie Royale de Musique, which you published in the *Mercure* of last October and of which the opera *Iphigénie* is the subject; if, I say, after testifying to my gratitude to the author of that letter for the praises which he has been pleased to lavish upon me, I did not hasten to declare that his friendship and a prejudice too greatly in my favor have without doubt carried him away and that I am very far from flattering myself that I deserve the eulogies which he bestows on me. I should bring against myself a still graver reproach if I permitted the attribution to myself of the invention of a new style of Italian opera of which the success has justified the endeavor. It is to M. de Calzabigi that the principal merit belongs; and if my music has had a certain éclat, I believe that I must recognize that it is to him that I am indebted for it, since it is he who has made it possible for me to develop the resources of my art. This author, full of genius and talent, has in his poems of *Orfeo*, of *Alceste*, and of *Paride* followed a path little known to the Italians. These works are filled with those happy situations, those terrible and pathetic strokes, which furnish to the composer the means of expressing the great passions and of creating a music energetic and touching. Whatever the talent of the composer, he will never compose any but mediocre music if the poet does not arouse in him that enthusiasm without which the productions of all the arts are feeble and languid; the imitation of nature is by general agreement their common object. It is this which I

---

1 Text: *Mercure de France*, Février 1773, pp. 182–184.

seek to attain. Always simple and natural, so far as is within my power, my music is directed only to the greatest expression and to the reinforcement of the declamation of the poetry.

This is the reason why I never employ the trills, the passages, or the cadenzas of which the Italians are profuse. Their language, which easily lends itself to them, has therefore in this respect no advantage for me. It has without doubt many others; but, born in Germany, whatever study I have been able to make of the Italian language, as well as of the French, I do not believe that it is permitted to me to appreciate the delicate distinctions which can give the preference to one of the two, and I think that every foreigner should abstain from judging between them. But what I believe it is permitted me to say is that the one which will always suit me the best is the one in which the poet will furnish me the greatest number of different means of expressing the passions. This is the advantage which I believe I have found in the words of the opera *Iphigénie*, of which the poetry had seemed to me to have all the energy proper to inspire me to good music.

Although I have never had occasion to offer my works to any theater, I cannot bear ill will to the author of the letter to one of the Directors for having proposed my *Iphigénie* to your Académie de Musique. I admit that I should have produced it in Paris with pleasure, since by its effect and with the aid of the famous M. Rousseau of Geneva, whom I was planning to consult, we might perhaps together have been able, by searching for a melody noble, affecting, and natural, with an exact declamation according to the prosody of each language and the character of each people, to determine the means which I have in view of producing a music suitable for all the nations and of causing the ridiculous distinctions of national music to disappear.[2] The study which I have made of the works on music of that great man, among others the letter in which he analyzes the monologue in Lully's *Armide*,[3] proves the sublimity of his attainments and the sureness of his taste, and has filled me with admiration. From it I have retained the profound conviction that if he had chosen to apply himself to the practice of that art, he would have been able to accomplish in reality the marvelous effects which antiquity attributed to music. I am charmed to find here the opportunity of rendering to him publicly the tribute of praise which I believe him to merit.

---

2 This is in direct and deliberate contrast to the reference to Rousseau in Du Roullet's letter. Rousseau's opinion of Gluck's music is set forth at some length in his "Fragmens d'observations sur l'*Alceste* italien de M. le Chevalier Gluck," appended to a letter of his to Dr. Burney and included in most editions of his writings on music.
3 See above, pp. 638–654, where Rousseau's analysis is, however, omitted.

I pray, Sir, that you will consent to insert this letter in your next *Mercure*.

I have the honor to be, etc.

Chevalier Gluck

XVI

The European Scene

74. Charles Burney

Born in 1726, Burney was appointed organist at St. Dionis-Backchurch, London, in 1749 and in 1769 received the degrees of Mus.Bac. and Mus.Doc. from Oxford University. Following this, Burney made extensive studies and journeys to the Continent to assemble the materials for his general history of music. In 1770 he went for this purpose to France and Italy; a trip to the Low Countries, Germany, and Austria followed in 1772.

The impressions gathered in the course of these tours are set down in two valuable books: *The Present State of Music in France and Italy* (1771), and *The Present State of Music in Germany, the Netherlands and United Provinces* (1773). The first volume of Burney's *General History of Music* appeared in 1776, but it was not until 1789 that the fourth and final volume was published. Burney also wrote a number of books of lesser importance, among them a biography of Metastasio, the librettist, and an *Account of the Musical Performances in Westminster Abbey in Commemoration of Handel* (1785). He died in 1814.

From The Present State of Music in France and Italy [1]

[*1771*]

Naples

I ENTERED this city, impressed with the highest ideas of the perfect state in which I should find practical music. It was at Naples only that I expected to have my ears gratified with every musical luxury and refinement which Italy could afford. My visits to other places were in the way of *business*, for the performance of a *task* I had assigned myself; [2] but I

---

1 Text: The original edition (London, 1771), pp. 291–293, 298–304, 305–307, 316–319, 324–330, 335–340, 352–358.

2 The collection of materials for his *General History of Music.*

came hither animated by the hope of pleasure. And what lover of music could be in the place which had produced the two Scarlattis, Vinci, Leo, Pergolesi, Porpora, Farinelli, Jommelli, Piccinni, and innumerable others of the first eminence among composers and performers, both vocal and instrumental, without the most sanguine expectations. How far these expectations were gratified, the reader will find in the course of my narrative, which is constantly a faithful transcript of my feelings at the time I entered them in my journal, immediately after hearing and seeing, with a mind not conscious of any prejudice or partiality.

I arrived here about five o'clock in the evening, on Tuesday, October 16,[3] and at night went to the Teatro de'Fiorentini to hear the comic opera of *Gelosia per gelosia*, set to music by Signor Piccinni. This theatre is as small as Mr. Foote's in London,[4] but higher, as there are five rows of boxes in it. Notwithstanding the court was at Portici, and a great number of families at their *villeggiature*, or country houses, so great is the reputation of Signor Piccinni, that every part of the house was crowded. Indeed this opera had nothing else but the merit and reputation of the composer to support it, as both the drama and singing were bad. There was, however, a comic character performed by Signor Casaccia, a man of infinite humor; the whole house was in a roar the instant he appeared; and the pleasantry of this actor did not consist in buffoonery, nor was it local, which in Italy, and, indeed, elsewhere, is often the case; but was of that original and general sort as would excite laughter at all times and in all places.

The airs of this burletta are full of pretty passages, and, in general, most ingeniously accompanied: there was no dancing, so that the acts, of which there were three, seemed rather long.

．　·　．　．　．

Thursday 18. I was very happy to find, upon my arrival at Naples, that though many persons to whom I had letters were in the country, yet Signor Jommelli and Signor Piccinni were in town. Jommelli was preparing a serious opera for the great theatre of S. Carlo, and Piccinni had just brought the burletta on the stage which I have mentioned before.

This morning I visited Signor Piccinni, and had the pleasure of a long conversation with him. He seems to live in a reputable way, has a good house, and many servants and attendants about him. He is not more than four or five and forty; looks well, has a very animated countenance, and

---

3 Burney had left Rome for Naples on Sunday, October 14, 1770.

4 The "New" Theatre in the Haymarket, opened in 1767.

is a polite and agreeable little man, though rather grave in his manner for a Neapolitan possessed of so much fire and genius. His family is rather numerous; one of his sons is a student in the University of Padua. After reading a letter which Mr. Giardini [5] was so obliging as to give me to him, he told me he should be extremely glad if he could be of any use either to me or my work. My first enquiries were concerning the Neapolitan conservatorios; for he having been brought up in one of them himself, his information was likely to be authentic and satisfactory. In my first visit I confined my questions chiefly to the four following subjects:

1. The antiquity of these establishments.
2. Their names.
3. The number of masters and scholars.
4. The time for admission, and for quitting these schools.

To my first demand he answered that the conservatorios were of ancient standing, as might be seen by the ruinous condition of one of the buildings, which was ready to tumble down. [a]

To my second, that their names were S. Onofrio, La Pietà, and S. Maria di Loreto.

To my third question he answered that the number of scholars in the first conservatorio is about ninety, in the second a hundred and twenty, and in the other, two hundred.

That each of them has two principal *maestri di cappella,* the first of whom superintends and corrects the compositions of the students; the second the singing and gives lessons. That there are assistant masters, who are called *maestri secolari;* one for the violin, one for the violoncello, one for the harpsichord, one for the hautbois, one for the French horn, and so for other instruments.

To my fourth inquiry he answered that boys are admitted from eight or ten to twenty years of age; that when they are taken in young they are bound for eight years; but, when more advanced, their admission is difficult, except they have made a considerable progress in the study and practice of music. That after boys have been in a conservatorio for some years, if no genius is discovered, they are dismissed to make way for others. That some are taken in as pensioners, who pay for their teaching; and others, after having served their time out, are retained to teach the rest; but that in both these cases they are allowed to go out of the conservatorio at pleasure.

a I afterwards obtained, from good authority, the exact date of each of these foundations; their fixed and stated rules, amounting to thirty-one; and the orders given to the rectors for regulating the conduct and studies of the boys, every month in the year.

5 Felice de Giardini, an Italian composer and violinist resident in London.

I inquired throughout Italy at what place boys were chiefly qualified for singing by castration, but could get no certain intelligence. I was told at Milan that it was at Venice; at Venice that it was at Bologna; but at Bologna the fact was denied, and I was referred to Florence; from Florence to Rome, and from Rome I was sent to Naples. The operation most certainly is against law in all these places, as well as against nature; and all the Italians are so much ashamed of it that in every province they transfer it to some other.

> Ask where's the North? at York, 'tis on the Tweed;
> In Scotland, at the Orcades; and there,
> At Greenland, Zembla, or the Lord knows where.
> —Pope, *Essay on Man.*

However, with respect to the conservatorios at Naples, Mr. Gemineau, the British consul, who has so long resided there and who has made very particular inquiries, assured me, and his account was confirmed by Dr. Cirillo, an eminent and learned Neapolitan physician, that this practice is absolutely forbidden in the conservatorios, and that the young *castrati* come from Leccia in Apuglia; but, before the operation is performed, they are brought to a conservatorio to be tried as to the probability of voice, and then are taken home by their parents for this barbarous purpose. It is, however, death by the laws to all those who perform the operation, and excommunication to everyone concerned in it, unless it be done, as is often pretended, upon account of some disorders which may be supposed to require it, and with the consent of the boy. And there are instances of its being done even at the request of the boy himself, as was the case of the Grassetto at Rome.[6] But as to these previous trials of the voice, it is my opinion that the cruel operation is but too frequently performed without trial, or at least without sufficient proofs of an improvable voice; otherwise such numbers could never be found in every great town throughout Italy, without any voice at all, or at least without one sufficient to compensate such a loss. Indeed all the *musici* [b] in the churches at present are made up of the refuse of the opera houses, and it is very rare to meet with a tolerable voice upon the establishment in any church throughout Italy. The virtuosi who sing there occasionally, upon great festivals only, are usually strangers, and paid by the time.

· · · · ·

[b] The word *musico*, in Italy, seems now wholly appropriated to a singer with a soprano or contralto voice, which has been preserved by art.

[6] "*Il Grassetto*, a boy who submitted to mutilation by his own choice and against the advice of his friends for the preservation of his voice, which is indeed a very good one." (Burney)

From hence I went directly to the comic opera, which, tonight,[7] was at the Teatro Nuovo. This house is not only less than the Fiorentini, but is older and more dirty. The way to it, for carriages, is through streets very narrow, and extremely inconvenient. This burletta was called the *Trame per Amore*, and set by Signor Giovanni Paesiello, *Maestro di Cappella Napolitano*. The singing was but indifferent; there were nine characters in the piece, and yet not one good voice among them; however, the music pleased me very much; it was full of fire and fancy, the ritornelles abounding in new passages, and the vocal parts in elegant and simple melodies, such as might be remembered and carried away after the first hearing, or be performed in private by a small band, or even without any other instrument than a harpsichord.[c] The overture, of one movement only, was quite comic, and contained a perpetual succession of pleasant passages. There was no dancing, which made it necessary to spin the acts out to rather a tiresome length. The airs were much applauded, though it was the fourteenth representation of the opera. The author was engaged to compose for Turin, at the next carnival, for which place he set out while I was at Naples. The performance began about a quarter before eight, and continued till past eleven o'clock.

．　．　．　．　．

Friday 26. This morning I first had the pleasure of seeing and conversing with Signor Jommelli, who arrived at Naples from the country but the night before. He is extremely corpulent, and, in the face, not unlike what I remember Handel to have been, yet far more polite and soft in his manner. I found him in his night-gown, at an instrument, writing. He received me very politely, and made many apologies for not having called on me, in consequence of a card I had left at his house; but apologies were indeed unnecessary, as he was but just come to town, and at the point of bringing out a new opera that must have occupied both his time and thoughts sufficiently. He had heard of me from Mr. Hamilton.[8] I gave him Padre Martini's letter, and after he had read it we went to business directly. I told him my errand to Italy, and showed him my plan, for I knew his time was precious. He read it with great attention, and conversed very openly and rationally; said the part I had undertaken was much

---

c This is seldom the case in modern opera songs, so crowded is the score and the orchestra. Indeed Piccinni is accused of employing instruments to such excess, that in Italy no copyist will transcribe one of his operas without being paid a zechin more than for one by any other composer. But in burlettas he has generally bad voices to write for, and is obliged to produce all his effects with instruments; and, indeed, this kind of drama usually abounds with brawls and *squabbles*, which it is necessary to enforce with the orchestra.

7 The date is still October 18.
8 The British Minister to the Court of Naples.

neglected at present in Italy; that the conservatorios, of which, I told him, I wished for information, were now at a low ebb, though formerly so fruitful in great men. He mentioned to me a person of great learning who had been translating David's Psalms into excellent Italian verse; in the course of which work he had found it necessary to write a dissertation on the music of the ancients, which he had communicated to him. He said this writer was a fine and subtle critic; had differed in several points from Padre Martini; had been in correspondence with Metastasio, and had received a long letter from him on the subject of lyric poetry and music; all of which he thought necessary for me to see. He promised to procure me the book, and to make me acquainted with the author.[9] He spoke very much in praise of Alessandro Scarlatti, as to his church music, such as motets, masses, and oratorios; promised to procure me information concerning the conservatorios, and whatever else was to my purpose, and in his power. He took down my direction, and assured me that the instant he had got his opera [10] on the stage he should be entirely at my service. Upon my telling him that my time for remaining at Naples was very short, that I should even then have been on the road on my way home but for his opera, which I so much wished to hear; that besides urgent business in England, there was great probability of a war, which would keep me a prisoner on the continent: he, in answer to that, and with great appearance of sincerity, said, if after I returned to England anything of importance to my plan occurred, he would not fail of sending it to me. In short, I went away in high good humor with this truly great composer, who is indisputably one of the first of his profession now alive in the universe; for were I to name the living composers of Italy for the stage, according to my idea of their merit, it would be in the following order: Jommelli, Galuppi, Piccinni, and Sacchini. It is, however, difficult to decide which of the two composers first mentioned has merited most from the public; Jommelli's works are full of great and noble ideas, treated with taste and learning; Galuppi's abound in fancy, fire, and feeling; Piccinni has far surpassed all his contemporaries in the comic style; and Sacchini seems the most promising composer in the serious.

. . . . .

9 Saverio Mattei, whose biography of Metastasio was published in 1785. For Metastasio's letters to him see Burney's *Memoirs of the Life and Writings of the Abate Metastasio* (London, 1796), II, 378–420; III, 115–153.

10 His *Demofoonte;* see above, p. 688, and below, pp. 694–696. Actually, this was an old work; first performed in Padua on June 16, 1743, it had already been heard in London, Milan, and Stuttgart.

Wednesday, October 31. This morning I went with young Oliver [11] to his conservatorio of S. Onofrio, and visited all the rooms where the boys practise, sleep, and eat. On the first flight of stairs was a trumpeter, screaming upon his instrument till he was ready to burst; on the second was a French horn, bellowing in the same manner. In the common practising room there was a "Dutch concert," consisting of seven or eight harpsichords, more than as many violins, and several voices, all performing different things, and in different keys: other boys were writing in the same room; but it being holiday time, many were absent who usually study and practise in this room. The jumbling them all together in this manner may be convenient for the house, and may teach the boys to attend to their own parts with firmness, whatever else may be going forward at the same time; it may likewise give them force, by obliging them to play loud in order to hear themselves; but in the midst of such jargon, and continued dissonance, it is wholly impossible to give any kind of polish or finishing to their performance; hence the slovenly coarseness so remarkable in their public exhibitions; and the total want of taste, neatness, and expression in all these young musicians, till they have acquired them elsewhere.

The beds, which are in the same room, serve for seats to the harpsichords and other instruments. Out of thirty or forty boys who were practising, I could discover but two that were playing the same piece; some of those who were practising on the violin seemed to have a great deal of hand. The violoncellos practise in another room; and the flutes, oboes, and other wind instruments in a third, except the trumpets and horns, which are obliged to fag, either on the stairs, or on the top of the house.

There are in this college sixteen young *castrati*, and these lie upstairs, by themselves, in warmer apartments than the other boys, for fear of colds, which might not only render their delicate voices unfit for exercise at present, but hazard the entire loss of them forever.

The only vacation in these schools in the whole year is in autumn, and that for a few days only: during the winter, the boys rise two hours before it is light, from which time they continue their exercise, an hour and a half at dinner excepted, till eight o'clock at night; and this constant perseverance, for a number of years, with genius and good teaching, must produce great musicians.

After dinner I went to the theatre of S. Carlo, to hear Jommelli's new

---

11 "A young Englishman who has been four years in the Conservatorio of S. Onofrio." [Burney]

opera rehearsed. There were only two acts finished, but these pleased me much, except the overture, which was short, and rather disappointed me, as I expected more would have been made of the first movement; but as to the songs and accompanied recitatives, there was merit of some kind or other in them all, as I hardly remember one that was so indifferent as not to seize the attention. The subject of the opera was Demophontes; the names of the singers I knew not then, except Aprile, the first man, and Bianchi, the first woman. Aprile has rather a weak and uneven voice, but is constantly steady as to intonation. He has a good person, a good shake, and much taste and expression. La Bianchi has a sweet and elegant toned voice, always perfectly in tune, with an admirable portamento; I never heard anyone sing with more ease; or in a manner so totally free from affectation. The rest of the vocal performers were all above mediocrity: a tenor with both voice and judgment sufficient to engage attention; a very fine contralto; a young man with a soprano voice, whose singing was full of feeling and expression; and a second woman, whose performance was far from despicable. Such performers as these were necessary for the music, which is in a difficult style, more full of instrumental effects than vocal. Sometimes it may be thought rather labored, but it is admirable in the *tout ensemble*, masterly in modulation, and in melody full of new passages.[d] This was the first rehearsal, and the instruments were rough and unsteady, not being as yet certain of the exact time or expression of the movements; but, as far as I was then able to judge, the composition was perfectly suited to the talents of the performers, who, though all good, yet not being of the very first and most exquisite class, were more in want of the assistance of instruments to mark the images, and enforce the passion, which the poetry points out.

The public expectation from this production of Jommelli, if a judgement may be formed from the number of persons who attended this first rehearsal, was very great; for the pit was crowded, and many of the boxes were filled with the families of persons of condition.

The theatre of S. Carlo is a noble and elegant structure: the form is oval, or rather the section of an egg, the end next the stage being cut. There are seven ranges of boxes, sufficient in size to contain ten or twelve persons in each, who sit in chairs, in the same manner as in a private house. In every range there are thirty boxes, except the three lowest ranges, which, by the King's box being taken out of them, are reduced to twenty-nine. In the pit there are fourteen or fifteen rows of seats, which are very roomy and commodious, with leather cushions and stuffed backs, each

d Jommelli is now said to write more for the *learned few* than for the *feeling many*.

separated from the other by a broad rest for the elbow: in the middle of the pit there are thirty of these seats in a row.

. . . . . .

Sunday 4. At night I went to the first public representation of Signor Jommelli's opera of *Demofoonte,* in the grand theatre of S. Carlo, where I was honored with a place in Mr. Hamilton's box. It is not easy to imagine or describe the grandeur and magnificence of this spectacle. It being the great festival of St. Charles and the King of Spain's name-day, the court was in grand gala, and the house was not only doubly illuminated, but amazingly crowded with well-dressed company.[e] In the front of each box there is a mirror, three or four feet long by two or three wide, before which are two large wax tapers; these, by reflection, being multiplied, and added to the lights of the stage and to those within the boxes, make the splendor too much for the aching sight. The King and Queen were present. Their majesties have a large box in the front of the house, which contains in height and breadth the space of four other boxes. The stage is of an immense size, and the scenes, dresses, and decorations were extremely magnificent; and I think this theatre superior, in these particulars, as well as in the music, to that of the great French opera at Paris.

But M. de la Lande, after allowing that "the opera in Italy is very well as to music and words," concludes with saying "that it is not, in his opinion, quite so in other respects, and for the following reasons:

"1. There is scarce any machinery in the operas of Italy.[f]

"2. There is not such a multitude of rich and superb dresses as at Paris.

"3. The number and variety of the actors are less.[g]

"4. The choruses are fewer and less labored. And

"5. The union of song and dance is neglected." [h]

To all which objections, a real lover of music would perhaps say, So much the better.

M. de la Lande, however, allows that the hands employed in the orchestra are more numerous and various, but complains that the fine voices in an Italian opera are not only too few, but are too much occupied by the music and its embellishments to attend to declamation and gesture.

With regard to this last charge, it is by no means a just one; for whoever remembers Pertici and Laschi, in the burlettas of London, about twenty

---

e The fourth of November is likewise celebrated as the name-day of the Queen of Naples and the Prince of Asturias.

f The Italians have long given up those puerile representations of flying gods and goddesses, of which the French are still so fond and so vain.

g If the characters are fewer, the dresses must be so, of course.

h *Voyage d'un François.*

years ago, or has seen the *Buona figliuola* [12] there lately, when Signora Guadagni, Signor Lovatini, and Signor Morigi were in it; or in the serious operas of past times remembers Monticelli, Elisi, Mingotti, Colomba Mattei, Mansoli, or, above all, in the present operas has seen Signor Guadagni, must allow that many of the Italians not only recite well, but are *excellent actors*.

Give to a lover of music an opera in a noble theatre, at least twice as large as that of the French capital, in which the poetry and music are good and the vocal and instrumental parts well performed, and he will deny himself the rest without murmuring; though his ear should be less stunned with choruses, and his eye less dazzled with machinery, dresses, and dances than at Paris.

But to return to the theatre of S. Carlo, which, as a spectacle, surpasses all that poetry or romance have painted: yet with all this, it must be owned that the magnitude of the building and noise of the audience are such, that neither the voices or instruments can be heard distinctly. I was told, however, that on account of the King and Queen being present, the people were much less noisy than on common nights. There was not a hand moved by way of applause during the whole representation, though the audience in general seemed pleased with the music: but, to say the truth, it did not afford me the same delight as at the rehearsal; nor did the singers, though they exerted themselves more, appear to equal advantage: not one of the present voices is sufficiently powerful for such a theatre, when so crowded and so noisy. Signora Bianchi, the first woman, whose sweet voice and simple manner of singing gave me and others so much pleasure at the rehearsal, did not satisfy the Neapolitans, who have been accustomed to the force and brilliancy of a Gabrieli, a Taiber, and a De Amici. There is too much simplicity in her manner for the depraved appetites of these *enfants gâtés*, who are never pleased but when astonished. As to the music, much of the *claire obscure* was lost, and nothing could be heard distinctly but those noisy and furious parts which were meant merely to give *relief* to the rest; the mezzotints and background were generally lost, and indeed little was left but the bold and coarse strokes of the composer's pencil.[13]

· · · · ·

Wednesday 7. Today I was favored at dinner with the company of Signor Fabio, the first violin of the opera of S. Carlo; he was so obliging and so humble as to bring with him his violin. It is very common in the

---

12 By Piccinni.

13 Leopold Mozart, in a letter written in Milan on December 22, 1770, says that the opera "failed so miserably that people are even wanting to sub-

stitute another" (*The Letters of Mozart & His Family,* tr. by Emily Anderson [London, 1938], I, 258).

great cities of Italy to see performers of the first eminence carry their own instruments through the streets. This seems a trivial circumstance to mention, yet it strongly marks the difference of manners and characters in two countries not very remote from each other. In Italy, the leader of the first opera in the world carries the instrument of his fame and fortune about him, with as much pride as a soldier does his sword or musket; while, in England, the indignities he would receive from the populace would soon impress his mind with shame for himself and fear for his instrument.

I obtained from Signor Fabio an exact account of the number of hands employed in the great opera orchestra: there are 18 first and 18 second violins, 5 double basses, and but 2 violoncellos; which I think has a bad effect, the double bass being played so coarsely throughout Italy that it produces a sound no more musical than the stroke of a hammer. This performer, who is a fat, good-natured man, by being long accustomed to lead so great a number of hands, has acquired a style of playing which is somewhat rough and inelegant, and consequently more fit for an orchestra than a chamber. He sang, however, several buffo songs very well and accompanied himself on the violin in so masterly a manner as to produce most of the effects of a numerous band. After dinner, he had a second to accompany him in one of Giardini's solos, and in several other things.

I spent this whole evening with Barbella,[14] who now delivered to me all the materials which he had been able to recollect, relative to a history of the Neapolitan conservatorios, as well as anecdotes of the old composers and performers of that school: besides these, I wrote down all the verbal information I could extract from his memory, concerning musical persons and things. During my visit, I heard one of his best scholars play a solo of Giardini's composition very well; he was the most brilliant performer on the violin that I met with at Naples.

And now, having given the reader an account of the musical entertainment I received at Naples, I hope I shall be indulged with the liberty of making a few reflections before I quit this city; which has so long been regarded as the center of harmony, and the fountain from which genius, taste, and learning have flowed to every other part of Europe that even those who have an opportunity of judging for themselves take upon trust the truth of the fact, and give the Neapolitans credit for more than they deserve at present, however they may have been entitled to this celebrity in times past.

M. de la Lande's account of music at Naples is so far from exact, that

---

14 Emanuele Barbella, an Italian composer and violinist, at one time resident in London.

it would incline his reader to suppose one of two things, either that he did not attend to it, or that he had not a very distinguishing ear.

Music [says this author] is in a particular manner the triumph of the Neapolitans; it seems as if the tympanum in this country was more braced, more harmonical, and more sonorous, than in the rest of Europe; the whole nation is vocal, every gesture and inflection of voice of the inhabitants, and even their prosody of syllables in conversation, breathe harmony and music. Hence Naples is the principal source of Italian music, of great composers, and of excellent operas.[1]

I am ready to grant that the Neapolitans have a natural disposition to music; but can by no means allow that they have voices more flexible and a language more harmonious than the inhabitants of the other parts of Italy, as the direct contrary seems true. The singing in the streets is far less pleasing, though more original than elsewhere; and the Neapolitan language is generally said to be the most barbarous jargon among all the different dialects of Italy.[J]

But though the rising generation of Neapolitan musicians cannot be said to possess either taste, delicacy, or expression, yet their compositions, it must be allowed, are excellent with respect to counterpoint and invention, and in their manner of executing them, there is an energy and fire not to be met with perhaps in the whole universe: it is so ardent as to border upon fury; and from this impetuosity of genius, it is common for a Neapolitan composer, in a movement which begins in a mild and sober manner, to set the orchestra in flames before it is finished. Dr. Johnson says that Shakespeare, in tragedy, is always struggling after some occasion to be comic; and the Neapolitans, like high bred horses, are impatient of the rein, and eagerly accelerate their motion to the utmost of their speed. The pathetic and the graceful are seldom attempted in the conservatorios; and those refined and studied graces which not only change but improve passages, and which so few are able to find, are less sought after by the generality of performers at Naples than in any other part of Italy.

---

[1] *Voyage d'un François.* The inaccuracy with which M. de la L. speaks about music and musicians runs through his work. He places Corelli and Galuppi among the Neapolitan composers; whereas it is well known that Corelli was of the Roman school, and he himself says in another place that Galuppi was of the Venetian.

[J] A sufficient proof of the Neapolitan language being only a *patois* or provincial dialect is that it remains merely oral, the natives themselves, who are well educated, never daring to write in it.

75. J. F. Reichardt

Born at Königsberg in 1752, Reichardt began as a student of philosophy and music. He spent the years 1771–1774 traveling in Germany and set down his impressions in his *Reisebriefe* of 1774–1776. In 1775 he became Capell-meister at the court of Frederick the Great, but left this position in 1785 to go to London and Paris; his sympathetic view of the French Revolution un-doubtedly had something to do with this. After Frederick's death he returned to Berlin, but was forced to leave again. He died at Halle in 1814.

Reichardt's literary production is a considerable one. He was a man of broad culture who handled his pen with great skill. The books in which he collected his impressions of Germany (1774–1776), Paris (1804–1805), and Vienna (1810) are valued, not only because of the information they con-tain but also because of their pleasant style.

From the Briefe eines aufmerksamen Reisenden [1]

[*1774*]

FIRST LETTER

TO HERR SCH[RIFTSTELLER] KR[EUZFELD] [2]

BERLIN

SAD AND lonely as is the way to Elysium, the more splendid, the more charming is its aspect. And yet, my friend, were the shade of Homer or Virgil to appear to you in the moment of your first rapture, would you

---

1 Text: The original edition (Frankfort & Leip-zig, 1774), 1–31. Reichardt's title ("Letters of an *Attentive* Traveller") is aimed, of course, at Dr. Burney. In his autobiography (H. M. Schletterer, *Johann Friedrich Reichardt* [Augsburg, 1865], I, 140), Reichardt says: "About this time [1772–1773], Bode's translation of Burney's journal of his musical tour made its appearance, and the intensely patriotic citizens of Berlin were offended by the offhand and (as they thought) one-sided way in which Burney had treated their music.

When Nicolai saw that I had this matter very much at heart, he proposed that I should write something against this journal, and not even the compliments on my violin-playing and on my be-ginnings as a composer which Burney had paid me in his book could make me hesitate to take up the work at once."

2 J. G. Kreuzfeld (1745–1784), Professor of Poetry and Librarian in Königsberg, Reichardt's birthplace.

then continue your stroll through the attractive fields and valleys or would you not rather hasten to the embrace of the blessed spirits? This was my experience too. Scarcely had I arrived in this beautiful royal city,[a] my greedy gaze—which flits from one object to another and wishes to consume everything that meets it—directed toward its many beauties, not yet had I quite thought out one thought, when I learned that the opera was to begin in two hours and that it would be an opera by Hasse. Need I tell you that I thought no longer of beautiful buildings,[b] nor yet of anything else,[c] but, once I had embraced our mutual friend S., I hastened immediately to the opera house? It was almost two hours before the opera was to begin, but these I by no means lost, devoting them to an inspection of the inner arrangements of the beautiful and lofty building. Solemn majesty is the character of this model of the noblest taste in architecture.

All at once I was startled by a warlike sort of music coming down from above; I looked for the musicians at first in the niches built into the sides of the proscenium; they were, however, less poetically situated, standing in the box nearest the stage in the highest gallery. I have always heard it said that music sounds very confused and unharmonious just before a battle—for then fear causes hands and lips to tremble—and such music seemed here to be imitated.[3] It did not last long, however, and there followed a beautiful and fiery symphony by the late Concertmeister Graun,[4] [d]

---

a The author has here the honor to assure his readers that henceforth he will never again be charmed by any great city, no matter how beautiful it may be. Having seen many great cities and finding in all of them much unhappiness and incurable disorder, he has come to agree with his friend Rousseau that all the splendor and all the amusements of the great cities are as nothing in comparison with a green meadow and a merry harvest dance and that all the art of a thousand artists is as nothing in comparison with the charm of laughing nature. And he who is insensible to this when it is sung by Weisse and Hiller is, in the author's opinion, heartily to be pitied.

b It is true; Berlin has buildings which few of those in other great cities can rival in beauty and taste. The great Schloss, the Opera House, the Catholic Church, St. Peter's, the Zeughaus, and many palaces are models of the noblest, most luxurious, and highest taste.

c The Tiergarten, made up of various sorts of trees and containing within itself little forests of fir, spruce, and oak, groves of beeches, etc., is a special ornament of the city. The Spree, inhabited by swans, flows beside it, reflecting the firs and spruces in its clear waters. Countless hewnout paths and several reservoirs intensify its beauty and bear witness that art has here proffered a cordial hand to nature. Unfortunately, however, there are also many beauties as yet unexploited which reveal that art, ordinarily so helpful, has had her hands tied. To sum up the great beauties of the Tiergarten in one word, I shall say that it deserves to be celebrated by Ramler. With its cool shadows it would be more grateful to him

for this than is the hero of many of his admirable odes, who would not envy a certain Roman his singer if he but really knew the immortalizer of his own deeds.

d Mr. Burney, in his musical journal, has sinned grievously against this admirable man. He does not find in his symphonies that fire which I, a more careful observer, have found in very few other symphonies; they need, however, to be performed as I have heard them performed by the composer himself. Mr. B. also refuses to allow his violin concertos to be accounted the masterpieces of their kind which they really are. In invention—in the precise point wherein those who know him best admire him most—in invention, he says, he is wholly wanting. Has Mr. B. then heard anything of his works? Actually not. Just as he noted down all his opinions from the words of the first person he met, so presumably this is also something said to him, and said to him by someone envious of this great man. [For Burney's estimate of the brothers Carl Heinrich and Johann Gottlieb Graun, see his *Present State of Music in Germany*, II, 224-229.—Ed.]

3 Dr. Burney, who was in Berlin from September 28 to October 5, 1772, also speaks of this "warlike sort of music" (*The Present State of Music in Germany* [London, 1773], II, 99): "Her Majesty is saluted at her entrance into the theatre, and at her departure thence, by two bands of trumpets and kettledrums, placed one on each side of the house, in the upper row of boxes."

4 Carl Heinrich Graun (1701-1759).

of which only the first movement was played. The curtain went up and one saw a most artistic and splendid scene by the master hand of the Turinese artist Signor Gagliari. I did not look at it long, however, for my attention was now claimed by music which wholly distracted me and made me all ears. It was the first opera of Hasse's [5] that I had seen performed, although I was thoroughly familiar with them all through reading the scores and comparing them with those of Graun. To avoid becoming altogether too prolix, I shall not analyze the beauties of the opera here, but shall merely say that it made the most lively impression on me and that I noted, as an indisputable proof of its general effect, that almost every listener had made mental notes of some of the ideas and that on leaving the theater these were being sung by nearly everyone. If a *melody* leaves an impression on one who is not a connoisseur and remains in his memory, this is an unfailing proof that it is *natural* and *unforced*. Such melody is not peculiar to Hasse; Graun and many others have it also. But something I find only in Hasse is this: once an idea has made an impression, one can never forget it. Wherein lies the cause of this? In this, it seems to me: that the idea is so perfectly suited to the point in the action at which it stands and to the person by whom it is sung that, each time we recall it or sing it, it represents to us at the same time the action and the person. By this means, then, the idea is graven deeper and deeper in our hearts with each repetition; after this, who can forget it? I shall now tell you no more about the composition of this great master, for I shall later on attempt to make a *comparison* between him and the immortal Graun.

But how shall I describe to you the charming singing of a Schmeling [e] and a Concialini? [6] Whatever I could tell you would always express most imperfectly the feeling that she inspired in me the first time I heard her. In view of the great compass of her voice, her delicacy, and her dexterity, one can say of her what the author of a beautiful work says of Voltaire: "He is a migrating swallow who neatly and delicately brushes the surface of a broad river, drinking and bathing himself in flight." Her singing,

---

e Mlle. Schmeling, now more correctly Mme. Mara, has improved uncommonly during the five years she has been in Berlin. Her voice, her execution, her acting—all has changed to her great advantage. Her voice, which formerly had a certain clarity bordering almost on the sharp, on the pointed, has now become more mellow and agreeable. To the connoisseurs of instruments I cannot express this better than by saying that, while she had at first the tone of a Stainer violin, she now has more that of a Cremona, although it is not quite this, but rather a beautiful blend of the two which I have for a long time been trying to transmit to my violin and have finally succeeded. In her execution she has formed herself on Concialini and on her husband, both of them perfect Adagio singers, the latter quite as much so on his violon-

cello as the former with his mellow throat. In acting, Porporino and even her husband (who is certainly one of the greatest geniuses) have been the best models for her that she could have; everyone knows this singer's art, while those who have seen Herr Mara function at Prince Heinrich's private performances grant him the title of a perfect actor.

5 His *Arminio*, libretto by G. B. Pasquini, first performed in Dresden, December 7, 1745. The first performance of the revival to which Reichardt refers took place on December 24, 1773.

6 Cf. Burney, *op. cit.*, II, 107–112, 206–208, and 98, for his impressions of Mlle. Schmeling and Concialini.

however, is often expressive and affecting, although she is surpassed in this by Concialini, whose singing is pure melting delicacy. Porporino, who sings a beautiful and unusual contralto, distinguished himself by admirable execution in singing and likewise as a perfect actor, a virtue one seldom meets with among singers, men or women.

The orchestra played very evenly and often with considerable emphasis; one recognizes by the unusual co-ordination of their performance that they are nearly all of them from the school of our great Benda and Graun. But if I am to speak wholly in accordance with my feelings, I found an insufficient precision with respect to forte and piano.

On this point I must explain myself more clearly.

For perfect precision with respect to forte and piano it is not enough to make the ritornellos loud and to play softly from the point where the voice begins. This much was done perfectly here, but one missed the finer shadings of the loud and soft. Both forte and piano are in Adagio very different from what they are in Allegro; the painter, similarly, uses very different degress of light and shade in depicting a sad or gentle situation and in a merry banquet scene or furious battle piece. Each of these shadings has again a special shading as the voice rises and falls. The significance of each movement, the situation of the character, even the natural voice of each singer and the very key of the aria—all these considerations must be most precisely weighed. For this, however, is required the correct and superlatively fine feeling and the untiring industry of a Pisendel,[f] who, to Hasse's great astonishment, never mistook the tempo of an aria and gave himself almost incredible pains to write into all the parts, of every opera and every piece of church music performed under his direction, the forte and piano, their various shadings, and even the single strokes of the bow, so that in the extremely well-chosen orchestra which the court at Dresden had in his time the most perfect order and precision necessarily prevailed.

Of the increasing and diminishing [g] of a long note or of many notes following one on another, which, if I may so express myself, passes through the whole shading of a light or dark color and which in Mannheim is executed in so masterly a fashion—of this I shall not speak here at all, for neither Hasse nor Graun ever employed it. Why not? This I have never been able to account for. But why they never employed the

---

f Pisendel was Concertmeister in Dresden during the time when Hasse was still there.

g It is said that when Jommelli caused this to be heard in Rome for the first time, the audience gradually rose from their seats with the crescendo and did not breathe again until the diminuendo, when they first noticed that they were out of breath. This last effect I have in Mannheim observed myself.

now so fashionable rapid alternations of forte and piano, in which every other note is either strong or weak—this I can readily explain as due to their proper feelings or fine taste. Only he whose taste is wholly dulled and spoiled asks for strong spices in the food he wishes to enjoy. What sort of taste can that be which takes pleasure in the lifelike portrait of a sick man who, in a burning fever, makes violent contortions? Yet what is this musical effect but violent contortions? Would the painter, who knows that the beauties of nature are the only subject he ought to represent to us on his canvases and that good taste has banished everything loathsome from the arts—would he treat such a subject? Ought not the musician, quite as much as the poet and painter, to study nature and his Ramler and Watteau? In nature he can study man, its noblest creature, but in our art we have unfortunately no Ramler or Watteau as yet. Everyone calculates, everyone broods over harmony— well and good! I readily admit that we can never sufficiently thank a Bach, a Marpurg, a Kirnberger for their supremely instructive writings. But one ought also to attend to the chief and final aim of music; one ought also to investigate its melody, its expression, and above all its effect. We have, to be sure, excellent practical works of every description, and from these a Bach, a Schwanenberger, an Agricola, a Homilius, and many others might derive and, insofar as the diversity of man permits, establish the most admirable and unfailing rules. How easy this would be for Capellmeister Schwanenberger, whose eight-year stay in Italy provided him with a store of knowledge and experience without making of him—what a blessing—a partisan. For thus far neglecting this he deserves to be and has been punished. For behold, an English gossip comes flying along and tells us things, most of which do not even deserve to stand in the footnotes of a good book of this kind; alas for him who, not knowing with whom he has to deal, may read his forthcoming little history,[h] which threatens us poor Germans with double punishment! The punishment, I should think, was already severe enough for the good man. Should it, however, still be insufficient to set him to writing, we shall have to conceal from him for the moment that he is one of the best and most agreeable composers of our day and at the same time a complete virtuoso of the clavier. Perhaps this will stir him to prove to us, from resentment at least, that he has still other means of eliciting our applause which only his gracious modesty has prevented him from showing us before. As to you, gentlemen —you will forgive me if I take you all together—you who seek to win

---

h Mr. Burney has promised a history of music, which will no doubt consist, as does his journal, of little anecdotes; unfortunately, two translating factories in Germany are already waiting for it.

general acclaim and the applause of the whole nation with a beautiful opera or piece of church music, which, thanks to your prodigal genius, costs you less pains—at first, to be sure, only a small number would thank and honor you in due measure for such a laborious book. But—without too much offense to your excellent works—it would give you far greater assurance of immortality than they do, for these, as has ever been the way with beautiful works, will have to submit to the melancholy fate of fashion, at least for a time. But the passions and feelings of mankind have always been and will always remain the same. And was it not after all from these, gentlemen, that you wished to derive your rules?

Forgive me this digression. I now return again to my letter.

The following week an opera by Graun was given; [7] it had much that was agreeable and attractive, but did not have the same effect as Hasse's, although it was more carefully worked out and still better performed. Herr Agricola, who now supplies the place of the late Capellmeister Graun, had contrived a masterly aria expressly for the voice of Mlle. Schmeling, and for Signor Concialini a superlatively affecting aria had been borrowed from Hasse's setting of the same libretto.[1] [8] In these, both singers revealed their full stature. Several arias composed by the *great and inspired author of the history of Brandenburg* [9] were likewise incorporated in the opera, and among these one gave evidence of great talent.

Why was it, however, that despite all this, the opera had less *effect* than Hasse's?

With Hasse, it seems to me, there was *more boldness and strength in the expression, more variety in the melody, and more sagacity, if less science, in the accompaniment.* Inasmuch as these, in my opinion, are in all of Hasse's dramatic works the characteristics distinguishing him from Graun, they deserve, it would seem, to be investigated more particularly.

If one takes the trouble to place side by side the settings by Hasse and Graun of one and the same libretto, one will find that in the expression of the violent passions, such as pride, hate, anger, fury, despair, and so on, Hasse invariably surpasses Graun, while on the other hand Graun

1 It is said, however, that this was done because the King was overly affected by Graun's setting.

7 His *Demofoonte*, first performed in Berlin on January 17, 1746. The first performances of the revival to which Reichardt refers took place during the carnival of 1774.

8 Hasse's *Demofoonte* was first performed in Dresden on February 9, 1748; a single aria, "Padre, perdona," is published in F. A. Gevaert's *Les gloires d'Italie*, I, 94–97.

9 Frederick the Great.

invariably surpasses Hasse in the gentle and affecting. Hasse retains, even in complaint and affliction, a certain lofty energy peculiar to him, and he can never descend to perfectly plain and unaffected lamentation or tenderness. Graun, on the contrary, is in such melodies so simple and so affecting that each affected listener—and who, listening to him, is not affected to the point of tears?—believes that he sings himself and that the personal interest he takes in the affliction of the character is dictating the melody to him. In this appears to be reflected the whole character of these two great men, for all those who have known them long and intimately are agreed that Hasse, in his youth a passionate lover, is at all times vehement and that Graun, on the contrary, was humane and a most loving friend. Hasse has a livelier and more fiery gift for invention; one recognizes in most of his works that, in composing, he is more the actor than Graun and that he enters more actively into the situation of the hero whose pain, whose anger, whose despair he is to translate into sounds. Who does not recognize in the admirable and altogether masterly monologue of Artemisia,[j] at the end of the piece, that the composer himself is tortured here by the extremity of pain, and that he is himself frantic, then complaining, then again frantic, until in the end, already almost out of breath, he invokes the gods in the aria "Rendetemi il mio ben, numi tiranni, etc."? A composer who was not himself an actor, that is, who had not, while writing, experienced the whole action, perhaps even singing and acting it out, would have made of this aria an *aria di bravura*. But in the foregoing recitative it has wholly worn itself out—has exhausted its whole suffering in hurling at the gods every reproach that its utterly unhappy situation could suggest. Hasse, too, works for the theater with a greater zest, while Graun invariably neglected his operas until the last moment, composing them then with the utmost rapidity. Graun, we know, first finished the individual arias, either in his head or at the clavier, and afterwards wrote them out in clear copies without changing a single note; his first score was also the one used at the performances. Having harmony at his command, he could do this the more easily. Hasse, in his scores, often strikes things out. But with what intention? Although it is not at all my purpose to suggest that Hasse is the equal of Graun in theoretical knowledge,[k]

---

j "Sarete paghi alfin, implacabili dei?" In Leipzig, I have often heard Mme. Schröter sing this recitative with such consummate expression that, sensitive singer, she drew from me each time cold shivers and warm tears!

k By how much Graun excels Hasse in harmonic science is evident even from the duets, trios, etc., in his operas. These are the best models we have, and the public cannot sufficiently thank

Herr Hartung in Königsberg and Herr Decker in Berlin for having made them more closely acquainted with these masterpieces, an honor to the German nation. It is now up to the public to show that they know how to repay a favor and how to appreciate the excellence of this music. How anxious I am—how anxious every friend and admirer of music must be—that such men should be encouraged to continue with the publication of

he has in any case knowledge enough to work as Graun did. But aside from every composer's having his own individual method,[1] Hasse has always the effect[m] in mind, and to this he devotes himself with tireless energy, sacrificing to it everything, so far as consistent with good taste and correct harmony. To this must also be added innumerable circumstances of their lives, all of which must be exactly inquired into if one would avoid doing Graun an injustice in comparing him to Hasse. For although it is beyond question that both are geniuses, yet in their genius very different, there must also be considered many circumstances disadvantageous to Graun where his dramatic works are concerned. With these I shall acquaint you to the best of my ability.

Hasse became known in Italy almost from his first opera and was soon admired, something which gave him no little encouragement; how much, too, the affection of his present wife, Signora Faustina, at that time one of the first singers in Italy, must have contributed to this later on! When he came to Dresden, he found there perhaps the most magnificent court that then existed in Europe; here he received great remuneration and still greater honor. He worked freely and, unhampered by the taste or will of any person, wrote as he felt and as he wished. Difficulties for the singers and the orchestra he had no reason to avoid, for he could rely on them all. At the same time he had also the proud, stimulating satisfaction of knowing that his works were being performed in Italy and at nearly all the German courts with precisely the same success as at Dresden. Thus he wrote rather for his contemporaries than for his King.

Graun, on the other hand, less generally known, worked only according to the taste of his King; what failed to please him was stricken out, even though it were the best piece in the opera. For, to some extent one-sided and arbitrary in his taste, the King permitted Graun neither liberty nor variety in his operas—qualities which after all are most essential to an agreeable, three-hour entertainment—and, what is still more strange, at all times heartily approved these same qualities in Hasse. As regards the singers and the orchestra, excellent as those at Berlin have been at all

outstanding works and that the compositions of a Handel, a Homilius, an Agricola, a Rolle, etc., should thereby become more generally known.

[Four volumes of duets, trios, quintets, and sextets from the operas of Graun, with a few choruses, had been published by Decker and Hartung, of Berlin and Königsberg, in 1773 and 1774.—Ed.]

[1] Graun's method would assuredly be uncongenial to Hasse's fiery genius, for when Hasse has at length grasped the central idea of a situation, has read the scene repeatedly, and now, almost without reflecting on it, begins to sing it, surrenders himself to its musical inspiration, and grasps his pen, the flow of his ideas is far too violent to be as it were measured and divided off in order that harmony may be added to the melody measure by measure and line by line.

[m] One cannot help being astonished when one hears this admirable man speak about the theater. Never, to my knowledge, has a composer had more experience than he; never has effect been studied more assiduously and with greater success. And this, presumably, is the point distinguishing him above all from every other composer—the point wherein he is the greatest who has ever written. For his slightest works often have more effect than the best and most labored works of others.

times, the greatest connoisseurs who have known them both have always given the preference to those at Dresden, under the direction of Concert-meister Pisendel. What must have been a further heavy blow to Graun was that he saw the operas of Hasse performed at the court of his own King with great applause, often greater than that accorded to his. Yet, despite this, he was in many works obliged to avoid all similarity to Hasse. If now, to all these circumstances, one adds a difference in the genius of these two great men, can one ask any longer why it is that Hasse has more *boldness and fire in his expression?*

But Hasse has also *more variety in melody*. Into this again there enter circumstances which prevent our ascribing, *without qualification*, greater power of invention to Hasse than to Graun. Hasse went often to Italy; there he heard on each visit new works; from these he extracted, as does the busy bee from buds and blossoms, the finest nectar, preparing then from this, as does the bee, a dainty honey which one consumed with pleasure, without concern for the fields and flowers from which it was prepared. For when one looks closely at the operas written and performed in Italy at a given time, one finds whole passages, indeed whole similar movements, which Hasse has used and in using improved. For when he noted in these operas this or that melody, he noted also, and with con-siderable penetration, what was wrong with it; this being corrected, he used the melody in a perfect form, thus making it, so to speak, his own. Graun did not have this good fortune. Almost continuously in *one* spot, he studied, to be sure, the best works, but one knows what a difference there is in music between *hearing* and *reading*, especially with respect to melody, still more especially with respect to effect. By this means Graun could make himself one of the greatest harmonists of our time, and he did so; for theatrical works, however, this helps little more than it helps the landscape painter to have a complete understanding of architecture. Assuredly it gives us pleasure to see a beautiful temple in a background or to see, surmounting a steep crag at whose foot a rushing stream whirls past, the castle of an ancient German prince; if, however, the artist neglects the meadows and valleys, the hills and forests, and the overhang-ing sky, we give him little thanks for his fine buildings, which ought only to stand there as contrasts to laughing nature, but which in this case ob scure it and make it tedious.

To this is to be added still another circumstance. No one can precisely condemn Graun for having neglected his secondary characters, like the painter who places his secondary figures in the shade in order that his principal figure may stand out the more. But one may ask whether, on this account, the secondary characters need all resemble one another. On the other hand, no one can help commending Hasse for having given attractive melodies and some variety even to his secondary characters and for having done this with well-nigh inexhaustible liberality in every aria, always retaining, at the same time, the noble and lofty for his principal characters alone. It is for this reason that, with Hasse, each listener remains continuously attentive and always finds fresh enjoyment, so that the hours slip by for him without his knowing how. With Graun, on the contrary, the so-called amateur often complains of monotony; having no knowledge of harmony—for Graun is always the man for him who has this—he often says, "I have heard this opera before," even though it is being performed for the first time.

Take the score of any one of Hasse's operas, compare it with one by Graun, and you will be persuaded of the truth of all these observations. Then, inasmuch as you have the two scores in hand, look also for a moment at the accompaniment of the voices. In their general style you will find them in this respect almost identical. But at this point observe Hasse's shrewdness. Here, from the very beginning, the two violins proceed in unison. Why is this? To impress the subject on the listener the more effectively. The bass proceeds in notes of larger value; the upper voice is to be clearly heard. "Well, no doubt the viola will so fill things out that at least a closely woven three-part pattern will emerge." So one would think. But look here—it only touches here and there a few notes not present in the upper and lower voices; for the rest it proceeds with the bass. "Well, that must sound very thin." Do you think so? Do you not also know that the composer of operas is in this not very different from the painter of scenery, who must paint everything with great sweeping strokes of his brush in order that, at the distance from which the beholder perceives it, it may for the first time seem to be that which it would represent? Now look for a moment at this aria by Graun. What a fine piece of work! How beautifully the voices imitate one another here! Look at this passage which you liked so much in the ritornello; now the voices have it in three-fold imitation; it is a joy to hear them contending in this way. But we have entirely forgotten the singer! Let us look to him again—heavens, what a face he is making! "Don't you understand it? He is angry that the accompanying voices have more than he has and that they so cover him up that one does not hear him." How did the melody go? Don't you recall it any more? "No—everything has been confused and obscured for me."

In this connection, the story of the two Greek sculptors is in point. Each is asked to make a goddess to be set up in a temple at a considerable height. This being done, the two figures are exhibited to the crowd. Scarcely have they been unveiled when everyone runs to the one figure, shouting: "This is beauty! This is art! With what industry and pains all this is worked out! As to that other one—fie on its distorted face! What a broad high forehead it has! What a nose, and what a big space between it and the mouth! Who ever saw such a face on a goddess?" The shrewder artist is silent and asks only that the two figures be placed in position. His is the first to be elevated. As it rises further and further from the floor it seems to undergo a transformation; astonishment overcomes the crowd and confused mutterings are heard. At length it stands in position, and the crowd grows still, standing as though rooted to the spot, blinded by its beauty. Then the other figure is elevated in its turn. It too is transformed, for no one can any longer recognize it. Its features are confused one with another; although one still perceives the beautiful harmony of its larger proportions, the expression—the soul which had seemed at first to hover about its face—is lost. The one artist recognizes his mistake and disappears, while the other, surrounded by the crowd, is crowned with the triumph, honor, and praise that accompany him for the remainder of his life.

I have attempted here, insofar as the shortness of the time and my insignificant talents permitted, to make a *comparison* between Hasse and Graun in their dramatic works. But you still do not know these men by half, especially Graun. You have seen how many circumstances were unfavorable to him—the lack of opportunity to hear different kinds of music, the sole means by which one can study effect; the confining influence of his King; the want of zest for the theater arising therefrom; the insufficient remuneration and appreciation of his merits—all these and still other private circumstances could not fail to bring it about that Hasse, to whom every circumstance was favorable, should surpass him in this department. Now, however, we shall leave the theater and listen to the two men in the *church*, where nothing is unfavorable to Graun and where indeed his great musical learning is rather an advantage to him. Here for the first time you see Graun in all his greatness. And he who does not admire him here with deep veneration is uninformed, insensible, and prejudiced. Today, however, I have perhaps already abused your patience; I shall accordingly spare you this voluminous material until another letter. Besides, in a few days I hope to hear Graun's masterpiece.[10] Inspiring me, through this, with ardor for him, he will perhaps himself dictate the words in

10 *Der Tod Jesu.*

which I am to sing his praises, I who would not have presumed to pass judgment on him, too far removed from him till now, had nature not given me good instincts and had fortune not led me to a man who, correcting my good instincts, has filled my whole being with love, respect, and gratitude toward him.

76. A. E. M. Grétry

Grétry was born at Liége, Belgium, in 1742. He had little real training. In 1759 he went to Rome, where he stayed for five years without ever settling down to solid work in counterpoint. Eventually Grétry went on to Paris, where at first he met with difficulties; soon, however, his music won favor and he became extraordinarily successful as a composer of comic operas.

In the history of French *opéra comique* Grétry is an outstanding figure. Among his many works the following are particularly outstanding: *Le tableau parlant* (1769); *Les deux avares* (1770); *Zémire et Azor* (1771); *La rosière de Salency* (1773); *Colinette à la cour* (1782); *Richard Coeur-de-Lion* (1784)—perhaps his masterpiece; *Raoul Barbe-Bleue* (1789). In his *Mémoires; ou Essais sur la musique* (1789, in one volume, and 1797, in three volumes), Grétry expounds his views on dramatic composition. His influence on the younger generation—Isouard, Boieldieu, Auber—was strong and persistent. He died near Paris in 1813.

From the Mémoires [1]

[1797]

JEAN JACQUES ROUSSEAU says that to educate oneself one should travel on foot, enjoying at the same time good health and the delightful sensations which the varied spectacle of nature offers at every moment. I left Rome on the first of January, 1767; I saw nothing on my way; I felt neither pleasure nor pain; I was in a good carriage.

Arriving in Turin, I found there a German baron whom I had known in Rome. He proposed that we should travel together to Geneva. He was

---

1 The second edition (Paris, 1797), pp. 127-128, 129-134, 136, 140, 142-145, 146-151, 155-172, 429-433.

in a hurry and we set out the next day. When we were out of the city, I wanted to say to him, "Ah, Baron, how delighted I am to——"

He interrupted me and said bluntly, "Sir, I do not talk in a carriage."

"Very well," I answered.

At the inn that evening he had a great fire lighted, put on his dressing gown, and came toward me with outstretched arms, saying, "Ah, my dear friend, how glad I am to——"

In my turn I interrupted him to say, dryly, "Sir, I do not talk in inns."

He began to laugh like a madman, and gave me the details of a cruel malady from which he was suffering, and complained bitterly of the Roman fair sex, who, he said, had shown him no indulgence.

.   .   .   .   .   .

At Geneva I parted company with my baron, consoling myself with the knowledge that I should see Voltaire there. After I had been presented at the best houses by my friend Weiss, I found that I had accepted twenty women as pupils. I had been preceded by a little reputation, and the magistrates allowed me to set a higher price for my lessons than that fixed by the government.

The trade of singing master did not please me, besides fatiguing my chest, but it was necessary for me to prepare for the expense which a stay in Paris involves.

The quarrel between the givers of theatrical performances and their opponents was then at its height. The ambassadors of France, Zurich, and Berne arrived in the capacity of mediators, and the Republic caused a theater to be built to amuse their Excellencies and the rebellious citizens. I heard French comic operas for the first time. *Tom Jones*,[2] the *Maréchal*,[3] and *Rose et Colas*[4] gave me great pleasure after I had become used to hearing French sung, which had at first seemed disagreeable to me.

It also took some little time to accustom me to hearing spoken dialogue and singing in the same piece;[5] nevertheless I already felt that it is im-

---

[2] By François André Danican Philidor (1726–1795), the most famous member of a family prominent in French musical life for over a century. Philidor was a celebrated chess player as well as a composer of genuine talent. It was at the suggestion of Diderot and his circle that Philidor returned from one of his tours as a chess player and devoted himself to composition. *Tom Jones* was first produced at Versailles in 1765 and the next year at the Comédie Italienne.

[3] *Le Maréchal ferrant*, a one-act piece also by Philidor, first produced in Paris at the Opéra Comique in 1761.

[4] By Pierre Alexandre Monsigny (1729–1817), a native French composer of meager musical training, but who, with Philidor and others, is ranked among the founders of the *opéra comique*. *Rose et Colas* was first heard at the Opéra Comique in 1764. All three comic operas were performed in Geneva for the first time in 1766 where they were produced in the original language by a French company.

[5] Like the German Singspiel, French comic opera consisted essentially of spoken declamation and closed arias. This distinguished the *opéra comique* from other varieties of opera played in Paris: the *tragédie lyrique* with its *recitativo accompagnato*, and Italian *opera buffa* with its *recitativo secco*.

possible to make a recitative interesting when the dialogue is not. If the poet wishes to build up or develop a character, he has to provide an exposition and to work out his scenes. In that case what can recitative do? Tire by its montony and slow up the dialogue. It is only the young poets who hurry their scenes in the fear of being too long; the man who has a better knowledge of nature knows that effects are produced only by preparing them and gradually working them up to their highest pitch. So let the stage use spoken dialogue. Let us form at the same time actors who declaim and musicians who sing; otherwise our dramatic works will lose the merit which they have and that which they can further acquire. I should like to set to music a genuine tragedy with spoken dialogue; I imagine that it would produce a greater effect than our operas which are sung from beginning to end.

I soon longed to try my talents upon the French language, and this trial was not useless before dreaming of the capital of France. I asked everywhere for a poem, but, although there are many talented men in Geneva, they were too much occupied with public affairs [6] to give audience to the Muses. I took the course of writing to Voltaire, substantially in these terms:

SIR:

A young musician arriving from Italy and for some time established in Geneva would like to try his feeble talents on a language which you daily enrich with your immortal productions. I vainly request the men of talent of your community to come to the aid of a young man filled with emulation; the Muses have fled before Bellona. They have without doubt taken refuge with you, sir; and I implore your intercession with them, persuaded that if I obtain this grace from you, they will from that moment be favorable to me and will never abandon me.

I am with respect, etc.

Voltaire sent me word by the person who had borne my letter to him that he would not reply in writing because he was ill, and that he would see me at his house as soon as I could come.

I was presented to him the following Sunday by his friend Madame Cramer.[7] How flattered I was by his gracious reception! I sought to excuse myself for the liberty I had taken in writing to him.

"Not at all, sir," said he. "I was enchanted with your letter. I have been told about you a number of times; I wanted to see you. You are a

---

6 At this time Geneva was a refuge for advanced thinkers of the French school. The Helvetic Society, founded in 1762, was an effective force in the spread of progressive ideas.

7 Presumably the wife of Sr. Cramer, Voltaire's Geneva printer.

musician and you have wit! The combination is too rare, sir, for me not to take the liveliest interest in you."

I laughed at the epigram and thanked Voltaire.

"But," said he, "I am old and I hardly know the comic opera which is today the fashion in Paris and for which they are abandoning *Zaïre* and *Mahomet*.[8] Why shouldn't you," he said, addressing Madame Cramer, "write a pretty opera for him to work on until I feel like writing one? For I am not refusing you, sir."

"He has begun something of mine," said the lady to him, "but I am afraid it is bad."

"What is it?"

"*The Cobbler Philosopher*."

"Ah, it is as if one were to say, 'Fréron the philosopher.'" [9]

·   ·   ·   ·   ·

Later on, he said to me that I must hasten to go to Paris. "It is there," said he, "that one takes flight for immortality."

"Ah, sir," said I, "with what ease you speak of immortality. That charming word is as familiar to you as the thing itself."

"As for me," said he, "I would give a hundred years of immortality for a good digestion."

Was he speaking the truth?

·   ·   ·   ·   ·

My opera with Madame Cramer made only slow progress, and with works of wit and imagination that is almost always a bad sign. At that time the actors of Geneva were giving the opera of *Isabelle et Gertrude*,[10] which had shortly before been performed at the Italian theater in Paris. The poem pleased, but the music seemed weak. I determined to make my first trial with this poem of Favart.[11] I did not encounter too great difficulty. It is true that I was unaware of the rigidity of the language and

---

8 *Zaïre* (1732), inspired by Shakespeare's *Othello*, and *Mahomet* (1741), two tragedies by Voltaire.

9 Elie Catherine Fréron (1719–1776), a conservative critic of encyclopedic thought who singled out Voltaire for an especially virulent measure of abuse. Voltaire was equally caustic: in a play on words, he alluded to *L'Année littéraire*, a journal published by Fréron, as *L'Ane littéraire*; and his minor but pungent farce, *L'Ecossaise*, is aimed directly at Fréron. By comparison the offhand remark above is mild indeed.

10 *Isabelle et Gertrude, ou Les Sylphes supposés*, a one-act *opéra comique* based on Voltaire's *Gertrude ou l'Education d'une Fille*, mu-

sic by Adolphe Blaise, a bassoonist at the Paris Comédie Italienne, performed in 1765. According to Clément et Larousse (*Dictionnaire des Opéra*, Paris, 1905), the authors introduced airs by Gluck into their "mince partition." The work was first heard in Geneva during the season of 1766–67.

11 Charles Simon Favart (1710–1792), the most successful comic-opera librettist of the period. The diffusion of his plays throughout Europe is a cultural fact of great social importance; it accounts in considerable measure for the spread of the intellectual tone of the French Enlightenment. Cf. Alfred Iacuzzi, *The European Vogue of Favart*, New York, 1932.

that I wrote florid passages on all the vowels. I did not know that one must wait for some such word as "chain," "flight," "warbling," or "triumph" before indulging in them.[12] I perceived, however, as I worked, that the French language is as capable of accent as any other.

. . . . . .

This first French opera had a success that was encouraging to me; the public thronged to it for six performances, and that is a great deal for a small city like Geneva.

One of the musicians of the orchestra, a dancing master, came to me to tell me that the young men of the city, following the Parisian custom, would call me out after the performance.

"I have never seen that done in Italy," said I.

"You will see it here," said he, "and you will be the first composer to have received this honor in our republic."

In spite of my protests, he insisted on teaching me how to make a bow gracefully. At the end of the opera I was in fact repeatedly called out and was obliged to appear and thank the public. My man in the orchestra kept calling to me, "That's not the way . . . no, no, no . . . go on, go on . . ."

"What's the matter with you?" his fellows asked.

"He drives me crazy; I went to his house this morning on purpose to teach him how to present himself to the public nobly. Look; could anybody be more awkward and stupid?"

I felt that it was time to go to Paris. I paid a parting call on Voltaire; I saw him moved by the thought of what might befall me, yet at the same time he seemed to envy me. No doubt I was renewing in his mind the time of his own youth, when he launched upon the artistic career in which one sometimes finds glory along with fortune, but much oftener discouragement followed by despair.

He said to me, "You will not return to Geneva, sir, but I hope to see you again in Paris."

I did not enter that city without an emotion on which I had not counted; it was the natural consequence of the plan which I had formed of not leaving it without having overcome all the obstacles that should oppose my desire to establish my reputation there. This was not the work of a day, for during more than two years, I had, like so many others, to combat the hundred-headed hydra which everywhere opposed my efforts.

Word went to Liége that I had come to Paris to compete with Philidor,

---

12 See above, p. 649.

Duni, and Monsigny. The musicians of Liége blamed my parents for my excessive temerity. This menace did not discourage me; on the contrary it enflamed my emulation, and I said to myself, "If I can gain a place near these three skillful musicians, I shall have the pleasure of surpassing the composers of Liége, who recognize that they are at a great distance from them."

I went twice to the Opéra, fearing that I had deceived myself the first time, but I did not understand French music any the better. They gave Rameau's *Dardanus;* [13] I sat beside a man who was expiring with pleasure, and I was obliged to go out because I was bored to death. Since then I have discovered beauties in Rameau, but at that time I had my head too full of the Italian music and its forms to be able to go back all at once to the music of the preceding century. I felt as if I heard certain Italian airs which had become old-fashioned and whose too familiar turns of phrase my master Casali used sometimes to cite to me as evidence of the progress of his art. [14]

.   .   .   .   .

I went at most four times to the Théâtre des Italiens. I knew their best pieces, and I went only to acquaint myself with the talents and the voices of the actors. The range of Cailleau's voice surprised me. [15] I saw him in the *Nouvelle troupe;* the Actor presents himself as singing alto, tenor, and bass, and actually he could have sung any one of the three equally well. It was this first impression of Cailleau's voice which led me to compose the part of the Huron [16] in too high a register. It will perhaps seem extraordinary that the theater which I frequented assiduously was the Français. I did not wish to write the music of anyone else; for that reason I took good care not to study the music of any of the composers that I have cited. The declamation of the great actors seemed to me the only fitting guide, and I believed that a young musician may be proud to have had that idea, the only one which could lead me to the goal I had set for myself; namely, to be myself, taking as my model beautiful declamation.

---

13 First produced at the Opéra in 1739; it was followed by a parody at the Comédie Italienne called *Arlequin Dardanus* in which Favart had a hand. The version heard by Grétry was Rameau's second revision of the original score.
14 Giovanni Battista Casali (c. 1715–1792), *maestro di cappella* of San Giovanni in Laterano (Rome) from 1753 to his death. It is a little difficult to take very seriously Grétry's account of his arduous contrapuntal studies with this con-servative musician, a follower of the Roman school.
15 Perhaps the leading male singer of French comic opera. "All these talents [other performers of the Comédie Italienne] are eclipsed by that of Cailleau" (*Mémoires secrets,* ed. Bachaumont, I:51, 28 février 1762).
16 The title role of Grétry's first Paris comic opera, *Le Huron.* The libretto was by J. F. Marmontel and it is based on Voltaire's *Ingénu.*

None the less, in order to work, I needed a poem, and to find one I went about knocking at all doors. I neglected no opportunity of forming relations with dramatic authors. If one of them read an opera to me, I made bold to say that I was in a position to undertake it, perhaps to astonish him; but I was put off with pretexts, and I learned without astonishment that some well-known musician had been preferred to me. Philidor and Duni,[17] however, strove in good faith to obtain a poem for me. Men of ability are naturally kind and generous. The educated man observes with so great an interest what it costs a genuine talent to make itself known that even the fear of protecting a rival cannot prevent him from actively favoring it.

At last Philidor announced that he had answered for me and that a poet had consented to confide to me a work designed for him. On the day appointed I hurry to his house; the author reads his work; at each scene my mind is so exalted that I find instantly the motive and the character befitting each number. I pledge my word that the work would not have been my worst. When after long studies the soul takes command with such impetuosity, it does not leave the mind the time to go astray. I found the poem only mediocre and cold, but the flame which burned in me could have warmed it up. I embraced the author; how did he fail to see in my eyes that so beautiful an ardor could not be without value for his success? No, he did not see it, for on the second day following, instead of my receiving the manuscript, Philidor informed me that the author had changed his mind. He was willing, however, to have me work on his poem, provided that I worked with Philidor, if that was agreeable to us both.

"Come now, courage, my friend," said that honest man to me. "I do not fear to join my music to yours."

"For my part, I must fear it," said I, "for if the piece succeeds, it will be by you; if it fails, the public will see only me."

One year later Philidor gave the public his *Jardinier de Sidon*, and it is well known that it had little success.

Some days later I presented myself of my own accord to an actor of the Comédie Italienne; he did not conceal how difficult it would be for me

---

17 Egidio Romoaldo Duni (1709–1775), Italian *buffa* composer who, upon securing a post at the court of Parma where French taste prevailed, adapted Italian comic opera to the French language. The first of these works, a play by Favart parodying Carlo Goldoni's *Bertoldo, Bertoldino e Cacasenno* (Ciampi's setting had been given by the Bouffons in Paris in 1748), is *Le Caprice amoureux,* and Sonneck has shown that it is a pasticcio from the works of more than a half-dozen other Italian composers. Better known as *Ninette à la cour,* it was most successfully performed at the Comédie Italienne in 1755. Duni's later operas were his own compositions. Although the *opéra comique* can be traced to sources in the late seventeenth century, Duni, Monsigny, and Philidor are rightly regarded as having defined its shape and style. Grétry's works are a direct issue of their efforts.

to succeed in competition with the three musicians who worked for their theater. He sang to me the entire romance of Monsigny, "Jusques dans la moindre chose, etc."

"There is song, sir," said he, "that is what you need to write, but it is very difficult."

As I left him I was composing melodies for romances which I compared with the melodies of Monsigny.

I made the acquaintance of a young poet, a member of fashionable society, who spent his nights gambling and his days writing verses.[18] I urged him to compose a poem for me as a favor; he promised without hesitation. I paid him thirty visits to encourage him in this good work, and as likable libertines often have a kind heart, he let himself be moved and set to work. The subject he chose was the *Mariages samnites*.[a] I went every morning to inform myself of the state of his health; he read to me what he had written; I wrested it from him scene by scene. I had to wait a long time, but no matter; my eagerness to work gave me a patience which could endure any test.

I knew Suard and the Abbé Arnaud.[19] I had them listen to what I had composed of the *Mariages samnites*. The citizens judged me favorably; the Abbé Arnaud especially applauded me with the enthusiasm of the educated man who has no need of the judgment of others to dare to approve.

If I was flattered by this success, my poet was no less encouraged to finish his piece. The citizens I have mentioned announced me in literary circles, and a few days later I was invited to a dinner given by Count Creutz, at that time the Swedish envoy. I executed the principal scenes of my opera; for the first time I heard my art discussed with infinite intelligence. I was struck by this, for I had observed, during my stay in Rome, that the Italians feel too intensely to reason long. An "O Dio!" and a hand placed over the heart are ordinarily the flattering signs of their approbation. Without doubt, that is saying much; but if in this case one sigh includes a rhetoric, one must agree that it is hardly instructive.

Among the men of letters present at this dinner, I observed that Suard and the Abbé Arnaud discussed music with that genuine feeling which the artist, who has felt everything during his labors, knows so well how to

---

a This piece was not the one with the same title given in 1776, of which I shall speak later.

18 Barnabé Farmian de Rozoy, who also wrote the libretto to Martini's *Henri IV* (1774) and a parody on Anfossi's *L'incognita perseguitata* with music arranged by J. B. Rochefort that was performed at the Opéra (1781).

19 Jean Baptiste Suard (1733–1817) and the Abbé François Arnaud (1721–1784), two critics, who together founded a progressive journal called *Variétés littéraires*. They followed the lead of the Encyclopedists in their aesthetic tendencies.

appreciate. Vernet [20] talked to me as if he had composed music all his life. I saw that he would have been nature's musician if he had not been her painter. After all, what matters the path one takes, whether that of the eyes or of the ears, provided that one reaches the heart?

. . . . .

Everything was going as I wished. It only remained for me to find, in my actors, judges as indulgent as the celebrated men whose approbation I had just obtained. I was seeking the means of having them hear my music when my poet informed me that our piece had been refused. We decided that our work should be recast and arranged for the Opéra, for the comedians, and especially Cailleau, had judged it to be too noble for their theater, and they were right. One month sufficed the poet and myself for this metamorphosis. The patrons of my talent (and in Paris one needs patrons if one is unknown) had spoken of my work to the late Prince de Conti, who ordered Trial, the director of his musicians and of the Opéra,[21] to have the *Mariages samnites* performed in his mansion. I copied out nearly all the parts myself, the state of my fortunes not permitting me to meet the cost of giving them out.

When the day arrived which was to decide my fate, Trial sent me word to come in the morning to the warehouse of the Opéra for the rehearsal of the choruses. At this point a practiced pen would be needed to describe all the hostility that I detected in the expression of the assembled musicians. An icy chill reigned everywhere. If I attempted, during the singing, to reanimate that indolent mass by my voice or my gestures, I heard laughter on all sides, and no one listened to me.

I shuddered still more that evening to see all the French court assembled at Prince de Conti's mansion to judge me. From the overture (which today is in part that of *Sylvain*) to the end of the opera, nothing produced the least effect; the feeling of boredom was so universal that I wanted to go after the first act. A friend held me back. The Abbé Arnaud pressed my hand; he seemed furious.

"You are not being judged this evening," he said. "It seems that all the musicians are leagued together to flay you. But you will survive it; I swear it upon my honor."

The Prince had the extreme kindness to say to me, "I did not find ex-

---

20 Claude Joseph Vernet (1714–1789), a French painter especially known for his marines and for the brilliant light quality he simulated on canvas.

21 Jean Claude Trial (1732–1771), a composer of but modest talents whose four operas are less important than the dance airs in the Italian style which he wrote for his aristocratic employer. He was co-director of the Opéra with Pierre Montan Berton (1727–1780).

actly what your friends had announced to me, but I am distressed that nobody applauded a march which I found charming." It was the one which I afterwards placed in the *Huron*.

I must here do justice to one of my singers, who in the middle of the most soporific rendition, displayed all the energy of a great talent and an honest man. If his role had been more important, or, to put it better, if he alone had sung the whole opera, I should have had a success; but as boredom had already overpowered the audience by the time he began, he was unable to rouse it from its lethargy. This distinguished artist, who beyond doubt had never had a soul base enough to oppose the success of rising talents, is Jélyotte.[22]

*   *   *   *   *

As one may imagine, I did not ask the director Trial whether my opera would be given; the question would have been absurd. The men of letters who were interesting themselves in me, seeing that I was planning to leave Paris, engaged Marmontel [23] to write a poem for me. He came to see me and told me frankly that he had given a piece to the Italians (the *Bergère des Alpes*), and that in spite of its little success, he was about to work on a tale by Voltaire, just published, the *Ingénu, ou Le Huron*.

"You restore me to life," I said, "for I love this charming country where they treat me so badly."

This work was composed, words and music, in less than six weeks. The Swedish envoy, who even after my disaster had declared himself my most zealous partisan, begged Cailleau to come and dine with him to hear a work in which a great role was destined for him; he told me later that he was on the point of refusing the invitation, having already so often compromised himself in the interest of poor works. He accepted only out of regard for the Swedish envoy and for Marmontel. He listened to the first numbers with distrust, but when I sang for him, "Dans quel canton est l'Huronie," he showed the greatest satisfaction. He told us that he would take charge of the whole matter, and that we should be played without delay. "And that," said he, "is the man whose talents I have heard so horribly torn to pieces."

From what I have just said, the young composer will perceive how important it is to leave nothing neglected in his first trial, which will either

22 Pierre Jélyotte (1713–1797), the leading French tenor of the period. He was also a chanson composer, wrote a ballet produced at the court, and was an accomplished performer on the guitar.

23 Jean François Marmontel (1723–1799), a member and later perpetual secretary of the Aca- démie des Beaux-Arts, a *littérateur* and critic as well. He wrote librettos for Piccinni and took his side in the Gluck-Piccinni controversy. Marmontel's *Essai sur les révolutions de la musique en France* (Paris, 1777) is one of the chief documents of the time.

make him known or hold back his progress for several years. A young painter is a hundred times more fortunate. A picture is easily placed in its true perspective, but the rendition of music requires preliminary attentions which are hardly bestowed on a little-known artist.

Cailleau conducted me to Madame La Ruette's,[24] where I found the principal actors gathered. I played alone on the harpsichord all the music of the piece. Some days later we had a rehearsal at the theater. When Cailleau sang the air, "Dans quel canton est l'Huronie," and came to the words, "Messieurs, messieurs, en Huronie . . ." the musicians stopped playing to ask him what he wanted. "I am singing my part," he answered. Laughing at their mistake, they began the number again. The opera was rehearsed with zeal, and I felt my hope of succeeding in Paris revive.

On the day of the first performance I was in such perplexity that it had hardly struck three before I was posted at the corner of the Rue Mauconseil; my gaze was fixed upon the carriages and seemed to be appealing for spectators and asking their indulgence. I did not enter the theater until the first piece had been played, and when I saw that they were about to begin the overture to the *Huron,* I went down to the orchestra. My intention had been to recommend my cause to the first violin, Lebel. I found him ready to give the first stroke of his bow. His eyes were inflamed; his features were so changed as to be hardly recognizable. I withdrew without saying a word, and I was seized by a feeling of gratitude of which I have never lost the remembrance. I have since then obtained his nomination as musician of the King, with a pension of twelve hundred francs.

The public behaved like Cailleau; it listened to the first number with distrust. It believed me to be an Italian because my name ends in *i.* I have since learned that the parterre said, "Now we are going to hear florid passages and *fermate* without end." They were deceived and made amends for their premature judgment. The duet, "Ne vous rebutez pas, etc.," removed their prejudice. Cailleau appeared and made the audience love the engaging Huron, who was long regretted at the Comédie Italienne. Madame La Ruette sang the role of Mademoiselle de Saint-Yves with her always finely restrained sensibility; La Ruette, as Gilotin, displayed his comic pantomime without overemphasis; the excellent actor Clairval,[25] always animated by the desire of being useful to his comrades and to the arts, did not disdain to undertake the small part of the French officer. The success of the piece was indicated at the end of the first act

---

24 A singer at the Comédie Italienne, better known as Vilette before her marriage to La Ruette in 1762.

25 J. B. Clairval, a tenor at the Comédie Italienne. Contemporary accounts speak of a small voice but one of unusual quality.

and confirmed at the end of the second. The authors were called for. Clairval named me, and said that the author of the text was anonymous.

If I have ever passed an agreeable night, it was the one which followed that happy day. My father appeared to me in a dream and held out his arms to me; I rushed toward him with a cry which dissipated the sweet illusion. Dear author of my life, how painful it was for me to think that you would not enjoy my first success! God, who reads the secrets of the heart, knows that the desire to procure for you the comfort which you lacked was the first motive of my ambition. But at the very moment when I was struggling against the storm with some hope of success, when cruel friends explained to my unhappy father how rash my efforts were, when, finally, I was the sole object of his anxiety, and, with a voice almost extinguished, he said, "I shall never see my son again. Will he succeed?" death came to end his long-menaced days, which I was about to make happier.

One of my friends, a painter, came to see me the next day. "I want to show you something that will please you," said he.

"Let's go," said I, "for I am tired of hearing pieces read."

"What, already? No!"

"You see before you a man to whom since this morning five pieces accepted by the Italians have been offered. 'All or nothing' is an adage which holds good especially in Paris. The poets who have honored me with their visits are the ones from whom I had vainly solicited a work."

"Ah!" said my friend. "I had a good laugh in the amphitheater yesterday. I was surrounded by these gentry, and at the end of each number they cried out, 'Ah! he will compose my piece; you will see, gentlemen, the work that I destine for him.' If a singer finished a comic number: 'Ah! I have gaiety in my work, too; bravo! bravo! that's my man!' Finally," continued the painter, "have you accepted any of these gentlemen?"

"No; I told them that Marmontel deserved the preference, because he had been willing to take a risk with me."

I went out with my friend; he led me to a little street behind the Comédie Italienne and stopped me in front of a shop. I read, "The Great Huron, N. Tobacconist." I entered and bought a pound, for I found it, of course, better than anywhere else.

If I was delighted with the success of the *Huron*, I was no less delighted with another event which I had been far from expecting. Could anyone have believed, indeed, that at the time of my arrival in Paris, when I was fruitlessly begging, in that great city, for poems to set to music, and when indeed I had no claim to inspire the Parisians with much confidence, Voltaire would keep the word which he had given and on which I did not dare count, by writing comic operas for me? In truth, he, as well as his niece Madame Denis, had shown great indulgence for the numbers I had performed in his presence at Fernay, but a few detached numbers and the music which I had rewritten for Favart's opera *Isabelle et Gertrude* seemed to me to be insufficient claims to excite the attention of such a man as Voltaire and to merit his encouragement. When, in order to persuade me to come to Paris, he assured me that he would work for me, I believed him to be joking, and I was far from imagining that Voltaire could for some moments relinquish the scepter of Melpomene for the bauble of Momus.

None the less he did so, and amused himself by composing the *Baron d'Otrante* and the *Deux tonneaux*. I received the former while the *Huron* was still being played as a novelty. Voltaire's tale entitled *L'Education d'un prince* furnished him with the subject of the *Baron d'Otrante*. I was directed to present the piece to the Comédie Italienne as the work of a young provincial poet. The subject was judged comic and moral and the details pleasing, but they were unwilling to accept the work unless the author made some changes. What shocked them, perhaps, was that one of the principal roles, that of the Corsair, is written in Italian and all the rest in French. This mixture of the two languages is not rare in their theater in the so-called Italian comedies, but it was a novelty in comic opera, and they were unwilling to hazard it, especially as they had no Italian singer. For all that, they distinctly saw in the *Baron d'Otrante* a talent which could be useful, and they engaged me to induce the anonymous young author to come to Paris. I promised to do my best. One can well believe that the proposal made Voltaire laugh, and that he easily consoled himself for his rejection by the actors. As for myself, I was greatly annoyed by this untoward incident, which made me renounce setting his piece to music, as he on his part renounced comic opera.

The public was not slow in placing me in the rank of the composers worthy of its encouragements; but people conceded me too much or else not enough. They began by denying me the comic genre, although there was an element of comedy in the *Huron*. Others attempted to arrange my songs according to the system of the fundamental bass, and it or I now and then failed to meet the requirements.

"I have tried in vain," said one man to me, "to find the fundamental bass of the horn note in the accompanied recitative of Mademoiselle de

Saint-Yves in the second act. What explanation would you offer me for the progression there from one key to another, with no relation between the harmonies?"

"Here it is," said I. "It is because the Huron, whose accents Mademoiselle de Saint-Yves imagines herself to be hearing, is too far from the place of the scene to know in what key they are singing there."

"And if the fundamental bass cannot justify this deviation?"

"So much the worse for the fundamental bass. But it is none the less true that one cannot sing a duet in thirds when one singer is half a league from the other."

"You have reason on your side, but what of the rule?"

I met my man again some time later; "Let your mind be at rest," said he. "I have found the fundamental bass of your note."

Woe to the artist who, imprisoned by the rules, dares not allow his genius to soar unhampered. Deviations are necessary if he is to express everything; he must know how to depict the sensible man who goes through the door and the madman who leaps through the window.

If you cannot be faithful to the truth except by creating a combination never before used, do not fear to enrich theory by one rule more; other artists will perhaps make more appropriate use of the license which you have allowed yourself and will force the most severe to adopt it. The precept has almost always followed the example. It is, however, only the man familiar with the rule who is sometimes authorized to violate it, because he alone can perceive that in a given case the rule has not sufficed.

Now let us try to see why my music slowly established itself in France, without raising up enthusiastic partisans for me and without exciting puerile disputes such as we have seen. I believe that I owe that advantage to my studies and to the manner which I have adopted.

I heard much discussion of music, and as in most cases I did not agree with anybody, I adopted the policy of keeping still. At the same time I asked myself, Is there no way of satisfying almost everybody? I answered, One must be faithful to the truth in declamation, to which the French are very susceptible. I had remarked that a frightful distortion did not disturb the pleasure of the average auditor at the performances of dramatic music, but that the least false inflection at the Théâtre-Français caused a general murmur. I therefore aimed at truth in declamation; after which I believed that the musician who knew best how to transform it into song would be the most skillful. Yes, it is at the Théâtre-Français, from the lips of the great actors, that declamation, accompanied by theatrical illusions, gives us ineffaceable impressions which the best-analyzed precepts will never replace.

It is there that the musician learns to interrogate the passions, to sound the depths of the human heart, to get a clear idea of all the impulses of the soul. It is in that school that he learns to recognize and to reproduce their true accents, to mark their nuances and their limits. It is therefore useless, I repeat, to describe here the sentiments by whose action we have been struck; if sensibility does not preserve them deep within our soul, if it does not rouse tempests there and restore calm, all description is vain. The cold composer, the man without passions, will never be anything but the servile echo which repeats sounds; and true sensibility, listening to him, will be unmoved.

Persuaded that each interlocutor had his own tone, his own manner, I studied to preserve for each his own character.

I soon perceived that music has resources which declamation, being alone, has not. A girl, for instance, assures her mother that she does not know love, but while she affects indifference by means of a simple and monotonous melody, the orchestra expresses the torment of her amorous heart. Does a fool wish to express his love or his courage? If he is really animated, he must have the accents of passion, but the orchestra, by its monotony, will show us the tip of the donkey's ear. In general, the sentiment must be in the melody; the spirit, the gestures, the expression must be distributed through the accompaniment.

Such were my reflections and my studies. I will not say that the actors whom I found in Paris were more actors than singers, and that I was obliged, for that reason, to adopt the system of musical declamation; no, I shall be more faithful to the truth; I shall say that as the music of Pergolesi had always affected me in livelier fashion than any other music, I followed my instinct, which conformed to that part of the public which even in the enjoyment of its pleasures likes to light its way with the torch of reason. The sex endowed with sensibility furnished my first partisans; the impulsive young men credited me with cheerfulness and finesse; the critical said that my music was eloquent; the elderly partisans of Lully and Rameau found in my melody certain relations to that of their heroes. But while the public may be willing to applaud the efforts of an artist, how far he is from being satisfied with his work! He soon comes to feel that the declamation is lost in vague and pleasing melodies, or that a beautiful melody excludes a complete harmony; that he is always bringing out one part by sacrificing another. He sees, as he works, the source of the different systems and the quarrels to which they give rise; but, oblivious of opinion, he must be guided only by the sentiment which dominates him.

· · · · ·

After my arrival in Paris I gave successively the *Huron, Lucile,* the *Tableau parlant, Sylvain, L'Amitié à l'épreuve,* the *Deux avares, Zémire et Azor,* the *Ami de la maison, Céphale et Procris,* and the *Rosière de Salenci.*[26] It was at that period of my career that the Chevalier Gluck brought us his club of Hercules, with which he laid forever low the old French idol,[27] already weak from the blows given it by the Italian Bouffons and then by Duni, Philidor, and Monsigny.

Beyond doubt we owe much to the Chevalier Gluck for the master-pieces with which he has enriched our theater. To his truly dramatic genius should have been confided the administration of a form of enter-tainment to which he had given a new birth by his immortal productions and of which he would have maintained the order and the vigor by his intelligence and by that transcendence which the superiority of talents confers. It is especially by encouraging men of letters, by having referred to himself the different poems that they compose, that it would be easy for a director like Gluck to employ each musician in his own genre. It often happens that a young composer or performer loses several years, perhaps his whole life, seeking what is suitable for him, whereas he could have been settled in a moment.[b]

I know that it is hard to establish subordination among the subjects who subjugate us by the charm of pleasures, but the small merit of those who command them is often the source of their discouragement.

If nature had endowed Lully with the creative genius of Gluck, how brilliantly would he not have made the Opéra of Paris flourish from its birth, being showered with the personal favor of Louis XIV? But that King, a friend of the useful and consolatory arts, could not make a better choice, since Lully was the first musician of his time. It was he who was permitted to create a Royal Academy of Music, of which he was sole di-rector.

Without doubt the courtiers immediately sought to gain authority over entertainments, a sinister authority, which oftener seduces the lover of the fair sex than the lover of the arts; but what could they do against an artist who, like Molière, had the honor of approaching his master to con-

---

b See the chapter relating to music in the *Instruction publique,* Vol. 3.

26 Grétry's comic operas produced between the years 1768 and 1773 and listed in an approxi-mately chronological order.

27 J. B. Lully.

sult him about his pleasures? It is said, I know, that too much jealousy reigns among artists to permit too great power to be confided to any one of them. Vain prejudices, vain lies, used to keep the man of talent out of his true place! The mediocre musician, once he has gained a place by his importunate solicitations and his baseness, will doubtless tremble at the sight of genuine talents, whom he will get rid of by affronts; but choose an artist whose deserved reputation guarantees a noble disinterestedness, whose celebrity, that charming phantom, would repulse envy and cupidity if they dared to tempt him; choose the artist who after numerous successes still loves to prolong his glory by lighting the way of young talents by his experience; choose the man, finally, who has the right to say to the famous man, his equal, "Your genius has known how to open to you, in Italy, a new route to truth; why lose yourself in the brilliant path which you have traced for your rivals by pursuing the genre which you cannot attain? Give up those terrible choruses, those dance tunes, of which nature has not revealed to you the animating power; do not deprive Europe of the touching scenes which you produce without effort."

To another he will say, "You, always correct and proud, who have only an inflexible style which cannot lend itself to the infinite gradations of the passions—you should depict only on a grand scale, upon a text of vague meaning."

Finally, to me Gluck would have said, "Nature has given you the melody suited to the occasion, but this talent was given to you at the expense of a severer and more complicated harmony."

It is only at the cost of efforts that we sometimes succeed in departing from the genre to which we have been called; most commonly one overshoots the mark or one falls short of it; the fault is the same.

It would be revolting to self-respect if ignorance should undertake to use this language, but the truth, presented in interesting fashion by an educated man, has always been well received by genuine talents, especially when the director, in order to fill his place well, has an interest in the successes of others.

77. J. F. Reichardt

From the Briefe geschrieben auf einer Reise nach Wien [1]

[*1810*]

FOR EVERYONE, surely, who can enjoy the good things of life, especially for the artist, perhaps quite especially for the musical artist, Vienna is the richest, happiest, and most agreeable residence in Europe. Vienna has everything that marks a great capital in a quite unusually high degree. It has a great, wealthy, cultivated, art-loving, hospitable, well-mannered, elegant nobility; it has a wealthy, sociable, hospitable middle class and bourgeoisie, as little lacking in cultivated and well-informed gentlemen and gracious families; it has a well-to-do, good-natured, jovial populace. All classes love amusement and good living, and things are so arranged that all classes may find well provided and may enjoy in all convenience and security every amusement that modern society knows and loves.

·   ·   ·   ·   ·

In the city and in the suburbs five theaters of the most varied sort give performances all the year round. At the two court theaters in the city itself, one sees everything outstanding in the way of grand and comic opera, comedy, and tragedy that Germany produces—and, in some measure, Italy and France as well; the same is true of the great suburban Theater an der Wien, where in addition the great romantic magic operas are given with unusual magnificence. At all three theaters, great pantomimic ballets, heroic and comic, are often given also. Two smaller theaters in the Leopoldstadt and Josephstadt play popular dramas of the jolliest

---

1 Text: The original edition (Amsterdam, 1810), II, 138–139, 143–144, 146–150; I, 161–168, 204–210, 218–222, 254–258, 450–454.

kind. On days when no play is scheduled, all these theaters give great concerts and performances of the most important ancient and modern music for church and concert hall. Aside from this, all winter long there are frequent public concerts, by local and visiting musicians, and excellent quartet and amateur concerts by subscription.

For dancing, Vienna makes the greatest and most varied provisions that any city in the world can boast of. The large and small Redoutensaal, the Apollosaal, the Mehlgrube, the Neue Welt, and countless others are dance halls which offer to all classes the gayest, most elegant, and most convenient resorts. The dance music is everywhere outstanding, the service with everything in the way of food and drink is perfect. And with all these amusements, there prevails the best and most jovial spirit, with never a trace of oppressing distinctions.

.   .   .   .   .

Viennese society is, moreover, so rich and so agreeable that, as regards hospitality, good living, freedom, and general merriment, Vienna has no equal in all Europe. He who enjoys the good fortune, in Vienna, of coming to know the societies of the various classes, from the higher nobility down to the petite bourgeoisie, enjoys in the highest degree and in the freest and most agreeable way everything charming, delightful, and satisfying that Europe has to offer. At the same time to have everywhere before one's eyes ladies who are beautiful, cheerful, and merry, who are neither affected nor yet impudently forward, is a pleasure one experiences nowhere in the world to the extent one does in Vienna.

To these countless and inexhaustible attractions of Vienna is further to be reckoned that thousands of strangers from all parts and countries of Europe have residences here and travel constantly back and forth, while some have established themselves with taste and not infrequently on a grand scale and live here in great splendor and hospitality. This applies especially to Russians and Poles, who bring the good sociable spirit with them and amalgamate themselves with the Viennese the more easily. Aside from them, the great Bohemian, Moravian, and Hungarian families, like the Austrians, live regularly all winter long in Vienna, giving it the brilliance and magnificence that make it the great splendid imperial city, for the court itself prefers a retired family life to external pomp and show. Yet the court appears also with great dignity and no little brilliance at the few public festivities which it still maintains. The greatest brilliance consists, however, in the rich background provided by the higher nobility of the crown lands.

In the mild and imperceptible gradations from the higher princely nobility, with an annual income of a million, a half million, or a quarter of a million gulden, to the lesser courtly nobility, with an income of a hundred thousand gulden or over; from thence to the petty new nobility, who not infrequently have and spend as much, if not still more—the bankers and great landowners and manufacturers are included here; and so on through the bourgeoisie proper down to the well-to-do petite bourgeoisie; in the way that all the great public diversions and amusements are enjoyed by all classes without any abrupt divisions or offending distinctions—in these respects, Vienna is again quite alone among the great cities of Europe. If, with respect to the first part of this observation, London shows certain similarities, with respect to the second, it is after all very different. In London, an ordinary citizen does not venture into the parterre of the great Italian opera—the drama of the nobility and the great rich world—without having at least marked himself as an elegant and wealthy gentleman by some outward sign—a fine, expensive ring, or something of the sort—and he can in no way obtain admission to a concert or any other sort of entertainment offered by subscription to the nobility—the Concerts of Ancient Musick, for example—unless he is at least related to the great noble families.

Through the utter banishment of all splendor and affectation in everyday costume, even in the greatest houses and circles, Viennese society has gained still more, and I do not know what one could wish added to it to make it perfectly agreeable.

Thus I had the good fortune to spend in Vienna a whole winter, richer in amusements and pleasures of every kind than any winter I have ever before experienced, for all my good fortune in my many earlier travels. If I have one regret it is that the winter continued severe too long to permit my again enjoying to my heart's content the great public art treasures, which, with the utmost liberality, stand free and open to everyone winter and summer and from which, on my first visit to Vienna, I derived so much pleasure and profit. My own work and the hope of being able to remain in Vienna undisturbed throughout the lovely spring season, so endlessly rich in pleasures here, caused me to put off many things, the more so since the extraordinary hospitality of the highest and most noble as well as greatest and most agreeable houses and families offered me daily so rich a social life.

·   ·   ·   ·   ·

[November 30, 1808] I have been anxiously awaiting a wholly free and quiet moment to describe faithfully for you a touching scene which

I had with old Haydn. Fräulein von Kurzbeck, whom he loves like a father,[2] and Frau von Pereira, full of admiration for him, as for everything great and beautiful, were my guides. As a fitting overture to the scene, Fräulein von Kurzbeck played for me beforehand on her fortepiano a big and difficult sonata by our late Prince Louis Ferdinand. A pupil of Clementi's, she played it in quite masterly fashion, with delicate expression and equally perfect execution which left nothing whatever to be desired in point of purity and clarity.

In one of the outlying suburbs we had to drive nearly an hour into the remotest alleys and corners. Here, in the small but quite attractive garden house which belongs to him, we found the splendid old man, seated at a table covered with a green cloth. Fully dressed in a simple but neat gray-cloth suit with white buttons and an elegantly groomed and powdered curly wig, he sat there quite stiffly, almost rigid, drawn up close to the table, both hands resting on top of it, not unlike a lifelike wax figure. Fräulein Kurzbeck first explained to him that she would like to introduce me; I was almost afraid he would not know my name, or would perhaps not recall it in this state of apathy, and I was really taken aback and (I may honestly say) ashamed when the old hero opened his eyes wider— they still have an animated sparkle—and said: "Reichardt? A —— man! Where is he?" I had just come in, and with outstretched arms he called to me from across the table: "Dearest Reichardt, do come! I must embrace you!" With that he kissed me, pressing my hand tightly and convulsively, then ran his thin hand three or four times over my cheeks, saying to the others: "What pleases me is that the —— artist also has such a good honest face." I sat down beside him and retained his hand in mine. He looked at me for a time, deeply affected, then added: "Still so fresh! Alas, I have put too great a strain on my powers—already I am altogether a child"— and wept bitter tears. The ladies were about to interrupt in order to spare him. "No, let me go on, children," the dear old man exclaimed; "this does me good; these are in reality tears of joy over the man beside me; he will fare better." I was seldom able to bring forth a friendly word of gratitude and could only fervently kiss his hand.

Frau von Pereira, whom he had at first not recognized with his feeble memory, reminded him in a childlike, playful way of various jokes, and

---

2 Magdalene von Kurzböck, to whom Haydn dedicated his piano trio in E-flat minor and the Viennese edition of his piano sonata in E-flat (No. 52). Reichardt, who had already met Fräulein von Kurzböck at Baron von Arnsteiner's, has this to say of her (I, 145): "One of the most interesting acquaintances I made was Fräulein von Kurzböck, who was presented to me as the greatest pianist among the ladies of the local musical world, and that is saying a good deal. For a long time I had been hearing about her great talent, and I had just heard about it again in Dresden and Prague; I had thus been looking forward particularly to making her acquaintance. She received me as well and as graciously as if she had been looking forward in the same way to meeting me."

he presently joined her in this style, of which he is said to have always been very fond. With this the ladies thought we ought to leave the weak old man, lest in the end he be too much affected, and we took our farewell. Scarcely had we gotten out the door, however, when he called us back, exclaiming: "After all, I must show Reichardt my treasures too!" At that a servant girl brought in all sorts of beautiful things, some of them quite valuable. The most interesting among them was a rather large flat box which Princess Esterhazy, the wife of the now reigning prince [3]—the son of the prince who was for the greater part of Haydn's life his master— had had made for him after her own express design. It was of black ebony, heavily mounted in gold and ornamented with a gold bas-relief.[4] On the lid had been painted the beautiful affecting scene in the Akademiesaal, which, on the occasion of the last great performance of Haydn's *Schöpfung*, proved a veritable apotheosis for the composer.[5] (Collin recently recited to me a really beautiful descriptive poem on this scene.[6]) In the box lay a magnificent big autograph album, likewise black and gold, signed on the cover by the Princess, most cordially inscribed within by the whole princely family. I should be the first artist to inscribe myself, the old man said, and he would have the book sent to me. The whole box, incidentally, was filled on either side with the most dainty writing things and with all sorts of pleasant and useful instruments of gold and fine English steel-work.

Then he showed me further a great number of gold medals—from the musical society in St. Petersburg, from the Paris concerts, for which he wrote several symphonies expressly, and from many others—also a perfectly magnificent ring from the Russian Czar, a diploma from the National Institute in Paris, another from Vienna, conferring honorary citizenship on him, and many other things of this sort. In them the kind old man seems to live again quite happily.

When after a full hour we took leave in earnest, he detained me alone, holding my hand firmly, and told me, while kissing me repeatedly, that I should visit him at least once a week as long as I remained here. I shall not soil this recital with the little anxious touches of avarice he betrayed, in the midst of treasures he could no longer even use—but they went straight to my heart.

The excellent Beethoven I have also called on, having found him out at

---

[3] Marie von Lichtenstein, Princess Esterhazy, wife of Prince Nicholas II.

[4] For the later history of this box, see Pohl-Botstiber, *Joseph Haydn*, III (Leipzig, 1927), 258–259.

[5] This miniature, by Balthasar Wigand, is reproduced in Karl Geiringer, *Joseph Haydn* (Potsdam, 1932), p. 144. The performance in question had taken place on March 27, 1808, some months before Reichardt's arrival in Vienna.

[6] Reprinted in Pohl-Botstiber, *op. cit.*, III, 395–396.

last. People here take so little interest in him that no one was able to tell me his address,[7] and it really cost me considerable trouble to locate him. I found him finally in a great deserted and lonely house. At first he looked almost as gloomy as his surroundings, but presently he grew more cheerful and appeared to take quite as much pleasure in seeing me again as I in seeing him, commenting also, openly and cordially, on many things about which I needed information. His is a powerful nature, outwardly Cyclops-like, but in reality sincere, friendly, and kind. He lives much of the time with a Hungarian Countess Erdödy, who occupies the front part of the great house,[8] but he has broken off completely with Prince Lichnowsky, who lives upstairs and with whom for several years he spent all his time. I wanted also to call on the Prince, who is an old acquaintance, and on his wife, a daughter of the excellent Countess von Thun, to whom I owe the greater part of the amenities of my previous stay in Vienna,[9] but I found neither one at home and soon afterwards learned that the Princess lives in virtually complete retirement.

Salieri, who occupies a fine-looking house of his own, I found sitting with a cloth greatcoat over his clothes and frock coat among the music and musical instruments which quite fill his big room, for he never heats it; he wanted me to put on again my own greatcoat, which I had left in the anteroom, but at the moment I was not so chilled, although I cannot ordinarily be as tough as this coarse Italian nature. He has aged, to be sure, since I last saw him, but for all that is still, as he always was, the quite extraordinarily elegant and adroit Italian gentleman in his physiognomy and manner. He too spoke to me in a friendly and confidential way about many things and characterized for me the singers and orchestras of the various theaters with equal frankness and precision. I took leave of him with a sense of pleasure and gratitude.

·　·　·　·　·

[December 10, 1808] Today I must speak to you about a very fine quartet series that Herr Schuppanzigh, an excellent violinist in the service of Prince von Rasoumowsky, the former Russian envoy to the imperial court, has opened by subscription for the winter. The concerts will take place in a private house every Thursday from twelve to two. Last Thursday we heard the first one; there was as yet no great company in attendance, but what there was consisted entirely of ardent and attentive friends

---

7 Krugerstrasse, 1704.
8 To Countess Erdödy, Beethoven dedicated the piano trios, Opus 70, on one of which he was still working at the time of Reichardt's call, also the two sonatas, Opus 102, for 'cello and piano.
9 During his travels between 1771 and 1774.

of music, precisely the proper public for this most elegant and most congenial of all musical combinations. Had Haydn given us only the quartet, inspiring other genial artists to follow his example, it would already have been enough to make him a great benefactor of the whole world of music. Difficult as it is to bring this sort of music to perfection in performance—for the whole and each of its single parts are heard in their entirety and satisfy only in the most perfect intonation, ensemble, and blending—it is the first variety to be provided wherever good friends of music meet to play together. And since it is charitably rooted in the human make-up that expectation and capacity as a rule keep more or less in step and go hand in hand, each one takes at least some degree of pleasure in the performance, once he has brought to it all that he can offer it individually or through his immediate background. On this account the exacting connoisseur and critic not infrequently finds such groups working away with great enthusiasm, perfectly at home, when he himself, spurred by his overtrained artistic nature, would like to run away.

Here, however, such was not the case. The quartet is on the whole well balanced, although some say that last year, when Herr Kraft [10] played with them, the balance was better. Herr Schuppanzigh himself has an original, piquant style most appropriate to the humorous quartets of Haydn, Mozart, and Beethoven—or, perhaps more accurately, a product of the capricious manner of performance suited to these masterpieces. He plays the most difficult passages clearly, although not always quite in tune, a consideration to which the local virtuosi seem in general to be superior; he also accents very correctly and significantly, and his cantabile, too, is often quite singing and affecting. He is likewise a good leader for his carefully chosen colleagues, who enter admirably into the spirit of the composer, though he disturbed me often with his accursed fashion, generally introduced here, of beating time with his foot, even when there was no need for it, sometimes out of habit alone, at other times only to reinforce the forte. Generally speaking, one seldom hears a forte here—let alone a fortissimo—without the leader's joining in with his foot. For me this ruins the pure free enjoyment, and every such beat interrupts for me the co-ordinated and perfected performance which it is supposed to help bring about and which I had expected from this public production. At rehearsal, where one must continue practicing and assist oneself by all possible means of direction until the piece goes together perfectly, there one may beat time and even shout as much as one pleases. At the per-

---

10 The 'cellist Anton Kraft. Reichardt will have heard the quartet with Joseph Linke as 'cellist. Kraft subsequently formed a quartet of his own: Reichardt heard their first concert early in 1809 (I, 368).

formance itself, repose in all things is the chief requirement; all pre-liminary scaffolding must now disappear altogether, and it is far better to let a mistake pass without censure, whether actually committed or only feared, than to try to help matters by using strong measures. Not to mention that the inexperienced and uninformed listener will probably not notice the mistake in any case, while the more competent will notice it no less and be doubly offended. Furthermore, an attentive and con-scientious colleague ought never to be disconcerted by such shameful public prompting—it can only disturb his repose and control, on which above all the perfection of the performance depends; an inattentive and sluggish colleague ought not to count on so ordinary a means of assistance and stimulation. Each one must help with all his senses and his entire attention; he who is incapable of this cannot be trained to it by beating time.

At this first quartet morning there was performed—besides a very naïve and charming quartet by Haydn, full of good humor and innocence, and a more powerful, more elaborate one by Mozart—Beethoven's clear and beautiful Sextet with wind instruments, which made a fine vigorous effect.[11] In this a horn player from the orchestra of the Theater an der Wien gave me quite special pleasure, reminding me, with his beautiful tone and accurate, positive intonation of the half-tones, of our late excel-lent Türschmidt.

I shall certainly not willingly neglect this agreeable quartet series, to which Herr Schuppanzigh has given me a ticket.

A few days later, Beethoven gave me the pleasure of inviting this same pleasing quartet to Countess von Erdödy's in order that I might hear something of his new works. He played himself in a brand new trio of considerable force and originality for fortepiano, violin, and violoncello, altogether excellent and resolute.[12]

The quartet played further several of his older and extremely difficult quartets. Herr Schuppanzigh revealed a quite special skill and dexterity in the performance of these difficult Beethoven compositions, in which the violin frequently competes with the piano in the execution of the most difficult keyboard figures, the piano with the violin in singing tone.

The dear Countess, a touchingly cheerful invalid, with a friend of hers, a Hungarian lady also, took such keen and enthusiastic pleasure in each beautiful bold stroke, in each fine well-turned inflection, that the sight of

11 Opus 81b, an early work not published until 1810.

12 Probably the trio in D major, Opus 70, No. 1, the first of the pair to be completed.

her did me almost as much good as Beethoven's masterly conceptions and performance. Fortunate artist, who can count on such a listener!

. . . .

The Liebhaberkonzerte [18] have begun here for the winter, and the one I have just attended was nearly the death of me, for all that the company was very agreeable. In three rather small rooms, the like of which I have scarcely seen here before, a great crowd of listeners of all classes and an almost equally great one of musicians were so crammed together that I lost both my breath and my hearing. Fortunately, however, I did not also lose my sight, for a part of the company consisted of very attractive fine ladies, some of whom also sang very nicely. But even excellent things by Beethoven, Romberg, Paër, and others could have no effect, since in the narrow space one was quite deafened by the noise of the trumpets, kettle-drums, and wind instruments of all sorts. At the same time I was offered something quite perfect to listen to—something that was also thoroughly appropriate here and for this reason did me the more good. It was a Neapolitan guitarist, who played so well that he recalled to me the good old days of the real lute playing; never have I heard anything so perfect from so imperfect an instrument. Two Italians, with agreeable tenor and bass voices, then sang with him a little French romance, "La Sentinelle": facing the enemy in the moonlight, a soldier stands on guard, confiding to the winds for his sweetheart that he watches, lives, fights, and dies for her alone. The elegant Italian, into the bargain a quite handsome young man, a regular Antinoüs, had very cleverly arranged for the guitar a wholly delightful marchlike melody, enriching it with lively interludes. This was perfectly suited to the room and to the company, which was likewise enchanted by it and appeared not to notice that the whole agreeable impression was destroyed again by Beethoven's gigantic and overpowering overture to Collin's *Coriolanus*. In the narrow rooms, my head and heart were nearly burst with the vigorous blows and crackings which each one strained himself to the utmost in augmenting, for the composer himself was present. It gave me great pleasure to see the excellent Beethoven not only on hand but much made of, the more so since he has in mind and heart the fatal hypochondriac delusion that everyone here persecutes and despises him. To be sure, his stubborn outward manner may frighten off some of the jolly good-natured Viennese, and many of those who acknowl-

---

[18] The orchestra of the Liebhaberkonzerte was made up of amateurs, with a few professional players for the wind instruments.

edge his great talent and merits may perhaps not employ sufficient humanity and delicacy to so offer the sensitive, irritable, distrustful artist the means of enjoying life that he may accept them gladly and also take satisfaction in them as an artist. It often pains me to the quick when I see this altogether excellent and splendid man gloomy and unhappy, although I am at the same time persuaded that it is only in his willful mood of deep discontent that his best and most original works can be produced. Those who are capable of appreciating these works ought never to lose sight of this or to take offense at any of his outward peculiarities or rough corners. Only then are they true, genuine admirers of his.

. . . . .

[December 25, 1808] The past week, during which the theaters were closed, the evenings filled with public concerts and musical performances, caused me no little embarrassment in my ardent resolve to hear everything. This applies particularly to the twenty-second, when the local musicians gave the first of this season's great performances at the Burgtheater for their deserving widows' fund, while on the same day Beethoven also gave at the great suburban theater a concert for his benefit, at which only his own works were played. This last I could not conceivably miss; that morning, accordingly, I accepted with many thanks the kind invitation of Prince von Lobkowitz to join him in his box. There we sat, in the most bitter cold, from half past six until half past ten, and confirmed for ourselves the maxim that one may easily have too much of a good thing, still more of a powerful one. Nevertheless—though many a mishap in performance tried our patience to the limit—I was no more willing to leave before the final conclusion of the concert than was the extremely polite and good-natured Prince, whose box was in the first balcony, quite near the stage, so that the orchestra, with Beethoven conducting in the midst of it, was almost on top of us. Poor Beethoven, who had from this concert his first and only ready profit of the whole year, found considerable hostility and only feeble support in the arrangements and performance. The singers and orchestra were made up of very heterogeneous elements, and it had not even been possible to arrange one full rehearsal of all the pieces on the program, every one of which was filled with the greatest difficulties. How much of the output of this fruitful genius and tireless worker was none the less performed during the four hours will astonish you.

To begin with, a pastoral symphony, or recollections of country life.

First movement: Agreeable impressions awakening in man on arrival in the country. Second movement: Scene by the brook. Third movement: Joyous amusements of the country folk. Fourth movement: Thunder and storm. Fifth movement: Benevolent feelings after the storm, joined with thanks to the Divinity. Each number was a very long and fully worked-out movement, filled with the liveliest images and the most brilliant ideas and figures; as a result, this one pastoral symphony alone lasted longer than an entire court concert is allowed to last with us.

Then followed, as the sixth piece, a long Italian scena,[14] sung by Mlle. Killizky, the beautiful Bohemian with the beautiful voice.[15] That today this pretty child rather shivered than sang could not be taken amiss, in view of the bitter cold; in our box near by, we too were shivering, wrapped in our furs and greatcoats.

Seventh piece: A Gloria, with choruses and solos, whose performance, unfortunately, miscarried altogether.[16]

Eighth piece: A new concerto for fortepiano, terribly difficult, which Beethoven played astonishingly well in the fastest possible tempi.[17] The Adagio, a masterpiece of beautiful sustained melody, he actually sang on his instrument with a deep melancholy feeling which awakened its response in me.

Ninth piece: A great symphony,[18] very elaborate and too long. A cavalier sitting near us reported having observed at the rehearsal that the violoncello part, busily occupied, amounted alone to thirty-four sheets. But the copyists here are quite as expert in spreading things out as are at home our lawyer's clerks and court recorders.

Tenth piece: A Sanctus, again with choruses and solos,[19] unfortunately —like the Gloria—a complete failure in performance.

Eleventh piece: A long fantasy, in which Beethoven revealed his full mastery.

And finally, by way of conclusion, another fantasy, in which the orchestra presently came in and was actually followed at the end by the chorus.[20] This strange idea met with disaster in performance as the result of an orchestral confusion so complete that Beethoven, with the inspired ardor of the artist, thinking no longer of his public or of his surroundings, shouted out that one should stop and begin over again. You can imagine

14 "Ah, perfido!" Opus 65.
15 Mlle. Killizky (Josephine Killitschgy), Schuppanzigh's sister-in-law, was a last-minute substitute.
16 From the Mass in C, Opus 86.
17 The Concerto in G, Opus 58.
18 The Symphony in C minor, Opus 67.
19 Again from the Mass in C.
20 The Choral Fantasy, Opus 80, a work subjected to further revision before its publication in 1811.

how I and all his other friends suffered at this. In that moment, indeed, I wished that I had had the courage to leave earlier after all.[21]

.   .   .   .   .

[February 25, 1809] Dear father Haydn I am still unable to see again; as often as we send out word to him, asking after his health and for an appointment agreeable to him, we receive from his people the invariable answer that he is very weak and can see no one. Clementi too is most desirous of seeing him again; since his arrival, he has still to succeed in doing so.[22] I fear that his noble spirit will soon depart from us. Although strictly speaking he has for some years been as good as morally dead for the world,[23] one still fears always the final extinguishing of the divine flame which, throughout a half century, has so magnificently lighted the way for us.

Not without being deeply touched can I recall how one of his first "cassations," as he called his cheery, youthful quartets, gave me my earliest artistic joy and was at the same time the chief display piece of my boyish virtuosity; [24] how his quartets, constantly increasing in inner content and character, offered me the best of nourishment and training as well as the most delightful enjoyment; how, on my many visits to England, and especially in France, his superb symphonies were almost everywhere the greatest and the most beautiful that I heard played; how later on his larger choral works for the church and concert hall brought me the keenest and most varied pleasure; and how, after all this, because of a combination of circumstances, I was never able to meet this hero—this patriarch of music—never able to imprint upon his lips or fatherly hand my ardent thanks for all this instruction and enjoyment—until the utmost weakness of mind and body made this for him, as for me, almost a torture. Nearly and deeply affected, I wrote soon after this into his handsome album a choral setting of these magnificent lines from Goethe's "Euphrosyne": [a]

---

a This is now published in the third number of my *Goethe's Lieder, Oden, Balladen und Romanzen* (Leipzig, 1809).

21 The announcement of this concert in the Wiener Zeitung for December 17 describes the program as consisting entirely of new works, not previously heard in public. With the exception of the scena "Ah, perfido!" and the movements from the Mass in C, which had already been heard in performances away from Vienna, this seems to have been strictly true.

22 Clementi had been in Vienna since the latter part of 1808.

23 In a letter to Breitkopf & Härtel written on June 12, 1799, Haydn himself refers to a falling-off of his mental powers; his last significant work was the "Harmoniemesse," completed during the summer of 1802; his death occurred on May 31, 1809, only a few months after the date of this entry in Reichardt's journal.

24 The quartet in B-flat, Opus 1, No. 1; in his autobiography (Schletterer, *Johann Friedrich Reichardt* [Augsburg, 1865], I, 161) Reichardt tells us that this was his boyhood "show piece."

Cliffs stand firmly based; the water eternally plunges;
  Down from its cloudy cleft foaming and roaring it falls.
Ever the pines are green, and even in winter the copses
  Foster on leafless twigs buds that are hid from the eye.
Each thing arises and passes by law; a wavering fortune
  Governs the life of man, treasure of priceless worth.
Not at the brink of the grave does the father, departing contented,
  Nod farewell to his son, blooming and splendid heir;
Nor is the old man's eye closed always by hand of the younger,
  Willingly parting from light, weak giving place to the strong.
Ah, more often does fate perversely order man's life-days:
  Helpless an old man mourns children and grandsons in vain,
Standing, a desolate tree, round which all shattered the branches
  Lie upon every side, ravaged by tempest of hail.

To this I added, from the bottom of my heart: "Also to see the shell of
the spirit that will live on among us forever and that created for us a new
life, rich in joys and destined—so long as harmony shall remain the highest expression of the endless—to outlive all posterity; also to see the shell
so soon demolished filled my innermost being with that deep melancholy
which sprang from the heart of the poet and which, in memory of a
solemn, never-to-be-forgotten hour, I dared to set to music. For I regard
myself as fortunate in having gazed deeply into the soul-filled eye—in
having pressed passionately to my heart and to my lips the loving, consecrating hand."

•   •   •   •   •

XVII

Literary Forerunners of Musical Romanticism

78. Jean Paul

"The highest criticism is that which leaves an impression identical with the one called forth by the thing criticized. In this sense Jean Paul, with a poetic companion-piece, can perhaps contribute more to the understanding of a symphony or fantasy by Beethoven, without even speaking of the music, than a dozen of those little critics of the arts who lean their ladders against the Colossus and take its exact measurements."

Strange to say, this observation of Schumann's is not altogether wide of the mark. A self-taught amateur whose piano-playing did not go beyond the improvisation of extravagant rhapsodies, Jean Paul responded almost as a clairvoyant to the poetic side of musical composition; a musical writer who never wrote on music, he exerted a compelling influence on the music and musical criticism of his time. By 1800, thanks to the musical episodes and allusions in his early novels, his name had become so closely identified with music in the minds of his readers that a sentimental ode by Andreas Kretschmer could win immediate and widespread popularity simply by being printed under the title "Jean Paul's Favorite Song." Two well-known writers on music sought him out and recorded their impressions of his personality—J. F. Reichardt, who spent an evening with him in 1796, and Ludwig Rellstab, who called on him in 1822 with a letter from Tieck. For many of his contemporaries he was the literary counterpart of Beethoven. August Lewald, who knew them both, found that they had much in common and reports that the resemblance extended even to physical characteristics. "Beethoven was somewhat smaller," he wrote in 1836, "but one noticed at once the same powerful nature, the same indifference to external appearance, the same kindliness, the same simplicity and cordiality. If we look at their works we find the same profundity, the same sharp characterization, the same painting of details; quiet states of temperament are described and sudden outbursts of extreme passion; ideas that might have been drawn from the most commonplace reality alternate with the highest flights into the sublime. I am confident that I can rediscover in Beethoven's symphonies the Swedish country parson's Sunday (*Flegeljahre*), the unfortunate's dream (*Herbst-Blumine*), Natalia Aquilana's letter (*Siebenkäs*), and the most magnificent episodes of the *Titan*. Only in Jean Paul's improvisation, however, did his kinship with Beethoven become truly evident."

The son of a musician whose father had been a musician before him, Jean Paul (properly Johann Paul Friedrich Richter) was born at Wunsiedel in

743

the Bavarian Fichtelgebirge on March 21, 1763. After attending the university in Leipzig he lived for a time in Hof and later in Weimar; in 1804 he settled in Bayreuth, where he continued a resident until his death on November 14, 1825. Two of Jean Paul's shorter writings, *Quintus Fixlein* and *Des Feldpredigers Schmelzle Reise nach Flätz*, were translated into English by Carlyle.

From the Vorschule der Aesthetik [1]

[2d ed., 1813]

22. THE NATURE OF ROMANTIC POETRY

THE SOUTHERN AND THE NORTHERN DISTINGUISHED

"THE ORIGIN and character of all recent poetry is so readily derived from Christianity that one could quite as well call this poetry Christian as romantic." With this assertion the author of the present paragraphs opened fire some years ago; [2] refuted and instructed, however, by more than one worthy critic of the arts, he has felt called upon to alter some details, removing them as one might remove a suburb to protect a fortification or a city as a whole. The first question is: Wherein does the romantic style [a] differ from the Greek? Greek images, stimuli, motives, sensations, characters, even technical restrictions are easily transplanted into a romantic poem without the latter's surrendering on this account its universal spirit; in the other direction, however, the transplanted romantic stimulus finds no congenial place in the Greek art work, unless it be a stimulus of the exalted sort, and then only because the exalted, like a borderline divinity, links the romantic with the antique. Even the so-called modern irregularity, for example that of the Italian opera or the Spanish comedy, may—since mere technique has not the power to

---

[a] Schiller calls it the *modern*, as though everything written since Grecian times were modern and new, irrespective of whether one or two thousand years old; likewise the *sentimental*, an epithet which the romanticists Ariosto and Cervantes would not have taken over-seriously. [In Schiller's "Über naive und sentimentalische Dichtung," first published in *Die Horen* for 1795 and 1796.—Ed.]

[1] Text: *Sämtliche Werke*, I. Abteilung, XI (Weimar, 1935), 75–81. I have made some use of the notes of Eduard Berend, the editor of this volume of Jean Paul's collected works.

[2] The first edition of the *Vorschule* was published in 1804

divide the spiritual sphere of poetry into an old world and an American new one—be pervaded and animated with the spirit of Antiquity; this is nicely supported by the observation of Bouterwek,[3] who says that Italian poetry, for all its lack of ideas, through its clarity, simplicity, and grace follows and approaches the Greek model more nearly than any other modern sort, and this though the Italian forms have traveled further from the Greek than either the German or the English. And with this correct observation Bouterwek refutes that other one of his,[4] according to which romanticism is precisely to be found in an un-Greek community of the serious, indeed tragic, and the comic. For this is as little a necessary characteristic of the romantic, where it is often absent, as its opposite is of the antique, where it is frequently present, for example, in Aristophanes, who sternly and crassly blends the exaltation of the choruses with the humiliation of the gods themselves, as though blending an intensification of an emotion with its comic relaxation.

Rather let us ask feeling why, for example, it calls even a countryside romantic. A statue, through its sharp, closed outlines, excludes everything romantic; painting begins to approach it more closely through its groups of human figures and, without them, attains it in landscapes, for example in those of Claude.[5] A Dutch garden seems only to deny everything romantic, but an English one, reaching out into the indefinite landscape, can surround us with a romantic countryside, that is, with a background of imagination set free amid the beautiful. What is it, further, that confers on the following poetic examples their romantic stamp? In the tragedy *Numantia* of Cervantes, the citizens, in order not to fall victims to hunger and the Romans, dedicate themselves in a body to a common death. When they have carried this out and the empty city is strewn with corpses and funeral pyres, Fame appears on the walls and proclaims to the enemy the suicide of the city and the future brilliance of Spain. Again, in the midst of Homer, the romantic passage in which Jupiter surveys from Mount Olympus, at one time and under one sun, the warlike upwrought Trojan plain and the far Arcadian meadows, filled with men of peace.[6] Or, although it sparkles less brightly, the passage in Schiller's *Tell* in which the eye of the poet sweeps down from the towering chain of mountain peaks to the long, laughing cornfields of the German lowlands.[7] In all these examples, the decisive element is not that of *exaltation*, which, as we

3 *Geschichte der Poesie und Beredsamkeit* (Göttingen, 1801–19), II, 544.
4 In his review of the *Vorschule*.
5 Claude Lorrain (Claude Gellée), French landscape-painter of the seventeenth century.

6 *Iliad*, xiii, 1.
7 *Wilhelm Tell*, III, iii.

have said, readily flows over into the romantic, but that of *expanse*.[8] Romanticism is beauty without bounds—the beautiful infinite, just as there is an exalted infinite. Thus Homer, in the example we have given, is romantic, while in the passage in which Ajax prays to the gods from the darkened battlefield, asking only for light,[9] he is merely exalted. It is more than a simile to call romanticism the wavelike ringing of a string or bell, in which the tone-wave fades into ever further distances, finally losing itself in us so that, while already silent without, it still resounds within. In the same way, the moonlight is at once a romantic image and a romantic example. To the Greeks, who defined things sharply, the half-light of the romantic was so remote and foreign that even Plato, so much the poet and so close to the Christian upheaval, in treating a genuinely romantic-infinite subject—the relation of our petty finite world to the resplendent hall and starry roof of the infinite—expresses it only through the confined and angular allegory of a cave, from out which we chain-bound ones see passing in procession the shadows of the true beings who move behind us.[10]

If poetry is prophecy, then romanticism is being aware of a larger future than there is room for here below; romantic blossoms float about us, just as wholly unfamiliar sorts of seeds drifted through the all-connecting sea from the New World, even before it had been discovered, to the Norwegian shore.

Who is the author of this romanticism? Not in every land and century the Christian religion, to be sure; to this divine mother, however, all its others are somehow related. Two un-Christian varieties of romanticism, historically and climatically independent of one another, are those of India and the Edda. Old Norse romanticism, bordering more nearly on the exalted, finds for the ghostly Orcus in the shadowy realm of its climatically darkened and awe-inspiring natural environment, in its nights and on its mountains, a boundless spirit world in which the narrow sensual world dissolves and sinks from sight; here Ossian [b] belongs, with his

---

b Great as are the advantages of Ahlwardt's translation, thanks to the discovery of the purer text, it seems to me nonetheless that far too little of the praise that is its due has been accorded to the lightness, the fidelity, and the euphonies of the translation by Jung. [James Macpherson's pretended translations from "Ossian" had been translated into German by F. W. Jung in 1808 and by C. W. Ahlwardt in 1811.—Ed.]

8 For further illustrations of the application of this thoroughly romantic principle, see the excerpts from Jean Paul's *Hesperus* (p. 769 below: "The harmonica tones flowed like radiating echoes," or p. 773: "And thou, reëchoing sound

of the harmonica") or, for examples drawn from music, Liszt's *Ce qu'on entend sur la montagne* (after Victor Hugo) or Wagner's

In des Wonnemeeres
wogendem Schwall,
in der Duft-Wellen
tönendem Schall,
in des Welt-Atems
wehendem All—
ertrinken—
versinken—
unbewusst—
höchste Lust!

9 *Iliad*, xvii, 645.
10 *Republic*, vii (514–521B).

evening and night pieces in which the heavenly nebulous stars of the past stand twinkling above the thick nocturnal mist of the present; only in the past does he find future and eternity.

Everything in his poem is music, but it is a distant and hence a doubled music, grown faint in endless space like an echo that enchants, not through its crudely faithful reproduction of a sound, but through its attenuating mitigation of it.

Hindu romanticism has as its element an all-enlivening religion which, through animism, has broken away the confines from the sensual world; this world has become as expansive as the spirit world itself, yet it is filled, not with mischievous spirits, but with cajoling ones, and earth and sky reach out toward one another as they do at sea. To the Hindu a flower is more alive than to the Norseman a man. To this, add the climate, that voluptuous bridal night of nature, and the Hindu himself, who, like the bee reposing in the honey-filled calix of the tulip, is swung to and fro by tepid west winds and takes his rest in a delightful rocking. Precisely for this reason, Hindu romanticism had inevitably to lose itself more and more in the magic of the senses, and if the moonlight and the echo are characteristics and images of other romantic kinds, the Hindu kind may be characterized by its dark perfume, the more so since this so frequently pervades its poetry and its life.

Through its predilection for the exalted and the lyric, through its incapacity for drama and characterization—above all, through its Oriental mode of thought and feeling—Oriental poetry is related less to the Greek than to the romantic. This mode of thought and feeling—namely, the sense of the mortal futility of our night's shadows (shadows cast, not by a sun, but as though by moon and stars—shadows that the meager light itself resembles); the sense that we live our day of life under a total eclipse filled with horror and the flying things of night (like those eclipses in which the moon quite swallows up the sun and stands alone before it with a radiant ring)—this mode of thought and feeling, which Herder, the great delineator of the East, has so exactly painted for the North,[11] could but approach romantic poetry by the path by which a kindred Christianity quite reached and formed it.

We come at length to Christian romanticism, respecting which we must first show why in the South (particularly in Italy and Spain) it took on and created other forms than in the North, where, as was shown above, the very soil made of the heathen outer-court a romantically Christian

---

11 Above all in his *Älteste Urkunde* (Riga, 1774), p. 95, and *Zerstreute Blätter*, IV (Gotha, 1792), 131.

Holy of Holies. In its natural environment, and then because of manifold historic connections, the South presents an aspect so very different from the North that such reflections as derive romanticism from sources wholly distinct from Christian ones must be considered or corrected.

For the southerly and earliest variety, Bouterwek names these sources: [12] first, the heightened respect for womankind, brought in by the ancient Goths, then, the more spiritualized form of love.

But it was the Christian temple that gave shelter to romantic love, not the prehistoric German forest, and a Petrarch who is not a Christian is unthinkable. The one and only Mary ennobles every woman; hence, while a Venus can only be beautiful, a Madonna can be romantic. This higher form of love was or is precisely a blossoming and blooming from out Christianity, which, with its consuming hatred of the earthly, transformed the beautiful body into the beautiful soul that one might love the other—beauty, then, in the infinite. The name "Platonic love" is borrowed, notoriously, from another sort of love, from that pure unsullied friendship between youths in itself so innocent that the Greek lawgivers counted it a duty, so fanatical that the lover was punished for the errors of the loved one; here, then, simply directed toward another sex, we have again as with the ancient Goths the same deifying love, held—to prevent its profanation—as far as possible from nature, not the love that sanctifies through Christianity and clothes the loved one with the luster of romance.

The spirit of chivalry—which, apart from this, embroidered side by side upon its banners love and religion, Dame and Notre Dame—and the Crusades, named sires of romanticism as second choices, these are children of the Christian spirit. . . . To enter the promised land, which two religions at once and the greatest being on earth had elevated for the imagination to a twilight realm of holy anticipation and to an isthmus between the first world and the second, to enter this land was to glorify oneself romantically and with two strengths, with valor and with faith, to make oneself master, literally and poetically, of one's baser earthly nature. What comparable result could the heroic ages and the voyages of the Argonauts bring forth?

As servants and silent creatures of romanticism we reckon further the ascending centuries which, allying all peoples more and more closely with one another, round off their sharp corners from without, while from within, through the rising sunlight of abstraction, like a form of Christianity, they break up more and more the solid material world. All this emboldens one to prophesy that, as time goes on, the writing of poetry

---

[12] *Geschichte der Poesie und Beredsamkeit*, I, 22.

will become more and more romantic, freer from rules or richer in them, that its separation from Greece will become wider and wider, and that the wings of its winged steed will so multiply that, precisely with the crowd, it will experience greater and greater difficulty in maintaining a steady course, unless, like Ezekiel's seraphim, it uses certain wings merely to cover its face.[13] But as for that, what concern have aestheticians and their prolegomena with time and eternity? Is only creeping philosophy to make progress, and soaring poetry lamely to gather rust? After three or four thousand years and their millions of horae is there to be no other division of poetry than Schiller's dull division of it into the horae [14] of the sentimental and the naïve? One might maintain that every century is romantic in a different way, just as one might, in jest or in earnest, place a different sort of poetry in every planet. Poetry, like all that is divine in man, is fettered to its time and place; at one time it must become Carpenter's Son and Jew, yet at another its state of abasement may begin on Mount Tabor and its transfiguration take place on a sun and blind us.[15]

Aside from this, it follows of itself that Christianity, although the common father of all romantic children, must in the South beget one sort of child, in the North another. The romanticism of the South—in Italy, climatically related to Greece—must blow more gently in an Ariosto, flying and fleeing less from the antique form, than that of the North in a Shakespeare, just as in turn the same southern variety takes on a different and orientally bolder form in torrid Spain. The poetry and the romanticism of the North is an aeolian harp through which the tempest of reality sweeps in melodies, its howlings resolved in tones, yet melancholy trembles on these strings—at times indeed a grief rends its way in.

. . . . .

---

13 Ezekiel, 1:11; Isaiah, 6:2.

14 Jean Paul is using the word "horae" (*Horen*) both in its literal sense and in reference to the periodical *Die Horen*, edited by Schiller and published monthly from 1795 to 1797; see Note a above.

15 An ancient tradition makes Mount Tabor the scene of the Transfiguration.

79. W. H. Wackenroder

Born at Berlin in 1773, Wackenroder was one of the first of the German romanticists. He was a fellow student of Ludwig Tieck's at Erlangen and Göttingen and inspired his friend with his own enthusiasm for the art of the Middle Ages. Wackenroder sought with romantic fervor to penetrate the mystery of music and emphasized in his writings the close relationship between religious feeling and artistic creation. This is the main theme of his *Herzensergiessungen eines kunstliebenden Klosterbruders* (1797). Wackenroder's premature death at the age of twenty-five was a great blow to Tieck, who completed and published his friend's posthumous *Phantasien über die Kunst für Freunde der Kunst* (1799).

The Remarkable Musical Life of the Musician Joseph Berglinger [1]

[*From* Herzensergiessungen eines kunstliebenden Klosterbruders]

[*1797*]

I have often looked backward and gathered in for my enjoyment the art-historical treasures of past centuries; but now my inclination impels me to tarry for once with the present time and to try my hand at the story of an artist whom I knew from his early youth and who was my most intimate friend. Alas, to my regret you soon departed this world, my Joseph, and not easily shall I find your like again! But I shall console myself by retracing in my thoughts the story of your genius, from the beginning, and by retelling it for those to

1 Text: *Kunstanschauung der Frühromantik,* ed. by Andreas Müller (Leipzig, 1931), 89–105.

whom it may give pleasure—just as, in happy hours, you often spoke of it to me at length, and just as I myself came inwardly to know you.

JOSEPH BERGLINGER was born in a little town in the south of Germany. His mother was taken from the world as she brought him into it; his father, already a somewhat elderly man, was a doctor of medical science in straitened circumstances. Fortune had turned her back on him, and it was only by dint of much perspiration that he got along in life with his six children (for Joseph had five sisters), the more so since he was now without a capable housekeeper.

The father had formerly been a tender and very kindhearted man who liked nothing better than to give such help, counsel, and alms as he could afford; after a good deed, he slept better than usual; deeply moved and grateful to God, he could long thrive on the good works of his heart; he nourished his spirit in preference with affecting sentiments. Indeed, one cannot but give way to a profoundly melancholy admiration when one contemplates the enviable simplicity of these souls who discover in the ordinary manifestations of a kindly heart a source of grandeur so inexhaustible that it becomes the whole heaven on earth that reconciles them to the world at large and preserves them in constant and comfortable contentment. When he considered his father, Joseph was entirely of this mind; but Heaven had once and for all so constituted him that he aspired steadily to something higher; he was not content with mere spiritual health or satisfied that his soul should carry out its ordinary earthly tasks —to work and to do good; he wanted it to dance as well in exuberant high spirits—to shout to Heaven, as to its source, for joy.

His father's temperament, however, comprised still other elements. He was a hard-working and conscientious doctor and had known no other diversion, his whole life long, than the curious knowledge of things hidden in the human body and the vast science of all the wretched ills and ailments of mankind. As often happens, this intensive study became a secret enervating poison which penetrated his very artery and gnawed, in his breast, through many a responsive cord. To this was added his discontent with his wretched poverty, and finally his age. All these things served to undermine his former kindliness, for, where the soul is not strong, whatever a man comes into contact with is absorbed into his blood and alters his inner nature without his knowing it.

The children of the old doctor grew up under his care like weeds in a deserted garden. Joseph's sisters were some of them sickly, some of them feeble-minded, and, in their dark little room, they led a pitiable and lonely life.

In such a family no one could have been more out of place than Joseph, whose whole life was a beautiful fantasy and a heavenly dream. His soul was like a delicate young tree whose seed a bird has dropped into a ruined wall, where, among the rough stones, it springs up like a maiden. He was always by himself, alone and quiet, feeding only on his inner fantasies; on this account, his father considered him too a little foolish and unbalanced. He was sincerely fond of his father and his sisters, but most of all he prized his inner life, keeping it secret and hidden from others. Thus one secretes a jewel casket, to which one gives no one the key.

Music had from the first been his chief joy. Occasionally he heard someone play the piano and could even play a little himself. In time, by means of this often-repeated pleasure, he developed himself in a way so peculiarly his own that his being became thoroughly musical and his temperament, lured on by the art, wandered about continually among the shady bypaths of poetic feeling.

An outstanding chapter in his life was a visit to the episcopal residence, whither a well-to-do relation, who lived there and had taken a fancy to him, carried him off for a few weeks. Here he was really in his element; his spirit was fascinated by beautiful music, thousand-sided, and, not unlike a butterfly, it fluttered about in the congenial breeze.

Above all he visited the churches to hear the sacred oratorios, cantilenas, and choruses resounding in the full blast of trumpet and trombone beneath the vaulted roofs; from inner piety, he often listened humbly on his knees. Before the music began, as he stood there in the tightly packed and faintly murmuring congestion of the crowd, it seemed to him as though he heard buzzing about him, unmelodiously confused, as at a great fair, the commonplace and ordinary life of man; his brain was paralyzed with empty earthly trivialities. Full of expectation, he awaited the first sound of the instruments; as this now broke forth from out the muffled silence, long drawn and mighty as the sigh of a wind from heaven, and as the full force of the sound swept by above his head, it seemed to him as though his soul had all at once unfurled great wings—he felt himself raised up above the barren heath, the dark cloud-curtain shutting out the mortal eye was drawn, and he soared up into the radiant sky. Then he held his body still and motionless, fixing his gaze steadfastly on the floor. The present sank away before him; his being was cleansed of all the pettiness of this world—veritable dust on the soul's luster; the music set his nerves tingling with a gentle thrill, calling up changing images before him with its changes. Thus, listening to certain joyous and soul-stirring songs in praise of God, he seemed quite plainly to see David in his royal mantle, a crown upon his head, dancing toward him and shouting psalms before the Ark of the Covenant; he saw all his enthusiasm, all his movements, and his heart leapt in his breast. A thousand sensations latent within him were liberated and marvelously interwoven. Indeed, at certain passages in the music, finally, an isolated ray of light fell on his soul; at this, it seemed to him as though he all at once grew wiser and was looking down, with clearer sight and a certain inspired and placid melancholy, on all the busy world below.

This much is certain—when the music was over and he left the church, he thought himself made purer and more noble. His entire being still glowed with the spiritual wine that had intoxicated him, and he saw all passersby with different eyes. Now, when he chanced to see a group of people standing together on the pavement and laughing or exchanging gossip, it made a quite peculiarly disagreeable impression on him. As long as you live, he thought, you must hold fast, unwavering, to this beautiful poetic ecstasy, and your whole life must be a piece of music. When he went to lunch at his relation's and had thoroughly enjoyed his meal in a company not more than usually hearty and jovial, it displeased him that he had let himself be drawn again so soon into the prosaic life and that his rapture had vanished like a gleaming cloud.

His whole life long he was tormented by this bitter dissension between his inborn lofty enthusiasm and our common mortal lot, which breaks in daily on our reveries, forcibly bringing us down to earth.

When Joseph was at a great concert he seated himself in a corner, without so much as glancing at the brilliant assembly of listeners, and listened with precisely the same reverence as if he had been in church—just as still and motionless, his eyes cast down to the floor in the same way. Not the slightest sound escaped him, and his keen attention left him in the end quite limp and exhausted. His soul, eternally in motion, was wholly a play of sounds; it was as though, liberated from his body, it fluttered about the more freely, or even as though his body too had become a part of his soul—thus freely and easily was his entire being wound round with the lovely harmonies, and the music's foldings and windings left their impress on his responsive soul. At the lighthearted and delightful symphonies for full orchestra of which he was particularly fond, it seemed to him quite often as though he saw a merry chorus of youths and maidens dancing on a sunny meadow, skipping forward and backward, single couples speaking to each other in pantomime from time to time, then losing themselves again amid the joyous crowd. Certain passages in this music were for him so clear and forceful that the sounds seemed words.

At other times again, the music called forth a wondrous blend of gladness and sadness in his heart, so that he was equally inclined to smile and weep—a mood we meet so often on our way through life, for whose expression there is no fitter art than music. And with what delight and astonishment he listened to that sort of music which, beginning like a brook with some cheery, sunny melody, turns imperceptibly and wonderfully, as it goes on, into increasingly troubled windings, to break at last into a loud and violent sob, or to rush by, as though through a wild chasm, with an alarming roar! These many-sided moods now all of them impressed upon his soul new thoughts and visual images, invariably corresponding—a wondrous gift of music, the art of which it may be said in general that the more dark and mysterious its language, the greater its power to affect us, the more general the uproar into which it throws all forces of our being.

The happy days that Joseph had spent in the episcopal residence came to an end at last, and he returned again to his birthplace and to his father's house. How sad was this return—how doleful and depressed he felt at being once more in a household whose entire life and strife turned only on the bare satisfying of the most essential physical needs and with a father who so little approved of his inclinations, who despised and detested all the arts as servants of extravagant desires and passions and as flatterers of the elegant world! From the very first it had displeased him that his Joseph had so fastened his heart on music; now that this inclination in the boy was growing by leaps and bounds, he made a determined and serious effort to convert him, from a harmful propensity for an art whose practice was little better than idleness and which catered merely to sensual excess, to medicine, as the most beneficent science and as the one most generally useful to the human race. He took great pains to instruct his son himself in its elementary principles and gave him books to read.

This was a truly distressing and painful situation for poor Joseph. Secretly he buried his enthusiasm deep in his breast, not to offend his father, and sought to compel himself, if possible, to master a useful science on the side. Yet in his soul there was a constant struggle. In his textbooks he could read one page ten times over without grasping what he read; unceasingly within, his soul sang its melodious fantasies on and on. His father was much distressed about him.

In secret his passionate love of music came to dominate him more and more. If for several weeks he heard no music, he became actually sick at heart; he noted that his feelings dried up, an emptiness arose within him, and he experienced a downright longing to be again inspired. Then even ordinary players, on church festival and consecration days, could with their wind instruments move him to feelings which they themselves had never felt. And as often as a great concert was to be heard in a neighboring town, he rushed out, ardent and eager, into the most violent snow, storm, or rain.

Scarcely a day went by without his calling sadly to mind those wonderful weeks in the episcopal residence, without his soul's reviewing the priceless things that he had heard there. Often he repeated to himself from memory the lovely and touching words of the sacred oratorio which had been the first that he had heard [2] and which had made a particularly deep impression on him:

> Stabat mater dolorosa
> Juxta crucem lacrymosa,
>   Dum pendebat Filius
> Cujus animam gementem,
> Contristantem et dolentem,
>   Pertransivit gladius.
>
> O quam tristis et afflicta
> Fuit illa benedicta
>   Mater Unigeniti!
> Quae moerebat, et dolebat,
> Et tremebat, cum videbat
>   Nati poenas inclyti.

And so forth.

But alas for those enchanted hours, in which he lived as in an ethereal dream or had just come quite intoxicated from the enjoyment of a splendid piece of music; when they were interrupted for him—by his sisters, quarreling over a new dress, by his father, unable to give the eldest daughter enough money for her housekeeping or telling the story of a thoroughly wretched and pitiable invalid, or by some old beggar-woman, all bent over, coming to the door, unable to shield herself in her rags from the wintry frost—alas, there is in all the world no feeling so intensely bitter and heart-rending as that with which Joseph was then torn. Dear God, he thought, is this the world as it is—and is it Thy will that I should plunge into the turmoil of the crowd and share the general misery? So it seems, and, as my father constantly preaches, it is the destiny and duty of man to share it, to give advice and alms, to bind up loathesome wounds, to heal odious diseases. And yet again an inner voice calls out to me quite clearly:

---

2 Wackenroder is probably thinking of the setting by Pergolesi.

"No! No! You have been born to a higher, nobler end!" With thoughts like these he often tormented himself for hours at a time, finding no way out; before he knew it, however, there vanished from his soul those unpleasant pictures which seemed to pull him by force into the mire of this life, and his spirit floated once more unruffled on the breeze.

In time he became thoroughly convinced that God had sent him into the world to become a really distinguished artist, and it may sometimes have occurred to him that, in view of the gloomy and confining poverty of his youth, Providence might be going to reward him all the more brilliantly. Many will consider it a novelesque and unnatural invention, but it is none the less strictly true that in his loneliness, from an ardent impulse of his heart, he often fell on his knees and prayed God to so guide him that he might some day become an altogether splendid artist in the sight of God and man. At this time, his pulse often violently agitated by the pressure of ideas directed steadily toward one point, he wrote down a number of shorter poems, setting forth his state of mind or the praise of music, and these, without knowing the rules, he set joyously to music after his childish heartfelt fashion. A sample of these songs is the following, a prayer which he addressed to music's sainted patron:

> See me comfortless and weeping,
> Solitary vigil keeping,
>   Saint Cecilia, blessed maid;
> See me all the world forsaking,
> On my knees entreaty making;
>   Oh, I pray thee, grant me aid.
>
>   .   .   .
>
> Let the hearts of men be captured,
> By my music's tones enraptured,
>   Till my power has no bound,
> And the world be penetrated,
> Fantasy-intoxicated,
>   By the sympathetic sound.

Perhaps for more than a year poor Joseph tormented himself, brooding alone over the step he wished to take. An irresistible force drew his spirit back to that splendid city which he regarded as his paradise, for he was consumed by the desire to learn his art there from the ground up. But it was his relations with his father that weighed particularly on his heart. Having no doubt observed that Joseph was no longer at all willing to apply himself seriously and industriously to his scientific studies, his father had indeed already half given him up, withdrawing himself into his displeasure which, with his advancing age, increased by leaps and bounds. He no longer paid much attention to the boy. Joseph, meanwhile, did not on this account give up his childlike feeling; he struggled continually against his inclination and still had not the heart to breathe, in his father's presence, a word of what he had to reveal. For whole days at a time he tortured himself by weighing one course against another, but he simply could not extricate himself from the horrible abyss of doubt; his ardent prayers were all to no avail—this almost broke his heart. To the utterly gloomy and distressed state of mind in which he was at this time, these lines, which I found among his papers, bear witness:

> Ah, what are these forces that surround me
> And in their embrace have tightly bound me,
> Calling me away—shall I obey them?
> Urging me from home—can I gainsay them?
> I must bear, though guiltless of transgression,
> Torture and temptation and oppression.
>
> That Thou'lt deign to save me, I implore Thee;
> Bury me in earth, call me before Thee;
> Otherwise I cannot long withstand it,
> Must live at the will (if it demand it)
> Of that unknown force whose awful power
> Governs me more fully every hour.

From day to day his distress grew more and more acute, the temptation to escape to the splendid city stronger and stronger. But, he thought, will not Providence come to my aid—will it give me no sign at all? His suffering finally reached its highest peak when his father, in connection with some family disagreement, addressed him sharply in a tone quite different from his usual one, afterwards consistently repulsing him. Now the die was cast; from now on he turned his back on all doubts and scruples; he would now consider the matter no further. The Easter holiday was at hand; this he would celebrate with the others at home; but as soon as it was over—out into the wide world.

It was over. He awaited the first fine morning, for the bright sunshine seemed to lure him on as though by magic; then, early in the morning, he ran out of the house and away—one was used to this in him—but this time he did not come back. With delight and with a pounding heart he hastened through the narrow alleys of the little town; hurrying past everything he saw about him, he could scarcely keep from leaping into the open air. On one corner he met an old relation. "Why in such a hurry, cousin?" she asked. "Are you fetching vegetables for the table from the market again?" Yes, yes, called Joseph to himself, and, trembling with joy, he ran out through the gates.

But when he had gone a little distance into the country, he looked about and burst into tears. Shall I turn back, he thought. But he ran on, as though his heels were on fire, and wept continually, so that it looked as though he were running away from his tears. His way led now through many an unfamiliar village and past many an unfamiliar face; the sight of the unfamiliar world revived his courage, he felt strong and free—he came nearer and nearer—and at last—Heavens, what delight! —at last he saw lying before him the towers of the splendid city.

PART TWO

I return to my Joseph a number of years after we left him; he has become Capellmeister in the episcopal residence and lives in great splendor. His relation, having received him very cordially, has been the author of his good fortune, has seen to it that he was given the most thorough training in music, and has also more or less reconciled Joseph's father, little by little, to the step his son had taken. By exceptional application Joseph has worked his way up, to attain at length the highest rung of success that he could possibly wish.

Yet the things of this world change before our very eyes. On one occasion, after he had been Capellmeister for several years, he wrote me the following letter:

DEAR PATER:

It is a miserable life I lead—the more you seek to comfort me, the more keenly I am aware of it.

When I recall the dreams of my youth—how blissfully happy I was in those dreams! I thought I wanted to give my fancy free rein continuously and to let out my full heart in works of art. But how strange and austere even my first years of study seemed to me—how I felt when I stepped behind the curtain! To think that all melodies (although they had aroused the most heterogeneous and often the most wondrous emotions in me) were based on a single inevitable mathematical law—that, instead of trying my wings, I had first to learn to climb around in the unwieldy framework and cage of artistic grammar! How I had to torture myself to produce a thing faultlessly correct with the machine-like reason of ordinary science before I could think of making my feelings a subject for music! It was a tiresome mechanical task. But even so, I still had buoyant youthful energy and confidence in the magnificent future. And now? The magnificent future has become the lamentable present.

What happy hours I spent as a boy in the great concert hall, sitting quietly and unnoticed in a corner, enchanted by all the splendor and magnificence, and wishing ever so ardently that these listeners might some day gather to hear my works, to surrender their feelings to me! Now I sit often enough in this same hall, even perform my works there, but in a very different frame of mind indeed. To think I could have imagined that these listeners, parading in gold and silk, had gathered to enjoy a work of art, to warm their hearts, to offer their feelings to the artist! If, even in the majestic cathedral, on the most sacred holiday, when everything great and beautiful that art and religion possess violently forces itself on them, these souls are not so much as warmed, is one to expect it in the concert hall? Feeling and understanding for art have gone out of fashion and become unseemly; to feel, in the presence of an art-work, is considered quite as odd and laughable as suddenly to speak in verse and rhyme in company, when one otherwise gets through one's life with sensible prose, intelligible to all. Yet for these souls I wear out my spirit and work myself up to do things in such a way that they may arouse feeling! This is the high calling to which I had believed myself born.

And when on occasion someone who has a sort of halfway feeling seeks to praise me and to commend me critically and to propound critical questions for me to answer, I am always tempted to beg him not to be at such pains to learn about feeling from books. Heaven knows, when I have enjoyed a piece of music—or any other delightful work of art—and my whole being is full of it, I should paint my feeling on the canvas with a single stroke, if only a single color could express it. I cannot bestow false praise, and I can bring forth nothing clever.

To be sure, there is a little consolation in the thought that perhaps—in some obscure corner of Germany to which this or that work of mine may penetrate some day, even though long after my death—there may be someone whom Heaven has made so sympathetic to my soul that he will feel on hearing my melodies precisely what I felt in writing them—precisely what I sought to put in them. A lovely idea, with which, no doubt, one may pleasantly deceive oneself for a time!

Most horrible of all, however, are those other circumstances with which the artist is hemmed in. To speak of all the loathsome envy and spiteful conduct, of all the untoward petty customs and usages, of all the subordination of art to the will of a court—to speak a word of this is repugnant to me; it is all so undignified, so humiliating to man's soul, that I cannot bring a syllable of it past my lips. A threefold misfortune for music that the mere existence of a work requires such a number of hands! I collect myself and lift up my entire soul to produce a great work—and a hundred unfeeling empty-headed fellows put in their word and demand this and that.

In my youth I thought to avoid the misery of earthly life; now, more than ever, I have sunk into the mire. This much seems certain, sad to say—for all our exertion of our spiritual wings we cannot escape this earth; it pulls us back by force, and we fall again into the common human herd.

They are pitiable artists, those I see about me, even the noblest ones so petty that, for conceit, they do not know what to do once a work of theirs has become a general favorite. Dear God, is not one half our merit due to art's divinity, to nature's eternal harmony, the other half to the gracious Creator who gave us the power to make use of this treasure? Those charming melodies which can call forth in us the most varied emotions thousandfold, have they not sprung, all of them, from the unique and wondrous triad, founded an eternity since by nature? Those melancholy feelings, half soothing, half painful, which music inspires in us, we know not how, what are they after all but the mysterious effect of alternating major and minor? Ought we not to thank our Maker if he now grants us just the skill to combine these sounds, in sympathy from the first with the human soul, so that they move the heart? Art, surely, is what we should worship, not the artist—he is but a feeble instrument.

You see that my ardor and my love for music are no less strong than formerly. And this is just the reason why I am so miserable in this . . . but I shall drop the subject and not annoy you further by describing all the loathsome reality about me. Enough—I live in a very impure atmosphere. How far more ideally I lived in those days when I still merely enjoyed art, in youthful innocence and peaceful solitude, than I do now that I practice it, in the dazzling glare of the world, surrounded only by silks, stars and crosses of honor, and people of culture and taste! What should I like? I should like to leave all this culture high and dry and run away to the simple shepherd in the Swiss mountains to play with him those Alpine songs which make him homesick wherever he hears them.

From this fragmentarily written letter one can realize in part the situation in which Joseph found himself. He felt neglected and alone amid the buzzing of the many unharmonious souls about him; his art was deeply degraded in his eyes in that, so far as he knew, there was no one on whom it made a lively impression, for it seemed to him created only to move the human heart. In many a dark hour he was in utter despair, thinking: How strange and singular is art! Is then its mysterious power for me alone—is it to all other men mere sensual pleasure and agreeable amusement? What is it really and in fact, if it is nothing to all men and something to me alone? Is it not a most absurd idea to make this art one's whole aim and chief business and to imagine a thousand wonderful things about its great effects on human temperament—about an art which, in everyday reality, plays much the same role as card-playing or any other pastime?

When such thoughts occurred to him, it seemed to him that he had been the greatest of visionaries to have striven so hard to make a practical artist of himself for the world. He hit on the idea that the artist should be artist for himself alone, to his own heart's exaltation, and for the one or two who understand him. And I cannot call this idea wholly incorrect.

But I must sum up briefly the remainder of my Joseph's life, for my memories of it are beginning to depress me.

For a number of years he continued to live on in this way as Capell-meister, and, as time went on, his discouragement increased, as did his uneasy realization that, for all his deep feeling and intimate understanding of art, he was of no use to the world, less influential than a common tradesman. Often and regretfully he recalled the pure ideal enthusiasm of his boyhood and with it how his father had tried to make a doctor of him so that he might lessen man's misery, heal the unfortunate, and thus make himself useful in the world. This had perhaps been better, he thought more than once.

His father, meanwhile, had at his age grown very weak. Joseph wrote regularly to his eldest sister and sent her something toward his father's support. He could not bring himself to pay him an actual visit and felt that this would be beyond him. He became more despondent; his life was far spent.

On one occasion he had performed in the concert hall a new and beautiful piece of music of his own composition; it seemed the first time that he had made any impression on the hearts of his listeners. The general astonishment, the silent approval, so much more welcome than noisy applause, made him happy in the thought that this time he had perhaps been worthy of his art; once more he was encouraged to begin work anew. But when he went out on to the street, a girl, dressed very miserably, crept up and sought to speak to him. Heavens, he cried; it was his youngest sister and she was in a wretched state. She had run on foot from her home to bring him the news that his father was about to die and had insistently demanded to speak with him before the end. At that, the music in his breast broke off; in a heavy stupor he made his preparations and set off in haste for his birthplace.

The scenes which took place at his father's bedside I shall not describe. But let the reader not believe that there were any melancholy long-drawn-out debates; without wasting many words they understood each other fully—in this respect, indeed, it seems that nature mocks us generally, men never understanding one another properly until these critical last moments. At the same time, he was smitten to the heart by all that he saw.

His sisters were in the most deplorable circumstances; two of them had fallen from grace and run away; the eldest, to whom he regularly sent money, had wasted most of it, letting his father starve; in the end his father died miserably before his eyes; alas, it was horrible, the way his poor heart was wounded through and through and torn to bits. He did what he could for his sisters and went home, for his affairs recalled him.

For the impending Easter festival he was to write a new passion music; his envious rivals were eagerly awaiting it. Yet, as often as he sat down to work, he burst into a flood of tears; his tortured heart would not let him recover himself. He lay deeply depressed, buried among the leavings of this world. At length, by an effort, he tore himself free, stretching out his arms to heaven in an impassioned prayer; he filled his soul with the most sublime poetry, with a full and exultant hymn, and, in a marvelous inspiration, but still violently shaken emotionally, he set down a passion music which, with its deeply affecting melodies, embodying all the pains of suffering, will forever remain a masterpiece. His soul was like that of the invalid who, in a strange paroxysm, exhibits greater strength than the healthy man.

But after he had performed the oratorio in the cathedral on Easter Sunday, straining himself to the utmost in feverish agitation, he felt faint and exhausted. Like an unhealthy dew, a nervous weakness attacked all his fibers; he was ill for a time and died not long afterwards, in the bloom of his years.

Many a tear have I offered to his memory, and a strange feeling comes over me when I review his life. Why did Heaven ordain that the struggle between his lofty enthusiasm and the common misery of this earth should make him unhappy his whole life long and in the end tear quite apart the twofold nature of his mind and body?

The ways of Providence are hidden from us. But let us marvel once again at the diversity of those inspired beings whom Heaven sends into the world to serve the arts.

A Raphael brought forth in all innocence and artlessness works of the utmost ingenuity in which we see revealed the whole of Heaven; a Guido Reni, leading a wild gambler's life, created the gentlest and most sacred paintings; an Albrecht Dürer, a simple citizen of Nuremberg, in that same cell in which his wicked wife abused him daily, produced with the antlike industry of the mechanic art-works highly spiritual in content; yet Joseph, in whose harmonious music lies such mysterious beauty, differed from them all.

Alas, his lofty fantasy was what destroyed him. Shall I say that he was perhaps created rather to enjoy art than to practice it? Are those in whom art works silently and secretly, like an inner genius, not hindering their doings upon earth, perhaps more fortunately constituted? And must the ceaselessly inspired one, if he would be true artist, perhaps not weave his lofty fantasies, like a stout strand, boldly and firmly into this earthly life? Indeed, is not perhaps this incomprehensible creative power something altogether different and—as it now seems to me—something still more marvelous and godlike than the power of fantasy?

The spirit of art is and remains for man eternally a mystery, and he grows dizzy when he seeks to plumb its depths; at the same time, it is eternally an object for his highest admiration, as must be said of all the great things in this world.

But after these recollections of my Joseph I can write no more. I conclude my book—in the hope that it may have served to awaken good ideas in some one or other of my readers.

80. Jean Paul

From the Hesperus [1]

[*1795*]

I. GARDEN CONCERT BY STAMITZ

I SHOULD not have allowed the hairdresser [2] to sing and carry on so long, had I been able to use my hero, this entire Sunday, for anything more than a figurant; but the whole day he did nothing of any account except that, out of charity perhaps, he obliged our old friend Appel—by himself unpacking her boxes and chests of drawers—to prepare, printed with typographical splendor, the regular Sabbath edition of her body, which preferred dressing hams to dressing itself, as early as three o'clock in the afternoon; ordinarily she did not deliver this till after supper. The Jews believe that on the Sabbath they get a new Sabbath soul; into girls there enters at least one; into Appel there entered at least two.

But why should I today expect more action from my hero—from him, who today—absorbed in his dream-night and in the coming evening—moved by each friendly eye and by the urns of the spring which he had dreamed away—gently dissolved by the peaceful tepid summer which lay smiling and dying on the incense-burning altars of the mountains, on the

---

1 Text: *Sämtliche Werke*, 1. Abteilung, III (Weimar, 1929), 289–294. The scene is the garden of Chamberlain Le Baut in St. Lüne, an imaginary watering-place not far from Flachsenfingen, the capital of a likewise imaginary principality; the supposed date is Sunday, October 21, 1792. Chamberlain Le Baut has arranged a garden concert in honor of the birthday of his daughter Clothilde. Besides Clothilde, the assembled company includes Pastor Peter Eyman and his wife, their daughters Agathe and Apollonia (Appel), Chamberlain Le Baut and his second wife, and Victor (also called by his middle name, Sebastian), the hero of the novel, supposedly the heir of Lord Horion, an English peer, but actually the son of Pastor Eyman. Jean Paul admits that Victor is to some extent a self-portrait. Throughout the evening Victor is under the spell of a dream which had come to him the night before: in this he stands beneath the evening star upon a plain covered with forget-me-nots and encircled by pyramids of ice, tinted by the setting sun; Clothilde appears to him, deathlike and serene, led by winged children; flower-covered funeral mounds are seen to rise and fall; into these mounds Clothilde sinks to the heart; forget-me-nots cover her; butterflies, doves, and swans with outspread wings cling to the purple peaks; at the summit of the highest peak he sees Clothilde again, transfigured, her arms outstretched.

2 Meuseler, the local wig-maker, a member of the village choir.

meadows draped in muslin, and beneath the receding funeral procession of the birds, now hushed, and which, as the first cloud rose against the foliage, departed—from Victor, I repeat, who today, smiled upon sadly by one tender recollection after another, felt that till now he had been far too merry. He could only look upon the good souls about him with loving, shimmering eyes, turn these away again still more shimmering and say nothing and go out. Over his heart and over his every note stood the word *tremolando*. No one is more deeply sad than he who smiles too much; for if once this smiling stops, then anything has power over the compliant soul, and a foolish lullaby, a flute concerto—whose d- and f-sharp keys and embouchures are but two lips with which a shepherd boy is piping—sets free the well-remembered tears as a slight sound the threatening avalanche. It seemed to him as though the morning's dream did not at all allow him to address Clothilde; she seemed to him too sacred, still led on by winged children and seated by them on thrones of ice. Because today he simply had no tongue or ears for Le Baut's conversations in the realm of the morally dead, he would listen unobserved in the great leafy garden to Stamitz's concert [3] and, at the most, allow himself to be presented by chance. His second reason was his heart, created as a sounding board for music; by preference this absorbed the fleeting sounds undisturbed, hiding their effects from ordinary men, who in truth can no more do without the works of Goethe, Raphael, and Sacchini (and for no less important reasons) than without those of Löschenkohl.[4] It is true that emotion lifts us above the shame of showing emotion; but in his emotional moments he shunned and hated all attention to the attentions of others, for the devil smuggles vanity into the best of feelings, one often knows not how. In the night, in the shadow, tears fall more easily and evaporate more slowly.

The parson's wife encouraged him in everything; for she had secretly —sent to town, invited her son,[5] and trumped up a surprise in the garden.

At length the parson's family elevated itself to the leafy concert hall, little knowing how much they were looked down on by the family Le Baut, who accepted only noble metals and noble birth as tickets of admis-

---

3 In August 1792, Carl Stamitz played in concert at Hof, where Jean Paul lived during the writing of the *Hesperus* (see Hans Bach's introduction to Vol. 3 of the *Sämtliche Werke*, p. xxxiv).

4 Johann Löschenkohl, Viennese engraver and art dealer. "His things were thrown on the market with the utmost haste, yet despite their faulty drawing and coloring—time did not permit better workmanship—people actually fought over them. Of his engraving 'Maria Theresia on Her Death Bed,' 7,000 copies at two gulden each were sold within a few days. With his restless industrial activity he produced without tiring and was always offering something new—silhouettes, portraits in miniature, calendars; he opened a factory for the manufacture of boxes, of fans, of buttons, and was responsible for setting many fashions" [Wurzbach, *Biographisches Lexikon des Kaiserthums Oesterreich*].

5 Flamin, actually the illegitimate son of the local prince and of Le Baut's first wife, Clothilde's mother.

sion and who rated the parson's family highly as friends of milord [6] and Matthieu,[7] but would have rated them still more highly as their lap dogs.

Victor remained behind a moment in the garden of the parsonage, because it was still too light, also because he felt sorry for poor Apollonia; the latter, in gala attire, lonely and unobserved, was gazing out into space from the window of the little garden house and rocking his godchild [8] straight up and down, holding him now above her head, now below her waist. Like a small-town worthy Victor kept on his hat in the garden house, hoping to stimulate her courage by politeness. The child in arms is, as it were, the prompter and bellows treader of the nursemaid; the young Sebastian lent Appel sufficient reinforcement against the old one, and at length she ventured to speak and to observe that the godchild was a dear, good, beautiful "Bastel." "But," she added, "the *gnädige Frölen* (Clothilde) mustn't hear me say so; she wants us to call him Victor when she hears Father say 'Bastel.' " Then she made much of how Clothilde loved his godchild, of how she took the little rascal from her and smiled at him and kissed him; and everything she praised the panegyrist repeated with the little one. Nay, even the grown-up Sebastian imitated it, but on the tiny lips he sought only another's kisses; and perhaps in Appel's case his own were among the things for which she sought. A happier man took leave of a happier woman; for Cupid now sent one bright hope after another to his heart as messengers and every one bore the same message: "We do not belie thee, truly; have faith in us!"

At last Stamitz began to tune, a thing the grand-chamberlain's tenacious purse would certainly not have bothered about, since there were today no strangers present, if Clothilde had not asked to have this garden concert as the sole celebration of her birth night. Stamitz and his orchestra filled a lighted arbor—the noble auditorium sat in the nearest, most brightly lighted niche and wished it were already over—the common one sat further off and the chaplain, afraid of the catarrhal dewy floor, twined one leg around the other over the thigh—Clothilde and her Agathe rested in the darkest leafy box. Victor did not steal in until the overture announced to him the seat and the sitting of the company; in the furthest arbor, at the true aphelion, this comet found a place. The overture consisted of that musical scratching and scrawling—of that harmonious phraseology —of that firework-like crackling of passages sounding one against another —that I so highly recommend, if it is only in the overture. There it belongs; it is the fine rain that softens the heart for the bigger drops of the

---

6 Lord Horion.
7 Matthieu von Schleunes, son of the prince's Minister.

8 Sebastian, the Eymans' youngest child.

simpler sounds. Every emotion requires its exordium; and music clears the way for music—or for tears.

Stamitz climbed gradually—following a dramatic plan not drawn up by every capellmeister—from the ears into the heart, as though from Allegros into Adagios; this great composer sweeps in narrower and narrower circles about the breast that holds a heart until he finally reaches it and in ecstasy embraces it.

Without seeing his beloved, Horion trembled alone in the dark arbor into which a single dried-up branch let in the light of the moon and of its driving clouds. Nothing ever moved him more, while listening to music, than to watch the clouds course by. When, with his eyes and with the music, he followed these nebulous streams in their eternal flight about our shadow orb, when he relinquished to them all his joys and his desires; then, as in all his joys and sorrows, he thought of other clouds, of another flight, of other shadows than those above him, then his whole soul longed and yearned; but the music stilled the longing as the bullet in the mouth stills thirst, and harmony loosed the flooding tears from his full soul.

Faithful Victor! in man there is a great desire, never fulfilled; it has no name, it seeks no object, it is nothing that you call it nor any joy; but it returns, when on a summer's night you look toward the north or toward the distant mountains, or when there is moonlight on the earth, or when the heavens are bright with stars, or when you are very happy. This great monstrous desire exalts our spirit, but with sorrows: Alas, prostrate here below, we are hurled into the air like epileptics. But this desire, to which nothing can give a name, our songs and harmonies name it to the human spirit—the longing spirit then weeps the more vehemently and can control itself no longer and calls amid the music in sobbing rapture: Truly, all that you name, I lack.

The enigmatic mortal likewise has a nameless, monstrous fear that has no object, that is awakened when one hears ghostly apparitions, and that is sometimes felt when one but speaks of it. . . .

With silent tears whose flowing no one saw, Horion abandoned his battered heart to the lofty Adagios, which spread themselves with warm eider-down wings over all his wounds. All that he loved came now into his shadow-arbor, his oldest and his youngest friend—he hears the raging of life's thunderstorms, but the hands of friendship reach out to one another and clasp and in the second life they still hold one another incorrupt.

Each note seemed a celestial echo of his dream, answering to beings whom one did not see and did not hear. . . .

He could not possibly stay longer in this dark enclosure with his burning fantasies and at this too great distance from the pianissimo. He approached the music—almost too boldly and too closely—through a leafy corridor, leaning far forward through the foliage in order at last to see Clothilde in the distant green shimmer. . . .

Ah, he did see her! But too lovely, too celestial! He saw, not the pensive eye, the cold mouth, the tranquil form that forbade so much and desired so little; for the first time he saw her mouth enveloped by a sweet harmonious pain in an indescribably touching smile—for the first time he saw her eyes weighed down under a great tear, like forget-me-nots bent under a tear of rain. Oh, this kind creature indeed concealed her finest feelings most of all! But the first tear in a beloved eye is too much for an overly tender heart. . . . Victor knelt down, overpowered by reverence and bliss, before the noble soul and lost himself in the shadowy weeping figure and in the weeping sounds. And then, when he saw her features grow pale, for the green foliage cast upon her lips and cheeks a deathlike reflection from the lanterns—and when his dream appeared again and in it the Clothilde who had sunk beneath the flowery mound— and when his soul dissolved in dreams, in sorrows, in joys, and in desires for the creature who was consecrating her birthday feast with pious tears, then was it still necessary to his dissolution that the violin ceased sounding and that the second harmonica, the *viole d'amour*, sent forth its sphere harmonics to his naked, inflamed, and throbbing heart? Oh, the aching of this bliss appeased him, and he thanked the creator of this melodic Eden for having relieved his bosom, his sighs, and his tears with the harmonica's highest notes, which with an unknown force split into tears the heart of man, as high notes burst a glass; amid such sounds, after such sounds, there was no further place for words; the full soul was enshrouded by leaves and night and tears—the swelling speechless heart absorbed the tones unto itself and took the outer tones for inner ones—and at the end the tones played only softly, like zephyrs, about his listless rapture, and only within his expiring inner self did there still falter the overly blissful wish: "Alas, Clothilde, if only I might today give up to you this mute and glowing heart—alas, if only I might, on this memorable heavenly evening, sink dying at your feet with this trembling soul and speak the words, 'I love thee!'"

And when he thought of her festival, and of her letter to Maienthal,[9]

---

[9] In this letter to her tutor, Clothilde had written: "Today in the garden I thought of your Maienthal with a longing that was almost too sad; Herr Sebastian often reminds me of it, for he appears to have had a teacher much like my own." Victor now knows that Clothilde's tutor Emanuel and his own tutor Dahore are one and the same.

which had paid him the high compliment of calling him Emanuel's pupil,
and of little signs of her respect for him, and of the beautiful companionship of his heart and hers—then amid the music there came to him vividly
and for the first time the bright hope of winning this ennobled heart, and
with this hope the harmonica tones flowed like radiating echoes far over
the whole future of his life. . . .

* * * * *

2. FRANZ KOCH'S DOUBLE MOUTH-HARMONICA [10]

I jumped to my feet at the name Franz Koch.[11] If one of my readers
is a guest at Carlsbad for the waters, or His Majesty King William II
of Prussia, or a member of his court, or the Elector of Saxony, or the Duke
of Brunswick, or some other princely personage, he will have heard the
excellent Koch, a modest soldier on half pay who travels about everywhere, playing his instrument. This last, which he calls "double mouth-
harmonica," consists in an improved pair of simultaneously played Jew's
harps, which he exchanges after every piece of music. His way of playing
the Jew's harp compares with the old way as do the bells of musical glasses
with a servant's bell. It is my duty to persuade those of my readers whose
imaginations have wren's wings, or who are lithopaedic (stillborn), at
least from the heart out, or who have eardrums only to drum on, to persuade such readers, with what few oratorical powers I have, to throw
the said Franz out of doors if he should come and offer to hum before
them. For there is nothing to him, and the most miserable viola or straw-
fiddle screams, in my opinion, more shrilly; indeed, his music is so delicate
that in Carlsbad he never strikes up before more than twelve customers
at one time, it being impossible to sit close enough to him, and when he
plays his best pieces he actually has the light carried out so that neither
eye nor ear may disturb the fantasy. But should one reader be otherwise
disposed—a poet, perhaps—or a lover—or very delicate—or like Victor—

---

10 Text: *ibid.*, IV (Weimar, 1929), 52–58.
The scene is the house of Chamberlain Le Baut;
the supposed date is Tuesday, April 2, 1793.

11 "Franz (Paul) Koch, celebrated German
virtuoso on the Jew's harp, was born in 1761 at
Mittersill near Salzburg and as a boy learned
the book-binding trade. In 1782 recruiting officers
induced the itinerant worker to come to Magdeburg, where he was at once pressed into service
as a grenadier. In this capacity an officer chanced
to hear him play his Jew's harp (mouth harmonica) and spoke to others of his amazement at
Koch's skill, so that the soldier's reputation soon
spread even as far as Berlin and Potsdam. King
Friedrich Wilhelm II sent for Koch, listened to
him play, and ordered him discharged from his
involuntary service in the army. Encouraged from
every quarter, Koch now went on tour and attracted uncommon attention, so that even Jean
Paul (in his *Hesperus*) took note of him. The
year of his death is not known. A more detailed
account of his life appears in Schummel's al-
manac for 1793 (p. 322)" [Mendel, *Musikalisches
Conversations-Lexikon*]. Like Stamitz, Koch
played in concert at Hof in August 1792.

or like myself, then let him hearken unhesitatingly, his soul at peace and ready to melt, to Franz Koch—or—since at this precise moment he is not to be had—to me.

My witty English friend [12] had sent this harmonist to Victor with a card: "The bearer is the bearer of an echo which he keeps in his pocket." Victor, on this account, preferred to take him over to Clothilde, the friend of all musical beauty, in order that her departure might not deprive her of this hour of melody. He felt as though he were going down a long aisle in a church when he entered Clothilde's Santa Casa; her simple room, like Our Lady's, was enclosed within a temple. She had already finished her black finery. A black costume is a lovely darkening of the sun, in the midst of which one cannot take one's eyes off it. Victor, who with his Sinese awe of this color brought to this magic a defenseless soul, a kindled eye, grew pale and confused at Clothilde's sympathetic features, over which the trace of a recently fallen rain of sorrow hovered like a rainbow against a bright blue sky. Hers was not the serenity of diversion—which every girl derives from dressing herself—it was the serenity of a pious soul filled with love and patience. He was embarrassed at having to walk among thistles of two sorts—the painted ones on the parquet, on which he was continually stepping, and the satiric ones of the nice observers about him, against which he was continually pricking himself. Her stepmother [13] was still busied with the plastering and painting of her body corruptible, and the evangelist [14] was in her dressing room as toilet acolyte and collaborator. Hence Clothilde had still time to hear the mouth-harmonist; and the chamberlain offered himself to his daughter and to our hero—for he was a father who knew what to do where his daughter was concerned—as a part of the audience, although he could make little of music, dinner music and dance music excepted.

Not until now did Victor gather, from Clothilde's joy over the musician he had brought with him, that her harmonious heart vibrated gladly to music; altogether, he was often wrong about her because she—like you, dearest ———, expressed with silence both her highest praise and highest blame. She asked her father, who had heard the mouth-harmonica before in Carlsbad, to give her and Victor an idea of it—he gave one: "It expresses in masterly fashion both the fortissimo and the piano-dolce and, like the single harmonica, it lends itself most readily to the Adagio." To this she replied—on Victor's arm, which was guiding her to a quiet room, darkened for the music—"Music is perhaps too good for drinking songs

---

12 "Cato the Elder," an illegitimate son of the local prince.

13 Le Baut's second wife.
14 Matthieu von Schleunes.

and for the expression of merriment. Just as suffering ennobles a man, unfolding him by the little pricks it gives him as regularly as one splits open with a knife the bud of a carnation that it may bloom with bursting, so music, as a sort of artificial suffering, takes the place of the genuine variety." "Is genuine suffering so unusual?" Victor asked, in the darkened room, lighted only by a single wax candle. He sat down next to Clothilde, and her father seated himself opposite them.

Blissful hour that thou once broughtest to my soul with the echoing music of thy harmonica—speed by once more, and may the reverberations of that echo again sound about thee!

Scarcely had the modest quiet virtuoso laid the implement of enchantment to his lips than Victor felt that (while the light still shone) he might not, as he usually did, paint scenes of his own to each Adagio and adapt to each piece particular inspirations from his poems. For an infallible means of giving music the omnipotence that belongs to it is to make of it an accompaniment to one's own inner melody, turning instrumental music into vocal, as it were, inarticulate sounds into articulate ones, not permitting the lovely succession of tones, to which no definite object lends alphabet or language, to glide from our hearts, leaving them bathed but not made tender. Hence, when the loveliest sounds that ever flowed from human lips as consonants (or consonances) of the soul began to flutter from the trembling mouth-harmonica; when he felt that these tiny rings of steel, as though the frame and fingerboard of his heart, would make their convulsions his; he forced his feverish heart, whose every wound bled afresh today, apart from the music, to contract itself against it and to paint itself no pictures, merely so that he might not burst into tears before the light was taken away.

Higher and higher rose the dragnet of uplifting tones, carrying his captive heart aloft. One melancholy reminiscence after another, in this spectral hour of the past, called out to him: "Do not suppress me, give me my tear." All his pent-up tears collected about his heart, and his whole inner self, lifted off the bottom, swam gently in them. Yet he composed himself: "Canst thou not yet deny thyself (he asked), not even a moistened eye? No, with a dry eye receive this muffled echo of thy whole breast, receive this Arcadian resonance and all these tearful sounds into your distraught soul." In the midst of this veiled distillation, which he often took for fortitude, it always seemed to him as though there were addressing him, from distant parts, a breaking voice whose words had the rhythm of verse; once again the breaking voice addressed him: "Are not these tones composed of faded hopes? Do not these sounds run one into another, Horion, like the days of man? O look not on thy heart! There, as it turns to dust, the shimmering days of yore have etched themselves as in a mist!" Nevertheless he replied, still quietly: "Life is after all too short for the two tears—for the tear of woe and for the other." . . . But now—as the white dove that Emanuel saw falling in the cemetery [15] sped through the images of his recollection—as he thought: "In my dream of Clothilde this dove was already fluttering and clinging to the iceberg; alas, it is the image of the fading angel beside me!"—as the music fluttered more and more quietly and at length stole back and forth among the whispering foliage of a funeral wreath—and as the breaking voice returned and said: "Dost not recall the familiar sounds? Lo, before her birthday feast they were already in thy dreams and there they lowered to the heart into the grave the sick soul beside thee, and she left thee but an eye filled with tears, a soul filled with grief!"—"No, more than that she did not leave me," his weary heart repeated haltingly, and all the tears he had held back came rushing to his eyes in streams. . . .

But, since the light had just been carried from the room, the first stream fell unnoticed into the lap of night.

The harmonica began the melody of the dead—"Wie sie so sanft ruhn." [16] Alas, in sounds like these the spent waves of the sea of eternity beat against the hearts of the somber watchers standing on the shore and yearning to put forth! Now, Horion, shalt thou be wafted by a sounding breeze out of the rainy mist of life into the clear hereafter. What sounds are these that fill the far-off fields of Eden? Do they not hark back, dissipated as breath, to distant flowers and flow, swollen by the echo, about the swanlike breast that, blissfully expiring, swims on pinions and draw it from melodic tide to tide and sink with it into the distant flowers that a mist of perfumes fills, and, in the dark perfume, does not the soul catch fire like a sunset before it blissfully departs?

Ah, Horion, does the earth still rest beneath us that bears its funeral mounds around the breadth of life? Is it in earthly air that these sounds vibrate? O Music, thou who bringest past and future so near our wounds with their flying flames, art thou the evening breeze from this life or the morning air of the life to come? In truth, thine accents are echoes, gath-

---

[15] A reference to an earlier letter in which Emanuel gives an account of a conversation between himself and the blind Julius, Lord Horion's son, and foretells the circumstances of his own death. " 'Now a white dove flies over the deep blue like a great dazzling snowflake . . . Now it circles about the sparkling golden tip of the lightening-rod, as though about a glimmering star hung in the sunlit sky—it weaves and weaves and sinks and disappears among the tall flowers of the cemetery . . . Julius, didst thou feel nothing as I spoke? Alas, the white dove was perhaps thy angel [Clothilde]; perhaps this is why thy heart dissolved today at its approach" (ibid., III, 400).

[16] "The Cemetery" (Der Gottesacker), words by A. C. Stockmann, music by Pastor F. B. Beneken (1787); cf. Max Friedländer, Das deutsche Lied im 18. Jahrhundert (Stuttgart, 1902), I, 318; II, 130; Musikbeispiel 181.

ered by angels from the joyous sounds of a second world to bring to our mute hearts, to our deserted night, the faded spring song of the soaring heavens! And thou, re-echoing sound of the harmonica, thou comest to us truly from a shout that, ringing from heaven to heaven, dies out at last in that remotest, stillest heaven of them all, consisting only of a deep, broad, eternally silent rapture. . . .

"Eternally silent rapture," repeated Horion's melted soul, whose delight I have in the foregoing made my own, "yes, there the country lies, there where I lift up mine eyes to the all-benevolent and hold out my arms to her, to this weary soul, to this great heart—then, Clothilde, will I fall on my heart, then will I cling to thee forever, and the flood of that eternally silent rapture shall envelop us. Breathe once again toward life, ye earthly tones, between my breast and hers, then let there float toward me over your clear waves a tiny night, an undulating silhouette, and I will look on it and say: 'This was my life'—then will I say more softly, weeping more intensely: 'Indeed, man is unhappy, but only on the earth.' "

Oh, if there be a mortal over whom, at these last words, memory draws great rain clouds, then I say to him: Beloved brother, beloved sister, I am today as touched as thou, I respect the grief thou hidest—ah, thou forgivest me and I thee. . . .

The song stopped and died away. How silent now the darkness! All sighing was clothed in halting breath. Only the nebulous stars of feeling sparkled brightly through the gloom. No one could see whose eyes had wept. Victor gazed into the still black air before him, which a few moments earlier had been filled with hanging gardens of sound, ebbing air castles of the human ear, miniature heavens, and which remained there as a naked, blackened scaffolding for fireworks.

But the harmonica soon filled this gloom again with a mirage of other worlds. Ah, why did it have to hit precisely on "Vergissmeinnicht," the melody that gnawed at Victor's heart,[17] repeating the lines to him as though he were himself repeating them to Clothilde: "Forget me not, now that relentless fate calls thee from me—Forget me not, if loose and cooling earth engulf this heart that gently beat for thee—Think it is I, if echo answers in thy soul: 'Forget me not.' " . . . Oh, if after this these sounds entwine themselves in waving flowers, flow back from one past time into another, run more and more softly through the departed years

---

17 Words by Franz von Knebel, music by Lorenz Schneider (1792); cf. Friedländer, *op. cit.,* II, 448. Schneider's music was at first generally attributed to Mozart and repeatedly published un-der his name (cf., Köchel, Anhang 246). In the continuation of our first excerpt (omitted above), Victor and Clothilde had heard the melody played by Stamitz.

that lie behind mankind—finally murmur beneath the morning dawn of life—roll on unheard below the cradle of mankind—grow cold in our chill twilight and dry up in the midnight where no one of us has been; then, deeply moved, man ceases to conceal his sighs and his unending sorrows.

The silent angel beside Victor could no longer veil them, and Victor heard Clothilde's first sigh.

Then he took her by the hand, as though to support her, hovering, above an open grave.

She let him keep it, and her pulse beat tremulously in unison with his.

At length the last note of the song projected its melodious circles in the ether and flowed expanding over all past time—then a distant echo wrapped it in a fluttering breeze and wafted it through deeper echoes to that last echo lying round about the heavens—then the sound expired and sped as a soul into Clothilde's sigh.

At this, her first tear fell, like a burning heart, on Victor's hand.

.   .   .   .   .

81. E. T. A. Hoffmann

A standard-bearer of German romanticism, Hoffmann was born in 1776 at Königsberg and died in 1822 at Berlin. His talents were manifold: he was a poet, a critic, a composer, a theater manager, a draftsman, and a public servant. Best remembered for his fantastic novels, Hoffmann was deeply devoted to music and for some time made music his profession. Among his works for the stage the most important is the opera *Undine* (1813–1814). Hoffmann was one of the fathers of modern musical journalism and in this field opened the way to Schumann and Wagner. His literary works testify to the deeply musical nature of his poetic inspiration. In turn, Hoffmann's poetic visions have inspired musical works of the most disparate character. Schumann's *Kreisleriana*, Offenbach's *Les Contes d'Hoffmann*, Busoni's *Die Brautwahl* are cases in point.

Beethoven's Instrumental Music [1]

[1813]

WHEN WE speak of music as an independent art, should we not always restrict our meaning to instrumental music, which, scorning every aid, every admixture of another art (the art of poetry), gives pure expression to music's specific nature, recognizable in this form alone? It is the most romantic of all the arts—one might almost say, the only genuinely romantic one—for its sole subject is the infinite. The lyre of Orpheus opened the portals of Orcus—music discloses to man an unknown realm, a world that has nothing in common with the external sensual world that surrounds

---

[1] Text: *Sämtliche Werke*, ed. by C. G. von Maassen, I (Munich & Leipzig, 1908), 55–58, 60–61, 62–64. As published in 1814 among the "Kreisleriana" of the *Fantasiestücke in Callot's Manier* (and earlier, anonymously, in the *Zeitung* *für die elegante Welt* for December 1813), this essay combines and condenses two reviews published anonymously in the *Allgemeine musikalische Zeitung* (Leipzig) for July 1810 and March 1813.

him, a world in which he leaves behind him all definite feelings to sur-render himself to an inexpressible longing.

Have you even so much as suspected this specific nature, you miserable composers of instrumental music, you who have laboriously strained your-selves to represent definite emotions, even definite events? How can it ever have occurred to you to treat after the fashion of the plastic arts the art diametrically opposed to plastic? Your sunrises, your tempests, your *Batailles des trois Empereurs*,[2] and the rest, these, after all, were surely quite laughable aberrations, and they have been punished as they well deserved by being wholly forgotten.

In song, where poetry, by means of words, suggests definite emotions, the magic power of music acts as does the wondrous elixir of the wise, a few drops of which make any drink more palatable and more lordly. Every passion—love, hatred, anger, despair, and so forth, just as the opera gives them to us—is clothed by music with the purple luster of romanticism, and even what we have undergone in life guides us out of life into the realm of the infinite.

As strong as this is music's magic, and, growing stronger and stronger, it had to break each chain that bound it to another art.

That gifted composers have raised instrumental music to its present high estate is due, we may be sure, less to the more readily handled means of expression (the greater perfection of the instruments, the greater virtuosity of the players) than to the more profound, more intimate recognition of music's specific nature.

Mozart and Haydn, the creators of our present instrumental music, were the first to show us the art in its full glory; the man who then looked on it with all his love and penetrated its innermost being is—Beethoven! The instrumental compositions of these three masters breathe a similar romantic spirit—this is due to their similar intimate understanding of the specific nature of the art; in the character of their compositions there is none the less a marked difference.

In Haydn's writing there prevails the expression of a serene and child-like personality. His symphonies lead us into vast green woodlands, into a merry, gaily colored throng of happy mortals. Youths and maidens float past in a circling dance; laughing children, peering out from behind the trees, from behind the rose bushes, pelt one another playfully with flowers. A life of love, of bliss like that before the Fall, of eternal youth; no sor-row, no suffering, only a sweet melancholy yearning for the beloved object

---

2 Perhaps Hoffmann is thinking of Louis Jadin's "La grande bataille d'Austerlitz," published in an arrangement for the piano by Kühnel of Leip-zig in 1807 or earlier.

that floats along, far away, in the glow of the sunset and comes no nearer and does not disappear—nor does night fall while it is there, for it is itself the sunset in which hill and valley are aglow.

Mozart leads us into the heart of the spirit realm. Fear takes us in its grasp, but without torturing us, so that it is more an intimation of the infinite. Love and melancholy call to us with lovely spirit voices; night comes on with a bright purple luster, and with inexpressible longing we follow those figures which, waving us familiarly into their train, soar through the clouds in eternal dances of the spheres.[a]

Thus Beethoven's instrumental music opens up to us also the realm of the monstrous and the immeasurable. Burning flashes of light shoot through the deep night of this realm, and we become aware of giant shadows that surge back and forth, driving us into narrower and narrower confines until they destroy *us*—but not the pain of that endless longing in which each joy that has climbed aloft in jubilant song sinks back and is swallowed up, and it is only in this pain, which consumes love, hope, and happiness but does not destroy them, which seeks to burst our breasts with a many-voiced consonance of all the passions, that we live on, enchanted beholders of the supernatural!

Romantic taste is rare, romantic talent still rarer, and this is doubtless why there are so few to strike that lyre whose sound discloses the wondrous realm of the romantic.

Haydn grasps romantically what is human in human life; he is more commensurable, more comprehensible for the majority.

Mozart calls rather for the superhuman, the wondrous element that abides in inner being.

Beethoven's music sets in motion the lever of fear, of awe, of horror, of suffering, and wakens just that infinite longing which is the essence of romanticism. He is accordingly a completely romantic composer, and is not this perhaps the reason why he has less success with vocal music, which excludes the character of indefinite longing, merely representing emotions defined by words as emotions experienced in the realm of the infinite?

The musical rabble is oppressed by Beethoven's powerful genius; it seeks in vain to oppose it. But knowing critics, looking about them with a superior air, assure us that we may take their word for it as men of great intellect and deep insight that, while the excellent Beethoven can scarcely be denied a very fertile and lively imagination, he does not know how to bridle it! Thus, they say, he no longer bothers at all to select or to shape his ideas, but, following the so-called daemonic method, he dashes every-

---

[a] Mozart's Symphony in E-flat major, known as the "Swan Song."

thing off exactly as his ardently active imagination dictates it to him. Yet how does the matter stand if it is *your* feeble observation alone that the deep inner continuity of Beethoven's every composition eludes? If it is *your* fault alone that you do not understand the master's language as the initiated understand it, that the portals of the innermost sanctuary remain closed to you? The truth is that, as regards self-possession, Beethoven stands quite on a par with Haydn and Mozart and that, separating his ego from the inner realm of harmony, he rules over it as an absolute monarch. In Shakespeare, our knights of the aesthetic measuring-rod have often bewailed the utter lack of inner unity and inner continuity, although for those who look more deeply there springs forth, issuing from a single bud, a beautiful tree, with leaves, flowers, and fruit; thus, with Beethoven, it is only after a searching investigation of his instrumental music that the high self-possession inseparable from true genius and nourished by the study of the art stands revealed.

Can there be any work of Beethoven's that confirms all this to a higher degree than his indescribably profound, magnificent symphony in C minor? How this wonderful composition, in a climax that climbs on and on, leads the listener imperiously forward into the spirit world of the infinite! . . . No doubt the whole rushes like an ingenious rhapsody past many a man, but the soul of each thoughtful listener is assuredly stirred, deeply and intimately, by a feeling that is none other than that unutterable portentous longing, and until the final chord—indeed, even in the moments that follow it—he will be powerless to step out of that wondrous spirit realm where grief and joy embrace him in the form of sound. The internal structure of the movements, their execution, their instrumentation, the way in which they follow one another—everything contributes to a single end; above all, it is the intimate interrelationship among the themes that engenders that unity which alone has the power to hold the listener firmly in a single mood. This relationship is sometimes clear to the listener when he overhears it in the connecting of two movements or discovers it in the fundamental bass they have in common; a deeper relationship which does not reveal itself in this way speaks at other times only from mind to mind, and it is precisely this relationship that prevails between sections of the two Allegros and the Minuet and which imperiously proclaims the self-possession of the master's genius.

How deeply thy magnificent compositions for the piano have impressed themselves upon my soul, thou sublime master; how shallow and insignificant now all seems to me that is not thine, or by the gifted Mozart or that mighty genius, Sebastian Bach! With what joy I received thy seventieth work, the two glorious trios, for I knew full well that after a little practice I should soon hear them in truly splendid style. And in truth, this evening things went so well with me that even now, like a man who wanders in the mazes of a fantastic park, woven about with all manner of exotic trees and plants and marvelous flowers, and who is drawn further and further in, I am powerless to find my way out of the marvelous turns and windings of thy trios. The lovely siren voices of these movements of thine, resplendent in their many-hued variety, lure me on and on. The gifted lady who indeed honored me, Capellmeister Kreisler,[3] by playing today the first trio in such splendid style, the gifted lady before whose piano I still sit and write, has made me realize quite clearly that only what the mind produces calls for respect and that all else is out of place.

Just now I have repeated at the piano from memory certain striking transitions from the two trios.

. . . . .

How well the master has understood the specific character of the instrument and fostered it in the way best suited to it!

A simple but fruitful theme, songlike, susceptible to the most varied contrapuntal treatments, curtailments, and so forth, forms the basis of each movement; all remaining subsidiary themes and figures are intimately related to the main idea in such a way that the details all interweave, arranging themselves among the instruments in highest unity. Such is the structure of the whole, yet in this artful structure there alternate in restless flight the most marvelous pictures in which joy and grief, melancholy and ecstasy, come side by side or intermingled to the fore. Strange figures begin a merry dance, now floating off into a point of light, now splitting apart, flashing and sparkling, evading and pursuing one another in various combinations, and at the center of the spirit realm thus disclosed the intoxicated soul gives ear to the unfamiliar language and understands the most mysterious premonitions that have stirred it.

That composer alone has truly mastered the secrets of harmony who knows how, by their means, to work upon the human soul; for him, numerical proportions, which to the dull grammarian are no more than cold, lifeless problems in arithmetic, become magical compounds from which to conjure up a magic world.

Despite the good nature that prevails, especially in the first trio, not even excepting the melancholy Largo, Beethoven's genius is in the last

---

3 The eccentric, half-mad musician from whose literary remains Hoffmann pretends to have taken his "Kreisleriana." Schumann borrows the title of his Opus 16 from these sketches of Hoffmann's (published in two groups as a part of his *Fantasiestücke in Callot's Manier*).

analysis serious and solemn. It is as though the master thought that, in speaking of deep mysterious things—even when the spirit, intimately familiar with them, feels itself joyously and gladly uplifted—one may not use an ordinary language, only a sublime and glorious one; the dance of the priests of Isis can be only an exultant hymn. Where instrumental music is to produce its effect simply through itself as music and is by no means to serve a definite dramatic purpose, it must avoid all trivial facetiousness, all frivolous *lazzi*. A deep temperament seeks, for the intimations of that joy which, an import from an unknown land, more glorious and more beautiful than here in our constricted world, enkindles an inner, blissful life within our breasts, a higher expression than can be given to it by mere words, proper only to our circumscribed earthly air. This seriousness, in all of Beethoven's works for instruments and for the piano, is in itself enough to forbid all those breakneck passages up and down for the two hands which fill our piano music in the latest style, all the queer leaps, the farcical capriccios, the notes towering high above the staff on their five- and six-line scaffolds.

On the side of mere digital dexterity, Beethoven's compositions for the piano really present no special difficulty, for every player must be presumed to have in his fingers the few runs, triplet figures, and whatever else is called for; nevertheless, their performance is on the whole quite difficult. Many a so-called virtuoso condemns this music, objecting that it is "very difficult" and into the bargain "very ungrateful."

Now, as regards difficulty, the correct and fitting performance of a work of Beethoven's asks nothing more than that one should understand him, that one should enter deeply into his being, that—conscious of one's own consecration—one should boldly dare to step into the circle of the magical phenomena that his powerful spell has evoked. He who is not conscious of this consecration, who regards sacred Music as a mere game, as a mere entertainment for an idle hour, as a momentary stimulus for dull ears, or as a means of self-ostentation—let him leave Beethoven's music alone. Only to such a man, moreover, does the objection "most ungrateful" apply. The true artist lives only in the work that he has understood as the composer meant it and that he then performs. He is above putting his own personality forward in any way, and all his endeavors are directed toward a single end—that all the wonderful enchanting pictures and apparitions that the composer has sealed into his work with magic power may be called into active life, shining in a thousand colors, and that they may surround mankind in luminous sparkling circles and, enkindling its

imagination, its innermost soul, may bear it in rapid flight into the faraway
spirit realm of sound.[4]

---

4 Hoffmann's essay was brought to Beethoven's
attention in February or March 1820 by someone
who wrote, during a conversation with him: "In
the *Fantasiestücke* of Hoffmann there is much
talk about you. Hoffmann used to be the music-
director in Bromberg; now he is a state coun-
sellor. They give operas by him in Berlin." On
the strength of this, evidently, Beethoven wrote
the following letter to Hoffmann on March 23,
1820:

Through Herr ———, I seize this opportunity
of approaching a man of your intellectual attainments. You have even written about my humble
self, and our Herr ——— showed me in his album
some lines of yours about me. I must assume,
then, that you take a certain interest in me. Permit me to say that, from a man like yourself,
gifted with such distinguished qualities, this is
very gratifying to me. I wish you the best of
everything and remain, sir,
              Your devoted and respectful
                         Beethoven.

82. E. T. A. Hoffmann

The Poet and the Composer [1]

[1819–1821]

[From Die Serapions-Brüder]

THE ENEMY was at the gates, cannons thundered all about, and grenades, spouting fire, cut whistling through the air. The citizens, their faces pale with fear, ran to their lodgings, and the empty streets echoed with the clattering hoofs of the cavalry patrols, charging hither and yon, cursing and driving from the rear those soldiers who had been left behind. Only Ludwig sat in his back room, completely immersed in the magnificent, varicolored world that his fancy had revealed to him before the piano; he had just finished a symphony in which he had endeavored to fix in black and white all the music of his innermost self, a work which, like Beethoven's compositions in this vein, was to speak in god-like language of the sublime wonders of that faraway romantic land in which we live perishing in inexpressible yearning; indeed, which was itself, like one of those wonders, to enter into our narrow, needy life and to entice out of it, with a lovely siren song, those willingly surrendering to it. Just then his landlady came into the room, reproaching him that in the midst of the general distress and emergency he could only play the piano and asking him whether he wanted to be shot to death there in his attic room. Ludwig really did not understand the woman until at that moment a grenade, roaring by, tore away a piece of the roof and broke in the windowpanes with a clatter; then the landlady ran screaming and howling down the stairs to the cellar with Ludwig hastening after her, carrying under his arm his most precious possession, the score of his symphony. Here the entire company of the house was assembled. In an attack of generosity otherwise by no means characteristic, the innkeeper who lived on the ground floor had sacrificed a couple of dozen bottles of his best wine; the women, trembling, hesitant, but as usual mindful of the needs and nourishment of the body, had brought in knitting-baskets many a dainty morsel from their

---

1 Text: *Sämtliche Werke,* ed. by C. G. von Maassen. The *Serapions-Brüder,* a collection of short tales set in the framework of a connecting narrative, is named for a little group of friends who meet once a week to exchange stories. The original members of this "club" are Lothar, Theodor (a composer), Ottmar, and Cyprian; the present story is told by Theodor.

kitchen surplus; one ate, one drank, one was soon transported from a state exalted by fear and anxiety to that sociable, comfortable state in which one neighbor, pressing himself against another, seeks security and thinks he has found it, and in which, as it were, that mincing, formal dance step which convention teaches is swallowed up in the great waltz to which the bronze fist of destiny beats time. Forgotten was the precarious situation, even the apparent mortal danger, and lively scraps of conversation poured from eager lips. Inmates of the house who, meeting one another on the stairs, scarcely touched their hats, sat side by side, hand in hand, revealing their innermost selves in hearty, mutual interest. The shots fell more sparingly, and some were already speaking of going upstairs, since the street seemed to be becoming safe. An old veteran went further and, after obliging by way of introduction with a few instructive words on the art of fortification among the ancient Romans and on the effect of catapults and, from more modern times, touching approvingly on Vauban, was on the point of demonstrating that fear was entirely uncalled for, since the house lay quite beyond the line of fire, when a bullet, striking the bricks that shielded the ventilator, hurled them into the cellar. No one was hurt, however, and when the old soldier sprang, glass in hand, upon the table, from off which the bricks had knocked the bottles, and defied the absent bullet, all took courage anew.

This, incidentally, was the last alarm; the night passed quietly, and the next morning one learned that the army had occupied a new position, voluntarily evacuating the city to the enemy. While one was leaving the cellar, hostile troops were already roaming through the town, and a public notice promised the inhabitants peace and security of possession. Ludwig threw himself into the motley crowd which, curious as to the new drama, was going to meet the approaching hostile general, who presently rode through the gate, heralded by the merry calls of trumpets and surrounded by brilliantly dressed guards.

Scarcely could Ludwig believe his eyes when, among the adjutants, he caught sight of Ferdinand, his dearly beloved academic friend, who, wearing a plain uniform and carrying his left arm in a sling, curvetted by quite close to him on a magnificent dun horse. "It is he—it is truly, surely he himself!" Ludwig called out involuntarily. Having vainly sought to follow his friend, whose flying steed had carried him quickly away, Ludwig thoughtfully hurried back to his room; but no work would move from the spot; the appearance of his old friend, whom he had entirely lost sight of for years, filled his thoughts, and as though in a bright glow there came back to him that blissful youth which he and the sociable Ferdinand had wasted together. In those days Ferdinand had not shown the slightest inclination toward the military life; he had lived solely for his muse, and many a gifted piece of writing had borne witness to his poetic vocation. For this reason, his friend's transformation was the less understandable to Ludwig, who burned with desire to talk with him without knowing how to set about looking for him.

Now the place became more and more lively, a large division of the hostile troops passed by, and at their head rode the allied princes, who were granting themselves at this point a few days of rest. But the greater the turmoil became at main headquarters, the less hope Ludwig retained of seeing his friend again, until at length, in an out-of-the-way, little-patronized café where he was in the habit of taking his frugal supper, his friend, with a loud cry of the utmost joy, fell unexpectedly into his arms. Ludwig remained silent, for a certain disquieting feeling had made the longed-for moment of reunion a bitter one. He felt as one sometimes does in a dream when one embraces loved ones only to have them at once strangely change themselves, keenest joys giving way in an instant to mocking illusions.

The gentle son of the muse, the poet of many a romantic stanza which Ludwig then had clothed with harmony, stood before him in his high, plumed helmet, his heavy, clanking saber at his side, denying even his own voice, calling out in a harsh, rough tone. Ludwig's gloomy gaze fell on Ferdinand's wounded arm and from that passed upward to the medal of honor which he wore at his breast. Then Ferdinand embraced him with his right arm, pressing him violently and passionately to his breast.

(FERDINAND) I know what it is that you are thinking, what it is that you feel at this reunion!

The Fatherland called, and I dared not hesitate to answer. With the joy, with the burning enthusiasm which a sacred cause kindles in every breast that cowardice does not brand a slave's, this hand, otherwise used only to the quill, grasped the sword! I have shed my blood, and only the chance which brought it about that I did my duty under the eyes of the prince, won me this medal. But believe me, Ludwig, those lyre strings which have so often sounded within me, whose tones have so often spoken to you, are still unharmed; indeed, after horrible and bloody battling, on my lonely post, while the horsemen lay in the bivouac about the watchfire, I wrote with high enthusiasm many a song that uplifted and strengthened me in my glorious calling, the defense of honor and freedom.

At these words, Ludwig's inner hostility gave way; and, when Ferdinand had stepped with him into a private room and had laid aside helmet and saber, it seemed to him as though his friend had merely tried his patience with a strange disguise that he had now thrown off. Now, while the two friends consumed the modest repast that had been brought in to them in the meantime, and while their glasses clinked merrily one against another, a joyous mood came over them, the good old days, with all their bright lights and colors, surrounded them, and all those bewitching fancies which their common artistic urge had as it were conjured up with powerful spell returned once more in the resplendent brilliance of their renewed youth. Ferdinand inquired incidentally as to what Ludwig had composed in the meanwhile and was most astonished when the latter confessed to him that he had still not yet managed to write an opera and have it produced on the stage, since thus far, in subject matter and execution, no poem had proved at all capable of stirring him to composition.

(F) Why you have not long since written a libretto for yourself, I cannot understand, for you have an adequate command of language and, with your unusually lively imagination, you ought surely not to be at a loss for subject matter.

(Ludwig) My imagination, I will admit, may well be lively enough for the invention of many a good subject; especially at night, when a light headache puts me into that dreamy condition that is as it were a battle between waking and sleeping, not only do right good, genuinely romantic operas indeed occur to me, but these are actually performed before me with my own music. Yet, as concerns the gift of retaining such things and writing them down, I believe I lack it; and after all, you can scarcely ask us composers, in order that we may write our own verses, to acquire that mechanical technique, essential to success in any art and attainable only by constant application and steady practice. But even if I had the knack of turning an invented theme correctly and with taste into scenes and verses, it is not likely that I would decide to write myself a libretto.

(F) Yet no one, after all, can enter into your musical tendencies as you can yourself.

(L) That is doubtless true; at the same time it would seem to me that the composer who sits down to the task of turning an invented opera subject into verse must be affected very much as a painter would be, if, before being allowed to begin his painting in live colors, he were first obliged to make a meticulous engraving of the image his imagination had conceived.

(F) You think that the fire needed for composing would burn itself out and be smothered in the work of versification?

(L) Actually, that is it! And in the end even my verses would seem to me miserable things, like the paper wrappers of the rockets which only yesterday were crackling through the air in fiery life. Seriously, though, it seems to me that, for the success of a work, it is in no art as necessary as it is in music to conceive the whole, with all its parts, down to the smallest detail, in the first and liveliest glow of inspiration; since nowhere is filing and altering more useless and more harmful, and also since I know from experience that the melody first brought to life, as though by magic, right while reading a poem, is always the best, perhaps indeed, from the composer's viewpoint, the only true one. It would be quite impossible for the composer not to busy himself, even while writing his poem, with the music which the situation called forth. Quite transported and working only on the melodies flooding toward him, he would search in vain for words, and, should he succeed in forcing himself to it, that stream, however powerfully its great waves might roar along, would all too soon run dry on the sterile sands. Indeed, to express my inner conviction still more forcefully, in the instant of musical inspiration all words—all phrases—would strike him as inadequate—insipid—contemptible, and he would have to climb down from his height to be able to beg in the lower region of words for the means of his existence. But would not his wings soon be lamed here, like those of the captive eagle, and would he not attempt in vain the flight to the sun?

(F) That, to be sure, is quite reasonable; but do you know, my friend, that you are not so much convincing me as excusing your unwillingness to first clear the way for musical creation with all the necessary scenes, arias, duets, etc.?

(L) That may be; but I shall renew an old complaint by asking why it was that, when a common artistic urge bound us together closely, you would never give in to my ardent wish that you should write a libretto for me.

(F) Because it seemed to me the world's most thankless task.

You will grant me that no one could be more self-centered in his requirements than you composers are; and if you maintain that I ought not to ask a musician to acquire the technique essential to the mechanical work of versification, then I shall on the other hand insist that for a poet to concern himself so exactly with your needs, with the structure of your trios, quartets, finales, etc., would add so much to his burden that he would, as indeed happens only too often, sin at every moment against the form which you have somehow adopted—with what justification I trust you know yourselves. And if, extending ourselves to the utmost, we have sought to fix each situation of our drama in genuine poesy and to depict it in the most inspired language and in perfectly rounded verses, then the way you often mercilessly cut out our finest lines and often mistreat our grandest phrases, turning them in the wrong way, inverting them, even drowning them in melody, is truly horrible.

I say this only of the vain task of working the poem out carefully. But even as to subject, many a magnificent one that has come to us as poetic inspiration and which we have brought to you, proud in the belief that we were conferring a great favor, you have refused point-blank as insignificant and unworthy of musical treatment. This, after all, is often mere conceit, or whatever you please to call it, for often you set your hands to texts that are beneath contempt, and . . .

(L) Stop, my good friend!

To be sure, there are composers to whom music is as foreign as poetry is to many a verse-carpenter; these, then, have often set music to texts that actually are in every respect beneath contempt. Genuine composers, living in and from their sublime and sacred art, choose only poetic texts.

(F) But Mozart . . . ?

(L) . . . chose in his classical operas only poems genuinely suited to music, paradoxical as this may seem.

But, putting this question aside for the moment, I believe it possible to specify quite precisely what sort of subject is suited to opera, so that a poet may never be in danger of erring in this.

(F) I confess that I have never reflected on it, and, in view of my want of musical knowledge, I should also have lacked the necessary premises.

(L) If by musical knowledge you mean the so-called theory of music, you will not need it to judge correctly of a composer's wants; for without it you can have so grasped the nature of music and so made it a part of you that, from this point of view, you may be a far better musician than one who, having in the sweat of his brow worked through the whole theory of music in all its labyrinthine detail, worships the dead letter, like a fetish he has carved himself, as the living spirit, and whom this idol-worship bars from the joys of a higher realm.

(F) And you believe that, without the school's having admitted him to those lower orders, the poet may penetrate the true nature of music?

(L) I do.

Indeed, in that faraway country, which surrounds us often with the strangest presentiments and from which wondrous voices call down to us, wakening all the echoes that sleep in our restricted breasts, which echoes, awakened now, shoot joyfully and gladly up, as though in fiery rays, making us sharers in the bliss of that paradise, there poets and musicians are members of a faith, related in the most intimate way; for the secret of word and tone is one and the same, and has admitted them to highest orders.

(F) I hear my dear Ludwig endeavoring to grasp, in deep parables, the mysterious nature of art; and, in truth, I already see the gap diminishing which formerly I thought divided the poet from the musician.

(L) Let me attempt to express my idea of the true nature of opera. In a word, it would seem to me that only that opera in which the music arises directly from the poem as its inevitable offspring is a genuine opera.

(F) I will confess that I do not yet quite follow you.

(L) Is not music the mysterious language of a faraway spirit world whose wondrous accents, echoing within us, awaken us to a higher, more intensive life? All the passions battle with one another, their armor shimmering and sparkling, perishing in an inexpressible yearning which fills our breasts. Such is the indescribable effect of instrumental music. Now, however, music is to come fully to life, is to take hold of life's phenomena and, beautifying word and deed, to speak of particular passions and situations. Can one then speak of the commonplace in elevated language? Can music then reveal anything to us beyond the marvels of that country from out which it calls?

Let the poet prepare himself for a bold flight into the faraway land of romance; there he will find the marvel that he is to bring to life, alive and gleaming with fresh color, so that one willingly believes in it, so indeed that one wanders as in a blissful dream among the flowery paths of romantic life, superior to the needs of everyday existence, so that one understands only the language of romance, words becoming sounding music.

(F) You would preserve, then, only the romantic opera, with its fairies, spirits, marvels, and transformations?

(L) Of course I regard the romantic opera as the only genuine one, for only in the land of romance is music at home. At the same time, you are, I dare say, ready to believe that I thoroughly despise those poverty-stricken medleys in which childish, spiritless spirits are conjured up and in which without regard for cause or effect marvel is piled on marvel, merely to flatter the eye of the indolent crowd. A genuinely romantic opera is written only by a gifted and inspired poet, for only such a one can bring to life the wondrous phenomena of the spirit world; on his wings we are lifted over the chasm which otherwise divides us from it, and, grown accustomed to the strange country, we believe in the marvels which, as inevitable effects of the action of higher natures on our being, take place visibly and bring about all the strong, powerfully affecting situations which fill us, now with awe and horror, now with the highest bliss. It is, in a word, the magic force of poetic truth which the poet representing the marvelous must have at his command, for only this can transport us; and a mere capricious succession of aimless fairy pranks which, as is usual in medleys of this kind, are only there to harass Pagliasso in his knight's costume, will, as farcical and stupid, leave us always cold and uninterested.

So, my friend, in an opera the action of higher natures on our being must take place visibly, thus opening up before our eyes a romantic existence in which language, too, is raised to a higher power, or rather, is borrowed from that faraway country—from music, that is, from song—where action and situation themselves, vibrating in powerful harmonies, take hold of us and transport us the more forcefully.

(F) Now I understand you fully, and I think of Ariosto and Tasso; yet it will, I think, be difficult to form the musical drama to your specifications.

(L) This is the task of the gifted, genuinely romantic poet.

Think of the incomparable Gozzi. In his dramatized fairytales he has succeeded perfectly in what I ask of a librettist, and it is incredible that this rich vein of operatic subjects has not thus far been more exploited.

(F) I confess that Gozzi, when I read him some years ago, appealed to me in the most lively fashion, although my point of view was naturally a different one from that which you have adopted.

(L) One of his finest tales is undoubtedly that of the raven.[2]

. . . .

(F) Now I recall the splendid, fantastic piece quite exactly and still feel the deep impression that it made on me. You are right; here the marvelous seems to be necessary, and it is poetically so true that one willingly believes in it. It is Millo's deed, the murder of the raven, which as it were knocks at the gates of the gloomy spirit realm; now they open sonorously, and the spirits stalk into life, ensnaring mankind in the wondrous, mysterious destiny that governs them.

(L) Quite so; and now consider the strong, splendid situations which the poet knew how to spin out of this conflict with the spirit world. Jennaro's heroic self-sacrifice, Armilla's heroic deed—in these things lies a grandeur of which our moralizing playwrights, burrowing into the miseries of everyday life as though among the sweepings thrown from the state hall into the dust cart, have no idea at all. How magnificently, too, the comic characters of the masks are woven in!

(F) Yes indeed!

Only in the genuinely romantic do the comic and tragic combine so naturally that they blend as one in the total effect, laying hold of the feelings of the audience in a wonderful way of their own.

(L) This even our opera hacks have dimly perceived. For hence, pre-

---

2 *Il Corvo*, "Fiaba teatrale tragicomica," first performed in Venice on October 24, 1761. An opera on this subject, by the Danish composer J. P. E. Hartmann, was performed for the first time in Copenhagen on October 29, 1832; Schu- mann has a long account of it in his *Gesammelte Schriften*, III, 247–255. Another tale of Gozzi's supplied Richard Wagner with the subject of *Die Feen*.

sumably, have arisen the so-called heroic-comic operas in which so often it is the heroic that is really comic, while the comic is heroic only insofar as it heroically rides rough-shod over everything that taste, decency, and good morals require.

(F) According to the specification which you have laid down for the opera libretto, we have very few genuine operas indeed.

(L) Quite so!

Most of our so-called operas are only stupid plays with music, and the utter lack of dramatic effect which is blamed, now on the libretto, now on the music, is to be attributed to the dead weight of scenes strung together without inner poetic connection, without poetic truth, to which music could not give the spark of life. Often the composer has unconsciously worked quite for himself, and the miserable libretto runs alongside, unable to make any contact with the music. Then the music can in a certain sense be quite good, that is, without inner depth, without forcibly laying hold of the audience as though by magic, it can arouse a certain feeling of comfort, like a joyous, brilliant play of colors. Such an opera is a concert, given on a stage with costumes and scenery.

(F) Inasmuch as you are in this way admitting only the romantic opera, in the strictest sense of the word, how about the musical tragedies, and finally, the comic operas in modern costume? Must you discard these altogether?

(L) By no means!

In most of the older, tragic operas, such as are unfortunately no longer being written and composed, it is again the genuinely heroic in the action, the inner strength of characters and situations, which lays hold of the beholder so powerfully. The mysterious and somber force that governs gods and men stalks visibly before his eyes, and he hears revealed in strange, foreboding tones the eternal, unalterable decisions of fate which even rule the gods. From these purely tragic subjects the fantastic proper is excluded; but in the connection with the gods, who have awakened men to higher life, indeed to godlike deeds, there must be heard, in music's wondrous accents, a more elevated language. Incidentally, were not the antique tragedies already musically declaimed? And does this not right clearly argue the need for a higher means of expression than that which ordinary speech affords?

In a way all their own, our musical tragedies have inspired gifted composers to a sublime, shall I say, sacred style, and it is as though man were drifting, in a miraculous ecstasy, on sounds from the golden harps of cherubim and seraphim, into the realm of light, where is revealed to him the mystery of his own being.

I wished, Ferdinand, to suggest nothing less than the intimate relation of church music to tragic opera, from which the older composers formed a magnificent style of their own, of which the moderns—not excepting Spontini, boiling over in luxuriant abundance—have no idea. The incomparable Gluck, standing there like a hero, I prefer not to mention at all; but to perceive how even lesser talents have grasped that genuinely grand and tragic style, think of the chorus of the priests of Night, in Piccinni's *Didon*.

(F) Now I feel as I did in the earlier, golden days of our life together; in speaking inspiringly of your art, you lift me up to views otherwise beyond my range; and you may believe that at the moment I imagine that I understand a good deal about music.

Indeed, I believe that no good line can form itself within me except it come forth as music.

(L) Is this not the true enthusiasm of the librettist?

I maintain that he must from the first set everything to music inwardly, just as the musician does; and that only the clear consciousness of particular melodies, even of particular sounds of the instruments taking part, in a word, the ready control over the inner realm of sound, distinguishes the one from the other. But I still owe my opinion of the *opera buffa*.

(F) You will scarcely admit this, least of all in modern costume?

(L) For my part, I confess, dear Ferdinand, not only that, precisely in the costume of our time, it is most congenial to me, but that it seems true to me in this guise alone, true to its character, true to the intention of the animated, excitable Italians who created it. Here it turns now on the fantastic, which arises, in part from the reckless abandon of single characters, in part from the bizarre play of chance, and which impudently forces its way into everyday life, turning everything upside down. One has to admit: "Yes, it is Master Neighbor in his familiar, cinnamon-colored, Sunday suit with its buttons of spun gold; what in the world can have happened to the man to make him behave so foolishly?"

Imagine a respectable company of cousins and aunts with a languishing daughter; add to these some students, who sing to the cousin's eyes and play the guitar beneath her window. To these enters Hobgoblin Droll with a tantalizing spell, and in the ensuing confusion all is movement, and we have absurd fancies, strange pranks of every description, and outlandish contortions. A special star has risen, and everywhere chance stretches nets in which the most respectable people are caught, if they poke out their noses ever so little.

Precisely in this intrusion of the adventurous into everyday life, and in the contradictions arising from it, lies in my opinion the nature of the true *opera buffa;* and it is precisely this grasp of the otherwise remote fantastic, now entered into life, that makes the acting of the Italian comedians so inimitable. They understand the poet's implications, and their acting brings to life the skeleton, which is all that he could give, in flesh and color.

(F) I think I have understood you perfectly.

You believe, then, that in the *opera buffa* it is essentially the fantastic that replaces the romantic, your indispensable requirement of opera, and the poet's art consists for you in this: that he brings his characters on the stage, not only perfectly rounded and poetically true, but taken straight from everyday life and so individual that one at once says to oneself: "Look! There is the neighbor I talk with every day! There is the student who goes to class every morning and sighs so terribly beneath the cousin's window, etc.!" And now the reckless action, which they set in motion as though suffering from some strange delirium, or of which they are the victims, affects us, you think, as surprisingly as though a crazy hobgoblin were to go through life, irresistibly driving us all into the charmed circle of his laughable mischief-making.

(L) You express my idea exactly, and I need scarcely add how now, according to my principle, music readily accommodates itself to the *opera buffa,* and how here too a special style arises of itself which in its own way lays hold of the temper of the audience.

(F) But has music the power to express the comic in all its nuances?

(L) Of this I am thoroughly convinced, and gifted artists have demonstrated it hundreds of times. So, for example, there may lie in music the expression of the most entertaining irony, like that which predominates in Mozart's incomparable *Cosi fan tutte.*

(F) Here you force on me the comment that, according to your principle, the despised libretto of this opera is in reality genuinely operatic.

(L) Just this is what I had in mind when I maintained before that Mozart in his classical operas chose only poems genuinely suited to music, for all that the *Marriage of Figaro* is more of a play with music than a true opera. The fruitless attempt to transplant the tearful type of play into the opera house can only miscarry, and our "orphan asylums," [3] "eye

---

3 *Das Waisenhaus,* comic opera by Joseph Weigl (1808); Hoffmann reviewed this for the *Allge-* *meine musikalische Zeitung* (Leipzig) in September 1810.

doctors," [4] etc., will surely be forgotten soon. Nothing can be more contemptible and foreign to true opera than that whole series of *Singspiele*, like those Dittersdorf turned out,[5] though I energetically defend such operas as the *Sonntagskind* and the *Schwestern von Prag*.[6] They may be called real German *opere buffe*.

(F) These operas, at least, when well performed, have always entertained me thoroughly, and what goes straight to my heart is what Tieck has the poet say to the audience in the *Gestiefelter Kater:* [7] "If this is to entertain you, you must put aside whatever culture you have and actually become children, to enjoy and entertain yourselves as children do."

(L) Unfortunately these words, like many others of their kind, fell on hard, sterile soil, where they could not penetrate and take root. But the *vox populi*, as a rule an outright *vox Dei* in affairs of the theater, drowned out the individual sighs which superfine natures gave vent to, horrified at the lack of naturalness and taste exhibited in these—to their minds, childish—pieces, and there is reason to believe that, as though carried away by the folly that had laid hold of the common people, many a superior person, in the midst of his dignified behavior, broke into a shocking laugh, at the same time protesting that he could not understand his own laughter.

(F) Ought not Tieck to be the poet who, if he chose, could give the composers romantic librettos, agreeing exactly with the specifications you have laid down?

(L) Quite possibly, for he is a genuinely romantic poet, and as a matter of fact I recall having had a libretto of his in hand which was laid out in a genuinely romantic way, though overcrowded with material and too lengthy. If I am not mistaken, it was called the *Ungeheuer und der bezauberte Wald*.[8]

(F) You remind me yourself of one difficulty with which you obstruct your librettists.

I have in mind the incredible brevity which you prescribe. All our effort to grasp and present properly, in really significant language, this or that situation, the outburst of this or that passion, is in vain; for the whole

---

4 *Der Augenarzt,* comic opera by Adalbert Gyrowetz (1811); this too was reviewed by Hoffmann (*Allgemeine musikalische Zeitung,* December 1812).

5 Perhaps the most familiar are *Doktor und Apotheker* (1786) and *Das rote Käppchen* (1790).

6 *Das Neusonntagskind* (1793) and *Die Schwestern von Prag* (1794), comic operas by Wenzel Müller.

7 *Der gestiefelte Kater* ("Puss in Boots"), satiric comedy in three acts, first published in Tieck's *Volksmärchen von Peter Lebrecht* (Berlin, 1797).

8 "Musical Fairytale in Four Acts" (1798), written for J. F. Reichardt, who did not set it to music.

must be dispatched in a couple of lines which, into the bargain, must permit your turning and twisting them according to your good pleasure.

(L) May I say that the poet, like the scene painter, must cover his whole canvas, after designing it properly, in bold, powerful strokes, and that it is music which now places the whole in so correct a light and in such proper perspective that everything stands out as though alive and individual, apparently arbitrary brush strokes blending in figures that stride forth boldly.

(F) We ought then to supply only a sketch, not a poem?

(L) By no means. It is obvious, after all, that the librettist, with respect to the arrangement and management of the whole, must be guided by the rules of drama derived from the nature of the problem; at the same time he actually does need to make a special effort to arrange the scenes in such a way that the story unfolds clearly and plainly before the beholder's eyes. Almost without understanding a word, the beholder must be in a position to form an idea of the plot from what he sees happening. No dramatic poem needs this to such an extreme degree as does the opera, for, aside from the fact that, even when the words are sung most clearly, one still understands them less than when they are spoken, the music too entices the audience all too easily into other regions, and it is only by constant firing at the point in which the dramatic effect is to concentrate that one succeeds in hitting it. Now as regards the words, these will be most acceptable to the composer if they express the situation to be presented tersely and forcefully; no special elegance is required and above all no images.

(F) How about the everlasting similes of Metastasio?

(L) True, that man actually had the peculiar idea that a composer, especially in an aria, has always first to be stimulated by some poetic image or other. Hence his eternally repeated opening lines: "Come una tortorella, etc.," "Come spuma in tempesta, etc.," and often there actually occurred, at least in the accompaniment, the cooing of the dove, the foaming of the sea, etc.[9]

(F) Are we then, not only to avoid poetic elegance, but to be barred also from every detailed delineation of interesting situations? For example, the young hero goes off to war and takes leave of his stricken father, the old king, whose kingdom a conquering tyrant is shaking at its foundations; or a cruel fate separates an adoring youth from his beloved; are then the two to say nothing but "Farewell"?

---

[9] This variety of aria is ridiculed by Metastasio himself in the second intermezzo of his *Didone* *abbandonata*. Hoffmann's examples seem to be invented.

(L) Though the former may speak briefly of his courage, of his confidence in his just cause, though the latter may say to his beloved that life without her is but slow death, the composer, who is inspired, not by words, but by action and situation, will be satisfied if the inner state of the young hero's or parting lover's soul is depicted in bold strokes. To keep to your example, in what accents, penetrating deep into one's innermost self, have the Italians, countless times already, sung the little word "Addio"! Of what thousands and thousands of nuances musical expression is capable! Is not this precisely the secret of music's miraculous power, that, just where plain speech runs dry, it opens up an inexhaustible spring of means of expression?

(F) According to this, so far as the words are concerned, the librettist ought to aim at the most extreme simplicity, and it should suffice merely to suggest the situations in a bold and noble way.

(L) Exactly; for, as I said, subject matter, action, situation must inspire the composer, not showy language, and, aside from the so-called poetic images, each and every reflection is for him a real mortification.

(F) But surely you believe that I feel quite keenly how difficult it will be to write a good libretto to your specifications? In particular, that simplicity of expression . . .

(L) For you who are so given to word painting, it will no doubt be difficult enough. But just as Metastasio, in my opinion, has shown in his librettos precisely how an opera ought *not* to be written, so there are many Italian poems which might be cited as perfect models of what song texts ought to be. What could be simpler than stanzas like this one, known all over the world:

> Almen se non poss'io
> Seguir l'amato bene,
> Affetti del cor mio,
> Seguitelo per me! [10]

What a suggestion of a nature torn by love and grief lies in these few simple words, a suggestion which the composer can lay hold of, presenting then the suggested inner state of the affections with the full force of musical expression. Indeed the particular situation in which these words are to be sung will so stimulate his imagination that he will give his melody a character all its own. For this same reason you will also find that the most poetic composers have often set poetry that is even downright bad quite magnificently to music. But in this case it was the genuinely operatic,

---

10 Metastasio, *La Clemenza di Tito,* II, v.

romantic subject matter that inspired them. As an example I give you Mozart's *Zauberflöte*.

Ferdinand was on the point of replying when in the street, right outside their windows, there was a call to arms. He seemed surprised; Ludwig, with a deep sigh, pressed his friend's hand to his breast, exclaiming:

Alas, Ferdinand, faithful, dearly beloved friend! What is to become of art in these rude, stormy times? Will it not perish, like a delicate plant vainly turning its head toward the dark cloud behind which the sun has vanished?

Alas, Ferdinand, for the golden days of our youth! Where have they gone? Everything worth while is being swept under in the swift stream that floods by, devastating the fields; from out its inky waves peer bloody corpses, and in the horror that converges on us we are carried along—we have no supports—our cry of terror echoes in empty space—a sacrifice to unbridled fury, we sink, past help, to the bottom!

Ludwig was silent, lost in thought. Ferdinand got up; took saber and helmet; stood before Ludwig, who gazed at him in bewilderment, like the god of war, armed for battle. Then an inspired expression passed over Ferdinand's features; his eyes shone with burning fire, and, raising his voice, he said:

Ludwig, what has become of you? Has then the dungeon air you have breathed here so long so wasted you that, ill and sickly, you would no longer feel the stimulating spring breeze that sweeps outside through clouds that shine in morning's golden glow?

Nature's children wallowed in brutish idleness, despising the finest gifts she offered them, treading them under foot in wanton obstinacy. Then angry Mother Nature wakened War, long asleep in her fragrant flower garden. Like a bronze giant he strode into the midst of the dissolute who, fleeing before his terrible voice, sought the protection of the mother in whom they had lost faith. But faith brought with it knowledge: Only in strength is health—from battle springs immortality, as life from death!

Yes, Ludwig, a fateful time has come; and, as though in the awe-inspiring depths of the old sagas which murmur to us strangely, like thunder in the distant gloaming, we plainly hear again the voice of Force, the eternally ruling passion—indeed, striding visibly into our lives, it stirs in us a faith to which the secret of our being is revealed.

The dawn is breaking, and inspired singers soar already in the fragrant breezes, announcing the godlike, praising it in song. The golden gates are open, and art and science kindle in a single ray the sacred impulse which brings mankind together in one faith. Hence, friend, turn your gaze heavenward—courage—confidence—faith!

Ferdinand embraced his friend. Ludwig picked up his full glass: "Eternally pledged to the higher existence in life and death!" "Eternally pledged to the higher existence in life and death!" Ferdinand repeated, and in a few moments his flying steed was already carrying him to the throngs which, lusting furiously for battle, cheering wildly, were advancing toward the enemy.

Composer-Critics of the Nineteenth Century

83. C. M. von Weber

In Carl Maria von Weber (1786–1826) we meet the prototype of the nineteenth-century composer-critic. Burney and Reichardt were observers of the musical scene—Weber seeks to mold public opinion; with Burney and Reichardt, writing on music was an end in itself—with Weber it is merely a means. Nowhere is this more apparent than in the two little essays with which Weber introduced to the opera-going public of Prague (1815) and Dresden (1817) his "Dramatic and Musical Notices" of the new operas to be performed under his direction. The undertaking, he says, is novel and even somewhat daring. Yet the attempt has to be made, and it is his duty to make it: "The good old days when the blessings of general and lasting peace invited every man to dedicate his free time to the arts and sciences—those good old days were rudely ended long ago, and with them disappeared, of course, the sympathetic interest of the public, essential to the work of art."

The novel character of Weber's literary activity, and of the literary activity of those who followed him, will stand out no less clearly if we contrast it with that of such eighteenth-century musicians as Quantz, C. P. E. Bach, and Leopold Mozart, or with that of Fux and Rameau. On the one hand, technical essays addressed to the musical fraternity; on the other, *feuilletons* addressed to the general public. Such things as Weber's analyses of the chorale harmonizations of J. S. Bach, as revised by Vogler, or his exchange with the poet Adolf Müllner, who had criticized Weber's setting of one of his poems, such things as the Berlioz treatise on instrumentation or Wagner's pamphlet on conducting —these are, for the nineteenth century, the exception and not the rule.

Himself the author of an unfinished novel, one fragment from which is incorporated in the review translated below, Weber counted among his friends many of the leading writers of the day: E. T. A. Hoffmann, whom he had met in Bamberg as early as 1811 and with whom he maintained the most cordial relations for ten years; Wieland, whom he had learned to know in Weimar in 1812 and to whom he owed the subject of his *Oberon;* Tieck, to whose circle he belonged during his years in Dresden; Brentano and Arnim, the compilers of *Des Knaben Wunderhorn;* and Jean Paul, whose writings he had known from childhood and whom he was to meet at last during the summer of 1822, at the time of his work on *Euryanthe.* Gerald Abraham contributed a first-rate account of Weber's literary activity to the *Musical Quarterly* for January, 1934 ("Weber as Novelist and Critic," XX, 27–38).

On the Opera "Undine" [1]

[1817]

Adapted from the fairy tale of the same name by Friedrich, Baron de La Motte Fouqué, set to music by E. T. A. Hoffmann, and performed for the first time at the Royal Theatre in Berlin.[2]

No sooner had I decided to say something publicly about this beautiful work than the possible forms of notices, reviews, or whatever one pleases to call them, passed involuntarily before my mind's eye, and I became aware of how uncommonly difficult it is to obtain from them a definite picture of the object appraised or anything like the impression that it is itself capable of making. For the most part, it seems to me, they either coincide with the ordinary judgments of society, where, without further demonstration, one party finds a thing good, another bad, while the more moderate neither condemn nor commend, the whole deriving weight and credibility only from the personality of the judge and from the confidence placed in him (again a partisan consideration); or they waste themselves, dissolved into tiny particles, entering, from a technical point of view, into details of the musical construction of such large works as do not come at once into everyone's hands. The greatest effects and beauties proceed solely from the manner of their disposition and combination; detached from their context, they nearly always lose their whole character, often, indeed, bearing witness seemingly against themselves in that, thus considered apart, they become well-nigh meaningless. Only very rarely can even the liveliest description make fully intelligible their true, organically connected coexistence with the remainder. It goes without saying that this opinion also is subject to various restrictions, and that especially where art works already matters of common knowledge are concerned, analysis of form and structure can only be salutary to those seeking improvement. In the present case, however, where the sole object is to call public attention to a work by attempting to suggest the intellectual sphere within which it moves and to represent in its distinctive outlines the shape that the composer has given it, it seems to me necessary that the critic begin by explaining how he himself sees, believes, and thinks, from which, then,

---

1 Text: *Allgemeine musikalische Zeitung,* XIX (1817), 201–208.

2 The first performance took place on August 3, 1816; by July 27, 1817, when the theater was destroyed by fire, the opera had been given four-teen times. An edition of the vocal score (edited by Hans Pfitzner) was published in 1908. In recent years there have been revivals in Aachen (1922), Bamberg (1926), and Leipzig (1933). [Loewenberg]

his readers can easily infer the extent to which they can subscribe to criticisms originating therein. With this in mind I think it wise to introduce my actual notice of the opera with the following fragment from one of my larger works,[a] the more so since it corresponds closely to the tendencies of the opera *Undine*.

For the proper appraisal of an art work moving in time there is needed that calm, dispassionate state of mind which, susceptible to every kind of impression, is to be carefully shielded from definite opinion or tendency of feeling, a certain receptivity for the material being treated alone excepted. Only thus is there given to the artist the simple power to draw our affections with *his* feelings and figures into the world which *he* has created and in which *he*, a powerful master of every passionate stimulus, causes us with *him* and through *him* to feel pain, pleasure, horror, joy, hope, and love. It will then be demonstrated clearly and almost at once whether he is capable of creating a great design which we will retain permanently in our hearts or whether, a creature of restlessly changing strokes of genius, he will let us be attracted by details while we forget the whole.

In no variety of art work is this so difficult to avoid—and consequently so often present—as in the opera. By opera I understand, of course, the opera which the German desires—an art work complete in itself, in which the partial contributions of the related and collaborating arts blend together, disappear, and, in disappearing, somehow form a new world.

As a rule a few striking numbers determine the success of the whole. Only rarely are these numbers, agreeably stimulating in the moment of their hearing, swallowed up at the end, as they properly should be, in the great general impression. For one must come first to admire the whole; then, on closer acquaintance, one may take pleasure in the beauty of the separate parts of which the whole is composed.

The nature and inner disposition of opera, a whole composed of wholes, gives rise to this great difficulty, which musical heroes alone succeed in overcoming. As a result of the form which is its right, each musical composition gives the impression of an independent, organic, self-contained unit. Yet, as a part of the whole, it must disappear when the whole is beheld; at the same time, displaying several surfaces simultaneously, it can and

---

a *Künstlerleben.* [Also called *Eine musikalische Reise* and *Tonkünstlers Leben.* Weber worked on this half-humorous, half-autobiographical novel intermittently from 1809 until 1820, but left it unfinished and published only fragments. It was to have run to 23 chapters; the present fragment is a part of Chapter 5. The most complete text is that in Georg Kaiser's edition of Weber's *Sämtliche Schriften* (Berlin & Leipzig, 1908), pp. 437–510.—Ed.]

should be many-sided (especially if it is an ensemble piece), a Janus head to be taken in at a glance.

In this lies the great, mysterious secret of music, a secret to be felt but not to be expressed; here are united the fluctuating and resisting natures of anger and of love, of ecstatic suffering; here sylph and salamander intermingle, embracing one another. In a word, what love is to man, music is to the arts and to mankind, for it is actually love itself, the purest, most ethereal language of the emotions, containing all their changing colors in every variety of shading and in thousands of aspects; *true only once,* but to be understood simultaneously by thousands of differently constituted listeners.

Though it appear in new and unusual forms, this truth of musical speech will in the end affirmatively assert its rights. The fate of every epoch-making and significant art work proves this sufficiently. What, for example, could have seemed more strange than Gluck's works at the time when everyone was overwhelmed and enervated by the sensual sea of Italian music? At this moment there are artistic errors that are on the point of overwhelming us again—in quite another way, to be sure, but perhaps in a not less dangerous way. As ruling principles the all-powerful conditions of our time have set up only the extremes—death and pleasure. Oppressed by the horrors of war, grown callous to misery of every sort, we have sought amusement only in aesthetic pleasures of the crudest kind.[3] The theater has become a puppet show at which, studiously avoiding the delightful, delighting emotional disturbance that accompanies the real enjoyment of an art work, we cause to be unwound before us a succession of scenes and are content to be tickled with trivial jests and melodies or to be taken in by inappropriate mechanical effects with neither point nor sense. Accustomed to the striking in everyday life, we are here too affected only by the striking. To follow the gradual development of a passion or an ingeniously motivated intensification of interest is called exhausting, tiresome, and—as the result of inattention—unintelligible.

As to the opera *Undine,* I had had to listen to judgments contradictory in every respect, prompted by the conditions just touched on. I sought as best I could to attain complete impartiality, although I could not at once prevent myself from looking forward to something significant, an expectation fully justified by Herr Hoffmann's literary writings. He who

3 The defeat of Napoleon in 1815 had brought real peace to the German states for the first time in Weber's memory. Until then he had lived always in the troubled environment reflected in his settings of poems from Theodor Körner's *Leyer und Schwert,* Opus 41, 42, and 43 (1814 to 1816) and in his cantata *Kampf und Sieg,* Opus 44 (1815), on the victory at Belle Alliance (Waterloo).

can penetrate Mozart's intention as he did, with his ardent flow of imagination and deep temperament, in the essay on *Don Giovanni* [4] (*Phantasiestücke in Callot's Manier*, Part I), can produce nothing downright mediocre; at the worst, he will beat against and even reshape the boundaries—he will not walk about within them idly.

The adaptation impressed the writer as a dramatized fairy tale in which many an inner connection might well have been more definitely and distinctly clarified. Herr von Fouqué knew the story only too well, and in such case there often occurs a sort of self-deception in which others, while recognizing it, believe. Still, it is by no means, as some allege, unintelligible.

The composer has brought the opera to life the more distinctly and clearly, with definite colors and outlines. It is actually *a single cast,* and after repeated hearings the writer recalls no passage which dispelled for him, even for a moment, the magic of the cycle of pictures which the composer had conjured up for him. Indeed, from beginning to end, he arouses so powerfully the interest in musical development that with the first hearing one has actually grasped the whole, while the detail disappears in genuinely artistic innocence and modesty.

With unusual self-denial, the greatness of which can be fully appreciated only by him who knows what it means to sacrifice the glory of momentary applause, Herr Hoffmann has disdained to enrich single numbers at the expense of the whole, so easy to do if one calls attention to them by broadening and enlarging their execution beyond that proper to them as members of the artistic body. He proceeds relentlessly, obviously led on by a desire to be always *true* and to intensify the life of the drama instead of retarding or arresting it in its rapid progress. Varied and strikingly portrayed as the many-sided characters of the persons of the action seem to be, they are all encircled by—or better, creatures of—that ghostly, fabulous world whose awesome stimulations are the peculiar property of the fairylike. Kühleborn stands out most prominently (the writer, like Fouqué, assumes a familiarity with the story) as a result of melodic selection and instrumentation which, remaining faithful to him throughout, announces his sinister presence. [5] Since he appears, if not as Destiny herself, then as the immediate agent of her will, this is after all quite correct. After him comes the lovely water sprite Undine, whose tonal waves now swirl and ripple, now, mightily threatening, assert their sovereign

---

[4] An excellent English translation, by Abram Loft, appeared in the *Musical Quarterly,* XXXI (1945), 504–516.

[5] As in *Don Giovanni*, and still to some extent in *Der Freischütz* and *The Flying Dutchman*, the use of the principle of the *leitmotiv* in Hoffmann's *Undine* is restricted to the supernatural.

power. A highly successful piece, her aria in Act II seems to the writer to sum up her whole character; uncommonly pleasing and ingeniously handled, it will serve as a small foretaste of the whole and is accordingly published here as a supplement.[b] The ardently fluctuating and unsteady Huldebrand, giving in to every lover's impulse, and the simple, pious Man of God, with his grave chorale melody, are then the most important. Berthalda, the Fisherman and Fishermaid, and the Duke and Duchess remain more in the background. The chorus of Attendants breathes joyous, pulsating life and in single numbers takes on an uncommonly satisfying freshness and gaiety, contrasting with the awesome choruses of the Spirits of Earth and Water, with their cramped and unusual progressions.

Most successful and quite grandly conceived seems to the writer the end of the opera, where the composer, as crown and capstone, has at length spread out the whole fullness of harmony in a pure eight-part double chorus and has pronounced the words "Now farewell to earthly care and pomp" with a real sense for their deeper meaning in a devoutly heartfelt melody that has a certain grandeur and melancholy sweetness, whereby the actually tragic ending leaves behind it a magnificent feeling of tranquillity. Enclosing the whole, overture and final chorus here join hands. The former builds up and discloses the wonder world, beginning quietly, then passionately storming along with growing intensity, immediately thereafter plunging directly into the action without coming to a full stop; the latter soothes and is perfectly satisfying. The whole work is one of the most ingenious that our day has given us. It is the magnificent result of the most perfect familiarity with, and grasp of, the subject, brought about by profoundly considered reflection and calculation of the effects of all the means of art, marked as a work of fine art by its beautiful and intimate melodic conception.

From all this it follows of itself that there are herein contained big instrumental effects, a knowledge of harmony, combinations often new, a correct declamation, with other necessary devices that are at the disposal of every real master, without a ready command of which there can be no freedom of thought.

And now, an observation as to what follows (for there must of course be blame as well as praise): The writer will not conceal certain wishes, although in *Undine* he would have *nothing* different, since everything, as it stands there, is necessary exactly as it is and not otherwise; one must needs wait to see whether the same things will reveal themselves in another work; one can, however, learn in a general way, by listening even

b It is to be supplied in a few weeks. [The promised supplement never appeared.—Ed.]

to *one* work, what those favorite devices are against which real friends ought to warn the composer, lest in the end they become mannerisms.

The writer, then, is struck by and wishes avoided: the partiality for little short figures which not only tend to become monotonous but easily oppress and obscure the melody, which, if it is to stand out, demands great experience and care on the part of the conductor; then, the partiality for the violoncellos and violas, for diminished-seventh chords, and for endings that are often too quickly broken off, which, at least on first hearing, are somewhat disturbing and, while by no means incorrect, for all that, inadequate; finally, certain inner voices which, because of their repeated employment by Cherubini, invite the vulgar to hunt for reminiscences.

As regards scenery and costume the performance may be pronounced splendid, and as regards singing and acting, a success. Regular capacity houses demonstrate the undiminishing, indeed constantly increasing interest that the opera has for the public. The prejudiced ascribe much to the scenery. But when the writer observes that in other pieces where this is the case people wait only for these moments and then leave, while here they remain, continuously and uniformly attentive, from beginning to end, the interest that the thing itself arouses in them is sufficiently proved. Tumultuous applause the composer could procure for nearly all the musical numbers by expanding a little the concluding measures; here the contrary obtains, and everything occurs swiftly and is constantly impelled forward.

May Herr Hoffmann soon give to the world again something as solid as this opera is, and may his many-sided talent, which within a short space of time brought him fame as an author and assured him the respect of his colleagues as a man of affairs (Councilor of the Royal Prussian Court of Appeals), become actively influential and productive in this branch of art also.

Written in Berlin, January, 1817.
Carl Maria von Weber.[6]

---

[6] At the time of the publication of this review, Hoffmann and Weber were still fast friends. Later on, after Hoffmann's work on the German libretto for Spontini's *Olimpie*, Weber's friendliness toward Hoffmann cooled, and the publication in the *Vossische Zeitung* of Hoffmann's masterly but distinctly critical review of *Der Freischütz* ended their association for good.

84. Hector Berlioz

In 1856, on Berlioz's election to the Institute, his friends were outraged and his enemies consoled by a malicious bon mot put into circulation by the music critic of the *Revue des deux mondes:* "Instead of a musician, the Institute has chosen a journalist." Yet a casual reader of the Parisian press of those days might almost have believed this true. Since 1823, Berlioz had been a regular contributor to one musical or literary review after another; by 1864, when he gave up his long-standing association with the *Journal des débats,* he had published more than 650 separate pieces—leading articles, letters from abroad, humorous sketches, fictitious anecdotes, imaginary conversations, *causeries* and *feuilletons* of every sort and description. Only a small part of this enormous production is assembled in his three volumes of collected writings—*Les soirées de l'orchestre* (1852), *Les grotesques de la musique* (1859), and *À travers chants* (1862); other pieces were salvaged in his *Voyage musical* (1844) and in the two volumes of his memoirs, printed in 1865 but not published until after his death.

"Music is not made for everyone, nor everyone for music"—this is perhaps the central article of Berlioz's critical creed, and in the essay translated below it recurs again and again with the persistence of an *idée fixe.* But in writing on *William Tell,* Berlioz also reveals many of the other facets of his critical personality—his preoccupation with the poetic and the picturesque, his capacity for enthusiasm and for indignation, his horror of the mediocre and his impatience with all that fails to measure up to the very highest standards, his contempt for everything academic, his intense dissatisfaction with the commercial and official aspects of musical life. Above all, he reveals his sense of justice and his readiness to acknowledge merit, even in the camp of the enemy. From the first, Berlioz had taken his stand with the opponents of Rossini and "the party of the dilettanti." But he has undertaken to review *William Tell* and he does so without *parti pris* and without hypocrisy.

Rossini's "William Tell" [1]

[*1834*]

TIRED OF hearing perpetual criticism of his works from the point of view of dramatic expression, still more tired, perhaps, of the blind admiration of his fanatical adherents, Rossini has found a very simple means of silencing the one and getting rid of the others. This has been to write a score—one seriously thought out, considered at leisure, and conscientiously executed from beginning to end in accordance with the requirements imposed upon all time by taste and good sense. He has written *William Tell.* This splendid work is thus to be regarded as an application of the author's new theories, as a sign of those greater and nobler capacities whose development the requirements of the sensual people for whom he has written until now have necessarily made impossible. It is from this point of view that we shall examine—without favor, but also without the least bias—Rossini's latest score.

If we consider only the testimonials that it has earned, the applause that it has called forth, and the conversions that it has made, *William Tell* has unquestionably had an immense success—a success that has taken the form of spontaneous admiration with some and of reflection and analysis with many others. And yet one is obliged to admit that to this glory it has not been able to add that other glory of which directors, and sometimes even authors, are more appreciative than of any other— popular success, that is, box-office success. The party of the dilettanti is hostile to *William Tell* and finds it cold and tiresome. The reasons for such a difference of opinion will become clear, we hope, in the course of the examination of this important production which we invite the reader to make with us. Let us follow the author step by step as he hur- ries along the new path that he has chosen, one that he would have reached the end of more rapidly and with a steadier pace if the force of deeply rooted habit had not caused him to cast an occasional glance behind him. These rare deviations once again bear out the old proverb: "In the arts one must take sides; there is no middle ground."

---

1 Text: *Gazette musicale de Paris,* I (1834), 326–327, 336–339, 341–343, 349–351. Berlioz's essay was not written until five years after the first performance of the opera, which took place in Paris on August 3, 1829.

For the first time Rossini has sought to compose an overture meeting the dramatic requirements recognized by every nation in Europe, Italy alone excepted. In making his debut in this style of instrumental music, entirely new to him, he has enlarged the form, so that his overture has in fact become a symphony in four distinct movements instead of the piece in two movements usually thought to be sufficient.

The first movement depicts most successfully, in our opinion, the calm of profound solitude, the solemn silence of nature when the elements and the human passions are at rest. It is a poetic beginning to which the animated scenes that are to follow form a most striking contrast—a contrast in expression, even a contrast in instrumentation, this first part being written for five solo violoncellos, accompanied by the rest of the basses and contrabasses, while the entire orchestra is brought into play in the next movement, "The Storm."

In this, it seems to us, our author would have done well to abandon the square-cut rhythms, the symmetrical phrase-structures, and the periodically returning cadences that he uses so effectively at all other times: "often a beautiful disorder is an effect of art," as an author says whose classical reserve is beyond question.[2] Beethoven proves this in the prodigious cataclysm of his Pastoral Symphony; at the same time he attains the end which the Italian composer lets us expect but does not give us. Several of the harmonic devices are remarkable and ingeniously brought in; among others, the chord of the minor ninth gives rise to effects that are indeed singular. But it is disappointing to rediscover in the storm scene of *William Tell* those staccato notes of the wind instruments which the amateurs call "drops of rain"; Rossini has already used this device in the little storm in the *Barber of Seville* and perhaps in other operas. In compensation he manages to draw from the bass drum without the cymbals picturesque noises in which the imagination readily rediscovers the re-echoing of distant thunder among the anfractuosities of the mountains. The inevitable decrescendo of the storm is handled with unusual skill. In short, it is not arresting or overpowering like Beethoven's storm, a musical tableau which will perhaps remain forever unequalled, and it lacks that sombre, desolate character which we admire so much in the introduction to *Iphigenia in Tauris*, but it is beautiful and full of majesty. Unfortunately the musician is always in evidence; we never lose sight of him in his combinations, even in those which seem the most eccentric. Beethoven on the other hand has known how to reveal himself wholly to the attentive listener: it is no longer an

2 Boileau, *L'Art poétique*, ii, 72.

orchestra that one hears, it is no longer music, but rather the tumultuous voice of the heavenly torrents blended with the uproar of the earthly ones, with the furious claps of thunder, with the crashing of uprooted trees, with the gusts of an exterminating wind, with the frightened cries of men and the lowing of the herds. This is terrifying, it makes one shudder, the illusion is complete. The emotion that Rossini arouses in the same situation falls far short of attaining the same degree of . . . But let us continue.

The storm is followed by a pastoral scene, refreshing in the extreme; the melody of the English horn in the style of the *ranz des vaches* is delicious, and the gamboling of the flute above this peaceful song is ravishing in its freshness and gaiety. We note in passing that the triangle, periodically sounding its tiny pianissimo strokes, is in its right place here; it represents the little bell sounded by the flocks as they saunter quietly along while the shepherds call and answer with their joyful songs. "So you find dramatic meaning in this use of the triangle," someone asks us; "in that case, pray be good enough to tell us what is represented by the violins, violas, basses, clarinets, and so forth." To this I should reply that these are musical instruments, essential to the existence of the art, while the triangle, being only a piece of iron whose sound does not belong to the class of sounds with definite pitch, ought not to be heard in the course of a sweet and tranquil movement unless its presence there is perfectly motivated, failing which it will seem only bizarre and ridiculous.

With the last note of the English horn, which sings the pastoral melody, the trumpets enter with a rapid incisive fanfare on b, the major third in the key of G, established in the previous movement, and in two measures this b becomes the dominant in E major, thus determining in a manner as simple as it is unexpected the tonality of the Allegro that follows. This last part of the overture is treated with a *brio* and a verve that invariably excite the transports of the house. Yet it is built upon a rhythm that has by now become hackneyed, and its theme is almost exactly the same as that of the Overture to *Fernand Cortez*. The staccato figuration of the first violins, bounding from C-sharp minor to G-sharp minor, is a particularly grateful episode, ingeniously interpolated into the midst of this warlike instrumentation; it also provides a means of returning to the principal theme and gives to this return an irresistible impetuosity which the author has known how to make the most of. The peroration of the saucy Allegro has genuine warmth. In short, despite its lack of originality in theme and rhythm, and despite its somewhat vulgar use of the bass drum, most disagreeable at certain moments, constantly pounding away on the strong beats as in a *pas redoublé* or the music of a country dance, one has to admit that the piece as a whole is treated with undeniable mastery and with an elan more captivating, perhaps, than any that Rossini has shown before, and that the Overture to *William Tell* is the work of an enormous talent, so much like genius that it might easily be mistaken for it.

Act I opens with a chorus that has a beautiful and noble simplicity. Placid joy is the feeling that the composer was to paint, and it is difficult to imagine anything better, more truthful, and at the same time more delicate than the melody he has given to these lines:

> How clear a day the skies foretell!
> Come bid it welcome with a song!

The vocal harmonies, supported by an accompaniment in the style of the *ranz des vaches*, breathe happiness and peace. Towards the end of the piece, the modulation from G to E-flat becomes original because of the way in which it is presented and makes an excellent effect.

The *romance* that follows ("Hasten aboard my boat") does not seem to us to be on the same level. Its melody is not always as naive as it should be for the song of a fisherman of Unterwald; many phrases are soiled by that affected style that the singers with their banal embellishments have unfortunately put into circulation. Besides, one scarcely knows why a Swiss should be accompanied by two harps.

Tell, who has been silent throughout the introduction and the fisherman's first stanza, comes forward with a measured monologue full of character; it sets before us the concentrated indignation of a lover of liberty, deeply proud of soul. Its instrumentation is perfect, likewise its modulations, although in the vocal part there are some intervals whose intonation is quite difficult.

At this point the general defect of the work as a whole begins to make itself felt. The scene is too long, and since the three pieces of which it consists are not very different in their coloring, the result is a tiring monotony which is further accentuated by the silence of the orchestra during the *romance*. In general, unless the stage is animated by a powerful dramatic interest, it is seldom that this kind of instrumental inactivity does not cause a fatal indifference, at least at the Opéra. Aside from this, the house is so enormous that a single voice, singing way at the back of the stage, reaches the listener deprived of that warm vibrancy that is the life of music and without which a melody can seldom stand out clearly and make its full effect.

After the intoning of a *ranz des vaches* with its echoes, in which four horns in G and E represent the Alpine trumpet, an Allegro vivace revives the attention. This is a chorus, full of impassioned verve, and it would be admirable if the meaning of the text were just the opposite of what it actually is. The key is E minor and the melody is so full of alarm and agitation that at the first performance, not hearing the words, as usually happens in large theatres, I expected the news of some catastrophe —at the very least, the assassination of Father Melchthal. Yet, far from it, the chorus sings:

> From the mountains a summons
> To repose sounds a call;
> A festival shall lighten
> Our labors in the field.

It is the first time that Rossini has been guilty of this particular kind of incongruity.

After this chorus, which is the second in this scene, there follows an accompanied recitative and then a third chorus, *maestoso*, chiefly remarkable for the rare felicity of the scale from the b in the middle register to the high b which the soprano spreads obliquely against the harmonic background. But the action does not progress, and this defect is made still more glaring by a fourth chorus, rather more violent than joyous in character, sung throughout in full voice, scored throughout for full orchestra, and accompanied by great strokes of the bass drum on the first beat of each measure. Wholly superfluous from the dramatic point of view, the piece has little musical interest. Ruthless cuts have been made in the present score, yet great care has been taken to delete nothing here; this would have been too reasonable. Those who make cuts know only how to cut out the good things; in castrating, it is precisely the noblest parts that are removed. By actual count, then, there are four fully developed choruses here, to do honor to "the clear day" and "the rustic festival," to celebrate "labor and love," and to speak of "the horns that re-echo close by the roaring torrents." This is an awkward blunder, especially at the beginning, this monotony in the choice of means, wholly unjustified by the requirements of the drama, whose progress it aimlessly brings to a standstill. It appears that the work has been dominated at many points by the same unfortunate influence which led the composer astray at this one. I say "the composer," for a man like Rossini always gets what he wants from his poet, and it is well known that for *William Tell* he insisted on a thousand changes which M. Jouy did not refuse him.

Lack of variety even affects the melodic style: the vocal part is full of repeated dominants, and the composer turns about the fifth step of the scale with tiresome persistence, as though it held for him an almost irresistible attraction. Here are some examples from Act I. During the fanfare of the four horns in E-flat, Arnold sings:

> Have a care! Have a care!
> The approach of the Austrian tyrant
> Is announced by the horns from the mountain.

All these words are on a single note—b-flat. In the duet that follows, Arnold again resorts to this b-flat, the dominant in E-flat, for the recitation of two whole lines:

> Under the yoke of such oppression
> What great heart would not be cast down?

Further on, after the modulation to D minor, Tell and Arnold sing alternately on a, the dominant of the new key:

> TELL: Let's be men and we shall win!
> ARNOLD: What revenge can end these affronts?
> TELL: Ev'ry evil rule is unstable.

Against this obstinate droning of the dominant, the five syllables on d, f, and c-sharp at the ends of the phrases can barely be made out. The key changes to F, and the dominant, c, appears again immediately:

> ARNOLD: Think of all you may lose!
> TELL: No matter!
> ARNOLD: What acclaim can we hope from defeat?

And later on:

> ARNOLD: Your expectation?
> TELL: To be victorious,
> And yours as well; I must know what you hope.

Nor is this all; the dominants continue:

> When the signal sounds for the combat,
> My friend, I shall be there.

The E-flat fanfare of the horns begins again and Tell exclaims:

The signal! Gessler comes.
Even now as he taunts us,
Willing slave of his whim, are you waiting
To entreat the disdain of a favoring glance?

These four lines are entirely on the dominant, b-flat. True to his favorite note, Tell again returns to it in order to say, near the end of the movement:

The music calls; I hear the wedding chorus;
Oh, trouble not the shepherds at their feast
Nor spoil their pleasures with your sad lament!

A defect as serious as this does immense harm to the general effect of the fine duet. I say "fine," for despite this chiming of dominants, it is really admirable in all other respects: the instrumentation is treated with unusual care and delicacy; the modulations are varied; Arnold's melody ("Oh Mathilda, my soul's precious idol") is suave in the extreme; many of Tell's phrases are full of dramatic accents; and except for the music of the line "But at virtue's call I obey," the whole has great nobility.

The pieces that follow are all of them more or less noteworthy. We cite in preference the A minor chorus:

Goddess Hymen,
Thy bright feast day
Dawns for us.

This would have a novel, piquant effect if it were sung as one has the right to demand that all choruses should be at the Royal Academy of Music. The pantomimic Allegro of the archers also has great energy, and several *airs de danse* are distinguished by their fresh melodies and the exceptional finish of their orchestration.

The grand finale which crowns the act seems to us much less satisfactory. The beginning brings in the voices and orchestra a return of the dominant pedal-points which have been absent for some time. After a few exclamations by the chorus of Swiss, one hears Gessler's soldiers:

The hour of justice now is striking.
The murd'rer be accursed!
No quarter!

All this is recited on b, the dominant in E minor, which has already been used as a pedal by the basses of the orchestra during the first nineteen measures of the introduction. Confronted by this persistent tendency of the composer's to fall back on the most familiar and monotonous of musical formulas, one can only suppose it to be due to sheer laziness. It is very practical indeed to write a phrase for orchestra whose harmony turns about the two fundamental chords of the key and then, when one has a left-over bit of text to add to it, to set this to the dominant, the note common to the two chords—this saves the composer much time and trouble. After this introductory movement there follows a chorus ("Virgin, adored by ev'ry Christian"); the tempo is slow—I might say, almost dragging—and the piece is accompanied in a very ordinary fashion, so that its effect is to hold up the action and the musical interest most inappropriately. Little is added by the syllabic asides of the soldiers' chorus during the singing of the women:

> How they tremble with fright!
> Do as we bid!
> Your own lives are at stake!

The music for these words is neither menacing nor ironic—it is simply a succession of notes, mere padding to fill out the harmonies, expressing neither contempt nor anger. At length, when the women have finished their long prayer, Rudolf—Gessler's most ardent satellite—breaks out in a violent rage. The orchestra takes a tumultuous headlong plunge, the trombones bellow, the violins utter shrill cries, the instruments vie with one another in elaborating "the horrors of plundering and pillage" with which the Swiss are threatened; unfortunately, the whole is a copy of the finale of *La Vestale*. The figuration of the basses and violas, the strident chords of the brass, the incisive scales of the first violins, the syllabic accompaniment of the second chorus beneath the broad melody of the soprano—Spontini has them all. Let us add, however, that the *stretta* of this chorus contains a magnificent effect due wholly to Rossini. It is the syncopated descending scale for the whole chorus, singing in octaves, while trebles, flutes, and first violins forcefully sustain the major third e to g-sharp; against this interval the notes d-sharp, a, and f-sharp of the lower voices collide in violent agitation. This idea alone, in its grandeur and force, completely effaces all previous sections of the finale. These are now wholly forgotten. At the beginning one was indifferent—in the end one is moved; the author seemed to lack invention—he has redeemed himself and astonished us with an unexpected stroke. Rossini is full of such contrasts.

The curtain rises on Act II. We are witnesses of a hunt; horses cross the stage at a gallop. The fanfare which we heard two or three times during the preceding act resounds again; it is differently scored, to be sure, and linked to a characteristic chorus, but it is a misfortune that so undistinguished a theme should be heard so frequently. The development of the drama imposed it, the musician will tell us. Nevertheless, as we have said before, Rossini might have obtained from his librettist a different arrangement of the scenes and thus have avoided these numerous chances of monotony. He failed to do so and, now that it is too late, he regrets it. Let us go on. Halfway through the chorus just mentioned there is a diatonic passage played in unison by the horns and the four bassoons that has an energy all its own, and the piece as a whole would be captivating were it not for the torture inflicted upon the listener who is at all sensitive by the innumerable strokes of the bass drum on the strong beats, whose effect is the more unfortunate since they again call attention to rhythmic constructions that are completely lacking in originality.

To all this I am sure that Rossini will reply: "Those constructions which seem to you so contemptible are precisely the ones that the public understands the most readily." "Granted," I should answer; "but if you profess so great a respect for the propensities of the vulgar, you ought also to limit yourself to the most commonplace things in melody, harmony, and instrumentation. This is just what you have taken care not to do. Why, then, do you condemn rhythm alone to vulgarity? Besides, in the arts, criticism cannot and should not take account of considerations of this kind. Am I on the same footing as an amateur who hears an opera once every three or four months, I who have occupied myself exclusively with music for so many years? Haven't my ears become more delicate than those of the student whose hobby it is to play flute duets on Sundays? Am I as ignorant as the shopkeeper on the Rue Saint-Denis? In a word, do you not admit that there is progress in music, and in criticism a quality that distinguishes it from blind instinct, namely taste and judgment? Of course you do. This being the case, the ease or difficulty with which the public understands new departures counts for little; this has to do with material results, with business, while it is art that concerns us. Besides, the public—especially in Paris—is not as stupid as some would like to think; it does not reject innovations if they are presented with the right sort of candor. The people who are hostile to innovations are—need I name them?—the *demi-savans*. No, frankly; excuses of this kind are inacceptable. You have written a commonplace rhythm, not because the public would have rejected another, but because it was easier and above all quicker to repeat what had already been used over and over again than to search for more novel and more distinguished combinations."

The distant "Bell Chorus," a contrast in style to the chorus that preceded it, seems to bear out this opinion of ours. Here the whole is full of charm—pure, fresh, and novel. The end of the piece even presents a chord-succession whose effect is delightful, although the harmonies succeed one another in an order prohibited by every rule adopted since the schools began. I refer to the diatonic succession of triads in parallel motion which occurs in connection with the fourfold repetition of the line, "The night has come." A Master of Musical Science would call this kind of part-writing most incorrect: the basses and first sopranos are continually at the octave, the basses and second sopranos continually at the fifth. After the C major triad come those in B major and A minor and finally that in G major, the prevailing tonic. The agreeable effect resulting from these four consecutive fifths and octaves is due, in the first place, to the short pause that separates the chords, a pause sufficient to isolate the harmonies one from another and to give to each fundamental the aspect of a new tonic; in the second place, to the naive coloring of the piece, which not only authorizes this infraction of a time-honored rule, but makes it highly picturesque. Beethoven has already written a similar succession of triads in the first movement of his Eroica; everyone knows the majestic nobility of this passage. Believe then, if you must, in absolute rules!

Hardly has this evening hymn died away like a graceful sunset when we are greeted with another return of the horn fanfare with its inevitable pedal-point on the dominant:

> There sounds a call, the horn of Gessler.
> It bids us return; we obey it.

The chief huntsman and the chorus recite these two lines in their entirety on b-flat. Our earlier observations have here a more direct and a more particular application.

With the following number the composer begins a higher flight; this is quite another style. Mathilda's entrance is preceded by a long ritornello doubly interesting as harmony and as dramatic expression. There is real passion in this, and that feverish agitation that animates the heart of a young woman obliged to conceal her love. Then comes a recitative, perfect in its diction and admirably commented upon by the orchestra, which reproduces fragments of the ritornello. After this introduction follows the well-known *romance*, "Sombre forests."

Rossini has, in our opinion, written few pieces as elegant, as fresh, as distinguished in their melody, and as ingenious in their modulations as this one: aside from the immense merit of the vocal part and the harmony, it involves a style of accompaniment for the violas and first violins that is full of melancholy, also—at the beginning of each stanza—a pianissimo effect for the kettledrum that rouses the listener's attention in a lively manner. One seems to hear one of those natural sounds whose cause remains unknown, one of those strange noises which attract our attention on a clear day in the deep forest and which redouble in us the feeling of silence and isolation. This is poetry, this is music, this is art—beautiful, noble, and pure, just as its votaries would have it always.

This style is sustained until the end of the act, and from henceforth marvel follows marvel. In the duet between Arnold and Mathilda, so full of chevaleresque passion, we mention as a blemish the long pedal of the horns and trumpets on g, alternately tonic and dominant, the effect of which is at certain moments atrocious. Then too we shall reproach the composer for having blindly followed the example of the older French composers, who would have thought themselves disgraced if they had failed to bring in the trumpets at once whenever the words made any mention of glory or victory. In this respect Rossini treats us like the dilettanti of 1803,[8] like the admirers of Sédaine and Monsigny.

> Ah, return to war and to glory,
> Take wing and make me proud once more!
> One gains a name if one's a victor;
> The world will then approve my choice.

"Out with the obbligato fanfare," Rossini will have said on reading this in his libretto; "I am writing for France." Finally, it seems to us that this duet, which is developed at considerable length, would gain if there were no repetition of the motive which the two singers have together, "The one who adores you." Since the tempo of this passage is slower than the rest, the repetition necessarily brings with it two interruptions which break up the general pace and detract from the animated effect of the scene by prolonging it uselessly.

But from this point until the final chord of the second act, this defect does not recur. Walter and Tell enter unexpectedly; Mathilda takes flight, Arnold remains to listen to bitter reproaches on his love for the daughter of the Helvetian tyrant. Nothing could be more beautiful, more expressive, more noble than this recitative, both in the vocal parts and in the orchestra. Two phrases are particularly striking in the verity of their expression. One is Walter's counsel:

8 The year in which Berlioz was born.

> Perhaps, though, you should alter
> And take the pains to know us better.

The other is Tell's apostrophe:

> Do you know what it is to feel love for one's country?

At length, the tragic ritornello of the trio is unfolded. Here we confess that, despite our role as critic and the obligations that it brings with it, it is impossible for us to apply the cold blade of the scalpel to the heart of this sublime creation. What should we analyze? The passion, the despair, the tears, the lamentations of a son horrified by the news of his father's murder? God forbid! Or should we make frivolous observations about details, quibble with the author over a *gruppetto* or a solo passage for the flute or an obscure moment in the second violin part? Not I! If others have the courage for it, let them attempt it. As for me, I have none at all—I can only join the crowd in shouting: "Beautiful! Superb! Admirable! Ravishing!"

But I shall have to be sparing of my enthusiastic adjectives, for I am going to need them for the rest of the act, which remains almost continuously on this same high level. The arrival of the three cantons affords the composer an opportunity to write three pieces in three wholly different styles. The first chorus is in a strong, robust style which paints for us a working people with calloused hands and arms that never tire. In the second chorus and the chaste sweetness of its melody we recognize the timid shepherds; the expression of their fears is ravishing in its grace and naïveté. The fishermen from the canton of Uri arrive by boat from the lake while the orchestra imitates as faithfully as music can the movements and the cadenced efforts of a crew of oarsmen. Hardly have these late-comers disembarked when the three choruses unite in a syllabic ensemble, rapidly recited in half voice and accompanied by the pizzicati of the strings and an occasional muffled chord from the wind instruments:

> Before you, Tell, you see
> Three peoples as one band,
> Our rights our only arms
> Against a vile oppressor.

First recited by the chorus of fishermen and then taken up by the two other choruses, who mingle with it their exclamations and their laconic asides, this phrase is dramatically most realistic. Here is a crowd in which each individual, moved by hope and fear, can scarcely hold back the sentiments that agitate him, a crowd in which all wish to speak and each man interrupts his neighbor. Be it said in passing that the execution of this *coro parlato* is extremely difficult, a fact that may in part excuse the choristers of the Opéra, who usually recite it very badly indeed.

But Tell is about to speak and all grow silent—*arrectis auribus adstant.*[4] He stirs them, he inflames them, he apprises them of Melchthal's cruel death, he promises them arms; finally he asks them directly:

> TELL: Do you agree to help?
> CHORUS: We one and all agree.
> TELL: You will join us?
> CHORUS: We will.
> TELL: Even in death?
> CHORUS: We will.

Then, uniting their voices, they swear a grave and solemn oath to "the God of kings and of shepherds" to free themselves from slavery and to exterminate their tyrants. Their gravity under these circumstances, which would be absurd if they were Frenchmen or Italians, is admirable for a cold-blooded people like the Swiss, whose decisions, if less precipitate, are not lacking in steadfastness or in assurance of attainment. The movement becomes animated only at the end, when Arnold catches sight of the first rays of the rising sun:

> ARNOLD: The time has come.
> WALTER: For us this is a time of danger.
> TELL: Nay, of vict'ry!
> WALTER: What answer shall we give him?
> ARNOLD: To arms!
> ARNOLD ⎫
> TELL   ⎬ To arms!
> WALTER ⎭

Then the whole chorus, the soloists, the orchestra, and the percussion instruments, which have not been heard since the beginning of the act, one and all take up the cry: "To arms!" And at this last and most terrible war cry which bursts forth from all these breasts, shivering in the dawn of the first day of liberty, the entire instrumental mass hurls itself like an avalanche into an impetuous Allegro!

Ah, it is sublime! Let us take breath.

We left Arnold in despair, thinking only of war and vengeance. His father's death, imposing new obligations upon him, has torn him abruptly from the attraction that had lured him little by little towards the ranks

---

4 They stand by with attentive ears.—Vergil. *Aeneid.* i. 152. [Fairclough]

of his country's enemies. Filled with gloomy thoughts, his words to Mathilda at the beginning of Act III reveal his fierce and sombre pre-occupation:

> ARNOLD: I tarry to avenge my father.
> MATHILDA: What is your hope?
> ARNOLD: It is blood that I hope for;
>   I renounce Fortune's favors all,
>   I renounce all love and all friendship,
>   Even glory, even marriage.
> MATHILDA: And I, Melchthal?
> ARNOLD: My father's dead.

The expression of these agitated sentiments dominates the whole of the long ritornello which precedes and prepares the entrance of the two lovers. After a short but energetic recitative, in which Arnold sings an-other five-measure phrase on a single note, an e, the great agitato aria of Mathilda begins.

At the outset, this piece is not as happy in its choice of melody and in its dramatic expression as we find it at the end. The composer seems to have begun it in cold blood and to have come to life by degrees as he pene-trated his subject. The first phrase is what we might call "a phrase in compartments" (*une phrase à compartimens*); it belongs to that vast family of melodies consisting of eight measures, four of them on the tonic and as many on the dominant, examples of which occur at the be-ginning of nearly every concerto of Viotti, Rode, Kreutzer, and their imitators. This is a style in which each development can be foreseen well in advance; in composing this, his latest and perhaps his most important work, it would seem to us that Rossini ought to have abandoned it once and for all. Aside from this, the two lines that follow cry out for an expressive musical setting:

> In my heart solitude unending!
> Shall you never be at my side?

Rossini has failed to give it to them. What he has written is cold and commonplace, despite an instrumentation that might have been less tor-tured in its superabundant luxuriousness. As though to efface the memory of this somewhat scholastic beginning, the peroration is admirable in its originality, its grace, and its sentiment. The liveliest imagination could not have asked the composer for a style of declamation more truthful or more noble than that in which he has caused Mathilda to exclaim, with melancholy abandon:

To the land of the stranger
Whose shore you seek, I may not follow
To offer you my tender care,
And yet all my heart shall be with you,
To all your woes it shall be true.

We are not as satisfied with the ensemble for the two voices which closes the scene. As the farewell of two lovers who separate, never to see one another again, it should have been heart-breaking; apart from Mathilda's chromatic vocalization on the word "Melchthal," it is only brilliant and overscored for the wind instruments, without contrasts or oppositions.

At the same time, it is greatly to be regretted—even if only because of the fine flashes of inspiration which we have mentioned—that the scene is entirely suppressed in the performances being given today. At present the act begins with the chorus of Gessler's soldiers, who are engaged in a brutal and arrogant celebration of the hundredth anniversary of the conquest of Switzerland and its addition to the German Empire.

After this there is dancing, of course; at the Opéra, an excuse for a ballet would be found, even in a representation of the Last Judgment. What difference does it make?—the *airs de danse*, all of them saturated with the Swiss melodic idiom, have rare elegance and are written with care (I except only the Allegro in G called the "Pas de soldats"). It is in the midst of this ballet that we meet the celebrated Tyrolienne, so popular nowadays, remarkable for its modulations and for the vocal rhythm which serves as its accompaniment. Before Rossini, no one writing for the stage had thought of using an immediate succession of chords having the character of contrasted tonic harmonies, such as the one that occurs in the thirty-third measure, where the melody outlines an arpeggio within the major triad on b, only to fall back at once into the one on g, the true tonic. This little piece, doubtless written one morning at the breakfast table, has had a truly incredible success, while beauties of an incomparably higher order have won only very limited approval, although this approval is, to be sure, of quite another sort than that which has welcomed the pretty Tyrolienne so graciously. With some composers, the applause of the crowd is useful but scarcely flattering—for these artists, only the opinion of the discriminating has real value. With others it is just the opposite—only quantity has value, while quality is almost worthless. Until their more frequent dealings with Europeans taught them the value of money, the American Indians preferred a hundred sous to a single gold piece.

After the dances comes the famous scene of the apple. Its style is in general nervous and dramatic. One of Tell's phrases in his dialogue with Gessler seems to us to have real character:

> GESSLER: My captive shall he be.
> TELL: Let us hope he may be your last.

On the other hand, a movement that seems to us absolutely false in sentiment and expression is that in which Tell, concerned for his son, takes him aside, embraces him, and orders him to leave:

> My heart's dearest treasure,
> Receive my embraces,
> Then depart from me.

Instead of this, it would have been enough to have made him a sign and to have uttered quickly these two words: "Save thyself!" To elaborate upon this idea in an Andante would perhaps have done no harm in an Italian opera, a really Italian one, but in a work like *William Tell,* where reason has been admitted to full civic rights, where not everything is directed towards permitting the singers to shine, such a piece is more than an incongruity—it is an outright nonsense.

The recitative that follows exactly meets the requirements that we have just laid down:

> Rejoin your mother! These my orders:
> That the flame on the mountains now be lighted
> To give to our allies the command to rebel.

This precipitate utterance throws an even more glaring light on the faulty expression that shocked us when this idea was presented before. In compensation, the composer offers us Tell's touching instructions to his little son:

> Move not a muscle, be calm and fearless,
> In prayer bend a suppliant knee!

How admirably the accompaniment of the violoncellos weeps beneath the voice of this father whose heart is breaking as he embraces his boy! The orchestra, almost silent, is heard only in pizzicato chords, each group followed by a rest of half a measure. The bassoons, pianissimo, sustain long plaintive notes. How filled all this is with emotion and anguish—how expressive of the anticipated great event about to be accomplished!

> My son, my son, think of thy mother!
> Patiently she waits for us both.

These last phrases of the melody are irresistibly lifelike; they go straight to the heart.

Let the partisans of popular opinion say what they please. If this sublime inspiration arouses only polite and infrequent applause, there is something about it that is nobler, higher, worthier for a man to take pride in having created, than there is in a graceful Tyrolienne, even though it be applauded by a hundred thousand and sung by the women and children of all Europe. There is a difference between the pretty and the beautiful. To pretend to side with the majority, and to value prettiness at the expense of that which addresses itself to the heart's most intimate sentiments, this is the part of the shrewd businessman, but not that of the artist conscious of his dignity and independence.

The finale of this act includes, in its first section, an admirably energetic passage which is invariably annihilated at the Opera by the inadequacy of the singer; this is the sudden outburst of the timid Mathilda:

> I claim him as my ward in the name of the sov'reign.
> In indignation a people is watching,
> Take care, take care, he is safe in my arms.

This general indignation is skillfully portrayed, both in the vocal part and in the orchestra; it is as lifelike as Gluck and Spontini. As an accompaniment to the ingeniously modulated melody of the sopranos, the syllabic theme of the men's chorus ("When their pride has misled them") makes an excellent effect. On the other hand, the *stretta* of this chorus consists only of furious cries; to be sure, they are motivated by the text, but they arouse no emotion in the listener, whose ears are needlessly outraged. Here again, it would perhaps have been better to change the wording of the libretto, for it would be difficult if not impossible to set the line, "Curséd be Gessler's name," except as a savage vociferation having neither melody nor rhythm and paralyzing by its violence all feeling for harmony.

Act IV re-establishes the individual passions and affords a needed relaxation after the uproar of the preceding scenes. Arnold revisits his father's deserted cottage; his heart filled with a hopeless love and with projects of vengeance, all his senses stirred by the recollections of bloody carnage always before his mind's eye, he breaks down, overcome by the enormity of the affecting contrast. All is calm and silent. Here is peace —and the tomb. And yet an infinity separates him from that breast upon which, at a moment like this, he would so gladly pour out his tears of filial piety, from that heart close to which his own would beat less sadly. Mathilda shall never be his. The situation is poetic, even poignantly melancholy, and it has inspired the musician to write an air which we do not hesitate to pronounce the most beautiful of the entire score. Here the young Melchthal pours out all the sufferings of his soul; here his mournful recollections of the past are painted in the most ravishing of melodies; harmony and modulation are employed only to reinforce the melodic expression, never out of purely musical caprice.

The Allegro with choruses, which follows, is full of spirit and makes a worthy crown for an equally fine scene. At the same time, the piece has only a very indifferent effect upon the public, to judge from the applause with which it is received. For the many it is too refined; delicate shadings like these nearly always escape their attention. Alas, if one could only reduce the public to an assembly of fifty sensible and intelligent persons, how blissful it would be to be an artist!

Since the first performance, the trio accompanied only by the wind instruments has been suppressed, also the piece immediately following it, the prayer sung during the storm. The cut is most inopportune, particularly in view of the prayer, a masterpiece in the picturesque style, whose musical conception is novel enough to have warranted some allowance being made in its favor. Aside from the *mise en scène*, considerations having to do with the decor or the stage machinery were no doubt responsible for the suppression of this interesting part of the score. The thing was accordingly done without hesitation—everyone knows that at the Opéra the directors *support* the music.

From this moment until the final chorus, we shall find nothing but padding. The outbursts of the orchestra while Tell struggles on the lake with the storm, the fragments of recitative interrupted by the chorus—these are things that the musician writes with confidence that no one will listen to them.

The final chorus is another story:

> About us all changes and grows.
> Fresh the air!

This is a beautiful harmonic broadening-out. The *ranz des vaches* floats gracefully above these massive chords and the hymn of Free Switzerland soars upward to heaven, calm and imposing, like the prayer of a just man.

85. Robert Schumann

In contrast to Weber, the practical propagandist, and Berlioz, the professional man of letters, Schumann brings to his critical writing romantic idealism and a high purpose. As he tells us himself in his introductory essay, the founding of the *Neue Zeitschrift* in 1834 was a direct outgrowth of his dissatisfaction with the existing state of music and of his desire to bring about a rehabilitation of the poetic principle, "the very thing," as he said later on, "by which we should like to have these pages distinguished from others." The editorial position of the new journal is perhaps most forcefully summed up in Schumann's "speech from the throne" for 1839: "A stern attitude towards foreign trash, benevolence towards aspiring younger artists, enthusiasm for everything masterly that the past has bequeathed." On the whole, these aims are not so very different from those implicit in Berlioz; it is simply that Schumann has less self-interest and less worldly wisdom and that he goes about his task in a more serious way, more humbly and more charitably, if also with greater chauvinism.

"The present is characterized by its parties," Schumann writes in another connection (1836). "Like the political present, one can divide the musical into liberals, middlemen, and reactionaries, or into romanticists, moderns, and classicists. On the right sit the elderly—the contrapuntists, the anti-chromaticists; on the left the youthful—the revolutionaries in their Phrygian caps, the anti-formalists, the genially impudent, among whom the Beethovenians stand out as a special class; in the *Juste Milieu* young and old mingle irresolutely—here are included most of the creations of the day, the offspring which the moment brings forth and then destroys."

In his day, Schumann stood at the very center of the romantic movement in German music, yet he makes little effort to define its aims and aspirations for us. To him, clearly, these were self-evident: "It is scarcely credible that a distinct romantic school could be formed in music, which is in itself romantic." But in his review of Stephen Heller's Opus 7 (1837) Schumann comes as close as he ever does to a definition and in so doing defines for us also his own personal style. "I am heartily sick of the word 'romanticist,' " he says; "I have not pronounced it ten times in my whole life; and yet—if I wished to confer a brief designation upon our young seer, I should call him one, and what a one! Of that vague, nihilistic disorder behind which some search for romanticism, and of that crass, scribbling materialism which the French neoromanticists affect, our composer—thank Heaven!—knows nothing; on the contrary, he perceives things naturally, for the most part, and expresses himself clearly and judiciously. Yet on taking up his compositions one senses that there is something more than this lurking in the background—an attractive, individual half-light, more like dawn than dusk, which causes one to see his otherwise clear-cut configurations under an unaccustomed glow. . . . And do not let me overlook the dedication—the coincidence is astonishing. You recall, Eusebius, that we once dedicated something to the Wina of the *Flegeljahre*; the dedication of these impromptus also names one of Jean Paul's constellations —Liane von Froulay [in Jean Paul's *Titan*]. We have in general much in common, an admission that no one should misinterpret—it is too obvious."

Davidsbündlerblätter [1]

INTRODUCTORY

[*1854*]

NEAR THE end of the year 1833 there met in Leipzig, every evening and as though by chance, a number of musicians, chiefly younger men, primarily for social companionship, not less, however, for an exchange of ideas about the art which was for them the meat and drink of life—Music. It cannot be said that musical conditions in Germany were particularly encouraging at the time. On the stage Rossini still ruled, at the piano, with few rivals, Herz and Hünten. And yet only a few years had elapsed since Beethoven, Weber, and Schubert had lived among us. Mendelssohn's star was in the ascendant, to be sure, and marvelous reports were heard of a Pole, one Chopin—but it was not until later that these exerted lasting influence. Then one day an idea flashed across the minds of these young hotheads: Let us not sit idly by; let us attack, that things may become better; let us attack, that the poetic in art may again be held in honor! In this way the first pages of a "New Journal for Music" came into being. But the joy of the solid unanimity of this union of young talents did not continue long. In one of the most cherished comrades, Ludwig Schunke,[2]

---

1 Text: *Gesammelte Schriften über Musik und Musiker* (Leipzig, 1854); for the essay "New Paths," *Neue Zeitschrift für Musik*, XXXIX (1853), 185–186.

2 Talented composer and pianist, friend of Schumann's, co-editor of the *Zeitschrift* during its first year, Schunke died on December 7, 1834, shortly before his twenty-fourth birthday.

death claimed a sacrifice. As to the others,[3] some removed from Leipzig altogether for a time. The undertaking was on the point of dissolution. Then one of their number, precisely the musical visionary of the company, one who had until now dreamed away his life more at the piano than among books, decided to take the editing of the publication in hand; [4] he continued to guide it for nearly ten years, to the year 1844. So there arose a series of essays, from which this volume offers a selection. The greater part of the views therein expressed are still his today. What he set down, in hope and fear, about many an artistic phenomenon has in the course of time been substantiated.

Here ought also to be mentioned another league, a more than secret one in that it existed only in the head of its founder—the "Davidsbündler." In order to represent various points of view within the view of art as a whole, it seemed not inappropriate to invent contrasted types of artist, among which Florestan and Eusebius were the most significant, between whom Master Raro stood as intermediary. Like a red thread, this "Davidsbündler" company wound itself through the journal, humorously blending "Wahrheit und Dichtung." [5] Later on, these comrades, not unwelcome to the readers of that time, disappeared entirely from the paper, and from the time when a Peri enticed them into distant climes, nothing further has been heard of their literary efforts.

Should these collected pages, while reflecting a highly agitated time, likewise contribute to divert the attention of those now living to artistic phenomena already nearly submerged by the stream of the present, the aim of their publication will have been fulfilled.

. . . . . .

AN OPUS TWO [a]

[1831]

Not long ago Eusebius stole quietly in through the door. You know the ironic smile on his pale face with which he seeks to arouse our expectations. I was sitting at the piano with Florestan, who, as you know, is one of those rare men of music who foresee, as it were, all coming, novel, or extraordinary things. None the less there was a surprise in store for him

a This essay was published as early as 1831 in the *Allgemeine musikalische Zeitung*. As the one in which the Davidsbündler make their first appearance, it is given a place here also.

3 In addition to Schunke, Schumann's chief collaborators during the first year were Friedrich Wieck and Julius Knorr.

4 During its first year, the *Zeitschrift* described itself as "published by a society of artists and friends of art"; with the first number of the second volume this is changed to read "published under the direction of R. Schumann in association with a number of artists and friends of art."

5 An allusion to the title of Goethe's autobiography.

today. With the words "Hats off, gentlemen, a genius!" Eusebius placed
a piece of music on the stand. We were not allowed to see the title. I leafed
about absentmindedly among the pages; this veiled, silent enjoyment
of music has something magical about it. Furthermore, as it seems to me,
every composer has his own special way of arranging notes for the eye:
Beethoven looks different on paper from Mozart, very much as Jean
Paul's prose looks different from Goethe's. In this case, however, it was
as though unfamiliar eyes were everywhere gazing out at me strangely—
flower-eyes, basilisk-eyes, peacock-eyes, maiden-eyes; here and there
things grew clearer—I thought I saw Mozart's "Là ci darem la mano"
woven about with a hundred harmonies; Leporello seemed to be actually
winking at me, and Don Giovanni flew past me in a white cloak. "Now
play it!" Florestan suggested. Eusebius obeyed; huddled in a window
alcove, we listened. As though inspired, Eusebius played on, leading past
us countless figures from the realest of lives; it was as though the inspiration of the moment lifted his fingers above the usual measure of their
capabilities. Florestan's entire approval, except for a blissful smile, consisted, to be sure, in nothing but the remark that the variations might perhaps be by Beethoven or Schubert, had either of them been piano virtuosi
—but when he turned to the title page, read nothing more than:

Là ci darem la mano
varié pour le pianoforte par
Frédéric Chopin
Oeuvre 2

and both of us called out in amazement "An opus two!"—and when every
face glowed somewhat with more than usual astonishment and, aside from
a few exclamations, little was to be distinguished but: "At last, here's
something sensible again—Chopin—the name is new to me—who is he?—
in any case a genius—isn't that Zerlina laughing there or perhaps even
Leporello?"—then, indeed, arose a scene which I prefer not to describe.
Excited with wine, Chopin, and talking back and forth, we went off to
Master Raro, who laughed a great deal and showed little curiosity about
our Opus 2—"for I know you and your new-fangled enthusiasm too well
—just bring your Chopin here to me some time." We promised it for the
next day. Presently Eusebius bid us an indifferent good night; I remained
for a while with Master Raro; Florestan, who for some time had had no
lodgings, fled through the moonlit alley to my house. I found him in my
room at midnight, lying on the sofa, his eyes closed.

"Chopin's variations," he began, as though in a dream, "they are still
going around in my head. Surely the whole is dramatic and sufficiently

Chopinesque; the introduction, self-contained though it is—can you recall Leporello's leaping thirds?—seems to me to belong least of all to the rest; but the theme—why does he write it in B-flat?—the variations, the final movement, and the Adagio—these are really something—here genius crops up in every measure. Of course, dear Julius, the speaking parts are Don Giovanni, Zerlina, Leporello, and Masetto. In the theme, Zerlina's reply is drawn amorously enough. The first variation might perhaps be called somewhat elegant and coquettish—in it, the Spanish grandee toys aimiably with the peasant maid. This becomes self-evident in the second, which is already much more intimate, comic, and quarrelsome, exactly as though two lovers were chasing each other and laughing more than usual. But in the third—how everything is changed! This is pure moonshine and fairy spell—Masetto watches from afar and curses rather audibly, to be sure, but Don Giovanni is little disturbed. And now the fourth —what is your idea of it? Eusebius played it quite clearly—doesn't it jump about saucily and impudently as it approaches the man, although the Adagio (it seems natural to me that Chopin repeats the first part) is in B-flat minor, than which nothing could be more fitting, for it reproaches the Don, as though moralizing, with his misdeeds. It is bold, surely, and beautiful that Leporello listens, laughs, and mocks from behind the shrubbery, that the oboes and clarinets pour out seductive magic, and that the B-flat major, in full blossom, marks well the moment of the first kiss. Yet all of this is as nothing in comparison with the final movement—is there more wine, Julius?—this is Mozart's whole finale—popping corks and clinking bottles everywhere, in the midst of things Leporello's voice, then the grasping evil spirits in pursuit, the fleeing Don Giovanni—and finally the end, so beautifully soothing, so truly conclusive." Only in Switzerland, Florestan added, had he experienced anything similar to this ending; there, on a fine day, when the evening sun climbs higher and higher to the topmost peak where finally its last beam vanishes, there comes a moment in which one seems to see the white Alp-giants close their eyes. One feels only that one has seen a heavenly vision. "Now Julius, wake up, you too, to new dreams—and go to sleep!"

"Florestan of my heart," I answered, "these private feelings are perhaps praiseworthy, if somewhat subjective; but little as Chopin needs to think of listening to his genius, I still shall also bow my head before such genius, such aspiration, such mastery."

With that we fell asleep.

Julius.[6]

---

6 This essay was Schumann's first published writing.

FLORESTAN'S SHROVE TUESDAY ADDRESS
DELIVERED AFTER A PERFORMANCE OF BEETHOVEN'S LAST SYMPHONY

[*1835*]

Florestan climbed on to the piano and spoke as follows:

Assembled Davidsbündler, that is, youths and men who are to slay the Philistines, musical and otherwise, especially the tallest ones (see the last numbers of the *Comet* [7] for 1833).

I am never overenthusiastic, best of friends! The truth is, I know the symphony better than I know myself. I shall not waste a word on it. After it, anything I could say would be as dull as ditch water, Davidsbündler. I have celebrated regular Ovidian Tristia, have heard anthropological lectures. One can scarcely be fanatical about some things, scarcely paint some satires with one's facial expression, scarcely—as Jean Paul's Giannozzo [8] did—sit low enough in the balloon for men not to believe that one concerns oneself about them, so far, far below do these two-legged creatures, which one calls men, file through the narrow pass, which one may in any case call life. To be sure, I was not at all annoyed by what little I heard. In the main I laughed at Eusebius. A regular clown, he flew impertinently at a fat neighbor who inquired confidentially during the Adagio: "Sir, did not Beethoven also write a battle symphony?" "Yes, that's the 'Pastoral' Symphony," our Euseb replied indifferently. "Quite right, so it is," the fat one expanded, resuming his meditations.

Men must deserve noses, otherwise God would not have provided them. They tolerate much, these audiences, and of this I could cite you magnificent examples; for instance, rascal, when at a concert you were turning the pages of one of Field's nocturnes for me. Unluckily, on one of the most broken-down rattle-boxes that was ever inflicted upon a company of listeners, instead of the pedal I stumbled on the Janizary stop [9]—piano enough, fortunately, so that I could yield to the impulse of the moment and, repeating the stroke softly from time to time, could let the audience believe some sort of march was being played in the distance. Of course Eusebius did his part by spreading the story; the audience, however, outdid themselves in applause.

Any number of similar anecdotes had occurred to me during the Adagio

---

7 An "Unterhaltungsblatt" published in Altenburg from 1830 to 1836. In its issue for August 27, 1832, it had printed Schumann's "Reminiscences from Clara Wieck's Last Concerts in Leipzig."

8 Principal character in Jean Paul's "Des Luftschiffers Giannozzo Seebuch," one of the humorous supplements to the second volume of his *Titan* (1801).

9 A pedal producing the effect of bass drum and cymbals or triangle, much favored during the vogue of "Turkish music."

when we came to the first chord of the Finale. "What is it, Cantor," I said to a trembling fellow next to me, "but a triad with a suspended fifth, somewhat whimsically laid out, in that one does not know which to accept as the bass—the A of the kettledrum or the F of the bassoons? Just have a look at Türk, Section 19, page 7!" [10] "Sir, you speak very loud and are surely joking." With a small and terrifying voice I whispered in his ear: "Cantor, watch out for storms! The lightning sends ahead no liveried lackeys before it strikes; at the most there is first a storm and after it a thunderbolt. That's just its way." "All the same, such dissonances ought to be prepared." Just at that moment came the second one. "Cantor, the fine trumpet seventh shall excuse you." I was quite exhausted with my restraint—I should have soothed him with a sound blow.

Now you gave me a memorable moment, conductor, when you hit the tempo of the low theme in the basses so squarely on the line that I forgot much of my annoyance at the first movement, in which, despite the modest pretense of the direction "Un poco maestoso," there speaks the full, deliberate stride of godlike majesty.

"What do you suppose Beethoven meant by those basses?" "Sir," I replied gravely enough, "a genius often jests; it seems to be a sort of night-watchman's song." Gone was the exquisite moment, once again Satan was set loose. Then I remarked the Beethoven devotees—the way they stood there goggle-eyed, saying: "That's by our Beethoven. That's a German work. In the last movement there's a double fugue. Some reproach him for not excelling in this department, but how he has done it— yes, this is *our* Beethoven." Another choir chimed in with: "It seems as though all forms of poetry are combined in the work: in the first movement the epic, in the second the humorous, in the third the lyric, in the fourth—the blend of them all—the drama." Still another choir really applied itself to praising: "It's a gigantic work, colossal, comparable to the pyramids of Egypt." Still another went in for description: "The symphony tells the story of man's creation: first chaos, then the divine command 'Let there be light,' then the sun rising on the first man, who is delighted with such splendor—in short, it is the whole first chapter of the Pentateuch."

I became more frantic and more quiet. And while they were eagerly following the text and finally applauding, I seized Eusebius by the arm and pulled him down the brightly lighted stairs, smiling faces on either hand.

Below, in the darkness of the street lamps, Eusebius said, as though to himself: "Beethoven—what depths there are in the word, even the deep

---

10 D. G. Türk, *Kurze Anweisung zum Generalbassspielen* (Halle, 1791).

sonority of the syllables resounding as into an eternity! For this name, it is as though there could be no other characters." "Eusebius," I said with genuine calm, "do you too condescend to praise Beethoven? Like a lion, he would have raised himself up before you and have asked: 'Who, then, are you who presume this?' I do not address myself to you, Eusebius; you mean well—but must a great man then always have a thousand dwarfs in his train? They believe they understand him—who so aspired, who struggled against countless attacks—as they smile and clap their hands. Do those who are not accountable to me for the simplest musical rule have the effrontery to evaluate a master as a whole? Do these, all of whom I put to flight if I drop merely the word 'counterpoint'—do these who perhaps appreciate this and that at second hand and at once call out: 'Oh, this fits our corpus perfectly!'—do these who wish to talk of exceptions to rules they do not know—do these who prize in him, not the measure of his gigantic powers, but precisely the excess—shallow men of the world —wandering sorrows of Werther—overgrown, bragging boys—do these presume to love him, even praise him?"

Davidsbündler, at the moment I can think of no one so entitled but the provincial Silesian nobleman who recently wrote to a music dealer in this fashion:

Dear sir:

At last I have my music cabinet nearly in order. You ought to see how splendid it is. Alabaster columns on the inside, a mirror with silk curtains, busts of composers—in short, magnificent! In order, however, to give it a final touch of real elegance I ask you to send me, further, the complete works of Beethoven, *for I like this composer very much.*

What more there is that I should say, I should, in my opinion, scarcely know.

ENTHUSIASTIC LETTERS [b]

[*1835*]

1. Eusebius to Chiara

After each of our musical feasts for the soul there always reappears an angelic face which, down to the roguish line about the chin, more than

---

b These letters might also have been called "Wahrheit und Dichtung." They have to do with the first Gewandhaus concerts held under Mendelssohn's direction in October, 1835.

[The concerts in question were the first four in the subscription series; their dates were October 4, 11, 22, and 29. They are also covered in more conventional reviews published in the *Allgemeine musikalische Zeitung* for October 14 and 21 and for December 16, with the help of which it is possible to supply certain details passed over in Schumann's account.—Ed.]

resembles that of a certain Clara.[12] Why are you not with us, and how may you have thought last night of us Firlenzer, from the "Calm Sea"[13] to the resplendent ending of the Symphony in B-flat major?[14]

Except for a concert itself, I know of nothing finer than the hour before one, during which one hums ethereal melodies to oneself, the finger on the lips, walks up and down discreetly on one's toes, performs whole overtures on the windowpanes. . . . Just then it struck a quarter of. And now, with Florestan, I mounted the polished stairs.

"Seb," said he, "I look forward tonight to many things: first to the whole program itself, for which one thirsts after the dry summer; then to F. Meritis,[15] who for the first time marches into battle with his orchestra; then to the singer Maria,[16] with her vestal voice; finally to the public as a whole, expecting miracles—that public to which, as you know, I usually attach only too little importance." At the word "public" we stood before the old chatelain with his Commendatore face, who had much to do and finally let us in with an expression of annoyance, for as usual Florestan had forgotten his ticket. As I entered the brightly lighted golden hall I may, to judge from my face, have delivered perhaps the following address:

"With gentle tread I make my entrance, for I seem to see welling up here and there the faces of those unique ones to whom is given the fine art of uplifting and delighting hundreds in a single moment. There I see Mozart, stamping his feet to the symphony until a shoe-buckle flies off; there Hummel, the old master, improvising at the piano; there Catalani, pulling off her shawl, for the sound-absorbing carpet has been forgotten; there Weber; there Spohr; and many another. And there I thought also of you, my pure bright Chiara—of how at other times you spied down from your box with the lorgnette that so well becomes you." This train of thought was interrupted by the angry eye of Florestan, who stood, rooted to the spot, in his old corner by the door, and in his angry eye stood something like this:

"Think, Public, of my having you together again at last and of my being able to set you one against another . . . Long ago, overt ones, I wanted to establish concerts for deaf-mutes which might serve you as a pattern of how to behave at concerts, especially at the finest . . . Like Tsing-Sing,[17] you were to have been turned to a stone pagoda, had you

---

12 Quoted from an earlier letter to Clara (*Jugendbriefe* [Leipzig, 1885], p. 266). At the time of the writing of these letters, Clara Wieck was just sixteen.

13 Mendelssohn's overture.

14 Beethoven's "Fourth."

15 Mendelssohn.

16 Henriette Grabau.

17 A character in Auber's opera *Le Cheval de bronze* (1835).

dared to repeat anything of what you saw in music's magic realm," and so forth. The sudden deathlike silence of the public broke in on my reflections. F. Meritis came forward. A hundred hearts went out to him in that first moment.

Do you remember how, leaving Padua one evening, we went down the Brenta; how the tropical Italian night closed the eyes of one after another? And how, in the morning, a voice suddenly called out: "Ecco, ecco, signori —Venezia!"—and the sea lay spread out before us, calm and stupendous; how on the furthest horizon there sounded up and down a delicate tinkle, as though the little waves were speaking to one another in a dream? Behold—such is the wafting and weaving of the "Calm Sea"; [c] one actually grows drowsy from it and is rather thought than thinking. The Beethovenian chorus after Goethe [18] and the accentuated word sound almost raw in contrast to the spider's-web tone of the violins. Toward the end there occurs a single detached harmony—here perhaps a Nereid fixes the poet with her seductive glance, seeking to draw him under—then for the first time a wave beats higher, the sea grows by degrees more talkative, the sails flutter, the pennant leaps with joy, and now holloa, away, away, away. . . . Which overture of F. Meritis did I prefer, some artless person asked me; at once the tonalities E minor, B minor, and D major [19] entwined themselves as in a triad of the Graces and I could think of no answer better than the best—"Each one!" F. Meritis conducted as though he had composed the overture himself, and though the orchestra played accordingly, I was struck by Florestan's remarking that he himself had played rather in this style when he came from the provinces to Master Raro as an apprentice. "My most fatal crisis," he continued, "was this intermediate state between nature and art; always ardent as was my grasp, I had now to take everything slowly and precisely, for my technique was everywhere found wanting; presently there arose such a stumbling and stiffness that I began to doubt my talent; the crisis, fortunately, did not last long." I for my part was disturbed, in the overture as in the symphony, by the baton,[d] and I agreed with Florestan when he held that, in the symphony, the orchestra should stand there as a republic, acknowledging no superior. At the same time it was a joy to see F. Meritis and the way in which his eye anticipated every nuance in the music's intellectual windings, from the most delicate to the most powerful, and in which, as the most blissful one, he swam ahead of the rest, so different from those conductors

---

c The overture by Mendelssohn.
d Before Mendelssohn, in the days when Matthai was in charge, the orchestral works were performed without a conductor beating time.

18 Beethoven's Opus 112.
19 *A Midsummer Night's Dream, Fingal's Cave, Calm Sea and Happy Voyage.*

on whom one sometimes chances, who threaten with their scepter to beat score, orchestra, and public all in one.

You know how little patience I have with quarrels over tempi and how for me the movement's inner measure is the sole determinant. Thus the relatively fast Allegro that is cold sounds always more sluggish than the relatively slow one that is sanguine. In the orchestra it is also a question of quality—where this is relatively coarse and dense the orchestra can give to the detail and to the whole more emphasis and import; where this is relatively small and fine, as with our Firlenzer, one must help out the lack of resonance with driving tempi. In a word, the Scherzo of the symphony seemed to me too slow; one noticed this quite clearly also in the restlessness with which the orchestra sought to be at rest. Still, what is this to you in Milan—and, strictly speaking, how little it is to me, for I can after all imagine the Scherzo just as I want it whenever I please.

You asked whether Maria would find Firlenz as cordial as it used to be. How can you doubt it? Only she chose an aria which brought her more honor as an artist than applause as a virtuosa.[20] Then a Westphalian music director [21] played a violin concerto by Spohr [22]—good enough, but too lean and colorless.

In the choice of pieces, everyone professed to see a change in policy; if formerly, from the very beginning of the Firlenzer concerts, Italian butterflies fluttered about the German oaks, this time these last stood quite alone, as powerful as they were somber. One party sought to read in this a reaction; I take it rather for chance than for intention. All of us know how necessary it is to protect Germany from an invasion by your favorites; let this be done with foresight, however, and more by encouraging the youthful spirits in the Fatherland than by a needless defense against a force which, like a fashion, comes in and goes out.

Just at midnight Florestan came in with Jonathan, a new Davidsbündler, the two of them fencing furiously with one another over the aristocracy of mind and the republic of opinion. At last Florestan has found an opponent who gives him diamonds to crack. Of this mighty one you will hear more later on.

Enough for today. Do not forget to look in the calendar sometimes for August 13, where an Aurora links your name with mine.

Eusebius.

---

20 Weber's "Was sag ich? Schaudern macht mich der Gedanke!" for Cherubini's *Lodoïska*.

21 Otto Gerke.

22 No. 11 in G major, Opus 70.

2. To Chiara

The letter carrier coming toward me blossomed out into a flower when I saw the shimmering red "Milano" on your letter. With delight I too recall my first visit to the Scala, just when Rubini was singing there with Méric-Lalande. For Italian music one must listen to in Italian company; German music one can enjoy under any sky.

I was quite right in not reading into the program of the last concert a reactionary intention, for the very next ones brought something Hesperidian. Whereat it was Florestan who amused me most; he finds this actually tiresome, and—out of mere irritation with those Handelians and other fanatics who talk as though they had themselves composed the Samson in their nightshirts—does not exactly attack the Hesperidian music, but compares it vaguely with "fruit salad," with "Titian flesh without spirit," and so forth, yet in so comical a tone that you could laugh out loud, did not his eagle eye bear down on you. "As a matter of fact," he said on one occasion, "to be annoyed with Italian things is long since out of fashion, and, in any case, why beat about with a club in this flowery fragrance which flies in and flies out? I should not know which world to choose—one full of nothing but refractory Beethovens or one full of dancing swans of Pesaro. Only two things puzzle me: our fair singers, who after all never know what to sing (excepting everything or nothing)—why do they never chance on something small, say, on a song by Weber, Schubert, Wiedebein; and then our German composers of vocal music, who complain that so little of their work reaches the concert hall—why do they never think of concert pieces, concert arias, concert scenas, and write something of this kind?"

The singer [23] (not Maria), who sang something from _Torvaldo_,[24] began her "Dove son? Chi m'aita?" in such a tremble that I responded inwardly: "In Firlenz, deary; aide-toi et le ciel t'aidera!" Presently, however, she showed her brighter side, the public its well-meant approval. "If only our German songbirds," Florestan interposed, "would not look on themselves as children who think one does not see them when they close their eyes; as it is, they usually hide themselves so stealthily behind their music that one pays the more attention to their faces and thus notices the difference between them and those Italian girls whom I saw singing at one another in the Academy at Milan with eyes rolling so wildly that I feared their artificial passion might burst into flames; this last I exag-

23 Fräulein Weinhold, from Amsterdam.   24 Rossini's _Torvaldo e Dorliska_.

gerate—still, I should like to read in German eyes something of the dramatic situation, something of the music's joy and grief; beautiful singing from a face of marble makes one doubtful of inner advantage; I mean this in a sort of general way."

Then you ought to have seen Meritis playing the Mendelssohn Concerto in G minor! Seating himself at the piano as innocently as a child, he now took captive one heart after another, drawing them along behind him in swarms, and, when he set you free, you knew only that you had flown past Grecian isles of the gods and had been set down again in the Firlenzer hall, safe and sound. "You are a very happy master in your art," said Florestan to Meritis when it was over, and both of them were right. Though my Florestan had spoken not a word to me about the concert, I caught him very neatly yesterday. To be precise, I saw him turning over the leaves of a book and noting something down. When he had gone, opposite this passage in his diary—"About some things in this world there is nothing to be said at all—for example, about Mozart's C major Symphony with the fugue, about many things in Shakespeare, about some things in Beethoven"—I read, written in the margin: "And about Meritis, when he plays the concerto by M."

We were highly delighted with an energetic overture of Weber's,[25] the mother of so many of those little fellows who tag along behind her, ditto with a violin concerto played by young ———,[26] for it does one good to be able to prophesy with conviction of a hard worker that his path will lead to mastery. With things repeated year in and year out—symphonies excepted—I shall not detain you. Your earlier comment on Onslow's Symphony in A [27]—that, having heard it twice, you knew it by heart, bar for bar—is also mine, although I do not know the real reason for this rapid commission to memory. On the one hand I see that the instruments still cling to one another too much and are piled on one another too heterogeneously; on the other hand the melodic threads—the principal and subsidiary ideas—come through so decidedly that, in view of the thick instrumental combination, their very prominence seems to me most strange. The principle ruling here is a mystery to me, and I cannot express it clearly. Perhaps it will stir you to reflection. I feel most at home in the elegant ballroom turmoil of the minuet, where everything sparkles with pearls and diamonds; in the trio I see a scene in an adjoining sitting room,

---

25 Either the Overture to the *Beherrscher der Geister,* played at the third concert on October 22, or that to *Euryanthe,* played at the fourth concert on October 29, probably the former.

26 Wilhelm Uhlrich, who played a concerto by L. W. Maurer.

27 No. 1, Opus 41, played at the fourth concert, on October 29.

into which, through the frequently opened ballroom doors, there penetrates the sound of violins, drowning out words of love. What do you think?

This brings me very conveniently indeed to the A major Symphony of Beethoven [28] which we heard not long ago. Moderately delighted, we went, late in the evening as it was, to Master Raro. You know Florestan—the way he sits at the piano and, while improvising, speaks, laughs, weeps, gets up, sits down again, and so forth, as though in his sleep. Zilia sat in the bay window, other Davidsbündler here and there in various groups. There was much discussion. "I had to laugh"—thus Florestan began, beginning at the same time the beginning of the symphony—"to laugh at a dried-up notary who discovered in it a battle of Titans, with their effectual destruction in the last movement, but who stole quietly past the Allegretto because it did not fit in with his idea; to laugh in general at those who talk endlessly of the innocence and absolute beauty of music in itself—of course art should conceal, and not repeat, the unfortunate octaves and fifths of life—of course I find, often in certain saintly arias (for example, Marschner's), beauty without truth and, sometimes in Beethoven (but seldom), the latter without the former. But most of all my fingers itch to get at those who maintain that Beethoven, in his symphonies, surrendered always to the grandest sentiments, the sublimest reflections, on God, immortality, and the cosmos, for if that gifted man does point toward heaven with the branches of his flowering crown, he none the less spreads out his roots in his beloved earth. To come to the symphony, the idea that follows is not mine at all, but rather someone's in an old number of the *Cäcilia* [29] (the scene there changed—out of a perhaps exaggerated delicacy toward Beethoven which might well have been spared—to the elegant hall of a count or some such place).

"It is the merriest of weddings, the bride a heavenly child with a rose in her hair—but with one only. I am mistaken if the guests do not gather in the introduction, do not greet one another profusedly with inverted commas—very much mistaken if merry flutes do not remind us that the whole village, with its Maypoles and their many-colored ribbons, takes joy in Rosa, the bride—very much mistaken if the trembling glance of her pale mother does not seem to ask: 'Dost not know that we must part?' and if Rosa, quite overcome, does not throw herself into her mother's arms, drawing the bridegroom after her with one hand. Now it grows very quiet in the village outside (here Florestan entered the Allegretto, break-

---

[28] Played at the third concert, on October 22.   [29] A musical journal published in Mainz by Schott, beginning in 1824.

ing off pieces here and there); only from time to time a butterfly floats by or a cherry blossom falls. The organ begins, the sun stands at its height, occasional long diagonal beams play through the church with bits of dust, the bells ring diligently, churchgoers gradually take their places, pews are opened and shut, some peasants look closely at their hymnbooks, others up into the choir loft, the procession draws nearer—at its head choir boys with lighted tapers and censers, then friends—often turning around to stare at the couple accompanied by the priest—then the parents and friends of the bride, with the assembled youth of the village bringing up the rear. How everything arranges itself, how the priest ascends to the altar, how he addresses, now the bride and now the fortunate one, how he speaks to them of the duties of the bond and of its purposes and of how they may find happiness in harmony and love of one another, how he then asks for her 'I do,' which assumes so much forever and forever, and how she pronounces it, firm and sustained—all this prevents my painting the picture further—do as you please with the finale"—thus Florestan broke off, tearing into the end of the Allegretto, and it sounded as though the sexton had so slammed the doors shut that the whole church re-echoed.

Enough. In me, too, Florestan's interpretation has stirred up something, and my alphabet begins to run together. There is much more for me to tell you, but the outdoors calls. Wait out the interval until my next letter with faith in a better beginning.

Eusebius.

DANCE LITERATURE

[*1836*]

J. C. Kessler: [30] Three Polonaises, Opus 25
Sigismund Thalberg: [31] Twelve Waltzes, Opus 4
Clara Wieck: Valses romantiques, Opus 4
Leopold, Edler von Meyer: [32] Salon (Six Waltzes), Opus 4
Franz Schubert: First Waltzes, Opus 9, Book 1
The same: Deutsche Tänze, Opus 33

"And now play, Zilia! [33] I wish to duck myself quite under in the harmonies and only occasionally to poke out my head in order that you may not think me drowned from melancholy; for dance music makes one

---

[30] Joseph Christoph Kessler, concert pianist and composer for the piano, piano teacher in Lemberg, Warsaw, Breslau, and Vienna.

[31] Sigismund Thalberg, composer for the piano and concert pianist of the first rank, Liszt's chief rival, toured the United States in 1857 together with Vieuxtemps.

[32] Pupil of Czerny, concert pianist, toured the United States from 1845 to 1847 and again in 1867 and 1868.

[33] Clara Wieck.

sad and lax, just as church music, quite the other way, makes one joyful and active—me at least." Thus spake Florestan, as Zilia was already floating through the first Kessler polonaise. "Indeed it would be lovely," he continued, half-listening, half-speaking, "if a dozen lady-Davidsbündler were to make the evening memorable and would embrace each other in a festival of the Graces. Jean Paul has already remarked that girls ought really to dance only with girls (though this would lead, indeed, to there being some weddings fewer); men (I add) ought never to dance at all."

"Should they do so none the less," Eusebius interrupted, "when they come to the trio, he ought to say to his partner-Davidsbündler, 'How simple and how kind you are!' and, in the second part, it would be well if she were to drop her bouquet, to be picked up in flying past and rewarded with a grateful glance."

All this, however, was expressed more in Euseb's bearing and in the music than in anything he actually said. Florestan only tossed his head from time to time, especially at the third polonaise, most brilliant and filled with sounds of horn and violin.

"Now something livelier, and do you play the Thalberg, Euseb; Zilia's fingers are too delicate for it," said Florestan, who soon interrupted to ask that the sections be not repeated, since the waltzes were too transparent—particularly the ninth, which remained on one level, indeed on one measure—"and eternally tonic and dominant, dominant and tonic. Still, it's good enough for those whose ears are in their feet." But, at the end, the one who stood at the foot (a student) called out "Da capo!" in all seriousness, and everyone was obliged to laugh at Florestan's fury at this and at the way he shouted him down, telling him that he might be on his way, that he should interrupt with no further encouragements of this sort or he would silence him with an hour-long trill in thirds, and so forth.

"By a lady, then?" a reviewer might begin, seeing the *Valses romantiques.* "Well, well! Here we shan't need to hunt long for fifths and for the melody!"

Zilia held out four short moonlit harmonies. All listened intently. But on the piano there lay a sprig of roses—Florestan always had vases of flowers in place of the candelabras—and, shaken by the vibration, this had gradually slid down onto the keys. Reaching out for a note in the bass, Zilia struck against this too violently and left off playing, for her finger bled. Florestan asked what the matter was. "Nothing," said Zilia; "as in these waltzes, there is as yet no great pain, only a drop of blood charmed forth by roses." And may she who said this know no other.

A moment later, Florestan plunged into the midst of the brilliant countesses and ambassadresses of the Meyer *Salon*. How soothing this is —wealth and beauty, the height of rank and style, with music at the summit; every one speaks and no one listens, for the music drowns all out in waves! "For this," Florestan blurted out, "one really needs an instrument with an extra octave to the right and left, so that one can properly spread out and celebrate." You can have no idea of how Florestan plays this sort of thing and of how he storms away, carrying you along with him. The Davidsbündler, too, were quite worked up, calling in their excitement (musical excitement is insatiable) for "more and more," till Serpentin [34] suggested choosing between the Schubert waltzes and the Chopin boleros. "If, throwing myself at the keyboard from here," Florestan shouted, placing himself in a corner away from the piano, "I can hit the first chord of the last movement of the D minor symphony,[35] Schubert wins." He hit it, of course. Zilia played the waltzes by heart.

First waltzes by Franz Schubert: Tiny sprites, ye who hover no higher above the ground than, say, the height of a flower—to be sure, I don't care for the *Sehnsuchtswalzer*, in which a hundred girlish emotions have already bathed, or for the last three either, an aesthetic blemish on the whole for which I can't forgive the author—but the way in which the others turn about these, weaving them in, more or less, with fragrant threads, and the way in which there runs through all of them a so fanciful thoughtlessness that one becomes part of it oneself and believes at the last that one is still playing in the first—this is really first-rate.

In the *Deutsche Tänze*, on the other hand, there dances, to be sure, a whole carnival. " 'Twould be fine," Florestan shouted in Fritz Friedrich's [e] ear, "if you would get your magic lantern and follow the masquerade in shadows on the wall." Exit and re-enter the latter, jubilant.

The group that follows is one of the most charming. The room dimly lighted—Zilia at the piano, the wounding rose in her hair—Eusebius in his black velvet coat, leaning over her chair—Florestan (ditto), standing on the table and ciceronizing—Serpentin, his legs twined round Walt's [36] neck, sometimes riding back and forth—the painter à la Hamlet, parading

---

e The deaf painter. [The painter J. P. Lyser.— Ed.]

34 Carl Banck, music critic and composer of songs.

85 See above, p. 833.

86 The pianist Louis Rakemann, who emigrated to America in 1839.

his shadow figures through the bull's-eye, some spider-legged ones even running off the wall on to the ceiling. Zilia began, and Florestan may have spoken substantially to this effect, though at much greater length:

"No. 1. In A major. Masks milling about. Kettledrums. Trumpets. The lights go down. Perruquier: 'Everything seems to be going very well.' No. 2. Comic character, scratching himself behind the ears and continually calling out 'Pst, pst!' Exit. No. 3. Harlequin, arms akimbo. Out the door, head over heels. No. 4. Two stiff and elegant masks, dancing and scarcely speaking to one another. No. 5. Slim cavalier, chasing a mask: 'At last I've caught you, lovely zither player!' 'Let me go!' She escapes. No. 6. Hussar at attention, with plume and sabretache. No. 7. Two harvesters, waltzing together blissfully. He, softly: 'Is it thou?' They recognize each other. No. 8. Tenant farmer from the country, getting ready to dance. No. 9. The great doors swing open. Splendid procession of knights and noble ladies. No. 10. Spaniard to an Ursuline: 'Speak at least, since you may not love!' She: 'I would rather not speak, and be understood!' . . ."

But in the midst of the waltz Florestan sprang from the table and out the door. One was used to this in him. Zilia, too, soon left off, and the others scattered in one direction and another.

Florestan, you know, has a habit of often breaking off in the very moment when his enjoyment is at its height, perhaps in order to impress it in all its freshness and fullness on the memory. And this time he had his way—for whenever his friends speak to each other of their happiest evenings, they always recall the twenty-eighth of December, 18—— . . .

NEW PATHS

[1853]

Years have passed—nearly as many as I devoted to the former editorship of this journal, namely ten—since last I raised my voice within these covers, so rich in memories. Often, despite my intense creative activity, I have felt myself stimulated; many a new and signficant talent has appeared; a new musical force has seemed to be announcing itself—as has been made evident by many of the aspiring artists of recent years, even though their productions are chiefly familiar to a limited circle.[f] Following the paths of these chosen ones with the utmost interest, it has seemed to

---

f Here I have in mind Joseph Joachim, Ernst Naumann, Ludwig Norman, Woldemar Bargiel, Theodor Kirchner, Julius Schäffer, Albert Dietrich, not to forget that profoundly thoughtful student of the great in art, the sacred composer C. F. Wilsing. As their valiant advance guard I might also mention Niels Wilhelm Gade, C. F. Mangold, Robert Franz, and Stephen Heller.

me that, after such a preparation, there would and must suddenly appear some day one man who would be singled out to make articulate in an ideal way the highest expression of our time, one man who would bring us mastery, not as the result of a gradual development, but as Minerva, springing fully armed from the head of Cronus. And he is come, a young creature over whose cradle graces and heroes stood guard. His name is *Johannes Brahms*, and he comes from Hamburg where he has been working in silent obscurity, trained in the most difficult theses of his art by an excellent teacher who sends me enthusiastic reports of him,[g] recommended to me recently by a well-known and respected master. Even outwardly, he bore in his person all the marks that announce to us a chosen man. Seated at the piano, he at once discovered to us wondrous regions. We were drawn into a circle whose magic grew on us more and more. To this was added an altogether inspired style of playing which made of the piano an orchestra of lamenting and exultant voices. There were sonatas—veiled symphonies, rather; lieder, whose poetry one could understand without knowing the words, although a deep vocal melody ran through them all; single piano pieces, in part of a daemonic nature, most attractive in form; then sonatas for violin and piano; string quartets—and every work so distinct from any other that each seemed to flow from a different source. And then it seemed as though, roaring along like a river, he united them all as in a waterfall, bearing aloft a peaceful rainbow above the plunging waters below, surrounded at the shore by playful butterflies and borne along by the calls of nightingales.

Later, if he will wave with his magic wand to where massed forces, in the chorus and orchestra, lend their strength, there lie before us still more wondrous glimpses into the secrets of the spirit world. May the highest genius strengthen him for what expectation warrants, for there is also latent in him another genius—that of modesty. His comrades greet him on his first entrance into the world, where there await him wounds, perhaps, but also palms and laurels; we welcome him as a valiant warrior.

In every time, there reigns a secret league of kindred spirits. Tighten the circle, you who belong to it, in order that the truth in art may shine forth more and more brightly, everywhere spreading joy and peace.

R. S.

---

g Eduard Marxsen, in Hamburg.

86. Franz Liszt

On November 17, 1852, Berlioz's fourteen-year-old *Benvenuto Cellini,* which had not been heard since its dismal failure at the Opéra in 1838 and 1839, was brilliantly revived in Weimar under Liszt's direction. This was neither the first nor the last of Liszt's generous gestures in behalf of his old friend. Years earlier, in Paris, Liszt had been one of Berlioz's most zealous and most effective partisans. In February 1855 he was to arrange a second "Berlioz Week" in Weimar, and at this time the essay on Berlioz's *Harold,* an old project, began to take definite shape. A third series of concerts, in January 1856, led indirectly to the writing and composition of *Les Troyens.*

Since the publication of the collected letters of Liszt to Princess Caroline von Wittgenstein (1900–1902) and of the collected letters of Peter Cornelius (1904–1905), it has been generally recognized that Liszt was only in a very limited sense the author of the later writings published under his name. More recently, the publication of the memoirs of the Countess Marie d'Agoult (1927) and of her correspondence with Liszt (1933 and 1934) has made it clear that this is also true of the earlier writings. The *Lettres d'un bachelier-ès-musique* are largely the work of the Countess; the writings published from 1850 on—and these include the monographs on Wagner's *Tannhäuser* and *Lohengrin,* on Chopin, on Berlioz, and on the music of the gypsies—owe at least their literary form to the Princess. How much more they owe is not easy to say. Emile Haraszti ("Liszt—Author Despite Himself," *Musical Quarterly,* XXXIII, 490–516) does not hesitate to reduce Liszt's part in the collaboration to the vanishing point and to put the Princess in charge of "an editorial office that published under the name of Liszt" and whose output, except for the *Bohémiens,* is "without interest, either for Liszt's evolution or as literature." Surely this goes too far. That it was the Princess who first suggested the essay on Berlioz is clear from the published correspondence. But from this it is also clear that Liszt was to provide sketches for her to "develop." The correspondence shows further that Liszt spoke out when "developments" of this kind displeased him, that in the case of the essay on Berlioz he corrected a proof of the first installment, and that the Princess was obliged to consult him before she could cancel a trifling change that he had made in her wording of the title. Whether Haraszti is justified in calling the essay on Berlioz's *Harold* "obscure, idle balderdash," the reader may judge for himself. But if he agrees, Liszt must bear his share of the blame.

From Berlioz and His "Harold" Symphony [1]
[*1855*]

IN THE realm of ideas there are internal wars, like those of the Athenians, during which everyone is declared traitor to his fatherland who does not publicly take one side or the other and remains an idle spectator of the evil to which the struggle leads. Persuaded of the justice of this procedure, which, if rigorously observed, can only help to put an end to differences and to hasten the victory of those destined for future leadership, we have never concealed our lively and sympathetic admiration for the genius whom we intend to examine today, for the master to whom the art of our time is so decidedly indebted.

All the pros and cons of the noisy quarrel that has sprung up since the appearance of his first works can be reduced to one main point, to suggest which will suffice to show that the consequences inherent in his example go far beyond the pronouncements of those who consider themselves infallible arbitrators in these matters. The blunt antipathies, the accusations of musical high treason, the banishments for life which have been imposed on Berlioz since his first appearance—these have their explanation (why deceive ourselves about it?) in the holy horror, in the pious astonishment which came over musical authorities at the principle implicit in all his works, a principle that can be briefly stated in this form: *The artist may pursue the beautiful outside the rules of the school without fear that, as a result of this, it will elude him.* His opponents may assert that he has abandoned the ways of the old masters; this is easy—who wishes to persuade them of the contrary? His adherents may give themselves the greatest pains to prove that his way is neither always nor yet wholly and completely different from that to which one was formerly used; what do they gain thereby? Both parties remain convinced that Berlioz adheres no less firmly to the creed which we have just pronounced, whether this is demonstrated in fact by one or by one hundred corroborating circumstances. And for the authorities who have arrogated to themselves the privileges of

---

1 Text: *Neue Zeitschrift für Musik*, XLIII (1855), 25–26, 40–46, 49–55, 77–79, 80–81. The essay was published in five installments; the present abridged translation includes the beginning of the first installment, the latter part of the second, all of the third, and the beginning of the fourth.

As printed in 1855, the text is a translation into German, by Richard Pohl, from the French original of Liszt and the Princess Wittgenstein. The later German "translation," by Lina Ramann (*Gesammelte Schriften*, IV [Leipzig, 1882], 1–102) is simply a fussy revision of the earlier one.

orthodoxy this is a more than sufficient proof of his heresy. Yet since in art no sect maintains a dogma on the basis of revelation and only tradition is authoritative; since music in particular does not, like painting and sculpture, recognize or adhere to an absolute model; the deciding of disputes between orthodox and heresiarchs depends not only on the court of past and present science, but also on the sense for art and for the reasonable in the coming generation. Only after a considerable lapse of time can a final decision be handed down, for what verdict of the present will be acceptable on the one hand to the older generation,[a] which has borne from youth the easy yoke of habit, and on the other hand to the younger generation, who gather belligerently under any banner and love a fight for its own sake? Old and young must then entrust the solution of problems of this sort to a more or less distant future. To this future is alone reserved the complete or partial acceptance of those *violations of certain rules of art and habits of hearing* with which Berlioz is reproached. One point, however, is now already beyond all question. The representatives of the development to come will entertain a quite special respect for works exhibiting such enormous powers of conception and thought and will find themselves obliged to study them intensively, just as even now contemporaries approach them *nolens volens* step by step, their admiration only too often delayed by idle astonishment. Even though these works violate the rules, in that they destroy the hallowed frame which has devolved upon the symphony; even though they offend the ear, in that in the expression of their content they do not remain within the prescribed musical dikes; it will be none the less impossible to ignore them later on as one ignores them now, with the apparent intention of exempting oneself from tribute, from homage, toward a contemporary.

·   ·   ·   ·   ·

Heaven forbid that anyone, in holding forth on the utility, validity, and advantage of the program, should forswear the old faith and assert that the heavenly art does not exist for its own sake, is not self-sufficient, does not kindle of itself the divine spark, and has value only as the representative of an *idea* or as an exaltation of language. The choice between such an offense against the art and the complete renunciation of the pro-

---

a "The majority would like to see themselves benefited but do not wish their cherished ways of living disturbed, just as the sick man would gladly regain his health but gives up unwillingly that which has made him sick. . . . When an original work appears, demanding that the listener assimilate its ideas instead of appraising its new spirit in the light of traditional concepts and that he adopt the new concept absolutely essential to new ideas, the majority, in the midst of their fervent longings for the 'new,' shrink from the difficulty and find consolation in the warmed-over old, persuading themselves, wherever possible, that it is new."—Marx, *Die Musik des 19. Jahrhunderts* (2d ed., Leipzig, 1873), pp. 154–155.

gram cannot remain in doubt, and it would be better to allow one of its most prolific sources to dry up than, by denying its independent existence, to sever its vital nerve. Music embodies *feeling* without forcing it—as it is forced in its other manifestations, in most arts and especially in the art of words—to contend and combine with *thought*.[b] If music has one advantage over the other means through which man can reproduce the impressions of his soul, it owes this to its supreme capacity to make each inner impulse audible without the assistance of reason, so restricted in the diversity of its forms, capable, after all, only of confirming or describing our affections, not of communicating them directly in their full intensity, in that to accomplish this even approximately it is obliged to search for images and comparisons. Music, on the other hand, presents at one and the same time the intensity and the expression of *feeling*; it is the embodied and intelligible essence of feeling; capable of being apprehended by our senses, it permeates them like a dart, like a ray, like a dew, like a spirit, and fills our soul. If music calls itself the supreme art, if Christian spiritualism has transported it, as alone worthy of Heaven, into the celestial world, this supremacy lies in the pure flames of emotion that beat one against another from heart to heart without the aid of reflection, without having to wait on accident for the opportunity of self-assertion; it is breath from mouth to mouth, blood flowing in the arteries of life. Feeling itself lives and breathes in music without representational shell,[c] without the meditation of action or of thought; here it ceases to be cause, source, mainspring, moving and energizing principle, in order to reveal itself directly and without intercessory symbols in its indescribable totality, just

---

b "Music is spirit or soul, sounding without mediation for itself alone and finding satisfaction in its self-recognition; . . . the language of the soul, which pours out the inner joy and the sorrow of temperament in sound and in this outpouring raises itself in alleviation above natural emotional forces, in that it transforms the momentary state of affection in the inner self into one of self-recognition, into a free introspection, and in this way liberates the heart from oppression and suffering. . . . If now, speaking generally, we have already been able to regard activity in the realm of the beautiful as a liberation of the soul, as a renunciation of affliction and constraint, . . . then music carries this liberation to its extreme limit. . . . The special task of music is that, in presenting any content to the mind, it presents it neither as it is latent in consciousness as a general *concept*, nor as definite external *form* offers itself elsewhere to observation or is through art more completely represented, but rather in the way in which it becomes alive in the sphere of *subjective inwardness*.

". . . If we refrain from mere intellectual analysis and listen without restraint, the musical art work absorbs us completely and carries us along with it, independent of the power which art as art in general exerts on us. The peculiar power of music is an *elemental* power, that is to say, it lies wholly in the element of *sound* in which the art here moves."—Hegel, *Aesthetik,* III, iii, 2.

c "Let us readily concede that our art is incapable of immediately presenting a character picture or any other object clearly and completely to the eye, as do poetry and painting. As compensations, it transcends the latter in having the power of progressive development, the former in being able to present the simultaneous speech of distinct and contrary characters. It cannot call by name, cannot define who you are, but it can successively exhibit, as they become perceptible, all the impulses of your temperament. And it assembles you, with your likes and opposites, and presents you all to us just as you live, breathing and echoing out your lives, so that from the nature and being of the many we fully comprehend the one. It is a progressive monologue, filled to the full with a dialogue-like, dialectic content, two-sided and many-sided as Plato's dialogues aim to be, but treated artistically with the emphasis on genuinely dramatic contrasts and conflicts."—Marx, *loc. cit.,* p. 54.

as the God of the Christians, after having revealed Himself to the chosen through signs and miracles, now shows Himself to them through visions in the beatific aura of His substantial presence. Only in music does feeling, actually and radiantly present, lift the ban which oppresses our spirit with the sufferings of an evil earthly power and liberate us with the white-capped floods of its free and warmth-giving might from "the demon Thought," brushing away for brief moments his yoke from our furrowed brows. Only in music does feeling, in manifesting itself, dispense with the help of reason and its means of expression, so inadequate in comparison with its intuition, so incomplete in comparison with its strength, its delicacy, its brilliance. On the towering, sounding waves of music, feeling lifts us up to heights that lie beyond the atmosphere of our earth and shows us cloud landscapes and world archipelagos that move about in ethereal space like singing swans. On the wings of the infinite art it draws us with it to regions into which it alone can penetrate, where, in the ringing ether, the heart expands and, in anticipation, shares in an immaterial, incorporeal, spiritual life. What is it that, beyond this miserable, paltry, earthly shell, beyond these numbered planets, opens to us the meadows of infinity, refreshes us at the murmuring springs of delight, steeps us in the pearly dew of longing; what is it that causes ideals to shimmer before us like the gilded spires of that submerged city, that recalls to us the indescribable recollections that surrounded our cradles, that conducts us through the reverberating workshops of the elements, that inspires us with all that ardor of thirsting after inexhaustible rapture which the blissful experience; what is it that takes hold of us and sweeps us into the turbulent maelstrom of the passions which carries us out of the world into the harbor of a more beautiful life; is it not music, animated by elemental feeling like that which vibrates in us before it manifests itself, before it solidifies and turns cold in the mold of the idea? What other art discloses to its adepts similar raptures, the more precious and ennobling in that they are veiled by a chaste and impenetrable mystery? What other art reveals to its votaries the heavens where angels lovingly hold sway and flies with them in Elijah's chariot through spheres of ecstasy?

As the Slavic poet [2] has it: "The word belies the thought, the deed belies the word." Music does not belie feeling, it does not deceive it, and Jean Paul could exclaim: "O Music! Thou who bringest past and future so near our wounds with their flying flames! . . . O Music! Reverberation from a distant world of harmony! Sigh of the angel within us! When the word is speechless, and the embrace, and the eye, and the tear; when

---

2 Mickiewicz.

our dumb hearts lie lonely behind the ironwork of our breasts—then it is Thou alone through whom they call to one another in their dungeons and through whom, in their desert habitation, they unite their distant sighs!" [3] To Hoffmann, music revealed "that faraway country which surrounds us often with the strangest presentiments and from which wondrous voices call down to us, wakening all the echoes that sleep in our restricted breasts, which echoes, awakened now, shoot joyfully and gladly up, as though in fiery rays, making us sharers in the bliss of that paradise. . . . Is not music the mysterious language of a faraway spirit world whose wondrous accents, echoing within us, awaken us to a higher, more intensive life? All the passions battle with one another, their armor shimmering and sparkling, perishing in an inexpressible yearning which fills our breasts." [4]

. . . . .

Who has the temerity to deny to our inspired art the supreme power of self-sufficiency? But need making oneself master of a new form mean forever renouncing the hereditary and historically inculcated one? Does one forswear one's mother tongue when one acquires a new branch of eloquence? Because there are works that demand a simultaneous bringing into play of feeling and thought, shall on this account the pure instrumental style lose its magic for those works that prefer to expend themselves and their entire emotional wealth in music alone without being hindered by a definite object in their freedom of feeling? Would it not amount to a lack of confidence in the vitality of the pure instrumental style were one to anticipate its complete decay simply because there arose at its side a new species, distinct from drama, oratorio, and cantata, but having none the less in common with these the poetic basis?

The dwellers in the antipodes of this new artistic hemisphere will perhaps think to advance a telling argument against it by saying that program music, through its apparent reconciliation of various subspecies, surrenders its own individual character and may not for this reason lay claim to independent existence within the art. They will hold that our art attains its purest expression in instrumental music and that it has in this form arrived at its highest perfection and power, revealed itself in its most kingly majesty, and asserted its direct character most impressively; that music, on the other hand, has from time immemorial taken possession of the word with a view to lending it, through song, the charm and force of its expression and has in consequence always developed in two forms

3 See p. 772 above.   4 See p. 787 above.

as instrumental and vocal; that these two forms are equally indigenous, equally normal; and that the inventive creator, when he wishes to apply music to definite situations and actual persons, can find sufficient motives in the lyric and dramatic vocal forms; so that there can accordingly be no advantage or necessity for him to cause the peculiar properties of that form of music which exists for its own sake and lives its own life to meet and continue on the same path with the development of that other form which identifies itself with the poetic structure of the drama, with the sung and spoken word.

These objections would be well taken if in art two distinct forms could be *combined*, but not *united*. It is obvious that such a combination may be an unharmonious one, and that the work will then be misshapen and the awkward mixture offensive to good taste. This, however, will be due to a fault of execution, not a basic error. Are not the arts in general, and the several arts in particular, quite as rich in variously formed and dissimilar phenomena as nature is in the vicissitudes of her principal kingdoms and their divisions? Art, like nature, is made up of gradual transitions, which link together the remotest classes and the most dissimilar species and which are necessary and natural, hence also entitled to live.

Just as there are in nature no gaps, just as the human soul consists not alone in contrasts, so between the mountain peaks of art there yawn no steep abysses and in the wondrous chain of its great whole no ring is ever missing. In nature, in the human soul, and in art, the extremes, opposites, and high points are bound one to another by a continuous series of various varieties of *being*, in which modifications bring about differences and at the same time maintain similarities. The human soul, that middle ground between nature and art, finds prospects in nature which correspond to all the shadings and modulations of feeling which it experiences before it rests on the steep and solitary peaks of contradictory passions which it climbs only at rare intervals; these prospects found in nature it carries over into art. Art, like nature, weds related or contradictory forms and impressions corresponding to the affections of the human soul; these often arise from cross currents of diverse impulses which, now uniting, now opposing, bring about a divided condition in the soul which we can call neither pure sorrow nor pure joy, neither perfect love nor thorough egoism, neither complete relaxation nor positive energy, neither extreme satisfaction nor absolute despair, forming through such mixtures of various tonalities a harmony, an individuality, or an artistic species which does not stand entirely on its own feet, yet is at the same time different from any other. Art, regarded generally and in the position it occupies in the history of mankind, would not only be impotent, it would remain incomplete, if, poorer and more dependent than nature, it were unable to offer each movement of the human soul the sympathetic sound, the proper shade of color, the indispensable form. Art and nature are so changeable in their progeny that we can neither define nor predict their boundaries; both comprise a host of heterogeneous or intimately related basic elements; both consist in material, substance, and endlessly diverse forms, each of them in turn conditioned by limits of expansion and force; both exercise through the medium of our senses an influence on our souls that is as real as it is indefinable.

An element, through contact with another, acquires new properties in losing old ones; exercising another influence in an altered environment, it adopts a new name. A change in the relative proportions of the mixture is sufficient to make the resultant phenomenon a new one. The amalgamation of forms distinct in their origins will result, in art as in nature, either in phenomena of quite new beauty or in monstrosities, depending on whether a harmonious *union* or a disagreeable *combination* promotes a homogeneous whole or a distressing absurdity.

The more we persuade ourselves of the diverse unity which governs the All in the midst of which man is situated and of that other unity which rules his very life and history, the more we will recognize the diverse unity which reveals itself in the destiny of art, the more we will seek to rid ourselves of our vicious inclination to carp at and curb it, like gardeners who hem in the vegetation in order to grow hedges in a row or who cripple the healthy tree for the sake of artificial shapes. Never do we find in *living* natural phenomena geometrical or mathematical figures; why do we try to impose them on art, why do we try to subject art to a rectilinear system? Why do we not admire its luxurious, unfettered growth, as we admire the oak, whose gnarled and tangled branches appeal in a more lively way to our imaginations than does the yew, distorted into the shape of a pyramid or mandarin's hat? Why all this desire to stunt and control natural and artistic impulses? Vain effort! The first time the little garden-artist mislays his shears, everything grows as it should and must.

Man stands in inverse relations to art and to nature; nature he rules as its capstone, its final flower, its noblest creature; art he creates as a second nature, so to speak, making of it, in relation to himself, that which he himself is to nature.[5] For all this, he can proceed, in creating art, only according to the laws which nature lays down for him, for it is from nature that he takes the materials for his work, aiming to give them then a life supe-

---

[5] Cf. Richard Wagner, *Das Kunstwerk der Zukunft*, I, 1 (p. 876 below).

rior to that which, in nature's plan, would fall to their lot. These laws carry with them the ineradicable mark of their origin in the similarity they bear to the laws of nature, and consequently, for all that it is the creature of man, the fruit of his will, the expression of his feeling, the result of his reflection, art has none the less an existence not determined by man's intention, the successive phases of which follow a course independent of his deciding and predicting. It exists and flowers in various ways in conformity with basic conditions whose inner origin remains just as much hidden as does the force which holds the world in its course, and, like the world, it is impelled toward an unpredicted and unpredictable final goal in perpetual transformations that can be made subject to no external power. Assuredly, the scholarly investigator can follow up the traces of its past; he cannot, however, foresee the final purpose toward which future revolutions may direct it. The stars in the heavens come and go and the species inhabiting our earth appear and disappear in accordance with conditions which, in the fruitful and perpetual course of time, bring on and again remove the centuries. Thus it is also with art. The fecundating and life-giving suns of its realm gradually lose their brilliance and warmth, and there appear on its horizon new planets, proud, ardent, and radiant with youth. Whole arts die out, their former life in time recognizable only from the skeletons they leave behind, which, like those of antediluvian races, fill us with astonished surprise; through crossbreeding and blending new and hitherto unknown arts spring up, which, as a result of their expansion and intermingling, will perhaps someday be impelled toward their end, just as in the animal and vegetable kingdoms whole species have been replaced by others. Art, proceeding from man as he himself proceeds, it appears, from nature, man's masterpiece as he himself is nature's masterpiece, provided by man with thought and feeling—art cannot escape the inevitable change common to all that time begets. Coexistent with that of mankind, its life principle, like the life principle of nature, does not remain for long in possession of the same forms, going from one to another in an eternal cycle and driving man to create new forms in the same measure as he leaves faded and antiquated ones behind.

·   ·   ·   ·   ·

Like loving gifts of a nature infinitely exalted above his own, like traces within himself of elements that lie without him, man carries in his mind the concepts *eternity* and *nonexistence*. Kant first observed the enigmatic contradiction with which the mind, capable of grasping neither the one nor the other, accepts them both. These concepts constitute the two opposite poles of the axis about which man revolves, the idea of existence without beginning or end, and that of nonexistence. Ceaselessly he circles about these two points of reference, inclining now toward the one, now toward the other, shrinking back from the thought of annihilation, horrified by the thought of the immutable. Man's whole environment is but end and beginning, life after death and death before life. Nevertheless he is seized instinctively and inexplicably with an aversion to the weaknesses of all beginnings, to the painful character of every end, while a no less instinctive and inexplicable impulse urges him to destroy in order to re-create. Experiencing disgust once he has reached the saturation point and provoked to desire by his eagerness for novelty, he feels himself impelled in perpetual alternation by an innate and sovereign longing for a satisfaction to which he cannot give a name, but which every change seems to promise him. From the struggle between these two exertions arise conflict and sorrow, our common, inevitable lot.

These two contradictory impulses, which suspend man's mind oscillating and fluctuating between permanence and instability, recur on every hand: in the physical world as centripetal and centrifugal force, in chemistry as formation and disorganization, in morality as improvement and deterioration, in politics as conservation and reform. A hidden power, which we call providence or destiny, regulates their equilibrium by raising or lowering the one scale or the other until, in unforeseen moments, it brings them both into equal oscillation. Struck by the wondrous equilibrium of these so contradictory principles, an equilibrium wise beyond comprehension, manifest in the destinies of mankind as in the worlds of space, Newton exclaims: "Were centripetal and centrifugal forces equal, they would destroy the cosmic mechanism; were they unequal, they would engender chaos; God's finger must hold them in check!" In art and in its oscillation between sterile, outworn forms which continue to vegetate, bearing no new types, and the progress of evolving forms which are still imperfect there is revealed *the finger of God* which Newton speaks of, that mysterious impulse, that unseen law, which maintains harmony among the most disparate elements, governing our progression in time and beyond time through the agency of *genius*. Like the conquering Gaul, it casts its shining sword into the scale of the attracting and repelling forces which, on the one hand, draw art toward renewal, betterment, and transformation, on the other seek to keep it in the old ruts, forms, and modes of procedure. So long as genius fails to speak its magic word, this dualism begets a more or less rapidly alternating ebb and flow, a deterioration or improvement of art and taste; sooner or later, however, genius draws art past its laboriously surveyed boundaries in order that its beacon may light the way for mankind, striving forward, like our sun, toward a goal hidden from our sight, not comprehended by our reason. The sun, to be sure, pursues its course with even, measured steps toward that point of the firmament whose constellation has strangely and, as it were, prophetically been named for Hercules, for the liberator of the Prometheus in whom the human race is symbolized; mankind and art approach their supreme and final transfiguration irregularly and haltingly, now with the slowness and patience characteristic of the mole's subterranean labors, now with a powerful spring, such as the tiger takes toward his prey.

From this variety in the tempo of artistic development proceeds the difficulty of recognizing it in its portents and precursors. One must have taken a step forward before one can recognize as such the progress one has made. As long as this progress remains remote, like an anchorage toward which we sail, only a sort of clairvoyance will enable us to assert positively that we are getting ahead as we approach it. We border here so closely on optical illusion that for skeptics, who regard what others take for progress as retrogressive movement, there can be no demonstrations *a priori*. At the same time it would be idle to wish to deny or dispute an upward tendency in the psychological development of the human mind, which, embodying itself in constantly nobler arts and forms, strives after constantly wider radiation, after a brighter light, after an infinite exaltation.[d] And it would be equally idle to consign an art or the least of its forms to the class of immovable objects by seeking to demolish the new forms in which it manifests itself or to destroy the shoots that spring from the seeds

---

[d] "One cannot reflect on the deeper significance of the three great (so to speak) cardinal arts—plastics, painting, and music—without being constantly reminded of the history of the three great (so to speak) cardinal senses—touch, sight, and hearing. Then quite unsought there come to light most remarkable relations between the evolution of these senses in the animate world of the planets and the evolution of these forces in the history of mankind. Just as touch is the first and altogether most indispensable means by which the living creature orientates itself, so some form of plastics is the first and most essential art of peoples, the earliest to attain to full development. Sight, that miraculous perception of the most delicate light-effects, appears for the first time at a higher level in the animal kingdom, exhibiting, moreover, a certain inconstancy, seating itself now in a single eye, now in thousands of eyes, again on occasion degenerating altogether, even in the highest animal forms. The flowering of painting falls accordingly in mankind's middle period, assuming the most varied forms, coming to the fore and on occasion retreating suddenly into the background. Still later, indeed last of all, hearing develops, merely prefiguring itself in the higher mollusks and only from the fishes on becoming a permanent property of the animal world, seating itself now with greater constancy and symmetry in two organs, no more, no less, a right one and a left one, and from henceforth never again wanting. In similar measure, genuine music appears only in the last centuries; firm in its basic laws, at the same time developing itself and only holding to these as though riding at anchor, capable of the most delicate and most inspired variation, it thus becomes the mystery in which, free from all imitation of the world of actuality, the spiritualized world of feeling is reflected. If those other arts have long since passed the high point in their development, the full flowering of the tonal world falls in most recent times, and here, hidden under a thin shell, there are still latent many secrets, ready assuredly to reveal themselves to the right rhabdomancer."—Carus.

of ripened fruit. These can never be stunted; no profane hand can restrain their seasonal impulse.

Strange contradiction! Nothing human stands still; cult, custom, law, government, science, taste, and mode of enjoyment—all change, all are constantly coming and passing away, without rest, without respite; no country is quite like any other, and no century ends in the same atmosphere with which it began; the endeavors, tendencies, improvements, and ideals of each generation plow up the hereditary fields in order to experiment with a new kind of crop. Yet in the midst of all these ferments, in this tempest of time, in this eternal world-rejuvenation, resembling the transformations of nature, if not in majesty then at least in universality, among all the paths of progress is one alone to remain untrodden —among all the manifestations of the human spirit is the development of the purest and most brilliant one to be forbidden, its mobility forever held in check? Among all the virtual forces, is it proposed to deny precisely to this force, to the supreme force, the possibility of perfection that spirit inspires in matter, which possibility, an echo of that first command of creation, forms, with its "Become!", a harmonious All from the reorganized elements of an embryonic chaos? Wondrous power, noblest sacred gift of existence! Where else but in art canst thou be found? However man employs himself on any path of life, however he discovers, invents, collects, analyzes, and combines—he *creates* only in the art work; only here can he out of free will embody feeling and thought in a sensual mold that will preserve and communicate their sense and content. Is art alone, from a given moment on, to remain unaffected by the ebb and flow of its soul, unmoved by the fluctuations of its hopes, unresponsive to all the changing of its dreams, to all the budding and weaving of its ideas? No, certainly not! Art, in general and in particular, sails with mankind down the stream of life, never to mount again to its source. Even when it appears to stand still momentarily, the tides which bear man and his life continue to remain its element. Art moves, strides on, increases and develops, obeying unknown laws, in cycles whose dissimilar return, recurring like the appearance of certain comets, at unpredictable intervals, does not permit the positive assertion that they will not again pass overhead in all their splendor or having passed will not return once more. Only it is not given us to foresee its unawaited reappearance or the undreamed-of glory in which it will then come forward.

. . . . .

When the hour of progress strikes for art, the genius is always found in the breach; he fulfills the need of the times, whether it be to bring a discovery from out a misty limbo fully and completely into the light or whether it be to combine single syllables, childishly strung together, into a sonorous word of magical power. It sometimes happens that art blossoms like the plant which gradually unfolds its leaves and that its successive representatives complement one another in equal proportion, so that each master takes only a single step beyond what his teacher has transmitted to him. In such cases, the masses, to whom this slow progress allows ample time, whose *niveau* is only gradually elevated, are enabled to follow the quest for more perfect procedures and higher inspiration. In other cases, the genius leaps ahead of his time and climbs, with one powerful swing, several rungs of the mystic ladder. Then time must elapse until, struggling after him, the general intellectual consciousness attains his point of view; before this happens it is not understood and cannot be judged. In literature, as also in music, this has often been the case. Neither Shakespeare nor Milton, neither Cervantes nor Camoëns, neither Dante nor Tasso, neither Bach nor Mozart, neither Gluck nor Beethoven (to cite only these glorious names) was recognized by his own time in such measure as he was later. In music, which is perpetually in a formative state (and which in our time, developing at a rapid tempo, no sooner accomplishes the ascent of one peak than it begins to climb another), the peculiarity of the genius is that he enriches the art with unused materials as well as with original manipulations of traditional ones, and one can say of music that examples of artists who have, as it were, leaped with both feet into a future time, are here to be found in greatest abundance. How could their anticipation of the style which they recognized as destined for supremacy fail to be offensive to their contemporaries, who had not sufficient strength to tear themselves loose, as they had done, from the comfortable familiarity of traditional forms? Yet, though the crowd turn its back on them, though envious rivals revile them, though pupils desert them, though, depreciated by the stupid and damned by the ignorant, they lead a tortured, hunted life, at death they leave behind their works, like a salutary blessing. These prophetic works transmit their style and their beauty to one after another of those who follow. It often happens that talents little capable of recognizing their significance are the very first to find ways of utilizing certain of their poetic intentions or technical procedures, whose value they estimate according to their lights. These are soon imitated again and thus forced to approach more closely to what was at first misunderstood, until, in the fumbling inherent in such imitations and tentative approaches, there is finally attained the understanding and glorification of the genius who, in his lifetime, demanded recognition in vain. Not until it has become used to admiring works analogous to his, but of lesser value, does the public receive his precious bequest with complete respect and jubilant applause. The old forms, thus made obscure, soon fall into neglect and are finally forgotten by the younger generation that has grown up with the new ones and finds these more acceptable to its poetic ideal. In this way the gap between the genius, gifted with wings, and the public which follows him, snail-like and circumspect, is gradually filled out.

* * * * *

The poetic solution of instrumental music contained in the program seems to us rather one of the various steps forward which the art has still to take, a necessary result of the development of our time, than a symptom of its exhaustion and decadence, for we cannot presume that it is now already obliged to resign itself to the subtleties and aberrations of *raffinement* in order that, after having drained all its auxiliary sources and worn out all its means, it may cover up the impotence of its declining years. If hitherto unused forms arise and, through the magic they exert, win acceptance for themselves with thoughtful artists and with the public, in that the former makes use of them while the latter shows its receptivity toward them, it is not easy to demonstrate their advantages and inconveniences in advance so exhaustively that one can strike an average on the basis of which to establish their expectation of longevity and the nature of their future influence. None the less it would be petty and uncharitable to abstain from inquiry into their origin, significance, bearing, and aim in order to treat works of genius with a disdain of which one may later have reason to be ashamed, in order to withhold due recognition to a widening of the field of art, stamping it, on the contrary and without further ado, as the excrescence of a degenerate period.

We shall forgo deriving advantage from a pronouncement of Hegel's if we can be convinced that great minds (those before whose Herculean intellectual labors every head is bowed, quite apart from sympathy for their doctrines) can characterize precisely those forms as desirable which reveal themselves as sickly and contributory to the downfall of art. Hegel appears to foresee the stimulation which the program can give to instrumental music by increasing the number of those understanding and enjoying it when he says, at the end of the chapter on music in his *Aesthetics,* the intuitive correctness of which as a general survey cannot be prejudiced by certain erroneous conceptions, such as its time brought with it:

The connoisseur, to whom the inner relationships of sounds and instruments are accessible, enjoys in instrumental music its artistic use of harmonies, interwoven melodies, and changing forms; he is wholly absorbed by the music itself and takes a further interest in comparing what he hears with the rules and precepts which he knows in order to appraise and enjoy the accomplishment to the full, though here the ingenuity of the artist in inventing the new can often embarrass even the connoisseur, to whom precisely this or that progression, transition, etc., is unfamiliar. So complete an absorption is seldom the privilege of the amateur, to whom there comes at once a desire to fill out this apparently meaningless outpour of sound and to find intellectual footholds for its progress and, in general, more definite ideas and a more precise content for that which penetrates into his soul. In this respect, music becomes symbolic for him, yet, in his attempts to overtake its meaning, he is confronted by abstruse problems, rapidly rushing by, which do not always lend themselves to solution and which are altogether capable of the most varied interpretations.

We would modify Hegel's opinion only to state it in a more absolute form, for we cannot concede that the *artist* is satisfied with forms that are too dry for the *amateur*. We assert, on the contrary, that the artist, even more insistently than the amateur, must demand emotional content in the formal container. Only when it is filled with the former does the latter have significance for him. The artist and the connoisseur who, in creating and judging, seek only the ingenious construction, the artfully woven pattern, the complex workmanship, the *kaleidoscopic* multiplicity of mathematical calculation and intertwining lines, drive music toward the dead letter and are to be compared with those who look at the luxuriant poetry of India and Persia only from the point of view of grammar and language, who admire only sonority and symmetrical versification, and do not regard the meaning and wealth of thought and image in its expression, its poetic continuity, not to mention the subject which it celebrates or its historical content. We do not deny the usefulness of philological and geological investigations, chemical analyses, grammatical commentaries—but they are the affair of science, not of art. Every art is the delicate blossom which the solid tree of a science bears at the tips of its leafy branches; the roots ought to remain hidden by a concealing coverlet. The necessity and utility of separating the material and substance in which art embodies itself into their component parts with a view to learning to know and to use their properties do not justify the confusing of science and art, of the study of the one with the practice of the other. Man must investigate art and nature; this is however not the goal of his relation to them—it is essentially a preparatory—if likewise important—moment in them. Both are given him primarily for his *enjoyment;* he is to absorb the divine harmonies of nature, to breathe out in art the melodies of his heart and the sighs of his soul. A work which offers only clever manipulation of its materials will always lay claim to the interest of the immediately concerned—of the artist, student, and connoisseur—but, despite this, it will be unable to cross the threshold of the artistic kingdom. Without carrying in itself the divine spark, without being a living poem, it will be ignored by society as though it did not exist at all, and no people will ever accept it as a leaf in the breviary of the cult of the beautiful. It will retain its value only as long as the art remains in a given state; as soon as art moves on to a new horizon and through experience learns improved methods, it will lose all significance save the historic and will be filed away among the archaeological documents of the past. Poetic art works, on the other hand, live for all time and survive all formal revolution, thanks to the indestructible life principle which the human soul has embodied in them.

If instrumental music calls itself the summit of our art, its least constrained and most absolute manifestation, it does so either by virtue of its capacity to give to certain feelings and passions an expression intelligible to the listener, affecting his soul while his mind follows a logical development agreeing with his inner one, or by virtue of the indescribable enjoyment of indefinable impressions which, by force or in alleviation, transform our whole being into a state, incomprehensible to the unresponsive, often called contemplation of the ideal, so aptly characterized by Hegel as a sort of *liberation of the soul,* since the soul actually believes itself released from all material fetters and resigns itself unhampered to emotion's endless sea. Each musical constitution recounts to itself, if not quite clearly then at least in an approximate way, the impression which an instrumental poem should transmit from the author to the listener and is conscious of the passions and feelings and their modifications which it unfolds. Even though, in accordance with the propensity of his imagination, the individual clothes these passions and feelings with images of his own, he will be unable to deceive himself about the sort of temperamental activity which the composer intended his work to evoke. Assuredly, one cannot judge a musician's character better than by defining the mood which he leaves in the listener. The difference between the tone-poet and the mere musician is that the former reproduces his impressions and the adventures of his soul in order to communicate them, while the latter manipulates, groups, and connects the tones according to certain established rules and, thus playfully conquering difficulties, attains at best to novel, bold, unusual, and complex combinations.[e] Yet, since he speaks to men neither of his joys nor of his sorrows, neither of resignation nor of desire, he remains an object of indifference to the masses and interests only those colleagues competent to appreciate his facility. The rest pronounce on him the most deadly sentence of all—they call him *dry*, meaning thereby that there flows in his work no vital sap, no noble blood, no burning passion, that it is a mere aggregation or crystallization of unorganic particles, comparable to those which scientists exclude from the science of life (biology), that is, from the realm of the living. But still—strange paradox—it is only the *tone-poet* who can widen the boundaries of the art by breaking the chains which restrain the free soaring of his fantasy. Only

> The Master can the moment choose
> With skillful hand to break the mold.[f]

---

[e] May we be permitted to quote once again from Hegel, who, in his appraisal and presentation of many important points in music, was led on by that keenness of instinct, often met with in talented constitutions, which deceives them less often than sophistry does in matters which they are incapable of regarding with the same impartiality. "It may be, on the one hand, that we enjoy mere sensuous sound and euphony without further inward participation; on the other hand, that we follow the harmonic and melodic succession which neither affects nor extends the inner self, observing it intellectually. Such a purely intellectual analysis, for which there is nothing in the art work beyond the ingenuity of skillful fabrication, is indeed present in music to an unusual degree. . . . To be sure, the composer can impart to his work a certain meaning, a content of ideas and emotions in organized and self-contained succession; conversely, without regard for such a content, he can concern himself with the purely musical structure of his work and with the ingenuities of such architectonic. In this case, however, the musical product can easily become something relatively devoid of thought and feeling, requiring otherwise no deep consciousness, cultivation, or temperament. As a result of this want of matter, we can frequently observe the development of the gift of composition in very young children, and talented composers often go through life the most inane and unobservant of men. The deeper implication, then, is that even in instrumental music the composer should devote equal attention to both sides—to the expression of an admittedly indefinite content and to musical structure—whereby he is once more at liberty to give the preference now to the melodic, now to the depth and complexity of the harmonic, now to the characteristic, and also to combine these elements one with another. . . . I have already observed that of all the arts, music possesses the greatest capacity for freeing itself, not only from any actual text, but also from the expression of any definite content, finding satisfaction in a mere self-contained succession of the combinations, modifications, contrasts, and transitions that fall within the province of the purely musical. Then, however, music remains empty and meaningless, and, lacking one of the chief sides of art in general, is not yet properly to be reckoned as art. Only when a spiritual content is adequately expressed in the sensual element of the sounds and their varied configurations does music rise to the level of genuine art, regardless of whether this content receives its more immediate identification expressly through words or whether it is in a less definite way perceptible in the sounds and their harmonic relationships and melodic animation." For all that Hegel is criticized for having spoken about music without possessing a wide knowledge of the art, we find his judgments on the whole to the point, as though dictated by that straightforward, healthy intelligence which coincides with the general conviction. He furthermore admits his lack of competence with a modesty which less important folk would do well to imitate and complains that his requests to be set right met with little response. "The sound and exhaustive treatment of the subject," he says, "presupposes a more exact knowledge of the rules of composition and a wholly different acquaintance with the masterpieces of musical literature than I possess or have been able to obtain at second hand, for one never hears anything detailed or definite about these matters from connoisseurs and practical musicians as such, from the latter, often the most unintelligent of people, least of all."

[f] Schiller, *Das Lied von der Glocke* (translated by J. S. Dwight, Boston, 1839).

The specifically musical composer, who attaches importance to the consumption of the material alone, is not capable of deriving new forms from it, of breathing into it new strength, for no intellectual necessity urges him —nor does any burning passion, demanding to be revealed, oblige him— to discover new means. To enrich the form, to enlarge it and make it serviceable, is granted, then, precisely to those who make use of it only as one of the means of expression, as one of the languages which they employ in accordance with the dictates of the ideas to be expressed; the formalists can do nothing better or more intelligent than to use, to popularize, to subdivide, and on occasion to rework what the tone-poets have won.

The program asks only acknowledgment for the possibility of precise definition of the psychological moment which prompts the composer to create his work and of the thought to which he gives outward form. If it is on the one hand childish, idle, sometimes even mistaken, to outline programs after the event, and thus to dispel the magic, to profane the feeling, and to tear to pieces with words the soul's most delicate web, in an attempt to *explain* the feeling of an instrumental poem which took this shape precisely because its content could not be expressed in words, images, and ideas; so on the other hand the master is also master of his work and can create it under the influence of definite impressions which he wishes to bring to full and complete realization in the listener. The specifically musical symphonist carries his listeners with him into ideal regions, whose shaping and ornamenting he relinquishes to their individual imaginations; in such cases it is extremely dangerous to wish to impose on one's neighbor the same scenes or successions of ideas into which our imagination feels itself transported. The painter-symphonist, however, setting himself the task of reproducing with equal clarity a picture clearly present in his mind, of developing a series of emotional states which are unequivocally and definitely latent in his consciousness—why may he not, through a program, strive to make himself fully intelligible?

.   .   .   .   .

If music is not on the decline, if its rapid progress since Palestrina and the brilliant development which has fallen to its lot since the end of the last century are not the preordained limits of its course, then it seems to us probable that the programmatic symphony is destined to gain firm footing in the present art period and to attain an importance comparable to that of the oratorio and cantata—in many respects to realize in a modern sense the meaning of these two species. Since the time when many masters brought the oratorio and cantata style to its highest brilliance, to its final perfection, its successful treatment has become difficult; for other reasons too, whose discussion would here be out of place, the two species no longer arouse the same interest as at the time when Handel animated them with the breath of the winged steer. Oratorio and cantata appear to resemble drama in their impersonation and dialogue. But these are after all external similarities, and close examination reveals at once that undeniable differences of constitution prevail. Conflicts of passions, delineations of characters, unexpected peripetias, and continuous action are in them even more noticeably absent than actual representation; indeed we do not for one moment hesitate to deny a close relation here and are on the contrary persuaded that in this form music approaches rather the antique *epos,* whose essential features it can thus best reproduce. Aside from dialogue, held together by a certain continuity in the action it presents, oratorio and cantata have no more in common with the stage than has the epos; through their leaning toward the descriptive, instrumentation lends them a similar frame. Episode and apostrophe play almost the same role in them, and the effect of the whole is that of the solemn recital of a memorable event, the glory of which falls undivided on the head of a single hero. If we were asked which musical form corresponded most closely to the poetic epos, we should doubt whether better examples could be brought forward than the *Israel, Samson, Judas Maccabaeus, Messiah,* and *Alexander* of Handel, the Passion of Bach, the *Creation* of Haydn, the *St. Paul* and *Elijah* of Mendelssohn.

The program can lend to instrumental music characteristics corresponding almost exactly to the various poetic forms; it can give it the character of the ode, of the dithyramb, of the elegy, in a word, of any form of lyric poetry. If all along it has been expressing the moods proper to these various species, it can by defining its subject draw new and undreamed-of advantages from the approximation of certain ideas, the affinity of certain figures, the separation or combination, juxtaposition or fusion of certain poetic images and perorations. What is more, the program can make feasible for music the equivalent of a kind of poetry unknown to antiquity and owing its existence to a characteristically modern way of feeling—the poem ordinarily written in dialogue form which adapts itself even less readily than the epos to dramatic performance.

It is our opinion that one does violence to the stage, to say the least, when one seeks to impose constructions on it that have taken root and flowered in other fields of poetry and literature and have gone through a development quite different from its own. For all this, the stage is always more receptive to the transplanting of motives from the classical epos than it is to those modern poems which, for want of a better name, we shall call *philosophical epopoeias;* among these Goethe's *Faust* is the colossus, while beside it Byron's *Cain* and *Manfred,* and the *Dziady* of Mickiewicz constitute immortal types. In the epos it is not the persons, but the action, that is unsuited to the theater; the genius, however, can overcome this difficulty, if not without effort, then the more brilliantly. In the epopoeia it is the persons themselves who fail to meet the requirements of the stage, for they are for the most part animated by feelings which, in their height and depth, are inaccessible to the majority who make up the bulk of the dramatic audience.

In the epos and in Homer, its inspired model, it is a hero, gifted with heroic human virtues, whose great deeds occupy the foreground, while a series of the figures of episodic narrative group themselves about him. Their great number is regarded as an enrichment of the work, the variety of their several appearances as one of its beauties. They are depicted with quick, bold strokes and exhibit their characters through actions and speeches without precise description or detailed portrayal. The play of their simple, natural passions is content with the presumptions granted by ordinary experience. The marvelous appears here as something quite as foreign and superior to man's will as natural force. Nature herself is depicted in her full coloring and admired as a power, as a drama. In the modern epopoeia she is rather celebrated than depicted; here her mysterious relations to the constitution of the human soul are unriddled; here she almost ceases to be an object and intervenes in the development as though an active person, in order to curb man by her example, sharing his impressions, consoling him, and lulling him to sleep with her dreams. Before her, the action and the event lose their importance, and the number of the episodic figures, apart from this sketched only lightly, shrinks together. The marvelous gives place to the fantastic; wholly exempt from the laws of probability, compressed and modified, the action acquires a symbolic luster, a mythological basis. No longer do supernatural beings disturb us by their intrusion into the development of human interests; they have to a certain extent become embodiments of passionate desires and hopes and appear now as personifications of our inner impulses. No longer does the poem aim to recount the exploits of the principal figure; it deals with affections active within his very soul. It has become far more important to show what the hero thinks than how he acts, and for this reason a limited concurrence of facts suffices to demonstrate how predominantly this or that feeling affects him. Dialogue becomes of necessity an excuse for monologue. To be sure, a hero is still celebrated, not however with a view to recalling his wanderings, for not even the choice of hero falls any longer on those who are patterns of extraordinary virtues. On the contrary, the modern hero often typifies rare and abnormal impulses, little familiar to the human heart. How these take root in the soul, mount flaming to the heavens, and, in subsiding, cast a flickering light on the ruins of the heart—all this is painstakingly and exhaustively depicted. While the antique epos exhibits to us the majority of mankind and, in its truthful and exact portrayal of character, causes us to admire its profound insight into the soul, the romantic species, as we shall call it, seeks out exceptional figures only; these it draws far beyond life-size and in unusual situations, so that there recognize themselves in them only those constitutions that are formed of a finer clay and animated by a warmer breath, that lead a more powerfully pulsating life than others, with a more responsive soul. Nevertheless they often exert an irresistible magic for all, idealizing in the eye of the plain man inclinations which he experiences and understands in a similar way, only more dully, less distinctly, less pervasively. The supreme charm and greatest merit of these art works lie in their eloquent expression of the most animated, most profound, and often most penitent feelings of great hearts.

If now, despite essential differences, we identify these two species of poetry and group them together under the common name *epopoeia*, we do so because of a similarity which seems to us more important than that of form and scale. Thanks to the cast which genius has given to their features, both species—small in number but great in value—reflect in the most lively manner the spirit of the age and nation which produced them. The antique epos offers us a typical, almost statuesque picture of ancient peoples. Formerly, in the poet's work, a people recognized themselves, as in a faithful mirror, with their morals, their religion, their politics, and their whole activity; today, however, when the distinguishing features of those peoples participating in the Christian civilization tend more and more to become obliterated, the poet naturally feels more drawn to characterize the century and the way of feeling which animates the man of the century (as Goethe and Byron have done in figures whose nationality one recognizes, so to speak, only from their costumes), to give permanent form to the ideal psychological impulse which in his time animates the cultivated man throughout Europe. Why should not music join in this new manifestation of the human spirit?

In literature, no one any longer denies that Goethe and Byron were justified in inventing or introducing the *philosophical epopoeia* as a narrative of inner events, of the fermentation, within the heart, of germs predominantly present in this or that nation or epoch, of exclusive psychological states which, when transferred to an individual being, impel it to actions sufficient to sign a destiny with the stamp of evil. No one any longer complains that these great poets chose as heroes exceptional natures, comparable to those legendary wonder-plants whose blossoms, responsive to the favorable or pernicious external conditions of their existence, distilled a corrosive poison, so that they either destroyed themselves or became fruits of paradise from which a single drop of ambrosia could reanimate the most withered lips. Is music unsuited to cause such natures to speak its language? To represent their origin and metamorphosis, their glorious ascent or downfall, their morbid outbreaks and redeeming powers, to portray their inspiring or awesome end? But could music do this in the drama? Scarcely. Literature itself cannot present upon the stage passions whose meandrine progress must be followed from their source to their disappearance in the eddies of the past. The interest which they arouse attaches itself far more to inner events than to actions related to the outer world.

Would perhaps the specifically musical symphony be better suited to such subjects? We doubt it. The conflict between its independent style and the one forced on it by the subject would affect us disagreeably, being without evident or intelligible cause. The composer would cease to conduct our imagination into the regions of an ideal common to all mankind and, without definitely announcing the particular path he wishes to choose, would only lead the listener astray. With the help of a program, however, he indicates the direction of his ideas, the point of view from which he grasps a given subject. The function of the program then becomes indispensable, and its entrance into the highest spheres of art appears justified. Surely we have no wish to question the capacity of music to represent characters similar to those the poet princes of our time have drawn. For the rest, we see music arrived at such a point in its relations of dependence on and correspondence with literature, we see at the same time all human feeling and thinking, aim and endeavor, so overwhelmingly directed toward profound inquiry into the sources of our sufferings and errors, we see all other arts, vying one with another in their efforts to satisfy the taste and needs of our time, consumed so specifically by the desire to give expression to this urge, that we consider the introduction of the program into the concert hall to be just as inevitable as the declamatory style is to the opera. Despite all handicaps and setbacks, these two trends will prove their strength in the triumphant course of their development. They are imperative necessities of a moment in our social life, in our ethical training, and as such will sooner or later clear a path for themselves. The custom of providing instrumental pieces with a program has already found such acceptance with the public that musicians cease to struggle against it, regarding it as one of those inevitable facts which politicians call *faits accomplis*. The words of an author previously cited will serve as proof of this.

Fine instrumental music must reckon with a much smaller number of competent listeners than opera; to enjoy it fully requires genuine artistic insight and a more active and experienced sensitivity. With the large audience, coloring will always pass as expression, for unless it consist of individuals capable of forming an abstract ideal—something not to be expected of a whole auditorium, no matter how select it may be—it will never listen to a symphony, quartet, or other composition of this order without outlining a program for itself during the performance, according to the grandiose, lively, impetuous, serenely soothing, or melancholy character of the music. By means of this trick, listeners identify most concerts of instrumental music with the expression of certain passionate feelings; they imagine an action differing from those imagined by others as individuals differ among themselves. I speak here of the most cultivated, since for many, frequently for the majority, instrumental music is only a sensual pleasure, if not indeed a tiresome enigma. For them, instrumental music has neither coloring nor expression, and I simply do not know what they look for in it.[g]

Is it not evident from this that it is merely a question of officially recognizing an already existing power with a view to allowing it greater freedom of action and assisting it in the removal of its liabilities, so that henceforward it may work toward its future, toward its fame, not secretly, but in the deliberate repose that comes with an established success?

. . . . .

Through song there have always been *combinations* of music with literary or quasi-literary works; the present time seeks a *union* of the two which promises to become a more intimate one than any that have offered themselves thus far. Music in its masterpieces tends more and more to appropriate the masterpieces of literature. What harm can come to music, at the height to which it has grown since the beginning of the modern era, if it attach itself to a species that has sprung precisely from an undeniably modern way of feeling? Why should music, once so inseparably bound to the tragedy of Sophocles and the ode of Pindar, hesitate to unite itself in a different yet more adequate way with works born of an inspiration unknown to antiquity, to identify itself with such names as Dante

---

g Fétis.

and Shakespeare? Rich shafts of ore lie here awaiting the bold miner, but they are guarded by mountain spirits who breathe fire and smoke into the faces of those who approach their entrance and, like Slander, whom Voltaire compares to coals, blacken what they do not burn, threatening those lusting after the treasure with blindness, suffocation, and utter destruction.

To our regret we must admit that a secretly smoldering but irreconcilable quarrel has broken out between *vocational* and *professional* musicians. The latter, like the Pharisees of the Old Law, cling to the letter of the commandment, even at the risk of killing its spirit. They have no understanding of the love revealed in the New Testament, for the thirst after the eternal, the dream of the ideal, the search for the poetically beautiful in every form. They live only in fear, grasp only fear, preach only fear; for them, fear (not precisely the fear of the Lord, however) is the beginning and end of all wisdom; they hang on the language of the law with the pettiness of those whose hearts have not taught them that the fulfillment of the prophecy lies in the abolition of the sacrifice, in the rending of the veil of the temple; their wisdom consists in dogmatic disputes, in sterile and idle speculation on subtleties of the rules. They deny that one may show greater honor to the old masters by seeking out the germs of artistic development which they embedded in their works than by servilely and thoughtlessly tracing the empty forms whose entire content of air and light they drained themselves in their own day. On the other hand the *vocational* musicians hold that to honor these patriarchs one must regard the forms they used as exhausted and look on imitations of them as mere copies of slight value. They do not hope to glean further harvests from fields sown by giants and believe that they cannot continue the work already begun unless, as the patriarchs did in their time, they create new forms for new ideas, put new wine into new bottles.

To Berlioz and his successes has been opposed from the beginning, like an insurmountable dam, that academic aversion to every art product which, instead of following the beaten path, is formed in accordance with an unaccustomed ideal or called up by incantations foreign to the old rite. But with or without the magisterial permission of the titulary and non-titulary professors—even without that of the illustrious director of the Paris Conservatoire, who visited Berlioz' concerts quite regularly in order, as he put it, "to learn how not to do it"—everyone who would keep up with contemporary art must study the scores of this master, precisely to see what is being done today and "to learn how to do it." And in truth, the so-called classicists themselves are not above making use of overheard and stolen ideas and effects and even, in exceptional cases, of conceding that Berlioz does after all show talent for instrumentation and skill in combining, since he is one of those artists, previously mentioned, who through the wider expression of their feelings and the freer unfolding of their individuality expand and enrich the form and make it serviceable. In the last analysis, however, the hypocrisy of his envious opponents consists in refusing to pay him the tuition they owe and have on their conscience while they publicly tread into the mire everything of his which they are not and never will be capable of imitating and privately pull out all feathers of his which they can use as ornaments themselves. We could name many who rise up against Berlioz, though their best works would be disfigured were one to take from them everything for which they are obliged to him. We repeat, therefore, that unusual treatment of form is not the supreme unpardonable error of which Berlioz is accused; his opponents will indeed concede, perhaps, that he has done art a service in discovering new inflections. What they will never forgive is that form has for him an importance subordinate to idea, that he does not, as they do, cultivate form for form's sake; they will never forgive him for being a thinker and a poet.

Strangely enough, that *union* of music and literature of which we have already spoken, constantly increasing in intimacy, developing itself with surprising rapidity, is gaining firm footing despite the equally lively opposition of *professional* musicians and men of letters. Both parties set themselves against it with the same vigor, with the same obstinacy. The latter, looking askance, see their property being taken over into a sphere where, apart from the value *they* placed on it, it acquires new significance; the former are horrified at a violation of their territory by elements with which they do not know how to deal. The tone-poets have hence to contend with a double enmity; they find themselves between two fires. But the strength of their cause compensates for the weakness of their position. Whether one recognizes it or not, the fact remains that both arts, more than ever before, feel themselves mutually attracted and are striving for inner union.

Through the endless variety of its forms, art reproduces the endless variety of constitutions and impressions. There are characters and feelings which can attain full development only in the dramatic; there are others which in no wise tolerate the limitations and restrictions of the stage. Berlioz recognized this. From the church, where it was for so many centuries exclusively domiciled and from whence its masterpieces scarcely reached the outer world, musical art moved by degrees into the theater, setting up there a sort of general headquarters or open house where anyone might exhibit his inspirations in any genre he chose. For a while it would scarcely have entered the head of any musician to regard himself as incapable of composing dramatic works. It seemed as though, on admission to the musical guild or brotherhood, one also acquired and accepted the ability, sanction, and duty to supply a certain number of operas, large or small, romantic or comic, *serie* or *buffe*. All hastened to the contest in this arena, hospitably open to everyone. When the terrain of the boards proved slippery, later on, some crept and others danced on the tightrope; many provided themselves with hammers instead of balancing poles and, when their neighbors struggled to keep their balance, hit them over the head. Some bound golden skates to their feet and with their aid left way behind them a train of poor devils, panting to no avail; certain ones, like messengers of the gods, had at their head and heels the wings given them at birth by genius, by means of which, if they did not precisely make rapid progress, they were able at least to fly on occasion to the summit. And, for all that these last remained, here as elsewhere, very much in the minority, they none the less imposed on their successors so great an obligation to surpass their accomplishment that a moment seems to have arrived which should cause many to ask themselves whether the sense of duty which urges them to join in this turmoil is not a prepossession. Those, indeed, who expect more of fame than a draft to be discounted by the present, more than a gilt-paper crown to be snatched at by fabricators of artificial flowers—let them ask themselves whether they were really born to expend their energies in this field, to course and tourney in these narrow lists; whether their temperament does not impel them toward more ideal regions; whether their abilities might not take a higher flight in a realm governed by fewer constraining laws; whether their freer fantasy might not then discover one of those Atlantides, blissful isles, or unknown constellations for which all students of the earth and sky are seeking. We for our part are persuaded that not every genius can limit his flight within the narrow confines of the stage and that he who cannot is thus forced to form for himself a new *habitaculum*.

To seek to import a foreign element into instrumental music and to domesticate it there by encroaching upon the independence of feeling through definite subjects offered to the intelligence in advance, by forcing upon a composer a concept to be literally represented or poetically formulated, by directing the attention of the listener, not only to the woven pattern of the music, but also to the ideas communicated by its contours and successions—this seems to many an absurd, if not a sacrilegious undertaking. Small wonder that before Berlioz they cover their heads and let their beards grow—before him who carries this beginning so far that, by symbolizing its presence, he causes the human voice to be heard in the hitherto wholly impersonal symphony; before him who undertakes to impart to the symphony a new interest, to enliven it with an entirely new element; before him who—not content to pour out in the symphony the lament of a common woe, to cause to sound forth in it the hopes of all and to stream forth from its focus the affections and shocks, sorrows and ardors, which pulse in the heart of mankind—takes possession of its powers in order to employ them in the expression of the sufferings and emotions of a specific, exceptional individual! Since the pleasure of listening to orchestral works has always been an altogether subjective one for those who followed the poetic content along with the musical, it seems to many a distortion, a violence done to its character, that the imagination is to be forced to adapt completely outlined pictures to that which is heard, to behold and accept figures in precisely the way the author wills. The hitherto usual effect of pure instrumental music on poetic temperaments may perhaps be compared to that which antique sculpture produces in them; in their eyes, these works also represent passions and forms, generating certain movements of the affections, rather than the specific and particular individuals whose names they bear—names, moreover, which are for the most part again allegorical representations of ideas. For them, Niobe is not this or that woman stricken by this or that misfortune; she is the most exalted expression of supreme suffering. In Polyhymnia they see, not a specific person engaged in specific speech or action, but the visible representation of the beauty, harmony, charm, and magic of that compelling, yet soft and placid persuasion whose eloquence can be concentrated in a single glance. Minerva, for them, is not only the divine, blue-eyed mentor of Ulysses, she is also the noblest symbol of that gift of our spirit which simultaneously judges and divines; who, provided with all the attributes of force, armed with all the weapons of war, is still a friend of peace; who, bearing lance and breastplate, causes her most beautiful gift, the olive tree, to sprout, promising peace; who, possessor of the terrifying aegis, loses nothing of the kindliness and attraction of her smile, of the slowly sinking cadence of her movements.

. . . . .

Just as marble presents artistic formulations of general concepts to the eye, so the ear, in instrumental music, desires something similar. For the cultivated listener, one symphony expresses to a supreme degree the several phases of passionate, joyous feeling, another—elegiac mourning, another—heroic enthusiasm, still another—sorrow over an irreparable loss. If, then, these cultivated listeners are accustomed to seek and find in an art work the abstract expression of universal human feeling, they must experience a natural distaste for everything that aims to lend this universality concrete character, to make it particular, to derive it from a specific human figure. They have admittedly the undeniable right, the inalienable duty, to wish to see this species of creative activity maintained; shall other species for this reason be scolded out of their right to existence? Shall those who feel driven by their genius and by the spirit of the age to discover new molds be bowed beneath the yoke of a uniform way of working? Or should one not rather fear to see them renounce ambitions which they would admirably succeed in realizing in order to deny their birthright in efforts not in agreement with the nature of their inspiration?

·　·　·　·

87. Richard Wagner

The Art Work of the Future belongs to the most critical period in Wagner's life, the first years of his exile and of his residence in Zurich, the years between the end of his work on *Lohengrin* (1847) and the beginning of his work on the *Ring* (1853). During this lull in his artistic productivity, Wagner endeavored to come to terms with the problem of the opera and with himself; the results of this soul-searching are his three capital essays—*Art and Revolution* (1849), *The Art Work of the Future* (1850), and *Opera and Drama* (1852)—and in a larger sense, the great music-dramas of his maturity and old age. Three times, later on, he attempted to summarize the contents of these essays—first in *A Communication to My Friends* (1852), then in *"Music of the Future"* (1860), finally in *On the Destiny of Opera* (1869); in 1879, near the end of his life, he returned to the problem once more in a series of three further essays—*On the Writing of Poetry and Music, On the Writing of Operatic Poetry and Music in Particular,* and *On the Application of Music to the Drama.*

It is well known that the three major essays of Wagner's earlier years in Zurich were written under the immediate influence of the philosopher Ludwig Feuerbach (1804–1872), author of *The Essence of Christianity* (1841), whose repeated attacks upon orthodox theology had attracted the interest of Marx and Engels and had made him, somewhat to his astonishment, the idol of the "Young German" intellectuals sympathetic to the uprisings of 1849. In his autobiography, Wagner tells us himself that his acquaintance with Feuerbach's reputation dates from his last years in Dresden; traces of Feuerbach's influence have even been detected in Wagner's *Jesus of Nazareth*, a dramatic synopsis sketched at just this time. As to *The Art Work of the Future*, this owes its very title to Feuerbach's *Principles of the Philosophy of the Future* (1843), and in its original edition as a separate monograph it was introduced by a letter from Wagner to Feuerbach, beginning: "To no one but you, my dear sir, can I dedicate this work, for with it I give you back your own property."

In later life, after his conversion to Schopenhauer and to a more prudent political philosophy, Wagner did what he could to play down the revolutionary character of his earlier writings and to represent his youthful enthusiasm for Feuerbach as an unimportant passing phase. This is already evident to some extent in the summary incorporated in his *"Music of the Future."* It became still more evident with the publication of the third and fourth volumes of his *Sämmtliche Schriften* in 1872; here the dedication to Feuerbach is silently suppressed, while the foreword to the third volume contains this apologia: "From my reading of several of the works of Ludwig Feuerbach, which held a lively interest for me at the time, I had taken over various designations for concepts which I then applied to artistic ideas to which they could not always clearly correspond. Herein I surrendered myself without critical reflection to a brilliant author who appealed to my mood of the moment, particularly in that he bade farewell to philosophy (in which he believed himself to have discovered nothing but disguised theology) and addressed himself instead to a view of human nature in which I was persuaded that I could recognize again the artistic man I had had in mind. Thus there arose a certain reckless confusion, which revealed itself in a hastiness and lack of clarity in the use of philosophical schemes." Wagner then goes on to criticize his earlier use of Feuerbach's terminology, particularly of the expressions "willfulness" (*Willkür*) and "instinct" (*Unwillkür*), for which he now suggests the substitution, by the reader, of Schopenhauer's "will" (*Wille*) and "conscious will" (*Verstandeswille*). Still more exaggerated is Wagner's account of his relation to Feuerbach in his posthumously published autobiography: "Before long," he says, "it had already become impossible for me to return to his writings, and I recall that his book *On the Essence of Religion*, which appeared soon after this, so repelled me by the monotony of its title that when Herwegh opened it for me I clapped it shut before his eyes." How far from the truth this is, can be gathered from Wagner's letter of June 8, 1853, addressed to the imprisoned Röckel, his fellow revolutionary, and accompanied by a copy of the book in question: "Feuerbach's book is to a certain extent a résumé of all that he has hitherto done in the field of philosophy. It is not one of his really celebrated works, such as *The Essence of Christianity* or *Thoughts upon Death and Immortality*, but it is a short cut to a complete knowledge of his mental development and of the latest results of his speculations. I should be glad to think of you as strengthened and encouraged by contact with this clear, vigorous mind."

In *A Communication to My Friends*, speaking of the contradictions between his new theories and his earlier scores, Wagner has this to say: "The contradictions to which I refer will not even exist for the man who has accustomed himself to look at phenomena from the point of view of their development in time. The man who, in judging a phenomenon, takes this developmental factor into consideration will meet with contradictions only when the phenomenon in question is an unnatural, unreasonable one, set apart from space and time; to disregard the developmental factor altogether, to combine its various and clearly distinguishable phases, belonging to different times, into one indistinguishable mass, this is in itself an unnatural, unreasonable way of looking at things, one that can be adopted by our monumental-historical criticism, but not by the healthy criticism of a sympathetic and sensitive heart. . . . Critics who make a pretence of judging my artistic activity as a whole have sometimes proceeded in this uncritical, inattentive, and insensitive way; taking as relevant to their judgment views on the nature of art which I had made known from a standpoint arrived at only after a gradual and deliberate development, they have applied these views to the very art-works in which the natural developmental process that led me to the standpoint in question began. . . . It does not occur to them at all, when they compare the newly acquired standpoint with the older one left behind, that these are in fact two essentially different points of view, each one of them logically developed in itself, and that it would have been much better to have explained the new standpoint in the light of the old one than it was to judge the one abandoned in the light of the one adopted."

Wagner's objection is well taken. Yet later on, as we have seen, he was himself guilty of an uncritical procedure very similar to the one complained of here. Wagner too endeavored to combine two clearly distinguishable phases of his development, the middle and the late, into one indistinguishable mass. But whereas his critics had sought, as he puts it, "to kill two flies at one blow," Wagner seeks to prove the essential identity of two points of view that are essentially opposed.

Nietzsche, in his *Genealogy of Morals* (1887), sums up Wagner's dilemma with telling irony: "Think of the enthusiasm with which Wagner formerly followed in the footsteps of the philosopher Feuerbach: Feuerbach's expression 'healthy sensuality'—to Wagner, as to many Germans ('Young Germans,' they called themselves), this sounded in the thirties and forties like the word of redemption. Did he finally *learn* a different view? For it seems at least that at the end he wished to *teach* a different one."

From Das Kunstwerk der Zukunft [1]

[*1850*]

MAN AND ART IN GENERAL

Nature, Man, and Art

As MAN is to nature, so art is to man.

When nature had of itself developed to that state which encompassed

---

[1] Text: *Sämtliche Schriften und Dichtungen*, 6th ed., Leipzig, 1912–14. Wagner divides the essay into five chapters; the present abridged translation includes I, 1 and 6; II, 1 and 4; IV, somewhat abbreviated.

the conditions for man's existence, then man arose of himself; once human life engenders of itself the conditions for the appearance of the art work, the art work comes into being of itself.

Nature begets and shapes aimlessly and instinctively, according to need, hence of necessity; this same necessity is the begetting and shaping force in human life; only what is aimless and instinctive arises from genuine need, and only in need lies the cause of life.

Natural necessity man recognizes only in the continuity of natural phenomena; until he grasps this continuity, he thinks nature willful.

From that moment in which man became sensible of his divergence from nature and thereby took the first step of all in his development as man, freeing himself from the unconsciousness of natural animal life to pass over into conscious life—when he thus placed himself in opposition to nature and when, as an immediate result of this, his sense of his dependence on nature led to the development in him of thought—from that moment, as the first assertion of consciousness, error began. But error is the father of knowledge, and the history of the begetting of knowledge from error is the history of the human race from the myth of primeval time to the present day.

Man erred from the time when he placed the cause of natural phenomena outside the state of nature itself, assumed for material phenomena an ideal origin, namely a willful origin of his own conceiving, and took the infinite continuity of nature's unconscious and purposeless activity for the purposeful behavior of will's noncontinuous, finite manifestations. Knowledge consists in the correction of this error, this correction in the perception of necessity in those phenomena for which we had assumed a willful origin.

Through this knowledge nature becomes conscious of self—to be precise, in man, who arrived at his knowledge of nature only through his distinction between self and nature, which he thus made an object. But this distinction disappears again at the moment when man recognizes nature's state as identical with his own; recognizes the same necessity in all that genuinely exists and lives, hence in human existence no less than in natural existence; and recognizes not only the connection of the natural phenomena with one another, but also his own connection with them.

If, through its connection with man, nature attains now to consciousness, and if the activity of this consciousness is to be human life itself—as though a representation, a picture, of nature—then human life itself attains to understanding through science, which makes of human life in turn an object of experience. But the activity of the consciousness won through science, the representation of the life made known through this activity, the copy of its necessity and truth is *art*.[a]

Man will not be that which he can and should be until his life is a faithful mirror of nature, a conscious pursuit of the only real necessity, *inner natural necessity*, not a subordination to an *outer* imagined *force*, imitating imagination, and hence not necessary but *willful*. Then man will really be man; thus far he has always merely existed by virtue of some predicate derived from religion, nationality, or state. In the same way, art too will not be that which it can and should be until it is or can be a faithful, manifestly conscious copy of genuine man and of the genuine, naturally necessary life of man, in other words, until it need no longer borrow from the errors, perversities, and unnatural distortions of our modern life the conditions of its being.

Genuine man, therefore, will not come into being until his life is shaped and ordered by true human nature and not by the willful law of state; genuine art will not live until its shapings need be subject only to the law of nature and not to the despotic caprice of fashion. For just as man becomes free only when he becomes joyously conscious of his connection with nature, so art becomes free only when it has no longer to be ashamed of its connection with life. Only in joyous consciousness of his connection with nature does man overcome his dependence on it; art overcomes its dependence on life only in its connection with the life of genuine, free men.

*   *   *   *   *

A Standard for the Art Work of the Future

It is not the individual mind, striving through art for fulfillment in nature, that has the power to create the art work of the future; only the collective mind, satisfied in life, has this power. But the individual can form an idea of it, and it is precisely the character of his striving—his striving for *nature*—which prevents this idea from being a mere fancy. He who longs to return to nature and who is hence unsatisfied in the modern present, finds not only in the totality of nature, but above all in *man's nature*, as it presents itself to him historically, those images which, when he beholds them, enable him to reconcile himself to life in general. In this nature he recognizes an image of all future things, already formed on a small scale; to imagine this scale expanded to its furthest compass lies within the conceptual limits of the impulse of his need for nature.

---

[a] Art in general, that is, or the art of the future in particular.

History plainly presents two principal currents in the development of mankind—the *racial-national* and the *unnational-universal*. If we now look forward to the completion of this second developmental process in the future, we have plainly before our eyes the completed course of the first one in the past. To what heights man has been able to develop, subjected to this first, almost directly formative influence—insofar as racial origin, linguistic affiliation, similarity of climate, and the natural character of a common native land permitted him to yield unconsciously to nature's influence—we have every reason to take the keenest pleasure in acknowledging. In the natural morality of all peoples, insofar as they include the normal human being—even those cried down as rawest—we learn for the first time to recognize the truth of human nature in its full nobility, its genuine beauty. Not *one* genuine virtue has been adopted by any religion whatever as a divine command which had not been included of itself in this natural morality; not *one* genuinely human concept of right has been developed by the later civilized state—and then, unfortunately, to the point of complete distortion!—which had not already been given positive expression in this natural morality; not *one* discovery genuinely useful to the community has been appropriated by later culture—with arrogant ingratitude!—which had not been derived from the operation of the native intelligence of the guardians of this natural morality.

That *art* is not an *artificial* product—that the need of art is not one willfully induced, but rather one native to the natural, genuine, unspoiled human being—who demonstrates this more strikingly than precisely these peoples? Indeed, from what circumstance could our mind deduce the demonstration of art's necessity, if not from the perception of this artistic impulse and its splendid fruits among these naturally developed peoples, among the people in general? Before what phenomenon do we stand with a more humiliating sense of the impotence of our frivolous culture than before the art of the *Hellenes?* To this, to this art of all-loving Mother Nature's favored children, those most beautiful human beings whose proud mother holds them up to us, even in these nebulous and hoary days of our present fashionable culture, as an undeniable and triumphant proof of what she can do—to the splendid art of the Greeks we look, to learn from intimate understanding of it how the art work of the future must be constituted! Mother Nature has done all she could—she has borne the Hellenes, nourished them at her breasts, formed them through her maternal wisdom, now she sets them before us with maternal pride and out of maternal love calls to us all: "This I have done for you; now, out of love for yourselves, do what you can!"

Thus it is our task to make of *Hellenic* art the altogether *human* art; to remove from it the conditions under which it was precisely a *Hellenic*, and not an altogether *human* art; to widen the *garb of religion,* in which alone it was a communal Hellenic art, and after removing which, as an egoistic individual art species, it could no longer fill the need of the community, but only that of luxury—however beautiful!—to widen this garb of the specifically *Hellenic religion* to the bond of the religion of the future—that of *universality*—in order to form for ourselves even now a just conception of the art work of the future. Yet, unfortunate as we are, it is precisely the power to close this bond, this *religion of the future,* that we lack, for after all, no matter how many of us may feel this urge to the art work of the future, we are *singular* and *individual.* An art work is religion brought to life; religions, however, are created, not by the artist, but by the *folk.*

Let us, then, be content that for the present—without egoistic vanity, without wishing to seek satisfaction in any selfish illusion whatsoever, but with sincere and affectionate resignation to the hope for the art work of the future—we test first of all the nature of the art varieties which today, in their dismembered condition, make up the present general state of art; that we brace ourselves for this test by a glance at the art of the Hellenes; and that we then boldly and confidently draw our conclusions as to the *great universal art work of the future!*

MAN AS ARTIST AND THE ART DIRECTLY DERIVED FROM HIM

Man as the Subject and Material of His Own Art

There is an *outer* and an *inner* man. The senses to which man presents himself as artistic subject are *sight* and *hearing;* to the eye he presents the outer man, to the ear the inner.

The eye apprehends *man's corporeal form,* compares it with its surroundings, and distinguishes it from them. The corporeal man and his instinctive manifestations, in physical pain and pleasure, of impressions received through external stimulation present themselves directly to the eye. Indirectly he communicates to it also, through facial expression and gesture, the sensations of the inner man, not directly perceptible to it; above all through the expression of the eye itself, which meets the beholding eye directly, he can communicate to the latter not only the feelings of his heart, but even the characteristic activity of his mind, and the more precisely the outer man can express the inner, the more clearly he reveals himself as artist.

Directly the inner man presents himself to the ear through the *tone of his voice*. *Tone* is the direct expression of feeling, as it has its physical seat in the heart, the starting and returning point for the circulation of the blood. Through the sense of hearing tone penetrates from heart to heart, from feeling to feeling; grief and joy communicate themselves directly, through the manifold tone of voice, from one man of feeling to another, and where the outer corporeal man's capacity for expression and communication finds its limit in the character of the inner feeling of the heart to be expressed and communicated to the eye, there steps in the decisive communication to the ear through the tone of voice, and through the ear to the feeling of the heart.

Moreover, where the direct expression of the tone of voice finds its limit in turn in the communication and exactly distinguishable definition, to the sympathetic and interested inner man, of the single feelings of the heart, there steps in, transmitted through the tone of voice, the expression of *speech*. *Speech* is the concentrated element of voice, word the consolidated *mass* of tone. In speech, feeling communicates through hearing to feeling, but to a feeling that is to be similarly concentrated and consolidated, to which it wishes to convey itself with a view to positive unmistakable understanding. It is accordingly the organ of the specific feeling which understands and would be understood—the understanding. For less definite, general feeling the direct character of tone sufficed; such feeling dwelt on tone, as the expression in itself already satisfying and pleasing to the senses; in the quantity of its expansion it had even the power to convey its own quality significantly. The specific need which seeks to make itself intelligible in speech is more decided, more imperious; it does not dwell comfortably on its sensual expression, for it must represent the feeling which is its subject and differentiate it from general feeling, hence portray and describe that which tone, as the expression of general feeling, conveyed directly. For this reason the speaker must derive his images from related, but at the same time differentiated objects and assemble them. For this complex mediating process he must, generally speaking, enlarge upon his subject; on the other hand, dominated by his principal aim—to promote understanding—he hastens the process by dwelling on tone as briefly as possible, by leaving its general capacity for expression wholly out of account. Through this necessary renunciation, through this giving up of his pleasure in the sensual element in his own expression—this giving up, at least, of that degree of pleasure which the man of body and the man of feeling were able to take in their manner of expression—the man of understanding becomes able, by virtue of his organ, to give to speech that positive expression in which the men of body and feeling progressively found their limits. The power of the man of understanding is unlimited; he collects and singles out the general; he divides and connects the images which his senses transmit to him from the outer world in accordance with his need and preference; he joins and looses the particular and the general as he sees fit, to satisfy his desire for a positive, intelligible expression of his feeling, his view, his will. Only there does he find his limit in turn, there in the agitation of his feeling, in the animation of joy or in the violence of grief—there where the particular and willful retire before the general and instinctive in the dominant feeling itself, where, leaving behind the egoism of his restricted personal sensation, he finds himself again in the communism of the great all-embracing sensation, hence of the unrestricted truth of feeling and of sensation in general—there where he must subordinate his individual arbitrary will to necessity, whether of grief or of joy, and has accordingly, not to command, but to obey—there where he desires the one appropriate direct expression of his infinitely intensified feeling. Here he must once again avail himself of general expression and must retrace his steps in order, passing through the same stages by means of which he arrived at his particular standpoint, borrowing from the man of feeling the sensual tone of feeling, from the man of body the sensual gesture of body; for where there is required the most direct and at the same time most positive expression of the highest and truest that man can possibly express, there must be indeed united the whole, complete man: the man of understanding, bound through the most intimate, all-pervading love to the men of feeling and body—no one of them for self alone.

The progress of the outer man of body through the man of feeling to the man of understanding is one of constantly increasing mediation; the man of understanding, like speech, his organ of expression, is the most mediate and dependent of all, for all the qualities subordinated to him must be normally developed before the conditions of *his* normal quality are present. But the most restricted capacity is at the same time the most intense, and his joy in self, which comes from recognition of his higher, pre-eminent quality, drives him to the arrogant presumption that he may employ the qualities basic to him as slaves of his arbitrary will. This arrogance, however, gives way before the omnipotence of physical sensation and the feeling of the heart the moment they manifest themselves to him as common to all mankind, as sensations and feelings of the species. The individual sensation and the individual feeling, as they reveal themselves in him as an individual through this one particular and personal contact with this one particular and personal object—these he has the power to suppress and to control in favor of a richer combination, which he conceives, of many-sided objects; the richest combination of all the objects perceptible to him finally sets before him *man as species and in his connection with nature as a whole*, and before this great all-powerful object his arrogance breaks down. Thenceforward he can will only the universal, the true, the absolute—his own absorption, not in the love of this or that object, but in love *in general*; thus the egoist becomes communist, the one —all, the man—god, and the art variety—art.

. . . . .

The Art of Tone

The sea divides and connects the continents; thus the art of tone divides and connects the two extreme antitheses of human art, the arts of dancing and of poetry.

It is man's *heart*; the blood, circulating from this center, gives to the flesh, turned outward, its warm, lively color—at the same time it nourishes the brain nerves, tending inward, with waves of resilient energy. Without the activity of the heart, the activity of the brain would remain a mere mechanical performance, the activity of the body's external organs equally mechanical and unfeeling. Through the heart, the intellect is made sensible of its relation to the body as a whole—the mere man of the senses attains to intellectual activity.

But the organ of the heart is *tone*, and its artistically conscious speech is the *art of tone*. This is the full, flowing heart-love that ennobles sensual pleasure and humanizes spiritual thought. Through the art of tone, the arts of poetry and dancing understand each other; in the one there blend in affectionate fusion the laws governing the manifestations natural to the others—in the one the will of the others becomes instinctive will, the measure of poetry and the beat of dancing become the inevitable rhythm of the heartthrob.

If music receives from its sister arts the conditions of its manifestation, it gives these back to them, made infinitely beautiful, as the conditions of their manifestation; if dancing supplies music with its law of motion, music returns it in the form of rhythm, spiritually and sensually embodied as a measure for ennobled and intelligible movement; if poetry supplies music with its meaningful series of clear-cut words, intelligibly united through meaning and measure as material bodies, rich in idea, for the consolidation of its infinitely fluid tonal element, music returns this ordered series of quasi-intellectual, unfulfilled speech-sounds—indirectly representative, concentrated as image but not yet as immediate, inevitably true expression—in the form of *melody*, directly addressed to feeling, unerringly vindicated and fulfilled.

In musically animated *rhythm* and *melody*, dancing and poetry regain their own being, sensually objectified and made infinitely beautiful and capable; they recognize and love each other. But rhythm and melody are the *arms* with which Music encircles her sisters in affectionate entwinement; they are the *shores* by means of which she, the *sea*, unites two continents. Should the sea recede from the shores, should the abysmal waste spread out between it and them, no jaunty sailing ship will longer range from the one continent to the other; they will forever remain divided—unless mechanical inventions, perhaps railroads, succeed in making the waste passable; then, doubtless, one will also pass clean across the sea in steamships; the breath of the all-animating breeze will give place to the puff of the machine; what difference need it make that the wind naturally blows eastward?—the machine clatters westward, precisely where we wish to go; thus the ballet maker sends across the steam-conquered sea of music to the poetry continent for the program of his new pantomime, while the stage-piece fabricator fetches from the dancing continent as much leg seasoning as he happens to need to liven up a stale situation. Let us see what has happened to Sister Music since the death of all-loving Father *Drama!*

Not yet may we give up our figure of the *sea* as music's being. If *rhythm* and *melody* are the shores at which the tonal art meets with and makes fruitful the two continents of the arts primevally related to it, then tone itself is the primeval fluid element, and the immeasurable expanse of this fluid is the sea of *harmony*. Our eye is aware only of its surface; its depth only our heart's depth comprehends. Up from its bottom, dark as night, it spreads out to its mirroring surface, bright as the sun; from the one shore radiate on it the rings of rhythm, drawn wider and wider—from the shadowy valleys of the other shore rises the longing breeze which agitates the placid surface in waves of melody, gracefully rising and falling.

Into this sea man dives to yield himself again, radiant and refreshed, to the light of day; he feels his heart expand with wonder when he looks down into these depths, capable of unimaginable possibilities, whose bottom his eye is never to fathom, whose fathomlessness fills him accordingly with astonishment and forebodings of the infinite. This is the depth and infinity of nature itself, which veils from man's searching eye the impenetrable mystery of its budding, begetting, and longing, precisely because the eye can comprehend only what has become visible—the budded, the begotten, the longed for. This nature is in turn none other than the *nature of the human heart itself*, which encompasses the feelings of love and longing in their most infinite being, which is itself love and longing, and which—since in its insatiable longing it desires itself alone—grasps and comprehends itself alone.

If this sea rises of itself from its own depths, if it derives the cause of its motion from the primeval cause of its own element, this motion is also endless, implacable, eternally returning to itself unsatisfied, eternally longing and rousing itself anew. But should an object situated outside the monstrous abundance of this longing enkindle it; should this defining object draw near it from the positive, concrete, phenomenal world; should man himself, radiant with sunlight, moving sinuously and vigorously, enflame this longing with a glance of his burning eye and agitate with his swelling breath the elastic mass of the sea crystal; then—no matter how high the towering glow, no matter how powerfully uprooted the surface by the storm—once the fierce glow has subsided, the flame will burn at last as a mildly shining light; once the giant waves have broken in spray, the surface will be ruffled at last only by the innocent play of the ripples; and man, happy in the sweet harmony of his whole being, will surrender himself in a frail shell to the trusted elements and will steer secure, guided by that familiar, mildly shining light.

The *Hellene*, when he set sail on his sea, never lost sight of the coast; this was for him the safe current which bore him from strand to strand, on which, between the familiar shores, he rode along to the melodious measure of the helm, now watching the dance of the wood nymphs, now listening to the hymn of the gods, whose ingeniously melodious word-round the breezes bore to him from the temple on the mountain top. On the surface of the water there lay faithfully reflected before him, framed in a blue ethereal border, the shore country with its rocks, valleys, trees, flowers, and men, and he took this charmingly weaving reflection, attractively animated by the fresh fanning of the breezes, for *harmony*.

The *Christian* bade the shores of life farewell. He sought a wider and less restricted sea, to be at last absolutely alone on the ocean between sea and sky. The *word*, the word of *faith*, was his compass, directing him steadfastly toward heaven. This heaven floated above him; at each horizon it sank down to bound the sea; the sailor, however, never reached this boundary; from century to century he drifted unredeemed toward the new homeland always hovering before him but never reached, until, seized with doubt as to the virtue of his compass, he grimly threw this too overboard as man's last illusion and now, free of all ties, gave himself up,

helmless, to the inexhaustible willfulness of the sea waves. In the unsatisfied, exasperated fury of his love he stirred up the depths of the sea against
the unattainable sky; he incited the insatiability of its very desire for love
and longing, which without an object must forever and ever love and long
for itself alone—this deepest, least redeemable hell of the most restless
egoism, which expands without end, wishes and wills, and forever and
ever can wish and will itself alone—against the abstract blue heaven-
generality, against the supremely object-needing general desire—against
absolute inobjectivity itself. To wish to be blissful, absolutely blissful, *blissful* in the widest and most unlimited sense, and at the same time to remain
wholly *itself*—this was the insatiable desire of the Christian temperament.
Thus the sea rose up from its depths to the sky, thus it sank back, again
and again, from the sky to its depths, eternally itself and hence eternally
unsatisfied—like the boundless, all-sovereign longing of the heart, self-
condemned to be forever unable to give itself or to be absorbed in an object, self-condemned to be *itself* alone.

But in nature everything immeasurable seeks its measure, everything
limitless draws limits for itself, the elements concentrate themselves at
last as definite phenomena; thus also the boundless sea of Christian longing found the new coastland against which it might break its impatience.
There on the far horizon, where we had fondly imagined the entrance
into the limitless heaven-space, always sought but never found, there at
last the boldest of all navigators discovered land—inhabited by peoples—
actual, blissful land. Through his discovery the wide ocean was not only
measured, but also made for mankind an inland sea about which the coasts
spread themselves out only in inconceivably wider circles. But if Columbus
taught us to sail the ocean and thus to connect all the earth's continents;
if through his discovery the short-sighted national man has, from the
point of view of world history, become the all-seeing universal man—has
become man altogether; so through the hero who sailed the wide shoreless
sea of absolute music to its limits were won the new undreamed-of coasts
which now no longer divide this sea from the old primevally human continents, but *connect* them for the newborn fortunate artistic humanity of
the future. This hero is none other than—*Beethoven.*[2]

When Music freed herself from the round of her sisters—just as her
frivolous sister, Dancing, had taken from her the rhythmic measure—she
took with her from her brooding sister, Poetry, as an indispensable, immediate life condition, the *word;* not by any means, however, the man-

---

2 See *Oper und Drama*, I, 5 (or, as translated by Edwin Evans, I, 116–117, §§ 208–210), where Wagner returns to this comparison of Beethoven to Columbus and develops it further.

creative, ideally poetic word, but only the materially indispensable word, the concentrated tone. If she had relinquished the rhythmic beat to her parting sister, Dancing, to use as she pleased, she now built herself up solely through the word, the word of Christian faith, that fluid, spineless, illusive thing which soon, gladly and unresistingly, placed itself altogether in her power. The more the word took refuge in the mere stammering of humility, the mere lisping of implicit, childlike love, the more inevitable was Music's recognition of her need to shape herself from the inexhaustible depths of her own fluid being. The struggle for such a shaping is the building up of *harmony*.

Harmony grows from the bottom up as a true column of related tonal materials, fitted together and arranged in strata laid one above another. The ceaseless changing of such columns, constantly rising up anew, each one adjoining another, constitutes the sole possibility of absolute harmonic movement on a horizontal plane. The perception of the need to care for the beauty of this movement on a horizontal plane is foreign to the nature of absolute harmony; harmony knows only the beauty of the changing play of the colors of its columns, not the charm of their orderly arrangement as perceived in time—for this is the work of rhythm. The inexhaustible many-sidedness of this changing play of colors is, on the other hand, the eternally productive source from whence harmony, in boundless self-satisfaction, derives the power to present itself unceasingly as new; the breath of life, moving and animating this restless change—which, in its turn, is willfully self-conditioning—is the nature of tone itself, the breath of the impenetrable, all-powerful longing of the heart. The realm of harmony, then, knows no beginning or end; is like the objectless and self-consuming fervor of the temperament which, ignorant of its source, remains itself alone; is desiring, longing, raging, languishing—*perishing*, that is, dying without having satisfied itself in an object—dying, in other words, without dying; and hence, again and again, returns to self.

As long as the word was in power, it ruled beginning and end; when it sank to the fathomless bottom of harmony, when it remained only a "groaning and sighing of the soul"—as at the fervent height of Catholic church music—then, at the topmost stratum of those harmonic columns, the stratum of unrhythmic melody, the word was willfully tossed as though from wave to wave, and harmony, with its infinite possibilities, had now to lay down for itself self-derived laws for its finite manifestation. The nature of harmony corresponds to no other capacity of man as artist; it sees itself reflected, neither in the physically determined movements of the body, nor in the logical progression of thought; it can conceive its just measure, neither, as thought does, in the recognized necessity of the world of material phenomena, nor, as bodily movement does, in the presentation, as perceived in time, of its instinctive, richly conditioned character; it is like a natural force, apprehended, but not comprehended, by man. From out its own fathomless depths, from an outer—not inner—necessity to limit itself for positive finite manifestation, harmony must shape for itself the laws it will obey. These laws of harmonic succession, based on relationship, just as the harmonic columns, or harmonies, were themselves formed from the relationship of tonal materials, combine now as a just measure, which sets a beneficial limit to the monstrous range of willful possibilities. They permit the widest possible selection from out the sphere of harmonic families, expand to the point of free choice the possibility of connections through elective relationship with members of distant families, demand above all, however, a strict conformity to the house rules of the family momentarily chosen and an implicit acceptance of them for the sake of a salutary end. To postulate or to define this end—in other words, the just measure of the expansion of the musical composition in time—lies beyond the power of the innumerable rules of harmonic decorum; these, as that part of music which can be scientifically taught or learned, while they can separate the fluid tonal mass of harmony, dividing it into bounded smaller masses, cannot determine the just measure of these bounded masses in time.

If music, grown to harmony, could not possibly go on to derive from itself its law of expansion in time, once the limiting power of speech had been swallowed up, it was obliged to turn to those remnants of the rhythmic beat that dancing had left behind for it; rhythmic figures had to enliven the harmony; their alternation, their return, their division and union had to affect the fluid expanse of harmony as the word had originally affected tone, concentrating it and bringing it to a definitely timed conclusion. This rhythmic enlivening, however, was not based on any inner necessity, crying out for purely human presentation; its motive power was not the man of feeling, thought, and will as he reveals himself in speech and bodily movement, but an *outer* necessity which harmony, demanding an egoistic conclusion, had made its own. This rhythmic alternation and shaping, not motivated by an inner necessity, could therefore be enlivened only according to willful laws and discoveries. These laws and discoveries are those of *counterpoint*.

Counterpoint, in its various progeny, normal and abnormal, is the artificial play of art with art, the mathematics of feeling, the mechanical rhythm of egoistic harmony. With its discovery abstract music was so pleased that it gave itself out as the one and only absolute and self-sufficient art—as the art owing its existence, not to any human need whatever, but simply to *itself*, to its divine and absolute nature. Quite naturally, the willful man considers himself the one man absolutely justified. Music, to be sure, owed to its arbitrary will alone only its seeming independence, for these tone-mechanical, contrapuntal pieces of art handiwork were altogether incapable of filling a *spiritual need*. In its pride, then, music had become its own direct antithesis; from a concern of the *heart* it had become a concern of the *mind*, from an expression of the boundless spiritual longing of the Christian it had become a balance sheet of the modern money market.

The living breath of the human voice, eternally beautiful and instinctively noble as it burst forth from the breast of the living folk, always young and fresh, blew this contrapuntal house of cards to the four winds. The *folk tune*, still true to self in undistorted grace—the *song* with positive limits, intimately entwined and one with poetry—lifted itself up on its elastic pinions into the regions of the scientifically musical world, with its need for beauty, and announced a joyous redemption. This world wished once more to set forth *men*, to cause men—not reeds—to sing; to this end it took possession of the folk tune and constructed from it the *operatic aria*. Just as the art of dancing had taken possession of the folk dance, to refresh itself, as it required, at this source and to employ it, as fashion dictated, in artistic combination, so also the elegant art of opera dealt with the folk tune; it now grasped, not the *whole* man, to indulge him artistically to the full according to his natural need, but only the *singing* man—and in the tune he sang, not the folk poem with its innate creative power, but only the melodious tune, abstracted from the poem, to which it now adapted as it pleased fashionably conventional, intentionally meaningless literary phrases; it was not the throbbing heart of the nightingale, but only its throbbing throat, that it understood and sought to imitate. Just as the art dancer trained his legs in the most varied and yet most uniform bends, twists, and whirls to vary the folk dance, which he could not of himself develop further, so the art singer trained his throat in endless ornaments and scrollwork of all sorts to paraphrase and change the tune taken from the lips of the folk, which he could from its nature never create anew; thus the place which contrapuntal cleverness had vacated was taken only by a mechanical dexterity of another kind. Here we need not characterize at greater length the repulsive, indescribably disgusting perversion and distortion of the folk tune as manifested in the modern operatic aria—for it is in point of fact only a mutilated folk tune, not by any means an original invention—as, in derision of all nature, of all human feeling, it frees itself from any linguistically poetic basis and, as a lifeless, soulless toy of fashion, tickles the ear of the idiotic world of the opera house; we need only admit with sorrowful sincerity that our modern public actually takes it for the whole of music.

But remote from this public and the makers and sellers of fashionable wares who serve it, the innermost being of music was to soar up from its bottomless depths, with all the undiminished abundance of its untried capacity, to a redemption in the radiance of the universal, *single* art of the future, and was to take this flight from that bottom which is the bottom of all purely human art—that of *plastic bodily movement*, represented in musical *rhythm*.

If, in the lisping of the stereotyped Christian word, eternally and eternally repeated to the point of utter thoughtlessness, the *human voice* had at length completely taken refuge in a merely sensual and fluid tone device by means of which alone the art of music, wholly withdrawn from poetry, continued to present itself, the tone devices, mechanically transmitted at its side as voluptuous accompaniments of the art of dancing, had developed an increasingly heightened capacity for expression. To these devices, the bearers of the dance tune, *rhythmic melody* had been assigned as an exclusive possession, and since, in their combined effect, these readily absorbed the element of Christian harmony, all responsibility for music's further development *from within itself* devolved on them. The *harmonized dance* is the basis of the richest art work of the modern *symphony*. This dance made in its turn an appetizing morsel for the counterpoint machine, which freed it from its obedient devotion to its mistress, the corporeal art of dancing, and caused it now to leap and turn at *its* command. Yet the warm life breath of the natural folk tune had only to inspire the leather harness of this dance, trained up in counterpoint, and it became at once the living flesh of the humanly beautiful art work. This art work, in its highest perfection, is the *symphony of Haydn, Mozart, and Beethoven*.

In the symphony of *Haydn*, the rhythmic dance melody moves with all the fresh serenity of youth; its interweavings, dissolvings, and recombinings, though carried out with the utmost contrapuntal skill, reveal themselves scarcely any longer as products of a thus skillful process, but rather as proper to the character of a dance governed by highly imaginative rules, so warmly are they permeated by the breath of genuinely and joyously human life. The middle movement of the symphony, in a more moderate tempo, we see assigned by Haydn to the swelling breadth of

the simply melodious folk tune; following the rules of melos peculiar to singing, he expands this, intensifying it in higher flights and enlivening it in repetitions many-sided in their expression. The melody thus conditioned was elemental to the symphony of *Mozart*, with his wealth of song and delight in singing. He inspired his instruments with the ardent breath of the *human voice*, to which his genius was overwhelmingly inclined. The rich, indomitable tide of harmony he brought to bear on melody's heart, as though restlessly anxious to give synthetically to the purely instrumental melody that depth of feeling and fervor which, in the innermost heart, makes of the natural human voice an inexhaustible source of expression. As to all those things in his symphonies which lay more or less remote from the satisfying of this, his primary aim, if Mozart to a certain extent merely dispatched them with uncommonly skillful contrapuntal treatment according to the traditional usage, becoming stable even in him, he intensified the capacity of the purely instrumental for singing expression to such a point that it could encompass, not only serenity and placid easy intimacy, as had been the case with Haydn, but also the whole depth of the heart's infinite longing.

The immeasurable capacity of instrumental music for the expression of impulses and desires of elemental intensity was opened up by *Beethoven*. He it was who released to unrestricted freedom the innermost being of Christian harmony, that fathomless sea so boundlessly vast, so restlessly mobile. Borne by instruments alone, the *harmonic melody*—for thus we must call the melody isolated from the spoken line, to distinguish it from the rhythmic dance melody—was capable of the most unlimited expression and of the widest possible treatment. In long connected sequences and in larger, smaller, indeed smallest fragments, it became, under the poetic hands of the master, the sounds, syllables, words, and phrases of a language which could express the unheard, the unsaid, the unuttered. Each letter of this language was an endlessly spiritual element, and the measure of their fusion was a measuring as free and unrestricted as a composer desiring the most immeasurable expression of the most impenetrable longing could possibly exercise. Rejoicing in the unspeakably expressive possibilities of this language, yet suffering under the burden of his artist-soul's desire, which, in its boundlessness, could have no object but itself and might not seek to satisfy itself outside it—the overly happy yet unhappy sailor, loving the sea yet weary of it, sought a sure anchorage from the rapturous storms of fierce impatience. If the possibilities of the language were endless, so also was the longing that inspired it; then how proclaim the end—the satisfaction—of this longing in the same language

which was no more than its expression? If in this absolute and quasi-elemental language we call up the expression of immeasurable heart's longing, then, like the endlessness of longing itself, the *endlessness* of this expression is its only necessary end; a finite *end*, as a stilling of longing, could be only willful. With the definite expression borrowed from the rhythmic dance melody, instrumental music can represent and end a mood in itself at rest and precisely limited, for it takes its just measure from bodily movement, an object lying originally outside itself. If from the first a piece of music surrenders wholly to this expression—which more or less inevitably must be understood as an expression of serenity—then, even when all the possibilities of tonal language are richly and luxuriously developed, satisfaction of every sort will be rooted necessarily in this expression; if in the end, however, this precisely limited expression even so much as approaches the storms of endless longing, this satisfaction can be only purely willful and hence actually unsatisfying. The transition from a mood of endless agitation and longing to one of joyous satisfaction cannot take place necessarily, except through absorption of the longing in an *object*. This object, in keeping with the character of endless longing, can only be one presenting itself as finite, concrete, and moral. In such an object, absolute music finds none the less its definitely determined limits; unless it adopts the most willful measures, it cannot now or ever bring of itself alone the concretely and morally determined man to exactly perceptible and clearly distinguishable presentation; in its endless intensification, it is still only *feeling* after all; it makes its appearance in the *train* of the moral deed, not as *the deed itself*; it can set moods and feelings side by side, but cannot in a necessary way develop one mood from another; it lacks *moral will*.

What inimitable art Beethoven employed in his C minor Symphony to guide his ship out of the ocean of endless longing into the harbor of fulfillment! He succeeded in intensifying the expression of his music almost to the point of moral resolve, yet was unable to proclaim this resolve itself. Without moral support, after each exertion of will, we are alarmed at the prospect that we may quite as well be headed, not for victory, but for relapse into suffering; indeed, such a relapse must seem to us rather more necessary than the morally unmotivated triumph, which—not a necessary achievement, but a willful gift of grace—can hence not lift us up or satisfy us *morally*, after the longing of the heart, as we require.

Who was less satisfied by this victory than Beethoven himself, may we presume? Was he tempted to another of this kind? The thoughtless army of his imitators, no doubt, who, having survived the tribulation of minor,

concoct continual triumphs for themselves out of the glorious jubilation of major—but not the chosen master who was in his works to write the *world history of music*.

With reverent awe he refrained from plunging himself again into that sea of boundless and insatiable longing, bending his steps rather toward those lighthearted, vigorous beings whom he saw jesting, dancing, and making love in the green meadows at the edge of the fragrant woods, spread out under sunny skies. There, in the shadow of the trees, to the rustling of the foliage and the familiar rippling of the brook, he made a salutary covenant with nature; there he felt himself a man, his longing driven back deep into his breast before the power of the sweet inspiring *prospect*. In gratitude to this prospect, in faith and all humility, he named the single movements of the composition thus inspired for the scenes from life whose aspect had summoned them forth; the whole he called *Recollections of Country Life*.

And yet they were in truth no more than recollections—images, not immediate and concrete reality. Toward this reality, however, he was impelled with all the force of necessary artist's longing. To give his tonal forms that concentration, that immediately perceptible, sure, and concrete solidity, which, to his joy and comfort, he had observed in natural phenomena—this was the generous spirit of that joyous urge that created for us the incomparably magnificent A major Symphony. All violence, all longing and storming of the heart, have turned here to the rapturous exuberance of joy which carries us along in bacchanalian insistence through all the realms of nature, through all the streams and seas of life, self-confidently exultant everywhere we tread to the bold measure of this human dance of the spheres. This symphony is the very *apotheosis of the dance*; it is the highest being of the dance, the most blissful act of bodily movement, ideally embodied, as it were, in tone. Melody and harmony fill out together the bony frame of rhythm with firm human figures, slender and voluptuous, which almost before our eyes, here with supple giant limbs, there with delicate elastic flexibility, join the round to which the immortal melody sounds on and on, now charming, now bold, now serious,[b] now boisterous, now thoughtful, now exultant, until, in the last whirling of desire, a jubilant kiss brings to an end the last embrace.

---

b To the rhythm of the second movement, solemnly striding along, a secondary theme lifts up its longing plaint; about that rhythm, whose steady step is heard unceasingly throughout the whole, this yearning melody entwines itself, as does about the oak the ivy, which, but for its encircling of the powerful trunk, would curl and wind chaotically along the ground, luxuriantly forlorn, but which now, as a rich ornament of the rough oak's bark, gains sure and substantial form from the solidity of the tree itself. With what want of discernment this deeply significant discovery of Beethoven's has been exploited by our modern composers of instrumental music, with their eternal "secondary theme-making."

And yet these blissful dancers were but tonally represented, tonally imitated beings! Like another Prometheus, forming men from *clay* (*Thon*), Beethoven had sought to form men from *tone* (*Ton*). Neither from clay nor tone, however, but from both substances at once must man, the likeness of life-giving Zeus, be created. If the creatures of Prometheus were present to the *eye* alone, Beethoven's were so only to the *ear*. *But only there where eye and ear mutually assure each other of his presence do we have the whole artistic man.*

Where indeed should Beethoven have found those beings to whom he might have offered his hand across the element of his music? Those beings with hearts so open that he might have let the all-powerful stream of his harmonious tones flood into them? With forms so vigorously beautiful that his melodious rhythms might have *borne* them, not *tread* them under foot? Alas, no brotherly Prometheus, who might have shown such beings to him, came to his help from any side! He had himself to begin by discovering the *land of the man of the future.*

From the shores of dancing he plunged again into that endless sea from out whose depths he had once saved himself on these same shores, into the sea of insatiable heart's longing. But on this stormy voyage he set out aboard a strong-built ship, firmly joined as though by giant hands; with a sure grasp he bent the powerful tiller; he *knew* his journey's goal and was resolved to reach it. What he sought was not the preparation of imaginary triumphs for himself, not to sail back idly into the home port after boldly surmounted hardships; he sought to bound the limits of the ocean, to find the land which needs must lie beyond the watery wastes.

Thus the master forced his way through the most unheard-of possibilities of absolute tonal language—not by hurriedly stealing past them, but by proclaiming them completely, to their last sound, from his heart's fullest depths—until he reached that point at which the navigator begins to sound the sea's depths with his lead; at which he touches solid bottom at ever increasing heights as the strands of the new continent reach toward him from afar; at which he must decide whether to turn about into the fathomless ocean or whether to drop anchor in the new banks. But it was no rude hankering for the sea that had urged the master on to this long voyage; he wished and had to land in the new world, for it was to this end that the voyage had been undertaken. Resolutely he threw out his anchor, and this anchor was the *word*. This word, however, was not that willful, meaningless word which the fashionable singer chews over and over as the mere gristle of the vocal tone; it was the necessary, all-powerful, all-uniting word in which the whole stream of full heartfelt emotion is poured out; the safe harbor for the restless wanderer; the light lighting the night of endless longing; the word redeemed humanity proclaims from out the fullness of the world's heart; the word which Beethoven set as a crown upon the summit of his creations in tone. This word was—"*Joy!*" And with this word he called to all mankind: "*Be embraced, ye countless millions! And to all the world this kiss!*" And *this* word will become the language of the *art work of the future*.

This *last symphony* of Beethoven's is the redemption of music out of its own element as a *universal art*. It is the *human* gospel of the art of the future. Beyond it there can be no *progress*, for there can follow on it immediately only the completed art work of the future, *the universal drama*, to which Beethoven has forged for us the artistic key.

Thus from within itself music accomplished what no one of the other arts was capable of in isolation. Each of these arts, in its barren independence, helped itself only by taking and egoistic borrowing; not one was capable of being *itself* and of weaving from within itself the all-uniting bond. The art of tone, by being wholly *itself* and by moving from within its own primeval element, attained strength for the most tremendous and most generous of all self-sacrifices—that of self-control, indeed of self-denial—thus to offer to its sister arts a redeeming hand. Music has proved itself the *heart*, connecting head and limbs, and, what is not without significance, it is precisely music which, in the modern present, has spread to so unusual an extent through every branch of public life.

To form a clear conception of the *thoroughly inconsistent* spirit of this public life, we must consider, first of all, *that it was by no means a collective effort of the artists, as a body, and the public—indeed not even a collective effort of the musical artists themselves*—which brought to completion that tremendous process which we have just seen take place; *quite the other way, it was purely a superabundant artist individual* who individually absorbed the spirit of that collectivity wanting in the public, who actually began, indeed, by producing this collectivity in himself, out of the abundance of his own being, joined to the abundance of musical possibility, as something he himself longed for as an artist. We see that this wondrous creative process, as it is present in the symphonies of Beethoven as an increasingly determining, living force, was not only achieved by the master in the most complete isolation, but actually was not *understood* at all—or rather, was *misunderstood* in the most shameful way—by the company of artists. The forms in which the master proclaimed his artistic, world-historical struggle remained for the composers of his and the succeeding age mere *formulas*, passing through mannerism into fashion, and although no composer of instrumental music was so much as able to reveal the slightest originality, even in these forms, there was not one who lacked the courage to keep on writing symphonies and similar pieces, not one who even suspected that the *last* symphony had already been *written*.[c] Thus too, we have had to stand by while Beethoven's great voyage of world discovery—that unique, altogether inimitable feat which we saw accomplished in his "Symphony of Joy" as the final and boldest venture of his genius—was after the event reundertaken, with the most idiotic naïveté, and, without hardship, successfully weathered. A new genre, a "symphony with choruses"—this was all one saw in it. Why should not this or that composer also write his Symphony with Choruses? Why should not "God the Lord" be resoundingly praised at the end, after He has helped to conduct the three preliminary instrumental movements to the most facile of possible conclusions? [3] Thus Columbus discovered America only for the fulsome petty profiteering of our time.

The cause of this revolting *phenomenon* is deeply rooted in the very nature of our modern music. Detached from the arts of poetry and of dancing, the art of tone is no longer an art instinctively necessary to mankind. It has had to construct itself, following rules which, derived from its own peculiar nature, find their related and clarifying just measure in no purely human phenomenon. Each of the other arts held firm to the just measure of man's outward form, of man's outward life, or of nature itself, however willfully it might distort this unconditionally existing and accepted measure. The art of tone, which found its outward human measure in the timid ear alone, subject to fancies and deceptions of all sorts, had to form more abstract laws, combining these into a complete and scientific system. This system was the basis of modern music; on it one built, on it one piled tower upon tower, the bolder the construction, the more indispensable the foundation—a foundation in itself by no means that of nature. The sculptor, the painter, or the poet learns about *nature* from the rules of his art; without an intimate understanding of nature he can create nothing beautiful. The musician learns the rules of harmony

---

c He who specifically undertakes to write the history of instrumental music since Beethoven will no doubt have within this period to report on isolated phenomena, capable, assuredly, of arousing a particular and interested attention. But he who considers the history of the arts from a point of view as broad as is here necessary has to restrict himself to its chief moments alone; whatever departs from or derives from these moments he must leave out of account. And the more unmistakably such isolated phenomena reveal great talent, the more strikingly do precisely these phenomena prove—in view of the general sterility of the whole artistic impulse behind them—that, once there has been expressed in their particular art variety what Beethoven expressed in music, whatever is left to be discovered has to do with technical procedures, perhaps, but not with the living spirit. In the great universal art work of the future it will be possible to keep on making new discoveries forever—but not in the individual art variety which, after having been conducted into universality as music was by Beethoven, perseveres in its isolated development.

3 An allusion to Mendelssohn's *Lobgesang.*

and counterpoint; his learning, without which he can erect no musical structure, is an abstract scientific system; attaining skill in its employment, he becomes a member of a guild and now, from the point of view of the guild member, looks into the world of actuality, which of necessity must seem a different world to *him* than to the worldly non-guild member— the *layman*. The uninitiated layman stands nonplused in turn before art music's artificial work, in which he quite correctly grasps nothing but what in general stirs his heart; this comes to him from out the marvelous structure solely in the form of melody immediately pleasing to the ear; everything else leaves him cold or disturbs him in a confused way, because he simply does not and cannot understand it. Our modern concert public, pretending to be satisfied and cordial toward the art symphony, is simply lying and dissembling, as we may verify at any moment if, after such a symphony—as is usual even in the most celebrated concert institutes—a melodious piece from any modern opera is played, for in this case we hear the real musical pulse of the auditorium beating at once with undissembled joy.

That there is any connection, conditioned by the public, between it and our art music must be flatly denied; wherever such a connection seeks to reveal itself, it is either affected and untrue or at least uncertain—as in the popular audience which occasionally succeeds in being carried away, without affectation, by the drastic side of a Beethoven symphony—and the impression made by these compositions is assuredly incomplete and fragmentary. Yet, where such a connection is lacking, the connection, as a guild, of the company of artists can be but superficial; the growth and shaping of art from within cannot be conditioned from out the artist community, which after all is mere artifice and system; only in the single artist, from out the individuality of the particular being, can there be active a natural impulse to shape and develop, governed by inner, instinctive laws. Denied its nourishment in external nature, the art-creative impulse can obtain it only in the peculiar character and abundance of an individual artist nature; only such an individuality—in its particularity, its personal view, its peculiar desiring, longing, and willing—can supply to the artistic substance the form-giving matter denied it in external nature; only in the individuality of this one particular human being does music become a purely human art; this individuality it consumes in order to attain, from out the fluidity of its very element, to concentration and to an individuality of its own.

Thus we see in music—as in the other arts, but for quite different reasons —that mannerism or so-called schools proceed as a rule exclusively from out the individuality of a particular artist. These schools were the guild companies which, in imitation, indeed in mimicry, grew up about a great master in whom was individualized the nature of the art. As long as music had not yet fulfilled its world-historical artistic task, the widespread branches of these schools, made fruitful by this or that relationship, could grow together as new seedlings; once this task had been completely fulfilled by the greatest of all musical individualities, once music from out its deepest abundance had through the force of this individuality destroyed the ultimate form in which it could remain an egoistically independent art —in a word, once *Beethoven* had written his last symphony—the musical guild companies could patch and mend to suit themselves in their effort to produce their absolute-musical man; from out their workshop there could now come forth only a patched and mended, pieced-together man of fantasy, not a sinuously stalwart man of nature. After Haydn and Mozart it was possible and necessary for a Beethoven to follow; music's genius needed him—without keeping music waiting, he was there; who now would be to Beethoven what he was to Haydn and Mozart in the realm of absolute music? Here the greatest genius could do nothing further, for the genius of absolute music has no further need for him.

You exert yourselves to no purpose when, to still your own childishly egoistic longing for productivity, you seek to deny the destructive, world-historical, musical significance of Beethoven's last symphony; not even the stupidity which enables you actually to misunderstand the work can save you! Do as you please; take no notice of Beethoven whatever, grope after Mozart, gird yourselves with Bach, write symphonies with or without voices, write masses, oratorios—those sexless operatic embryos!—make songs without words, operas without texts; you produce nothing that has real life in it. For behold—you do not have the *faith!*—the great faith in the necessity of what you do! You have only the faith of the foolish— the superstitious faith in the possibility of the necessity of your egoistic willfulness!

Surveying the busy desolation of our musical art world; becoming aware of the absolute impotence of this art substance, for all its eternal ogling of itself; viewing this shapeless mess, of which the dregs are the dried-up impertinence of pedantry, from which, for all its profoundly reflecting, ever-so-musical, self-arrogated mastery, can finally rise to the broad daylight of modern public life, as an artificially distilled stench, only emotionally dissolute Italian opera arias or impudent French cancan dance tunes; appraising, in short, this complete creative incapacity, we look about us fearlessly for the great destructive stroke of destiny which will put an end to all this immoderately inflated musical rubbish to make room for the art work of the future, in which genuine music will in truth assume no insignificant role, to which in this soil, however, air and room to breathe are peremptorily denied.[d]

. . . . . .

FUNDAMENTALS OF THE ART WORK OF THE FUTURE

If we consider the situation of modern art—insofar as it is actually *art* —in relation to public life, we recognize first of all its complete inability to influence this public life in accordance with its high purpose. This is because, as a mere cultural product, it has not grown out of life, and because, as a hothouse plant, it cannot possibly take root in the natural soil and natural climate of the present. Art has become the exclusive property of an artist class; it gives pleasure only to those who *understand* it, requiring for its understanding a special study, remote from real life, the study of *art connoisseurship*. This study and the understanding it affords are thought today to be within the reach of everyone who has the money to pay for the art pleasures offered for sale; yet if we ask the artist whether the great multitude of our art amateurs are capable of understanding him in his highest flights, he can answer only with a deep sigh. And if he now reflects on the infinitely greater multitude of those who must remain cut off, as a result of the influence of our social conditions, unfavorable from every point of view, not only from the understanding, but even from the enjoyment of modern art, the artist of today cannot but become conscious that his whole artistic activity is, strictly speaking, only an egoistic self-complacent activity for activity's sake and that, in its relation to public life, his art is mere luxury, superfluity, and selfish pastime. The disparity, daily observed and bitterly deplored, between so-called culture and the lack of it is so monstrous, a mean between them so unthinkable, their reconciliation so impossible, that, granted a minimum of honesty, the modern art based on this unnatural culture would have to admit, to its deepest shame, that

---

d Lengthily as I have spoken here about the nature of music, in comparison with the other art varieties (a procedure fully justified, I may add, by the peculiar character of music and by the peculiar and truly productive developmental process resulting from this character), I am well aware of the many-sided incompleteness of my discussion; not one book, however, but many books would be needed to lay bare exhaustively the immorality, the weakness, the meanness of the ties connecting our modern music and our modern life; to explore the unfortunate overemotional side of music, which makes it subject to the speculation of our education maniacs, our "improvers of the people," who seek to mix the honey of music with the vinegar-sourish sweat of the mistreated factory worker as the one possible mitigation of his sufferings (somewhat as our sages of the state and bourse are at pains to stuff the servile rags of religion into the gaping holes in the policeman's care of society); and finally to explain the saddening psychological phenomenon that a man may be not only cowardly and base, but also *stupid*, without these qualities preventing him from being a perfectly respectable musician.

it owed its existence to a life element which in turn could base *its* existence only on the utter lack of culture in the real mass of humanity. The one thing that, in this, its allotted situation, modern art should be able to do —and, where there is honesty, does endeavor to do—namely, *to further the diffusion of culture*—it cannot do, for the simple reason that art, to have any influence on life, must be itself the flowering of a *natural* culture —that is, of one that has grown up from below—and can never be in a position to rain down culture from above. At best, then, our cultured art resembles the speaker who seeks to communicate with a people in a language which it does not understand—all that he says, his most ingenious sayings above all, can lead only to the most laughable confusions and misunderstandings.

Let us first make apparent how modern art is to proceed if it would attain *theoretically* to the redemption of its uncomprehended self from out its isolated situation and to the widest possible understanding of the public; how this redemption can become possible only through the *practical* mediation of the public will then be readily apparent of itself.

•   •   •   •   •

Man as artist can be fully satisfied only in the union of all the art varieties in the *collective* art work; in every *individualization* of his artistic capacities he is *unfree,* not wholly that which he can be; in the collective art work he is *free,* wholly that which he can be.

The *true* aim of art is accordingly *all-embracing;* everyone animated by the true artistic impulse seeks to attain, through the full development of his particular capacity, not the glorification of *this particular capacity,* but the glorification *in art of mankind in general.*

The highest collective art work is the *drama;* it is present in its *ultimate completeness* only when *each art variety, in its ultimate completeness,* is present in it.

True drama can be conceived only as resulting from the *collective impulse of all the arts* to communicate in the most immediate way with a *collective public;* each individual art variety can reveal itself as *fully understandable* to this collective public only through collective communication, together with the other art varieties, in the drama, for the aim of each individual art variety is fully attained only in the mutually understanding and understandable co-operation of all the art varieties.

•   •   •   •   •

Not *one* of the richly developed capacities of the individual arts will remain unused in the collective art work of the future; it is precisely in the collective art work that these capacities will attain to full stature. Thus especially the art of tone, developed with such singular diversity in instrumental music, will realize in the collective art work its richest potentialities—will indeed incite the pantomimic art of dancing in turn to wholly new discoveries and inspire the breath of poetry no less to an undreamed-of fullness. For in its isolation music has formed itself an organ capable of the most immeasurable expression—the *orchestra*. Beethoven's tonal language, introduced through the orchestra into the drama, is a force wholly new to the dramatic art work. If architecture and, still more so, scenic landscape painting can place the dramatic actor in the natural environment of the physical world and give him, from the inexhaustible font of natural phenomena, a background constantly rich and relevant, the orchestra—that animate body of infinite harmonic variety— offers the individual actor, as a support, what may be called a perpetual source of the natural element of man as artist. The orchestra is, so to speak, the soil of infinite universal feeling from which the individual feeling of the single actor springs into full bloom; it somehow dissolves the solid motionless floor of the actual scene into a fluid, pliant, yielding, impressionable, ethereal surface whose unfathomed bottom is the sea of feeling itself. Thus the orchestra resembles the *earth*, from which *Antaeus*, once he touched it with his feet, gathered renewed and deathless vital energy. Although by nature diametrically opposed to the actor's natural scenic environment and hence, as local color, placed very rightly in the deepened foreground outside the scenic frame, it also constitutes the perfect complement of scenic environment, expanding the inexhaustible natural element of the *physical* world to the no less inexhaustible emotional element of *man* as artist; this composite element encircles the actor as with an atmospheric elemental ring of nature and of art; in this he moves assured, as do the heavenly bodies, in ultimate completeness, at the same time sending forth in all directions his views and feelings, endlessly expanded, as do the heavenly bodies their rays, into the infinite distances.

Thus completing one another in their ever-changing round, the united sister arts will show themselves and bring their influence to bear, now collectively, now two at a time, now singly, as called for by the need of the dramatic action, the one determinant of aim and measure. At one moment plastic pantomime will listen to thought's dispassionate appraisal; at another the will of resolute thought will overflow into the immediate expression of gesture; at still another music will have to utter the flood of feeling, the awe of apprehension; finally, however, all three, in mutual entwinement, will exalt the will of drama to immediate active deed. For there is one thing which all three united art varieties must will, would they be free to act—this is the *drama;* all three must be concerned for the attainment of the dramatic aim. If they are conscious of this aim, if all direct their will to its accomplishment, each will receive the strength to lop off on all sides the egoistic offshoots of its particular nature from the common trunk, in order that the tree may grow, not shapelessly in all directions, but to the proud summit of its branches, twigs, and leaves—to its crown.

Human nature, like the art variety, is in itself multiform and many-sided; the soul of the *individual* man—the activity most necessary to him, his strongest instinctive urge—is a *single* thing. If he recognizes this single thing as his basic nature, he can, to further its indispensable attainment, suppress each weaker, subordinate desire, each feeble longing whose satisfaction might hinder him in this attainment. Only the weak and impotent man discovers in himself no supremely strong and necessary soul's desire; at every moment he is subject to chance appetite, stirred up incidentally from without; precisely because this is mere appetite, he can never satisfy it; tossed willfully back and forth from one appetite to another, he never even attains to real enjoyment. But if this man, knowing no need, has might enough obstinately to pursue the satisfaction of these chance appetites, then there arise in life and art those horrible and monstrous phenomena which—as excrescences of mad egoistic impulses, as murderous debaucheries of despots, or as lascivious modern operas—fill us with such unspeakable disgust. If, on the other hand, the individual man discovers in himself a strong desire, an urge repressing every other longing that he feels, in other words, that necessary inner impulse which makes up his soul and being, and if he bends all his energy to satisfy it, then he exalts his might, and with it his particular capacity, to a strength and height he cannot otherwise attain.

The individual man, given perfect health of body, heart, and mind, can experience no higher need than that common to all men similarly constituted, for, as a *real* need, it can only be such as he can satisfy in the community alone. But the strongest and most necessary need of the perfect artist is to communicate himself in the ultimate completeness of his being to the ultimate community, and he attains this with the universal intelligibility necessary to it only in the *drama*. In the drama he expands his particular being to general being by representing an individual personality other than his own. He must wholly forget himself to comprehend another personality with the completeness necessary to representation; he attains this only when he explores this individuality with such precision in its contact, penetration, and completion with and by other individualities—hence also the being of these other individualities themselves—when he apprehends this individuality so accurately that it is possible for him to become conscious of this contact, penetration, and completion in his own being; the perfect representative artist is therefore the individual expanded to the *being of the species* in accordance with the ultimate completion of his own particular being. The scene in which this wondrous process is accomplished is the *theatrical stage;* the collective art work which it brings to light is the *drama.* To force his particular being to the highest flowering of its content in this *one* highest art work, the individual artist, however, like the individual art variety, has to repress each willful egoistic inclination to untimely expansion useless to the whole in order to be able to contribute the more actively to the attainment of the highest collective aim, which is in turn not to be realized without the individual and his periodic limitation.

This aim—the aim of the drama—is at the same time the only genuinely artistic aim that can be possibly *realized;* whatever is remote from it must necessarily lose itself in the sea of the uncertain, the unintelligible, the unfree. And this aim is attained, not by *one art variety for itself alone,*[e] but only by *all collectively,* and therefore the *most universal* art work is at the same time the one art work that is real and free—in other words, universally *intelligible.*

. . . . . .

---

[e] The modern *playwright* will be the one least inclined to admit that the drama is not to belong exclusively even to *his* art variety, the *art of poetry;* in particular he will be unable to persuade himself to share the drama with the tone poet—or, as he would put it, to allow the play to be absorbed by the opera. As long as the opera exists, the play—and, with as much right, the pantomime—will unquestionably continue to exist also; as long as argument on this point is thinkable, the drama of the future will remain unthinkable. If, however, the poet's doubts lie deeper, and he objects that he cannot understand how *singing* is once and for all to take over the place of spoken dialogue, the reply will be that, in two respects, he has not yet come to a clear understanding as to the character of the art work of the future. In the first place, he does not stop to consider that music, in this art work, is to be given a place altogether different from its place in the modern opera; that it is to unfold its full breadth only where its capacity is greatest, while, in all places where dra-matic speech, for example, is what is needed most, it is to subordinate itself completely to this; and that music, without becoming altogether silent, has the capacity to adapt itself to the thoughtful element of speech so imperceptibly that, while supporting speech, it scarcely interferes with it at all. Having recognized this, the poet has in the second place to realize that those ideas and situations, in connection with which even the slightest and most restrained support of music must seem burdensome and importunate, can arise only from the spirit of the modern play, a spirit which, in the art work of the future, will find no further breathing space whatever. The man whom the drama of the future will represent has no longer anything at all to do with that prosaic intriguing hodgepodge, dictated by state and fashion, which our modern poets have so circumstantially to tangle and untangle; his action and speech, dictated by nature, is Yes and No; all else is evil, that is, modern and superfluous.

Index

Acciajoli, Cavaliere Filippo, 488
Achillini, G. F., 671
Addison, Joseph, 511-17
Aeolia, 48
Aeschylus, 52, 54
Agazzari, Agostino, 424-31
Agenor of Mitylene, 29
Agricola, Alexander, 211n.
   "Allez regrets," 205n., 216n.
   "Si dedero," 206n., 217n.
Agricola, Johann Friedrich, 703, 704, 706n.
Ahlwardt, C. W., 746n.
Albinus (4th cent. A.D.), 92
Alcaeus, 52, 332
Alcibiades, 284
Alcman, 48, 86n.
Alembert, Jean Le Rond d', 670n.
Alexander the Great, 282, 287, 319, 328, 408, 574
Alfonso I, Duke of Ferrara, 334
Algarotti, Francesco, 657-72
Allison, Richard, 353n.
Alsace, 443
Altenburg, 832
Alus, John, 226
Alypius, 92
America, 662, 823, 841n., 843n.
Ammonius, 250
Amphion, 59, 61, 62n., 94, 194, 522
Ananius, 49
Anaxilas, 47
Anerio, Felice, *Missa Vestiva i colli*, 268n.
Anfossi, Pasquale, *L'incognita persegui-tata*, 718n.
Angares (musician), 55-56
Animuccia, Giovanni, *Missa Ad coenam Agni providi*, 268n.
Anonymous:
   Medieval writers:
   Anonymous I, 153n.

Anonymous IV, 140n., 158n., 159n.
Anonymous VI, 172n.
De musica libellus (Anonymous VII), 142n., 152n.
   Compositions:
   "Beata Dei Genetrix" (*Motetti C*), 205n., 217n.
   "C'est possible" (*Canti B*), 206n., 217n.
   "Disant adieu madame" (*Odheca-ton*), 206n., 217n.
   "La dicuplaisant," 206n., 212n.
   "E la la la" (*Canti B*), 206n., 217n.
   "Hélas m'amour," 206n., 212n.
   "Je cuide si ce temps" (*Odhecaton*), 206n., 218n.
   "Je suis amie" (*Canti B*), 206n., 217n.
   "Mittit ad Virginem" (*Motetti C*), 206n., 218n.
   "Myn morgen ghaf" (*Canti B*), 206n., 217n.
   "Ne l'oserai je dire" (*Odhecaton*), 206n., 218n.
   "Nunca fué pena mayor" (*Odheca-ton*), 206n., 215n.
   "O Maria rogamus te" (*Motetti C*), 206n., 215n.
   "Or quà conpagni," 171n.
   "Pourquoi fut fuie cette emprise" (*Canti B*), 206n., 212n.
   "Le serviteur" (*Odhecaton*), 206n., 212n.
   "Thoma tibi obsequia," 178n.
Ansbach, 596
Antigenedes, 53, 282n.
Apelles, 328
Apollonius of Rhodes, 288
Aprile (singer), 694
Apuleius, 92
Apulia, 333
Aquinas, St. Thomas, 198n.

Arcadelt, Jacob, 288n., 289
Arcadia, 50-51, 63, 337
Archilei, Vittoria, 371, 375
Archilochus, 52, 53
Archytas, 20, 198
Arigoni, Cardinal Pompeo, 393
Arion, 59, 61, 62n., 82-83, 288, 433, 529
Ariosti, Attilio, *Il Coriolano*, 529n.
Ariosto, 316n., 335n., 519, 662, 744n., 748, 789
Aristides Quintilianus, 4n., 5n., 88n., 292, 293n.
Aristophanes, 745
Aristotle, 4n., 13-24, 25, 26, 41n., 44n., 45n., 53n., 85, 89n., 161n., 166n., 178, 179n., 182n., 184n., 188n., 194, 198, 223n., 246, 249n., 282, 292, 294, 296, 300, 312, 314, 319n., 333, 413n., 521
Aristoxenus, 5n., 25-33, 41n., 44, 48, 49n., 54, 194, 198, 297, 374n., 402, 413n.
Arnaud, Abbé François, 718, 719
Arnsteiner, Baron von, 731n.
Aron, Pietro, 195, 205-18, 224n., 252n.
Artemon, 81n.
Artusi, G. M., 393-404, 405n., 406-12
Asclepiades, 92, 293
Asola, Matteo, 269
Asopodorus of Phlius, 53
Astyages, 55-56
Athenaeus, 47-56, 81n., 283n., 297n., 306n., 337n.
Athens, 21, 499, 847
Auber, Daniel, *Le Cheval de bronze*, 835n.
Augsburg, 445, 449, 450
Augustus Caesar, 121, 289
Austria, 443
Auvergne, Antoine d', 676n.

Bach, C. P. E., 609-15, 703
Bach, Johann Christian, 591n.
Bach, Johann Sebastian, 596, 778, 858, 898
    St. Matthew Passion, 864
Bacilly, Benigne de, 501
Ballard, Robert, 288
Banck, Carl, 843n.
Barbella, Emanuele, 697

Bardi, Giovanni de', 290-301, 303n., 303-4, 305, 307n., 308n., 322, 363, 370-71, 372, 378, 408
Bardi, Pietro de', 363-66
Bargiel, Woldemar, 844n.
Bassani, G. B., 481
Bateson, Thomas, 337
Bavaria, 443
Beauchamps, Pierre, 476
Beethoven, 732-33, 734, 735-39, 775-81, 782, 810, 828, 830, 833-34, 838, 839, 840, 858, 886-90, 891-96, 897, 898, 901
    "Ah perfido," 738, 739n.
    Battle Symphony, 832
    Cantata, *Calm Sea and Happy Voyage*, Op. 112, 836
    Choral Fantasy, 738
    Concerto No. 4, 738
    Mass in C, 738, 739n.
    Overture, *Coriolanus*, 736
    Sextet, Op. 81b, 735
    Sonatas, Op. 102 ('cello and piano), 733n.
    Symphony No. 3, 818
    Symphony No. 4, 835
    Symphony No. 5, 738, 778, 892
    Symphony No. 6, 737-38, 810, 832, 893
    Symphony No. 7, 840-41, 893
    Symphony No. 9, 832-34, 843, 895-96, 898
    Trios, Op. 70, 733n., 735, 779-80
Belli, Giulio, *Missa Vestiva i colli*, 268n.
Benda, Georg, 702
Beneken, F. B., "Wie sie so sanft ruhn," 772
Bergamo, 276
Berlin, 596, 662n., 699-704, 705n., 706, 781n., 802
Berlioz, Hector, 808-26, 847-48, 869, 872
    Harold in Italy, 847
Berton, Pierre Montan, 719n.
Bianchi (singer), 694, 696
Binchoys, Gilles, 195, 199
Blaise, Adolphe, *Isabelle et Gertrude*, 714
Blancks, Edward, 353n.
Boësset, Antoine, 504
Boethius, 79-86, 88n., 99n., 125, 134, 140, 186, 194, 198, 201, 202, 203,

204n., 251, 252, 289, 293n., 402, 413

Bohemia, 443, 619-20, 728

Boileau, Nicolas, 491n., 513, 810n.

Bologna, 481, 663, 677, 690

Boncompagni, Giacomo, 323n.

Bonnet, Jacques, 480n., 489n.

Bononcini, G. B., 481
   "Mai non si vidde ancor" (*Camilla*), 479

Bordoni, Faustina, 706

Boschetti, Girolamo, 336

Botta, Bergonzo, 658

Bottrigari, Ercole, 409

Boucher, François, 633n.

Bouterwek, Friedrich, 745, 748

Brahms, Johannes, 845

Brandi, Antonio, 375

Bromberg, 781n.

Brossard, Sébastien de, 565n.

Bruhns, Nikolaus, 595

Brumel, Antoine, 221
   "Je dépite tous," 206n., 214n.
   Missa de Beata Virgine, 221n., 225
   Missa Ut re mi fa sol la, 268n.

Brussels, 336

Burney, Charles, 139n., 269n., 303n., 591n., 633n., 666n., 682n., 687-98, 699n., 700n., 701n., 703n.

Busnoys, Antoine, 195, 199
   "Je ne demande," 206n., 216n.
   "Pourtant si mon," 206n., 214n.

Buxtehude, Dietrich, 595

Byrd, William, 327-30, 334-35, 336
   Cantiones sacrae, 335
   Gradualia, 327-30, 335
   "The Nightingale," 336n.
   Psalms, Sonnets, & Songs, 335
   "Susanna fair," 335n.
   "La virginella," 335

Byron, 865, 866

Caccini, Giulio, 290-91, 364, 365, 368n., 370-72, 376, 377-92, 408
   Aria di romanesca, 388, 391
   "Deh, dove son fuggiti," 379n., 389-90, 391
   "Dovrò dunque morire," 371, 379
   Euridice, 370-72, 376
   "Itene all'ombra," 370, 379
   "Perfidissimo volto," 371, 379
   "Vedrò il mio sol," 371, 379

Caen, Arnold:
   "Judica me Deus," 206n., 212n.
   "Nomine qui Domini," 206n., 212n.

Caffarelli, 653n.

Caillot (Cailleau), Joseph, 716, 719, 720-21

Caldara, Antonio, *Achille in Sciro*, 662n.

Calvin, 345-48

Calzabigi, Ranieri de', 674, 677n., 681

Camoëns, Luis de, 858

Campra, André:
   Hésione, 500
   Tancrède, 488n.

Capella, Martianus, 88n., 194, 293n.

Carissimi, Giacomo, 481, 495n., 670

Carlsbad, 769

Caron, Philippe (Firmin), 195, 199
   "Hélas que pourra devenir," 206n., 216n.

Carus, Carl Gustav, 856n.

Casaccia (singer), 688

Casali, G. B., 716

Casella, 300

Cassani (singer), 513

Cassiodorus, 87-92, 127n., 134n., 135n., 250

Castiglione, Baldassare, 281-85

Catalani, Angelica, 835

Cavaliere, Emilio del, 373, 408

Cavendish, Michael, 353n.

Censorinus, 87, 92, 293n.

"Centoventi, La" (singer), 659

Cerone, Pietro, 229n., 262-73

Certon, Pierre, 288n., 289

Cervantes, 744n., 745, 858

Cesena, G. B., *Missa Vestiva i colli*, 268n.

Cesti, Marc' Antonio, 670

Chamaeleon of Pontus, 47

Charlemagne, 593

Charles, Cardinal of Lorraine, 289

Charpentier, Marc Antoine, 495

Chassé, Claude de, 625n.

Cherubini, Luigi, 807
   Lodoïska, 837n.

Chevalier (Fesch), Marie Jeanne, 624n.

Chiabrera, Gabriello, 379

Chopin, Frédéric, 828, 830-31
   Boléro, 843
   Variations on "Là ci darem," Op. 2, 830-31

Christian IV of Denmark, 434n., 439
Christian, Prince (son of Christian IV),
    434-36, 437
Ciampi, Legrenzo, *Bertoldo in corte*,
    717n.
Cicero, 82, 194, 197, 198, 199, 246,
    283n., 312, 319n., 333, 513
Cini, Francesco, 375
Clairval, J. B., 721-22
Claudian, 221
Cleinias of Tarentum, 47
Clemens non Papa, 408
    Missa En espoir, 268n.
    Missa Virtute magna, 268n.
Clement of Alexandria, 59-63, 87
Clementi, Muzio, 731, 739
Cleonides, 28n., 34-46, 374n.
Clermont, Conte de, 629n.
Cobbold, William, 353n.
Cocchi, Gioacchino, 641
Colasse, Pascal, *Thétis et Pélée*, 492
Collin, Heinrich Joseph von, 732, 736
Columbus, 886, 896
Compère, Loyset:
    "E d'en revenez vous," 206n., 217n.
    "Mes pensées," 206n., 218n.
    "Si mieux," 206n., 213n.
    "Virgo caelesti," 206n., 213n.
    "Vôtre bargeronette," 206n., 216n.
Concialini (singer), 701-2, 704
Conti, Louis François, Prince de, 719
Corax, 317
Corelli, Arcangelo, 449, 481, 487, 506,
    698n.
Corneille, 492
Corsi, Jacopo, 365, 368, 373, 375
Cramer, Mme. (librettist), 713-14
Cranmer, Archbishop Thomas, 350-51
Crecquillon, Thomas, 288n., 408
Crete, 50, 52, 283
Creutz, Count Gustaf Philip, 718, 720
Croce, Giovanni, 275, 336n.
    Penitential Psalms, 336
Cynaetha, 51
Cyrus, 55-56
Czerny, 841n.

Damon, 5n., 6, 7, 292
Dante, 300, 301, 364, 368, 519, 858,
    868
David, King, 62, 63, 69, 70, 92, 94,
    113, 194, 332, 348, 353, 356, 752

De Amici, Anna, 696
Deering, Richard, 337
Delphi, 60
Demetrius of Byzantium, 55
Demetrius of Phalerum, 246
Democritus, 83
Demodocus, 522
Demosthenes, 312
Dentice, Fabrizio, 320
Descouteaux, Philibert, 475n.
Diderot, Denis, 649n., 712n.
Dietrich, Albert, 844n.
Dinon, 55
Dio Cassius, 121n.
Dio Chrysostom, 282n.
Dittersdorf, Carl Ditters von, 793
    Doktor und Apotheker, 793n.
    Das rote Käppchen, 793n.
Domitian, 334
Doni, G. B., 290n., 303n., 363, 365-66
Dorians, 48
Dowland, John, 336, 353n.
Dresden, 596, 701n., 702, 704n., 706,
    707
Dryden, John, 512n.
Dürer, Albrecht, 762
Dufay, Guillaume, 195, 199
Dumény (singer), 485
Duni, Egidio Romoaldo, 716, 717, 726
    Ninette à la cour, 717n.
Dunstable, John, 195, 199
Du Roullet, F. L., 676-80, 681, 682

East, Michael, 337
East, Thomas, 352-54
Egypt, 63
Elisi, Filippo, 696
Empedocles, 83, 293
England, 195, 278, 336, 376n., 513,
    514, 517, 596, 637, 697, 739
Epaminondas, 194, 283
Ephorus, 50, 306
Epicharmus, 53
Erasmus, 224, 333
Erdödy, Countess Marie, 733, 735
Esterhazy, Princess Marie, 732
Esterhazy, Prince Nicholas II, 732n.
Euclid, 92
Eumolpus, 288
Eunomus of Locria, 59-60
Eupolis, 47
Euripides, 16, 521, 658, 662

Eustachio:
"Benedic anima mea," 205n., 215n.
"Laetatus sum," 206n., 215n.

Faber Stapulensis, 252
Fabio (violinist), 696-97
Farinelli, 688
Farmer, John, 353n.
Farnaby, Giles, 353n.
Faugues, Guillaume, 199
Favart, Charles Simon, 632n., 714, 716n., 717n., 723
Fel, Marie, 624n., 631, 632, 633, 640
Felis, Stefano, 336
Ferabosco, Alfonso I, 275, 335-36
   "I saw my lady weeping," 336
   "The Nightingale," 336
   "Susanne un jour," 335n.
Ferabosco, Alfonso II, 337
Ferdinand I of Naples, 193, 194-95, 197, 199
Ferinni (singer), 486
Ferrara, 393n., 394n.
Ferrara, Benedetto, 438n.
Ferretti, Giovanni, 275, 336
Festa, Costanzo, "Gaude Virgo," 206n., 214n.
Fétis, François Joseph, 868n.
Févin, Antoine de, 221
   "Egregie Christi," 206n., 216n.
   "Nobilis progenie," 206n., 213n.
   "Sancta Trinitas," 206n., 216n.
   "Tempus meum," 206n., 216n.
   "Vulnerasti cor meum," 206n., 213n.
Ficino, Marsilio, 407n., 410n.
Field, John, 832
Fiorini, Hippolito, 394
Florence, 291, 303, 363, 364, 365, 371, 378, 379, 481, 627
Fogliano, Lodovico, 204n., 252
Fontanella, Count Alfonso, 375, 408
Fontenelle, Bernard Le Bovier de, 491n., 637
Fracastoro, Girolamo, 316n.
France, 166-71, 195, 277-78, 334, 411, 442-43, 449, 473-89, 491n., 496, 498-99, 502, 504n., 505-7, 580-81, 588, 592, 593-95, 596-97, 610, 612, 613, 623-54, 659, 660, 661, 671, 676-77, 695, 696, 712-13, 724-27, 728, 739, 819, 898

Franco of Cologne, 139-59, 161n., 181, 183, 185
François II of France, 286, 288-89
Frangipane, Cornelio, 658n.
Franz, Robert, 844n.
Frederick the Great, 662n., 674n., 704n.
Freneuse, Le Cerf de La Viéville, Seigneur de, 480n., 484n., 488n., 489-507
Fréron, Elie Catherine, 714
Froberger, Johann Jakob, 595
Fux, Johann Joseph, 535-63

Gabrieli, Andrea, 336, 400
Gabrieli, Giovanni, 433
Gabrieli (singer), 696
Gade, Niels Wilhelm, 844n.
Gaetani (lutenist), 487
Gafori, Franchino, 252, 303
Gagliano, Marco da, 365n.
Gagliari (artist), 701
Galen, 408
Galilei, Galileo, 363
Galilei, Vincenzo, 252n., 257n., 291n., 297n., 302-22, 363-64
Galliard, J. E., 473n.
Gallus, Jacob, "Ecce quomodo moritur justus," 265n.
Galuppi, Baldassare, 641, 672, 692, 698n.
   "Voi che languite," 640
Gastoldi, Giovanni Giacomo, 276, 400
Gaudentius, 87, 89n., 92
Gaul, 337
Gellius, Aulus, 293
Geminiano (16th cent.), 336
Geneva, 711-15
Gerke, Otto, 837n.
Germany, 276, 277, 436-37, 439, 442-43, 444, 447, 448, 449, 457, 459, 469-70, 588, 595-98, 610, 612, 613, 622, 628, 629, 637, 699-710, 728, 793, 803, 828, 833, 837, 838-39
Gesualdo, Carlo, Prince of Venosa, 333, 408
Ghizeghem, Hayne von:
   "A l'audience," 205n., 216n.
   "De tous biens plaine," 206n., 213n., 222n.
   "D'un autre amer," 206n., 213n.
   "La regretée," 206n., 216n.

Giacomelli (Jacomelli), G. B., 375
Giardini, Felice de', 689, 697
Giovanelli, Ruggiero, 275, 400
  Missa Vestiva i colli, 268n.
Giusti, Jacopo, 376
Glarean, Heinrich, 219-27, 240n.,
  244n., 253n., 255n., 303
Gluck, C. W. von, 673-83, 714n.,
  720n., 726, 727, 791, 804, 825, 858
  Alceste, 673-75, 677n., 681
  Iphigénie en Aulide, 677-82
  Iphigénie en Tauride, 810
  Orfeo ed Euridice, 677n., 681
  Paride ed Elena, 677n., 681
Goethe, 739, 765, 830, 836, 865, 866
Gogava, Antonius, 402n.
Goldoni, Carlo, 717n.
Gombert, Nicolas, 288n., 408
  "En espoir," 268n.
Goretti, Antonio, 394
Goths, 364, 748
Goudimel, Claude, 349
Gozzi, Carlo, 789
Grabau, Henriette ("Maria"), 835, 837
Graun, Carl Heinrich, 700, 701, 702,
  704-10
  Demofoonte, 704n.
  Montezuma, 662n.
  Der Tod Jesu, 709n.
Graun, Johann Gottlieb, 700n., 704
Greece, 302, 306, 363, 367, 371, 374,
  375, 409, 519, 521, 593, 658, 666,
  744-45, 746, 748, 879-80, 885
Gregory I, Pope, 104, 118, 140, 194
Gregory XIII, Pope, 323-24, 357-59
Grétry, André, 649n., 711-27
  L'Ami de la maison, 726
  L'Amitié à l'épreuve, 726
  Céphale et Procris, 726
  Les Deux avares, 726
  Le Huron, 716, 720-22, 723, 726
  Isabelle et Gertrude, 714-15
  Lucile, 726
  La Rosière de Salenci, 726
  Sylvain, 719, 726
  Le Tableau parlant, 726
  Zémire et Azor, 726
Grimm, F. W. von, 619-35, 654
Guadagni, Gaetano, 696
Guadagni, Mme. (singer), 696
Guarino Veronese, 401
Guerrero, Francisco, 263

Guido, Abbot of Pomposa, 123
Guido of Arezzo, 106n., 117-25, 140,
  171, 186, 194, 204, 263n., 304
Gyrowetz, Adalbert, *Der Augenarzt*,
  793n.

Hamburg, 845
Handel, George Frederick, 513, 588,
  691, 706n., 838, 864
  Alexander's Feast, 864
  Agrippina, 526n., 528n.
  Amadigi, 511n.
  Israel in Egypt, 864
  Judas Maccabaeus, 864
  The Messiah, 864
  Il Pastor fido, 529n.
  Rinaldo, 511n., 512-13, 514
  Rodelinda, 529n.
  Tamerlano, 622
  Samson, 864
Hanover, 596
Hartmann, J. P. E., *Ravnen*, 789n.
Hasse, Johann Adolph, 596n., 672n.,
  700-1, 702, 704-9
  Arminio, 701n.
  Artemisia, 705
  Demofoonte, 704n.
Hawkins, Sir John, 473n.
Haydn, Joseph, 731-32, 734, 735, 739-
  40, 776-77, 778, 890-91, 898
  The Creation, 732, 864
  Harmoniemesse, 739n.
  Quartet, Op. 1, No. 1, 739
  Sonata in E-flat, No. 52, 731n.
  Trio in E-flat minor, 731n.
Hegel, 849n., 859-61, 862n.
Heller, Stephen, 844n.
Henri II of France, 287-88
Henri III of France, 658
Henry VIII of England, 333, 350-51
Heracleides of Pontus, 48, 49n.
Herder, 747
Hermogenes, 246
Herodotus, 52, 63n.
Herz, Henri, 828
Hesiod, 529
Hill, Aaron, 513n.
Hiller, Johann Adam, 700n.
Hippocrates, 83, 408
Hipponax, 48, 49
Hoby, Sir Thomas, 281-85

Hoffmann, E. T. A., 775-97, 804-5, 851,
Undine, 802-3
Homer, 10, 15, 48, 52-53, 54, 55, 61n., 199, 221, 288, 333, 368, 699, 745, 746, 865
Homilius, Gottfried August, 703, 706n.
Hooper, Edmund, 353n.
Horace, 196, 221, 229, 246, 256, 399, 401, 403, 406, 446, 511, 521
Hotteterre family, 475n.
Hünten, Franz, 828
Hugo, Victor, 746n.
Hummel, Johann Nepomuk, 835
Hungary, 729
Hyagnis, 48

Ingegneri, Marc' Antonio, 408
Ion, son of Creusa, 44
Ionia, 48
Isaac, Heinrich, 221
Tulerunt Dominum meum, 224n.
Isabella of Aragon, 658n.
Isidore of Seville, 93-100, 198, 293n.
Ismenias of Thebes, 83, 293
Isocrates, 317
Italy, 165, 166-71, 269, 276, 277, 303, 334, 376n., 411, 436, 439, 440, 442, 444, 449, 451-52, 469, 473-89, 491n., 495n., 502, 505-7, 513, 517, 580-81, 583, 588, 592, 593-95, 596-97, 601n., 603, 607, 613, 622n., 624n., 627, 631, 633, 637n., 638-54, 656-77, 682, 687-98, 703, 706, 707, 716, 718, 727, 728, 747, 749, 791, 804, 810, 824, 837, 838, 898

Jacob of Liége, 152n., 175n., 180-90
Jacotin:
    "Interveniat pro rege nostro," 206n., 214n.
    "Michael archangele," 206n., 214n.
    "Rogamus te Virgo Maria," 206n., 212n.
Jadin, Louis, *La grande bataille d'Austerlitz*, 776n.
James I of England, 328, 329
Jannequin, Clément, 289
Japart, Jean, "Hélas qu'il est à mon gré," 206n., 214n.

Jean de Muris, 172-79, 182n., 183n., 185n., 194
Jélyotte, Pierre, 624n., 631, 632, 633, 640, 720
Joachim, Joseph, 844n.
Johann Georg I, Elector of Saxony, 432, 434n.
Johann Georg II, Elector of Saxony, 432-34, 438-40
John XIX, Pope, 122
John of Garland, 140n., 141n., 142n., 148n., 152n., 158n.
Johnson, Edward, 353n.
Johnson, Samuel, 698
Jommelli, Niccolo, 639n., 641, 672, 688, 691-92, 694n., 702n.
    Demofoonte, 692n., 694, 695
Josquin Desprez, 219-27, 263, 288n., 289, 408
    "Alma Redemptoris," 205n., 216n.
    "Cela sans plus," 206n., 212n.
    "Comment peut," 206n., 218n.
    "De profundis," 222-23
    "L'homme armé," 206n., 214n.
    Liber generationis Jesu Christi (Luke), 223-24, (Matthew), 223
    "Madame hélas," 206n., 218n.
    "Miserere," 206n., 215n.
    Missa ad fugam, 221
    Missa Ave maris stella, 206n., 213n.
    Missa de Beata Virgine, 206n., 211n., 221, 225
    Missa D'un autre amer, 206n., 213n.
    Missa Faisant regrets, 412
    Missa Fortuna desperata, 224
    Missa Hercules dux Ferrariae, 206n., 214n.
    Missa L'homme armé s. v. m., 221
    Missa La sol fa re mi, 221, 268
    "O admirabile commercium," 206n., 216n.
    "O Venus bant," 206n., 217n.
    "Planxit autem David," 226-27
    "La plus des plus," 206n., 213n.
    "Stabat mater," 206n., 216n.
    "Victimae paschali laudes," 221-22
Jouy, Étienne, 814
Jubal, 62, 194
Julian the Apostate, 337
Jung, F. W., 746n.
Juvenal, 99

Kant, 854
Kerle, Jacob de, 355-56
　Missa Ut re mi fa sol la, 268n.
Kessler, Joseph Christoph, Polonaises,
　Op. 25, 841-42
Killizky, Josephine, 738
Kirbye, George, 337, 353n.
Kirchner, Theodor, 844n.
Kirnberger, Johann Philipp, 703
Knorr, Julius, 829n.
Koch, Franz, 769-74
Königsberg, 705n.
Körner, Theodor, 804n.
Kraft, Anton, 734
Kreutzer, Rodolphe, 822
Kreuzfeld, J. G., 699n.
Krünner, Christian Leopold, 446
Kurzböck, Magdelene von, 731

La Barre, J. C., 506
La Borde, Jean Benjamin de, 624n.
La Bruyère, Jean de, 495, 504n.
Laconia, 81, 189n.
Lactantius, 198
La Fosse, Antoine de, 503n.
Lalande, Joseph Jérome de, 695, 697-98
Lambert, Magister, 141n., 142n., 181
Lambert, Michel, 504
La Motte Fouqué, Baron Friedrich de,
　802, 805
Lanfranco, G. M., 252n.
Lapi, Giovanni, 375
La Rochoix (singer), 485
La Rue, Pierre de, 221, 408
　"Ce n'est pas," 206n., 213n.
　"Fors seulement," 206n., 214n.
　Missa de Beata Virgine, 206n., 216n.
La Ruette, Jean Louis, 721
La Ruette, Mme. (singer), 721
Laschi, Filippo, 695
Lasso, Orlando di, 288n., 289n., 316n.,
　325-26, 335, 400
　Penitential Psalms, 335
　"Susanne un jour," 335
Lasson, Mathieu, "Virtute magna,"
　268n.
Lassus, Rudolf, Missa Vestiva i colli,
　268n.
Lasus of Hermione, 49, 88n.
Lebel (violinist), 721
Lecce (Leccia), 690
Legrenzi, Giovanni, 481

Leipzig ("Firlenz"), 620-21, 828, 829,
　835, 837
Leo, Leonardo, 639, 688
Leopold I, Emperor, 445, 488n.
Le Petit, Ninot, "Hélas hélas," 206n.,
　217n.
Le Roy, Adrian, 288
Lesbos, 316
Leschenet, Didier, 288n.
Lichnowsky, Prince Carl, 733
Liége, 715-16
Linke, Joseph, 734n.
Linus, 94, 194
Liszt, 841n., 847-73
　Ce qu'on entend sur la montagne,
　746n.
Livy, 197
Lobkowitz, Prince Josef Franz, 737
Löschenkohl, Johann, 765
London, 692n., 695, 697n., 730
Lorenzani, Paolo, 506
Lorrain, Claude, 745
Louis XIV, 505, 726
Louis XV, 653n.
Louis Ferdinand, Prince of Prussia, 731
Lovatini, Giovanni, 696
Lucan, 221
Lucian, 337
Lully, Jean Baptiste, 443, 447, 449,
　476, 480, 481, 482, 489n., 491n.,
　492-95, 498, 504, 505-6, 588, 593,
　622n., 627-28, 630n., 639, 648,
　652, 665, 725, 726n.
　Acis et Galatée, 492-93, 496, 630n.
　Alceste, 659n.
　"Amour que veux-tu" (Amadis),
　496, 498
　Armide, 496, 499, 507, 682
　Atys, 476
　"Bois épais" (Amadis), 495, 496
　Cadmus, 506, 659n.
　Isis, 476, 498n.
　Persée, 476, 494, 499-500
　Phaëton, 494
　Proserpine, 498
　Roland, 498n., 661n.
　Thésée, 497-98, 659n.
Luther, 341-42
Luynes, Charles Philippe, duc de, 653n.
Luzzaschi, Luzzasco, 394, 408
Lycurgus, 283, 333
Lydia, 50, 52, 80

Lyser, J. P., 843n.
Lysippus, 329

Macpherson, James, 746n.
Macrobius, 198, 300
Maillard, Jean, 288n., 289
Mainz, 840n.
Malvezzi, Cristofano, 364
Mancini, Francesco, L'Idaspe fedele, 514n.
Manelli, Pietro, 629, 632-33
Mangold, C. F., 844n.
Mannheim, 702
Mansoli (singer), 696
Mantua, 658n.
Mara, J. B., 701n.
Marburg, 334
Marcello, Benedetto, 518-31, 666n., 672
  Cassandra, 672
  Estro poetico-armonico, 672n.
  Timoteo, 672
Marchand, Jean Baptiste, 506
Marchetto da Padua, 160-71
Marenzio, Luca, 275, 335, 408
  "Cantava la piu vaga," 335
  "Che fa hogg'il mio sole," 335
  "Io partirò," 335
  "Tirsi morir volea," 335
  "Veggo dolce mio bene," 335
Maria Medici, Queen of France, 367, 376
Marmontel, Jean François, 716n., 720, 722
Marpurg, Friedrich Wilhelm, 703
Marschner, Heinrich, 840
Martial, 514
Martini, Padre Giambattista, 691, 692
Martini, Jean, Henri IV, 718n.
Marx, Adolf Bernhard, 848n., 849n.
Marxsen, Eduard, 845n.
Mary, Queen of Scots, 288n.
Masson, Charles, 492n.
Mattei, Colomba, 696
Mattei, Saverio, 692n.
Matthäi, Heinrich August, 836n.
Mattheson, Johann, 529n.
Maurer, L. W., 839n.
Mazarin, 659
Mei, Girolamo, 303, 308n.
Melani, Jacopo, 481
"Memphis" (philosopher), 297

Ménage, Gilles, 504
Mendelssohn, Felix ("F. Meritis"), 828, 834n., 835-36, 839
  Concerto in G minor, 839
  Elijah, 864
  Lobgesang, 896n.
  Overture, Calm Sea and Happy Voyage, 835, 836
  Overture, Fingal's Cave, 836n.
  Overture, A Midsummer Night's Dream, 836n.
  St. Paul, 864
Méric-Lalande, Henriette, 838
Merula, Tarquinio, 438n.
Merulo, Claudio, 400
  Proteo, 658n.
Metastasio, Pietro, 641, 662, 665, 666n., 671, 692, 794-95
Mexico, 662
Meyer, Gregor, 225-26
Meyer, Leopold von, Salon, Op. 4, 841, 843
Mickiewicz, Adam, 850n., 865
Milan, 481, 677, 690, 692n., 838
Miletus, 49
Milton, John, 858
Mingotti, Regina, 696
Miriam, 332
Mocenigo, Girolamo, 414
Molière, 493n., 497n., 504n., 634, 726
Mondonville, Jean Joseph, Le Carnaval du Parnasse, 634
Monsigny, Pierre Alexandre, 712n., 716, 717n., 718, 726, 819
  "Jusques dans la moindre chose," 718
  Rose et Colas, 712
Montalvo, Don Grazia, 375
Montausier, Charles de Sainte-Maure, duc de, 492
Monte, Philippe de, 336, 400
Monteverdi, Claudio, 4n., 5n., 336, 365, 394-404, 405-15, 436
  "Anima mia perdona," 394n., 395
  Arianna, 365n.
  "Armato il cor," 437, 438n.
  "Cruda Amarilli," 394n., 395, 396-98, 401-4, 406, 407
  "O Mirtillo," 411
  "Zefiro torna," 438n.
Monteverdi, G. C., 405-12
Monticelli, Angelo Maria, 696
Moors, 298

Morales, Cristóbal, 263
  Magnificat in Tone I, 271
  Magnificat in Tone V, 403
  Magnificat in Tone VIII, 271n.
  Missa Ut re mi fa sol la, 268
Moravia, 729
Morigi, Andrea, 696
Moritz, Landgrave of Hesse-Cassel, 334, 433n.
Morley, Thomas, 256n., 274-78, 337
Moses, 61, 70, 94, 194, 332, 342
Moulu, Pierre, 289
Mouret, Jean Joseph, 629
Mouton, Jean, 288n., 289, 408
  "Beata Dei Genetrix," 205n., 212n.
  "Celeste beneficium," 206n., 216n.
  "Congregati sunt," 206n., 212n.
  "Gaude Barbara," 206n., 214n.
  "Illuminare Hierusalem," 206n., 216n.
  Missa Ut sol, 206n., 217n.
  "Peccata mea Domine," 206n., 212n.
  "Quaeramus cum pastoribus," 206n., 216n.
Mozart, Leopold, 599-608, 696
Mozart, W. A., 734, 735, 773n., 776-77, 778, 787, 792, 805, 830, 835, 858, 890, 891, 898
  Bastien und Bastienne, 632n.
  Cosi fan tutte, 792
  Don Giovanni, 805, 830-31
  Le Nozze di Figaro, 792
  Symphony in E-flat, 777n.
  Symphony in C, 839
  Die Zauberflöte, 796
Müller, Wenzel:
  Das Neusonntagskind, 793n.
  Die Schwestern von Prag, 793n.
Muffat, Georg, 442-52
Munich, 450, 596
Musaeus, 17, 194
Mutianus, 87, 92

Nanino, G. M., 400
  Missa Vestiva i colli, 268n.
Naples, 275, 481, 663, 677, 679, 687, 690
Napoleon, 804n.
Naumann, Ernst, 844n.
Neantius, son of Pittacus, 316
Neri, Nero, 379

Nero, Pier del, 303n.
Netherlands, 596
Newton, Sir Isaac, 855
Nicomachus, 198
Nicolai, Christoph Friedrich, 699n.
Nicolini, 511, 514-17
Niedt, Friedrich Erhardt, 453-70
Noblet, Charles, 645
Norman, Ludwig, 844n.
Northampton, Henry Howard, Earl of, 327-29
Nucius, Johannes, *Missa Vestiva i colli*, 268n.

Obrecht, Jacob, 221
  "Si sumpsero," 206n., 216n.
Ockeghem, Joannes, 195, 199, 408
  "D'un autre amer," 222n.
  "Malheur me bat," 206n., 214n.
Odo of Cluny, 103-16, 120n., 125n.
Olympus (musician), 299
Onslow, George, Symphony No. 1, 839
Orléans, Louise Henriette, Duchesse d', 629n.
Ornithoparcus, Andreas, 195n.
Orpheus, 54, 59, 61, 62n., 91, 98, 194, 288, 316, 368, 513, 515, 529, 775
Orto, Marbriano de:
  "D' un autre amer," 206n., 213n.
  "Mon mari m'a diffamée," 206n., 217n.
Ossian, 746
Ott, Johannes, 256n.
Otto, Johann, Bishop of Augsburg, 325-26
Ovid, 221, 256, 832

Pachelbel, Johannes, 595
Paciani (singer), 486n.
Padovano, Annibale, 320
Padua, 689, 692n., 836
Paër, Ferdinando, 736
Pagin, André Noël, 633
Paisiello, Giovanni, *Le trame per amore*, 691
Palantrotti, Melchior, 375
Palestrina, Giovanni Pierluigi da, 263, 323-24, 358-59, 400, 430, 535n., 862
  "Aegypte noli flere," 265n.
  Magnificat in Tone II, 271n.

Missa Ad coenam Agni, 268n.
Missa Ecce sacerdos magnus, 268n.
Missa Papae Marcelli, 430
Missa Ut re mi fa sol la, 268n.
Missa Vestiva i colli, 268n.
Missa Virtute magna, 268n.
"Surge Petre," 265n.
"Vestiva i colli," 268n.
Pallavicino, Benedetto, 336
Palle, Scipione del, 377
Paris, 443, 499, 506n., 621, 630n., 712, 714-23, 725, 726, 732, 809n., 817, 869
Parma, 677
Pasquini, Bernardo, 449, 487
Pasquini, G. B., 701n.
Passau, 442, 443, 445, 449, 450
Paul, Jean (J. P. F. Richter), 743-49, 764-74, 830, 832, 842, 850
Pausanias, 81n., 292, 529
Pauson, 19
Peacham, Henry, 331-37
Pecci, Tomaso, 408
Penet, Hylaere, "Ascendens Christus," 205n., 217n.
Pepusch, John Christopher, *The Beggar's Opera*, 529n.
Pereira, Frau von, 731
Perez, Davide, 641
Pergolesi, G. B., 630, 639, 672, 688, 724
    La Serva padrona, 630n., 671
    Stabat mater, 755n.
Peri, Jacopo, 305n., 364, 365, 371n., 373-76, 408, 665-66
    Dafne, 365, 368, 373
    Euridice, 368, 371n., 373-76, 665
Periander, 54
Pericletus of Lesbos, 316
Perrault, Charles, 491n.
Perrault, Claude, 491
Pertici, Pietro, 695
Pesaro, 838
Petrarch, 274, 294n., 296n., 300, 301, 315, 316, 519, 671, 748
Petre, Lord John, 330
Petronius, 121n.
Petrus de Cruce, 185, 186n.
Philammon, 522
Philbert (flutist), 475n.
Philetaerus, 56

Philidor, Anne, 475n.
Philidor, François, 712n., 715, 717, 726
    Le Jardinier de Sidon, 717
    Le Maréchal ferrant, 712
    Tom Jones, 712
Philip the Good, 178n.
Philippe de Vitry, 167n., 173n., 178n., 187n., 188n.
Philips, Peter, 336
Philochorus, 53
Philolaus, 198
Philoxenus of Cythera, 23, 51
Phinot, Dominique, 263
Phocylides, 54
Phrygia, 48, 50, 63, 80, 97
Piccinni, Niccolo, 688-89, 691n., 692, 720n.
    La Buona figliuola, 696
    La Didone, 791
    Gelosia per gelosia, 688
Pindar, 50, 331, 529, 868
Pisendel, Johann Georg, 702n., 707
Plato, 3-12, 18n., 19n., 25, 80, 81, 86n., 194, 198, 246, 252, 255-56, 258, 282, 287, 292-93, 295, 298, 300, 333, 347, 378, 406-7, 409, 410, 413, 414n., 746, 849
Playford, John, 377-92
Pliny, 121n., 197, 522
Plutarch, 4n., 5n., 81n., 88n., 223n., 282n., 283n., 284n., 289, 293, 321n., 522
Pohl, Richard, 847n.
Poland, 335, 729
Poliziano, Angelo, 658
Polybius, 50, 306, 337
Polygnotus, 19
Ponzio, Pietro, 269
    Missa Ut re mi fa sol la, 268
Pope, Alexander, 690
Porpora, Niccolo Antonio, 641, 688
Porporino, 701n., 702
Porta, Costanzo, 400
Pradon, Nicolas, 634
Prague, 620-21, 623, 625n.
Pratinas, 49, 55
Pronomus of Thebes, 53
Pseudo-Aristotle; *see* Lambert, Magister
Ptolemaeus Philadelphus, 334
Ptolemy, 92, 194, 198, 202, 252, 291n., 296n., 402

Puckering, Sir John, 352-53
Pythagoras, 29, 54, 82, 83, 87, 94, 106n.,
    182, 194, 198, 285, 292, 293, 297n.,
    298
Pythermus, 49-50

Quantz, Johann Joachim, 577-98, 665n.
Quinault, Philippe, 474, 494, 628, 665
Quintilian, 246, 282n., 283n.

Racine, 505n., 634, 652, 677-78
Raguenet, François, 473-88, 491n., 504
Rakemann, Louis, 843
Ramann, Lina, 847n.
Rameau, Jean Philippe, 499n., 564-74,
    624n., 628n., 630n., 640, 646, 716,
    725
    Dardanus, 716
    Hippolyte et Aricie, 640n.
    Zoroastre, 634n.
Ramler, Karl Wilhelm, 700n., 703
Ramos, Bartolomé, 200-4
Raphael, 762, 765
Rasi, Francesco, 375
Rasoumowsky, Prince Andreas, 733
Rebel, François, 622n.
Rebel, Jean Ferry, 622
Regis, Jean, 195, 199
    "Clangat plebs flores," 206n., 212n.
Reichardt, Johann Friedrich, 699-710,
    728-40, 793n.
Reincken, Jan Adams, 595
Reni, Guido, 762
Rich, Christopher, 514
Richafort, Jean, 289
Richter, J. P. F., see Paul, Jean
Rinaldi, Giulio, 336
Rinuccini, Ottavio, 365, 367-69, 373,
    658
Rochefort, J. B., 718n.
Rode, Pierre, 822
Rolle, Johann Heinrich, 706n.
Romberg, Andreas, 736
Rome:
    Ancient, 302, 306, 364, 367, 374,
        375, 409, 519, 521, 593
    Modern, 335, 365, 379, 421, 430,
        431, 449, 481, 486, 487, 488,
        495, 497, 663, 690, 698n., 702n.,
        711, 716n.
Ronsard, Pierre de, 286-89

Rore, Cipriano de, 295, 305, 336, 400,
    407, 408, 409
    "Crudel acerba," 407
    "Dalle belle contrade," 407
    "Di virtù, di costume, di valore," 295
    "Et se pur mi mantieni amor," 407
    "Musica dulcisono," 300n.
    "Non gemme, non fin'oro," 403
    "O sonno," 295
    "Poichè m'invita amore," 295, 407
    "Quando signor lasciaste," 412
    "Schietto arbuscello," 295
    "Se bene il duolo," 295, 407
    "Un altra volta la Germania stride,"
        295, 407
Roscius Gallus, 319n.
Rossi, Giacomo, 513n.
Rossi, Luigi, 481, 506n.
Rossini, Gioacchino, 809-26, 828
    Il Barbiere di Siviglia, 810
    Torvaldo e Dorliska, 838
    William Tell, 809-26
Rousseau, Jean Jacques, 499n., 603n.,
    622n., 624n., 636-54, 677n., 682,
    700n., 711
    Le Devin du village, 632, 640n.
Rozoy, Barnabé Farmian de, 718n.
Rubini, G. B., 838
Rudolph II, Emperor, 334
Russia, 729, 732

Sacchinni, Antonio, 692, 765
St. Ambrose, 194
St. Athanasius, 74
St. Augustine, 73-75, 92, 93n., 95n.,
    137-38, 194, 346, 348
St. Basil, 64-66, 282n.
St. Hilary of Poitiers, 194
St. James, 187
St. Jerome, 71-72, 182, 332
St. John Chrysostom, 67-70, 283n., 333,
    348
St. Paul, 68-69, 70, 71, 122, 341-42,
    346, 347, 348
St. Peter, 187
St. Petersburg, 732
Saint Real, Abbé de, 495
St. Thomas; see Aquinas, St. Thomas
Saint-Yves, Mlle. (singer), 724
Salieri, Antonio, 733
Salzburg, 442, 443, 450
Sannazaro, Jacopo, 370, 379

Sappho, 332
Sarro, Domenico, *Didone abbandonata*, 662n.
Sartorio, Antonio, *Orfeo*, 488n.
Saul, 63, 72, 92, 94
Saxony, 433
Scarlatti, Alessandro, 667, 688, 692
Scarlatti, Domenico, 688
Schäffer, Julius, 844n.
Schiller, 744n., 745, 749, 862n.
Schmeling, Gertrud, 701-2, 704
Schneider, Lorenz, "Vergissmeinnicht," 773
Schröter, Corona, 705
Schubert, Franz, 828, 830, 838, 843
    Deutsche Tänze, Op. 33, 841, 843-44
    Waltzes, Op. 9, No. 1, 841, 843
Schütz, Heinrich, 432-41
    "Es steh Gott auf," 437
Schumann, Clara Wieck ("Zilia"), 835, 840, 841-44
    Valses romantiques, 841-43
Schumann, Robert, 779n., 789n., 827-45
Schunke, Ludwig, 828
Schuppanzigh, Ignaz, 733-35, 738n.
Schwanenberger, Johann Gottfried, 703
Sédaine, Jean Michel, 819
Segrais, Jean Regnauld de, 505
Seneca, 188, 282n.
Sermisy, Claudin de, 289
Servandoni, Giovanni Niccolo, 633
Sforza, Gian Galeazzo, 658n.
Shaftesbury, 3rd Earl of, 638n.
Shakespeare, 698, 749, 778, 839, 858, 869
Silas, 69
Simonides, 50
Simplicius, 180
Socrates, 4-12, 23, 24, 182, 194, 252, 256n., 282, 285, 292, 293, 297
Solon, 54
Sophocles, 368, 521, 658, 868
Soriano, Francesco, *Missa super voces musicales*, 268n.
Soto, Pietro, 355
Spain, 269, 276, 298, 637, 662, 747, 749
Sparta, 17, 21, 48, 50, 52, 53, 54-55, 81-82, 189, 283, 316, 333, 663
Spohr, Louis, 835

Concerto No. 11, Op. 70, 837
Spontini, Gasparo, 791, 825
    Fernand Cortez, 811
    Olimpie, 807n.
    La Vestale, 816
Stamitz, Carl, 764, 765, 766-67, 773n.
Statius, 83, 221
Stockmann, A. C., 772n.
Stokhem, Johannes, "Brunette," 205n., 216n.
Strabo, 522
Striggio, Alessandro, "Nasce la pena mia," 412
Strozzi, Leone, 379
Strozzi, Pietro, 305, 375
Stuck, Jean Baptiste, 506n.
Stuttgart, 692n.
Suard, Jean Baptiste, 718
Suetonius, 334
Suidas, 282n., 319
"Susanna fair," 335n.
Sweelinck, Jan Pieters, "Susanne un jour," 335n.
Swift, Jonathan, 491n.
Switzerland, 826, 831

Tagliazucchi, G. P., 662n.
Taiber, Elisabeth, 696
Taormina, 82
Tartini, Giuseppe, 633
Tasso, 414, 513n., 662, 789, 858
Telemann, Georg Philipp, 588, 589, 630n.
Telestes, 50
Temple, Sir William, 491n.
Terpander, 44, 82, 89n., 288, 309, 522
Terradellas, Domenico, 641
Thales of Miletus, 189, 293, 300
Thaletas of Gortyn (Crete), 81, 293n.
Thalberg, Sigismund, *Waltzes*, Op. 4, 841-42
Themistocles, 283
Theophilus, 47
Theophrastus, 48
Theopompus of Chios, 52
Thessaly, 48
Thrace, 81
Thrasippus, 21
Thun, Countess Elizabeth von, 733
Tieck, Johann Ludwig, 793
Timotheus, 51, 81-82, 189n., 194, 282n., 287, 319, 408

Tinctoris, Joannes, 193-99, 209n., 212n.
Titian, 838
Torelli, Giuseppe, 583
Tortona, 658
Trent, Council of, 355-56, 358
Trial, Jean Claude, 719, 720
Tubal Cain, 94, 98, 181
Türk, D. G., 833
Türschmidt, Carl, 735
Tunstede, Simon, 153n.
Turco, Giovanni del, 408
Turin, 481, 488, 691, 711

Uhlrich, Wilhelm, 839n.

Vanneo, Stefano, 252n.
Vannius, Joannes, 225
Varro, 91
Vauban, Sébastien Le Prestre de, 783
Vecchi, Orazio, 275, 336, 375
    "Fa una canzone," 336
    "Io catenato moro," 336
    "S'io potessi raccor'i mei sospiri," 336
    "Vivo in fuoco amoroso," 336
Vega, Lope de, 267n.
Venice, 276, 295, 336, 414, 433, 436, 481, 487, 488, 658, 663, 690, 698n., 836
Venturi, Stefano, 275
Verdelot, Philippe, "Si bona suscepimus," 254
Vergil, 95n., 97, 98, 199, 220, 221, 246, 513, 662, 667, 699, 821n.
Vernet, Claude Joseph, 719
Vespasian, 487
Viadana, Lodovico Grossi da, 419-23
    "O sacrum convivium," 422n.
Victoria, Tomás Luis de, 263, 335
Vienna, 450, 488n., 596, 728-40
Vieuxtemps, Henri, 841n.
Vinci, Leonardo (composer), 665, 672, 688
    Didone, 667
Vinci, Pietro, Missa Ut re mi fa sol la, 268
Viotti, G. B., 822
Vitello, Erasmus, 396

Vivaldi, Antonio, 622
Voltaire, 701, 712-15, 716n., 723, 869

Wackenroder, W. H., 750-63
Wagner, Richard, 746n., 853n., 874-903
    Die Feen, 789n.
    Der fliegende Holländer, 805n.
Walther, Johann (1496-1570), 343-44
Watson, Thomas, 335n.
Watteau, Jean Antoine, 703
Watzdorff, Volrad von, 434
Weber, C. M. von, 801-7, 828, 835, 838
    Der Freischütz, 805n., 807n.
    Kampf und Sieg, 804n.
    Leyer und Schwert, 804n.
    Overture, Beherrscher der Geister, 839n.
    Overture, Euryanthe, 839n.
    "Was sag ich?" 837n.
Weelkes, Thomas, 337
Weigl, Joseph, Das Waisenhaus, 792n.
Weinhold, Fräulein (singer), 838n.
Weiskern, F. W., 632n.
Weisse, C. E. F., 700n.
Wert, Giaches de, 400, 408
Wieck, Friedrich, 829n.
Wiedebein, Gottlieb, 838
Wigand, Balthasar, 732
Wilbye, John, 337
Willaert, Adrian, 261, 263, 288n., 289, 400, 408, 409
    "Aspro core e selvaggio," 258, 315n.
    "Giunto m'ha Amor," 258
    "I vidi in terra angelici costumi," 258
    "Ne projicias nos," 412
    "O invidia nemica," 254
    "Ove ch'i posi gli occhi," 258
    "Quando fra l'altre donne," 258
Wilsing, C. F., 844n.
Wittgenstein, Princess Carolyne, 847n.
Wotton, Sir Henry, 491n.

Xenophanes, 54
Xenophantes, 282n.

Yonge, Nicholas, 335n., 336n.

Zanetto, 214, 215, 216, 217
  "Multi sunt vocati," 206n., 217n.
Zannettini, Antonio, *Temistocle in bando*, 486n.
Zarlino, Gioseffe, 204n., 223n., 224n., 228-61, 303, 307n., 309n., 311n., 315n., 316n., 318n., 319n., 408, 409, 410, 412, 565, 567, 568, 572, 574, 658
Zethus, 94, 194
Zoilo, Annibale, 358-59
Zoroaster, 194

 Books That Live